HISTORY
OF
HUMANITY

Scientific and Cultural Development

History of Humanity
Scientific and Cultural Development

Volume I   *Prehistory and the Beginnings of Civilization*

ISBN 92–3–102810–3 (UNESCO)
ISBN 0–415–09305–8 (Routledge)

Volume II   *From the Third Millennium to the Seventh Century BC*

ISBN 92–3–102811–1 (UNESCO)
ISBN 0–415–09306–6 (Routledge)

Volume III   *From the Seventh Century BC to the Seventh Century AD*

ISBN 92–3–102812–X (UNESCO)
ISBN 0–415–09307–4 (Routledge)

Volume IV   *From the Seventh to the Sixteenth Century*

ISBN 92–3–102813–X (UNESCO)
ISBN 0–415–09308–2 (Routledge)

Volume V   *From the Sixteenth to the Eighteenth Century*

ISBN 92–3–102814–6 (UNESCO)
ISBN 0–415–09309–0 (Routledge)

Volume VI   *The Nineteenth Century*

ISBN 92–3–102815–4 (UNESCO)
ISBN 0–415–09310–4 (Routledge)

Volume VII   *The Twentieth Century*

ISBN 92–3–102816–2 (UNESCO)
ISBN 0–415–09311–2 (Routledge)

In memory of Paulo E. de Berrêdo Carneiro,
President of the first International Commission
for a Scientific and Cultural History of Mankind
(1952–1969) and of the present Commission from
1979 to 1982

HISTORY OF HUMANITY

Scientific and Cultural Development

Volume II
From the Third Millennium to the
Seventh Century BC

EDITED BY

A. H. Dani
J.-P. Mohen

CO-EDITED BY

J. L. Lorenzo	M. B. Sakellariou
V. M. Masson	B. K. Thapar
T. Obenga	Zhang Changshou

CONSULTANT
S. J. De Laet

First published in 1996
by the United Nations Educational, Scientific and Cultural Organization
7 Place de Fontenoy, 75352 Paris 07 SP
and
Routledge
11 New Fetter Lane, London EC4P 4EE

Simultaneously published in the USA and Canada
by Routledge
a division of Routledge, Chapman and Hall, Inc.
29 West 35th Street, New York, NY 10001

Typeset by 🅰 Tek-Art, Croydon, Surrey
Printed in Great Britain by Clays Ltd, St Ives plc

♾ Printed on acid-free paper

Index compiled by Indexing Specialists
202 Church Road, Hove, East Sussex BN3 2DJ

British Library Cataloguing in Publication Data
A catalogue record for this book is available on request

Library of Congress Cataloging in Publication Data
A catalogue record for this book is available on request

ISBN 92-3-102811-1 (UNESCO)
ISBN 0-415-09306-6 (Routledge)

PREFACE

Federico Mayor
Director-General of UNESCO

'Our civilization is the first to have for its past the past of the world, our history is the first to be world history.'[1] As we approach the year 2000, the phenomenon described over fifty years ago by Jan Huizinga becomes an ever more sensible reality. In a bounded and increasingly interconnected world, we necessarily find ourselves a part of that emerging global civilization that constitutes the matrix of our collective destinies.

The years immediately following the Dutch historian's assertion were indeed to illustrate, and in the most horrific manner, the interdependence of the world community. The planet on which millions of humans wished for nothing more than to live in peace and well-being presented the unnatural spectacle of a world at war. Land, sea and air routes were patrolled day and night by armadas venting fury on all that was most precious and vital to the inhabitants. The dreadful hurt that the populations sustained, physically and morally, dispelled *in perpetuum* a number of illusions and faced humanity with a stark choice – that of being, in the words of Albert Einstein, 'one or none'.

Thenceforth the grave danger attendant on inter-racial, and consequently inter-cultural, ignorance was conspicuous to thinking minds. A flawed consciousness of our common humanity must be incompatible with the survival of a world armed with knowledge of such awesome potential. Clearly the only course of action, the only way forward lay in building bridges between peoples, in forging a resilient awareness of the unity inherent in human diversity.

Such was the background to UNESCO's decision in 1947 to produce a truly universal work of international co-operation that would provide 'a wider understanding of the scientific and cultural aspects of the history of mankind and of the mutual interdependence of peoples and cultures and of their contributions to the common heritage'.[2] That initiative, which was one of UNESCO's earliest projects, sprang from the Organization's fundamental principles and was widely acclaimed, although not a few saw in it a Sisyphean undertaking at which past attempts had signally failed.

Three years later, in 1950, the first International Commission for a History of the Scientific and Cultural Development of Mankind began the task of fashioning a history that

– in the words of René Maheu – would 'present to man the sum total of his memories as a coherent whole'. As the distinguished international team of collaborators took shape and as the first results of its work began to appear in the Commission's review the *Journal of World History*, it became clear that new ground was being broken in pursuit of this ambitious goal. When some fifteen years later the first edition began to appear in six languages, the reception accorded to the work confirmed – some inevitable reservations apart – the success of this 'first attempt to compose a universal history of the human mind from the varying standpoints of memory and thought that characterize the different contemporary cultures'.

The compilers of the first edition of the *History of Mankind* were conscious that all historiography is 'work in progress', that in the continuous flux of history nothing is fixed, neither facts nor interpretations. In 1969, Paulo de Berrêdo Carneiro declared: 'The day will come when what we have written . . . will, in its turn, have to be replaced. I like to think that our successors will attend to this, and that a revised edition of the work we have begun may be published at the dawn of a new millennium.'

That day is now with us. The General Conference of UNESCO decided in 1978 that the work should be revised, and two years later the Second International Commission met to formulate its aims.

Much has changed since the publication of the first edition. In recent years, the historical sciences have been enriched by contributions from many disciplines, giving rise to new methods of investigation and bringing to light new facts, particularly in the realm of 'prehistory'. At the same time, a heightened awareness of cultural identity has intensified the demand for a corresponding decentralization of historical viewpoints and interpretations. UNESCO has both heeded and nurtured this trend by undertaking a series of regional histories, one of which – *The General History of Africa* – is on the point of completion while others are in active preparation. Finally, history itself has moved on, altering in the process the perspectives from which the past is viewed.

For all these reasons and to take account of some valid criticisms of the original version, it was decided that the new edition to be called simply the *History of Humanity*, should not be merely a revision, but rather a radical recasting of its predecessor. Its goal – to provide an account of the history

1 HUIZINGA, J. 1936. A Definition of the Concept of History. In: KLIBANSKY, R.; PATON, H. J. (eds), *Philosophy and History*. Oxford. p. 8.
2 UNESCO. 1947. *General Conference; Second Session*. Paris. Resolution 5.7.

of humanity in terms of its varied cultural and scientific achievements – remains unchanged, but the view it offers of its subject is – it is hoped – more detailed, more diverse and broader in scope.

Ten years after the launching of the project, it is my privilege to present this new *History* which has built upon and extended the pioneering work of those dedicated scholars responsible for the first edition. I should like to express my admiration and deep gratitude to the members of the Second International Commission and to the some 450 distinguished specialists from all geocultural backgrounds who have contributed to this historic undertaking. Readers will, I feel sure, make known their own views in the years to come. In committing this work to their scrutiny, the International Commission – and, through it, UNESCO – is taking the final step in the task entrusted to it by the community of Member States represented at the General Conference. Each of us, I am sure, stands to benefit from this concerted testimony to our common past and act of faith in our shared future.

CONTENTS

Preface   v
Federico Mayor, Director-General of UNESCO

Foreword   ix
Charles Morazé, former President of the International Commission

General Introduction   xv
Georges-Henri Dumont, President of the International Commission

The International Commission   xvii

History of Humanity (Scientific and Cultural Development) in Seven Volumes   xviii

List of figures   xix

List of maps   xxi

List of plates   xxii

The contributors   xxiv

Acknowledgements   xxvii

A Introduction   1

  Prehistory to history   3
  Sigfried J. De Laet
  Main trends of the new period   6
  Ahmad Hassan Dani and Jean-Pierre Mohen

B Thematic section   13

1   Technical aspects   15
  Jean-Pierre Mohen

2   From empirical to scientific knowledge   23
  2.1   From empirical knowledge to the beginnings of scientific thought   23
    Walter F. Reineke
  2.2   The measurement of time and the establishment of calendars   27
    Jean Leclant and Jean-Pierre Mohen

3   Economic and socio-political developments   30
  Mario Liverani

4   Sedentary agricultural and nomadic pastoral populations (3000–700 BC)   37
  Andrew Sherratt

5   From state to empire   44
  Vladimir A. Jakobson and Muhammad A. Dandamaev

6   The development of long-distance trade and the emergence of a merchant class   52
  Jean-Pierre Mohen

7   The beginning of the Iron Age: invention of ironwork and its consequences   58
  Pierre Villard

8   The dawn of writing and the principal linguistic families   65
  8.1   From the origins of writing to the alphabet   65
    Monica Rector
  8.2   The most ancient languages revealed by writing   70
    Stephen A. Wurm
  8.3   The Indo-European phenomenon: linguistics and archaeology   80
    J. P. Mallory

9   Oral traditions and literature, religion and art   92
  9.1   Oral traditions and literature   92
    9.1.1   The oral tradition   92
      Jean-Pierre Mohen
    9.1.2   Writing and literature   95
      Monica Rector
  9.2   Religion and art   98
    9.2.1   The development of religion   98
      Julien Ries
    9.2.2   Art and architecture   107
      Jean-Pierre Mohen
    9.2.3   Song, music and dance   112
      Jean-Pierre Mohen

C Regional section   115

  Editor's note   116

1. Regions for which written sources are available   117

10   Africa   118
  10.1   The Nile Valley (3000–1780 BC)   118
    Christiane Ziegler
  10.2   The Nile Valley (1780–700 BC)   133
    10.2.1   Egypt   133
      Gamal Mokhtar
    10.2.2   Nubia and its relationship with Egypt (1780–700 BC)   138
      Théophile Obenga

11 Europe 145
  11.1 The Aegean world 145
    Michel Sakellariou
    11.1.1 The Early Bronze Age 146
      (3000–1500 BC)
      Christos Doumas
    11.1.2 The Middle and Late Bronze Age 152
      (2100–1100 BC)
      Michel Sakellariou and Christos Doumas
    11.1.3 Decline and Recovery 159
      (1100–700 BC)
      Michel Sakellariou
  11.2 Cyprus 167
    Vassos Karageorghis
12 Asia 170
  Editor's Note 170
  12.1 Mesopotamia 171
    12.1.1 The Tigris and Euphrates valley 171
      (3000–1500 BC)
      C. C. Lamberg-Karlovsky and R. Wright
    12.1.2 The Kassite period (1500–700 BC) 182
      Georges Roux
  12.2 Syria and Palestine 191
    12.2.1 The Early and Middle Bronze Age 191
      (3000–1600 BC)
      Dominique Beyer
    12.2.2 The Late Bronze Age and the Early 198
      Iron Age (1600–700 BC)
      Horst Klengel
  12.3 Anatolia 205
    Ekrem Akurgal
  12.4 Iran 224
    Reinhard Dittmann
  12.5 Afghanistan 232
    Victor I. Sarianidi
  12.6 The Arabian Peninsula 238
    Abdul Rahman Al-Ansary
  12.7 The Indus Valley (3000–1500 BC) 246
    B. K. Thapar and M. Rafique Mughal
  12.8 The Post-Indus Cultures (1500–700 BC) 266
    B. K. Thapar and Abdul Rahman
  12.9 China
    12.9.1 China (3000–1600 BC) 280
      An Zhimin
    12.9.2 China (1600–700 BC) 289
      Zhang Changshou

**II Regions for which only archaeological and 297
anthropological sources are available**

Editor's Note
13 Africa, excluding the Nile Valley 299
  Louise M. Diop-Maes
  Aboubacry M. Lam
  Massamba Lam
  Théophile Obenga
  David W. Phillipson
  Babacar Sall

14 Europe 320
  Editor's Note 320
  14.1 Introduction 321
    Jean-Pierre Mohen
  14.2 Southern Europe 334
    Renato Peroni
  14.3 South-Eastern Europe 345
    Roumen Katincharov and Nikola Tasić
  14.4 Central Europe 350
    Istvan Ecsedy and Tibor Kovács
  14.5 Eastern Europe (Fourth millennium to 357
    seventh century BC)
    Nikolai J. Merpert
  14.6 Western Europe 364
    Jacques Briard
  14.7 Northern Europe 373
    Henrik Thrane
  14.8 Religion and art 382
    Lili L. Kaelas
15 Asia 392
  15.1 Central Asia 392
    Vadim M. Masson
  15.2 South-East Asia and the Pacific 401
    Charles F. W. Higham and Wilhelm G.
    Solheim II
  15.3 Korea 415
    Tadashi Nishitani
  15.4 Japan (3000–700 BC) 418
    Tatsuo Kobayashi
  15.5 Northern Asia and Mongolia (3000–700 BC) 421
    Anatoly P. Derevyanko
16 Australia 432
  Josephine Flood
17 The Americas 439
  Editor's Note 439
  17.1 An overview of the cultural evolution 440
    Mario Sanoja Obediente
  17.2 Religion and art 446
    José Alcina Franch
  17.3 North America 453
    Melvin L. Fowler
  17.4 Mesoamerica: Genesis and first developments 462
    Christine Niederberger
  17.5 South America 476
    17.5.1 The north-east and eastern region 476
      Mario Sanoja Obediente
    17.5.2 The eastern region 486
      Osvaldo R. Heredia
    17.5.3 The western region 492
      Luís Guillermo Lumbreras
    17.5.4 The south-west region 510
      Lautaro Nuñez

Afterword 524
  Jean-Pierre Mohen

Chronological table 526

Index 529

FOREWORD

Charles Morazé, former
President of the International Commission

Among the great tasks assigned to UNESCO by the Constitution is the duty to promote and encourage mutual knowledge and understanding throughout the world. While many of the divergences which divide people date from a distant past, an analysis of their historical antecedents discloses links which draw them nearer to one another, brings to light their contributions to a common patrimony of humanity, reveals the ebb and flow of cultural exchanges and emphasizes their increasing tendency to become integrated into an international community.

This is how Paulo E. de Berrêdo Carneiro, President of the International Commission (1952–69), expressed himself in the opening paragraph of the Preface to the *History of the Scientific and Cultural Development of Mankind* in 1963. Today, it would be difficult to say anything about humanity's 'increasing tendency to become integrated into an international community', unless an attempt is made to assess the outcome of this 'tendency' as reflected in the state of the world since. Today, few events remain local. Information on any minor or major occurrence is communicated to almost everyone immediately and an action undertaken in one part of the world inevitably has its repercussions on the others. Those who experience fully this 'planetarization' sense the 'integration' of all human beings into an international community less as a 'tendency' than as a *fait accompli*. But what about the subordinates who are more or less associated or the vast excluded majority of people? These others, put the question in completely different terms. What they seem to ask is: can a 'common patrimony of humanity' be achieved solely through an integration based on scientific and technical developments? What then can we do to ensure an equal access to such means for all when the more fundamental task of reducing existing differences in the very standards of living lags far behind?

The idea of writing a history of the development of humankind was first put forward by Julian Huxley, the Executive Secretary of the Preparatory Commission of UNESCO. In 1946 Huxley wrote that 'the chief task before the Humanities today would seem to be to help in constructing a history of the development of the human mind, notably in its highest cultural achievements'. He underscored the major role that historians would play in the realization of what he called a 'gigantic enterprise'. Huxley later out-

lined a project which was to be submitted to the future UNESCO. In 1950, in accordance with a resolution passed by the General Conference of UNESCO, an International Commission was set up and the publication of a *History of the Scientific and Cultural Development of Mankind* in six volumes was approved. The first volume appeared in 1963.

What was this 'gigantic enterprise', conceived by Huxley worth? Critics received the volumes more often badly than well. They did not question the data included. What they objected to mainly were the criteria of the selection of data and the interpretations offered. Yet a closer look at these criticisms revealed that, skilled as they were at pointing out certain flaws and misconceptions, these commentators hardly ever came up with concrete suggestions that would lead to any improvement of the work in the future. On the whole, however, we were left with the impression that notwithstanding its shortcomings, a very large number of readers found the work commendable, particularly as a first step towards the achievement of an 'essential task'.

No elucidation, rational or otherwise, of the origins or the evolution of human beings can be offered once and for all, as if by divine revelation. Writing a history of the development of humankind necessarily constitutes a work that one has to return to over and over again. Nearly thirty years passed by before UNESCO decided to take up once more a work that could by no means be regarded as finished. Requested by the new Member States, a recasting of the first edition deserved the wholehearted support of all those who helped establish the Organization. The changes which have taken place over these last thirty years rendered necessary and amply justified a revision and revaluation of history, and the members of the International Commission were the first to acknowledge such a need. There were, of course, other and more imperative reasons. Two of these should be pointed out here.

The first concerns the developments in the area of research methodology since the 1960s. Over the last three decades historical knowledge has increased considerably and has turned from factual history to greater interest in anthropological research. Although they still remain far from being fully capable of answering all the questions that we ask today – or for that matter the more serious of those posed thirty years ago – the added insight that present studies offer us deserves to be transmitted to a larger public. The second,

ix

and perhaps less obvious, reason springs from the very role that the writing of history can, and is meant to, play in increasing our level of awareness. A writing or, as in the present case, a rewriting of the history of human scientific and cultural evolution signifies not only taking stock of the new data available but also helping one and all in evaluating and assessing the various implications, positive and also negative, of all the changes. Justifying science in the name of all its benefits and advantages amounts to refusing to accept the damaging effects it can have. We have gradually accustomed ourselves to the presence of many latent nuclear volcanoes without compensating for the technological risks. Not enough has been done to counterbalance the excessive monetary investments needed to build up such arsenals with sufficient funds to help confront the problems and miseries afflicting one section of humanity and which is on the way to becoming a danger for the other. Technological development has also begun seriously to endanger animal and plant life on this planet. Factors such as these plead for greater vigilance.

Universal histories and histories of the world abound. So many have already been published and continue to be published that one could question the need to bring out yet another one. No doubt many readers will be surprised at this venture. Each in his own way will of course judge this work better or worse than another of its kind. There is however one major difference. Other works of history enjoy a certain freedom that has in a sense been denied to the present one. They are free to choose themes, periods and regions that suit best the demands of a particular readership and a specific conception of history. Such works can thereby claim a certain cohesion of the elements introduced; a cohesion which also helps establish a certain uniformity of expression and style. The present work is founded on an entirely different principle: a maximum of diversity. This diversity proves to be, on the one hand, so great that it is difficult to stop it from becoming disparate and, on the other, not great enough to allow for a convenient regrouping of elements into types. The fault lies not in the venture itself nor in those who took up the task. It lies mainly in the present state of historical knowledge. The analytic nature of historical research today blocks the way to synthesis, to the kind of approach required in the writing of a history that can be considered truly universal.

This work can serve only as a history of the world and not as a universal history. This, of course, is already a great deal. We should not count on the diffusion of a universalism, which is the subject of reflection by a very small, privileged minority, as long as all cultures are not equally represented and historians from all parts of the world are not endowed with the same means and cannot claim the same status, social and otherwise.

Not claiming to attain the unattainable does not, however, mean renunciation. The roads to universalism are full of bends and curves. But, they all lead to the same destination: one history for one united world. Since this history could not reach the highest common factor, it had to tend towards the lowest common multiple. And in this respect, the present work has not failed in its mission.

In 1950 we opted in three days for a plan that would take thirteen years to complete. With a view to ensuring a unity of style and presentation, we decided that each of the six volumes would be written by a single author. Such ideas had to be abandoned. Some thirty years later, the New Commission decided to take more time over the distribution of the work to be done among seven and not six volumes, each well co-ordinated with the other and allowing free play to as many authors as would be necessary to cover a maximum of domains. The selection of the criteria on which the new history would be based first led to a detailed examination of the comments made by the readers of the first edition. After many debates and discussions, all agreed that it would not do simply to juxtapose a series of regional histories one after the other. Then one of the two possible solutions had to be chosen: dividing history either into themes or into periods and analysing each according to themes and regions. The first option – an idea that had already been put forward before 1948 – would perhaps have helped bring out in a more significant manner the factors which render manifest the common destiny of mankind. But the present state of historical research, which in most cases and owing to an ever-increasing acquisition of skills, proceeds in the form of temporal as well as regional specializations, constituted a real obstacle to the realization of such a scheme. It was therefore decided that each of the seven volumes would be devoted to a single period and would contain a thematic and regional section.

Yielding to the constraints imposed by the state of knowledge and research today does not, however, solve all probable problems. Let us take a look at the issue point by point.

The idea of splitting up into periods a past that the mission of all historians is to revive as an organic whole pleased no one. But, taking everything into consideration, had the objective been to separate one cultural component from another or, for example, the physical from the cultural or the religious from the profane, this surgery would have turned literally into a vivisection. Opting for the lesser evil, the Commission thus decided to work on chronological sections. This, at least, allowed for the preservation of a certain unity within each group.

Already in the 1950s it had become evident that the form of periodization upheld by the European tradition loses its signification when applied to the other parts of the world. Terms such as 'Antiquity', 'the Middle Ages' or 'modern times' do not correspond to much in so far as Asia is concerned, and perhaps even less for what concerns Africa. Admittedly we continue using such words for the sake of convenience. We cannot totally discard them, but we should try at least not to trust them fully.

The importance of each period is measured more in terms of what humankind has contributed to each than in terms of a duration defined by astronomy. The 'Grand Discoveries' of the sixteenth and the seventeenth centuries led to some spectacular changes in the history of the world. A sudden growth of ideas and of commercial capitalism accompanied by or resulting from military conquests gave rise to migrations that brought about the creation of a new map of the world and new conceptions of humanity's destiny. This moment marks a turning point that we have ever since sensed as an acceleration of history. It was, therefore, decided that three volumes of the present work would be devoted to the period succeeding these significant changes and transformations as against only four which would cover the entire preceding period, starting from the origins of humankind and leading up to the sixteenth century. The Commission also decided to devote more and more pages to the more recent years. The fifth volume thus covers three centuries; the sixth, one and a half; and the seventh only about seventy-five years.

A word of caution is, however, necessary. We often make use of a concept of progress that is based on the quantitative and not the qualitative value of what has been achieved. Manufactured goods, consumer items and exchanges, whether they concern concrete objects or ideas, can be more or less quantified. But, as we do not possess any means of measuring happiness or well-being, we cannot infer therefrom that the quantitative and the qualitative values of this progress are the same, particularly in so far as the world in general is concerned. This notion of progress should not, moreover, hinder a proper appraisal of all that was contributed to history by our ancestors, to whom we owe our existence and our way of living.

Great care was taken to avoid putting an undue emphasis on what could be considered as being only the European landmarks of history. The years 1789 and 1914, although highly significant in the history of Europe, served only nominally as points of reference. It was understood that, depending on the case, the ethnocentrism implied by these dates would be reduced as much as necessary through a proper and adequate treatment of the issues preceding or following them. Similarly, to avoid falling into the traps of Western traditionalism, it was considered necessary to cease using the Christianization of the Roman Empire as a mark of the end of the Ancient World and the beginning of the Middle Ages and, therefore, to include the first years of the Hegira in the third volume, which covers the period from 700 BC to AD 700, the middle of which comes before the beginning of the era acknowledged – belatedly – also by the Muslims.

The Commission's choice does not conflict very much with the Chinese system of dating, because around the same epoch the same phenomenon appeared in both the east and west of Eurasia: the awakening of tribes in these Central Steppes who until then had been restricted to a disorderly, Brownian form of movement of particular groups, henceforth united together and set off to conquer the largest empire that the world has ever known. Events such as this draw our attention to the advantages of following a calendar determined not according to the permanent aspects of the planets but according to the variations of climate. Indeed, the Mongols would not have reached such a high degree of power had the climate not favoured the humidification of the pasture lands which nourished their horses. However, it will be a good while before we have available a calendar based on climatic variations. We still lack information on some vital factors: the evaluation of harvests, the extension or the regression of lacustrine and forest areas, phytographical analyses, etc. Only when we have obtained such necessary data can we think of establishing a new type of periodization that can be verified through metereological calculations extrapolating and applying to the past our present conjectures about the influence of solar explosions on the atmosphere.

The period to be treated in the fourth volume was therefore set by the end of Volume III (the seventh century) and the beginning (the sixteenth century) of Volume V. Volumes I and II have been devoted to the many thousands of years constituting the origins of humanity. The richness of the new data at our disposal made it necessary to treat separately the period spreading from the third millennium to the beginning of the seventh century before our era.

This division into seven volumes, dictated by a combination of factors ranging from the abstract to the practical – amongst the latter, being that of ensuring the more or less equal size of the volumes – is more or less in keeping with historical facts. Beyond all specific differences, five principal stages can be recorded in human evolution: the use of material tools accompanied by the emergence of cultures destined to be full of meaning for a long time to come; the moulding of a geo-politics or a geo-culture signalled by the appearance of major works of all kinds, all of which were to be of lasting value; partitive convulsions that forced in advance the distinction of cultural identities through the play of mutual influences; conceptions resulting from a closed human universe whose planetary course lies within a limitless space; the intensification of centres of development under the pressure of a capitalism that has become industrial and an industry that is becoming scientific – phenomena which push to the outskirts the excess of constraints from which the thus privileged zones escape. The seventh volume will thus deal with the issue of these new currents and the tidal waves that they provoke; facets that lead to the birth of a new type of polarization and as a result of which traditional cultures fall into abeyance.

Such bird's-eye views as those offered here are not misleading because they are crude; they seem questionable because they escape our sight when we keep ourselves too close to the ordinary facts. And it is in this that we mainly confront the limitations of our methods of research. No one is unaware of the difficulties that continue to affect all attempts to provide a synthetic view of humankind's common destiny. There is no answer to these difficulties from which the present subdivision of each volume into themes and regions suffers; into themes to bring out what all human beings share in common; into regions to mark the diversities.

In each volume, the thematic parts should have been the easiest to work out. Several problems were, however, encountered. In order to ensure that the cultures that benefit from the spectacular development that we witness today be no longer favoured beyond measure, it was considered necessary to reduce the importance granted to theoretical innovations and their applications and therefore to refrain from using scientific discoveries as chronological pointers. Had this not been the case, the distribution of themes would have been a simple matter. It would have sufficed to begin with a survey of the scientific and technical knowledge acquired over a given period of time and then retrace the causes in their sequential order.

Now, from the moment when it becomes necessary for history to tone down the privileges conferred on some by the process of evolution – and, more particularly, to question a system of values rooted in an overly univocal notion of progress – it also becomes necessary to standardize the distribution of themes by including more 'ordinary' references, for example, by starting with a description of the physical and natural conditions in order to arrive at the scientific through the demographic and the cultural. This not only increased the uniformity of the volumes but also offered the major advantage of emphasizing the ways of living. Whatever they are, these must first satisfy the basic physiological needs – a vital minimum dictated by the instincts of survival and rendered partially relative by the differences of climate. Each culture responds to this in its own manner and according as much to its natural environment as to the habits that it inherits. Certain acquired needs are then added to this vital minimum – superfluous needs turned into necessary ones and established in varying degrees according to the social hierarchies and geohistorical differences. Moreover, as human beings are not only biological but also thinking and feeling entities, each material culture is accompanied by a culture that can be called 'spiritual' in the widest sense of the term and that also varies according to the situation already mentioned. Finally, even though the conditions are not identical, material culture and spiritual culture are interrelated.

This enunciation of the common grounds on which all human lives are established stands to reason and would seem evident to any lay person. It could also, however, lead us to think that it is easy to find historians ready to develop each theme. The present state of historical knowledge proves that it is not so and, as always, for the same reason. Insignificant as this problem may be, the solution lies in turning one's back on analytical methods and adopting an approach that would be one of synthesis.

Undoubtedly, current research and investigations help us in our evaluation of material and spiritual cultures, but separately. We are completely ignorant about the interconnections between the two. Where does this notorious deficiency come from? Two main reasons can be put forward.

The first concerns the elaboration of a global history. Indeed, when it comes to local or regional histories, each confined to a particular epoch, the data that we possess help us either to deal with some of the problems or to contribute by offering some information. But when one or the other problem needs to be looked at from a global point of view, then we confront a major difficulty: which elements of the data available should be included in an inventory of an absolutely common heritage? In other words, what advances made at one place or the other, or at one point of time or another, effectively contributed to what can be called 'general progress'? The workshops of historians can boast of few if any historians at all who specialize in the evaluation of 'generalities'! When the need for one arises, then it has to be admitted that the courageous few who have undertaken such a task suffered from the absence of sufficient information and were compelled to work in conditions that rendered their merits highly eminent but curbed considerably their influence.

This first reason leads to the second, the absence of criteria that would make it possible to distinguish effectively the subjective from the objective as much in the work accomplished as in the reputations won. Here we touch upon an issue that is too important to dismiss without fuller attention.

The studies on primitive or savage societies, particularly those conducted over the last fifty years, carried anthropology to a high degree of what must be called the 'intelligence' of cultures. Indeed, in these societies, myth plays a fundamental role. It legitimizes matrimonial and social behaviour as well as customs and ways of living – the way one eats, dresses and organizes one's life inside and outside one's own dwelling. In an even more significant manner, it legitimizes humankind's spiritual behaviour as much in times of war as in peace. This global aspect of myth itself leads us to the heights from which, at one glance, we can view not only the various behaviours as a whole, but also, and as a result, the very logic that sustains them.

Historical evolution disperses myth, without however abolishing the mythological function. It provokes the growth of branches and favours ramifications. What had been thanks to myth, at one and the same time, religion and literature, moral and political, art and technique, breaks up later into more and more subdivided areas of knowledge; differentiations that led namely to the belief that the logic of myth or of the sacred is gainsaid by that of science. 'Science': this word which obstructs more than all others what we term historical intelligence. In the original sense of the word, science means knowledge, with no distinction implied between knowledge and know-how. Today this same word has taken on such a specific meaning that for a vast majority of the most highly informed minds, science denotes truth, as against the falsity of myth. Yet, many eminent scholars acknowledge that this 'truth' contains a part of myth and that it is indeed thanks to this that methods and knowledge advance. It is by working within the mythological that we reduce the part of myths, something of which always survives in the very heart of science.

The barriers that have been most resolutely built against the 'intelligence' of history have their sources in the gradual formation of separate enclaves of investigation. Social, economic, political, literary history and so on: each domain follows its won path and rarely meets the other, or never enough to allow for the establishment of criteria common to all that could constitute the basis for a truly universal history of scientific and cultural developments. The worst form of such separations can be found in the cosmic distance that has been introduced between the history of religion and that of science, and this, in spite of some highly remarkable, though rare, attempts to make them move towards each other via the social and the philosophical. No significant results should be expected until the gaps between ordinary language and scientific language are bridged, particularly when the latter makes use of mathematical terms so fully exploited by the initiated few and so little accessible to the secular mass.

This brings us back to the question of the limitations of this edition referred to earlier: limitations concerning the basic logical presuppositions on which a truly universal history of humankind should be founded. It is only on the basis of certain common features that one culture can comprehend something that is part of another culture and that the people of today can understand a little of what lies in the past. But then, given the present state of our knowledge and the manner in which the basic logical presuppositions are handled, our history will remain beyond the reach of the general public, however enlightened, for which it is intended.

None the less, a certain merit – perhaps less significant than hoped for – makes this second edition worthy of our attention. By eliminating the notion that the cultures rendered marginal by 'progress' represent groups of people 'without history', the study of cultures wherein myth is dispersed among all kinds of domains could only gain from the experience of those whose lives are, even today, steeped in a mythology that they all consider fundamental. We have not as yet reached our goal, but the step taken marks a sure improvement in terms of our understanding of history. And, as the readers will themselves find out, it is this aspect of the thematic part of each volume that makes this work truly exceptional.

We now come to the question of the treatment of regions in each volume. To begin with, let us look at a major ambiguity which threatened the very conception of these sections. An example will suffice. To which region does Newton belong? To Cambridge? England? Europe? The West? The world? There is no doubt that the universality of his law of gravitation makes him a part of the common heritage of humanity. Yet, undoubtedly this law discovered by a particular man, at a particular place and point of time, would seem to have miraculously descended from the skies, if we did not take into account the facts of the discovery, the circumstances leading to it and the manner in which the law was adopted by all. Should we have then talked about

Newton in one way in the thematic chapter and in another in the regional? Although the difficulties involved in solving such a problem are great, they turn out to be less so when confronted with yet another problem that would have resulted from any attempt to merge the two parts into one: for, in that case, the question would have been, which one? A fusion of all into the regional would, to a great extent, have simplified the task, given that we are dealing with specializations in different fields. But it would have led to the very unpleasant need to emphasize the merits of one culture at the cost of the others. A fusion of all into the thematic? In that case, Newton's law would have been stripped of its socio-cultural characteristics and this would have led to some kind of sanctification of the 'genius'. Needless to say, what has been noted as regards Newton applies to all thinkers, discoverers and to all that humankind has created.

Some readers will perhaps regret the fact that this history, whose dominant note is certainly transcultural, does not succeed better in overcoming certain problems resulting from habits and preconceived notions. We all talk about Asia, Africa and Europe. Originally, these were names given to Greek nymphs and were used to distinguish the three principal, cardinal points of the world perceived by the Mediterranean navigators: the south, the east and the north, respectively. To these seafarers the west was nothing but a vast indecipherable stretch, presumably a part of the legendary Atlantis. As for the continent of America, its name was curiously given to it by a cartographer who, while outlining a map of this continent, used the information supplied to him by Amerigo Vespucci – thus depriving Christopher Columbus of the recognition he deserved. In the case of the nymphs as well as in that of the cartographer, we can no longer distinguish the subjective from the objective. What was in fact a very subjective decision in the first place now appears to be very objective because it is commonly accepted by everyone. We cannot change something that has been so firmly established over the years, but the often very serious problems and disadvantages that result from the ethnocentrism implied by such customs need to be pointed out.

Depending on the epochs, Egypt is at times best understood when considered as African and at others when its civilization is regarded as having acquired much of its significance from a dual Nile-Euphrates identity. Similarly, instead of remaining Mediterranean, southern Europe became continental when the centre of gravity of exchanges and developments shifted to the Atlantic. China constitutes another example. This Middle Kingdom felt the effects of the existence of other continental regions when its Great Wall no longer protected it from the conquerors it tried later to assimilate, or when it yielded, perhaps for too long a period, to the attacks of the seamen and naval forces coming from the other end of the world, that is, from Europe.

Geographical perspectives change from one era to the other. But it is difficult to incorporate such changes and align them with the periodization adopted for a work on history. Those responsible for planning the seven volumes had to devise the ways and means of solving such problems. At times they had to have recourse to certain subterfuges so as to prevent the periodization from turning into some kind of a jigsaw puzzle and requiring a frequent arrangement and rearrangement. This entailed, however, the risks of introducing certain anachronisms.

Such risks are in no way negligible. To a modern mind, for example, the commerce or the conquests in ancient times across the deserts of Sinai appear as manifestations of the hostilities existing between Africa and Asia. This distinction between the two continents becomes nonsensical when applied to the period when Egypt did not see itself as African nor Assyria as Asian. Each region thought of itself first as constituting in itself the whole universe or as representing in itself the whole universe as defined by its own gods. We must be aware of the dangers of accepting such ideas, which still survive in the unconscious, affect our conscious minds, and foster notions of rights and privileges detrimental to the development of universalism.

The need to determine the number of pages to be devoted to each 'contingent' arose from certain customs that, although anachronic, generate at times very strong emotions and influence our decisions. It also arose from the fact that the distrust of ethnocentrism expressed itself in terms that were very ethnocentric. Including Cro-Magnon man in an inventory of 'European' sites amounts to attributing to him a label that contradicts all that was felt in times when existence could not be conceived of except in terms very different from those related to our planetary territoriality. Similarly, the concept of Africa was itself foreign to the African empires or kingdoms, each constituting for each a world in itself and, at the same time, a world which belongs to all. The readers will themselves correct such imperfections, which have resulted from a need to adopt a pragmatic approach.

Applying modern notions of geography to any period of the past relieves us of the dizziness felt when we look down into the immense depths of time, yet it is in these depths that cultural but also natural interactions, direct or indirect, multiplied: a swarming mass much too indecipherable to allow for the delineation of linear ancestry. It is, therefore, better to avoid distinguishing overmuch our distant common ancestors. Physical evolution leads perhaps to the formation of races. But as the human species can be known through its customs, faculties and cerebral activities, this privilege common to all reduces practically to nothing the particularisms that some not always disinterested viewpoints defined formerly as racial.

The human species cannot really be differentiated except as ethnic groups and through customs that defy any simplistic typology. A strong capacity for adaption, peculiar to humans, enables them to invent a practically limitless number of solutions to the problems posed by all kinds of environments, and even more so by circumstances that the smallest events modify and great events transform altogether. In this lies the most amazing aspect of history: the infinite variety of answers that each individual or collectivity finds to the questions put to it by destiny. The more history accelerates its pace and becomes more specific, the more our destiny becomes enigmatic. This is because every human being is a human being and no single one resembles another.

The end of the colonialisms that believed or claimed themselves to be the civilizers of this world led to the birth of many new nations and many new Member States of international organizations. 'New' in what sense? The establishment of a 'New World Order' is bound to remain a Utopian idea as long as history has not explained how a local body of historical cultures finally engendered what it has over the centuries referred to as 'civilization'; a word full of contradictions. Intended as universal and respectful to other cultures, this civilization turned out to be materialist and destroyed many cultures as a result of the superiority that it attributed to its own system of laws and rights. Two heavy tasks thus face historians: acknowledging the universalism that lies hidden beneath all particularisms and agreeing among themselves on what should be made generally known in this respect.

An elucidation of the past requires personal as well as collective efforts. This two-fold process should therefore have found spontaneous expression in a work meant to aid the advancement of knowledge. The Commission recommended therefore that, in addition to the thematic and regional parts, a third part be added that would have comprised specific supplements on details that needed developing, problems that needed solving, and finally an exposition of different and opposing opinions on interpretations in dispute. This project met with overwhelming difficulties and some explanation is called for!

This international history, which had been conceived as a result of dialogues and discussions, would evidently have gained considerably from an exposition of the differences in interpretation in their proper dimensions. It would have been more lively and instructive and have given readers more food for thought. Unfortunately, the dispersion of authors to be included and chosen from the whole world demanded means and time that we did not have. The Editors, who already had a heavy task, could not have undertaken this extra work without assistance, in particular from committees specifically chosen and brought together in the light of the subjects to be discussed. Taking into account the costs of travel and accommodation, the already high cost of the operation would have almost doubled. No doubt a day will come when, debates on themes and regions being easier than they are now, it will be possible to expound history as it is revealed by a confrontation of knowledge and viewpoints on particular questions concerning all humanity.

Until the state of knowledge and of historical research in the world has reached this convergent point, we are obliged to give up the idea of showing the divergences that future workshops of historians will have to face. We have, however provided notes at the end of articles, which have been written so as to ensure maximum diversity and the broadest possible participation. A certain arbitrariness persists, of course. But this will remain unavoidable as long as the excesses that analyses lead to are not minimized through the elaboration of syntheses based on criteria derived from irrefutable logical presuppositions – presuppositions that help establish universal certitudes. Let us not forget, however, that innovations originate only within the gaps of certitude.

One of the merits of this work lies in that it has succeeded in enlisting the collaboration of a very large number of people, representing a large number of regions and cultures. The Commission also encouraged the formation of local working groups responsible for obtaining and organizing the data to be included in the various chapters. This present work marks perhaps only the beginning of such collective efforts. Nevertheless, it permits us to anticipate satisfactory results. Knowing oneself well in order to make oneself better known constitutes a major contribution to mutual understanding. In this respect, historical research resembles an awareness of unconscious phenomena. It brings into the daylight what in the nocturnal depths of individual or collective existences gives them life, so to say, in spite of themselves or against their will.

This publication will no doubt give rise to many criticisms. If these turn out to be harsh, they will justify the project, whose main objective is to arouse us from our dogmatic slumber. Historical events take care of this much more efficiently, but at a much higher price.

GENERAL INTRODUCTION

Georges-Henri Dumont, President
of the International Commission

Societies are making greater demands than ever on history, but urgent as they might be, these demands by various groups are not altogether straightforward. Some societies look to historians to define their identity, to buttress the development of their specific characteristics or even to present and analyse the past as confirming a founding myth. Conversely, other societies, influenced both by the *Annales* school of historiography and by the geographical, chronological and thematic enlargement of history, aspire to the building of bridges, the ending of self-isolation and the smoothing out of the lack of continuity that is characteristic of the short term.

In 1946 those attending the meeting of the first Preparatory Commission of UNESCO agreed that it was part of the fundamental mission of the United Nations Educational, Scientific and Cultural Organization to lay the foundations for a collective memory of humanity and of all its parts, spread all over the world and expressing themselves in every civilization. The International Scientific Commission came into being four years later with the apparently gigantic task of drafting a *History of the Scientific and Cultural Development of Mankind*. Publication of the six volumes began in 1963, marking the successful conclusion of an international endeavour without parallel, but not without risks. Success with the general public was immediate and lasting, notwithstanding the reservations expressed by the critics, who often found certain choices disconcerting but were not consistent in the choices and interpretations they proposed as alternatives.

For its time – not the time of its publication but that of its long preparation – the first edition of the *History of the Scientific and Cultural Development of Mankind* must be seen as a daring achievement, having a number of faults inherent in the very nature of historical knowledge but opening up new avenues and encouraging further progress along them.

In 1978, the General Conference of UNESCO decided to embark on a new and completely revised edition of the *History of the Scientific and Cultural Development of Mankind* because it realized that the considerable development of historiography, the improvement of what are called its auxiliary sciences and its growing links with the social sciences had combined with an extraordinary acceleration of day-to-day history. What it did not know, however, was that the pace of this acceleration would continue to increase until it brought profound changes to the face of the world.

It scarcely needs saying that the task laid upon the International Scientific Commission, under the chairmanship of the late Paulo de Berrêdo Carneiro and then of my eminent predecessor, Professor Charles Morazé, was both enormous and difficult.

First of all, international teams had to be formed, as balanced as possible, and co-operation and dialogue organized between the different views of the major collective stages in the lives of people, but without disregarding the cultural identity of human groups.

Next, attention had to be given to changes in chronological scale by attempting a scientific reconstruction of the successive stages of the peopling of our planet, including the spread of animal populations. This was the goal pursued and largely attained by the authors of the present volume.

Lastly, steps had to be taken to ensure that traditional methods of historical research, based on written sources, were used side by side with new critical methods adapted to the use of oral sources and contributions from archaeology, in Africa for the most part.

To quote what Professor Jean Devisse said at a symposium in Nice in 1986 on 'Being a historian today': 'If we accept that the history of other people has something to teach us, there can be no infallible model, no immutable methodological certainty: listening to each other can lead to a genuine universal history.'

Although historians must be guided by a desire for intellectual honesty, they depend on their own views of things, with the result that history is the science most vulnerable to ideologies. The fall of the Berlin Wall a few weeks after I assumed office symbolized the end of a particularly burdensome ideological division. It certainly makes the work of the International Scientific Commission easier whenever it has to come to grips with the past–present dialectic from which history cannot escape.

In a way, the impact of ideologies will also be lessened by the fact that the Chief Editors of each volume have sought the invaluable co-operation not only of experienced historians but also of renowned specialists in disciplines such as law, art, philosophy, literature, oral traditions, the natural sciences, medicine, anthropology, mathematics and economics. In any event, this interdisciplinarity, which helps dissipate error, is undoubtedly one of the major improvements of this second edition of the *History of Humanity, Scientific and Cultural Development* over the previous edition.

Another problem faced was that of periodization. It was out of the question systematically to adopt the periodization long in use in European history, i.e. Antiquity, the Middle Ages, modern times, because it is now being extensively called into question and also, above all, because it would have led to a Eurocentric view of world history, a view whose absurdity is now quite obvious. The seven volumes are thus arranged in the following chronological order:

Volume I   Prehistory and the beginnings of civilization
Volume II   From the third millennium to the seventh century BC
Volume III From the seventh century BC to the seventh century AD
Volume IV   From the seventh to the sixteenth century
Volume V   From the sixteenth to the eighteenth century
Volume VI   The nineteenth century
Volume VII The twentieth century.

It must be stated at once that this somewhat surgical distribution is in no way absolute or binding. It will in no way prevent the overlapping that there must be at the turn of each century if breaks in continuity and the resulting errors of perspective are to be avoided. Indeed, it has been said that we are already in the twenty-first century!

In his preface, Professor Charles Morazé has clearly described and explained the structure of each of the volumes, with a thematic chapter, a regional chapter and annexes. This structure, too, may be modified so as not to upset the complementarity of the pieces of a mosaic that must retain its significance.

When the International Scientific Commission, the Chief Editors of the volumes and the very large number of contributors have completed their work – and this will be in the near future – they will be able to adopt as their motto the frequently quoted saying of the philosopher Etienne Gilson:

We do not study history to get rid of it but to save from nothingness all the past which, without history, would vanish into the void. We study history so that what, without it, would not even be the past any more, may be reborn to life in this unique present outside which nothing exists.

This present will be all the more unique because history will have shown itself to be, not an instrument for legitimizing exacerbated forms of nationalism, but an instrument, ever more effective because ever more perfectible, for ensuring mutual respect, solidarity and the scientific and cultural interdependence of humanity.

THE INTERNATIONAL COMMISSION

for the New Edition of the History of the Scientific and Cultural Development of Mankind

President: G.–H. Dumont (Belgium)

Members of the International Commission:

I. A. Abu-Lughod (United States of America)
A. R. Al-Ansary (Saudi Arabia)
J. Bony (Côte d'Ivoire)
E. K. Brathwaite (Barbados)
G. Carrera Damas (Venezuela)
A. H. Dani (Pakistan)
D. Denoon (Australia)
M. Garašanin (Yugoslavia, Fed. Rep. of)
T. Haga (Japan)
F. Iglesias (Brazil)
H. Inalcik (Turkey)
S. Kartodirdjo (Indonesia)
J. Ki-Zerbo (Burkina Faso)
C. Martinez Shaw (Spain)
E. Mendelsohn (United States of America)

E. M'Bokolo (Zaire)
K. N'Ketia (Ghana)
T. Obenga (Congo)
B. A. Ogot (Kenya)
Pang-Pu (China)
W. Sauerlander (Germany)
B. Schroeder-Gudehus (Ms) (Canada)
R. Thapar (Ms) (India)
I. D. Thiam (Senegal)
K. V. Thomas (United Kingdom)
S. L. Tikhvinsky (Russian Federation)
N. Todorov (Bulgaria)
G. Weinberg (Argentina)
M. Yardeni (Ms) (Israel)
E. Zürcher (the Netherlands)

Bureau of the International Commission:

A. R. Al-Ansary (Saudi Arabia)
E. K. Brathwaite (Barbados)
G. Carrera Damas (Venezuela)
A. H. Dani (Pakistan)
E. Mendelsohn (United States of America)

R. Thapar (Ms) (India)
I. D. Thiam (Senegal)
K. V. Thomas (United Kingdom)
S. L. Tikhvinsky (Russian Federation)
N. Todorov (Bulgaria)

Honorary Members:

S. A. Al-Ali (Iraq)
P. J. Riis (Denmark)
T. Yamamoto (Japan)

Former Presidents:

P. E. B. Carneiro (Brazil) (deceased)
C. Morazé (France)

Former Members:

E. Condurachi (Romania) (deceased)
G. Daws (Australia)
C. A. Diop (Senegal) (deceased)
A. A. Kamel (Egypt) (deceased)
M. Kably (Morocco)
H. Nakamura (Japan)
J. Prawer (Israel) (deceased)
S. Zavala (Mexico)

HISTORY OF HUMANITY
SCIENTIFIC AND CULTURAL DEVELOPMENT
IN SEVEN VOLUMES

VOLUME I

Prehistory and the Beginnings of Civilization

Editor: S. J. De Laet (Belgium)
Co-Editors: A. H. Dani (Pakistan)
           J. L. Lorenzo (Mexico)
           R. B. Nunoo (Ghana)

VOLUME II

From the Third Millennium to the Seventh Century BC

Editors: A. H. Dani (Pakistan)
          J.-P. Mohen (France)
Co-Editors: C. A. Diop (Senegal) (deceased)
           J. L. Lorenzo (Mexico)
           V. M. Masson (Russian Federation)
           T. Obenga (Congo)
           M. B. Sakellariou (Greece)
           B. K. Thapar (India)
           Xia Nai (China) (deceased)
           Zhang Changshou (China)

VOLUME III

From the Seventh Century BC *to the Seventh Century* AD

Editors: E. Condurachi (Romania) (deceased)
          J. Herrmann (Germany)
          E. Zürcher (the Netherlands)
Co-Editors: J. Harmatta (Hungary)
           J. Litvak (Mexico)
           R. Lonis (France)
           T. Obenga (Congo)
           R. Thapar (India)
           Zhou Yi-Liang (China)

VOLUME IV

From the Seventh to the Sixteenth Century

Editors: M. A. Al-Bakhit (Jordan)
          L. Bazin (France)
          S. M. Cissoko (Mali)
          A. A. Kamel (Egypt) (deceased)

Co-Editors: M. S. Asimov (Tajikistan)
           P. Gendrop (Mexico) (deceased)
           A. Gieysztor (Poland)
           I. Habib (India)
           J. Karayannopoulos (Greece)
           J. Litvak/P. Schmidt (Mexico)

VOLUME V

From the Sixteenth to the Eighteenth Century

Editors: P. Burke (United Kingdom)
          H. Inalcik (Turkey)
Co-Editors: I. Habib (India)
           J. Ki-Zerbo (Burkina Faso)
           T. Kusamitsu (Japan)
           C. Martinez Shaw (Spain)
           E. Tchernjak (Russian Federation)
           E. Trabulse (Mexico)

VOLUME VI

The Nineteenth Century

Editors: P. Mathias (United Kingdom)
          N. Todorov (Bulgaria)
Co-Editors: S. Al Mujahid (Pakistan)
           A. O. Chubarian (Russian Federation)
           F. Iglesias (Brazil)
           Shu-Li Ji (China)
           Iba Der Thiam (Senegal)

VOLUME VII

The Twentieth Century

Editors: E. K. Brathwaite (Barbados)
          S. Gopal (India)
          E. Mendelsohn (United States of America)
          S. L. Tikhvinsky (Russian Federation)
Co-Editors: I. A. Abu-Lughod (United States of America)
           Iba Der Thiam (Senegal)
           G. Weinberg (Argentina)
           Tao Wenzhao (China)

LIST OF FIGURES

1 Smelting bronze in a crucible before it is poured into moulds
2 Earliest iron objects
3 Table of the earliest analysed iron objects in the Ancient Classical world
4 Workers cutting, weaving and braiding thongs (tomb of Rekh-Mi-Re, Thebes, Egypt)
5 Examples of the use of cords in antiquity from Egyptian reliefs
6 Early Egyptian and Babylonian numerals
7 The changing design of the scratch-plough in northern Europe, shown in two rock engravings from Tanums Parish (Sweden)
8 The first evidence for the horse-drawn chariot in central Eurasia: a tomb-chamber under a burial mound at Sintasha (Russia)
9 Small votive model boats in gold leaf from Nors (Denmark)
10 Reconstruction of the boat from North Ferriby (United Kingdom)
11 Rock stippling of an archer on skis pursuing an elk (Russian Federation)
12 Skiing equipment of circumpolar Europe, Stone Age
13 Pictographs in proto-literate script, fourth millenium BC from Uruk (Iraq)
14 Scale drawings of a wagon, second millenium BC, from Barrow II, Lchashen (Armenia)
15 A slab carving of a horse-drawn chariot (Sweden)
16 Wheeled vehicles (Spain)
17 Wooden wheels in three segments (Italy)
18 Rock carvings of ox-drawn wagons and carts (Armenia)
19 Grave-slab with warrior, sword, spear, shield and chariot (Spain)
20 Bronze Age and Early Iron Age warriors
21 Hieroglyphic script
22 Pictographic origin of the cuneiform signs
23 West Semitic scripts and their descendants
24 Examples of Chinese pictograms and ideograms
25 The 'centre of gravity' of the Indo-European languages
26 Plan of a palatial building at Kalavassos-Ayios Dimitrios, 13th century BC (Cyprus)
27 Plan of the palace at Kish
28 Tablet with the first known Sumerian 'freedom' law
29 The obelisk temple of Byblos
30 Mari. Reconstitution of the Amorite palace viewed from a north-western angle.
31 Bronze plaque representing a prince wearing a Syrian cloak
32 Troy I-IX. Restored plan (Turkey)
33 Troy II c-g. Restored plan (Turkey)
34 Boghazköy (Hattusas). Restored plan (Turkey)
35 Relief of Tuthalia IV (1250–1220 BC) in the embrace of the god Sharruma (Turkey)
36 Axonometric projection of the round temple in Dashli-3, north Afghanistan
37 General table of the Bactrian culture
38 Principal buildings at the citadel mound of Mohenjo-daro
39 Harappan metropolis Kalibangan; period II
40 Typical mature Harappan pottery
41 The Indus bronze and copper vessels
42 The bronze and copper tools from Harappa and Mohenjo-daro
43 The cemetery H pottery and painted designs from Harappa
44 Chariot-and-horse pit in the Yin ruins (China)
45 Reconstruction of a large-sized house of the Western Zhou period (China)
46 Saharan rock painting of horse-drawn chariot
47 Relief carving of an Egyptian trading expedition to the 'Land of Punt'
48 Stone rasp and potsherd from Kintampo sites (Ghana)
49 Neolithic pottery from Okala (Gabon)
50 Rock painting at Genda Biftu (Ethiopia)
51 Rock painting of ox-drawn plough, Ba'ati Facada near Adigrat
52 Artefacts from Njoro River Cave (Kenya)
53 Wooden artefacts of the Late Stone Age from Gwisho Hotsprings (Zambia)
54 Rock painting showing people in trance, Barkly East (South Africa)
55 Similaun Man: reconstruction of his leather garment and shoes
56 Similaun Man: reconstruction of the jacket made of different coloured leather strips
57 Similaun Man: reconstruction of his leather cap and raffia cape
58 Man's and woman's costumes. Bronze Age. (Denmark)
59 Diagrammatic section of the flint-mining area of Spiennes (Belgium)

60 Flint extraction: mines and quarries at Saint-Mihiel (France)
61 Flint mine galleries radiating outwards from the main shaft, Grime's Graves (United Kingdom)
62 Deer-antler 'pick', Grime's Graves (United Kingdom)
63 Cores and blades: flints from Grand-Pressigny (France)
64 Copper Age: Malta and Sicily
65 Copper Age: Italian peninsula and Sicily
66 Copper Age: Sardinia, Spain, southern France
67 Early Bronze Age: Italy and Spain
68 Types of Middle Bronze Age dwellings
69 Historico-cultural area of timber-frame culture. Materials of artefacts from Volga region and Ukraine
70 Bell-shaped pottery (France)
71 Early Bronze Age tumulus and collared urns (United Kingdom)
72 Middle Bronze Age urns (France)
73 Middle Bronze excised pottery west-central France
74 Reconstruction of the settlement at Ilford Hill, Sussex (United Kingdom)
75 Warrior stelae, Estremadura (Spain)
76 Red Corded-ware culture pottery
77 Central Honshu Middle Jomon elaboratly decorated pottery
78 Early Yayoi burial types, varieties of double jars
79 Carved animal figures of the Upper Ob Neolithic culture (Russian Federation)
80 Fishhooks and daggers found in the Kitoi burials (Russian Federation)
81 Artefacts of the Neolithic tribes on the Lower Amur (Russian Federation)
82 The Afanasievo culture in southern Siberia (Russian Federation)
83 The Okunev culture in southern Siberia (Russian Federation)
84 Bowls and jars of the Andronovo pottery (Russian Federation)
85 The Karasuk culture in southern Siberia (Russian Federation)
86 The Glazkovo culture in eastern Siberia (Russian Federation)
87 Reconstruction of the clothing of a woman of the Glazkovo culture (Russian Federation)
88 Bronze artefacts of the Shiversky stage, eastern Siberia (Russian Federation)
89 The Formative period
90 Figurines from Tlatilco, Valley of Mexico
91 Olmec art: colossal axes and plaque-like axes
92 Suggested reconstruction of the Temple of Cerro Sechin, Chavín culture (Peru)
93 Eagle from the 'New Temple' at Chavín de Huántar (Peru)
94 Basalt sculpture from San Lorenzo (Veracruz)
95 Reproductions of excised motifs on the body of pottery of the Olmec civilization
96 Olmec civilization: symbols and styles of Period II (900–700 BC)
97 Monumental art from the La Venta site, Tabasco
98 Chronological table with radiocarbon datings from the westernmost ports of South America
99 Semi-sedentary encampment of hollowed-out circular dwellings with cemented stone walls, Huelén-42 (Chile)
100 Sequence of settlements (Chile)
101 Sequence of dated settlements in the central-southern Andean region (Chile)
102 The emergence of cultural complexity and food production in Chile
103 South American members of the Camelidae family

LIST OF MAPS

1 Map of the principal means of food procurement in the world *c.* 1500 BC

2 The effects of improved varieties of maize and irrigation technology on the productivity of the Oaxaca Valley, Mexico, between 1300 and 300 BC

3 Language distribution in ancient Africa; written languages in ancient Mesoamerica and China

4 Written languages in the ancient western Asia and North Africa

5 The distribution of the major branches of the Indo-European languages, *c.* 500 BC

6 Various recent solutions to the homeland problem for Indo-Europeans

7 Egypt and Nubia (3000–700 BC)

8 The Aegean world: 2000–1100 BC

9 The Greek world: 1100–700 BC

10 Cyprus. Major archaeological sites (3000–700 BC)

11 Mesopotamia: archaeological sites of modern towns

12 Syria and Palestine (3000–700 BC)

13 Anatolia during the time of the Hittites

14 Distribution of Indus civilization during the mature and later periods, *c.* 2500–1500 BC

15 Post-Indus civilization: Chalcolithic cultures and copper hoards

16 Post-Indus civilization: Megalithic cultures

17 Post-Indus civilization: distribution of Painted Grey Ware

18 China (1600–700 BC)

19 Map of Africa, showing sites mentioned in text

20 Distribution of rock paintings in eastern and southern Africa

21 Europe

22 Principal areas of Chalcolithic and Bronze Age Rock Art

23 Island South-East Asia

24 Korea

25 Australia

26 Outline map of North America, showing the location of various archaic cultures and traditions

27 Mesoamerica: principal sites of the Olmec civilization (1250–600 BC)

28 The Andean empires

29 Centre-south, southern and far south Andean areas and Patagonian archipelago region. Location of the main sites mentioned in text

LIST OF PLATES

1 Palace of Sargon II at Khorsabad
2 Late Bronze Age hoard of tools and jewellery (Hungary)
3 Bronze foundry debris from Fort-Harrouard (France)
4 Stonehenge: trilithons (United Kingdom)
5 Stonehenge from the North East (United Kingdom)
6 Egyptian painted bas-relief containing many figures from the hieroglyphic numbering system
7 The cubit (525 mm), an ancient Egyptian measure of length
8 Egyptian scribes drawing up the accounts for a burial ground; 5th dynasty
9 Tree crops in Mesopotamia: relief from the palace of the Assyrian king Sennacherib
10 Fortifications of the Hittite Empire, 1450–1200 BC.
11 Statue of Goudea seated
12 Rock stippling of Bronze Age ships (Sweden)
13 Bronze armour from Marmesse (France)
14 Detail from the Book of the Dead of Nebqued (Egypt)
15 Statue menhir, Mas d'Azaïs (France)
16 Rock design in Magnificent Gallery (Australia)
17 The pyramids of Giza (Egypt)
18 Volcanic-rock portrait of Amenemhat III
19 Egyptian scribe sitting cross-legged
20 Seated alabaster statuette of Abikhil
21 Stela of Djedkhonouioufankh: Amon's musician playing the harp
22 Narmer Palette (Egypt)
23 Detail from the Book of the Dead of Nebqued (Egypt)
24 Collar from the Middle Kingdom found at Illahun (Egypt)
25 Model of soldiers from the 11th dynasty, found at Asyût (Egypt)
26 A-Group culture, Nubia
27 Fortress of Buhen, Nubia
28 King Hor, 13th dynasty (Egypt)
29 Statue of Thuthmosis III (Egypt)
30 The famous scribe and architect Amenhotep (Egypt)
31 Gilded chapel from the Tutankhamen treasuries (Egypt)
32 Alabaster head rest from the Tutankhamen treasuries (Egypt)
33 Great Temple, Abu Simbel
34 Temple of Wadi es Sebua, Nubia
35 Ramses II crowned by Horus and Set (Egypt)
36 Statue of Ramses V offering a *naos* (Egypt)

37 Early Cycladic marble figurine of a harp-player (Greece)
38 Early Cycladic marble statue of a female figure (Greece)
39 Early Cycladic marble vase (Greece)
40 Early Cycladic clay container with painted linear decoration (Greece)
41 The Phaistos Disk with hieroglyphic writing (Greece)
42 Clay tablet with inscriptions in the Linear A script (Greece)
43 Wall-painting of a woman from Mycenae (Greece)
44 Golden funerary mask from Mycenae (Greece)
45 Golden cup from Vapeio (Greece)
46 Wall-painting of the flotilla from Thera (Greece)
47 Middle Cycladic clay jug with painted decoration of swallows from Thera (Greece)
48 Middle Minoan clay crater with flowers in relief (Greece)
49 Wall-painting of bull-leaping (Greece)
50 Late Minoan faience statuette of the 'Snake Goddess' (Greece)
51 Late Minoan ritual vessel in the shape of a bull's head (Greece)
52 Late Minoan ritual vessel of rock-crystal (Greece)
53 Middle Geometric krater from Kerameikos (Greece)
54 Middle Geometric ivory statuette (Greece)
55 Late Geometric krater from Dipylon (Greece)
56 Bronze horse found at Olympia (Greece)
57 Late Geometric bronze statuette from Olympia (Greece)
58 Late Geometric bronze statuette found at Olympia (Greece)
59 Tabular idol from Cyprus, red lustre ware, end of third millennium
60 Group of clay figures surrounding a trough; Middle Bronze Age
61 Bronze statue from Enkomi of an armed god (Cyprus)
62 Ivory throne from a 'Royal Tomb' at Salamis (Cyprus)
63 Bronze head from Nineveh depicting Naram-Sin
64 Sandstone 'Victory stela' of Naram-Sin
65 Aerial photograph of the Sumerian city of Ur
66 The ziggurat of the moon god Nana
67 Gypsum statuette of a man holding a goblet from Eshnunna
68 Akkadian cylinder seal
69 The so-called 'Standard of Ur'
70 The sun god Shamash presenting the 'law of the land' to Hammurabi

71 Ebla (Tell Mardikh): stone ritual basin from temple D
72 Syrian cylinder seal with gold moundt
73 Impression of a cylinder of Sumirapa, king of Tuba
74 Impression of Syrian cylinder seal
75 Impression of Syrian cylinder seal of Hyksos period
76 Pectoral in Egyptian style from Byblos
77 Bronze statuette, probably from Qatna
78 Ivory seated goddess of fertility from Ugarit
79 Relief of Kilamuwa with a Phoenician inscription
80 Ritual standard in the form of a stag. Hattian style (Turkey)
81 Ritual standard representing the cosmos. Hattian style (Turkey)
82 Golden clasp with fitted pin. Hattian style (Turkey)
83 Twin idol; sheet gold. Hattian style (Turkey)
84 Golden flagon. Hattian style (Turkey)
85 Jug and the view of its base; gold. Hattian style (Turkey)
86 Hattian female statuette (Turkey)
87 Jug; clay with reddish-brown slip. Hittite style (Turkey)
88 Beaker-jug; clay with reddish-brown slip. Hittite style (Turkey)
89 Pair of ritual vessels in the form of bulls. Hittite imperial style (Turkey)
90 Orthostat relief from the city walls of Alaca Hüyük. Hittite style (Turkey)
91 Rock reliefs of the Hittite open-air sanctuary in Yazilikaya, Boghazköy (Turkey)
92 Hittite ritual silver vessel in the form of a stag (Turkey)
93 The Goddess Kupaba; fragment of an orthostat relief. Neo-Hittite art (Turkey)
94 Detail from an orthostat relief of a chimaira. Neo-Hittite art (Turkey)
95 Tomb stela of Tarhunpias. Neo-Hittite Aramaean art (Turkey)
96 Orthostat relief of nursing mother with child from Karatepe. Neo-Hittite Phoenicianizing style (Turkey)
97 Silver Urartian situla (Turkey)
98 Clay Phrygian vessel. Transitional style (Turkey)
99 Clay Phrygian vase. Ripe Phrygian style (Turkey)
100 Bronze Phrygian fibulae. Ripe Phrygian style (Turkey)
101 Gold seal from Bactria, north Afghanistan
102 Stone cylinder seal from Bactria, north Afghanistan
103 Rock art from Jubba (Saudi Arabia)
104 Dilmun-type seals from Failaka (Kuwait)
105 Lihyanite inscription from Hereibh (Saudi Arabia)
106 Kalibangan: excavated thoroughfare in the lower city
107 Kalibangan: cylinder-seal and its impression
108 Kalibangan: grave with extended skeleton and pottery
109 Large-sized tomb at Taosi (China)
110 Pottery gui and li from Keshengzhuang (China)
111 Palace foundation in the ruined Shang city, Yanshi (China)
112 Aerial view of the Yin ruins near Anyang city (China)
113 Bronze ritual vessel from the Yin ruins (China)
114 Mould of a bronze vessel from the Yin ruins (China)
115 Squatting jade human figurine from the Yin ruins (China)
116 Jade elephants from the Yin ruins (China)
117 Ivory cup inlaid with turquoise from the Yin ruins (China)
118 Oracle bone with inscriptions from the Yin ruins (China)
119 Yin bronze axe with human mask (China)
120 Foal-shape zun vessel (China)
121 Western Zhou jade animal mask (China)
122 Western Zhou glazed pottery jar (China)
123 Restored Western Zhou laquer dou (China)
124 Rubbing of the inscription on a basin, Western Zhou dynasty (China)
125 Western Zhou bronze vessel with inscription (China)
126 Pottery li with patterns painted after baking (China)
127 Huge bronze human figure from Guanghan County (China)
128 View in the Ahaggar highlands of southernmost Algeria
129 Rock-painting of cattle-herders, Sefar, Tassili
130 Rock painting at Arakoukam, Algeria
131 Rock engraving of boat, animals and people in the Wadi el-Barramiya (Egypt)
132 Neolithic stone houses at Dhar Tichitt, Mauritania
133 Neolithic potsherds with seed-impressions of cultivated cereals (Mauritania)
134 Rock shelters at Ele Bor, northern Kenya
135 Nderit ware pottery bowl from central Kenya
136 Rock painting of eland and hunter in the Transkei region (South Africa)
137 Rock engraving of a farming scene, Val Camonica (Italy)
138 Late Bronze Age stone mould for casting bronze sceptre shafts
139 Cart from Dupljaja (Federal Republic of Yugoslavia)
140 Idol from a cremation cemetery at Korbovo (Federal Republic of Yugoslavia)
141 Early Bronze Age clay hanging vessel (Hungary)
142 Early Bronze Age clay bell-shaped vessel (Hungary)
143 Middle Bronze Age clay vessel with handle (Hungary)
144 Middle Bronze Age horn disk, possibly the base of a whip handle (Hungary)
145 Middle Bronze Age disc-shaped gold ornament (Romania)
146 Bracelet decorated with bulls' heads; gold and silver
147 Middle Bronze Age clay four-handled footed vessel (Hungary)
148 Middle Bronze Age carved horn bit branch
149 Middle Bronze Age clay vessel with base in the form of human feet (Hungary)
150 Late Bronze Age wide bracelet in gold plate (Hungary)
151 Late Bronze Age gold chain (Romania)
152 Late Bronze Age cast bronze pendant (Hungary)
153 Late Bronze Age clay urn (Hungary)
154 Late Bronze Age bronze object, possibly the hub-cap from a funeral car (Slovakia)
155 Hoard from Stockhult, Scania (Sweden)
156 Rock painting from Val Camonica (Italy)
157 Anthropomorphic stela with symbolic composition, Val Camonica (Italy)
158 Bronze Age engravings from the Vallée des Merveilles (France)
159 Rock painting of Bronze Age ships (Sweden)
160 Class 2 tools and Jomon pottery (Japan)
161 Rock engravings from Tasmania
162 A mimi hunter in a rock painting in Kakadu (Australia)
163 Stencil art and an engraved vulva in the Carnavon Gorge National Park (Australia)
164 A dingo painted in red ochre with white outline (Australia)
165 Copper artefacts of the Old Copper Culture (USA)
166 Jadeite celt from Oaxaca (Mexico)
167 Jadeite head from Tenango del Valle (Mexico)
168 Monument 34 of San Lorenzo (Mexico)
169 Black vessel from Tlatilco with Olmec excised motifs (Mexico)

THE CONTRIBUTORS

Akurgal, Ekrem (Turkey); spec. archaeology and history of Anatolia, Dr.h.c.; Holder of The Goethe Medal; Visiting Professor, Universities of Princeton, USA, Berlin and Vienna; Member of 7 foreign academies.

Al-Ansary, Abdul Rahman (Saudi Arabia); spec. pre-Islamic history and archaeology of the Arabian Peninsula; Dean, College of Arts, King Saud University.

Alcina Franch, José (Spain); spec. archaeology and ethnohistory of Mesoamerica and the Andean area. Complutense University, Madrid.

An Zhimin (China); spec. Neolithic archaeology of China; Chief, Section I (Neolithic) and Deputy Director, Archaeology Institute of the Chinese Academy of Social Sciences.

Beyer, Dominique (France); spec. Syro-Mesopotamian archaeology, formerly Curator, Department of Oriental Antiquities, Musée du Louvre, Paris; Professor, University of Strasbourg II.

Briard, Jacques (France); spec. European Bronze Age, Megalithism of Britanny, Palaeometallurgy. Research Director C.N.R.S.; Director, Laboratory Anthropology Université Rennes l, Professor, University Haute-Bretagne (Prehistory).

Dandamaev, Muhammad A. (Russian Federation); spec. history of the Ancient Near East; Head of the Department of Ancient Oriental Studies, Institute for Oriental Studies, Saint Petersburg.

Dani, Ahmad Hasan (Pakistan); spec. archaeology; Professor, University of Islamabad; Director, Centre for the Study of Central Asian Civilizations. Member of numerous national and international academic bodies.

De Laet, Sigfried Jan (Belgium); spec. Roman history, European archaeology and prehistory; Chief Editor, History of Scientific and Cultural Development of Humanity, Volume I. Member of the Royal Academy of Sciences, Letters and Fine Arts of Belgium.

Derevyanko, Anatoly P. (Russian Federation); spec. prehistory of Siberia. Corresponding member of the Russian Academy of Sciences.

Diop-Maes, Louise Marie (France and Senegal); spec. demogeography and historical demography of sub-saharan Africa; Doctor of anthropogeography (University of Paris I).

Dittmann, Reinhard (Germany); spec. archaeology of the ancient Near and Middle East; Professor, Free University, Berlin.

Doumas, Christos (Greece); spec. archaeology of the Aegean world; Supervisor, Antiquities in various regions of Greece; Director, Antiquities at the Ministry of Culture; Professor, University of Athens.

Ecsedy, Istvan (Hungary); spec. Neolithic Period and Copper Age of Central and South-East Europe; Director, Janus Pannonius Museum, Pécs.

Edens, Christopher (USA); spec. Bronze Age and Iron Age of Western Asia, especially Arabia; Research Associate, Peabody Museum, Harvard University, Cambridge, Massachusetts.

Flood, Josephine M. (Australia); spec. cultural heritage of the Aborigines; Principal Conservation Officer, Australian Heritage Commission in Canberra.

Fowler, Melvin L. (USA); spec. archaeology of Central and Southern United States and Central Mexico; Professor of Anthropology, University of Wisconsin-Milwaukee.

Heredia, Osvaldo Raimundo, deceased 1989 (Argentina); spec. archaeology of South America.

Higham, Charles (New Zealand); spec. archaeology of mainland South-East Asia; Professor of Anthropology, University of Otago, Dunedin, New Zealand; Fellow, Society of Antiquaries of London, Royal Society of New Zealand; Former fellow, St John's College, Cambridge.

Jakobson, Vladimir A. (Russian Federation); spec. history of the Ancient Near East, cuneiform law; Head of the Group of the Philology of Ancient Orient, Oriental Institute, Saint Petersburg.

Kaelas, Lili (Sweden); spec. European Neolithic, megaliths, post-glacial rock art; Guest Professor, Universities of Gothenburg and Oslo and the University of California (Los Angeles). Member, Göteborgs Kungl. Vetenskaps och Vitterhets Samhälle (Royal Society of Arts and Sciences in Gothenburg).

Karageorghis, Vassos (Cyprus); spec. Classical archaeology; Visiting Professor, Universities of Laval, Oxford, Princeton, Ecole Française des Hautes Etudes; Member, Royal Swedish Academy, Académie des Inscriptions et Belles Lettres; Foreign member, Academy of Athens.

Katincharov, Roumen (Bulgaria); spec. archaeology of prehistoric Bulgaria; former Scientific Secretary of the Archaeological Institute, Bulgarian Academy of Sciences; Director-General of the State Culture Historical Heritage Union of the Committee of Culture.

Klengel, Horst (Germany); spec. ancient Oriental history, Assyriology, Hittitology. Professor, Humboldt University Berlin.

Kobayashi, Tatsuo (Japan); spec. prehistory of Japan and ethnoarchaeology of north-west coast native peoples of North America; Professor, Kokugakuin University in Tokyo.

Kovacs, Tibor (Hungary); spec. Bronze Age archaeology of Central and South-East Europe; Deputy Director General, Hungarian National Museum, Budapest.

Lam, Aboubacry M. (Senegal); spec. relations between ancient Egypt and Black Africa, Université Cheikh Anta Diop de Dakar.

Lam, Massamba (Senegal); spec. Neolithic civilizations of Africa; former Director of the Department of Prehistory and Protohistory, Institut Fondamental d'Afrique Noire; Director of the Museum of African Arts, Dakar.

Lamberg-Karlovsky, C. C. (USA); spec. archaeology of ancient Near East, Stephen Phillips Professor of Archaeology; Curator of Near Eastern archaeology, Peabody Museum, Harvard University.

Leclant, Jean (France); spec. Egyptology; Honorary Professor at Collège de France; Permanent Secretary of the Académie des Inscriptions et Belles-Lettres, Paris.

Liverani, Mario (Italy); spec. history of the Ancient Near East; Professor, University of Rome; Member, Academia Europaea.

Lumbreras Salcedo, Luis Guillermo (Peru); spec. Pre-Columbian archaeology of the Andean region; Professor, Universidad Nacional Mayor de San Marcos in Lima.

Mallory, J. P. (UK); spec. archaeology of Indo-European-speaking peoples; Senior Lecturer, Department of Archaeology and Palaeoecology, Queen's University, Belfast.

Masson, Vadim M. (Russian Federation); spec. history of Central Asia; Corresp. member, Academy of Sciences of Turkmenia, Deutsches archäol. Institut and IsMEO (Rome); Member, Royal Danish Academy of Sci. and Lit., Society of Antiquaries (London), Institute of Archaeology of the Russian Academy of Sciences.

Merpert, Nikolai J. (Russian Federation); spec. Neolithic and Bronze Age in the European part of the Russian Federation; Professor, Chief of Neolithic and Bronze Age Section at the Institute of Archaeology, of the Russian Academy of sciences.

Mohen, Jean-Pierre (France); spec. Neolithic and Metal ages; Director of the Musée des Antiquités Nationales, Saint Germain-en-Laye, Director Unity CNRS; Director, Laboratoire de Recherche des Musées de France.

Mokhtar, Gamal (Egypt); spec. history and archaeology of Ancient Egypt; formerly President of the Egyptian Organisation of Monuments, Professor at Alexandria University.

Mughal, Mohammad Rafique (Pakistan); spec. protohistory of South Asia; General Director of Archaeology and Museums, Government of Pakistan; formerly Archaeological Advisor to the Government of Bahrain; Visiting Scholar and Lecturer, Universities of California, Berkeley and Pennsylvania, Philadelphia.

Niederberger, Christine (France); spec. human relations with the palaeo-environment, traditional agrarian techniques and economic systems; socio-political and iconographic aspects of early Mesoamerica and the Olmec civilization at the Centre of Mexican and Central American Studies, Mexico.

Nishitani, Tadashi (Japan); spec. East Asian archaeology; Professor, Department of Archaeology, Faculty of Literature, Kyushu University at Fukuoka.

Núñez Atencio, Lautaro (Chile); spec. prehistoric archaeology of the southern part of South America; Professor and co-founder of the Institute of Archaeological Research at the Northern University in Atacama. Member, Chilean Academy of Social Sciences.

Obenga, Théophile (Congo); spec. ancient history of Africa and civilizations of the Nile Valley; Professor, University of Brazzaville; Member of the Société Française d'Egyptologie.

Peroni, Renato (Italy); spec. of European and Mediterranean Bronze and Iron Age; Professor for European Protohistory, University of Rome.

Phillipson, David W. (UK); spec. archaeology of East and Southern Africa; Curator, Archaeology and Anthropology Museum, University of Cambridge.

Rahman, Abdul (Pakistan); Professor of Archaeology, University of Peshawar; contributed to studies on Shahi Dynasty; excavated many archaeological sites in Swat, Dir and Peshawar valley; catalogued coins in the Peshawar Museum; presently working in advisory capacity for archaeology with North-West frontier government.

Rector, Monica (Brazil/USA); spec. linguistics and communication, Universidade Federal Fluminense, Rio de Janeiro; presently Associate Professor, Department of Romance Languages, University of North Carolina, Chapel Hill.

Reineke, Walter F. (Germany); spec. Egyptology and ancient history of sciences; Professor, Berlin-Brandenburgian Academy of Sciences, Berlin Dictionary of Egyptian Language.

Ries, Julien (Belgium); spec. history of religions; Prof. Emeritus, University of Louvain-la-Neuve (Belgium); Director of Centre d'histoire des religions, Louvain-la-Neuve.

Roux, Georges (France); Doctor; spec. Assyriology.

Sakellariou, Michael (Greece); spec. ancient Greek history; formerly Professor, University of Thessaloniki, and Director, Centre for Greek and Roman Antiquity, Athens. Member, Academy of Athens; foreign member, Accademia Nationale dei Lincei; corresp. member Académie des Inscriptions et Belles Lettres and Accademia Pontaniana. President, Foundation for Hellenic Culture.

Sall, Babacar (Senegal); spec. ancient civilizations of the Nile Valley; Dept. of History, University C. Anta Diop, Dakar.

Sanoja Obediente, Mario (Venezuela); spec. archaeology and anthropology of the northern part of South America; Research Fellow, Smithsonian Institution, U.S. National Museum in Washington D.C.; Member, National Academy of History, Venezuela.

Sarianidi, Victor (Russian Federation); spec. archaeology of Central Asia; Member, Institute of Archaeology, Russian Academy of Sciences.

Sherratt, Andrew (UK); spec. Old World archaeology and history, especially prehistoric Europe; Senior Keeper, Ashmolean Museum, University of Oxford.

Solheim II, Wilhelm G. (USA); spec. prehistory of South-East Asia; Professor Emeritus, Department of Anthropology, University of Hawaii Manoa, Honolulu.

Tasić, Nikola (Federal Republic of Yugoslavia); spec. prehistory of Central and South-East Europe; Director, Institute for Balkan Studies, Member of the Serbian Academy of Sciences and Arts; Active member of the European Academy of Sciences and Arts.

Thapar, B. K. (India); spec. archaeology of West and South Asia, particularly the Neolithic and Chalcolithic periods. Former Director-General, Archaeological Survey of India; presently Chairman, Centre for Cultural Resources and Training; Secretary, Indian National Trust for Art and Cultural Heritage, New Delhi.

Thrane, Henrik (Denmark); spec. Bronze Age and settlement archaeology; Curator Fyns Oldtid, Hollufgård; member of Dan. Research Council for the Humanities.

Villard, Pierre (France); spec. Assyriology; Assistant Professor, University of Paris I.

Wright, Rita (USA); spec. archaeology of Iran, Indus Valley and analysis of ceramic technology. Associate Professor of Anthropology, New York University.

Wurm, Stephen A. (Australia); spec. linguistics of the Pacific area, East, North and Central Asia, ancient and modern Near East, and Arctic areas; Language in society, language and culture; Professor of Linguistics, Australian National University; Research Director, and Immediate Past President, Australian Academy of the Humanities; President of CIPSH-UNESCO.

Zhang, Changshou (China); spec. archaeology of Shang and Zhou periods in China. Former Deputy Director of the Institute of Archaeology, Chinese Academy of Sciences.

Ziegler, Christiane (France); spec. Egyptian archaeology; General Curator, Department of Egyptian Antiquities, Musée du Louvre; Professor of Egyptian Archaeology, Ecole du Louvre.

ACKNOWLEDGEMENTS

The UNESCO International Commission for a New Edition of the History of the Scientific and Cultural Development of Humanity elaborated, following a decision of the General Conference in 1978, the concept of this 'new edition'.

The UNESCO International Commission, the authors and the publishers wish to thank all those who have kindly given permission for the reproduction of the plates in this book.

The Chief Editors of this volume wish to pay tribute to the support received from the Presidents of the Commission, Professor Paulo E. de Berrêdo Carneiro, until his death in 1982, Professors Charles Morazé and Georges-Henri Dumont; from their Co-Editors, Zhang Changshou, José Luis Lorenzo, Vadim M. Masson, Théophile Obenga, Michael B. Sakallariou, B. K. Thapar, the late Cheikh A. Diop and the late Xia Nai; from all the authors of chapters, from the members of the Reading Committee, and finally from all the members of the UNESCO Secretariat involved in the venture. They would especially like to thank Professor S. J. De Laet for acting as consultant.

UNESCO also wishes to express its gratitude to the Islamic Call Society for its generous financial assistance to this project.

A

INTRODUCTION

PREHISTORY TO HISTORY

Sigfried J. De Laet

Towards 3100 BC, at the start of the period dealt with in this volume, humanity already had a past which stretched back to some two and a half million years, and it had gone through 99.5 per cent of its existence from the emergence of the first being who can be classified under the genus *Homo* to the present day.

We shall not return here to the distinction usually drawn between the prehistoric age – the period before the appearance of writing – and the historical period in the strict sense of the word, or to the vast, almost unimaginable, duration of this most ancient of human adventures. The reader will find further details on this subject in the General Introduction to Volume I. It should nevertheless be pointed out that Volume I, in spite of the length of time it covers, restricts itself to the period when all populations were still ignorant of writing, and prehistory was still far from nearing its end. In the two and a half thousand years covered by this volume, the knowledge of writing was in fact limited to a handful of regions, and the great majority of populations were still in the prehistoric stage.

Volume III will continue to deal with preliterate populations. Even today, in certain regions of the world, there survive some rare tribes who do not seem to have gone past the Neolithic or even the Palaeolithic stage. These tribes provide material for cultural anthropology and ethnology; their cultures, with their specific values, will naturally feature in the later volumes of the present work.

The unspecialized reader will perhaps be surprised by the enormous chronological disproportion between the different volumes of this *History of Humanity*: two and half million years are condensed into a single volume, whereas the last five millennia are given six volumes. Two reasons can be advanced for this difference in treatment.

In the first place, the scientific study of prehistory is still relatively young (barely one and a half centuries old); it is moreover founded mainly on unwritten sources (mostly archaeological and anthropological), whose interpretation is difficult and often unreliable; finally, each year leads to new discoveries which cast old interpretations into doubt. Prehistory is today therefore still in constant evolution, and resembles a jigsaw puzzle in which many pieces are missing and others have not yet fallen into place. The Afterword to Volume I points out some of the main gaps in our knowledge and indicates some of the fresh problems confronting prehistorians. It will be noted that the space allocated to prehistory in the *History of Humanity* is more than double the amount it received in the 1963 edition, which clearly reflects

the progress achieved in a quarter of a century. Furthermore, it is clear that most of the information pertaining to preliterate times is still buried in the ground, awaiting new excavations to bring it gradually to the surface.

The second consideration stems from what is generally called 'the acceleration of history'. For hundreds of millennia, indeed millions of years, the cultural progress achieved by the ancestors of *Homo*, and later by humans themselves, was extremely slow, certain periods giving the impression of stagnation and of even being at a complete standstill. However, as we draw nearer to our present state of civilization, the intervals between the main stages of progress become shorter, and the dates representing historical milestones come closer to each other. An outline of this development is provided in the Afterword to Volume I; it will therefore suffice to recall here some of these stages along with their approximate dates:

- the first primates appeared some 60 million years ago;
- *Kenyapithecus* seems to have been the first primate to *use* tools (*tool-user*) some 14 million years ago;
- the dichotomy between the Panini (ancestors of the gorilla and chimpanzee) from the hominids (ancestors of *Australopithecus* and *Homo*) took place about 5 or 6 million years ago;
- bipedalism appeared in the hominids about 4.5 million years ago;
- the first traces of the manufacture of tools go back 2 to 2.5 million years; this *tool-maker*, the earliest being to be classified under the genus *Homo*, is *Homo habilis*;
- a more developed human, *Homo erectus*, appeared around 1.8 million years ago;
- after remaining confined to southern and eastern Africa for more than half a million years, *Homo erectus* began to move outwards 1 million years ago: specimens are to be found in temperate Europe 900,000 years ago, in China 700,000 years ago, and in Java a little later;
- the mastery of fire by *Homo erectus* goes back half a million years;
- after a long existence of nearly 1.5 million years, *Homo erectus* developed through different regional phyletic lines into *Homo sapiens* (*H. sapiens* with Mongoloid features in East Asia; *H. sapiens* with Australoid features in Indonesia, *H. sapiens neanderthalensis* in Europe and West Asia and, finally, *H. sapiens sapiens* about 130,000 to 100,000 years ago in Africa).

The emergence of *H. sapiens* was accompanied by a considerable acceleration of progress. Instead of counting in millions of years, prehistorians start to count in thousands.

The Middle Palaeolithic (which in Europe and West Asia corresponds to the Neanderthal age) and the Middle Stone Age (which in Africa is the period of the first *H. sapiens sapiens*) spanned about 65,000 years at least, from 100,000 years (and even earlier in Africa) to about 35,000 years ago. It was during this period that humans, now in possession of an articulate language and able to form abstract ideas, began to bury their dead with a certain amount of ceremonial, denoting eschatological concerns, and executed their first few 'artistic' drawings.

Towards the end of this period, about 40,000 years ago, groups of people, who were already permanently occupying the periglacial regions of Europe and Asia, extended their zone of habitation to other continents; certain groups from Eastern Asia crossed the isthmus ('Beringia') which then linked Asia and America, and via Alaska gradually colonized the whole of America south to Tierra del Fuego. During the same period other groups from Indonesia colonized New Guinea, Australia and Tasmania.

The Upper Palaeolithic and Epipalaeolithic, which span the last part of the last glacial period and the beginning of the Holocene, lasted 'only' about 23,000 years, from approximately 35,000 to about 12,000 years ago. This began with a period when groups of advanced hunters used new weapons to pursue the large herbivores living in herds in the tundra, the steppes and the savannah; their spiritual culture was highly developed and their entire life was dominated by magical and religious beliefs and practices which were expressed in rock art, both engravings and paintings, small statuettes of female or zoomorphic figures, and funeral rites. Later, after the ice had receded, their way of life had to be adapted to the new environmental conditions and was thereafter based on specialized and selective hunting, fishing, and the gathering of edible plants, in short on the optimal use of their biotope. This mode of life required an empirical knowledge of the ethology, biology and physiology of game, and of the biological cycle of plants.

After this period, there was a gradual transition from 10,000 BC onwards to the Neolithic, characterized by the production of food (agriculture and stock-rearing). This transition, made possible by the knowledge of animal and plant biology acquired during the preceding period, was very gradual, but the consequences of the new mode of life were so important that the switch to food production is rightly considered to be one of the major turning-points in the development of human civilization. We shall not repeat here all these consequences which led to the formation of highly hierarchic social structures and to the birth of the first states (see Vol. I, Chapter 29). However, in the present context emphasis should be laid on a new and substantial acceleration of history, with barely 7,000 years separating the first village of farmers from the first city-state, and barely 5,000 years separating the latter from our own times.

The Neolithic saw the beginning of what we called (Vol. I, General Introduction) 'the diachronic development of civilizations'. It will therefore not be amiss, at the start of this volume, to take stock and consider the stage of civilization reached by the different populations of the world at the turn of the fourth millennium BC.

It should first of all be noted that practically all the inhabitable regions, even those which seemed the most inhospitable, as for example the arctic regions, were occupied. Only a few archipelagos and isolated islands in the Pacific were still uninhabited, the main one being the New Zealand archipelago.

Many populations of hunter-gatherers, well adapted to their environment and therefore under no pressure to alter their mode of life, perpetuated traditions dating back to the Epipalaeolithic. Towards the end of the fourth millennium BC these hunter-gatherers were still freely occupying vast regions, in particular all Africa south of the Sahara, North America north of central Mexico, South America excluding the equatorial and subtropical Andes, Australia and Tasmania, certain regions of South Asia (as for example the centre of southern India and Sri Lanka) and South-East Asia, and the arctic regions of Eurasia. Moreover, it cannot be ruled out that in certain regions which had already moved into the Neolithic age, groups of hunter-gatherers still existed in areas unsuited to stock-rearing and agriculture, living in symbiosis with the Neolithic peasants of neighbouring regions. It is worth remembering that some of these populations of hunter-gatherers were to adopt the Neolithic way of life during the period covered by this volume, whereas others perpetuated their ancestral customs sometimes even up to the present day. At the time those who switched to agriculture and stock-rearing probably did not, at least initially, consider this as a form of progress, but rather as a grim necessity in certain periods of crisis, for example when it was necessary to adapt to a new environment. At the beginning of the period covered by this volume, the communities engaged in agriculture and/or stock-rearing had reached highly unequal levels of development. In Meso-America, for example, although corn, beans and calabash were already being cultivated, these crops had not yet become the staple food, as their subsistence was still largely based on hunting and gathering. It was only towards the middle of the third millennium BC that the populations of these regions became completely sedentary.

The stage of sedentariness and village life had nevertheless been reached in very many regions. In the villages, houses in wattle and daub, sometimes even partly in stone, had replaced the caves and huts of previous eras. The two inventions of pottery and weaving usually appeared at the same time, to within a few centuries, as the switch to food production; this led to growing specialization of the activities of the inhabitants of these early villages. It was obviously necessary to regulate the relations between the inhabitants, for example between the farmers and the first artisans (potters, stone-cutters, weavers, carpenters, and so on) whose work had to be paid for in kind. It was also necessary to make arrangements for the inhabitants to collaborate in performing certain types of work in common (for example the erection of fortifications or irrigation works): hence the appearance of established practices, accepted by all, amounting to a sort of unwritten law. Agriculture and stock-rearing also brought an end to the system practised by groups of hunter-gatherers of equally sharing the proceeds of hunting and gathering: this solidarity and its cycle of reciprocity gave way to competition to possess as many resources as possible individually. The emergence of ownership accelerated the occurrence of theft, pillage and war. Wars between villages to appropriate the property of a neighbouring community were frequent, as indicated by the fact that most of the Neolithic villages were fortified. The social structure of these early Neolithic communities was still very simple, but the power of both the chief and the former shaman-magician had increased considerably. The erstwhile chief of the hunters became a 'king', with hereditary functions. It was he who regulated relations between the villagers according to the aforementioned unwritten code, and led the warriors in the event of war. The shaman-magician became the priest, regarded as the intermediary between the villagers and the gods, on whom the yield of the harvests and the fertility of the herds depended.

While the stage of development sketched above was still characteristic of many regions towards the end of the fourth millennium BC, it had nevertheless become a thing of the past elsewhere, with new forms of material progress gradually leading to the birth of the first city-states. A first consideration to be taken into account was a series of discoveries and technical achievements in stock-rearing (domestication of new species, beginnings of genetic engineering – castration), and agriculture (new food and textile crops, invention of the swing-plough, beginnings of irrigation and drainage which enabled vast stretches of too dry or too humid land to be brought under cultivation). All this resulted in large food surpluses, which provided the economic basis needed for the creation of the first city-states. The invention of the wheel (and thus of the cart) and of the sail made possible long-distance transportation and trade. Finally, metallurgy was discovered in West Asia, and later, independently, in the Balkans, Spain, Italy, China and South-East Asia.

The economic self-sufficiency of the Neolithic villages was disrupted by the production of food surpluses which could be used to establish trade between different communities for the procurement of consumer goods, raw materials, and soon also of luxury and prestige goods. Kings and priests appropriated these surpluses for themselves: they and their direct collaborators were responsible both for the furtherance of peaceful trading relations and for wars of conquest to procure raw materials (for example to build monumental palaces and temples) or precious objects to enhance their prestige.

It was during this transition period, which might be described as 'pre-urban', that the social stratification developed which was to reach its full extent only in the first city-states, though its beginnings and development can be traced from the archaeological remains of the sixth, fifth and fourth millennia BC. At the start of the period covered by this volume, stratification had been practically completed in Egypt and in Mesopotamia; it was already well advanced at the time in China and the Aegean world and to a lesser degree in South-East Europe, Spain and Italy. These cultural, social and economic developments will be dealt with at length in the present volume.

NOTE

Due to unavoidable circumstances certain texts, which were written in the mid-1980s, do not contain the most up-to-date data.

MAIN TRENDS OF THE NEW PERIOD

Ahmad Hassan Dani and Jean-Pierre Mohen

The great civilizations of this period have always been known through world-famous monuments such as the pyramids of Egypt or through texts such as those in the Bible. As early as the period of the Romantics, Heinrich Schliemann (1822–1890) began to read the *Iliad* in an attempt to discover Troy. He did indeed discover Troy, under the hill of Hissarlik in Anatolia. He then sought and found Mycenae, Tiryns and Orchomenus. Sir Arthur Evans in 1890 discovered Knossos, which he partially restored. Sir William Flinders Petrie (1853–1942) became famous throughout Egypt as a result of his excavation of the necropolises of Nagada and Abydos, and later excavations in Palestine. In 1922, Howard Carter uncovered, under rubble from a later period, the first of the sixteen steps which led down to the tomb of Tutankhamen who died around 1344 BC. Carter was working for Lord Carnarvon, who hastened out to Egypt to witness this fabulous discovery. In the period which followed, Sir Mortimer Wheeler (1890–1976) devised a method of excavation which divided the ground up into squares separated by earth walls. This method, which he used in England at Maiden Castle and in India at Harappa, was adopted by many archaeologists throughout the world to explore the sites of the period with which we are concerned. Meanwhile, the Abbé Breuil, that indefatigable traveller, revealed the rock art of Spain and South Africa. Matching the great monuments from this period which were already well known, and the famous prehistoric sites, was emerging a more recent prehistory covering every continent.

In 1949, the invention by an American chemist, Willard Libby (1908–80), of a dating system based on the radioactive traces of ^{14}C revolutionized archaeology thanks to its 'absolute' dating of organic traces in charcoal or bone. Exact chronological references were then obtained and pinned down by the 'calibration' of dates, according to a scale established through the study of the growth rings of trees, dendrochronology. The use of this type of analysis inaugurated an 'archaeometry' which made laboratory findings, in the widest sense of the term, essential for the period which concerns us: findings relating to physico-chemical dating, the definition of materials and the understanding of their chemical evolution, and the statistical processing of data.

In the 1970s and 1980s L. Binford and the Anglo-Saxon 'New Archaeology' established the historical study of processes, such as the settlement of a region, the domestication of plant and animal species, neolithization, the development of metallurgy, the sedentarization of activities and increasing trade. Meanwhile, the Marxist approach to archaeology kept as its objective the reconstitution of historical ethnology. Other points of view, whether topological or ecological or even those linked to specific events, provided a starting point for interesting overall views of the period.

Although archaeology provides the most common source of knowledge, other sources – philological, literary and historical – are available in certain regions and shed new light on the evolution of societies. The wide variety of approaches and of sources for study has led us to adopt two attitudes towards the contributions which follow.

First, we respect the views of each author, even if all the arguments they put forward do not concur. Often the different authors' views are complementary rather than mutually exclusive. For example, several more or less independent explanations have been put forward to take into account the coming of the Iron Age. Some attribute a key role to the Hittites, who invented iron metallurgy and were thus responsible for one of the major technical revolutions of the ancient world, giving rise to the Iron Age. Others tend rather to favour a social explanation for the new age, attributing it to a caste of horsemen coming from the steppes of Central Asia and spreading westwards the great metal sword. Egyptian specialists argue that it was the 'People of the Sea', sweeping down over the Nile Delta with their horses and iron swords who brought about the changes marking the beginning of the Iron Age.

Another vast problem which fuels passionate debate is that of the arrival of the Indo-Europeans. Some authors identify Indo-European units from the sixth millennium onwards. Others, more cautiously, link certain archaic linguistic aspects to the archaeological events of the Bronze Age of the second millennium BC, and even then speak only of a degree of Europeanization.

Secondly, we decided in this volume to take into account the written and literary sources which are available from 3000 BC onwards. These epigraphic records are of such importance that they enable us to have a well-rounded view of the past of certain regions, from historical, diplomatic, legal and economic standpoints.

One of the most original features of Volume II is the attempt to describe the beginning of history as defined by its written sources while also implying a sociological context and a conception of historical time of which the prehistoric period leaves no evidence. This difference seemed to us significant, bringing historians and prehistorians together, and we bore it in mind in our ordering of the articles in this volume. Thus the summary shows, after a section dealing with subject areas, a regional section which is divided into two parts; in the first subdivision we group together the first historical civilizations and in the second we review the civilizations which are known only from archaeological and anthropological evidence.

The beginnings of history introduce us to ancient history which is dated in relation to the birth of Christ. It is easy to understand why prehistorians talk of their period in relation to the present. They say that the skeleton known as Lucy is three-and-a-half million years old, that the use of fire goes back over 400,000 years or that the Lascaux caves were painted approximately 18,000 years ago. In these examples, reference to the historical period and in particular to the date of Christ's birth which historians use as a convenient baseline would be pointless. With this second volume, however, we reach the dawn of Western history, which we regard as beginning around 3000 BC with the appearance of writing, and it is customary to express this date in relation to the birth of Jesus Christ. Even though this custom is not shared by certain countries, it seemed logical to adopt throughout this volume and those that are to follow the most widely used historical system, namely that of dating before and after Christ.

We should also say that the chronological dividing lines chosen for this volume are perhaps more applicable to Western Asia, Egypt and Europe than to other parts of the world, such as sub-Saharan Africa, America or Oceania, and this should be borne in mind. Any division of historical time is artificial and, whatever the country, will require some refocusing, which is not always easy. The significant dates used in this volume are listed in the general chronological table at the end of the work.

TRADITIONS AND INNOVATION

Now that the basic features of the study have been described, we must outline the major innovations in the history of humanity from 3000 to 700 BC.

From a slow process of cultural development in the preliterate period of prehistory to a rapid rise to civilization is a phenomenal human achievement. How such a qualitative cultural change occurred and what actually took place in the first stages of urban development form the main subject of the present volume. The phenomenal change has been termed an 'urban revolution' by the Australian prehistorian Professor V. Gordon Childe (*Man Makes Himself: Man's Progress Through the Ages*, 1951), in contrast to the 'Neolithic revolution', seen in the emergence of a productive agricultural society during the last stages of prehistory. However, the term 'revolution' is hardly appropriate in either case, as development has unfolded through a long process of human activity. On the other hand, the word 'urban' overemphasizes the role of the city in the development of a civilization, appearing as it does in the early Neolithic (at Jericho, see Volume I) and is just one feature, present in some but not all the examples of world civilizations known today. Cultural development is an all-round combination of human activities. When all these activities lead on to a new complex process, that complex stage is referred to as civilization. It is a new way of living, thinking and acting – the whole system of human achievement from this period onwards – that is termed civilization.

Although many peoples and human societies of the period presented here continued to be non-literate, the progress achieved by a community now primarily depended upon some of its members' ability to read and write, and to disseminate knowledge through written works to their contemporaries and to future generations. Literacy is the chief feature of civilized people which distinguishes them from their prehistoric ancestors. It is this characteristic which opened a new world of advancement not only in material terms but also in scientific, cultural, spiritual and moral fields. The surviving literary records enable us not only to reconstruct the political, social and economic history of the period but also to fathom the minds of those alive at that time, the direction that they gave to their life, the motivation that inspired them to work and their ultimate view of the universe and their place in it. For the first time it is possible to fathom human philosophic ideas, poetic fancies, myths and mythologies, legal and moral codes and many other features that were earlier concealed behind purely archaeological sources. In definitive terms real history now begins, in which both literary records and material remains play an equal role in interpreting human activity on the basis of the geography, ecology and resources of the time and the ways in which they were exploited by people's skill and experience.

This development was not uniformly achieved by all human societies of the period. There were great variations among human groups. Apart from literate and non-literate groups in different parts of the world and even in the same region, there were strong differences in human experience and heritage which constitute the variant cultural traditions that differentiate one human society from another. Even so the age is marked by the emergence of states and civilizations and interplay between them by conscious human effort. Isolation of human societies now was an exception. More important was the interrelation between them, whether literate or non-literate, urban or non-urban, city-centred states or rurally oriented peoples; whether endowed with new technology or surviving with their older tools and techniques; whether with conscious ideas revealed in writing, art and religion or continuing in their traditional beliefs in magic, sorcery and unexplained or unexplainable forms of art. This human commingling among non-equals in cultural achievement is the chief characteristic of human civilizations of the period. It is the growth of this cultural phenomenon that distinguishes history from prehistory and marks out civilization as the main characteristic from this period onward.

It is because of the wide differences in advancement that ideas about higher civilizations versus barbarian societies became popular, and views were expressed indicating that it was from the former that new elements, techniques or technologies flowed to the latter. Hence the flow of new ideas from one community to another was seen as a legitimate base for the propagation of the diffusionist principle for levelling out variant human cultures. Although diffusion of certain features from one to the other is not ruled out, human societies continued to develop in their own particular style and tradition even after accepting external cultural traits. Common features in any two societies need not be achieved only by a process of borrowing. The same feature may have originated in two or three societies at different times. This is particularly true in this period when the knowledge of copper metallurgy is seen simultaneously in different areas but producing different results. Societies in Western Asia, South-East Asia or the Americas in the Bronze Age materially differed from one another. The old idea that Western Asia had the monopoly of higher civilization and that its cultural traits then affected cultural change in other areas is gradually disappearing. Even northern Europe, with its dissimilar cultural milieu, was not necessarily always at the receiving end. The old concept of civilized and barbarian societies is now giving way to one of common human interrelations among variant cultural groups in different ecological zones, many of them interacting during the stage of human civilization presented in this volume.

It is none the less important to emphasize the new feature of urban growth. Populations concentrated in cities can be divided into several social groups on the basis of craft, trade, religion, ritual, custom, tradition and other known or unknown factors that compel us to treat them as more than homogeneous bands and use such terms as 'social stratification'. There does not appear to be one uniform pattern for such societies, nor do we know how they developed a power base for the amicable management of their common problems. How all these factors integrated to form states is another big question. There may be several answers, depending upon the local pressures and experiences. As experience varies with the complex growth of material culture, communities do not all evolve into one uniform society. The data now diverge so much in content and in quantity that they become relevant only when understood in the perspective of each society as it developed within its own environment and ecology. And yet all of them combine to present a picture that is far different from that which we find even in the centuries of incipient town building discussed in the first volume.

In the following chapters we present the various combinations and permutations that go to make up one or other cultural whole. Amidst competing systems people still live to maintain themselves and build a growing cultural personality. They grow in complexity, and when faced with different environments they react differently. Is it possible for us to measure the human factor in relation to the environment?

The human factor is divisible into various forms of mental activity – thoughts, ideas, ideology, philosophy, imagination, emotion, feeling and so on. Is it possible for us to evolve a coefficent that can be applied to personality so that we may quantify human genius? The attempt would be futile for it would lead to infinity. Nor is it necessary as we are dealing with human beings in society wherein they build their own particular world. It is the reconstruction of these worlds that is the subject matter of history. Here we limit ourselves mainly to the Bronze and Iron Ages and try to define each society's particular world at the critical stage of human history when cultures advanced to build a new world of their own.

TRANSFORMATION INTO A NEW ORDER

The common denominator of the new world order was bronze (alloy of copper and tin) technology. It affected in varying degrees the life patterns of all major human societies. But copper was already mined and used in the last stage of prehistory, when the development of towns and the beginnings of the notion of state took place. That was but a transitional stage, when new cultural traits began to appear, whose real significance was felt only when they integrated into the new system termed here civilization. Though living patterns had varied in the past, however little the differences might have been, the gaps between them now widened. Marked variation is seen between those societies which took advantage of the favourable conditions of the agricultural plains and plateaux and fully utilized the new bronze technology, and those others which continued with their pastoral or agricultural economies because of local environmental conditions. It is this differential production and the common need for the exploitation of mineral and forest resources that established mutual relations between these

two groups of societies. The need led to exchange, war or invasions – a peaceful trade among neighbours or an explosive demand by one group upon another. This was true not only between two distinct societies but also among the members of the same group, creating new social situations that led to stratified societies. The trading of goods has to be based on certain accepted or acceptable norms and for that one must have measures and weights – an agreed standard which would also define the value of goods. This necessity led, on the one hand, to symbolic writing and, on the other, to counting by numbers. Writing and enumeration are the two great inventions of this period, but they can hardly be pinned down to one source in any one region. The present evidence shows that different regions evolved symbols for writing and enumeration that followed different patterns, in one place the number system being based on fours, in another on scores, and in yet another on a sexagesimal system. Just as in the earlier prehistoric age spoken languages had simultaneously developed in different regions of the world, in the Bronze Age writing and enumeration followed patterns according to the genius of the local communities. What was required was communication within the group and between different societies. It is the development of this interaction, assisted by understanding the symbols and enumeration of other societies, that forms the fundamentals of civilization.

So far we have limited our ideas of cultural change to the economic aspect, and its consequences on social stratification. However, even economically we have not exhausted all its implications. Trade evolves not only because there is a demand for one or other material but also because of surplus production. Whatever the need, whether for simple living or luxury, surplus production is the minimum base – a condition already created in the earlier Neolithic, when a simple form of trade already existed. It led to the creation of the whole system of trade in which laws governing exchange, relative market values, a balanced economy and many other aspects became fully understood, accepted and finally codified.

In addition to external material relations came the problem of social relations within a given society. The surplus produce was after all created by the society's own efforts, using the new technology and the natural facilities available in a given region. Who enjoyed this surplus or who disposed of it? Some writers, particularly those having a Marxist bias, have talked of primitive communism and hence equal distribution of the surplus among the producers. Even if we accept this principle in the earlier Neolithic stage, it changed in the period after 3000 BC. In many regions not all food producers shared the produce equally. In fact there was growing diversity among the producers, distributors and consumers. This diversity led to new concepts of labour and to labourers – agricultural, industrial and technical – who could be distinguished from those who had a stake in the land and its production. This latter class assumed the responsibility of the ownership of land. In the first edition of *The History of the Scientific and Cultural Development of Mankind* (1963–6), Sir Leonard Woolley opined that such ownership of land was vested in the temple managers or priests, particularly in Mesopotamia. But a new study of the Babylonian documents has clarified the issue and there is a growing consensus among scholars that there was a system of management in which more than one class had a direct stake in land, even in Mesopotamia. If the situation in other regions is taken into account, the issue becomes more complicated. The question of ownership is complex and varied. Wherever documentary evidence is available, it shows that there gradually developed a system in which both the owners and actual producers developed rules or codes by which they lived, and by which they determined their means of sustenance. Such codification is seen for the first time in this period.

However, it was not a universal codification. The nature of production differed, the means of production, and even control over production were not the same everywhere. The laws, whether written or customary, were also multiple. A difference existed between agricultural laws and those obtaining for animal production and still more complicated were the rules that obtained in those societies which were dependent on agricultural and pastoral production, or which were changing from one to the other. Whatever their activities societies were not necessarily isolated; they were often affected by conditions obtaining in other societies. The disparity between societies was often a cause of conflict. Both strife and peaceful harmony led to the establishment of human relations. The documents of the period mirror the position and show how interrelations between communities was a necessity. From this period onwards human beings have been consciously trying to improve the conditions of such a relationship.

People engaged in the actual process of production had to live close to the land, but what about those who had less to do with production but more with produce – the distributors and the non-agricultural consumers? Among the distributors are included those engaged in trade, traversing long distances searching for places of demand, collecting the surpluses of one or the other place and making them available in a third place, for those versed in marketing; people in such occupations could be recognized as falling within the mercantile class. Such merchants and businessmen developed a special position for themselves in society, becoming an indispensable part of the social structure. If we add to them exploiters of mineral resources, the community of labourers who specialized in the handling of bronze tools and developed the technology to improve such tools, and who evolved other uses of the metal, we have a whole group of skilled persons who were set apart from the process of production. This is true also in the case of those handling animals. They too needed specialists. In this period we thus distinguish different human communities – those in the process of production and hence living near the place of production, and those in the process of distribution or in some specialized work. Such commonality of interests multiplied in the course of time but all interests remained attached to the needs of the group. This was the crucial stage in the development of communal living. The commonality of interests brought larger numbers of people to one centre of habitation, leading to the development of cities, as in Mesopotamia and in the Indus Valley. Alternatively, groups might be dispersed and yet have close ties of relationship, as in the non-urban civilization of the Americas. In either case the new development in this period has now to be viewed in the much broader context of community of interests rather than in the limited sense of urban growth occasioned by setting apart merchants and specialists of various kinds. The growth of cities is not an indispensable feature of civilization, nor need the monuments and other paraphernalia that go with them be prerequisites of civilization. Similarly, many consequent institutions that accompany these features, or that precondition them, as many anthropologists believe, should now be viewed in a different light. Such institutions were created because they were needed to solve the problems of

the varying interests of societies as they began to live in one or another environment. The growth of a town was one method by which certain communities found a solution to their problems. Human communities are the agents of civilization, towns are not the main catalyst. Civilization is much more than urbanism. The latter is only a material means of concentrated living while the former is the growth of a higher system in which communities find a better solution for establishing relations among the groups which make up their society. The beginning of this whole process of civilization is seen in the period under review.

Such common interests in a group of individuals in a given society lead to the formation of strata, and not vice versa. Hence, social stratification is the recognition of the expression of diverse communal interests, which bring people together into groups; such group living gives rise to social classes which may be equal or unequal in status; but all stratification results from the creation of differential groups. Stratified societies are the natural consequence of the complications of living that developed in this period. It has been generally interpreted that social stratification at this time was sanctified and social disparities were dictated by temple managers. While temples are institutions that have more than simple sociological implications, stratification, whether urban or non-urban, follows the simple principle of sociology. New reading of Babylonian texts makes it clear that stratified societies were not dictated by temple priests but that the priests were part and parcel of the stratification. This interpretation clearly interrelates temples in urban centres with religious centres in a non-urban society. In both cases managers or priests had a role to play. As their own interests were based on the unexplainable supernatural wishes and demands of the people in general, they rose higher in status and their place of work, that is the temples, received greater attention. They became magnificent buildings. Temple centres had a mystical appeal to the people and hence all lavished expenditure on maintaining them or worked in their service. Whether such lavish gifts were ever appropriated by the managers for their own use is another matter. In any case, the managers did not dictate living conditions in the communities as they were themselves part of the same structure.

Rising above these common interests, we have to find an overall institution that brings them all into one order, without which there can be no communal living. But that order need not follow one pattern. What is necessary is an agency – source of power – for the enforcement of commonly accepted rules in the interests of all communities. Then each community must recognize the necessity of sharing its power with others in order to maintain tolerably amicable living conditions. The origin of this sharing of power may lie deep in prehistory but its formal institutional development is recognized in this period in the origin of state.

The state is an organization which, like a city, is a feature of civilization but not civilization itself. State as a coercive agency cannot create civilization but civilization as a process of higher human development builds institutions that satisfy the interests of its members. The state establishes political and social relations among individuals, and groups of individuals, not only within its borders but also externally, with members of different states. On the basis of the study of Mesopotamian examples it has often been held that city-states were paramount. But this is not true everywhere. In the socio-geographic environment of Mesopotamia city-states were common, but in other areas there were no cities, although the inhabitants created states that suited their own particular needs.

Are such states simple administrative organisms for governing the interests of different communities? This would be only a partial definition. According to some, the state deals only with political relations, but according to others it has a wider role, embracing the whole of life. Whichever interpretation we accept, the state is a progressive organism that brings into play common interests in the developing process of human relations. As these relations are based on certain accepted laws, the state appears to be the enforcer of laws, while in fact it only manages or controls those laws already accepted by humanity for its own survival. These laws appertain to all spheres of life, whether sacerdotal or temporal.

Who is in control of the state? Just as priests may appropriate to themselves properties belonging to the temple, similarly a ruler may usurp the power of the state and use it to his own advantage. The forms of state may vary from society to society and from region to region. The state authorities may also quarrel among themselves or may oppress their own people. Whatever form their manipulation takes, they have to establish inter-state relations, whether peaceful or war-like. As the community of interests expands, so the authority of the state extends, and may transgress one zonal boundary and spread over another. This process of expansion may or may not be peaceful, but wherever states expand they have to establish another order to meet the demands of the new configuration. This growth process results in the formation of empires. From state to empire is a step towards bringing together a greater number of communities into one political spectrum. Such a development took place in the later stage of our period. The expansionist policy of one group often upsets the amicable and harmonious growth of another. On the other hand, expansion does not necessarily mean that a group tramples on the interests of others; climatic circumstances may force one people to seek better prospects in a better environment. Migrations and movements of peoples are a necessary consequence of seeking a more congenial life in a greener land. Such displacement of populations, voluntary or involuntary, is seen in our period as well.

The settled agricultural communities of the river valleys have usually been regarded as the main architects of civilization because it is there that we note the development of alphabetic writing, the creation of plastic art and monumental buildings, the preservation of cultural traditions, astronomical calculations, the measurement of time by means of solar and lunar calendars and, above all, the creation of myths and mythologies based on physical experience and folk memory. There are many other features that may be attributed to one or other civilization of these lands. In contrast the steppe land, desert areas, and colder regions of the world offered fewer facilities for settled life. Nomads and pastoral communities were more often on the move than attached to a fixed territory, although nomads generally returned annually to particular areas where suitable climatic conditions attracted them. It was in this process of return that older traditions survived and became integrated into new myths and mythologies, as we find in the case of the Alpine tribes and the Mongols. Nomadic groups established relationships not only between themselves but also between humans and animals. In this biotic symbiosis they adjusted themselves fairly comfortably to a particular natural surrounding. The whole technology of animal domestication, if it did not originate here, at least had a great opportunity for further development. This particular association of people and animals led to better management and to an understanding of the power that was potential in animals. By harnessing this power for their own purposes, herders took another step forward towards progressive civilization. The bull or horse was harnessed to the plough and the horse or camel was used for a quicker ride across the grassy steppe land or sandy deserts. The horse was a great source of power towards the later stage of our period. It was the close companion of the Indo-Europeans who spread out through Eurasia in a bid for a new world order.

Although other regions relied on other animals, the horse has retained its value right up to very recent times. Its domestication, training and proper use and its companionship with its owner have left lasting memories in art, in certain rituals and in Shamanistic practices and ceremonies. As the food crop is the base of agricultural civilizations, so the horse is the mainstay of the nomadic way of life and all that implies in the process of nomadic cultural growth to steppe civilization. The horse was a means of controlling other animals and placing them too in the service of human beings, just as the growing of crops enabled them to produce a surplus and head for new ventures towards civilization. From the juxtaposition of these two processes towards the concluding stage of our period there dawned a new order that is discussed in Volume III: empire building. This was greatly accelerated as a result of horse power.

An understanding of the different features of civilization can also be gained from the many documents that have now been recovered from numerous archaeological sites. Although their interpretation may not be uniformly acceptable to all scholars, the data contained in these documents portray the various sequences in the history of humanity, including the contemporary concept of the universe and an individual's place in that universe, human destiny and, above all, not only the advantage taken of the materials and powers available in this world but also the notion of supernatural powers supposed to bestow extra benefits upon supplicants, so as to better their prospects in the future. We know from the written sources that belief in such supernatural forces existed; hence representations of their imagined likeness were made in sculpture and painting. Such gods and goddesses have been named and stories about them narrated. In the written documents they are easy to read; in the oral traditions of the nomads and other non-literate communities they inspired succeeding generations with heroic legends of the past, whose appeal was so great that they have had an abiding influence on the minds of men and women up to the present time. With the Bronze Age commenced the conscious appreciation of a clear distinction between belief in magic and sorcery and faith in the new forms of religion that related humankind to the universe.

The clay tablets of Mesopotamia narrate the creation of humans out of clay, their fall from heaven, the golden age in the past and the various flood legends. They list ruling kings and dynasties, and record their warring. Administrative, economic, legislative and other transactions throw light on the extent and content of these activities. Although the time-scale of the ruling kings is often more fable than fact, yet the legends are not pure legends. They have their roots in history and are understood as such. This can be compared with the prophetic history of sacred literature. Here the concept of the prophet is new and the history is woven round the person of the prophet; but even in this narration there is movement and a clear perception of cultural change. In the Indian world we have the traditions of the ancients (the *Puranas*). Here again the concept of *yugas* (ages) and the state's legendary history is duly subdivided into different dynasties. As pointed out by F. E. Pargiter, the Pauranic history is not pure fiction. It is a narration of worldly events, written down much later, but told in the future tense as if the events were destined to happen by the will of the gods. And hence these *Puranas* are named after the gods. On the other hand, in the Chinese annals monarchy is a tacit assumption. It is within the life-span of a monarch, or a series of monarchs, that world events are presented year by year so as to focus on the majesty of that monarch and the grandeur of the civilization over which he presided. In the Americas, mythical concepts dominate the human mind and all humans play their role under the spell of such concepts. Such varying ideas of history are presented to us for the first time in this period.

Historians, such as Sir Arnold Toynbee, have tried to understand each civilization's historical role in the changing perspective of the world. Scholars have also talked of the cradle, or cradles, of civilization and tried to measure the variation in a scale of higher or lower rungs of achievement. Regional disparities can often be explained on the basis of varying natural features. The concepts of high or low civilization, main or periphery, developed or sophisticated, nomadic or barbarian are but relative terms of reference. With few exceptions, all humans participate in the forward march of humanity; all contribute in their own way to the building of civilization. They share the effort as well as the fruits, although in varying ways. The bonds of relationships are maintained and hence their 'togetherness' becomes the main catalyst for further activity. The rise and fall of one particular form of civilization does not bring to an end the pace of humanity; in other regions other forms gain ascendancy. Hence, in the longer perspective of history civilization is a perpetual summation of all human striving for a higher and higher way of life.

If this concept of onward movement in history is something that cannot be denied, the meaning of progress – the development of humanity – should be understood as the continuum of universal human betterment. Human achievements, so well documented in the Bronze Age, made great strides forward and their momentum has never stopped, but has accelerated into our own life-time. It is this civilizational springboard that is the abiding legacy of the Bronze Age and which provides a link between the efforts of our prehistoric ancestors and those of succeeding generations.

Within this general principle of progression, different groups contributed in different ways; within this analytical framework we try to place them side by side in order to consider the part they played in the building of world history.

First to be considered is the geographical world of the time, its physical features and ecology and how people could take advantage of them and their resources on the basis of their technical knowledge and experience. We normally make the division between the Old World and the New World. Opinions differ as to whether there was any cultural contact between the two, and some similarities in cultural traits have been emphasized. In the Old World chances of contact were more favourable, though natural barriers caused great disparities even in the same continent, such as, for example, between the Nile Valley and the rest of Africa, or between the Greco-Roman world and the rest of Europe, or even the western and southern regions of Asia and China in contrast to the temperate zone of northern Asia.

During the period under review proper names appeared for the first time in documents. It is no longer necessary for us to name the peoples according to the tools they made or the areas they occupied. Now we can talk of the Sumerians, Babylonians, Hittites, Meluhhans, Minoans, Kassites, Medians, Egyptians or Aryans. The demography of the then known world can be calculated for the first time and all these peoples described according to their physical characteristics. They could perhaps be divided into different ethnic groups, though ethnic groups in the course of time may lose their identity as historical tribes appear and then gradually disappear into larger communities. For instance, the tribes enumerated in the earliest book of the Aryans, the *Rigveda*, had coalesced by the time of the Indian epics. This changing pattern of humanity is for the first time presented in this period.

An important feature of this period is the concept of time, which makes a distinction between legendary tales and historical records. The time concept is applicable not only to the hours of day and night but also to the periods of weeks, months and years. What is more important is the fixing of a year's duration because of a recurring event, such as the annual flood coinciding with the appearance of a star in Egypt; and also the invention of a solar calendar in the New World. This simultaneous discovery of time-measurement led to the concept of chronology – one of the most revolutionary processes in unlocking the secrets of the planetary system.

We are now able to analyse human activities – material, spiritual, philosophic, sociological, economic, political – all the institutional or personal fields in which people acted within a given society. Although Egypt, Sumer and the Indus complex all fall within the category of river valley civilizations, they materially differ one from the other. When we compare their cultures with those of the peoples living in the neighbouring zones, the difference is great, but according to the definition adopted here they all fall within the same world of human relations. It is their mutual aspirations that affect future movement in history, as we find when nomadic and pastoral peoples later impinge on the sedentary population of the agricultural plains. This was a natural consequence of past relations among human groups. So far the emphasis has been one-sided. The contribution of marginal peoples has been overlooked. But from the available evidence it is possible to fathom the whole process of growth and assess the way in which it affected different peoples. In the study of past communities it is not just material objects that are important but also the techniques involved in their production which affect the life of the entire community. This technological aspect brings into play all the different strata of society, which are for the first time presented in the records.

Two other important aspects of human behaviour can be expressed. One concerns the imaginative but impelling inspiration that motivates humankind. It is in this imagination that one discovers one's place in the universe and tries to relate oneself to the entire universal creation. Imagination and inspiration lead people to develop various concepts of what we call today religion; people create ceremonies and perform rituals that tie them to this mystic world of their own conception. Such religious institutions, whose ancient forms probably appeared from as far back as the Upper Palaeolithic period, are certainly important features of the conscious progress towards civilization.

The second aspect concerns the political world, in which people-in-society try to adjust themselves within a framework of rights and duties. This political awareness, which results in the creation of states, is built up stone by stone into the edifice of civilization. The political framework may differ and the role of individuals or groups in that framework may vary from place to place or from time to time. But such political relations are the greatest levellers of social groups into one integrating system.

Human achievements during the Bronze Age are phenomenal, and qualitatively far different from those seen in the prehistoric period. Their legacy is fundamental in placing us on the road of scientific and cultural progress. The seeds that were sown in the Bronze Age ripened to bear fruit right down to today.

NOTE

1 The ten criteria of civilization according to Professor Gordon Childe are: (1) Urbanization; (2) Writing and enumeration; (3) A large population; (4) Monumental buildings; (5) A stratified social structure; (6) The presence of a ruling class; (7) Surplus to feed the city people; (8) Long-distance trade; (9) Full-time artists; (10) The development of predictive sciences such as arithmetic, geometry and astronomy.

B

THEMATIC SECTION

I

TECHNICAL ASPECTS

Jean-Pierre Mohen

Technical domains are, as one can see in the first volume of this *History*, the basis of our knowledge of prehistoric worlds. In the period covered by this volume, technical innovations acquire tremendous importance in certain regions, to the point of 'giving birth' to the scientific ideal. This evolution can be observed in Western Asia, in Egypt, and generally in the eastern basin of the Mediterranean; it appears in Eastern Asia, for example in China since the beginning of the third millennium BC and in America throughout the period with which we are concerned, and, among other countries, in Mexico and Peru. All the techniques of everyday life are concerned, including those necessary for the acquisition and production of food, agriculture and pastoralization, exploitation and transformation of materials, exchange, and so on. We can select certain spectacular aspects of the technical evolution, which progressed all the more rapidly in that its social and demographic context was dynamic.

The demographic increase plays an essential role in the development of the different techniques which are elaborated, calling for specialization in working methods and in the distribution of products. It is important to find a way to measure the demographic evolution. The transition from prehistory to history may in fact coincide with the formation of large population groups the like of which had never been seen before. If we are to grasp fully the demographic situation that was to exert so great an influence on the evolution of societies, we must bear in mind that throughout the Palaeolithic millennia the population was very small indeed, of the order of a few thousand individuals scattered over vast areas (Masset, 1989); the density was estimated at one inhabitant per 11 km² in France around 7000 BC. With the emergence of the urban phenomenon in Western Asia in the early Neolithic period, fairly dense concentrations of inhabitants are attested in Jericho and Çatal Hüyük. Cities proliferated and expanded in both area and population from the time when the first large states began to appear around 3000 BC. Babylon is said to have had some 80,000 inhabitants. Major construction works for public or religious monuments required thousands of labourers (Plate 1). The most famous of them were the Egyptian pyramids of Giza. It has been calculated that at the end of the reign of Cheops, around 2528 BC, the site of the Great Pyramid, the most imposing of antiquity that this pharaoh caused to be constructed, was built at a rate of over 185 blocks of stone – of an average weight of 2.5 tons – every day, which amounts to more than 100,000 per year. The site employed a minimum of 3,000 workers, and certainly more if, as some think, the work was

seasonal. The size of the population engaged solely in the construction of the Great Pyramid amounts to at least 10,000 individuals, including women, children and old people. All the great monuments of this period testify to increased population densities. J. Cauvin (1978) has conjectured that the spectacular rise in population was one of the most important factors in the evolution of societies, their way of life and their economic and political systems.

The fundamental changes which took place from the third millennium BC onwards, covering a vast area which stretched from India to Greece, were both the cause and the consequence of the development of a group of techniques which attained a high degree of specialization, as well as a level of production that merits the term industrial. Workshops were often grouped together and protected in the vicinity of palaces, within the confines of cities. Slaves worked in them, using raw materials often collected in remote areas to which official expeditions were sent. The development of metallurgy is the finest example of this nascent skilful technique. It formed part of a new world which also saw the advent of writing and the development of systems of weights and measures which were the foundation stones of developed economies, and the emergence of an urban, state-based society which was buttressed by theocratic religion. All the most advanced techniques were under the control of the king, the pharaoh or the stewards directly employed by them. It should also be borne in mind that during this same period in rural areas traditional domestic activity persisted in the making of pottery, stone and wooden tools, textiles and esparto grass goods, to name only a few. This production was often a family activity and involved the use of local materials. Production was therefore restricted to immediate needs.

COPPER AND BRONZE METALLURGY

Copper working, signs of which appear in Anatolia in the seventh millennium BC in Çatal Hüyük, was at that time confined to the hammering of the native metal. It was not until 3800 BC that there is evidence of the reduction of copper ore (copper melts at 1,052°C) by heat treatment in Tepe Yahya in Iran. Then the Copper Age had really begun. It is interesting to note that neither Egypt nor Mesopotamia possessed natural copper deposits. Copper, malachite and chrysocolla ores were mined by gangs of slaves in the eastern Sinai desert at Timna and in the upper valley of the Tigris in Arghana Maden.

South-western Anatolia was rich in copper, silver and gold. Very soon afterwards, metallurgical centres also developed in Eastern Europe, based on the copper ores extracted from the mines of Ali Bunar in Bulgaria and Rudna Glava in Serbia (Plate 2).

In recent years the metallurgical installations of Timna have been explored by a team led by B. Rothenberg. He discovered the stone mallets used to prise the ore from the rock-face and crush it, and the reducing furnaces with their blast pipes. The metal was refined in melting pots and cast in ingot moulds or moulds of other types. Ingots were exported to centres for recasting and shaping by founding or hammering. It was there, too, in most instances in the plain, that the work of finishing the objects, that is, removal of rough edges, polishing, and hammering of edges to harden them, was carried out. Ornaments such as pins, rings and bracelets, weapons such as daggers and axes, and tools such as picks and adzes were also obtained.

In addition to pure copper, copper alloys which may or may not have been intentionally produced are also found. Copper containing arsenic is frequently found in the Caucasus, where there are copper ores which are naturally rich in arsenic, but high percentages of arsenic, sometimes as high as 23 per cent, indicate the enrichment of the alloy. This arsenic-based metallurgy, using techniques which remain largely unknown to us, was widespread in Europe during the third millennium BC. The Copper Age was a period of prosperity. Metallurgy was under the dominance of kings and smelters' moulds are to be found in their citadels in Troy, Ali§ar Hüyük, Boghazköy, Kultepe and, further west, in Lipari, Kastri on the island of Syros, and Thermi, among others. Tin poses a complex problem, as its origins remain a mystery in the context of the metallurgy of arsenical copper: in Troy I, the percentage of tin ranges from 0.16 to 1.65, although a pin containing as much as 13.1 per cent has been found; in Troy II, tin is more frequent; and a ring of pure tin has even been found in Troy IV. During the same period, bronze containing 10 per cent tin also existed alongside objects made of pure copper in Ali§ar Hüyük. The royal tombs of Ur (in about 2800 BC) contained among the offerings a large number of bronze weapons and tools with a fairly constant tin content (8 to 10 per cent). It was only from 2000 BC onwards that bronze, containing a small percentage of tin, spread into Egypt. The famous scene in a Theban tomb, in about 1500 BC, portrays all the stages of the bronze-founder's work (Fig. 1). The situation was approximately similar in the Aegean where, particularly in Cyprus – the island of copper – mineral exploitation began in earnest in about 2000 BC, while the use of bronze was spreading (the Alambra dagger) (Plate 3). There are no minerals in the Indus Valley, and yet a few objects made of copper exist in the Harappan culture. They contain small quantities of nickel (up to 1.5 per cent, and sometimes even tin, as much as 27 per cent!) whose origins remain unknown, as do the origins of the copper ingots found in Mohenjo-daro.

THE DEVELOPMENT OF GOLD-WORKING

Gold, a native metal washed from river beds or mined from rock seams, does not appear to be the first metal to have been worked. The first major gold-working centre was situated at the mouth of the Danube, on the shores of the Black Sea in Bulgaria in the region of Varna. Highly stylized ornaments, beads, appliquéd ornaments and pendants in the shape of bulls and female idols were in existence from the fifth millennium to the third millennium BC in Eastern Europe and Anatolia (Alaca Hüyük, Sardis and Troy). The first gold beads found in Egypt date back to the fourth millennium BC and show no signs of having been elaborately worked. Starting in about 3000 BC, skilful gold-working techniques are seen in the jewels of the Egyptian King Djer, buried in Abydos, as well as in the ornaments and furniture of the royal tombs of Ur. Mention should also be made of the existence, no doubt somewhat later in time, of the tableware, statuettes and ornaments of Troy and Alaca Hüyük in Anatolia and of Maïkop in the northern Caucasus. In these places, silver and gold were both appreciated as precious metals. Gold, because of its unchanging brightness, soon came to signify the eternal radiance of the king or the pharaoh. Its role was more symbolic than economic. It was mined in the Arabian desert and Nubia (in the Egyptian language, *nub* means gold), and in Anatolia in the Valley of Pactolus, famous for its wealth of nuggets. Two silver mines are mentioned in Bulgar and Bereketli in the Konya plain. Smelting, hammering, chasing, stamping, granulation, soldering and wire-making were known techniques. A recent study of the metallurgy of Susa shows just how wide a variety existed of bracelets, rings, earrings, beads, pendants in the shape of dogs, and many other

Figure 1 Smelting bronze in a crucible before it is poured into moulds – after an Egyptian tomb painting in Thebes (*c.* 1500 BC). On the right the ingots are being carried in, on the left the metal is being melted down and in the centre the bronze is being poured into moulds (after Mohen, 1990).

head and chest ornaments. Susa's copper and bronze statuettes represent kings and gods. The god 'with the golden hand' from the beginning of the second millennium BC is a fine example of the royal and religious side of the goldsmith's craft. Another example, and one belonging to the same period, is that of Byblos, where King Abi Shemou (eighteenth century BC) was buried in a vault 10 m deep. He was placed in a sarcophagus hollowed out of a single huge block of limestone covered by a slab. Around his neck he wore a large gold plaque decorated in repoussé, representing a falcon with outspread wings holding two palm leaves in its talons: a Phoenician emblem. A gold medallion and pectoral in cloisonné enamel and precious stones are inspired by pharaonic decorations in a very free local style. Moreover, the king's crown and his gold and bronze sceptre show signs of contacts with Mesopotamia; his knife is made of gold and silver, and a vase in the shape of a teapot is made of silver. Other gold objects, such as a dagger with a storiated sheath bearing stamped decorations and an axe with a granulated design bear eloquent testimony to skilful craftsmanship which drew its inspiration from the various royal courts of the period. These luxury objects were later to be found only in the Cyclades and later in Greece: the gold and silver tableware of Euboea, the Peloponnese and Crete was similar in shape to that of Troy. Fifteenth-century Minoan vases are reminiscent of Egyptian shapes. The golden bowl with a handle, from a tomb in Dendra, seems to have been hammered out of a single sheet before being decorated with stamped motifs. The gold jewellery also reveals elaborate techniques: witness the famous stamped leaf pendant from Mallia in Crete representing two bees, face to face and gathering nectar from a flower decorated with granulations. It dates back to about 2000 BC. Minoan gold working foreshadowed that of Mycenae, which came a little later. The iron used during this period is probably of meteoritic origin, with a high percentage of nickel. It is a precious metal that was used to make beads found in Gerzeh (3500 BC), the blade of a dagger found in Ur (2800–2000 BC) and a knife discovered in Deir el Bahari (2000 BC).

IRON WORKING

The writers of antiquity, such as Pliny and Lucretius, made a value judgement about the development of metal working by distinguishing a golden age, the earliest and most congenial for humankind; a bronze age, in which life became more laborious; and an iron age, the most recent and the most disastrous, because the new metal was of the greatest service to humanity through the high quality of the instruments forged from it, yet led to very tragic situations when it was used as the most effective weapons – those made of tempered steel – for criminal purposes. Authorities on early metallurgy, such as R. Tylecote and R. Pleiner, attribute the late development of iron and steel manufacture to its complexity. Specialists in the history of antiquity point to the consequences of the invention of this new metallurgy.

As long ago as 1783, Buffon drew attention to the difficult nature of various stages in the iron-making process. In fact, with the exception of the Chinese who had been able to produce cast iron in the sixth century BC, none of the metal workers elsewhere in antiquity were able to achieve temperatures as high as 1,500°C in their furnaces so as to obtain molten iron. In ancient times, iron was reduced by the furnace to a semi-solid state, in the form of nodules mixed in with the slag. The delicate stages in the operation consisted in removing these impurities by hammering, or nobbling, and in the hot self-welding of each of the particles of pure iron, also called soft iron by reason of its malleability, in order to create an ingot. Iron bars and plates were then hot-forged from the ingot – a process for which the mechanical and thermal conditions had to be just right – and could then be formed into artefacts. The final stage would be to subject these to a process of annealing or quench-hardening, which improves the quality of the metal by giving it a homogeneous internal structure, or by hardening certain parts of it, such as the tip or cutting edge of a tool. The most important phase of these processes is the converting of pure iron into steel by the introduction of carbon, a process known as cementation or carbonizing, which involves repeated hammering in charcoal. Steel, or carbonized iron, is harder and it alone can rival other metals in the manufacture of weapons and tools.

According to legend, the country of the Hittites was the centre of innovation in iron working and there is much evidence to support this. In fact, the whole area along the eastern edge of the Black Sea contains sand rich in iron ores and especially hematite. They were being mined at the beginning of the second millennium BC to supply a thriving iron and steel industry. According to Aeschylus and Strabo, it was in this area, Paphlagonia, between Samsun and Trabzon, that

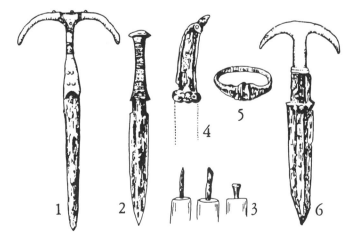
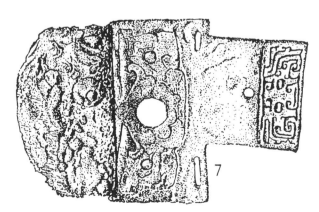

Figure 2 Earliest iron objects: 1, Alaca Hüyük (Turkey); 2, Thebes, Tutankhamen's dagger (Egypt); 3, Thebes, Tutankhamen's chisels (Egypt); 4, Ganovce (Slovak Republic); 5, Vorwohlde (Germany); 6, Ur, iron blade with gold handle (Mesopotamia); 7, *Qi* Chinese axe with bronze sleeve and iron blade (after Mohen, 1990).

iron making was invented. This information from antiquity relates to the early development of iron metallurgy but iron itself was known in even earlier times. Around 500 iron artefacts dating from the end of the Bronze Age (third millennium and first half of the second millennium BC, according to location) were catalogued by J. Waldbaum (1980). They include unique specimens, such as the blade of a tool from Ur, the blade from Tutankhamen's dagger, and a mace found among treasure at Troy, all forged from meteoric iron with a high nickel content; and a certain number of weapons and tools formed from smelted terrestrial iron, including, for example, the blade of a dagger from Tell Ahmar and one from Alaca, and a tool found in the pyramid of Cheops (Fig. 2). The fact that ferrous metal could be smelted in ancient times can be understood when one realizes that in the smelting of certain copper ores the metallurgists used a 'flux', which facilitated the separation of the metal and its impurities, and which may have been an oxide of iron. If overheating occurred, it is probable that nodules of iron were formed. But although iron smelting was practised, the technique of steel making by cementation and hammering remained unknown. Iron itself was still a rarity and the preserve of important personages. We know from ancient documents the relative value of iron; in the nineteenth century BC iron was worth forty times the value of silver. By the end of the seventh century BC, when silver coinage was introduced in Greece, a silver coin weighing 6 g would fetch 12 kg of iron. So the price ratio of iron to silver had changed to 1/2,000. As J. D. Muhly (in Maddin, 1988) has pointed out, this spectacular development shows to what extent the new metal had become assimilated into the society of antiquity (Fig. 3). The progress of this assimilation can be traced, starting with Anatolia.

In Hittite society, iron was originally used solely for ceremonial purposes and ritual, as was lapis lazuli, cornelian and rock crystal. The widely held belief that the Hittites had a monopoly on the production of iron does not seem to be based on very solid evidence. It is true that, according to a document called 'the iron letter', the Hittites were constrained to send, as a gift to the Assyrian kings, iron from Cilicia, a region which straddled the border between Anatolia and the Caucasus, the cradle of the future civilization of Urartu. But we do have from other sources firm evidence of iron making elsewhere in Western Asia. In I Samuel 13: 19–21 there is mention of the Israelites going to have work done by Philistine ironsmiths. Another interesting piece of evidence was provided by the discovery at Ras Shamra (Ugarit) of an iron-bladed axe with a gold encrusted bronze handle, apparently, from the inscription, a gift from Tusratta, king of Mitanni, to the pharaoh. From the twelfth century BC iron making became firmly established in the countries bordering the Eastern Mediterranean, and this has given rise to speculation as to a possible link between the expansion of this new technology, with its quickly realized potential for weapon making, and the irruption of the 'maritime peoples'. We have evidence dating from that time in the shape of a pickaxe, discovered on Mount Adir in the north of Israel, in which the iron of the pick had been carbonized, indicating that the principle of the mastery of iron making and its future improvement was assured. The fact that this technology was well established is demonstrated by analysis of an Egyptian knife dating from the ninth century BC. From that time onwards there is a veritable plethora of iron artefacts, and several thousand weapons have been discovered at Hasanlu in the north-west of Iran. At the same time, in Luristan, it appears that iron had been used for swords, daggers, knives and the points of lances. Sites such as Gordion in Phrygia and Nimrud in Iraq also contain thousands of artefacts. A. Snodgrass (1980), using the example of offerings, or weapons left for the most part in the graves of a Greek cemetery, has demonstrated how the use of iron was widespread in Hellenic society in the tenth century BC. Out of twenty-one swords, one is bronze, the other twenty are iron. Out of thirty-eight lance points, eight are bronze and thirty iron; all fifteen knives are made of iron.

The technical innovations of quench-hardening and annealing meant that iron became the most highly processed and the most useful material in antiquity. Quenching is described by Homer in the eighth century BC and various artefacts found at Nimrud in Iraq are among the first to show signs of this hardening process. Evidence of annealing, which renders the metal homogeneous, has been found at Al Nina, a Greek trading-post on the Anatolian coast in the fourth century BC. If to this is added the advantage of plentiful and cheap supplies of iron ore in almost every region, which is not the case with copper and especially tin ores, it is easy to understand why the ancient world adopted iron and steel in the course of a few centuries and why it was used by the great nations of the time as weaponry for their armies. The military use of iron is evident from the very beginning of the Iron Age and this reinforces its reputation among the writers of antiquity as the 'worst age'. Bronze, on the other hand, was used almost exclusively for ornaments, domestic and ceremonial receptacles and for statues of gods and kings.

Although the numbers of iron objects increased in Central and Western Europe between the twelfth and ninth centuries BC, the use of iron did not become widespread until the eighth century, in those areas where Greek colonies made a significant contribution to the spread of iron and steelmaking technology, whether directly in the cases of Sicily, Italy, the south of France and eastern Spain, or indirectly in Meseta, Aquitaine, Burgundy, Bavaria, Austria, Bohemia, and so on. In the bay of Populonia, 2 million tonnes of slag bear witness to the many tonnes of iron produced between the eighth and fifth centuries BC. This location was worked in conjunction with the island of Elba, famous at the time for its high-grade, pure hematite ore. Iron-working centres then began to expand more or less everywhere in the temperate zones of Europe with the advantage of large reserves of wood. Their remains, however, have not been extensively studied, although one exception is the site at the Moravian cave of Byči-Skala, which contains ironsmiths' tools dating from the sixth century BC. In these regions, the advent of iron brought with it a certain economic and political independence and at the same time the emergence of the ethnic groups first mentioned by ancient historians and geographers such as Hecataeus of Miletus (sixth century BC) and, above all, Herodotus (around 400 BC). So the tribes as described to us in history – the Celts, Iberians, Etruscans, Illyrians, Dacians, Thracians and Scythians – are the archetypal Iron Age peoples.

In Asia we find a variety of situations, which have sometimes given rise to speculation that iron making was invented in isolated independent locations. In India, iron and gold are to be found side by side in the Megalithic tombs of Bhandara, Nagpur and Chandrapur in Maharashtra, which has iron and manganese deposits. We still have no very remote dates for these remains, which are estimated to have come from the early years of the sixth century BC, the very end of the period under discussion.

SITE	DEFINITION	DATE B.C.	NICKEL	CONCLUSION
Prehistoric: before 3000 BC				
Iraq: Samarra	instrument, tomb A	5000	no	reduced ?
Iran: Tepe Sialk	three balls	4600-4100	yes	meteorite
Egypt: El Gerzeh	bead		7,50%	meteorite
Early Bronze Age: 3000–2000 BC				
Mesopotamia:				
Ur	blade of tool, tomb PG/580		10,9%	meteorite
Uruk	fragment	3100-2800	yes	meteorite
Tell Asmar	blade of dagger with Cu handle	2450-2340	no	reduced
Tell Chagar Bazar	fragment No. 5, tomb G.67		no	reduced
Anatolia:				
Troy	mace of treasure L	2600-2400	3,02	meteorite
			6,34	
Alaça	dagger blade, tomb K	2400-2100	no	reduced
	gold-headed pin, tomb MA	2400-2100	5,08	meteorite
	plate, tomb MC	2400-2100	4,30	meteorite
Egypt:				
Giza	rust, Valley of the Temple M	2565-2440	no	reduced
	rusted tool, Pyramid of Cheops	2565-2440 ?	no	reduced
Abydos	lump of rust	2345-2181	no	reduced
Deir el Bahari	amulet, tomb Aa Shait	2133-1991	10%	meteorite
Middle Bronze Age: 2000–1600 BC				
Egypt: Buhen	lance-head	1991-1786 ?	no	reduced
Cyprus: Lapithos	rough bead, tomb 313	1800-1750	no	reduced
Late Bronze Age: 1600–1200 BC				
Syria Palestine: Ugarit	axe with sleeve in Cu and Or	1450-1350	3,25%	0,41% of C
Egypt: Thebes	amulet, dagger, sixteen small chisels, tomb of Tutankhamen	1350	yes	meteorite

Figure 3 Table of the earliest analysed objects in the Ancient Classical world (after Mohen, 1990).

Iron working in China poses different questions due to the unique nature of its development. Following a very early period when meteoric iron was used, terrestrial iron was first smelted in 1100 BC. Could it be that knowledge of iron-working techniques developed in Western Asia had found its way to Eastern Asia? From the seventh century BC there was wide use of iron, both forged and enhanced by reheating, quenching and hammering into a form of steel. Then in the sixth century BC the technique of casting made its first appearance (something the Western world did not discover until the sixteenth century AD!) – the result of a perfectly controlled process of heating and preparing the ore. This process was made possible by the presence of particularly rich iron-ore deposits in Shanxi and Shaanxi. Soon, too, the

Chinese were burning coal in furnaces perfectly adapted for iron founding.

On the other hand, around 600 BC, iron seems to have been unknown in Japan and Indonesia, and in all the Pacific Islands and Australia. Again, in Africa the situation is unique. As stated, a number of iron artefacts have been found in Egypt, dating from the end of the second millennium BC, but the conservative nature of the Egyptian character would seem to explain the relatively late acceptance of the new metal. A few items reinforce what was written by the historian Herodotus, who stated that iron had been in everyday use around 400 BC. Further up the Nile Valley the kingdom of Kush rapidly developed a prosperous iron-working industry whose place of origin, called Napata, goes back to the eighth century BC. To this period belong the artefacts in tombs of prominent people of the reign of Piankhy (747–716 BC), which include the oldest iron items found in that part of the world, such as arrowheads, triangular blades, axes, knives, hooks and tongs. At that time shapes with sockets were not in evidence in Egypt, which would indicate either a certain degree of technical independence in the metallurgy of Kush, or direct contact with Arabia and possibly the Mediterranean, where sockets were known. From the sixth century BC the capital of this kingdom, Meroë, expanded as a result of the prosperity which iron working brought. Could it be that the kingdom of Kush was the source of the spread of iron making across central, western and southern Africa? The question has been raised often enough. It is linked to the question of the expansion of the Bantu peoples, whose tribal languages spread throughout the same areas at about the same time. Yet another kind of metallurgy, however, took root in northern Africa following the foundation of the Phoenician city of Carthage in 814 BC. According to Herodotus, Mediterranean techniques then spread along the Atlantic Coast to Mauritania and from there as far as Timbuctu; and from the gulf of Sidra in Libya across the Sahara to Gao on the Niger. Whatever the case, iron was the first metal to become established in equatorial Africa from the seventh century BC onwards. In the area of Nok, in Nigeria, it seems that the manufacture of iron became known before that of bronze or gold. The centuries which followed saw the great expansion to the south and east of iron working, agriculture and the Bantu languages.

In the case of America, Australia and the Pacific, it was the Europeans who introduced iron and steel. With the possible exception in North America of some knife blades hammered out by Eskimos from meteoric iron, there are therefore no iron artefacts in those regions dating from the period under discussion.

OTHER SPECIALIZED CRAFTS

The large-scale exploitation of some other types of raw materials called for the use of special techniques by kings and pharaohs. The arts requiring the use of fire, of which metallurgy is one, also came to include the making of glazes and glass which needed sophisticated draught-induced high-temperature ovens. 'Egyptian faience', of a blue akin to turquoise or lapis lazuli, is a composite material consisting of a nucleus and a glazed surface. The former is obtained at high temperature by combining pulverized particles of quartz mixed with lime or alkali. The glaze is produced by the fusion of lime and soda, quartz and a copper-based dye. This technique, which was very widespread in Egypt, especially during the 18th and 19th dynasties, was imitated throughout Europe for making 'segmented beads'. In Mesopotamia, ceramic cylinders with a variety of colours were used to make the scroll-shape mosaics which decorate the courtyard walls of a temple in Uruk dating from the end of the fourth millennium BC. Bricks with faience decorations came into use only during the first millennium BC. The beginning of the industrial production of ceramics was contemporaneous with the use of high-temperature ovens and of the tournette, a mobile tray fixed on a pivot and worked by hand, which seems to have preceded the wheel. In the middle of the fourth millennium BC thrown vases began to appear in Uruk. The potter's wheel was used in the Aegean only in the middle of the second millennium BC. As we have seen, native ores and metals were obtained in many cases from far-away areas, as were the high-quality polished stones used in architecture and sculpture, which came from the best quarries, often situated at a considerable distance. Lapis lazuli was one of the most sought-after semi-precious stones introduced into Egyptian, Mesopotamian and Phoenician jewellery. Deposits are said to have existed in Afghanistan, and the Standard of Ur (about 2800 BC) is a magnificent example of the royal use of this material. Turquoise may have come from Sinai, and cornelian and amethyst from Nubia. Fine limestone was mined in Tura, sandstone in Silsila, and granite in Aswan, in the area of the Nile cataracts, for Egyptian sculptures. Alabaster and diorite came from the Arabian desert. We know some of the quarries from which these blocks of stone were obtained. The most spectacular example is the granite obelisk which was found unfinished in its Aswan quarry. It is 42 m long and weighs 1,168 tonnes. It was sculpted on the spot, using round stone hammers wielded by a multitude of slaves. Transport was by rafts and sledges drawn by thousands of men. Two other impressively weighty monoliths are the colossi of Memnon ordered by Pharaoh Amenhotep III (fourteenth century BC) to be positioned in the plain of Thebes. Each weighs 1,000 tonnes. The use of building materials, such as stone in Egypt and brick in Mesopotamia, brings to mind the vast sites for the construction of official buildings such as palaces and temples. The three great pyramids of Giza, of Mycerinus, Chephren and Cheops, built in about 2700 BC, remain somewhat mysterious as regards the symbolism of their architectural form. The Ur-Mammon ziggurat, with its temple at the top, is slightly earlier than the pyramids. It is a solid mass of sundried bricks overlaid with impermeable burnt bricks coated with bitumen. These forms of architecture are among the most impressive to have come down to us from the ancient world. The building techniques used remain unknown; among other things, the scarcity of wood in these countries would have made scaffolding a problem. Lebanese wood was sought after by the Egyptian cabinet makers who worked for the pharaohs. The royal tombs contain carved and painted chests, chairs and thrones, chariots and coffins. It would thus appear that Egypt depended on imports for most of its specialized crafts, with the exception of two branches: linen textiles, whose fine quality was famous in the ancient world; and papyrus, which was used as protective wrapping for preservation, transport and, above all, for writing, knowledge of which conferred authority on the scribes. Sculptures in elephant ivory were a Phoenician speciality which spread to all the royal courts of the ancient world. Finally, mention must be made of the large-scale engineering works to channel rivers and provide irrigation for the surrounding countryside. The 350 km of canals and dams built in Mesopotamia alone symbolize the organizing power of the king in the interests of a profitable economy. Devices had been invented which could carry water uphill!

TRANSPORT

The first states were established solely as a result of international relations, which guaranteed the supply of raw materials, new technologies and the relative economic unity achieved through competition. New transport techniques were therefore of crucial importance, although traditional means were also developed and a road network protected by trading-posts was built from kingdom to kingdom. Illustrations from the period show the frequent use of slaves and donkeys to carry merchandise, since they were best suited to regions where the landscape varied from plain to desert to mountainside. Dromedaries were rare and found only in the desert. Overland transport was not initially improved by the invention of the wheel, which appeared at the end of the fourth millennium BC in Ur and Susa. Four-wheeled vehicles and, a little later, two-wheeled chariots drawn by oxen, donkeys, and eventually, horses, were initially set apart for use by royalty. Later, they are found again in the army. The use of this invention in the economic sphere seems to have been progressive, which is borne out by Egyptian wall paintings. On the other hand, sledges drawn over a layer of clay lubricated by regular watering were used to transport the huge blocks of stone for the pharaonic palaces and temples, as is illustrated by the bas relief of the tomb of Djutihetep in El-Berschi. It also illustrates the importance of the use of ropes, the manufacture of which is described in another relief in the tomb of Ueh-hetep in Meir (Fig. 4). Ropes were also of the utmost importance on boats. The regions of the Nile, Mesopotamia, the mouth of the Indus, the eastern coast of the Mediterranean and the Aegean developed as a result of intense maritime activity. The saying that the Nile gave birth to Egyptian civilization finds strong confirmation here: the river gave political and economic unity to the country and, through its mouth, connected it to the world of the Eastern Mediterranean. Reliefs, those of the tomb of Mereruka in Saqqara for example, show boats with sails or oars. At an early date, the Phoenicians seem to have begun to play

Figure 4 Workers cutting, weaving and braiding thongs (tomb of Rekh-Mi-Re, Thebes, Egypt).

the role of intermediaries in maritime trade (Fig. 5).

TECHNIQUES, WEIGHTS AND MEASURES AND WRITING

The new techniques could be developed only where there was some degree of trade regulation and control over the systems of weights and measures. The traditional barter system was replaced by exchanges which were measured with

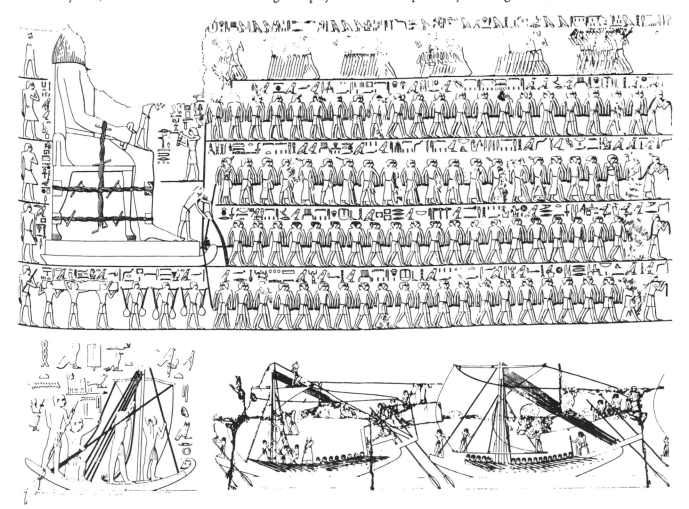

Figure 5 Examples of the use of cords in antiquity from Egyptian reliefs: a, El Berschi, tomb of Djutihetep; b, Saqqara, tomb of Mereruka.

references to abstraction whose symbols are to be found on the earliest written tablets. The detailed accounts of the economic wealth of the king or the pharaoh seem to have had a role which was at least as important as that played by legal and religious texts in the development of writing. Moreover, the use of scales and their weights, one example of the latter consisting of polished and calibrated stone ducks, made it possible to assess the equivalent quantities of certain products: in some Sumerian cities, a *gur* (120 litres) of barley was equal to two-and-a-half sheepskins and a *shekel* (8 g) of silver. A live sheep cost between 1 and 5 shekels, an ox between 6 and 18 shekels, and a pack donkey between 17 and 33 shekels. A shekel of silver was worth 20 shekels of tin or between 50 and 200 shekels of copper, whereas a shekel of gold was worth 8 shekels of silver. Judging by the Babylonian texts, a system based on multiples of six seems to have been the norm. In the code of Eshnunna (eighteenth century), the silver shekel seems to have been the unit reference of a price-fixing system, since it was worth one gur of grain, 3 sila of refined oil, 16.4 sila of ordinary oil, 15 sila of lard, 6 minas of wool or 2 gur of salt. The quantitative precision of their alloys and architectural forms proves that the technologies of the kings and pharaohs were based on scientific knowledge. The primacy of the Egyptian intellectuals, the scribes, offers revealing proof of the high degree of technical skill of these civilizations, whose vitality was derived from these collective undertakings. When Sesostris I decided to send a slave expedition to quarry stone in the Wadi Hammamat, he despatched 17,000!

BIBLIOGRAPHY

CAUVIN, J. 1978. *Les premiers villages de Syrie-Palestine du IXème au VIIème millénaire avant J. C.* Lyon.

COGHLAN, H. H. 1961. *Notes on the Prehistoric Metallurgy of Copper and Bronze in the Old World.* Oxford.

—— 1977. *Notes on Prehistoric and Early Iron in the Old World.* Oxford.

DE JESUS, P. 1980. *The Development of Prehistoric Mining and Metallurgy in Anatolia.* Oxford. (BAR Int. Ser., 74.)

DESHAYES, J. 1969. *Les civilisations de l'Orient ancien.* Paris.

ELUERE, C. 1990. *Les secrets de l'or antique.* Paris.

FORBES, R. J. 1964–72. *Studies in Ancient Technology.* Leiden. 9 vols.

JOVANOVIC, B. 1982. *Rudna Glava.* Beograd.

KOVÁCS, T. 1977. *A Bronzkor Magyarovszágon (L'âge du bronze en Hongrie).* Budapest.

MADDIN, R. (ed.). 1988. *The Beginning of the Use of Metals and Alloys.* Cambridge, Mass.

MASSET, 1989. La démographie préhistorique. In: MOHEN, J. P. (ed.), *Le temps de la préhistoire.* Société préhistorique française. Paris. pp. 30–2.

MOHEN, J.-P. 1990. *Métallurgie préhistorique.* Paris.

MUHLY, J. 1973. *Copper and Tin: The Distribution of Mineral Resources and the Nature of the Metal Trade in the Bronze Age.* New Haven, Conn.

MUHLY, J.; MADDIN, R.; KARAGEORGHIS, V. (eds). 1982. *Early Metallurgy in Cyprus, 4000–500 BC.* Nicosia.

PLEINER, R. (ed.). 1989. *Archaeometallurgy of Iron.* Praha.

RENFREW, C. 1972. *The Emergence of Civilization, the Cyclades and the Aegean in the Third Millennium BC.* London.

ROTHENBERG, B. 1972. *Timna: Valley of the Biblical Copper Mines.* London.

SEFERIADES, M. 1985. *Troie I, Matériaux pour l'étude des sociétés du Nord-Est égéen au début du bronze ancien.* Paris. (Rech. Civilis., 15.)

SNODGRASS, A. M. 1980. Iron and Early Metallurgy in the Mediterranean. In: WERTIME, T.A.; MUHLY, J. D. *The Coming of the Age of Iron.*

TALLON, F. 1987. *Métallurgie susienne I, de la fondation de Suse au XVIIIè avant J.C.* Paris.

TREUIL, R. 1983. *Le néolithique et le bronze ancien égéens.* Paris.

TYLECOTE, R.F. 1976. *A History of Metallurgy.* London.

—— 1987. *The Early History of Metallurgy in Europe.* London/New York.

WALDBAUM, J. C. 1980. The First Archaeological Appearance of Iron. In: WERTIME, T. A.; MUHLY, J. D. *The Coming of the Age of Iron,* pp. 68–98.

WERTIME, T. A.; MUHLY, J. D. (eds). 1980. *The Coming of the Age of Iron.* New Haven, Conn./London.

2

FROM EMPIRICAL TO SCIENTIFIC KNOWLEDGE

2.1

FROM EMPIRICAL KNOWLEDGE TO THE BEGINNINGS OF SCIENTIFIC THOUGHT

Walter F. Reineke

'Modern science and industry not only go back to the period when bronze was the dominant industrial metal, their beginnings were in a very real sense conditioned and inspired by the mere fact of the general employment of bronze or copper', wrote Professor V. Gordon Childe (1930). In fact, the foundations of many modern sciences and disciplines were laid in this period.

In this context, by science is meant the particular form of social labour that by observing, collecting, analysing and systematizing empiric material, by trial and experiment – including the occasional use of special devices and equipment – obtains results which are useful and efficient for the interaction of man with his material and social environment, and represents the highest generalization of practice. These results establish a system of knowledge fixed in terms, statements, theories, hypotheses, rules and laws that retain the accumulated heritage of the past; this system is objectively, that is with regard to reality, relatively true. The results of scientific work serve to keep up and develop production and reproduction, but they are also instruments for exercising power. Some of them are services for the benefit of the entire society, few serve exclusively to develop science itself which, originally having been a social phenomenon, began in this period to institutionalize and develop its autonomous laws and to evolve specific methods.

Anticipatory forms of scientific activities and their preconditions can be followed long before the third millennium BC. Already in the Neolithic age environmental phenomena were observed, observation results were collected and handed down orally. Thus, sometimes remarkably precise knowledge of nature was obtained, especially of spheres that were useful to society as, for example, species of plants and animals, minerals, drugs and cures, but also of planets that were significant for religious purposes and for the determination of days, months and years. In the production process, in building and construction activities as well as in primitive barter, skills in counting and arithmetic developed, and a system of measures was established by which areas and bodies could be calculated. These arithmetical skills were both fostered and challenged by various kinds of games that go back to pre-literate civilizations, where number memory games, board games, and games with throwing sticks were played; all of them demanded an ability to count and calculate.

The most impressive manifestation of this early knowledge based on the collection of long-term observation data is the astronomically oriented cult centres as, for example, the henges, the most well-known of which is Stonehenge in Wiltshire (southern England), with its earliest stage of construction being about 5,000 years old. By simple observation with a sight rod and determination of a certain direction by wooden posts, the axis of the henge was set in such a way that it runs towards the very point of the horizon where the sun is rising at the summer solstice (Plates 4, 5). In 2772 BC, long-term observations of the beginnings of the Nile flood in Egypt and the early rise of Sirius led to the establishment of the Egyptian civil calendar with the heliacal rise of Sirius as New Year's Day. Corresponding to the exactly known vegetation periods the year was subdivided into three seasons of four months each. Every month had thirty days. Five so-called 'days above the year' completed the Egyptian year. This calendar, derived from mere observation data, was, as the renowned science historian O. Neugebauer (1957, p.81) put it, 'the only intelligent calendar which ever existed in human history'. However, neither the henge cult centres nor the Egyptian calendar nor the frequently changed lunar months calendars with their manifold difficulties of aligning them to the solar year are results of scientific work. In fact, all these achievements were attained by evaluation of observation data. The step towards analysis and recognition of the inherent laws and rules was still to be done. The Peruvians' knowledge of astronomy at the time of Chavín indicates a similar quasi-empirical approach to the world.

23

The development of script as a means of lasting and unequivocal recording and handing down of data was the precondition for the evolution of a proper science. During the Copper/Bronze Age script seems to have developed more or less independently in Mesopotamia, Egypt, the Indus Valley, and finally in Crete and China. In these areas there existed a prosperous agriculture with a stable surplus product, craft and trade, but also a division of the society, mostly into a class of rural producers and a ruling class that claimed a share of the surplus product for itself. It was this claim on taxes in the shape of natural produce – money did not yet exist – that, together with certain demands of distribution and trade, literally forced the evolution of script.

Undoubtedly, there must have been a fairly long process of collecting, evaluating, analysing and experimenting to form a real script, and this process seems to have been one of continual creative and critical examination of administrative practice. The Egyptian and Sumerian cultures are the only ones for which we are able to get an exact idea about the scientific development which took place there, as for them we have the text evidence necessary to do so. There is no doubt that also in the highly developed Indus Valley culture scientific knowledge must have existed. Without mathematics, how could large cities have been planned, built and maintained? Without a certain amount of astronomical knowledge, how could shipping have been possible? Many of the achievements attained here may have survived in India or in ancient Iran, though we have evidence only from later periods. The same also applies to the Cretan-Mycenean culture, a civilization from which the Greeks profited. In China, where the first evidence of the existence of script – oracle texts on bones and sacral inscriptions on bronze vessels – goes back to the mid-second millennium BC, much of what we know from later texts on mathematics, astronomy, medicine and historiography has been developed undoubtedly in an earlier period.

After a thorough analysis of the Chinese evidence, Joseph Needham and Wang Ling (1959, pp. 13–15) conclude:

In general, therefore, it will be seen that the Shang numeral system was more advanced and scientific than the contemporary scripts of Old Babylonia and Egypt. All three systems agreed in that a new cycle of signs began at 10 and at each of its powers. With the exception already noted, the Chinese repeated all the original 9 numerals with the addition of a place-value component, *which was not itself a numeral*. The Old Babylonian system, however, was mainly additive or cumulative below 200, like the later Roman, and both employed subtractive devices, writing 19 as 20–1 and 40 as 50–10. But the multiplication process was also introduced, for example 10 × 100 representing 1,000. Only in the sexagesimal notation of the astronomers, where the principle of place value applied, was there better consistency, though even then special signs were used for such numbers as 3,600, the subtractive element was not excluded. Moreover, numbers less than 60 were expressed by 'piled-up' signs. The ancient Egyptians followed a cumulative system, with some multiplicative usages. It seems therefore that the Shang Chinese were the first to be able to express any desired number, however large, with no more than 9 numerals. The subtractive principle of forming numerals was never used by them. It will thus be seen that behind the 'Hindu' numerals, as the West subsequently knew them, there lay two thousand years of place value in China.

In Western Asia and North Africa, particularly in Sumer

and in Egypt, the early-state phase at the beginning of the third millennium BC is the period when science went through its most important stage of development. Obviously, in the following period efficiency and empirical experience grew and procedures and methods became more sophisticated, but as far as scientific progress itself is concerned it seems to have been less productive. This evaluation is today considered a certain fact, irrespective of the question of when the frequently complex complications and series of scientific texts, some of them probably based on much older ones that originate from the mid-third millennium BC, were recorded.

The mathematical texts from Western Asia and Egypt are closely connected with practical problems such as debit-and-credit calculations, field measurement and calculation of bodies, though exercises of arithmetic rules with numbers that rarely occur in practice show a certain scientific interest. Moreover, from the arrangement of the texts in the compilations some conclusions may be drawn: the exercises were supposed to explain certain logarithms without the underlying law being formulated, which makes the decisive difference compared with Greek science which is almost 2,000 years younger. The latter did not deny that it was to ancient Oriental knowledge that Classical Antiquity went back; the Greeks especially considered Egypt the source of mathematics (Plates 6–8).

In the ancient Oriental writings we find two types of text: tables and problem texts, the latter being the proper exercises. Sometimes the content of the tables is closely connected to the system of measures, as for example conversion tables of simple fractions into parts of the measure of capacity, square tables of measures of length, and so on. Other tables are mere calculation aids. Thus, from Western Asia where a sexagesimal numerical system with incomplete position notation was used, we know of multiplication tables that give the products of the nominal numbers resulting from their multiplication with the numbers 1 to 20, 30, 40 and 50. By reduction into factors and addition of single results with these tables every kind of multiplication could be made. Furthermore, there are tables for quadratics and square and cube roots. Particularly important were the so-called reciprocal tables that served to facilitate division, which in Western Asia was considered a multiplication with the reciprocal value of the divisor.

In Egypt a decadic numerical system was usual in which every tenth power had its own hieroglyph. As far as fractions are concerned, except $\frac{2}{3}$ and $\frac{3}{4}$, the ancient Egyptians knew only stem fractions with 1 for denominator. Thus, contrary to the elegant sexagesimal fraction in Western Asia, this type of calculation was awkward and not very easy. Every simple fraction had to be reduced to a series of stem fractions with 1 for denominator and ascending values of denominators, and could not be expressed otherwise. Therefore, fraction tables were a necessity for every scribe. There were fraction tables of the stem fraction series for 2 divided through an odd number, from $\frac{2}{3}$ to $\frac{2}{101}$. The construction of these calculation aids for values in common practice and their completion demonstrates a mathematical interest. Various possible solutions were tried until a generally accepted result was found (Fig. 6).

The problem texts convey an impression of mathematical thinking in Western Asia and Egypt. There is no doubt that the stage of a primitive calculation technique had been passed, and there were foundations of an elementary mathematical logic. Although most of the exercises are meant for practice and neither theorems nor probes nor proofs are

Early Egyptian and Babylonian numerals

These two groups of symbols show how scribes of ancient Egypt and Babylon would have written 1989 using their respective number systems.

Egypt

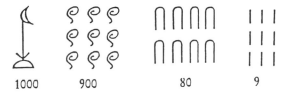

| 1000 | 900 | 80 | 9 |

The Egyptian numeral system, here shown in hieroglyphic writing, was based on 10. We see *one* sign for thousands, *nine* signs for hundreds, *eight* signs for tens, and *nine* signs for ones.

Babylon

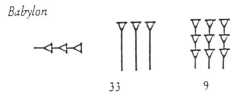

33   9

The Babylonian numeral system was based on 60. Using base 60, one thousand nine hundred and eighty-nine would be written as *thirty-three* sixties and *nine* ones. The position of the nine to the right indicates that it constitutes the ones, while the 33, one place over to the left, represents the sixties.

Figure 6 Early Egyptian and Babylonian numerals (after Ritter, 1989).

recorded, they represent an early form of mathematics. Out of the abundance of material available, some evidence is reported here: based on maintaining the basic types of calculation, equations with one or more unknowns, square and cubic equations, interest and compound interest problems, most complicated distributions and mixtures (some of them with numerical values that never occur in practice) as well as arithmetical progressions were calculated. Geometrical and stereometrical calculations could be made and even the volume of the truncated pyramid could be calculated. In the so-called pyramid exercises the batter of a pyramid was defined as a tg-proportion. The value of the cyclometrical factor π of 3.124 in Western Asia and 3.16 in Egypt was remarkably exact. The Pythagorean triples and the golden section (or the Fibonacci numbers) were known; the evidence from practice also suggests knowledge of the Pythagorean theorem.

Despite all these achievements in mathematics, most of which were fruits of human thinking in the third millennium BC, from the mid-second millennium BC on there was no notable further development of ancient Oriental mathematics. The reason is that the knowledge acquired was suf-

ficient in terms of economy and practice, and society did not need additional knowledge. Individuals may have engaged in further research but the results of their efforts are lost, as society recorded and handed down only what it could directly exploit.

Whereas mathematics in Western Asia and Egypt during the Copper/Bronze Age reached its climax, astronomical knowledge was rather poor. It was much later and only in Western Asia that mathematical methods were applied to calculate or, in connection with oracles, forecast celestial phenomena. Early astronomy is exact in long-term observation of the stars. The evaluation of these observation series resulted, for example, in the above-mentioned introduction of the Egyptian civil calendar and in the permanently necessary corrections of the calendar in Western Asia. How a calendar year of 354 days was evolved here is given below.

However, the regular and exact observation and recording of celestial phenomena was the only contribution to the development of astronomy the ancient Oriental civilizations made until the mid-second millennium BC.

There is also evidence of the beginnings of medical science in Western Asia and Egypt during the Copper/Bronze epoch. It may be suggested that the persons skilled in the art of healing at the rulers' courts collected the experiences in surgical treatment and curing of diseases that had been made and handed down since the Neolithic age. One has only to recall the fractures on long bones and the trepanations on skeletons of the fourth-third millennia BC in Western Europe. The ossified rim of the cranial perforation proves in many cases that patients survived the operation. In Western Asia and in Egypt the fairly comprehensive medical compilations that give us an impression of the then existing medical knowledge were written. Of course, it is difficult to find out the real effects of many drugs, as a number of them are only known by their names.

However, there are remedies that we know for certain have been applied for 5,000 years now. Also it is difficult to demarcate the difference between medicine and magic. After all, religious thinking dominated everything and in the treatment of diseases magical procedures were quite common and consequently became part of medical texts. Good anatomical knowledge, the ability to diagnose with certainty a variety of diseases, the medical terminology, the beginnings of the formation of theories as, for example, the Egyptian theory of the vessels of the human body, and the specialization of the early physicians in particular fields belong to the heritage of that epoch. At that time reflections started on the purposes of the various organs.

What was said about the rigidly systematic construction of the mathematical texts is valid also for the medical compilations. The material compiled was arranged according to a theoretical concept. The description of diseases runs from head to foot. At the same time the texts are written according to a precise scheme – obviously a result of both an intensive preoccupation with the subject and a fairly long tradition. First, there is an introduction of the case with its symptoms; it is followed by the diagnosis combined with remarks on whether the respective disease could be treated and what the prognosis is. Then treatment instructions and prescriptions are set down, and finally the composition of the medicine is given. This rational and empirical part is sometimes supplemented by magic spells.

It is the greatest achievement of ancient Oriental science to have collected, systematized and handed down the social treasure of experience. Certain laws or regulations and rules were recognized, although reasons were not asked for and no theoretical generalizations were made. All answers were provided by religion alone, the power of which was unlimited. Thus every finding was considered to be an expression of the just order in macro- and microcosm that was initiated by the gods in the act of creation. The main task of man was to guarantee this order forever, and permanent experience of the gods' will was considered a necessity.

In Western Asia and Egypt the learned scribes collected the existing knowledge of the natural and social environment and systematized it by categories as plants, animals, minerals, countries, rivers, gods, groups of individuals, professions and so on. In so doing they repeated an intellectual process that had been significant already when script developed at the end of the fourth millennium BC when, for example, in the Egyptian hieroglyphic script determinatives were created in order to assign a word to a certain complex. The arrangement of the environment by classes of terms, sometimes called 'list-science', is the subject of many texts that might have served as teaching material for schools. They look like the cue record of an encyclopaedia of the knowledge of that time. In Mesopotamia, where up to the beginning of the second millennium BC apart from Sumerian Akkadian was also spoken, Akkadian explanations were added to these records written in Sumerian – a procedure that resulted in a kind of dictionary, a philological aid.

The order of the world was conceived to be static and just, and it included both nature and society. In this scheme there was no concept of evolution; all rules and laws were considered part of this order. Myth gave the answer, explained the causes. Social phenomena were interpreted as a permanent new setting and implementation of the order itself; every ruler had to observe this principle as if it were a rite. Thus, historiography in a modern sense could not develop, although the reigns of the kings and their particular deeds, especially in terms of cult and war, were recorded in the annals. There is evidence that such annals have existed since the end of the fourth millennium BC. First attempts to systematize history were made in the mid-second millennium BC when the historical data recorded were arranged and structured; for example, the well-known list of kings in Egypt.

BIBLIOGRAPHY

ARCHIBALD, R. C. 1949. *Outline of the History of Mathematics*. Menasha.

BECKER, O. 1966. *Das mathematische Denken der Antike*. 2nd ed. Göttingen.

CANTOR, M. 1880. Vorlesungen über die Geschichte der Mathematik. Leipzig. Vol. 1.

CHILDE, V. G. 1930. *Bronze Age*. Cambridge.

FARRINGTON, B. 1969. *Science in Antiquity*. 2nd ed. Oxford.

GILLAIN, G. 1927. *La science égyptienne – l'arithmétique au Moyen Empire*. Bruxelles.

GILLINGS, R. J. 1974. *Mathematics in the Time of the Pharaohs*. Cambridge, Mass./London.

GOLTZ, D. 1974. *Studien zur altorientalischen und griechischen Heilkunde*. Wiesbaden. (Sudhoffs Archiv, 16.)

GRAPOW, H. et al. 1954–73. *Grundriss der Medizin der alten Ägypter*. Berlin. Vols 1–9.

KÖCHER, F. 1963. *Die babylonisch-assyrische Medizin in Texten und Untersuchungen*. Berlin. Vol. 1.

LECA, A. P. 1971. *La médecine égyptienne au temps des pharaons*. Paris.

NEEDHAM, J. 1959–87. *Science and Civilization in China*. Cambridge. Vols 1–6.

NEEDHAM, J. with the collaboration of WANG LING 1959. *Science and Civilisation in China*, Vol. 3: *Mathematics and the Science of Heavens and the Earth*. Cambridge, pp. 13–15.

NEUGEBAUER, O. 1957. *The Exact Sciences in Antiquity*. 2nd ed. Providence.

—— 1975. *A History of Ancient Mathematical Astronomy*. Berlin. Vols 1–3.

NEUGEBAUER, O.; PARKER, R. A. 1962–4. *The Egyptian Astronomical Texts*. London. Vols 1–2.

PARKER, R. A. 1972. *Demotic Mathematical Papyri*. London.

REINEKE, W. F. 1984. Technik und Wissenschaft. In: EGGEBRECHT, A. (ed.), *Das alte Ägypten*. München.

RITTER, J. 1989. Les Sources du nombre. *Le courrier de L'UNESCO*, pp. 12–17.

SANTILLANA, G. de. 1970. *The Origins of Scientific Thought*. 2nd ed. Chicago, Ill.

SARTON, G. 1959–66. *A History of Science*. Cambridge, Mass. Vols 1–2.

SEIDL, E. 1957. *Einführung in die ägyptische Rechtsgeschichte*. Glückstadt, Hamburg, New York.

SETHE, K. 1916. *Von Zahlen und Zahlworten bei den alten Ägyptern*. Strasbourg.

SIGERIST, H. E. 1951. *A History of Medicine*, Vol. 1: *Primitive and Archaic Medicine*. New York.

SOLLA PRICE, D. de. 1975. *Science Since Babylon*, 2nd ed. New Haven, Conn./London.

VAN DER WAERDEN, B.L. 1966–8. *Erwachende Wissenschaft*. Basel/Stuttgart. Vols 1–2.

—— 1983. *Geometry and Algebra in Ancient Civilizations*. Berlin/Heidelberg/New York/Tokyo.

WUSSING, H. 1965. *Mathematik in der Antike*. 2nd ed. Leipzig.

2.2
THE MEASUREMENT OF TIME AND THE ESTABLISHMENT OF CALENDARS

Jean Leclant and Jean-Pierre Mohen

History, it has been written, begins at Sumer, the actual date of its commencement being tentatively set at 3100 BC. In point of fact, unanimity is far from having been reached between the specialists working on the various lists of dynasties that reigned in ancient Mesopotamia. Another matter of dispute concerns observations relating to lunar and solar eclipses and occultations of the planet Venus during the reign of Ammizadugga, the tenth king of the 1st dynasty of Babylon, which are preserved in relatively recent tablets recording astrological omens. Like the planets, the sun and the moon were divinities that exercised a direct influence on human destiny; hence the study of their movements was of the very greatest importance. Astronomical observations properly so called were recorded alongside astrological predictions.

Under the sway of the moon-god Nannar the Sumerian calendar was based on the lunar month, of 29 or 30 days, whose alternance was not regular but was determined by observation of the new moon. The names of the months, designated in accordance with some memorable religious festival, varied from one city-state to another. A uniform system was adopted under Hammurabi: the phases of the moon led to a division of the month into four 7-day weeks, with additional public holidays being intercalated. A parallel system in which the month was divided into six weeks of 5 lunar days developed concurrently.

With the triumph of the sun-god Shamash the Babylonian year became a solar year. It began in the spring and comprised twelve months of 29 or 30 days, making a total of 354 days, to which a further 11 days had to be added; this was done by intercalating an extra month every two or three years. Thus Hammurabi was able to announce: 'This year is too short. The next month will therefore be regarded as a second Ululu.'

During the Early Dynastic period each city-state gave different names to the year. It was only under the reign of Ur Nammu (c. 2120 BC) that a uniform nomenclature came into being. The year took its name from some outstanding event: a victory or religious festival. It could not therefore be named until it was under way or actually over. In certain eras the year was also named by reference to a reigning sovereign, which sometimes led to its having a twin appellation: for example, 'Year 5, year during which Anshan was destroyed.'

Comparable methods, resulting in the same complications, were adopted in Egypt. It is indeed generally supposed that the ancient Egyptians used a lunar calendar in prehistoric times. However, the difficulties encountered – in particular the need to intercalate an extra month at certain moments – caused them to abandon this method. All that survived were certain liturgical uses: for example, according to an Illahun papyrus, priests took up office for alternate periods of 29 and 30 days, which means that the monthly service was calculated on the basis of the lunar cycle. Two observations of a purely empirical nature no doubt made an impact upon the Egyptians. One was that the annual return of the Nile floods, upon which the fertility of the entire valley depended, occurred almost regularly, every 365 days – the length of a year. The other was that the floods began on a date close to that of the heliacal rising of Sothis. At dawn on 19 July the star Sothis, our Sirius, following a period of invisibility due to its conjunction with the sun, once again becomes visible, shortly before sunrise. As an ivory tablet dating from the 1st dynasty indicates, Sirius is 'the harbinger of the new year and of the floods'.

Eduard Meyer's theory that the Egyptian calendar was established around 4242 BC, that is, right in the middle of the Aeneolithic period – the so-called 'long chronology' – has long since been abandoned. It is the 'short chronology' that has now been adopted, albeit with a number of minor variants. Today, it is generally considered that the division of the year into twelve months of 30 days – to which would have been added 4, 5 or 6 days, the so-called 'epagomenal' days – lasted until c. 2773 BC, the date when the 365–day year was definitively adopted. It then comprised three seasons, each divided into four 30–day months: these were the floods or inundation (*akhet*), the Going Forth or seedtime (*péret*) and the Deficiency or harvest time (*shémou*). This civil year, supplemented by the five 'epagomenal' days, was one day late every four years, in relation to the Julian calendar year of 365 ¼ days. As a result, the first day of the civil year coincided with that of the solar year only once every 1,460 years. The oldest recorded date for a heliacal rising (1882–1879 BC) occurs during the 12th dynasty, more precisely under the reign of Sesostris III. This enables historians to date the beginning of the reign of Amenemhat I from c. 2000 BC (some opt for 1991 BC).

As regards earlier periods, account must be taken of the fact that, for the Egyptians, each reign formed as it were a self-contained era: the different events were considered by reference to the year of the reign in which they had occurred. In order to assign absolutely accurate dates it would therefore be necessary to know the order of succession of all the kings of Egypt and the exact length of each of their reigns. To be sure, 'king lists' were drawn up during the New Kingdom on the orders of sovereigns wishing to know the names of their venerated predecessors: examples include the ancestors' chamber at Karnak, the Abydos table, the Saqqara table and above all the magnificent royal papyrus preserved in the museum of Turin, on which Champollion had the privilege of working. These extremely precious documents are in fragments, however, and above all, for the very early periods they are both incomplete and unconfirmed. During the Ptolemaic period, around 300 BC, a priest by the name of Manethon – known from various sources such as Leo Africanus and Eusebius – drew up a list of the pharaohs, classifying them according to thirty dynasties. He assigns 253 years to the 1st dynasty and 302 (or 297) years to the 2nd dynasty, that is approximately 550 years for the first two dynasties. Thus it is by means of deductions of varying reliability that the institution of the pharaohs is situated slightly before 3000 BC. This is the period during which, according to convention, the kings Scorpion and Ka, then Narmer, who is equated with the legendary Menes, reigned in succession. Accordingly, the reign of Djoser, the founder of the 3rd dynasty, is dated around 2624–2605, and the glorious 4th dynasty, that of the builders of the great pyramids of Giza, between 2575 and 2465 BC.

To return to the 12th dynasty and the later periods, there is a far greater wealth of documents available, documents that can moreover be interpreted more reliably. The chronology can thus be established with greater certainty, although it is true that the Second Intermediary Period itself remains extremely obscure. The dynasty of the Theban 'restorer' kings (17th dynasty) is considered to cover the years 1650–1551 BC, the date on which Ahmose, the first sovereign of the 18th dynasty, inaugurated the New Kingdom. Some writers however prefer to continue to date this 'turning-point' of history from 1580 BC.

As can be gauged, questions of chronology constitute a weak point of Egyptology. The fact is that, basically, Egypt did not possess our own sense of history. Nothing in its traditions resembles our desire to arrive at a rational narration of events, according to a chain of cause and effect, occurring within the framework of our experience of life: it had no continuous history and scarcely any systematic will to address posterity. The theatre of what we call history is trapped in the grand play of cosmic forces, whose only worthwhile spectators are the gods. The link between these and the Egyptians is formed by the pharaohs. Hence it is not surprising that Egypt recorded nothing but the succession of reigns, the years being designated by reference to their sequence within each of these reigns.

To be sure, as that exceptional hieroglyphic record, the Palermo Stone, attests, for the earliest times the years were characterized by memorable events, frequently of a religious nature. Later, reference was made also to censuses and to years when taxes were levied, as a general rule every two years. Later still, the years of each of the reigns were recorded. Moreover, it would seem that while, during the Middle Kingdom, the year of reign extended from one New Year to the next, in the New Kingdom by contrast it was the date of the king's accession to the throne that was recorded.

Cross-references are also provided by the genealogical records. In some cases, lists of ancestors extend for up to sixty generations, with all the uncertainties that such documents may entail. Another question that has given rise to lengthy debate is that of the possible synchronisms with the history of Western Asia in general and of Mesopotamia in particular. Even for the much later reign of Ramesses II

(1290–1224 BC), during which the mingling together of peoples had become intense, unanimous agreement has not always been reached.

This explains why great hopes have been placed, in regard both to the history of Egypt and to that of Mesopotamia, in ^{14}C dating and in other techniques such as thermoluminescence and dendrochronology.

In fact, the interpretation of physico-chemical dating raises new problems, such as that of the correction of so-called 'calibrated' ^{14}C dates, on account of the non-constant level of ambient radioactivity. As for dates regarded as being absolute, for example those obtained through dendrochronology, these only concern specific samples which have to be placed in their proper context if the date of the event is to be established correctly: in a king's tomb, the wood of the sarcophagus indicates the date when the tree was felled and not that of the king's death!

Our present concern with chronological exactitude must take into account all the data, with more or less satisfactory results. In this work we refer to a number of these chronological debates which arise frequently in the study of this period and which we have deliberately left unsettled. These uncertainties are illustrated in the dating of a famous event in the following example.

The Exodus of the Hebrews, for which no contemporary corroboration is available, in fact concerned only half of one single tribe, that of Joseph, out of the twelve tribes which were later to constitute Israel. It certainly took place in the reign of Ramesses II (c. 1290–1224 BC): a group of habirus, a generic term designating certain nomadic people in western Asia who were requisitioned either for the army or for the great construction works, succeeded in escaping from the vast building site of Pi-Ramesse, the capital of Ramesses II in the Delta (now Tell el-Daba-Qantir), by taking a roundabout path to avoid the Egyptian border posts. The crossing of the Sea of Reeds (Red Sea) episode may doubtless be situated in the present 'Baudouin Lagoon', on the Mediterranean shore, which was indeed subject to sudden and unheralded changes of water level. The path then followed by the Hebrews was determined by the fact that the peoples already inhabiting the area would not let them enter Palestine and forced them to make a long detour south as far as the Gulf of Aqaba before going back northwards through Transjordan, culminating in the taking of Jericho and their settlement in the 'Promised Land'. In year 5 of the reign of Pharaoh Merenptah, in about 1219 BC, the 'Israeli stela' confirms that they actually settled there.

Another significant example is that of the taking of Babylon for which authors in this volume propose dates varying over a period of one and a half centuries (from 1750 to 1595 BC). In countries without written traditions, the ^{14}C calibrated dates have given good arguments for the high chronological scales. Other debates have had important repercussions which C. Renfrew has not hesitated to describe as 'revolutions'. These concern the dating of the Necropolis of Varna (Bulgaria) and the sites of Western Europe, dated to the fifth millennium BC. This places further back in time the origins of the metallurgic and megalithic phenomena which henceforth fall outside the period with which we are concerned. The overall result is to limit the effects of the diffusion theory and to give arguments for a better understanding of the evolution in place following different processes of local innovation. It would be a significant improvement if archeological dated (^{14}C calibrated) confirmed other historical calendars which are hardly known.

It is probable that during the same period, 3000–700 BC other systems were developed for establishing chronology. In China, for example, what we know of the highly sophisticated science of chronology under the Han emperors, during the last centuries BC, proves that this science was rooted in very ancient knowledge. This was also true among the Peruvians of the Chavín period.

BIBLIOGRAPHY

AURENCHE, O.; EVIN, J. (eds) 1987. Liste des dates C-14 des sites du Proche Orient de 14000 à 5700 B.P. In: *Chronologies in the Near East. CNRS International Symposium, Lyon (France), 24–28 November 1986.* Oxford. (BAR Int. Ser., 379.)

BARTA, W. 1983. Zur Entwicklung des ägyptischen Kalenderwesens. *Z. ägyptisch. Sprache Altert. kd.* (Leipzig), Vol. 110, pp. 16–26.

BRINKMAN, J. 1977. Appendix. In: OPPENHEIM, A. L. (ed.), *Ancient Mesopotamia: Portrait of a Dead Civilization.* Chicago/London. 2nd ed. pp. 335–52.

CLOSE, A. 1980. Current Research and Recent Radiocarbon Dates from Northern Africa. *J. Afr. Hist.* (Cambridge), Vol. 21, pp. 145–67; Vol. 25, pp. 1–21.

DERRICOURT, R. M. 1971. Radiocarbon Chronology for Egypt and North Africa. *J. Near East. Stud.* (Chicago, Ill.), Vol. 30, pp. 271–92.

EDWARDS, I. E. S. 1970. Absolute Dating from Egyptian Records and Comparison with Carbon-14 Dating. *Philos. Trans. R. Soc.,* Ser. A, Vol. 269, pp. 11–18.

HASSAN, F. A. 1980. Radiocarbon Chronology of Archaic Egypt. *J. Near East. Stud.* (Chicago, Ill.), Vol. 39, pp. 203–7.

—— 1985. Radiocarbon Chronology of Neolithic and Predynastic Sites in Upper Egypt and the Delta. *Afr. Archaeol. Rev.* (Cambridge), Vol. 3, pp. 95–116.

HORNUNG, E. 1978. *Grundzüge der ägyptischen Geschichte.* Darmstadt.

KRAMER, S. N. 1975. *L'histoire commence à Sumer.* Grenoble.

KRAUS, R. 1985. *Sothis– und Monddaten. Studien zur astronomischen und technischen Chronologie Altägyptens.* Hildesheim.

LIBBY, W. F. 1952. *Radiocarbon Dating.* Chicago, Ill.

LONG, R. D. 1976. Ancient Egyptian Chronology, Radiocarbon Dating and Calibration. *Z. ägyptisch. Sprache Altert. kd.* (Leipzig), Vol. 103, pp. 30–48.

NEUGEBAUER, O.; PARKER, R. A. 1960. *Egyptian Astronomical Texts,* Vol. I. Providence, R.I./London.

PARKER, R. A. 1950. *The Calendars of Ancient Egypt.* Chicago, Ill.

RENFREW, C. 1973. *Before Civilization: The Radiocarbon Revolution and Prehistoric Europe.* London.

SÄVE-SÖDERBERGH, T.; OLSSON, I. V. 1970. In: OLSSON, I. V. (ed.). *Radiocarbon Variation and Absolute Dating.* Stockholm. pp. 35–55.

SUESS, H. E. 1986. Radiocarbon and Egyptology, In: DAVID, A. R. (ed.), *Science in Egyptology.* Manchester, pp. 61–5.

WEILL, R. 1926. *Bases, méthodes et résultats de la chronologie égyptienne.* Paris.

3

ECONOMIC AND SOCIO-POLITICAL DEVELOPMENTS

Mario Liverani

The basic socio-economic structure of the Bronze Age in western Asia is the result of the great revolutionary changes of the strong development of 'first urbanization' (the 'urban revolution' of Gordon Childe; Uruk period: *c.* 3500–3000 BC), that is the birth of the city, the (temple) state, the centralized (redistributive) administration, bureaucracy and writing, especially in the original core of lower Mesopotamia and then in Egypt; and of the 'second urbanization' (*c.* 2700–2200 BC) with the diffusion of the state structures all over the ancient Orient and the shaping of a system of regional states in mutual interaction. Somewhat later in time, the growth of the Harappa/Mohenjo-daro civilization in the Indus Valley, and the passage from the Neolithic to the Bronze Age in China, follow similar lines of development – yet the lack of written records is an obstacle to precise historical reconstructions.

In western Asia, as a result of these changes, a threefold partition of society takes place in relation to the central political power and in relation to the ownership of the means of production. The centre of society and of the political structure is provided by the 'great organizations' (Oppenheim, 1967), that is, the temples and the royal palaces where, in addition to religious and political activities, entire sections of the economy concentrate: in particular those related to the transformation of goods, redistribution, exchange, services. Craftsmanship, trade, cults, administration, war, and all other specialized activities are largely monopolized by the 'great organizations' and carried on by people who do not own the means of production, which belongs in fact to the temple or the king, but work for them and receive from them their recompense. Since the authority commanding all these activities is the same as the political power, political dependence is coterminous with economic dependence. The members of the palace (or temple) sector are economically 'servants' of the king (or his symbolic hypostasis, the god); at the same time they are his political subjects. In the redistributive system administered by the Bronze Age states, the palace dependants receive a real profit: in exchange for specialized services, their maintenance is provided for, even well beyond the simple subsistence levels.

A second category is composed of the peasantry, deriving from the pre-urban (that is Neolithic and Chalcolithic) mode of production. Peasants are devoted to food production (agriculture and animal husbandry), and located in village communities as opposed to the palace dependants who are centred in the city. They have no working specialization, and are owners of the relevant means of production (fields, cattle) according to their family and kin structure. This group is linked to the political and economic core, the palace, by a tributary relationship. A percentage of the produce (the 'tithe') and of the work (the corvée) is sent to the palace in order to maintain the managing personnel and the specialized (non-food-producing) workers, and in order to finance public works (for example the canals) and the display hoarding (to begin with, the building of the palace and the temples themselves), so necessary for the cohesion of the state. As a return for the food provided, the peasantry receive from the palace basic productive, religious and military services. Quite often, however, a kind of 'mutation' takes place inside the redistributive system, where the forwarding of food from the villages to the palace continues, but the return is reduced to merely ideological expressions (religious and political propaganda). This second group is tributary and politically subject to the palace; but it is economically 'free', since the peasants own their means of production.

Lastly, a third element has a tenuous link to the palace and the town (and therefore the state). It consists of tribal groups, mainly devoted to transhumant sheep-rearing, in the two variant forms of 'vertical' transhumance in hilly countries (Anatolia, Armenia, Iran) and 'horizontal' transhumance in the semi-arid plateaus. This third group is free not only economically – as owner of the means of production and not even subject to consolidated tribute – but also politically, not recognizing the authority of the king, who has serious problems in establishing his power upon a rarified demographic texture and a mobile organization. The urban states and their agricultural hinterland are concentrated (and isolated) in the most profitable farming lands; the nomadic belt often separates them by occupying the intermediate areas (mountains or steppe). The urban states brand the nomads as 'brigands', dangerous because of their aggressiveness and mobility. While it is true that pastoral tribes may covet the goods stored in the town, the economic and military pressure exerted by the urban state on the nomads is more burdensome: by trying to subdue them to a tribute relationship, by exploiting the raw materials in the peripheral areas, by reducing the pasture-lands to the advantage of the tillage-lands.

From a strictly social point of view (family and kin structure, inheritance of the means of production), basic differences exist between the two groups. In the palace (and temple), the individual worker (generally a specialized one) has a direct link with the central administration: in exchange for his service the palace dependant receives a personal recompense, originally in the form of rations and eventually (in the period here analysed) in the form of land allotment. The allotment is personalized, subject to conditions, and reversible in the event that the service is no longer performed. The personal nature of work and recompense, the relevance of personal skill, the non-transferability (at least in theory) of lands (whose ownership belongs to the palace or temple) produce a reduction of kinship relations to the advantage of the personal relationship with the central agency. In the palace group, therefore, the characteristic features are: nuclear families, positive evaluation of personal merits, small relevance of inheritance procedures, and the disappearance of larger kin ties.

For the peasants in the village the situation is quite different. The productive unit is the nuclear family, but kinship roles are very important, and the inheritance of land is basically automatic. From birth, any member of a given family has a destiny largely fixed not so much by his personal skill as by his position in the inheritance order, and by possible marriage ties. The solidarity of the extended family is moreover effective in maintaining the relationship among the various families stable over time, consequently reducing the risk of dispossession and marginalization.

Lastly, also in the pastoral/tribal sphere, the relevance of the extended family, the owner of the means of production (herds, pastures, transhumance tracks), and the basic political structure are determined by the method of production. The tribe is a complex of extended families, bound together by economic interests (use of the same pastures) and by ideological motivations centred on the presumed descent from a common ancestor, eponym of the tribe and venerated in cult.

THE LATE BRONZE AGE

Towards the middle of the second millennium BC, these basic structures undergo a process of change, partly due to the inner socio-economic dynamics, and partly to external factors. In comparison to the Early and Middle Bronze Age periods, the Late Bronze Age is characterized by a contraction of urban settlements and agricultural exploitation, now limited to the areas better provided with water (irrigation or rainfall). It is also possible that a middle-term worsening of climatic conditions plays a role; in any case it is certain that large semi-arid regions previously settled by towns and villages are progressively abandoned – especially in inner Syria, Transjordan, and central Iran. This trend leaves larger space for the pastoral sphere, and increases the difficulties experienced by the extant urban centres in maintaining high standards of consumption and conspicuous display while drawing on a reduced productive base. The demographic trend remains a positive one in some areas not affected by the settlement crisis (Egypt and the Aegean reach their peaks for all the Bronze Age); but all over western Asia the population undergoes an evident decrease.

In the Indus Valley, after the sudden collapse of the Indus civilization, a difficult recovery of the old demographic levels and settlement system is slowly taking place. In far-away China, on the contrary, the general trend is quite different (and unconnected): by the middle of the second millennium

BC the first large towns and political structures of regional extent are finally emerging, and with the Shang dynasty we have for the first time a sound connection between archaeological remains and historical records.

During this time of demographic and productive disturbance, important changes in political ideology and in technology are effective in modifying the socio-economic structure. The Middle Bronze Age kingship paid special and steadfast attention to the preservation of the social balance. Thanks to the periodical issue of royal edicts of debt remission, 'free' peasants (always running the risk of losing their freedom and their lands for irreversible indebtedness) receive some relief in times of difficult economic conditions. In the Late Bronze Age, however, remission edicts are no longer issued, indebtedness is unlimited, and the king – far from seeking a remedy – takes advantage of the current process with a stronger taxation and exploitation policy. The 'just and righteous' king of the Middle Bronze Age is succeeded by a kingship characterized by personal bravery and belonging to a privileged class devoted to luxury and ostentation.

It should be emphasized that the shift from the Middle to the Late Bronze Age is marked in particular by the spread of horses, reared and trained to draw the light two-wheeled chariot for war and hunting. The peasant infantry loses its traditional importance, while a class of 'war specialists' acquires a new pre-eminence. The chariot-warriors are maintained by the palace in order that they may raise horses, acquire a sophisticated armour, and train in brave and knightly war. Besides the king, the chariot-warriors build up a kind of military aristocracy, hold large real properties in exchange for their service and subdue the indebted peasantry to the condition of 'serfs' (still tilling fields that are no more their own). The same reduction of the geographical space controlled by the royal palace, in addition to the centralization of wealth and political power in the hands of the military aristocracy, gives the palace a new character. It is no longer only the managing centre for its own territory; it is now also a link in the interregional network (with clear class connotations), which monopolizes high-value specialized craftsmanship, freezes an enormous amount of wealth in expensive equipment and keeps in contact through inter-dynastic marriages, exchange of gifts, and exchange of messages.

The different specialized groups are mostly dependent on the palace (temples being now economic agencies subordinated to the palace). The proportion is quite different from area to area, but we may guess that 20 per cent of the population was composed of palace dependants, classified in various groups ('guilds' would be a very misleading term in this period), with different ranks, social prestige and economic recompense. The top of the social and economic ranking is occupied by warriors, scribes, priests and merchants. The warriors – that is, the chariot-warriors (maryannu is the technical term, Indo-Iranian in origin) – hold large estates, are related by marriage or descent to the king, and share his heroic and élite ideology. Horses and chariots, probably originating from central Asia, reach upper Mesopotamia (Mitanni), lower Mesopotamia (Cassites), Syria-Palestine, Anatolia (the Hittite kingdom and others), the Aegean (Myceneans) and Egypt (New Kingdom); in the same period they also reach northern India and China. Besides the chariot-warriors, the palace maintains lower-rank military personnel, mainly as guards.

Priests are generally reduced to the rank of king's dependants, the central (political and economic) role of the temple having by now faded out. They keep a high prestige, however, even in regions where the temples are small buildings devoted to cult activities only. Elsewhere the temples maintain large estates and groups of serfs: this is especially true of Egypt and Babylonia, as a legacy of the first urbanization that took place under the impetus of temple-building. Scribes and administrative personnel also have a high social prestige and economic recompense, since they monopolize a technical skill (the logo-syllabic writing) very difficult to acquire and necessary for the management of palace activities.

The merchants' prestige is not particularly high, but their wealth is noteworthy. In general terms, they are trade agents of the palace, acting by the king's order and using the king's financial support. Yet the relationship between palace and merchants, and the very role of the merchants, undergoes important changes from the third millennium BC to the Late Bronze Age period. In the third millennium BC merchants received from the palace or the temple an endowment (in silver or in goods) and went away to remote lands in order to acquire materials not available at home. On their return they settled accounts with the central administration, checking that the value of the imported materials was the equivalent of the original endowment. In the Late Bronze Age the theoretical principle is still the same, with two important changes. First, the merchants add their own private activities to the institutional one. Moreover, they are the only social group provided with 'cash' money (silver) and credits, and become increasingly more involved in loan activities (for interest, personal pledges, mortgage), thus acquiring additional wealth. This financial activity is carried out in the intervals – so to say – of the commercial activity proper: accounts are settled one year after the endowment has been received, a year that can be partly spent in travelling, but partly also in lending money in the home country.

The craftsmen, although skilled in refined techniques and authors of the artistic pictures so characteristic of ancient Oriental societies in the Late Bronze Age, get lower profits. They work inside the palace organization, receive (as a result of the trade activities of the palace) raw materials of distant origin and high value (wood and ivory, metals and precious stones), their main client being the palace. They are even 'lent' from palace to palace, so spreading the working procedures and the artistic tastes, but partly losing their personal freedom.

Food production belongs mainly to the sphere built up of 'free' peasants, engaged especially in dry-farming. Agricultural and pastoral activities may also be accomplished by palace dependants (serfs) in farms belonging to the king or the temples, as is the case in lower Mesopotamia and also (in different forms) in Egypt and Anatolia, but much less in Syria-Palestine and in upper Mesopotamia. Whereas the palace receives only a tribute from the free villages, it receives much more from its own farms (the total produce, with deduction of the seed for the next season and rations for the serfs). But the palace cannot increase direct exploitation too much, because palace farms can only function profitably with peasant work service (corvée). The peasants provide a necessary reservoir of manpower which is exploited in the most intensive seasonal work, and allows the palace to keep only a limited number of permanent serfs. (This obviously increases the problems of the village sphere.)

In contemporary China, some basic features are different: the agricultural technology and management seem more backward, the social structure is strongly dependent on kinship ties, and the social ideology is consequently dominated

by an ancestor cult. Yet the relationship between town and countryside is basically the same, with a concentration of specialized craftsmen (bronze working is especially highly developed) in the palace circle, and a large tributary population of peasants ensuring the production of food and the availability of a work-force for the public enterprises of canal digging and temple building. Even the role of the chariotry in warfare characterizes the Shang dynasty as being on a par with the Late Bronze Age period in western Asia and the 'heroic age' of India – a coincidence hardly to be imputed to independent development. Unfortunately, the available written records do not allow us to reconstruct Chinese society of the mid-second millennium BC with the detail possible for western Asia.

EVOLUTIONARY TRENDS

The close connection between the palace and the free sphere (including the pressure of the palace on the free sphere) produces an exchange of influences in both directions which changes the social structure of western Asia. Under the influence of the 'free' peasantry, with its model of family coherence and family transmission of properties, the inheritance of personal position and service in the palace sphere also becomes more and more widespread. Father is succeeded by son, and consequently the land parcel given as payment for service remains in the possession of the same family, gradually losing the character of a conditional and time-limited grant and merging with the family lands. Once the holdings are so consolidated, the palace dependants tend to release their service relationships. In some cases the service becomes a sinecure or a mere title; in others the king gives the dependant an 'exemption' from service; in still other cases he prefers to substitute for personal service a payment in silver – a yearly one or a one-off payment. At the end of this process, here described in a theoretical pattern not always followed in reality, the palace remains deprived of land and of service, receiving occasional profits in cash, but its survival in the long run is seriously endangered.

On the other hand, the palace model of individual property and the positive evaluation of the personal merits influences the traditional family structure in the village sphere. Hereditary transmission is no longer automatic (with a privileged share for the first-born), but is now conditioned by the behaviour of sons toward parents. The father can disinherit, or he can prefer one son to another; adoptions grow in number, and also the freeing of domestic (female) slaves. Summing up, the family is more than in the past subject to personal events to the detriment of its pre-conceived structure. Moreover, economic necessity increases the sale of lands. In the Middle Bronze Age customs existed which tried to keep every family in its ancestral lands. These customary norms are no longer in use in the Late Bronze Age, when the sale of land is free (or disguised as 'false adoption' or other juridical fictions). The changes within the traditional family, and the end of solidarity in the extended family lead to a generalized process of expropriation of lands in the 'free' sphere, to the advantage of money-lenders (merchants and other palace officials). During the Late Bronze Age the number of fleeing indebted peasants and slaves increases, and in some areas reaches the dimension of a social trend. The palace (that is the state), in agreement with the creditors, organizes a judicial (and police) structure for the pursuit and delivery of runaways. Neighbouring states enter into treaties for the mutual return of refugees, who sometimes had a political motive for fleeing but more often are simply debtors and slaves.

Within the framework of these evolutionary trends, the pastoral tribe – little involved in palace activities during the Late Bronze Age – takes the role of an alternative state model, or at least an alternative focal point, attracting runaways (isolated or in groups), and even villages which, although still keeping their physical position, may move from a tributary relationship to the palace to an inclusion in the kin-structure of the tribe. This kind of process takes place only where suitable geographical preconditions exist. In the large alluvium of Mesopotamia and Egypt the control exerted by the state is quite strict, and the political administration is unified over a large area. But in regions such as Syria, Palestine, and the mountain valleys of Anatolia and Iran, the political fragmentation and the coexistence at short distances of both elements (palace and tribe) make the situation more open and movable, allow the runaways an easier escape, and produce greater trouble for the urban states.

THE EARLY IRON AGE: CRISIS AND NEW STRUCTURES

The inner factors of crisis, so characteristic of the final phase of the Bronze Age, receive a sudden acceleration by external pressure at the beginning of the twelfth century BC. The eastern Mediterranean is involved in migratory movements that throw the political system into confusion, destroy many palaces and produce a void in local organization, thus making the emergence of new socio-economic models easier. The crisis and subsequent rearrangement are more intense in the Aegean, in Anatolia, Syria, Palestine and Cyprus. In the Nile Valley and in the lands east of the Euphrates, untouched by immigrants, the states already existing (Egypt, Assyria, Babylonia, Elam) can resist, but their international and inner relationships become affected.

West of the Euphrates, the eclipse of the royal palaces is almost total for a while and specialized craftsmanship (basically centred in the palace) collapses, as does the international network (exchange of gifts, inter-dynastic marriages, diplomacy, and so on). Merchants, artisans, scribes and administrative officials, chariot-warriors, all lose their economic base and their (almost unique) client. Some groups (for example the *maryannu*) simply disappear from the documentary record: their role, already transformed into a sinecure, is by now finished. Other groups (for example the merchants) on the contrary are able to reorganize their activities in a different framework with private enterprise, private ownership of the means of production, plurality of clients and technological improvements.

The destruction of the Late Bronze Age palaces has some kind of freeing effect on various aspects of culture and technology, here relevant for its impact on the socio-economic order. Iron metallurgy and alphabetic writing, whose bases were already established in the Late Bronze Age, can now become more widespread due to the collapse of the palace bronze-workers, the interruption of the long-distance metal (tin) trade, and the disappearance of the specialized scribes controlling the complex and time-honoured logo-syllabic (cuneiform) writing. Other technological improvements (large-scale breeding of camels and dromedaries, irrigation of semi-arid lands, terracing of the hilly slopes) produce a change in the settlement pattern. When compared to the Late Bronze Age, the Iron Age has a much more widespread settlement: in addition to the coasts and valleys, the arid plateaus and the hills are settled anew; even the desert oases are reached and the interregional network is reshaped and considerably widened. The neat distinction during the Bronze Age between large fortified towns (the seat of the palace, that is political power, specialized crafts, ceremonial activities) and small open villages devoted to food production partly disappears in the Iron Age. Towns are now smaller, large villages are fortified, and the distribution of specialized functions throughout is more varied. In this new scene, an important role is played by the pastoral tribes – both the old 'half nomads' (sheep-breeders) and the new 'full nomads' (camel-breeders). In some regions they assume their (already mentioned) role as political focal points, an alternative to the palace. Peasant villages, formerly the administrative units of the palace state, become clans of the tribe dominating the area. The dichotomy of nomads and sedentary people becomes less evident. The tribe becomes in some cases politically dominant. The sedentarization of nomads is archaeologically visible in the new settlements in previously void areas (inner Syria, Transjordan, central Iran); the 'full nomads' spread into areas (especially northern Arabia) previously unimportant from an historical viewpoint.

The collapse of the palace-centred states and the increased importance of the pastoral tribe give birth to a new state model. The state in the Bronze Age was a purely territorial and administrative unit (an area controlled by a royal city). In the Iron Age state, the political membership is the result of ethnic, kinship and religious factors. Differences in language and religion become politically important, and are symbolically linked with the descent from a common ancestor and the cult of a 'national' god.

At the socio-economic level, the collapse of the palace and the new role of the tribe lead to the increased importance of the 'free' sphere of village communities to the detriment of the 'king's servants'. Some Late Bronze Age evolutionary trends (for example the transformation of family relationships) are for the moment halted. But other trends continue their progress, especially those related to personal responsibility, individual property and the shaping of human personality. Some groups, previously belonging to the palace sphere (for example merchants and craftsmen) find a new setting, separate themselves from the political élite, and constitute in some cases a true counterpart to the royal palace. The palace receives a new impetus (especially from the tenth century BC on), but the city assemblies and the councils of elders retain a political (not only judicial) role. In the large and traditional kingdoms of Egypt and Babylonia, kept apart from the most acute factors of crisis but also from the most promising features of the new order, socio-economic changes continue. The previously 'free' peasants undergo a kind of generalized serfdom. The groups of scribes, priests and specialized craftsmen centred on the temples look for a new status in their relations with the palace, based on grants of 'freedom', tax and corvée exemptions, and 'guild' organization, thus protecting their autonomy and serving a more varied clientele.

In China, the shift from the Shang to the (western) Zhou dynasty seems to take place as a consequence of inner struggles, with no major social upheaval marking the end of the second millennium BC. Also, the role of nomadic peoples, which will become so important in the following stages of Chinese history, remains for the moment outside the historical record – with the dynamics between an 'inner' country and the 'outer' lands still basically contained in the very core of Chinese civilization.

THE IMPACT OF THE EMPIRES

The differences between a 'western' area affected by collapse and restructuring in the Early Iron Age and an 'eastern' area keeping a more traditional order is to some extent eliminated by the imperial expansion of Assyria in the ninth and in the eighth-seventh centuries BC. This is a mainly political phenomenon (in its various elements: military, administrative, and so on); but it has relevant effects in the field of culture (towards unification but also impoverishment), and in its socio-economic structures.

At the core of the empire, in the Assyrian capital cities, management, administrative and ceremonial activities and specialized work are concentrated, but in new forms and on a larger scale. The scale is much larger because the Assyrian capital cities are able to draw from an extended hinterland (encompassing the entire western Asia), which is exploited in its human and material resources according to procedures much more violent than in the Bronze Age. In the Assyrian towns the concentration of people is unprecedented, and inside the towns the palace sphere is abnormally expanded. The high officials of court and state, civil governors and military officers, reach high economic positions, based on large estates granted by the king, abundant manpower obtained from war campaigns and fiscal privileges. Their fortunes are subject to the king's arbitrary acts, however, so that substantial patrimonies can be accumulated and lost in a short time, following the failure of personal relationships, or by reason of slander and internal struggles severing family loyalty ties. It is not by chance that the class privileged by the king is that of the eunuchs, which is characterized by a peculiar personal loyalty and the inability to transmit position and wealth to natural heirs.

Even stronger is the impact of the Assyrian empire on the surrounding, conquered regions. The political and military 'imperialism' of the Bronze Age led to a tributary relationship, but left untouched the local political structures, their productive apparatus and their cultural characteristics. The Assyrian conquest, on the contrary, especially from the mid-eighth century BC, leads to physical destruction and political annexation, transforming the autonomous states into provinces of the empire. The local palaces are destroyed, the local specialized personnel (scribes, craftsmen, merchants and so on) are either eliminated or deported to Assyria, with the twofold aim of breaking any possibility of political recovery and of acquiring for the central city competences particularly appreciated for their exotic nature. The capital of the empire, ideally located at the centre of the world, is the beneficiary of a centralization not only of food and raw materials, but also of technologies and art styles from the conquered states, which were until recently the seat of cultural activities and whose populations are now brutally enslaved and homogenized.

Partly similar is the condition of the countryside and the food-producing population. Here violent destruction leads to a collapse of human settlements in the conquered regions, as can be appreciated from the archaeological record. Also in this case massive deportations take place, both towards the Assyrian countryside and between different provinces, with the double aim of homogenizing the conquered peoples (depriving them of any 'national' character) and repopulating Assyria, whose depopulation (as a result of constant

military involvement) was no less serious than that in the conquered regions. The decimation of the inner class of free peasants, and their substitution with deportees, bring about a radical change in the social landscape of Assyria. Village communities become settlements of serfs who are the property of the king or of the great officials (landowners), and who are often deprived of their original family setting, in addition to their religion, language and culture.

At the end of the process, the impression we get, equal to that of the Greeks when they entered into contact with the Oriental empires, is one of 'generalized serfdom' (or even of 'generalized slavery'). The old class of palace dependants, structurally 'servants' of the king, improve their economic position but are still dependent on the king and subject to his arbitrary acts. The old class of 'free' (but economically depressed) peasants in the village communities, on the other hand, loses its economic autonomy (that is the ownership of the means of production) as a result of long-term indebtedness, and also as a result of the new imperialistic policy of enslavement and deportation.

While this process reduces most of western Asia to a generalized serfdom, the elements of innovation and of freedom in the Early Iron Age find a new impetus in marginal areas, external to the empire but destined to a new centrality in an enlarged arena. The Greek *poleis* of the archaic period and the Phoenician city-states increase their trade and craftsmanship, consolidate the relevance of non-royal political structures (city assemblies and the like), and attain a more widespread and differentiated participation in the decisional responsibility and in the social distribution of resources. In a quite different socio-economic and political environment, something similar can be said of pastoral nations in the Syro-Arabic and Iranian areas. These too remain external to the empire; these too develop forms of political organization and economic activity less subject to the burden of a central palace. Transhumant pastoralism, a caravan trade and emerging mining activities acquire in the Later Iron Age a new centrality and relevance, granting the entire western Asia area a higher standard of socio-economic complexity.

Different again is the case of the great traditional centres of civilization, Egypt and Babylonia. They are still, in the Iron Age, the largest 'markets' of western Asia, because they have the largest concentrations of population, and they produce the largest amounts of food. The same holds true for the Indus Valley in the Indian subcontinent and for the river valleys in China. Egypt and Babylonia are partly involved in imperial conquest, but they are better provided with a time-honoured cultural tradition. The cultural trends to archaism and traditionalism have their parallel, at the socio-economic level, in the revival of the temples as centres of productive and redistributive activities, still using the old administrative tools of the logo-syllabic writing. The temple-cities, which had been the core of the state at the time of the first urbanization, are now in some way the local counterpart, attached to their fiscal exemptions, organized in 'guild' structures. They are part of an economic system that can be labelled 'market' only in the sense that goods are obtained not simply as a return for a service, but in the frame of a network where labour, salary and goods are exchanged among a plurality of agencies of different juridical status.

In different ways, according to their relationship to the imperial unification, the burden of tradition and their participation in the reorganization of the Early Iron Age, all the component parts of western Asia are well on the way at the end of the seventh century BC towards a socio-economic system quite different from that of the Bronze Age. At this point, however, the process confronts two different and almost opposed issues. In the marginal environments – be they politically and geographically so, like the Greek city-states, or socially so, like the Hebrew deportees inside the empire – the great changes of the 'axial age' take place. These innovations go in the direction of rational science, of ethical religions, individualism and (in the economic field) a pluralistic structure where the state is only one of the components. On the other hand, in the traditional environments of Egypt and Mesopotamia (by now included in the Achaemenian empire), the trends to conservatism prevail, leading to a substantial re-establishment of the central role of the royal court over an enslaved population not even provided (as it was in the Bronze Age) with an inner 'vertical' (that is, social) and 'horizontal' (that is, geographical) diversification.

In China, the development of the earlier (western) Shou dynasty is only very superficially parallel to that of the Assyrian empire. Certainly a process of consolidation and enlargement of the state structures takes place, but the image of a true and proper Chinese 'empire' seems to be an anachronistic projection of a later (Han) situation. It is only toward the middle of the first millennium BC that some degree of co-ordination can be suggested for historical development throughout all the Eurasiatic territories. The 'axial age' of the seventh century BC will be characterized by widespread social and cultural trends, partly similar all over the area: from the emergence of the Yonian philosophers and scientists in archaic Greece, and the activity of the Hebrew prophets, to the ethical religions known by the names of Zoroaster in Iran, of Buddha in India, of Confucius in China. These spiritual movements are linked with substantial changes in social and economic relations as well; but this is the subject for a new chapter in the development of human history.

BIBLIOGRAPHY

ADAMS, R. MCC. 1981. *Heartland of Cities*. Chicago, Ill.

AERTS, A.; KLENGEL, H. (eds) 1990. *The Town as Regional Economic Centre in the Ancient Near East*. Leuven.

ARCHI, A. (ed.) 1984. *Circulation of Goods in the Non-Palatial Context in the Ancient Near East*. Roma.

BALKAN, K. 1986. *Studies in Babylonian Feudalism of the Kassite Period*. Malibu, Calif.

BOROWSKI, O. 1987. *Agriculture in Iron Age Israel*. Winona Lake, Ind.

BRENTJES, B. (ed.) 1988. *Das Grundeigentum in Mesopotamien*. Berlin.

BRIANT, P. 1982. *Etat et pasteurs au Moyen Orient ancien*. Paris/Cambridge.

BUCCELLATI, G. 1967. *Cities and Nations of Ancient Syria*. Roma.

BULLIET, R. W. 1990. *The Camel and the Wheel*. New York.

COGAN, M. 1971. *Imperialism and Religion*. Pittsburg, Pa.

DIAKONOFF, I. M. 1967a. Die hethitische Gesellschaft. *Mitt. Inst. Orientforsch.*, Vol. 13, pp. 313–66.

—— 1967b, 1968. [Problems of Economics. The Structure of Near Eastern Society before the Middle of the Second Millennium BC] *Vestn. Drevnej Istor.*, No. 4, pp. 13–35, 1967; No. 3, pp. 3–27, 1968; No. 4, pp. 3–40, 1968 (translated into English in *Oikumene*, Vol. 3 (1982), pp. 7–100).

—— 1969. Agrarian Conditions in Middle Assyria. In:——(ed.), *Ancient Mesopotamia*. Moscow. pp. 204–34.

—— (ed.) 1991. *Early Antiquity*. Chicago, Ill./London.

FALES, F. M. 1973. *Censimenti e catasti de epoca neo-assira*. Roma.

—— 1975. Popolazione servile e programmazione padronale in tarda età neo-assira. *Oriens antiq.* (Roma), Vol. 14, pp. 325–60.

—— 1990. The Rural Landscape of the Neo-Assyrian Empire: A Survey, *State Arch. Assyria, Bull.*, Vol. 4, pp. 81–142.

FRICK, F. 1985. *The Formation of the State in Ancient Israel*. Winona Lake, Ind.

GARELLI, P. 1967. Le problème de la 'féodalité' assyrienne du XVème au XIIème siècle av. J. C. *Semitica*, Vol. 17, pp. 5–21.

GELB, I. J. 1967. Approaches to the Study of Ancient Economy. *J. am. Orient. Soc.* (New Haven, Conn.), Vol. 87, pp. 1–8.

GEUS, C. de. 1976. *The Tribes of Israel*. Amsterdam.

GIBSON, MCG. 1974. Violation of Fallow and Engineered Disaster in Mesopotamian Civilization. In: DOWNING, T. E.; GIBSON, MCG. (eds), *Irrigation's Impact on Society*. Tucson, Ariz. pp. 7–19.

GOBLOT, H. 1979. *Les qanats*. Paris.

GOTTWALD, N. K. 1979. *The Tribes of Yahweh*. New York.

HELTZER, M. 1976. *The Rural Community in Ancient Ugarit*. Wiesbaden.

—— 1982. *The Internal Organization of the Kingdom of Ugarit*. Wiesbaden.

HELTZER, M.; LIPINSKI, E. (eds) 1988. *Society and Economy in the Eastern Mediterranean (c. 1500–1000 BC)*. Leuven.

HOPKINS, D. C. 1983. *The Highlands of Canaan*. Winona Lake, Ind.

JACOBSON, V. 1969. The Social Structure of the Neo-Assyrian Empire. In: DIAKANOFF, I. M. (ed.), *Ancient Mesopotamia*. Moscow. pp. 277–95.

JANSSEN, J. J. 1975. Prolegomena to the Study of Egypt's Economic History During the New Kingdom. *Stud. altägypt. Kult.*, Vol. 3, pp. 127–84

—— 1981. Die Struktur der pharaonischen Wirtschaft. *Gött. Misz.*, Vol. 48, pp. 59–77.

KLENGEL, H. 1972. *Zwischen Zelt und Palast*. Leipzig.

—— (ed.) 1989. *Kulturgeschichte des alten Vorderasien*. Berlin.

KRAUS, F. R. 1969. Erbrechtliche Terminologie im alten Mesopotamien In: DAVID, M.; KRAUS, F. R.; PESTMAN, P.W. (eds.). *Essays on Oriental Laws of Succession*. Leiden. pp. 1–57.

LEMCHE, P. 1982. *Early Israel*. Leiden.

LIPINE, L. A. 1960. The Assyrian Family in the Second Half of the Second Millennium BC. *Cah. Hist. mond.*, Vol. 6, pp. 628–43.

LIPINSKI, E. (ed.) 1979. *State and Temple Economy in the Ancient Near East*. Leuven. 2 vols.

LIVERANI, M. 1975. Communautés de village et palais royal dans la Syrie du II millénaire. *J. econ. soc. Hist. Orient* (Leiden), Vol. 18, pp. 146–64.

—— 1976. Il modo di produzione. In: *L'alba della civiltà*. Torino. Vol. 2, pp. 1–126.

—— 1984. Land Tenure and Inheritance in the Ancient Near East: the Interaction between 'Palace' and 'Family' Sectors. In: KHALIDI, T. (ed.), *Land Tenure and Social Transformation in the Middle East*. Bairūt. pp. 33–44.

—— 1986. The Collapse of the Near Eastern Regional System at the End of the Bronze Age. In: ROWLANDS, M.; LARSEN, M. T.; KRISTIANSEN, K. (eds), *Centre and Periphery in the Ancient World*. Cambridge. pp. 66–73.

—— 1988. *Antico Oriente, Storia, società, economia*. Roma.

—— 1990. *Prestige and Interest*. Padova.

MALBRAN-LABAT, F. 1982. *L'armée et l'organisation militaire de l'Assyrie*. Genève.

MELLINK, M. (ed.) 1964. *Dark Age and Nomads c. 1000 BC*. Istanbul.

MENU, B. 1970. *Le régime juridique des terres et du personnel attaché à la terre dans le Papyrus Wilbour*. Lille.

MUSTI, D. (ed.). 1985. *Le origini dei Greci: Dori e mondo egeo*. Roma.

OATES, D. 1968. *Studies in the Ancient History of Northern Iraq*. London.

ODED, B. 1979. *Mass Deportation and Deportees in the Neo-Assyrian Empire*. Wiesbaden.

—— 1992. *War, Peace and Empire*. Wiesbaden.

OPPENHEIM, A. L. 1967. A New Look at the Structure of Mesopotamian Society. *J. econ. soc. Hist. Orient* (Leiden), Vol. 10, pp. 1–16.

PESTMAN, P. W. 1968. Burial and Inheritance in the Community of the Mecropolis Workmen at Thebes. *J. econ. soc. Hist. Orient* (Leiden), Vol. 11, pp. 137–70.

POSTGATE, J. N. 1974. *Taxation and Conscription in the Assyrian Empire*. Roma.

POWELL, M. (ed.). 1987. *Labor in the Ancient Near East*. New Haven, Conn.

READE, J. 1978. Studies in Assyrian Geography. *Rev. Assyriol.* (Paris), Vol. 72, pp. 47–72, 157–80.

REVIV, H. 1972. Some Comments on the Maryannu. *Israel Explor. J.*, Vol. 22, pp. 218–28.

SANDERS, N. 1978. *The Sea Peoples*. London.

SAPIN, J. 1981, 1982. La géographie humaine de la Syrie-Palestine au deuxième millénaire av. J.C. *J. écon. soc. Hist. Orient* (Leiden), Vol. 24 (1981), pp. 1–62; Vol. 25 (1982), pp. 1–49, 114–86.

SCHACHERMYER, F. 1982. *Die Levante im Zeitalter der Wanderungen*. Wien.

STAGER, L. 1985. The Archaeology of the Family in Ancient Israel. *Bull. am. Sch. Orient. Res.* (New Haven, Conn.), Vol. 260, pp. 1–35.

STRANGE, J. 1987. The Transition from the Bronze Age to the Iron Age in the Eastern Mediterranean and the Emergence of the Israelite State. *Scand. J. Old Testam.*, Vol. 1, pp. 1–19.

WALDBAUM, J. 1978. *From Bronze to Iron*. Göteborg.

WALSER, G. (ed.) 1964. *Neuere Hethiterforschungen*. Wiesbaden.

WERTIME, T.A.; MUHLY, J. (eds) 1980. *The Coming of the Age of Iron*. New Haven, Conn.

ZACCAGNINI, C. 1973. *The Rural Landscape of the Land of Arraphe*. Roma.

—— 1981. Modo di produzione e Vicino Oriente antico. *Dialoghi Archaeol.*, Vol. 3, No. 3, pp. 3–65.

—— 1984. Proprietà fondiaria e dipendenza rurale nelle Mesopotamia settentrionale (XV-XIV sec. A.C.). *Stud. Stor.*, Vol. 25, pp. 691–723.

—— (ed.) 1989. *Production and Consumption*. Budapest.

4

SEDENTARY AGRICULTURAL AND NOMADIC PASTORAL POPULATIONS (3000–700 BC)

Andrew Sherratt

When European writers first began to systematize their observations on the diversity of the world's peoples, in the eighteenth century AD, they created a set of categories which have dominated discussion ever since: hunters, pastoralists, farmers and city-dwellers (Schnapp, 1993). From the mobile life of the wandering hunter, to the stability of urban settlement, the continuing theme seemed to be one of increased sedentism – a gradual process of 'settling down'.

Today, through the growth of archaeological fieldwork and investigation (Flon, 1985), a different picture has emerged. The image of 'Man the hunter' seems too simple a characterization of the diversity of pre-agricultural populations. Sedentism is no longer synonymous with farming, since coastal foraging can also sustain dense, sedentary populations; while the mobility of Arctic and desert hunters can be seen as a sensitive adaptation to life in demanding environments at the limits of human occupation – as great an achievement, and as specialized a mode of existence, as the increasingly arduous life of populations dependent on the yearly commitment to tending growing crops. So, too, with pastoralism: no longer a transitional phase between the wandering life of the hunter and the settled existence of the farmer, it now appears rather to be a specialized offshoot of the balanced plant and animal husbandry practised by the first farmers – the result of an adjustment to the demands of gaining a livelihood from the harsh and often unpredictable regions of the steppes and semi-deserts, or among mountains and upland valleys. The same argument can be applied to the supposedly 'primitive' forms of agriculture characterized by swiddening (shifting agriculture or 'slash-and-burn' farming), in which patches of land are temporarily cleared and cultivated, before being abandoned for fresh fields carved from the forest. Such systems of cultivation are not relics of a primeval form of simple farming, but rather represent a delicate adjustment to the soils of tropical or Boreal forests, which are subject to severe degradation if cropped by more intensive methods (as is increasingly evident in the world today). This ethnographic diversity must therefore be seen as part of a pattern of increasing specialization and adaptation to a range of global environments which was taking place during the later Holocene; and such developments occurred in parallel with the emergence of more intensive systems of food production which were associated with the emergence of urban life.

It is salutary, therefore, to remember that cultures such as those of the Inuit or the inhabitants of Polynesia were created on the same timescale as those of the civilizations of Mesopotamia, China and the Americas; and that the evolution of farming systems in Europe, or the emergence of pastoral populations on the steppes of central Asia and the desert regions of North Africa, must be seen within the same framework as the growth of large-scale irrigation systems and the intensive cultivation of tree crops – dates, olives and vines – grown to supply the burgeoning needs of cities and their specialized consumers.

It is even more relevant to see the emergence of these different forms of subsistence economy as a set of parallel and largely contemporaneous developments when it is realized that in some cases they formed a related and mutually dependent set of specializations, which were historically connected. It has often been observed, for instance, that a pastoralist lifestyle in western Asia is dependent for many aspects of its existence on the acquisition of supplies – either of grain or of items of technological equipment – from neighbouring sedentary agriculturalists; and moreover that demographically the two groups together form part of a single system, within which constant flows of surplus population take place as members of pastoral communities, who cannot accumulate the flocks and herds needed for successful stock-raising, become accommodated to agricultural groups – sometimes even changing their language and ethnic affiliations to do so (Barth, 1969). In many cases, such pastoral groups are best regarded as forming a zone of specialist production on the edge of urban and farming populations in more fertile conditions for cultivation. Such examples challenge the stereotypes of simple, set 'lifeways' correlated with clear ethnic and cultural distinctions, and instead provide a picture of inter-dependent communities in a complex mosaic of social groups and productive practices.

Even when the links are not so immediate, the existence of intensive farming economies often provides opportunities which alter the effective environment of their neighbours, through the transmission of new domesticates or features of diet and technology to groups which would not otherwise acquire them. The appearance of new elements in the farming economies of Europe and central Asia, such as wool-bearing sheep, the preparation of alcoholic drinks and the use of the plough, can all be related to the influence of emerging urban cultures in areas further south. The chain reaction continues further, in the transmission of livestock-raising techniques from pastoralists to northern hunters, resulting in the emergence of reindeer-herding economies. Tropical agriculture, too, incorporated techniques developed in more central regions, and there was a continuing spread of farming economies on the southern margins of the zones where agriculture began: in sub-Saharan Africa, south Asia and tropical South America. Even on the outermost margin, in the Arctic and the Polynesian islands, the appearance of specialized hunting and farming economies in these remote parts of the earth's surface must be related to population pressures generated nearer to the centres of global population, and to processes of out-migration. The human populations of the world form parts of a vast, interacting network, in which no region can exist in isolation for very long.

The processes of global economic development in the later prehistoric period, therefore, show a pattern of increasing diversification but also inter-connectedness, in which new lifeways constantly emerged and adjusted to each other. At the same time as they explored the diversity of local environmental opportunities, they were subjected to influences from faster developing regions, and on a constantly increasing scale. The historical irruption of European industrial societies and their intrusion into the furthest areas of the globe from the sixteenth century AD onwards was only the last episode in a process whose origins lay deep in the preceding millennia, and in the potential which agriculture provided for the increasing aggregation and impact of human numbers.

THE PERSPECTIVE OF THE WORLD

The reasons for the rapid development of human cultures and economies in the Holocene lay in the biological changes of the preceding glacial period – the emergence of anatomically modern humans and their capacity for complex language, exchange, social organization and planning. This change was global in its effects: the human inhabitants of all the world's continents possessed the same anatomical and mental capacities. Nevertheless the Holocene saw the rise of greater regional contrasts in human cultures than ever before, with the emergence of localized foci of development such as western Asia and north-west Africa, China, and central America (including Mexico) and the central Andes. These were the nuclear regions where farming was independently developed, on the basis of crops such as wheat, millet or rice and maize, in the western and eastern Old World and the New World respectively. It was in these areas that city life made its appearance, some two or three millennia after the appearance there of village farming.

These developments exhibit a striking degree of parallelism, but they were not simultaneous in the three major regions where they appeared. The New World had been more recently occupied by human populations than the other two; in the western Old World, a particular combination of environmental features, such as the close juxtaposition of Mediterranean, oasis and sub-montane zones, led to an especially fast rate of growth. The period from 3000 to 700 BC, therefore, saw different stages of this process in operation in different areas. While farming had begun in the Levant at the very beginning of the Holocene, and urban life had appeared in Mesopotamia in the middle of the fourth millennium BC, village-based farming in the Americas developed only during the third millennium BC, and complex societies with elaborate temple-centres only made their appearance at the end of the period in question. In China, where village farming had been known from at least the sixth millennium BC, the first dynasties of the Chinese state began in the early second millennium BC, contemporary with the first civilizations of the Bronze Age Aegean and Anatolia (Map 1).

Outside these nuclear regions, similar contrasts are evident. Farming practices had spread early to Europe and the north African littoral, but were still expanding into the more northerly parts of Eurasia. Most of sub-Saharan Africa was still the province of hunters and foragers, with farming only to spread in the context of the use of iron, after the end of this period. The great extension of farming in Polynesia was also yet to come, though a remarkable cultural complex in Melanesia, associated with the use of Lapita pottery, demonstrated already in the second millennium BC the seafaring skills that were to carry cultivators over the Pacific horizon. In the Americas, only a tiny fraction of the New World land mass was affected by the localized growth of farming populations.

While these processes of economic and cultural development were still exerting their initial effects, the natural environment was also in course of change. Although the immediate adjustments of the post-glacial, such as the rise in sea-levels and the spread of forests, had already taken place (and the major environmental impacts of farming were still to become apparent), longer-term changes were making themselves felt (Roberts, 1989, pp. 88–91). Regions such as the Sahara, which had benefited from increased rainfall in the early Holocene, now began to experience increased desiccation; and this environmental pressure speeded the transition to a greater emphasis on pastoralism, and the substitution of native plants (notably tropical millets and yams) for the introduced crops of west Asiatic origin. Farming in the Sahel belt, on the southern margin of the Sahara, came to have an increasingly indigenous character – producing the conditions for the major expansion of farming that was to come about in the next period with the dispersal of iron-using populations speaking Bantu languages.

The beginnings of African (and Arabian) pastoralism, however, are considerably less well understood than those of the other part of the great arid zone which stretches across the Old World: that of central Asia. It was during the period from 3000 to 700 BC that societies in the arid zone of Eurasia made the successive adjustments which led to the emergence of truly nomadic pastoralism, and to a mobile way of life capable of covering vast distances. These societies therefore came to form an important link between the civilizations of the western and eastern Old World. Unlike the pastoral populations which grew up over this time in the interstices of the alluvial civilizations of the Nile Valley, Mesopotamia, and their Levantine neighbours, these groups initially had less immediate contacts with urban communities and followed a more independent existence; though they, too, were to irrupt into the territories of their more settled neighbours during the course of the Iron Age. For this area, as for the sub-Saharan zone, the third and second millennia BC comprised a formative period in which the potential was accumulated for a much wider impact on human affairs.

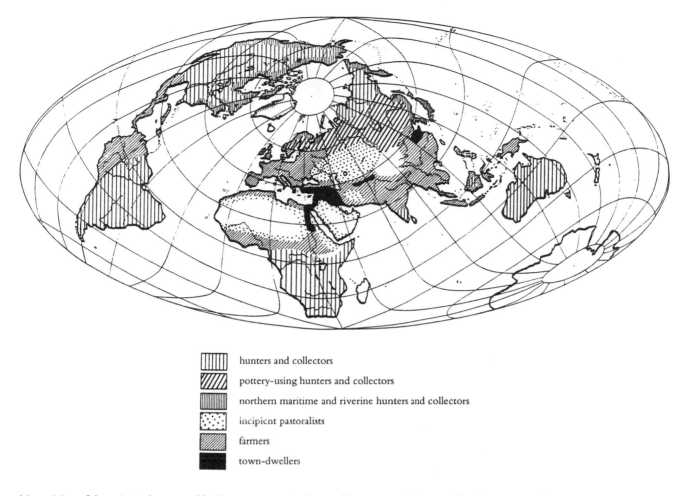

‖‖‖	hunters and collectors
⫽⫽⫽	pottery-using hunters and collectors
‖‖‖	northern maritime and riverine hunters and collectors
∵∵∵	incipient pastoralists
⫽⫽⫽	farmers
▬	town-dwellers

Map 1 Map of the principal means of food procurement in the world *c.* 1500 BC (redrawn after Sherratt, 1980b).

THE NEW WORLD

Unlike the heartlands of Old World agriculture, where villages appeared simultaneously with the cultivation of crops, New World crop plants were for a long time simply one component of a foraging existence, and did not necessitate either sedentism or the concentration of population in larger communities. One reason may have been the smaller range of animals suitable for domestication, and hunting, fishing or collecting continued to be necessary to supply animal protein, supplemented by crops such as beans and chenopods. The cultivated plants, too, were slower to evolve into varieties with a higher yield; and since they were plants adapted to the photoperiodicities of southern latitudes, they did not spread into the temperate areas of North America until much later – even though maize and quinoa achieved a remarkable altitudinal range in the Andes. For all these reasons, the pattern of New World farming was radically different from that of the Old World.

It was during the third and second millennia BC, however, that village communities with economies based on high-yielding crop plants first appeared, both in Central America (including Mexico), the central Andean region, and northern Amazonia. Different parts of this whole area contributed their own innovations: maize, beans, root crops such as potato and manioc, squashes, chenopods, peppers, gourds, cotton – though many plants and varieties, adapted to local conditions, were only of regional or local significance. Pottery was apparently pioneered in the zone between the main

nuclear centres, in northern Brazil, Venezuela and Colombia; cotton textiles were a notable contribution of the Andean coastlands; ornamental shells were widely traded. From this interregional mixture a new pattern was precipitated, as settlements (often, in the Andean region, centred on ceremonial buildings on platforms) grew up near the fertile alluvial bottomlands that provided the bulk of their crops – either in plains or montane valleys. It was this commitment to fine, well-watered soils that brought communities together in farming villages; and the extension of this system of horticulture was closely dependent on the development of raised fields or simple irrigation systems (Map 2). These permitted the growth of the urban civilizations which grew up largely in the first millennium BC. Such intensive horticulture contrasts markedly with the widespread pattern of slash-and-burn cultivation which came to characterize many of these areas in post-contact times, partly because of the displacement of populations from fertile bottomlands. Of the domestic animals, llamas and alpacas (which were initially herded on the high grasslands) became especially important in providing transport and secondary products, and in allowing the vertical integration of contrasting altitudinal zones in the Andes (Murra, 1972).

THE EASTERN OLD WORLD

The only urban society in the eastern Old World at this time was China, relatively isolated from the other contem-

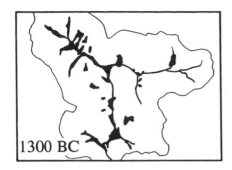
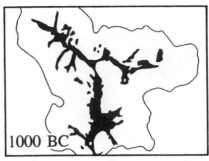
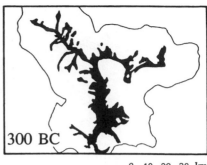

Map 2 The effects of improved varieties of maize and irrigation technology on the productivity of the Oaxaca Valley, Mexico, between 1300 and 300 BC; areas in black show soils capable of producing 200 kg per hectare (redrawn after Kirby, 1973).

porary Bronze Age civilizations. The civilization of the Indus Valley, which flourished in the second half of the third millennium BC, must – although distinctively Indian in its culture – be counted among those of the western Old World with which it shared its basic crop complex and its closest trading contacts. In between, in eastern India, South-East Asia and southern China lay a mosaic of stone-, copper-, and bronze-using cultures not unlike those of temperate Europe: not yet urban, but loosely linked by trade and technology to more complex neighbours. These largely tropical areas cultivated mainly rice, but also tree crops like bananas. (In southern India, where largely stone-using cultures relied heavily on cattle pastoralism, some tropical millets of African origin were cultivated – as a result of contacts with Arabia and east Africa.) As in the early farming systems of the Americas, floodplain horticulture was the basic technique of cultivation, rather than the slash-and-burn systems using hill-rice that were later to become characteristic of this area (Gorman, 1977). Irrigation systems, as yet still small in scale, were the basis for further intensification, using the water-buffalo as a traction animal. Pigs were the main form of domestic livestock, along with chickens. Other crops suitable for growing in wet areas were melons and water-chestnuts. Root crops, too (notably taro), were increasingly important in island South-East Asia, and cultivated in New Guinea with irrigation and drainage ditches. Maritime contacts from south China to Indonesia are shown in the later second millennium BC by the distribution of ritual bronze drums, some decorated with scenes showing boats and houses raised on piles. Further east lay the equally extensive sites of the Lapita complex, whose elaborate pottery may represent a set of vessels for the ritual consumption of the fermented *kava* drink, made from the pepper *Piper methysticum*.

The civilization of Bronze Age China was very different from that of succeeding periods, in that it remained confined to northern China (the valley of the Huanghe), and was thus part of the zone of (temperate) millet and hemp cultivation. Rice at this period was less important, though Chinese cabbage (*Brassica sinensis*) was grown from an early date. Wheat and barley, like sheep, were western introductions brought along the steppe route by groups also responsible for the introduction of wheeled vehicles in the early second millennium BC. Millet was also cultivated further north, in Korea and Manchuria, though in more remote areas fishing and foraging were more important resources which still allowed a degree of sedentism in rich coastal and lacustrine areas. In China, the millet was fermented to make

the 'wine' served warm in the elaborate cast-bronze containers characteristic of the Shang and Zhou periods.

THE WESTERN OLD WORLD

The heartlands of western Old World civilization, in the Nile Valley and Mesopotamia, combined simple irrigation techniques with use of the plough to produce surpluses of primary staples such as wheat and barley – used not only for bread but also beer. Equally important in the area of the Fertile Crescent were the tree crops: date, fig, pomegranate, olive and vine (Plate 9). These could be used not only for direct consumption, but also for manufactured oil and wine, and such products were important contributions of the surrounding Mediterranean areas to which urban life spread in the second millennium BC. Animals, too, yielded products for industry: notably wool, on which specialized textile manufacturing industries developed. Exports of these products ensured supplies of other raw materials on which urban civilizations depended. These complex economies had their own inbuilt dynamic, which explains why this way of life spread outwards from its initial centres to occupy an area from the Aegean to southern Iran and the Indus Valley.

Beyond this nuclear area, the farming systems of temperate Europe were slowly transformed by innovations which could be transferred to the belt of woodland and steppe outside the zone of immediate urban contacts in the eastern Mediterranean. These innovations included both new varieties of older domesticates, like the new wool-bearing breeds of sheep, and new uses of old ones, such as the employment of cattle to pull carts and ploughs. Equally significant were dietary innovations which arose from the sugar-rich fruits now available in the Mediterranean, and gave rise to an interest in fermented alcoholic drinks. Entirely new species of domestic livestock also made their appearance; and while donkeys and camels remained largely confined to western and central Asia, the horses that had been domesticated on the Eurasian steppes were widely welcomed when they arrived both in western Asia and in Europe. The combined effect of these new features was to produce a second generation of farming economies over much of western Eurasia, in which animals had a greater importance than before: types of farming which can now be described as 'agriculture' rather than 'horticulture' (Sherratt, 1981).

Central to these new farming systems was the use of the plough, which was the first technological device to use animal energy and provided a functional link between animal keeping and crop production (Fig. 7). This required an appropriate balance between pastureland and arable, and offered the incentive to clear woodland on a larger scale than heretofore. It also made viable the cultivation of drier areas, where the amount of grazing land available to support draught animals could compensate for the poor quality of the arable. The keeping of cattle in larger numbers, as well as the new forms of livestock, affected both patterns of settlement and forms of social organization. With the clearance of larger tracts of woodland, farmers were no longer so closely tied to small areas of fertile soil; and the accumulation of herds introduced new forms of competitive aggrandisement which found expression also in the acquisition of mobile forms of material culture suitable for display – notably items of metal. The concept of a 'Bronze Age' is thus more than a technological label, but denotes a whole way of life with a distinctive agro-pastoral basis. The use of horses and wheeled vehicles, woollen textiles and alcoholic drinks, played an important part in defining the culture of the élites to which this system gave rise.

These changes did not initially produce a uniformity of practice within later Neolithic and Copper Age Europe; indeed, their initial effect was to exaggerate its diversity. The village farming populations of south-east and central Europe, where simple copper metallurgy had long been practised, adopted most readily the appurtenances of Aegean civilization, copying its metal vessels in the shapes of their pottery. Northern and western Europe, where a substantial proportion of the population consisted of indigenous groups who had only recently taken up farming, was more resistant to change: less nucleated patterns of settlement, centred on megalithic monuments, continued to exist for at least another millennium. This way of life was increasingly challenged, however, by a more fluid pattern of social organization based on extensive forest clearance, livestock raising and warrior

burials in round, earthen mounds: the pattern associated with distinctive beaker-shaped drinking vessels often decorated wih impressions of twisted cord that provide a convenient archaeological label as 'Corded-ware' and 'Bell-beaker' cultures. These were not simple reflections of new types of farming; rather, they demonstrate the range of cultural responses to new opportunities in the sphere of subsistence economy. What the new patterns had in common was an increased fluidity in settlement pattern, replacing the stability and longevity of older patterns based either on mudbrick tell settlements or massive stone monuments: a mobility made possible by the increased importance of animal keeping in the farming systems of temperate Europe.

This description should make clear that there was no simple progression from 'horticulture' to 'agriculture' or 'pastoralism', but rather a spectrum of responses in which the cultural valuation given to animals was as important as its rationality as a form of exploitation of the environment. Nevertheless there was a considerable degree of convergence in the way of life of European populations, which by 2000 BC had produced two broad zones – one south of the Carpathian Mountains, the other occupying much of the north European plain and west-central Europe – united by a common range of material items such as bronze weapons or woollen clothing, but with regional contrasts in their forms of settlement and burial. Where land was extensive but of relatively low quality it was rapidly cleared, cropped and abandoned. Livestock probably provided the primary form of agricultural wealth. Burials occupied a prominent place in the landscape. Where arable farming was more permanent, landholding was probably more important, and settlements – now often fortified – were more prominent. Both forms of economy, however, participated in the circulation of bronze, and probably also items such as textiles which survive less well in the archaeological record; and both types of community maintained loose contacts with the civilizations of the Aegean, through the exchange of valuable materials such as amber and perhaps metals such as gold and tin.

In the centuries after 1300 BC, when Mediterranean urban economies experienced recession and collapse, the surrounding areas of Europe, the Pontic steppes, the Caucasus and Iran seem to have undergone a new resurgence – most evident in the thriving bronze industries of these regions, but predicated upon the successful expansion of agriculture and pastoralism (Chernych, 1992). The pastoral element, involving extensive transhumance, was probably more important in the mountainous areas of the Caucasus and Iran, and perhaps in the Alps; but in other parts of Europe more intensive forms of agriculture are likely to have been involved. One possibility is a more widespread use of winter-grown crops, rather than the spring-grown ones which were still common among later prehistoric farmers in Europe; and the alternation of winter-grown crops and fallow was to be the basis of temperate European farming down to the introduction of three-course rotations in the medieval period (Sherratt, 1980a). The growing permanence of European agriculture is reflected in the extensive fossil field systems from this time onwards, which survive in many parts of the continent and are especially well documented from the United Kingdom.

THE CENTRAL OLD WORLD

The combination of the horse (domesticated during the fifth millennium BC in Ukraine and Kazakhstan) and the ox-

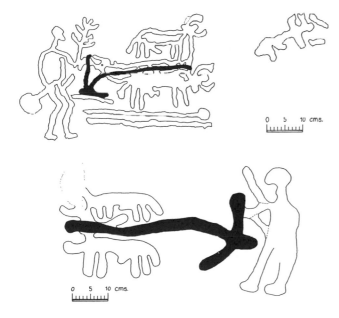

Figure 7 The changing design of the scratch-plough (ard) in northern Europe, shown in two rock engravings from Tanums Parish, Bohuslän, western Sweden. Top: simple crook-ard (based on a hoe design), earlier Bronze Age. Bottom: bow-ard (based on a spade design), later Bronze Age. The implements themselves are shown here in black for clarity (redrawn after Glob, 1951).

drawn wheeled vehicles which spread from northern Mesopotamia to the Caucasus and Pontic steppe region in the later fourth millennium BC, provided new opportunities for the exploitation of the steppe belt which extends from the Carpathians to the Altai. Successive cultural groups, marked by their burials in pits or chambers under round tumuli (*kurgany*), spread across this region in the third and second millennia BC. It is likely that they were associated with the eastward spread of populations speaking Indo-European languages (Mallory, 1989).

Although livestock keeping (especially for milk) was the most fundamental aspect of their subsistence economies, it is unlikely to have been the sole one, and wheat, barley and millet cultivation with the light plough was also practised. (Hemp was also grown, and its narcotic properties were already appreciated.) Nor were they fully nomadic, and substantial settlements of timber-built villages are known. Camels, as well as horses, were used for riding and traction. While horses were used by the early second millennium BC to pull light, spoke-wheeled vehicles (Fig. 8), these chariots were probably used as much for the purposes of social display as practical conveyences in everyday life; and these steppe groups were very similar to contemporary bronze-using groups in east-central Europe, with whom they were in contact (and to whom the use of the chariot soon spread). Nevertheless, their ability to make use of the landscapes of the arid zone allowed them increasingly to expand into the adjacent semi-desert regions to the south, where they largely absorbed the small communities of irrigation farmers in the oases of Turkestan and northern Iran, and as far as northern India. Indeed their effects spread further, and can be seen in the introduction of spoke-wheeled vehicles to China during the Shang dynasty (Piggott, 1992). This chain of populations thus came to form a set of links across the whole breadth of the Old World.

The transformation of these groups into the classic nomads of the Eurasian steppes took place in the later centuries of the second millennium BC and the early centuries of the first (Khazanov, 1984). It was associated both with a mixing of the biologically Europoid populations of the steppes with Mongoloid populations of the Altai and Sayan mountains and northern Mongolia, and with the use of larger breeds of horses for riding. The social and cultural effects of this transformation are seen in the emergence of a lively 'animal style' of applied art, well exemplified in bronze bridle-bits and other items of decorated horse-gear, and in the elaborate burials under tumuli which were accompanied by human and horse sacrifices as well as copious grave goods. Such populations were now truly nomadic, living in tents as much as in permanent villages, and capable of covering vast distances on horseback. The social structures were correspondingly complex, since individual dynasties could come to dominate huge areas by their economic success and military might. The pattern of population movements now came to be reversed, with raids and migrations spreading from east to west. Indo-European groups, at the western end of the chain, were to enter history as the Cimmerians and Scythians – the first of a long succession of steppe peoples to affect the fortunes and character of both eastern and western Old World civilizations.

CONCLUSION

The effects of recent archaeological work around the world have been an emancipation from the categories of comparative ethnography, which has allowed the archaeological record to tell a more dynamic, historical story. The result is less of an evolutionary account of the replacement of the primitive by the more advanced, than an appreciation of the diversity of previous modes of human existence. Terms such as 'agriculture' or 'pastoralism' are always relative ones, whose content is constantly being redefined as circumstances change. One effect of this is that the story can no longer be told simply in terms of calories: the simple succession of more effective forms of food-getting. Farming is more than just the technology of growing crops; it is a mode of organization with its own structures of family life, material culture and consumption rituals, in which human populations are intimately bound both to each other, to their lands, and to the material world which they create. Each of these aspects is mutable and subject to alteration. Pastoralism, too, is not just an automatic adaptation to climatic extremes, but a new set of relationships to humans and animals in which culturally created values are as important as physical survival in explaining new patterns of existence. Ceremonial centres, elaborate bronze artefacts or burial monuments are therefore an integral part of the account which has been presented here: not just a cultural superstructure erected on an economic base, but parts of the same acts of creation. Control of calories is not an end in itself, but part of the realization of human goals and objectives – which, because of their often unintended consequences, impart a constant dynamic to human affairs.

BIBLIOGRAPHY

BARTH, F. 1969. *Ethnic Groups and Boundaries.* London.

CHERNYCH, E. N. 1992. *Ancient Metallurgy in the USSR: The Early Metal Age.* Cambridge.

FLON, C. (ed.) 1985. *Le grand Atlas de l'Archéologie.* Paris.

GLOB, P. V. 1951. *Ard og Plov i Nordens Oldtid.* Arhus, Universitetsforlaget. (Jysk Arkäol., selsk. Skr., 1.)

GORMAN, C. 1977. A Reconsideration of the Beginnings of Agriculture in South-east Asia. In: REED, C. A. (ed.), *Origins of Agriculture.* Paris/La Haye, pp. 321–56.

KHAZANOV, A. M. 1984. *Nomads and the Outside World.* Cambridge.

KIRKBY, A. V. T. 1973. *The Use of Land and Resources in the Past and Present Valley of Oaxaca, Mexico.* Ann Arbor, Mich. (Mem. Mus. Anthropol., 5.)

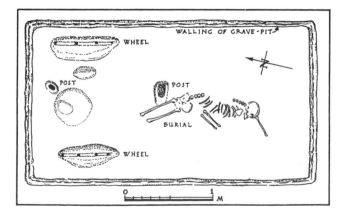

Figure 8 The first evidence for the horse-drawn chariot in central Eurasia: a tomb-chamber under a burial mound at Sintashta near Chelyabinsk, Russia, with impressions of spoked wheels in pits sunk to accommodate a vehicle in the grave (redrawn after Piggott, 1992).

MALLORY, J. P. 1989. *In Search of the Indo-Europeans*. London.

MURRA, J. V. 1972. El 'control vertical' de un máximo de pisos ecológicos en la economía de las sociedas andinas. In: —— (ed.), *Visita de la Provincia de Léon de Huanáco (1562) por Iñigo Ortiz de Zuñiga*. Huanáco (Peru): Universidad Nacional Hermilio Valdizan. (Doc. Hist. Enol. Huanáco Selva central, Vol. 2.)

PIGGOTT, S. 1992. *Wagon, Chariot and Carriage: Symbol and Status in the History of Transport*. London.

ROBERTS, N. 1989. *The Holocene: An Environmental History*. Oxford.

SCHNAPP, A. 1993. *La conquête du passé: aux origines de l'archéologie*. Paris.

SHERRATT, A. G. 1980a. Water, Soil and Seasonality in Early Cereal Cultivation. *World Archaeol.* (Oxford), Vol. 11, No. 3, pp. 313–30.

—— 1980b. *The Cambridge Encyclopaedia of Archaeology*. Cambridge.

—— 1981. Plough and Pastoralism: Aspects of the Secondary Products Revolution. In: HAMMOND, N.; HODDER, I.; ISAAC, G. (eds), *Pattern of the Past: Studies in Honour of David Clarke*. Cambridge, pp. 261–305.

5

FROM STATE TO EMPIRE

Vladimir A. Jakobson and Muhammad A. Dandamaev

The human evolutionary process to the stage of state formation is seen in terms of societal development as people began to build a better and better organization to institutionalize their social relations on the basis of material, technological, scientific and ideological progress in a given natural background.

From the stage of tribal formation to that of state building was a great advance achieved in different ways in different societies. How tribes coalesced into a higher integral system is hypothecized by different historians using different theoretical models; and similarly the way in which tribal chiefs succumbed to the authority of a state government of any form, either monarchical or otherwise, can be viewed from different angles. Yet it is fair to assume the evolution of a higher 'ethos' on the basis of either fusion of tribes into a bigger whole or the break-up of tribes whose members reunite under different socio-ethnological principles. The state as a coercive organ of political management may not limit itself to a single ethnic cohesion; when it transgresses beyond its ecological boundary either peacefully by trade or by cultural penetration, or by war, it has taken a step towards building a still higher system of integration that is characterized as empire. In this process of empire building several states may join or lose their individual identity to create one big power that holds superior authority over the whole empire. What line of action this process assumes in Mesopotamia and what elements constitute the state therein are described below on the basis of the available records.

STATES AROUND THE WORLD
(EXCLUDING MESOPOTAMIA)

In Egypt the state developed independently. Unlike Mesopotamia where, from the start, geographical conditions created the natural boundaries of the first states and predetermined their long independent existence, Egypt consisted of an extremely narrow inhabited strip of territory along the Nile. There were no natural boundaries to separate the first small states from one another and the Nile was a convenient communication route running the full length of Egypt. In these circumstances the wars that ineluctably arose with the beginning of civilization were bound to lead very rapidly to the unification of the entire Nile Valley under a single power. The only alternative to unification would have been mutual annihilation. The exact manner in which a single ruling power arose in Egypt remains unknown, since it took place

before 'recorded' history, that is, prior even to the most ancient extant writings. Because autocracy arose so early in such a vast and rich country, the state sector of the economy absorbed virtually all the other sectors. In ancient Egypt it is possible to observe only faint traces of a primitive communal organization; the country was divided into 'nomes', which seem to have corresponded roughly to primitive communal organizations and states. The nomes were stable entities that sought to assert their independence whenever the central power weakened. The fact that Egyptian towns retained some corporate attributes (in that they exercised rights of ownership over their own property) and enjoyed a semblance of self-government (a council attached to the town governor) may be ascribed to remnants of communal organization. The history of Egypt shows a constant striving by the private sector of the economy to break away from the royal sector, although it was precisely in the royal sector that the private sector had arisen (in the form of hereditary offices with attached landholdings, for instance). Furthermore, it was in the royal (state-temple) sector economy that 'secondary' communities (such as those of necropolis functionaries) were constantly emerging. In antiquity the community was the only possible form of social organization. These 'secondary' communities, being small, were unable to constitute any kind of serious counterweight to royal power. The Egyptian pharaohs stood at the apex of a vast, ramified and well-organized bureaucratic system that embraced all areas of social life. Their power and ideological roles were so great that they were regarded as rulers by divine right from a very early stage until the end of the existence of ancient Egypt as an independent state.

In the Indus Valley the geography is more varied and encompasses extensive areas of uneven development. State formation in the beginning was confined to small river plains, such as the Gomal plain, the Bannu plain, the Hakra or Beas Valley and the Kacachi plain in the lower Indus region. In each plain towns cropped up to harness the economy into one socio-political order. These towns were no doubt centres of administration as well as having a religious function. It is, however, not clear who managed their affairs, because the records are absent. This multicentred pattern continued even when the Indus civilization matured, and many common factors of socio-economic life prevailed all over the land (see Chapter 12.7). These factors include the system of weights and measures, the style of many of the metal objects, the ceramic corpus if taken as a whole, architectural features such as the use of baked bricks, drains, and the diversity of building forms, town planning and the distinctive, but normative, organization of settlements with a high mound to the west and a lower habitation mound to the east, and finally the development of a settlement hierarchy (Possehl, 1979, p. xi). Earlier it was believed that the entire land was managed from the twin capitals of Mohenjo-daro and Harappa, but now it has been shown that cities sprang up in different areas and continued the subregional patterns under an overall system of politico-economic control that imposed uniformity in cultural development (Mughal, 1990). This multi-growth is akin to empire building, which was sustained as long as its overseas trade and distant overland supplies continued to enrich the coffers of the state system. The nature of the managerial system is difficult to determine because of the non-decipherment of contemporary writing. But when the whole system broke down because of hydrological dislocation, the subregional patterns resumed their own particular ways of living. In these subregions the Aryans later adapted their own living conditions to what they found. The Aryan clan system did not alter the essentials of politico-economic living in the regions, with the result that regionalism has survived in the Indus Valley, giving a different power boost to the state or states that grew up all over the land in historic times. The pull of the countryside is greater than that of the cities in the different subregions. The power of the people is more important than that of a single head of state, even if such a head assumes authority on their behalf in order to carry out their wishes. It is this concept that gave rise to a republican system rather than a monarchical system, as is noted in later Indian (Sanskrit) literature. However, in the development of urban civilization the city plays a dominant role and its pattern is set by such examples as Mohenjo-daro.

China's cultural development is best illustrated by the archaeological data recovered from the upper and lower reaches of the Huanghe – a Neolithic cultural pattern in which the high land was transformed into a complex of interrelated villages under the control of a monarchical order, and spread its influence from the lower Huanghe plain as far south as the Changjiang. The importance of a village economy is an essential feature of Chinese civilization, but this stage of civilization differs from the earlier Neolithic stage in that the developing economy is related to a system of interdependence and is under the control of the head of the state. During the first historic period, the Shang dynasty, the state occupied a central place, for example, at Cheng-Chou or Anyang, as an administrative and religious fountain-head. These towns acted as political and ceremonial centres, although they could not reach the level of development of Mohenjo-daro in the Indus Valley. In the walled enclosure of Cheng-Chou the royal family and the nobles lived. They served as the nucleus of the entire social group and dictated the political and economic life of the whole kingdom. It is around this nucleus that industrial quarters with high degrees of specialization and farming villages clustered. Village requirements were met apparently through the administrative centre, which also managed redistribution. The Shang city was divided into three major social groups: the aristocracy, the craftsmen and the farmers. Thus the whole population, which was considerably larger in quantity and complexity than previously, was socially stratified and given to industrial specialization. The main Shang sites performed all the essential functions of cities, indicating a definite break from the Neolithic community pattern and leading to an urban civilization. This pattern continued in the later historical periods when the main sites grew into large commercial and political urban centres (Kwang-chih, 1974, p. 460).

Another path for state development can be observed in the regions beyond the major river civilizations. Here, where there was no need to build and maintain major irrigation systems and where large centralized states came into existence only much later, the private sector was more important than the state-temple sector. From the end of the third millennium BC all the societies of Anatolia, western Asia, the Balkans and Italy (with the exception of the above-mentioned examples) conformed to this pattern of development. The strong states that emerged (Hittite, Achaean and so on) were not *imperia*, as they are frequently cited, and not even centralized states, but unions or confederations *sui generis* under the hegemony of a single state to which all the member states provided military assistance and paid tribute while otherwise remaining independent.

The unique variety of this pattern of development was exemplified by the ancient *polis*. Strictly speaking, the *polis* was not a state, since its people ruled directly and constituted the army. For various reasons a sort of revival of the primitive community took place in the first millennium BC, but at a higher level of development of productive forces that not only allowed one person's work to be exploited by another but necessitated it. In this region the *polis* replaced the earlier kingdoms, which had in no way differed from those that existed elsewhere. Since the *polis* was a 'community of equals' it was considered degrading for a free person to work for another. This applied not only to work for hire but even to the renting of another person's land. In these circumstances it was possible to exploit only foreigners (including the citizens of other *poleis*), who for one reason or another had been enslaved. In the ancient *polis* the antithesis between freedom and slavery was particularly marked, found its purest expression and had its own terminology.

The free-born person knew no master or chief, apart from his commander during military campaigns. But even the commander could be called to account at the end of the campaign for having abused his power. In the other ancient societies there were complex hierarchical structures, the lower level of which was occupied by a large category of personally dependent individuals and the top level by the ruler. To the Greeks these societies were the epitome of slavery.

In the New World the origin of civilization and state has a distinctive character of its own, having apparently no links with developments in the Old World. The entire evolutionary process has been traced to a background of differing environments in the different subregions. Contrast is made between the lowland and highland areas of southern Mexico, where the one produced the classic Mayan non-urban civilization, and the other led to the urban civilization of the Teotihuacan Valley. The climax of the Maya classic period is marked by a population peak in the south, greater construction of dwelling houses, a rise in the number of ceremonial centres, the peak of artistic endeavour, ceremonialism and calendries, more hieroglyphic inscriptions, and above all a transformation of the Mayan socio-political structure. This became complex and hierarchic, leading to the rise of a truly stratified or class society and presaging a pattern of hereditary aristocracy. In sum, 'the non-urban civilization is linked to a redistributive economy in the hands of an aristocracy, to a social ranking system, to corporate or kin ownership of land and to a theocratically oriented leadership. It is the setting of a chiefdom' (Willey, 1974, p. 97). On the other hand, in the Teotihuacan Valley both irrigation and a symbiotic pattern were the prime factors in the evolution of civilization. The latter replaced the simple town-village-hamlet by the growth of a gigantic city, the influence of which on other Mesoamerican regional cultures is closely related to its huge size and to its extraordinary level of socio-economic integration (Sanders, 1974, p. 128).

Further south the example of the central Andes shows three stages of human development: the first of early hunting, the second, food collecting and incipient cultivation, and finally of agriculture. The last is again marked by three periods. First, the formative, when central Andean technology, religion and art were established. The community consisted of several villages, gradually increasing in number but remaining small. The ceremonial centres were also small and simple, although the associated religious cult spread widely. In the economic field irrigation expanded, agricultural produce became more varied, and painting on pottery and ornaments of copper and copper-gold alloy were common. In the second or classic period, we find intensive agriculture based on extended irrigation, a population increase, craft specialization and plenty of luxury goods, enormous temple construction, the use of a variety of metals for ornaments, tools and weapons, a class-structured society, a state under priest-kings and organized warfare. In brief, few towns clustered round temple pyramids. Thirdly, the post-classic period was marked by increased warfare, progressive urbanization, overproduction of goods and political unification under the Inca empire. It is in this last period that planned urban centres, enclosed by defensive walls, appeared and reached a climax in Chanchan, the Chimu capital. However, even in this period writing was completely absent, and this resulted in lack of development in mathematics, astronomy and calendrics. And yet the Incas maintained government bureaucracy and constructed many public works (Collier, 1974, p. 175).

The most characteristic form of state organization in ancient times was monarchy. The only exceptions to this rule were the ancient *poleis* and a few republics in India. Even in these societies, however, a monarchy was eventually established – and always, apparently, in the same way: a victorious military leader backed by a popular assembly would seize power for himself against the will of the council of elders (*gerousia*, senate and so on) and other ruling bodies. This was how the transition from warrior democracy to monarchy took place in ancient Sumer and, considerably later, how the Greek tyrannies and imperial power in Rome arose.

The traditional definition of this royal power as 'oriental despotism' does not mean anything and should be discarded. Royal power, like other social institutions, evolved in the course of a state's historical development. But rulers always had to conform to definite rules and were also subject to the psychological pressure exerted by society. In ancient times the ruler was not, as in the Middle Ages, God's representative on earth but on the contrary represented his people before the gods. The royal charisma (*nam lugal* in Sumer, *khvarnah* in Persia, the royal *dharma* in India, the Mandate of Heaven in China) was given to the ruler by the will of the gods on certain conditions, and could be taken away from him if he failed to respect those conditions. The constant references in ancient writings to the ruler as a shepherd watching over his flock, a defender of the weak and a protector of widows and orphans, or a promulgator of *dharma* are not mere demagogy. This was exactly how the ruler was perceived and how he perceived himself. The king contin-

ued for a very long time as a kind of communal leader who, although the ruler, was under an obligation to take care of all members of the community. It will be recalled that the monarch emerged from an elective ruling body, and hence the principle of a hereditary monarchy was established only with great difficulty. Contrary to a widely held opinion among contemporary scholars, right up to the very end of an independent Mesopotamian state, the royal power was not, in principle, hereditary. The ruler was considered to be the chosen representative of the great gods, who had sometimes marked him out for the task 'while he was still in his mother's womb'. Of course in practice the heir to the throne usually belonged to the royal family and was designated by the reigning king, but it was still necessary to confirm the king's choice by ascertaining the will of the gods (probably by drawing lots). Furthermore, the royal power in Mesopotamia was far from being absolute. Once a year, at the time of the New Year festival, the Babylonian ruler, after having removed his regalia, had to enter the 'holy of holies' of Marduk's temple and swear before his statue that he had never violated the privileges of the citizens of the towns that had temples, infringed their honour or encroached upon their property. The high priest then gave him a slap on the cheek, and it was then, and only then, that he received the staff and tiara, which signified that his investiture had been renewed. In Assyria, during the solemn procession and sacrifice at the New Year festival, 'Ashur rules' was proclaimed repeatedly. It is not clear whether this referred to the god Ashur or to the town of Ashur, but obviously the ceremonial was intended to remind the king of his true position. Lastly, and again contrary to a widely held opinion, the king in Mesopotamia was not the supreme judge, although he did possess the right of pardon.

Such a limitation of the power of the monarch is known in other societies, even though monarchy may not have originated from an elective system. The king in ancient India was limited by his adherence to *dharma* and in China he was subject to the Confucian model of morality. In the New World the forces of tradition and of religion were binding on the chief.

The idea of royal power unbounded by any rules or institutions took shape fully only towards the end of antiquity. It was most clearly formulated in Justinian's *Digest*: 'the will of the *princeps* has the force of law'. The principle of a hereditary monarchy was also formulated in Byzantium. Both principles found expression in the titles of the Byzantine emperors 'autokrator' and 'porphyrogenite'.

FUNDAMENTAL STAGES IN THE DEVELOPMENT OF THE STATE IN MESOPOTAMIA

Eventually the development of the tribal and kinship structure led to inequalities and hence to internal conflicts. These threatened the very existence of the society, and the state arose as a new system of societal organization designed, if not to eliminate those conflicts, then at least to keep them within bounds. The emergence of the state was usually preceded by tribal alliances, some of which were very large and occupied vast areas; structurally, they could be equal or unequal, with one or more tribes dominating the other members of the 'alliance'. But primary states were always small in size and included one, two or three (but rarely more) cities. Here we must stipulate that by a city we mean a centre with a self-sufficient population in which surplus products are concentrated, redistributed and marketed. It is from this, the city's fundamental function, that all its others – in respect of politics, culture, commerce and the crafts – spring.

Arising as the central point of a neighbourhood commune, whose production and trading resources it contained, together with its temples, the magistrates' and temple servants' homes and the public assembly place or hall, the city grew and developed together with the commune and was its embodiment. We call such primary states 'city-states' or 'nome states'. It is their emergence that denotes the beginning of civilization, when the productivity of social labour reached a level at which society could use the surplus product to maintain a considerable number of people who were not themselves engaged in productive labour, but fulfilled functions of great importance to society: as administrators, warriors, priests and the 'intelligentsia' – scholars, artists, poets and so on.

The further development of society called for more such people and, consequently, for a growth in the surplus product. But until the turn of the second and first millennia BC (when iron came into use), labour productivity grew very little – and in Mesopotamia it even fell as soil salination brought declining harvests. Therefore the surplus product could only grow extensively through robbing neighbours, capturing slaves, enlarging one's territory and so increasing one's population, or else through unequal trade with neighbouring peoples. All this could be done only through war, and war now became a constant factor in the life of society.

Successful conquerors united a number of city-states (nomes) beneath their rule and established territorial states that eventually occupied the whole or virtually the whole of a given ethno-cultural region. Within such states the former nome centres generally remained staunchly separatist. In economic terms they were, after all, rivals, competitors rather than partners capable of uniting in a common interest. Further, each had as good a claim as the others to be the metropolis and could be kept in the status of a province only by force of arms. That is why, for instance, division characterized Mesopotamia in the last three millennia BC and why the unitary state that embraced the entire country was short-lived. The stability of the unitary state in Egypt was due to particular geographical circumstances: the only alternative to union for the nomes located along the narrow strip of the Nile Valley, with no natural boundaries between them, was mutual annihilation.

The economic imperative prompted continual warfare through which there arose, by trial and error, a new type of state: the empire (Plate 10). This went far beyond the boundaries of a single ethno-cultural region, uniting different and economically complementary regions and linking them with trade routes. The component parts of the empire were generally at different levels of social and political development and the metropolis was not always the foremost in this regard. Imperial peace promoted trade and generally reinforced economic ties, as well as making for a syncretic, super-ethnic culture. Conversely, it was the empire that first gave rise, in addition to the already commonplace distinction between freemen and slaves or, on a broader footing, between citizens and foreigners, to a distinction among freemen in the guise of a difference between citizens and subjects, that is, between conquerors and conquered. This in turn led to the emergence and spread of ethnic warfare which was hitherto virtually unknown. Clearly, the stability of the empire depended on how well its component parts complemented

each other, which was, of course, a matter of chance. And when, through the inevitable levelling out of economic and cultural conditions, these component parts became rivals rather than partners, the empire's further development lost all point and it perished. Of course, not every empire survived to reach this natural end, the only one that did being that of Rome.

On the basis of these theoretical considerations, we consider the first empire in humanity's history to be the Assyrian state of the ninth to seventh centuries BC. To describe as 'empires' the Akkadian kingdom, the kingdom of the Ur III dynasty (c. 2112–2003 BC) or Hammurabi's Mesopotamian kingdom is to court theoretical and terminological confusion. Neither, for the same reasons, can the political structures established by the Mayas or the Aztecs in the New World be viewed as 'empires', although some regard the later political development of the Incas as 'empire'.

THE EARLY DYNASTIC PERIOD IN MESOPOTAMIA

Characteristic of this period (c. 2750–2315 BC) were small 'nome states', generally occupying less than 100 km², located along the Euphrates, its natural tributaries or artificial canals. Modern science employs the terms 'primitive' or 'military democracy' to describe their political structure. Such a state was a neighbourhood commune centred around the temple of the local tutelary god; in this was stored the contingency reserve in case of crop failure or other natural disasters, and also the reserve for trading (Mesopotamia had virtually no mineral resources and the local civilization could only exist by importing metals, timber and even stone.) Around the temple, the commune's economic centre, lived the priests, the members of the communal administration, the craftsmen and so on. Obviously, the temple stores were a tempting prize for neighbouring nomes and because of the increased military danger states began to protect the temple area and the surrounding settlement with a wall. The supreme authority was the assembly of the people, which comprised all adult male warriors; day-to-day affairs were run by a council of elders headed by the chief priest who bore the title ensi (a Sumerian term) or iššiakum (the Akkadianized form of the word). Other communal magistrates were responsible for foreign trade (the chief merchant), the court, the laying and maintaining of canals or for temple affairs. In the city-state of Ashur a key figure was the limmu, an official who was the city treasurer and who gave his name to the year. Lastly, an important role was played by the military chief or lugal, who appears originally to have been selected only for the space of a single military campaign: usually the ruler himself was chosen. As war grew in importance, the military leader increasingly came to take pride of place and the office was made permanent rather than temporary. More and more frequently rulers discarded ensi in favour of the title lugal as being more prestigious. Disposing of a considerable share of the spoils of war and commanding both the temple guard and the levy of citizens, the lugal concentrated ever greater power in his hands and increasingly pushed such traditional institutions as the council of elders and other offices to the second rank. The Sumerian epic poem Gilgamesh and Agga tells how Gilgamesh, the ruler of Uruk (here he bore the title en), when that city was besieged by the host of Agga, the lugal of Kish, asked the Uruk council of elders whether to resist or to submit to Agga. But when the elders counselled submission, Gilgamesh turned to the assembly of the people which called for war and proclaimed Gilgamesh *lugal*; the war ended with the defeat of Kish. Regardless of the historical accuracy of this story, this train of events is emphatically typical of many later periods: a successful military commander, drawing on the support of the masses and flouting the traditional authorities (the council of elders, areopagus or senate), seizes personal power. This is just how the tyrannies arose in Greece and the constant dictatorships, later to become the empire, in Rome. So too the monarchy arose in Mesopotamia. The word *lugal*, which originally meant a 'big man', 'chief' or 'owner', later became a royal title. The ruler, subsequently the king, gradually handed over his religious functions to the priests since, with his constant involvement in warfare, it became ever harder for him to preserve ritual purity (see I Chronicles, 28: 3, where God refuses to accept a temple from the warrior David: 'Thou shalt not build an house for my name, because thou hast been a man of war, and hast shed blood'). Gradually a structure of civil and military officials that no longer coincided with the temple administration took shape around the king. Through successful wars that structure's authority might be extended to several nomes and thereby automatically take precedence over the local institutions. But within his own nome the ruler relied on the assembly of the people and tried to prevent the growth of property differentiation (and the consequent intensification of internal contradictions) by reforms to protect the weak against the strong. Such legislative acts, later styled 'edicts on justice', were periodically issued until the Persian conquest of Mesopotamia in 539 BC.

The ruler was deemed to be appointed by the great gods, particularly by the nome's tutelary deity. In practice he was probably appointed by lot or by oracle. The ruler's power was originally neither hereditary nor even lifelong: although it later became virtually hereditary, all the kings of Mesopotamia (to the very end of its history as an independent land) ruled in theory by divine appointment. In the third millennium BC rulers and kings were also held to be the sons or descendants of gods; not literally, as for instance were the heroes of the Greek myths, but rather in the abstract sense: each Mesopotamian considered himself in some sense the 'son of his god', but that did not prevent him from having earthly parents. Contrary to the commonly-held view, the ruler or king of the nome state was not the representative of the gods on earth; he was rather the commune's spokesman to the gods, passing its wishes on to them and obeying their commands on its behalf.

THE FORMATION OF TERRITORIAL STATES

Ancient Mesopotamia passed through several stages in this process, the first being the establishment of a given nome's hegemony over a greater or smaller number of neighbouring nomes without forming a unitary state. It must be emphasized that, contrary to the universally accepted opinion, the country did not unite because of economic necessity. The irrigation systems of most nomes were more or less independent of each other; the establishment of a single irrigation system was as yet neither possible nor necessary. The cities of Mesopotamia were not and could not be trading partners, since their products were identical in kind; they tended consequently to be rivals. The purpose of warfare was to achieve an extensive increase in surplus product

through territorial expansion with a corresponding rise in population, and through plain plundering. Each nome centre had an equal claim to be the metropolis, and military fortune was fickle. But titles that reflected the position of the hegemonic ruler were already appearing, the most important being that of *lugal* of Kish. This title was not necessarily borne by the ruler of Kish itself: history records no more than one '*lugal* of Kish' at any one time, so that the title could only be acquired by the common consent of all other rulers or, possibly, by oracular decision (divination or lots) emanating from Nippur, the chief religious centre of Mesopotamia.

Many scholars hold that the title is evidence of a prehistoric 'empire' whose capital was at Kish. But this must be rejected both on theoretical grounds (see above) and because in historical times the city of Kish itself enjoyed no special prestige. A more plausible conjecture is that there was a prehistoric tribal alliance or amphictyony whose religious centre was Nippur but whose political and commercial centre was Kish. The *lugal* of Kish was probably at first the military leader of this alliance: in historical times he was the arbitrator in border conflicts and possibly the military commander of the alliance.

And so the territorial expansion of the state brought the fortunate conqueror a greater surplus product, first and foremost due to the increase in the ruler's possessions and also in the temple holdings, which the rulers were gradually bringing under their control. This enabled them to show 'generosity' towards full citizens of the large or revered temple cities, rescinding either wholly or in part their taxes and obligations. The first, albeit contested, instance of this is recorded in an inscription of Entemena, ruler of Lagash (*c.* 2360–2340 BC) (Plate 11).

However, the first to achieve truly large-scale, though short-lived, success in the unification of Mesopotamia was the ruler of Umma, Lugalzaggesi (*c.* 2336 BC). The state he established was a kind of confederation: almost all the nomes that it incorporated kept their own lords but recognized Lugalzaggesi's superior might and probably paid tribute. None the less, Lugalzaggesi was very soon attacked by Sargon of Akkad (2316–2261 BC), who prevailed and established a state that embraced the whole of Mesopotamia. Sargon did not see fit to choose an ancient and renowned city as his capital but set himself up in little Akkad: he wished to be free of the influence of the powerful local aristocracies and priests of particularly revered temples, and also to make a clean break with the tradition of the city-state. Subsequently, all others who founded major states in Mesopotamia did likewise, for similar reasons, either selecting as their capitals small or at least relatively unimportant cities (Isin, Babylon, Nineveh), or building themselves special capitals (Dur-Kurigalzu, Kar-Tukulti-Ninurta, Dur-Sharrukin). The only exception was Ur, capital of the kingdom of the Ur III dynasty. Characteristically, however, even this dynasty, which originated in Uruk, did not choose its native city as its capital but established itself in Ur where the highly revered local temple of the moon god was headed by a high priestess who enjoyed enormous esteem but played no political role.

Sargon's choice was inevitably construed as disrespect towards the great gods, their cities and their temples. Later priestly tradition is clearly hostile to Sargon and the dynasty he founded, accusing these kings of sinful arrogance. Sargon bore the traditional titles of 'king' (*lugal*, Akkadian *sharrum*), 'king of the land' and 'king of Kish', which in Akkadian became *shar kishshiatim*, meaning 'king of the multitudes'. His empire retained a nome structure and most of these nomes were governed by representatives of local dynasties as *ensis*: they played an important part in local cults and were given the appropriate initiation, which was tantamount to a coronation. The local *ensis* not only wanted independence but also dreamed of the opportunity of establishing their own states. Consequently, the entire period of this dynasty (over 100 years) was characterized by uprisings. Sargon's grandson Naram-Sin, who won brilliant victories over his internal and external enemies, was deified. No matter where the initiative for this really came from, it was presented as an 'honorary decree', an expression of the will of Akkadian citizens in gratitude to their fellow-citizen and supreme magistrate and 'requesting' that the great gods give him to them as 'the god of their city'. The uprisings none the less continued under the later kings and this led to the downfall of the state and the reign of the Gutians. Mesopotamia once again became a conglomeration of city-states.

The empire of the third dynasty of Ur (*c.* 2112–2003 BC), that was established after the Gutians had been driven out, was far smaller than that of Sargon and of Naram-Sin. Like Naram-Sin, however, its kings bore the title 'king of the four quarters of the earth' and Shulgi, the second king of the dynasty, was even deified. On the other hand, they emphasized that they merely headed the council of rulers of the city-states in at least three cities – Nippur, Ur and Uruk. It follows that not even Ur III was a genuine centralized state. Conversely, in this period an important step was taken towards the formulation of such a state's ideology: the compilation of what was called the Sumerian King List, which was designed to furnish the ideological justification for a sole and single kingdom that had, it was claimed, always existed in Mesopotamia, merely moving from one capital city to another. Here we encounter for the first time the concept of the charisma of a monarch (*nam-lugal* or kingship) that exists independently, regardless of its bearer, and that came down from heaven 'at the dawn of time'. However, it must be said that the ideology of the city-state is proclaimed even here, in a document established to justify autocracy: the 'kingship' is given to the city and only thereby to a person. In other words, there are no 'dynastic rights' and any city may claim the status of metropolis.

Indeed, this did happen. Ishbi-Erra transferred the 'kingship' of Sumer and Akkad to Isin (first dynasty of Isin, 2017–1794 BC), and his name began to be written with the determinative of divinity. In practice, however, Mesopotamia fell apart into a mosaic of mutually hostile kingdoms, each of which claimed primacy. The problem of relations between the kings and the cities again arose, and the latter were granted privileges (the oldest example is an inscription by the fourth king of Isin, Ishme-Dagan, granting privileges to Nippur). This began the process whereby the cities of Mesopotamia became civil and religious communities deprived of political independence but free of state taxes or duties and enjoying internal autonomy. Gradually they gave up their attempts to win back their political independence, but they zealously pursued this new status and jealously defended it. The kings, meanwhile, abandoned their claims to divinity but consolidated their rule – although this reached its full fruition only with the reign of Hammurabi (1792–1750 BC). The sixth representative of the so-called first Babylonian dynasty, he used refined diplomacy and successful wars to subjugate the whole of Mesopotamia. In the political structure of Hammurabi's state there was no longer any room for nomes. In the Prologue to his famous laws Hammurabi enumerates the benefits he has bestowed upon the most important cities of Babylonia, but carefully avoids any suggestion of a personal link with any city other than Babylon: they were all merely parts of a single state. That state was divided on purely administrative grounds into districts, and the post of *ensi* was completely abolished. In ideological terms, all this was underpinned by a break with the fundamental concept of the Sumerian King List. Babylon was proclaimed the eternal habitation of the monarchy. Although resistance, in the shape of hostile propaganda and uprisings, occurred even during Hammurabi's lifetime, the Babylonian state endured, albeit in a truncated form, for more than a thousand years. In the fourteenth century BC, several city-states in the north of Mesopotamia came together to form the territorial state of Assyria whose centre was Ashur. The interests of the further consolidation of the centralized state caused the Kassitic kings of Babylonia to leave Babylon for a specially built capital, Dur-Kurigalzu, and the Assyrian king Tukulti-Ninurta I to move to Kar-Tukulti-Ninurta. On this occasion Babylon was given privileges. The élite of Ashur declared the king mad, dethroned him and killed him. Subsequently, the Assyrian kings none the less left Ashur, but the city received privileges. The Babylonian kings returned each year to Babylon during the New Year festival and solemnly confirmed the city's privileges.

In the privileged cities the communal bodies for self-government – the council of elders headed by the city chief – again came to the forefront: for a time an important role was also played by the *karum*, the organization of merchants.

THE FIRST EMPIRES

Late in the second millennium BC Aramaean nomads of Western Semitic stock began to penetrate Mesopotamia. This unorganized horde could not be stopped by armed force. Although the Aramaean desert nomads could not capture cities, sooner or later the cities found themselves completely surrounded, with no alternative but submission to the conquerors. As a result Assyria, which had advanced its borders to the Euphrates, was able to keep only its own indigenous territory: a narrow strip to the west of the Tigris and, to the east of the river, the lands between the Great and the Little Zab – but even here, the Aramaeans came in. However, Assyria was able to preserve an advantageous strategic position, an important role in international trade and a powerful military organization. Other 'great powers' of the time either perished as the tribesmen advanced (the Hittite empire) or were seriously damaged and weakened (Babylonia and Egypt). Meanwhile, Assyria had to wait until the movement of the Aramaeans stopped. In Syria and northwestern Mesopotamia a large number of petty Aramaean, or rather Aramaicized, kingdoms arose, while in Babylonia proper, which was taken by a particular branch of the Aramaeans known as the Chaldaeans, the kingship was seized by Chaldaean leaders. With these events the old languages began to be pushed out by Aramaic, which in the course of several centuries became the common colloquial tongue of the whole region, including Mesopotamia.

Only towards the end of the tenth century BC did Assyria go over to the offensive with the aim of gaining control over the trade routes and where possible over sources of raw material. The traditional method of utilizing these was 'compulsory exchange' – or, in other words, plain plunder. This method was always advocated by the military and bureaucratic élite. The other method, preferred by the urban élite and the priestly class, was the 'correct exploitation' of the subjugated lands, the maintaining of 'imperial peace' that furthered normal economic relations. In time this led to a struggle between two 'parties' corresponding to these groups, with the kings either acting in the interests of one or other party or attempting to manoeuvre between the two.

Originally, however, only the first method was used. Assyria once again pushed its frontiers far to the west and the south and also mounted successful campaigns into Syria and Media. A great part of the occupied territories, however, was razed to the ground and depopulated. The Assyrians took virtually no prisoners since they did not yet need an influx of slaves. And the political situation had also begun to change for the worse: in the north the fragmented tribes of the Armenian highland united to form the powerful state of Urartu; the petty Syrian kingdoms began to establish anti-Assyrian coalitions; and the internal situation in Babylonia was becoming somewhat more stable. Even within Assyria itself, separatist tendencies on the part of the provincial governors posed a considerable threat. These difficulties could only be overcome by radical reforms, and these were implemented by Tiglath-Pileser III (744–727 BC), the founder of the Assyrian empire.

Tiglath-Pileser III broke the provinces down into smaller units, formed a standing army that was maintained by the king and made a practice of the mass deportation of the population of captured countries. These people were driven off together with their families, their property and even 'with their gods', settled as far as possible from their homelands and incorporated into 'the people of Assyria'. In time they did indeed come to form the bulk of Assyria's rural population, adopting the Aramaic language and living in a state of semi-slavery. In the towns, meanwhile, there lived a privileged minority. A series of successful campaigns made Tiglath-Pileser III lord of an empire that stretched from the Mediterranean to western Iran and from the Armenian highlands to the Persian Gulf. However, Babylonia's prestige was so great that when he conquered it, Tiglath-Pileser III kept it as a separate kingdom and had himself crowned its monarch, thereby joining Assyria and Babylonia by a personal bond. Most of his successors followed this example (the rest appointed 'vice-kings' – governors – in Babylonia). In the seventh century BC Assyria even took Egypt, albeit for less than two decades.

Although the Assyrian kings succeeded in establishing quite an effective administrative system (which was largely copied by later empires), their empire was nevertheless a fragile edifice. Its component parts by no means fully met the requirements set out above. Consequently, forcible methods prevailed, and the response to them was separatism. The privileged cities acted in some measure as a counterweight to the royal power. They were, of course, interested in the 'imperial peace' and in the preservation and expansion of their privileges; they were ready to defend the unity of the empire, but only on certain conditions. Kings who encroached on the privileges of the holy cities lost their thrones and their lives: Shalmaneser V (726–722 BC) for trying to strip Ashur of its privileges; Sennacherib (704–681 BC) because, in anger at its perpetual revolts, he ordered the destruction of Babylon (his successor Esarhaddon immediately took steps to have it rebuilt). But Babylon again became the centre of an uprising between 652 and 648 BC – although even after the cruel suppression of that uprising the Assyr-

ian king deemed it necessary to confirm his respect for Babylon. For the rural population it did not matter who held power, but the cities – as has been said – were largely favourable to the empire. That is why Nabopolassar (626–605 BC), who restored the independence of Babylonia, was obliged to subdue Nippur and other ancient Babylonian cities by force of arms. The Assyrian empire fell as a result of the coincidence of several unfavourable circumstances: the gradual disintegration of some of its parts, the growth of internal feuds and the establishment of the powerful and hostile kingdom of Media in direct proximity to Assyria proper. In 614 Ashur fell beneath the blows of the Medians, in 612 a Median and Babylonian army took and destroyed Nineveh and in 609 BC the last remnants of the Assyrian army were wiped out near Harran, a city in Upper Mesopotamia.

Assyria's successor in west Asia was the Neo-Babylonian empire, which held all the land west of the Euphrates to the Egyptian border and lasted for less than ninety years. Its last king, Nabonidus (556–539 BC), also tried to strip the Mesopotamian cities of their privileges (this was, in fact, the thrust of his 'religious reformism'). Thus it was that the Persians were able to enter Babylon without battle. In the minds of later generations (such as the authors of the later books of the Old Testament or the father of history, Herodotus), Assyria and Babylonia often became confused.

The political events of the sixth to first centuries BC gave a fresh development to the ancient concepts of royal power. As was said earlier, ideas of 'kingship' moving from one city to another were replaced by that of Babylon as the eternal habitation of the monarchy. Under the influence of later events (such as the Persian conquest of Babylonia or the coming of the Greeks), the idea of the primacy of cities was transformed into that of the primacy of states as expressed in the Old Testament Book of Daniel, which relates the consistent transfer of worldly power to Assyria (Babylonia), Persia, Greece (meaning the empire of Alexander and his successors) and finally to Rome. St Jerome then took the idea to European soil, where the theory of *translatio imperii* reigned among the historians of the Middle Ages. Its influence on the historical and political thought of Europe was profound.

BIBLIOGRAPHY

ADAMS, R. MCM. 1960. The Origin of Cities. *Sci. Am.* (New York), Vol. 203, No. 3, pp. 163–8.
—— 1966. *The Evolution of Urban Society. Early Mesopotamia and Ancient Mexico.* Chicago, Ill.
BRIANT, P. 1982. *Rois, tribus et pays. Études sur les formations tributaires du Moyen-Orient ancien.* Paris.
CHENG Te-K'UN. 1959. Archaeology in China. In: *Prehistoric China.* Cambridge. Vol. 1.
COLLIER, D. 1974. The Central Andes. In: SABLOFF, J. A.; LAMBERG-KARLOVSKY, C. C. (eds), *The Rise and Fall of Civilizations.* Seattle, Wash.
EISENSTADT, S. K. 1973. *The Political Systems of Empires.* London/New York.
KWANG-CHIH, CHANG. 1974. The Emergence of Civilization in North China. In: SABLOFF, J. A.; LAMBERG-KARLOVSKY, C. C. (eds), *The Rise and Fall of Civilizations.* Seattle, Wash.
LARSEN, M. T. (ed.) 1979. *Power and Propaganda. A Symposium on Ancient Empires.* København. (Mesopotamia, 7.)
MUGHAL, M. R. 1990. The Harappan 'Twin Capitals' and Reality. *J. Cent. Asia* (Islamabad), Vol. 13, No. 1., pp. 155–62.
POSSEHL, G. L. (ed.). 1979. *Ancient Cities of the Indus.* New Delhi.
SABLOFF, J. A.; LAMBERG-KARLOVSKY, C. C. (eds) 1974. *The Rise and Fall of Civilizations.* Seattle, Wash.

SAKELLARIOU, M. B. 1989. *The Polis-State, Definition and Origin*, Athens, Research Centre for Greek and Roman Antiquity, National Hellenic Research Foundation.

SANDERS, W. I. T. 1974. Hydraulic Agriculture, Economic Symbiosis and the Evolution of States in Central Mexico. In: SABLOFF, J. A.; LAMBERG-KARLOVSKY, C. C. (eds), *The Rise and Fall of Civilizations*. Seattle, Wash., p. 128.

SYMPOSIUM ON URBANISATION AND CULTURAL DEVELOPMENT IN THE ANCIENT NEAR EAST, 4–7 December 1958. *City Invincible*. Chicago, Ill., 1960.

WILLEY, G. R. 1974. Commentary on the Emergence of Civilization in the Maya Lowlands. In: SABLOFF, J. A.; LAMBERG-KARLOVSKY, C. C. (eds), *The Rise and Fall of Civilizations*. Seattle, Wash., p. 97.

YOFFEE, N.; COWGILL, G. L. (eds) 1988. *The Collapse of Ancient States and Civilisations*. Tucson, Ariz.

6

THE DEVELOPMENT OF LONG-DISTANCE TRADE AND THE EMERGENCE OF A MERCHANT CLASS

Jean-Pierre Mohen

The period which concerns us in this volume is also one of technological innovations resulting in improved means of transport that greatly broadened the horizons of certain communities, with all the economic, military, diplomatic and social consequences that this entailed. Considerable use had been made of inland waterways since prehistoric times, and the Nile, the Tigris, the Euphrates, the Indus and the Huanghe became crucial links in the development of great states. But these states also devised new overland communication systems to transport armies, goods and, especially, messages. New trades grew up and merchants began to engage in international commerce.

River and maritime routes played a major role in extending humanity's reach to the farthest corners of the world. By the beginning of this period, much of the globe had been explored, with the exception of the Pacific islands, and they, too, gradually became known to seafarers from the West. Expeditions reached Vanuatu, New Caledonia and Fiji in about 1000 BC and even ventured as far as Samoa in western Polynesia. The vessels used for these ocean voyages were probably large dugout canoes, sometimes coupled, catamaran-style, similar to those seen by the first European travellers in Polynesia in the eighteenth century. We know a little more about the vessels of classical antiquity from Egyptian or Assyrian iconography and from certain famous descriptions such as those of Homer's *Odyssey*, in which he recounts the return to Ithaca in Greece of Ulysses, one of the victors of the Trojan War, along the Anatolian coast. The Mediterranean craft had a mast and a sail. It was not unduly large or heavy, and Ulysses' companions were able to haul the boat up on to the beach at night. These vessels transported warriors, their provisions and their booty. There were also merchantmen plying their wares, as we know from the study of a number of wrecks.

The Cape Gelidonya wreck discovered in 1959 off the southern coast of Anatolia was carrying a cargo of copper and tin ingots weighing about a ton, which went down with the ship *c.* 1200 BC. The owner was a Phoenician on his way to the Aegean. It is likely that the Syrian seal found on board belonged to him and that he used it for official transactions. Egyptian-type scarabs, Syro-Palestinian imitations, were worn by the members of the crew. The clay vessels for everyday use and the cabin lamp also came from Syria-Palestine.

The weights used correspond to a system common in western Asia and in the Aegean, evidence of sustained economic relations between the two regions.

Another Anatolian wreck discovered in 1982 at Ulu Burun off the Lycian coast was carrying a royal cargo dating from the fourteenth century BC. The ship, 15 to 17 m long, was transporting 6 tons of copper ingots and a quantity of tin ingots. There were about a hundred Canaanite amphorae filled with a ton of turpentine resin, possibly intended for making perfumes. Another amphora contained olives. There were slabs of cobalt-blue glass with the same composition as Mycenaean amulets and Egyptian lachrymal vases dating from the 18th dynasty. Ivory from hippopotamus teeth and elephant tusks, and ostrich eggs were also found, possibly of western Asian origin. Amber from the Baltic, ebony from equatorial Africa, Cypriot pottery, gold Canaanite jewellery, two pieces of Egyptian gold jewellery, a ring and a scarab which, according to the inscription, had belonged to Queen Nefertiti, and a Mycenaean sword convey some idea of the quality and variety of the goods traded during stopovers along the shores of the Eastern Mediterranean. The cargo is of the kind sent by western Asian rulers to the pharaoh, as is attested, for example, by the tablets discovered at El Amarna in Egypt.

Sunken vessels laden with metal have also been located at Rochelongue (Hérault, France), where 1,700 fragments of bronze objects and 800 kg of copper ingots dating from the eighth century BC have been recovered, and off the coast of England, at Dover and Plymouth, where bronze weapons and tools dating from about 1200 BC have been found. We now have a better idea of such vessels after the discovery at Dover in 1992 of a large wooden version.

Further north, away from the Mediterranean world, boats were needed for contact with the numerous British, Danish and other islands. The Cassiterides, thought to be situated somewhere off the coast of Cornwall or closer to Brittany, are a good example of the island trading-posts that nurtured a flourishing maritime trade, the commodity in this case being cassiterite or tin ore (Figs 9, 10).

In addition to the dugout canoes commonly used in these temperate and northern regions of Europe, mention may be made of the umiak or coracle, with a keel and a skin-covered wooden frame, of the kind depicted in the Rodoy and Forsely rock paintings in Norway.

The abundant iconography of the Nordic Bronze Age cave settlements represents peaceful fishing or whaling boats, but also others apparently reserved for warriors in battle gear or blowing lurs, the great musical horns of Nordic proto-history. The oldest engraved designs show a horizontal line curved up at either end to indicate the prow and stern. The most recent depict a second horizontal line, which is quite simply the keel equipped with a ram. The prow is curved up and outwards to form a post with a figurehead representing a dragon, a serpent or, in the White Sea region, a moose. These vessels were propelled by oars; up to twenty pairs of oarsmen have been counted. Sails were not used in the northern regions, unlike the Mediterranean. Were oars used to steer the boats? This seems likely from the Ekjeberg design (Plate 12).

Another ship-building technique could have been recorded around 1000 BC, the lashed-plank. It was commonly used during the Iron Age (400 BC at North Ferriby in the United Kingdom) and the Late Middle Ages by the Vikings who ventured out on to the open seas in this kind of vessel.

Among the protohistoric boats found in temperate marshy lands, some were no doubt ferries used to cross the rivers.

A fair number of bog roads made of logs have been cleared and identified in England and northern Germany. They are typical of this period and of the following periods, during which overland routes were also developed to facilitate communications and trade.

In the far north, various methods were evolved for travelling over snow. In 1955, J.G.D. Clark recorded the vestiges of skis and sledge runners found in Norway, Finland and Sweden and depicted in rock engravings at the Zalavruga site near the White Sea. Examples are the Riihimaki ski in Finland and the Kalvträsk ski in Sweden, used with a ski-pole resembling a paddle. Sledge runners from Heinola in Finland and Marjarv in Sweden date from the third to the second millennia BC (Figs 11, 12).

The invention of the wheel and wheeled vehicles completely revolutionized overland transport, even though its impact was felt only gradually. Pictographic characters from Uruk in Iraq show for the first time the transition from chariots on runners to wheeled chariots. This was at the end of the fourth millennium BC (Fig. 13). Specimens of wooden wheels, terracotta models of chariots, drawings on vases or rock faces and actual chariots found buried in tombs provide evidence of the rapid development of this invention, both in western Asia and in eastern and central Europe. The frieze of chariots adorning a chest from Ur is a spectacular example, as are the wooden vestiges of the funeral chariots of Tri Brata between the Caspian Sea and the Black Sea, dating from the third millennium BC (Fig. 14). During the second millennium BC, the stippled Val Camonica drawings in northern Italy, and those found on stelae in the south-west of the Iberian Peninsula and again on the megalithic tomb of Kivik (Sweden), show how magnificent such vehicles could be, some of them four-wheeled (processional carriages) and some two-wheeled (war chariots), there being few representations of goods vehicles (Figs. 15, 16).

Wheel design changed as technology advanced. The earliest wheels were solid and made of wood (for example, the De Exe wheel, Netherlands) and usually in three segments (Armenian and Georgian funeral chariot wheels from the second millennium and the Zurich wheel from the third millennium BC) (Fig. 17).

These were supplanted by spoke wheels; hence the

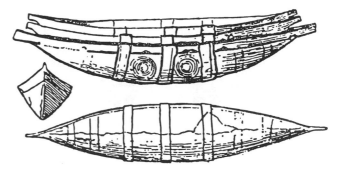

Figure 9 Small votive model boats in gold leaf from Nors, Thy, Denmark (after Clark, 1955).

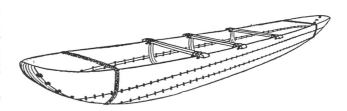

Figure 10 Reconstruction of the boat from North Ferriby, Yorkshire, United Kingdom (after Clark, 1955)

Figure 11 Archer on skis pursuing an elk. Rock engraving from Zalavruga, north-west Russia (after Clark, 1955).

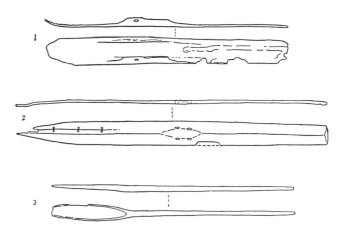

Figure 12 Skiing equipment of circumpolar Europe, Stone Age. 1, 'Southern' ski from Riihimaki, south Tavastlan, Finland; 2 and 3, 'Arctic' ski and stick from Kalvträsk, Burträsk, Västerbotten, Sweden (after Clark, 1955).

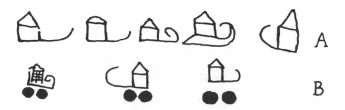

Figure 13 Pictographs in proto-literate script, fourth millennium BC, from Uruk, Iraq. A, sledge symbols; B, sledge-on-wheel vehicle symbols (after Piggott, 1983).

growing importance of the hub as a support for the spokes. Four spokes were common in the second millennium BC (votive chariot from Dupljaya in the former Yugoslavia, votive chariot from Trundholm in Denmark); wheels of this kind were sometimes made of bronze. Subsequently, the number of spokes increased (funeral chariots from the beginning of the Iron Age), with parts made of wood and metal, either bronze or iron.

The main features of chariot design seem to have been established from the earliest times, with the widespread use of a forked shaft attached to one of the axles supporting the wheels. This kind of shaft had the drawback of not being articulated, making the chariot difficult to steer. It was not until the beginning of the Iron Age that some technical improvements were made to overcome the problem.

Another important development in the history of carts and chariots was the use of draught animals. The earliest wheeled vehicles, in western Asia, were drawn by asses and later by a yoke of oxen.

Harnessed wagons of this kind are depicted in cave art at sites such as Syunik in Armenia or on stelae such as in the Longundo stela in Italy (Fig. 18).

The domestic horse made its appearance from the fifth millennium BC on the steppelands of eastern Europe. When horses were introduced to western Asia, around 2000 BC, they were used for war chariots. Evidence of the use of the horse as a draught animal is to be found, for example, in the Val Camonica engravings and the Trundholm votive chariot. For the slower wagons used for transporting goods, there was, however, no match for the reliable ox, with its steady pace and strength.

It should not be forgotten that the horse was primarily a saddle animal, a means of rapid locomotion which changed the nature of human relations. For the aristocracy of central Asia and Europe it was a status symbol. Not infrequently it would be sacrificed at its master's funeral and placed alongside him in his tomb. Many examples of this are to be found at the end of this period to the north of the Black Sea, among the ancient Scythians described by Herodotus, but also in Central Europe, in the Danube Valley, at Szentes-Vekerzug, in the south of France, at la Française and Cazals, and even in Spain, at Vallfogona de Balaguer. It was also quite common practice at the end of the Bronze Age and the beginning of the Iron Age for a person of note to be laid to rest surrounded by parts of his horse's harness in addition to all his finery and weapons. Examples are to be found in

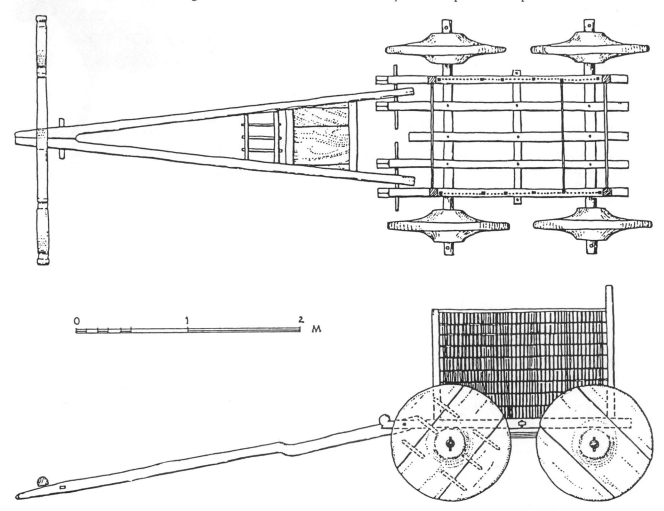

Figure 14 Scale drawings of a wagon, second millennium BC, from Barrow 11, Lchashen, Armenia (after Piggott, 1983).

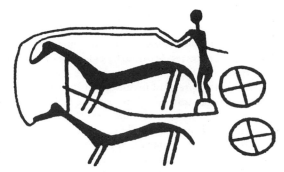

Figure 15 Horse-drawn chariot. Carving on a slab from the burial chamber at Kivik, Skane, southern Sweden (after Clark, 1955).

Figure 16 Wheeled vehicles. Chalcolithic rock paintings from Los Buitres, Penalsordo, Badagoz, Spain (after Clark, 1955).

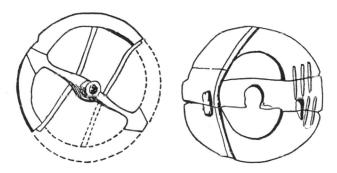

Figure 17 Wooden wheels in three segments from Mercurago, near Ancona, Italy (after Clark, 1955).

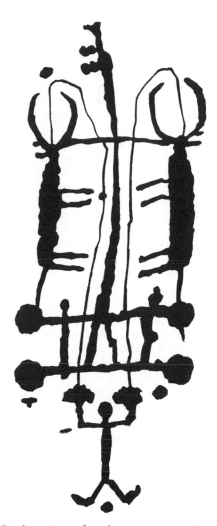

Figure 18 Rock carvings of ox-drawn wagons and carts, second millennium BC, Syunik, Armenia (after Piggott, 1983).

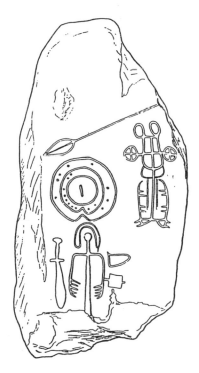

Figure 19 Grave-slab with warrior, sword, spear, shield and chariot, eighth-seventh century BC, from Cabeza de Buey, Spain (after Piggott, 1983).

Southern Germany, at Beilngries and Gernlinden. On the battlefield, horses and soon the cavalry as such were to play a decisive role, for instance when the 'Peoples of the Sea' swept over an awestruck Egypt around the thirteenth to twelfth centuries BC (Fig. 19).

Carts and chariots called for better roads, primarily a feature of the great centralized empires which needed a network of speedy communications to convey information and messages, to transport weapons, troops and baggage – for which horse-drawn wagons were used from 1500 BC – and to supply the large urban centres with foodstuffs for their inhabitants and basic materials for their craft workers. The earliest goods to be transported over long distances were luxury items, precious stones, metals, perfumes, timber and spices. Subsequently, products for everyday use were also imported into the capital cities; they included wheat, olive oil, wine, and so on. Some of the merchandise came from very far afield – amber, gold, furs and slaves from northern Europe, Russia and Asia. Salt, silk, tin and gold were brought across the Saharan, Nubian and Arabian deserts by caravans of dromedaries and camels.

With these two animals, it became possible for the first time and for economic reasons to cross these vast expanses of land that were otherwise difficult of access. Antiquity initially made no distinction between the two-humped Bactrian camel and the single-humped Arabian dromedary, which has led to some confusion today in retracing the history of their domestication. Archaeological discoveries are of some help. Among the Aeneolithic vestiges found in Turkmenia, at Altyn-depe, several sculpted terracotta statuettes representing camels or rather protome (heads and necks) attached to the front of four-wheeled chariots have been found. These statuettes dating from the third millennium BC suggest not only that the camel was domesticated but also that it was used as a draft animal in the regions of central Asia. This did not yet mean that the camel was used for crossing deserts, for there had to be precise economic and political reasons for undertaking such long journeys and these did not materialize until about 1100 BC, when the Assyrians brought camels from Media for mountain travel. It was they, too, who started using the dromedary for international transport across the Arabian desert, around 700 BC. It was not until a single political power, the Persian empire, held sway over the vast region of the Fertile Crescent that the great caravans could be organized, providing a direct link between the two tips of the Crescent. Dromedaries were introduced very much later in the Libyan desert and in the Sahara.

The construction of roads greatly facilitated these exchanges. From the third millennium BC, the Egyptians built roads so that the massive blocks of stone hewn for the construction of the pyramids or temples or for the sculpting of obelisks and colossi, the temple guardians, could be hauled from the stone quarries to the building sites. In Crete, traces of the road linking Gortyna to Knossos during the same period have been found. A major coastal road connecting Egypt with Gaza was of slightly later construction. Steps hewn in the rock where the road passes through the Nahr-el-Kelb gorges suggest that it could not be used for wheeled traffic. The Assyrians, under the reign of Tiglath-Pileser I (c. 1100 BC), had an engineering corps, the 'Ummani', who were responsible for road building, bridge construction and sapping.

There were staging posts along the roads where animals and people could rest and find running water, food and vehicle repair workshops. The administration was thus able to monitor the goods in circulation and levy taxes. The speedy, regular transmission of information was crucial to the great empires; the Assyrians, for instance, improved their communication system under the reign of Sennacherib (c. 700 BC), who developed a signalling system with lights along the roads, in order to convey messages. This technique was known in Israel and in Mesopotamia. The royal road from Sardis to Ephesus and to Susa, completed by Darius I in about 500 BC, had all these characteristics.

The empires that grew up between 3000 and 700 BC wielded considerable economic power as a result of the technological advances in transport. In every palace (Knossos) and city, lofts and storerooms were filled to overflowing with grain and olive jars.

Special districts were set aside for the various crafts, metal working or pottery (Enkomi). Trade in precious materials flourished not only in the Egyptian, western and central Asian states but also in the village civilizations of northern Europe (trade in green slate from Olonetz in Karelia, Baltic amber and tin from the Cassiterides off the British Isles). In the states of classical antiquity, graded systems of weights and measures were introduced (some examples of the technical aspects of such systems have been given in Chapter 1). The existence of such units of measurement, some of them imitated in distant countries, seems to be evidence of the importance of trade and other exchanges in the relations among peoples and in the spread of inventions. One example is the mina, a Phoenician unit weighing 0.727 g, which seems to have been current in several countries of western Europe (Switzerland and France) around the ninth century BC. Currency as such did not make its appearance until later (the earliest Rhodian coins dating from the fifth century BC).

Not only the land empires but also the maritime powers benefited from improved means of transport and the broadening of economic horizons. In the Mediterranean, the Phoenicians are a good example of intermediaries trading in wares of very different origins. The founding of Carthage in 814 BC was a sign of the opening up of the western shores of Africa and Europe.

Another fine example of a sea power was that of Greece, established before 700 BC and later to expand with the Greater Greece of the fifth century BC, stretching westwards to the Atlantic and eastwards to the Black Sea.

The great spheres of cultural influence which formed across the globe were not always based on political unity like the empires, but on economic factors brought about by human contacts or long-distance trade. This accounts for the spread of Celtic culture towards western and eastern Europe, the vast sphere of influence of Arctic culture, the relative unity of Andean cultures in which certain types of shell were exchanged from one village to the next, and the dissemination in Melanesia and western Polynesia of Lapita pottery cultures.

In this economic context, merchants tended to specialize. One might own a ship in the Eastern Mediterranean and sail from port to port offering his wares. Another might obtain a royal commission and thus transport gold objects and, often, carry messages. Yet another might act as middleman and take a consignment of tin oxide from England to the continent for onward shipment to a more southerly destination.

Some products had to be carried across the desert by camel or dromedary, travelling in caravans. Over rough terrain, as in mountainous regions, they were more commonly transported by pack asses or porters. Certain precious raw materials such as amber from the north, Chinese jade or certain shells from the Pacific were sometimes transported over great distances, several thousand kilometres from their place of origin. Merchants would follow the imperial armies, which steadily increased in number and were constantly on the move. With the growth of contacts and international trade, certain peoples – the Phoenicians, for example – hired out their services and controlled the flow of trade over such huge areas as the southern Mediterranean seaboard.

BIBLIOGRAPHY

BASS, G. F. et al. 1989. The Bronze Age Shipwreck at Ulu Burun: 1986 Campaign. *Am. J. Archaeol.* (Boston, Mass.), Vol. 93, pp. 1–29.

CLARK, J. G. D. 1955. *L'Europe préhistorique, les fondements de son économie.* Paris.

COLES, B.; COLES, J. 1989. *People of the Wetlands: Bogs, Bodies and Lake Dwellers.* London/New York.

FORBES, R. J. 1965. *Studies in Ancient Technology.* 2nd rev. ed. Leiden, Vol. 2.

LEE, N. E. 1955. *Travel and Transport through the Ages*. 2nd ed. Cambridge.

PARKES, P. A. 1986. *Current Scientific Techniques in Archaeology*. London/Sydney.

PIGGOTT, S. 1983. *The Earliest Wheeled Transport from the Atlantic Coast to the Caspian Sea*. London.

POLANYI, K.; ARENSBERG, M.; PEARSON, H. (eds) 1957. *Trade and Market in the Early Empires*. Glencoe, Ill.

SABLOFF, J.; LAMBERG-KARLOVSKY, C. C. (eds) 1975. *Ancient Civilisation and Trade*. Albuquerque, N.M.

STEINMAN, D. B.; WATSON, S. R. 1957. *Bridges and their Builders*. New York.

VIGNERON, P. 1968. *Le cheval dans l'antiquité*. Nancy, Annales de l'Est.

WALTZ, R. 1951, 1954. Zum Problem des Zeitpunktes der Domestikation der Altweltlichen Kameliden. *Zeitschrift der deutschen morgenlänändischen Gesellschaft*. Leipzig. pp. 29–51 (1951); pp. 45–87 (1954).

WILL, E. 1957. Marchands et chefs de caravane à Palmyre. *Syria* (Paris), Vol. 24, pp. 262–7.

WRIGHT, E. V. 1976. *The North Ferriby Boats: A Guide Book*. London. (Marit. Monogr. Reports, 23.)

7

THE BEGINNING OF THE IRON AGE: INVENTION OF IRONWORK AND ITS CONSEQUENCES

Pierre Villard

The period which extends from the fifteenth century to the eighth century BC saw the gradual introduction of iron into Western Asian societies and the confirmation of the position in this region of Assyria, a resolutely militaristic power, all of whose efforts seem to have been directed towards establishing a formidable war machine to use as an instrument of permanent conquest.

In fact, the political situation in the ancient Orient in the middle of the second millennium BC was one of relative equilibrium – which did not exclude expansionist designs – between several large states: Egypt, Kassite Babylonia, the Hittite kingdom and the Mitanni confederation, which extended from the shores of the Mediterranean to the foothills of the Zagros. On the borders of these kingdoms there continued to exist, particularly in Syria-Palestine, a number of small buffer states whose military weakness was offset by a prosperity based on trade and manufacturing, from which their more powerful neighbours also benefited. The decline of Mitanni and the simultaneous emergence of Assyria as a major power in the succeeding centuries did not fundamentally upset this dynamic equilibrium.

However, this regional pattern was radically changed about 1200 BC, when the invasion of the 'Peoples of the Sea' (a generic name given to peoples of very different origins) put an end to the Hittite kingdom and laid waste the Syro-Palestinian regions, from which Egypt was expelled. Subsequently, taking advantage of the weakness of the longer established states, new Semitic groups (the Aramaeans) gradually settled in the countries of the Fertile Crescent, overwhelming Babylonia about the middle of the eleventh century BC, before establishing a series of principalities in the Syrian regions.

These political and ethnic upheavals coincided with the real beginnings of the Iron Age in the ancient Orient and it has been suggested that the military superiority of the newcomers was partly due to their mastery of the new technologies. However, if there was a relationship between these technological advances and political developments at the beginning of the first millennium BC, it would inevitably be a complex one since, paradoxically, it was Assyria – the heir to the Bronze Age states – which in the ninth century BC initiated a policy of reconquest and expansion leading to the formation of the neo-Assyrian empire, which from the end of the eighth century and throughout the seventh century BC established and maintained its ascendency over practically all the countries of western Asia. In fact, although we should not minimize the importance of the spread of iron technology, it was only one factor in a whole series of more complex technological and economic changes which, while they cannot in themselves explain political developments, clearly brought about radical changes in long-established societies, in particular by strengthening their military capacities. Thus, the introduction of the horse not only revolutionized methods of warfare, but affected the whole economic and social structure.

Obviously, such changes only affected certain aspects of economic activity in these states, having a very limited impact on basic manufacturing sectors of the economy such as the textile sector. Likewise, whatever may have been the strategic importance of iron working or the new techniques connected with the use of horses, they were far from being the only reasons for the power of a state. To take only one example, Assyria's control of the cereal-growing lands of northern Mesopotamia, extending from the wider valleys of the Zagros to the Euphrates, was undoubtedly a decisive factor in its ability to build a lasting empire.

Due to the limited space at our disposal, greater attention will be given to the more dynamic sectors of the economy than to the many features which remained unchanged, partly because in most countries these sectors depended on access to imported raw materials and called for economic policies designed to ensure regular supplies.

THE INTRODUCTION OF IRON

It is sometimes difficult to make an accurate assessment of the impact which the introduction of iron-working techniques had on the economies of the states of the ancient Orient on account of the relative scarcity of archaeological finds in this field. However, in general terms it is possible to identify three main phases in the emergence of this technology, corresponding to the growing importance of the new metal in the economy as a whole. During the initial phase the existence of objects made of iron shows that the techniques of iron working were not unknown, although advantage was not really taken of the new metal's particular characteristic. It was still a rarity which, on account of its extremely high price, was used mainly for prestige items. During the second phase, the metal's special qualities began to be recognized and exploited for practical uses (tools and weapons), although bronze was still by far the most common metal in use. Finally, during the third phase, most tools and weapons were made of iron, although it did not necessarily replace bronze completely.

The first evidence of iron objects dates from relatively early in the ancient Orient (at least as early as the fourth millennium BC), but for a long time the metal was used on an extremely limited scale; in the middle of the second millennium BC the main purposes for which iron was used (in particular the manufacture of votive weapons intended as royal presents or for sanctuaries) clearly indicate that the ancient Orient was still in the first phase. Examples are the iron-bladed dagger discovered in the tomb of Tutankhamen (about 1350 BC) and a battleaxe, which is probably from a sanctuary at Ugarit (fourteenth century BC?): mounted in a copper socket inlaid with gold, the iron head of this axe contains a significant amount of nickel, which suggests that at least some of the metal was of meteoritic origin. This was true for a large proportion of objects of the early period and gives some indication of the difficulty of extracting this metal from mineral ores, which of course was why it was so rare.

If iron working was to make real progress and advance into the second phase, ways had to be found of producing the metal in sufficient quantities from the ore. In fact, the high degree of technical skill which metal workers had already acquired in working copper and bronze was not directly transferable, mainly because the temperatures obtained in primitive furnaces were not, barring accidents, high enough to produce cast iron.

The first step in extracting the iron probably consisted in processing the ore (usually haematite or magnetite) in a furnace (initially probably just a hole in the ground) with charcoal. Careful control of the heating process (possibly with the help of bellows) made it possible to obtain a temperature which was probably not in excess of 1,200°C. This temperature was lower than the melting point (1,540°C) of pure iron, but was high enough, as a result of chemical reactions with the charcoal, to reduce the ore to a spongy, doughy mass which cooled down in the form of porous blocks. These had to be heated up again and then the remains of the scoriaceous material had to be hammered off, so as to obtain ingots which could then be used to manufacture objects.

The adoption of such techniques not only requires ores which could be exploited by the methods known in the ancient world, but also plentiful supplies of fuel: eight tons of charcoal were needed to process one ton of ore. In western Asia the most favourable areas were north-west Iran and, above all, the Armenian mountains and the ranges of the Taurus and Anti-Taurus mountains. The absence of written documentation for these regions makes it difficult to reach any definite conclusions about the origin of these techniques or the activities of the miners and prospectors who first attempted to process the ore. It should of course be clearly understood that the actual manufacture of finished objects could be carried out in other places to which the iron ingots had been exported.

However, the metal obtained by this method was less resistant than well-worked bronze. The decisive step was the discovery of the processes of iron carburization. The repeated heating of an iron object lying on a bed of charcoal to a temperature above 900°C, so that it becomes white hot, makes it absorb a certain amount of carbon, which has the effect of transforming it superficially into steel. The metal then acquires physical characteristics – it becomes more resistant or can be given a cutting edge – which are likely to increase its usefulness. Finally, tempering (rapid cooling in water or oil), a process which had no place in bronze metallurgy, made it possible to combine hardness with strength, which gave iron a real superiority.

However, we should not forget the extremely gradual and empirical nature of the discovery of the processes mentioned above. It is possible that the techniques of iron carburization first appeared in the fourteenth or thirteenth centuries within the sphere of influence of the Hittite or Mitanni kingdoms, but it is significant that the Assyrian kings of the thirteenth century BC (Shalmaneser I and Tukulti-Ninurta I) buried iron tablets as votive offerings in the foundations of the buildings of their capital, Ashur, which indicates that it was still, in their eyes, a metal of particular value.

We should not underestimate the technological obstacles to the spread of iron, which mainly arose from the variety of processes which had to be followed in order to achieve acceptable results. It took some time to produce iron objects, while copper or bronze objects could be made in a single operation, casting, and required little finishing. Above all, however, the craftsmen had to control a considerable number of different factors at each stage of the operation. To take only one example, the processes of carburization depended both on the temperature of the furnace – which was very difficult to judge – and on the length of time the metal was left there. In any case, as iron objects have to be hammered while they are still hot in a charcoal furnace, carburization must frequently have taken place accidentally and only long experience would enable blacksmiths to identify the technique. Incidences where it can be shown with some certainty that carburization was intentional and properly controlled hardly appear in Mesopotamia before the seventh century BC.

The observation helps to give us a clear idea of the circumstances in which ancient Oriental societies advanced into the Iron Age proper, that is to say, the third of the phases described above. Both archaeological finds and the written evidence indicate that this process occurred relatively rapidly, although the chronology differed from region to region. Thus, it is probable that the transition first occurred at the end of the second millennnium BC in the Mediterranean region (Cilicia, north-west Syria and then Palestine). In Assyria, the process was delayed until the end of the ninth century, while in Egypt it probably did not take place before the seventh century BC.

As we have seen, this transition could not have been due wholly to the technological advantages of the new metal. The theory of the technological superiority of the Philistines (who are generally considered to be related to the 'Peoples of the Sea'), thanks to the jealously-guarded secret of iron metallurgy (for example I Samuel, 13), should no doubt be discarded, together with the idea that the Hittite kingdom had a 'monopoly of iron' several centuries earlier. We should take into account the information available on trade routes and the migration of craftsmen, which may be connected with the political upheavals that occurred at the end of the second millennium BC. The proximity of sources of supply (particularly in the Taurus Mountains) may partly explain the lead taken by the western regions, although it has also been suggested that disruption of the routes supplying copper and tin accelerated the introduction of iron. It is also probable that the capture of craftsmen and the seizure of raw materials, during the great campaigns towards the west by the Assyrian rulers of the ninth century BC (Ashurnasirpal II and Shalmaneser III), were factors in the spread of iron into

Assyria. Subsequently, the Assyrian army's considerable need for weapons and tools must have led to a greater use of iron, if only because supplies of tin were probably insufficient, a situation which might in itself have contributed to the gradual discovery of the potential of the new metal. It is clear, therefore, that the adoption of iron as the most commonly used metal does not need to be attributed to one single cause. It seems, however, that the reasons were as much economic as technological, although iron was probably not very much cheaper than bronze before the neo-Babylonian period (sixth century BC).

Thus, it is easy to understand why, at the end of the period under review, the two metals – iron and bronze – existed side by side. An examination of early iron objects shows that metalworkers often tried to copy forms typical of the Bronze Age, and up to the Achaemenid period we find objects made of a combination of the two metals (for example a sword with an iron blade and a bronze hilt). The greater precision made possible by casting techniques encouraged the use of bronze for anything which was ornamental. There was thus a degree of specialization, different metals being used for different purposes. The sword benefited more than any other weapon from the use of iron, as blades made of bronze were of limited strength. However, bronze weapons did not disappear entirely: for example, bronze helmets, which were lighter, continued to be used alongside iron helmets, which offered better protection (Plate 13).

The use of iron for non-military purposes led to the invention of new and the improvement of some existing tools (picks, axes, hammers, chisels, files, saws, and so on), which had a marked effect on the working methods of craftsmen and particularly on building techniques. However, it was agriculture, which was still the basis of the economy, which seems to have benefited most from the spread of iron working, as improvements to the tools had been long delayed as a result of the relative scarcity of metal. The ploughshares and hoes which have been discovered in Mesopotamia are all made of iron from the end of the eighth century BC onwards and Sennacherib (704–681 BC), describing in his annals the irrigation works which extended the area of cultivation in the region of Nineveh, states that he used iron tools to cut canals through the mountains.

THE STRENGTHENING OF MILITARY POWER

Although the spread of iron technology did not only affect weaponry, it nevertheless clearly illustrates the dynamic role played by military factors in technical development in the formation of economic structures. The introduction of the horse into the countries of western Asia provides perhaps an even better example of this phenomenon, since it shows how the emergence of new techniques in the art of war was associated with the rise of a social group consisting of specialized warriors and with the reorientation of certain sectors of the economy (Fig. 20).

Probably first domesticated in the Euro-Asiatic steppes, the horse is known to have existed in western Asia as early as the beginning of the second millennium BC, although at that time it was of marginal importance. Similarly, the chariot was used as early as the Sumerian period. Apparently drawn by onagers, but mounted on four solid wheels which were fixed directly to the body, it was too cumbersome to play a really effective tactical role. It was improvements

enabling the chariot to play a real military function which boosted demand for horses in western Asia. The new type of chariot had both a lighter and a stronger body, formed of pieces of wood joined together by leather straps and supported by an axle with two spoked wheels. Harnessed with throat collars to two horses controlled by a bit, it was extremely easy to handle and its devastating charges could easily rout infantry.

Clearly, the effectiveness of this new piece of equipment depended on the quality and manoeuvrability of the horses, which in itself presented a dual problem: first, the animals, which were not native to western Asia, had to be acclimatized, and secondly, they had to be properly trained. A treatise which was probably written in the fourteenth century by a person of Mitanni origin, Kikkuli, deals specifically with these two questions. This text is known in a Hittite version, discovered at Boghazköy, which supports the view that this new instrument of warfare was probably first developed within the Hittite-Mitanni sphere of influence. The many technical terms in Kikkuli's treatise which appear to be of Indo-Aryan origin seem to indicate that these methods had been devised by newcomers to western Asia.

Be that as it may, these discoveries spread rapidly, both into Assyria and into the Syro-Palestinian regions, as is shown by an Assyrian treatise of another king and by a veterinary text from the Mediterranean port of Ugarit, both of which were written about a century after the work of Kikkuli.

During the first centuries of the first millennium BC, when the Assyrian army was becoming the dominant force in western Asia, chariots seem to have become heavier and acquired a new tactical role. More sturdily built and harnessed to four horses, they were no longer launched forward in order to rout the enemy troops, but instead were deployed alongside the foot soldiers. The cavalry became a light, fast-moving force, the Assyrian army comprising several cavalry contingents from the ninth century BC onwards. The Assyrians may well have been copying the nomad peoples they were fighting (there are pictoral representations dating from as early as the tenth century BC of mounted Aramaean warriors), although it took them some time to assimilate these new techniques completely. Bas-reliefs of the ninth century BC show two horsemen operating side by side, one fighting and the other holding the reins of the two horses: this teamwork was a straight transfer to this new instrument of warfare of the combat roles associated with the light chariot. Under Sargon II (721–705 BC), however, the horsemen operated individually, a tactical change which was made possible by the adoption of a type of rein which could, when required, leave both the rider's hands free for fighting, and by a new bit which made it possible to rein the horse in more effectively. During this period the Assyrian army had several thousand horsemen, divided into small groups of about a hundred each.

These developments were bound to bring about changes in the methods of breaking in and raising horses. It seems that the Assyrians used different breeds or sizes of animals for different purposes. Seventh-century texts make a distinction between draught horses (for chariots) and those intended for riding, and also between the breeds from Kush (probably from Nubia originally) and from Mesu (northwest Iran). About the same period, a passage in the annals of Sargon II relates that the king of Urartu (present-day Armenia) employed Mannaeans (a people living on the eastern borders of his kingdom) to allocate young horses from his stud-farms for different uses.

Figure 20 Bronze Age and Early Iron Age warriors. Rock art from Fossum, Sweden (1 and 3), Vitlycke I, near Tanum, Sweden (2 and 4), and Val Calmonica, Italy (5, 6 and 7) (after Mohen and Bailloud, 1987).

It should be clearly understood that during the period in question the horse appears to have been used for strictly military purposes; it was far too expensive to be used as a draught animal in agriculture. It is therefore not surprising that the horse came to be associated, in western Asia, with power and royalty. A significant example of this is provided by the story of Idrimi, a Syrian ruler who was a vassal of the Mitannian king, who is described in an inscription carved on his statue as having come back from exile to regain possession of his kingdom, bringing only his horse, his chariot and his squire. This myth of the warrior king setting out to conquer his kingdom with his horse as his only possession was to take deep root throughout western Asia, since several centuries later Sargon II, recounting his campaign against the Urart-

ian king, Rusa, mentions among the booty a statue of his defeated enemy bearing the proud inscription: 'with my two horses and my charioteer, my hands have conquered the kingdom of Urartu'. It is also interesting that the sovereign's horses and chariots were associated with the royal family in the conventional formulae of greeting used in diplomatic exchanges between the most powerful rulers during the El Amarna period (fourteenth century BC).

This conception of power, principally based on military strength, is also apparent in the social structure which is known to have existed to the west of the Mitanni kingdom and in some Syro-Palestinian states at the end of the Bronze Age. There, in addition to the nobles of royal blood, the group of *Maryannû* formed a kind of military aristocracy.

This term, derived from an Indo-European word which originally meant 'young man', was used to describe the chariot troops, who formed the professional warrior élite.

In the Hittite world, too, it seems that the charioteers were solely engaged in military activities: they, together with their families, horses and servants, were maintained at the king's expense through concessions of land belonging to the palace. However, it should be noted that there are no known instances of this social élite acquiring autonomous power. The work of supplying the army, with both food and equipment, was organized by the palace thanks to a system of taxation. The possession of horses and chariots seems to have been a matter for the royal administration. Military power thus remained under the close control of the ruler.

The army of the Neo-Assyrian empire provides another example of the growing professionalization of warfare. In addition to those forced to enter the royal service (in a military or civilian capacity) for a specific period of time, there was a standing army organized as a central force directly under the sovereign and large provincial forces, whose troops should probably be numbered in hundreds of thousands. In fact, this army was not composed exclusively of Assyrians. The use of Aramaean mercenaries in the infantry is well attested. There is also clear evidence, as early as the reign of Ashurnasirpal II, of the inclusion in the Assyrian chariot forces of soldiers from the states of northern Syria, who were regarded as particularly skilled in this kind of warfare. In addition, following the capture of Samaria (722 BC), Sargon II drew on the best officers of this city to form a chariot corps which was incorporated into the central army, although it preserved its identity as a national force. It might seem surprising to see men serving in this way in their conqueror's army, but it seems likely that the total professionalism of such soldiers, together with a long-standing tradition in the use of mercenaries, made them completely trustworthy.

While the economic consequences are apparent as early as the middle of the second millennium BC, it is the Neo-Assyrian empire which provides the best example of the repercussions of the growth of a class of professional soldiers and the huge expansion in the numbers of military (and administrative) personnel. Clearly, the Assyrian army played an economic role of its own, particularly through pillage in foreign countries, but its need for equipment and supplies led to the organization of an internal system which was firmly based on the system of provinces and whose main function was to obtain from the private sector of the economy the resources needed to maintain the civil administration and, above all, the military administration.

The main obligation, whose fulfilment the governors of the Assyrian provinces were responsible for supervising on behalf of the central military administration, was the *ilku*. This term, which is known to have been in use as early as the Old Babylonian period (beginning of the second millennium BC), referred to both the land granted by a superior authority and the duties related to it, for example, military service in the case of lands held from the king. During the second half of the second millennium BC, the word appears at Nuzi (a vassal principality to the east of the Mitanni) and also in the Assyrian kingdom: it was usually used to refer to military service performed for the state, but sometimes it also referred to the supplying of horses for the army. In the Neo-Assyrian empire, while the basis of the institution seems to be the same, it emerges, first, that the relationship between the *ilku* and landholding is not an inherent part of the system (city-dwellers were compelled to take part, unless

exempted) and, secondly, that the idea of personal service was modified: while some of those subject to this obligation did in fact enter the royal service, others fulfilled their obligations by directly providing various kinds of supplies, ranging from agricultural products to certain metals, to the soldiers stationed in their province (there is evidence of this particularly in the case of the chariot troops). A similar practice is attested at Ashur: during the winter months preceding the assembly of the army in springtime for the annual campaign, horsemen took their horses back with them to their villages, which were apparently responsible for maintaining them. Finally, there is the example of the incorporation of teams of craftsmen (sometimes belonging to the conquered peoples) into the 'royal contingent' (*kisir sarrûti*); a word normally used to describe the central army. While any attempt to draw a rigid distinction between civil and military administrations is somewhat anachronistic, it seems that one of the aims of these teams was to provide the army with equipment and specialized services. These different examples illustrate the way in which the productive forces of the country were incorporated into a system designed to maintain an increasingly onerous and specialized war machine.

Thus, while there was a general tendency towards militarization in these societies, it is Assyria which provides the best example of this trend. The only survivor, together with Egypt, of the ancient Oriental states of the Bronze Age, it possessed a higher degree of social cohesion and national unity than its rivals. Therein lies, perhaps, the reason for the resounding success which it achieved at any rate for a certain period of time.

THE STATES AND THE CONTROL OF STRATEGIC RESOURCES

One of the major economic problems facing most of the states of ancient western Asia was how to ensure supplies of the various resources essential for the needs of the army and also for many of the key sectors of the economy. In fact, these products (wood, metals, horses and so on) mainly came from the mountainous areas bordering the Fertile Crescent, which were only intermittently controlled by the large urbanized states, or occasionally by more distant countries. International exchanges of goods and resources therefore became a necessity. Understood in its widest sense, this meant not only trade as such, but also the downright plundering of neighbouring countries whenever circumstances allowed or demanded.

As far as trade is concerned, the direct sources date mainly from the middle of the second millennium BC (fifteenth to thirteenth centuries), at a time of political equilibrium between several major powers. At that time merchants and traders were clearly subordinate to royal authority. In Nuzi, for example, we find merchants mentioned in lists of palace servants, while another person is described as a 'merchant of the queen', which does not mean, of course, that such men could not have also carried on business on their own account. In fact, diplomacy and trade were closely linked. Thus, in a message to the pharaoh, the king of Alashiya (Cyprus) introduces the men whom he has sent to the court of Egypt not only as his messengers, but also as his merchants. We might also mention the famous letter in which the Hittite king, Hattusilis III (1289–1265 BC), apologizes to his correspondent, an Assyrian sovereign, because the iron blades which the latter had requested, probably in exchange for bronze armour, had not yet been finished. Royal initiatives in the international exchanges of goods are clearly illustrated by such practices, in which gifts from one sovereign to another – which obviously required gifts in return – masked what were, in fact, commercial relations.

This system, in which the functions of ambassador and commercial representative were often confused, found its clearest expression in Egypt, where foreign trade seems to have been a royal monopoly. The relative rigidity in international trade which ensued (particularly as a result of the restrictions imposed on private initiatives) undoubtedly increased the role of the cities of the Mediterranean Levant as commercial intermediaries. The merchants of these ports, partly organized as private firms, were also able, thanks to their knowledge of navigational techniques, to gain direct access to various kinds of raw materials which were vitally important to their powerful neighbours. The economy which they developed, based on a rapid turnover of trade and on the substantial profits resulting from the manufacture of luxury goods from imported materials, was complementary to the mainly palace-based economies of the major inland powers which accumulated reserves and wealth. That explains the close relations between Egypt and the Canaanite cities, particularly Byblos. The relationship of vassalage, which was expressed in the payment of tribute, in fact involved a situation of interdependence and alliance from which both parties benefited. Further north, Ugarit had a similar relationship with the powers controlling its hinterland. Evidence of this is provided by the treaty containing commercial clauses concluded between the Hittite king, Hattusilis III, and his vassal Niqmepa, the ruler of Ugarit, and also the agreements reached about the same time between Ugarit and the kingdom of Carchemish, which made provision for indemnities to be paid if a merchant was murdered on the other party's territory.

It is clear, therefore, that while the most powerful rulers depended on merchants, either from their own countries or from abroad, for supplies of many essential goods, they provided them with both political protection and opportunities for international contacts. It is this symbiotic relationship which most clearly characterizes commercial activity during this period.

During the early centuries of the first millennium BC, information about commercial activities becomes much more scanty at a time when Assyria from the ninth century BC onwards was gradually becoming, despite some setbacks, the dominant power in western Asia. In fact, the official inscriptions of the Assyrian sovereigns, which give self-congratulatory accounts of the fabulous booty obtained during their campaigns, give the impression of an economy based on pillage much more than on trade. Although this picture contains part of the truth, it is subject to some qualifications: it is highly probable that numerous commercial documents of the first millennium BC, written in Aramaic (the language which was used to write on perishable materials such as parchment), have not come down to us. In fact, there are clear signs that major commercial activities continued during this period, but operated under new conditions resulting from the expansion of the Neo-Assyrian empire.

In order to understand how the desire to obtain essential strategic resources could influence the direction taken by conquest, we need to assess the economic significance of the levies imposed on foreign countries by the Assyrians. These might take two main forms.

Assyrian victories usually ended with the plundering of the conquered country or with the payment of a heavy tribute in recognition of its subjugation. While precious objects were not disdained, this practice also formed a way of providing for the needs of the artisans and the army: wood, horses and, above all, metals headed the lists of the booty obtained. To take only one example, the Syrian pricipalities, such as Carchemish and Damascus, supplied not only considerable amounts of gold and silver, but also tin, copper and iron, and it would seem that the location of these regions, at the end of important trade routes along which metals were imported, partly explains the frequency of the Assyrian campaigns directed against them. The stocks accumulated over several generations, particularly in the palaces and temples, were thus put into circulation for the benefit of the conqueror's economy.

Another form of levy, although it was much more modest in volume, was the annual tribute imposed on the vassal states which recognized Assyrian suzerainty, but which were left a certain amount of political and economic independence. It was much more modest in amount and usually consisted of luxury products that were normally shared among the principal members of the Assyrian court. The goods demanded (for example, dyed wool and luxury textiles in the case of a Phoenician ruler) are often the same as those mentioned in some of the commercial documents of this period, and it is possible that the annual tribute, which served to provide the Assyrian élite with luxury goods, was also symbolic of the reorientation of the economic activity and trade of the vassal countries towards Assyria.

In the absence of full documentary evidence, it is clearly difficult to state accurately the exact proportion of Assyria's needs which was met by such levies. It should, however, be remembered that Assyrian practices varied in this respect from one period and place to another.

The early conquests often took the form of raids the purpose of which was the acquisition of substantial loot, and they did not always result in the permanent occupation of the conquered countries, which simply became tributary states. The resulting indirect control was precarious and constantly threatened by rebellions or changes of alliance. At the end of the ninth century BC and the beginning of the eighth, Assyria went through a period of temporary decline, partly caused by internal crises, and this endangered its access to essential resources (horses from the high valleys of the Zagros to the east, metals from Syria in the west). The reign of Tiglath-Pileser III (744–727 BC), which decisively marked the restoration of Assyrian military power, inaugurated a more systematic policy of annexation. The regions brought under provincial administration were mainly extended towards the west, beyond the traditional frontier on the Euphrates which had been established during the first period of expansion in the second millennium BC. The Syro-Palestinian regions, together with the vital trade routes which crossed them, thus became an integral part of the empire. Nevertheless, most of the mining regions remained outside Assyrian control. However, a passage in the annals of Sargon II, recounting an expedition into the Taurus Mountains, describes the mining activities, making particular mention of copper and iron, and there can be little doubt that this area, which provided Assyria with one of its only direct means of access to mineral ores, was of particular strategic importance.

The system of indirect control was maintained for peoples other than Babylonia, whose cultural and religious prestige gave it a particular status, either as a matter of policy or because it was impossible to control them more directly. Thus, the Assyrian sovereigns frequently organized raids on the Iranian plateau, mainly to rustle horses needed to equip the army, but they were never able to control these regions on a permanent basis. In another case, the autonomy granted by the Assyrians to peoples situated on the fringes of their empire reveals a desire to tap part of the traffic on trade routes which it was beyond their capacity to control directly. Thus, Sargon II forced Egypt to open its doors to Assyrian trade by establishing on its frontier a 'quay' (*kâra*), at which the Assyrians enjoyed preferential treatment and dues were levied. This trade, which must have been mainly in horses from Nubia, was probably carried on through Arab tribes, who alone were able to follow the trails through Sinai. The Assyrians, who were largely ignorant of the techniques of navigation, also drew upon the services of the Phoenician cities which took over from Canaanite cities during the first millennium BC. In exchange for tribute and preferential terms of trade for their powerful neighbour, as indicated by the opening of a *kâra* at Arwad and the treaty imposed on Tyre by Esarhaddon (680–669 BC), these cities were able to maintain a certain amount of freedom. In addition, it is possible that Assyrian demands for metal and other raw materials contributed towards the extension of Phoenician commercial influence towards the western Mediterranean.

Despite the apparent brutality of the methods used, the Neo-Assyrian economic system thus had a certain coherence. There was, however, a heavy concentration of economic activity in certain cities – royal or provincial capitals – towards which most resources were directed. The political centre was therefore extremely vulnerable to any breakdown in external supplies, on which it was heavily dependent. Everything depended, in fact, on military force and well-organized central administration. While there is no proof that a crisis in the supply of goods and materials, accompanying political upheavals, played a direct part in the relatively sudden collapse of the Neo-Assyrian empire in 612 BC, it is clear that the political and military eclipse of Assyria and of the central regions of the empire put an end to their prosperity and their economic vitality for a considerable period.

BIBLIOGRAPHY

DALLEY, S. 1985. Foreign Chariotry and Cavalry in the Armies of Tiglath-Pileser III and Sargon II. *Iraq* (London), Vol. 47, pp. 31–48.

EBELING, E. 1951. *Bruchstücke einer mittelassyrischen Vorschriftensammlung für die Akklimatisierung und Trainierung von Wagenpferden.* Berlin.

ELAT, M. 1978. The Economic Relations of the Neo-Assyrian Empire with Egypt. *J. am. Orient. Soc.* (New Haven, Conn.), Vol. 98, pp. 20–34.

—— 1982. The Impact of Tribute and Booty on Countries and People within the Assyrian Empire. *Arch. Orientforsch.* (Graz), Vol. 19, pp. 244–50.

FORBES, R. J. 1964. *Studies in Ancient Technology.* Leiden, Brill. Vols 8–9.

FRANKENSTEIN, S. 1979. The Phoenicians in the Far West: A Function of Neo-Assyrian Imperialism. In: LARSEN, M. T. (ed.), *Power and Propaganda.* København. pp. 263–94.

HANCAR, F. 1956. *Das Pferd in prähistorischer und früher historischer Zeit.* Wien/München.

HOLMES, Y. L. 1973. Egypt and Cyprus: Late Bronze Age and Diplomacy. In: HOFFNER, H. A. (ed.), *Orient and Occident.* Neukirchen-Vluyn. pp. 91–8.

JANKOWSKA, N. B. 1969. Some Problems on the Economy of the Assyrian Empire. In: *Ancient Mesopotamia. Socio-Economic History.* Moskva. pp. 253–75.

KHLOPINA, L. I. 1982. Das Pferd in Vorderasien. *Orient. Iovan. Period.* (Leuven), No. 13, pp. 5–24.

LITTAUER, M. A.; CROUWEL, J. H. 1979. *Wheeled Vehicles and Ridden Animals in the Ancient Near-East.* Leiden.

LOON, M. van. 1966. *Urartian Art.* Istanbul. Nederlands Historisch-archaelogisch Institut.

MAXWELL-HYSLOP, K. R. 1974. Assyrian Sources of Iron. *Iraq* (London), Vol. 36, pp. 139–54.

MOHEN, J. P.; BAILLOUD, G. 1987. *La vie quotidienne à l'âge du Bronze: les fouilles du Fort-Harrovard.* Paris. (Vol. 4: *L'âge du Bronze en France.*)

MOOREY, P. R. S. 1985. *Materials and Manufacture in Ancient Mesopotamia.* Oxford. (BAR Int. Ser., 237.)

OPPENHEIM, A. L. 1967. Essay on Overland Trade in the First Millennium BC. *J. Cuneif. Stud.* (New Haven, Conn.) Vol. 21, pp. 236–54.

PARDEE, D. 1985. *Les textes hippiatriques (Ras-Shamra-Ougarit II).* Paris.

POSTGATE, J. N. 1974. *Taxation and Circonscription in the Assyrian Empire.* Rome. (Studia Pohl, Ser. maior, 3.)

—— 1979. The Economic Structure of the Assyrian Empire. In: LARSEN, M. T. (ed.), *Power and Propaganda.* København. pp. 193–222.

POTRATZ, H. A. 1938. *Das Pferd in der Frühzeit.* Rostock.

—— 1965. *Die Pferdetrensen des Alten Orient.* Roma. (Analecta Orient., 41.)

SINGER, C.; HOLMYARD, E. J.; HALL, A. L. 1979. *A History of Technology.* 8th ed. Oxford. Vol. 1.

ZACCAGNINI, C. 1977. The Merchant at Nuzi. In: *Trade in the Ancient Near East.* London, British School of Archaeology in Iraq. pp. 171–89.

8

THE DAWN OF WRITING
AND THE PRINCIPAL LINGUISTIC FAMILIES

8.1

FROM THE ORIGINS OF WRITING
TO THE ALPHABET

Monica Rector

Humanity has throughout the centuries followed a long path in order to obtain information, to store it and to pass it on. In the first place, humans had to discover the means by which thought could be transformed into language. Language-thought is linked to bipedalism, or rather to the transformation of *Homo erectus* into *Homo sapiens*. A strong hemispheric differentiation of the brain occurred, an expansion of the occipital area shifting to a higher centre of gravity (and the beginning of frontal expansion) (Haworth, 1984, p. 265), which changed human behaviour.

The representation of thought was achieved by means of oral signs, mutually understood by the group, who recognized the same system of representation. This oral manifestation was later on preserved in the form of drawings and writings, so that each community left behind a record of its culture. But writing is not only a way to preserve memory, it is also the symbol of a culture. This can be clearly observed in the systems of writing which were historically developed. Writing was later developed into artistic and aesthetic forms of knowledge and communication, and wherever it developed so did calligraphy. Not in the same manner in all cultures, however: the Chinese, Koreans and Japanese, for example, by juxtaposing poetry and painting, achieved a balance between aesthetics and functionality.

'Writing is not language, but merely a way of recording language by means of visible marks' (Coulmas, 1981, p. 39). This does not mean, however, that every society has a written form of representing its culture. There are still many societies who only communicate orally. The non-existence of writing is only a socio-cultural phenomenon.

Writing is nothing more than a secondary graphic representation of speech, a written message being relatively permanent, whereas speech is ephemeral. Once uttered, the oral message, unless it is recorded electronically or otherwise, is lost forever. Events and ideas can be transformed into writing, and thus cease to be a burden on the memory. A great

advantage, too, is that written messages can be read by different people in different places and times.

The written form of language sometimes becomes so important that it influences the spoken form, especially in the so-called orthographic pronunciation. For example, in English the word *often* is pronounced without the 't', but one frequently hears it pronounced with the sound of this letter, due to its spelling.

REPRESENTATION

Thoughts have to be represented, and representation means a 're-presenting' or a 'giving again'. But one cannot represent the thing itself. That which is represented 'must be made present indirectly, through an intermediary; it must be made present in some sense, while nevertheless remaining literally absent' (Pitkin, 1969, p. 16).

Anything which is represented has the advantage of being referred to even if it is not present, either if it existed in the past and no longer exists, or if it never existed and is only a product of our imagination.

In order to interact, we need language which functions as a representation of our thoughts and as a means of communication. Language is represented either orally or written, as we have seen, by means of discrete units, restricted in number (words), limited in size (how much of the event is represented), and repeatable in a text (Baron, 1981, p. 162). Therefore, writing is a visual representation in a conventionalized ordering of elements, a digital communication that follows a sequence in which the elements can be depicted. 'Picture-writing' is a mode of expressing thoughts or noting facts by marks which at first were confined to the portrayal of natural or artificial objects (Baron, 1981, p. 163).

However, there is a difference between 'embryo-writing' and 'writing proper'. Some recorded petroglyphs are unordered and non-conventionalized drawings, characteristically arbitrary and unsystematic; on the other hand, the North American Indian pictographs represent a sequential picture-writing, like a comic-strip; speechless stories, with image-situations or object-signs.

The distinction between 'drawing' and 'writing' is fundamental. Drawing is iconic representation, where graphic forms are important because they reproduce the form of the objects. Writing is beyond iconicity: the graphic forms reproduce neither the form nor the outline of the objects, nor their spatial order.

Writing is, in the first place, the representation of language and secondly a code made up of the graphic transcription of sound units. Any system of representation consists of recognizing the elements and relations present in the object that is to be represented, and the selection of those elements and relations which will be retained in the representation. But no representation is equal to the reality it presents. Historically, writing has been a process of building up a pragmatic system of representation.

THE SIGN

Ideas, in order to be communicated, have to be materialized. The representation of ideas is made through signs. A sign implies two aspects, according to Ferdinand de Saussure: the form called a *signifier* and the content called the *signified*. The Danish linguist, Louis Hjelmslev, remarks that 'it appears more appropriate to use the word "sign" as the name for the unit consisting of the content-form and the expression-form and established by the solidarity that we have called the sign-function' (Hjelmslev, 1961, p. 58). For him, a sign-function is realized by the mutual correlation of expression and content. For example, the expression item 'bank': the English language provides many content items for it, such as 'slope', 'institution that safeguards and issues money', 'row or tier of oars', and so on. In this example, for an expression, there are at least three sign-functions.

Moreover, according to Charles S. Peirce's theory, the sign is conceived as an element in a signifying process: 'A sign, or *representamen*, is something which stands for something in some respect or capacity. It addresses somebody, that is, creates in the mind of that person an equivalent sign, or perhaps a more developed sign. That sign which it creates I call the *interpretant* of the sign. The sign stands for something, its *object*. It stands for that object, not in all respects, but in reference to a sort of idea, which I have sometimes called the *ground* of the representation' (1931–58, 2, p. 228). Thus, if a person says *tree*, this is something (a sequence of sounds) which stands for something (a vegetal object, with roots, trunk, a crown with branches and green leaves) for somebody (this person) in some respect or capacity (the object selected is perennial, of a certain height and shape).

Since writing is a second order representation, it is the transcription of spoken language (a first sign) into an approximate permanent representation utilizing written signs (a second sign generated from the former one).

Letters are signs of signs. The difference between speech and writing as two systems of signs is their specific function. Speech is a system of signs, that symbolizes a signification. Writing is a system of signs that symbolizes another system of signs, either by another system (optic system of writing), or by another structure (for example, Morse code).

Alphabetic scripts are systems which represent the difference between signifiers. Ideographic scripts are systems of representation whose main purpose is to represent the signifiers. No writing system, so far, has been able to represent in a balanced way the dual nature of the sign.

Writing allowed spoken utterances to be available even outside the situation in which they took place, overcoming the contextual dependency of speech. Alphabetic scripts have an advantage over other systems in their economy of signs. Each alphabetic script has basic signs. There is, however, a direct relation between the effort of learning and the effort of performance of these signs. Logographic scripts, such as Chinese, demand an enormous learning effort, but since Chinese uses in most cases only one sign for each word, the text is generally short. Syllabic scripts are limited to about 1,000 basic signs, which in languages such as Japanese decrease to about 100. But this reduction of learning effort demands a greater performance effort (Posner, 1985, pp. 69–70). Alphabetic scripts have from 20 to 50 basic signs obtained by codifying syllables in a sequence of letters. However, in languages using alphabetic scripts, the length of the word increases.

How long ago did writing begin? There is no archaeological discovery of written documents before the year 4000 BC. We may conclude that writing is not so indispensable for living, because its history is only 5,000 years old, and it is still not universal. Only about half of the world's population uses it. In the eleventh century AD writing was legitimized as a support for oral tradition. It was the Church which, through the reforms of Luther, defeated oral authority and declared the Bible to be available in the vernacular. From that date, the ability to read meant one could return to the primary and original written source. With writing, humanity gained the accumulation of organized knowledge, but lost in the process much oral participation in the transmission of knowledge.

WRITING: A SYSTEM OF REPRESENTATION AND COMMUNICATION

There are three principal ways of looking at writing: (1) as a *code*. One can study its internal structure, its relation to the spoken content, and its relation between content and expression on several levels; (2) as *communication*, that is, as a process that is able to relate two people, by means other than oral (visual, auditive, and so on); (3) as a *cognitive dimension*, that is, the capacity and ability of the writer to affect the reader.

This leads on to three basic elements in the representation: (1) the *content*, a real or imagined experience; (2) the *shape*, the material means of representation, such as sounds or letters in the linguistic representation and forms and colours in the visual representation; (3) the *participants* and/or interpreters.

As we have seen, the process began with the communication of ideas and feelings by means of visible signs, understood not only by the author of the signs but also by the receiver who shared the same system. Therefore, 'writing is clearly *a system of human intercommunication by means of conventional visible marks*' (Gelb, 1963, p. 12).

Does writing derive from one unique system of representation? It is difficult to say if there existed a proto-writing. The oldest writing system goes back to the Sumerian civilization, around 3100 BC. Was there nothing systematic before that? Specialists affirm that writing developed due to stimulus from cultural contact and that it progressed quickly under foreign influence. Common among today's most important writing systems is the principle of phonetization: signs are written by expressing words that are similar in sound. (However, writing never expresses exactly the spoken language.)

In the historical evolution of representation writing took into consideration several linguistic elements (see Table 1).

Table 1 Linguistic Elements in Writing

	Written signs	System of signs
Single sound (phoneme)	Letter or alphabetic sign	Alphabet or alphabetic writing
Syllable	Syllabogram or syllabic sign	Syllabary or syllabic writing
Word	Lologram or word sign	Lolography or word writing
Phrase	Phraseogram or phrase sign	Phraseography or phrase writing
Prosodic feature	Prosodic sign or mark	Prosodic writing

Source Reproduced from Gelb, 1963, fig. 2, p. 14.

This system of written signs is conventionally treated on several levels: (1) the representation of the sign; (2) the categorization in minimal units; (3) a set of rules which represent the system and allow the learning of the forms and principles of writing.

A provisional typology of writing systems can be set up as follows: '(a) *narrative* (or syntagmatic) writing, in which each drawing corresponds to a narrative utterance (Innuit and Alaskan Indians); (b) *morphematic* (or analytical) writing, where a morpheme sign corresponds to a grapheme sign (Chinese, Egyptian); and (c) *phonematic* writing, which establishes a correspondence between graphemes and phonemes (Western languages)' (Greimas; Courtes, 1982, pp. 375–6).

In these systems, there is a symmetry between aesthetics and functionality, in drawings as well as in written representation. This symmetry can be depicted in the Egyptian hieroglyphs, a collection of small images, stylized, but drawn with great care to preserve the beauty of the characters. These hieroglyphs maintain the same elements as in wall decoration in monuments and tombs, a way of better communicating with illiterate peoples.

Indic, the Harappan system

Apart from the complete systems of writing which are taken up further on, some as yet undeciphered systems refer to principles that were to have no follow-up, thus making it difficult to understand them. An example of this is the written documents of the Indus Valley and those later assembled in Greece under the name of 'Linear A'.

The prehistoric culture of north-western India can be divided into urban civilization (Harappan) and diverse peasant cultures. Linguists suggest that various Indic writings are derived from a prototype, at present unknown, cognate with proto-Sumerian (Diringer, 1968, p. 49). Proto-Indic writing appeared in the second half of the third millennium BC. Most of the writings found are on inscriptions on seals, pottery and copper tablets from the excavations of Harappa and Mohenjo-daro. They remain mostly undeciphered.

Indic as a full writing system appears in the third century BC in the edicts of Aśoka. They are of two types: Kharosthi and Brāhmī. Kharosthi is derived from Aramaic. Each sign has a consonant plus *a*; the other vowels are represented with short strokes. Brāhmī evolved a further step. It follows the Kharosthi system, but with other signs to indicate the initial or syllabic vowels.

The best documentation to explain the Indic script is based on the Mohenjo-daro and Harappa excavations. Hunter (1934) thought that there was a connection between Indus and Brāhmī characters. He saw a similarity between certain Indus signs and Proto-Elamite and Sumerian characters. Several specialists believe that Sumerian was enciphered in the Indus inscriptions. They base their conclusions on the evidence of trade links with the Indus Valley in the third and second millennia BC (Mitchener, 1978, p. 3). The seals found in Mesopotamia provide more evidence of a link between the Indus cities of Lothal and Mohenjo-daro, the Makran and southern Iran, Bahrain and Sumer. There is some evidence that the peoples of Sumer and the Indus Valley were trading partners.

Another language believed to be involved in the Indus inscription is a form of Proto-Dravidian. There is no doubt that the Indus civilization extended beyond the Indus Valley and that the Indus people knew a form of Proto-Dravidian as well as a form of Proto-Elamite. Both languages are Finno-Ugric. In addition to the Proto-Dravidian and the Proto-Elamite, there was the Proto-Indoaryan, which resembles the Indo-European.' Most of the information about these languages is based on seal-inscriptions, which are connected with trade, and contain personal names, names of offices or titles, royal epithets, and votive formulae.

THE ALPHABET AND OTHER MODERN TYPES OF WRITING

An alphabet is a system of signs which express single speech sounds. The word 'alphabet' comes from the first two letters of the Greek alphabet, *ālpha* and *bêta*, which correspond to the Semitic *āleph* and *beth*, that mean 'ox' and 'house'.

The alphabetic script used nowadays has its origin in the Greek system, which the Greeks adapted from Phoenician. However, the Phoenicians represented only the consonants, while the Greeks added vowels. It is this development of the Greek alphabet, expressing single sounds by means of consonant and vowel signs, which is the last important step in the history of writing. The alphabet has not changed since.

The symbols of an alphabet should represent, up to a certain point, the phonemes of a given language. Among the best known alphabetic systems are Latin, Cyrillic and Greek. However, these are not phonetic, representing the sounds of the language, but phonemic, representing something which is functionally meaningful. This explains similar vowel-signs being used for different sounds: thor*ough* [ou], thr*ough* [u], c*ough* [o]. In fact, there is a distortion between the alphabet, or orthography and phonetics. For this reason, linguists established the International Phonetic Alphabet (IPA), which is a system of sounds that really represents the single sounds of speech, in any language. In IPA, [ð] stands for 'th' in 'this' (English), for 'd' in *cada* (Spanish), for 'd' in *gade* (Danish), and for δ in Greek.

The Latin (Roman) alphabet has 26 symbols, plus such

punctuation marks as the dot, hyphen, apostrophe, and so on. These marks help to indicate the limits between the components of a sequence of words in a sentence, transcribe the different intonations, and represent the breathing pauses.

The Latin alphabet is in itself not sufficient to represent all the sounds of a language. Several cultures added diacritics and developed other conventions to change the basic sound of a letter. For example, c is sounded as k in the French *cadavre*, but with a cedilla the sound becomes s as in *façade*. The n with a tilde (ñ) represents the palatalized nasal, as in Spanish *mañana*.

The first Latin script used what today we call capital letters. In the fourth and fifth centuries AD, a cursive script was developed with lower-case letters. With the decadence of the Roman empire, several cultures developed their national script: the Spanish West-Gothic, the English and Irish insular, and the French 'Merovingian' script. In the Middle Ages, Charlemagne introduced the Carolingian or lower-case letters to France in about AD 800.

In the twelfth century AD the Gothic script was introduced in Germany. The round Carolingian form gave place to a broken and vertical form. The Gothic script gave origin to the current writing, adopted later on as the common system.

Nowadays, the alphabet used is the cursive form, with capital letters taken from the Roman 'Capitalis Quadrata', and lower-case letters from the Carolingian period.

The evolution of writing is also linked to the improvement and modification of the materials used to write on: papyrus gave place to parchment and to paper.

Besides the Latin script two other systems deserve mention: Korean and Cyrillic.

Korean, with an orthography based on phonemics, was created by King Seijong (AD 1417–50). This king realized that the 30,000 Chinese characters discouraged people and that without simplification illiteracy would continue. The Korean alphabet, called *hankul*, first had 11 vowels and 17 consonants, and was then reduced to 10 vowels and 14 consonants.

The Cyrillic alphabet was named for St Cyril and is used for Slavic languages such as Russian, Ukranian and Bulgarian. Most people in the Russian Federation and Mongolia use it. It has 32 letters, 20 of which are consonants. It is directly derived from Greek and from an ancient alphabet called 'glagolitic'.

ORTHOGRAPHY

The pronunciation of a word is its linguistic form; spelling or orthography is the written representation. If writing represented the spoken language perfectly, there would be no need for reforms. However, there are many irregularities between graphemes (letters) and phonemes. In English, the main differences are: (1) a different spelling used for the same sound, that is: ay occurs in 'eye', 'buy', 'tie'; (2) the same spelling used for different sounds: an æ occurs in later [ei], Mary [ɛ]; (3) silent letters as in ni*g*ht, com*b*, du*e*; (4) pronounced sounds without a corresponding letter [y]: use/yuz/, furor/fyu'rɔ/.

Time and space are also responsible for differences: late Middle English pronunciation compared to Modern English and English, American and Irish pronunciations. For example *four*: British [fɔ:], Midwest USA [fɔr], South [foð].

In the Renaissance, fifteenth and sixteenth centuries AD,

a spelling reform took place, in order to change English spelling to match original Latin and Greek etymologies. Spelling is more conservative than pronunciation and a slower changing process, but modifications always continue.

Writing, as we have seen, is a basic tool for civilization. From semasiography, making developed to phonography. First there was the picture writing, which used pictograms and represented objects. Nowadays, there are three main writing systems: (1) word-writing in which every symbol represents a word: Chinese, (2) syllabary writing in which every syllable is represented by a sign: Japanese, and (3) the most common one, alphabetic writing, which represents each phoneme by a different symbol: English. In the history of writing, every culture has to pass through the stages of logography, syllabography and alphabetography in this order. A writing can stop in one stage, but the capacity of dividing a word into syllables, and then into single sounds shows a consciousness about language, an intellectual development and a capacity of abstraction and of reconstructing a speech process. Writing was a great contribution to the development of humanity and this process will continue throughout the centuries to improve understanding among human beings.

NOTE

1 This term 'denotes primarily groups of people sharing a common language-base with distinct dialectical peculiarities between different groups...' (Mitchener, 1978, p. 9).

BIBLIOGRAPHY

BARON, N. S. 1981. *Speech, Writing and Sign. A Functional View of Linguistic Representation*. Bloomington, Wis.
—— 1985. From Universal Language to Language Origin: The Problem of Shared Referents. *Semiotica* (Den Haag), Vol. 57, No. 1/2, pp. 13–32.
BARTHES, R. 1971. Ecrivains, intellectuels, professeurs. *Tel Quel* (Paris), Vol. 47, autumn, pp. 3–18.
COHEN, M.; GARNOT, J. S. F. 1968. *La escritura y la psicología de los pueblos*. Trans. Juan Almela. Mexico, Siglo Veintiuno.
COULMAS, F. 1981. *Über Schrift*. Frankfurt am Main.
—— 1980. Einleitung. *Z. Semiot*. Tübingen, Vol. 2 (4), pp. 313–17.
DIRINGER, D. 1968. *The Alphabet, A Key to the History of Mankind*. New York. Rev. ed. London.
DUBOIS, J. 1973. *Dictionnaire linguistique*. Paris.
EHLICH, K. 1980. Schriftentwicklung als gesellschaftliches Problemlösen. *Z. Semiot*. Tübingen, Vol. 2, No. 4, pp. 335–59.
FROMKIN, V.; RODMAN, R. 1974. *An Introduction to Language*. New York.
GELB, I. J. 1963. *A Study of Writing*. 2nd ed. Chicago, Ill.
GRACE, W. 1965. *Response to Literature*. New York.
GREIMAS, A. J.; COURTES, J. 1982. *Semiotics and Language: An Analytical Dictionary*. Trans. Larry Crist. Bloomington, Wis.
HAWORTH, K. A. 1984. The Origin of Language-based Thought: A Synthesis of Cognitive Science and Semiotics. In: DEELY, J. (ed.), *Semiotics 1984*. New York, N.Y., pp. 261–5.
HJELMSLEV, L. 1961. *Prolegomena to a Theory of Language*. Madison, Wis.
HOLENSTEIN, E. 1980. Doppelte Artikulation in der Schrift. *Z. Semiot*. Tübingen, Vol. 2, No. 4, pp. 319–33.
HOOKER, J. T. 1990. Introduction. In: *Reading the Past, Ancient Writing from Cuneiform to the Alphabet*. Berkeley/Los Angeles, Calif.
HUNTER, G. R. 1934. *The Script of Harappa and Mohenjo Daro and its Connections with Other Scripts*. London.

KRISTEVA, J. 1971. Comment parler à la littérature. *Tel Quel* (Paris), Vol. 47, autumn, pp. 27–49.

MACKAY, E. J. 1938. *Further Excavations at Mohenjo Daro*. New Dehli.

MALHERBE, M. 1983. *Les langages de l'humanité*. Paris.

MARSHALL, J. 1931. *Mohenjo Daro and the Indus Civilization*. London.

MITCHINER, J. E. 1978. *Studies in the Indus Valley Inscriptions*. New Delhi/Oxford.

MOODY, H. L. B. 1977. *The Teaching of Literature*. 4th ed. London.

OPPENHEIM, A. L. 1977. *Ancient Mesopotamia*. Rev. ed. Chicago, Ill.

PEIRCE, C. S. 1931–58. *Collected Papers*. Cambridge, Mass.

PITKIN, H. 1969. *Representation*. New York.

POSNER, R. 1985. Língua falada, língua escrita, língua planeada. *Cruzeiro Semiót.* (Porto), Vol. 2.

SAMPSON, G. 1985. *Writing Systems, A Linguistic Introduction*. Stanford.

SAUSSURE, F. de. 1916. *Cours de linguistique générale*. Paris.

SILVERMAN, D. P. 1990. *Language and Writing in Ancient Egypt*. Pittsburgh.

TOYNBEE, A. J. 1956. *An Historian's Approach to Religion*. New York.

VATS, S. M. 1940. *Excavations at Harappa*. New Delhi.

8.2

THE MOST ANCIENT LANGUAGES REVEALED BY WRITING

Stephen A. Wurm

Several of the most ancient civilizations of the world, the history of their peoples and the languages which they spoke, are reasonably well known to us for the reason that their citizens developed and used writing systems from very early days, with varied amounts of relevant text materials from ancient times preserved until today, more and more of which are coming to light. Most of the scripts have been deciphered, and the languages understood to a point where much, most or all of the texts' contents are at least relatively, if not completely, intelligible. This opens windows for us on the history of the writers of such texts, the nature, development and functioning of their cultures, as well as on the nature of their languages and the place of such languages within language families. Outstanding examples of such peoples are the ancient Egyptians, the Sumerians, the early Chinese, speakers of various ancient Semitic languages such as Akkadian (Assyrian and Babylonian), Ugaritic, Phoenician, Old Hebrew and Old Aramaic. Speakers of ancient Indo-European languages, such as the Hittites, and speakers of several other languages closely related to it, ancient Indians whose language was Sanskrit, and speakers of other languages of Western Asia such as the Elamites and the Hurrians, also belong to this category. Of all these languages, Chinese and the Semitic languages will be dealt with here in addition to others such as the non-Semitic Sumerian whose fate was inextricably linked with that of the Semitic Akkadian.

THE EGYPTIAN LANGUAGE (MAP 3)

According to the currently most generally accepted classification of the languages of Africa (Greenberg, 1963; Heine et al., 1981), Egyptian belongs to the so-called Afroasiatic languages in which Egyptian, Berberic, Cushitic, Semitic, Chadic (and probably also Omotic in Ethiopia) constitute five (or six) hierarchically coordinated genetically related language families. The formerly widely accepted inclusion of Egyptian into the Hamito-Semitic language group is now superseded. Egyptian had strong contacts with the ancient Semitic languages and probably also with Berberic (Heine et al., 1981).

In contrast to the Sumerians in Mesopotamia, who are believed to have entered the later historical habitat where their cuneiform script developed some time in the second half of the fourth millennium BC, the Egyptians can be assumed to have lived in Egypt well before the invention of

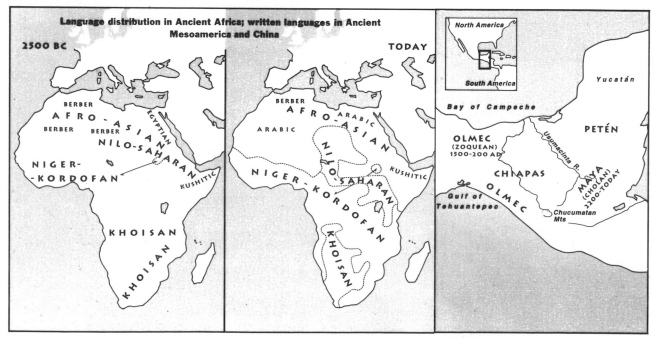

Map 3 Language distribution in ancient Africa; written languages in ancient Mesoamerica and China.

70

their hieroglyphic (from Greek 'sacred carved letters') script, of which the oldest written records date back to around 3000 BC. As was the case with the ancestral form of cuneiform in Mesopotamia, the Egyptian hieroglyphic was a pictographic writing, with the individual picture symbols originally representing only the object depicted and the word for it in Egyptian, for instance, picture symbols for 'face', 'eye', 'house', and so on. The symbol for 'face' also indicated words denoting the action of seeing. As a further step (and again similar to the Sumerian cuneiform script system), picture symbols denoting concrete objects whose names were similar to words which indicated other concepts were employed to denote these other concepts too – they were often more abstract and difficult to represent by separate pictorial symbols. For instance, the word for 'face' was ḥr (ḥ was probably similar to Arabic ḥ). The word for 'upon, on' was also ḥr, and represented in writing by the pictorial symbol for 'face', usually with a vertical stroke underneath. (Vowels are not indicated and are usually not known to us. Egyptologists have adopted certain conventions enabling them to pronounce Egyptian words through putting e or a between consonants – but this is purely artificial and probably bears no relation to the vowels as spoken by the Egyptians themselves.) In view of this, ḥr 'face' and ḥr 'upon' may have had quite different vowels, but this does not seem to have affected the process of using one pictorial symbol for several quite different concepts denoted by words containing the same consonants. Words for which no suitable pictorial symbols could be found were rendered by compounding their written forms from two or several hieroglyphic pictorial signs, the sum of whose pronunciations produced that of the word required, for example nḥt 'strong' was written by a combination of the hieroglyphic signs for 'surface of water; water' (pronounced n and 'tree' (pronounced ḥt) (ḥ corresponds to Arabic ḥ). Further extensions of this principle resulted in individual hieroglyphs becoming symbols for groups of consonants rather than symbols for words and concepts. This was taken further so that certain hieroglyphs only indicated single consonants, which made a part of the hieroglyphic writing a letter script. This allowed the writing of any word

and also of grammatical elements. A very important separate development was the addition of determinatives to written words, that is signs indicating the general semantic class to which the noun or verb to which they were added belonged, such as men, women, gods, birds, concepts of running, concepts of action involving the mouth such as eating and speaking, concepts of fire and burning or abstract concepts. Such determinatives were themselves usually the *signs* for individual objects and concepts – man, woman, god, bird, running, mouth, and so on. Thus the sign for god was added to names of deities, that for bird to different kinds of birds, and so on. This system of determinatives is in principle very similar to that found in cuneiform and to that of the radicals in Chinese. Thus, the developed hieroglyphic writing system contained (1) pictorial symbols which indicated individual words or concepts, (2) symbols which denoted the class or category of a noun or verb to whose basic symbol (or form written in consonant groups or letters) they were added, and finally (3) symbols which indicated groups of consonants or individual consonants.

In contrast to the Sumerian cuneiform script and the Chinese script, which both moved away from the pictorial nature of their symbols, Egyptian hieroglyphs remained pictorial right through the thousands of years of their use. The monumental hieroglyphic script was essentially used on the stone walls of temples and tombs, on gravestones, stelae, obelisks, monuments, and also on paintings and objects of daily use. Hieroglyphic writing runs predominantly from left to right, sometimes also from right to left, with the individual symbols always looking towards the beginning of the lines. Lines can be horizontal and vertical (Fig. 21).

However, already during the 1st dynasty, around 2900 BC, a cursive form of writing adapted from hieroglyphic developed, written with ink on a flat surface, mainly papyrus, with a brush-pen. It consisted of cursive transcriptions, sign by sign, of hieroglyphic symbols, with most of them retaining little or hardly any of the original hieroglyphic pictures, and with many signs linked together and forming ligatured groups of symbols (Diringer, 1968, p. 34). This cursive script, whose direction was originally vertical and later horizontal, and

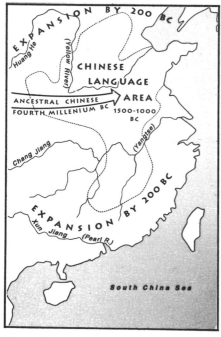

Map 3 (continued)

Chinese Script

2200+ BC	Proto Chinese. Earliest pictographs and ideograms, written with bamboo stylus. Later haphazard changes to the system of writing
500	Archaic Chinese
250	Invention of Chinese writing brush: script changes to angular strokes of different thickness
213	Revision and systematization of script by Li Si. Radicals and phonetic elements
103	Invention of paper
0	Ancient Chinese
500 AD	First phonetic methods to indicate the pronunciation of Chinese characters
600 AD	Middle Chinese
1100 AD	Modern Chinese

Egyptian Script

3000+ AD	Early Egyptian. First hieroglyphic writing. Gradual development of use of some signs for words with different meanings, but similar pronunciations. Compounding of symbols to indicate the pronunciation of certain words. Certain hieroglyphs are beginning to indicate single consonants making part of the writing a letter script. Addition of determinators
2900	Development of cursive form of writing (hieratic) in addition to the continuing hieroglyphic
2600	Old Egyptian
2100	Middle Egyptian
1550	Late Egyptian
700	Demotic cursive script develops
300 AD	Beginning of Koptic as daughter language of Egyptian
500 AD	Knowledge of the three Egyptian writing systems, hieroglyphic, hieratic and demotic, is lost

which ran from right to left, was used for any cursive writing of a sacred or profane character. It was later called hieratic (from Greek 'sacred, priestly') when in the seventh century BC another cursive writing, the demotic (from Greek 'popular, vulgar'), came into being. Hieratic script then became essentially a script of the priestly class. Demotic was a highly cursive derivative of hieratic, though its appearance was quite different. Many associated groups of hieratic symbols are fused into single demotic signs. It was written horizontally from right to left (Diringer, 1968, pp. 34–6).

Knowledge of the hieroglyphic script, including its two cursive forms, was lost in the fifth century AD, with the story of the great Egyptian empire and culture hidden from humanity until the decipherment of hieroglyphic writing in the early nineteenth century. This was made possible by the discovery of the famous Rosetta Stone, found in the fort of Saint Julien de Rosetta by the French captain M. Boussard in 1799 during Napoleon's attempted conquest of Egypt. It

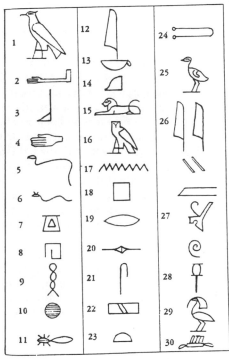

1 white-headed vulture	18 stool of reed matting
2 forearm	19 mouth
3 foot	20 bolt
4 hand	21 folded cloth (?)
5 cobra in repose	22 garden pool
6 horned viper	23 bread
7 ring-stand for jars	24 hobble rope for tethering
8 reed shelter in fields	animals
9 wick of twisted flax	25 quail chick
10 human placenta	26 two flowering reeds
11 animal's belly showing teats and tail	27 two diagonal strokes; the two ribs of an oryx; spiral; crown of lower Egypt
12 flowering reed	28 chisel
13 wickerwork basket	29 crested ibis
14 sandy hill-slope	30 portion of backbone with spinal cord issuing at both ends
15 recumbent lion	
16 owl	
17 vibratory energy, fluid	

Figure 21 Hieroglyphic script (after Rossini, 1989). The hieroglyphs of the ancient Egyptians, a mainly ideographic writing, independent of cuneiform and occasional phonetic signs, were already in use three thousand years before our era. Most of the characters, although symbols, are already recognizable depictions of real objects, often executed with elaborate naturalism.

contains a priestly decree from 197/6 BC in two languages and three scripts: in Egyptian in hieroglyphic and demotic script, and in Greek. The first decipherment was achieved by the French Egyptologist J. F. Champollion in 1822. Today, only very few of the more than one thousand hieroglyphic symbols remain a mystery. This decipherment constituted a key to our understanding of Egyptian which in turn opened a window for us on the history and culture of the Egyptians and gave us detailed knowledge of both.

The life of the ancient Egyptian language spans the entire period of concern to this volume, and it lived beyond it for more than a millennium, to continue afterwards in its descendant, Coptic, until the fifteenth century AD as a spoken language, and to the present day as the liturgical language of the Coptic Christian church in Egypt. During its long history, the language underwent considerable changes in its grammar and vocabulary, which makes it possible to distinguish several periods in its development. The earliest known form of Egyptian, called *Early Egyptian*, was the language form encountered in the 1st and 2nd dynasties (2900–2600 BC). This was followed by the *Old Egyptian* of the 3rd to the 8th dynasties (2600–2100 BC) (of which the first known writings on papyrus are extant, in addition to many hieroglyphic inscriptions). *Middle Egyptian* was characterised by an increasing content of colloquial forms and elements. Its use first covered the periods from the 9th to the 12th dynasties, that is 2100 to 1800 BC, but its use as a classical literary language continued well beyond that period. In the course of the 18th to 25th dynasties (1550–700 BC) and beyond, the spoken language first moved gradually towards being used in writing and, as *Late Egyptian*, became the literary language under Amenhotep IV (Akhnaten), who ruled from 1364 to 1348 BC. The Egyptian language shows its most significant changes, including syntactic ones, between the Middle Egyptian and Late Egyptian stages.

A sketch of some of the features of (Middle) Egyptian may be given here. In nouns, pronouns and verbs, two genders (masculine and feminine) and two numbers (singular and plural) are distinguished. Adjectives follow the nouns to which they belong. There is no case marking on nouns. Prepositions ('to') and linking words ('belonging to') express concepts such as those referred to as *dative* and *genitive* in traditional grammars. The personal pronouns are suffixed to nouns to indicate possession. They are also added to verb stems (or to verb stems + tense or aspect markers) to indicate the subject. Passive forms of verbs are marked by suffixes added to the verb stem. Negation is indicated by a particle placed before the verb. The word order is verb-subject-direct object-indirect object-other elements. Relative clauses follow the main clause without a relative marker, or with one occurring in masculine, feminine and plural forms.

OTHER AFRICAN AND ANCIENT AMERICAN LANGUAGES (MAP 3)

With one marginal exception mentioned below, we have no written records of African languages for the time span covered by this volume. However, the now well advanced study of African linguistics makes it possible to make some suggestions as to the probable location, at about 2500 BC, of the ancestors of the four main African language families recognized today (Brunner et al., 1990, I, p. 37; Möhlig et al., 1977). It appears that the *Khoi-San* language family which today consists of remnant languages in southern Africa and

Tanzania, occupied vast tracts of land in southern Africa and extended into eastern Africa. The Berberic languages of the present-day *Afroasiatic* language family, which occupy scattered areas of north-western African today, were widespread in northern Africa and the Sahara. It is assumed that the entire *Afroasian* language family, of which several Semitic languages entered Africa only during the last two millennia from Asia, had its original roots in Africa perhaps as long as 15,000 years ago. The *Nilosaharan* language family, whose members are scattered in an area extending from the western parts of the Sudan to Kenya and Tanzania, was probably widespread in the general Sudan area. The *Nigerkordogan* family, which occupies today a small area in the Nuba Mountains in the Sudan and a very large part of sub-Saharan Africa, was restricted to some areas in western Africa, as well as to the Nuba Mountains.

The marginal case mentioned above is Meroitic, the language of a Nubian kingdom south of Egypt, which became independent from Egyptian domination in the eighth century BC. At first, Egyptian was used as a written language, but a Meroitic written language was developed later - the earliest records known to us are from the third century BC. The writing consists of a monumental hieroglyphic type and a cursive demotic type, both obviously descended from Egyptian scripts, though the symbols show differences, especially in their phonetic values. The Meroitic symbols are purely phonetic and alphabetical (except for two syllabic signs). There are no ligatures, and the total number of signs is twenty-three which includes signs for vowels (Diringer, 1968, pp. 140–1). Meroitic was first believed to be the ancestor of the present-day Nubian languages, but this is now known not to be the case. Like Nubian, Meroitic does appear to belong to the Nilosaharan language family, but bears no close relationship to any other known language within that group. For that reason, most of the Meroitic written records, though easily legible and transcribable, are not yet understood to any great extent. Lengthy bilingual inscriptions have not yet been discovered (Heine et al., 1981, pp. 301–4).

Of the languages of ancient America, Maya may be briefly mentioned here. On the basis of linguistic prehistory, it has been hypothesized that proto-Mayan was spoken in the Chucumatan Mountains in today's Guatemala at about 2200 BC. After the diversification of proto-Mayan into several languages, speakers of them moved down the Usumacinta River into the Petén region about 1000 BC, and later into the Chiapas Highlands of Mexico (Campbell, 1992, p. 403) and the highlands around today's Guatemala City. Maya is the only language in ancient America which later had a complete script (and a very complex calendar notation). At points on the Pacific slope of Guatemala, the oldest Maya calendar dates appear, fully written out and dated just before 230 BC. It appears that the Mayan script itself was invented by speakers of the Cholan language of the Maya family. The Mayan script, brought to its peak of development centuries later in the Classic Maya period, is a mixture of ideographic and phonetic elements and also has determinatives, and is therefore similar in principle to the Egyptian and Sumeric scripts. It was usually read in double columns from left to right and descending from top to bottom. It was carved on stone surfaces or written on pages in folding screen books of bark paper. About 50 per cent of the extant texts can now be understood (Coe et al., 1986, pp. 114, 118–20).

Latest research (1993) has shown that the carriers of the ancient Olmec culture centre around the Bay of Campeche and the Pacific coast area east of the Gulf of Tehuantepec in south-eastern Mexico spoke Zoquean, a language ancestral to four languages in that part of Mexico, and had hieroglyphic writing predating Mayan script, which gives us further insights into the Olmec culture.

SEMITIC LANGUAGES (MAP 4)

Our present knowledge of the culture and history of the oldest Semitic peoples is the result of the very early use of cuneiform by them and by the Sumerians before them, with the latter apparently its inventors. The Sumerians are believed to have entered southern Mesopotamia some time in the second half of the fourth millennium BC, coming from the north, possibly from the Caspian Sea region (Kramer, 1963, pp. 42 ff). Their ethnicity has not yet been established, and their language, though typologically somewhat reminiscent of Altaic and having perhaps also some Caucasian features, is still regarded as isolated. It seems now, contrary to scholars' views up to the 1950s, that the land they entered had already been occupied by other people whose ethnicity is not known, but who spoke a language different from Sumerian. From that language, according to Landsberger (1944), came the names of the earliest and most important Sumerian urban centres which cannot be explained through the Sumerian language - the same is true of the names of the Euphrates and Tigris as used by the Sumerians. Landsberger calls these people the Proto-Euphrateans, and they are known as Ubaids to archaeologists. It appears from further linguistic evidence that these people were agriculturalists, founded a number of towns and developed a notable rural economy (Kramer, 1963, pp. 41 ff). Also, very importantly, there are circumstances permitting us to assume that Semitic nomads coming from the Arabian peninsula infiltrated the country of the Proto-Euphrateans, and that the cross-fertilization of their two cultures resulted in the first relatively high civilization in the area before the arrival of the Sumerians (Kramer, 1963, p. 42). Even the oldest Sumerian inscriptions contain Semitic loanwords, and the oldest Sumerian dynasty begins with rulers who have Semitic names.

Written records, however, do not begin until after the arrival of the Sumerians, with the oldest known inscriptions, all in the Sumerian language, dating from about 3000 BC. They are in the ancestral form of cuneiform which was probably invented by the Sumerians, or at least developed by them into an effective writing system in the third millennium BC (Kramer, 1963, p. 302). Gradually, the surrounding peoples (Akkadians, Elamites, Hurrians, later also Old Persians and so on) took it over and adapted it to their languages. By the second millennium BC it was widespread in ancient western Asia.

The ancestral form of the cuneiform script was a pictographic writing, with each symbol a picture of one or several objects (Fig. 22). Its meaning was that of those objects or something associated with them, so that, for example, one symbol denoted 'mouth' and 'speak'. The signs appear to have originally been written on wood or leaves, but clay tablets came into use very early. On them, the pictographs were soon turned at an angle of 90° and were lying on their back, whereas in inscriptions scratched into stone or metal they remained upright for centuries more. The signs were gradually simplified and conventionalized, and their numbers reduced, largely through substituting phonetic values for the original meanings of pictographs, with the pictographs not only denoting objects and concepts related to them, but

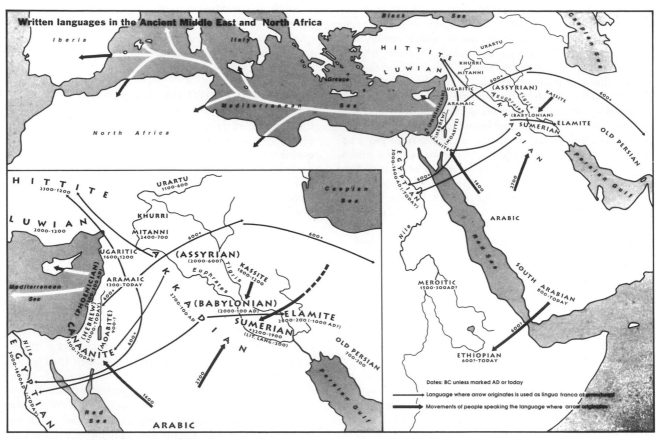

3000+	BC Sumerian pictographs	1850	Old Babylonian period begins
2900–	Pictographs turned 90% to lie on their backs. Signs simplified, conventionalized, their numbers (originally 2000) reduced through signs beginning to indicate phonetic values of words and one sign having several meanings	1600	Extensive use of Sumerian as literary language ends. Limited use continues until 200 BC. Kassite period begins. C. script adopted for Ugaritic as alphabetic script with 30 signs
2500+	Linear drawing of signs broken up into series of strokes. Adding of grammatical elements and determinatives	1500	C. script adopted for Urartu
2450	Early Akkadian. Cuneiform script adopted	1200	Assyrian period begins
2300	C. script adopted for Elamite (later 113 signs), Khurri and Hittite	800	C. script adopted for Old Persian as syllabic script with 41 signs.
2000	C. script adopted for Luwi	700	Signs for Assyrian-Babylonian down to about 600
1900	Summerian no longer a living spoken language. Continues strongly as literary language	600	Neo-Babylonian period begins. C. script becomes practically a syllabic script
		300	Revival of cuneiform writing
		100 BC	End of cuneiform writing

Map 4 Written languages in ancient western Asia and North Africa.

also the phonetic values of the words indicating such objects, irrespective of the original meaning of the pictographs. For instance, the Sumerian word *ha* means 'fish' and also 'may'. The pictograph for 'fish' was therefore used also to indicate 'may' (Kramer, 1963, p. 306). A very important development, about 2500 BC or earlier, was the breaking up of the linear drawing of signs into a series of wedge-shaped strokes impressed upon soft clay tablets with the edge of a square broad-headed stylus, with the tablets subsequently dried in the sun or baked in a kiln. The script, which was written from left to right, became gradually simplified, with many of the symbols indicating sound values only, and grammatical elements being added by further symbols. Another important development was the addition of so-called determinatives to nouns. As in Egyptian, these signs indicated the general semantic class to which a noun belonged. The function of these determinatives in the cuneiform script is similar to that of the radicals in Chinese (see below). Determinants were probably not spoken, even when a text was read out loud (Hayes, 1990, p. 14). To sum up, the same cuneiform sign may stand for an object or concept by itself, or it may indicate the class of a noun to whose sign it is added, or it may stand phonetically for a simple syllable or vowel which constitutes a grammatical element (Diringer, 1968, p. 18). Nev-

ertheless, the Sumerian script remained essentially a mnemonic system, an aid to memory in which an exact rendering of the pronunciation was not aimed at (Diakonoff, 1976, p. 112). However, the number of distinct signs was still very great.

Of profound influence upon the further development of cuneiform and the fate of the Sumerian language was the increasing influence of the Semitic Akkadians in the Sumerian area. There had been long periods of close contact between the Sumerians and Akkadians who had come up from the south, from the Arabian peninsula, like earlier Semitic speakers even before the arrival of the Sumerians (see above). These contacts led to the adoption of loanwords in both languages, and Sumerian influence brought about changes in the structure of Akkadian, such as the introduction of the word order subject-object-verb, which is unusual for a Semitic language (Thomsen, 1984, p. 16), a far-reaching simplification of the rich Semitic consonantal system, and a notable assimilation of consonants which gives Akkadian clearly the appearance of a language taken over by a population speaking an unrelated language, Sumerian (Bergsträsser and Daniels, 1983, p. 26). It appears from the sources that there was a rather large number of bilingual speakers in the northern part of the Sumerian heartland, called Sumer, around

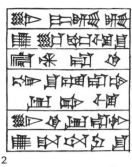

BIRD				
FISH				
DONKEY				
OX				
SUN				
GRAIN				
ORCHARD				
PLOUGH				
BOOMERANG				
FOOT				

Figure 22 Pictographic origin of the cuneiform signs: 1, Sumerian pictographic inscription; 2, Babylonian cuneiform text; 3, pictographic origin of ten cuneiform signs (after Naveh, 1982).

ing of the Semitic people in Mesopotamia (Akkadians who spoke two distinct dialects, Assyrian and Babylonian):

> Early Akkadian, and Akkadian writings in the so-called Ur III Sumerian period (about 2450–1850 BC)
> Old Babylonian period (eighteenth to sixteenth century BC)
> Kassite period (sixteenth century to 1171 BC)
> Assyrian period (twelfth to seventh century BC)
> Neo-Babylonian period (sixth century BC)
> Revival and end of cuneiform writing (third century BC to first century AD).

The periods of the greatest flourishing of cuneiform writing were the periods of Hammurabi (1792–1750 BC) and the ninth to the seventh centuries in Assyria.

In the middle of the second millennium BC, the cuneiform script and the Akkadian language became the international language of the ancient civilized world. The script was used by a number of other nations, mostly non-Semitic, such as the Elamites, Kassites, Hittites, Mitannis and Hurris, and the Urartus, the Luwis, the Old Persians, and to some extent also by the Semitic Canaanites - there is even an extant inscription in Egyptian in cuneiform script (Diringer, 1968, p. 24).

After AD 75, the cuneiform script was forgotten and only rediscovered in the early seventeenth century by European travellers in the area of ancient Western Asia. Its decipherment had to wait for the efforts of English, French, German, Danish and Irish scholars during the nineteenth century; they succeeded in deciphering various scripts and their different languages, with Henry C. Rawlinson, Edward Hincks and Jules Oppert playing a leading role in these efforts (Kramer, 1963, pp. 13 ff). They were greatly aided in this by the existence of trilingual inscriptions on stone, such as the very extensive Old Persian, Elamite and Babylonian inscription on the Behistun rock near Kermanshah in Persia. The first script to be deciphered was Old Persian, which was used between the end of the sixth to the middle of the fourth century BC. It was the most recent, and the simplest, semi-alphabetic form of cuneiform with only about forty characters, and the language was known (Diringer, 1968, p. 139). This was followed by that of the rather more complex Babylonian script which had over 640 signs, written in a Semitic language and therefore relatively easily accessible to a Semiticist. The neo-Elamite cuneiform script, which had only 113 signs, over 80 of them syllabic, was next, but the language was hitherto unknown. The decipherment of the Sumerian script came last - not only was the language unknown, but its very existence and that of the Sumerians themselves had been entirely unsuspected. The bilingual Sumerian-Akkadian dictionaries mentioned above were of help in this work. The decipherment of Babylonian and Assyrian scripts made possible the decipherment of the remaining cuneiform scripts and the understanding of the languages which employed them.

This lengthy discussion of a scenario of which Semites constitute only one, though in many ways a very important, part, demonstrates that a discussion of the earliest scripts and earliest known Semitic languages is not possible by itself in view of the close nexus between them and other languages and the scripts used for them.

At this point a sketch of the features of Semitic languages may be appropriate. It has been pointed out that under Sumerian influence, Akkadian (both Assyrian and Babylonian) developed features atypical for Semitic languages, while

2500 BC, with Akkadian spreading from the north. By 2300 BC, Sumerian as a spoken language began to recede, with at least a part of the Sumerian population becoming bilingual, though it was continuing strongly as a written language (Gelb, 1960). About 1900 BC or so, Sumerian appears to have ceased to be a living spoken language in daily use and to have been replaced by Akkadian, though it may have continued to survive for a while in pockets in the south. After that time, Sumerian was still used extensively as a written language until the end of the Old Babylonian period in 1594 BC. As Sumerian became a foreign, dead language to the scribes, the earlier mnemonic writing was replaced by a more and more elaborate writing of grammatical forms (Thomsen, 1984, p. 23). After that time, some limited types of Sumerian text continued to be written until the second century BC.

At the same time, Akkadian came more and more to the fore in writing, with the cuneiform system being gradually simplified down to the Assyrian period (twelfth to seventh centuries BC), though still having about 570 signs. Even later, the Assyrian cuneiform script became practically a syllabic script and the Old Persians even developed it into a quasi-alphabetic script (Diringer, 1968, pp. 19 ff). With the taking over of the cuneiform script by the Akkadians and the continued use of both languages in writing over a long period, dictionaries became necessary which contained Sumerian cuneiform signs with their Akkadian equivalents, and whole Sumerian sentences with Akkadian translations (Diringer, 1968, p. 21).

Six periods can be distinguished in the cuneiform writ-

much of their structure remained characteristically Semitic and similar to that of other Semitic languages.

All Semitic languages are quite closely related, to a similar extent as are languages of the Indo-European family, such as the Romance languages. Aberrant features in some of them, as in Akkadian and Ethiopic, are attributable to the influence of non-Semitic languages. The typical Semitic consonant system contains both several laryngeals and so-called emphatics. Vowels are generally restricted to a, i, u. Generally speaking, the meaning of a root lies exclusively in its consonants, of which there are usually three in a root, with no more than one each from the same point of articulation. The vowels (and lengthening of consonants) serve only to modify the root meaning through the formation of nominal and verbal stems and their inflection. In pronouns, verbs and nouns, three numbers (singular, dual and plural) and two genders (masculine and feminine) are present, the latter in the second and third persons in pronouns and verbs. The apposition between nouns and verbs is quite unusual: there is a small number of forms which are strictly nominal and do not correspond to the rule of a consonantal root, and a very large number of nominal-verbal roots which do. Inflection is carried out through prefixes, suffixes and vowel changes, and the formation of derived verb-stems, with a great variety of modifications of the root meanings. Numerals are substantives with two genders, 20 is the dual of 10, 30–90 the plural of 3–9. There are complex concordances, especially with numerals.

While Akkadian, which constitutes East Semitic, has a number of peculiarities of its own (see above), the remaining Semitic languages, which constitute West Semitic, underwent a further period of common development (Bergsträsser and Daniels, 1983, pp. 2 ff). West Semitic can be further subdivided into North Semitic which includes Ugaritic, the Canaanite group containing Hebrew with Phoenician and a few minor languages, Aramaic; and South Semitic, which includes North and South Arabic and Ethiopic. Hebrew and Aramaic are sometimes regarded as belonging closer together as North-west Semitic. It seems possible (Bergsträsser and

Daniels, 1983, p. 1, c) to regard North Arabic as not belonging to South Semitic, but to a Central Semitic which has affinities with both North-west and South Semitic.

The speakers of West Semitic languages are believed to have penetrated into the western coastal areas, Syria, Phoenicia and Palestine, coming from northern Arabia, a long time after the Akkadians had entered Mesopotamia. The penetration occurred in several successive waves, and in the course of time different languages were superimposed upon each other (Fig. 23).

Here again, it is the written sources that give us information on this second large group of Semitic languages and on their speakers, their culture, society and history. The scripts in which these languages were written were alphabets, and virtually all alphabets found in most parts of the world are ultimately derived from them. The common ancestor of the alphabets is a form which appears first in the graffiti of Canaanite mine workers in the Sinai area from about the sixteenth century BC. The next stages of it are found in Phoenician and Aramaic inscriptions from about 1300 BC onwards, and by the sixth century BC a Canaanite and Aramaic script could be clearly distinguished.

The Phoenician forms survived only in Samaritan, but the Aramaic became more widely used and developed and by 400 BC or so had nearly reached today's square Hebrew letters in form (Bergsträsser and Daniels, 1983, p. 236). These alphabets, which together constitute the North Semitic alphabets, had 22 letters, all consonants. This might have been the result of influence from the Egyptian script which only indicates consonants, and was also supported by the relative predictability of the placement and nature of vowels in Semitic languages. The direction of writing was from right to left.

The simple Ugaritic cuneiform alphabet of 30 letters, of the fourteenth century BC, constitutes somewhat of a mystery. It was clearly impressed upon clay tablets with a stylus and runs from left to right like the Mesopotamian cuneiform script. Unlike the North Semitic alphabets mentioned above, it contains three vowel symbols for a, i, u, and eight of its letters are similar to North Semitic letters which have the

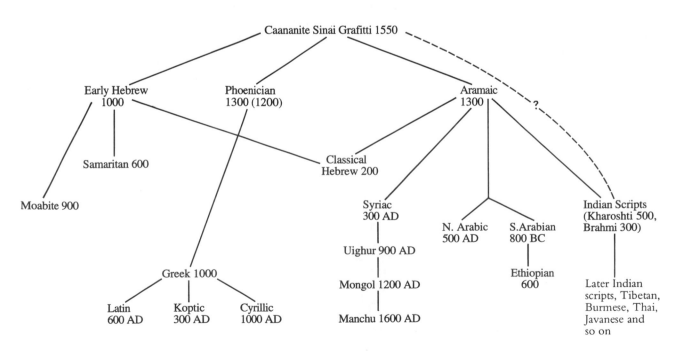

Figure 23 West Semitic scripts and their descendants (drawn by S. Wurm).

same phonetic value (Diringer, 1968, p. 150).

The alphabet of South Arabic inscriptions is closest to the Ugaritic script in the form of the letters, but it is much younger, with the oldest inscriptions dating from 500 BC or perhaps two or three centuries earlier (Bergsträsser and Daniels, 1983, p. 238).

To sum up, there were essentially three branches of the alphabet used for West Semitic languages: the Canaanite branch (Early Hebrew, Phoenician), the Aramaic branch, and the South Semitic branch (South Arabic and Ethiopian). The Greek alphabet developed as a fourth branch and became the point of origin of the western alphabets (Diringer, 1968, p. 170).

Of these, the Early Hebrew alphabet was used in Israel from about 1000 BC onwards until the sixth (or fifth) century BC. The Samaritan alphabet is a descendant of Early Hebrew and still survives today for the liturgical purposes of the Samaritans, an ancient sect of a few hundred people (Diringer, 1968, p. 188). Other descendants of the Early Hebrew alphabet were the Moabite (middle of the ninth century BC), Ammonite and Edomite (eighth-seventh centuries BC) scripts.

The Phoenician alphabet existed in a number of varieties in Phoenicia and in the Phoenician trade centres (Cyprus, Greece, northern Africa, Malta, Sicily, Sardinia, the present Marseilles area and Spain). The whole time-span of this script is from about 1200 BC to the last Punic inscriptions belonging to the third century AD (Diringer, 1968, pp. 189 ff), but the language itself continued until the seventh century AD (Spuler, 1953, p. 27).

The Aramaic language and script played a particularly important role in the first millennium BC and beyond. The first mention of Aramaeans in history dates back to the fifteenth and fourteenth centuries BC, and the end of the great Aramaean migration into northern Syria was in the twelfth and eleventh centuries BC when the great powers of the time, the Egyptian, Assyrian, Hittite and Minoan empires, were on the wane or had ended. The Aramaeans settled in Mesopotamia and Syria, only to succumb to the newly strengthened Assyrians by the middle of the eighth century BC. However, their fall was followed by a meteoric rise of Aramaean cultural and economic power in western Asia, with all Syria and a large part of Mesopotamia thoroughly influenced by it. Aramaic became the supreme lingua franca. It was one of the official languages of the Achaemenid empire, and the main lingua franca of traders from Egypt and Anatolia to India. It became the language of Israel for more than a thousand years. The Aramaic script constitutes one of the two main branches of the North Semitic alphabet - it was used from about the tenth or ninth centuries BC onwards to rise to its very great role and become the official administrative script and language of the Persian empire. Its downfall was mainly caused by the spread of Arabic and Islam, though a few villages in Syria and elsewhere have preserved the Aramaic language until the present day (Diringer, 1968, pp. 196 ff).

The classical Hebrew alphabet developed from Aramaic, but was strongly influenced by the early Hebrew alphabet. The earliest documents in the alphabet date from the second century BC.

The earliest inscriptions in the ancient South Arabic alphabet belong probably to the eighth century BC or so. There are some links between that alphabet and the North Semitic alphabet. South Arabian colonies were established in Ethiopia in the second half of the first millennium BC and their language and script were introduced there. The Ethiopic script

appears to be the result of a gradual development from the South Semitic script, with vocalization introduced into it (Diringer, 1968, pp. 173 ff).

The decipherment of all these alphabetic Semitic scripts and scholars' understanding of the respective languages has been a prerequisite for our knowledge of the history and culture of these people. We know now that the Western Semites entered their areas in a succession of waves, coming from northern Arabia, with the first wave, the Ugarites, arriving about the fifteenth century BC. The next wave was the Canaanite, a few centuries later, apparently with the Phoenicians coming first and spreading far and wide in colonies in Europe and northern Africa, followed by the Moabites and ultimately the Hebrews. After the Canaanite immigration, the Aramaeans penetrated the area and eventually assumed a role of great cultural and linguistic importance, eventually ousting most of the other Semitic languages of the area until the ascendancy of Arabic in the first millennium AD (Spuler, 1953, pp. 24 ff).

CHINESE LANGUAGES (MAP 3)

Chinese is a member of the Sino-Tibetan group of languages to which also the large Tibeto-Burman language family belongs. It is now believed by the majority of linguists outside China that the Thai (Thai-Kadai) and Miao-Yao languages of southern China and South-East Asia are not genetically related to Chinese, though in China itself a number of scholars still adhere to the belief that they are (Wurm et al., 1987-90).

It appears that during the third millennium BC, a people related to the Tibetans and coming from the west penetrated into north-western China, into an area which today is Henan with the adjoining parts of Gansu, Shanxi and Shaanxi, which lay on a busy trade route in Neolithic times, with their language an ancestral form of Chinese (Forrest, 1973, p. 82). It seems that they did not occupy a compact territory, but expanded along the rich cultivable ground in the river valleys, with the original non-Chinese population living in the remaining areas and undergoing gradual sinicization. This had a strong influence on the ethnic composition of the Chinese people, of which many living south of the Changjiang are sinicized Thai and other people, and also left its mark in the formation of the modern Chinese language.

The earliest written records of the Chinese language date back to about 2000 BC (Diringer, 1968, p. 67), and it is thought likely that the Chinese were familiar with writing as early as 2200 BC (Forrest, 1973, p. 38). The earliest pieces of Chinese writing known to us are already far removed from a purely pictorial representation of objects which may well be regarded as the earliest forms. The earliest known specimens are inscriptions on bronze vessels, and perhaps some of many inscriptions in very ancient forms of Chinese characters on oracle bones. The Chinese script is essentially an ideographic script - a character represents a word. While the script has its origin in pictures of objects and many Chinese ideograms can still be recognized as such today, the script went through developments on additional lines. Reference to vocabulary items indicating actions, more or less abstract ideas and so on had to be represented by logical compounds or special symbols (for example, 'action of lifting' = 'hand' + 'vessel', 'profit' = 'wheat' + 'knife', two horizontal bars = 'two'). Ideograms falling into disuse were employed to represent quite different concepts whose spoken representation happened to be the same or similar in sound to the one of the obsolete ideograms. While these developments proceeded somewhat haphazardly for well over a millennium and a half, leading to increasing confusion in the system of writing, a major revision and systematization was conducted in 213 BC by Li Si at the order of the emperor Shi Huangdi. He codified and systematized the use of the so-called radicals which indicate, or at least suggest, a class of ideas to which the word represented by a Chinese written character belongs, for example, 'water', 'fire', 'woman', 'mouth', 'tree, 'wood'. Another part of a character is what is called the *phonetic element,* which indicates the approximate pronunciation of the character with the help of a common character which in isolation has, or more correctly had in the far past, a certain accepted spoken representation or pronunciation in the spoken language. Sound changes over time have since obscured this in many instances. However, this systematized method of writing has largely remained unchanged until recent days - the one major recent change being the creation and introduction of a very large number of abbreviated and simplified Chinese characters (Fig. 24).

The earliest Chinese pictograms and ideograms were written with a narrow bamboo stylus on silk and pieces of bamboo or wood and had equally thick lines and flowing curves. This period lasted from the beginning to about the end of the third century BC, with several types of characters emerging. The invention of the Chinese writing brush of elastic hair in the third century BC resulted in a new type of script with angular strokes of different thickness, square shapes and sharp angles. The invention of paper in AD 105 caused a further development in the shape of the Chinese characters, which have remained largely unchanged since that time.

With Chinese characters not indicating the sound value of the words represented by them, except in a very vague way for a proportion of them, it has not immediately been clear how different, in terms of sound structure and pronunciation, old forms of Chinese were from modern Chinese dialects. It must be understood that present-day Chinese writing is based on and represents the forgotten speech forms of several thousand years ago (Diringer, 1968, p. 72). Also, modern Chinese has many mutually unintelligible dialects (Wurm et al., 1987–90), but Chinese who cannot understand each other's spoken language can read Chinese books and communicate with each other through writing.

However, as from about AD 500, phonetic methods began to come into use in China to indicate the pronunciation of characters in lexical works, presumably stimulated by efforts of Buddhist missionaries from India who were translating their sacred books into Chinese. This gives us an insight into the sound system of Chinese around that time, which is an important basis for the reconstruction of earlier stages. The history of the Chinese language has been divided by sinologists into five periods, Proto-Chinese, Archaic Chinese, Ancient Chinese (which should more correctly be called Old Chinese), Middle Chinese and Modern Chinese. Of these, Proto-Chinese extends from the earliest monuments and information to about 500 BC and is of special interest here. Archaic Chinese extends approximately from that date to the beginning of our era, Ancient (or Old) Chinese from then to AD 600, Middle Chinese from AD 600 to the middle of the eleventh century AD, which marks the beginning of Modern Chinese (Forrest, 1973, p. 48).

The methods by which the sound structures and pronunciation of older forms of Chinese were step by step established constitute scholarly achievements comparable to the decipherment of the Egyptian hieroglyphs and the cuneiform

scripts. This work has been greatly helped by the fact that the Chinese language and script have continued to live to the present day, in sharp contrast to the ancient Egyptian and cuneiform scripts and the languages for which they were used and which both had to be rediscovered after thousands of years of oblivion. The concern of Chinese scholars with their language in the past and their extensive work with some aspects of it has been indispensable in this work.

Research into older forms of Chinese had to be carried out in reverse chronological order. The modern forms and sounds are directly observable, and older forms can be inferred and reconstructed from them step by step through the comparative study of modern Chinese dialects (Forrest, 1973, pp. 50 ff). A lot of additional insights can be gleaned from the forms of Chinese words which were introduced as loanwords in very large numbers into Korean about the third century AD, into Japanese shortly afterwards, and into Vietnamese in the ninth century AD. Old Chinese rhyme tables and pronouncing dictionaries provide additional information, as well as the Chinese transliteration of the large number of Sanskrit words whose Sanskrit pronunciation is well known to us and which were introduced into Chinese by

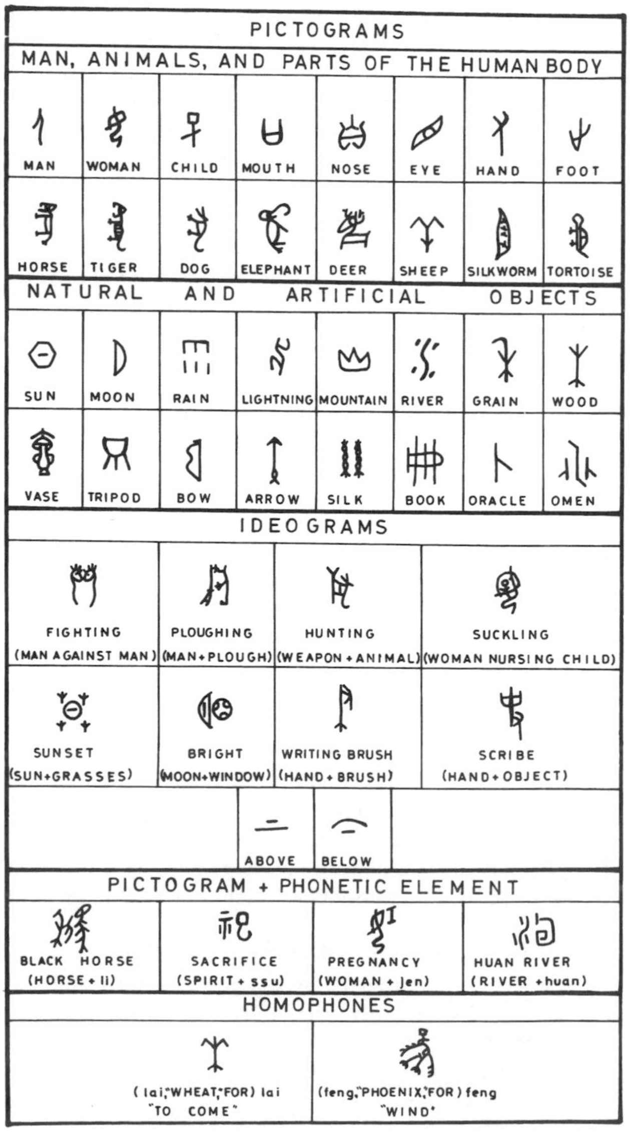

Figure 24 Examples of Chinese pictograms and ideograms, combined with phonetic elements and homophones (after Diringer, 1968).

Buddhists from the first century AD onwards. Within the Archaic Chinese period, most of the present Chinese characters consisting of radicals and phonetic elements were established, and their study and that of rhymes allowed the eminent Swedish scholar B. Kalgren (1940) to establish the Archaic Chinese sound system. From there, inference allows us to come to conclusions regarding the sound system of Proto-Chinese. From that, and the extant inscriptions, we can obtain a picture of what the Chinese language was like from the earliest documented beginnings to the middle of the first millennium BC.

The nature of the Chinese language as we know it throughout its documented history is briefly as follows: in its oldest known form it was a fully monosyllabic language in a phonetically, relatively elaborate form; it gradually changed to a contemporary standard form which has largely moved away from being monosyllabic and is a language amongst those in the world which have the smallest number of phonetically different base words. More so in earlier periods than today, base words function as nouns, verbs, adjectives and adverbs, and each has a semantic tone (see below). There is a very small number of distinct syllables in Chinese even when the tonal differences are taken into consideration. In old forms of Chinese, each base word consisted of a single syllable, and was, and today still is, completely invariable. In more recent forms of Chinese, monosyllabic base words have been combined often inseparably, to form compounds of varying length, but denoting single concepts. Each syllable has a tone, and syllables identical in sound but differing in their tones have quite different basic meanings. Old forms of Chinese (and conservative modern dialects which reflect older forms of the language) had six or more tones, whereas others, such as modern standard Chinese, have only four. Stress also plays an important part in compounds. Grammatical functions are expressed by auxiliary means such as word order, use of base words in auxiliary functions (for example, of noun-functioning base words to express the concepts rendered in English by prepositions). Between numerals and demonstratives, and the nouns determined by them, classifiers or determinants are interposed which are different according to the shape or nature of the object or concept denoted by the respective nouns.

Turning more specifically to Proto-Chinese, it must be noted that classifiers appeared to have been absent in it. Similarly absent is the auxiliary indication of the prepositional auxiliary function of nouns mentioned above. Most interesting is the possibility that some time before our earlier records of Proto-Chinese the language had an inflectional stage and word formation like Tibetan which has prefixes and suffixes (Kalgren, 1920, 1931, 1934).

Our understanding of the Chinese language and script throughout its documented history has allowed us to gain some general to more detailed understanding of the culture, society and history of the Chinese from the time of the earliest written records onwards with increasing clarity as we move towards the middle of the first millennium BC.

BIBLIOGRAPHY

BERGSTRÄSSER, G.; DANIELS, T. 1983. *Introduction to the Semitic Languages*. Winona Lakes, Ind.

BRUNNER, H.; FLESSEL, K.; HILLER, F. (eds) 1990. *Lexion Alte Kulturen*. Mannheim. Vol. 1.

CAMPBELL, L. 1992. Mayan Languages. In: BRIGHT, W. (ed.), *International Encylopedia of Linguistics*. New York/Oxford. Vol. 2, pp. 401-6.

COE, M.; SNOW, D.; BENSON, E. 1986. *Atlas of Ancient America*. Oxford.

DIAKONOFF, I. M. 1976. Ancient Writing and Ancient Written Language: Pitfalls and Peculiarities in the Study of Sumerian. *Assyriological Studies* (Chicago), Vol. 20, pp. 99–121.

DIRINGER, D., 1968. *The Alphabet: A Key to the History of Mankind*. 3rd edn. 2 Vols. London.

FORREST, R. A. D. 1973. *The Chinese Language*. 3rd ed. London.

GELB, I. J. 1960. Sumerians and Akkadians in their Ethno-Linguistic Relationship. *Genava* (Genève), No. 8, pp. 258–71.

GREENBERG, J. H. 1963. The Languages of Africa. *Inter. Am. Linguist.* (Bloomington, Wis.), No. 29, Pt 2.

HAYES, J. L. 1990. *Manual of Sumerian Grammar and Texts*. Malibu, Calif.

HEINE, B.; SCHADENBERG, T. C.; WOLFF, E. 1981. *Die Sprachen Afrikas*. Hamburg.

KALGREN, B. 1920. Le proto-chinois, langue flexionelle. *J. asiat.* Ser. 11, Vol. 15, pp. 205–32.

—— 1931. Tibetan and Chinese. *T'oung Pao* (Leiden), Ser. 2, Vol. 28, pp. 25–70.

—— 1934. Word Families in Chinese. *Bull. Mus. Far East. Antiq.* (Stockholm), No. 5, pp. 175–83.

—— 1940. Grammata Serica, Script and Phonetics in Chinese and Sino-Japanese. *Bull. Mus. Far East. Antiq.* (Stockholm), No. 12, pp. 1–471.

KRAMER, S. N. 1963. *The Sumerians, their History, Culture, and Character*. Chicago, Ill./London.

LANDSBERGER, B. 1944. Die Anfänge der Zivilisation in Mesopotamien. *J. F. Lang. Hist. Geogr.* (Ankara), No. 2, pp. 431–7.

MOHLIG, W. J. G.; ROTTLAND, F.; HEINE, B. (eds) 1977. *Zur Sprachgeschichte und Ethnohistorie in Africa. Neue Beiträge afrikanistischer Forschung*. Berlin.

NAVEH, J. 1982. *Early History of the Alphabet: an Introduction to West Semitic Epigraphy and Palaeography*. Leiden. The Hebrew University. Jerusalem.

ROSSINI, S. 1989. *Egyptian Hieroglyphics: How to Read and Write Them*. New York.

SPULER, B. 1953. *Der semitische Sprachtypus*. In: SPULER, B. (ed.). *Handbuch der Orientalistik* (Leiden-Köln), Vol. 3, pp. 3–25.

THOMSEN, M-L. 1984. *The Sumerian Language*. Kobenhavn.

WURM, S. A. et al. (eds) 1987–90. *Language Atlas of China*. Hong Kong.

8.3
THE INDO-EUROPEAN PHENOMENON: LINGUISTICS AND ARCHAEOLOGY

J. P. Mallory

Three-quarters of the member states of the United Nations recognize an Indo-European language as an official language of state. That the Indo-European languages now comprise a truly global language family is largely the result of west European colonizations during the past 500 years with some additional extension of the Russian language into Asia. There are, for example, more than seven times the number of native speakers of English and Spanish and sixteen times the number of Portuguese-speakers outside of Europe than in their countries of origin. Prior to these relatively recent expansions, the borders of the Indo-European family in Eurasia were confined to an area little different from the one it occupied two thousand years ago in the Iron Age.

In order to summarize the distribution of the Indo-European languages, it is convenient to imagine a rough map of Eurasia at about AD 500 (Map 5). The Celtic languages, which had dominated much of western and central Europe dur-ing the Hallstatt and La Tène Iron Ages (c. 700 BC), would have now been confined largely to the British Isles. At about this time, the Gaelic language had begun spreading to both Scotland and the Isle of Man (Manx), while the British language would eventually evolve into Welsh, Cornish and, in a migration to northern France, Breton. By now the Roman conquest had spread Latin over much of its former empire from which, in a few centuries, there would emerge the earliest

documents in the Romance languages of French, Spanish, Portuguese, Sardinian, Italian and Romanian. It was only in the early centuries BC that Latin came to predominate in Italy and replace both closely related Italic languages such as Osco-Umbrian and other extinct Indo-European languages such as Venetic in the north-east of the peninsula and Messapic in the south-east. North of the western Roman empire Germanic tribes had begun their drive to the south. From this Germanic group arose the Scandinavian languages that are today represented by Icelandic, Faeroese, Norwegian, Swedish and Danish; west Germanic languages such as English, Dutch, Flemish, Friesian and German; and in the east the Gothic language, a variant of which survived in the Crimea until the sixteenth century. East of the Germanic-speakers of North-ern Europe were the Balts, who once occupied a much larger area of north-east Europe than is comprised by their linguistic legacy: Old Prussian (extinct), Lithuanian and Latvian, all attested in written form from only the sixteenth century. At AD 500 the Slavic languages were both expanding and diverg-ing to eventually form a western block of Polish, Czech and Slovakian, a southern group of Slovenian, Croatian, Serbian, Macedonian and Bulgarian, and the eastern group of Russ-ian, Belarusian and Ukrainian. South Slavic incursions car-ried them through the Balkans over the earlier territories of the extinct Dacian, Thracian and Illyrian languages that had

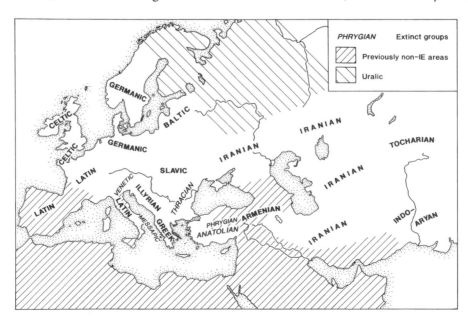

Map 5 The distribution of the major branches of the Indo-European languages, *c.* 500 AD.

dominated this region when the Celts held sway in the west. The only modern survivor of the Balkan languages is Albanian, possibly a descendant of Illyrian, itself only attested in written form from about AD 1500. Further south lay Greek, earliest known in the thirteenth century BC in the Linear B tablets of Crete and Mycenaean Greece.

The linguistic composition of Anatolia has fluctuated throughout the period of written records. In the later Bronze Age (c. 2000–1000 BC) we recover texts of the earliest representatives of the Anatolian group – Hittite, Luwian and Palaic; by the Iron Age Anatolian is represented by only marginally attested languages such as Lycian before these completely die out. The Phrygian language appeared in the heart of Anatolia, presumably by immigration from somewhere further west, by c. 800 BC but by AD 500 it too had become extinct. To the east lay Armenian-speakers who emigrated into the previous non-Indo-European kingdom of Urartu to survive today in the southern Caucasus and eastern Turkey. The Iranian-speaking tribes are attested from c. 1000 BC and were by no means confined to the modern territory of Iran, as many of the Iron Age nomads of the Eurasian steppe also appear to have spoken an Iranian language. Although they made incursions into and through Europe, nothing remains today of the languages of the earlier Scythians, Sarmatians and Alans except for Ossetic, preserved by those Alans who took refuge in the Caucasus. There was also Iranian settlement in central Asia (Sogdian) and on the western fringes of China (Saka). To the south expanded the Indo-Aryans, linguistically so similar to their Iranian cousins that we may imagine an earlier period when a common Indo-Iranian language was spoken. By AD 500 the primary Indo-Aryan literary and liturgical language of Sanskrit had already given way to more vernacular forms of the Indic language, the Prakrits, which would in turn set the stage for the rise of the modern languages of Bangladesh, India, Nepal, Pakistan and Sri Lanka, such as Hindi, Urdu, Punjabi, Marathi and Gujarati. To their north in the Tarim basin on the frontiers of the Chinese empire settled other Indo-European speakers, who left us translations of Buddhist religious texts in Tocharian A (Turfanian) and Tocharian B (Kuchean) before they became extinct by the tenth century.

Our earliest written documents suggest that the borders of the Indo-European-speaking world were not always as large as those we find in the Iron Age or later. Again, moving from west to east, we find in Spain inscriptions in earlier non-Indo-European languages, termed Tartessian and Iberian, while the modern Basques presumably occupied their home in northern Iberia and southern France before the arrival of Indo-Europeans. In central Italy we find remains of the Etruscan language, which is held by general but not all scholarly opinion to be a non-Indo-European language. Traces of other putatively non-Indo-European languages have been attributed to other parts of Italy. The earliest records of the Hittites reveal that they established their state in the territory of the Hatti, a non-Indo-European-speaking people whose very name the Hittites adopted. Both Luwians and Armenians pushed into territories otherwise occupied by Hurrio-Urartian-speaking peoples in eastern Anatolia, while a segment of Indo-Aryans appears to have briefly ruled the Hurrian-speaking Mitanni of north Syria. The southward expansion of the Iranian language carried it over the earlier state of Elam, which has also left its own non-Indo-European documents. Finally, the expansion of the Indo-Aryan languages in India was obviously at the expense of the Dravidian languages, which still predominate in the southern third of the subcontinent. All of this suggests that the distribution of Indo-European languages in the Iron Age was a result of earlier linguistic expansions from somewhere beyond this southern border (Mallory, 1989). The questions of when and from where these earlier linguistic expansions took place comprise what is generally known as the search for the Indo-European homeland.

THE HOMELAND PROBLEM

For more than 150 years scholars have sought to locate the homeland of the Indo-Europeans and trace their migrations across Eurasia to their historic seats (Mallory, 1973). Whenever there has appeared sufficient agreement among scholars to suggest consensus, new theories diametrically opposed have always arisen to challenge though seldom destroy any previous 'solution'. Indo-European homelands have been found everywhere between the Atlantic and Pacific Oceans and at both the North and South Poles! Temporally, the Proto-Indo-Europeans have been assigned to anywhere between the Neanderthals c. 80,000 years ago to as recently as c. 1600 BC. Today, most scholars argue whether the homeland lay in Anatolia-Armenia or in one of a number of proposed European venues. Ironically, our knowledge of the Indo-Europeans seems to be just great enough to deny us any easy solution.

In considering the homeland problem, several basic factors must be emphasized. First, as there exists no direct evidence of a Proto-Indo-European language any arguments as to the time and place of Proto-Indo-European must involve some form of indirect inference. Second, the homeland problem is essentially a prehistoric linguistic question and although the evidence of archaeology must play an important role, it is helpless to do so unless the linguistic evidence itself can be translated into a form that an archaeologist can see in the ground. Third, although the linguistically reconstructed language demands a real Proto-Indo-European, it does not necessarily require that all of the elements of those reconstructions be set to a discrete place or time. Linguists reconstructing the Romance languages, for example, may posit forms that in reality were several hundred years apart and this problem is greatly magnified with respect to the reconstruction of Proto-Indo-European. The proto-language is best imagined as an artificial slice out of a continuum with respect to both space and time and neither of these borders can be precisely determined. Fourth, both the evidence of observable linguistic behaviour and that of the earliest linguistic record of Eurasia suggest that the Proto-Indo-Europeans occupied an area more confined than that of c. AD 500. Language is always in a state of change, and the larger the area, the smaller the likelihood that different communities will experience similar changes in phonetics, grammar and vocabulary. From at least the beginning of settled communities, we should imagine that Eurasia was occupied by speakers of many different languages and language families and that even those sharing a common ancestral language, after expansion, would be expected to diverge over time. The search for the Proto-Indo-Europeans is a search for the location of a language immediately prior to its divergence.

WHEN WAS PROTO-INDO-EUROPEAN SPOKEN?

Our earliest historical records of Indo-European languages, be it clay tablets in Anatolia and Greece or the presumed date of earlier oral texts such as the Rig Veda of India or the Avesta in Iran, all fall within the Bronze Age and none before *c.* 1900 BC. We already have distinctly Anatolian names in Akkadian records from *c.* 1900 BC and the differences between Late Bronze Age Greek and our earliest record of the Indo-Iranian languages would seem to be sufficiently strong by *c.* 1300 that they too must surely have diverged by *c.* 2000 BC (Zimmer, 1988). Consequently, the concept of a Proto-Indo-European language should be confined to a period before 2000 BC. On the other hand, we must recall that we do not have any evidence concerning the linguistic state of the rest of the Indo-European-speaking world at this time. In much of temperate Europe, for example, where we do not have written records until long after the process of differentiation had occurred, we have no way of knowing whether the Indo-European languages presumably spoken there would have yet undergone the types of sound shifts or grammatical change by which we might distinguish an Italic, Celtic, Germanic, Baltic or Slavic language. We observe, for example, that various Indo-European groups such as Italic and Celtic, or Germanic, Baltic and Slavic, frequently share words or grammatical features between one another and not with any other Indo-European group. An extremely vague stage of 'late Indo-European' is proposed to accommodate certain shared linguistic features that cannot be set to Proto-Indo-European because they are confined to a few geographically adjacent languages but which may be otherwise indistinguishable from Proto-Indo-European reconstructions. Therefore, we must be conscious that the 'historical event' of the separation of the Indo-European languages is not necessarily the same as the collapse of the reconstructed proto-language which is an abstraction which yields no precise dates.

While we may lack direct testimony of the age of Proto-Indo-European, there are other indirect though less conclusive approaches to the problem. One of these is lexico-cultural reconstruction or linguistic palaeontology, whereby the cultural content of the reconstructed language may indicate the final period of its existence. While there are procedural problems involved in such reconstructions, such as the isolation of borrowed from inherited words, linguists are still able to produce a general outline of Proto-Indo-European culture.

The reconstructed Proto-Indo-European vocabulary makes it clear that the speakers of the proto-language had a settled mixed agricultural economy. We are able to reconstruct words for cattle, sheep, goat, pig and, of course, dog. Agriculture is attested by a shared vocabulary for grain, plough, yoke and sickle. Architectural terms are limited but indicate stable dwellings with words for house, door, door-post, post, and wattling, to which may be added a term for some type of fortified settlement. Technologically, we have terms for pottery and some basic metal, presumably copper or bronze. All of these terms suggest that we are dealing at least with a Neolithic society which should not predate the seventh millennium BC no matter where in Eurasia it was situated.

So far we are able to compress Proto-Indo-European somewhere between *c.* 7000 and 2000 BC and any attempt to constrain the date any further risks sacrificing some confidence for the sake of precision. The concept of a 'secondary products revolution' in Europe, for example, proposes that the plough, wheeled vehicles, dairy products and wool did not spread from western or central Asia until the later Neolithic, *c.* 4000 BC or later (Sherratt, 1983). But the evidence for all of these changes will generally be perishable or indirect and, consequently, dates for their initial appearance in the archaeological record will not be very precise. Nev-

ertheless, many of these economic phenomena are first dated to *c.* 4000–2500 BC across much of Eurasia. Moreover, evidence for all of these pursuits can be attributed to the Proto-Indo-European vocabulary. We have words for wool, the wheel and several other parts of the wagon, and the plough. Silver may also have been a part of the Proto-Indo-European vocabulary and it too begins to appear in Eurasia in the fourth millennium BC. A consequence of this is that the lexical items attributed to Proto-Indo-European would appear to contain terms that seem to be less congruent with what we know of the early Neolithic than the later, and, therefore, on archaeological grounds there has generally been a presumption that initial Indo-European expansions and divergence was likely to fall between the fifth and third millennia BC rather than earlier.

Linguistic evidence alone provides no precise technique for dating Proto-Indo-European. Technically, we may only date the terminal existence of any mother language with the initial appearance of its daughter languages. Notionally, linguists examining the Indo-European languages and arguing from the degree of divergence seen between the earliest historically attested language have presumed roughly 2,000 years of separation (for example, Cowgill and Mayrhofer, 1986). This generally sets the proto-language to between the fifth millennium and 2000 BC when individual Indo-European languages are confidently assumed to have emerged. Glottochronology, the system of estimating the divergence between related languages according to their loss of a 'basic' vocabulary, is regarded by many as both theoretically doubtful and, at least in the case of the Indo-European languages, almost impossible to implement with proper rigour. The dates it yields tend to fall around the fifth to third millennia as well (Tischler, 1973; Ehret, 1988), although many would argue that such a questionable technique cannot provide additional support for such a date.

The general state of opinion then concerning the date of the Proto-Indo-European language is that it was spoken some time before *c.* 2000 BC and there is some evidence that the proto-language began to expand and fragment after *c.* 5000 BC rather than before it. But it is necessary to emphasize that a number of both linguists and archaeologists are convinced that the expansions began with the initial spread of agriculture from south-west Asia *c.* 7000 BC.

LINGUISTIC APPROACHES TO THE HOMELAND

Although the Indo-European language family and a Proto-Indo-European language are essentially linguistic concepts, linguistics alone seems unable to determine the location of the homeland and indeed many linguists would regard the search as idle and beyond anyone's competence. Nevertheless, there are a series of procedures that linguists have employed to help determine the location of Proto-Indo-European and are widely used in the investigation of the world's other language families.

As is the case with individual languages, language families may also have external relations with other language families. Broadly speaking these may be of two types – contact relations between two families and genetic relations where two or more language families are themselves believed to derive from a common ancestor. Some argue that if Proto-Indo-European can be shown to be related in some way with another language family, this should provide an indication of its geographical location. Linguistic relations have been proposed between Proto-Indo-European on the one hand and the Semitic languages of western Asia, the Kartvelian language group of the south Caucasus, the north Caucasian languages, the Uralic language family of the north European forest-zone and other even more long-distant connections with the Altaic (Turkic and Mongolian) languages of Asia or the Dravidian languages of southern India. On the basis of such proposed relationships the Proto-Indo-Europeans are set in the vicinity of one or more of these other language families. For example, relations with the Uralic and north Caucasian languages have been used to suggest that the Proto-Indo-Europeans lived north of the Black and Caspian Seas, while contacts with Kartvelian and Semitic have suggested homelands in south-west Asia, usually Anatolia. Some propose that all of these languages are derived from a single presumably Palaeolithic language known sometimes as Nostratic, all of which Colin Renfrew has recently suggested may possibly have spread from south-west Asia with the expansion of agriculture (Renfrew, 1991).

The problems with employing external contacts to locate the Proto-Indo-Europeans are substantial. In general, the comparisons that support the notion of external linguistic relations are not of the same quality as those that support a proto-language for a single family, and frequently there is hardly an item that has not been refuted by another linguist, for example: for Proto-Indo-European relations with Semitic and Kartvelian (Gamkrelidze and Ivanov, 1984); against such relations (Diakonoff, 1985; Harris, 1990). When the small number of linguists engaged in the analysis of extra-familial relationships is so divided, even after over a century of research and debate, there seems no compelling reason for anyone

outside this group to be certain of any of the arguments proposed. Second, the positioning of a homeland on the basis of another language family presumes that its speakers are securely anchored in the prehistoric record. Third, it is not all that certain that the nature of relationship between language families can be correctly identified and dated so that one may distinguish between deep genetic relationships between different language families and later contacts. Fourth, any proposed similarities are essentially founded on the notion that the comparisons are between adjacent languages rather than via other unattested languages. It would seem that proposed correspondences between Proto-Indo-European and other language families are as debatable as the homeland problem itself and can themselves hardly resolve it.

Another approach is to propose that the internal relationship of the different Indo-European languages with one another provides a clue to the earlier location of the parent language. It is frequently argued that, where we have the greatest level of differentiation among the Indo-European languages, we may expect to find the centre of its original distribution. This 'centre of gravity' principle proposes that where we find a single linguistic group widely dispersed, we may presume that its expansion has been relatively recent, while considerable linguistic diversity among related languages suggests longer occupation to account for the degree of such divergence. Hence, the very wide distribution of the Indo-Iranian languages across Asia would be interpreted as a relatively recent expansion and possibly the same could be said for the spread of the Celtic languages that covered western and central Europe during the Iron Age. Far greater linguistic variety is found when we approach the area between about 20° and 40° longitude (Fig. 25). On this principle,

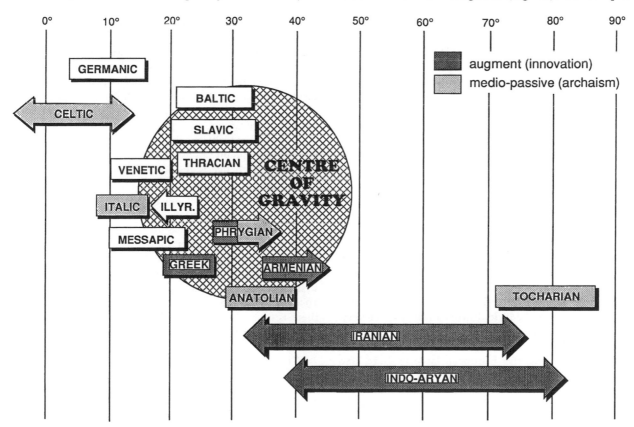

Figure 25 The 'centre of gravity' of the Indo-European languages. An isogloss such as the augment links Greek, Armenian, Iranian and Indo-Aryan together as 'innovating' languages while the retention of the old medio-passive ending in Celtic, Italic, Anatolian and Tocharian suggests that they were spared some of the later innovations. Note that Phrygian appears to participate in one of the innovations while generally it behaves conservatively (drawn by J. P. Mallory).

then, it is easier to explain the earliest historically attested distribution of the Indo-European languages from a centre that lay somewhere between a line from Poland to Albania on the west and from the Dnieper to central or eastern Turkey on the east. These borders are hardly precise since much depends on when one measures the number of different languages; and if this exercise were set to the period c. 1000 BC, the centre of gravity would shift further to the east, since Greek would be the sole representative of the European languages as we are totally ignorant of the linguistic situation in the rest of Europe. Moreover, this approach appears to presume that languages diverge solely because of distance or time and it ignores other factors, such as contacts with speakers of other languages, that might also influence the distribution of linguistic divergence. Nevertheless, the area marked out by the centre of gravity principle does broadly include all of the major current theories on Indo-European origins and it seems improbable that the homeland lay either on the extreme European or Asian distribution of the language family.

While the internal distribution of the Indo-European languages does not permit us to select from among the conflicting theories in vogue today, it does have one very important bearing on their location and expansion. Any solution to the homeland problem should be able to explain the dialectal relationships between the different Indo-European subgroups. For example, we know that the similarities between Indo-Aryan and Iranian are so great that it is possible to reconstruct a Proto-Indo-Iranian stage between Proto-Indo-European and the two subgroups. Any solution to the homeland problem that placed the immediate ancestors of the Indo-Aryans somewhere totally removed from the ancestors of the Iranians would be linguistically improbable. Germanic, Baltic and Slavic share certain grammatical features and items of vocabulary that are not found elsewhere; however, here such common developments can be explained by the fact that the ancestors of these languages were geographically contiguous from the late Indo-European period onwards. Similarly, Celtic and Italic share a number of features but they too would be major representatives of presumably adjacent western European languages. The dialectal links become more important when the associations are not between geographical neighbours. For example, there seem to be closer links between Greek and Armenian (which were separated by Anatolian and Phrygian) and between these two subgroups and Indo-Iranian than between themselves and any other Indo-European language (Fig. 25), and any solution to the homeland problem must somehow explain such connections.

The two most controversial links involve Tocharian and Anatolian. The Tocharians appear to be far more closely related to their western cousins (Adams, 1984) than their Indo-Iranian neighbours and, therefore, their location on the eastern periphery of the Indo-European languages is very difficult to explain. There are two possible but mutually opposed solutions. The first suggests that the similarities between Tocharian and the European languages are best explained by a long-distance migration from Eastern Europe or Anatolia to China. The second argues that the similarities between Tocharian and the European languages rest not on shared innovations but rather on the conservation of archaic features in Indo-European (Fig. 25) that were replaced by the 'central' or 'southern' dialects, that is Greek-Armenian-Indo-Iranian (Crossland, 1971). Therefore, the Tocharians may have always been on the periphery of Indo-European

expansions. In any event, any solution to the homeland problem should explain how the Tocharians reached their historical seats with so little in common with their Indo-Iranian neighbours.

Anatolian also offers problematic relations with the other Indo-European groups. It is not only the earliest attested Indo-European group but it is also extremely archaic in structure, lacking some features found in all other Indo-European languages. The archaic appearance of Anatolian has been explained in one of two, again totally opposed, manners. The first explains it as due to the very early separation of Proto-Anatolian from the other Indo-European groups, some proposing that it was not so much a descendant of Proto-Indo-European but a sister of it, both derived from a Proto-Indo-Hittite. The second suggests that the differences between Anatolian and the other Indo-European languages can be best explained by the impact of substrates, that is, the Indo-European language that moved into central Anatolia was very severely affected by local languages and lost a number of its Indo-European features through 'simplification'. Either explanation requires a separation of Anatolian from the Indo-European continuum before 2000 BC.

That contacts between Indo-Europeans and non-Indo-Europeans might accelerate language diversity has not only been suggested for Anatolian but also for other Indo-European languages as a means of determining the earlier borders of the proto-language. Here one assumes that the centre of Indo-European expansions should be located where we find the least change from the reconstructed proto-language, since this will indicate which Indo-European group has moved the least, that is, been least affected by foreign substrates. Conversely, the greater deviance from the reconstructed proto-language, the greater the likelihood that the speech community has moved from its place of origin and absorbed non-Indo-European substrates. As with all other linguistic principles, this one, too, suffers from both theoretical and methodological problems. In theory, it relates language change to the impact of substrate languages, a phenomenon that is exceedingly difficult to predict. Old English, for example, was spoken by a population that had absorbed earlier Celtic speakers, yet the impact of the ancient British language on English seems negligible. Measurement of degree of change is also very difficult since no one has ever objectively scored each Indo-European language against the reconstructed proto-language or determined which features have greatest importance. There is no doubt that a language such as Lithuanian has been remarkably conservative in preserving many earlier Indo-European features; however, this is hardly proof that the homeland was in the Baltic region. Indeed, recent research into the entire field of 'substrate' influences in Indo-European (for example, Polomé, 1986; Markey, 1989; Huld, 1990; Hamp, 1990) suggest that there is no such thing as an Indo-European language that does not reveal foreign (non-Indo-European) substrate features.

While the concept of Indo-European is fundamentally a linguistic one, it seems clear that purely linguistic procedures are insufficient to determine where the prehistoric Proto-Indo-Europeans were situated. This is not to say that there are not many advocates of the techniques reviewed above, but that none of the arguments alone compels us to select one homeland over another. To go beyond this requires that we translate a linguistic concept into a phenomenon retrievable from the archaeological record.

THE CULTURE OF THE PROTO-INDO-EUROPEANS

Any attempt to convert the concept of Proto-Indo-European speakers into an archaeological context should adhere as closely as possible to the linguistic data. Only in this way can one avoid compounding unwarranted assumptions regarding their culture or physical type or, worse, creating an archaeological solution that ignores the linguistic requirements of the problem. Lexico-cultural analysis, the technique which provides us with broad dates for Proto-Indo-European, is one obvious procedure for translating linguistic information into archaeological data. Such an approach cannot possibly provide a complete picture of a prehistoric culture but it can identify some categories of material culture, environment or social behaviour by which an archaeologist may hope to distinguish between one prehistoric culture and another.

The climate known to the Proto-Indo-Europeans is not particularly distinctive although they clearly knew snow as well as heat. Their environment contained rivers, forests, and an assortment of trees (Friedrich, 1970), which should at least have included the birch, oak, willow and ash and perhaps yew and pine. The presence of the beech, only attested in European languages and even there with its original meaning in some doubt, was once regarded as of great importance, since the common beech did not grow east of a line from the Baltic to Odessa on the Black Sea. This was supposed to argue for a homeland in Central or Northern Europe; however, other varieties of beech are known from along the shores of the Black Sea and the Caucasus while the word itself may be of late rather than Proto-Indo-European origin.

The wild animals commonly attributed to the Proto-Indo-Europeans include riverine animals such as the otter and beaver, and the wolf, fox, bear, lynx, elk, red deer, hare, hedgehog, mouse and perhaps roe deer. The most important fish term reconstructed was traditionally assumed to refer to the sea salmon (*Salmo salar*) and hence again to point to a North European homeland (Thieme, 1954), but the original meaning may well have been the salmon trout, a species which is fairly ubiquitous across Eurasia (Diebold, 1976).

The domestic livestock includes cattle, which is very well reconstructed under a number of different roots, such as cow, ox and steer, and both Indic and Greek even share the same term for a cattle sacrifice. Sheep and lambs are also well attested and the goat, marked by a number of linguistic cognates, should probably be included along with the domestic pig and dog. The horse is clearly reconstructible with the same term occurring in many different linguistic groups (for example, Old Irish *ech*, Latin *equus*, Mycenaean Greek *i-qo*, Hieroglyphic Luwian *asuwa*, Old Indic *ásva-* and Tocharian B *yakwe*). It is potentially the most diagnostic species since the distribution of both the wild and domestic horse was restricted in Eurasia during the Neolithic and Early Bronze Age. In general, it is not known south of the Caucasus before *c.* 4000 BC and not much before *c.* 2500 BC in Iran or India, which makes it extremely difficult to conceive of a homeland on the south-eastern periphery of the Indo-Europeans. Likewise, it is so far unknown from Anatolia earlier than the second half of the fourth millennium BC and it is not known in Greece earlier than *c.* 2000 BC. Traces of horse have been recovered from further north in south-east Europe but these have generally been associated with the spread of domestic horses from the Ukraine.

There is a traditional view of the Proto-Indo-Europeans as a horse-centred society, which rests considerably on the assumption that the horse they knew was domesticated. This is the sense in which the term is generally taken and while it cannot be proved that Proto-Indo-European *ekwos* meant 'domestic horse', there is supplementary evidence to support this. By the time of our earliest historical records, the cognate words for horse all, naturally, refer to domestic horses. There is also a correspondence between Lithuanian and Old Indic for the 'tail of a horse' and both Latin *domitor* and its cognate Sanskrit *damitár-* describe one who 'breaks horses' while the verbal form indicates 'horse breaking' in Old Irish and other languages. Extra linguistic evidence derives from an inauguration ceremony, attested in ancient India, Rome and Ireland, which involves the coupling of a king with a horse, and the element 'horse' plays a prominent role in Indo-European personal names. There is, therefore, a case to be made that before marked linguistic divergence, those occupying the Indo-European continuum were very well acquainted with the domestic horse. In general, the centre of horse domestication is set in the steppe and forest-steppe between the Dnieper and the Urals, *c.* 4000 BC.

The economy also included agriculture, although the identification of crops by species, other than a general word for grain, is difficult. There are terms for barley and oats among the European languages but these lack cognates in Asiatic languages. There are also implements associated with the harvesting and processing of plants, the sickle, grinding stone, and perhaps most diagnostic, the plough, which is generally assumed to reflect the somewhat more advanced agricultural techniques of the later Neolithic.

The vocabulary relating to settlement and architecture, unfortunately, is not particularly diagnostic. The Proto-Indo-Europeans clearly had houses, for we have for example Latin *domus*, Russian *dom*, Armenian *tun*, Old Indic *dáma-* that were organized into larger settlements or villages. Several terms suggest the concept of enclosure, for example, Old Norse *gardr* 'fence', Russian *gorod* 'town', Hittite *gurtas* 'citadel', Old Indic *grhí-* 'house', Tocharian B *kerciyi* 'palace'; possibly fortified sites such as Lithuanian *pilis* 'fort', Greek *pólis* 'town', and Old Indic *púr* 'fort', or Thracian *bría* 'fort' and Tocharian B *riye* 'town' from a root suggesting an elevated place.

Evidence for craft production is limited but includes ceramics and wood working as well as some individual tools such as the awl and whetstone, or ornaments such as beads: for example, Albanian *varg* 'string of beads', Tocharian B *warke* 'beads'; and naturally various garments such as Latin *vestis* and Tocharian B *wastsi*; for clothes, Lithuanian *juosmuo* and Avestan *yah* 'belt'. Metals are not strongly attested but correspondences such as Latin *aes* 'bronze', Gothic *aiz* 'ore' and Old Indic *áyas-* 'metal, iron' suggest acquaintance with at least one metal, presumably copper, while a good case can be made for a knowledge of both gold (Latin *aurum*, Tocharian B *wäs*) and silver. While copper and to a lesser extent gold are known from sites across much of Eurasia from the Neolithic onwards, silver appears to have been confined to the Caucasus, Black Sea region and south-east Europe, including the Aegean, prior to *c.* 3500 BC (Mallory and Huld, 1984).

There are a number of technological terms that may pertain to either domestic pursuits or warfare. These include words for knife, spear (Old Irish *gae* 'spear' and Old Indic *hésas-* 'missile'), the bow (Greek *biós* 'bowstring', Old Indic *jyá* 'bow string') and arrow (Greek *iós* and Old Indic *ísu-*), and the axe (*tekso-). The one item more probably associated with warfare is the *(h)nsi- 'sword', which is attested with this meaning in Latin *ensis* and Sanskrit *asi-*. The word poses some problems of interpretation since no swords are known from the Neolithic and this weapon is generally attributed to the Later Bronze Age. It is not easy to imagine a referent for Proto-Indo-European swords prior to the divergence of Proto-Indo-European, although the recent discovery of a copper sword from a grave near Novosvobodnaya in the northern Caucasus, which would date to the late fourth millennium BC, does provide an isolated possibility. More likely, however, is the evolution of an original meaning such as 'knife', a process to be seen in individual Indo-European languages, for example, Old English *seax*, both 'knife' and 'sword', and it receives some support here due to a Pali cognate of *asi-* which also means 'knife'.

Transportation among the Proto-Indo-Europeans would include both the boat (Old Irish *náu*, Latin *navis*, Old Norse *nor*, Old Indic *nau-* and so on) and wheeled vehicles (words for wheel, *thill*, to ride in a wagon) and yoke. It is generally presumed that these words pertain to heavy wheeled wagons or carts pulled by oxen rather than much lighter spoke-wheeled chariots drawn by horses. Wheeled vehicles are attested from the fourth millennium BC from central Europe across the steppe into Mesopotamia.

Indo-European kinship and marriage terminology suggests a patrilineal society where women were acquired through some form of gift exchange to live in the homes of their husbands. There is strong emphasis on the male role but although the word patriarchal is frequently employed, it suggests little in the absence of evidence for strictly matriarchal societies. There is some evidence for leaders in society although it is difficult to specify their precise social role. The coincidence of meanings for settlement and clan suggests that the Proto-Indo-European *wik- referred to some larger unit of kinship such as the clan. The often cited correspondence between Old Irish *rí*, Latin *rex* and Old Indic *raj-*, all indicating 'king', has been challenged on grounds that the Indic term may not form a true correspondence with the West European words associated with kingship (Scharfe, 1985). There are also several terms apparently associated with military institutions: for example, Proto-Indo-European *qor- underlies such terms as Middle Irish *cuire* 'troop', Old Norse *herr* 'army', Lithuanian *kãras* 'war, army', Greek *koíranos* 'commander' and Old Persian *kara-* 'army, people'.

Terms associated with divinities and the general sphere of religion are also reconstructible and include a sky god, the Indic *Dyaupitár*, Greek *Zéus patér*, and Latin *Jup-piter*, general spirits (Old Norse *ass* 'god' Old Indic *ásu-* 'powerful spirit'; Old Norse *draugr* and Old Indic *dru-* 'phantom') as well as general concepts of 'awe', 'reverence', 'sacred' and socio-religious concepts concerning law, order, obligation, and so on. Actual religious rites may be suggested by such correspondences as Latin *daps* 'sacrificial meal', Old English *tiber* 'sacrifice', Armenian *taun* 'feast' and Tocharian A *tap-* 'eat', while liquid rituals are attested in Greek *kheuma* and Old Indic *hóman-* 'libation'.

ARCHAEOLOGICAL EVIDENCE

The utility of archaeology in examining the homeland problem and the expansions of the different Indo-European groups is effectively limited to establishing plausible rather than certain results, since it is fundamentally impossible for archae-ology, without the aid of texts, to demonstrate what language was spoken purely from the evidence of material culture, economic remains or social behaviour. Moreover, while evidence for migrations is obviously to be welcomed, the process of linguistic expansion need not result in clear breaks in the archaeological record. Originally, it was thought that the various 'branches' of the Indo-European peoples crystallized in the homeland with, for example, the Celts moving off to the west and the Indo-Iranians marching to the south and east. Today, the model of Indo-European expansions requires a linguistic continuum growing in size until the processes of divergence fragmented it into increasingly more specific groups. This expansion need not have involved only long distance and well marked migrations but also minor population displacements or less marked contacts, where the periphery gradually absorbed their non-Indo-European neighbours. A consequence of this billiard-ball effect would be the absence of any single diagnostic traits marking the course of Indo-European migrations from their homeland to their historical seats. Each progressively assimilated population could conserve enough of its own culture that language change might not be very difficult to perceive in the archaeological record.

It would seem useful to consider briefly the process of language change from first principles. The Indo-European languages were spread into new areas by social groups whose relationship to the surrounding population might vary considerably. In some cases, expansion may have been into areas with such low population densities that Indo-Europeans rapidly became the majority. Such a process might be envisaged, for example, in the spread of steppe pastoralists into the Asiatic steppe region, where the economy could support far greater populations than native hunter-fisher-gatherers. Another example is Colin Renfrew's (1987) suggestion that the Indo-European languages were spread by the first farmers in Europe, who progressively would have assimilated any Mesolithic populations because of their more productive economy and higher birth rate.

A second manner of expansion would involve Indo-European minorities moving into fully occupied territories. Where this results in the spread of the new language, this is sometimes referred to as élite dominance, the minority subjugating by either force or economic prestige the native population who then adopt the language of the intruders. If this model was totally symmetrical with archaeological remains we would expect to find evidence of Indo-Europeans shown in special contexts, such as élite burials or hierarchical settlements. Unfortunately, the expansion of a minority language need not be so closely tied in with simple archaeological models. What seems most probable is that linguistic assimilation is invariably preceded by societal bilingualism, a period in which the native population speak both their own tongue and that of the intruders. The progressive assimilation of the native population occurs because they begin to employ the new language in an increasing number of social domains, contexts in which one must select which mode of speech or language is appropriate. It might be expected that the language of the intruders would spread in a variety of different social domains over time. For example, an Indo-European language might be employed initially in contexts of exchange or trade, where the Indo-Europeans controlled exchange links with their linguistic relations. It might also serve as the language of warrior sodalities for which we have some evidence as an Indo-European institution. Prestigious religious ceremonies might also be expected to be carried out in an

Indo-European language. Eventually, the domains of the native language would recede until it was only spoken in the household by the elderly and then no one. As this process might well last the course of many generations, we can hardly expect that the material culture retrieved from the archaeological record would always mirror such gradual social changes; indeed, the common use of the native material culture by intrusive Indo-Europeans might mask the entire event. All of these caveats, of course, still do not remove the archaeological burden of producing some concrete evidence that a people moved from one point to another and spread their language.

CURRENT HOMELAND SOLUTIONS

Although there is no wholly satisfactory solution to the homeland problem, there are at present a number of basic homeland areas proposed for the Indo-Europeans that enjoy widespread support (Map 6). One argues for a homeland in Asia, specifically Anatolia-Armenia, while the others suggest some form of European homeland. None of these solutions is new; in fact, they were all originally suggested in the nineteenth century BC, which indicates how truly persistent (and intractable) the homeland problem is. It should also be emphasized that there is so much variation in detail that even those supporting the same homeland territory may contradict rather than support one another.

Until the late nineteenth century BC, the preferred homeland lay in Asia, an hypothesis supported by the Bible (where the Indo-Europeans were believed to derive from Japhet the son of Noah), by the popular belief of *ex oriente lux* 'light from the east', a view of history that always looked to Asia for innovations in human culture, and by the notion that man, or at least the so-called Caucasian race, originated in the highland regions of western Asia, generally between the Caucasus and the Pamirs. This theory was also stimulated by the scholarly excitement that accompanied Europe's first acquaintance with the ancient writings of India and Iran and, to some extent, early Iranian texts themselves, that indicated a belief in an Aryan homeland situated in the highlands of western Asia. There were other more specific reasons that now include the main arguments of those who support an Asiatic homeland. These comprise the belief that the earliest Indo-Europeans introduced agriculture to Europe and that the Indo-European languages had been in contact with those of western Asia, specifically Semitic but also Sumerian. In general, the nineteenth-century BC model associated Indo-European expansions either with a superior race spreading the gifts of civilization from Asia to Europe or a primarily pastoral people immigrating in tribes comparable to both the Semitic tribes of western Asia and the Turkic tribes of Asia.

Today, the Asiatic homeland is supported in the works of linguists such as the Georgian Tomas Gamkrelidze and the Russian Ivan Ivanov (1984), the Israeli (formerly Russian) Aron Dolgopolsky (1987), and archaeologists such as the Russian Vladimir Safronov (1989), Colin Renfrew (1987) and Andrew and Susan Sherratt (1988) from Great Britain, and the classicist Robert Drews (1988) in the United States, as well as other scholars. Although all argue that Indo-European dispersals are connected with Anatolia-Armenia, their arguments are not always mutually compatible. Gamkrelidze, Ivanov and Dolgopolsky, for example, regard proposed linguistic relations between Proto-Indo-European and Proto-Semitic (and Proto-Kartvelian) as major factors in locating the Indo-Europeans in Anatolia, while Safronov, following the work of the Russian linguist Nikolay Andreev (1986), argues that Proto-Indo-European was a 'Boreal' language, that is, it is genetically linked to the Uralic and Altaic languages, and any similarities between Indo-European and Semitic derive from exchange relations.

A number of these scholars also propose primary and secondary homelands. While all agree that the earliest Indo-Europeans are to be placed in Asia, Gamkrelidze and Ivanov argue an Asian homeland only for Anatolian, Greek, Armenian and Indo-Iranian and a secondary homeland for the European languages which dispersed from north of the Caucasus. Similarly, Aron Dolgopolsky suggests that while the earliest (Anatolian) stage of Proto-Indo-European lay in Asia, the 'centre of gravity' principle points to the Balkans as the dispersal point for all of the other Indo-European languages. Vladimir Safronov also places only the earliest stage of the Indo-Europeans in Anatolia but regards their actual point of dispersal in late Indo-European to have been north of the Carpathians, since Asia fails to meet the criteria for the environment reconstructed by lexico-cultural means. Safronov goes so far as to suggest that even the Hittites and the Luwians both immigrated into Anatolia from Europe. The Sherratts suggest a central or western Anatolian homeland for pre-Proto-Indo-European associated with the spread of early farming communities; however, the actual formation and spread of Indo-European, again with the exception of Anatolian, is based on the periphery of the Black Sea where Proto-Indo-European languages developed, possibly as pidgins associated with developing exchange systems.

Two of the proponents of an Anatolian homeland offer clear-cut models of Indo-European origins and expansions, although again they are so different in detail that they must be regarded as mutually opposed. Colin Renfrew suggests

Map 6 Various recent solutions to the homeland problem for Indo-Europeans.

that the Proto-Indo-Europeans should be associated with the origins of agriculture in Anatolia and that the spread of the Indo-European languages, beginning *c.* 7000–6500 BC, is due to human population increase and expansion over generations, as farmers entered Europe and carried the more productive economy in a 'wave of advance' to both the Atlantic and around the Black Sea eastwards into Asia. Robert Drews also posits the Indo-Europeans in Anatolia-Armenia, but links them with the spread of chariot warfare in the centuries around 1600 BC.

It is immediately apparent that an Asian, specifically Anatolian, homeland for the Indo-Europeans does not mean the same thing to each of its supporters and the divergence of timescales is so great as to render many of them contradictory. For example, while it is obviously correct to suggest that the English language came from England, it is only valid if one suggests that it was England *c.* AD 1100–1900, and it would be wholly inaccurate to derive the language spoken in the United States, Canada, Australia or India from Late Bronze Age England. Yet the differences between those who associate Indo-European expansions with the beginnings of the Neolithic, such as Renfrew and Safronov, and those who support a later date, such as Gamkrelidze and Ivanov, propose theories whose dates differ by a similar order of magnitude and an even greater interval separates them from Robert Drew's proposal.

In general, the positive aspects of the Asian argument rest primarily on two supports: such a location is convenient to the Semitic and other south-west Asian languages should connections with such languages be required. More importantly, in linking Indo-European expansions to the spread of agriculture, as Colin Renfrew has done, a homeland in south-west Asia offers a suitable vehicle for language spread and one that can be traced in the archaeological record.

The various Asian theories, on the other hand, also have deficiencies, some minor but others quite serious. To begin with, an expansion of the Proto-Indo-Europeans *c.* 1700–1600 BC and its association with chariot warfare as proposed by Drews is unlikely (although it may well have been associated with early Indo-Iranian expansions). Although there are terms associated with wheeled vehicles, wagons and carts, there is no linguistic evidence that the Proto-Indo-Europeans shared a common vocabulary concerning light-wheeled vehicles such as chariots, and any model that sees the Indo-Europeans beginning their expansion only *c.* 1700 BC seems much too recent to explain the differences between the earliest attested Indo-European languages. Finally, this theory lacks any compelling archaeological evidence. The hypothesis advanced by Gamkrelidze and Ivanov, that draws the Indo-Europeans from eastern Anatolia-Armenia, situates the Proto-Indo-Europeans in an area where we find it virtually surrounded by non-Indo-European languages (Caucasian, Hurrian, Hattic); it requires the proto-Greeks to somehow go around the Anatolian languages to reach their historical seats, and in the absence of any evidence for migrations from this area, it too seems archaeologically unsustainable.

One of the reasons that linguists have suggested secondary homelands is the failure of an Aegean-Anatolian homeland to meet the lexical-cultural requirements of the reconstructed vocabulary: for example, Anatolia would seem to be beyond the range of the beaver and birch, which are credited to Proto-Indo-European (Dolgopolsky, 1987). Unfortunately, the written evidence of Anatolian is not sufficient to test fully whether it possesses a purely native vocabulary, that is, an early local Neolithic vocabulary that could have evolved

into Anatolian, or whether it should be derived from either outside Anatolia or from a more recent period. What evidence we do have, however, makes it very difficult to associate the Proto-Indo-Europeans (or Proto-Anatolians) with the origins of agriculture in the seventh millennium BC in this region. The word for horse, for example, is solidly reconstructed to Proto-Indo-European, yet there are no remains of horses known from Anatolia prior to the fourth millennium BC and also none from Greece, where this theory would have Proto-Greeks by *c.* 6500 BC. If the homeland were to be situated in Anatolia, we would be at a loss to explain why both Luwians and Greeks share the same Indo-European word for an animal they would not know for thousands of years. In terms of secondary products, Hittite also shares a cognate of the term for 'wool' with the other Indo-European languages. On the basis of such words and other evidence of a non-Indo-European 'substrate' across the East Mediterranean, the Indo-European inheritance in Anatolian would appear to derive from no earlier than the fourth millennium BC or from outside Anatolia rather than any native early Neolithic culture. Moreover, the expansion of Proto-Indo-Europeans with the spread of agriculture should have initiated language shifts far earlier than many linguists believe probable: for example, the earliest Greek and Indo-Aryan languages, presumed to be relatively closely tied by shared linguistic innovations, would be separated by about 5,000 years according to the Neolithic model, rather than about 1,000–2,000 years as linguists suggest. Moreover, if Proto-Indo-European actually developed on the western frontier of the Kartvelian, Hattic or Hurrian languages, we might expect far better correspondences between these languages and Proto-Indo-European than any that have been so far proposed. Finally, a model such as Renfrew's, which appears to demand purely demic, that is, population, movements originating from Anatolia, permits neither secondary movements of Indo-Europeans nor allows for the appearance of acculturated Neolithic populations in Europe. This, however, is not a critical flaw since it can be easily mitigated by recognizing an initial expansion of farmers as far as the Danube and then assuming a more complicated and somewhat later spread of language through the rest of Europe (Zvelebil and Zvelebil, 1988).

Although not so old as the Asian hypothesis, the argument for a homeland in Europe has been proposed since the nineteenth century. Initially, a European homeland was suggested on the 'centre of gravity' principle but only received widespread acceptance due to the now disgarded notions that the 'original' Indo-Europeans were blonde Aryans who must have come from northern Europe. By the twentieth century archaeological evidence was added to support this theory, especially in the works of the German archaeologist Gustav Kossinna. A broadly central European homeland was championed by more recent monographs, such as that of the Italian linguist Giacomo Devoto (1962), while the Hungarian archaeologist János Makkay (1991) has also emphasized the important (although not exclusive) role of the Linearbandkeramik culture in the spread of Indo-European languages. Finally, the Balkans has also been supported as the homeland region, particularly on linguistic grounds such as the 'centre of gravity', by, for example, the Russian linguists Boris Gornung (1964) and Igor Diakonov (1985), or as the 'secondary homeland' according to Aron Dolgopolsky (1987). It should be noted that all of these homelands fall to the west of the Dnieper River.

The case for a European homeland finds support among

those linguists who regard the relationship between Proto-Indo-European and Uralic or, perhaps, North Caucasian (Starostin, 1988), to be far closer than any connections with West Asian languages. The proposed European homelands also fall within the middle of the dispersal area of the Indo-European languages, towards the 'centre of gravity', and with Anatolian separating early they afford a reasonable model for the dialectal relationships within Indo-European. In terms of the reconstruction of Indo-European environment and society, the existence of Proto-Indo-Europeans in Central or Northern Europe *c.* 5000–2500 BC is relatively congruent with the archaeological evidence for this period: for instance, within this general area there appears the horse, both wild and domesticated, wheeled vehicles by the fourth millennium BC, secondary products, and any supposedly diagnostic item of environment or material culture.

There are, however, strong objections to some of the proposed European homelands. Even if one rejects the Indo-European languages spreading from Anatolia with the expansion of farming, it is difficult to deny some population movement from Asia to south-east Europe in the seventh millennium BC. Hence, it seems incongruous to hold that the first farmers of south-east Europe were Proto-Indo-European but those of Anatolia were not when, as Renfrew rightly proposes, they are likely to have spoken the same language. The Neolithic cultures of the Danubian region have been occasionally isolated as Proto-Indo-European, to the exclusion of their southern neighbours on the assumption that while the south-east European Neolithic was the result of Asiatic (presumably non-Indo-European) colonists, the Linearbandkeramik culture that is known from Holland and France to the western Ukraine was a result of an acculturated native population. Hence, János Makkay has emphasized how a single ethos might account for the rapid spread of the Linearbandkeramik rather than actual population movement. However, many would still regard the 'Danubian' culture as also an extension of the Anatolian-southeast European Neolithic (for example, Zvelebil; Dolukhanov, 1991).

Obviously, the further north one feels impelled to seek the Proto-Indo-Europeans, for example in the Linearbandkeramik or northern Neolithic culture, such as the TRB (Funnel-necked Beaker) culture and later Corded Ware culture, the more difficult it is to explain the presence of Indo-Europeans in the Mediterranean and Asia, since it is very difficult to find any evidence for archaeological expansions from this area south and eastwards at the relevant time. Especially critical is the highly debatable relationship between Europe west of the Dnieper and the cultures of the Ukrainian and Russian steppe which, no matter where one sets the homeland, are universally agreed to have embraced at least the Indo-Iranian languages.

If primary and secondary homelands are major features of some of the Asia hypotheses, many who support a European homeland do so on the basis of a bi-partite homeland. By this is meant that the homeland of the European languages is seen to lie in either northern or central-eastern Europe, while the Indo-Iranians are assigned to the steppe and forest-steppe regions of the Ukraine and south Russia. This model is impelled by what is widely regarded as a cultural watershed between essentially agricultural populations west of the Dnieper and primarily pastoral tribes east of the river, both of whom should be recognized as early Indo-European speakers. Hence, there have been attempts to combine both zones into a single homeland. For example, both the Span-

ish (Mexican) archaeologist Pedro Bosch-Gimpera (1960) and the Polish (British) archaeologist Tadeusz Sulimirski (1968) argued that the homeland may have stretched from Central Europe to the steppe region. Similar territories have been suggested by more recent authors, such as the German archaeologist Lothar Killian (1983).

If the steppe cultures must be included within the area of the homeland in association with the central-east European cultures, then there are three possible ways they can be related. The first suggests that the Mesolithic substrate across both central Europe and the steppe region was essentially pre-Proto-Indo-European and that the two regions evolved to form the Proto-Indo-Europeans, the steppe representing the eastern branch. This is a very dubious compromise, since it does not explain why such distant communities should have been linguistically virtually identical for so many thousands of years and achieved the same vocabulary for both natural phenomena and environment as well as late Neolithic innovations. The second explanation recognizes that there must be an historical connection between the two regions (if they are both to be regarded as Indo-European) and suggests that it derives from south-east Europe. Here, as also argued by Colin Renfrew in his Asiatic hypothesis, the food-producing economy spread from the west to the east, hence so presumably did human populations that formed the steppe cultural zone. In this way, all would share the same language. On a later horizon, Safronov has argued that the steppe cultures, specifically the Yamnaya culture, originated from the TRB culture and thence spread across the steppe in the fourth millennium BC. The problem with these theories is that the existing archaeological evidence does not support the progressive spread of a food-producing economy, much less a population shift from the Balkans or central Europe across the steppe region; but rather we find a clear break between settled agriculturalists with ultimately south-east or central European affinities, for example, Tripolje, and economically autonomous steppe and forest-steppe cultures beyond the Dnieper who underwent a very different transition to agriculture (Zvelebil and Dolukhanov, 1991). Indeed, the most recent examination of the economic foundations of the steppe cultures (Shnirelman, 1993) suggests that it was from the Caucasus that they derived their food-producing economy.

The third possible association between central-eastern Europe and the steppe constitutes another major homeland solution, the so-called Kurgan theory. In this model the directions of migration are reversed and the homeland is set on the steppe and forest-steppe between the Dnieper and the Urals among primarily pastoral tribes, who buried their dead under a tumulus (Russian *kurgan*). From the southern Ukraine and Russia, it is argued, Indo-European populations travelled east into Asia, perhaps south through the Caucasus into eastern Anatolia, and west into central and northern Europe.

The steppe theory was first advanced in 1890 by the German Indo-Europeanist Otto Schrader, who proposed south Russia as the homeland since this area was the only one that satisfactorily explained why we have many specifically European shared terms for trees and economic features that are absent in Indo-Iranian. Schrader's theory remained 'isolated' and attacked for a number of years until Sigmund Feist provided additional support in 1913. The steppe theory was then taken up by George Poisson (1934) and at least contemplated by the famous British (originally Australian) archaeologist V. Gordon Childe (1926). Linguistic support for a homeland that embraced both Indo-Iranian pastoralists and

European cultivators was also emphasized in the works of Wilhelm Brandenstein (1936). Today, the theory of steppe invasions is most closely connected with the writings of the American (originally Lithuanian) archaeologist Marija Gimbutas (most recently, 1991). Gimbutas has argued that an Indo-European pastoral society emerged in the Volga steppe and spread westward to burst upon the settled non-Indo-European agriculturalists of the lower Danube region and beyond. In three waves, c. 4500–4000 BC, 3500 BC and 3000 BC, the relentless pressure of steppe pastoralists introduced a patrilineal and patriarchal society that employed the horse, built and ruled from hillforts, buried their dead under *kurgans* and worshipped solar deities. This resulted in a progressive amalgamation of the matri-centred, peaceful, agriculturalist communities of her 'old Europe' and the Indo-Europeans, who as a ruling élite, altered the linguistic trajectory of Europe.

The Kurgan theory posits a homeland slightly east of the centre of Indo-European distributions and provides the most plausible link between the historical Indo-Iranians of Asia and their European cousins. Indeed, almost all solutions to the Indo-European problem would link the steppe cultures with the later Indo-Iranians, so there is at least broad consensus on this issue. Moreover, as with central Europe, the Kurgan hypothesis has no difficulty in fulfilling the requirements painted by lexico-cultural reconstruction, since it is the homeland of horse domestication, includes evidence for early wheeled vehicles and the other supposedly Indo-European markers, and even utilizes these to explain the success of Indo-European expansions.

As with the other theories, the Kurgan solution has its weaknesses. While Kurgan incursions as far west as the Tisza River in Hungary are supported by the type of specific archaeological evidence that draws wide agreement (Anthony, 1990), arguments for any further Kurgan 'movements' outside south-east Europe tend to rest on more generic similarities, for example, the spread of the domestic horse, wheeled vehicles, defensive architecture, tumulus burial, battle axes and animal burial, for which diffusion or common social response may suffice to explain. The evidence for steppe intrusions into central Anatolia, Greece or indeed anywhere else along the Mediterranean is not very strong and proposed links between the steppe and the Corded Ware horizon, seen by many as the ancestor of many of the North and West European languages, is a constant topic of debate. In short, while few if any would deny that the cultures of the steppe were the ancestors of the Indo-Iranians, many would question whether they were the linguistic ancestors of all Indo-Europeans.

It should be obvious then that each current solution to the homeland problem has both its supporters and opponents not only locked in a debate over a century old but often competing with arguments of similar antiquity. It is naturally possible to draw the borders of the prehistoric Indo-Europeans so large that they encompass western Anatolia, central and eastern Europe, and the steppe regions extending into Western Asia, an area which would include most of the homelands proposed. Unfortunately, the larger the homeland area (or greater the compromise between competing homelands), the less satisfactory the solution since it must either propose areas of increasingly implausible size or archaeological cultures with little or no conceivable interrelationship that might impel us to accept an underlying linguistic identity. The specific origin of the world's largest language family still remains very much open.

BIBLIOGRAPHY

ADAMS, D. Q. 1984. The Position of Tocharian Among the Other Indo-European Languages. *J. am. Orient. Soc.* (New Haven, Conn.), Vol. 104, pp. 395–402.

ANDREEV, N. D. 1986. *Ranne-Indoevropeyskiy Prayazyk* [The Early Indo-European Basic Language]. Leningrad.

ANTHONY, D. 1990. Migration in Archeology: The Baby and the Bathwater. *Am. Anthropol.* (Washington, D.C.), Vol. 92, pp. 895–914.

BOSCH-GIMPERA, P. 1960. *El Problema Indoeuropeo.* Mexico.

BRANDENSTEIN, W. 1936. *Die erste 'Indogermanische' Wanderung.* Wien.

CHILDE, V. G. 1926. *The Aryans: A Study of Indo-European Origins.* London.

COWGILL, W.; MAYRHOFER, M. 1986. *Indogermanische Grammatik.* Heidelberg.

CROSSLAND, R. A. 1971. Immigrants from the North. In: EDWARDS, I.E.S.; GADD, C.J.; HAMMOND, N.G. (eds), *Cambridge Ancient History.* Cambridge, Vol. I, Part 2, pp. 824–76.

DEVOTO, G. 1962. *Origini Indeuropee.* Firenze.

DIAKONOFF, I. 1985. On the Original Home of the Speakers of Indo-European. *J. Indo-European Stud.*, Vol. 13, pp. 92–174.

DIEBOLD, D. 1976. Contribution to the Indo-European Salmon Problem. In: CHRISTIE, W. (ed.), *Current Progress in Historical Linguistics.* Amsterdam. pp. 348–87.

DOLGOPOLSKY, A. 1987. The Indo-European Homeland and Lexical Contacts of Proto-Indo-European with Other Languages. *Mediterr. Lang. Rev.*, Vol. 3, 1987, pp. 7–31.

DREWS, R. 1988. *The Coming of the Greeks.* Princeton.

EHRET, C. 1988. Language Change and the Material Correlates of Language and Ethnic Shift. *Antiq.* (Cambridge), Vol. 62, pp. 564–74.

FEIST, S. 1913. *Kultur, Ausbreitung und Herkunft der Indogermanen.* Berlin.

FRIEDRICH, P. 1970. *Proto-Indo-European Trees.* Chicago, Ill.

GAMKRELIDZE, T.; IVANOV, I. 1984. *Indoevropeyskiy yazyk i idoevropeytsy* [Indo-European Language and Indo-Europeans]. Tbilisi.

GIMBUTAS, M. 1991. *Civilization of the Goddess.* San Francisco, Calif.

GORNUNG, B. 1964. *K Voprosu ob Obrazovaniy Indoevropeyskoy Yazykovoy Obshchnosti* [Creation of an Indo-European Language Community]. Moskva.

HAMP, E. 1990. The Pre-Indo-European Language of Northern (Central) Europe. In: MARKEY, T. L.; GREPPIN, J. A. C. (eds), *When Worlds Collide.* Ann Arbor, Mich. pp. 291–309.

HARRIS, A. 1990. Kartvelian Contacts with Indo-European. In: MARKEY, T. L.; GREPPIN, J. A. C. (eds). *When Worlds Collide.* Ann Arbor, Mich., pp. 67–100.

HULD, M. 1990. The Linguistic Typology of the Old European Substrate in North Central Europe. *J. Indo-Eur. Stud.* (Washington, D.C.), Vol. 18, pp. 389–423.

KILLIAN, L. 1983. *Zum Ursprung der Indogermanen.* Bonn.

MAKKAY, J. 1991. *Az Indoeurópai Népek Östöorténete.* Budapest.

MALLORY, J. P. 1973. A Short History of the Indo-European Problem. *J. Indo-Eur. Stud.* (Washington, D.C.). Vol. 1, pp. 21–65.

—— 1989. In Search of the Indo-Europeans. London.

MALLORY, J. P.; HULD, M. 1984. Proto-Indo-European 'Silver'. *Z. Vgl. Sprachforsch.*, Vol. 97, pp. 1–12.

MARKEY, T. 1989. The Spread of Agriculture in Western Europe: Indo-European and (Non) Pre-Indo-European Linguistic Evidence. In: HARRIS, D. R.; HILLMAN, G. (eds), *Foraging and Farming.* London. pp. 585–606.

POISSON, G. 1934. *Les Aryens: Étude linguistique, ethnologique et préhistorique.* Paris.

POLOMÉ, E. 1986. The Non-Indo-European Component of the Germanic Lexicon. In: ETTER, A. (ed.), *O-o-pe-ro-si: Festscrift für Ernst Risch.* Berlin. pp. 661–72.

RENFREW, C. 1991. Before Babel: Speculation on the Origins of Linguistic Diversity. *Cambridge Archaeol. J.*, Vol. 1, pp. 3–23.

—— 1987. Archaeology and Language. London.

SAFRONOV, V. A. 1989. *Indoevropeyskie Prarodiny* [Indo-European homelands]. Gorky.

SCHARFE, H. 1985. The Vedic Word for 'King'. *J. am. Orient. Soc.* (New Haven, Conn.), Vol. 105, pp. 543–8.

SCHRADER, O. 1890. *Prehistoric Antiquities of the Aryan Peoples.* London.

SHERRATT, A. 1983. The Secondary Exploitation of Animals in the Old World. *World Archaeol.* (London), Vol. 15, pp. 90–104.

SHERRATT, A. and SHERRATT, S. 1988. The Archaeology of Indo-European: An Alternative View. *Antiq.* (Cambridge), Vol. 62, pp. 584–95.

SHNIRELMAN, V. 1993. The Emergence of a Food-Producing Economy in the Steppe and Forest-Steppe Zones of Eastern Europe. *J. Indo-Europ. Stud.* (Washington, D.C.).

STAROSTIN, S. A. 1988. Indoevropeysko-Severnokavkazskie izoglossy. Drevniy Vostok Etnokul'tu [Indo-European language of the northern Caucasus]. Svyazi, Vol. 80, pp. 112–63.

SULIMIRSKI, T. 1968. *Corded Ware and Globular Amphorae Northeast of the Carpathians.* London.

THIEME, P. 1954. *Die Heimat der indogermanischen Grundsprache.* Wiesbaden.

TISCHLER, J. 1973. *Glottochronologie und Lexikostatistik.* Innsbruck.

ZIMMER, S. 1988. On Dating Proto-Indo-European: A Call for Honesty. *J. Indo-Europ. Stud.* (Washington, D.C.), Vol. 16, pp. 371–5.

ZVELEBIL, M.; DOLUKHANOV, P. 1991. The Transition to Farming in Eastern and Northern Europe. *J. World Prehist.*, Vol. 5, No. 3, pp. 233–78.

ZVELEBIL, M.; ZVELEBIL, K. 1988. Agricultural Transition and Indo-European Dispersals. *Antiq.* (Cambridge), Vol. 62, pp. 574–83.

9

ORAL TRADITIONS AND LITERATURE, RELIGION AND ART

9.1
ORAL TRADITIONS AND LITERATURE

9.1.1
THE ORAL TRADITION

Jean-Pierre Mohen

From the work of German scholars at the end of the eighteenth century it is known that oral tradition can be as highly structured as written sources; however, certain obstacles hinder the study of oral tradition, especially when it is associated with a distant past that has left no trace of any original sources. What remains today of the words of the songs, poems and epics, of the laws and ordinances, of the prayers recited by children and the religious codes of the many societies that were not literate or used writing only for limited or particular purposes? Oral tradition commands attention, first, by the fact that people acquired the use of modern language 100,000 years ago. Certain oral forms can be discerned from a number of indicators, associated mainly with the earliest written signs.

ORAL TRADITION AND RELIGIOUS PRACTICES

In some early writings religious formulae are transcribed from oral traditions. About thirty baked clay models of animal livers, dating from the nineteenth century BC, were found with the Mari tablets. Each model bears a divine inscription – a transcription of what the priest had read from the surface of the liver, a vital organ whose appearance was thought to reflect the cosmic harmony hidden from humankind and known only to the gods. The oracles' practice of divining and reading signs was fundamentally an oral exercise, as were the prophecies to which the Bible makes such frequent reference. The same impulse inspired the Chinese, in the twelfth

century BC, to inscribe symbols on the underside of a tortoise-shell. These are graphic representations of what the seer has grasped in his observation of the cosmos. The many shades of meaning expressed by the calligraphy indicate that the Chinese had mastered a vast domain, the oral tradition of which must have reached far back into the past.

Writing existed then to serve the 'divine word'. A stone sculpture from the fifteenth century BC depicts the Egyptian god Thoth conveying his words to the scribe Nebmerutef. Yahweh, 'the Word', transmitted his law to Moses, symbolizing the passage from a uniquely oral tradition to a literate culture constructed from rules handed down orally.

In Greece, according to an ancient concept of the world described by Hesiod (800 to 700 BC), the harmony of the cosmos arose from sound, and Muses could thus inspire poets as they declaimed their verses. More than any other form of expression, the voice, especially when exalted by Eros, was of divine essence.

ORAL TRADITION AND RHETORIC

Ancient Greece and Rome remained faithful to the oral tradition and, in particular, to the use of rhetoric, one of the principles of democratic life, which appeared in its early form around 750 BC. In the Greek agora, or market-place, free citizens gathered to debate the city's affairs, creating figures of speech that enhanced their powers of persuasion. We therefore have the intentional paradox that democracy in Athens arose from the combination of public debate and the introduction of writing, a political measure taken at the end of the seventh century BC to establish the law.

Rhetoric was also frequently used for didactic purposes, as for example in the maieutic method employed by Socrates and the philosophical arguments of the Sophists. Rome borrowed from Greek rhetoric in developing its social and political life. At the forum, the Roman equivalent of the agora, speakers commented on public affairs and defended particular points of view. The forum was also the place where a deceased citizen would be displayed, upright, while a relative praised him and his ancestors.

Many societies have preserved the oral tradition, which is the most effective form available for social relations and, above all, for teaching.

ORAL TRADITION, RITES AND THE THEATRE

In all rites associated with life and death, in theatrical representations and in productions with song, the participants express themselves orally, and the voice itself plays a particular and fundamental role.

Every funeral ceremony is accompanied by cries, lamentations, prayers, entreaties and expressions of mourning and consolation. The ceremony is always held against a backdrop appropriate to the circumstances, with particular lighting, colours, symbolic objects and orientation. Those gathered at the ceremony, including the relatives of the deceased, priests and mourners, enter on cue with gestures – acrobatic at times – songs, and set forms of words. Traces of these oral ceremonies have been found in the tombs of all societies. The most spectacular occurred in Egypt, which has also given us the words of prayers and invocations. Numerous other examples of tombs depicting majestic ceremonies have been found in Mesopotamia, India, China and Mexico.

Homer, the first to describe these ceremonies, writes of one organized by Achilles in tribute to his friend Patroclus, who had been slain in combat. Following the funeral ceremony and oration and the cremation, athletic games, with prizes, were held in memory of the deceased. The same religious and funerary rituals gave rise to the Etruscan games. Both the Olympic Games and the dramatic form of tragedy appear to have their origins in the funeral ceremonies and religious festivals held in honour of heroes. Oral tradition played an essential role in both, particularly in the theatrical tradition that developed in the Greek city-state.

THE ORAL ORIGIN OF THE GREAT WRITTEN SOURCES

Most of the first great written sources appear to represent the final stage of a long oral tradition. The transition from oral to written can be illustrated by a few examples.

The Egyptian texts, some of them long, such as the biographies of the deceased and the magic formulae assembled in the *Book of the Dead*, were works addressed to the gods rather than to the living. The scribes were not poets but artisans who set down in writing the many utterances made in religious services. On the other hand the person reading the text, like the gods, in particular Thoth, the god of writing, was seen as inspired with a special gift of wisdom that enabled him to understand the written word (Plate 14).

In Mesopotamia, the oral tradition of epic poetry relating to the god Marduk was probably written down for two interrelated reasons, a religious one – to spread the influence of Marduk – and a political one – to extend the boundaries of the empire. The great 'Creation' epic was probably written at the end of the twelfth century BC. In it, the power of Marduk, the tutelary god of Babylon, extends throughout the universe. He becomes a propaganda instrument for an empire seeking to justify its political and religious expansion.

Although the Biblical prophets interpreted the word of God and long kept to their habits of oral communication, on Mount Sinai Yahweh engraved the law upon tablets of stone so that Moses could spread it abroad, since the written word of God, clear and strong, was superior to the interpretations of soothsayers. The written law, timeless, could be likened to a divination whose author, being himself divine, was at once present and inaccessible. The great codes of Mesopotamia also satisfy this dual requirement of universalism and religion.

The first Chinese texts were also concerned with divination. Each emperor promulgated his own laws and calendar, which were prepared by soothsayers and presented to the subjects of the Celestial Empire as the revealed law.

For the Greeks of the classical period, Homer was the poet-author of an oral work that was secular rather than religious in character and was learnt and recited by every citizen; but does not this work derive its very perfection from the fact that it was written down?

The Greek alphabetic system of writing was borrowed from the Semites in the eighth century BC, although other systems such as the Linear A and Linear B scripts had been used for several centuries. At the time when the Greek alphabet was adopted, the principal means of literary communication were words declaimed or sung, as in the *kleos* ('good report, fame') conferred by bards on the heroes of an epic. Their power was great since it was those words that gave life to the heroes. It is thought that, in adopting the alphabetical system, the Greeks wished to increase the power of the *kleos*, especially in a religious or funerary context, and it is true that Orphic inscriptions on gold leaf were often placed in tombs and that inscriptions were engraved on stone stelae, bearing witness to eternity. Writing did not so much compete with as come to the aid of the oral tradition. The Homeric poems were probably given their written form in the eighth century BC, whereas the events recorded and probably the oral tradition go back to three or four centuries earlier. Hesiod, who lived in the eighth or seventh century BC, began to write down reflections on the nature of inspiration and on the interpretation of written texts. He singled out three primordial divinities, Chaos (the chaotic Universe), Gaia (the Earth) and Eros (Love), carrier of the lyre, symbol of creative inspiration. He introduced into the oral tradition a breadth of scope and soundness of interpretation which were indissociable. The Muses, daughters of Zeus, guaranteed the reliability of knowledge and Mnemosyne, the goddess of memory, considered to be their mother, ensured the immortality of events of former times. The introduction of writing prompted a transition from poetry to philosophy among pre-Socratic philosophers, especially Hesiod, Heraclitus and Parmenides. Pericles recommended the reading of Homeric poems as a democratic exercise, and reading in general was associated with the ability to reason. Socrates, the wise, inspired by his 'demon', was replaced by Plato, the philosopher, and then the Sophists.

BIBLIOGRAPHY

DETIENNE, M. (ed.) 1988. *Les Savoirs de l'écriture en Grèce ancienne*. Lille.

FONAGY, I. 1983. *La vive voix*. Paris.

GOODY, J. 1977. *The Domestication of the Savage Mind*. Cambridge.

LEROI-GOURHAN, A. 1964. *Le geste et la parole*. Paris.

QUINSAT, G. et al. 1990. *Le grand atlas des littératures*. Encyclopaedia Universalis.

ZUMTHOR, P. 1987. *La lettre et la voix*. Paris.

9.1.2
WRITING AND LITERATURE

Monica Rector

The printing of the alphabet and, as a consequence, the possibility of repeating the text, gave humans a revolutionary dimension, giving rise to consciousness of their individuality, in opposition to the common personality and feelings which prevailed up to then. There is a displacement in the relationship between the individual and the group. Now knowledge, information, communication can take place through the eyes, by means of written 'paper', multiplied and distributed, without the need of oral languages, of voices. Here, only the book, the reader and the silence are necessary to transmit the written message.

The material used and the form of the book caused several transformations. In the fifteenth century AD competition arose, on one side between *papyrus* (material made from the stems of the *Cyperus papyrus* plant by the ancient Egyptians) and *parchment* (material made of animal skin) and, on the other, between *volume* and *codex*. The volume was a large rolled up sheet written on only one side; whereas the codex was formed by a series of written 'booklets', placed one after the other and tightened together in a kind of folder. The codex achieved a faster development in the Occident as it was easier to handle. It was similar to the book used nowadays.

LITERATURE

If we look up the meaning of the word 'literature' in a dictionary, we notice that it originates from Latin *litteratura* (letter); under this heading there are the following entries: (1) writings that have artistic merit; (2) a body of writings, as of a particular period, country, language or style; (3) writings dealing with a particular subject: the *literature of science*; (4) activity or profession of writing; (5) printed matter of any kind. So there is a narrow relation between the word *literature* and the notion of written language. This notion of writing is implicit or explicit in the various meanings of literature.

Literature is a social object, which involves somebody who writes and somebody who reads. Therefore, literature only exists as social interaction, it creates among these two individuals an attraction, an aesthetic interaction.

Not every text, however, is considered a literary one. A naïve classification has been to consider 'literary' those texts which are of a 'good' quality. Tradition is one factor: classical works are considered literary because their value continues throughout the ages. In fact, what really defines the literary or non-literary nature is the relation between a situation of production and reception established by words. In the interaction of the world symbolized by words in the 'state' of literature with man's daily reality, literature becomes a force of transformation. The world presented and represented in literature is born out of the writer's experience of a social and historical reality. The author and the reader are thus able to share time and space of this world, created by the former and recreated by the latter. Although until the present we have been referring mostly to writing, literature has also been present. Why? Because literature is language, either spoken or written; that is, literature consisting of certain selected and specialized forms of language. Literature, first of all, is a creative work of art that expresses experiences 'to be contemplated', living experiences, or in Aristotelian terms, mimesis, art of a higher imitation of experience. As it is a qualified selection among the multiple experiences, according to a code of values, it is also criticism. So, the function of literature is 'to make a heightened or selective imitation of life through the medium of literary art' (Grace, 1965, p. 6). In the second place, it is a means of communicating thoughts and ideas, which are considered socially or intellectually significant. By transmitting, the receiver is gaining experience, an imaginary experience, analogous to reality. Third, as literature is re-creation of experience through signs, these signs are drawn from any area of cultural knowledge, each with its respective concept of truth, so valuable to human nature. But literature is not experience in itself; experience is the description of a perceived reality, while literature is the imagined and idealized reality.

As the function of language refers to experiences, the works of literature are more than the language used to shape them. These experiences are elaborated forms of retaining certain aspects of the world: (1) knowledge (every work of literature is about something); and (2) sensorial faculties (intellectual, affective, social, religious). In this sense, literature also has a didactic function; that is, to produce comprehensive awareness of the human being about himself as well as about others.

Literature hence can be viewed as experience and as language. Since writing is language and literature is language, both are closely related in their verbal written manifestation. Literature is fundamentally language in operation, in a verbal text.

Therefore, a writer is someone who manipulates the written side of language. For Barthes (1971, p. 3), 'writing starts there where speech becomes impossible' [l'écriture commence là où la parole devient impossible]. Speech is irreversible, like a bicycle rolling forward, one cannot 'go back' to a spoken word. The written word can be taken back, transformed, corrected as a work of art, until perfection is achieved. When the language is uttered, the sound disappears but we retain the image, we 'feel' the utterance (Barthes, 1971, pp. 11–12). The written word, on the other hand, is detached from the writer's body, it is a separate piece.

For this reason, speech can be more effective than a written text. In speech my 'self' is present, in the text my 'imaginary self' replaces my 'self'. To write spoken language is an imposed act, cultural and political. Oral language tries to be clear and transparent, adequating expression and experience; writing, on the contrary, is an opaque language, mediating between the 'self' and 'oral expression'. Orality is movement, action; while writing is stability, paralysis. This does not mean, however, that one is more real than the other; they are different fields of experience. Writer and reader establish a reciprocal contract: each one accepts his role and allows seduction to take place, as in a love relationship.

For this reason, literature succeeds where common language is often inefficient, 'because literature presents an explicit referent which can be shared by individuals who themselves lead disparate lives' (Baron, 1985, p. 28).

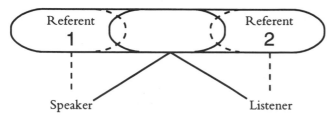

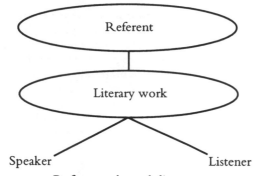

Reference through ordinary language

Reference through literature

In literature, the shared reference is obtained by the writer's creativity and skills, which make the referent understandable. The content clarifies the doubts, because action and environment are made comprehensible through detail. Misunderstanding is reduced through inferences which shorten the distance between writer/reader. The high degree of understanding is obtained by means of representation, of referring indirectly to shared referents, which do not need to be present or to have been experienced beforehand.

'The emergence of human civilization and culture can be interpreted as the move towards greater and greater precision in making indirect reference' (Baron, 1985, p. 31). This can be observed in literary discourse, in which the referent is imaginary. The discourse, itself already being a multi-layered organization, is constituted by several levels, superimposed on each other, as, for example, in concrete poetry, which combines words and drawing. Verbal and visual elements are complementary in that they overlap in this kind of literature. The verbal element is placed in a secondary position and the visual element allows a constant evolution of the possibilities of reading a poem. The reader can observe that the reproducibility of the text is never lost, but the consumer/creator/participant makes his own versions, according to his background. Creator (author) and consumer (reader/viewer) are placed on the same level, each one contributing and being co-author. In a sense, it is a return to hieroglyphs, to the sign-word: for example, the hieroglyph for house (a rectangular space, with one door, seen from the top). The visual and verbal elements are placed together, the lines are simplified on purpose, just the outline and the essential details are maintained.

WRITING AND LITERARY FORMS OF KNOWLEDGE

Writing is linked to every form of human knowledge: to its history and the preservation of its memory, to its future progress and development. 'Writing exists only in a civilization and a civilization cannot exist without writing' (Gelb, 1965, p. 222). Writing and speech are also closely connected. As writing is more conservative, the older oral forms are preserved by it. Writing and art interact; writing is not only functional and utilitarian, but aesthetic elements play a great role.

Literary writing has centred on all fundamental areas of human life. There is religious, social and personal literature. The religious forms of expressions are present in prayers and praises. Once accessible only to a privileged few, such as priests and monks, the mystic element gained weight through written texts. Books and other literary documents were feared, because they contained the secrets of the past and had the magic power of predicting the future.

A second area concerns the social impulse, which expresses behaviour and relationships among individuals, and among these and their community. Literature is concerned here with social and individual well-being, as can be observed, for example, in the ethics of the fable.

The third area deals with the exploration of personal elements: biographies and autobiographies, in the form of novels, plays and poems, from King Lear to Madame Bovary; forms of enjoying and sharing individual words. The reader either projects himself into the life of the character and dreams the undreamable dreams or he identifies aspects of his life with that of the other and receives an imaginary feedback. Every literary work, belonging to any area of knowledge, is also history; it contains the notion of abstraction, it enhances the future of humanity and is an activity of reconstructing the past. Writing then becomes art, because it embraces a situation of communication.

Writing becomes literature, in this sense, because the discourse is always open to the laws of literary practices, and it is the exercise of this operation, the process itself, which produces literature; it implies not only language by itself, but also and simultaneously meta-language, a language about itself.

BIBLIOGRAPHY

BARON, N. S. 1981. *Speech, Writing and Signs. A Functional View of Linguistic Representation*. Bloomington, Ind.
—— 1985. From Universal Language to Language Origin: The Problem of Shared Referents. *Semiotica* (Den Haag), Vol. 57, No. 1/2, pp. 13–32.
BARTHES, R. 1971. Ecrivains, intellectuels, professeurs. *Tel Quel* (Paris), Vol. 47, autumn, pp. 3–18.
COULMAS, F. 1981. *Über Schrift*. Frankfurt am Main.
GELB, I. J. 1965. *A Study of Writing*. Rev. ed. Chicago, Ill.

GRACE, W. 1965. *Response to Literature*. New York.

GREIMAS, A. J.; COURTÈS, J. 1982. *Semiotics and Language: An Analytical Dictionary*. Trans. Larry Crist et al. Bloomington, Ind.

HAWORTH, K. A. 1985. The Origin of Language-Based Thought: A Synthesis of Cognitive Science and Semiotics. In DEELY, J. (ed.), *Semiotics 1984*. New York. pp. 261–5.

HJELMSLEV, L. 1961. *Prolegomena to a Theory of Language*. Madison, Wis.

KRISTEVA, J. 1971. Comment parler à la littérature. *Tel Quel* (Paris), Vol. 47, autumn, pp. 27–49.

MOODY, H. L. B. 1977. *The Teaching of Literature*. 4th ed. London.

PEIRCE, C. S. 1931–58. *Collected Papers*. Cambridge.

PITKIN, H. 1961. *Representation*. New York.

POSNER, R. 1985. Língua falada, língua escrita, língua planeada [Spoken Language, Written Language, Planned Language]. *Cruzeiro Semiót.* (Porto), pp. 69–79.

SAUSSURE, F. de. 1916. *Cours de linguistique générale*. Paris.

9.2
RELIGION AND ART

9.2.1
THE DEVELOPMENT OF RELIGION

Julien Ries

This period of human history corresponds roughly to the Bronze Age. However, the Hittites created an iron industry as early as the second millennium BC, and they were exporting its products from the fourteenth century BC on. The Neolithic ancestors of Bronze Age people had endowed them with a significant religious heritage: the art of symbolic representation of the divinity in statuettes, figurines and frescoes; prayer with hands raised to the sky; funerary rites, megaliths and hypogea (underground burial chambers); altars and sanctuaries, and pictograms. Neolithic *Homo religiosus* had not only had religious experiences; a spiritual edifice had been erected, consisting of myth, rites, symbols and ideas concerning transcendence, the mystery of the hereafter, the cosmos, man and life.

OVERVIEW

Several main religious themes can be considered as characteristic of the period 3000–700 BC.

Solar beliefs and astral cults

The great sky-gods began to emerge at the end of the Neolithic period as the inhabitants of the Fertile Crescent increasingly turned their gaze to the heavens. This religious movement gathered impetus throughout subsequent millennia and developed into the great solar and lunar cults of Mesopotamia and Egypt. The religious shift towards sun and moon worship was accompanied by the establishment of calendars. The astral cult intensified from the beginning of the Early Bronze Age, with its new sanctuaries, gods, myths, rituals and feasts.

The movement spread to the Mediterranean and the Atlantic world, although the debate over the religious significance of megalithic monuments such as menhirs has by no means been concluded: they were already being erected in the Neolithic period and the tradition continued into the Bronze Age. Most experts now agree about one of these megalithic monuments, namely Stonehenge on Salisbury plain in Wiltshire, whose perfect alignment to the rising sun at the summer solstice makes it likely that this remarkable sanctuary was a temple to the sun.

Abundant further Bronze Age evidence of related religious symbols is provided by the enormous number of engravings in rocks facing the rising sun, which can be found in Scandinavia, the valleys of the Alps, Spain, Africa and elsewhere. Figures with arms and hands raised to the sun are shown worshipping, whilst others carry their tools or weapons as if they were offerings. Recent discoveries of new examples of cave art seem to indicate a significant expansion of solar cults at this time.

Sacred royalty and priesthood

From the beginning of the third millennium BC we find the same form of government from India to the Atlantic, both among nomadic peoples and ethnic groups settled in one place: they had at their head a leader who was acknowledged to have divine powers. Historians call this sacral kingship.

In Egypt, a royal theology was established from the 1st dynasty, whose influence lasted until the Ptolemies. The 'Memphite theology' of the Shabaka stela (BM No. 797) confirms that Menes, the founder of the dynasty, is Horus, the divine king. Under the 5th dynasty, the solar revolution of Heliopolis added 'great god, son of Re' to the pharaoh's titles and later the 12th dynasty (2000–1788 BC), based at Thebes, added 'son of Amon'. Over the centuries the priests developed the doctrine of theogamy, the divine birth of the pharaoh, whereas in the beginning the coronation alone had invested the pharaoh with the responsibility of building temples and leading the daily act of worship. The pharaoh appointed an imposing hierarchy of officials 'of the house of god' to run the temples, with often hereditary duties. Over time, this 'priesthood' acquired such economic and political power that it felt able to challenge royal decisions, as in Thebes during the 12th dynasty.

From the fourth millennium BC in Mesopotamia each Sumerian city-state was headed by a leader who was called *lugal*, 'big man', or *ensi*, 'prince-priest'. He was appointed by the god to rule the city and was supposed to live in his temple. Texts describe royalty as power coming from the gods, a tradition passed on to the Semites as it crops up again in Babylon and Assyria, where the kings' names had similar meanings. They derived their power from their enthronement and coronation. An extensive vocabulary referring to divine light and divine splendour was used to describe their attributes. Since the king was responsible for building temples, organizing offerings to the gods, worship, sacrifices and feasts, functionaries gradually replaced him and various duties were delegated to priests. Gradually, the priests were called upon to act as seers and exorcists.

In the archaic Indo-European world, the organic unity of the different components of society, *brahmans, kshatriyas* and *vaishyas*, was personified by the king, *rajan*, who came from the warrior aristocracy. His consecration by a *brahman* conferred upon him the charisma of the two latter functions but linked him mystically to the first, hence the old term *reg,* which signifies that first function and which has been preserved in the Indian, Latin and Celtic languages. The king 'set the line' in both political and religious life. Dumézil (1958) demonstrated the ambiguity of this function. In India the king and the *brahman* formed a pair equivalent to that of the king and the druid for the Celts. However, harmony does not last for ever and so in India, at the time of the *Brahmana,* the priestly caste imposed its will on society. In contrast, the religious function among the Germanic peoples was absorbed by the warriors, relegating the priesthood to a secondary role. The Indo-European legacy reappears in the early history of Rome and in Iran, where it was favoured by the Achaemenids.

Indo-European regal ideology and Mesopotamian theologies converged in Anatolia in the second millennium BC. At the time of the Hittite empire (fourteenth and thirteenth centuries BC) the great king of Hattusas was at the apex of the priestly hierarchy. Numerous stone bas-reliefs portray the royal couple exercising priestly prerogatives. However, the king's time was taken up with politics and military campaigns and he handed over responsibility for worship to the numerous, well-educated, and very hierarchical clergy, who, given the wealth of the temples and the hereditary privileges of the priestly class, eventually made incursions into economic and diplomatic affairs.

In Israel the monarchy was established late, on the Western Asian model, and was, according to the Uppsala School, a 'divine kingship'. The Biblical titles of the Davidic monarchy situate the king in relation to Yahweh: he is chosen by Yahweh, anointed by Yahweh, son of Yahweh, priest of the order of Melchisedech and saviour of his people. These various titles would be taken up again in references to the Messiah. Although they did not assume the title of priest, the kings had authority in respect of worship, appointed priests and blessed the people at major feasts. Abraham paid a tithe to Melchisedech, the priest-king.

Before the Exile the question of the priesthood was complicated in Israel. It was the head of the family who offered up sacrifices and blessed the children. At the time of the Covenant, Moses was a mediator and sprinkled the blood of the sacrifices over the people. Aaron, his brother, was a priest and the tribe of Levi had a special mission, particularly after the settlement in Palestine. The transfer of the Ark of the Covenant to Jerusalem by David ensured the pre-eminence of the priests attached to the new sanctuary. From that time onward the hierarchy and functions of the priesthood were clarified, but the real organization of the priesthood in Israel occurred after the Exile.

Death, the after-life and funerary rituals

The Bronze Age saw a substantial development in beliefs in human after-life. Egypt provides the most abundant evidence, ranging from the Old Kingdom mastabas and

pyramids to the New Kingdom *Book of the Dead* and including tombs of every era. The necropolises were hymns to life and the after-life. The Vedic symbolism of immortality is centred on the sun, Agni (fire) and Soma, an elixir of life from heaven. Brahmanism enriched this symbolism by according the sacrificial rite the power to surmount death. Going still further, Upanishadic thought tried to disengage India from brahmanic ritualism by conferring upon human acts a force that would bear fruit after death.

One of the social characteristics of the western Neolithic period was the introduction of communal tombs. According to archaeologists, the Early Bronze Age saw a return to individual burial north of the Alps and throughout Northern Europe: this is the tumulus culture with princely tombs rich in grave goods in which the bodies were placed in coffins hollowed out of the trunks of oak trees. During the Late Bronze Age, an innovation appeared in central Europe, along the Rhine and in France, Spain and Italy, that of the 'urnfields', involving the cremation of the dead. This new funerary rite must be seen in connection with specific religious beliefs: freeing the spiritual essence that is locked in the body so that it can easily reach the heavens. Solar symbols also occur in the context of cremation. These burial practices recurred in the Achaian kingdoms up to the fourth century BC.

THE SUMERIAN AND BABYLONIAN RELIGIONS AND THEIR INFLUENCE IN THE EAST

The Sumerian and Akkadian deities

Arriving in Mesopotamia in the fourth millennium BC, the Sumerians exerted a strong influence over the people of the region, through their city states of Nippur, Eridu, Uruk, Lagash, Ur and Mari. The Akkadians, a Semitic people from the west, blended with the Sumerians. The Sumerian cuneiform script was invented in *c.* 3000 BC, after various attempts; the script was to become the medium in which the two peoples' thinking was expressed. A Mesopotamian religion developed, formulated in Sumerian and Akkadian texts. From 2000 BC on, these were augmented by the Babylonian texts, and today we have access to some half-million documents.

In the Sumerian language, the name of the divine being was *dingir,* in Akkadian it was *ilu* – two words for which we have no etymology, although the sense of the words is revealed thanks to the star ideogram that always preceded the name of the deity, indicating that he/she lived in heaven. Thus the divine was conceived of as the celestial: the terrestrial world was a reflection of the heavens. Another emblem of the divine being was a horned crown, symbolizing the bull, found as early as 8000 BC at Mureybet on the Euphrates, as both representation of the deity and symbol of the fecund woman. This dual notion of power and fertility is found throughout the history of the Mesopotamian pantheon, which was composed of gods and goddesses. One also sees the monarchical principle transferred from the government of the country and reflected in the divine world, which was ruled by a triad: An, greatest of the gods, Enlil, god of the atmosphere, and Enki, lord of earth. It is clear that the Sumerians linked their concept of the divine with the workings of nature and their culture.

The Sumerians and Semitic peoples endowed their deities with human form, attributing light and brilliance to them as their chief characteristics. This brilliance manifested itself as a glitter radiating from the statue or temple of the deity; sometimes it was like a sparkling mantle. The light could also become a halo surrounding the statue's head, and India, Iran and the West adopted this Mesopotamian representation of divinity. In the Babylonian ritual the crowning of statues of divinities was of great importance, since it was considered to confer supernatural power upon them.

Humankind, the human condition, and royalty

The origins of human beings on earth are explained in four mythic tales whose conclusions are identical: the gods created human beings to serve them. Divine decrees (*me* in Sumerian) governed the functioning of the cosmos and of society: they determined each being's fate and ensured that a person or function conformed to the model the gods desired. The concept of the model was developed by the Akkadians into that of a rite to be practised. Service to the gods was composed of the totality of human tasks, including worship. Controlled by divine decrees, human life was lived in linear time, ending in death, which led the deceased to the kingdom of Nergal, where the dead were only shadows. Believing that fate is revealed in natural phenomena, the Mesopotamians organized a highly developed and diverse science and practice of divination.

To benefit humanity, the sovereign lord An sent royalty down to earth. The god An selected the Sumerian king at a glance and invested him with his office, pronouncing his name aloud. He conferred the tiara and throne on the king, along with the insignia of his functions as leader of his people and servant of the gods. King and priest, he conducted services of worship every day in the dwellings of the gods, which were placed in his care.

Forms of worship: the service of the gods; prayer: the service of humankind

Awed by the vault of the heavens, the Mesopotamians regarded it as the celestial abode of their great gods. Yet the king also built earthly homes for them: the temples and sanctuaries, settings for the daily sacrifices and offerings, whose splendour is described in the tablets, around the statue of the deity. The gods were fed, clothed and covered with jewels and perfumes. At the major festivals of the new moon, celebrating the celestial light, and during the festival of *akitu* marking the New Year, the priests set out to seek their god descending from heaven, by climbing up the ziggurats, the great stepped towers with staircases linking the different levels. A large procession was organized in order to obtain the renewal of vegetation. This mythico-ritual rehearsal of cosmic processes was taken over by the Hittites, at Ugarit and in Iran.

In the first religiously inspired history – the repository of the memory of ancient western Asia – we find a mythic account of the Flood, a work of Semitic genius on the quest for immortality (the epic of *Gilgamesh*) as well as a Babylonian poem on the Creation, *Enuma Elish*, probably written in the twelfth century BC in honour of the god Marduk and making him lord of all the gods and of humankind. In the religious sphere, the Mesopotamian tablets have preserved for us the first large collections of prayers. The Sumerian prayer, *siskur*, was accompanied by offerings and a special

gesture: the supplicant put his hand to his mouth, or raised it. These prayers were very short, and hymns were usually litanies in praise of the god. Most of the prayers are in the Akkadian language: hymns, penitential prayers, prayers for deliverance from harm, prayers to accompany offerings, royal prayers for the country. Alongside the official cult celebrated in the temples, the prayers of individuals give us a more intimate view of Mesopotamian religion, a consciousness of the greatness of the gods to whom one turned in times of distress.

Influence and spread of Mesopotamian religions

The Hittites

As early as the sixth millennium BC, Anatolia was very active in the religious sphere, as can be seen in the cities of Çatal Hüyük, Erbaba and Haçilar: sanctuaries, frescoes, goddess-and-bull as divine figures, altars and funerary rites. When Indo-European nomads called Hittites invaded the country in the third millennium BC they adopted several of the local Hattic cults, which were already fairly sophisticated. The resulting syncretism gave rise to cults of the sun, mountains and springs. Subsequently the Syrian Hurrians influenced the theologians and scribes of Hattusas, capital of the Hittite empire (1380–1180 BC), introducing them to the religious concepts and rites of Babylon, which were incorporated into the national cult. Side by side with local pantheons there existed a hierarchical imperial pantheon in which, as in Mesopotamia, the world of the gods was conceived in the image of the royal court. At the summit reigned the two celestial beings of the sun and the storm (justice and war). The priesthood was governed by a priest-king, the great god's vicar. The idea of a body of priests as functionaries originates in Sumerian-Babylonian religion. These officials were responsible for the organization of the temples in which daily offerings were made to the gods and goddesses, where cleanliness had a sacred value. The Hattusas tablets have preserved for us many texts of hymns and prayers used in the liturgy or at royal ceremonies. In the Assyrian-Babylonian world, hymns were mainly in praise of the god, whereas the Hittites' hymns served a markedly utilitarian purpose: it would seem that the prayer of pure adoration was unknown to them. Sumerians and Hittites turned to their deities when in dire straits: the former submitted to their whims, while the Hittites adopted a freer attitude to their deities, which may have been an Indo-European influence.

The cults of the western Semites: Phoenicia and Canaan

The common name of the divinity was *el* or *ilu*, probably indicating strength or power. El became the supreme deity of the Canaanites. At the end of the third millennium BC the Amorites – Semites from the mid-Euphrates region – brought Mesopotamian influence into Syria and Palestine. The goddess Anat and the god Hadad thus made their appearance: female deities played an important role in the fertility cults. The gods had their dwelling places: a temple in the city, a simple stone elsewhere, the *beyt-el* in the middle of a courtyard. The sacrifice was the banquet in honour of the deity. It was the king who presided over the great liturgical ceremonies in which the statues signified the divine presence. The funerary cult of the Neolithic era was intensified, and demonstrated the continuing belief in life after death.

The tablets of Ras Shamra are the only collection of western Semitic myths we have, and they give us a rough idea of the religious thought of the fourteenth to thirteenth centuries. Like the Mesopotamians, the western Semites believed that agriculture must support the existence of gods and men.

Pre-Vedic religion in India and Pakistan

Thousands of seals, a range of decorated ceramics, male and female figurines, religious scenes and tombs found at Mohenjo-daro and Harappa (in Pakistan) and in India could be a sign of Mesopotamian influence at the end of the third millennium BC. The great goddess and great god indicate a fertility religion. Horns symbolizing power, the crown representing the sun, the throne as the mark of majesty – the symbolism of representation of the Babylonian gods is also found on the Indus Valley seals. We now know that there was trade between the Euphrates and the Indus regions as early as the third millennium BC. One day the 3,500 inscriptions will be deciphered and provide an answer to these enigmas of the Indus Valley religion.

THE RELIGION OF PHARAONIC EGYPT

In the course of the fourth millennium BC, Egypt had contacts with Syria and Palestine and the Sumerian world. From Sumeria, Egypt inherited the cylinder seal, the art of building in brick, and boat construction. In c. 3000 BC Menes unified the country and built Memphis, the capital city. The inhabitants of Egypt were constantly marvelling at the wonders of nature: each day's dawn; the annual rise in level of the Nile; the impressive regularity of its flooding; water in abundance without rain; fertile silt; luxuriant vegetation beneath a luminous sky. Creation was seen as a Golden Age that gave rise to the earth, light, humankind, and the transformation of Chaos into Cosmos.

The origins: the gods and the world

For the Memphis theologians, creation was the work of the god Ptah, who gathered around him the eight primordial gods he had created (ennead). With his words and his heart he created the universe, visible and invisible. He introduced living creatures and established justice and the arts, the cities and sanctuaries of Egypt, royalty, Memphis and its temple. Royalty was a feature of the world of the gods and of that of men. Thus Ptah was the shaper of living beings, the author of all creation, brought into being by the force of the divine word.

During the 3rd dynasty Djoser based the royal power on the sun cult, associating the priesthood of Heliopolis with his government. This doctrine appears in the Pyramid Texts which present Atum-Re as creator of the world and father of the other gods. He began by creating the primordial hill on which he placed the stone benben. He drew this creative power from his consciousness, symbolized by the sun. The god Re was the first king of Egypt and the father of the divine ennead.

In the theology of Hermopolis, linked with the capital of the fifteenth nome of Upper Egypt, the god Thoth (creator of the eight gods – the ogdoad – who merged with him) was the primordial god who deposited an egg on the hillock of Hermopolis. In a variation of this story, the calyx of the blue lotus emerged from the primordial swamp.

For three millennia the theological concepts and the religious life of Egypt were to be guided by these doctrines on origins developed in the priestly colleges of Memphis, Heliopolis and Hermopolis during the first dynasties. There were 753 deities: local gods, gods and goddesses of the cosmos, gods of the sages. All of them possessed a power – neter – which Egypt attempted to express by means of images, symbols or signs which make their representations appear so strange.

The pharaoh and religious observance

The Egyptians' wonderment in the face of nature enabled them to perceive the mystery of life and its sacred character: life was the supreme creation of the gods, and was represented by the mysterious sign – ankh – found as early as prehistoric times and adopted by the Coptic Christians. This sign was carved on temple walls, funerary stelae and statues. Gods and goddesses offered the sign to the pharoah and to the dead. Royalty was a divine institution with the pharoah as its trustee by virtue of the coronation ceremony at Memphis. The sovereign's mission was to ensure the continuity of life, the stability of the cosmos and the harmonious working of the world. Every temple sanctuary (naos) contained the statue of the god, before whom the pharoah (through his priestly deputy) worshipped at dawn, midday and evening, with purifications, food offerings and perfumes. By means of this ceremony the priest called the divine power down into the statue each day. Every temple was a house of god, but it was also a symbolic construction identified with the primordial hill, its function being the maintenance of creation. The construction of a temple was a royal privilege.

Human beings and their destiny

Humanity is in the hands of the gods. The Egyptians were aware of the vicissitudes of fortune, but they had a feeling for the sacred and a love of life. They were perfectly conscious of the linear form of existence, stretching towards the immortality symbolized by the mummy. Full of the joy of life, they wanted to carry into the next world the things that had made for their earthly happiness. In the meantime they took every possible measure to prolong life: the djed column erected to celebrate thirty years of the pharaoh's reign; the life sign; the house of life attached to every temple; statuettes of Osiris. Embalming gave the dead an everlasting body. The doctrine of the pyramids spoke of the heavenly calling of the king, who was reunited with the gods. From the time of the New Kingdom on, every believer became an Osiris at death, and the ritual of embalming was generalized. The Book of the Dead, begun under the 18th dynasty (beginning in 1580 BC) and continuously enlarged up to 650 BC, was wrapped, sealed and deposited on top of the mummy: it was to be the eternal companion of the deceased.

Akhenaten, prophet of the one God and creator

The New Kingdom (1580–1085 BC) was based on the worship of the god Amon; Thebes became the political and religious capital of Egypt, and the priesthood played a pre-eminent role. Amenhotep IV abandoned Thebes to build Akhetaten (Akhet-Aten, Tell el-Amarna), assuming the name Akhenaten – 'splendour of Aten' – and made himself the priest-king and prophet of the one god, creator of all things, lord of all peoples. A universal religion of the sun, that of the god Aten, represented by the sun disc, supplanted that of the dynastic god Amon. The two Amarna hymns that have been preserved show how the ancient doctrine of Heliopolis was transferred from Re to Aten, the one God, universal creator. At one stroke this eliminated traditional doctrine, the royal theology, and all other gods. The death of Akhenaten in 1352 BC marked the end of Amarna's break with the past.

With the close of the New Kingdom the religious creativity of pharaonic Egypt came to an end; thereafter the country was content to maintain its old traditions.

The religion of Israel

Our knowledge of the history and religion of Israel comes mainly from the Bible, but over the last century excavations in western Asia have provided a great deal of very valuable information on the emergence of this people, who have always focused their national identity on their God.

Patriarchal religion

In the beginning there was a tribal religion, dating back to the end of the third millennium BC. The tribes worshipped the god El, also called Shaddai, the protector. They frequented local sanctuaries where the patriarchs raised altars on which offerings were made. The name Abram belongs to the system of names found in the second millennium BC in Mesopotamia. From the time he settled in Mamre, his name became Abraham (Genesis 17: 5). Various traditions make him the father of Israel's belief in one god. Later Biblical tradition urges the importance of circumcision as the sign of Abraham's covenant and his heroic obedience. A religion for all the tribes came into being. It was based upon recognition of Abraham's personal god, protector of the individual, surety for intertribal treaties and alliances. This religion implied particular forms of worship and a priesthood – local guardians of the sacred place, the god's territory. There developed, alongside this religion of sanctuaries, an Israelite cult of the warrior god Sebadt or Sabaoth, who gathered the tribes for victory over their enemies.

Moses and the religion of the covenant

When the Israelites, having left Egypt, stopped to camp near Mount Sinai, the mountain of God, Yahweh made a covenant with the people, revealing ten commandments to Moses. From this time on the covenant occupies the central place in relations between Yahweh and Israel. The supreme virtue is loyalty, fidelity – *khéséd* – of which Yahweh is the model. God's own divine fidelity means mercy and grace for the people, for God is the father of Israel. Seen in the context of the covenant, Yahweh's law forms its basis. To serve any other god would mean that Israel was subject to other laws and had lost its independence. An original component of the Israelite religion is the ban on sacred images: it constitutes an absolute prohibition of idolatry.

Israel associates Moses and his work with its own establishment as an independent nation. Historians place these events in the fourteenth century BC. The phrase 'the God who brought Israel out of the Land of Egypt' was to punctuate Yahweh's interventions in the history of the Israelites, and certain ritual practices, such as the celebration of the Passover, and rest on the seventh day – the Sabbath – are linked to this deliverance. The Ark of the Covenant enclosing the tables of the law came to symbolize the power of Yahweh among the chosen people. Worship was organized at Shiloh and at other sanctuaries such as Bethel and Gilgal.

Israel's religion under the monarchy

When the tribes were first established in Palestine they had judges who enjoyed a limited authority. Royalty on the dynastic model began with Saul (*c.* 1030–1010 BC). Chosen by God, the king was responsible for the sanctuaries and the organization of worship: his decrees were as God-given. David (1010–970 BC) seized Jerusalem, making it the tribes' capital, and he had the ark installed there in order to give his rule the aura of the divine presence and to elevate Zion to the rank of chosen abode of Yahweh. It was this ark that Solomon had installed in the temple he had built. It was consecrated at the autumn festival, henceforth to be the great royal festival: waiting for the rains that ensured prosperity. The age of David and Solomon saw the large-scale assimilation of Canaanite sanctuaries. Adjoining the temple, the royal palace signified the divine nature of the king's rule. The priesthood remained faithful to Mosaic ritual.

There were several strands within this monarchic religion. The king was Yahweh's servant, responsible for organizing the worship of the national god. Yet there was also a popular religion, focusing on high places and still influenced by Canaanite rites, especially those connected with fertility. The prophetic religion was to react against both these elements: it would develop the personal and moral features in the religion of the God of Abraham. With Elijah (ninth century BC) the conflict between king and prophets came into the open and opposition to the Phoenician gods intensified. The prophetic movement gained impetus. Elisha, Amos, Hosea and Isaiah came forward to criticize the royal religion and purify it. They recalled the tradition of Moses and the ten commandments, and did their best to eradicate the local sanctuaries.

THE DEVELOPMENT AND EXPANSION OF THE INDO-EUROPEAN RELIGIONS

In the course of the third millennium BC, groups of conquering peoples roamed between India and the Atlantic. During the second millennium BC they gradually settled in Europe, on the western fringes of Asia, in Iran and on the Indo-Gangetic plain. They spoke different dialects of a common ancestral language, now lost, which can be called Indo-European. This common base was to give rise to many ancient and modern languages, including the Indo-Iranian, Greek, Slav, Germanic, Italian and Celtic languages. Language being the medium of thought, the French historian and linguist Georges Dumézil (1898–1986) undertook a huge comparative work which enabled him to determine the mechanisms and balances that shaped Indo-European religion and society, and thus the fundamental structures of thought in the pre-historic era: a theology dividing the gods into three categories, with functions involving either over-lordship, power, or fertility. This theology is homologous with a tripartite division of society. The religious vocabulary used in all Indo-European languages closely associates the idea of a god with the heavens: light, transcendence, sovereignty, paternity.

Vedic and Brahmanic India

The Indo-Europeans reached the basin of the Indus, then the Ganges basin, in about 2000 BC. Their society consisted of three classes: the *brahmans*, priests, responsible for religious matters; the *kshatriya*, warriors and defenders; and the *vaisya*, who raised livestock and worked the land. The compilation of their knowledge, known as the Veda, drawn from immemorial traditions, treats of thirty-three guardian deities of the cosmic order. Mitra and Varuna were the supreme gods, Indra and the Maruti the warrior gods, and the Nasatyas or Asvins the gods of fecundity and fertility. Hymns, the *Rig Veda*, were sung in praise of the gods during sacrifices, the living flame being the god Agni. After a millennium the conquest of India was complete: the Vedic oral traditions were committed to writing. The priests began to impose the treatises on sacrifice, the *Brahmana*, and they directed the whole of religious activity towards the quest for immortality by means of sacrificial rites. The god *soma* was the drink of 'non-death'.

In a reaction against the imposition upon all of this path of ritual, the way of the *Upanishads* emerged in about 700 BC. This advocated salvation by bringing together the identities of Brahman and the Atman, the 'I' with pure Being, pure Consciousness and Bliss. Liberation (*moksha*) is the escape from *samsâra*, the eternal return to this earth as the result of one's actions in a previous life. The cycle of Karma must be broken to prevent the transmigration of the soul. Knowledge, meditation and mysticism prepare the way for salvation. In place of ritual, India advocated development of the experience of the internal light. Brahman was revealed as both immanent and transcendent.

Zoroaster and Mazdaism

The name Iran comes from Iran-shahr, 'country of the Aryans'. In India, as in Iran, the invaders considered themselves to be Aryans (nobles). Before their arrival, between 1200 and 1000 BC, the various regions of eastern Iran observed the religions of Central Asia: a female pantheon consisting of goddesses, but one in which the symbol of the bull is also found; funerary rites attesting to belief in a life after death; the worship of a great goddess from the second half of the third millennium BC; and the gradual introduction of a male pantheon with temples and sanctuaries.

In the ninth century in eastern Iran, Zoroaster (Zarathushtra), a *zaotar* – priest and prophet – embarked on important religious reforms, substituting the worship of Ahura Mazda for the Aryan cult. These reforms are known to us through analysis of the Gathas, a collection of hymns composed by the reformer himself and preserved in the *Avesta*, the sacred book of Mazdaism. Here Zoroaster declares his faith in one supreme god, creator of light, beginning and end of creation, wise lord and king of heaven, guardian of the laws.

The three existing couples of functional deities – those of sovereign authority, of power, and of fertility – were replaced by six archangels constituting the heavenly court of Ahura Mazda. They are Bohu Manah, Righteous Thinking; Asha, Justice; Khshathra, Dominion; Armaiti, Devotion; Haurvatât, Health; Ameretât, Immortality. The relations of the supreme God with mankind are conducted by these six Entities.

Alongside this monotheism there is a dualism, with two spirits struggling for control of the world: a spirit of good, Spenta Mainyu, originator of life, giver of salvation and immortality, and his adversary Ahra Mainyu, the spirit of evil, corrupter, liar, originator of death. Human beings are free to choose between good and evil, and this choice determines the salvation of each after death and judgement. It is no longer a question of reincarnation, but one of reward in the 'House of Praise', or punishment by a sojourn in the 'House of Shadows'. Zoroaster also taught the idea of a renewal of the world and he substituted linear times for cyclical times.

The Mazdean community was formed shortly after the prophet's death. Its credo was faith in Ahura Mazda, but during this period it was mingled with popular beliefs deriving from the ancient Aryan religion. The Mazdean wore the belt, reminder of the Brahmanical thread. The main focus of worship came to be the fire ritual: fire symbolized the ancestral sacrifice, but also the Wise Lord's light. Mazdaism constituted both a community of believers and a solemn commitment to good and justice. The community practised endogamous marriage as a means of preserving the purity of its doctrine and the ideal of its fight for the truth.

The Indo-Europeans in Europe

We have little information on Bronze Age Indo-Europeans in Europe: the Celts constituted the most easterly branch, and are found in Gaul and the British Isles in the tenth to ninth centuries BC. When the Romans conquered these regions they found a clearly tripartite social and religious structure: the class of druids – who were priests, legal experts and guardians of tradition; the military aristocracy who owned the land; and the stock-raisers who owned herds. This categorization corresponds to that of Indo-Iranian societies, and is reflected in all Celtic religious traditions.

A series of statue-stelae from the third millennium BC found in the Alpine valleys of Italy – Valtelina, Val Camonica and Alto-Adige – carry a carved, three-tier decoration. On the uppermost register the artist carved either a sun symbol or a human figure; on the middle register, representations of daggers; on the lowest register scenes connected with stock-rearing, agriculture or the symbols for water and vegetation. Are these not traces of an Indo-European presence in the Alpine valleys at the beginning of the third millennium BC?

Georges Dumézil's research has led to the discovery, at Rome, of a trifunctional ideology dating from the archaic period. This ideology had three main figures: Romulus, the divine son of Jupiter, to whom his promises are made; Lucumon, his Etruscan ally, military strategist; and Titus Tatius, chief of the Sabines. This has given a new twist to the study of the origins of Roman religion, and highlights the importance of the Indo-European heritage in the emergence of that religion as early as the founding of Rome in 753 BC.

It remains now to discuss the Indo-Europeans in Hellas during the Bronze Age, within the special context of their encounter with Cretan religion.

MEDITERRANEAN RELIGIONS

The Minoan religion

Towards the middle of the third millennium BC in Crete, peoples arriving from the south and east developed bronze-working techniques. This was the beginning of the Minoan culture (the term 'Minoan' comes from the name of the legendary king Minos). During the Middle Minoan period (2000–1580 BC) culture and religion were dependent upon the palaces of Knossos and Mallia. This period saw the appearance of a hieroglyphic script, and the arrival of the first groups of Indo-Europeans into the area. The civilization reached its peak in the Late Minoan phase (1580–1450 BC). Cretan culture began to decline with the rise of Mycenae and Greek hegemony.

Ancient Minoan sanctuaries were on hill and mountain tops, and in caves and labyrinths, suggesting that initiation into mysteries played an important role, and this was subsequently confirmed. The main focuses of symbol worship were the goddess of fertility and the bull. The 'Mistress of Wild Beasts' was to live on in Greek mythology. With the construction of the palaces, the worship of the goddess developed much more significance in the sacred dwelling assigned to her; the presence of the king-priest leading the ritual; her throne as an object of veneration; her epiphany; initiation rites, celebration of the mysteries of life, death and rebirth; sacred dances and bullfights. The religion observed in the Cretan temple-palace was a full synthesis of the goddess and bull cults which spread through western Asia and the Mediterranean world from the Neolithic period on.

The Achaean and Mycenaean religion

At the beginning of the second millennium BC successive waves of Indo-Europeans invaded Hellas, where they found the fertility cults of the Mediterranean world. The Achaeans brought the horse, their sophisticated ceramics, and a heavenly pantheon of male gods ruled over by Zeus, the Dyaus of the Aryans. A second large-scale invasion gave rise to the brilliant Mycenaean civilization, which was to come into its own in the Peloponnese, Boeotia and Attica, and extended as far as Crete. This civilization lasted from 1580 to 1100 BC.

The tablets found at Knossos, Pylos and Mycenae refer to Zeus, Hera, Athene, Poseidon and Dionysus. A large priestly class developed around the king at Pylos: its functions were specialized and divided among both sexes, and ran from the priest responsible for sacrifices to the wardens of the treasury and down to the baker. The gods and goddesses of the two civilizations met, but Indo-European society underwent significant Cretan influence. The Mycenaean period laid the foundation of Greek religion: the main deities, cults and myths, the sanctuaries of Delphi, Olympia, Eleusis and Delos and the Acropolis at Athens. The very impressive Mycenaean tombs bear witness to a firm belief in life after death. Even in this period, initiation ensured this blessing.

From Cretan-Mycenaean religion to the religion of the city

The Cretan-Mycenaean civilization disappeared in c. 1100 BC. Indo-European warrior tribes arrived in the area and occupied Hellas, the coastal regions of Anatolia and the Aegean islands. They were to build the first cities under a tyrant's supervision. Indo-European features in the pantheon were accentuated, with Zeus occupying the first rank. The Lycian god Apollo appeared in the sanctuaries of Delos and Delphi. Aphrodite, a transformation of the Phoenician goddess Astarte, reached Greece via Crete. Hecate the Carian goddess was adopted, together with the Phrygian goddess Cybele. The initiation of adolescents and young people was increasingly important.

There was a profound change in Greece in about 800 BC. The policy of urbanization led to the creation of cities, which caused the uprooting and transplantation of local cults, and the transformation of religious architecture. The ancient sanctuaries gave place to temples in which the city's prestige took precedence over faith. The constitution of the *polis* – the Greek city – gave rise to a political cult: it was the task of the guardian deities to watch over people, property, and the city. Popular religion turned to Dionysus and equally to Demeter and Core, whose mysteries were celebrated at Eleusis.

Two religious currents developed: on the one hand the official cult of the gods of the *polis*; on the other, the mysteries and initiations. The first was political and associated with the city. The second was mystical: it sought personal salvation and immortality. The basic documents for a new trend in Greek religious thought appeared in the eighth century. The *Iliad* and the *Odyssey*, attributed to Homer, portray the vast pantheon of Greek deities in their relationships with human beings. Hesiod, in his *Works and Days*, presented Zeus as protector of humankind and chief of judges. His *Theogony* is the oldest account of Greek mythology.

CHINESE RELIGION IN THE BRONZE AGE

The oldest evidence of religion in China dates from the Neolithic culture of Yangshao in the fifth millennium BC, the utensils and foodstuffs found in tombs indicating belief in an after-life. We have more evidence for the Bronze Age under the Shang dynasty (1751–1028 BC): decorated vases, royal tombs, oracular inscriptions on animal bones. The supreme god Shang-Ti governed the rhythms of the cosmos and natural phenomena. He gave the king victory in battle and ensured an abundant harvest. He was worshipped in two contexts: in the sanctuaries of the ancestors, and in the countryside. These were agrarian cults, whose two pillars were the king's authority and that of the ancestors. The king's first ancestor was believed to have descended from Shang-Ti. The normal sequence of the seasons was ensured thanks to sacrifices. In the royal tombs, archaeologists have discovered animal bones, but also the remains of human victims, probably sacrificed so that they might accompany the king to the other world. Tombs were the houses of the dead. When a palace or temple was built, human sacrifices ensured its solidity and endurance.

In 1028 BC, the Chou dynasty witnessed the beginning of a prestigious period under the auspices of the celestial deity T'ien (Heaven) or Shang-Ti (Lord of the Heavens) who from his position in the centre of heaven saw and heard all things. He protected the dynasty because the king was his son, and as such was the only person entitled to offer sacrifices to the god. The worship of the ancestors continued; the tablet was now placed in the ancestors' temple, rather than in the former urn-house.

Besides the supreme god there was a multitude of other deities: the gods of the earth, of the village and the manor. Texts and myths describe this as a period in which the Chinese raised their eyes to the heavens, speculated on the nature of the cosmos and on the place of humankind within it, and invented symbols and rites which represented the universal harmony of the triad formed by heaven, the earth and humankind. The originality of their conception of the sacred resides in the alternation of, and complementarity between, the two poles *yin* and *yang*, opposed and correlated principles whose interaction wove the fabric of life. This concept made its appearance in the fifth century BC.

CONCLUSION

The Bronze Age was crucial in the history of religion. It saw the development of the great religions of western Asia and the Mediterranean world: Sumer, Babylon, Egypt, Israel, India, Iran and Greece. The founders of these religions, such as Abraham, Moses or Zoroaster, were sometimes personalities who left their mark on the history of their peoples. The first large-scale religious systems to emerge would continue to provide models for millennia to come. First of all there was the divinity of the sovereign, which took slightly different forms in Egypt, Mesopotamia, India and the Indo-European world, Israel and Crete. The priesthood was also associated with the various cultures, yet everywhere it performed a dual function: on the one hand to develop a theological system explaining God, human beings and the world, and on the other, to devise rituals to worship the gods in a way that was worthy of them.

In addition, these two millennia bequeathed a very rich heritage to humanity: the first great theologies and cosmogonies; a series of coherent doctrines on the human condition, on the value of actions on judgement after death and the after-life, on the meaning of human destiny. The invention of writing was to be one of the most important events of this era: from then on it would give humanity its sacred books as well as its sanctuaries and temples. Religion and culture became inseparable.

However, the central event of the Bronze Age was the creation of Israel. Conscious of the revelation vouchsafed to Abraham by the one God, and of the covenant between Yahweh and Moses at Sinai, the people of Israel would assume their specific destiny among the peoples of ancient western Asia.

In recent decades the study of cave art has developed significantly. We see that metal working made possible the manufacture of chariots and weapons, the new symbols of power, which resulted in far-reaching cultural changes. The study of the Chalcolithic period and the Bronze Age should therefore interest historians of religion. The first studies of Bronze Age art, in particular stone engravings in Europe and Africa, revealed a series of signs indicating new attitudes: a predilection for weapons, an impressive number of combat scenes, a multiplicity of symbols of strength and war. Although there is much evidence of solar cults, the fertility rites which were so common in the Neolithic period are far less prominent. The invention of the chariot and weapons made fighting and combat seem more important than agriculture. Female symbols became less common. One wonders whether this represents a shift to the myths of the warrior and the hero.

BIBLIOGRAPHY

ANATI, E. (ed.) 1975. *Les religions de la préhistoire. Valcamonica Symposium 72.* Capo di Ponte.

—— (ed.) 1983. *Prehistoric Art and Religion. Valcamonica Symposium 79.* Milano.

BARGUET, P. 1967. *Le livre des morts des anciens Egyptiens.* Paris.

BARUCQ, A.; DAUMAS, F. 1980. *Hymnes et prières de l'Egypte ancienne.* Paris.

BERGAIGNE, A. 1963. *La religion védique d'après les hymnes du Rig-Veda.* 2nd ed. Paris.

BONNEFOY, Y. (ed.) 1981. *Dictionnaire des mythologies.* Paris.

BOTTÉRO, J. 1987. *Mésopotamie. L'écriture, la raison et les dieux.* Paris.

BOTTÉRO, J.; KRAMER, S. N. 1989. *Lorsque les dieux faisaient l'homme. Mythologie mésopotamienne.* Paris.

BUDGE, E. A. W. 1961. *Osiris, the Egyptian Religion of Resurrection.* 2nd ed. New York.

BURKERT, W. 1977. *Griechische Religion der archaischen und klassischen Epoche.* Stuttgart.

CASAL, J. M. 1969. *De la Mésopotamie à l'Inde. La civilisation de l'Indus et ses énigmes.* Paris.

CASSIN, E. 1968. *La splendeur divine. Introduction à l'étude de la mentalité mésopotamienne.* Paris.

CAZELLES, H. 1985. La religion d'Israël. In: PIROT, L; ROBERT, A. (eds), *Catholicisme hier, aujourd'hui, demain,* Vol. X, Paris, col. 240–277.

—— 1989. *La Bible et son Dieu.* Paris.

DE VAUX, R. 1961. *Les institutions de l'Ancien Testament.* 2nd ed. Paris.

DI NOLA, A .M. (ed.) 1970–6. *Enciclopedia delle religioni.* Firenze.

DUCHESNE-GUILLEMIN, J. 1962. *La religion de l'Iran ancien.* Paris.

DUMÉZIL, G. 1958. *L'idéologie tripartie des Indo-Européens.* Brussels, Latomus 31.

ELIADE, M. 1958. The Sky and Sky Gods. In: ELIADE, M., *Patterns in Comparative Religion.* London/New York, Ch. 2.

—— 1974. *Traité d'histoire des religions.* Paris.

—— 1976. *Histoire des croyances et des idées religieuses.* Vol. I. *De l'âge de la pierre aux mystères d'Eleusis.* Paris.

—— 1978. Les religions de la Chine ancienne. In: ELIADE, M. (ed.), *Histoire des croyances et des idées religieuses.* Vol. II, *De Gautama Bouddha au triomphe du christianisme,* Paris. Vol. 2, pp. 9–46.

—— (ed.) 1987. *The Encyclopedia of Religion.* New York/London.

ERMAN, A. 1968. *Die Religion der Ägypter.* 2nd ed. Berlin.

FAULKNER, R. O. 1969. *The Ancient Egyptian Pyramid Texts.* Oxford.

FRANKFORT, H. 1978. *Kingship and the Gods. A Study of Ancient Near Eastern Religion.* Chicago, Ill.

GARELLI, P. 1969. *Le Proche-Orient asiatique des origines aux invasions des peuples de la mer.* Paris.

GONDA, J. 1960. *Religionen Indiens.* Vol. I. *Veda und älterer Hinduismus.* Stuttgart.

GOYON, J. C. 1972. *Rituels funéraires de l'ancienne Egypte.* Paris.

GRANET, M. 1980. *La religion des Chinois.* Paris.

GUIART, J. 1979. *Les hommes et la mort. Rituels funéraires à travers le monde.* Paris.

INTERNATIONAL CONGRESS FOR THE HISTORY OF RELIGIONS, Roma, April 1955. 1959. *La regalità sacra. The Sacred Kingship.* Leiden.

JACOBSEN, T. 1976. *The Treasures of Darkness. A History of Mesopotamian Religion.* New Haven, Conn.

JAMES, E. O. 1963. *The Worship of the Sky-God. A Comparative Study in Semitic and Indo-European Religion.* London.

KEES, M. 1941. *Der Götterglaube im alten Ägypten.* Leipzig.

KLIMKEIT, H. J. 1978. *Tod und Jenseits im Glauben der Völker.* Wiesbaden.

KÖNIG, F. 1964. *Zarathustras Jenseitsvorstellungen und das Alte Testament*. Wien.

LABAT, R. et al. 1970. *Les religions du Proche-Orient. Textes et traditions sacrés babyloniens, ougaritiques, hittites*. Paris.

LAGRANGE, J. M. 1903. *Études sur les religions sémitiques*. Paris.

LEBRUN, R. 1980. *Hymnes et prières hittites*. Louvain-la-Neuve, Centre d'histoire des religions.

LITTLETON, C. S. 1982. *The New Comparative Mythology. An Anthropological Assessment of the Theories of Georges Dumézil*. 3rd ed. Berkeley, Calif.

MASPERO, H. 1950. *Les religions chinoises*. Paris.

—— 1971. *Le taoïsme et les religions chinoises*. Paris.

MORENZ, S. 1960. *Ägyptische Religion*. Stuttgart.

MYLONAS, G. 1956. *Ancient Mycenae, the Capital City of Agamemnon*. Princeton.

NILSSON, M. P. 1981. *Geschichte der griechischen Religion*. Vol. I. *Die Religion Griechenlands bis auf die griechische Weltherrschaft*. Vol. II. *Die hellenistische und römische Zeit*. 3rd ed. München.

NOTH, M. 1954. *Geschichte Israels*. 2nd ed. Göttingen.

NYBERG, N. S. 1966. *Die Religionen des alten Iran*. 2nd ed. Osnabrück.

POUPARD, P. et al. (eds) 1993. *Dictionnaire des religions*. 3rd ed. Paris.

PUECH, H. C. (ed.). 1970. *Histoire des religions*. Paris.

RENOU, L.; FILLIOZAT, J. 1985. *L'Inde classique. Manuel des études indiennes*. 2nd ed. Paris.

RINGGREN, H. 1966. *Israelitische Religion*. Stuttgart.

RIVIÈRE, J. C. 1979. *Georges Dumézil à la découverte des Indo-Européens*. Paris.

SETHE, K. 1930. *Urgeschichte und älteste Religion der Ägypter*. Leipzig.

SEUX, M. J. 1976. *Hymnes et prières aux dieux de Babylonie et d'Assyrie*. Paris.

STEPHENSON, C. 1980. *Leben und Tod in den Religionen*. Darmstadt.

WATSON, W. 1966. *Early Civilization in China*. London.

WIDENGREN, G. 1968. *Die Religionen Irans*. Stuttgart.

9.2.2
ART AND ARCHITECTURE

Jean-Pierre Mohen

Artistic expression was present in all the cultures of the period between 3000 and 700 BC. There were great centres of art linked to ambitious architectural achievements in Egypt, Babylon, Iran, Crete, Greece, China and Mexico. Archaeological exploration also reveals the richness and variety of rock art throughout the world, in regions now mainly uninhabited. Everywhere, excavations of houses, sanctuaries and tombs bring to light stone and terracotta statuettes, decorated objects, stone and sometimes wooden tools or ceramic vases. Artistic creation was a living and universal reality in that period, but we know very little about it, because organic remains have almost all vanished – with a few exceptions: those of the Egyptian tombs have survived on account of the dry, stable atmosphere, while those of the Danish peat bogs and the Swiss lakes have been preserved through constant humidity.

WIDELY SPREAD TRADITIONAL ARTS

In regions where there were no great state structures, such as non-Mediterranean Europe, Africa with the exception of Egypt, northern Asia and large parts of America and Australia, art remained traditional, collective and religious in inspiration. Small anthropomorphic and zoomorphic representations, modelled or sculpted in styles specific to each culture, are interpreted as amulets or votive figures: the bronze chariot of Trundholm in Denmark, with its horse drawing the solar disc decorated with sheet gold, the bronze chariot of Strettweg in Austria, with a goddess surrounded by deer hunters, the terracotta chariot of Dupljaya in Serbia, with its bird-headed divinity. Painted on the rocks or hollowed out of their surface, these figures are juxtaposed and sometimes even grouped together in tableaux. Deep-sea fishing and deerstalking are favourite themes picked out on the rocks of Zalavruga in Karelia; hunting and fighting scenes decorate the stone slabs of the Val Camonica in northern Italy (Plates 137, 156, 157); praying figures with their arms raised to heaven are to be found at Mont Bégo (Monte Bego), in the south of France. None of these representations appears to be anecdotal: all seem to evoke heroic or mythical events. From these many thousands of representations emerges a stereotyped male figure, most often a warrior mounted on a horse-drawn chariot, who appears on the stelae of southwestern Iberia. He undoubtedly represents the prince, the dominating figure of the societies of the time (see Chapter 14.6, Fig. 75). Monumental art is rare in these regions, with the exception of the famous circle of standing stones at Stonehenge (Plates 4, 5) built in the western European megalithic tradition that flourished during the Neolithic period.

Terracotta and stone statuettes were also widespread outside Europe, replacing the earlier ones that were in the form of a highly stylized woman, sitting or standing, evoking generosity and prosperity (Plate 15). Around 3000 BC the Egyptian female dancers with raised arms were painted black and red; other fusiform ivory statuettes date from the same period. During the third millennium BC, in Cyprus, Syria, Sumer, Iran and Turkmenia, there were female clay figures, many with the arms cut off below the shoulders, ornamented with necklaces and elaborate hairstyles. Each detail is typical of a local style. From between 2500 and 2000 BC, for example, Cycladic idols in marble with triangular heads, wide shoulders and feet placed together are to be found (Plates 37, 38). Further stylization produced the 'violin-idol'. These statuettes were still widespread throughout the second millennium BC. Some in Iran and Syria are decorated with stamped ocellations suggesting eyes, breasts and knees; others are wearing an ear-ring in bronze wire; their joined hands are clasped to the breast in an attitude of devotion; some hold an offering. A few are in bronze, silver or gold – the richer materials reserved for temples and royal funeral offerings, such as the Maikop bulls. Bronze statuettes are also to be found in greater numbers in metal-bearing regions such as Sardinia and Luristan.

These figurines, which are the expression of local religions, are to be found in their hundreds in the Indus Valley, China and Japan. They are also present in America, particularly in the Olmec culture of Mexico and in the Chavín culture of Peru. Comparison of the various centres of rock art also reflects the need, across the continents, to express – through signs and animal and human figures – a whole mythical realm specific to each region. We have already mentioned the European, Scandinavian, Alpine and Iberian centres. The other great areas of rock art are difficult to situate in time. They have in common the fact of having been inhabited since the Neolithic period, from the sixth and fifth millennia BC onwards, since when paintings or engravings have been added until the beginning of our era and even sometimes up to the present day, among the Australian Aborigines, for example.

There are, however, reference points for some regions: in the Sahara, giraffes, rhinoceroses and elephants disappeared at the end of the last humid phase, around the third millennium BC. Thus we may be certain that depictions of these animals antedate desertification. On the other hand, the horses and their chariots appeared in the region towards the end of the second millennium BC. They were then found throughout the first millennium BC from the Moroccan Atlas, along the Atlantic coast of Mauritania to the interior mountains of the Sahara – Tassili des Ahaggar, Adrar des Iforas and Air.

In South Africa the rock art of the San peoples is also perhaps of Neolithic origin: thousands of paintings with the Cape eland as their dominant theme cover the rocks of Barne, Game Pass and Bragaliesberg. In Asia there are paintings and engravings representing harnessed horses and metal weapons – axes, halberds, lances and swords – of types that are recognizable as dating from the second and first millennia BC. These are often intermingled with pre-existent and therefore older animal motifs. This succession may be seen in central India, China, the Gobi Desert, and in the Lena and Karachstan sites. Some caution must be observed in interpreting these designs. It was in fact easy to make a systematic distinction between representations of hunting scenes and those of agricultural life, assuming that the first came before the second. It was then observed, however, that these two types of representation could be contemporaneous. Many figures in the recent phase of prehistory, among which the shaman can be discerned, are still being found in the Angara Valley.

In Australia, rock-art sites such as that of Dampier in the western part of the continent were inhabited for a very long time. Paintings of mythical animals, fish, kangaroos, lizards and phantom 'dream figures' are superimposed, and from prehistoric times onwards it is difficult to distinguish which works belong to any specific period in these sanctuaries, which are still regarded as sacred places by the Aborigines of today. A highly geometric style, common to Australia and Tasmania, might belong to the period that concerns us (Plate 16).

In America, also, the rock sites as they are excavated reveal thousands of signs and animal and human figures. Whole areas of painted rocks and cliffs may be found both in the north and in the south of the continent. The most ancient decorated surfaces date back more than 20,000 years, and a long prehistoric tradition was established. Archaeologists distinguish as being more recent than the hunters paintings of a geometrical style that date from the period with which we are concerned. This style includes many regional features, some characterized by the exclusive use of red, others using red, yellow and black. The geometrical figures became more numerous and the animal and human forms increasingly stylized. The Brazilian sites of Piaui date from 2000 BC. Others appeared in Patagonia at about the same time. Towards 1000 BC agricultural themes gradually predominated.

MONUMENTAL ARCHITECTURE AND ART PIECES, THE PRINCIPAL EXPRESSION OF GREAT STATES

Monumental architecture, of which we have examples from the early Neolithic period (such as that of Jericho) became the most original expression of certain civilizations, in particular those linked to great states.

Egypt

In Egypt, first of all, the famous pyramids, of which the architectural origins are still uncertain, certainly seem to have been developed from the mastaba. The pyramids of Giza and the necropolis of Memphis are sanctuary tombs where the living came to place their offerings for the eternal salvation of the sovereign. On the same site, around 2700 BC, the funerary function of the pyramid was separated from the function of worship, which was reserved for the temple, a separate building. The Great Pyramid of Giza, with its smooth sides, is the most celebrated of them all and covers an area of 45,000 m²; it was built by a team of about 10,000 men commanded by Cheops, the pharaoh who ordered the building of this symbol of eternity. The temple is linked to the pyramid by a causeway (Plate 17). The Sphinx, 20 m high, faces the visitor at the entrance to the necropolis. Another form of pyramid, the stepped pyramid, existed at Saqqara at a very early period – around 2800 BC. The funerary monuments of the third millennium BC were designed to glorify the power of the divine sovereign. The temples that are to be found scattered in large numbers along the Nile are grandiose reflections of the fervour of the people towards the gods and the divine pharaoh.

In Egypt, monumental sculpture was used to invoke power and immortality in the vicinity of royal tombs and temples. The Sphinx at Giza is adorned with the head and portrait of the pharaoh Chephren. Twenty-metre-high colossi stand guard at the entrance of the temple of Ramesses II. These monuments, designed for eternity, were built of hard stone: basalt, diorite and granite. Each figure has certain social realism. Chephren, a pharaoh carved in diorite, is shown in idealized form with his attribute, the falcon Horus, behind his head. Ranefer, the high priest of Memphis (around 2500 BC), is known thanks to a statue made of him, with an official facial portrait and the rigid pose characteristic of representations of the ruling class (Plate 18).

Later, during the Middle and New Kingdoms, the royal tombs were hidden in labyrinths hollowed out of the mountainside. It would appear that this was for reasons of security and to protect the offerings. The best known of these subterranean necropolises is the Valley of the Kings near Thebes. At that period the temple was built in a separate place. That of Khonsu in Karnak has an older part constructed with pylons, and a monumental gateway flanked by two massive towers and surrounded on each side by obelisks and statues. Inside there is a peristyle, a hypostyle hall and a sanctuary reserved for the priests. The sanctuary temple of Amon Re in Karnak, dating from the 19th dynasty, represents a summit of architectural achievement, with its pillars and its lotus-shaped, bell-shaped or palm-shaped capitals based on floral patterns. The function of each architectural part is emphasized by abundant decoration, that of the hypostyle hall, for example, evoking the creation of the world. Riverside and water plants and birds in bas-relief symbolize the crossing of the great marshes that separate the terrestrial world from the world of the hereafter. Hieroglyphic inscriptions record the names of the human and divine actors in this grandiose performance. Later, the temples also were to become subterranean, like that of Ramesses at Abu Simbel. Official and religious architecture in Egypt, built of stone blocks or hewn out of the rock in the hope that it would last forever, contrasts with the transitory architecture of the brick-built palaces and houses.

The priest Ka-aper, a contemporary of Ranefer's but lower in rank, is shown in a more realistic manner, sculptured in wood: the fleshy face is a magnificent portrait. This same period also produced the well-known seated scribe from Saqqara, in painted limestone, who holds his head in a submissive, attentive manner. His rolls of excess stomach fat attest to his largely inactive life-style (Plate 19). Art historians have often drawn attention to the rigid canon of Egyptian sculpture, which is characterized by a frontal presentation of the human figure, arms close to the body, one foot forward, with a fully rendered anatomy owing to the use of just a loincloth as clothing, and occasionally a kneeling oblatory position, such as that of the statue of Tuthmosis III (fifteenth century BC).

The two traditions found in both tombs and temples are that of relief sculpture and that of painting. The god Amon and Queen Hatshepsut (around 1500 BC) are represented in the temple of Amon in Karnak in negative relief, which is sunken and does not project above the level of the stone's surface. Another technique used was bas-relief, which brings out the figures in slight relief from a smooth, recessed background. Two outstanding examples are the god Horus in the temple of Seti I in Abydos (approximately 1300 BC) and the sister-in-law of Ramose, in the Theban tomb of the latter, who served as vizier under Amenhotep III and Amenhotep IV (1370 BC).

Painting was another technique used for the specific purpose of glorifying the pharaoh's power, providing a memorial to his achievements on earth, and invoking his pharaonic status in the after-life. Here again, certain aesthetic canons were observed: the men were painted red, and the women an ochre yellow; black was used for the hair and eyes, and green and blue were reserved for costumes, birds and plants. Human figures, animals and various other motifs were represented in profile and positioned in such a way as to be clearly understood. It is no doubt for this reason that no shadows are shown.

The size of the figures depicted varied according to their importance in the social structure. The pharaoh was often the biggest, but could in turn be towered over by a divinity. There are many well-known examples of this. The frieze at Maidum (2700–2600 BC), which depicts geese having one foot forward, neck stretched out and beak open, ready to snap at some morsel of food, demonstrates the painter's skill in rendering the birds' plumage and their movement. The mourning women in the fresco at Ramose's tomb in Thebes provide an example of funerary rites. The hunting scene with a boomerang painted on the tomb of Nakht in Thebes (around 2400 BC) and the other bird-hunting scene, at the tomb of Menna in Thebes (around 1420 BC), illustrate the mythically charged marshlands; a place half-way between the world of the living and that of the dead. The musicians of the tomb of Nebanom in Thebes (around 1370 BC) combine frontal and profile presentation in a lively composition wherein the artist was able to use the rigid conventions to the best advantage.

Hieroglyphics were carved, engraved and painted on most of the decorated walls, the sarcophagi, the mummy's bandages and on papyrus deposited in the tomb, which imparted a visual unity as well as profound religious meaning to these compositions.

One of the most highly developed forms of artistic expression in Egypt at the time of the pharaohs was the goldsmith's art. The treasure of Tutankhamen (1350 BC) comprises offerings made to the young pharaoh and placed in his tomb. The pharaoh's sarcophagus and famous death mask were made using the repoussé process with gold leaf. Cloisonnés made of strips of soldered gold leaf surround precious stones, lapis lazuli, turquoise and carnelian. Tutankhamen's bracelets and breast ornaments represent the cloisonné form at its height. Other pharaohs and dignitaries wore remarkable gold pieces, as well. Statuettes cast in gold were worn as amulets.

Owing to the extreme variety of pharaonic art, we can give only a brief overview of it here. Ivory statuettes in the Neolithic tradition, amulets in blue glaze, and many every-day objects such as make-up palettes, decorated spoons and musical instruments make direct or indirect reference to the religion of the god-king.

Mesopotamia

In Mesopotamia, there were many cities, including Ur, Eridu, Uruk and Larsa. The only building material was brick, used for walls, arches and vaults to support the superstructure. There were no monumental tombs as in Egypt. The temple and palace were juxtaposed, forming an architectural whole. In the religious precinct, the ziggurat, or stepped temple mound, was reminiscent of the Egyptian pyramid, except that it had no funerary function. The ziggurat of Ur dates from 2700 BC; that of Choga Zanbil, near Susa, was built in the thirteenth century BC, near the palace. The most significant site is that of Sargon II at Khorsabad, which dates from the seventh century BC and includes a vast palace, a royal sanctuary and a ziggurat with seven storeys linked by a ramp. At the end of the period with which we are concerned the palaces of the Assyrian kings were characterized by the military aspect of their walls. In 500 BC Herodotus described the ramparts of Echatana, in Persia, which was built several centuries earlier using enamelled bricks in bright colours – white, black, red, blue, orange, silver and gold. It has been said that the taste for juxtaposed colours came from the great tradition of making carpets and tapestries. It is known that these were hung on the walls and laid on the floors of the palace rooms. The design on the paving stone at the entrance to the palace of Sennacherib at Kuyunjik is doubtless an imitation on a hard surface of the shimmering effect of the carpet one would expect to find in that place.

In Mesopotamia, the various arts depict the feats of the monarchs in the hunting and battle grounds. The Stela of Vultures is a bas-relief of the victory of the ruler of Lagash in the twenty-ninth century BC. In another bas-relief in the palace of Nimrud, Ashurnasirpal (ninth century BC) is shown laying siege to a city. Two centuries later, and using the same technique, Ashurbanipal appears in a hunting scene at his palace at Nineveh.

The king and his dignitaries were also sculptured in the round in hieratic poses characterized by a frontal posture, wearing long sheath-like garments, their arms close to their bodies and hands joined. The material most often used was hard, black stone. The faces of the oldest statues – those from Ur, Mari and Lagash – are also the most realistic (Plate 20). The best known are of Gudea, the neo-Sumerian prince of Lagash, who appears in highly idealized form in his statues (Plate 10).

Bronze statues were also cast in the image of the sovereigns. The head of the Akkadian king believed to be Sargon or his grandson Naram-Sin is one of the most striking and dates back to 2500 BC.

Ivory was used for small sculptures, such as the statuette of a female singer discovered in the temple of Ishtar in Mari (2500 BC), or for facings, such as those found on the Standard of Ur, which depicts the victory of a 1st dynasty king (Plate 64).

One of the most original forms of Mesopotamian art was the making of cylinder seals, which were incised so that when applied to soft clay they would leave a design in relief. The design thus obtained featured the name of the owner associated with the king's protective divinities, which were often depicted in scenes such as the resurrection of the god of the plant kingdom, or a variety of processions. These miniature masterpieces are in many ways the key to our understanding of Mesopotamian religion.

At the opposite end of the spectrum from the miniature art of the cylinder seals, monumental art, fashioned of enamelled brick, ornaments the outer walls of the major cities. Fabulous animals – winged bulls with human heads and beards – decorate the palace of Sargon II in Khorsabad (eighth century BC). This is part of the mythology surrounding the king, designed to show him as a god-like hero.

The mediterranean world and Anatolia

Is there a link between the Mesopotamian palace and the Cretan palace of Knossos (1700–1500 BC)? Although the general plan of rooms arranged around a central courtyard is common to both types of palace, they are different in other ways. In Crete the basic building material is stone covered by painted stucco, and the sanctuary does not hold a place of central importance as in Mesopotamia. The great sculptured horns in Knossos nevertheless prove that religion played its part in the palace. The plan of the Cretan palace has some original features, such as suites of rooms forming apartments. The palace of Knossos had two upper storeys that are reached by staircases. The Cretan palaces at the height of their glory were not fortified, as their king depended on maritime power to protect both the territory and the palace.

A century later in Anatolia, with the Hittite city of Boghazköy, and in continental Greece with Tiryns, Mycenae and Pylos, great fortified palaces were built in stone, those in Greece enclosing a special building, however, called a megaron, consisting of a rectangular hall with a porch. Their princes were conquering heroes. Those of the Hittite countries attacked Babylon, Assyria and Egypt; those of Greece laid siege to Troy, on the Aegean coast of Anatolia, as we know from Homer's *Iliad*. These palaces were undoubtedly military in nature. Ramparts were raised, using large close-fitting stones in what is called Cyclopean masonry. The gate was reinforced by great monoliths. The Lion Gate at Mycenae is a typical example of the strength of this architecture. Near the citadel of Agamemnon there are a number of monumental beehive-shaped tombs with stone corbelling, dating from the fourteenth century BC. The tomb of Clytemnestra and the Treasury of Atrius are two of the best-known examples. Hittite sanctuaries such as that of Yazilikaya, hewn out of the mountainside, are closely linked to royal power, according to iconographic sources.

If we turn to Crete, the Aegean world and Greece, we first encounter the famous Cycladic idols in marble, most often in hieratic postures, but in somewhat more animated positions as well: the seated figure with a harp, and the *aulos* (double pipe) player. The originality and refinement of the civilization of the Minoan palaces that emerges from an architectural study is confirmed by its highly 'legible' and graceful fresco painting. Specialists have identified characteristics of Egyptian painting in the flat, clearly outlined areas of colour, but a scene like that of the bull-ring in Knossos renders both the strength of the animal in mid-charge and the skilful and precise movement of the acrobats. The position of the hands and legs, the curly hair and the use of empty background space to introduce floral detail make the compositions of the Cretan frescoes of the fifteenth century BC less austere than their Egyptian counterparts (Plate 49). Examples of this abound, such as 'The prince with lilies', who was

possibly a royal priest. Plants, flowers and birds are arranged in the background, surrounding the figures' profiles. 'La Parisienne' wears make-up, and her curly hair enhances the elegance of her silhouette. Excavations at the city of Thera, on the island of Santorini, have yielded the most extraordinary frescoes featuring human figures (wrestlers and fishermen) and scenes set against landscaped backgrounds (Plate 46). Baroque compositions with free curves decorate spherical shaped vessels such as the one depicting an octopus stretching out its tentacles (Late Minoan period). Terracotta sarcophagi of Hagia Triada serve as a support for painted funerary scenes. Cretan sculpture was sober by comparison, apart from bulls' horns carved in stone (symbols of prosperity in the palace of Knossos) and carved stone vessels and statuettes, like the one in ivory of a goddess brandishing gold snakes (Plate 50). Outstanding examples of the goldsmith's craft include a pendant representing two bees, a duck and bulls' heads ornamented with patterns of raised dots and double hatchets with handles.

Cretan innovations found their way to Greece, where they were at the origin of Mycenaean civilization, which is known for its rich tradition of gold work. The gold masks and crowns found in Mycenae immediately spring to mind (Plate 44), but there are also daggers with gold leaf-covered handles whose bronze blades are decorated with hunting scenes featuring human and animal silhouettes inlaid in gold leaf. The two Vaphio cups are masterpieces of Mycenaean gold work, which also produced rings with historiated settings, pendants and appliqué work. Carved and polished hard stone was used for seals with figurative motifs and vessels like the one found in Mycenae, which is decorated with a duck's head carved in rock crystal. Some of the frescoes discovered in 1970 in Mycenae rival in beauty the Minoan frescoes, but others, adorning the palaces of Tiryns and Pylos, lack the brilliance of the preceding period. The Pylos fresco depicts warriors wearing helmets crowned with boars' tusks, like those appearing in paintings in the museum at Heraklion. Small carved ivory pieces were produced in Greece with materials imported from Western Asia. This was a period of extensive trade flows throughout the eastern Mediterranean and the exchanging of valuable diplomatic gifts. There were also obvious links between Greece, Crete, Cyprus and Ugarit, on the Syrian coast. Mycenaean pottery was widely used, and most probably imitated locally. Trade relations fostered development of the arts in all these regions. The example of Cyprus is significant, with its historiated terracotta pottery – occasionally enamelled (for example, the Kition vase) – ivory sculptures, and statuettes in terracotta and bronze (the horned deity of Enkomi), which reveal it as a hub of creative endeavour. With the archaic Greek period (1100–700 BC), an extremely coherent vision of artistic expression – that of 'geometric' art – was born. Pottery became of extremely fine workmanship and was adorned with friezes of stylized warriors on foot or in chariots. Sculpture in cast or engraved bronze observed the same canon of slender and noble proportions, the Apollo in the Boston Museum being the classic model of the *kouros*.

The empires of the east

In the Indus Valley we find great brick-built cities at Mohenjo-daro that are reminiscent of Iranian sites such as Tepe Yahya. Despite a highly organized overall plan, which was made possible through strong political power, we have no traces of any monumental public building, palace or temple.

If we limit ourselves to indicating a few major centres for the development of original arts, we cannot neglect to mention the Indus Valley where new archaeological finds are constantly being made. The quality of three limestone sculptures (2400–2000 BC), comprising two male torsos from Mohenjo-daro and a dancing girl from Harappa, points to a grand tradition of masterpieces of which we are familiar with only an infinitely small percentage. Other small works reveal a partiality for precious rather than spectacular pieces. A series of steatite seals is carved in negative relief, with symbolic designs that parallel early writing in this region. Valuable stones – lapis lazuli from Afghanistan, turquoise from Iran and Tibet, and jade from Central Asia – were widely used in pendants and beads for necklaces.

In China, large cities were built in about 1300 BC under the Shang dynasty, such as the one at Anyang in Honan Province, on the Anyang Ho, a tributary of the Wei Ho, north of the Huanghe, on the site of present-day Zhengzhou. The houses were built of clay. The walls of the fortress were 18 m thick in some places and protected a temple palace situated in the centre of the city. The royal tombs were separate from the other tombs and were beginning to resemble the enormous tumuli of the subsequent era.

Under the Xia dynasty (2000–1500 BC) the art of Chinese bronze was to attain an apogee that would influence all of Chinese civilization. It appeared simultaneously with the introduction of writing, the traditional worship of ancestors, and the establishment of a social hierarchy ruled by a sovereign with absolute powers. In the treasure-laden tombs of the Shang dynasty (1500–1000 BC) ritual, often epigraphic, bronze vessels and musical instruments were found, along with bells and chimes in wood and bronze. Bronze vessels had a sacred as much as a social function. Although reserved initially for offerings made to the ancestors of the royal clan, they were later given as gifts and rewards. Under the Chou dynasty, the feudal nobility claimed for itself the exclusive privilege of owning bronze vessels, which were classified into three categories of use: for food, alcoholic beverages and water. Their concealed geometric and animal motifs and shapes were moulded with remarkable craftsmanship. The Chou also introduced zoomorphic bronze vessels. Another original feature of Chinese art was its use of jade for ornamentation and votive statuettes.

America

Monumental art reflects the emergence of great states throughout the world. Each of these has its own characteristics. The monument provides a spectacular and eternal reflection of the institution. In America, temples, pyramids and monumental sculptures were grouped together in religious and ceremonial places, constituting the focal point of what amounted to states formed of scattered villages. In Mexico the great cities Tikal, Teotihuacán and Monte Albán

were established around such focal points at the end of our period. Towards 1300 BC Xochipala, in the province of Guerrero, about 100 km from the Pacific coast, was undoubtedly a religious and political capital. In the region of Veracruz and Tabasco, the monumental art of the Olmecs spread throughout this area, which as yet had no main cities. The site of La Venta is particularly spectacular.

In Peru, at Chuquitanta, the ruins of a temple with stone-faced mud walls, at the top of an artificial hill, are said to be the traces, dating from 2000 to 1800 BC, of a religious centre similar to those of Mexico. At the beginning of the first millennium BC the impressive sanctuary of Chavín de Huántar, built at an altitude of 3,000 m, with sculptured and decorated stone blocks, also reflects a predominantly religious state organization. In the centre of the most ancient part of the sanctuary stands a monolith known as 'el Lanzón', a stone idol engraved to represent a half-human, half-feline creature.

The Olmec art of Mexico bears certain similarities to Chavín art in Peru. It appears that exchanges of traditions, which date back to ancient times, featuring shells, strombs and spondyls, decorated with curvilinear designs, form the basis of a certain stylistic community. In Chavín art, the motif of the human/feline figure is omnipresent, and it appears on the monolith erected in the middle of the oldest sanctuary. It is flanked by secondary figures such as jaguars, birds of prey, snakes and fish. These symbolic decors are on stone or ceramic bases. Whatever the origin of Chavín art, autochthonous or northern (Olmec), it is the result of a powerful cultural, and no doubt political and religious, unity.

This brief review of art and architecture from 3000 to 700 BC reveals that while aesthetic expression is universal, our knowledge of it is extremely partial. The variety of designs and forms makes itself felt at the regional – and even local – levels, and it is here that creativity lies: in the case of traditional art, it is the language of a community, but it can be used by a monarch of a large state to disseminate an institutional and religious message. The nature of this ideal image of the vitality of the state, its iconography and the media specific to it form the very essence of its cultural identity.

BIBLIOGRAPHY

Le grand atlas de l'archéologie. 1985. Paris, Encyclopaedia Universalis.

Le grand atlas de l'art. 1993. Paris, Encyclopaedia Universalis, 2 vols.

L'univers des formes. Collection founded by André Malraux and Gallimard. Paris. Several volumes consulted: La Préhistoire; Sumer; Assur; les Hittites; Perse; Parthes et Sassamides; les Phéniciens; le Temps des Pyramides; L'Empire des Conquérants; l'Egypte du Crépuscule; Naissance de l'art grec; Grèce archaïque; le Mexique des origines aux Aztèques; les Andes de la Préhistoire aux Incas; l'Océanie.

The Pelican History of Art. Several volumes consulted: Prehistoric Art in Europe; The Arts in Prehistoric Greece; The Art and Architecture of Ancient America; The Art and Architecture of Ancient Egypt; The Art and Architecture of Ancient Orient; The Art and Architecture of China.

9.2.3

SONG, MUSIC AND DANCE

Jean-Pierre Mohen

In the most ancient cosmogonies, sounds and rhythms are part of the primal universe. For the Veda, 'the world burst forth like a cry' in order to exist. The Greek *logos* and the 'And God said' in the Book of Genesis proclaim the pre-eminence of the divine word, which is repeated and praised in hymns.

As far as may be ascertained, song was linked to oral tradition in that most declamations were chanted and often accompanied by musical instruments, as were other community activities such as dancing, funerals, and religious feasts in general.

The scanty information available in this field leaves many questions unanswered, but a few major discoveries confirm that music was an important feature of life at the earliest royal courts. A richly decorated harp is one of the most prestigious funerary offerings found in the tombs at Ur.

Quite a lot is known about the place of music in ancient Egypt. Tomb paintings show musicians playing various instruments (Plate 21); the goddess Hathor shakes sistra while a young girl holds a lute; some men blow pipes or trumpets while others pluck harps; dancers sway to the sound of clappers and rattles; priests beat drums and tambourines during ceremonies; a lover pays court to his beloved to the sound of pan-pipes, and even monkeys are shown with a double oboe-like instrument and a lyre. A few of these instruments have been found in tombs and are now on display in our museums, but about the music itself we know nothing at all.

Only a few hints may be gleaned from the abundant silent vestiges of this period in other regions. Two of the most famous of the white marble Cycladic sculptures, from Keros (Greece), portray a man playing an *aulos* or double pipe and another playing a harp (Plate 37). A fresco in the Mycenaean palace at Pylos shows a woman playing a lyre, and some fragments of ivory are believed to have come from an instrument of this type. A decorated sarcophagus from Hagia Triada in Crete shows us a scene of sacrifice during the Minoan period with a female figure playing a lyre and a male a double pipe. A little later, in Greece, we find a few interesting clues about musical transcription. In the sixth century BC, Pythagoras drew a parallel between musical notation and mathematics.

In Stockholm, research in palaeomusicology has shown the existence, between 3000 and 700 BC in temperate northern Europe, of a series of traditional percussion instruments (drums, lithophones, and so on), wind instruments (flutes, bird calls, and so on) and humming instruments (bull-roarers) made of bone, stone or ceramic. Metal, particularly bronze, has sonorous qualities which were turned to account in instruments for shaking and in wind instruments.

The development of a liking for ostentatious jingling sounds was linked to the emergence of a horse-riding aristocracy. It seems that the clinking pendants (Rattle pendant) of the Atlantic regions were attached to horses' breastplates. The 'tintinnabula' of La Ferté-Hauterive (Allier) and Vaudrevanges (Sarre) are large hollowed-out discs about 30 cm long which would clink against two disc-shaped mobile pendants. They were also probably parts of harness fittings. Decorated bronze tubes, with jingling rings attached, are thought to have played the same role. Such instruments have been found in France in Autun, Mâcon and Boissy-aux-Cailles, near Paris.

Other sound instruments seem to have been associated more with religious ceremonies. It has been suggested that small, 10 cm bells and rattles found in Irish sites like Dooresheath were linked to the cult of the bull. Metal horns or trumpets from Ireland and Britain consist of a bent cone up to 1 m long. Some of them, with a lateral mouthpiece, produce a single note (between D sharp and G). The others, with an axial mouthpiece, produce, in addition to the single notes, a number of harmonics, such as fifths, sevenths, octaves or tenths. The development of this kind of instrument undoubtedly derived from the use of the horns of animals for musical purposes, suggesting again the cult of the bull.

The lurs found in Scandinavia, Denmark and north Germany are exceptional pieces. Made of three or four parts, cast by the *cire perdue* method and fitted together, they have a long conical bore in a bent S-shape. The bell of the horn is in the shape of a disc, decorated with small embossments or engraved circles. The near end consists of the mouthpiece. Pendants attached by a ring to the main part of the instrument jingle against one another. Specialists assert that in theory the lur can produce up to twenty-two tones within a range of four octaves. In practice, the player confines himself to the fundamental note and its harmonics over three octaves. Lurs are found in marshes in symmetrically curved pairs. The fact that they were left in areas where offerings were made to the water gods suggests that they were used during ceremonies. Lurs are also known through rock art where they are shown being played in Kalliby, in the Swedish province of Bohuslän, or in the context of funerary or 'sacrificial' scenes on one of the decorated tombstones of Kivik, in Swedish Scania.

Sistra, which are rarer, seem identical to those of Egypt, as attested by the one found in the necropolis of Hochborn, in Rhine-Hesse. It is 35 cm long, in the shape of a two-pronged fork with a crossbar that was probably hung with pendants.

The remains of a nine-piped pan-pipe were found in a tomb in the necropolis of Przeczyce, in Poland, calling to mind engravings from the area north of the Adriatic, dating from the Early Iron Age. Lastly, the lyre, known in western Asia since the third millennium BC, is depicted on a Spanish stele from Valpamas in Extremadura and seems to have had fourteen strings strung between two symmetrical uprights.

In China, bronze bells were the forerunners of a whole series of metal percussion instruments, drums and gongs which spread throughout eastern Asia. In 1976, the discovery was made in the tomb of Fu Hao, one of the wives of the sovereign Wu Ding, at Anyang in Honan province (late fourteenth-early thirteenth century BC), of five bells of decreasing size, which confirmed the existence of a pentatonic system. As early as the Shang dynasty, terracotta whistles, resembling ocarinas, were producing sounds on a heptatonic scale which is subsequently referred to in written sources.

For the Americas and other parts of the world information is limited, but there is no reason to believe that music, from bird calls for hunting to music as a form of instrumental expression, was unknown in those regions.

It is difficult to consider dance outside the context of music, which in most cases provides an accompaniment to rhythmical movements of the body. Yet the iconographic sources sometimes show female or male dancers without accompanying musical instruments. In fact these may be no more than little bells tied to their feet, and castanets or tambourines in their hands. Dancing must be considered as an art in its own right.

Certain figures depicted in rock art in, for example, the Spanish Levant, Tassili and South Africa seem to be dancing. A line of armed warriors appears to be leaping in the Cueva Remigia (Spain), while naked women make swaying movements on a rock in Upper Mertoutek, in Ahaggar. Further information is available in certain countries such as Egypt. The terracotta statuettes known as the 'dancing women' with their arms raised above their heads from the late prehistoric era (Nagada period) remain shrouded in mystery, but subsequent representations of dancing, from the beginning of the third millennium BC, point to a specific religious context.

Thus, in Tutankhamen's time (fourteenth century BC), during the celebration of *opet*, Amon, the national god, is shown sailing to the temple of Luxor to visit his 'southern harem', preceded by a dancer playing the tambourine to drive away evil spirits. In the procession that follows, Nubian dancers clad in animal skins and banging on their tambourines move to the rhythm of the darabukka, a terracotta drum with a stretched membrane. On the quay, the god is welcomed by a group of female dancers bowing and stepping backwards in time to the sistrum. This was the *keby* dance or 'lively dance', depicted here for the first time.

Ritual dances were performed on other occasions. There was, for instance, the Feast of the Valley when Amon came to the left bank to visit Hathor, the goddess of the west. In his honour, twelve female dancers arching backwards formed a great bridge with their bodies. The feast of the god Minh celebrated fertility and fecundity with frenzied whirling. Before the pharaoh, priests are shown moving forward to

the sound of the tambourine, hands clasped against their chests, while female dancers perform cartwheels and others genuflect. For the dead, dance symbolized vitality and survival. At the entrance to the tomb, Mouou priests dance with arched arms while the list of offerings is read out.

Among the Assyrians, the tradition of the armed dance continued over a long period. Dancers wore masks and lion skins. A number of figures performed precise choreographic routines with one knee on the ground. In all the earliest Assyrian and Hebrew written sources, allusion is made to dances in a line, in a ring and following a circling pattern. One of these, around the Golden Calf was considered dangerous by Moses because of the trance state that it induced, which distanced the dancer from Yahweh. But David expressed his religious fervour by twirling and leaping with all his might before the Ark of the Covenant.

Cretans modelled statuettes of women forming a circle around a female figure playing a lyre, and three female worshippers with arms outstretched dancing around a goddess are engraved on the bezel of a ring found at Isopata. Cretan women danced bare-breasted, clad in a long skirt from the hips down. Men danced in arms before the gods as they would at a later date in Greece before Zeus and Artemis. Associated with each god and each event of whatever importance were one or more dances. For Homer, even a ball game was a dance and Nausicaä, when surprised by Ulysses, was leading the 'chorus' of this sportive dance. Greek thinking, from Pythagoras to Plato, saw order and rhythm as the principles governing the world. The god of the life force, Dionysus, who came from the East, inspired and drunk, led a procession of disorderly, writhing and dancing Bacchantes and Satyrs, who were celebrating a form of worship through dance known as the 'dithyramb'.

Less is known about the dances of other regions in this period. It is difficult to understand the precise attitudes of the dancing statuettes and the figures carved on seals from the Indus Valley. In China, a vase from the third millennium BC, found at Shanju-Jiazhai in the province of Quigkai, is decorated on the inside with women dancing in a ring but, here again, we can only deplore the scantiness of our documentary evidence in a part of the world where terpsichorean expression was so highly developed as far back as the closing centuries BC. Our present ignorance precludes any discussion of dance in the rest of the world.

BIBLIOGRAPHY

Archaeologia Musicalis, No. 1, 1987–98, Celle.

BOURCIER, P. 1989. *Danser devant les dieux. La recherche en danse.* Paris.

COLES, S. 1973. Irish Bronze Age Horns and their Relations with Northern Europe, *Proc. prehist. Soc.*, Cambridge, Vol. 39, pp. 326–56.

L'HELGOUACH, J. 1989. La musique préhistorique. In: MOHEN, J. P. (ed.)., *Le temps de la Préhistoire*. Paris. Vol. 2, pp. 254–6.

ZIEGLER, C. 1979. *Les instruments de musique égyptiens au Musée du Louvre*. Réunion des musées nationaux. Paris.

C

REGIONAL SECTION

EDITOR'S NOTE

The most striking feature of the period covered by Volume II is the transition from prehistoric to historical times in regions whose civilizations helped to shape the development of humanity. In the thematic section, we have assessed the importance of writing; this is one of several criteria for defining what is meant by historical times, a distinguishing feature of which is the desire to keep a written record of economic activities, reflections on ethics and the law, epic tales and divine injunctions. As a result we are now able to make use of written sources which, though incomplete because not all have been preserved, are of rich historical interest. We have chosen to abide by the principle of distinguishing between the regions where writing was known, which happen to correspond to the major states, and regions where it had not yet made its appearance. Equal treatment has been given to the latter, which have all too often been overlooked but have been rediscovered thanks to the methods of archaeology and anthropology. They provide examples of brilliant material cultures that developed into or strongly influenced historical civilizations.

I Regions for which written sources are available

10

AFRICA

10.1
THE NILE VALLEY
(3000–1780 BC)

Christiane Ziegler

EGYPT (MAP 7)

In a natural setting, where climatic variations eventually led to the desertification of most of the country, was born a civilization whose existence was tied to the pattern of the rising and falling water-levels: each summer the floodwaters from the high Ethiopian plateaus brought down the black, fertile silt on which agricultural prosperity depended. Yet the picture of a primitive valley with luxuriant vegetation is somewhat altered by recent geomorphological studies and the prospecting of desert areas. Vast deserts stretch as far as the eye can see: to the east, the high plateaus of Arabia and Sinai, whose black schists and purple granites are cleft by deep valleys and watered irregularly; to the west, the pale plateau of the Libyan desert with its dunes and rocky wastes, whose aridity is relieved by a few oases, which enable the population to move around the country. This inhospitable landscape, a natural protection from neighbouring invasions, also conceals mineral wealth. The building stones for timeless architecture are to be found here: fine limestone from Tura, pale sandstone from Silsile, veined alabaster from Hatnub and pink granite from Aswan. These regions are full of metals – gold, copper, galena, malachite – and semi-precious stones – turquoise, jasper and cornelian. Yet this wealth never isolated Egypt from other countries. On the contrary, as part of the desert belt which crosses Africa from the Red Sea to the Atlantic, Egypt soon became a crossroads of cultures. There were many points of contact: the eastern desert and Sinai were passages to the Levant and Mesopotamia with their sophisticated civilizations; the western desert with the Sahara and its as yet little-known tribes, and lastly the Nile, which linked the Mediterranean world to Nubia and formed a corridor to Equatorial Africa.

The prelude to history (c. 3300–3100 BC)

Pharaonic society, regulated by the Nile, was descended from the Naqada culture of the fourth millennium BC, from which it inherited social and ideological structures. Naqada III witnessed the rapid changes which heralded pharaonic Egypt. Three of these are of considerable importance: urbanization; the establishment of a hierarchical society with the emergence of sovereigns who already bore the attributes of the pharaoh; and the adoption of a single culture – that of southern Egypt – for the whole area stretching from the Mediterranean to south of the First Cataract. The first great urban centres, some fortified, others not, appeared in southern Egypt, the best-known being at Abydos, Ombos (Naqada), Coptos, Elkab and Hierakonpolis.

The Hierakonpolis site shows the most ancient traces of monumental architecture in dried mudbrick, whether religious in origin such as the platform of the archaic temple, or funerary, in the case of the great tombs; one of these measures 6.5 m by 3.5 m and is attributed to the 'Scorpion king'. The stepped architecture which appeared around this period seems to have come from the East: an ivory casket found in the necropolis of Minshat Abu Omar, in the eastern Delta, shows an outstanding example of this style. All along the Nile Valley there are smaller tombs whose richness distinguishes them from the other necropolises.

This rise of an élite, which is reflected in an accumulation of wealth, reached a peak with the necropolis of Abydos, where recent excavations have identified the tombs of kings whose names are inscribed within the image of a royal palace, the *serekh*, surmounted by a falcon.

In Naqada III, the first royal names emerge from anonymity to form what is now termed the 'O dynasty'. This marks Egypt's entry into history. Attested by very brief inscriptions, the kings' power stretched through the region of Memphis to Tura, Tarkhan, Heluan, Abu Roach, and as far as the Second Cataract. Their names, incised or painted on pottery, are surmounted by the falcon Horus, the first symbol of royalty.

Did these kings really reign over a politically unified Egypt? This point is still open to debate. The later texts provide some indications of the royal succession. The 'Turin canon' and the 'Annals of Manetho' make several references to Menes as the first pharaoh; but between the mythical reign of the gods and the reign of Menes there were a number of kings designated by a collective name – the 'Followers of Horus'. The series of kings who bore the name of Horus in Upper and Lower Egypt and whose tombs have been recently identified at Abydos give, in succession, Ka, Narmer, Aha; some names are incorporated in scenes illustrating the concept of triumph, sculpted on ceremonial objects, such as the mace of the 'Scorpion king', and the mace and pallet of Narmer. Concordances between the name of Horus of Aha, under whose reign work began on the great cemetery of Saqqara, and that of Men-Menes, designate him as the most

likely candidate to have been first king of this historic period. It seems clearly established that before him Narmer reigned over a unified Egypt, as did the 'Scorpion king'. However belligerent and violent the representations of the acts leading to unification may have been – they often refer to 'smiting Lower Egypt' – they are more the expression of a concept, that of pharaonic power, than of a historical reality. The cultural unity of the Nile Valley was by then already well established.

The Thinite period (c. 3100–2700 BC)

The first two dynasties which formed the period known as 'Thinite' lasted for more than 400 years. During this ancient period, civilization organized itself around a single monarch, the pharaoh, the keystone of an ideological system which became firmly established. The art of writing spread widely, while monumental, brick-built architecture, the traces of which are mainly funerary, developed in the great cities: in the south, the ancient city of Abydos; and Memphis which had been constructed at the apex of the Delta, doubtless to control the newly integrated regions. Besides inscriptions, these tombs yield a wealth of information about a prosperous, centralized state, with an efficient and outward-looking system of administration.

The birth of the pharaonic state

There are virtually no surviving records of the pharaohs of the 1st dynasty, apart from their names inscribed on tablets, cylinders, seals and funeral slabs, but the Palermo Stone, a fragment of the royal annals, provides brief indications of events during this period. The best-known reigns are those of Djer, Den and Semerkhet, whose tombs figure among the many necropolises of Abydos. We know something of their economic activity through the census and the measurement of the Nile floods; we follow the process of the political unification of Upper and Lower Egypt, the assertion of the dual nature of royalty, the celebration of ritual feasts and the victorious expeditions outside the Nile Valley against Asians, Nubians and Libyans. We have much less information on the 2nd dynasty, which apparently followed on without a break. Very few royal tombs have been discovered, and only the reign of Nineter is well documented by the Palermo Stone. The decorated monuments of Khasekhem, most of which were discovered at the Hierakonpolis site, depict essentially war-like exploits; perhaps Khasekhem may be identified with Khasekhemui, who had the largest tomb in the royal cemetery of Abydos and who was the last of the Thinites.

Despite political conflicts, the details of which have not come down to us, the main features of the pharaonic institution were stabilized by this time. The king – or pharaoh (from the Egyptian per-aâ, denoting the palace) – held supreme power at the hub of the world. The nature of his power was reflected in his titulary, which, at the end of the period, was composed of three names as compared with five during the classical period: the name of Horus, the falcon-divinity spreading its wings over the heavenly vault, which made the pharaoh the earthly heir to the gods; the name of the king of Upper and Lower Egypt, representing his sovereignty over the whole country; and lastly the name of the 'two goddesses', the vulture and the cobra. Only the reigning pharaoh was Horus; when he died, the continuing existence of the

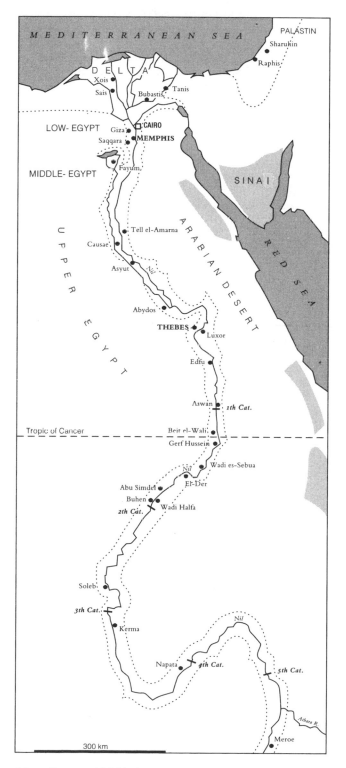

Map 7 Egypt and Nubia (3000–700 BC)

pharaonic institution was assured only by the advent of a new Horus, chosen from among his sons or his male relations. The royal attributes, which were to survive without a break for 3,000 years, were inherited from the predynastic period and in some cases became merged with those of the gods. Like the latter, the king wears an animal's tail attached behind his loincloth (*chendjit*), and holds a sceptre and a flail. The red crown of Lower Egypt and the white crown of Upper Egypt were combined to form a double crown, the *pschent* – in Egyptian 'the two powers' – symbolizing his dual sovereignty. Already the image of the *nemes* appears, a head-dress in front of which is affixed the *ureus*, the sacred cobra which protected the king. The pharaoh, bearing a mace and a dagger, is depicted as a warlord.

Such a sovereign left his mark on the whole of society. Imbued with divine royalty, he was responsible for the kingdom, and he governed by enforcing universal laws. All events were recorded, not yearly or by reign as in later periods, but by reference to an established list of the achievements of each pharaoh: the year in which a shrine or a divine statue was erected, the year in which a royal ritual was performed, the biannual census, the year marking a victorious expedition, and so forth. Whether in the economic or the religious spheres, the state institutions functioned only through delegates who had been invested with a part of the royal power. There were many of these high officials, who were well organized in a number of institutions employing countless scribes: the vizier, whose title is already attested, did not seem to have as much power as he did later, from the 4th dynasty onwards. He was still part of the closed circle of royal counsellors whose responsibility remains obscure: 'controller of the two thrones', 'he who stands at the king's head', 'secretary'. The royal chancelleries of Upper and Lower Egypt, each with a chancellor at its head, were responsible for the census, the organization of irrigation and the cadastre, tax-collection and the redistribution of consumer goods to the civil service and the temples. This transfer was effected by the grain officials in the granary administration. The treasury took charge of manufactured products. The royal estate produced oil and wine. In the provinces, royal power was represented by authorities such as the 'magnate of the Tens of Upper Egypt' or the 'governor of Buto and Nekhen'. This degree of organization could not have been achieved without the use of a new means of communication: writing.

The advent of hieroglyphs

The first written records that have come down to us may be dated to around 3200 BC. They appear on large historiated palettes which replaced the earlier ivory tablets and are contemporary with the first pharaohs: the most famous of these, the 'Bull Palette', bears the name of Narmer (Plate 22).

Analysis of the seventy private stelae in the reign of Djer reveals the presence of twenty-one uniliteral phonograms out of the thirty known in Egypt, as well as a number of other phonograms which resemble ideograms and determinatives. It may therefore be legitimately concluded that Egypt moved in a short space of time from a system based on images to the use of signs corresponding to sounds.

Was this system of writing invented by one person? This hypothesis was recently defended by the American Egyptologist H. G. Fischer. It may be, as the French philologist P. Vernus suggests, that the creation and rapid development

of hieroglyphs was encouraged by the early kings as an instrument of management and control, and also as a means of expressing and presenting royal and religious ideology.

The very fine 'Serpent king' stela from Abydos, as well as the many private stelae, are not only marks of property but also religious monuments and, in the first case, the expression of royal power. From this period onwards, the dual role of writing, both functional and formal, becomes apparent.

Yet do the signs that we observe really constitute a form of writing? Composed of isolated or juxtaposed words, a succession of titles and proper names, this 'proto-writing' does not yet have any linguistic syntax.

The possibility that other types of texts may have existed, which have since vanished because they were written on perishable materials, nevertheless leads us to revise our ideas to some extent. At Saqqara, the tomb of Hemaka, a contemporary of King Den, yielded two blank papyrus scrolls. With this medium, which was essential for a highly evolved form of writing, the Thinite period therefore had the means of establishing archives and recording events of major importance, such as those related on the Palermo Stone. Perhaps traditional scientific and religious texts also existed but, according to our present knowledge, it was only at the beginning of the 4th dynasty, when autobiographical texts appeared, that the hieroglyphic system became established as a properly structured means of recording speech.

The first examples of pharaonic art

One of the most important innovations of the period was the spread of monumental art. Works such as the Serpent king stela (Louvre) have preserved for us the image of vanished palaces. Their dried mudbrick façade is reminiscent of a fortified enclosure with defensive towers; the walls with their high doors are composed of a series of 'stepped' sections which alternately jut out or are set back, surmounted by a cornice. At the same period, similar stepped walls were to be found in Mesopotamia.

At the beginning of the third millennium BC, as often in Egypt, we know more about the realm of the dead than that of the living. At the end of the nineteenth century, the French archaeologist E. Amélineau discovered at the Abydos site a series of tombs with stelae bearing the names of the kings of the 1st dynasty. Other excavations then revealed the existence of some thirty other necropolises, the largest being situated on the plateau of Saqqara. It was there that the British archaeologists discovered monuments so imposing that they thought they had found the genuine royal tombs of the 1st dynasty, those of Abydos being only false sepulchres (cenotaphs).

The tombs of Saqqara still have the quadrilinear brick slab which surmounted them and traces of a surrounding enclosure. They are imposing in size (from 35 to over 50 m long by about 20 m wide) and their bench-like form explains the origin of the term 'mastaba', by which the Egyptologists designated them (from the Arabic *mastaba*, 'bench'). They are decorated with stepped façades which still bear traces of plaster painted to look like coloured reeds. In the tomb attributed to King Ka, a funerary chapel was identified which presaged the temples adjacent to the pyramids.

It was not before the end of the Thinite period that the first examples of dressed stones built up in regular patterns were found in the tomb of King Khasekhem. It is probable that a desire to economize on costly materials led to the development of new techniques; arched, dried-brick vaults and corbelled vaults appeared in the more modest tombs of El Amra and Tura.

Although they are mainly famous for their architectural remains, the Thinite necropolises also revealed statues, mostly small ivories like that of the 'Leaning king' (British Museum), as well as a number of female statuettes.

Two statues of King Khasekhem (one in limestone, the other in schist in the Cairo Museum) stand out among these stone works of art. Seated on a square throne, wearing a ceremonial garment and the crown of Upper Egypt, the king already has all the austere forward-facing dignity typical of Egyptian statuary.

The first royal annals mention copper statues. The royal stelae of Abydos, tall slabs with a curved top, bear the name of the sovereign inscribed within the walls of a palace. It is still unclear whether these were originally set up in pairs at the entrance to the funeral monument: the finest of these, that of the Serpent king, seems to have been found inside the tomb. The name of the king, accompanied by the depiction of a rising cobra, is surmounted by the falcon Horus, protector of royalty. The other royal stelae are very unequal in craftsmanship. Those belonging to private individuals are smaller and take a different form: they may be curved stones or rectangular slabs bearing the name and title of the deceased, or four-cornered panels depicting the funeral repast, with indications as to the dishes served. The decorative reliefs from the same period show considerable differences: they range from a plain, chiselled out silhouette, to finely carved reliefs. The furniture from the funerary stores shows greater refinement: earthenware crockery or precious dishes in alabaster, crystal or diorite sometimes decorated with gold; in the Thinite tombs, hundreds of bowls containing offerings were discovered. Among the treasures found in the tomb of the minister Hemaka, steatite disks inlaid with alabaster bear images of animals pursuing one another. Many pieces are of carved ivory: pieces for games sets, in the shape of caskets, marbles and lions, items of toiletry or supports for furniture in the form of bulls' feet. The gazelles of Naga el-Deir and the turquoise, amethyst and gold bracelets found in the tomb of Djer testify to the craftsmanship of the jewellers of the time and are forerunners of the precious gold cockleshells found in the tomb of Sekhemkhet (3rd dynasty).

The old kingdom: 3rd to 6th dynasties (*c.* 2700–2200 BC)

Although historians usually place the beginning of the Old Kingdom, which succeeded the Early Dynastic period, at around 2700 BC, the transition from one to the other took place without any major upheaval. Family links united the first king of the 3rd dynasty with the last Thinite king, Khasekhemui. This was a period of internal stability and peace.

Religion and politics

Many of the kings of the Old Kingdom bore names well known to us: Djoser, founder of the 3rd dynasty, who erected the first pyramid; under the 4th dynasty, Snefru, whose wife Hetepheres had a brief moment of glory at the beginning of this century with the discovery of her inviolate tomb; then Cheops, Chephren and Mycerinus, who chose the plateau of Giza to erect one of the seven wonders of the world; finally, Unas, the last king of the 5th dynasty, whose tomb contained the most ancient version of the Pyramid Texts. Other, less well-known kings, such as Userkaf, Sahure or Neferirkare, raised temples dedicated to the sun in the 5th dynasty.

This period has left documents which enable us to build up a clearer picture of the pharaoh. We have seen how, from the start, the king of Egypt was imbued with divine power. The Old Kingdom enriched this concept through epithets – the king was known as 'god' or 'perfect god' – or through new additions to his title: among royal names, that of the 'son of Re', the sun-god, appears during the 4th dynasty. This divinity is also reflected in the royal court: thus the royal spouse is described as 'she who sees Horus and Seth' and there are also references to a 'chancellor of god'.

From 2350 BC, the Pyramid Texts appeared, inscribed upon walls. These, the most ancient religious texts known to history, include magic formulae, hymns, rituals and legends juxtaposed in no apparent order. Preserved from the reign of Unas onwards, they assert the supremacy of the deceased king as a deity, after his admission to another world of which there are many different depictions. Although the myth of Osiris and his son Horus predominates, the texts also identify the king with Re and evoke a cosmic after-life in heaven.

Throughout the period, the divine king, established in his capital Memphis at the apex of the Delta, governed a unified country which was regarded as the centre of the universe. Egypt did not, however, become inward-looking. Recent excavations at Balat show that the oasis of Dakhla, in the western desert, was part of the kingdom. In the south, Lower Nubia was rigorously controlled and contacts with Africa were established as far as Dongola. To the east, Byblos and the Lebanese coast remained important trading partners. The type of government and court culture established during the Old Kingdom reached a peak of effectiveness and achievement from the 3rd dynasty onwards. This system was to function for more than 500 years.

The art of measurement

Scribes, officials and educated people now possessed instruments whose existence followed logically from the advent of writing. The monuments and texts of the Old Kingdom reveal a grasp of figures and concepts which permitted the development of the art of measurement.

Arithmetic and geometry seem to have developed mainly from practical necessity: stocktaking of raw materials, the annual measurement of the Nile floods, the construction of buildings and the establishment of a cadastre as a basis for taxation. The decorated palettes of the Naqada III period already included the writing of certain figures, whole numbers which were to remain in use throughout pharaonic civilization. Under the Old Kingdom, this system appears to have developed all its potential. It was a system which was both decimal and additive: a vertical line was used for the units, and special signs for the different powers of 10, from 100 to 1 million. When noting a figure, the higher values were inscribed before the lower values, and in indicating numbers between 1 and 10, the vertical line was repeated as many times as necessary; the same applies to the writing of the various other powers of 10. This system makes addition and subtraction easy. In order to multiply by 10, one has merely to replace the figure by the sign which indicates its tenfold increase. The other multiplications were presented as a series of duplications, and division was achieved by the opposite process. It seems that the calculation of area and volume was facilitated by the empirical knowledge of the squares and square roots of certain numbers. As for fractions, which were essential for the proportional distribution of goods, the Egyptians' knowledge was limited. They used only fractions whose numerator was equal to one figure, breaking down complex fractions into a sum of fractions with different denominators.

When applied to simple figures, surveyors' formulae made it possible to calculate the surface area of a trapezium and to discover the relationship between the area of a triangle and that of a rectangle. These formulae, which were obviously known at the time when the pyramids were built, are collected together in the Middle Kingdom papyri. An architect's sketch discovered inside Djoser's pyramid and dating probably from the 3rd dynasty defines a curve, which seems to correspond to the roof of a chapel, in terms of equidistant vertical lines, accompanied by marks indicating their length. Although the horizontal line is not drawn in, the system seems to be based on definition by co-ordinates. The most spectacular discovery by the Egyptians is undoubtedly that of the relationship between the diameter of a circle and its area, with an estimation of the value of *pi* which is not far from its true value: 3.16. Probably the calculation of certain volumes, which we know from later papyri, was dictated by the characteristic features of the architecture of the Old Kingdom: the pyramid, the frustum of the pyramid and the cylinder.

Although the Egyptian numerical system was decimal, the system of units of length, surface or weight was mixed. These units varied from one region or one period to another and sometimes we still do not know their value. From the Old Kingdom onwards, one of the most frequently used units of measurement was the royal cubit, 52.3 cm long. This was subdivided into twenty-eight fingers of 1.86 cm grouped together into a palm of four fingers or digits, each measuring 7.47 cm. There were also fractions of fingers ranging from half a finger to one-sixteenth of a finger. It was with this unit that the documents of the period measured items that ranged from the height of the Nile flood and that of the divine statues to the perimeter of a garden. The most ancient papyri known today, the Abusir Papyri, which came from the funerary temple of Neferirkare, mainly provide vast quantities of accounts: daily accounts; monthly accounts; accounts for offerings; meat rations; sacks of grain or fabrics; recapitulatory accounts; employees' attendance registers, and so on. The figures are noted on lines corresponding to the days of the month, separated by red lines into three decades, for the measurement of time was also an essential feature of pharaonic society.

The Egyptians do not seem to have been outstanding astronomers, although the orientation of their monuments reflects a very precise observation of certain constellations, such as the Great Bear: the sides of the pyramid of Giza are in fact fairly strictly aligned with the four points of the compass, with a maximum of precision for the pyramid of Cheops, which shows an error of 5'30" for the east side and 1'57" for the south side; to obtain such a result it may be assumed that the sighting was determined by the 'bisecting line of the angle of the directions of the rising or setting of a circumpolar star on an artificial horizon'. Although the Egyptians first used a calendar based on the phases of the moon, in the predynastic period the year was divided into 365 days, distributed into three seasons of four months. Each month contained 30 days, 5 additional days, known as epagomenal days,

being added at the end of the year. The seasons reflect the natural cycle and that of the Nile on which it depended: they are known as *akhet*, 'flood', *peret*, 'germination' and *chemu*, 'harvest'. It seems that when the Egyptian calendar was created, the first day of the year corresponded to two natural phenomena, which occurred almost simultaneously in the region of Memphis around 19 July in our calendar: the annual flooding of the Nile and the reappearance on the horizon of the star Sirius. Theoretically the rise of Sirius was supposed to take place on 'the first day of the first month of the season of the flood'. Unfortunately, as there were no leap years, every four years the calendar fell one day behind, thereby creating an increasing discrepancy. By the end of the Old Kingdom, this discrepancy amounted to about five months, and the date expressed in seasons, months and days of the civil calendar no longer bore any relation to the natural cycle. In fact it was only after 1,460 years (365×4) that the beginning of the year again fell on 19 July. References to the reappearance of Sirius are highly important in establishing Egyptian chronology. They are valuable reference points around which it is possible to situate the successive dynasties. Unfortunately, these references are very rare: five for the whole of Egyptian history.

From the Thinite period onwards, each new king marked the starting-point of a new chronology. In the Old Kingdom, dates were first fixed in relation to the census, carried out every two years by the pharaoh. At the end of the period a dating system based on the year of the king's reign was adopted and retained until the end of the pharaonic period.

The spread of stone-built architecture: the reign of Djoser

The reign of Djoser, the first pharaoh of the 3rd dynasty, marked the beginning of the era of stone monuments, when the royal tomb began to take on a form which distinguished it from the private sepulchre: the pyramid, with its accompanying buildings designed to assist the king in the after-life.

It was on the plateau of Saqqara, near Memphis, the new capital, that the first pyramid was built. History has handed down to us the name of the architect who invented the art of dressed-stone building: Imhotep, whose name is engraved on the base of a statue of Djoser, and whose 'teachings' have been imparted to thousands of generations. Patron of the scribes, he was later to become identified with the Greek god of healing, Asclepios.

Besides the systematic use of limestone, Djoser's tomb differs from those of his predecessors in its massive proportions and in its shape, which was apparently designed in several stages. Constructed on a foundation of limestone rubble, the pyramid rises up within a 15–hectare enclosure. Initially, the edifice was a 60 m² square mastaba, which was extended to encompass the family tombs. On this original structure Imhotep raised four terraces; then another two, whose six steps mounting towards the heavens formed the first step pyramid. Its base measures 109 × 121 m. This gigantic staircase, 60 m high, could be seen for miles around. Symbolizing the aspiration to the after-life, it invites the king's soul to join the eternal stars among which it must take its place. The shape of the monument also recalls the original mound from which the sun emerged: an evocation of genesis, as taught at Heliopolis, but also an allusion to the inexorable course of the sun, with which death seeks to become one.

The underground level contains storehouses from which have been extracted thousands of alabaster vases, as well as an apartment with a room decorated in blue ceramic tiles.

On the limestone walls, fine reliefs show the king accomplishing ritual acts. Similar scenes are to be found in the 'South tomb' which belongs to the series of monuments adjacent to the pyramid. These are enclosed by a monumental surrounding wall, 10 m high, made of carefully dressed limestone blocks decorated with bastions. The wall has a single door giving access to a remarkable pillared gallery opening on to a great courtyard bounded on the west by the splendid 'Cobra Wall'.

Patiently reconstructed, Djoser's eternal resting-place rises up today as it did 4,500 years ago. The pharaoh communicated with the world of the living through a statue: enclosed in a small chapel built at the foot of the pyramid, it received the quickening breath of the north wind through narrow slits in the masonry. This painted limestone statue, whose inlaid eyes have vanished, is the first example of a life-size royal effigy.

The few contemporary statues of private individuals obviously draw their inspiration from this royal model. The granite *bedjmes* is a significant example and the painted limestone statues of Sepa and his wife Nesa (Louvre) are a continuation of this archaic tradition.

Pyramids and temples of the 4th to the 6th dynasties

In their quest for immortality, the sovereigns of the Old Kingdom built the most imposing monuments in history: the pyramids. Before attaining the perfect regularity of the Giza pyramids, however, the royal tombs went through various shapes. Those of Saqqara, Zauet el Aryan, built by Djoser's successors, are still giant staircases. The last of this type, built at Maidum, was later redesigned. At Dahshur, Snefru, the father of Cheops, built a double-sided pyramid whose silhouette resembles the top of an obelisk; this is the first real pyramid. We do not know why the same king built another tomb to the north of this one. From then on, in Giza, Saqqara and Abusir, the pharaohs raised similar monuments to heaven.

The interior design of the pyramid was simple. A shaft or corridor running from the north face led to the funeral chamber where the mummy lay in a sarcophagus. It seems that for the sarcophagus of Cheops three successive chambers were designed, the first of which was underground. The ramps and corridors needed for manoeuvres and ventilation were hewn out of the central mass of the monument. Once the funeral ceremonies were completed, these were filled in with supposedly impenetrable blocks of granite, designed to prevent access to the tomb. These efforts were unfortunately confounded by tomb-robbers from ancient times onwards. Mere figures give only a faint idea of the colossal proportions of the pyramids. The highest, which bears the name of 'Horizon of Cheops', was that king's last resting-place: it is 146.5 m in height and 235 m square, with an inclination of 51°56'; that of Chephren is comparable at 143.5 m in height, 215.25 m square with an inclination of 52°21'. The third great pyramid of Giza, that of Mycerinus, marks the start of a period of smaller monuments: 62 m high, 108.4 m square and 51° inclination. The four sides are aligned with the four points of the compass.

Only the pyramid of Mycerinus has retained its outer facing of carefully adjusted hewn granite. Under the mass of stone above them, the ceilings of the room and corridors threatened to cave in. To avoid this danger, Snefru's architects built high corbelled vaults, and Cheops did the same for his majestic 'Great Gallery'. Weight is discharged from the horizontal ceiling of his upper burial chamber by means of smaller chambers with supporting slabs arranged in chevron patterns. This solution was adopted frequently during the later dynasties.

The pyramids were not built by thousands of slaves straining under the tyrant's whip. The plateau of Giza attracted masses of peasants who could not work on the land during the flood period. The floods themselves facilitated transport of the immense blocks of stone to the building site. The Tura limestone, the granite for decorating the funeral chamber and for facing the outside of the pyramid and the dark basalt or diorite for the statuary arrived by boat. The stone blocks were dragged along on round logs or hauled on sledges as far as the clay ramps flanking the rising pyramid. Kept constantly wet, these ramps facilitated the raising of the blocks and constituted a kind of scaffolding where all the different craftsmen could work.

Boats made of brick, stone and wood accompanied the dead king on his last journey. Five of these were found in the pyramid of Cheops, built in Lebanese cedarwood and laid in pits to the east and south of the pyramid. One of these boats, 43 m long, was recovered in a perfect state of preservation. Flanking the eastern side of the pyramid is the high temple linked to a covered causeway running down to the Nile as far as the low or valley temple, where the cult of the king was apparently celebrated before his death. The beauty of the temple of Chephren, which is well preserved, lies in the sobriety of its square pillars, carved out of single blocks of granite. The remains of twenty-three statues of the king were found here: carved in diorite, the finest of these, conserved in the Cairo Museum, provides a striking portrayal of the majesty of the king-gods of the Old Kingdom. Seated on a throne, flanked by two lions, the king holds the symbol of the union between Upper and Lower Egypt; behind his impassive features the divine falcon Horus spreads its protective wings.

The reliefs, which thereafter no longer appeared inside the pyramids, cover the walls of the temple and the causeway with their magic images. The rituals which they depict were intended to assist the dead king on his journey to eternity. One of the most remarkable of these shows a procession of the dead king's 'estates', personified in the shape of young women bringing the pharaoh Snefru the produce of the land, and the transport of the palm-shaped pillars which decorated the high temple of pharaoh Unas. These reliefs are also found in the divine temples, many of which are associated with the pyramids. One of these stood before the famous Sphinx of Giza; the sculptors transformed a huge rock into a monstrous beast, a lion with human features evoking the power of Chephren and symbolizing an aspect of the sun, the heavenly body more particularly venerated during the 5th dynasty.

It was in the pyramids and their dependencies that most of the royal statues of the Old Kingdom were found, reflecting the majestic gravity of a son of the gods. By an ironic quirk of history the only statue of Cheops that has come down to us is an effigy 9 cm high, representing the builder of Giza holding the royal whip. In a very different style we have the quartzite head of his son Didufri (Louvre) whose face, framed by the symmetrical head-dress, evokes the severity of Djoser, though with a hint of melancholy. The Sphinx of Giza and the statues of the valley temple are reminiscent of the stern features of Chephren. No sovereign of ancient Egypt has left so many effigies as his successor, Mycerinus. All have the same roundness and benevolent expression which renders the sovereign more human. The schist triads representing the pharaoh beside the goddess Hathor and the personification of the Egyptian provinces show a precision hitherto unequalled in the portrayal of the human body. The great royal couple in the Boston Museum, with the queen standing beside her husband, is of a majesty equal to that of the statue of Chephren. The kings of the 5th dynasty have left few statues. One of them, carved in red granite, is the first example of a colossus: the head alone measures nearly 70 cm. At the end of the Old Kingdom, the effigies of Pepi I and that attributed to his son are exceptional because of the material used: copper. Although the metal has become dulled by corrosion, Pepi I remains an impressive figure with his inlaid eyes. Some parts of the statue seem to have been cast, but most of the work is made of riveted plates on a supporting wooden base.

The private sepulchres

The pharaoh was not to be alone in the after-life, and around each pyramid stretched a veritable city of the dead. Beside the royal tomb stood small pyramids, apparently the resting-place of the dead queens; not far away, princes and courtiers had secured the privilege of building their stone or brick mastabas, lining the avenues. Similar tombs were built in the provinces for the high officials; these have been discovered as far away as the distant southern oases. The sarcophagus and funeral furniture were deposited in a subterranean chamber reached by a vertical shaft. The whole structure was surmounted by a mastaba with slightly sloping walls.

Hollowed out of the inside of the mastaba or built partly outside it, the chapel displays decorations evoking life on earth. On the walls are successions of scenes carved, painted or inlaid in coloured paste, which ensure, through the magic of their images and texts, that the dead will enjoy an after-life similar to their earthly existence, surrounded by a loving family and diligent servants. They portray a picturesque tableau of daily life at the time of the pyramids. Important events in agricultural life are depicted: the sowing and the harvest, the grape harvest, and the fattening of domestic animals. On the walls of the tomb of Ti, a herdsman tries to drive his recalcitrant cattle across a ford; at Maidum, geese with beautiful plumage are set against a background of greenery.

The main scene, however, is the funeral repast, towards which all other scenes converge. As in previous periods, this scene is to be found on the stela which bears the name of the deceased; the stela is either set into the masonry or else surmounts the 'false door'. One of the most beautiful examples is that of Nefertiabet, who is thought to be the sister of Cheops. It portrays the princess seated before a table heaped with golden loaves of bread. The bas-relief is painted in colours which have retained all their freshness; on the table are arranged savoury meats, wine and fruit, together with linen and unguents to dress the mummified body of the princess. The inscription ensures that for all eternity she will receive 'a thousand pieces of beef, fowl, loaves of bread and jugs of beer'. One of the essential purposes of the stela is to supplement the offerings in kind which must be left regularly to provide sustenance for the dead.

Egyptian art is intended above all for the glorification of the gods and the dead. Reliefs and paintings are not mere decorations: they either perpetuate religious themes designed to conciliate the gods on whom the stability of the world depends, or they provide the deceased with everything that they will need in the after-life. Statues often represent substitute bodies which are vehicles for the vital force of the god or of the dead person, and are subjected to reanimation rites. Statues of private individuals have been found in the chapels or bricked up in a small storeroom, the *serdab*, which communicates with the world of the living by a narrow slit. As indestructible substitute bodies they are placed at the service of the dead person, of whom they provide an idealized representation. Already at the time of the pyramids these figures had fallen into certain stereotyped categories: the standing figure, immobile or striding forward, the seated scribe, the couple or the family group.

Here we have Prince Rahotep seated beside his beautiful wife, Nefret (Cairo Museum). This group in painted limestone is the idealized image of a royal couple preserved forever in their eternal youth. Their inlaid eyes were so bright that the workmen who discovered them were seized with panic.

The statue of Shayak al-Balad, in the Cairo Museum, is one of the earliest examples (5th dynasty) of the great wooden sculptures which were to become famous a hundred years later with the statue of Metchetchi (Kansas City Museum). Here, the figure, which is standing upright holding a staff of authority, is deliberately imposing; the face and body show a slight plumpness which in no way detracts from the dignity of this high official. Although the body is treated in the same way as the famous 'Seated scribe' in the Louvre, this statue is in striking contrast, with its alert face tilted as if listening to an unseen interlocutor, and the bright eyes in crystal and quartz set in rings of copper (Plate 19). As for the many statues of groups, these reflect the affection which unites Egyptian families and brings them so close to us. The most outstanding of these groups is that representing the dwarf Seneb sitting beside his wife, clasping her affectionately in his arms (Cairo Museum).

Funeral rites and beliefs

Through the monuments and works of art, most of which are connected with funeral rites, we can perceive a whole set of beliefs inherited from earlier periods and which are made clearer for the first time through the texts.

Despite the highly cryptic nature of these texts, it may be assumed that already in the Old Kingdom there was a distinction between the different subtle components of the human being: *akh*, the principle of light which opened the way to the stars; *ka*, the vital force which must be constantly sustained; *ba*, the immaterial principle expressing the power of its owner; the name, which through the magic power of the word enabled the individual to live again. The practice of mummification is well attested from this period onwards: examples include the mummy of King Merenre, preserved in the Cairo Museum, and that of the courtesan Nefer, still in place in its burial chamber at Saqqara.

The canopic jars discovered in the tomb of Hetepheres testify to the practice of ablation of the viscera, which were then deposited in special receptacles. The saline solution, traces of which were found *in situ* by the excavators, was doubtless prepared with the help of natron in which, in the classical period, the corpse was immersed for about ten days. Thereafter priests and embalmers took it in turns to officiate, reciting incantations over the body and applying the embalming techniques. Once washed, purified, duly annointed with oils and filled with aromatic herbs, the body was covered with a mask, enveloped in linen bandages and winding sheets, and adorned with jewellery and amulets. Objects used during the 'opening of the mouth' ceremony were placed in small containers and deposited in the tombs, thus recalling the importance of this ritual, which magically restored to the deceased the use of their senses. There are a few rare scenes in the mastabas which portray some parts of the funeral ceremonies, such as the halt in the purification tent, the voyage of the dead by boat, accompanied by official mourners, ritual dances, and so forth. The more complex burial rites of the pharaoh are evoked in the Pyramid Texts. After these ceremonies the mummy, protected by a heavy stone sarcophagus often decorated with a stepped design, was surrounded by the necessary furniture (headrest, mirror, razor, scribe's palette, jars containing food and ointments and, in ideal circumstances, a bed and armchairs) and placed at the foot of an inaccessible vertical shaft or a sealed chamber. But in the temples surrounding the pyramids or in the chapels above the mastabas, the soul of the dead came to breathe in the perfumed incense and enjoy the offerings regularly left by the living. The statues provided a substitute body for this purpose; they were placed in the sealed chambers of the *serdab* or in the chapels where the funerary cult was celebrated. At regular intervals, the heirs and the priests came to recite incantations and deposit the offerings essential for life after death, which were recorded in the offering-list: loaves of bread, beer, wine, meat, fruit, green and black cosmetics, ointments, fabrics, and so on. The chapel, linking the realm of the dead and the living, could be a mere niche in a stela, or it could be a small room. For the kings, this room was the innermost chamber of the temple abutting on the pyramid. Everywhere the main element was the stela, often carved in the form of a door or gate. Symbolizing the passage between the worlds of the living and the dead, its images and texts through their magic power ensured constant renewal of the offerings needed for the survival of the dead in the after-life.

The mere building of a tomb was not enough, however. Arrangements for the funeral cult must also be made: how should the deceased's table be kept regularly garnished? How should the invocations essential for life after death be perpetuated? Already in the 4th dynasty, the Egyptians had an answer to this fundamental question. The inscriptions show that the tombs might be supplied from many different sources: the 'offerings given by the king' which came from the royal properties or royal cult institutions; donations of land; 'castles of *ka*' granted by the pharaoh, from which the produce went to deck the offering table; the 'reversion' of the offerings initially intended for the temples or tombs and which, by contract, could be redistributed to other beneficiaries. A funerary foundation intended for the cult of the deceased was often composed of several types of property, land or villages, together with the people who lived there and the cattle belonging to them.

With its administrators, its farmers, craft-workers and priests, the foundation took care of the service of the deceased for centuries to come. It is understandable that its image was immortalized on the walls of the tomb.

Although we are well informed about burial rites, we know little of how the people of the Old Kingdom conceived of life after death. We are more familiar with the destiny of the dead pharaoh. The Pyramid Texts, the oldest version of which is that of the pyramid of Unas, are a compilation of still older writings intended to guarantee the best possible after-life for the pharaoh. With their innumerable verses they form the oldest funeral ritual known to humanity. In his quest for eternity the pharaoh seeks to join the great cosmic galaxies and the gods who have their being there. The pharaoh becomes in turn an imperishable star or constellation, Orion or Sirius, or the sun, as a son of the god, Re. To reach heaven and take his place among the gods, he uses the most unexpected methods: changing into a winged scarab or into incense smoke, or climbing a gigantic ladder (Plate 23). He invokes the power of the gods to assist him in overcoming the many obstacles placed in his way, and does not hesitate to threaten them if they refuse their help. To preserve his body in its entirety, he places each part of it under the protection of a god. He is also divine by virtue of his identification with the god of the dead, Osiris.

The first intermediate period and the middle kingdom: 7th to 12th dynasties (c. 2200–1785 BC)

After the long reign of Pepi II, Egypt declined into a period of disorder during the First Intermediate Period under the pressure of social unrest which some have described as a 'revolution': the weakening of pharaonic power, a stronger claim from the provinces, climatic changes, the upheavals that occurred towards the end of the Old Kingdom – all these factors combined to bring about a period of instability. Bedouin tribes took advantage of the situation to invade the Delta, spreading terror before them. Since the 5th dynasty the changes in pharaonic society had become perceptible: a state governed by a divine king gave way to a form of feudalism; the governors of the provinces gradually succeeded in passing on their office to their sons, thus forming local dynasties, which the king had to strive to keep under control.

Attempts to achieve unification were made successively by the princes of Herakleopolis on the edge of the Faiyum and by those of Thebes in the south, leading to a conflict from which the Theban princes emerged victorious in about 2500 BC. Egypt was again reunified under the reign of Mentuhotep the Great, marking the start of the Middle Kingdom, which is regarded as the classical age of Egyptian history during which contacts with neighbouring countries were strengthened. The pharaohs pushed back their frontiers by annexing Nubia, and their influence spread over Syria and Palestine. The kings bearing the name of Amenemhat and Sesostris, who formed the 12th dynasty, appear to have been true statesmen, reorganizing the economy and administration: the reclaiming of the marshlands of the Faiyum is the most famous example of their policy of major works.

The temples and the gods

We have some indications, mostly indirect, that shrines existed in the archaic period of pharaonic Egypt. Thus on Elephantine Island, at the First Cataract of the Nile, a series of predynastic votive offerings attest the sustained presence of a religious cult in a place where, from the Old Kingdom onwards, there was a succession of great building projects: upon the granite *naos* erected by Pepi I, stone monuments were superimposed on one another until the Late Period.

It is only from the Middle Kingdom onwards that we can really follow the extraordinary proliferation all along the Nile of divine temples which it was the pharaoh's mission to erect. They have come down to us in a very fragmented state. At Tôd, for instance, a few miles from Luxor, the foundations of a small temple dedicated to pharaoh Mutu suggest that it was once a building surrounded by a vestibule containing nine rooms; it was under its flagstones that the famous treasure of Tôd was discovered, a hoard of gold and silver ingots, precious plate and lapis lazuli.

At Karnak we may admire the finest example of the architecture of the period: a small kiosk or 'way-station' where the divine boat could rest as it went in procession, carrying the statue of the god. The carved stone blocks had been re-used as building materials to construct the third pylon of the Temple of Amon. Two thousand years later, archaeologists discovered them when dismantling the monument. Today the kiosk, entirely reconstructed, is one of the treasures of the Karnak open-air museum. It is a small rectangular building in fine limestone, crowned by a grooved lintel and standing on a platform which may be reached on both sides by a gently inclined ramp.

At Heliopolis, now a suburb of Cairo, the monument in honour of the sun-god, Re, built by Sesostris I, was doubtless the prototype of the great temples of the New Kingdom, but only one of the two obelisks which adorned its façade is still in existence. The building of the monuments of Abydos, the site of the necropolis of the Thinite kings, coincided with the spread of the cult of Osiris, of which it was regarded as the centre. Of its magnificent shrines to which the texts refer, only a few uninspiring traces remain.

Hitherto little-known gods eclipsed the patrons of Memphis, which had until then been the capital: Apis and especially Ptah and Re, around whom, perhaps as early as the 3rd dynasty, the priests had elaborated two competing versions of genesis which are known to us through later sources. In the beginning was *nun*, a vast, inert stretch of water from which emerged the original mound upon which the Creator took his place: a transcendent image of the Nile Valley where the only visible evidence of the lands submerged by the floods are a few muddy hillocks. For the theologians of Heliopolis, it was the god Atum, the solar principle, who first came into existence and created the other gods who became the powers of nature: Shu, god of the air; Tefnut, goddess of the life-giving moisture which gave birth to Gab, god of the earth; Nut, goddess of the sky, and so on. For the theologians of Memphis, it was Ptah who created the world through the Word, first conceiving all things in his heart and then creating them through his mouth.

The Middle Kingdom raised to the rank of national deities Montu and Amon, venerated at Thebes, the birthplace of the founders of the 11th dynasty, then the crocodile Sebek, patron of the swamps of the Faiyum. Osiris, whose legendary tomb was situated at Abydos, inspired new funeral rites. According to the legend, the god, assassinated and hacked to pieces by his brother, Seth, rose from the dead through the magical powers of his wife, Isis. The Middle Kingdom texts and monuments establish him clearly as the principal god of the dead. Many of the statues and stelae of the period came from his shrine in Abydos where they were deposited as votive offerings. His religion offers the reassuring ideal of a paradise open to all after a long and perilous journey through the underworld. For the first time in the history of humanity, the concept of a last judgement appears, when the deceased is weighed in the balance.

The Egyptian view of the world is essentially pessimistic. The harmony of the cosmos, the balance between heaven and earth, are under constant threat. Only the gods can maintain this fragile equilibrium. Even they are vulnerable and must be protected, nourished and sustained. The plan of the temple, the rites performed at its foundation ceremony, its building materials, decoration and inscriptions – all combine to construct a fortress for the god and thus perpetuate, through the power of magic, the rites which ensure the god's ever-renewed life. The omnipresent image of the king, in the bas-reliefs and statuary, highlights his essential role in maintaining the harmony of the world.

Through the royal statuary we seem to discern two schools of art with contrasting trends, that of the north and that of the south. Yet a distinction may also be drawn between the official representations of the sovereign, images used as propaganda to consolidate his authority, and the more peaceful images which adorn his funerary monuments. Although we cannot identify all the factors behind the emergence of the new style, it is possible to define those which gave it unity. The representation of figures clothed in short loincloths, who bear the stamp of eternal youth, gives way to that of men draped in cloaks or long tunics, who have lost the fine self-assurance of the past. The art of portraiture develops, but the expression on the faces is often meditative, or may even reflect pain or resignation. The choice of more static attitudes and the trend towards massive shapes give an impression of immobility. The sculptors abandon painted limestone and favour dark stone, polished to perfection.

During the 11th dynasty, Antef II had his effigy laid in a sanctuary in Elephantine, sculpted in the rigid style of the period. It is reminiscent of the better-known colossal statues erected by Mentuhotep in his funerary temple at Deir el Bahari. The pharaohs of the 12th dynasty left an abundance of statues, not only in their own tombs but in many shrines throughout Egypt. These sculptures express the power of the king of Egypt through their colossal proportions and hieratic appearance. Such works of propaganda are to be found along the Nile in the vicinity of the Second Cataract. The muscular strength of the king is accentuated to convey the impression of an athlete with the physical power to overcome his enemies, as can be seen in particular in one of the statues of Sesostris III, a royal portrait of dramatic intensity.

The statues of Sebektohep, originally from Karnak, are distinguished by the unusual size of the royal *nemes* and the extreme narrowness of the waists. Beside these effigies which, apart from a few details, reproduce the attitudes inherited from the period of the pyramids, the 'Osiran' colossi grew in number. From the reign of Sesostris I they take on a classical aspect: that of the pharaoh in the shape of the god Osiris, closely wrapped in a shroud, arms folded across the chest. Backed by pillars, these colossal statues form an integral part of the architecture of the religious and funerary temples; despite their imposing proportions, many of them give a faithful rendering of the features of the sovereign, such as the fragment belonging to Sesostris III recently discovered at Karnak.

In the statues of private individuals, new types also appear, corresponding to a change in the purpose of these works. Junior and senior officials had acquired the privilege of placing their statues in the divine temples. These works, which are a lasting tribute to their piety, show us figures in meditation, draped in long cloaks and wearing heavy wigs, the left hand often placed on the chest in a gesture of devotion. Some are of excellent craftsmanship, such as the seated Rehemuankh in the British Museum, the seated Knumhotep in the Metropolitan Museum, New York, or the remarkable kneeling Satsnefru. But many of the pieces from Abydos, where these votive offerings were placed near the 'staircase of the great god', were small and often of mediocre craftsmanship.

A similar trend may be observed in the relief of the temples of Abydos, Ermant and Thebes, where innumerable scenes show the dialogue between the king and the gods, or the long litany of rites.

These works of the 11th dynasty were succeeded by the new style of the 12th dynasty, of which the kiosk erected at Karnak by Sesostris I is the finest example. It shows in fairly high relief the king facing the deities which grant him their protection. The sobre composition blends with the pillared architecture associating two or three figures. The royal features are strangely similar to those of the gods, for is not the king the son of the gods? The hieroglyphs accompanying these scenes are treated with the same care and precision. The most famous block, from a sanctuary built by Sesostris III at Medamud, bears a double scene, carved in intaglio, showing the offering of bread; the pharaoh is portrayed twice, opposite the god Montu. The great originality of this relief is that it presents the sovereign at different ages. On the left the face of the king shows the roundness of youth, while on the right his features are gaunt and furrowed with age. This contrast, which is to be found in several other statues in the same temple, has been given different interpretations. Does it correspond to a new conception of the pharaoh who, like his subjects, experiences the vicissitudes of human life? Or do these contrasting images represent in a single, striking portrayal the ideal of an eternally renewed life-cycle?

The Middle Kingdom has left us more than the dwellings of the gods. At Kahun in the Faiyum, an entire city has been exhumed from the sand. The 'new town' was inhabited by the officials and workmen who were employed to build the pyramid of Sesostris II. Closely lining the small alleys which ran into the main streets, the workmen's houses had one or two storeys and a dozen rooms with small barred windows. Their terraced roofs, surrounded by a low parapet, provided space to enjoy the cool of the evening. The residential quarter, built along an avenue to the north-east of the town, comprised a number of vast properties (as many as 2,500 m²). These houses had colonnades decorated with plant motifs and a garden with trees, where a central pool with lotus flowers added a note of fresh coolness. This is the picture evoked by the models of the houses deposited in the tombs.

It was in the south of the country, where the Egyptian conquest was progressing, that the most outstanding examples of military architecture were found: the fortifications of the port of Elephantine, the massive brick buildings of Kerma and the small forts stretching from Lower Nubia to the Second Cataract of the Nile.

New necropolises

It was in the rocky cirque of Deir el Bahari on the west bank of Thebes that Mentuhotep the Great built his last resting-place. This vast complex, new in design, combines a burial chamber hewn out of the rock with a series of stone-built cult monuments. It was reached by a triumphal avenue lined with imposing statues of the king. Gently sloping ramps led to two stepped terraces bordered on three sides by a forest of square columns and many-sided pillars. The whole complex was crowned by a massive structure about 20 m square, the remains of which suggest that it may have been a small pyramid. However, the findings of recent excavations indicate that the central building was perhaps flat-roofed.

The kings of the following period, the 12th dynasty, moved their capital north and built their pyramids at the confines of the desert. Amenemhat I, the founder, selected the site

of Lisht, 60 km south of Memphis; Sesostris III chose to be buried at Dahshur, thus reviving the tradition of the sovereigns of the Old Kingdom, while Amenemhat III built the most gigantic monument of all time at Hawara, on the eastern edge of the Faiyum: did not the Greek writers believe that this was the site of the famous Labyrinth? Several hundred metres high, these pyramids hold their own in comparison with those of Giza, but although they had more ingenious systems for thwarting the tomb-robbers, their architecture has not withstood the ravages of time.

All these structures were decorated with monumental statues which were an integral part of the architecture. Those of Mentuhotep from the funeral buildings of Deir el Bahari, motionless and awesome, are in sharp contrast with the serenity of the sovereigns of the Old Kingdom. At Dahshur, Illahun and Hawara, the tombs of the royal princesses of the 12th dynasty have yielded magnificent jewellery. At no other period did the goldsmiths and lapidaries achieve such heights of technical perfection (Plate 24).

As in the Old Kingdom, the royal funerary complexes were surrounded by private tombs. There, members of the royal family and high officials lay at rest in stone or sun-dried brick mastabas, now in ruins. The most remarkable tombs, however, are to be found in the provinces – a reflection of changing social trends. Local governors and high dignitaries had magnificent tombs built for themelves near the cities.

At Qau el-Kebir, those of the princes Wahka and Ibu are inspired by royal monuments with their porticos, sloping causeways and staircases leading to funeral chambers hewn out of the rock. In Upper and Middle Egypt, the tombs lining the Nile were dug out of the cliffs overhanging the river. At Gya, from the reign of Mycerinus onwards, tombs were carved out of the quarries from which the stones for the pyramids were extracted. In the Middle Kingdom, similar sepulchres were made for members of the greatest families in Egypt.

Further south, the princes of Aswan who controlled the First Nile Cataract preferred the austerity of the quadrangular pillars which decorate the interior of their tombs. The succession of subterranean rooms is broken here and there by pillars carved out of the rock, the most elegant of which are those of the tomb of Kheti at Beni Hasan. Designed in the archaic style, they have the shape and colours of a lotus in bud.

This period witnessed the spectacular development of painting, which became an art in its own right. The walls of the tombs are first prepared with a coat of mud covered by a fine layer of plaster; in some cases, the plaster is applied directly to the stone.

The traditional scene of hunting in the marshes is given new life at El-Berschi by the masterly portrayal of many-coloured birds perched in an acacia with leaves so light as to be almost transparent. The well-known theme of fattening the animals is given a more refined dimension by the subtle use of colour. The pink of the oryxes' coat is set off by the blacks and whites of their slender pointed horns. The colour is spread in large patches, but with an attempt at gradual shading under the animal's throat. Other paintings are more remarkable for their anecdotal quality – for example, the transport of the colossal statue which adorned the tomb of Prince Djuti-hetep at El-Berschi, or the arrival of a caravan of Asians whose many-coloured clothes are rendered in faithful detail. Depictions of battles and the gymnastic training which took place before them are one of the creations of the period. The image of the besieged fortress or that of pairs of fighting wrestlers reveal an acute sense of composition and movement.

In the undecorated tombs it became customary to place models, which became increasingly numerous during the First Intermediate Period and the Middle Kingdom, replacing the sculpted representations on the walls, which became rarer. The models were made of wood, forming little scenes in miniature with several figures fitted carefully into a setting from everyday life: a workshop, a villa or an open-air scene. For example, a weaver's workshop in which the workmen are bending over their looms or unwinding skeins of linen thread, or fishermen bringing back a net full of fish, stretched between two boats. In the Asyût tombs, a veritable model army was discovered, with its marching soldiers brandishing shields and miniature spears and its troops of Nubian archers (Plate 25). There are also processions of servants carrying provisions, walking in single file across a supporting base, like those found in a tomb at El-Berschi, or there are tall women bearing offerings, moving forward one by one. The finest comes from the Theban tomb of Maketre, which contained other marvels such as the parade of troops before the master who sits under a canopy surrounded by his subjects. The 'Female bearer of offerings' in the Louvre is standing upright, swathed in a close-fitting dress; she is presenting a jug of beer, and on her head is balanced a basket containing a calf's leg. In the same category as the models are a number of other objects made of alabaster, or of unglazed or glazed earthenware found in the tombs. The most unusual are fashioned out of very fine Egyptian earthenware, a quartz paste coloured bright blue with copper oxide and depicting hippopotamuses. The female statuettes known as 'concubines of the dead' are often also made of earthenware. They were probably placed near the dead man in order to conceive an heir in the after-life, who would thus perpetuate the deceased.

Carved out of wood or stone, the first *ushabti* figures appeared at around this time, representing servants to attend the deceased.

The private tombs of Upper Egypt provide many clues to household goods by means of their funerary objects. The sepulchres of Wah and Meketre in Thebes, which were found intact, as well as a large group of tombs in Asyût, yielded a wealth of material: models, toilet articles, personal ornaments in silver and earthenware, miniature tools, dummy weapons and impressive lengths of fabric. Statues were also placed in the tomb, such as that of the chancellor Nahti, carved out of acacia wood.

The riches of the intellect

The Old Kingdom had known three literary genres: religious poetry, biography and moral doctrine. The first was illustrated by the Pyramid Texts. The second, which was to flourish, comprised what are known as the autobiographies, engraved on the walls of the tombs. These are mainly expressions of faith in the deceased, and while not relating personal exploits, list actions which correspond to a moral ideal: 'I gave bread to the hungry and clothes to the naked; I brought the boatless to land.' Sometimes at this period, well-known figures wished to leave for posterity an account of their exemplary career, glorifying their memory and placing them in high social esteem, this being the only means of not disappearing forever into anonymity. The story of the victories won by Uni over the Bedouins, and the expedition launched by Harkhuf far beyond Aswan, are examples

of this practice. These sober and precise accounts are the first examples of historical literature.

The third literary genre is that of wisdom literature, of which only one complete work remains, that of Ptahotep. These 'Instructions', as the Egyptians called them, are composed of a series of maxims. The most ancient example, that which bears the name of Hordjedef, begins with a sentence explaining that the work is intended for his son. This provides a context. The Instructions are generally attributed to wise men of the Old Kingdom, such as Prince Hordjedef, the viziers Ptahotep or Kagemeni, and take the form of advice given by a father to his son. Although no text of this period has come down to us directly, we can take it that the Middle Kingdom inherited an already well-established literary tradition. The works show a real attempt at style, with striking contrasts, parallel themes and balanced sentences. Intended originally for the aristocracy, they propose a rule of conduct applicable to all.

The qualities which an Egyptian must show in his path through life are varied: moderation, discretion, self-control, kindness, generosity, justice, loyalty, and so forth.

> Do not be proud of your knowledge,
> Do not be over-confident because of your learning.
> Consult the ignorant and the wise.
> The limits of art are not yet attained,
> No artist's skill is perfect.
> True words are hidden deeper than malachite,
> Yet may be found among the maids at the millstone.

As shown by this passage, which dates from the First Intermediary Period, these teachings illustrate one of the constant features of Egyptian culture, namely, the reference to the ancient models.

> Emulate your fathers, your ancestors;
> They have ruled by their knowledge.
> See, their words endure in books.
> Open, read them, copy their knowledge.
> One who is taught becomes skilled.

Some of the Instructions also have a political slant. Composed during the First Intermediate Period, the Instructions for King Merikare are both a historical document and a philosophical work. Describing the state of Egypt on the eve of the Theban attack on his capital, one of the kings of Herakleopolis, probably Kheti, tells his son what should be preserved or changed; he gives him advice on the art of government; he explains one by one the merits of clemency and firmness and the attitude to be adopted towards opponents.

> Do justice, then you will endure on earth;
> Calm the weeper, do not oppress the widow;
> Do not expel a man from his father's property.
> Do not reduce the nobles in their possessions.
> Beware of punishing wrongfully.

The Middle Kingdom saw the flourishing of a whole political literature, often of propaganda in favour of the reigning sovereign, such as the Instructions of Amenemhat I and The Prophecies of Neferti. Of the former, a work by the founder of the 12th dynasty, some strong dramatic fragments survive, consisting of political advice after an attempt at nocturnal assassination:

> Beware of subjects who are nobodies,
> Of whose plotting one is not aware;

Do not approach them alone;
Trust not a brother, know not a friend;
Make no intimates, it is worthless.

The second, which dates from the time of Snefru, describes a prophet announcing the advent of a saviour, Ameni, who will deliver Egypt from the disorders of revolution; for contemporaries, there is little doubt that the text refers to Amenemhat I.

'Loyalist teaching', which is presented in the form of instructions to young people, combines a glorification of the pharaoh, expressed in poetic terms recalling the great hymns of the period, with a series of maxims in the style of the scholars of the Old Kingdom. One of the most popular teachings of the time, the 'Kemit', seeks to raise Egypt to the heights of moral perfection. 'The Satire of the Trades', which exalts the function of the writer and cruelly lists the disadvantages of other trades, encourages young people to become scribes.

A set of texts known as 'pessimistic literature' doubtless reflects the social unrest during the collapse of the Old Kingdom. The best-known examples are 'The Maxim of Khakheperreseneb' and the 'Dispute between a despairing man and his *Ba*', in which the author, in magnificent verse, expresses his desire to leave this world:

Death is before me today
Like the fragrance of lotus,
Like sitting at the shore of drunkenness
Death is before me today
Like a well trodden way,
Like a man's coming home from warfare.

On an even more lyrical note, the 'Songs of the Harpists', of which there are traces on a few stelae, invite us to enjoy each passing moment.

This period has also left us many novels. The most famous, 'The Story of Sinuhe', recounts the misadventures of a courtier of Amenemhat I who was forced to flee to Palestine because he had overheard compromising information; before being able to return to Egypt he has many adventures. The 'Eloquent Peasant' follows the inextricable problem of an unfortunate fellah with the sinister high steward Rensi. Those who enjoy the fantastic will appreciate 'The Tale of the Shipwrecked Sailor', about a castaway on an island inhabited by a monstrous serpent. The tales from the Westcar papyrus, unfortunately only fragmentary, transport us to the court of Djoser and Cheops, where a clever magician shows off his skills; the last of these tales recounts the divine origins of the first kings of the 5th dynasty. The art of narration, the simplicity of the style, the varied verbal form, the alternation between narration and more picturesque modes, are the main features of a bona fide literature intended for a refined society which appreciated the perfection of the writing and the psychology of the heroes. These works also reflect the very high moral ideals which are already perceptible in the Instructions inherited from the Old Kingdom.

It cannot be said that science went through as significant a period of development as did literature. Despite the considerable knowledge traditionally attributed to them, the Egyptians do not seem to have conducted any pure, theoretical research. They nevertheless achieved certain important results. For example, the Middle Kingdom made a substantial contribution to medicine and mathematics. The titles of doctor, dentist and veterinary surgeon are attested as early as the Archaic period and those who bore such titles

also had links with magic. According to the Egyptian view of reality, most diseases would always remain the result of malign influences which should be exorcised by means of magic rituals. But in the case of corporeal accidents, practical remedies could be applied: milk, honey and the inhalation of plant essences, but also mouse, hippopotamus or pelican droppings. During the Middle Kingdom, medical treatises were compiled which have often come down to us through later copies. The most famous of these is the Edwin Smith papyrus, written in the Second Intermediate Period, which lists cases of bone surgery dating back to the early years of the Old Kingdom. Spinal bruising, dislocation of the jaw and various fractures are set out in order, following the order of the parts of the human body from the head downwards. The forty-eight cases are divided into three categories: curable, doubtful and incurable. The first two categories are accompanied by diagnoses and advice on treatment, such as 'you will give him a massage [in other cases 'apply a bandage'] every day until he is cured'. For the second category, which contained such disorders as lesions of the spinal cord, the entries are confined to a description and a purely theoretical diagnosis; the surgeon concludes gravely: 'an illness for which nothing can be done'. Other papyri, drafted along similar lines, deal with various diseases. One of these, found in Illahun, is a gynaecological treatise. Another, from the Rameseum, deals with muscular disorders, rheumatic pains and general ill-health. The examination of mummies reveals certain practices such as trepanation, draining of abscesses, dental fillings and the use of gold wire to hold loose teeth in place. However, despite his familiarity with the human body, resulting from the practice of mummification, the Egyptian doctor was ignorant of certain basic principles of anatomy: the heart, together with the blood vessels, which are so curiously studied in the Ebers papyrus, is regarded as the organ which produces all body fluids, from blood to tears.

The most important of the mathematics papyri, some of which were also found at the Illahun site, is the Rhind papyrus, copied during the Second Intermediate Period on a manuscript of the 12th dynasty, 2 m in length. This is not, as was long thought, a mathematical treatise, but a series of model problems with their solutions: arithmetical problems, calculations of volumes and of the surface of squares, circles and triangles, and division of odd numbers from 3 to 101. It was perhaps devised as a kind of slide-rule for use by the scribes.

NUBIA (3000–1780 BC)

The Greek geographer Strabo (XVII, 2, 3) was apparently the first person to use the word Nubia to describe the country to the south of Egypt. The hypothesis that the word originates from the Old Egyptian *nub* (nbw), a word meaning gold (Säve Söderbergh, 1992, p. 14) is uncertain although the country contained significant deposits of the precious metal that were being exploited in pharaonic times. The First Cataract on the Nile, south of the Egyptian town of Aswan, marks the northern edge of the country which stretches more than 700 km south as far as the Fourth Cataract, in the middle of the Sudan. The countryside is extremely varied. Today, Egyptian Lower Nubia is partly submerged beneath the waters of Lake Nasser, but once, after the labyrinth of the First Cataract through which the Nile struggles on its way, it possessed a fertile valley, enclosed by sandstone terraces, and formed a geographical unit distinct from Sudanese Upper Nubia. There, going south we find the bleak and desolate wastes of the Batn el Haggar, the 'stone belly', where the river bubbles between black rocks, and then the sandy stretches of the Abri-Delgo district, and finally the vast Dongola plain. The valley is bordered by immense deserts which produce an arid climate, with extreme temperatures (40°C and more in the shade is the daytime high in summer, while during winter nights it often falls below 0°C). It contains limited natural resources that enable only a sparse population to survive, living on fishing and the cultivation of the date-palm; in antiquity, tamarinds, acacias, sycamores and dum-palms, planted along the edges of fields, provided wood for building. In Lower Nubia, as soon as one moves away from the river, almost all life disappears. Clearly, before stabilizing at a level not very different from what it is today, the climate experienced humid phases, the fourth of which, between 5100 and 2200 BC, is known as the 'Neolithic subpluvial', but from the very remotest periods the Nile was the most reliable route linking Equatorial Africa to the Mediterranean world. Animals from tropical African countries, such as giraffes, cheetahs or monkeys, the skins of felines, ostrich feathers and eggs, ivory, ebony and gold all passed through Nubia on their way to Egypt and western Europe.

Nubia was the meeting place of different cultures. Original civilizations developed there from a very early date. Although it lacked writing, one Nubian kingdom, Kerma, was for a time the equal of the kingdom of the pharaohs. With Egypt, its more powerful neighbour, Nubia had relations that were at times peaceful commercial ones and at others involved military occupation.

Our knowledge of the country has been totally transformed by the discoveries made during the international campaign launched by UNESCO at the time of the construction of the Aswan high dam. The salvage of the main known sites and the archaeological excavations carried out in the 1960s in the area that the reservoir was to flood resulted in the birth of a new discipline, Nubiology, and scholars are today at work publishing and analysing the documentation that has been collected. The whole history of Nubia will eventually have to be revised. Yet the region between the Second and Fourth Cataracts and the desert areas have given rise to only a very few excavations. The picture that we give here can thus be nothing more than a provisional one.

In c. 3200 BC Lower Nubia and the Aswan region witnessed the prolongation of a culture that had appeared in the fifth millennium BC, known as the A-Group (Plate 26). It stretched over 1,500 years, and ended c. 2800 BC at the time of Egypt's first pharaonic dynasties. Although numerous objects dating from predynastic Egypt have been found in sites in Lower Nubia, the A-Group culture was purely Nubian and the old hypothesis advanced by the American scholar, G.A. Reisner, of an Egyptian migration southward must be abandoned. While it was close to the pharaonic civilization with which it was in contact from the beginning, it shows strong resemblances, especially in pottery, to the strictly Nubian cultures that preceded it. Buried under the thick alluvia of the Nile, the oldest A-Group sites are very difficult to study and do not yield an answer to the key question of the mutual influences between Egypt and Nubia, especially the appearance of a pottery that is found in both countries and that appeared in the fifth-fourth millennia BC: glossy, striated, black-topped red ware. In c. 3100–2800 BC society appears to have been hierarchical. The archaeolo-

gist, D. William, recently put forward the hypothesis, now disputed, of the existence of a pharaonic dynasty established at Qustul, south of Abu Simbel. The fact is that, like the tombs at Sayala, the very rich ones at Qustul (William, 1986), probably those of rulers, rival those of the Thinite kings with their gold jewellery, ivories and stone platters as well as hundreds of conical pots intended to contain foodstuffs; these are extremely thin, with reddish-orange decoration that imitates wickerwork. At Sayala, vast bird-head shaped palettes are found alongside pear-shaped maces; the handle of one of them, covered with gold leaf, was decorated with a series of animals reminiscent of Naqada ivories. A large number of objects are of Egyptian or Western Europe provenance (including wine or beer jars, copper implements and weapons), showing the intensity of commercial relations conducted by the A-Group. While the tombs at Sayala have a rectangular well covered by large sandstone slabs, many round-shaped burial places sometimes contain an offering chapel and occasionally an inscription stela. This evidence, combined with the presence of clay-modelled human and animal figures, shows a developed conception of the hereafter. Rock shelters, decorated with rock carvings, were found at Sayala, while the largest known village, Afiyeh, had large houses with stone foundations. The concentration of wealth observed at the end of the period doubtless reflects the commercial activities carried on by A-Group populations. In the 578 silos found at Khor Daoud, Egyptian jars and black-topped ware that once contained beer, wine or oil attest the role of the site as a place where goods were exchanged and redistributed (Midant-Reynes, 1992, p. 210). This first Nubian state, which the most ancient Egyptian texts call 'Ta Sety', 'the land of the bow', probably an allusion to the famous Nubian archers, disappeared about the end of the Egyptian 2nd dynasty for reasons that are not yet clear. Probably the raids made by the pharaohs of the 1st dynasty, such as that by Djer illustrated in a graffito at Jebel Sheikh Suleiman, contributed to it (Trigger, 1976, p. 46). But south of the Second Cataract, Nubian culture continued to evolve.

In the Old Kingdom, the Egyptian presence in Lower Nubia took the form of peaceful expeditions conducted by various rulers. Cheops caused to be brought back from the quarries at Toshka, near Abu Simbel, the precious diorite used for carving royal effigies. At Buhen, opposite the modern city of Wadi Halfa, the remains of a fortified town have yielded the names of 4th and 5th dynasty kings, while pottery and metal-working furnaces suggest that an Egyptian colony engaged in copper working there. Egyptian texts also suggest an aggressive policy. The Palermo Stone, a fragment of royal annals, lauds the exploits of King Snefru, of the 4th dynasty: 'Laid waste the land of the Nubians. Prisoners brought back: 7000; cattle and livestock: 200,000' (Roccati, 1982, p. 39). The biographical inscriptions in the necropolis at Aswan, composed at the end of the Old Kingdom, are more eloquent about pharaonic policy towards Africa. Harkhuf, the 'overseer of foreign troops', records his travels to the distant Nubian country of Yam, describing his various routes – along the valley or by the oasis roads – and his sometimes stormy encounters with various rulers, listing the products brought back: '300 donkeys loaded with incense, hekenu oil, grains, leopard skins, elephant tusks, javelins, and so on' and even a pygmy whose dancing would charm the young pharaoh Pepi II. Pepinakht, the 'overseer of the troops', boasted of the number and valour of his soldiers and recorded the destruction of the land of Wawat and Irthet where 'he massacred a large number of the princes' children and the best military leaders'. To find the body of his father, who had died on an expedition in the south, Sabni, prince of Aswan, gathered together an escort and headed into Nubia, accompanied by 'one hundred asses loaded with perfumed unguents, honey, fabrics and oil', intended for local rulers. Along with the precious body, Sabni brought back to Egypt exotic products including an enormous elephant tusk and a lion's skin 2.5 m long (Roccati, 1982, pp. 216 ff). These reports carved on tombs at Aswan, rich in information but sometimes obscure, indicate how great the demand in Egypt was for products from afar; they are evidence, too, of the growing resistance encountered by penetration into Africa.

This resistance coincided with the appearance of new Nubian cultures, which are surely related to population movements towards the valley consequent upon the desiccation of the terrain. One is the C-Group, the B-Group that archaeologists once thought to have identified never having existed. Without writing, the C-Group developed in Lower Nubia between 2000 and 1500 BC. The highest concentrations are to be found at the sites of Faras, Aniba and Dakka. Relations with Egypt seem to have been peaceable, the population exploiting the narrow alluvial plains and engaging in herding, which played an important part in their culture. Circular graves surmounted by a stone tumulus enclose the remains of domestic animals, dogs, gazelles and cattle, doubtless symbolizing the wealth of their owners. Standing outside, the great stone stelae that bear representations of cattle, sheep and goats probably have the same significance, as do the terracotta figures placed inside the tombs. Leather and linen clothes have belts and sandals to go with them. Leather head-dresses have been found, still with their decorative feathers. Men and women are arrayed with numerous items of coloured stone or faience jewellery; there are ear-rings, which were not worn in Egypt until the end of the Middle Kingdom. Hand-shaped pottery remains in the Nubian tradition, with black vases decorated with incised lines forming infinitely varied geometric patterns, picked out with white or coloured pigments. While little is known of the habitat, the remains of stone walls found in villages indicate a high degree of sedentarization. Although subject to Egyptian contact, the population retained its cultural identity but never formed a state of its own.

This is also true of the Pan-Grave Nubian culture, which appeared at the end of the First Intermediate Period and is attested all over Egypt and Lower Nubia. It owes its name to the shape of the round, shallow graves that archaeologists compared to frying pans. These contain small amounts of material, and often have weapons. Probably originally from the eastern desert, these skilled Nubian bowmen were used as mercenaries by the pharaohs who made grants of land to them. They have been identified as the Medja people referred to in Egyptian texts. A few rare representations, such as a painting on an ox skull, show us these dark-skinned soldiers who do not deign to have their image accompanied by any hieroglyphic inscription.

Around the modern town of Kerma, above the Third Cataract, another Nubian culture developed which constituted a threat to Egypt by the end of the Old Kingdom. Its origins are still unknown, the region having been little investigated, but its geographical situation made it, at the end of the Neolithic, an essential stage between the south Khartoum Neolithic and the Lower Nubia A-Group. As the French Egyptologist, B. Gratien, suggests, it may be that the transitional phase preceding 'early Kerma' 'is the direct suc-

cessor of the Lower Nubia A-Group' (Gratien, 1978, pp. 159, 320). By the end of the Old Kingdom there may well have existed south of the Second Cataract a well-organized population resistant to Egyptian penetration. That would explain the military expeditions that are recorded in the texts of the Aswan necropolis. A little later, the well-dated necropolises of 'early Kerma' reveal a hierarchical, essentially pastoral society, with chiefs possessing large herds of cattle and goats. The presence of one or two bows deposited near several bodies is evidence of a warrior tradition. While the pottery is African in type, close to that of the Ethiopian borders and the Khartoum region, objects using mother-of-pearl from the shores of the Red Sea and ivory from the Sudan reflect prosperous commercial activity. Strong Egyptian influence is shown in the abundance of bronze mirrors and jars, some of which bear hieroglyphics. The circular tombs are surmounted by stone tumuli or sandstone stelae arranged in a circle. Bowls, deposited outside at the time of the funerary ceremonies, are perhaps what is left of a meal shared with the deceased. The bodies, placed on ox skins, are equipped with an abundance of items – loin-cloths decorated with leather panels and multi-coloured beads, ivory bracelets and ear-rings, leather sandals, ivory and bronze daggers, bows, ostrich feather fans, and so on. Near sacrificed domestic animals, dogs, lambs and rams, sometimes wearing ornaments, from a very early date there are signs of human sacrifices, such as the adolescents wrapped in a sack discovered by the Swiss archaeologist, C. Bonnet (1986, p. 48). The period also saw an urban community come into being, protected by an enclosure inside which were mudbrick houses with granaries, and the development of industrial activity, as indicated by a recently discovered bronzesmith's workshop.

During the First Intermediate Period, Egypt's political difficulties must have favoured the growth of the Kerma culture. Taking its powerful neighbour as its model, the kingdom was organized around a sovereign and laid the foundations for a true state. Its army now constituted a threat to the pharaohs who called the new power the 'land of Kush'.

The reaction occurred in the Middle Kingdom, during which reunited Egypt subdued Lower Nubia and set its southern border at the Second Cataract. It was in this region that, in c. 1900 BC, Sesostris I built a series of powerful mudbrick fortresses along the Nile, the best-known being at Faras, Buhen (Plate 27), Mirgissa and Semna. Today they have disappeared under the waters of Lake Nasser but they were true fortresses equipped with crenellated ramparts, fortified gates and moats. The barracks and magazines of some of them could hold up to a thousand soldiers. Ingenious positioning enabled each fortress to communicate with its neighbours, watching over this strategic region, controlling the local population and protecting Egypt from the 'abominable enemy of Kush'. They also had an economic role since they functioned as trading posts and collected the gold extracted in large quantities from the Nubian deserts.

While military occupation and mineral exploitation continued in Lower Nubia until c. 1700 BC, the power of the kingdom of Kerma became established, its territory stretching from the Second to the Fourth Cataract.

The period corresponding to the Egyptian Middle Kingdom or 'classical Kerma' saw growing social disparities. This is revealed in the co-existence in the capital of districts made up of huts with vast residences and Egyptian-type one-room, one-door houses, grouped around a temple, and a circular wood and mudbrick hut over 16 m across. The necropolis shows the same disparity, with pits from 2 to 12 m in diameter surmounted by tumuli. While some of the urban constructions draw their inspiration from the Egyptian model, African influence predominates in the funerary customs and is expressed in certain buildings such as the great ceremonial hut. Relations with the Egyptians were indeed very strained, and a very small amount of pharaonic pottery reappears in tombs only at the end of the period, confirming what we are told by military archaeology and hieroglyphic texts. Terms of execration are used against the 'abominable ruler of Kush'. The kingdom of Kerma reached its zenith just as Egypt was sliding into the upheavals of the Second Intermediate Period, abandoning Lower Nubia; Upper Egypt itself was no longer safe from Kushite invasions. In an unexpected political turnaround, the ruler of Kerma came to regard himself as the equal of the pharaoh, ruled over regions where Egyptian populations lived and maintained friendly relations with the Hyksos who invaded Egypt.

BIBLIOGRAPHY

ADAMS, S.; VERCOUTTER, J. 1980. The Importance of Nubia: A Link between Central Africa and the Mediterranean. In: MOKHTAR, G. (ed.), *General History of Africa*, Vol. 2, pp. 226–43. Paris.

ADAMS, W. Y. 1984. *Nubia, Corridor to Africa. Africa in Antiquity. The Arts of Ancient Nubia and the Sudan.* Vols 1–2, 1978. Exhibition Catalogue, Brooklyn.

Africa in Antiquity. 1978. *The Arts of Ancient Nubia and the Sudan.* Vols 1–4. Exhibition Catalogue, Brooklyn.

AMÉLINEAU, E. 1985, 1987–9. *Les nouvelles Fouilles d'Abydos.* Paris. 3 vols.

ARKELL, A. J. 1961. *A History of the Sudan from the Earliest Times to 1821.* London.

ASSMAN, J. 1989. Maât, *L'Egypte pharaonique et l'idée de justice sociale.* Paris.

BARGUET, P. 1986. *Les textes des sarcophages égyptiens du Moyen Empire.* Paris.

BONHÈME, M. A.; FORGEAU, A. 1988. *Pharaon. Les secrets du pouvoir.* Paris.

BONNET, C. 1986. *Kerma. Territoire et métropole.* Cairo.

—— 1990. *Kerma, Royaume de Nubie.* Genève.

CENIVAL, J. L. de. 1971. *L'Egypte avant les pyramides.* Paris.

DREYER, G. 1990. Umm el-Qaab. *Nachuntersuchungen im frühzeitlichen.* Königsfriedhof. 3/4 Vorbericht, Vol. 46, pp. 53–89.

EDWARDS, I. E. S. et al. (eds). 1971. *Cambridge Ancient History*, Vol. I, Part 2. Cambridge.

EMERY, W. B. 1961. *Archaic Egypt.* Harmondsworth.

FAULKNER, R. O. 1969. *The Ancient Egyptian Pyramid Texts.* Oxford.

FISCHER, H. G. 1990. *The Origin of Egyptian Hieroglyphs.* Nebraska.

GEUS, 1984a. Excavations at el Kadada and the Neolithic of Central Sudan. In: KRZYZANIAK, L.; KOBUZIEWICZ, M. (eds), *Origin and Early Development of Food-Producing Cultures in North-Eastern Africa.* Poznan. pp. 361–72.

—— 1984b. *Rescuing Sudan's Ancient Cultures.* Khartoum.

GHALIOUNGHI, P. 1983. *The Physicians of Pharaonic Egypt.* Cairo.

GRATIEN, B. 1978. *Les cultures de Kerma: Essai de classification.* Lille.

GRIMAL, N. 1988. *Histoire de l'Egypte ancienne.* Paris.

HAYNES, J. L. 1992. *Nubia, Ancient Kingdom of Africa.* Boston, Mass.

HOFFMAN, M. 1980. *Egypt before the Pharaohs.* London.

HORNUNG, E. 1986. *Les dieux d'Egypte.* Monaco.

KAPLONY, P. 1964. *Die Inschriften der Ägyptischen Frühzeit.* Wiesbaden.

LAUER, J. P. 1988. *Le mystère des pyramides.* Paris.

LECLANT, J. (ed.) 1978. *Le temps des pyramides. L'Univers des formes, Les pharaons.* Paris.

—— 1980. The Empire of Kush: Napata and Meroe. In: MOKHTAR, G. (ed.), *General History of Africa.* Paris. Vol. 2, pp. 278–97.

LEXIKON der Ägyptologie. Wiesbaden.

LICHTHEIM, M. 1973. *Ancient Egyptian Literature.* Vol. 1: *The Old and the Middle Kingdom.* Berkeley, Calif.

MALEK, J. 1986. *In the Shadow of the Pyramids. Egypt during the Old Kingdom.* Cairo.

MIDANT-REYNES, B. 1992. *Préhistoire de l'Egypte. Des premiers hommes aux premiers pharaons.* Paris.

Naissance de l'écriture. 1982. *Cunéiformes et hiéroglyphes.* Exhibition catalogue. Paris.

POSENER-KRIEGER, P. 1976. *Les archives du temple de Neferirkaré Kakai (Les papyrus d'Abousir).* BdE 65. Le Caire.

REINOLD, L. 1982. Le site préhistorique d'El Kadada (Sudan central. La nécropole). Lille, Université de Lille III. (Doctoral thesis.)

REISNER, G. A. 1923. *Excavations at Kerma*, Vols 1–4. Cambridge, Mass. (Harvard African Studies, 4–6.)

ROCCATI, A. 1982. *La littérature historique sous l'ancien empire égyptien.* Paris.

SÄVE-SÖDERBERGH, T. 1992. *Temples and Tombs of Ancient Nubia.* Paris/London.

SHERIF, N. M. 1980. Nubia before Napata (-3100 to -750). In: MOKHTAR, G. (ed.), *General History of Africa.* Paris. Vol. 2, pp. 245–77.

STADELMANN, R. 1990. *Die grossen Pyramiden von Giza.* Graz.

TRIGGER, B. G. 1976. *Nubia Under the Pharaohs.* London.

TRIGGER, B. G. et al. 1983. Ancient Egypt. *A Social History.* Cambridge.

VALBELLE, D. 1990. *Les neuf arcs. L'égyptien et les étrangers de la préhistoire à la conquête d'Alexandre.* Paris.

VANDIER, J. 1952–64. *Manuel d'archéologie égyptienne.* Vols 1–4. Paris.

VERCOUTTER, J. 1992. *L'Egypte et la vallée du Nil.* Vol. 1. *Des origines à la fin de l'Ancien Empire.* Paris.

VERNUS, P. 1990. Les espaces de l'écrit dans l'Egypte pharaonique, *Bulletin de la Société Français d'Egyptologie.* No. 119. pp. 35–56.

WILDUNG, D. 1984. Sesostris und Amenemhet. *Ägypten im Mittleren Reich*, München.

WILLIAM, D. 1986. *The A-Group Royal Cemetery at Qustul: Cemetery L.* Chicago, Ill.

ZIBELIUS-CHEN, K. 1988. *Die ägyptische Expansion nach Nubien.* Wiesbaden.

10.2
THE NILE VALLEY
(1780–700 BC)

10.2.1
EGYPT

Gamal Mokhtar

This chapter deals with a period characterized by many social, economic and cultural changes which occurred when Egypt's previously isolated security was fractured and when it was opened to the outer world.

THE SECOND INTERMEDIATE PERIOD (c. 1784–1570 BC)

13th and 14th dynasties

Since the time of Amenemhat IV, the seventh king of the 12th dynasty, it was obvious that the royal family was beginning to lose its power. His short and uninteresting reign was followed by an even shorter reign, that of Queen Sebekne-fru, which ended the prosperous period of the Middle Kingdom. The Middle Kingdom probably had an internal weakness due to the fact that it began as a feudal government and was obliged to keep many aspects of provincial feudalism. This meant that the king would be respected as the head of the state only so long as he kept his strength and his ability. The last kings of the 12th dynasty, however, were weak and lacked both power and ability with the result that the central authority collapsed and Egypt passed into a dark and gloomy period. In addition, there were other factors contributing to the fracture: internal factors like the competition and struggle between the members of the royal family itself as well as external factors caused by the new large migrations and movements which at that time disturbed the whole of Western Asia. Evidence of the weakness of the kings of that period can be traced through the documents which we call the Execration Texts (Kemp, 1983). These texts can be dated to the end of the 12th dynasty and to the 13th dynasty and contain magical curses which the king used against his enemies.

The Egyptian state was divided between two competing dynasties over a period of time before the Hyksos invasion. A royal family at Thebes continued to rule Upper Egypt (Manetho's 13th dynasty), while there was a second native dynasty at Xois (modern Sakha) in the Delta which Manetho labelled the 14th dynasty. This dynasty collapsed at the time when the Hyksos succeeded in establishing their complete authority over the Delta. While the kings of Thebes, like

Sebekhotep and Khender, were trying unsuccessfully to reign all of Egypt, the migrations of Semitic groups (which we call 'the Hyksos') from north-west Asia to the Delta were increasing.

Although a number of monuments of the 13th and 14th dynasties have survived, the history of this period is not yet certain. We know about thirty-eight royal names for these dynasties from the Turin papyrus, the Karnak list and their own monuments, but the sequence of these names is still in doubt (Plate 28). All the indications are that in Upper Egypt the administrative and cultural aspects of the 12th dynasty continued during the 13th dynasty. Five out of six tombs from that period which have been discovered at Saqqara and its environs were pyramids, small in size and complicated in their internal composition. The funerary inscriptions and scenes of this period show a great decline in quality when compared with those of the 12th dynasty, although the Memphite school of art maintained its high standard of workmanship.

The Hyksos period (15th, 16th and 17th dynasties)

After their infiltration of the Delta, the Hyksos seriously began to challenge the authorities of the 13th and 14th dynasties during the eighteenth century BC. Manetho's word, Hyksos, is derived from the ancient Egyptian term *heka khasut*, which literally means 'rulers of the foreign lands'. Unfortunately there is an absence of contemporary written records concerning the Hyksos' conquest and their rule of Egypt before the war of liberation, as the Egyptians did not desire to record their great national humiliation until they began to drive the Hyksos out of the country. Nevertheless, there is some material dealing with the Hyksos rule which has come to us from later writings, while the archaeological remains, especially those in the Delta, can provide some additional information.

The purpose of the Hyksos invasion was to settle, dominate and rule Egypt. But in reality the Hyksos occupied only the Delta and Middle Egypt as far south as Cusae at the actual province of Asyût, while shadow pharaohs at Thebes continued to rule the rest of Egypt as far south as Aswan.

The Hyksos were composed of several ethnic groups, notably Semitic, who entered Egypt as a result of large population movements and migrations coming from Central Asia. Their culture was strongly influenced by the Middle Bronze Age in Palestine, as can be clearly seen from the remains of their tombs and settlements in both Egypt and Palestine.

Although they first ruled from Memphis (Kemp, 1983), the Hyksos soon built a great fortified city which Manetho called Avaris; the site of this city was probably that of Tell el-Daba in the eastern Delta. The Hyksos emerged as a well-equipped and war-like people who had a number of military advantages over the Egyptians. The speed and striking power of the horse and chariot, the advantage of body armour, and new types of weapons, especially the compound bow, gave them obvious superiority and increased their chances of victory.

Among the Hyksos remains are rectangular fortified camps which survive both in Egypt and in Palestine, certain kinds of jewellery and distinctive types of pottery. Some objects bearing the name of the Hyksos king Khyan were found outside Egypt.[1] This, however, does not mean that his authority extended into those regions, but indicates only some kind of commercial relations.

There is no doubt at all that the Hyksos occupation had deep and sad effects on the Egyptians. It was the first time in their history that they had been dominated by foreigners. Their hatred towards those foreigners was enormous since they viewed the Hyksos rule as a severe blow to national dignity. According to Manetho, the Hyksos ruled Egypt during two dynasties, the 15th and the 16th. The final dynasty of Hyksos rule coincided with the 17th dynasty, which was a dynasty of Theban kings. The pyramids of these Theban kings have been located at Dra Abu el-Naga in western Thebes.

Driven by their desire for liberation and revenge, the Egyptians began to learn to use the Hyksos weapons and after about a century they turned them on their Hyksos enemies. The war of liberation had begun. The earliest evidence of this war may be provided by a mummy, that of King Sekenenre, who was apparently killed in one of the first battles against the Hyksos. Following him, his son Kamose began a systematic and determined war against the enemy. It was a war of vengeance, as we know from the Carnarvon Tablet, of a pupil in a scribal school; this tablet was a copy of a royal text which recorded the serious events of that time. Two stelae from the reign of Kamose confirm his victory, although it was probably limited and the territory gained was only Middle Egypt. It was, however, the first major encounter in the war with the Hyksos which would eventually lead to complete victory.

THE NEW KINGDOM (c. 1570–1070 BC)

The 18th dynasty

The pharaohs of the 18th dynasty, which begins the New Kingdom, were the offspring of the kings who united Egypt and expelled the Hyksos. Although the culture of the 18th dynasty adopted and continued that of the preceding phases without much change, it is very clear that the habit of attending only to affairs within the Nile Valley had been replaced by an effective foresight towards the borders of Asia and Africa. Because the pharaohs of the New Kingdom had complete authority within Egypt, they had the liberty to lead armies out of Egypt. The first generations of the 18th dynasty carried on the old tradition of punitive raids, rather than the principles of conquest and empire-building which would typify the later dynasts.

Ahmose, who is considered the father of the New Kingdom and the founder of the 18th dynasty, was obviously a man of extraordinary force and great ability. In addition to the final expulsion of the Hyksos and the defeat of the independent Nubian kingdom to the south of Egypt, he succeeded in reorganizing the administration of the reunited country. Ahmose was succeeded by his son Amenhotep I, a worthy successor who continued and advanced his father's internal and external policies. After his death Amenhotep I, together with his mother Ahmose-Nefertari, became a divinity in the necropolis of Thebes (Cerny, 1927). His successor Tuthmosis I is considered to be the king who first established an Egyptian empire in Asia and Africa. His son, Tuthmosis II, was a weak ruler and was married to his energetic and ambitious sister, Hatshepsut.

Five years after the death of her husband, Hatshepsut was powerful enough to declare herself supreme ruler of the country, bypassing completely the heir to the throne, Tuthmosis III. Her monuments designated her as the actual king of Egypt and gave her all the official titles and attributes of a pharaoh. She had a very prosperous reign which concentrated on the internal affairs of Egypt. Her great achievements were her great temple at Deir el Bahari, her expedition to Punt, and the raising of two magnificent obelisks at Karnak.

At the time of Hatshepsut's disappearance, Tuthmosis III was already a mature man. He tells us that while his father was leading a ceremony in the temple of Karnak, the statue of the god Amon chose him, by means of an oracle, to be king of Egypt. This story was probably created to weaken Hatshepsut's claim to legitimization that her father was not Tuthmosis I but the god Amon Re himself.

Tuthmosis III's career shows him to be the greatest and most important pharaoh of ancient Egypt. He was an energetic warrior, a great builder and a gifted administrator. He began his military exploits by marching his army towards the east to face a coalition of the city-states of Syria-Palestine which had gathered at the city of Megiddo. He skilfully won the battle and invaded the city thereby placing the entire region as far as southern Lebanon under Egyptian control. By the time of his sixteenth campaign in western Asia, Egypt had been converted to a world power and had become responsible for a large empire stretching from northern Syria and Anatolia in the north to the Fourth Cataract in Upper Nubia in the south. In addition to his military victories, he achieved much internally and constructed temples throughout Egypt (Plate 29).

The reigns of Hatshepsut and Tuthmosis III provide interesting contrasts in the domain of activities and intentions. Hatshepsut recorded no military achievements, while Tuthmosis is considered the greatest warrior among all of the Egyptian kings. Her pride centred on the internal development of Egypt, while his pride was centred on Egyptian military supremacy.

Tuthmosis III was succeeded by two able and active pharaohs: Amenhotep II who possessed extraordinary muscular strength and athletic ability and Tuthmosis IV who showed an interest in the cult of the sun. Egypt attained the peak of its magnificence and prosperity during the reign of Amenhotep III, the son of Tuthmosis IV and a Mitanni princess. His reign was an era of peace and well-being; he did not establish his fame upon military accomplishments.

He was married to many wives, but his favourite was Tiye, a woman of amazing personality and the mother of his son, Amenhotep IV/Akhenaten. To Amenhotep III posterity owes the Luxor temple which is considered one of the most beautiful temples in Egypt, the avenue of the ram-headed sphinxes which leads from the Luxor temple to Karnak, and the two colossi of Memnon in western Thebes (Plate 30). But towards the end of his reign it is evident from the Tell el-Amarna letters that the absence of military force encouraged enemies in western Asia to plot against Egyptian authority.[2]

His son, Amenhotep IV, did not intend to become either a warrior or a statesman. He was interested only in things concerning religion, morality and intellectual matters. From the beginning he led a direct attack on the priesthood of Amon which had acquired great wealth and wide authority. He continued to live at Thebes during the first part of his reign and built a great temple for his new god 'Aten' at Karnak. A short time later he decided to leave Thebes and quickly founded a new residence and capital at Tell el-Amarna in Middle Egypt. In the sixth year of his reign he moved to the new capital with his wife Nefertiti, his daughters and a considerable number of officials. He named the new capital Akhetaten, 'The Horizon of the Aten', and lived there until his disappearance in the fourteenth year of his reign. He worshipped his god, the Aten, the creative power of the sun. He also changed his name to Akhenaten which means 'one who is useable to the Aten', ordered the name of Amon to be erased and decreed that the priesthood of Amon should be discriminated against and that the temple estates should be dissolved. The Aten religion gave special attention to truth and was bound up with a love of nature; nevertheless, it was simpler than the traditional one. Akhenaten emphasized a free naturalism in art and he permitted the artists to depict him and his family in informal attitudes: drinking, eating, playing, embracing and worshipping.

Akhenaten's revolution did not survive after his death. His successor, Smenkhare, began the process of reconciliation with the priests of Amon. He was succeeded after a short reign of three years by Tutankhaten who changed his name to Tutankhamen. Although he ruled for only nine years and died at about the age of eighteen, the spectacular discovery of his tomb was the most outstanding archaeological event of our century and has made Tutankhamen one of the most famous pharaohs of Egypt (Plates 31, 32). After a short reign of a King Ay, the throne of Egypt was achieved by Horemheb whose previous career as a commander of the army and whose administrative experience offered him the opportunity to abolish the corruption, dishonesty and immorality which had spread in Egypt since the reign of Akhenaten. His severe decrees and firm reforms helped to maintain order and discipline and to achieve a kind of 'renaissance' which paved the way for a new dynasty, the 19th, to return to Egypt its missing power and vanished glory.

THE RAMESSIDE PERIOD (19TH AND 20TH DYNASTIES)

The 19th dynasty

After the death of Horemheb, a new dynasty came into power. Its founder, Ramesses I, was an army officer who had been favoured by Horemheb; as preparation for the throne, Horemheb had appointed Ramesses I to be vizier. He was, however, already an old man and reigned only for about two years. He was succeeded by his son and co-regent Seti I. The new dynasty exhibited a peculiarity in its selection of names, apparently because its founder came from the north-eastern part of the Delta (modern Sharqia province). When forming their names, the kings of the 19th dynasty replaced the southern gods such as Thoth and Amon with northern gods such as Re, Seth and Ptah. Thus the names Tuthmosis and Amenhotep were replaced by Seti, Ramesses and Merenptah.

Seti I is the first of a line of warriors of the 19th dynasty who turned all their efforts to regaining Egypt's prominence and prestige. From the beginning of his reign he faced as great a threat from an alliance of Syrian city-states as had previously faced the kings of the 18th dynasty; this alliance of Syrian city-states was supported by the Hittites, while the earlier alliance had been directed by Mitanni kings. Seti I was able to defeat the Hittite-Syrian alliance and regain control over Palestine. After driving back a Libyan attack, he marched to northern Syria; at this time the Egyptian and Hittite armies confronted one another for the first time. Seti I succeeded in seizing the city of Kadesh, but the Hitties retained their influence and authority over northern Syria. The struggle between Egypt and the Hittites had not ended and the confrontation continued. The reign of Seti I has provided us with a decree which carries the same severity as the earlier decrees of Horemheb. It does, however, include a new element, that of a magical incantation which was supposed to support his orders. His unique temple at Abydos and his magnificent tomb in the Valley of the Kings are indicative of how art and architecture retained their glory during his reign.

Although Seti I had achieved some success in rebuilding the Egyptian empire in Asia, his successor and son, Ramesses II, still faced the Hittite challenge. In the fifth year of his reign, Ramesses II set out for Syria with four independent armies to rejoin the struggle against the strong alliance assembled by the Hittites. Although Ramesses II did direct two of his armies into a trap near Kadesh, he still succeeded in converting a disaster into a qualified success. Fortunately for posterity, he depicted his wars (including the battle of Kadesh) against the Syrians, the Libyans and the Nubians in his temples in Nubia (Plates 33, 34),[3] at the Karnak and Luxor temples, and in his funerary temple, the Ramesseum. His wars with the Hitties continued until the twenty-first year of his reign when he signed a remarkable peace treaty with the Hittite king, Hattusilis, whose eldest daughter he married. In addition to proclaiming peace between the Hittites and the Egyptians, this treaty also provided for a defensive alliance against any other power which challenged either of the two signatories. The achievements of Ramesses II during his reign of about sixty-seven years included the erection of temples, obelisks and statues throughout the land of Egypt (Plate 35); together with his proclamations of military triumph, these achievements have made him the most celebrated and famous pharaoh. They, moreover, have given him the appellation, 'Ramesses the Great'.

At the time of his death, twelve of Ramesses II's sons had already predeceased him with the result that he was succeeded by his thirteenth son, Merenptah, who was also somewhat advanced in age. In the fifth year of his reign, he found himself facing a very serious situation as a great number of 'Sea Peoples' were moving toward the western Delta in alliance with the Libyans. Merenptah was victorious and the results of the battle were recorded in a stela: 6,000 enemies were slain and more than 9,000 were taken captive. This stela also recorded his activities in Palestine; Israel is mentioned for the first time in Egyptian records.

At Merenptah's death a dynastic struggle began and the throne was occupied by five different kings within a period of twenty years. At the end of the dynasty, a Queen Twosret reigned with her husband Seti II. When he died, she assumed the titles of pharaoh, like Hatshepsut, and reigned in her own right for about two years. After her death the 19th dynasty collapsed and Egypt suffered disorder for some years until a man, Sethnakhte, gained the throne and established the 20th dynasty.

The 20th dynasty

This dynasty, which according to Manetho was composed of twelve kings, witnessed many events and contained at least one mighty king. Nevertheless, it is obvious that the former splendour of Egypt was waning. Papyrus Harris tells us that at the end of the 19th dynasty there was complete disorder and that a Syrian named Arsu had succeeded in putting the entire land under his authority. Order was restored by Sethnakhte who reigned for a short time and was succeeded by his son, Ramesses III.

Ramesses III was so impressed by the greatness of Ramesses II that he modelled his names after those of the 19th dynasty king. He also attempted to revive the glory of Egypt. In the fifth, eighth and eleventh years of his reign, he decisively defeated the enemies of Egypt from both the west and the north. The well-planned and systematic invasion by both land and sea during his eighth year was a major threat, but he succeeded in defending Egypt, in winning victory in the first sea battle in history and in sending the Libyans and Sea Peoples elsewhere. Defeat in any one of those three battles would have meant the occupation of Egypt by people who, in addition to their warriors, had brought with them their families and their herds. Ramesses III also succeeded in holding the Egyptian empire in Palestine where he built a temple to Amon. One of his statues has been found at Beth Shan and a record of his reign exists at Megiddo (Wilson, 1951, p. 259).

Ramesses III, however, was more effective at fighting and external affairs than in coping with the internal affairs of Egypt. Corruption spread all through the country. Labour troubles increased together with inflation and the frequency of tomb robbery. Decadence thrived during the reigns of his successors, Ramesses IV-XI, while the power of the priests of Amon multiplied (Plate 36). Finally the High Priest of Amon, Herihor, took royal titles, thus beginning a new period in Egyptian history, the Third Intermediate Period.

THE THIRD INTERMEDIATE PERIOD (1070–656 BC)

In about 1100 BC, when Ramesses XI was ending his reign, the effective rule of Egypt was divided between Herihor in Thebes and Smendes, the founder of the 21st dynasty, who ruled from Tanis in the Delta. Thus Egypt was governed from two separate capitals; what is truly astonishing is that relations between these rulers were friendly and co-operative. The expedition of Wenamon, on the other hand, illustrates the depths to which Egyptian prestige had fallen in western Asia by this period (Gardiner, 1964, pp. 306–13). Wenamon was a royal messenger who was sent to Byblos in Phoenicia to bring cedar for the divine boat of Amon Re and who faced extreme and unendurable humiliation during his trip abroad. Following the death of Herihor, Smendes seems to have taken control over all of Egypt. During the period of the 21st dynasty, trade and other contacts with neighbouring states survived; military struggle was, however, mostly avoided. Disorder, debauchery and dishonesty continued to increase.

During the period of the 21st dynasty a family from the Faiyum began to flourish. Originally the members of this family had been part of a contingent of Libyan mercenaries who had settled in Egypt and who called themselves 'the chiefs of the Meshwesh'. A member of this family, Shoshenq, seized the throne of Egypt and established the 22nd dynasty in 946 BC. He maintained peaceful relations with King Solomon of Jerusalem, but after Solomon's death he attacked Jerusalem and took away the treasures of the Temple of Solomon.[5]

By the end of the 22nd dynasty, Egypt was divided into several minor kingdoms. Internally, the country was beset with civil war and increasing fragmentation while externally it was being menaced by Assyria in the north and a powerful Nubian kingdom in the south. A Delta prince named Pedibast set up a rival Libyan dynasty, which Manetho calls the 23rd dynasty; its kings bear the names used by the 22nd dynasty. At the same time, yet a third Libyan dynasty (the 24th) was established at Sais in the delta. The 24th dynasty consisted of only two kings, Tefnakhte and his son, whom the Greeks called Bocchoris. During the reign of Tefnakhte, Egypt was invaded by the Nubian king Piankhy who became the nominal ruler over all of Egypt. This conquest from the south was the first successful invasion of Egypt in a thousand years; the previous invasion, that of the Hyksos, had come from the north-east. Piankhy was powerful enough to take the Egyptian throne and to establish the foundations of the Nubian domination of Egypt for the next seventy years.

The 24th dynasty, however, continued for a brief period of time as a kind of sub-dynasty, since it recognized the Nubian dynasts as the rulers of Egypt. The army of Bocchoris was defeated in 720 BC at Raphia by the Assyrian king Sargon II and at almost the same time Egypt was invaded by Piankhy's successor Shabako who placed all of Egypt under his control. The struggle between the Assyrians and the Nubians over Egypt soon began, and it finally came to an end with the defeat of the Nubian king Tanutamon by Ashurbanipal after an Assyrian raid on Thebes in 663 BC. The Nubian king returned to his capital at Napata, but continued to claim that he was still the real king of Egypt.

After the Assyrian king returned to his capital, his officials who retained real control over only the Delta were faced with continued resistance from the Egyptian populace. This resistance continued until the ruler of Sais, Psammetichus, succeeded in driving the Assyrians out of Egypt and in establishing the 26th dynasty.

NOTES

1 They comprise a small lion statuette bought in Baghdad and now in the British Museum, an alabaster vase lid from Knossos (Crete), a fragment of an obsidian vase from Boghazköy (Anatolia) and a seal from Palestine.

2 About 400 clay tablets were found in the ruins of Tell el-Amarna; they contain the letters Amenhotep III and IV exchanged with the kings and princes in the neighbourhood of Egypt.

3 Six of his temples in Nubia were saved through the International Campaign of Nubia: the two temples of Abu Simbel and the temples of Wadi es Sebua, Beit el Wali, El Der and Gerf Hussein.

4 Which was abbreviated as 'Chiefs of the Ma'.

5 Old Testament, 1 Kings 14: 16–26.

BIBLIOGRAPHY

ADAMS, W. Y. 1977. *Nubia, Corridor to Africa*. London.

ALDRED, C. 1968. *Akhenaten, Pharaoh of Egypt: A New Study*. London.

BARNETT, R. D. 1975. The Sea Peoples. In: EDWARDS, I. E. S. et al. (eds), *Cambridge Ancient History*. 3rd ed. Cambridge. Vol. 2, p. 2, Chapter 28.

BIERBRIER, M. L. 1975. *The Late New Kingdom in Egypt (c. 1300–664 BC). A Genealogical and Chronological Investigation*. Warminster.

BIETAK, M. 1968. Vorläufiger Bericht über die erste und zweite Kampagne der österreichischen Ausgrabungen auf Tell el-Dab'a im Ostdelta Ägyptens (1966–1967). *MDAIK*, Vol. 73, pp. 79–114.

—— 1975. *Tell el-Dab'a*. Wien. Vol. 2.

—— 1975. Die Hauptstadt der Hyksos und die Ramesesstadt. *Antike Welt*, Vol. 6, pp. 24–43.

BREASTED, J. H. 1909. *A History of Egypt*. 2nd ed. New York.

CERNY, J. 1873. *A Community of Workmen at Thebes in the Ramesside Period*. Cairo.

—— 1927. La culte d'Amenophis I chez les ouvriers de la nécropole thébaine. *BIFAO*, Vol. 27, pp. 159–203.

DAVIES, N. de G. 1947. *The Tomb of Rekhmire at Thebes*. New York.

DESROCHES-NOBLECOURT, C. 1963. *Tutankhamen: Life and Death of a Pharaoh*. London.

DRIOTON, E.; VANDIER, J. 1962. *L'Egypte*. 4th ed. Paris.

EMERY, W. B. 1965. *Egypt in Nubia*. London.

GABALLA, G. A. 1977. *The Memphite Tomb-Chapel of Mose*. Warminster.

GARDINER, A. H. 1964. *Egypt of the Pharaohs: An Introduction*. Oxford.

HALLO, W.; SIMPSON, W. K. 1971. *The Ancient Near East: A History*. New York.

HAYES, W. C. 1959. *The Scepter of Egypt*. Cambridge, Mass. 2 vols.

HELCK, H. W. 1968. *Geschichte des Alten Ägyptens: Handbuch der Orientalistik*. Leiden/Köln. Bd. 1.

HELCK, H. W.; OTTO, E. (eds) 1972 *Lexikon der Ägyptologie*. Wiegsbaden.

KEES, H. 1961. *Ancient Egypt. A Cultural Topography*. London.

KEMP, B. J. 1983. Old Kingdom, Middle Kingdom and Second Intermediate Period. In: TRIGGER, B. G. et al., *Ancient Egypt: A Social History*. Cambridge. pp. 149–74.

KITCHEN, K. A. 1973. *The Third Intermediate Period in Egypt (c. 1100–650 BC)*. Warminster.

—— 1982. *Pharaoh Triumphant: The Life and Times of Ramesses II*. Warminster.

LEFEBVRE, G. 1929. *Histoire des grands prêtres d'Amon de Karnak jusqu'à la XXI Dynastie*. Paris.

MOKHTAR, G. 1981. *General History of Africa: Ancient Civilization of Africa*. Paris, UNESCO, Vol. 2.

PRITCHARD, J. B. 1969. *Ancient Near Eastern Texts Relating to the Old Testament*. 3rd ed. Princeton, N.J.

READ, J. G. 1970. Early Eighteenth Dynasty Chronology. *J. Near East. Stud.* (Chicago, Ill.), Vol. 29, pp. 1–11.

REDFORD, D. B. 1967. *History and Chronology of the Eighteenth Dynasty of Egypt*. Toronto.

—— 1970. The Hyksos Invasion in History and Tradition. *Orientalia* (Roma), Vol. 39, pp. 1–51.

SÄVE-SÖDERBERGH, T. 1941. *Ägypten und Nubien: ein Beitrag zur Geschichte altägyptischer Aussenpolitik*. Lund.

—— 1956. The Nubian Kingdom of the Second Intermediate Period. *Kush* (Khartoum), Vol. 4, pp. 54–61.

SETERS, J. van. 1964. A Date for the Admonitions in the Second Intermediate Period. *J. Egypt. Archaeol.* (London), Vol. 50, pp. 13–23.

—— 1966. *The Hyksos: A New Investigation*. New Haven, Conn/London.

SMITH, H. S.; SMITH, A. 1976. A Reconsideration of the Kamose Texts. *Z. Ägyptische Sprache Altert. kd.* (Leipzig), Vol. 103, pp. 48–76.

TRIGGER, B. G. et al. 1983. *Ancient Egypt. A Social History*. Cambridge.

WENTE, E. 1975. Tuthmosis III's Accession and the Beginning of the New Kingdom. *J. Near East. Stud.* (Chicago, Ill.), Vol. 34, pp. 265–72.

WILSON, J. A. 1951. *The Culture of Ancient Egypt*. Chicago, Ill.

IO.2.2
NUBIA AND ITS RELATIONSHIP WITH EGYPT
(1780–700 BC)

Théophile Obenga

A precise chronological framework and a few essential preliminary definitions will enable us to identify more accurately the links between Nubia and Egypt in the period concerned, placing appropriate emphasis on scientific and cultural aspects.

CHRONOLOGY

In Egypt, our starting point coincides with the end of the Middle Kingdom (2040–1785 BC) and the beginning of the Second Intermediate Period (1785–1554 BC), while the date 700 BC corresponds to the Egyptian Late Period. In the case of Nubia, the period concerned extends from that of middle and classical Kerma culture to the age of Napata of the kingdom of Kush (ninth century BC), that is to say before the Meroë period (270 BC to AD 350) of the same Kushite state.

From 1970 to 1785 BC Egypt under the Sesostrids was omnipresent in Nubia, as it was to be again from 1500 to 1100 BC under the rulers of the New Kingdom. On the other hand, during the 25th dynasty it was the kings of Kush who established themselves in Egypt and ruled the country from 747 to 656 BC.

These dates are prompted by the need for some kind of historical perspective, rather than from any artificial concern with classification by periods, since the chronology of the civilizations of the Egypto-Nubian Nile Valley is not always easily grasped by a reader unacquainted or unfamiliar with the ancient history of the African continent.

A FEW DEFINITIONS

Today Nubia designates, ethnically and culturally, that part of the Nile Valley inhabited by peoples speaking the Nubian languages, which are related to the Negro African languages of north-east Africa and the languages of the populations inhabiting the plateaux of Kordofan and Darfur to the west of the Nile. Thus, the country of Nubia nowadays extends from Aswan to the village of Ed-Debba: this means that almost one-third of this territory, between the First and Second Cataracts, traditionally referred to as Lower Nubia, is situated in Egypt while the remaining two-thirds, Upper Nubia, is part of the Sudan.

In ancient times, however, Nubia was a much larger, more extensive country than it is today. In the sixth century we find the Nubians at the confluence of the White Nile and the Blue Nile at Khartoum. The ancient Greek and Latin authors, Homer, Herodotus, Diodorus of Sicily, Strabo,

Seneca and Pliny the Elder referred to the Nubians and Nubia as 'Ethiopians' and 'Ethiopia'.

The ancient Egyptians used the following terms to designate these 'southern lands': *Khent* during the Old Kingdom (2780–2280 BC); *Kas, Kash* or *Kashi* during the Middle Kingdom: hence the term *Kush*; *Ksh*, the form current during the New Kingdom (1567–1085 BC). The name *Kas* appears for the first time during the Middle Kingdom on the stela from Buhen now in the Florence Museum in Italy. This stela bears an inscription the date of which is the year 18 of the reign of Sesostris I (12th dynasty).

The land of Kush is the land of gold which, in the pharaonic tongue, is *nbw*, hence *Nubia* for the land of precious metal. The Nubians in ancient history had the same habitat as the Nubians of today. The uninterrupted physical presence of a people on its native soil from early antiquity to the present day is quite exceptional in the overall history of Africa where migrations and movements of peoples were relatively frequent in ancient and precolonial times. The middle stretches of the Nile in the earliest days of African history formed part of an essential artery of communication between the Mediterranean basin and the interior of the African continent, an artery which, of course, passed through Egypt.

It is appropriate at this point to draw attention to the historic and cultural importance of the Nile, which crosses the eastern part of the world's most formidable desert, the Sahara, on leaving the swamps of the African Great Lakes. The waters, silt and annual floods of the river have made human life possible in arid desert conditions. It is the river valley which is fertile. Nubia and Egypt are the gifts of the Nile, as Herodotus observed. The Nile also made possible the movement of goods (gold, ivory, skins, tortoise-shell, animals, wood, and so on), men (servants, slaves, warriors) and ideas (rites, institutions, beliefs) between the heart of Africa and the Egypto-Nubian Nile Valley and between that valley and the Mediterranean world. For example, the sacred status of royalty and the ritual wearing of leopard skins are quite distinctive cultural features which are specific to the Nile Valley and the rest of Black Africa.

It is difficult to know if the Nubians physically resembled their neighbours. Diodorus of Sicily made the following anthropological observation on some Ethiopians: 'and particularly those living on the banks of the river [the Nile] had black skin, flat noses and frizzy hair'.[1] Herodotus, the 'father of history', had already noted that the 'Egyptians' had 'dark skin'.[2]

These features, which come within the province of physical anthropology, provide arguments for the view that 'Nubians' and 'pharaonic Egyptians' were Black Africans like all the other Black Africans of the continent: Sara, Galla, Bantu, Yoruba, Mossi, Dogon, Wolof, Fulani, Malinke, Songhai, and so on.

NATURE OF THE EVIDENCE

Recourse to a number of different disciplines is necessary to write the history of the Egypto-Nubian Nile valley which, in reality, forms a single anthropological and cultural unit. A brief word should be said about these disciplines, from the standpoint of their relevance to methodology and historical criticism.

Archaeology, which is based on excavation, is central to a knowledge of Egypto-Nubian ancient history. This source of historical information seeks to resolve problems related to stratigraphy, the origin of centres of cultural influence, dating, cultural contacts in time and space between different cultural areas, and so on. Another vital technique for the history of the region is the deciphering of ancient texts, in this instance hieroglyphs, hieratic and demotic, and Meroitic. Egyptian hieroglyphs were deciphered by Champollion in 1822. The Meroitic script can be read but the language thus revealed remains unknown and undeciphered up to the present time. The deciphering of the Meroitic language will undoubtedly be one of the key cultural and scientific events[3] in the years or centuries to come.

Philology enables the historian to follow the evolution of ancient languages from the inside: their particular forms, borrowings, losses, archaisms, the dynamics of grammatical structures, and so on. Chronology, of course, assigns dates to civilizations in universal time: the Kerma culture in Nubia is divided into four stages: Old Kerma, Middle Kerma, Classical Kerma and Recent Kerma, this division being based on the differences – over time and space – in materials (particularly ceramics), funerary rites (the shape of graves, sacrifices) and the relationship with neighbouring Nilotic cultures – the A-Group (3000–2500 BC) in the case of Old Kerma, the C-Group (2000–1500 BC) in the case of Middle Kerma, and contemporary pharaonic Egypt for the entire duration of antiquity in the Egypto-Nubian Nile Valley. The Nubian cultural complexes known as the A-Group, C-Group and Kerma cultures belong to the pre-Kushite period – the Kushite period including Napata and Meroë as well as the X-Group or the Ballana culture, that is to say the transitional period between Meroë and the beginning of the Christian era (fourth and fifth centuries AD). Historians of antiquity thus work with extremely varied and difficult sources when dealing with these remote periods of African history.

In the history of Egypto-Nubian relations, from the end of the pharaonic Middle Kingdom to the Late Period in Egypt, and from the Middle and Classical Kerma culture to the Napatan period in Nubia, we shall focus on those facts of major relevance to the history of the scientific and cultural development of humanity.

THE KINGDOM OF KERMA

Technologies employed by the populations of Middle and Classical Kerma

Since the decisive excavations conducted in Nubia from 1907 to 1932 by the American Egyptologist George Andrew Reisner, the Nile Valley between the First and Second Cataracts has probably been the most thoroughly excavated region of the world. Where the Nubian Kerma sites are concerned, excavations have extended as far as the region of the Fourth Cataract. The Kerma culture, which takes its name from a modern town in the Sudan between the site of Tabo and the Third Cataract, is a complex culture extending over several centuries between the A-Group and the Egyptian domination of Upper Nubia at the beginning of the New Kingdom. Brigitte Gratien, in a work which is remarkable for its precise detail, gave an account in 1978 of some forty-seven known Kerma sites, describing and analysing the pottery, funerary rites and furniture (Gratien, 1978). Since 1980, Professor J. Leclant has made regular reports on the excavations and research on Kerma, notably that conducted by Professor G. Bonnet and his team at the University of Geneva (Leclant and Clerc, 1986), on which the following is essentially based.

The site of Kerma itself is the largest site of the culture, but other sites are equally important: thus Old Kerma has been identified with Sai, to the south of the Second Cataract, where almost sixty tombs have been excavated; Middle Kerma is mainly grouped around and to the south of the Second Cataract, with the necropolises of Semna (eleven burials excavated), Ukma, Aksha and those in the region of Amara; Classical Kerma is located between Middle Egypt and the Fourth Cataract – at Ukma, where there are several hundred tombs; at Aksha, with over a hundred burial sites; at Sai, which is the second centre of Classical Kerma in terms of its area; at Kerma itself with its several thousand tombs; and at Tabo, Bugdumbush and so on.

Chronologically, Old Kerma, which had only weak links with Egypt, appeared at the end of the Old Kingdom (around 2280 BC) and gave rise to Middle Kerma at the beginning of the Middle Kingdom (2052 BC). Middle Kerma culture, which is marked by a growth in relations with Egypt, gave way to Classical Kerma during the 18th dynasty before disappearing completely under Tuthmosis III (1504–1450 BC). Thus the Kerma period, which constitutes an entity in spite of its different stages of development, stretches in Nubia from the end of the Old Kingdom to the 18th dynasty.

Middle and Classical Kerma: their relations with Egypt

Middle Kerma already had stone silt-retaining dikes. The Nubians thus sought to meet the challenge of a formidable desert in order to cultivate the soil, which would have been extremely arid without such hydraulic engineering technology since the Nile floodwaters, depositing their fertilizing silt on the river banks, did not always reach the land further away from the river.

Large-scale mixed stock rearing was the principal resource of the population of Middle Kerma, who herded cattle, sheep and goats. Livestock was undoubtedly a factor of social differentiation and the animal sacrifices on tombs express a particular ideology, that of pastoral desert-dwellers. The many flocks of sheep and goats, pulling up the roots of plants and destroying young shrubs, must have impoverished the vegetation. Domestic animals thus contributed to the desertification of a country which was already condemned to drought.

While fans and mats continued to be produced in Middle Kerma, the handicraft industry developed and diversified to include wood working, leatherwork, pottery and clay enamelling. Most of the ceramics are rather crude. Bulbous wide-mouthed pots are the items most frequently encountered in the tombs. They are of average size, 30 cm high and 30 cm in diameter. The base is rounded and the body convex with a change of curve in the centre, a narrow neck, a wide bell-shaped mouth and a simple lip continuing the line of the walls. The clay is of variable quality, black in section, the colour of the surface varying from beige to red and black. The most common motifs on the shoulder, which bears an incised or printed geometric decoration in repeated horizontal bands, are the triangle, the lozenge and the rectangle. But fine well-made pottery also existed: red, black-rimmed bowls with a rounded base and convex body. The clay in this case is of even consistency, fine and extremely hard. The pottery is entirely glazed and black in section with an even rim. The interior surface is a deep black and the exterior an orange red. One particular form of pottery of Middle Kerma has a flat or slightly convex base, sides which are concave to varying degrees and a bell-shaped mouth with a simple rim. The clay is nevertheless of the same quality and colour as that used in the fine ware.

Great honour was shown to the dead, who were buried in cloth and leather, with personal possessions placed on or beside the body. Wooden footrests were placed at the feet and fans usually made from several sheaves of ostrich feathers were laid alongside; stone vessels and pottery toilet jars were placed near the skull. At Sai, G. A. Reisner excavated a spherical jar of veined alabaster which had a narrow neck and a small curving convex rim closed by an enamelled blue lid with a rosette decoration (Reisner, 1923, p. 59, pls. 38–42).

The bone needles are straight with very wide eyes. Large numbers of them were also found at Old Kerma placed close to the pelvis of the dead.

Red ochre, which was also used in Old Kerma burials, was found in nearly all the tombs, sprinkled finely over the entire body. In other parts of Black Africa, red kaolin or *tucula* powder, obtained from the bark of a red wood, was used in precolonial times. This is a custom of ontological significance everywhere in Black Africa: red signifies life. The colour has a protective effect and strengthens human virtues. It turns the dead man into a powerful being who continues to live. Essentially, life and death form a single organic whole in this African Negro ideology.

The use of metal began to spread during Middle Kerma: triangular-bladed knives, copper and bronze daggers with crescent-shaped ivory pommels resembling the type of daggers found during the Egyptian Middle Kingdom and described in 1917 by Flinders Petrie in his work *Tools and Weapons*.

Ivory, shells and enamelled clay were the materials most frequently employed in the making of jewellery. We find wrist and ankle bracelets made of bark and leather and large quantities of discoid beads made of enamelled clay or bone. The population of Kerma also worked cornelian and quartz which they coated in blue enamel.

The most common type of amulet was the falcon, sculpted from schist. Scarabs, which were rare, bore signs or inscriptions in the style of the Egyptian Middle Kingdom.

The culture of Middle Kerma has many features in common with that of the C-Group which flourished at the same time in Lower Nubia: circular superstructures, sacrificed animals, ox skulls deposited around the pits, incised semi-spherical bowls and so on. It is obvious that the funerary customs of the C-Group and Middle Kerma are identical. C-Group and Middle Kerma are perhaps no more than two local variants of a common earlier tradition, known as Old Kerma in

the case of Kerma, evidence of which is also found in the early sites of the C-Group. The C-Group is located to the north of the Second Cataract; to its south is Middle Kerma, which reached its apogee in Classical Kerma before the country was occupied by Egypt.

Classical Kerma appears to have been an important centre for commerce and crafts. Many seals for baskets, pots and boxes were found in the middle of the town of Kerma together with the raw materials necessary for the manufacture of objects, including red ochre, copper oxide, resin, blocks of mica, rock crystal deposits, pebbles of cornelian and fragments of ostrich eggs. Tools were found with these raw materials: grinders, polishers, pottery equipment. The dwellings of Classical Kerma were made of sun-dried bricks. Spreading north, the population occupied the old Egyptian fortresses of the Middle Kingdom, abandoned by their garrisons after the 18th dynasty, at Kuban, Kor, Buhen, Semna and Mirgissa.

At the site of Kerma in the ancient town near the religious district, the Swiss excavations of 1984–5 brought to light the foundations of a round structure organized around three rows of wooden supports. A round wall surrounding this inner area gives the building an inside diameter of 15.5–16.5 m. The masonry consists of sun-baked bricks. A few traces of an ochre wash suggest that part of the superstructure was painted. The foundation trench of a thick wall of baked bricks around the building underscores the importance of the complex. This surprising building constructed roughly between 2000 and 1800 BC appears to have been occupied for several centuries (Leclant and Clerc, 1986).

In the western part of the site of Kerma, the Swiss expedition discovered new houses of unbaked bricks, thereby completing the picture of the general layout of the town. Everyday objects were excavated in one dwelling: spindle whorls, fragments of the shell of ostrich eggs used in the production of beads, worn axe heads, polishing or grinding stones of ferruginous sandstone used in the decoration of ceramics. Men and women accompanied by giraffes are depicted on some fragments of ostrich eggs.

Agriculture developed at Classical Kerma in association with animal husbandry. A system of dikes and irrigation canals is present. Egyptian representations of the Middle Kingdom and the 18th dynasty show long-horned cattle in Nubian tributes. The craftsmen worked quartz, mica, copper, ivory, gold and pottery. This martial people (Nubia had been called *Ta-sety*, 'The Land of the Bow', since the period of the Egyptian Old Kingdom) made leather bonnets employing an original Nubian technique. Giraffe hair, ostrich feathers, ivory, stone and enamelled quartz were worked at Kerma. The pottery follows older traditions: black-rimmed red vases of black section with incised and impressed decoration. These black-rimmed red vases disappeared from Egypt after the predynastic period. Consequently, the specimens found later in Egypt were probably imported from Nubia where that form of pottery was produced from the prehistoric period until the fourth century of our era (Säve-Söderbergh, 1941, p. 5; Obenga, 1973, pp. 97–9).

Classical Kerma, which covers the end of the Middle Kingdom and the whole of the Second Intermediate Period, appears to have had a hierarchical society. A prince reigned at Kerma to the south of the Third Cataract. A form of central authority may have been based on this leader, something which appears to be confirmed by the existence of an important dignitary who governed the country's secondary centres. Huge tombs were built for these princes and dignitaries.

Animal and human sacrifice, a custom encountered elsewhere in Black Africa, in ancient Abomey for example, was practised. As ethnic unity usually implies linguistic unity in Black Africa, we must assume the ethnic and linguistic unity of all the populations of Kerma which occupied the valley as far as Egypt. Several distinct human groups which are geographically separate from each other may none the less belong to a single linguistic community. Writing was still unknown. The god, Horus, a deified falcon which is encountered in ancient Mali and in the Zimbabwe of Mwene Mutapa (Monomotapa), was an object of worship. The use of red ochre to cover the bodies of the dead is another old funerary custom typical of Black Africa.

Recent Kerma corresponds to a period of Egyptianization and the rapid disappearance of its characteristic features under Egyptian occupation.

To sum up, Kerma, an independent Nubian kingdom having trading contacts with Egypt, formed an organic whole in spite of its evolution and the changes and modifications it underwent during the different stages in its history. It had a specific social and ideological structure, practised agriculture, animal husbandry and handicrafts, and an original form of art was expressed in scenes on earthenware vessels, jewellery and decorated clothing. The villages were built on either the west or east bank of the river. The necropolises were dug on the edge of the desert and the graves were always placed on an east-west axis. The bodies of the dead lay in a contracted position. All sorts of objects have been found in the tombs: the people of Kerma believed in the world beyond.

The country of Kerma is therefore a remarkable cultural entity. The major centres, such as Ukma and Aksha, Sai and Kerma, were clearly linked and the prince of Kerma controlled the entire country, especially during the Second Intermediate Period. The reason the Hyksos kings of the 15th and 16th dynasties appealed to the king of Kush for assistance in his struggle against the Egyptian kings of Thebes was that there was a central authority in the country of Kerma, located precisely at Kerma.

The Kerma kingdom thus occupied Nubia to the south of the Second Cataract from roughly 2000 to 1550 BC. What, then, was its relationship with pharaonic Egypt?

Relations between Kerma and pharaonic Egypt

Kerma was extremely rich. The copper mines at Buhen had been exploited since the time of the Old Kingdom, as proved by the smelting furnaces found locally (Emery, 1962). There are also other deposits, stretching as far as the south of Darfur, at the mines of Afrat en-Naar. The crystalline substratum of Nubia contains outcrops of gold. Precious and semi-precious stones such as garnet, crystal, quartz, agate and obsidian were also among the coveted riches of Nubia. The diorite of Toshka in Lower Nubia was highly valued, as was the lilac-coloured amethyst and the orange-red cornaline which were worked to produce jewels. To these must be added the products of Upper Nubia: ivory, gazelle, oryx, ostrich feathers, leopard skins and living animals such as monkeys and baboons, leopards and giraffes. Ebony and gum were also supplied by Nubia, which was at the crossroads between Egypt and the other countries of Black Africa. Cattle was also a part of the great wealth of Nubia, which supplied the army and the desert police. Domestic servants were also supplied.

Nubia was accordingly a country coveted by Egypt for its many riches. The period which concerns us here saw the beginnings of the conquest of Nubia by Pharaoh Kamose (Vandersleyen, 1971), who made use of the forts established on the Second Cataract of the Nile during the 12th dynasty, during which the Egyptians penetrated beyond Kuban, Krosko and Toshka to the northern boundaries of the cataract, while consolidating Buhen which had been a centre of Egyptian activity under the Old Kingdom. Sesostris III (1878–1843 BC) had mounted no fewer than four expeditions to Nubia and extended the frontier south of the cataract near Semna, where his stelae have been found.

Kamose, the son of Sekenenre and brother of Ahmose, who was to wage a struggle for national freedom against the Hyksos under Apopi towards the middle of the sixteenth century BC, nevertheless admitted in his long account engraved on several stelae dedicated to Amon of Karnak that he had to divide the country between two rulers, an Asian ruler to the north and a king of Kush to the south. Lower Nubia between the First and Second Cataracts was, in fact, the territory of the princes of Kush, and Kerma close to the Third Cataract was the capital. At the time of Kamose the territory of Kerma was held by the Kushites but the Egyptian pharaoh appears to have advanced as far as Buhen.

The conquest of Nubia was continued under Ahmose, who advanced to Sai (Vercoutter, 1973). Tuthmosis I (1530–1520 BC), the great conqueror of the New Kingdom, progressed beyond the Fourth Cataract. Almost every pharaoh from Ahmose up to and including Tuthmosis III (1504–1450 BC) conducted campaigns in Nubia. The once powerful kingdom of Kush was thus ruined. Egypt then achieved control over the valley of the Nile from the Delta to the region of Jebel Barkal between the Fourth and Fifth Cataracts. Jebel Barkal is none other than Napata, which was an administrative centre under the 18th dynasty. The first temple of 'Amon of Napata, dweller of the sacred mountain' was founded by Tuthmosis III. Napata thus became the principal shrine of the kingdom of Kush.

During the New Kingdom, after the fall of Kerma, the administration of Nubia was entirely under the control of the 'royal son of Kush', the title of the Egyptian official who was directly responsible to the pharaoh. This high Egyptian official was assisted by a 'lieutenant' for Kush and for Wawat, that is to say for Upper and Lower Nubia. The 'son of Kush' was mainly resident at Aniba but also spent some time at Faras. Aniba was a town and fortress in Lower Nubia between the First and Second Cataracts in which there stood a temple of Horus. Under the New Kingdom it became the administrative centre of Lower Nubia. In the thirtieth year of his reign, Amenhotep III (1408–1372 BC) established a large temple of Amon, also intended for the worship of his own person, at Soleb to the south of the Third Cataract. Queen Tiye, who lived from c. 1415 to 1340 BC, the well-loved companion of Amenhotep III, 'great royal spouse', Queen Mother of Egypt for half a century, mother of the pharaohs Akhenaten and Tutankhamen and mother-in-law of Nefertiti, was herself a woman of the south, from Nubia-Kush. Another temple was built by Amenhotep III at Sedeinga, upstream of the Third Cataract on the west bank of the Nile.

During the Ramesside period, the 19th and 20th dynasties (1314–1085 BC), the 'chief of the countries of the South', 'royal son of Kush', was an extremely important person. Thus, Seti I and, for example, the royal son of Nubia, Amenemope, had sculpted on the rock above the valley at Qasr

Ibrim, a small distance downstream from the Second Cataract, a votive inscription which records the reconquered glory of Egypt: 'Perfect God who strikes the Nine Bows, mighty heart who crushes his enemies, laying waste the land of Kush, trampling underfoot the Tjenhenou [Libyans] and leading away their chiefs into captivity... To him [pharaoh] the strangers from the South come with lowered heads, while the peoples of the North [western Asia] prostrate themselves before his splendour ...' (Kitchen, 1969, pp. 98–9).

Seti I was indeed a great king who asserted the power of the pharaohs in Palestine, in the land of the Hittites, in ancient Libya and in Nubia: 'Thy frontiers henceforth stretch from the lands of the South to the limits of the winds of the North and the boundaries of the deep green [sea]' (Ibid.). The reign of Seti I, which was a time of renewed prosperity, was also an artistic high point of ancient Egypt, witnessing as it did the construction of the 'funerary temple' of Gourna and the hypostyle hall of Karnak, decorated with ritual scenes and pictures recalling the victories of the king over the Bedouins, the Libyans, the Amorites and the Hittites.

But in the eighth year of the reign of Seti I a revolt occurred in Nubia, in the land of Irem (Iram). The resulting campaign lasted over two months and a battle was fought which lasted seven days. This revolt by the Nubians of Irem must therefore have been serious (Kitchen, 1969, pp. 102–3). Another revolt broke out in Nubia, again in the land of Irem, between the fifteenth and eighteenth years of the reign of Ramesses II (1301–1235 BC). Ramesses II conducted a campaign in Nubia together with four of his sons in order to assist the royal son of Kush, who presumably was experiencing difficulties in collecting Nubian tribute. The Iram, one of the most important tribes in Upper Nubia, have been known among Sudanese rural communities since the time of the Egyptian Old Kingdom (Priese, 1974).

The reign of Ramesses II was very long. Like his father Seti I, he attempted to exploit the gold-bearing mines in the Nubian and Arabian deserts. The gold from the desert near Wadi Mia, to the east of the present-day town of Redisiyeh, and the gold from Wadi Akita, in the region of Wadi Allaki, with the fort at Kuban, swelled the Egyptian treasury.

Setaou was unquestionably the most powerful 'royal son of Kush' between the thirty-eighth and sixty-third years of the reign of Ramesses II. This great administrator, who received the encyclopaedic education of the scribes, became tax-collector of the kingdom and was assigned to the domain of Amon Re before being appointed 'royal son of Kush'. He ended his brilliant career as one of the august judges of the state tribunal. The construction of the Nubian temples at Abu Simbel, the most important sanctuary in Lower Nubia, at Gerf Hussein, roughly 90 km south of Aswan, and at Wadi es-Sebua, roughly 150 km south of Aswan on the west bank, was largely due to Setaou. His wife, Mut Nefert ('Mut the Beautiful') was 'superior of the harem of Amon', an eminent position in the female priesthood. Setaou administered Nubia with the assistance of other senior Egyptian officials: the 'lieutenant' of the region of Wawat, the 'lieutenant' of the region of Kush, the mayors of large towns such as Miam and Aniba in Lower Nubia, and the 'controller of the priests of all the gods of the lands of the South'. The administration recorded crops and inventoried cattle. The chief of the archers was also 'chief of the deserts of the gold of Amon in Nubia'. In that capacity he supervised the desert police and the extraction of the precious metal by local Nubian workers. The Egyptians in Nubia were therefore numerous and exploited Nubia like any colony.

As already noted, the presence of the Egyptians in Nubia did not go uncontested. Thus, Merenptah, the thirteenth son of Ramesses II who was crowned c. 1129 BC and who ruled Egypt for about ten years, had serious difficulties with Nubia as we learn from a text sculpted on a stela from the temple of Amada: 'The Medjai were led off to Egypt; their throngs were set alight in the presence of those who remained; their hands were cut off because they had revolted; others had their ears torn off and their eyes torn out; these were taken to the land of Kush and piled up in their towns so that Kush should never more rebel ...'

This strange and exceptional cruelty on the part of the Egyptians suggests that the suppressed revolt must have been dangerous for Egypt. Merenptah employed the same rather untypical force in dealing with the 'People of the Sea' in the fifth year of his reign. The hands of the dead were cut off on the battlefield as were the penises of dead Libyans and other uncircumcised peoples, Philistines, Shardanes, Siculi, Lycians, Achaeans, Etruscans and so on.

The last Ramesside, Ramesses XI, who had grown weak towards the end of his long reign, could not prevent the coup organized by the royal son of Kush, Panehesy, who rebelled and entrenched himself in Nubia, thus depriving Egypt of the resources of the Nile Valley to the south of Elephantine.

The break with Nubia was to have considerable political consequences.

Napata and Meroë: the kingdom of Kush

The ruling class in the kingdom of Kush was not the product of a line originating outside Nubia. In its southern half the area in which the Kushites first settled extended as far as the 'Island of Meroë' between the Atbara, the Nile and the Blue Nile rivers. Centres such as Musawwarat es-Sufra to the north-east of Khartoum must have been in existence from the Napatan period. A sphinx of King Aspelta (593–568 BC) was found close to Khartoum but the monument may have been moved there at a later date. Lower Nubia, on the other hand, was an integral part of the kingdom of Kush from its beginning. The Nubian tribes lived in the Bayuda, the great desert steppe which extends from south of Napata (Kerma) to the region of Meroë. In the eastern desert lived the Blemmyes, who were the ancestors of today's Beja peoples.

The oldest tombs in the cemetery at El-Kurru take us back five generations of rulers before Kashta (760–742 BC), almost to 900 BC. However, the earliest king of Kush known to us by name is Alara, who was probably the direct successor of Kashta. Alara is mentioned only in late inscriptions but in a context which suggests that he was the founder of the kingdom. Thus, Taharka proclaimed that he had received his power through the intercession of Alara on behalf of his grandmother.[4] Irike-Amanote (431–405 BC) hoped that his reign would be as long as that of Alara.[5] Nastasen (335–315 BC) spoke of a place on the road from Meroë to Napata where Alara 'emerged' and proclaimed that he himself had been invested at Napata with the 'power, the victorious power', of his ancestor. It should be borne in mind that the genealogy of the female ancestors of Aspelta ends with the two last generations before Alara.[6] Historical considerations therefore suggest that the foundation of Kush should be dated at around 800 BC.

The kingdom of Kush had two important centres:

Napata, at the foot of Jebel Barkal (the 'Holy Mountain'), and Meroë. Under the Egyptian New Kingdom, Napata was an Egyptian administrative centre with several small temples. The cemeteries of the kings of Napata at El-Kurru and Nuri (c. 900–300 BC) were quite close to each other. The Napatan dynasty of Kush would appear to have originated in the region of Napata as it remained the most important religious centre throughout, though the place indicated by Nastasen as the (political) birthplace of Alara cannot be pinpointed accurately. It may have been Sanam Abu Dom at the end of the road through the Bayuda between Meroë and Napata.

The other Kushite centre, Meroë, probably played a much more important role at an earlier date, contrary to what was formerly believed. Since the beginning of the fifth century BC Meroë was the permanent royal residence of the Kushite kings who travelled to Napata only for their 'coronation journey', investiture and burial. The royal palace at Napata was uninhabitable by the time of Harsiotef (404–369 BC) and the temples were in an appalling state.[7] It is generally accepted that the royal residence was transferred to Meroë in 591 BC, but some doubt is cast on this by the fact that only the kings, royal wives and mothers were buried near Napata from the time of Piankhy (747–716 BC) to that of the last ruler. The other members of the royal family were buried near Meroë. Furthermore, the text describing the coronation of King Tanutamon,[8] which took place in 664 BC, declares that the sovereign had only visited Napata on a journey to Egypt. Finally, excavations have uncovered human occupation on the edge of Meroë dating from the seventh century BC. It is therefore highly probable that the country of origin of the Meroitic kings was actually located in the region of Meroë itself.

Whatever the case may be regarding these questions of origin and of the transfer or otherwise of the kings from Napata to Meroë, it must be accepted that Egyptian culture and religion occupied a dominant position in the kingdom of Kush at the time of Kashta, that is to say, during the first period of the history of the kingdom of Kush. Inside Egypt itself the sovereign power of the 22nd and 23rd dynasties, two dynasties of Libyan origin, had disintegrated into several rival chiefdoms. And, perhaps to save Egypt from the nomadic invaders from the Libyan desert, Upper Egypt fell into the hands of Kashta in about 760 BC. The Kushite king took the title of pharaoh and entrusted to his daughter Amenirdis I the politically important position of 'Divine Lady of Amon'. This divine votaress of the Egyptian god-king was adopted by Shepenwepet I, the last representative of the Theban dynasty. Because of this, Kashta's successor, Piankhy, was clearly affected by the struggles for power in Egypt. His main rival was Tefnakhte, a prince from the western Delta, who was preparing to subjugate neighbouring chieftains. Piankhy was therefore forced to take action. He himself related in detail his struggle against Tefnakhte in the nineteenth and twentieth years of his reign and his account was reproduced on a magnificent stela erected in the Great Temple of Amon at Jebel Barkal.[9] Tefnakhte was defeated and a sort of status quo was temporarily observed in Egypt. The Nubian king saw himself as a restorer of the Egyptian monarchy while Piankhy emphasized his respect for the thousand-year-old traditions of Egypt by ordering offerings to be made in the temple of Amon at Karnak and by treating the local population humanely: 'The people of Memphis shall be unharmed and no child shall ever cry. Consider the southern provinces: not a single inhabitant has died,

except those enemies who had sinned against the god and were killed as rebels.'

Bocchoris, the son of Tefnakhte, resumed hostilities but he in turn was defeated and killed by Piankhy's successor, Shabako (715–702 BC), the first sovereign of the 25th dynasty of Egypt, known as the 'Ethiopian' dynasty, which also included Shabataka (702–609 BC), Taharka, undoubtedly the greatest sovereign of the dynasty, and Tanutamon (664–659 BC). It should be noted that the royal succession was matrilineal, kings generally being succeeded by the children of their sisters, their nephews. A Greek source (Nicholas of Damascus) specifically makes this point. Thus, Piankhy, who succeeded Kashta, was not his son and Shabako himself was the brother of Piankhy. Similarly, Shabataka, Shabako's nephew, reigned prior to Taharka, while Tanutamon, the son of Shabataka, succeeded Taharka.

The reign of these Kushite pharaohs was a period of economic and cultural revival for Egypt which lasted several decades. Construction and architecture received a new impetus. The old religious and philosophical literature was 'republished' and ancient motifs were rediscovered for the decoration of temples and tombs. These archaistic trends in literature and art were actively promoted by the Kushites not only in Egypt but in the land of Kush itself. Thus, Piankhy restored the old Temple of Amon at Napata. His brother and successor Shabako was extremely active in the area of Thebes: he was responsible for the flood-level markings or Nilometers, on the waterfront at Karnak, the stamped bricks in the walls of Madinat Habu, the construction of a pylon in front of the small temple of Madinat Habu (completed by Taharka), the reliefs in the passageway of the great pylon at Luxor, and the construction in front of the temple of a colonnade/propylaeum, a type of monument which the Kushite king also introduced at Medamud, 9 km to the north of Luxor. At Karnak, which is by far the largest religious complex in Egypt, Shabako renovated the gate at the fourth pylon with a fine coat of gold, having resumed activities in the eastern desert in the gold-bearing region of Wadi Hammamat. He also renovated the 'treasury' to the north of the Banqueting Hall of Tuthmosis III, and worked on a columned structure to the north of the third pylon.

At Memphis the most important achievement was the republishing of the famous text of Memphite philosophy.[10] This text is of genuine historical significance. Now dated to the Egyptian Old Kingdom, it is the very first philosophical text concerning the Creation in the Mediterranean basin. Through the Word, Ptah, god of Memphis, created everything which exists: plants, animals, people. Attention is thus drawn to the unity of all existing things and to the omnipotence of the creative word. Thus, before the Bible and the Koran, and even before the Greek philosophers themselves, the Egyptian philosophers of the Old Kingdom had clearly worked out a doctrine of the Word, of the logos, in the institution of Reality. 'In ancient Egypt, the demiurge created the world by uttering the names of things and beings. The sovereign word sufficed to create any reality simply by uttering its name'(Gusdorf, 1977, p. 16; Obenga, 1973). Under the Kushite kings Egypt experienced a cultural renaissance. The archaistic adoption of many ancient features does not detract from the remarkable quality of the works.

In the area of foreign policy, Shabako arguably made efforts to cultivate good relations with Assyria, which had just subjugated Syria and Palestine. Shabataka for his part supported the small states of Syria and Palestine which wished to be independent from Assyria, and in the year 701 BC a

Kushite army commanded by the future King Taharka met and gave battle to the Assyrians near Altaku in Palestine.

But Kushite rule in Egypt was not destined to endure, for the Assyrians advanced towards Egypt from the north-east. After many attacks, the Assyrian king Ashurhaddon arrived in Memphis in 671 BC. Taharka was forced to withdraw to the south. The Assyrians took away with them to Mesopotamia not only statues but also scholars and craftsmen.

Thus, at different times in the period from 1780 to 700 BC, one finds Nubia and Egypt developing independent endogenous kingdoms while maintaining trading links; the pharaonic empire extending its boundaries as far south as the Fourth and Fifth Cataracts, following the fall of the kingdom of Kerma; and Kushite Nubia being in full possession of the entire valley of the Nile from Napata to the Delta, with a return to the cultural, literary and artistic heritage of earlier periods of the Egyptian past. In reality, the two parts of the Nile Valley, Nubia and Egypt, were never completely cut off from each other. Kerma, Napata and Meroë clearly belonged to the valley of the Egypto-Nubian Nile and thus constitute the basis of Africa's 'classical antiquity'.

NOTES

1. Diodorus of Sicily, *Bibliotheca historica*, Vol. 3, para. 8.
2. Herodotus, Book II (*Euterpe*), para. 104. Note: this phase refers to the Colchians from the Caucasus who are akin to the Egyptians.
3. Barber (1974), in a highly technical work, does not even raise the question of Meroitic.
4. Khartoum stelae 2678, 2679.
5. Kawa IX inscription.
6. Cairo stela JE 48866.
7. Cairo stela JE 48864.
8. Cairo stela JE 48863.
9. Cairo JE 48862.
10. Breasted (1901). The stela, which is in poor condition, is now in the British Museum ('Shabaka Stone' No. 498).

BIBLIOGRAPHY

BARBER, E. J. W. 1974. *Archaeological Decipherment: A Handbook.* Princeton, N.J.

BREASTED, J. H. 1901. The Philosophy of a Memphite Priest. *Z. Ägyptische Sprache und Alter. kd* (Leipzig), Vol. 39, pp. 39–54.

EMERY, W. B. 1962. Preliminary Report on the Excavations at Buhen. *Kush*, Vol. 9, pp. 116–20.

GRATIEN, B. 1978. *Les cultures de Kerma: Essai de classification.* Lille.

GUSDORF, G. 1977. *La parole*, Paris.

KITCHEN, K. A. 1969. *Ramesside Inscriptions.* Oxford, Vol. 1.

LECLANT, J.; CLERC, G. 1986. Fouilles et travaux en Egypte et au Soudan, 1984–1985. *Orientalia* (Roma), Vol. 55, No. 3, pp. 123–319.

OBENGA, T. 1973*a*. Création des êtres d'après l'inscription de Shabaka. In:—— *L'Afrique dans l'antiquité.* Paris. pp. 129–61.

—— 1973*b*. *L'Afrique dans l'antiquité.* Paris.

PRIESE, K. H. 1974. 'rm und '3m, das Land Irame. Ein Beitrag zur Topographie des Sudan im Altertum. *Altorient. Forsch.* (Leipzig), Vol. 1, pp. 7–41.

REISNER, G. A. 1923. *Excavations at Kerma.* Vol. II. Cambridge, Mass., Harvard African Studies.

SÄVE-SÖDERBERGH, T. 1941. *Ägypten und Nubien: Ein Beitrag zur Geschichte altägyptischer Aussenpolitik.* Lund.

VANDERSLEYEN, C. 1971. *Les guerres d'Amosis, fondateur de la XVIIe dynastie.* Brussels, Fondation égyptologique Reine Elisabeth.

VERCOUTTER, J. 1973. La XVIIIe dynastie à Saï et en Haute Nubie. *Cah. rech. Inst. Papyrol. Egyptol.* (Lille), Vol. 1, pp. 7–38.

II

EUROPE

II.I

THE AEGEAN WORLD

Michel Sakellariou

SPACE AND TIME; REGIONS AND PERIODS

This chapter is devoted to the cultural history of Greece and the Aegean basin in the Bronze Age (*c.* 3000–1100 BC) and the Iron Age (*c.* 1100–700 BC). During this period Greece and the Aegean basin formed an area with a culture that was relatively homogeneous during the Bronze Age and markedly so in the Iron Age. During the Bronze Age, pockets with distinctive regional characteristics can be identified in various parts of the Greek mainland, but particularly in the south; in some of the Aegean islands, particularly in the Cyclades; and in Crete. From the beginning of the Iron Age, the area attained a very marked degree of cultural uniformity as a result of significant movements of Greek groups towards the eastern Aegean and Crete.

Archaeological data provide the basis for dividing the Bronze Age into three stages, and each stage into three periods: the Early Bronze Age I, II and III, in the third millennium BC; the Middle Bronze Age I, II and III, from about 2000–1900 BC until about 1600 BC; and the Late Bronze Age I, II and III, which came to an end in about 1100 BC. More specific designations are used for some regions, namely Early Helladic I, II and III, Middle Helladic I, II and III and Late Helladic (or Mycenaean) I, II and III for the southern part of the Greek mainland; Early Cycladic I, II and III, Middle Cycladic I, II and III and Late Cycladic I, II and III for the Cyclades; Early Minoan I, II and III, Middle Minoan I, II and III and Late Minoan I, II and III for Crete. The dividing line between successive stages varies from one cultural region to another. Specialists also draw a distinction between phases and sub-phases within certain periods, resulting in such references as Mycenaean IIIA1a.

Only in exceptional cases do the demarcations between stages, periods or phases correspond to historical upheavals. The exceptions are the transition from Early Helladic II to III, from Early Helladic III to Middle Helladic I, and from the end of the Late Bronze Age to the beginning of the Iron Age. The first two reflect the arrival of the Proto-Greeks in Greece. What occurred *c.* 1100 BC on the Greek mainland in the Aegean basin and Cyprus, and also in the Balkan lands and Anatolia, was not so much the transition from the Bronze Age to the Iron Age as the migratory movements, destruction of settlements, breaks in continuity and, generally speaking, profound upheavals. By contrast, the historical processes that began around 1100 BC did not come to a halt around 700 BC, but continued. Successive styles of pottery provide the basis for a distinction between the periods known as Sub-Mycenaean, from 1100 BC to *c.* 1050 BC, Protogeometric, from *c.* 1050 BC to 900 BC and Geometric, from *c.* 900 BC to 725 BC.

II.I.I

THE EARLY BRONZE AGE (3000–1500 BC)

Christos Doumas

As has been observed in Volume I, the distribution of Late Neolithic settlements shows a distinct preference for coastal sites and a marked increase in the importance of the southern reaches of the Hellenic peninsula. This shift in the siting and distribution of settlements reflects the gradual change effected in the economic basis of Aegean society. Trade and seafaring activities, already initiated in Neolithic times, increased in significance, as is attested by the intensive settlement of the islands – even the smallest – and Aegean littoral, throughout the Early Bronze Age.

Geographical and environmental heterogeneity in the Aegean also influenced cultural development and four distinct entities can be distinguished. The Early Helladic culture of the Greek mainland represents the most conservative among Aegean societies in the third millennium BC, with an economy mainly based on agriculture, founded in Neolithic traditions. It is divided chronologically into Early Helladic I (EH I), EH II and EH III. The Aegean islands cradled two cultures: one in the north, embracing the islands of Lemnos, Lesbos, Chios, Samos and so on, as well as the shores of the Troad; and one in the south centred on the Cyclades and extending to the coast of Attica and some of the islands of the Dodecanese. Both cultures share the characteristics – potentials and limitations – of island cultures: isolation due to the barrier of the sea, relative protection from external invasion or attack, factors which determine a kind of island conservatism both biological and cultural. Yet the islands are characterized by receptiveness to innovations, the conscious introduction and assimilation of new ideas, mainly fostered by the development of trade, and technological discoveries encouraged by limited availability of natural resources. The Early Cycladic culture is also conventionally divided into three stages, EC I, EC II and EC III. In Crete the Early Bronze Age culture, which Sir Arthur Evans dubbed Minoan, and in which he too distinguished three phases, EM I, EM II and EM III, is hybrid in nature. It combines the self-sufficiency typical of mainland regions with the isolation and conservatism of the islands.

The major technological innovation of this period is the introduction of metallurgy and consequent exploitation of the mineral resources of the area. Although it has been maintained that bronze working was introduced from the East (Theocharis, 1974, p. 41), recent archaeological discoveries have demonstrated that metallurgy developed in the Balkans much earlier than was previously believed (Renfrew, 1979, p. 381). Lead isotope analyses also point to a northern rather than eastern origin for bronze in the Aegean Early Bronze Age. Thus it is probable that metallurgy was introduced to this region from the north (cf. Renfrew, 1979, p. 103) and that the islands played a significant role in its dissemination

and expansion. In this respect, it is hardly fortuitous that the earliest proto-urban centre on European territory appeared in one of the Aegean islands, at the site of Poliochni on Lemnos, and the earliest evidence of mining and metallurgical activities comes from the Cycladic islands (Renfrew, 1972, pp. 308 ff).

THE GREEK MAINLAND

Despite the fact that there are only scant architectural remains from the Early Helladic I period (3000–2600 BC), it appears that there was a clear preference for low hills, close to the coast where possible, as settlement sites. This observation holds for almost the whole of the Greek peninsula, from Macedonia and Thrace in the north to the Peloponnese in the south. Sites such as Mihalic in Aegean Thrace, Sitagroi in eastern Macedonia (Renfrew, 1979, pp. 196–7) and Kritsana in Chalcidice (Caskey, 1971, p. 774) have shown that these regions were either in direct or indirect contact with both the north Aegean islands and the southern Balkan regions. Thus they may be qualified as 'melting pots' of Aegean and Balkan cultures or, as Renfrew characterized Sitagroi, Januses facing 'both to north and south' (1979, p. 197).

The development of the Helladic culture of central Greece and the Peloponnese was more rapid in the coastal area. Eutresis in Boeotia is a representative Early Helladic rural site with a well-documented chronological sequence. The site of Lerna in the Peloponnese, on the Argolic Gulf, has furnished convincing evidence of the establishment of foreign contacts and the growth of trade.

Although there is a dearth of building remains from the Early Helladic I period, the continued occupation of Neolithic settlement sites suggests that habitation was not subject to violent disruption. Moreover, the cultural level of these sites is generally low, more reminiscent of Chalcolithic tradition, with a closed agricultural economy (Theocharis, 1974, p. 94). The earliest houses of Early Bronze Age Thessaly were mudbrick, timber-framed structures, such as those unearthed at Argissa (Caskey, 1971, p. 776). Further south houses were constructed with stone foundations and socles. Red-burnished pottery, including bowls, small jugs and jars, is the characteristic ware of the period. In the ensuing EH II period (c. 2600–2300 BC) development is more rapid but there is a smooth transition from the preceding one. Some EH I sites were abandoned, some expanded and others founded. It was during this phase that the first tentative steps towards urbanization were made (Konsola, 1986), probably as a result of the establishment of a mercantile, maritime economy. Collective works, craft specialization and organized trade are significant new features of EH II society.

In architecture the small, two-roomed rectilinear house with courtyard was the norm. These dwellings, of mudbrick on stone foundations, were closely packed in the settlements, being clustered in quarters, circumvented by narrow streets. All had a hearth. Coastal settlements were frequently surrounded by stone-built enclosures (Manika, Asketario, Rafina in Attica), which in major centres (Aegina, Lerna) developed into true fortifications (Theocharis, 1974, p. 97). In many such centres a distinctive building, with an inner passage running parallel with its external walls, has often been qualified as an administrative and/or religious centre. Such edifices, also referred to as Early Helladic II megara, are known from Thebes in Boeotia, Lerna in the Argolid, Akovitika in Messenia and Aegina (Walter and Felten, 1981). With the exception of the insular settlement of Aegina, the geographical location of the others suggests that they controlled and exploited the fertile plains of their environs. Thus it is quite possible that the EH II megaron was intended for the collection of an agricultural surplus, for subsequent redistribution and exchange, as is strongly suggested by the large number of seals recovered from the House of the Tiles, the megaron at Lerna, which probably bespeak intense commercial activity (Theocharis, 1974, p. 97). These megara of the EH II period, whose ancestry may be traced to the megaron of Late Neolithic Thessalian settlements, are perhaps also indicative of a centralization of authority.

A similar rapid development is apparent in the sphere of technology during the EH II period. Metallurgy was by now a necessity, as attested by the wide distribution of metal objects, both in coastal and inland sites (Theocharis, 1974, p. 94; Branigan, 1974, pp. 105 ff). Though pottery was still hand-made, the repertoire was enriched with new shapes: sauce-boats, 'askoi', squat pyxides basins, two-handled jars and shallow bowls are the commonest, diffused throughout the Greek mainland, from Thessaly southwards. The absence of the sauce-boat is noted in the north, while high-spouted jugs, cups and tankards, and one-handed cups with spherical body and conical neck prevail, shapes reminiscent of those found in North Aegean culture. Decoration on pottery is rare, being mainly limited to raised bands around large pithoi, impressed with cylinder seals (Caskey, 1971, p. 785). The technique of Urfirnis (early glaze) is an innovation mainly observed in pottery from southern sites.

The final stage of the Early Helladic period (c. 2100–2000/1900 BC) seems to have been one of wretchedness and obscurity. Many of the sacked EH II settlements were abandoned; others, like Lerna, were resettled by newcomers (Lerna IV), perhaps those responsible for the destruction of the previous one (Lerna III). New pottery forms characteristic of EH III are: tankards, small cups, two-handled bowls with everted rim, round-bodied jars with flaring rim; and the sauce-boat, diagnostic of EH II, is absent. EH III pottery is black or brown burnished, some vases are decorated with rectilinear designs, 'usually in dark semi-lustrous paint on light ground, occasionally in light paint on dark surfaces' (Caskey, 1971, p. 786). A major technological innovation is the use of the potter's wheel, marks of which are sometimes present on pots. On the whole, it seems that the foundations of Middle Helladic culture (2000/1900–1500 BC) were laid down during the LH III period.

Early Helladic culture, as outlined above, was characteristic of the Aegean side of the Hellenic peninsula. As Caskey remarked, it was 'thinned out and altered when it first reached the west coast, coming into contact with other influences from the Adriatic sphere'. This is borne out not only by the absence of certain pottery shapes, such as the sauce-boat, but also by the fact that the upheavals and destructions experienced on the Aegean coast at the end of EH II evidently did not affect the Ionian coast. There is some evidence of contacts between the west coast of the Peloponnese, and Nydri on Lefkas, further north, with the Cyclades (Caskey, 1971, p. 793).

THE NORTH AEGEAN ISLANDS

Major Early Bronze Age (EBA) sites so far investigated in the North Aegean islands are: Poliochni on Lemnos (Bernabo Brea, 1964), Thermi on Lesbos (Lamb, 1936) and Emporio on Chios (Hood, 1981).

Archaeological exploration of these islands continues and new sites have been located, augmenting our knowledge of their prehistory. In its EBA phases, at least, Troy (Troy I–V), on the Anatolian coast of the Aegean, belongs to the same North Aegean culture, constituting its continental province. Because Troy was sung of by Homer and excavated by Schliemann it has tended to overshadow later discoveries on the islands in its vicinity, even though these are in fact the metropolis of the culture of the Troad. For not only was Poliochni on Lemnos founded before Troy, in the early third millennium BC, it was already a proto-urban settlement, though Troy remained to the last a fortified site (Renfrew, 1972, p. 129). Moreover, the nucleus of the North Aegean culture was the islands; its presence is much weaker in Thrace and the Troad, which should be regarded as its hinterland, a fact observed by other scholars who have remarked on the strong links of the Troad with the Aegean, as opposed to the mainland of Thrace or Anatolia (Blegen, 1963, pp. 5, 7–9; Hood, 1982, p. 716; Doumas, 1968, pp. 27–8).

In all probability the first settlers of the North Aegean islands arrived from the neighbouring Anatolia littoral, towards the end of the fourth millennium BC (Bernabo Brea, 1964, p. 683), as is inferred from the Oriental character of their culture, which was gradually 'westernized' as it came into contact with those of insular and continental Greece (Bernabo Brea, 1964). The Late Neolithic curvilinear, stone-built huts of the first settlers gave way to oblong, rectilinear houses (Bernabo Brea, 1964; Hood, 1981), organized in settlements embodying such urban features as defensive walls (Poliochni II, Blue period: Bernabo Brea, 1964; Thermi V: Lamb, 1936; and Emporio III: Hood, 1981); public wells (Poliochni: Bernabo Brea 1964; 1976; and Emporio: Hood 1981); paved streets (Poliochni: Bernabo Brea, 1976) or 'gravelled roadway' (Emporio: Hood, 1981); last but not least, a sewerage system (Poliochni: Bernabo Brea, 1976). All the above may be considered as public works, requiring coordinated communal effort for construction and maintenance, characteristic of urban settlements. In addition there is ample evidence of craft specialization, an agricultural surplus and trade (Lamb, 1936, pp. 12, 43; Bernabo Brea, 1964, p. 24).

Of all aspects of material culture, pottery is the best documented and most abundantly represented. It exhibits a wide variety of shapes, reflecting its long developmental process. Vessels of both coarse and fine fabric include storage jars, cooking pots, drinking cups, bowls, dishes, fruit stands, miniature vases and so on. The *depas amphikypellon* (two-handled tall cup) and jar with wing-like attachments, as well as anthropomorphic and theriomorphic vases, are the most distinctive shapes, being exclusive creations of North Aegean culture.

In addition to pottery, other objects fashioned from clay include spindle whorls and figurines, the latter being typical of Thermi (Lamb, 1936, pp. 149 ff). The ground stone industry includes mortars, querns, grinders, hammers and axes, while there is limited use of flint and obsidian for chipped stone tools.

The wide variety of metal objects recovered from the sites of the North Aegean: daggers, spearheads, axes, knives, saws, chisels, borers, hooks, needles, tweezers, razors, pins and so on, not only bear witness to the spread of metallurgical technology, they also furnish indirect evidence of other activities and occupations, such as carpentry and fishing. Although bronze was the metal used in the greatest quantity, lead, silver and gold were also worked. Pieces of lead were often used for mending broken pots and for modelling figurines; gold and silver were mainly used for fashioning ornaments, such as pins, pendants, finger and ear-rings, and other items of jewellery (Branigan, 1974).

The islands' limited potential for the development of an agricultural economy obliged the islanders to turn their attention to the sea and what it had to offer. This explains why settlement sites were selected on the east coast, facing the Anatolia littoral, which has always guaranteed the viability of island communities (cf. Cherry, 1985, p. 20). The channel between these islands and the coast of the mainland opposite facilitated the passage of ships from north to south and vice versa, and the rapid development of Poliochni into a thriving urban centre undoubtedly owes much to its strategic location at the mouth of the Dardanelles, controlling the traffic between the Aegean and the Black Sea. Furthermore, Lemnos is ideally placed for establishing contact with the southern Aegean, via the northern Sporades, Pagasetic Gulf, straits of Euboea, and thence the Argolid, via the Cyclades and the coast of Attica. For it was possible for ships to navigate the entire route, and back again, in lee of the coast, without being exposed to the open sea. Archaeological evidence supports such a proposed route.

In the North Aegean also, the end of the EBA came abruptly and violently, all the major sites being destroyed simultaneously: Troy, Poliochni, Thermi and Emporio. All, excepting Troy, which was rebuilt and reinhabited into the Middle Bronze Age, were abandoned and the islands apparently deserted. What caused this wholesale destruction is still a matter for debate, though it seems that it cannot be dissociated from that suffered by the east coast of mainland Greece, nor from the sudden appearence of small hill-forts in the Cyclades at about this time.

THE CYCLADIC ISLANDS

Situated in the central part of the Aegean sea, the Cyclades have evidently been inhabited since at least the end of the fifth millennium BC, as suggested by finds from Saliagos (see Vol. I). Their development during the EBA was rapid and it seems that the islanders' involvement in seafaring and trade contributed a great deal to laying the foundations of the entrepreneurial character of the Aegean economy, which is the legacy of the third millennium BC. The earliest representations of boats in the Aegean area come from the Cyclades; incised on pottery, rock carvings, lead models of ships (Basch, 1987, pp. 76 ff). The evidence suggests that the earliest ships were propelled by oars and that the keel had been invented, a significant contribution to marine technology.

There is no evidence of the use of sails before the end of the third millennium BC. As in the North Aegean islands the paucity of resources for agriculture presumably encouraged the islanders to engage in seafaring activities, particularly trade, for which they were admirably situated, between the Greek mainland, Crete and Anatolia. It has also been suggested that not only did the Cycladic islanders pioneer shipbuilding techniques and propulsion, but they also conceived methods of navigation, including pictorial representations of the constellations.

Very few settlement sites have been located in the Cyclades and even fewer excavated. Our knowledge of Early Cycladic society is derived mainly from cemeteries. These are generally small (10–30 graves), and the graves were for single inhumations, from which it is inferred that the settlements, still to be investigated, were also small in extent and population. In EC II there was probably an increase in population, since the burial grounds are larger and the graves accommodate multiple inhumations (Doumas, 1977, p. 31). Scant architectural evidence from this phase comes from isolated dwellings of flattish stones embedded in clay, insufficient for us to estimate the extent of settlements, though it seems there was a preference for coastal sites consonant with the increasingly maritime character of Cycladic society. During the third phase, EC III, large, proto-urban settlements emerged in places guaranteeing safe anchorage. Such sites have been excavated at Phylakopi on Melos, at Ayia Irini on Kea, at Paroikia on Paros. In the next period, the Middle Cycladic, these developed into real harbour towns and trading stations.

Besides these 'ports' there appeared in the Cyclades during the EC III period quite a different type of settlement; fortified installations on rather remote and easily defensible hilltops, such as Kastri on Syros, Kynthos on Delos, or Panormos on Naxos. Both pottery and metal objects found in these settlements display North Aegean associations and the indications are that their life was short and came to a violent end. It has been suggested that these Cycladic hillforts were founded by refugees from the North Aegean who fled southwards, intruding into the Cyclades, perhaps with the intention of resuming their maritime activities. The Cycladic islanders seem to have reacted to these interlopers, expelled them from the islands but evidently tolerated their settling on the coast of the Greek mainland and Aegina (Doumas, 1988, p. 28).

Concerning the material culture of the Early Cycladic period, there is an overt increase in sophistication in all spheres; architecture, pottery and, in particular, marble carving. Only one type of vessel is known from the EC I phase: the handmade, poorly fired pyxis, decorated with incised rectilinear patterns. From this the EC II vessels are derived, bearing incised or impressed decoration of curvilinear designs. During this phase the first painted pottery was produced, with rectilinear motifs in dark paint on a light ground. Themes from the animal kingdom (birds, fish, mammals) were also depicted, though very rarely, being either incised or painted. The pottery of the EC III period is of even better quality and likewise exhibits a wide range of shapes. Painted decoration predominates, at the expense of the old technique of incised which gradually disappears, but curvilinear motifs are retained.

The simplicity of forms and clear outlines of the Cycladic

environment are perhaps echoed in those of the Cycladic marble figurines (Doumas, 1968; Preziosi-Getz, 1985). Though we shall probably never know whether these artistic creations had a religious or secular function, their anthropocentric conception is indisputable. Could this reflect the ideology of the society which produced them?

Throughout the third millennium BC inhumation was the sole type of burial. The dead were interred in a highly contracted position and accompanied by grave goods, comprising pottery, marble vases, marble figurines, toiletry items and jewellery. The absence of domestic objects from the graves perhaps implies that only personal belongings were buried together with the dead, possibly indicating a belief in an after-life (Doumas, 1977) (Plates 37–40).

CRETE

The Early Bronze Age in Crete, also known as the pre-palatial period, is best documented in the east and the centre of the island, perhaps indicative of Crete's foreign contacts and extraneous influences. It seems that before the rise of the so-called palaces, in the Middle Minoan (MM) period, settlements in Crete were founded in locations difficult of access and easily defensible. Except for Mochlos, where traces of rectangular EM I houses have been observed, no other architectural remains can be attributed to this period. There is better evidence from the succeeding EM II phase when houses were built of stones and clay on coarse rubble foundations and covered with 'flat wooden rafter roofs with brushwood on top filled in with earth' (Hutchinson, 1950, p. 205). The completely excavated settlement at Phournou Koryphi, Myrtos (Warren, 1972) is the best known, followed by the site of Vasiliki, which has not yet been so thoroughly investigated. Both sites exhibit features which led the excavator of the former to suggest they are the precursors of the Middle Minoan palaces. They seem to have been planned to accommodate specific activities in specific areas, so that 'the origins of the palaces are to be sought here ... architecturally in part and economically in full' (Warren, 1972, p. 261). The architectural evidence from the EM III period is again scant, perhaps because of the overlying remains of the later periods (Hutchinson, 1962, p. 155), unless what is known as EM III pottery is just a local style developed in central Crete and does not represent a phase (Platon, 1981, I, p. 148).

There was a rapid development of pottery-making in EBA Crete, in both shapes and techniques (Hood, 1978, p. 30). The burnished pottery of the Neolithic period continued to be produced, though much less, in EM I Crete, with the introduction of new styles, such as pattern-burnished ware, slip-coated vases with linear decoration in red, white or dark paint (Betancourt, 1985, p. 23). The repertoire of shapes is small, comprising jugs, chalices, tankards, askoi and so on. Certain shapes and decorative styles seem to have been specific to certain regions (Pyrgos ware, Aghios Onouphrios ware and so on). Pottery of the EM II phase is characterized by a greater variety of shapes and innovations in decoration: Koumasa ware with hatched and cross-hatched decoration; Vasiliki ware with mottled decoration resulting from controlled firing conditions (Betancourt, 1985, p. 35 ff). The most distinctive class of EM III pottery is the so-called white-on-dark ware, in which there is a wide range of shapes and the decoration consists of white linear patterns on a dark ground. Patterns vary from plain lines, circles and spirals to complex geometric motifs (Betancourt, 1985, pp. 53 ff).

The manufacture of stone vases, an industry in which Crete excelled in the Aegean area, does not seem to have started before the EM II period (Hood, 1978, p. 139). Initially both the range of shapes and of materials was limited. Chlorite or chlorite schist were used to fashion pyxides, often bearing incised and relief spiral decoration. In the succeeding phases, through until the Middle Minoan, 'there is a great increase in the number of types and in the materials used' and the decoration is more elaborate than before (Warren, 1969, p. 183).

Very much in its infancy during the EM I period, metallurgy rapidly expanded during EM II. Bronze tools and weapons (daggers, spears, arrowheads, double-axes, knives, saws), as well as toilet implements (tweezers, scrapers, razors) were produced and there is evidence for the introduction of the cire perdue casting technique (Branigan, 1974, p. 106).

Gold and silver working also developed in EM II Crete, particularly along the island's north coast (Branigan, 1974, p. 107), perhaps indicative of the provenance of the raw materials, the objects, or even the techniques. Technological advances in metallurgy do not seem to have been affected by the devastation and turmoil attested in the Aegean towards the end of EBA II and development continued during the MM period.

Marble sculpting was not as popular in Early Minoan Crete as it was in the Cycladic islands, other materials being preferred for small figurines, such as clay, stone, shell and ivory (Hood, 1978, p. 90).

Although evidence of painting on plaster does exist from as early as the middle of the third millennium BC, it was only in the subsequent Middle and Late Bronze Age that wall paintings came into the ascendancy as a means of artistic expression (Hood, 1978, p. 48). In the domain of artistic activities, we should include seal-carving. From EM II onwards, soft stones, ivory, animal teeth and bone were used for carving seals, depicting a diversity of linear and pictorial themes (Hood, 1978, pp. 210–12; Yule, 1980). In Crete the Early Bronze Age did not end abruptly but evolved smoothly and gradually into the Middle Bronze Age, the period of the great palace complexes.

With regard to the burial customs of Early Minoan Crete, archaeological research has brought to light multiple burials in caves and rock shelters, virtually throughout the island and continued during EM II, being restricted to northern and central Crete. During this period built graves were introduced, of two types: one comprises complexes of an inner and one or more outer rectangular chambers, which were used as ossuaries for multiple inhumations; the other is encountered mainly on the Mesarà plain and consists of a circular structure of internal diameter from c. 4 to 13 m. Next to the entrance of this circular chamber, which always faces east, there were one or more compartments. It is not known exactly how they were roofed. The hundreds of burials associated with these tombs attest their protracted and communal use (Branigan, 1970b; Pelon, 1976). It is interesting that larnakes (baked clay coins) and cist graves also appeared during the EM II phase. EM III burial habits do not differ from those of the previous period and in many instances the same graves and tombs continued in use.

BIBLIOGRAPHY

ALEXIOU, S. 1969. [*Minoan Civilization*]. Irakleion.

BARBER, E. J. W. 1991. *Prehistoric Textiles: The Development of Cloth in the Neolithic and Bronze Ages with Special Reference to the Aegean.* Princeton, N.J.

BASCH, L. 1987. *Le Musée imaginaire de la marine antique.* Athènes.

BERNABO BREA, L. 1964, 1976. *Poliochni: Città preistorica nell'isola di Lemnos.* Roma.

BETANCOURT, P. P. 1985. *The History of Minoan Pottery.* Princeton, N.J.

BLACKBURN, E. 1970. *Middle Helladic Graves and Burial Customs, with Special Reference to Lerna in the Argolid.* Ann Arbor, Mich., Diss. Inaug. (microfilm).

BLEGEN, C. W. 1963. *Troy and the Trojans.* London.

—— 1973. Troy IV. In: EDWARDS, I. E. S. et al. (eds), *Cambridge Ancient History.* 3rd ed. Cambridge. Vol. 2, Part 1, pp. 483–5.

BOUZEK, J. 1985. *The Aegean, Anatolia and Europe: Cultural Interrelations in the Second Millennium* BC. Göteborg. (Stud. mediterr. Archaeol., 29.)

BRANIGAN, K. 1968. *Copper and Bronze Working in Early Bronze Age Crete.* Lund. (Stud. mediterr. Archaeol., 19.)

—— 1970a. *The Tombs of Messara.* London.

—— 1970b. *The Foundations of Palatial Crete: A Survey of Crete in the Early Bronze Age.* London.

—— 1974. *Aegean Metalwork of the Early and Middle Bronze Age.* Oxford.

CADOGAN, G. 1976. *Palaces of Minoan Crete.* London.

CARPENTER, R. 1968. *Discontinuity in Greek Civilisation.* Cambridge.

CASKEY, J. L. 1971. Greece, Crete and the Aegean Islands in the Early Bronze Age. In: EDWARDS, I. E. S. et al. (eds), *Cambridge Ancient History.* Cambridge. Vol. 1, Part 2, pp. 771–807.

—— 1973. Greece and the Aegean Islands in the Middle Bronze Age. In: EDWARDS, I. E. S. et al. (eds), *Cambridge Ancient History.* Cambridge. Vol. 2, Part 1, pp. 117–40.

CASSOLA GUIDA, P. 1973. *Le armi difensive dei Micenei nelle figurazioni.* Roma. (Incunabula Graeca, 56.)

CHADWICK, J. 1976a. *The Decipherment of Linear B.* 2nd ed. Cambridge.

—— 1976b. *The Mycenaean World.* Cambridge.

CHERRY, J. F. 1985. Islands out of the Stream : Isolation and Interaction in Early East Mediterranean Prehistory. In: KNAPP, A. B.; STECH, T. (eds), *Prehistoric Production and Exchange.* Los Angeles, Calif. (Monogr. 25.)

CROUWEL, J. 1981. *Chariots and Other Means of Transport in Bronze Age Greece.* Amsterdam.

DARQUE, P.; POURSAT, J.-C. (eds) 1985. *L'iconographie minoenne: Actes de la table ronde d'Athènes, 21–22 avril 1983.* Paris.

DARQUE, P.; TREUIL, R. (eds) 1990. *L'habitat égéen préhistorique: Actes de la table ronde internationale organisée par le Centre national de la recherche scientifique, l'Université de Paris I et l'École Française d'Athènes, 23–25 juin 1987.* Paris.

DAVIS, J. L.; CHERRY, J. (eds) 1979. *Papers in Cycladic Prehistory.* Los Angeles, Calif.

DESBOROUGH, V. R. d'A. 1964. *The Last Mycenaeans and their Successors: An Archaeological Survey c. 1200–1000.* Oxford.

DESBOROUGH, V. R. d'A.; HAMMOND, N. G. L. 1975. The End of Mycenaean Civilization and the Dark Age. In: EDWARDS, I. E. S. et al. (eds), *Cambridge Ancient History.* 3rd ed. Cambridge. Vol. 2, Part 2, pp. 658–712.

DESHAYES, J. 1960. *Les Outils de bronze de l'Indus au Danube.* Paris. (Inst. fr. Archéol. Beyrouth. Bibl. archéol. hist., 71.)

DICKINSON, O. 1977. *The Origins of Mycenaean Civilisation.* Göteborg. (Stud. mediterr. Archaeol., 49.)

DOUMAS, C. 1968. *The N. P. Goulandris Collection of Early Cycladic Art.* Athína.

—— 1977. *Early Bronze Age Burial Habits in the Cyclades.* Göteborg. (Stud. mediterr. Archaeol., 48.)

—— 1983. *Thera. Pompei of the Ancient Aegean.* London.

—— 1988. Early Bronze Age in the Cyclades: Continuity and Discontinuity? In: FRENCH, L.; WARDLE, K. *Problems in Greek Prehistory: Papers presented at the Centenary Conference of the British School of Archaeology at Athens. Manchester, April 1986.* Bristol.

DREWS, R. 1988. *The Coming of the Greeks: Indoeuropean Conquests in the Aegean and the Near East.* Princeton, N.J.

DUHOUX, Y. 1976. *Aspects du vocabulaire économique mycénien,* Amsterdam.

ECKSHMITT, W. 1986. *Kunst und Kultur der Kykladen,* Vol 1: *Neolithikum und Bronzezeit.* Mainz. (Kult. gesch. antiken Welt, 29).

EFFENTERRE, H. van. 1986. *Les Egéens. Aux origines de la Grèce: Chypre, Cyclades, Crète et Mycènes.* Paris.

EVANS, A. J. 1921–35. *The Palace of Minos at Knossos.* Vol. 1 (1921), Vol. 2 (1928), Vol. 3 (1930), Vol. 4 (1935). London.

FINLEY, M. I. 1970. *Early Greece. The Bronze Age and Archaic Ages.* London/Toronto.

FURUMARK, A. 1941. *The Mycenaean Pottery: Analysis and Classification.* Stockholm.

GRAHAM, J. 1962. *The Palaces of Crete.* Princeton, N.J.

GSCHNITZER, F. 1981. *Griechische Sozialgeschichte von der mykenischen bis zum Ausgang der klassischen Zeit.* Wiesbaden.

HÄGG, P. et al. (eds) 1988. *Early Greek Cult Practices: Proceedings of the Fifth International Symposium of the Swedish Institute at Athens, 26–29 June 1986.* Stockholm. (Skr. utg. Svenska Inst. Athen, 38.)

HÄGG, R.; KONSOLA, D. 1986. *Early Helladic Architecture and Urbanization.* Göteborg. (Stud. mediterr. Archaeol., 81.)

HÄGG, R.; MARINATOS, N. (eds) 1984. *The Minoan Thalassocracy: Myth and Reality.* Stockholm. (Skr. utg. Svenska Inst. Athen, 32.)

—— 1987. *The Function of the Minoan Palaces.* Stockholm. (Skr. utg. Svenska Inst. Athen, 35).

HAMMOND, N. G. L. 1976. *Migrations and Invasions in Greece and Adjacent Areas.* New Jersey.

HARDING, A. F. 1984. *The Mycenaeans and Europe.* London.

HELCK, W. 1979. *Die Beziehungen Ägyptens und Vorderasiens zum Ägäis bis 7. Jh. v. Chr.* Darmstadt.

HOOD, S. 1967. *The Home of the Heroes.* London.

—— 1971. *The Minoans: Crete in the Bronze Age.* London (Anc. Peoples Places, 75).

—— 1978. *The Arts in Prehistoric Greece.* Harmondsworth.

—— 1981–2. *Prehistoric Emporio and Ayio Gala.* London. 2 vols.

HOOKER, J. 1976. *Mycenaean Greece.* London/Boston, Mass.

—— 1980. *Linear B. An Introduction.* Bristol.

HUTCHINSON, R. W. 1950. *Prehistoric Town Planning in Crete. Town Plan. Rev.,* Vol. 21, No. 3.

—— 1962. *Prehistoric Crete.* Harmondsworth.

IAKOVIDIS, S. E. 1969–70. [*Perati*]. Athína.

—— 1983. *Late Helladic Citadels in Mainland Greece.* Leyden.

IMMERWAHR, S. A. 1990. *Aegean Painting in the Bronze Age.* University Park/London.

KAISER, B. 1976. *Untersuchungen zum minoischen Relief.* Bonn.

KNAPP, A. B.; STECH, T. (eds) 1985. *Prehistoric Production and Exchange.* Los Angeles, Calif.

KONSOLA, D. 1984. [*Early Urbanisation in the Early Helladic Settlements.*] Athína.

—— 1986. Stages of Urban Transformation in the Early Helladic Period, in *Early Helladic Architecture and Urbanisation.* Seminar held at the Swedish Institute, Athens, *Proceedings.* Göteborg.

LAFFINEUR, R. 1977. *Les vases en métal précieux à l'époque mycénienne.* Göteborg. (Stud. mediterr. Archaeol.)

—— (ed.) 1987. *Thanatos: les coutumes funéraires en Égée à l'Age du Bronze. Actes du Colloque de Liège, 21–23 avril 1986.* Liège.

—— 1989. Transition du monde égéen du Bronze Moyen au Bronze Récent: Actes de la deuxième rencontre, égéenne internationale de l'Université de Liège, 18–20 avril 1988. *Aegeaum,* Vol. 3.

LAMB, W. 1936. *Excavations at Thermi in Lesbos.* Cambridge.

LEHMANN, G. A. 1985. *Die mykenisch-frühgriechische Welt und der östliche Mittelmeerraum in der Zeit der 'Seevölker' – Invasionen um 1200 v. Chr.* Opladen. (Rhein. Westf. Akad. Wiss., Vortr., 176.)

LENCMAN, J. 1966. *Die Sklaverei im mykenischen und homerischen Griechenland.* Wiesbaden.

LEVY, E. (ed.) 1987. *Le système palatial en Orient, en Grèce et à Rome: Actes du colloque de Strasbourg, 19–22 juin 1985.* Leiden.

LINDGREN, M. 1973. *The People of Pylos, Prosopographical and Methodological Studies in the Pylos Archives.* Uppsala. (Acta Univ. Ups., 3).

MADDOLI, G. (ed.) 1977. *La civiltà micenea: Guida storica e critica.* Roma (2nd ed., 1981; 3rd ed., 1992). (Bibl. univers. Laterza, 384.)

MARAZZI, M.; TUSA, S.; VAGNETTI, L. (eds) 1986. *Traffici Micenei nel Mediterraneo, Atti del convegno di Palermo.* Taranto. (Magna Grecia, 3.)

MARINATOS, N. 1986. *Minoan Sacrificial Ritual: Cult Practice and Symbolism.* Göteborg. (Skr. utg. Svenska Inst. Athen, 9.)

MARINATOS, S.; HIRMER, M. 1973. *Kreta, Thera und das mykenische Hellas.* 2nd ed. München.

MATTHÄUS, H. 1980. *Die Bronzegefässe der kretisch-mykenischen Kultur.* München.

MATZ, F. 1962. *Kreta und frühes Griechenland.* Baden-Baden.

—— 1973a. The Maturity of Minoan Civilisation. In: EDWARDS, I. E. S. et al. (eds), *Cambridge Ancient History.* 3rd ed. Cambridge. Vol. 2, Part 2, pp. 141–64.

—— 1973b. The Zenith of Minoan Civilisation. In: EDWARDS, I.E.S. et al. (eds), *Cambridge Ancient History.* 3rd ed. Cambridge. Vol. 2, Part 2, pp. 557–81.

MOUNTJOY, P. 1986. *Mycenaean Decorated Pottery.* Göteborg. (Stud. mediterr. Archaeol.)

MYLONAS, G. 1977. [*Mycenaean religion, temples, altars and temene.*] Athína.

ONASSOGLOU, A. 1985. *Die 'talismanischen' Siegel.* Berlin.

PAGE, D. L. 1970. *The Santorini Volcano and the Destruction of Minoan Crete.* London. (Suppl. Pap., 12.)

PALAIMA, T. G. 1990. Aegean Seals, Sealings and Administration. *Aegaeum,* Vol. 5.

PELON, O. 1976. *Tholoi, tumuli et cercles funéraires.* Paris.

PLATON, N. 1981. *La civilisation égéenne.* Paris, 2 vols.

POURSAT, J.-C. 1977–81. *Les ivoires mycéniens.* Paris. (Bibl. Écoles fr. Athènes Rome, 230.)

PREZIOSI, D. 1983. *Minoan Architectural Design, Formation and Signification.* Berlin.

PREZIOSI-GETZ, P. 1985. *Early Cycladic Sculptures.* Malibu, Calif. Paul Getty Museum.

RENFREW, C. 1972. *The Emergence of Civilisation.* London.

—— 1979. *Problems in Prehistory.* Edinburgh.

—— 1987. *Archaeology and Language. The Puzzle of Indo-European Origins.* London.

—— 1991. *The Cycladic Spirit.* London.

RUIPEREZ, M. C.; MELENA, H. L. 1990. *Los Griegos micenicos.* Madrid. (Bibl. hist., 16.)

RUTKOWSKI, B. 1972. *Cult Places in the Aegean World.* Warszawa.

SAKELLARIOU, A. 1966. *Mykenaike Sphragidoglyphia* [Mycenaean Seal Carving]. Athína.

—— 1977. *Peuples préhelléniques d'origine indo-européenne.* Athína.

—— 1980. *Les proto-grecs.* Athína.

—— 1990. *Between Memory and Oblivion: The Transmission of Early Greek Historical Traditions.* Athína, Research Centre for Greek and Roman Antiquity. (Meletemata, 12.)

SAMUEL, A. E. 1966. *The Mycenaeans in History.* Englewood Cliffs, N.J.

SANDARS, N. 1978. *The Sea-Peoples.* London. 2nd ed. 1985. (Anc. Peoples Places, 89.)

SCHACHERMEYR, F. 1955. *Die ältesten Kulturen Griechenlands.* Stuttgart.

SCOUFOPOULOS, N. 1971. *Mycenaean Citadels.* Göteborg. (Stud. mediterr. Archaeol., 22.)

SINOS, S. 1971. *Die vorklassischen Hausformen in der Ägäis.* Mainz.

STAVRIANOPOULOU, E. 1989. *Untersuchungen zur Struktur des Reiches von Pylos: Die Stellung der Ortschaften im Lichte der Linear B-Texte.* Partille.

STELLA, L. A. 1965. *La civiltà Micenea nei documenti contemporanei.* Roma.

STUBBINGS, F. H. 1973. The Recession of Mycenean Civilization. In: EDWARDS, I. E. S. et al. (eds), *Cambridge Ancient History.* 3rd ed. Cambridge. Vol. 2, Part 2, pp. 338–58.

—— 1973. The Rise of Mycenaean Civilisation. In: EDWARDS, I. E. S. et al. (eds), *Cambridge Ancient History,* 3rd ed. Cambridge. Vol. 2, Part 2, pp. 627–58.

TAYLOUR, W. 1971. *The Mycenaeans.* London. 2nd ed. 1990.

THEOCHARIS, D. R. 1974. Early Helladic Civilisation. In: CHRISTOPOULOS, G. (ed.), *History of the Hellenic World.* Athína. Vol. 1.

TREUIL, R. 1983. *Le Néolothique et le Bronze Ancien égéens: les problèmes stratigraphiques, les techniques, les hommes.* Paris. (Bibl. Éc. fr. Athènes Rome, 248.)

TREUIL, R. et al. (eds) 1989. *Les civilisations égéennes du néolithique et de l'Âge du Bronze.* Paris.

TRIPATHI, D. N. 1988. *Bronzework of Mainland Greece from c. 2600 BC to c. 1450 BC.* Göteborg. (Stud. mediterr. Archaeol., 69.)

TSOUNTAS, C. 1889. Kykladika II. In: *Archaiologike Ephemeris.* Athína.

VERLINDEN, C. 1984. *Les statuettes anthropomorphes crétoises en bronze et en plomb du IIIe millénaire au VIIe siècle av. J.-C.* Providence/Louvain.

VERMEULE, E. 1964. *Greece in the Bronze Age.* Chicago, Ill./London. 3rd ed. 1972.

—— 1975. *The Art of the Shaft Graves of Mycenae.* Cincinnati, Ohio.

WALTER, H.; FELTEN, F. 1981. *Alt-Aegina.* Mainz. Vol. 3.

WARREN, P. 1969. *Minoan Stone Vases.* Cambridge.

—— 1972. *Myrtos: An Early Bronze Age Settlement in Crete.* London.

—— 1988. *Minoan Religion as Ritual Action.* Partille. (Stud. mediterr. Archaeol., 72.)

WARREN, P.; HANKEY, V. 1989. *Aegean Bronze Age Chronology.* Bristol.

YULE, P. 1980. *Early Cretan Seals: A Study of Chronology.* Mainz.

THE MIDDLE AND LATE BRONZE AGE (2100–1100 BC)

Michel Sakellariou and Christos Doumas

HISTORICAL SURVEY: ECONOMY, SOCIETY AND THE STATE (MAP 8)

Michel Sakellariou

As in the case of the rest of the Balkan peninsula and Anatolia, Greece was occupied by immigrants around the year 2000 BC; apart from ethnic changes, this led to a decline in the economy and in social structures. Several island sites also bore witness to upheavals. Crete, on the other hand, which had not been drawn into the maelstrom, was able to preserve its cultural attainments and it even made further strides.

The arrival of the immigrants left its traces, inasmuch as settlements were destroyed in their entirety and from their remains new cultural features emerged. An examination of the geographical distribution and chronology of these traces shows that there were two waves of immigration. The first occurred around 2100 BC and affected several coastal settlements in the Hellenic peninsula, while the second spread overland from Macedonia towards the year 1900 BC. The new developments that they brought to Greece at the time were already known in the rest of the Balkan peninsula. Some of these innovations came from the Danubian region, such as burials inside the settlement area, apsidal buildings and perforated axe hammers. Many more of them came from a culture known as the Kurgan culture in the Eurasian steppes. These included cist or shaft graves, which were sometimes covered with a burial mound, the custom of placing remains on an animal skin, the presence of ochre inside the tomb, as well as ellipsoidal edifices, corded ware, battleaxes and mace heads. These elements originating from two different places appeared simultaneously on the same sites; it may be presumed therefore, that those who brought the Kurgan and the Danubian cultures with them had merged before their arrival in Greece. The bearers of the Kurgan culture have been quite rightly identified with the peoples classed as Indo-Europeans. The characteristic features of this culture, which appeared in Greece between 2100 and 1900 BC, were linked to those of the Proto-Greeks. We have come to apply the term Greek exclusively to the language spoken in historical times and Greeks to the users of this language, whereas the terms Proto-Greek and Proto-Greeks have been created to designate the Indo-European language introduced in Greece around 2000 BC and those who spoke it, for the Greeks of historical times are the product of the merging of the Proto-Greeks and the Pre-Greeks; and the Greek used in historical times differs from Proto-Greek in two ways. It

Map 8 The Aegean world: 2000–1100 BC.

incorporated a large number of Pre-Greek appellatives, place-names, personal names and names of gods, and was itself responsible for the creation of a wide range of innovations (M. Sakellariou, 1980; Drews, 1988).

The immigrants were more dependent on pastoralism for their livelihood than on land cultivation. They settled in hamlets that were smaller and considerably fewer in number than the settlements they had destroyed. As soon as they arrived in Greece, they ceased making corded ware and using battleaxes; for some time at least, they continued to build ellipsoidal or apsidal structures, but as might logically be expected, they displayed considerable conservatism with regard to their buildings and burial customs, and this continued up until the sixteenth century BC (M. Sakellariou, 1980). Shortly before this date, a number of settlements situated close to the sea or at the crossroads of different routes abandoned their isolation and subsistence economy. Argolid was soon to set up links with the Cyclades and Crete in the south, with Troas and Chalcidice in the north of the Aegean basin, and with the island of Leucas in the Ionian Sea. A number of graves from the same period show signs for the first time of economic inequality. The appearance of graves in the sixteenth century BC containing weapons and articles of value confirm the existence of a warrior class who divided up the region's resources between them, attesting to the strengthening of monarchical power.

In contrast to the Greek continent, towards the year 2000 BC Crete was experiencing a calm period in its development and demonstrating considerable creativity in all areas. The Cretan states set up an administrative system which was capable of running all the economic activities on their territory. They built great palaces not only to house the royal family, dignitaries and troops of servants, but also the administrative offices, workshops and storehouses. At this point the elimination of the clans was in its closing phase, and society had reached an advanced stage of stratification and stability (Treuil et al., 1989, p. 214). The civilization as a whole had attained a level that placed it among the most sophisticated cultures of humankind.

Towards 1600 BC, the most advanced societies in continental Greece had attained a degree of maturity that enabled them to borrow from Cretan civilization. The Cretan models played a crucial part in the development of these societies at the time. Greece drew closer to Crete and shared certain aspects of its civilization. The Bronze Age Cretans are also known as Minoans and their culture is termed the Minoan civilization. The Minoan-influenced civilization on the continent is known as Mycenaean, a term which covers not only the inhabitants of Mycenae but also all the inhabitants of the continent belonging to this civilization, who are also known as 'Achaeans'.

The Mycenaeans soon began to compete with the Minoans in the Aegean Sea, and established contact with Egypt. Some consider these contacts, whose importance in fact they overestimate, to be the factor that led to the blossoming of the Mycenaean world. Around 1450 BC, Mycenaean troops landed in Crete, destroyed the Cretan palaces and established a Mycenaean state which held sway over eastern Crete from Knossos. At the beginning of the following century, this state was subjugated by Greeks from the continent.

From the Minoans the Mycenaeans borrowed, among other things, their system of production, social organization and political structure. Consequently, Crete and continental Greece (the latter from 1600 BC onwards) may be studied together in these particular domains. Each was divided into several states. There were four states in eastern Crete up to about 1450 BC – Knossos, Phaistos, Mallia and Zakro. This part of the island was subsequently unified and came under the rule of a Mycenaean dynasty. As far as western Crete is concerned, we have insufficient information at our disposal. In continental Greece, half a dozen states are known to have existed, namely Mycenae, Pylos, Thebes, Orchomenos and Iolcos, and there were presumably others. Messenia, which formed the territory of Pylos, had a surface area of 2,600 km². Boeotia was equivalent in size, and was divided up between the kingdoms of Thebes and Orchomenos. The size of the kingdom of Mycenae is difficult to assess, but it probably lay between 2,000 and 3,500 km². As far as the population was concerned, the kingdom of Pylos is thought to have had 50,000 inhabitants and the city of Pylos 2,500 (Chadwick, 1976b; Treuil et al., 1989; Ruipérez and Melena, 1990).

With regard to the system of land tenure, it is known that some land was set aside for deities, while some belonged to the monarch and the dignitaries, in addition to which there were individually owned properties, communal land, part of which was rented out to individuals, and land worked by groups in exchange for services rendered to the cult (Chadwick, 1976b; Ruipérez and Melena, 1990).

The entire production system was run by the palace, by means of a highly structured administrative system. The documentation available enables us to follow the meticulous work of the scribes, accountants and storekeepers. Crops and herds in both the royal and the private domains were kept under close supervision and the output of the latter was subject to levies. A list of free craftsmen and of slaves assigned to different workshops, even private ones, and to different tasks was kept up to date. These workshops were provided with raw materials, and the quantity and quality of the products manufactured in them were monitored. Care was taken to ensure that produce (raw materials and finished products) entered or left the storehouses in accordance with established rules. Masons or other craftsmen were supplied with the necessary materials, told what they were for, and sent out on jobs. Some of the workshops and storehouses were located in the palace, while others were housed in the annexes or were to be found in the provinces. It has been calculated that the palace of Pylos had in its employ 400 free bronzesmiths, 550 slaves who produced cloth and a further 200 who carried out the domestic chores. The slaves were female. An administrative department dealt with foreign trade. It may be assumed that the boats that plied this trade came under this department (Chadwick, 1976b; Duhoux, 1976).

The extent to which activities were specialized is astonishing. In the field of textiles alone there were two major categories of slaves, for work with wool and with flax; then came the spinners, the carders, the weavers and those responsible for the finishing; finally, there were the slaves who made specific types of materials, such as hair ribbons. We also know that cloth made in one workshop was embroidered in another. The same practice of the division of labour also prevailed on the domestic front: apart from those who served as servants, there were certain women who were given the sole task of milling the grain, others were assigned responsibility simply for the baths and so on (Lindgren, 1973; Stavrianopoulou, 1989, pp. 24 ff).

Trade networks were formed between the Greek continent and Crete, which also traded with the Aegean islands, the western coast of Anatolia, Cyprus, the Levant, Egypt, Sicily and southern Italy. Mycenaean products have been discovered in central Europe and in England. The Minoan and Mycenaean palaces imported gold, copper, tin, amber and manufactured articles. They exported olive oil, wine, wool, fabrics and vases. There are good grounds for thinking that the 400 bronzesmiths of Pylos, who were very much more numerous than the kingdom's needs warranted, worked to a large extent for the export market. The Minoans and Mycenaeans founded colonies in the Cyclades, in Rhodes and in Miletus. It is assumed that Mycenaean craftsmen and traders were also to be found in Cyprus. Finally, the existence of Minoan and Mycenaean trading-posts has been attested or may be assumed in the Levant, in Sicily and in southern Italy (Treuil et al., 1989). The Minoans and the Mycenaeans were responsible for many advances in ship building and navigation; they built networks of roads, dug canals in order to irrigate and also to drain land prior to drying out lakes, and built fortifications that the Greeks in historical times attributed to mythical beings who were more powerful than humans.

It was in order to facilitate the management of the enormous concerns that the Minoan and Mycenaean palaces represented that an ideographic-hieroglyphic script was developed in Crete during the Proto-Palatial period (the first centuries of the second millennium BC). In the period of the later palaces (from the seventeenth century onwards) this became a script that mainly used syllabic signs and in which ideograms took second place; finally, again in Crete – but for the Mycenaean palace in Knossos, where Greek was spoken after 1450 BC – a script was developed that was partly derived from the preceding one (Plates 41, 42). The syllabic scripts are known as Linear A and Linear B, on the basis of their chronological order. Regarding weights and measures, the situation seems somewhat complex, implying that much was borrowed from elsewhere at the same time as considerable conservatism prevailed. The largest unit of weight was divided into thirtieths, which were themselves subdivided into fourths. The solid measure contained tenths, each tenth being divided into sixths, and each sixth into fourths. In the case of liquids, the unitary measure was divided into thirds, which were again divided by three, then into sixths and subsequently into fourths (Chadwick, 1976a; Hooker, 1980; Treuil et al., 1989; Ruipérez and Melena, 1990).

Little is known about the social classes. In general the information at our disposal is limited to a few details concerning the slaves. We have seen what sort of work they did. It should be added that the women kept their children with them and were given food for them, just as they received food for themselves, consisting of wheat or barley and figs. The rest of the available information consists of quotations concerning the categories of notables or of those engaged in trades. Nothing is known about the intermediate classes, nor about the serfs who were bound to the land belonging to the king, dignitaries, individuals or even the communes (Lindgren, 1973; Treuil et al., 1989; Ruipérez and Melena, 1990).

Cretan women took part in social and religious events and, furthermore, played an important part in society. It would, however, be rash to conclude from this that Cretan society was matriarchal; at the very most, it conserved a few vestiges of an extremely ancient matriarchy.

In the Minoan states, the king is thought to have performed the functions of priest and judge but did not wield power of any note in other matters. However, the Mycenaean king, or *annax*, was required to be a great warrior. We have some data on the state dignatories of Pylos. The title *lawagetas* apparently designated a high-ranking officer, but did not apply to the commander-in-chief of the army, as was initially assumed somewhat hastily. It is thought that the *equetai* or 'companions' formed part of the king's entourage and were responsible for carrying out different missions and military operations. It seems likely, although it is not certain, that landowners known as *telestai* occupied posts in the administrative or military structure (Hooker, 1976; Platon, 1981, I, pp. 283 ff, II, pp. 83 ff, 342 ff).

Regarding the regional divisions of a Cretan or Mycenaean state and running of the administration at the different levels, the only documents we have concern Pylos. The territory of the kingdom was divided into two provinces, sixteen districts and several communes. The commune was known as the *damos* which, even in the Greek of historical times, conserved the meaning of 'commune, community' and 'territory of a commune or community'. In Ionic and Attic, *damos* became *demos*, giving *demokratia* or 'democracy'. In the kingdom of Pylos, the *damos* owned land and rented it out. In general it consisted of an association of people enjoying a certain degree of self-management. However, the *damokoros*, 'he who looks after the *damos*' was apparently appointed by the king, just as the *koreter* and *prokoreter* – governor and assistant-governor – of the district probably were (Ruipérez and Melena, 1990, pp. 107–29).

In the second millennium BC there were no fortifications in Crete, and the Minoan iconography depicts neither scenes of war nor even warriors. What is more, neither the graves nor the other Cretan environments of the time have yielded any weapons. However, the recollection of a Minoan thalassocracy was perpetuated in the traditions handed down to the Greeks by the Cretans. It is consequently assumed that an understanding prevailed among the Minoan states and that they were afforded protection against any seaborne attack by their fleet or that of their allies. This situation has been termed the *pax minoica*. The archives of Pylos throw some light on the staffing of the armed forces, which has already been touched on, detachment movements and defence measures. It may, furthermore, be assumed that the kingdom was in a position to mobilize some 200 chariots. The Mycenaean king of Knossos had a force of equivalent strength at his disposal.

SETTLEMENT AND ARCHITECTURE, ARTS AND CRAFTS, IDEOLOGY

Christos Doumas

After the end of the Early Bronze Age, which in many parts of the Aegean was marked by major catastrophes, civilization developed differently in different regions. Of the settlements in the North Aegean, only Troy survived and continued its splendid career until it was sacked and destroyed by the Achaeans. On the Greek mainland a cultural regression is evident, while in Crete the dawn of the second millennium BC ushered in its cultural floruit with the growth of the major palaces, and last but not least, the coastal settlements established in the Cyclades during the final phase of the Early Bronze Age evolved into thriving centres in the conveyancing trade. While the transition from Early to Middle Bronze Age was smooth in the Cyclades and Crete, in the north Aegean and on the Greek mainland it was accompanied by the appearance of entirely new elements strongly represented in the archaeological record, as much in the architecture and burial customs as in material culture and the economy. These, hitherto unknown, elements have been interpreted as indicative of the arrival of new populations in the Aegean (Blegen, 1973; Caskey, 1973; M. Sakellariou, 1980, pp. 32 ff).

The North Aegean

In both the islands and coastal regions of the North Aegean the archaeological data indicate a retardation in comparison with the Early Bronze Age. Islands such as Lemnos, Lesbos, Chios and Samos, on which important proto-urban centres had flourished, do not seem to have played a significant role in cultural developments in the Aegean during the Middle Bronze Age. This observation also holds for the shores of Macedonia and Thrace. Thus the whole of the Middle Bronze Age in this region is known solely from Troy (Caskey, 1973; see also this volume, Chapter 12.3).

Troy VI, which had a long life-span (*c.* 1800–1300 BC) represented by eight successive levels was built upon the ruins of the fifth city (EBA). In its early phase this city had many traits in common with those characteristic of the civilization of the Greek mainland, but as time elapsed these became differentiated and followed their own developmental course (Blegen, 1973). Even though the architectural remains from the early phases are rather scant, it seems that throughout its existence the city was fortified. The most monumental defensive structures are dated to the final phase (Blegen, 1963, p. 115), which probably coincides with the Late Bronze Age. Within the confines of this fortified hill, arranged in terraces, free-standing spacious houses had been built, probably belonging to officials or favourites of the king, whose palace was situated on its summit, on the site where the temple of Athena was erected in later times (Blegen, 1973). Where it has been possible to reconstruct the plan of these dwellings, it is apparent that they are of megaron type, that is an oblong, rectangular structure, already known in Troy in the Early Bronze Age. The city was rebuilt (Troy VII) in the wake of extensive destruction by earthquake, and its two levels comprise phases a and b respectively. Troy VIIa, razed to the ground by conflagration, is considered to be the city of Priam and its end is dated to the mid-thirteenth century BC.

Middle and Late Bronze Age Troy has yielded distinctive angular, greyish pottery, the so-called Minyan ware which is found in Middle Helladic centres on the Greek mainland and is tangible evidence of a technological innovation in the Aegean region: that is, the process of firing pottery 'under reducing conditions that produced so generally the even grey colour'. This type of pottery continued to be produced in Troy until the end of the city and the technique was also applied in the manufacture of purely Mycenaean vases (Blegen, 1963, pp. 140–1). There is a dearth of other artefacts, which include a few bronze spindle whorls and jewellery of gold, silver and electrum.

As during the Early Bronze Age, Troy maintained close relations with the other regions of the Aegean, in particular the Greek mainland, as attested by the common use of Minyan ware and by Helladic imports, initially of matt-painted ware and later of Mycenaean pottery, as well as objects of stone, ivory and bone. Troy's contacts with the outside world must have been via the sea, as confirmed by the presence of Cypriot pottery in Troy VII. In contrast to the situation in the Aegean, the relations of Troy VI and VII with the Anatolian hinterland, as in the Early Bronze Age, were virtually non-existent, despite the fact that Troy VI is contemporary with the mighty state of the Hittites.

Clues as to the beliefs and ideology of the inhabitants of Troy are limited to the discovery of a series of monolithic pillars, menhirs, thought to be associated with the religious life of the sixth city, and the finding of a small cemetery from its final period, in fact the only cemetery connected with prehistoric life in Troy. It is a cemetery of funerary urns containing the ashes and bones of children and adults (Blegen, 1963, pp. 139–43).

It is perhaps not without significance that the practice of cremation appears sporadically throughout the Aegean at this time (Iakovidis, 1970). The maintenance of relations with the Aegean, but primarily the simultaneous appearance of innovations in pottery making, the use of the horse as a beast of burden, the adoption of the same architectural forms, have been interpreted as evidence of the arrival of new population elements in the Aegean, branches of which settled on the Greek mainland and in the Troad respectively. Some scholars have interpreted this element as the 'first Hellenic peoples to set foot in the peninsula' (Blegen, 1963, p. 145).

Mainland Greece

The early stages of the Middle Helladic (MH) period are characterized by cultural regression; indeed in northern Greece – Macedonia and Thessaly – the stagnation is so pronounced that it seems as if the Early Bronze Age civilization is of extended duration (Caskey, 1973). Central Greece (Boeotia and Attica) and the eastern Peloponnese (Corinth and the Argolid) were the main centres of development. The early MH settlements were apparently unfortified and comprised humble buildings, simple architectural units probably intended to house extended families. The apsidal plan of the houses, without being an innovation in architectural tradition, co-existed with the rectangular, which actually predominated, though with local variants. These MH dwellings were the precursors of the house types which prevailed in the Mycenaean age (1550–1100 BC), distinguished by their simple regular plan. Mycenaean towns, as a rule extending over the slopes of fortified hills, consist of such houses, arranged in clusters around a royal palace, and their layout is reminiscent of that of medieval towns. Mycenae and Tiryns in the Argolid, Pylos in Messenia, Thebes in Boeotia *inter alia*, are cities of this type. The palace, on the summit of the citadel, was built according to a standardized plan, with local variants only with respect to its secondary and ancillary rooms: the tripartite nucleus comprises the *aithousa* (porch), *prodomos* (vestibule) and *domos* (megaron), in which there was a circular hearth surrounded by four columns. The megaron was the throne room in which official audiences and receptions were given by the king, and around this a complex of courts, porticoes and other auxiliary apartments was organized (Taylour, 1971, pp. 92–9).

Despite the fact that farming was the basis of the economy, technological innovations, such as, for example, the use of the potter's wheel and the introduction of the manufacture of Minyan ware by firing in a controlled, reducing environment occurred. Another innovation in pottery making was the decoration of vases with matt-painted motifs. Yet another new element in the economy of the MH period is the use of the horse – hitherto unknown in the Aegean – as a beast of burden (Caskey, 1973, pp. 135–6). Technological innovations did not cease during the succeeding phase either, when the wheeled vehicle made its appearance. Difficulty of communication, due to the high mountains of the Greek mainland, encouraged the establishment of sea routes and the growth of trade led to a more intensive exploitation of natural resources and so to further technological discoveries. One of the most important large-scale works in the prehistoric Aegean was the draining of the Copais lake, by digging canals and drainage tunnels through the mountain. The major fortifications with their Cyclopean walls which girt the Mycenaean acropolis, the laying of provincial roads and the construction of bridges are well attested archaeologically, being major public works characteristic of the Mycenaean world. In the sphere of technology, pottery making flourished and even today its products are outstanding on account of their excellent quality and wide variety of shapes (cf. Furumark, 1941). Progress in the sphere of metal working is confirmed not only from ancient texts but also from the impressive variety of tools, weapons, vessels and toreutic objects found in excavations (Hood, 1978; Chadwick, 1976b; Deshayes, 1960; Matthäus, 1980). At the same time, the contact and development of relations with Crete encouraged the exploration of new crafts and artistic spheres, such as ivory carving, gem carving for seal stones, sculpture and painting (Hood, 1978; Poursat, 1977; A. Sakellariou, 1966).

From the sixteenth century BC onwards, Mycenaean Greece gradually forged relations with the outside world, extending as far as the Aeolian islands in the west, and Egypt,

Syria and Palestine in the eastern Mediterranean (Marazzi et al., 1986; see also this volume, Chapter 14.2). The spread of trade in the Eastern Mediterranean, especially after Knossos had sunk into oblivion (c. 1400 BC), is also apparent from the founding of Mycenaean colonies in such far-flung islands as Rhodes and Cyprus.

Throughout the Middle and Late Helladic periods the common form of burial was inhumation. Only towards the thirteenth and twelfth centuries BC are sporadic instances of cremation observed. In the MH period the dead were usually interred in a contracted position, either inside the settlements or in special cemeteries outside. One or more burials were sometimes covered by a tumulus. But although there was variety in the type of burial ground, the form of the actual grave remained stable: a cist grave with lined walls. There were also burials in funerary urns, usually of children and much more rarely of adults. As time passed the graves became differentiated, both in size, number of interments and grave goods. Thus, alongside the small cist graves, usually intended for a single inhumation, larger shaft graves appeared, which housed multiple burials. Similarly, though the earlier burials are generally not furnished with grave goods, in about the sixteenth century BC burials accompanied by rich grave goods first appeared, such as the shaft graves of Mycenae. The variety of graves and differences in the value of the grave goods probably reflects the emergence of a hierarchical society in the MH world (see Sakellariou in this chapter). This developmental trend continued into Mycenaean times when the use of shaft graves was gradually abandoned. Chamber tombs cut into the hillside and used for multiple inhumations became the rule for the majority of the population, while kings were laid to rest in the monumental tholos tombs, frequently embellished with sculpted decoration. They were provided with precious vessels of gold and silver, weapons and armoury, and jewellery. Pottery vases and a few metal or other tools and minor objects accompanied the common mortals in the chamber tombs.

Even though the names of deities later found in the Greek pantheon (Athena, Demeter, Dionysos, Hephaistos, Poseidon, and so on) occur in the Linear B tablets, we have no information on the nature of Mycenaean religion or the rites of any cults. The gods are mentioned only as the recipients of offerings (Chadwick, 1976a, pp. 84–101). Some buildings, the arrangement of which precludes a domestic function, have also been associated with religion and worship. Furthermore, within their halls clay figurines, rhyta and other objects usually regarded as cultic or of ritual significance have been found. Such rooms or shrines have been revealed at Mycenae, on Kea, Melos, at Malthi and elsewhere. Some artistic impressions are also considered to depict religious or ritual scenes, such as those on seal stones and ring bezels. Finally, the circular hearth in the throne room or domos of the Mycenaean palace has also been attributed with a religious significance. For this reason it is maintained that the king was not only a political leader with temporal power, but a religious leader too (Taylour, 1971, pp. 60–74) (Plates 43–5).

The Cyclades and Crete

From the end of the third millennium BC onwards the history of the Cyclades runs parallel with that of Crete, even though society seems to have developed somewhat differently in the two regions. The development of major urban trading centres in the Cyclades – Melos, Thera, Paros –

bespeaks the maritime-mercantile character of the islands' economy, which presumably influenced the structure and development of Cycladic society. Both the layout of the settlements and distribution of wealth within these suggest that they were subject to a system of government very different from the concentrative palatial system of Crete. From the beginning of the second millennium BC a gradual infiltration of Minoan civilization to the Cyclades is observed, so that by the middle of the sixteenth century BC the Cycladic port-cities display a markedly Minoan aspect. Minoan traits abound in both their material culture – architecture, pottery making, metal working – and the intellectual sphere – their script, metric systems and religion. Nevertheless, these features do not seem to have been brought to the islands by Cretan colonists, as has been frequently maintained, but have been varied and modified in accordance with local needs and taste (Doumas, 1983).

Recent archaeological research has shown that the islands enjoyed a degree of economic, artistic and, presumably, political independence, probably as a result of their great experience in seafaring and the need to develop international trade imposed by the ever-increasing agricultural surplus in Crete and the Greek mainland. One of the most important urban trading centres of this period was Akrotiri on the island of Thera, a rich source of invaluable information on Aegean society during the seventeenth century BC, due to its preservation beneath deep layers of pumice and volcanic ash. The well-designed town plan, with a drainage system beneath the cobbled streets and large, multi-storeyed buildings decorated with wall paintings and with an abundance of vessels and utensils, furnish a picture of the affluence of the island world during this period.

Furthermore, the large quantities of carbonized grain, animal bones and other organic remains provide precious information on the climate of the period, the dietary habits of the inhabitants, the agricultural economy and methods of cultivation. A host of details on the day-to-day occupations of the islanders may be derived from their art, such as their voyages, ship-building techniques, fashions in hairstyles, dress and jewellery.

The city of Akrotiri was destroyed and buried beneath thick layers of pumice and pozzolana ejected by the Thera volcano which erupted in around 1625 BC. This eruption, estimated to have been four times greater in force and extent than that of Krakatoa in AD 1883, is often associated with events in the Bible, such as the crossing of the Red Sea and the plagues of the pharaoh, as well as with the myth of Atlantis. Without doubt, a geological occurrence of such magnitude must have disrupted life throughout the Aegean world, since the ash-fall reached as far as the African coast in considerable quantities. However, its effect on the civilization of Crete does not seem to have been as decisive as has hitherto been maintained (Doumas, 1983). In all likelihood this eruption accelerated processes which had already been initiated in the Aegean, with the emergence and eventual consolidation of the ascendancy of the Mycenaeans of the Greek mainland. Certainly, after the eruption the Minoan character of Cycladic settlements diminished appreciably and Mycenaean traits are increasingly apparent in both their architecture and artefacts.

The continued growth of the agricultural economy of Early Minoan Crete, and the need to collect the surplus for subsequent redistribution and exchange, led to the organization of a concentrative system. In the early years of the second millennium BC this manifested itself in the founding of the large, multi-storeyed building complexes known as palaces. From the time of their founding they were built according to a specific plan. Apartments, workshops, magazines, halls for public assemblies and cult places were arranged around a large rectangular court. This plan, with only minimal local variations probably dictated by topographical factors, was applied in all the palatial centres known so far: Knossos, Phaistos, Mallia and Zakro. The Proto-Palatial period ended between 1700 and 1624 BC when there was widespread destruction, usually attributed to earthquakes. The new palaces were rebuilt on the same sites and according to the same basic plan, perhaps slightly modified and improved. The Neo-Palatial period lasted until around 1450 BC, when the palaces were destroyed, excepting Knossos, which survived until around 1400 BC, though under another, Mycenaean, ruler. Although it is difficult to determine the kind of authority exercised, the role of the palaces seems to have been multifold: administrative, economic and religious (Alexiou, 1969; Hägg and Marinatos, 1987).

Around the periphery of the palaces spread the towns, very few traces of which have been brought to light to date. The most completely excavated town of Minoan Crete is Gournia, located on a hill overlooking the north coast of the island. Between the end of the Early Minoan (EM) period, to which the earliest remains belong, until its final destruction in around 1450 BC, Gournia developed into a small conurbation with a street network, drainage system and public buildings, spread out around a small palace. Palaikastro, on the east coast of Crete, is another such town, located on a flat tract of land and evidently better organized than Gournia, though it has not been fully investigated (Cadogan, 1976, pp. 129 ff). Of especial interest are the country houses or villas. These are large, isolated structures of Neo-Palatial times, built in the countryside on sites ensuring a view overlooking a plain or valley, perhaps over which the occupants exercised economic control. These villas closely resemble the palaces, both in architectural elements and household contents. This may signify that the occupants of the villas were persons in the higher echelons of the Minoan hierarchy, through whom the palaces exercised control – economic and administrative – over the whole of Crete (Cadogan, 1976, p. 42).

The burial customs do not exhibit noticeable changes from the EM period and many tombs were still in use during the Middle Minoan (MM) period. The use of larnakes and burials in pithoi become more common in Proto-Palatial times, while at the same time the precursors of the chamber tombs with niches for individual burials appeared (Alexiou, 1969, p. 24).

In Neo-Palatial times it was common practice to bury the dead in pithoi or clay sarcophagi which were placed within rock-cut chamber tombs. At the same time there is an overt tendency towards the construction of monumental tombs, such as the 'temple-tomb' at Knossos, which is a combination of a rock-cut chamber and an impressive two-storey structure situated on its façade. According to prevailing opinion, this monument was destined not only for the cult of the deceased inhumed within, but also for the related deity. Between the years 1450 and 1400 BC, when the palace of Knossos – the only one not destroyed – had become the seat of the Mycenaean conquerors, there was a change in funerary customs. The dead were still interred in chamber tombs, but placed inside brightly coloured, usually wooden coffins or sarcophagi. Grave goods were no longer limited to vases and jewellery, but included weaponry, such as helmets, daggers, swords, javelins and spears, indicative of the martial preferences of the new masters of Knossos (Alexiou, 1969).

During the Middle and Late Minoan periods Crete forged external relations and established contacts, in particular with lands in the eastern Mediterranean, as attested by archaeological finds. Trade between these countries, probably conducted on the basis of exchange of gifts between rulers, included such items as ivory from Syria, copper from Cyprus, gold materials, stone vessels and their contents, monkeys and chariots from Egypt, metal vessels and agricultural produce, such as oil, wine and saffron from Crete (Alexiou, 1969; Hägg and Marinatos, 1987, pp. 261 ff).

Exchange does not seem to have been confined only to material goods, but included technical knowledge and ideas. Thus, for instance, the technique of wall painting, which flourished in palatial Crete and was diffused throughout the Aegean, must have been introduced to Crete from Syria or Egypt. Palaces, villas and other important edifices were decorated with wall paintings and their thematic repertoire is a rich source of information on the daily life – public and private – of the Cretans (Hood, 1978; Platon, 1981, II).

Although coloured plaster was used in Crete from as early as the third millennium BC, wall paintings proper do not appear until the Middle Bronze Age, along with the Minoan palaces. Minoan wall paintings are not true frescoes, as they are frequently erroneously described. Perhaps the artists began painting while the stucco was still damp but no effort was made to maintain this state until the process was completed. For this reason the colours tend to flake, since they have not permeated the plaster, but the use of earth and mineral pigments (ochres, copper and iron oxides, malachite, azurite, limonite and so on) has contributed to their good state of preservation. Egypt and Syria are often cited as models for the development of wall painting in the Aegean region, but whatever the original provenance of the technique, the style, inspiration and execution are distinctively Aegean. In Crete and on the Greek mainland wall paintings are a characteristic feature of palaces and wealthy houses. In the Aegean islands, where there was also a remarkable development of this art form, they evidently served wider social strata and are more frequently encountered in the urban centres of Kea, Melos and Thera. The themes chosen for decorating the walls of Middle and Late Bronze Age buildings in the Aegean display considerable diversity. Geometric and abstract motifs, plants and animals individually or in combinations, landscapes, or even entire narrative scenes were used to adorn an equally wide variety of surfaces: door and window jambs, narrow zones above or below rows of openings, small free spaces, whole walls.

The rich repertoire of the wall paintings is an inexhaustible source of information on the flora, the fauna and the environment of the period, the dress, hairstyles, and various – economic, social, religious – activities of the inhabitants of the Aegean. Through these wall paintings the different nature of the two worlds, the Minoan and the Mycenaean, emerges: that of Crete and the islands is peaceful and happy, that of the Greek mainland martial and harsh.

There is a tendency for scholars involved in Aegean prehistory to attribute a religious meaning to almost all the wall paintings found so far. However, it should not be overlooked that the societies which created these works are distinguished by a secularism which could be qualified as proto-scientific. Thus, though the religious character of some of the assemblages cannot be excluded, particularly when the context and accompanying finds support such an interpretation, they may also have had a social, political or other aspect (Hood, 1978; Platon, 1981, II; Immerwahr, 1990).

Sculpture also achieved great heights in Crete during palatial times, especially small objects such as figurines, sealstones, gemstones and other miniature works of art. Materials sculpted were stone, ivory and bone (Hood, 1978; Poursat, 1977, 1981). Because these arts and crafts were under the direct control of the palace they were subject to certain conventions dictated by it. Several occupations took place within the palace, or at least on its behalf, such as stone cutting, metallurgy or pottery making, and the workshops in which the artisans laboured have been identified inside the palaces (Hägg and Marinatos, 1987).

Although the texts shed little light on the religion of Minoan Crete, much information can be gleaned from works of art, especially minor arts, and architecture. Thus cult sites have been located in the countryside and in caves, as well as in the palaces and dwellings. Certain unusual vessels are accorded religious or ritual significance, as are scenes represented in wall paintings, on gemstones or sealstones. Although much has been written about Minoan religion, neither the form of worship nor the nature of divinities and their attributes may be described with certainty. It seems that there was belief in life after death and perhaps in the fertility and fecundity of nature. The works of art also furnish an insight into various ceremonies of social, rather than religious, import, such as initiation ceremonies and puberty rites (Alexiou, 1969; Rutkowski, 1972).

The Minoan civilization came to an end after 1400 BC, though signs of its decline had appeared much earlier. Some scholars hold that its end was due to the eruption of the Thera volcano, or catastrophic earthquakes, or even foreign invasion (Page, 1970; Luce, 1970). However, the archaeological data in support of such hypotheses are very scant. It is highly unlikely that the demise of a civilization could be brought about by natural phenomena, since the human factor, the bearer of that culture, still continues to control acquired knowledge and experience, as well as the sources of raw materials. On the other hand, no traces of violence have been discovered, which discounts the proposed invasion from elsewhere. It is the contention of the author that the probable reason for the fall of the Minoan civilization was internal disintegration, the inability of the system to evolve in response to new needs; it had outlived its usefulness (Doumas, 1983) (Plates 46–52).

BIBLIOGRAPHY

See Chapter 11.1.1

II.I.3
DECLINE AND RECOVERY (1100–700 BC)

Michel Sakellariou

The societies belonging to the Mycenaean civilization collapsed around 1100 BC, leading to its utter and complete downfall. They were succeeded, in Greece and the Aegean basin, by societies whose standards of economic and social organization were lower than those of the Mycenaean age, but which nevertheless created a new civilization. After the year 1050 BC things should no longer be viewed in terms of 'an ending' but rather in terms of 'a beginning' in all spheres: technology, economics, social organization, types of state, political institutions, the figurative arts, religion, writing and literature.

Some historians have referred to the period from 1100 to 800 BC as the 'Dark Age' or the 'Greek Middle Ages'. The value of such descriptions is relative. Another widely used term is the 'Geometric' period, said to run from 1100 to 700 BC, but this applies only to figurative art.

ETHNIC MOVEMENTS; DEMOGRAPHIC AND ECONOMIC DECLINE (MAP 9)

Around the year 1100 BC, the Mycenaean world was invaded by Greek ethnic groups who lived beyond the confines of Mycenaean civilization and led a nomadic pastoral life. They are usually referred to as Dorians, but in fact this term applies to only some of them. Other invaders belonged to such peoples as the Boeotians, Phocians, Locrians, Aininians, Aetolians, Magnesians and Thessalians. Only Attica and Arcadia remained untouched by the newcomers. Some Greek peoples, however, held out in Epirus (Hammond, 1972), whereas the Macedonians, who were related principally to the Dorians and the Magnesians,' headed away from the Pindus Mountains towards the future Macedonia.

These invasions gave rise to further displacements of Greek populations. Groups that had hitherto been established in Greece proper fled their occupied or threatened homelands to seek refuge elsewhere. In this way the islands of Lesbos and Tenedos and the coast of Anatolia opposite were colonized by peoples speaking the Aeolian dialect. The island of Euboea, the Cyclades, Samos, Chios and a seaboard area of mainland Anatolia received immigrants who mainly spoke the Ionic dialect; some of them came from Attica (Sakellariou, 1958). Groups from Arcadia and other parts of the Peloponnese went to Pamphylia and Cyprus.

Some Dorian groups also took to the sea to settle in Crete, the islands of the Dodecanese, various places in south-west Anatolia beyond the Dodecanese and in Pamphylia. As a result, all the regions of Greece were depopulated and impoverished (Snodgrass, 1971).

RECOVERY (1050–800 BC)

Signs of recovery were not slow in appearing. Towards 1050 BC Crete, where some traces of Minoan artistic traditions still lingered, as well as Attica and Argolid, were importing objects made in Cyprus and assimilating techniques and styles originating in western Asia. As from 1000 BC, these places were using iron rather than bronze to manufacture weapons and tools, particularly since continental Greece and the Greek islands had their own iron-ore deposits, whereas they had to import bronze, copper and tin from abroad. Bronze working would only resume in continental Greece after 900 BC. Meanwhile, the Greeks were learning to extract silver from lead-rich alloys. Somewhere between 850 and 835 BC they began to work gold and ivory again. Commercial links between the Aegean basin and the outside world were few and far between from 900 to 800 BC. Furthermore, these links were maintained by the Phoenicians, whose boats brought from the Levant such raw materials as bronze, gold and ivory, goods made from these materials, and textiles, embroidery and perfume (Snodgrass, 1971).

TRADE AND THE BEGINNINGS OF GREEK COLONIZATION

Around 800 BC, Greek traders repulsed the Phoenicians and ventured up to the periphery of the Levant: Euboeans settled in a city on the Syrian seabord at a site now known as Al Mina. At the same time, the Greeks headed into the Tyrrhenian Sea in search of bronze.

It was here that people from Cyme, Eretria and Chalcis, (on the island of Euboea) founded the oldest Greek colonies: Pithecusa (on the island of Ischia) and Cumae (Cumes), around 770/760 and 760/750 respectively. Between 734 and 706 BC ten other colonies were set up in Italy and Sicily. Chalcidians, sometimes accompanied by other settlers, established themselves at Naxos (734), Zancle (730/725) and Rhegium (725/720). Naxos eventually became the metropolis of Catania (728) and Leotini (728), both of them in Sicily. The Corinthians founded Syracuse (733), after occupying Corcyra (Corfu) on the way. People from Megara founded Megara Hyblaea, which is also in Sicily (727). The Gulf of Tarentum attracted a number of settlers, some of them from Achaea, who set up colonies in Croton and Sybaris (720/715), others from Sparta, who founded Taras (708/706). Before the end of the eighth century BC, the Chalcidians, the Eretrians and certain Cycladean islanders had sent settlers to the

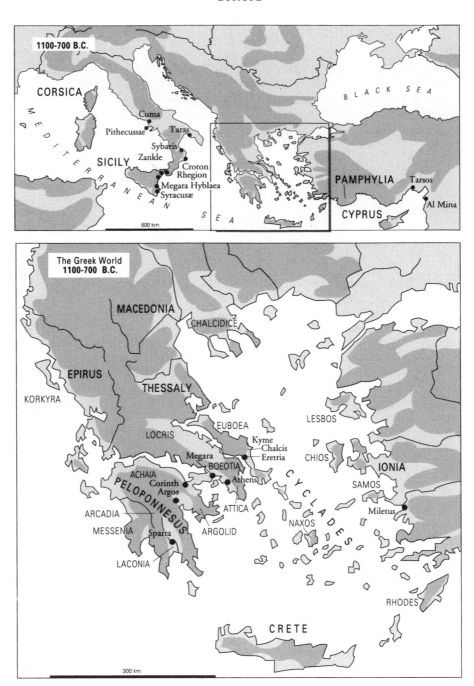

Map 9 The Greek world: 1100–700 BC.

north of the Aegean, to the peninsula which later became known as Chalcidice.

There were several reasons for this colonizing movement. Pithecusa and Cumae were established as trading posts for dealings with the bronze suppliers of the Tyrrhenian Sea, and incidentally to relieve overcrowding in the metropolises. Some decades later these same metropolises sent further settlers, this time for purely social reasons, although this did not prevent them from establishing new colonies on either side of the Strait of Messina in order to secure communications with the Tyrrhenian Sea. The exodus of Eretrians and Chalcidians to Chalcidice can also be attributed to socio-demographic pressures, although the host country attracted the metropolises because of its rich resources of metal and timber. The settlers sent by the Corinthians to Syracuse were mainly peasants, and the Achaean colonies were also agricultural. Taras (Tarentum) was founded by landless settlers without political rights, who had been exiled for stirring up a rebellion. A further

cause of colonization was the expulsion of certain population groups. This is the case of the Messenians who went to Rhegium and possibly of the Megarians who founded Megara Hyblaea (Bérard, 1957, 1960; Sakellariou, 1990, pp. 66–123; Ridgway, 1992). Greek colonization was to reach its peak in the seventh and sixth centuries BC.

DEVELOPMENT OF LONG-DISTANCE TRADE LINKS; TECHNICAL PROGRESS

In the course of the eighth century BC the Chalcidians and the Eretrians established a trade network centred on the Aegean basin, but extending towards Syria and the Tyrrhenian Sea. Like the seafarers from Rhodes, they carried merchandise from Al Mina, Tarsus and Cyprus to the Greek ports of the Aegean. The cargoes consisted of bronze, gold, ivory, precious and semi-precious stones and manufactured goods (such as vases, figurines, textiles and perfumes). However, the Chalcidians and Eretrians also bartered products manufactured in the East or in Greece for bronze from the Tyrrhenian Sea. As rivals in trade with the West they soon had to contend with the Corinthians, who did not need to circumnavigate Attica and Peloponnesus, besides having intermediate ports between the metropolis and Syracuse. The most famous builder of fighting ships at the end of the eighth century BC was a Corinthian. The Athenians, although they took no part in the colonizing movement, were nevertheless enthusiastic seafarers. Greek boats were small rudimentary craft built to hug the shore. When undertaking military operations, they carried warriors armed as for battle on land. Greek blacksmiths had very quickly mastered some Oriental methods, from iron working to the manufacture of tools and weapons. Bronze continued to be used for receptacles, tripods and luxury vases. The above is a brief summary of studies of archaeological evidence of the eighth century BC. Another source, the Homeric poems, dating from the second half of the eighth century BC, refer to products from the East – metals, fine textiles and garments, jewellery, knick-knacks – which were shipped to Greek ports by the Phoenicians. But this should be regarded, apparently, as typical of the period before the end of the ninth century BC or the first few decades of the era that witnessed the birth of the *Iliad* and the *Odyssey*.

LAND TENURE

Even in the economies of the most advanced cities, the importance of trade and the production of manufactured goods was insignificant by comparison with agriculture and stock-farming. The Homeric poems refer to three categories of property outside the public domain. The most common is the *kleros*. These are plots of land originally allocated by lot to the owners' ancestors who had just conquered a territory. On other occasions, property was offered to a god, king or some other individual for services rendered. The decision to offer property of this kind, *temenos*, was taken by the Elders or the public Assembly. Thirdly, population growth, that we can trace from the archaeological record, made it necessary to take over land which, for one reason or another, had still not been privatized. In this situation everyone could become the owner of the land that they had cleared and tilled.

Differences in land ownership gradually grew wider. The reason for these mounting disparities was the division of properties among direct heirs and the transmission of land to more distant relatives who already were landowners. By the eighth century BC, the percentage of people owning no more than a patch of land or without property at all had risen dramatically.

In some societies, the workers who tended the fields and the flocks were serfs from subject peoples. The best known examples are from Laconia (the *heilotes* or 'captives'), Argolis (the *gymnetes* or 'naked'), Thessaly (the *penestai* or 'poor') and Crete (the *klerotai* or 'those who till a *kleros*', the *aphamiotai* or 'rustics' and the *mnoitai* or 'captives, subjects'). Slavery as such was patriarchal in character and involved women more than men.

Every landowner was the head and an active member of a household comprising his family – hence the appellation *oikos*, 'house, family' – and possibly his slaves or serfs, as well as free agricultural labourers. Each *oikos* formed a single production and consumption unit and did its best to be self-sufficient. For this reason a great deal of effort went into diversifying rather than specializing production: the group produced all that was needed to feed its members and their beasts and to make cloth; simple tools, utensils and furniture were also manufactured.

BEGINNINGS OF THE CITY AND OTHER TYPES OF STATE

Between 1100 and 700 BC a very large number of states of different types and sizes were established.

The type of state known by the ancients as the *polis* appeared earlier, evolved more rapidly and spread more widely than the others – the *ethnos*, the *koinon* and the *systema demon*. A state of the first type was intimately linked to a community grouped in a *polis*, that is, an inhabited area protected by a fortified citadel or 'acro-polis'. An *ethnos* state was based on an *ethnos* or 'ethnic group'. The other terms refer to (con)federations: *koinon* – a confederation of *poleis* belonging to the same people, or *systema demon* – a federation of village communities. Thus all these types of state were based on population groups. In this respect, the Greek state differs from the modern state (Sakellariou, 1989; Musti et al., 1991). Around the year 700 BC, there were a hundred or so unitary states of the *polis* type in the area stretching from Cyprus to the Tyrrhenian Sea. Nowadays the word *polis* is usually translated as 'city'.

The Homeric poems show us a world in which the king and the elders (*geron* – 'elder') meet occasionally, and may discuss public affairs and take decisions at a banquet. The adult males of the community, both aristocrats and commoners, attend assemblies convened by the king and the elders, but only those of noble birth are allowed to speak (Vlachos, 1974; Deger-Jakoltzy, 1983; Drews, 1983; Ulf, 1990). However, at the time when the Homeric poems were taking shape, the type of government they depict was no longer current in Athens, Corinth or Sparta. In Athens, hereditary kingship for life was replaced in 752/1 by an elected ten-year magistrature. The first three or four individuals to have been appointed *archon* were members of the Codrid royal family; their successors belonged to families of the nobility. In Corinth, it was the royal clan of the Bacchiads who decided, in about 780 or 750 BC, to replace hereditary kingship for life by an elected annual magistrature, an office which was held by a member of the clan elected by the others. At a date that is uncertain but must be prior to 754 BC, the institutions of Sparta were modelled on the *rhetra* – 'enactment, oracle'. Among other things, this stipulated that (1) the Council of Elders should have thirty members, including the two kings (who belonged to different clans, the Agiads and the Euryponrids); (2) the public Assembly should meet at regular intervals at a clearly specified place; and (3) the kings and the elders should have the right to make proposals to the Assembly and to declare its meetings closed. The *rhetra* ends with a phrase that has given rise to several more or less debatable emendations and interpretations, including one that vests supreme authority in the Assembly. This interpretation is contradicted by other evidence and above all by subsequent events. The Assembly later did claim the right to modify proposals by the kings and the elders and, to put an end to this abuse, the kings submitted a constitutional amendment to the people in the form of another Delphic oracle. This amendment, issued well before the year 700 BC, gave the kings and the elders the right to dissolve the Assembly if the people, instead of saying yea or nay to a proposal, attempted to make it 'crooked'. In 754 BC, between the *rhetra* and the amendment, a new institution appeared, the body of the five *ephors*.

By the end of the eighth century BC, Sparta was regarded as the greatest territorial and military power in Greece. The Spartans had annexed to the territory of their *polis* some of the lands they had conquered in Laconia and Messenia; the rest of the land was left to *poleis* which were granted their autonomy and were peopled by *perioikoi* – 'fringe dwellers'. The land of Sparta, divided into *kleroi* or 'allotments' (4,500 of them in Laconia and as many again in Messenia), was tilled by the *heilotes*. Argos, the second largest territorial and military power, occupied part of the Argolid and Cynuria and bordered on Sparta, its rival.

THE FIGURATIVE ARTS

Turning their backs on the flowing shapes and stylized figures of sub-Mycenaean art, the Athenian potters created the Proto-Geometric style (1050–900 BC). The early vases already exemplify the aesthetic principles that were to govern Greek art in general: a sense of proportion, with priority given to the whole rather than the parts. The neck and the base stand out clearly from the body of the vase, which has become ovoid in shape; the form combines structural solidity with elegance. The decoration consists of straight, wavy or broken lines, arranged in circles, and later in meanders, within two narrow, sharply defined bands, one round the neck, the other round the belly, of the vase. The remainder of the surface is covered with a glossy black paint. In the early ninth century BC, the Proto-Geometric gave way to the Geometric style proper, which was to last until the end of the eighth century BC. In the course of these two centuries it went through successive stages. To begin with, the decorated bands widen and the decorative elements abound. Towards 800 BC, the alternation of bands of differing width begins to create rhythmic effects; the different parts of the vase become more harmoniously related. Soon, depictions of human beings and animals make their appearance, first in isolation and then in ever broader compositions – dancers, boxers, funerary scenes, chariot processions, warriors in combat, ships with oarsmen and other nautical scenes. Now the artists are attempting to capture movement and detail. Their style is vigorous and betrays a very marked inclination for precision and order, both external and internal. Some large vases became monumental in character. They were, incidentally, placed over tombs. The Athenian potters surpassed all others by the quality and refinement of their work. Their products circulated widely outside Attica and helped to propagate the thematic and stylistic ideas they embodied. After having fully assimilated these ideas, the Corinthians began to absorb Oriental influences in the late eighth century BC. Argos, on the other hand, remained subsidiary to Athens and Corinth, whereas Crete showed remarkable independence in some respects, particularly in its iconography, with human figures appearing as early as the Proto-Geometric period. At the same time, Cretan pottery displays traces of Minoan ancestry and Oriental influences (Ahlberg, 1971*a* and *b*; Coldstream, 1977; Boardman, 1982) (Plates 53–5).

Scenes depicting human figures (mortals or gods) in action also adorn the surface of bronze vases and brooches. The decoration is either in the form of bas-relief or is incised on the surface with lines and dots (Canciani, 1970; Naumann, 1976).

Figurines first appeared in the ninth century BC. Small in size, they were either moulded, in clay or bronze, or sculpted in ivory. Some were used to decorate vases – bronze cauldrons in particular – others were free-standing. They represent people or animals in various postures or actions: a warrior brandishing a javelin or shooting an arrow, a blacksmith forging a helmet, and also female figures. Sometimes they are in groups: boxers, musicians, hunters, horses and riders. From a stylistic point of view, the terracotta or bronze figures are rigid in form and somewhat stylized and abstract, although they also attempt to suggest natural postures or movements. Hence the artists were not attempting to capture fleeting moments, but to depict pure natural form. The workshops of Argos and Corinth excelled in the art of the figurine, with Sparta, Arcadia, Boeotia and Crete not far behind in quality. It was only towards the end of the eighth century BC that Athens was to make outstanding progress (Zimmermann, 1989; Morris, 1992) (Plates 56–58).

The goldsmith's art, known mainly from Athenian examples, takes the form of narrow headbands decorated with geometric patterns and human or animal figures, as well as necklaces and earrings.

ARCHITECTURE, TOWN-PLANNING, WALLS

From the end of the Mycenaean period to the closing decades of the ninth century BC, the only form of building was rudimentary dwellings made out of flimsy materials. The remains of these dwellings show more or less rectilinear ground plans or ground plans with an apse. The situation improved around 850 BC with the construction of surrounding walls, while temples made their appearance towards the year 800 BC. The temple, regarded as the dwelling-place of a god, was built on the pattern of human habitations. Thus, considering the ground plan only, we find temples with an apse, temples that are roughly square and others that are quadrilateral. Temples were, however, larger and better built than houses. Some had columns *in antis*, others were surrounded by an external colonnade, while yet others had an internal colonnade. At the present time we know of at least a dozen temples built before the year 700 BC, in continental Greece, in Crete and on the Aegean islands. On the other hand, walls dating from that period are rare. Smyrna (the archaeological site of Bayrakli) was the first Greek settlement, after those of the Mycenaean period, to be enclosed (in approximately 850 BC). Towards the end of the eighth century BC this same settlement was to construct an even more imposing wall. Carefully planned, with a lower facing of brick and an outer facing of stone, it is 4.75 m wide and is reinforced by bastions at various points. At the end of the eighth century BC, walls were built at Melia, near Smyrna, and at Emporio, on the island of Chios. These walls were erected in haste. To the best of our knowledge at this time Smyrna is also the first Greek settlement to have had an unmistakably urban appearance. With a surface area of 48,000 m², it had 400 to 500 stone-built houses of rectilinear shape (Coldstream, 1977; Fagerström, 1988).

RELIGION

Temples and votive figures are the tangible element, as it were, of our evidence on the religion of the Greeks between

1100 and 700 BC. Before building temples – from around the year 800 BC – the Greeks honoured the divine powers by making sacrifices to them on rudimentary altars erected in the open air. The idea of building a temple was a new one, as was the idea of regarding it as the dwelling-place of a god. *Xoana* – blocks of wood roughly carved with a cutting instrument and said to have fallen from the sky – are representations of the gods. Some less stylized figures, two- or three-dimensional, may be identified with the Olympian gods. The faithful offered sacrifices, figurines and other objects to the gods (Coldstream, 1977; Snodgrass, 1980; Boardman, 1982). But archaeological evidence is not our best source of information for the state of Greek religion before 700 BC. It pales before the great literary creations of the closing decades of the eighth century BC and the opening decades of the seventh – the *Iliad*, the *Odyssey*, the *Theogony* and the Homeric Hymns. These works depict a world inhabited by divine beings. Gods and goddesses have personalities; they are ruled by their passions and behave like humans. Each of them, male or female, has his own character as well as his own functions. Sometimes they are related to one another. It is a pantheon with a strict hierarchy and rules. Zeus is the king of the gods and lives on Mount Olympus, where he is surrounded by his family of gods and goddesses whom he summons from time to time for discussion, like a Council of Elders, before taking a decision. The Olympian deities are more human than other gods. They savour the delights of ambrosia and nectar (the food and drink of the gods), but also enjoy the scent of the burnt offerings made to them. Several deities intervene in the life of mortals and may grant favours to a king or people or, alternatively, heap disgrace on them. For the most part, they are fundamentally benevolent; they only lash out to punish a crime, censure an excess or exact vengeance. It is on the confines of the world familiar to the Greeks that certain more malevolent deities lie in wait for mortals who venture their way (Dietrich, 1974; Clay, 1983; Erbse, 1986).

ALPHABETIC WRITING

The Greeks ascribed the creation of their alphabet to an 'inventor', Kadmos, who was believed to have come from Phoenicia in very remote times, somewhere around the fifteenth century BC by our system of reckoning. In fact, however, the oldest documents testifying to the use of the Greek alphabet date from the second half of the eighth century BC and modern research has shown that the prototype adopted by the Greeks was a form of writing in use among the Phoenicians and other Semitic peoples in the tenth century BC. This Phoenician writing had signs for consonants only. The Greeks took over these signs and their order, but went a stage further. Feeling the need to represent the vowels too, they gave the values of a, e, i, o and u to five of the signs they had just borrowed. They also simplified the shape of the signs. Modern research has also pointed to the virtually simultaneous appearance of certain early local variants and postulates the existence of different centres responsible for their creation. As for identifying the places where the Greeks could have become familiar with Phoenician writing, attention has been drawn to contacts between Greeks and Phoenicians initially in the ninth century BC, at certain locations in the Aegean basin, and subsequently, early in the eighth century BC, on the coasts of Syria and Palestine (Jeffery, 1961; Powell, 1991).

POETRY

The first appearance of alphabetic writing among the Greeks preceded the composition of the epic poems traditionally attributed to Homer. This observation in itself, however, does not entail the conclusion that these poems were recorded in writing from the start. The existence in certain illiterate societies of people capable of reciting epic poems of a length comparable to that of the *Iliad* or the *Odyssey* has prompted several Homer scholars to uphold the view that these epics too could have been compositions that were communicated orally. However, they have an elaborate structure and a dense texture; a wealth of detail is made to serve the overall design and there are subtle textual echoes. Some scholars therefore maintain that the *Iliad* and the *Odyssey* were written down from the start, but as it took some time for the use of writing to spread, they do not exclude the possibility that bards may have passed the poems on orally in the early stages.

The *Iliad* and the *Odyssey* are composed in highly literary language. Based on the Ionic dialect, but with some Aeolic elements, both poems have a very wide-ranging vocabulary, including synonyms, and sometimes use parallel grammatical forms. The style is refined and natural at the same time. Homeric descriptions, images and comparisons have become exemplary models. All the lines are written in the same metre, the dactylic hexameter, which generally consists of five feet of three syllables (–◡◡ = long-short-short), and one foot of two syllables (–◡ = long-short). It is a metre of pre-Hellenic origin, and does not fit all combinations of Greek words, but the *Iliad* and the *Odyssey* employ a wide variety of devices to avoid lines that do not scan, to overcome the monotony inherent in the repetition of the same rhythm and to give the words a flowing, musical quality. The characters of the protagonists are sharply drawn; they are tragic figures struggling to escape from some divine wrath or the power of destiny. The moods of the main characters and the relationships between them are very intense. In both poems, the story begins *in medias res* and recounts the final weeks of an adventure that has lasted ten years. Against this backdrop, the poet skilfully introduces digressions – in the manner of flashbacks – in order to bring previous episodes or situations to life.

Some point to weaknesses in the *Iliad* and the *Odyssey* in support of the theory that they were composed in stages by different *rhapsodes* (professional singers) who expanded or combined already existing poems. Close study shows, however, that these weaknesses are no more numerous or significant than those occurring in any other masterpiece of similar length. The controversy between proponents of the 'piecemeal' theory and those who believe in the essential unity of the *Iliad* and the *Odyssey* has been going on for 200 years, though over the last few decades the latter have gained the upper hand.

Another debate – this time going back more than 2,000 years – concerns the authorship of the *Iliad* and the *Odyssey*: are they the work of the same person? There are, in fact, some quite marked differences between them. So some scholars attribute them to different authors, while others explain the differences by saying that, although by the same hand, the *Odyssey* is a much later work than the *Iliad*.

From antiquity the name of Homer has been associated with other poetic works, of which only the texts of the Homeric Hymns, addressed to various gods, have survived, but most of these remarkable works were produced after 700 BC. Information has also been handed down from antiquity about epics that are not attributed to Homer and researchers are attempting to establish their content and date.

The question of the sources and antecedents of the *Iliad* and the *Odyssey* is a very important and complex one. The poems reflect cultural features – principally in such areas as vocabulary, techniques, trade, weapons and warfare, geographical knowledge, religion and burial customs – of which the latest date from the early eighth century BC and the earliest go back to Mycenaean times. Since virtually all these features predate the alphabet, the poems are quite justifiably considered to have been passed down orally. The same poems speak of professional singers reciting hymns in praise of kings who were of outstanding valour or wisdom, and they frequently reveal the importance such kings attached to their reputation in posterity. So it is presumed that over the centuries the singers reworked and added to the epics they had learnt, while at the same time refining their powers of expression. The Homeric poems emerge at the end of this process and mark the transition of the art of poetry from the oral to the written stage. They influenced subsequent Greek literature very strongly, and in a variety of ways.[2]

DIVERSIFYING AND UNIFYING TRENDS

The Greek world during the eighth century BC was being pulled in two different directions: towards diversity and towards unity. Each state endeavoured to assert its independence and self-sufficiency. Each community formed a cultural entity. Technical and institutional progress occurred in certain states only. Local differences emerged in the sphere of artistic creation. On the other hand, as a result of the contacts they maintained, some Greeks began to be aware of a Pan-Hellenic cultural community in such matters as habits and customs, language as opposed to dialect, religion as opposed to local cults and myths, poems that came to be known throughout the Greek world, and finally the heroic legends and figures conveyed by these poems. Such Greeks fell into specific categories: seafarers, wandering bards, itinerant craftsmen or pilgrims.

Eventually, a fair number of these sanctuaries were to become meeting-places of wider significance. Pilgrimages to the sanctuary of Demeter near Thermopylae and to the sanctuary of Apollo at Delphi gave rise to the establishment in the early eighth century BC of the Pylaio-Delphic Amphictyony. Its members consisted of twelve *ethnei*: the Perrhaebi, Magnesians, Thessalians, Achaeans, Phthiotes, Dolopes, Aininians, Malians, Locrians, Phocians, Boeotians, Dorians and Ionians. Each *ethnos* had two votes in the Council that administered the Amphictyony. The city of Sparta was considered part of the *ethnos* of the Dorians, while the cities of Athens and those of Euboea shared the votes of the Ionian *ethnos*. Up to 700 BC, the Amphictyonic Council met at the sanctuary of Demeter, although by that time the Delphic oracle was already so famous that it was consulted by cities on religious and political matters. Also in the eighth century BC, the festival of Apollo at Delos was attended by the Ionians of Athens, Euboea, the Cyclades and Ionia. The sanctuary of Poseidon on Mount Mycale became a religious centre for the Ionian cities. The league established by these cities in about 700 BC – the *Panionion* – had only a limited and temporary existence at that time and later. Lastly, the sanctuary of Apollo at Triopion served as a religious centre for the cities of Doris.

ATHLETIC CONTESTS

The nobility, fired by a spirit of competition, aspired to excellence (*aristeia*), which it revered as the supreme value. The ethics of their class compelled nobles to excel in war, hunting and sports contests. Such contests accompanied ritual or lay ceremonies. Olympia, whose prestige as a religious centre never ceased to grow, added an institutional flavour to the athletic encounters that every four years brought in Greeks from neighbouring areas at first, and then from ever more distant ones, to compete for the glory of victory and the honour of being crowned with a wreath of olive leaves. In the year 776 the organizers of these games began to record the names of the victors and their homelands, which is why that year was henceforth regarded by the Greeks as that of the first Olympiad. The first thirteen Olympiads had only one event: the *stadion* (a 192-m race). It was at the fourteenth Olympiad, in 724 BC, that the *diaulos* (a two-length race) was introduced. Subsequently, in 720 BC, the *dolichos* (a four-length race) was added, and the *pentathlon* and wrestling in 700 BC. Yet other contests were subsequently included in the Olympic Games.

NATIONAL CONSCIOUSNESS

Before the year 700 BC, the Greeks held a considerable body of religious beliefs and legends in common together with the sense of a national bond. In the *Iliad*, this is reflected in the way in which the Trojan War is presented as an enterprise common to all Greeks resolved to face the challenge of an alliance of foreigners. The *Iliad* and the *Odyssey* use three equivalent ethnic descriptions to designate the Greeks: the Achaeans, the Danaeans and the Argives. The oldest example of the use of the name Hellenes is in a fragment of Hesiod, who refers to a legendary character named Hellen as the common ancestor of all the Greeks. The Italic peoples knew the Hellenes as *Grai* or *Graeci*, the name of a branch of the settlers who colonized Cumae.

NOTES

1. According to Hammond (1972, pp. 405–41 and 1979, pp. 1–70), and taken up again by Sakellariou (1983); a different point of view is expressed by Borza (1990).
2. These paragraphs summarize the present state of Homeric studies and the main views that have been put forward in this field (Wade-Gery, 1952, pp. 155–9; Bowra, 1955, 1972; Kakridis, 1971; Heuberck, 1974; Luce, 1975; Broccia, 1979; Clarke, 1981; Tsagarakis, 1982; de Romilly, 1985; Latacz, 1985, 1991; Vivante, 1985, 1991; Fenik, 1986; Edwards, 1987; Silk, 1987; Casewitz (ed.), 1989; Montuori, 1990; Tracy, 1990).

BIBLIOGRAPHY

AHLBERG, G. 1971a. *Prothesis and Ekphora in Greek Geometric Art.* Götenborg. (Stud. mediterr. Archaeol., 32.)
—— 1971b. *Fighting on Land and Sea in Greek Geometric Art.* Stockholm. (Skr. utg. Svenska Inst. Athen, 16.)
BAKHUIZEN, S. C. 1976. *Chalcis-in-Euboea, Iron and Chalcidians Abroad.* Leiden.
BERARD, J. 1957. *La colonisation grecque de l'Italie méridionale et de la Sicile dans l'antiquité.* 2nd ed. Paris.

—— 1960. *L'expansion et la colonisation grecques jusqu'aux guerres médiques*. Paris.

BOARDMAN, J. 1963. *Island Gems*. London.

—— 1970. *Greek Gems and Finger Rings*. London.

—— 1973. *The Greeks Overseas*. 2nd ed. Hamondsworth.

—— 1982. The Geometric Culture of Greece. In: EDWARDS, I. E. S. et al. (eds), *Cambridge Ancient History*. 2nd ed. Cambridge, Vol. 3, Part 1, pp. 779–93.

BORZA, E. N. 1990. *In the Shadow of Olympus. The Emergence of Macedon*. Princeton, N.J.

BOUZEK, J. 1969. *Homerisches Griechenland im Lichte der archaeologischen Quellen*. Praha.

BOWRA, C. M. 1952. *Heroic Poetry*. London.

—— 1955. *Homer and his Forerunners*. Edinburgh.

—— 1972. *Homer*. London.

BRELICH, A. 1961. *Guerre, agoni e culti nella Grecia arcaica*. Bonn.

BROCCIA, G. 1979. *La questione omerica*. Firenze.

CANCIANI, F. 1970. *Bronzi orientali e orientalizzanti a Creta nell' VIII e VII sec. a.C.* Roma.

CARPENTER, R. 1956. *Folktale, Fiction and Saga in the Homeric Epics*. 2nd ed. Berkeley, Calif. (Sather class. Lect., 20.)

CARTLEDGE, P. 1979. *Sparta and Lakonia: A Regional History 1300–362 BC*. London.

CASEWITZ, M. (ed.) 1989. *Études homériques*. Lyons. (Trav. Maison Orient, 17.)

CHARBONNEAUX, J. 1958. *Les bronzes grecs*. Paris.

CLARKE, H. 1981. *Homer's Readers: A Historical Introduction to the Iliad and the Odyssey*. University of Delaware Press.

CLAY, J. S. 1983. *The Wrath of Athena: Gods and Men in the Odyssey*, Princeton, N.J.

COLDSTREAM, J. N. 1977. *Geometric Greece*. London.

COOK, J. M. 1962. *The Greeks in Ionia and the East*. London.

COOK, R. M. 1960. *Greek Painted Pottery*. London.

DEGER, S. 1970. *Herrschaftsformen bei Homer*. Wien.(PhD Dissertationen.)

DEGER-JAKOLTZY, S. (ed.) 1983. *Griechenland, die Ägäis und die Levante während der 'Dark Ages' vom 12. bis 9. Jahrhundert v. Chr.: Akten des Symposions von Stift Zwettl (NÖ) 11.-14. Oktober 1980*. Wien.

DEMARGNE, P. 1947. *La Crète dédalique*. Paris. (Bibl. Éc. fr. Athènes Rome, 164.)

—— 1964. *La naissance de l'art grec*. Paris.

DESBOROUGH, V. R. d'A. 1952. *Protogeometric Pottery*. Oxford.

—— 1972. *The Greek Dark Ages*. London.

DIETRICH, B. C. 1974. *The Origins of Greek Religion*. Berlin/New York.

DIMOCK, G. E. 1989. *The Unity of the Odyssey*. Amherst, Mass.

DREWS, R. 1983. *Basileus, the Evidence for Kingship in Geometric Greece*. New Haven, Conn./London.

EDWARDS, M. W. 1987. *Homer: Poet of the Iliad*. Baltimore/London.

EFFENTERRE, H. van. 1985. *La cité grecque*. Paris.

ERBSE, H. 1986. *Untersuchungen zur Funktion der Götter im homerischen Epos*. Berlin/New York. (Unters. antiken Lit. Gesch., 24.)

FAGERSTRÖM, K. 1988, *Greek Iron Age Architecture: Development through Changing Times*. Göteborg. (Stud. mediterr. Archaeol., 81.)

FENIK, B. 1986. *Homer and the Nibelungenlied: Comparative Studies in Epic Style*. Cambridge, Mass./London. (Martin class. Lect., 30.)

FINLEY, M. I. 1966. *The World of Odysseus*. London.

FITTSCHEN, K. 1969. *Untersuchungen zum Beginn der Sagendarstellungen bei den Griechen*. Berlin.

GRIFFIN, J. 1987. *Homer, the Odyssey*. Cambridge.

HAMMOND, N. G. L. 1967. *Epirus*. Oxford.

—— 1972–9. *A History of Macedonia*. Oxford. 2 vols.

—— 1976. *Migrations and Invasions in Greece and Adjacent Areas*. New Jersey.

—— 1989. *The Macedonian State*. Oxford.

HAMPE, R.; SIMON, E. 1981. *The Birth of Greek Art*. London,.

HEUBERCK, A. 1974. *Die homerische Frage*. Darmstadt.

HIGGINS, R. 1961. *Greek and Roman Jewellery*. London.

HÖLSCHER, U. 1988. *Die Odyssee: Epos zwischen Märchen und Roman*. München.

HURWIT, J. M. 1985. *The Art and Culture of Early Greece 1100–480 BC*. Ithaca, N.Y./London.

HUXLEY, G. L. 1962. *Early Sparta*. London.

—— 1966. *The Early Ionians*. London.

JEFFERY, L. H. 1961. *The Local Scripts of Archaic Greece*. Oxford.

KAKRIDIS, J. 1971. *Homer Revisited*. Lund.

KELLY, T. 1976. *A History of Argos to 500 BC*. Minneapolis.

KUNZE, E. 1931. *Kretische Bronzereliefs*. Stuttgart.

LATACZ, J. 1985. *Homer*. München.

—— (ed.) 1991. *Zweihundert Jahre Homerforschung: Rückblick und Ausblick, Castalen, Aug. 16–19 1989*. Stuttgart.

LENCMAN, J. 1966. *Die Sklaverei im mykenischen und homerischen Griechenland*. Wiesbaden.

LUCE, J. 1975. *Homer and the Heroic Age*. London.

MATTUSCH, C. C. 1988. *Greek Bronze Statuary from the Beginning through the Fifth Century BC*. Ithaca, N.Y./London.

MONTUORI, F. 1990. *Introduzione a Omero con un appendice su Esiodo*. Firenze.

MORRIS, S. P. 1992. *Daidalos and the Origins of Greek Art*. Princeton, N.J.

MUSTI, D. et al. (eds) 1991. *La transizione dal Miceneo all'alto arcaismo, dal palazzo alla città*. Roma.

NAUMANN, U. 1976. *Subminoische und protogeometrische Bronzeplastik auf Kreta*. Berlin. (Beih. athenische. Mitt., 6.)

NILSON, M. P. 1963. *The Mycenaean Origin of Greek Mythology*. New York.

PAGE, D. L. 1955. *The Homeric Odyssey*. Oxford.

—— 1959. *History and the Homeric Iliad*. Berkeley, Calif.

PINSENT, J.; HURT, H. V. 1992. *Homer 1987: Papers of the Third Greenbank Colloquium*. Liverpool.

POWELL, B. B. 1991. *Homer and the Origin of the Greek Alphabet*. Cambridge.

RIDGWAY, D. 1992. *The First Western Greeks*. Cambridge.

ROMILLY, J. de. 1985. *Homère*. Paris. (Que sais-je?, 2218).

RUTKOWSKI, B. 1981. *Frühgriechische Kultdarstellungen*. Berlin.

SAKELLARIOU, M. B. 1958. *La migration grecque en Ionie*. Athènes.

—— 1983. The Nationality of the Macedonians. In: —— (ed.), *Macedonia*. Athina. pp. 48–63.

—— 1989. *The Polis-State: Definition and Origin*. Athens. (Meletemata, 4.)

—— 1990. *Between Memory and Oblivion: The Transmission of Early Greek Historical Traditions*. Athens. (Meletemata, 12.)

SCHWEIZER, B. 1969. *Die geometrische Kunst Griechenlands*. Köln.

SILK, M. 1987. *Homer, the Iliad*. Cambridge.

SNODGRASS, A. M. 1964. *Early Greek Armour and Weapons*. Edinburgh.

—— 1971. *The Dark Age of Greece*. Edinburgh.

—— 1977. *Archaeology and the Rise of the Greek State*. Cambridge.

—— 1980. *Archaic Greece at the Age of Experiment*. London.

STARR, C. G. 1961. *The Origins of Greek Civilisation, 1100–650 BC*. New York.

—— 1977. *The Economic and Social Growth of Early Greece, 800–500*. New York.

STYRENIUS, C. G. 1967. *Submycenaean Studies*. Lund. (Skr. utg. Svenska Inst. Athen, 7.)

TAPLIN, O. 1992. *Homeric Soundings: The Shaping of the Iliad*. Oxford.

THEMELIS, P. G. 1976. *Frühgriechische Grabbauten*. Mainz.

TOMLINSON, R. A. 1972. *Argos and the Argolid from the End of the Bronze Age to the Roman Occupation*. London.

TRACY, S. V. 1990. *The Story of the Odyssey*. Princeton, N.J.

TSAGARAKIS, O. 1982. *Form and Content in Homer*. Wiesbaden. (Hermes, 46.)

ULF, C. 1990. *Die homerische Gesellschaft: Materialien zur analytischen Beschreibung und historischen Lokalisierung*. München. (Vestigia, 43.)

VIVANTE, P. 1985. *Homer*. New Haven, Conn./London.

—— 1991. *The Iliad: Action as Poetry*. Boston, Mass. (Twayne's Masterwork Stud., 60.)

VLACHOS, G. 1974. *Les sociétés politiques homériques*. Paris.

WADE-GERY, H. T. 1952. *The Poet of the Iliad*. Cambridge.

WEBSTER, T. B. L. 1958. *From Mycenae to Homer*. London.

WHITLEY, J. 1991. *Style and Society in Dark Age Greece: The Changing Face of a Preliterate Society 1000–700 BC.* Cambridge.

WHITMAN, C. H. 1958. *Homer and the Heroic Tradition.* Cambridge, Mass.

WILL, E. 1955. *Korinthiaka.* Paris.

WILLETTS, R. F. 1977. *The Civilization of Ancient Crete.* London.

ZIMMERMANN, J.-L. 1989. *Les chevaux de bronze dans l'art géométrique grec.* Genève.

II.2
CYPRUS

Vassos Karageorghis

FROM c. 3000 BC TO c. 1900 BC

The insular character of the prehistoric civilization of Cyprus, which started in the Neolithic period, c. 7000 BC, continued until the end of the Chalcolithic (Map 10). The beginning of the third millennium BC corresponds to the floruit of the Chalcolithic, when the south-west part of the island in particular experienced important cultural developments. Settlements with impressive circular structures, some measuring over 10 m in diameter, appeared at sites such as Kissonerga-Mosphilia and Lemba-Lakkous. Natural copper was used for small tools and ornaments, hence the name 'Chalcolithic'. Economic and social developments, particularly in religious life, enhanced the artistic creations of the population. Richly painted (red-on-white) pottery was used in dwellings and deposited as tomb gifts; anthropomorphic and zoomorphic vases demonstrate an imaginative artistic spirit. Figurines of terracotta, limestone and picrolite, representing mainly female but also male human figures, have been found in 'sacred places' and in graves (Plate 59). They symbolize fertility, a notion which dominated religious ritual and was connected with human and animal fertility as well as with the fertility of the fields. Rituals associated with childbirth may have been practised, as suggested by the discovery at Kissonerga-Mosphilia of a clay model of a 'sacred building', in which terracotta and stone figurines were found, some of which represent pregnant women, one in the process of giving birth.

Dramatic cultural changes occurred c. 2500/2400 BC over a wide area in the Mediterranean, extending from the Cyclades to Anatolia and the Levant and including Cyprus. Cultural innovations in the island include the appearance of chamber tombs with multiple burials, the import of goods such as faience beads, the use of stamp seals, and so on. Such innovations point to the arrival of newcomers from Anatolia who caused the abandonment of Chalcolithic sites.

By c. 2300 BC a new cultural phase, the Early Bronze Age, appeared in Cyprus. Its earliest stages are to be found in the Morphou Bay area, in Nicosia and at Sotira-Kaminoudhia, a recently excavated settlement near the south coast. Buildings with rectilinear walls appeared for the first time. The pottery has strong Anatolian affinities both in shape and fabric (red polished). Gold and silver ear-rings of Anatolian type have been found in tombs.

Cemeteries with chamber tombs are located outside the settlements. Large numbers of tombs with rich grave goods have been excavated, dating mainly to the end of the period. Pots with imaginative shapes, often decorated with incised abstract patterns or figurative motifs in relief or in the round, have been found in large quantities. Plank-shaped terracotta

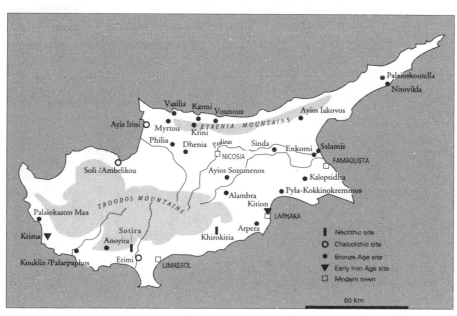

Map 10 Cyprus. Major archaeological sites (3000–700 BC).

figurines symbolizing a divinity of fertility demonstrate that old religious ideas continued; furthermore clay models of sanctuaries have been found in tombs, the best known being the model from Vounous. It represents a circular open-air sanctuary where a ritual ceremony is shown taking place in honour of divinities symbolized by the bull and the snake, and most likely connected with life and death. Male human figures attend the ceremony and bulls appear in pens. The bull as a religious symbol doubtless derived from Anatolia.

By the end of the Early Bronze Age or the beginning of the Middle Bronze Age the Cypriots must have started exploiting the copper resources and producing tin-bronze. Bronze tools and weapons were deposited in tombs. The profusion of weapons (daggers) both in bronze and in the form of clay models may suggest that the population was ready for any eventuality.

FROM c. 1900 BC TO c. 1600 BC

The Middle Bronze Age is a short, transitional period during which the island became widely populated. Ample evidence for the period comes from settlements scattered all over Cyprus such as Kalopsidha, Alambra and Episkopi-Phaneromeni. The houses comprise many rectangular rooms arranged around a courtyard. The beginning of the period is characterized by the appearance of some imported Cretan pottery, as well as pottery and other goods from Egypt and the Levant. If the equation Cyprus = Alashiya is accepted, then the first mention of the island appears on written documents from the palace of Mari in Mesopotamia, dating to the seventeenth century BC and referring to Alashiya as a copper-producing country. Cypriote goods, mainly pottery, have been found in the Levant, Egypt and some in Crete.

Though red-polished pottery continued to be produced, several new fabrics appeared, particularly white-painted ware with dark paint on a white surface. Middle Bronze Age material culture is however basically a development of Early Bronze Age culture and serves as a transition to the Late Bronze Age (Plate 60). The end of the Middle Bronze Age must have been marked by some unrest, the reasons for which have not yet been defined. Several fortresses were constructed in various parts of the island, either to protect it from external dangers or on account of local antagonisms between the various regions.

FROM c. 1600 BC TO c. 1050 BC

The Late Bronze Age is a period of interrelations in the Mediterranean of brisk trade and cultural exchanges, especially after the expulsion of the Hyksos from Egypt c. 1555 BC and the establishment of peaceful conditions in the East Mediterranean. Relations with the Aegean increased, no doubt because of the island's wealth in copper, enhanced by the commercial relations between Crete and Ugarit on the Syrian coast opposite Cyprus. About this time (c. 1500 BC) the Cypriots borrowed a linear script from Crete which they adopted for their own language and which is known as the Cypro-Minoan script. Several baked tablets of a west Asian form engraved with texts in this script have been found, but they are still undeciphered as the language of the texts is not known.

Development of the economy and trade encouraged the establishment of urban centres, especially near the east and

south coasts as at Enkomi, Kalavassos and Maroni. Relations with the Aegean increased even more from the beginning of the fourteenth century BC when the Mycenaeans succeeded the Minoans in trading with the Levant. There was an influx of Mycenaean goods in the island, especially pottery, and Mycenaean artistic styles influenced the art of Cyprus from the fourteenth century BC. Monumental palatial buildings constructed with large hewn stone blocks have been found at sites such as Kalavassos and Maroni. They may have been administrative buildings which regulated trade relations with the outside world (Fig. 26).

Radical cultural and political changes took place in the island c. 1200 BC after the collapse of the Mycenaean 'empire' and the fall of Troy. Invaders, known from Egyptian records as the 'Sea Peoples', appeared in the Eastern Mediterranean and caused turmoil before they settled both in Cyprus and along the Syro-Palestinian coast. Late Bronze Age centres in both these regions were abandoned or destroyed; some towns were rebuilt with Aegean elements in their art, architecture and even religious symbolism (such as the 'horns of conservation').

New waves of Aegeans must have come to the island c. 1050 BC. In the eleventh century BC Mycenaean funerary architecture and burial customs were introduced as well as new artistic styles. From a tomb dating to the mid-eleventh century BC comes the earliest evidence for the use of the Greek language in Cyprus (the Arcadian dialect) on a bronze skewer from Palaepaphos. Mythical tradition tells of the foundation of cities in the island by Greek heroes after the end of the Trojan War (Plate 61).

FROM c. 1050 BC TO c. 700 BC

The period known in the Aegean as the 'Dark Ages' of poverty and illiteracy was not so dark in Cyprus, no doubt as a result of the trade relations developed by the Mycenaean aristocracy among the newcomers. These Mycenaeans, having gained supremacy in political and cultural life in the main

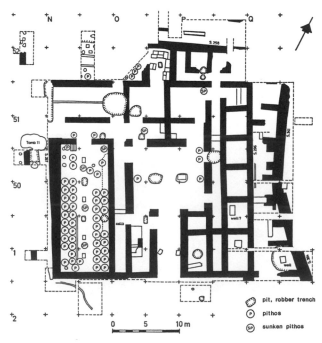

Figure 26 Plan of a palatial building (building X) at Kalavassos-Ayios Dimitrios, thirteenth century BC (after Karageorghis, 1990).

centres, may have caused the shifting of settlement from the old towns to new locations, such as Salamis which succeeded the nearby Late Bronze Age town of Enkomi (Plate 62).

By the end of the ninth century BC the Phoenicians had begun their westward expansion and Kition in Cyprus became their first established commercial colony. They soon attained political power, especially as a result of the political domination of successive foreign powers (Assyrians, Egyptians, Persians) over the island. Considerable Phoenician influence is observed on the art of this period in Cyprus and partly on the island's religion. But the old basic culture was retained by the conservative Cypriots. Salamis on the east coast developed into a major city of considerable wealth. Its 'royal tombs', where 'Homeric' burial customs were observed, illustrate the high cultural level attained during this period.

BIBLIOGRAPHY

BAURAIN, C. 1984. *Chypre et la Méditerranée orientale au Bronze Récent. Synthèse historique.* Paris.

KARAGEORGHIS, V. 1968. *Cyprus.* Génève.

—— 1982. *Cyprus from the Stone Age to the Romans.* London. (Anc. Peoples Places, 101.)

—— 1990. *Cyprus at the End of the Late Bronze Age.* Nicosia.

—— 1991a. *The Coroplastic Art of Ancient Cyprus,* Vol. 1: *Chalcolithic-Late Cypriote I.* Nicosia.

—— (ed.) 1991b. *Proceedings of the International Symposium on the Civilisations of the Aegean and their Diffusion in Cyprus and the Eastern Mediterranean, 2000-600 BC, 18-24 Sept., 1989.* Larnaca.

KARAGEORGHIS, V.; VERMEULE, E. 1982. *Mycenaean Pictorial Vase-Painting.* Cambridge, Mass.

12

ASIA

EDITOR'S NOTE

The data of archaeological research in Asia are today so abundant as to defy any attempt to summarize them. The Reading Committee, wishing to preserve the inputs of the individual authors, each of whom is a specialist in one or other of the major regions of Asia, asked Professor C. Edens to adapt and harmonize the contributions by C. C. Lamberg-Karlovsky, R. Wright, G. Roux, D. Beyer, H. Klengel, A. R. Al-Ansary and V. M. Masson so as to present a coherent picture of the continent's history from 3000 to 700 BC.

12.1
MESOPOTAMIA

12.1.1
THE TIGRIS AND EUPHRATES VALLEY
(3000–1500 BC)

C. C. Lamberg-Karlovsky and R. Wright

As described in Volume I, Mesopotamian civilization and state-level political organization had developed by the Late Uruk period. The accomplishments of the Late Uruk period still belong to the twilight of proto-history on which archaeological evidence sheds the most light. During the third millennium BC, however, the cuneiform writing system matured into a vehicle suited to detailed bureaucratic accounts, royal propaganda, religious literature, and private correspondence.

Though not without its difficulties, the textual evidence permits an increasingly detailed view of Mesopotamian political and social history beginning in the middle centuries of the third millennium BC (Edzard, 1968; Sollberger and Kupper, 1971). Even so, archaeology continues to provide important information about the physical realities of ancient Mesopotamia, and about the lives of ordinary people only dimly recorded in the textual evidence.

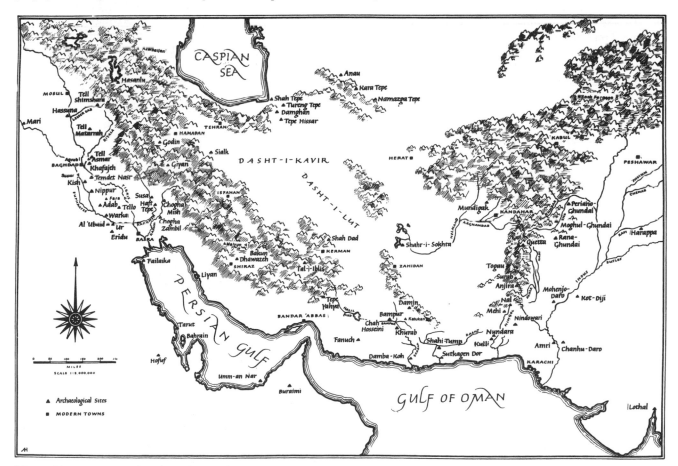

Map 11 Mesopotamia: archaeological sites of modern towns.

Although the inhabitants of Mesopotamia recognized themselves as belonging to the same civilization, the region contained considerable cultural and political diversity. Both the Sumerian and Akkadian languages were spoken in the region at least from the beginning of the Early Dynastic III period; initially Akkadian was more prevalent in the north (around modern Baghdad) but gradually replaced Sumerian as a spoken language in the south by the end of the third millennium BC. This linguistic diversity may correlate with subtle differences in the material culture (for instance, pottery forms) between the two parts of Mesopotamia, and perhaps also in details of social organization. And Mesopotamian political history was in some ways cyclical, in which short phases of regional integration (Akkadian, Ur III, Old Babylonian dynasties) punctuated the longer phases of regional fragmentation into city-states or petty kingdoms (Early Dynastic, post-Akkadian periods, Isin-Larsa periods). These political cycles, however, helped to spur changing relationships between socio-political institutions and the citizenry, and eventually led to more enduring regional kingdoms (the Kassite and Isin II dynasties of the later second millennium BC).

THIRD MILLENNIUM POLITICAL HISTORY

The political history of Mesopotamia remains poorly known for the first half of the third millennium BC. The Sumerian King List (Jacobsen, 1939) records the ruling dynasties of different cities, arranged in succession. Its opening lines report that Eridu was the first city to which 'kingship was lowered from heaven', and then passed to four other cities before the Flood; these dynasties contained several kings each of whose rule lasted tens of thousands of years. After the Flood, kingship was again lowered from heaven to the city of Kish, and subsequently passed to thirteen different dynasties in eight different cities, including Uruk, Ur, Mari, Kish and Adab. The character of these dynasties differs from that of the antediluvian rulers in several respects: the length of individual reigns shortens, eventually to plausible duration; kingship passes from city to city by force of arms; and some kings are recorded in documents written during or soon after their reigns. Even this section of the Sumerian King List is not historical, however. The List is conceived as the succession of kingship from city to city. But several of the successive dynasties actually existed simultaneously, and the List does not include dynasties that ruled other cities, notably Lagash. Moreover, the List excludes several kings who are independently known to have ruled in cities named in the succession of dynasties.

Nonetheless, the Sumerian King List does help to illuminate the themes of Early Dynastic political history. Kish formed an important centre in the north, and its kings seem to have exerted considerable if nebulous influence or even control over other places: inscriptions of the kings of Kish have been found in distant places, and kings of Kish regulated or referred in some way conflicts between other cities (such as Lagash and Umma). In the south, the cities of Uruk, Ur, Lagash and Umma were the regional powers, in which shifting relations of conflict and alliance between cities maintained a precarious balance of power (Lambert, 1952; Cooper, 1983). The best documented city-state was that of Lagash, in the deep south, during the Early Dynastic III period. Lagash contained three major centres, another twenty-two towns, and approximately forty villages within an area of approximately 1600 km² (Diakonoff, 1969). This city-state engaged in a border war with Umma, its neighbour to the north-west, over the course of several centuries, during which time neither was able decisively to defeat the other (Cooper, 1983).

Toward the end of the Early Dynastic III period, the efforts of several vigorous kings managed to overturn the balanced rivalries of Mesopotamian city-states. Lugalzagesi, a king of Uruk, was partially successful in subordinating a number of city-states within Mesopotamia. However, Sargon soon overturned his efforts. Sargon (2334–2279 BC), whom the Sumerian King List describes as the cupbearer of a king of Kish, established the first Mesopotamian imperial state by defeating the various Mesopotamian city-states and then expanding outward in a series of campaigns, or raids, northward into northern Mesopotamia and Syria and eastward into Elam and the Iranian mountains. Sargon founded a new capital at Agade (Akkad), and brought the wealth of trade, tribute and plunder to it (Plate 63). The reigns of his immediate successors, and especially of Naram-Sin (2254–2218 BC), continued Sargon's use of military force (Plate 64) and of diverting wealth to the new aristocracy of the Akkadian empire (Glassner, 1986). Despite Akkadian military successes, the city-states retained their traditional identity, and the leaders of the old aristocracy regularly rebelled against Akkadian rule.

The fragile Akkadian control disintegrated after the rule of Sharkalishari (2217–2193 BC), when local dynasties again reclaimed autonomy and when Gutian invaders from the mountains established control over parts of Mesopotamia. This post-Akkadian, or Gutian period, remains poorly known. Towards the end of the twenty-first century BC, Utu-hegal of Uruk began a process of driving out the Gutians and reforming a united Mesopotamia. Ur-Nammu (2112–2095 BC), the ruler of Ur, was initially subordinate to Utu-hegal, but soon emerged as the dominant power by founding the Ur III empire. Although it too expanded to control regions along the Tigris to the north and in the mountains to the east, the Ur III state had a very different character from the Akkadian empire. Shulgi (2094–2047 BC), Ur-Nammu's successor, instituted a series of sweeping reforms that created a bureaucratic rather than predatory empire (Steinkeller, 1987). However, this empire lasted an even shorter time than did its predecessor, and collapsed under the combined pressures of nomadic Amorite incursions from the north-west, rebellious governors, and a military invasion from Elam in the east.

INSTITUTIONAL LANDSCAPE OF THE THIRD MILLENNIUM

Cities and city-states formed the basic units of the Mesopotamian social landscape during the third millennium BC. Archaeological survey indicates that the majority of Mesopotamians were urban, living in towns and cities at least 40 hectares in size; in contrast, no more than 25 per cent lived in places less than 10 hectares in size (Adams, 1981). As Table 1 indicates, these proportions fluctuated somewhat over the course of the third millennium BC, and the urban character of the region peaked during the Early Dynastic III, in the middle centuries of the millennium. Following this peak urbanism, the proportion of rural population increased steadily until the early first millennium BC.

Table 2: Changing Mesopotamian urbanism

Period	Total settlement area (ha)	Non-urban settlements <10 ha	Urban settlements >40 ha
Late Uruk	583	50%	24%
Early Dynastic I	1,065	21%	57%
Early Dynastic III	1,659	10%	78%
Akkadian	1,416	18%	63%
Ur III	2,725	25%	55%
Old Babylonian	1,791	30%	50%
Kassite	1,308	57%	31%
Post-Kassite	616	64%	16%

The extreme degree of Mesopotamian urbanization is an unusual, and 'unnatural', phenomenon in the ancient world. The reasons for the great importance of cities in the Mesopotamian world were doubtless complex, having to do with the politics and economics of city-states. Adams has described the flow of resources between countryside and city as 'grain, domestic animals, other agricultural products, corvée labour ... spun wool, woven cloth, hides, dried fish, reed mats, and beer ... [in exchange for a reciprocal flow of] ... stone of various kinds, luxury goods to validate the status of subordinate local élites, copper tools, and weapons and vessels for utilitarian purposes as well as for conspicuous consumption' (Adams, 1981, p. 81). Thus cities, from their inception, served as market centres, and this factor would have been a primary motivating force in the migration of rural populations to them. Cities clearly maintained a primary role as centres for the production and distribution of crafts and, therefore, were significant attractions to rural settlements. And the intense inter-city warfare characteristic of the Early Dynastic period defined cities as places of relative security. Certainly by the Early Dynastic period, the city had become a symbol of both secular and non-secular authority, and among its major attractions would have been not only its role as a market centre, but also its role as a centre of local ritual and feasting.

The great 'organizations', Oppenheim's (1977) term for the temple and palace, dominated Mesopotamian societies, whether in times of competing city-states or of regional empires. Both of these institutions were arranged like households, headed by the god or king and run by household members. In addition to their political and cultic roles, these households contained concentrated economic power, in the form of large tracts of agricultural land and water, dependent labour forces for both agricultural and craft production, skilled craftsmen, and the traders who acquired raw materials for distant places. In addition to the public institutions, extended families and other kin groups formed important land-owning households that could also accumulate wealth and exert political power.

By the Early Dynastic period, the increased centralization of state power had produced a dependent labour force among temple and palace personnel, along with the slave and semi-free workers who provided services and production to the estates. Individuals of rural communities may also have been recruited for temporary labour on irrigation and construction work, and have been obliged to give tribute to the temple in the form of agricultural produce. These societies thus contained five major classes of people: nobility, among whom were counted royal administrators, merchants and priests; citizens or community members who held private property; clients of the temple or palace, like artisans, who temporarily held pieces of property in exchange for craft products; semi-free labourers who received payment by subsistence rations; and slaves, prisoners of war and other indigent members of the community (Diakonoff, 1972, 1982; Gelb, 1965, 1969).

The relative positions of temple, palace and private kin-groups changed significantly during the third millennium BC. These changes reflect the growing domination of palace over temple, and the public institutions over private groups.

Temple

Shrines formed a part of Mesopotamian communities since the Ubaid period, and grew into elaborate temple complexes by the Uruk period. Temples occupied, both literally and figuratively, the key positions in cities, and at the end of the fourth millennium BC formed the institutional organization of political authority. The oldest documents from the Late Uruk period show that land, draft animals and seed, although held by the temple, were turned over to the community for cultivation. Later, temples appeared more as self-contained socio-economic units with their own managers and labour personnel. The lowest-ranking members of the temple were enslaved women and children, some former prisoners of war and others donated to the temple as pious gifts (Gelb, 1972). Temple personnel were able masterfully to combine their function as caretakers of the physical homes of gods with overseeing and undertaking productive activities. These economic activities enabled the accumulation of the surpluses that provided the resources and capital with which to engage in trade and to develop further the temple's industries. Leadership in the temple thus required both religious skills and sacred knowledge, and the political ability normally associated with non-secular institutions.

The autonomy of the temples began to erode during the Early Dynastic period, when the palace assumed the primary political role. Moreover, many temples came under the control of relatives of ruling kings (often wives or daughters) during the Early Dynastic and Akkadian periods, and during the Ur III period the temples were placed under the jurisdiction of provincial governors, who siphoned off surplus production into the state treasury. Despite the declining autonomy of temple households, the conceptual connection between kingship and the gods guaranteed that religious architecture retained its prominent place in the urban fabric.

Many of the concepts of architectural design that characterized the Uruk period carried over into the third millennium BC, and embodied principles of formal symmetry. Temple construction exemplified these concepts (Crawford, 1977). Single-room shrines, usually with a bent-axis approach, were similar to earlier Ubaid-period buildings, and persisted through the Early Dynastic period. Two other formal types, the bipartite and tripartite plans, also had precedents in earlier buildings, and continued as dominant forms in the third millennium BC. A fourth type, the 'house-plan temple', consisted of a courtyard surrounded by several large rooms on each side. This temple form, which appeared during the Early Dynastic period, clearly reflected the concept of the temple as a residence of the god to whom it was dedicated.

Two of the most impressive types of monumental buildings in the third millennium BC, the oval temple and the ziggurat, also exhibited formal regularity in plan. The oval temple, best represented at Khafaje, was an innovation of the Early Dynastic period. While ziggurats had antecedents in the White Temple and platform at Uruk, construction became more elaborate during the third millennium BC. The most impressive example was the ziggurat at Ur, built during the Ur III period (Plates 65, 66). This ziggurat was constructed of a mud core faced with baked brick set in bitumen, forming the multiple terraces of the staged tower; three monumental staircases set parallel and perpendicular to the tower gave access to the terraces and to the shrine at the summit. Ziggurats were among the most spectacular and enduring forms of Mesopotamian architecture. Their massive form and great areal size must be correlated with the increased complexity of social and political organization, and the ability to marshal the labour and organizational skills necessary to build them.

Palace

The secular figure of the 'king' was a supreme political power that appeared early in the Mesopotamian sequence. The Sumerian word *lugal* (literally 'great man', that is, king) had occurred already in Late Uruk texts, while the word *en* in these same texts was a priestly title referring to both non-secular and secular authority; the word for palace, *e-gal*, or great household, appeared in Early Dynastic I texts from Ur. The archaeological evidence indicates that distinctly palace architecture may have appeared during the Jamdat Nasr period and certainly was present in Mesopotamian cities by the end of the Early Dynastic II period (Margueron, 1988). In other words, the palace as a distinctive organization and as an architectural component of the urban fabric appeared at the beginning of the third millennium BC. This textual and archaeological evidence correlates with certain inferences from Sumerian mythology and the indications of endemic conflict between cities.

Sumerian mythology may be used to reconstruct the rise of kingship from an early form of 'primitive democracy'. According to one interpretation (Jacobsen, 1970), during the period before the development of formal social and political institutions, decisions were made by the consensus of an assembly of free adult males. This body convened during times of stress, when temporary leaders were elected. The genesis of kingship was in the refusal of one 'temporary leader' at Uruk to relinquish his authority, and his success in rallying the support of the younger men in the community. This mythical first king was Gilgamesh, whose name appears in the Sumerian King List as an early ruler of Uruk. Gilgamesh is usually assigned to the Early Dynastic II period, the period when increasing conflict between city-states led to the construction of walls around cities (Nissen, 1972). The appearance during the Early Dynastic II both of distinctive palace architecture and of city walls lends credence to the idea that kingship as a powerful institution, separate from the temples and community organizations, emerged during the second quarter of the third millennium BC.

The gradual ascendancy of palace over temple has already been mentioned, as have some aspects of the decline of community councils. The economic position of the palace emphasized its rising political authority. Again the situation in Early Dynastic III Lagash provides the best example. Of the roughly 1,600 km² that belonged to the city-state, the palace owned approximately 25–35 per cent, the palace and the ten or more temples 25 per cent; the private kin-groups possessed the remaining 40–50 per cent (Diakonoff, 1969). Since the palace formed a single organization, the temples at least ten

distinct organizations, and the multiple kin-groups a much larger number, the palace concentrated agricultural and craft production to a degree unparalleled in any other single institution. Moreover, beginning in the Early Dynastic and accelerating sharply under the Akkadian dynasty, the palace purchased land from kin-groups, a process that further diminished the economic power of this social sector. By the Ur III period, the central government monopolized the entire system.

Palace architecture was a regular, if less salient, component of Mesopotamian cities. Like the temples, palace structures were based on geometric and regular plans (Margueron, 1982). The palace at Kish (Fig. 27), the most complete example for the Early Dynastic period, consisted of two large buildings separated by a narrow alley. Both buildings were fortified with impressive exterior walls, but one also contained an outer wall, gateway, and tower. The Kish palace had a monumental entrance with buttressed and recessed doorways and pillared halls. Interior space, for example in the Eridu palace, consisted of a reception room, square courtyards, and 'audience halls' or 'throne rooms' which became a standard in later palace architecture. Later palaces, including those of the early second millennium BC, became larger and more elaborate; the palace at Mari, for example, covered 2.5 hectares and contained well over a hundred rooms, halls, courtyards and corridors.

Kin-groups

The kin-groups outside the palace and temple organizations formed the majority of the population; in the example of Lagash during the Early Dynastic period, these groups accounted for perhaps two-thirds of the city-state's population. These groups varied considerably in their economic standing. Some owned large estates and managed to accumulate wealth, while others were impoverished and forced to sell their lands and to enlist their members as dependents of temples (Diakonoff, 1976; Gelb, 1979). The socio-economic pyramid is reflected in the distribution of wealth within the Royal Cemetery at Ur, of Early Dynastic III to Akkadian date (Adams, 1966, p. 100):

royal graves	5	extremely large, rich, with sacrificed attendants
rich, non-royal	20	abundant metals, semi-precious stones, other wealth
rich, common	434	some metal
common	825	pottery

As already mentioned, these groups owned land and participated in city councils, but even in the aggregate their position weakened considerably over time.

Relatively little is known of the more ordinary secular architecture, including the urban residents and village dwellers. The archaeological evidence and depictions on objects indicate that mudbrick, single-storied and flat-roofed houses were the principal form. These houses consisted of several rooms focused on a larger central area, which in Akkadian times became a courtyard. The excavations at places like Ur and Khafaje show that residences typically were densely packed together in blocks along streets and alleys, even up to the exterior walls of temples and other public buildings. Neighbouring houses shared party-walls through which new doorways could be cut when individual rooms

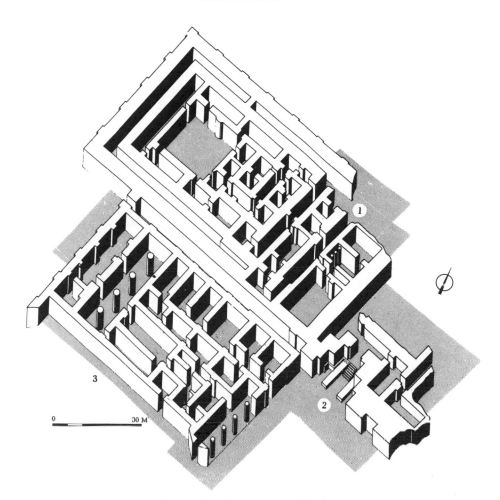

Figure 27 Plan of the palace at Kish, one of the earliest royal residences excavated in Sumer.

of a house were sold. Recent work at Abu Salabikh has revealed a significantly different pattern during the Early Dynastic I period, when perimeter walls created separate compounds of buildings; this pattern may reflect the residential extended kin-groups (Postgate and Moon, 1982). In addition to mudbrick architecture, reed huts of the type inhabited by Marsh Arabs today are represented on seals and other ornamental objects.

For both monumental and more ordinary architecture, the third millennium BC architectural features included vaults, domes, pillars, stairways and drainage systems.

Ideology

The changing relationship between temple and palace organization was also reflected in changing patterns of religious thought. The philologist Thorkild Jacobsen has characterized Mesopotamian religion as one in which the *numinous*, or 'wholly other', is experienced as immanent (in distinction from transcendent). In his words, the Mesopotamians viewed numinous power 'as a revelation of indwelling spirit, as power at the centre of something that caused it to be and thrive and flourish ..: and the external form given to encountered numinous power tended in earliest Mesopotamia to be simply the name and the form of the phenomenon in which the power seemed to reveal itself' (Jacobsen, 1976, p. 6). For example, the Sumerians used the word *an* for the sky overhead, but also applied the same name to the numinous power in the sky, the sky god. As a consequence, Mesopotamian religion was polytheistic, consisting of a mul-

titude of gods, each of whom was associated with different aspects of daily existence. Temples were the 'home' where gods were present, and the temple staff was responsible for the organization and management of the god's home (Plate 67). Since temples were sacred houses, they were imbued with the 'essence' of the numinous force that resided within them; accordingly, each temple differed from others.

Within the structure of these basic concepts, two aspects of Mesopotamian religion are relevant here: shifts in the ways in which gods and goddesses were perceived, and the rivalries among different Mesopotamian states. These factors are relevant because they reflect on the kinds of political changes described above. In the previous periods, the forms that the gods took were closely linked to the specific phenomenon that each represented: for example, a lion-headed bird represented the roaring thunder-cloud. Later, in the Jamdat Nasr and Early Dynastic periods, divine names took on the prefix *en*, indicating the gods and goddesses as rulers. A third metaphor came later, in the Old Babylonian period, when the gods were associated with parents. In other words, as the character of political leadership changed through time, so also the mythological representation of the gods changed.

The second factor, identification and rivalries between city-states, was directly related to religious concepts. In the earliest periods, the city gods were associated with their primary economies. Enki, the god of freshwater and marsh life, resided at Eridu, while sheep herders like Dumuzi resided in the central grasslands of Uruk and grain goddess Ninlil lived to the north at Shuruppak. Later, the total identification of a god with a particular city led to sharp rivalries, with important consequences. For political leaders aspiring to unite

Mesopotamia, these mythological rivalries mirrored political ones, and were an obstacle to the development of an integrated regional state. Not surprisingly, during the Old Babylonian period Hammurabi attempted to instal Marduk, the god of Babylon, as the supreme deity in mythology, a metaphor for the unification of the entire Euphrates and Tigris Valley. This attempt at harnessing theological reform to political goals is illustrated in the following hymn of the period:

> Ninurta is Marduk of the hoe,
> Nergal is Marduk of the attack,
> Zababa is Marduk of the hand-to-hand fight,
> Enlil is Marduk of lordship and counsel,
> Nabu is Marduk of accounting ...

Just as Marduk absorbed the identity of the gods associated with the different places of Mesopotamia, so too was Babylon claiming the loyalty of these same cities.

POLITICAL ECONOMY OF THE THIRD MILLENNIUM

The principal factors in the brilliant rise to power of the temple and palace organizations appear to have been the dual aspects of an agrarian economy combined with vigorous trade relations. Writing as a mechanism of accounting and bookkeeping took its place as a primary factor in the development of the Mesopotamian economy. Beginning with the Late Uruk period, documents reveal economic transactions concerning temple herds, and lists of professions and a hierarchically ordered labour force. Later, these systems were elaborated, so that by the Ur III period, virtually all aspects of the state-sector economy were recorded in an elaborate bookkeeping system. Documents recorded the supervision of crafts, management of an elaborate textile system, notations relating to foreign trade, and the quality control of products, all of which were inextricably intertwined with a flourishing economy (Zagarell, 1986). Moreover, writing contributed to the organizational power of the temple and palace institutions in other ways. Writing made possible the elaboration of sacred and literary texts; inscriptions also appeared on the seals that circulated both within and outside Mesopotamian communities, and on the stone sculptures that celebrated the military exploits of rulers. In sum, writing as an administrative technology underpinned the organizational power and the institutional memory of Mesopotamian societies.

Agriculture and animal husbandry

Irrigation figured as a factor in state control in a complex way; the individual city-state appears to have been more effective in exercising political leverage by controlling water than was the unified regional state. For example, the most common pattern in the third millennium BC was a local irrigation district controlled by individual cities. The question of whether this same pattern applied to agricultural and pastoral production is more difficult to answer.

The principal pattern was the near monopoly over agriculture and husbandry by temple, palace, and large private households. The first concrete evidence of state control occurs for the Ur III period, when the state controlled extensive agricultural lands and employed large numbers of work-ers. Moreover, the Ur III state conscripted workers from towns and cities. For example, the so-called 'harvest workers' migrated from south to north following seasonal variations in harvest times. The state also apparently took its share of local harvests; at Girsu, for example, the state and priesthood divided one quarter to one half of the harvest. And state-managed animal husbandry showed a heavy hand in the distribution of animals.

Major innovations in agriculture involved new tools and changes in irrigation technology (Salonen, 1968). Chipped stone 'hoes' figure in the archaeological record of the Uruk period, and pictographic representations of ox- or donkey-drawn ploughs belong to the same period. The seeder plough, a device that both saved labour and reduced seeding volume, was developed by the Early Dynastic period. Later Ur III texts reflect attempts to cut further seed volume by grading barley fields by seed volume/productivity ratios. Over the same thousand years, irrigation systems became increasingly linear, consolidated and integrated, with an expansion in cubic capacity. Where in earlier periods the land suitable to agriculture was patchy, the progressive integration of irrigation networks opened new land to the plough during Early Dynastic and Akkadian times, culminating in a latticework of canals during the Ur III period. These substantial irrigation works required more elaborate construction and more attentive maintenance, and at the same time they increased the food supply for an expanding population (Adams, 1981; Nissen, 1988).

The textual evidence indicates that the major crops included barley, emmer, wheat, peas and beans, all of which had been grown in earlier periods. Some important new crops also appeared, including date-palms and grapevines. Date-palm orchards were created on the high levees of the irrigation canals or river banks, where the trees could reach down into the underground flow of fresh water for added moisture. By the middle of the third millennium BC, the evidence indicates the processing of a number of foods: barley was processed into flour, malt and beer; sesame seeds were crushed for oil; and dates were made into wine.

The livestock of Mesopotamia included cattle, sheep, goat, pigs and donkeys; wild animals continued to be hunted. Livestock provided not just meat, but also a wide range of secondary products. These secondary products were key to the shift in agricultural and husbandry practices. Cattle, for example, were kept for dairy farming, and yielded butter and cheese with moderate success. The average Mesopotamian cow, according to best estimates, produced five dry quarts of butter and 7 ½ dry quarts of cheese a year, both low figures but compatible with production in twentieth-century India. Sheep became an invaluable asset for their wool, and while Mesopotamian sheep were less than half as productive as modern breeds, they still adequately supplied the massive textile industry of the third millennium BC. In addition to food, animals like cattle and donkeys provided traction and transportation.

Animal husbandry formed an important component of the regional economy, and fell under both private and state control. State records of the Early Dynastic III refer to a large staff of oxherds and shepherds, and mention the breeding of sheep, goat, oxen, pigs and donkeys. The Ur III archives reveal a detailed bureaucratic oversight of animal herds. The state clearing house at Drehem registered the receipt, maintenance and delivery of animals, an effort that encompassed livestock, wild animals, fowl, grain for fodder and reeds for bedding. This textual evidence suggests that experimentation with animal breeding was a concern of the state and other major institutions, since a sedentary population of animals was dependent upon pasturage or supplementary grain feeding. The practice of grazing livestock on fields of sprouting barley is common today and apparently also a practice of the third millennium BC, attesting to the interdependence of the agriculturalist and pastoralist economic sectors and also providing a potent source of conflict between them. Management of herds for their wool and hair was a central state concern. The scale of the textile industry is reflected in administrative documents that referred to 6,000 tons of wool and the employment of 9,000 female and male slaves in the manufacture of textiles. Ur III documents inventoried large numbers of garments and wools stored in warehouses, and tracked the disbursements of these stocks (Waetzoldt, 1972).

The economic rationale for the control of agriculture and animal husbandry involved religious as well as economic institutions. Animals and grain were brought as gifts to the palace, as temple offerings, and as taxes from conquered lands. These materials were subsequently disbursed as offerings and sacrifices, as partial payment of salaries to officials and soldiers, and as stipends to the royal household. The goods were also shipped to other cities, a destiny best reflected in the bureaucratic accounts from the Drehem office responsible for tracking shipments of animals to Shuruppak and Nippur.

Occupational specialization

Specialized production had become pervasive during the Uruk period, as reflected in the lists of craftsmen arranged into different ranks and occupation. The Early Dynastic period temple and palace institutions were involved in all aspects of the economy. Archaeological evidence reveals the presence of metal-working areas and the presence of kilns for pottery production in temple and palace compounds. Temple and palace commissioned the creation of certain objects like sculpture and elaborate art-works that both represented religious belief and political exploits, and stood as symbols of temple and palace authority. The wide variety of skills required to produce these extraordinary objects implies the organized collaboration of many specialized artisans such as seal cutters (Plate 68), sculptors, jewellers and others.

Technical innovations occurred within a variety of other industries, and especially craft production (Moorey, 1985). Many innovations in pyrotechnologies, stone working, and ornamental arts represented an extension of advances already underway in earlier periods. In potting, the adoption of the fast wheel by the Uruk period had greatly reduced the ornamentation of pottery; the third millennium BC wares continued to be relatively little decorated, though exceptions did occur, like the Jamdat Nasr polychrome and the Diyala scarlet painted wares. Metallurgy in the third millennium BC built on the massive Uruk-period advances, and both the scale and variety of metal production expanded considerably, especially for utilitarian items (Limet, 1960; Moorey, 1982). Metalsmiths worked copper, silver, gold and lead, using a variety of techniques such as the lost-wax method, gold-beating, casting, soldering and filigree. The Uruk-period explosion of the ornamental arts set the stage for continued advances in seal-cutting, stone-carving, and faience production. Of special interest is the ingenuity with which Sumerians used bitumen; these uses included bitumen cores for copper-covered works of art, and as the setting for inlays of shell and stone in a variety of objects (Plate 69).

Intra-regional and inter-regional exchange

A strong imperative existed to establish trading relationships with other regions. The lack of resources requisite to the development of a civilization forced Mesopotamians to look outward. And seemingly at some time in the Early Dynastic period, a conscious decision was made to develop trading partnerships, rather than continue the policy of colonization in order to acquire foreign materials. Even so, political leaders at various times did use military force to collect booty and a labour supply by conquest. In the Akkadian period, Sargon and his successors boasted of victories in far-off corners to the north-west, conquering Ebla, the Cedar Forest, and the Silver Mountains (the Amanus and Taurus Mountains). However, these campaigns were costly, and political leaders boasted as proudly of their trading relations. Sargon, for example, boasted that boats from Meluhha tied up at the quay in Agade. Thus Mesopotamian leaders successfully and confidently experimented with alternative forms of resource acquisition, and developed a system by which they were able to procure needed resources without the expense of extensive military operations.

Agricultural and pastoral products provided the primary basis for the development of extensive intra- and inter-regional trade. Sumerian myths make frequent allusion to temples as storehouses. Depots existed at estates, but also adjacent to fields and threshing floors. A centralized accounting agency supervised expenditures, clearing incoming and outgoing items from widely separated locations and for a variety of purposes. For example, an entry from a storage depot at the mouth of a particular canal shows barley disbursed as fodder for oxen and wages for labourers employed in digging. Administrative officials were concerned with maintaining canals both for irrigation and for transporting goods. In fact, canals were the major means by which materials were distributed between rural and urban centres. By the Ur III periods, textual accounts indicate that boats transported grain, fish and animals. One example records twenty-eight men employed for three days loading 1,550 bushels of barley onto a ship that sailed for four days on the canal until its arrival at a granary at Umma.

In addition to the intra-regional shipment of products, the temple and palace engaged in wide-ranging inter-regional trade (Lambert, 1953; Leemans, 1960; Neumann, 1979). These extensive trade contacts were an essential aspect of the Mesopotamian economy, for with rare exceptions, like pottery, virtually all craft production was dependent on the procurement of exotic raw materials. The tight supervision of craft specialists, grading of products, and quality control were important ingredients in the success of Mesopotamia in developing trading relationships.

The development of trade outside the Mesopotamian heartland was well underway by the Uruk period, but the scale and range of contacts greatly increased during the third millennium BC. Some evidence indicates the import of finished goods, the best documented of which are the carved chlorite vessels from the Iranian site of Tepe Yahya. However, raw materials were more important among Mesopotamian imports. The imported raw materials were then fashioned into products, which for the most part were consumed at home. This consumption of goods made from raw materials from outside the alluvium suggests that a major economic resource in Mesopotamia was labour and its organization.

By the Early Dynastic period, important trade networks

had been established, in which a variety of goods were traded between Mesopotamia and other regions. Products like pigs' fat, perfumes, textiles and agricultural goods were exchanged for commodities like copper, turquoise, lapis lazuli, carnelian, woods and shell. Trade to the east was by ship through the Persian Gulf or overland across the mountains, while traffic westward was by combinations of pack animals and river boats. Mesopotamia circulated goods from different areas, for example importing exotic oils or woods from the west, and passing some of these imports further eastward through Dilmun (modern Bahrain), or through mountain passes in exchange for materials not available from the west. By these means, Mesopotamia gained access to some very distant goods. For example, lapis lazuli came from the Badakhshan area of north-eastern Iran, arriving in Mesopotamia via staging posts such as Shahr-i Sokhta in eastern Iran, where workshops for making lapis lazuli beads have been found (Hermann 1968; Tosi and Piperno, 1973).

The consumers of these products varied according to the nature of the product. Since the temple and palace directed the production and distribution of many products, the possession of many objects and ornaments made from ornamented goods must have been confined to a few élites. Still, production overall was tied to societal demands, and for some products these demands included different sectors of society. Pottery, for example, maintained its place as a product in high demand, as the large quantities from archaeological excavations and grave lots attest. For example, in the last phases of the Early Dynastic period, pottery was the most ubiquitous material in the burials, both rich and poor, at the Royal Cemetery of Ur. This circumstance suggests that pottery and other products were available to all segments of society. Conversely, the rather limited nature of products crafted from imported raw materials, like lapis lazuli and copper, were restricted to fewer graves, suggesting a differential access to those resources.

Entrepreneurial activities

A last aspect of the Mesopotamian economy concerns the role of individual entrepreneurs and independent producers, whether in cities or the countryside. The obvious implications of the above are that segments of the population in rural areas exercised a degree of autonomy, especially those individuals who remained in or retreated to the numerous rural villages where they may have controlled their own means of production. In addition, some city dwellers carried out entrepreneurial activities, either as temple and palace emissaries or as agents independent of the palace and temple estates. Thus a commercially oriented sector of the economy co-existed with the palace and temple. In addition, both traders and independent specialists, such as potters and fishers, would have operated outside the formal organizations, engaging in what has been characterized as 'peddling and marketing' activities that were supplemental to the central redistributive economy.

THE OLD BABYLONIAN PERIOD

The Ur III empire ended abruptly under the combined weight of an invasion from Elam and massive infiltration by Amorite groups from the north-west. Whereas the Elamites soon withdrew, Amorite groups established control over some places in Mesopotamia, especially along the Tigris River, and founded ruling dynasties. In other places, Ur III governors and indigenous élites formed the ruling families. The result was the political disintegration of Mesopotamia into multiple competing city-states and petty kingdoms, the more important of which included Larsa, Isin, Eshnunna and Mari (Edzard, 1957). For most of the first two centuries of the second millennium BC, these small states maintained a rough balance of power, reminiscent of the situation during the Early Dynastic period. In the south of Mesopotamia, Larsa and Isin contended for control, while in the north, Eshnunna extended temporary control over its neighbours, and the Amorite dynasty at Babylon, founded at the beginning of the nineteenth century, began fitfully to stir. Mari occupied the intermediate position along the Euphrates between the Mesopotamian states to the south-east and the kingdoms of Qatna and Yamkhad in Syria to the north-west.

Around 1800 BC, the political situation began to change, as Rim-Sin of Larsa and Hammurabi of Babylon began to vie for regional control. Rim-Sin (1822–1763 BC) managed decisively to defeat Isin and to control southern Babylonia, while in the north Hammurabi (1792–1750 BC) began diplomatic manoeuvres in confronting both Eshnunna and Larsa. For a brief time, the rough parity of power held, as reported in a diplomatic report to the king of Mari: 'No king is powerful by himself: ten or fifteen kings follow Hammurabi, king of Babylon, as many follow Rim-Sin, king of Larsa, as many follow Ibalpiel, king of Eshnunna, as many follow Amutpiel, king of Qatna, and twenty follow Yarimlim, king of Yamkhad.' However, Hammurabi secured his position in the north, and created an alliance with Eshnunna and Mari to defeat Rim-Sin in the south; Hammurabi then turned northward, conquering Eshnunna and Mari.

Babylon's control of Mesopotamia, however, was fragile. The deep south of Mesopotamia (the 'Sealands') split off during the reign of Samsu-iluna (1749–1712 BC). And elsewhere the scope and strength of Babylon's direct control declined progressively after Hammurabi's death. Babylon's administrative troubles derived from the crown's difficulties in controlling local groups. The eventual collapse of the dynasty was due essentially to its inability to integrate these local and autonomous groups within the larger socio-political organization which the empire envisioned. Already in a weakened and much reduced state during the seventeenth century BC, the Hittite raid on Babylon put an end to the Amorite dynasty in 1595 BC.

The character of Mesopotamian society significantly changed during the Isin-Larsa and Old Babylonian periods. As has already been discussed, the degree of urbanism in southern Mesopotamia continued to decline from its Early Dynastic peak (see Table 2, p. 171); by the Old Babylonian period, roughly half of the population lived in cities (Adams, 1981). The urban decline may have been related to the gradual diffusion of technological innovations into the hinterlands. As these technologies spread in rural areas, the organization of work and economic control of products would have shifted, perhaps enough for markets to develop in rural areas as well. A significant shift in the predominant location of settlement also occurred during this period. The Old Babylonian military successes in the south led to the gradual dissolution of the traditional seats of southern power, and to the diversion of population and wealth to the new centres of power in the north, in and around Babylon. The problems of salinization in the south may have resulted in declining agricultural productivity, and thus contributed to this demographic shift towards the north (Jacobsen, 1982).

In contrast to the centrally administered economy of the Ur III period, the Isin-Larsa and Old Babylonian periods saw the emergence of a strong entrepreneurial ethic. The period was characterized by a continuation of foreign trade for the acquisition of luxury goods and staple commodities, although the mechanics of trade shifted. Whereas during the third millennium BC the temple and palace financed trade, and assumed the risks inherent to trade, now traders organized expeditions themselves and assumed personal responsibility for the risk of loss. Private investors provided the capital for the maritime trade through the Persian Gulf that brought large amounts of Arabian copper to Mesopotamia (Leemans, 1960). In Ashur to the north, private family firms established their factors in various towns in Cappadocia; in the best-known example, at Kanesh, Assyrian traders lived together in a large quarter of the lower town, forming an association that entered into formal agreements with the local government (Larsen, 1976). In effect, the period was one of increasing private enterprise, driven by the profit motive on a scale not apparent in earlier periods.

The new entrepreneurial spirit is also reflected in the economic and political relationships between the crown and the private sector (Diakonoff, 1982; Renger, 1979, 1984). As during the third millennium BC, the crown continued to own large tracts of land and large herds of animals, and to manage large numbers of semi-free but dependent workers. State officials received allotments of crown land, but could also amass private estates by purchase. Despite its holdings, the crown relied heavily on contracted private entrepreneurs to produce and circulate wealth, thereby helping to create a class of wealthy families. However, most private families possessed only small plots of land, and often could survive the vicissitudes of agricultural uncertainty by borrowing from palace or temple treasuries, or from rich officials and merchants. The result was increased debt slavery and alienation of land.

The crown's struggle for dominance over local groups is most evident in the documentation of local institutions that reflect independent power bases. In the city of Sippar, for example, we know of the *alum* institution, a local citizens' body the membership of which was restricted to males living within city walls and to heads of wealthy families. The group was led by an Overseer of Merchants, the office of which was selected by lot and changed annually. This office was consistently held by men from one of the wealthier families, and tended to be confined to a limited circle, or 'rotation among peers'. While the institution may have been organized as a service to the crown for the collection of taxes, it also served as an organized body of citizens against the state. Since crown acquisition of lands threatened the economic well-being of wealthy families and came at the expense of local groups, these community institutions may have focused active resistance to the state.

These facts notwithstanding, a strong ideology of justice permeated Hammurabi's rule, among the most enduring accomplishments of which was the development of a new law code. In fact, the Old Babylonian law code was not the first attempt to establish a formal system of justice, for codes appeared early in the Mesopotamian sequence. The codes of Urukagina (now read as Uruinimgina) during the Early Dynastic period marked the earliest formal code in which individual rights, authority and punishment were explicitly established. Later codes by Ur-Nammu (2112–2095 BC) and Lipit-Ishtar (1934–1924 BC) followed along these same lines.

While these codes reflected more on life within Mesopotamia itself, they also referred to its relations abroad. For example, Ur-Nammu set as one of his goals the restoration of sea trade, in which he started a system of standardized weights and measures. With respect to life at home, a strong tradition of kingship associates him with justice, protector of the weak against oppression and executor of punishment. Codes often specifically singled out those whom the king protected, for example the widowed, the orphaned, and occupational groups such as agriculturalists and merchants.

The Code of Hammurabi incorporated these ideas and motivations, but includes others (Plate 70). While much of the above would have been a standard in earlier codes, Hammurabi's was inscribed in a single black stone stela, and stands out as the single most significant written document of law. New provisions also were introduced in the code, addressing various agricultural reforms, the rights of specific sectors of society, questions of land tenure and the public affairs of *naditum* priestesses. Perhaps the most dramatic new policy was what appears as a reversion to the idea of an eye-for-an-eye (retaliation in kind), a departure from the earlier, and possibly more humane, monetary compensation for crimes known in previous codes. The rationale for instituting this retaliative form of punishment may reflect Hammurabi's own nomadic background and a new mood that resulted from the previous Amorite occupation.

The social and legal philosophy that has come down to us from the Old Babylonian period is among its most powerful legacies, as apparently for the first time we see a balance of the rights and obligations of the ruler and the ruled (Fig. 28). This balance is exemplified by the contrasting *misharum* ('equity, justice') and *andurarum* ('freedom'). Thus

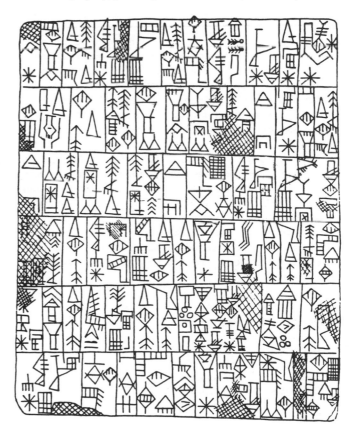

Figure 28 The first known Sumerian 'freedom' law (*am-ar-gi*) proclaiming debt cancellation and freedom from debt servitude. The tablet is dated to the reign of Entemena of the city-state of Lagash, c. 2402–2375 BC.

the Babylonian kings were obliged to protect the freedom and liberty of individuals in the context of equity and justice, the balancing of the rights and obligations of ruler and ruled. These concepts are unknown elsewhere in the ancient world, and were only seen again as concepts borrowed by the Hebrews in the Iron Age and in the later civilizations of the classical Mediterranean.

CONCLUSION

Just before the period addressed in this chapter, Mesopotamian society had successfully transformed a barren countryside into a vigorous state within a relatively short period. The development of ancient Mesopotamia during the third millennium BC leaves the impression of an innovative and aggressive society. The Mesopotamian landscape subjected its inhabitants to the risks of unpredictable seasonal inundations and other irregular environmental conditions. The Sumerians expressed this capricious quality of their landscape in the representation of the gods, who at times were erratic and unpredictable. We imagine that Mesopotamian leadership also embodied this quality, providing a degree of uncertainty to the ordinary citizen. Nevertheless, a certain playfulness is also apparent in Sumerian society, exemplified by the presence of mundane objects like a gaming board in the Royal Cemetery at Ur, and by the lavishly decorated musical instruments. Some of this playfulness would have trickled down to the ordinary citizens, as they participated in annual feasting and ritual displays. Life was not all work and no play.

An additional aspect that lends insight into the Mesopotamian character deserves special mention. Mesopotamian literature is replete with references to military exploits and conquests, the rationale for which was the acquisition of resources. At various points in its history, Mesopotamian leaders attempted to colonize and conquer distant regions. By the mid-third millennium BC, Mesopotamian military power must have had few equals. None the less, Mesopotamia appears to have rejected a pattern of conquest in favour of establishing extensive trading relationships. On balance, the prevalent pattern was mastery by control of trade, a peaceful solution to the problem of meeting the society's basic needs. Thus its political leaders confidently relied on their superior economic position. In doing so, Mesopotamian society actively sought and successfully achieved a position at the 'core' of a network of trading partnerships that covered virtually all of south-west Asia and the western margins of south Asia. Standing at the crossroads of several other civilizations, Mesopotamia figured as the hub of international relations, playing the dominant political and economic role.

BIBLIOGRAPHY

ADAMS, R. 1966. *The Evolution of Urban Society*. Chicago, Ill.
—— 1981. *The Heartland of Cities*. Chicago, Ill.
COOPER, J. 1983. *Reconstructing History from Ancient Inscriptions: The Lagash-Umma Border Conflict*. Malibu, Calif.
CRAWFORD, H. 1977. *The Architecture of the Third Millennium BC*. København.
DIAKONOFF, I. M. 1969. The Rise of the Despotic State in Ancient Mesopotamia. In: —— (ed.), *Ancient Mesopotamia: A Socio-Economic History*. Moskva. pp. 173–203.
—— 1972. Socio-Economic Classes in Babylonia and the Babylonian Concept of Social Stratification. In: EDZARD, D. O. (ed.),

Gesellschaftsklassen in Alten Zweistromland und im angrenzenden Gebiet. München. pp. 41–52. (Abhandlungen der Bayerischen Akademie der Wissenschaften, Phil.-Hist., Klasse 75).
—— 1976. The Rural Community in the Ancient Near East. *J. econ. soc. Hist. Orient* (Leiden), Vol. 18, pp. 121–33.
—— 1982. The Structure of Near Eastern Society before the Middle of the 2nd Millennium BC. *Oikumene* (Budapest), Vol. 3, pp. 7–100.
EDZARD, D. O. 1957. *Die 'Zweite Zwischenzeit' Babyloniens*. Wiesbaden.
—— 1968. *Sumerische Rechtsurkenden des III. Jahrtausends aus der Zeit vor der III. Dynastie von Ur*. München. (Abhandlungen der Bayerischen Akademie der Wissenschaften, Phil.-Hist., Klasse 76).
GELB, I. J. 1965. The Ancient Mesopotamian Ration System. *J. Near East. Stud.* (New Haven, Conn.), Vol. 24, pp. 230–43.
—— 1969. On the Alleged Temple and State Economies in Ancient Mesopotamia. In: GIUFFRE, A. (ed.), *Studi in onore di Edouardo Volterra*. Milano. Vol. 6, pp. 137–54.
—— 1972. The Arua Institution. *Rev. Assyriol.* (Paris), Vol. 66, pp. 1–32.
—— 1979. Household and Family in Early Mesopotamia. In: LIPINSKI, E. (ed.), *State and Temple Economy in the Ancient Near East*. Vol. 1. Leuven. pp. 1–97. (Orientalia Lovaniensia Analecta, 5.)
GLASSNER, J.-J. 1986. *La chute d'Agade: L'événement et sa mémoire*. Berlin.
HERMANN, G. 1968. Lapis Lazuli: The Early Phases of its Trade. *Iraq* (London), Vol. 30, pp. 21–57.
JACOBSEN, T. 1939. *The Sumerian King List*. Chicago, Ill.
—— 1970. *Toward the Image of Tammuz and Other Essays on Mesopotamian History and Culture*. Ed. by W. Moran. Cambridge, Mass.
—— 1976. *The Treasures of Darkness: A History of Mesopotamian Religion*. New Haven, Conn.
—— 1982. *Salinity and Irrigation Agriculture in Antiquity*. Malibu, Calif.
LAMBERT, M. 1952. La période présargonique: essai d'une histoire sumérienne. *Sumer* (Baghdad), Vol. 8, pp. 57–77, 198–216.
—— 1953. Textes commerciaux de Lagash (époque présargonique). *Rev. Assyriol.* (Paris), Vol. 47, pp. 57–69, 105–120.
LARSEN, M. 1976. *The Old Assyrian City State and its Colonies*. København.
LEEMANS, W. F. 1960. *Foreign Trade in the Old Babylonian Period*. Leiden.
LIMET, H. 1960. *Le travail du métal au pays de Sumer au temps de la IIIᵉ dynastie d'Ur*. Paris.
MARGUERON, J. 1982. *Recherches sur les palais mésopotamiens de l'âge du bronze*. Paris.
—— 1988. Quelques remarques concernant l'architecture monumental à l'époque 'Obeid'. In: HUOT, J.-L. (ed.), *Préhistoire de la Mésopotamie*. Paris,.
MOOREY, R. 1982. The Archaeological Evidence for Metallurgy and Related Technologies in Mesopotamia, *c*. 5500–2100 BC. *Iraq* (London), Vol. 44, pp. 13–38.
—— 1985. *Materials and Manufacture in Ancient Mesopotamia: The Evidence of Archaeology and Art*. Oxford. (BAR, Int. Ser., 237.)
NEUMANN, H. 1979. Handel und Handler in der Zeit der III. Dynastie von Ur. *Altorient. Forsch.* (Leipzig), Vol. 6, pp. 15–68.
NISSEN, H. 1972. The City Wall of Uruk. In: UCKO, P.; TRINGHAM, R.; DIMBLEBY, G. (eds), *Man, Settlement and Urbanism*. London. pp. 793–8.
—— 1988. *The Early History of the Ancient Near East, 9000–2000 BC*. Chicago, Ill.
OPPENHEIM, A. L. 1977. *Ancient Mesopotamia: Portrait of a Dead Civilization*. Rev. ed. completed by E. Reiner. Chicago, Ill.
POSTGATE, N.; MOON, J. 1982. Excavations at Abu Salabikh, 1981. *Iraq* (London), Vol. 44, pp. 103–36.
RENGER, J. 1979. Interaction of Temple, Palace, and Private Enterprise in the Old Babylonian Economy. In: LIPINSKI, E. (ed.), *State and Temple Economy in the Ancient Near East*. Vol. 1. Leuven. pp. 249–56. (Orientalia Lovaniensia Analecta, 5.)
—— 1984. Patterns of Non-Institutional Trade and Non-Commercial Exchange in Ancient Mesopotamia at the Beginning of

the Second Millennium BC. In: ARCHI, A. (ed.), *Circulation of Goods in Non-Palatial Context in the Ancient Near East*. Roma, pp. 31–123.

SALONEN, A. 1968. *Agricultura Mesopotamica*. Helsinki. (Annales Academiae Scientarium Fennicae, Series B, 149.)

SOLLBERGER, E.; KUPPER, J.-R. 1971. *Inscriptions royales sumériennes et akkadiennes*. Paris. (Littératures anciennes du Proche-Orient, 3.)

STEINKELLER, P. 1987. The Administrative and Economic Organization of the Ur III State: The Core and the Periphery. In: GIB-

SON, M.; BIGGS, R. (eds), *The Organization of Power: Aspects of Bureaucracy in the Ancient Near East*. Chicago, Ill. pp. 19–41.

TOSI, M.; PIPERNO, M. 1973. Lithic Technology Behind the Ancient Lapis Lazuli Trade. *Expedition* (Philadelphia, Pa.), Vol. 16, pp. 15–23.

WAETZOLDT, H. 1972. *Untersuchungen zur neusumerischen Textilindustrie*. Roma.

ZAGARELL, A. 1986. Trade, Women, Class, and Society in Ancient Western Asia. *Curr. Anthropol.* (Chicago, Ill.), Vol. 27, pp. 415–30.

12.1.2

THE KASSITE PERIOD

(1500–700 BC)

Georges Roux

THE KASSITE PERIOD

In 1595 BC a Hittite raid on Babylon destroyed the Amorite dynasty of Hammurabi. The political successors to the Old Babylonian line were Kassites, an ethnic group newly arrived in the area. The Kassites ruled Babylonia for about four centuries (1595–1157 BC). This long period may be divided into two parts, distinguished by the arrival of a revitalized and aggressive Assyria on the Mesopotamian political scene. The 'Middle Assyrian' period overlapped considerably with the 'Kassite' period but endured eighty years later. Babylonian and Assyrian relations were complex, involving on the one hand political rivalry and episodes of Assyrian domination of Babylonia, and on the other considerable Babylonian cultural influence on Assyria.

Political history

Mesopotamia from 1595 to 1330 BC

The Kassites were a mountain people, probably originating in the central Zagros where they continued to live during the first millennium BC. Although the Kassite language belongs to no known linguistic group of ancient western Asia, contact with Indo-European-speaking groups is evident in the names of some Kassite gods (for example, Buriash, the Greek Boreas; Marrutash and Shuriash, the Indian Maruti and Surya). The principal deities of the Kassites were Harbe, the paramount god, Shuqamuna and Shumalia, god and goddess of the mountains and patrons of the dynasty, and the moon-god Shipak.

Individuals with Kassite names began appearing in Babylonian labour rosters by Hammurabi's time. Several year formulae of Samsu-iluna (1749–1712 BC) and Abi-eshuh (1711–1685 BC) record military actions against Kassite forces in southern Mesopotamia. The Babylonian King List implies that Kassites controlled some part of Mesopotamia by around 1730 BC, a time when rulers with Kassite names (such as Kashtiliashu) led petty states on the middle Euphrates, notably Hana. The Hittite raid on Babylon in 1595 BC allowed the Kassites to seize political control of southern Mesopotamia (Brinkman, 1980a).

The early political history of the Kassite dynasty in Babylonia is obscure. Since the time of Samsu-iluna, the 'Sealand' dynasty had controlled the south of Babylonia. Very possibly this dynasty briefly occupied Babylon in the aftermath of the Hittite raid. According to the Kakrime inscription,

Agum II restored to Babylon the Marduk statue looted by the Hittites, implying that the Kassite dynasty had established itself in Babylon during the first quarter of the sixteenth century BC. The Sealand kings continued to hold southern Babylonia during the first century of Kassite rule; military action finally dislodged them around 1460. From this time until its final collapse in 1157 BC, the Kassite dynasty ruled all of Babylonia, or Karduniash; despite occasional brief episodes of foreign control, these three centuries represent the most durable period of political unity in the history of southern Mesopotamia.

The sixteenth and fifteenth centuries BC was the time when competing empires of the Late Bronze Age were formed. The Old Hittite kingdom disintegrated under the stresses of dynastic contention and other internal disorders during the sixteenth century. At the same time, two imperial powers emerged. The Hurrians, a people present in the far north of Mesopotamia since the third millennium BC, established the kingdom of Mitanni during the sixteenth century. This kingdom controlled, partially through vassal states, an extensive zone that stretched from Iraqi Kurdistan across northern Mesopotamia to north Syria. In the following century, Assyria gave obeisance to the Mitanni sovereigns Paratarna and Shaustatar I. And rulers of the Egyptian 18th dynasty, having evicted the Hyksos from the Nile Delta, now advanced into western Asia. Tuthmosis III (1490–1436 BC) capped this advance, establishing firm control over Palestine and southern Syria as far north as the Mitanni sphere of domination.

Mitanni and Egypt then arranged a condominium over Syro-Palestine, solemnified by royal gift exchanges and marriages. This balance of power was short-lived, however. Having re-established political order at home, the Hittite state expanded outward. By the middle of the fourteenth century BC, the Hittite king Suppiluliumas supplanted Mitanni domination over the petty kingdoms of north Syria, and installed two sons in the key cities of Aleppo and Carchemish. And Assyria, under the rule of Ashur-uballit I (1363–1328 BC) and his successors, completed the destruction of Mitanni power, and itself became a great power.

Babylonia did not directly participate in the imperial struggle for Syro-Palestine. However, the Kassite dynasty did have a keen interest in the outcome of these changing power relations, and Kassite diplomatic relations helped guarantee that no single power should grow too strong. On the occasion of their advances into Syria, Kassite kings sent embassies to Tuthmosis III and Amenhotep II, and then established a regular messenger service in the time of Karaindash (c. 1410

BC). The Kassite kings participated in the system of royal gift exchange that characterized the diplomatic and commercial interactions between the great powers, best seen in the Amarna archives of Egypt. The Kassite kings Kadashman-Enlil I (1374–1360 BC) and Burnaburiash II (1359–1333 BC) presented to their Egyptian contemporaries Amenhotep III and Amenhotep IV horses and chariots, lapis lazuli, oil and occasionally bronze and silver, receiving in return gold, ivory, precious woods and fine clothing. Babylonia acquired so much Egyptian gold in this way that the regional economy adopted the metal as the standard of value (Edzard, 1960). The same archives refer to a treaty between the two powers, and to the marriages of Kadashman-Enlil's sister and daughter to Amenhotep III. And Burnaburiash expressed concern about the stirring power in Assyria, begging Amenhotep IV not to enter into exchange relations with Ashur-uballit.

Ashur-uballit I was the first great king of Assyria since the time of Shamshi-Adad, over four centuries earlier. Confident and shrewd, Ashur-uballit corresponded directly with Amenhotep IV, claiming equal status, and married his daughter into the Kassite royal house. When dynastic quarrels overtook Hurri-Mitanni following the assassination of Tusratta (c. 1350 BC), Ashur-uballit lent support to Shuttarna against the Hittite candidate Mattiwaza. The resulting reconfiguration of power relations enabled Ashur-uballit to dominate the Mitanni heartland, including the capital Washshuganni (somewhere in the Khabur triangle), and to confine Mattiwaza to Khanigalbat, a petty state on the upper Khabur and Balikh rivers that provided the Hittites with a buffer against Assyrian aggression. Thus, by the end of the fourteenth century BC, Assyrian control extended from the borders with Karduniash in the south to the middle Euphrates in the west.

Karduniash between Assyria and Elam (1330–1157 BC)

The Hittite expansion into Syria early in the fourteenth century BC, and the Assyrian resurgence towards the end of that century, redefined the imperial power relations of western Asia. Conflict over Syrian possessions broke out between Egypt and Khatti toward the end of the fourteenth century, during the time of Seti I (1317–1304 BC); the confrontation continued until the inconclusive battle at Qadesh, after which Ramesses II and Hattusilis III established a peace treaty. The Assyrian successors to Ashur-uballit, notably Adad-nirari I (1305–1274 BC), Shalmaneser I (1273–1244 BC), and Tukulti-Ninurta I (1243–1207 BC) greatly extended Assyrian power. During this century, Assyrian armies campaigned to the north and east, fighting among others the Hurrian mountain peoples that later formed the Urartian state. In Mesopotamia, the Assyrians destroyed and absorbed Khanigalbat and directly confronted the Hittite state; to the south, intermittent wars characterized Assyrian-Babylonian relations, culminating in Tukulti-Ninurta's brief occupation of Babylonia. The end of the thirteenth century BC witnessed the general collapse of imperial power in western Asia, when widespread upheavals throughout the eastern Mediterranean destroyed the Hittite state, greatly diminished Egypt's role in Syro-Palestine, and threw Assyria into a period of weakness.

The thirteenth and twelfth centuries were a time of varied external threat to Babylonia. Ashur-uballit's grandson Kara-hardash (1333 BC) succeeded Burnaburiash, only to be assassinated in the same year. Enraged, Ashur-uballit set his own candidate Kurigalzu II (1332–1308 BC) on the throne, in place of the usurper Nazi-Bugash (1333 BC). Kurigalzu

inconclusively fought with Ashur-uballit's successor Enlil-nirari (1327–1318 BC), when the common border was set on the lower Zab. A generation later, the Kassite Nazi-maruttash (1307–1282 BC) and the Assyrian Adad-nirari I again fought, in consequence of which the frontier shifted southwards in favour of Assyria. On the diplomatic front, Babylonia reached an understanding with the Hittite rulers, especially Hattusilis III, probably in an effort to coordinate containment of Assyrian expansion.

The difficult relations between Assyria and Babylonia culminated during the reign of the Kassite king Kashtiliashu IV (1232–1225 BC), who undertook border raids on Assyrian possessions and perhaps supported Khanigalbat in resisting Assyrian domination. In response, Tukulti-Ninurta invaded and occupied Babylonia, naming himself king of Babylonia, and ruling through a series of puppet kings. He removed the Marduk statue from Babylon to Ashur, along with other treasure, medical and religious texts, and Kashtiliashu himself. Babylonian revolt broke the Assyrian domination after seven years, when Adad-shuma-usur (1216–1187 BC), Kashtiliashu's son, took the throne. In Assyria, Tukulti-Ninurta was himself murdered ten years later, and in the dynastic confusion that followed, the Babylonian king was able to advance his own candidate to the Assyrian throne.

Babylonian relations with Elam to the east are less well known, but ultimately more important. Middle Elamite political history remains poorly documented before the thirteenth century BC (Carter and Stolper, 1984). Some textual evidence points to conflict with Babylonia during the fourteenth century BC, leading to a (probably) brief occupation of Susa by Kurigalzu II. After this episode, Elam increasingly interfered in Babylonian affairs. The Elamite king Untash-Napirisha (c. 1250 BC) raided the area of Der, while Kidin-Hutran's two raids several decades later extended into the Babylonian heartland (including Nippur and Isin), and deposed one of Tukulti-Ninurta's puppet kings. In 1158 BC the Assyrian king Ashur-Dan I (1178–1133 BC) raided the northern Babylonian border. In the same year, the Elamite Shutruk-Nakhkhunte invaded northern Babylonia and deposed the Kassite king Zababa-shuma-iddina (1158 BC); continued Elamite campaigning soon overran southern Babylonia and captured the last Kassite king, Enlil-nadin-ahi (1157–1155 BC). The Elamite victors removed the Marduk statue from Babylon, having already seized many other Babylonian monuments (such as the Victory Stela of Naram-Sin; a statue of Manishtushu; a copy of Hammurabi's law code) that have since been discovered in archaeological excavations at Susa.

Social and economic conditions

Babylonia

Although the Kassites had a tribal (kinship) organization, they quickly adopted the language, religion and traditions of the local population. The king ruled through a bureaucratic apparatus controlled by various high officials, backed by a Kassite aristocracy of chariot-warriors; native Babylonians usually held the important administrative offices (Brinkman, 1974). Archaeological survey reveals a general reduction in regional population, and a shift toward town and village life from the more urban conditions of earlier periods (Adams, 1981). Land tenure included both private smallholdings and extensive estates attached to the crown, temples and court dignitaries (Brinkman, 1980b; Oelsner, 1982). The first *kudurrus* appeared during the time of Kurigalzu II, these being charters of royal land grants to important individuals or to communities. The industrial activities of Kassite Babylonia remain almost entirely unknown. Interregional trade flourished, and was largely but not completely in the hands of state institutions; Babylonian exchange relations extended from the Arabian Gulf to the eastern Mediterranean.

Assyria

Texts from Ashur and elsewhere document large estates owned by leading Assyrian families, many acquired by mortgage loans. The king granted certain smaller holdings in return for military duties. The palaces of the provincial governors served as agricultural as well as administrative centres (Garelli, 1969, pp. 209–15, 333–4). Little survives of a compendium of Assyrian laws, except some articles concerning the status of women. These Assyrian laws differ from Babylonian statutes with respect to certain social practices, such as the levirate and status of concubines; they are also remarkable for the severity of prescribed punishment, and for the strict discipline of the royal harem (Cardascia, 1969).

Mitanni

The Nuzi archives, from the Mitanni vassal state of Arraphe (Kirkuk), contain the only sources on Hurrian society in Mesopotamia (Morrison and Owen, 1981). These texts, which date to the late fifteenth and fourteenth centuries BC, provide glimpses of peasants and craftsmen working for the king and paid in rations, and of rich individuals in possession of estates, the latter often acquired by fictive inheritance under the terms of adoption in return for a gift. In Nuzi, women held a special position and enjoyed extensive rights.

Cultural development

Babylonia

Although of foreign origin, the Kassite sovereigns discharged the traditional duties of Mesopotamian kingship. The Kassite construction or restoration of cultic buildings in such places as Nippur, Larsa, Isin and Ur followed traditional lines. Karaindash built a more innovative temple for Inanna/Ishtar at Uruk, distinguished by its sharply projecting corner bastions and its deeply recessed façade with plastic images of deities pouring water from vases (Strommenger, 1962, fig. 170). The divine images were made from assembled molded brick, a technique previously applied to columns with geometric designs at sites in northern Mesopotamia earlier in the second millennium BC. The Kassite innovation in turn formed the basis for later Middle Elamite, Neo-Babylonian and Achaemenid glazed brickwork.

Kurigalzu I was the first king to build a royal residence bearing his name, a practice adopted by later Assyrian kings. Dur-Kurigalzu, modern 'Aqar Quf, is 30 km west of Babylon. At the foot of an enormous ziggurat (badly damaged, but still 57 m high) lay three temples and a palace, the central courtyard of which was framed with porticoes and the corridors decorated with frescoes. The many objects found within this complex attest to the artistic sophistication and skill of the Babylonian craftsmen; these objects include fragments of a colossal statue of Kurigalzu, beautiful jewellery, and life-like coloured terracotta figurines.

The *kudurrus* are a special class of Kassite period sculpture, a form that continued into Neo-Assyrian times. Made of hard stone, they bear lengthy records of royal grants (land, other possessions, privileges) over which are representations and/or symbols of gods, and occasionally the king himself, as witnesses to the grants (Seidl, 1968). Another special class of the lapidary's art are cylinder seals, which often carry long inscriptions giving the name and profession of their owner and usually an invocation or prayer. Seal decoration incorporates both geometrical and naturalistic designs, the latter including plants, flies, bees, grasshoppers, dogs and monkeys (Beran, 1958).

In addition to scientific (medical, astronomical or divinatory observations), didactic (lexical works) and traditional religious works, the literature of Kassite Babylonia explores questions of ultimate meaning, the relationship between humanity and the gods, and particularly the question of evil. Such works as *The Just Sufferer*, the *Dialogue of Pessimism*, and, to some extent, the legend of *Adapa*, counsel either a resignation that verges on despair, or a blind confidence in the gods, whose purpose is impenetrable (Lambert, 1960). During this time, Babylonian became the international language, used for diplomacy; Mesopotamian literature circulated throughout western Asia, and was translated into other languages. Very likely this wide circulation reached Mycenaean Greece, later to be absorbed into classical Greek mythology (for instance, stories of the Flood; the ascension of Etana as Ganymede; and Icarus).

Assyria

All the Middle Assyrian rulers were anxious to restore, renovate or rebuild temples, palaces and walls in Ashur, the capital. Tukulti-Ninurta was the most active, building a vast royal residence in Ashur as well as his new foundation at Kar-Tukulti-Ninurta. The latter town contained the royal palace, decorated with mural paintings and polychrome panels of enamelled brick, most of which bear the sacred tree motif (Eickhoff, 1985). Tukulti-Ninurta also transformed the Ishtar temple at Ashur into a double sanctuary, matching the existing temples of An (sky-god) and Adad (storm-god), and of Sin (moon-god) and Shamash (sun-god) (Andrae, 1938).

Little remains of the sculpture of the period. A few orthostats – large slabs laid along the base of walls – show battle scenes; two bas-reliefs on stone altars depict the king at worship, the gods themselves represented by symbols (for example, Ashur by the winged disc). Cylinder seals, on the other hand, are more abundant and skilfully made; often portraying combat between animals, monsters and humans, the seals are admirable for their sense of movement and simplicity of composition.

The annals, a characteristic Assyrian literary form that relates the king's military campaigns, first began taking shape during the rule of Adad-nirari I. The account of Tukulti-Ninurta's victory over Kashtiliashu is truly epic in its length and tone. In other genres, Assyria looked to Babylonia both for literary models and for looted texts; the library of Tiglath-Pileser I (1114–1076 BC) was founded on both the collection of Shalmaneser I and the booty of Tukulti-Ninurta. Babylonian scribes found employment in Assyria, and Babylonian influence extended to the foundation of a temple of Marduk, the 'national' god of Babylonia, in Ashur.

Mitanni

The evidence from Nuzi reveals architectural traditions, whether palace, temple or private houses, that differ very little from those of other Mesopotamian towns. Many decorative details, on the other hand, betray a Syrian and Egyptian influence that is most evident in the palace murals (garlands, acroters, bucrania, 'Hathor heads') and the glazed terracotta statuettes from the temple. These influences reflect the geography and foreign relations of the Mitanni state. The Mitanni style of cylinder seals has many affinities with Syrian glyptics, being over-elaborate in composition, and counting among the common motifs the sacred tree and griffins. Nuzi also yielded an elegant type of fine-ware pottery, painted with floral motifs and stylized animals in white on a dark grey background. This Mitanni pottery gained a wide distribution in northern Mesopotamia and Syria (Stein, 1984). In most artistic production, however, a specifically Hurrian or Mitanni style cannot convincingly be defined.

THE POST-KASSITE PERIOD

Political history

Extensive upheavals attended the end of the Late Bronze Age in western Asia and the eastern Mediterranean; the two centuries that followed 1200 BC, the early Iron Age, witnessed the creation of a considerably altered political and social landscape. The Hittite state disappeared under the pressure of local uprisings of subject peoples, harassment from the Pontic region of Anatolia, and the regional movements of the 'Sea Peoples'. New groups arrived to occupy various parts of Anatolia (for example, the Phrygians). Egypt, after the death of Ramesses III (1166 BC) increasingly withdrew into itself, and subsequently divided into two kingdoms, the beginning of the Third Intermediate period. In Syro-Palestine a number of petty kingdoms arose, under Aramaean, Neo-Hittite, Phoenician, Israelite and other newly defined ethnic identities. In the mountain country to the north, the Urartian state began to form among the Hurrian peoples that earlier had been involved in Mesopotamian political events during the Bronze Age.

These widespread changes in western Asia also affected Mesopotamia. The Assyrian and Babylonian chronicles and annals record the movement of aggressive peoples from the west, beginning in the eleventh century BC. The Ahlamu/Aramaeans, who first appear in historical sources during the fourteenth century, presented a military threat to Assyria, whose eleventh century BC rulers fought them on numerous occasions over wide reaches of northern Mesopotamia. Aramaeans also moved into Babylonia during the eleventh century BC, here occupying the districts along the Tigris and in the area of Nippur, where they maintained a kin-based social organization, a high degree of mobility, and a distinctive ethnic identity. The aggressive Aramaean arrival in Babylonia greatly disrupted the political unity and economic vitality of the region. The Chaldaeans, another tribal group, appeared in Babylonia during the nineteenth century BC, and settled along the southern Euphrates (especially in the area of Uruk and Ur). In contrast to the Aramaeans, the Chaldaeans became largely sedentary, adopted Babylonian customs, and formed powerful tribal polities; these groups would be central to the Babylonian resistance to Assyrian imperialism later in the first millennium BC (Dietrich, 1970).

In the aftermath of the Elamite destruction of the Kassite dynasty in Babylonia, Marduk-kabit-ahheshu (1157–1140 BC) founded the Isin II dynasty (Brinkman, 1968). While the question of an Elamite interregnum in some parts of Babylonia remains moot, Marduk-kabit-ahheshu probably controlled Babylon by the end of his reign, and his son claimed to rule the entirety of Babylonia. At this point, Babylonia reasserted its political power: the third king of the new dynasty, Ninurta-nadin-shuma (1131–1126 BC), raided deep into Assyria, and the fourth king, Nebuchadnezzar I (1125–1104 BC) defeated the Elamite Huteludush-Inshushinak and recovered the stolen Marduk statue. Nebuchadnezzar also skirmished with Assyrian forces, and fought various mountain peoples. The subsequent seven rulers of the dynasty continued the border conflicts with Assyria that included a raid by Tiglath-Pileser I deep into northern Babylonia (when he burned Marduk-nadin-ahhe's palace in Babylon itself). The dynasty weakened considerably during the eleventh century BC under the pressures of Aramaean incursion, as well as a series of failed crops and famines, and episodes of factional strife.

The political successors to the Isin II kings fall into a series of short-lived or unnamed dynasties under whom the regional disintegration accelerated during the tenth century BC. Although nominally kings of Babylonia, their effective power was increasingly limited by tribalized areas, independent cities and unrest in the countryside. Several rulers of early ninth century BC, notably Nabu-shuma-ukin I and Nabu-apla-iddina, briefly restored a measure of Babylonian power, and successfully confronted the growing imperial power of Assyria at the time of Adad-nirari II and Shalmaneser III (see below). Soon thereafter, however, the Assyrians gained the upper hand. Under the pressure of Shalmaneser's incursion and the military actions of later Assyrian kings, the centres of Babylonian power began to shift southward, into the hands of the Chaldaean tribes.

In Assyria, the dynastic troubles that followed Tukulti-Ninurta's assassination combined with the vanguard of the Aramaean incursions to produce a period of weakness. The situation stabilized during the long reign of Ashur-Dan I (1178–1133 BC), and Assyria considerably regained strength under his successors Ashur-resha-ishi I (1132–1115 BC) and Tiglath-Pileser I (1114–1076 BC). These two kings vigorously repulsed the nomadic threat from the west; Tiglath-Pileser swept deep into Syria, reaching the Mediterranean coast where he extracted tribute and returned home with cedar wood to adorn the An-Adad temple at Ashur. Tiglath-Pileser also pushed back the threat of the Mushki, a mountain people to the north, and then campaigned against the Nairi, in the Anatolian hills west of Lake Van; he also fought other peoples to the east, and in Babylonia.

Renewed Aramaean incursions troubled the reign of Ashur-bel-kala (1073–1056 BC), who beat off these nomadic groups again pushing into Syria. These pressures, from both west and north, continued to beset Assyria through the tenth century BC, and Aramaean groups occupied the Khabur area and much of the steppe between the Khabur and Ashur. As in Babylonia, these external threats combined with episodic famines to induce an extended period of Assyrian decline. Assyria did not rise to prominence again until the accession of Adad-nirari at the end of the tenth century BC.

Social and economic conditions

The few administrative documents available for this period reveal that Assyria and Babylonia were divided into provinces, each with its own governor (Brinkman, 1963, 1974). As at the time of Hammurabi, society consisted of three classes: free men, citizens dependent on the state (mushkenu) and slaves. In accordance with the practices of the Kassites, the kings of Babylon often made gifts of land to communities (temples, cities, villages, families) or to individuals deserving special reward. These estates had previously been the property of the crown or had been purchased from certain landowners by the crown. In these two essentially agricultural countries, the economic situation appears to have been satisfactory at first, but then deteriorated disastrously at the time of the Aramaean invasions.

Cultural development

In both Assyria and Babylonia, the kings tended to restore rather than to build during this period. The only form of sculpture is the finely chiselled figures on the Babylonian kudurrus, and the few extant Assyrian altars. The cylinder seals, for the most part Assyrian, are of poorer quality than earlier, but nonetheless remarkable for their variety of motifs.

Historical literature of the period includes the Assyrian annals, which were increasingly detailed, and short Babylonian notices of important events; royal hymns experienced a revival. Literary works reflect the considerable uncertainty of the time. The *Babylonian Theodicy* is a dialogue between a just sufferer and another person, and reaches the conclusion that deceit and oppression are divinely willed (Lambert, 1960). The *Epic of Erra* is a bleak and magnificent poem in which Erra, the god of death, temporarily dislodges Marduk from power, and gives free rein to his bellicose rage, ravaging Sumer and Akkad (Gossman, 1955).

THE ASSYRIAN EMPIRE

Political history

In three centuries, the Assyrian empire gradually developed, and then abruptly collapsed. Its history may be divided into four phases – two long periods of expansion separated by a brief retrenchment, and followed by a rapid decline and extinction (Olmstead, 1923; Vieyra, 1961; Saggs, 1984).

Liberation and foreign raids (911–783 BC)

Adad-nirari II (911–891 BC) freed Assyria from immediate foreign threat. He drove the Aramaeans out of the Tigris Valley back to the Khabur, crushed the mountain peoples to the east, recaptured Arraphe after a Babylonian raid, and signed a peace accord and exchanged daughters with the Babylonian king Nabu-shuma-ukin I. Tukulti-Ninurta II (890–884 BC), his son, consolidated these successes with a triumphant march along the Khabur and the middle Euphrates.

Ashurnasirpal II (883–859 BC) then launched a policy of annual campaigns and calculated brutality. He forced annual tribute, under penalty of terrible reprisals and torture, on the Aramaean kingdoms of the Jazirah and the petty mountain states of the Taurus and the Zagros. Then he crossed northern Syria and reached the Mediterranean; surprised by this action, the Phoenician, Neo-Hittite and Aramaean states of Syria ransomed their future with extravagant gifts.

Shalmaneser III (858–824 BC) pursued his father's policy less cruelly, and met stronger resistance. In the mountains to the north and east, Arame of Urartu avoided a decisive defeat, while the Medes (Madai) and Persians (Parsua) proved formidable opponents. In Syria, Shalmaneser successively defeated coalitions of Neo-Hittite and of Aramaean states. Though failing to take Damascus, he exacted tribute from the defeated cities. To the south, Shalmaneser assisted the Babylonian king Marduk-zaki-shumi I in putting down a brother's revolt, battling both Aramaean and Chaldaean adherents of the pretender and extorting tribute from them.

After a struggle over succession, Shamshi-Adad V (823–811 BC) continued military action in the mountainous north and also, with considerable success, in Babylonia (he styled himself king of Sumer and Akkad). Adad-nirari III (810–783 BC) took the throne in his minority, and his mother Sammuramat – the model for the legendary Semiramis – governed four years as regent. Both fought the Medes; Adad-nirari later campaigned in Syria, and succeeded in taking Damascus, whose king Ben-Hadad II surrendered his treasures to the Assyrian.

The Assyrian eclipse (782–745 BC)

Adad-nirari's three sons ruled in succession. Shalmaneser IV (782–773 BC) was effectively under the thumb of his general-in-chief, Shamshi-ilu, who warred in Urartu and Syria. The reign of Ashur-Dan III (772–755 BC) was marked by two plague years and by Syrian revolts. And Ashur-nirari V (754–745 BC) spent most of his time at home in Kalkhu, where the revolt broke out that brought Tiglath-Pileser to the throne.

During this period of Assyrian weakness, Urartu expanded considerably (Piotrovskii, 1967; Kroll, 1979). Under the kings Argisti I (787–766 BC) and Sardur II (765–733 BC), the kingdom incorporated the Ararat plain and expanded to the south-west along the upper Euphrates toward Syria. Containing this menace was one of the central tasks of Tiglath-Pileser and his successors.

Conquest and expansion (744–627 BC)

By the end of his reign, Tiglath-Pileser III (744–727 BC) had managed to restore the Assyrian empire, and to reorganize it along more stable lines than before. The administrative reform replaced the earlier system of annual campaigns and tribute extraction with a system of administrative provinces under Assyrian governors or closely watched vassal states. The new provinces included lands in some parts of the Zagros, several Neo-Hittite kingdoms in south-eastern Anatolia, and Syria, while the Phoenician and Philistine cities and lands in the southern Levantine interior (Israel, Judah, Ammon, Moab) formed vassal states. Elsewhere, particularly in the mountain areas to the north and north-east, raids served to keep enemies (the Medes, Urartu) at bay. And in the three years between 731 and 729 BC, Tiglath-Pileser invaded Babylonia, deposed the king Mukin-zeri (a Chaldaean of the Bit Amukani tribe), and himself took the Babylonian throne.

As part of his reorganization, Tiglath-Pileser built up a professional army with a substantial cavalry. He also introduced the practice of mass deportation of subject peoples, a system that helped reduce potential revolts, populated cities and colonized agricultural districts, and channelled labour – both skilled and unskilled – into state institutions. Since many populations of the empire spoke Aramaic by that time, this policy contributed to the Aramaicization of Assyria.

Although the immediate Urartian threat had been contained, other troublesome developments presented other dangers. Egypt and Elam, both having endured long periods of weakness, now began taking an interest in the affairs of empire; both joined Urartu in supporting revolt among Assyria's vassal states. Shalmaneser V (726–722 BC) put down the revolt of Hosea, and transformed Israel into an Assyrian province. The difficulties that attended the accession of Sargon II (721–705 BC) sparked several uprisings. Merodakh-Baladan, head of the Chaldaean Bit Yakin tribe, seized Babylon with the support of the Elamite king Humbannikash. Sargon managed to evict him from the Babylonian throne ten years later, but not entirely to suppress his revolt; Merodakh-Baladan remained a thorn in the Assyrian side for some time. Egypt supported the revolts of Hama and Gaza in 720 BC, and of Ashdod, Judah, Moab and Edom in 712; these ended unhappily for the Syro-Palestinian lands. And, with the support of both Urartu and Phrygia, Neo-Hittite Carchemish and Cilicia went into revolt in 717, which was put down in 712 BC. Sargon addressed the Urartu problem with his famous eighth campaign in 714, during which he took the Urartian stronghold at Musasir.

Sargon's son Sennacherib (704–681 BC) was also obliged to put down widespread revolt – in the Zagros, Cilicia, Phoenicia and Palestine – early in his rule. During his campaign in Palestine (in 701 BC), Sennacherib sacked Lachish and threatened Jerusalem, which escaped destruction by payment of heavy tribute. In Babylonia, Merodakh-Baladan had once more put himself on the throne (703 BC), but Sennacherib drove him off it again in the same year. The south of Babylonia still in unrest, abetted by Elam, Sennacherib continued to make war against both during the first decade of the seventh century BC, at first with very mixed results. He finally gained victory in 689 BC, and sacked Babylon with considerable brutality. Sennacherib also attempted to conquer Egypt, the supporter of Levantine revolts; the attempt failed when an epidemic decimated his army. Shortly thereafter a son, passed over in favour of Esarhaddon, assassinated Sennacherib.

Esarhaddon (680–669 BC) rebuilt Babylon, and the region remained relatively quiet throughout his reign. The king put down a revolt in Sidon, and repelled the Cimmerian and Scythian incursion into the Assyrian sphere, making peace with them. In the east, he fought the Mannaeans and the Medes. The Medes at this time had become a settled people, centered on Hamadan (Ecbatana); archaeological evidence for Median towns has been discovered at Nus-i Jan, where there are pillared halls and a fire temple (Stronach, 1969, 1973). Phraortes (Kashathrita), Esarhaddon's contemporary, united the Median tribes in a confederation, which the Assyrian king managed to split, making some of these tribes his vassals. Esarhaddon's major military accomplishment was his conquest of Egypt, then divided into multiple small kingdoms subject to Taharqa, king of Kush. In 671 BC the Assyrian army entered the Delta and captured Memphis; the rulers of Sais became Assyrian vassals. Taharqa retook Memphis two years later, and fomented revolt in the Delta. Esarhaddon died on his way to quelling the uprising.

Following Esarhaddon's wishes, his son Ashurbanipal (668–627 BC) sat on the Assyrian throne, while another son, Shamash-shuma-ukin (667–648 BC), occupied the Babylonian throne. Ashurbanipal's first business was Egypt. The Assyrians defeated Taharqa and, after putting down a revolt in the Delta, raided Thebes, carrying off much booty. The Saite king Psammetichus I then governed all Egypt in Ashurbanipal's name. Other military actions of Ashurbanipal's reign included the suppression of two revolts in Phoenicia, and dealing with another Cimmerian incursion. Assyrian-Elamite relations during the first part of the seventh century BC oscillated between entente and enmity, with occasional Elamite raids into Babylonia (such as Humban-haltash's sacking of Sippar in 675 BC). In 664 BC the Elamite king Urtak again raided Babylonia, and was driven off. Ashurbanipal invaded Elam in turn some twelve years later in 653 BC, and installed his clients in power. At the same time, he crushed the growing power of the Gambulu, the Aramaean tribe that lived in the marshy land in the south of Babylonia, on the Elamite border. When Ashurbanipal's attention diverted to the east, Psammetichus took the opportunity to drive the occupiers out of Egypt.

Shamash-shuma-ukin revolted in 652 BC. Ashurbanipal had kept his brother under close control, obliging him to follow instruction in matters both of foreign policy and of internal politics and religious observance; Shamash-shuma-ukin's revolt apparently was his response to the prospect of further restrictions. Within Babylonia, support for the revolt came from the northern Babylonian cities and most of the tribal areas in the south, that is, the pro-Chaldaean and/or anti-Assyrian factions within Babylonia; Elam and the Arabs lent external support. The Babylonian revolt lasted four years, before the Assyrian forces put it down in 648 BC. Ashurbanipal then launched, over the next three years, a series of punitive campaigns against Shamash-shuma-ukin's external supporters, devastating Elam and the Aramaean zone on the Babylonian border, and forcing Arab groups into submission.

Decline and collapse (627–609 BC)

The last decade of Ashurbanipal's life remains obscure. In Babylonia, Ashurbanipal's client Kandalanu had governed for two decades, during which the region regained its economic prosperity. Kandalanu died in 627 BC, the same year as Ashurbanipal himself, and Nabopolassar (625–605 BC) then claimed the Babylonian throne. In the upheavals of the next several years, Nabopolassar successfully contested with two of Ashurbanipal's sons, Sin-shar-ishkun and Ashur-etil-ilani, for control over Babylonia. Just as Babylonia broke away from Assyrian control, other parts of the empire also moved toward independence. At the same time, the Medes under Cyaxares (653–585 BC) were increasingly powerful, threatening the Mannaeans and Urartu.

Nabopolassar launched an offensive against Assyria in 616 BC, campaigning in that year up the Euphrates into the Khabur and along the Tigris to the Little Zab. In the following year the Medes joined the hunt, sacking Ashur. Nabopolassar and Cyaxares formed an alliance, and in 612 BC took Nineveh and killed Sin-shar-ishkun, the Assyrian king. Assyrian resistance, now led by Ashur-uballit II, continued from Harran in northern Syria until 609 BC, when the last Assyrian king disappeared. The great Assyrian empire, which had dominated western Asia for so long, had collapsed.

Organization and socio-economic conditions

Organization of the Assyrian empire

Although possessing absolute power in theory, the potential opposition of his family, courtiers, urban populations, and the people of Assyria obliged the king to temper its exercise (Garelli, 1973). The king thus attempted to achieve consensus on certain issues, such as designation of heirs, grants of tax exemption, or imposition of forced labour on communities or individuals. Responsible to the gods for his military actions and for the general welfare, the king did nothing without consulting soothsayers, underwent ritual humiliations, and resorted to royal substitutes to evade portended disasters (Labat, 1939; Frankfort, 1948).

The king appointed the high dignitaries, the hierarchy of which constituted the central government; among these dignitaries figured the general-in-chief (*turranu*), the great cupbearer, the palace herald, the head steward, the vizier and the *rab reshi* (general). The palace was the administrative nerve-centre of the country, and also disbursed the enormous loot garnered from the far reaches of the empire; the large palace staff of officials, scribes, soothsayers, physicians, storekeepers, cooks, guards and so on, supported the execution of these functions (Postgate, 1978).

Governors, *bel pikhati* or *shaknu*, headed the provinces; village chiefs (*rab alani*) led the constituent districts within each province. The governor's duties (Postgate, 1980) required him to keep order, mete out justice, recruit soldiers, supervise major construction projects, and receive tribute. He exercised a large measure of autonomy, but was nonetheless liable to review by financial inspectors (*qipu*) and, on occasion, by royal envoys (*qurbutu*). An excellent network of messengers linked the capital and the provinces.

The army, the central instrument of imperial power, consisted of professional standing units, of soldiers of the king (young men performing military service as a form of *ilku*, or state service, and called up for a campaign) and of reservists mobilized as needed (Malbran-Labat, 1982). In the professional army, Assyrians served in the cavalry or chariotry, while other imperial subjects, and especially Aramaeans, formed the heavy and light infantry. The army also included foreign auxiliaries (Medes, Arabs, Cimmerians, Elamites) who joined more or less voluntarily. While the structure and tactics of the army remain obscure, its sophisticated logistical support included an intelligence service and an engineering corps, the duties of the latter having mostly to do with siege weapons. Fortified and garrisoned outposts, arsenals and troop mobilization points existed at strategic points throughout the empire.

Social and economic conditions

For various reasons, including the growing use of Aramaic on perishable materials, knowledge of social and economic conditions under the empire remains incomplete. Agriculture was the basic activity; smallholdings existed alongside the large tracts of crown and temple lands and the estates of nobles. Agricultural production was subject to taxes in kind, used to feed the administration and army. Stock-breeding has left little trace in the surviving records, but must have been an important activity. Industrial production occurred on a small scale, divided between private craftsmen under contract and royal workshops. Empire gave the Assyrians ready access to the mineral resources of Lebanon, the Amanus, and eastern Anatolia. In commerce, both crown and private sectors probably existed, but these are difficult to distinguish. The king encouraged foreign trade, which dealt mostly with luxury goods (linen, cotton, dyes, precious stones, ivory), and also provided taxes to the state.

The Assyrian population could be divided into three categories: free men whatever their social status, dependents of the state or of wealthy households (corresponding to the

mushkenu of previous periods) and slaves (Garelli, 1972). Recruitment of the last was mostly by warfare, and slaves undertook large-scale construction work. Typical of the spirit of the times, official texts almost exclusively used such general terms as people, human beings or servants when referring to a population in service to the king.

Cultural development

Architecture and art

The Assyrian kings were even more grandiose builders than their second millennium BC predecessors. Many kings restored or remodeled the temples and palaces of Ashur, the ancient capital; some made radical changes to old cities or established new ones. Ashurnasirpal II founded Kalkhu (Calah, Nimrud) on the ruins of a small town, turning the inauguration of his palace into a display of imperial power; Shalmaneser III added a large complex that served simultaneously as palace, fortress, arsenal and barracks. Kalkhu remained the military capital of Assyria until Sargon constructed Dur-Sharrukin (Khorsabad) not far from Nineveh. Sennacherib transformed Nineveh into a metropolis, the walls of which, now four times longer than before, enclosed palaces of Sennacherib and Ashurbanipal and several sanctuaries. An immense royal garden of exotic plants extended to the foot of the walls, and an extensive system of canals and aqueducts irrigated the surrounding countryside. Other major construction included provincial royal residences at such places as Imgur-Enlil (Balawat) near Nimrud, and Til Barsip (Tell Asmar) and Hadatu (Arslan Tash) in Syria.

Assyrian palaces were remarkable for the variety and excellence of the materials used in their construction – beams and doors of rare woods, nails of bronze and copper, embossed bricks on the floor, and, especially, the carved stone decorations. Lions, winged spirits, and gigantic winged bulls with human heads guarded the doorways. Orthostats, ornamented with bas-reliefs, lined the base of walls in corridors and certain chambers. These bas-reliefs, executed with skill and vigour, depict scenes of combat or the hunt, royal processions and, occasionally, magico-religious observations; this artistic corpus has made the school of Assyrian sculpture one of the most renowned of the ancient world. Panels of enamelled brick or brilliantly coloured frescoes decorated the walls above stone plinths. The few surviving statues of kings or gods have less artistic merit. Other categories of sculpture are better represented: rock sculptures, inscribed stelae with sculptured tops, and obelisks (truncated tiered pyramids) with military scenes and accompanying texts.

The Assyrians also displayed expertise in metalwork. Apart from the splendid strips of embossed bronze that decorated the palace doors at Balawat, numerous small objects of molded bronze and some magnificent gold and silver jewellery have survived. Their craftswomen decorated carpets and clothing with delicate embroidery, faithfully reproduced in the orthostat bas-reliefs. The cylinder seals of the period are perfectly made, and possess a cold but fascinating beauty. The varied and expert decorative ivories, and particularly certain pieces of furniture, deserve special mention. The product of Phoenician, Syrian or Assyrian artists, these small masterpieces present exclusively peaceful motifs, in contrast to the huge exercises in personal propaganda (Reade, 1981) that are the architectural reliefs. The ivories reveal a refinement and sensitivity to charm that lay behind the more brutal public faces of the Assyrian kings (Gadd, 1936; Barnet and Forman, 1970; Parrot, 1969; Strommenger, 1962; Mallowan, 1978).

Sciences and literature

The Assyrian palaces housed both state archives and libraries. The archives, stored in labelled baskets, contained royal correspondence, and legal and administrative documents. The libraries, ordered on wooden shelves, encompassed historical, didactic, scientific and literary texts (Parpola, 1983). These works were usually written on clay tablets, but occasionally on wax sheets set in hinged wooden or ivory frames. Library collections also existed in temples and certain private households.

The libraries not only housed Assyrian scholarship, but also served to perpetuate that tradition, through scribal training. The texts used in the education of scribes included models of penmanship; lists of cuneiform signs together with their names, their phonetic values, and archaic orthography; Sumero-Akkadian vocabularies; paradigmatic guides to grammar and collections of stock expressions; models of textual genres (legal, epistolary, religious, and so on); and bilingual dictionaries for foreign tongues. These pedagogical instruments often took the form of lists.

Lists also epitomized scientific knowledge, a very old practice in the Mesopotamian tradition; such lists catalogued names for various plants, animals, stones, places (rivers, mountains, cities, temples), stars, gods and their symbols, manufactured objects, hierarchies of office and social standing, and so on. These lists usually gave equivalent terms in other languages, especially Sumerian (for example, the *HAR.ra = hubullu* bilingual series of twenty-two tablets). Procedural and problem texts were other characteristic ways of presenting scientific knowledge. The first presented recipes for making certain kinds of things, such as glass or alloys that look like silver; the second posed mathematical and astronomical problems which sometimes were highly abstract in character (Oppenheim, 1977).

Mesopotamian medicine took as its basic principle the notion that illnesses were punishments for various sins visited by the gods on the afflicted. Soothsayers (*baru*) assessed the nature of the sin that caused the ailment, and exorcists (*ashipu*) then attempted to remove the affliction by the appropriate rites and incantations. At the same time, a pragmatic medicine existed along with this ritual practice. The professional doctor (*asu*) was familiar with the etiology of certain natural agents, observed symptoms with great precision as the basis for diagnosis, and applied surgical or medical remedies that had nothing to do with magic. Medications contained plant- or mineral-based ingredients, some of which are still in use (Kocher, 1963–79).

The concept of illness as divine punishment was one facet of the more general idea that the gods directed individual and collective destiny. Thus both Babylonians and Assyrians searched desperately to learn about their immediate or more distant future. By the Neo-Assyrian period, divination had become an extremely complex discipline, codified in tens of thousands of texts often assembled into hugh treatises (Bottero, 1974). Two kinds of divination existed. In the intuitive or inspired type, the god responded to questions through an oracle, a vision or a special dream, obtained in a period of isolation, or by the mediation of prophets, sometimes in a state of trance. In deductive divination, the soothsayer (*baru*) sought a sign that expressed an omen. The *baru* used several methods, including observation of heavenly phenomena, of physical or behavioural anomalies in humans or animals, or of the entrails of sacrificial animals (extispicy) and especially their livers (hepatoscopy). Astrology, in the sense of the influence of the stars on individual lives, was a late and aberrant development of Mesopotamian divination taken over by the Greeks.

BIBLIOGRAPHY

ADAMS, R. MC. 1981. *Heartland of Cities*. Chicago, Ill.

ANDRAE, W. 1938. *Das Wiedererstandene Assur*. Leipzig.

BARNETT, R. D.; FORMAN, W. 1970. *Assyrian Palace Reliefs in the British Museum*. London.

BERAN, T. 1958. Die babylonische Glyptik der Kassitenzeit. *Arch. Orientforsch.* (Graz), Vol. 18, pp. 255–87.

BOTTERO, J. 1974. Symptomes, signes et écriture en Mesopotamie ancienne. In: VERNANT, J.-P. (ed.), *Divination et rationalité*. Paris. pp. 70–196.

BRINKMAN, J. A. 1963. Provincial Administration in Babylonia under the Second Dynasty of Isin. *J. econ. soc. Hist. Orient* (Leiden), Vol. 6, pp. 233–42.

—— 1968. *A Political History of Post-Kassite Babylonia (1158–722 BC)*. Roma.

—— 1974. The Monarchy in the Time of the Kassite Dynasty. In: GARELLI, P. (ed.), *Le palais et la royauté*. Paris. pp. 395–408.

—— 1980a. Kassiten. *Reallex. Assyriol.* (Berlin), Vol. 5, pp. 464–73.

—— 1980b. Forced Laborers in the Middle Babylonian Period. *J. cuneif. Stud.* (New Haven, Conn.), Vol. 32, pp. 17–22.

CARDASCIA, G. 1969. *Les lois assyriennes*. Paris.

CARTER, E.; STOLPER, M. 1984. *Elam: Surveys of Political History and Archaeology*. Berkeley, Calif.

DIETRICH, M. 1970. *Die Aramaer Südbabyloniens in der Sargonidenzeit (700–648)*. Neukirchen-Vluyn.

EDZARD, D. O. 1960. Die Beziehungen Babyloniens und Ägyptens in der mittelbabylonischen Zeit und das Gold. *J. econ. soc. Hist. Orient* (Leiden), Vol. 3, pp. 67–97.

EICKHOFF, T. 1985. *Dar Tukulti-Ninurta. Eine mittelassyrische Kult- und Residenzstadt*. Berlin.

FRANKFORT, H. 1948. *Kingship and the Gods*. Chicago, Ill.

GADD, C. J. 1936. *The Stones of Assyria*. London.

GARELLI, P. 1969. *Le Proche Orient Asiatique*. Paris. Vol. 1

—— 1972. Problèmes de stratification sociale dans l'empire assyrien. In: EDZARD, D. O. (ed.), *Gesellschaftsklassen im alten Zweistromland*. München, Bayerische Akademie der Wissenschaften. pp. 73–9.

—— 1973. Les sujets du roi d'Assyrie. In: FINET, A. (ed.), *La voix de l'opposition en Mesopotamie*. Bruxelles, Institut des Hautes Etudes de Belgique. pp. 189–213.

GOSSMAN, P. 1955. *Das Erra-Epos*. Würzburg.

KOCHER, F. 1963–79. *Die babylonisch-assyrische Medizin in Texten und Untersuchungen*. Berlin. Vols 1–6.

KROLL, S. 1979. *Urartu, das Reich am Ararat*. Hamburg, Helms-Museum.

LABAT, R. 1939. *Le caractère religieux de la royauté assyro-babylonienne*. Paris.

LAMBERT, W. G. 1960. *Babylonian Wisdom Literature*. Oxford.

MALBRAN-LABAT, F. 1982. *L'armée et l'organisation militaire de l'Assyrie*. Genève.

MALLOWAN, M. E. L. 1978. *The Nimrud Ivories*. London.

MORRISON, M. A.; OWEN, D. I. (eds) 1981. *Studies on the Civilization and Culture of Nuzi and the Hurrians*. Winoma Lake, Ind.

OELSNER, J. 1982. Zur Organisation des gesellschaftlichen Lebens im kassitischen und nachkassitischen Babylonien: Verwaltungsstruktur und Gemeinschaften. *Arch. Orientforsch.* (Graz), Vol. 19, pp. 403–10.

OLMSTEAD, A. T. 1923. *History of Assyria*. New York.

OPPENHEIM, A. L. 1977. Man and Nature in Mesopotamian Civilization. *Dict. sci. Biogr.* (New York), Vol. 15, pp. 634–66.

PARPOLA, S. 1983. Assyrian Library Records. *J. Near East. Stud.* (Chicago, Ill.), Vol. 42, pp. 1–29.

PARROT, A. 1969. *Assur.* 2nd ed. Paris.

PIOTROVSKII, B. 1967. *Urartu, the Kingdom of Van and its Art.* London.

POSTGATE, J. N. 1978. *The Governor's Palace Archive.* London.

—— 1980. The Place of the Saknu in Assyrian Government. *Anatol. Stud.* (London), Vol. 30, pp. 69–76.

READE, J. E. 1981. Neo-Assyrian Monuments in their Historical Context. In: FALES, F. M. (ed.), *Assyrian Royal Inscriptions: New Horizons in Literary, Ideological, and Historical Analysis.* Roma. pp. 143–67.

SAGGS, H. W. F. 1984. *The Might that was Assyria.* London.

SEIDL, U. 1968. Die Babylonischen Kudurru-reliefs. *Baghdader Mitt.* (Berlin), Vol. 4, pp. 7–222.

STEIN, D. 1984. Khabur Ware and Nuzi Ware: Their Origin, Relationship and Significance. *Assur* (Malibu, Calif.), Vol. 4, No. 1.

STROMMENGER, E. 1962. *Fünf Jahrtausende Mesopotamien.* München.

STRONACH, D. 1969, 1973. Excavations at Tepe Nush-i Jan. *Iran* (London), Vol. 7, pp. 1–20; Vol. 11, pp. 129–40.

VIEYRA, M. 1961. *Les Assyriens.* Paris.

12.2
SYRIA AND PALESTINE

12.2.1
THE EARLY AND MIDDLE BRONZE AGE
(3000–1600 BC)

Dominique Beyer

The physical geography, and particularly the absence of clear-cut natural boundaries (except for the Mediterranean coast), has always prevented the achievement of real political unity in the Syro-Palestinian regions. From west to east four to five types of region can be distinguished (Map 12).

In the west the presence of the sea permitted the development of a series of coastal cities, such as Ugarit and Byblos, which very early on became points of contact between western Asia and the Mediterranean or Egypt.

The mountains parallel to the coast, such as the Amanus, the Jebel el Ansariye and the Lebanon and Anti-Lebanon ranges, meant that the major routes ran north-south, with fruitful valleys enjoying a climate that remained Mediterranean (the Ghab, traversed by the Orontes, and the Bekaa, where the Jordan rises), communicating through gaps in the mountains with the coast or the interior. In the interior, plains of varying extent and watered to varying degrees gave rise in Syria to territorial units such as Hama or Aleppo, which played an important role in ancient times. Some territorial units, of which Damascus is an example, were already oases surrounded by desert steppe so arid that it could scarcely provide sustenance for any but nomadic herdsmen, whose wanderings were one of the constant features of the history of these regions. This Syrian steppe is traversed to the east and north-east by the Euphrates, which was very early a much-used transit route, linking Mesopotamia, Anatolia and Syria and making the northern half of Syria a hub of communications for western Asia.

Finally, in the south-west, Palestine, scored from north to south by the Ghor trench (valley of the Jordan), a country of hills that were more fertile in antiquity than they are today, was occupied by communities of farmers. Hemmed in to the east by the Syrian desert and to the west by a coast with few natural harbours, Palestine was accessible only from the north or, with more difficulty, from the south, where the Negev and Sinai deserts proved inadequate as barriers to conquest from Egypt.

These Syro-Palestinian regions gave sanctuary to several peoples, mainly Semitic, and it was long thought that Syria had never developed any civilization of its own. However, work that has been in progress for several decades in the area, particularly in northern Syria, is tending to bring to light an original Syrian contribution, nurtured by the richness of its contacts with neighbouring regions.

THE EARLY BRONZE AGE (THIRD MILLENNIUM BC)

Syria

The Euphrates and the Jazirah

On the bend of the Euphrates in Syria, the destruction and abandonment of the important colonies of the Sumerian type (Babuba-Qannas, Aruda) towards the end of the fourth millennium BC doubtless held back for a time the spread into Syrian lands of certain cultural achievements such as the Sumerian script. Little is known as yet of Syria's history at the beginning of the third millennium BC, but, one important city, Mari, on the middle Euphrates, destined to be the centre of one of the great Syrian states in the middle of that millennium, was founded at its beginning and on a large scale, it would seem, from the outset, as has been shown by the recent research of a French team under J. Margueron. Built on the Euphrates between the two poles of commerce constituted by Mesopotamia and northern Syria, Mari gradually grew rich through its control of trade in essential goods for a Mesopotamia lacking in basic products such as timber, metals and stone. This favourable position and the ample scope of its links with Mesopotamia explain why Sumerian-type traditions were so widely adopted in Mari by its Semitic population, examples being the cuneiform texts of the epoch, the Sumerian-type praying figures and the cylinder-seals. At the height of this civilization of the archaic dynasties, between 2600 and 2340 BC, a Mari dynasty was even recorded by the Sumerian scribes as the 'tenth after the Flood'. And in fact a gigantic palace belonging to that period, built of sun-dried brick in successive stages, bears witness to the solidity of power in Mari. Its excavation, begun by A. Parrot, is continuing. The presence of a large sanctuary in the interior of the palace complex, the 'sacred precinct', suggests that at the

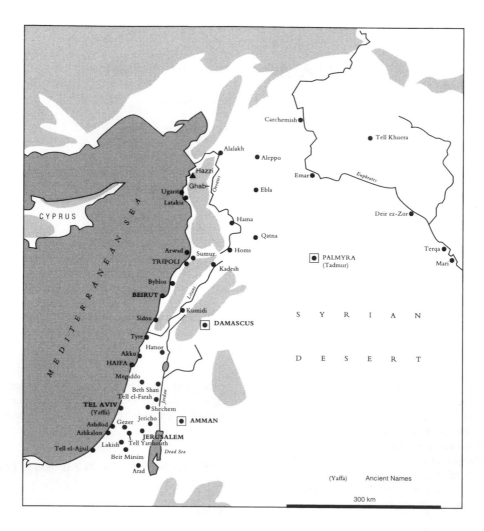

Map 12 Syria and Palestine (3000–700 BC).

time the religious and the profane were very closely linked and perhaps indissoluble.

In the architecture of the temples certain features are typical of the Syrian world, such as the existence of an open space associated with the sanctuary (temples of Ishtar, Ninhursag and pre-Sargon Dagan) or the use of betyls, standing stones in the centre of the temple (Ninni-Zaza).

Mari's profitable hold on trade down the Euphrates was the cause of its difficulties with the great powers of the time, Ebla in Syria and Akkad in Mesopotamia. Mari channelled off the trade not only of the Euphrates itself but also of its tributaries in Upper Syria, the Balikh and above all the Khabur. In those northern regions the German excavations of Tell Khuera have demonstrated that Sumerian influence had spread to the Jazirah in northern Syria from the archaic period onwards, as is shown by the stylized statuettes discovered in a small temple, whose layout, on the other hand, illustrated a specifically Syrian tradition: the little *templum in antis*, consisting of a single elongated room fitted out for worship, preceded by a vestibule with an anta on either side. It appears in the middle of the third millennium BC as the oldest example of the series of Syrian temples elongated to form a megaron, a design adopted at a much later date for Solomon's temple in Jerusalem.

The interior of Syria

The great revelation of Syrian archaeology in the past decade has been the discovery by the Italian expedition led by P.

Matthiae of the ancient city of Ebla, an important city previously known from the Sumerian and Akkadian cuneiform texts of Mesopotamia and imagined to be lying in southern Turkey until the Italian excavations found it at Tell Mardikh, 60 km south of Aleppo. While Mari is in many respects already a Mesopotamian city, Ebla is proving to be the epitome of the 'proto-Syrian' urban culture of inland Upper Syria. Part of a vast palace building (Palace G), roughly contemporaneous with that of Mari, has been uncovered, yielding an impressive harvest of archives consisting of about 15,000 clay tablets, covered with the cuneiform script of Mesopotamia and written in Sumerian but also in an Eastern Semitic language akin to Canaanite and dubbed Eblaite. These archives are those of a dynasty of 'lords' reigning over a vast state which had dealings with distant regions (northern Syria, Anatolia, the middle Euphrates and Mesopotamia) and to a lesser extent with the towns on the Syrian coast. Ebla's prosperity was based on establishing its hegemony over independent principalities for economic ends. Its basic resources came from agricultural revenue in the form of barley, olive oil and livestock. The very large number of sheep recorded on the tablets enabled a large textile industry to be developed. Trade in metals – copper, tin and precious metals – was also considerable.

The part of the Ebla palace already uncovered consists of a vast courtyard, bordered with porticoes, to the north and east, where the king gave audiences, as is suggested by the discovery of a dais in the centre of the north portico. A monumental staircase probably led to the private apartments. At the north-east corner of the courtyard a massive tower with a staircase consisting of three straight flights, richly decorated with incrustations of shells, emphasized the importance attached to the first floor. While affinities have been found between this palace and the Mesopotamian palace of Kish, for example, the one at Ebla appears above all to be the prototype of Syrian palace architecture. To the north, in the residential and administrative quarter, among other things precious and rare pieces of carved wooden furniture have been found. From what is known at the moment, the art of the court at Ebla seems to bear a highly original imprint, while also being akin to the art of Mesopotamia in the final phase of the archaic dynasties, before the establishment of the Akkadian empire towards 2340 BC. It is to these kings of Mesopotamia, and particularly Naram-Sin towards 2250 BC, that the capture and destruction of the proto-Syrian metropolis must be attributed. The two rivals, Mari and Ebla, represented for the Mesopotamian conquerors solid obstacles that had to be removed if they were to gain free access to the rich areas of northern Syria or the Mediterranean coast. After the fall of the Akkadian empire, the last century of the third millennium BC saw the kings of Ur's third dynasty impose Mesopotamian suzerainty anew on Mari, Ebla, and, it would seem, Byblos on the coast, before the nomadic Amorites came to disturb these regions and weaken urban civilization for a time.

The Syrian coast

The fate of the Syrian coastal towns throughout the third millennium BC was appreciably different.

Concerning the city of Ugarit, destined to be of great importance in the second millennium BC, the information available is unfortunately still vague. On the other hand Byblos on the Lebanese coast, isolated from the interior by high wooded mountains, truly represented in the Early Bronze Age the prototype of the Phoenician city, given over entirely to maritime trade. Byblos (the name given to the town later by the Greeks, its Semitic name being Gubla or Gebal) was protected by stone ramparts from 2900–2800 BC onwards but on the landward side only; this indicates that there was hardly any fear of invasion from the sea. Thanks to its two ports, one on the north and the other on the south, an arrangement dictated by the direction of the prevailing winds, the city had profitable trading links with Egypt very early, from the time of the second dynasty. In addition to other products, Byblos provided the pharaohs with the pine and precious cedarwood they were so fond of for building their great monuments. The gifts sent by Egyptian rulers were consecrated in the temple of Baalat Gebal, the great goddess of Byblos, whom the Egyptians identified with Isis-Hathor. The city thus went through a long period of prosperity, to which its wealth of monuments, well known as a result of the vast excavations carried out by the French expedition led by M. Dunand, bears witness.

In the centre of the city three temples stood round a body of water, the Sacred Lake. The temple to the west was that of Baalat Gebal, which was developed on several levels and is striking for its massive use of columns bearing the terrace roof. This design was also adopted for the city's vast residential buildings. The buildings were in stone with wooden superstructures. The city was burnt towards 2300 BC or a little later, probably in the course of incursions by the Amorites, Semitic nomads belonging to the same stock as the

Canaanites who lived in these regions. Byblos, however, did not take long to rise again from its ruins.

Palestine

The chronology of the whole of the Early Bronze Age – a term used for convenience only, since metal was still in only limited use and bronze was only slowly replacing copper – is linked to that of Egypt by the discovery of Egyptian artefacts in Palestine and also by the presence of pottery from Palestine in Egyptian tombs of the 1st dynasty. Egyptian contacts with Palestine were not pacific in nature like the trade between the pharaohs and Byblos. The villages founded at the foot of the Judaean and Samarian hills (Lakish, Gezer and so on) tried to protect themselves against the prevailing insecurity behind massive walls.

Palestine in the third millennium BC was characterized by a process of urbanization, though to a more modest degree than its neighbours in Syro-Mesopotamia and Egypt and without the critical cultural achievement of a written language. The people settled generally in the areas most favourable to the development of agriculture (the Jordan valley, the hills on the West Bank, the rim of the Jordanian plateau to the east). The country was made up of small city-states, each with its own limited area of farmland attached to it. The north seems to have been richer and more densely settled than the south. Beth Shan, Megiddo and Jericho were built with care and reflect continuous social and economic development, due in particular to the imperative needs for collective defence and collective efforts. The ramparts, first of brick then of stone, were strengthened (seventeen phases of repair at Jericho) and equipped with towers.

The Israeli excavation at Arad revealed a city of Early Bronze Age II, on the skirts of the Negev desert and the hills of Judaea, an example of a settlement at a point that, while arid, was at the junction of the caravan routes leading to the Sinai, Egypt and Arabia. The general layout of the town was that of ramparts, furnished with semicircular towers enclosing residential quarters, and a well-demarcated official centre with temples and probably public buildings. In the centre of the built-up area a reservoir collecting rainfall guaranteed the essential water supply. Elsewhere, as at the Jawa site in the basalt desert situated south of the Jebel Druze, in Transjordan, diversion channels made it possible to recover and store the precious water from a wadi.

According to recent excavations, one of the most important sites of the Early Bronze Age was at Tell Yarmouth in the hills to the west of Jerusalem, consisting of a completely fortified lower town dominated by an acropolis. The site, which has an area of more than 16 hectares (corresponding perhaps to a population of 7,000 inhabitants), was important in Early Bronze Age III: the old stone ramparts had been strengthened on the outside with a glacis and a second set of ramparts, the total width of the defensive works reaching almost 37 m. A monumental gateway contained a zigzag passage.

In the last centuries of the third millennium BC the urban settlements were destroyed or abandoned and, in contrast to Syria, where urban civilizations suffered no real interruption, Palestine saw a return to pastoral and village modes of life at the same time as the polished red slipware gave way to new types of pottery. In the same way individual burials seem to have replaced the great collective tombs. Without rejecting the traditional explanation of incursions by the

Amorite nomads, modern archaeology ascribes these upheavals to internal changes, particularly ecological ones.

MIDDLE BRONZE AGE (2000–1600 BC)

Syria

Whereas they had been quite quickly assimilated in Mesopotamia, the Amorite nomads who had disturbed the last centuries of the third millennium BC in Syro-Palestine were slow to settle down and adopt the civilization of the sedentary peoples. In addition to the native inhabitants the Semitic Amorites, who had come from the confines of the Syro-Arabian desert, came in contact in northern Syria with the Hurrians, an Asiatic people who had gradually filtered in from the north-east of western Asia and who spoke an agglutinative language, still quite obscure, to which they adapted the cuneiform script.

The interior of Syria, Ebla, Iamkhad

One of the first Syrian centres to be rebuilt at the beginning of the second millennium BC was Ebla. Powerful ramparts were built round it, reinforced with a glacis and pierced to the south-west by a monumental gateway with multiple *tenailles*, its walls lined with great stone orthostats. Italian excavations have shown the existence of two palaces. While Palace E, to the north of the acropolis, is only partly known, Building Q, discovered a few years ago to the west of the third-millennium palace, represents an important monumental ensemble. Its function seems complex by reason of the length of time for which it was used and the succession of alterations it underwent but it was administrative and residential as well as probably concerned with religious ceremonies connected with the burial there of the ancestors of the royal house. Among other important pieces of evidence a necropolis has been found, hollowed out of the rock under the palace and under two temples, containing the tombs of persons of high rank from the Middle Bronze Age II (c. 1800–1600 BC). The structural relationship between these underground chambers and the three buildings has been demonstrated; this calls to mind practices known to have taken place for example at Mari, or at Ur in Mesopotamia during the third Ur dynasty. Although they had been robbed, the 'tomb of the princess', the 'tomb of the lord with goats' and to a lesser extent the 'tomb of the water cisterns' still contained treasures: in addition to pottery and stone vases, important items of gold jewellery, a pharaonic sceptre and a relief in bone carved with religious scenes including a ritual banquet and, perhaps, the adoration of the bull.

Among the temples so far discovered at Ebla the most important is temple D, which is of the elongated type with the layout of a megaron. Preceded by a porch with antae opening into a vestibule, the elongated cella had at its far end a podium and a deep recess in the wall. In front of the podium stood a betyl, characteristic of the Semitic cults of the west, and consisting of a roughly dressed block of stone. In the south-east corner of the cella a rectangular basin, divided into compartments, was decorated with a bas-relief, like other examples of the same type (nineteenth century BC) (Plate 71). Among the themes represented in these stone basins is that of a ritual banquet, a theme that seems to have enjoyed particular favour, associated with mythological subjects. One such basin also shows a picture which has been

interpreted as a scene of alliance between kings. This typically Syrian theme is also found among the symbols on the cylinder-seals.

One of the temples in the lower town (N) belonged to the category of massive temples or temple-towers, like those of Baal and Dagan, the great Syrian gods, at Ras Shamra, formerly Ugarit.

In the eighteenth and seventeenth centuries BC Ebla had probably become subject to the 'great kingdom' of Iamkhad, whose capital was Aleppo and which dominated central Syria. While hardly any traces of ancient Aleppo are known, the British archaeologist Sir Leonard Woolley succeeded in uncovering the various levels of the city of Alalakh (Tell Atchana in the Antioch plain), where the palace of its king Iarim-Lim (at level VII, eighteenth century BC) is one of the most important Syrian buildings of the period. With the ramparts at its back it was an elongated edifice consisting of two wings separated by a central space. In the official part, to the north, the mudbrick base of the walls was strengthened with basalt orthostats, a design feature that was long to persist in Syrian architecture. The building had at least one upper floor, in one apartment of which are preserved the remains of wall-paintings which have been likened to those of the Cretan palaces.

The cuneiform texts found in Iarim-Lim's palace have retained imprints of cylinder-seals, particularly royal seals, representative of the 'classical' phase of Syrian glyptics. These clearly dated documents (end of the eighteenth and the seventeenth centuries BC) are valuable markers for the chronology of Syrian seals, whose exact place in the stratigraphic context is often unknown. Workshops, doubtless operating in the large urban centres such as Aleppo, Ebla, Ugarit or Qatna, created a very refined style using hard stone such as haematite, a style that was original despite borrowings from neighbouring Anatolia and Mesopotamia, from Egypt – particularly during the seventeenth century BC under the influence of the Hyksos – and from Minoan art. The mythological texts composed later at Ugarit in the fourteenth and thirteenth centuries BC enable us to a certain extent to decipher the dominant themes. These include a number of divinities, among whom the most popular is the god of the storm, associated as in the case of all the peoples of the Levant with the bull, and often represented on seals and in numerous bronze figurines in the form of a young god fighting. In a set of symbols recalling the natural order of the world and the alternation of the seasons, the appearance of the god of the storm, triumphing over the forces of evil, represented in the Levant by the serpent, heralds the onset of rain, guaranteeing the renewal of the vegetation in the dry crop-growing regions (Plates 72–5).

The Syrian coast

Egypt very quickly re-established intensive trade with the coastal towns – Ugarit, no doubt Tyre and Sidon, and above all Byblos, also the best known of these towns at the time and inscribed on the pharaohs' lists as an Egyptian city. As in the third millennium BC the pharaohs continued to send gifts but they also sent a certain number of officials whose functions covered at least the organization of trade. The kings of Byblos appeared then to be vassals of the 12th-dynasty pharaohs. They bore Egyptian titles and wrote in hieroglyphics, while trying out a pseudo-hieroglyphic script to represent their Phoenician language. Royal or princely tombs hollowed out of rock have yielded hoards of precious objects in which gifts from the pharaohs were found side by side with specimens of the local goldsmiths' art, strongly inspired by Egyptian models (Plate 76). Those discovered in the temple of Byblos are generally in a more local style: a dagger-hilt plated in gold with a design of goats charging each other, fenestrated axes richly decorated with filigree and granulations. Over 1,300 votive offerings were recovered from where they were hidden under the floor of the Obelisk Temple, that fine example from the nineteenth and eighteenth centuries BC of west Semitic architectural design and places of worship. The temple proper was of modest proportions. Its unroofed cella contained scarcely anything but a large betyl on its plinth. The courtyard surrounding the temple was more extensive, with more than thirty stelae, many of them shaped like obelisks. One of them had been dedicated by King Abi-Shemu to the Egyptian god Herishef-Re (Fig. 29).

The Syrian Euphrates: Mari, Terqa

In the part of Syria watered by the Euphrates, further to the east, the important city of Mari knew a second period of splendour up to the middle of the eighteenth century BC, when it became too great an obstacle to the hegemonic ambitions of Hammurabi the Great of Babylon and he swept if from his path. Its history is well documented in the 20,000 or so cuneiform tablets in the archives – which cover, however, a period of only forty years, roughly between 1800 and 1760 BC – discovered in the palace which King Zimri-Lim was the last to occupy. This monumental building, one of the most important in Middle Eastern antiquity, is impressive both in size – 300 courtyards, rooms and corridors on the ground floor alone – and in the fine state of preservation of its decoration and of what André Parrot's mission discovered in it – statues, wall-paintings, and everyday utensils, including a complete set of terracotta moulds for making cakes. Probably over 15 m high, at least in certain sections where there was an upper floor, and laid out around two large courtyards, the palace provided room on its ground floor for storehouses, kitchens and servants' lodgings as well as the official apartments with the throne room and, to the

south-east, a sanctuary on the site of the sacred portion of the third-millennium palaces. Determination of what the upper floor looked like and was used for is naturally a difficult problem but it is known that the king's private quarters and some administrative offices were situated there (Fig. 30).

After the fall of Mari, its position in the Euphrates area was taken over, but on a more modest scale, by its former vassal, Terqa, which had long housed a great sanctuary of the god Dagan. Round that city the kingdom of Hana was established, which seems to have played a part in the development, of which little is yet known, of the civilization of the Kassites, who reigned over Mesopotamia from the beginning of the sixteenth century BC.

Palestine

After the decline of urban civilization and the complex population movements that characterized the end of the Early and the beginning of the Middle Bronze Age, Egyptian sources show from the nineteenth century BC onwards a decrease in the number of tribes and an increase in permanent settlements. While several clans coexisted, as is shown *inter alia* by burial practices (shaft-and-chamber tombs and cist or dolmen passage graves with a barrow above them are both found), Palestine was gradually being rebuilt. The use of the fast potter's wheel, perhaps introduced by a new population group, led to the creation of fine pottery akin to that of Anatolia and north Syria.

It was between 1700 and 1550 BC, during the Hyksos period in Egypt, that the Canaanite civilization in Palestine enjoyed its golden age. The Hyksos, known in Egypt as the Princes of Foreign Lands, must have been a grouping of ambitious and turbulent landless princes who had gradually succeeded in obtaining a foothold in the Nile Delta and dominating at least Lower Egypt. What impact the Hyksos invasion had on the civilization of Palestine is not certain. Tradition attributes to them the introduction of the chariot and certain improvements in military architecture. It is a fact that to a greater extent than

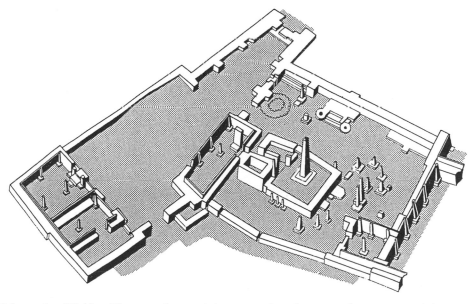

Figure 29 The obelisk temple of Byblos. The most characteristic part consists of a rectangular court containing some 30 stelae-obelisks with a raised open-air sanctuary in the centre. An obelisk or 'betyle' of the type traditionally found in Semitic sanctuaries probably stood here. The religious furnishings consisted of numerous basins and tables for offerings. The finds also included many stores of votive objects, often of precious materials: mostly bronze weapons and statuettes covered with fine gold leaf, but also earthenware animal figurines (after Amiet, 1977).

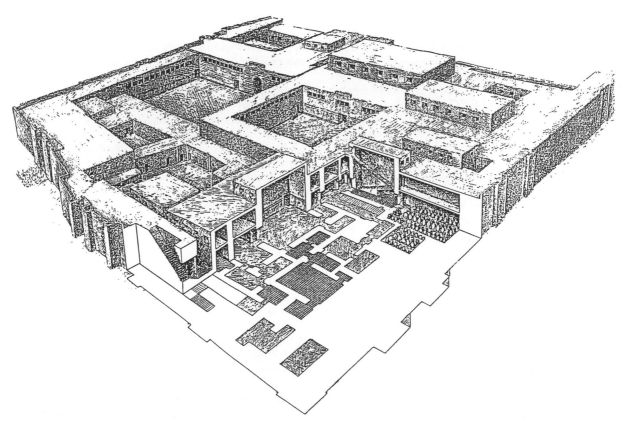

Figure 30 Mari. Reconstitution of the Amorite palace viewed from a north-western angle. Based on the work of Jean Margueron, this document shows, in particular, the importance henceforth assumed by the concept of storeys built around the central courtyards of the palace. While the throne room was on the ground floor, the king's private apartments must be visualized on a higher floor. This important palace, some parts of which date from the twenty-first century, was destroyed in about 1760 BC by the soldiers of Hammurabi of Babylon, founder of the palaeo-Babylonian empire.

in the third millennium BC powerful ramparts flanked by towers and reinforced with glacis began to protect the capitals of the little Canaanite kingdoms – Shechem, Hatsor, Megiddo, Beit Mirsim, Farah (in the north), El-Ajjul (on the coast) and Jericho. Access to them was protected by monumental gateways in double or triple *tenaille*, approached by ramps parallel to the ramparts and hence exposed to the defenders' missiles.

One of the most important towns at that time was Hatsor in upper Galilee at the crossroads of the routes leading from Syria to the Jordan Valley. Mentioned in the eighteenth century BC, both in the Egyptian Execration Texts and in the archives at Mari, in connection with the tin trade, the town must have housed official archives written in Akkadian, since it had commercial and diplomatic relations with Hammurabi's Babylon. It covered an area of 80 hectares; the lower town was surrounded by ramparts 9 m thick and there was an acropolis in which *inter alia* traces of an important palace are preserved. Excavations led by Y. Yadin have uncovered a temple in characteristic massive style, comparable with the temple at Alalakh, its contemporary. In the lower town a double temple has been uncovered, with burial chambers hollowed out of the rock beneath it. This temple featured two symmetrical sanctuaries, each with a small central courtyard, as in the dwelling-houses.

Most of the objects that bear witness to artistic activities come from burial hoards, which are particularly rich (an example is the recent excavations by Pella). Local goldsmiths' work (Tell El-'Ajjul) and metal objects are highly developed, whereas sculpture in the form of statues or reliefs is rare (Fig. 31, Plate 77). Egyptian importations (particularly scarabs, alabaster vases and inlaid caskets) called forth numerous imitations.

Figure 31 Syrian prince. This bronze plaque, cast in a mound, was probably part of a frieze attached to a wooden mount. The figure has assumed the habitual posture of a worshipper praying before a divinity. His elaborate costume, wrapped in several layers around the body and generously enveloping the shoulders, shows Syrian influence on the rich Galilean kingdom of Hatsor. Middle of the second millennium BC; bronze; h 9.5 cm; Ayelet Hashahar, Hatsor Museum (after Orthmann, 1975).

The defeat inflicted on the Hyksos by Amosis, the first pharaoh of the 18th dynasty in Egypt, swept them out of Palestine and put an end to this period. Towns like Jericho, Beit Mirsim and Megiddo were destroyed. Palestine moved into the orbit of New Kingdom Egypt.

BIBLIOGRAPHY

ALBRIGHT, W. F. 1963. *Archaeology of Palestine*. London.

AMIET, P. 1977. *L'art antique du Proche-Orient*. Paris.

AVI-YONAH, M. M.; KEMPINSKI, A. 1980. *Syrie-Palestine*, II. Genève (Archaeologia Mundi).

KENYON, K. 1965. *Archaeology in the Holy Land*. London.

KLENGEL, H. 1965, 1969, 1970. *Geschichte Syriens im 2. Jahrtausend v.u.Z.* Berlin. 3 vols.

MATTHIAE, P. 1962. *Ars Syra*. Roma.

—— 1975. Syrische Kunst. In: ORTHMANN, W. (ed.), *Der Alte Orient, Propylaen Kunstgeschichte*. Berlin, Vol. 14, pp. 466–93.

—— 1980. *Ebla, An Empire Rediscovered*. London,.

MELLAART, J. 1966. *The Chalcolithic and Early Bronze Ages in the Near East and Anatolia*. Bairūt.

ORTHMANN, W. 1975. *Der Alte Orient*. Propyläen-Kunstgeschichte. Vol. 14. Berlin.

PERROT, J. 1978. *Syrie-Palestine*, I. Genève (Archaeologia Mundi).

12.2.2

THE LATE BRONZE AGE AND THE EARLY IRON AGE
(1600–700 BC)

Horst Klengel

THE LATE BRONZE AGE (*c.* 1600–1200 BC)

Political developments

During the final period of the Middle Bronze Age, the political situation in Syria and Palestine changed. Successful Hittite campaigns reduced Iamkhad/Aleppo, the most important power among the Syrian states, to the status of a minor principality. After Mursili's decisive victory over Halab/Aleppo and a coalition of north Syrian princes (about 1595 BC), no political power in Syria existed to withstand the attacks of foreign aggressors. The Hittites themselves were unable immediately to take advantage of this weakness, however: conflicts within the ruling class of Hatti and a series of murders in the royal dynasty weakened the Hittite state for nearly a century. This situation encouraged the expansion of other states, and favoured the rise of Hurrian political influence in Syria. Judging by the onomastic contrasts between Alalakh VII and IV (Tell Atchana, near the mouth of the Orontes river), a large Hurrian element appeared in north-west Syria in the mid-second millennium (Astour, 1978; Wilhelm, 1982, pp. 9 ff). The Alalakh IV (fifteenth century BC) texts also point to the growing influence of Hurri-Mitanni, a newly arisen political power in northern Mesopotamia (Klengel, 1978a).

Hurrians and Mitanni

The so-called 'autobiography' of Idrimi, a king of Alalakh (*c.* 1480 BC), relates the flight of the royal family from Halab to Emar (Meskene) on the Euphrates (Dietrich and Loretz, 1981). The story then follows Prince Idrimi's ride through the Syrian desert to Ammiya in Canaan (near modern Tripoli). After an extended exile, Idrimi returned to Syria and took up residence in Alalakh. Before his installation as king, he swore an oath to the king of Hurri-Mitanni, 'the mighty king, the king of the Hurri people'. The story reveals the extension of Mitanni influence in Syria as far west as the Mediterranean coast, and implies a system of royal clientage. The Mitanni overlordship in most parts of northern Syria surely had its impact on the cultural development of the region. But identifying a specific Mitannian influence on the art of Syria is difficult, not least because the definition of Mitannian art remains moot (Barrelet et al., 1977; Hrouda, 1985).

The Egyptians in Syria

Egyptian influence at this time is more apparent. Egypt's commercial and political involvement with Syria, and especially with Gubla/Byblos and its hinterland, was already more than a thousand years old (Helck, 1962, pp. 5 ff). Prior to the Late Bronze Age, no evidence exists to suggest Egyptian military control over the Syrian interior. But the rise of the 18th dynasty profoundly changed the situation. Beginning with the reign of Amenhotep I (*c.* 1500 BC) (Krauss, 1985), the Egyptian textual sources refer to incursions into central and northern Syria.

Tuthmosis III (*c.* 1470 BC) records a series of progressively more distant campaigns. The first of these campaigns climaxed in his victory at Megiddo over a Syro-Palestinian coalition (which, according to the Egyptian tradition, involved 330 princes and tribal leaders). After strengthening the Egyptian military footholds on the coast, Tuthmosis in subsequent campaigns turned to northern Syria, warring with towns on the Akkar plain and with Tunip (the location of which is not certain); in his eighth campaign, Tuthmosis defeated a Mitannian force and reached the Euphrates. In the last years of his reign, Tuthmosis again warred in central and northern Syria, perhaps an indication of continued Mitannian suzerainty in these regions.

Amenhotep II (*c.* 1420 BC), the successor to Tuthmosis III, was also active in central Syria, in the land of Takhshi (the northern Bekaa Valley), near Qatna (in the area of modern Homs), and Qadesh (on the Orontes). Qadesh, it seems, remained the northernmost outpost of Egyptian military power in inland Syria. Amenhotep and Tuthmosis IV (*c.* 1400 BC) subsequently arranged peaceful relations with Hurri-Mitanni, strengthened by dynastic marriages and gift exchanges. The renewed strength of the Hittite state and the growing Hittite interest in Syria provides the background to this rapprochement between the former rivals, Egypt and Mitanni.

The Hittites in Syria

The cuneiform letters discovered in the royal residence at Amarna, in middle Egypt, give the clearest picture of Hittite intervention in Syria. Although not bearing dates, leaving their chronology in dispute (Rainey, 1978), these fourteenth-century BC letters address the political situation both in Syria and in Palestine. The Hittite records from the capital Hattusas (Boghazkale/Boghazköy) in central Anatolia and from Ugarit (Ras Shamra) provide additional archival sources (Klengel, 1965–70). The Egyptian topographical lists and other inscriptions (Helck, 1962; Ahituv, 1984), and some scattered cuneiform tables from various Syrian towns (Edzard, 1985, pp. 248–59) add supplementary evidence.

These rich sources contain valuable information about changing overlordship in central and northern Syria. Hittite domination replaced that of Mitanni, and a son of the Hittite great king Suppiluliumas occupied Carchemish (on the Euphrates) as viceroy for Syria. Egypt continued to control territories south of Ugarit and the Homs plain. Tensions and conflict between the Hittites and Egyptians after the so-called 'Amarna Age' did not substantially alter this partition of Syro-Palestine (Murnane, 1985; Kitchen, 1982). After avoiding open confrontation during the time of Mursilis II, the Egyptian Seti I began penetrating into Hittite central Syria, a pressure that culminated in the famous battle between the Egyptian Ramesses II and the Hittite Muwatallis at Qadesh (c. 1275 BC) (Kuschke, 1979; Kadry, 1981). A mood of reconciliation prevailed soon afterward, marked by a peace treaty between Ramesses II and Hattusilis III (Spalinger, 1981) that recognized the territorial status quo and spheres of domination in Syro-Palestine. Mutual awareness of the growing Assyrian threat in northern Mesopotamia probably contributed to the 'brotherhood' established between these two kings.

Socio-political developments

The most important centres documented in the textual sources included the following places: Carchemish, on the middle Euphrates, was the seat of a Hittite dynasty, while Emar (Meskene), at the great bend of the river, was an important harbour. Halab/Aleppo, in the north Syrian plain, contained a highly venerated temple of the weather-god and, for several years, the residence of another branch of the Hittite royal house; the land of Nukhashe lay in the fertile plain to the south. The Orontes river provided the setting for numerous places, notably Alalakh near the river's mouth, Niya and its hinterland in the Ghab Valley, Qadesh (Tell Nebi Mend), and Tunip (probably near Qadesh). Qatna (Mishrife), a forerunner of Homs on overland trade routes, lay adjacent to the Orontes. Other important stations of the interior included Tadmur (Palmyra) in the Syrian desert to the north, and Timashqi (Damascus) at the edge of the Anti-Lebanon mountain range to the south. Kumidi (Kamid el Loz), the temporary residence of a high Egyptian official, sat in the Bekaa Valley within the mountains. 'Canaanite' centres, such as Hazor and Megiddo, Shechem and Jerusalem, Gezer and Lachish, flourished in Palestine. The Mediterranean coast hosted a string of important places, including Ugarit, Arwad/Ruad, the land of Amurru with its town Sumur in the Akkar plain, Gubla/Byblos, Beruta/Beirut, Sidon, Tyre, Akko, Jaffa, Ashdod, Ashkalon and Gaza.

These cities and towns contained stratified societies, the precise nature of which is well known to any degree only at Ugarit, Emar and, slightly earlier, Alalakh. The Ugarit archives in particular reveal the dominance of the palace in the economic as well as political sphere. The economic activities of the palace extended to long-distance trade (a near if not total monopoly) and to craftsmen and craft production, and also to large agricultural holdings. A basic division of people into 'freemen' and 'men of the king' reflected the importance of the palace; the power of the palace extended over 'free' communities in administrative and fiscal ways. Even 'free' agricultural communities contained a hierarchical order, and by the Late Bronze Age nuclear families and readily alienable land had replaced the extended family organization of such villages. These changes placed communities under severe stress, resulting in high indebtedness and growing rates of flight; the more remote countryside seems to have experienced a degree of depopulation, as people turned to pastoralism and/or brigandage to escape oppressive relations with the palace and its representatives (Dietrich and Loretz, 1966; Liverani, 1974).

Better understood are the systems by which the Hittites and Egyptians dominated their Syro-Palestinian clients. These systems differed in the manner by which the metropoles controlled the political and economic affairs of the Syro-Palestinian lands. The Hittites relied mainly on vassal treaties, sworn by the various local leaders and supervised by the Hittite viceroy at Carchemish. In contrast, the Egyptians installed officials in places without local rulers, for example at Gaza, Kumidi and, for a time, Sumur; the Egyptian royal family owned land and estates in Palestine and Syria just as it did in the Nile Valley. Although the Egyptian and Hittite overlords were eager to suppress open local conflicts, continued polycentrism and local rivalries characterized the relations between the various principalities, cities and tribal units of Syro-Palestine. The classic example of local rivalry, expressed in the Amarna archives, is that between Rib-Addi of Byblos and Abdu-Ashirta and Aziru of Amurru, and the former's efforts to enlist active Egyptian support against his enemies. The part of the *apiru* in regional political affairs is much discussed, with this class of people being cast in the role of deracinated and turbulent groups that could act as mercenaries, factional clients or brigands.

Archaeological investigations document temple architecture with long or wide cellas, walled courtyards with altars and incense burners; statues of the gods were not freely visible to the public. Besides the temples, open-air cult centres also existed, located at holy stones or trees. Palace architecture is best seen at Ugarit, where the buildings had upper floors and contained both archives and workshops. The great palace at Ugarit covered nearly a hectare. Vaulted tombs lay below it, maintaining the royal family's connection to the past even after death. The rural communities in the farmlands surrounding these urban centres are largely unknown.

Agriculture, specialized handicraft and trade provided the economic foundations for these societies. The richest agricultural land lay in the fertile plains of northern and central Syria, in some small areas of Palestine, and in the Akkar plain and the Ugarit hinterland along the coast. Hilly regions supported vine and olives, the wine and oil from which was in part exported. The various Syro-Palestinian states also contained extensive pasturelands, especially in hill country and drier steppe; at least at Ugarit, most of the pasture belonged to the crown, which contracted out the herding of its large flocks. In drier and less reliably watered zones, nomadic sheep and goat herding dominated local economic activities. The relationships between nomadic and settled, tribal and urban state were extremely complex, and not limited to the antagonisms usually implied by this dichotomy, but also encompassed exchanges of specialized products, clientage, flexible responses to socio-political and environmental stresses, and so forth.

During the Late Bronze Age, craft products often betray a mingling of different styles and traditions. Local sculpture reveals a trend toward abstraction, at least for parts of Syria and Palestine. The more valuable bronzes, especially those of the coastal zone, reveal a strong Egyptian influence, and also a mastery of metallurgy. Syro-Palestinian ivory-carving was famous, and sometimes borrowed its motifs from Egypt. Some objects clearly show a combination of local and foreign elements, thus reflecting the composite culture of the eastern Mediterranean (Plate 78). The seals in particular give strong indications of the different elements that merged in the arts of Syria and Palestine: toward the end of the second millennium the use of scarabs, an Egyptian device, increased, while in northern Syria the Hittite stamp seal became common. Tyrian purple dye, derived from the murex sea snail and famous in classical antiquity, already existed in the Late Bronze Age; archaeological evidence documents this industry at places like Ugarit (Minet al-Beida), Sarepta, Akko, and elsewhere in the eastern Mediterranean.

Trade was an important source of wealth, particularly to coastal cities or those on established overland routes. Already, in the Middle Bronze Age, the eastern Mediterranean and the Levant had become a major sphere of interregional commercial exchange. During the Late Bronze Age, Mycenaean trade had a strong impact on Syro-Palestinian centres, as revealed both in the cuneiform texts from Ugarit and in archaeological evidence. The wide distribution of Mycenaean pottery and its local imitations (Hankey, 1967), and of oxhide copper ingots (Klengel, 1978b) reveal the close relationship between the Levant and the Aegean world; the copper ingots, most of which came from Cyprus, formed the basic commodity of this trade as revealed from shipwrecks (Bass, 1986). Palace households were the most important investors in trade, but private trade also existed, as demonstrated by documents from private houses as well as the palace (Courtois, 1979).

Writing

The texts from Ugarit were written not only in syllabic Akkadian, but also in a kind of alphabetic script with only thirty cuneiform signs; this alphabetic script was most commonly used for economic and literary documents. Other places in Syro-Palestine have provided examples of this writing, but the great majority of alphabetic texts occur at Ugarit. These 'Ugaritic' texts, with characters placed in a fixed order ('ABC') show that the Ugarit alphabet was one of the forerunners of the writing system now used in most parts of the world. Innovations in simplified scripts, suitable not only to clay and stone but also to papyrus and parchment, also occurred elsewhere in the Levant.   The invention of this alphabetic writing is one of the major achievements of Late Bronze Age Syria (Rollig, 1985; Bordreuil, 1979), a region where Mesopotamian and Egyptian influences met, and where multiple contacts with other peoples favoured a writing system more suitable for foreign toponyms and personal names. The archives from Ugarit reveal the formation of a literary tradition, built upon the existing oral mechanisms by which tradition passed from generation to generation. This literary development may have been a local response to the political situation of the Late Bronze Age – foreign domination.

Literature and religion

The Ugarit texts leave a record of the mythology and religion in coastal Syria, and they make possible comparisons with the religion and poetry of the Old Testament. The most interesting mythological texts come from libraries of priests, the scholars of the day, and some of the texts obviously were intended to be recited on different – not only cult – occasions (Rollig, 1978).

The pantheon of Ugarit focused on representations of the natural forces critical to fertility and agriculture in a dry-farming region. The most important of these gods was Baal, god of storm and rain. In contrast to El, father of the gods and head of the pantheon, Baal represented the active aspect of divinity, and the myths portray him as youthful and energetic. Among the goddesses, Ashirat had the highest rank; she was El's wife and responsible for the benevolent aspects of the ocean. Yam represented the ocean itself, and was the enemy of Baal, that is, of fertility. Ashtar was the god of water in the netherworld; Ashtarte, goddess of fertility, was his female counterpart, and was venerated in all Syro-Palestine throughout the ages (cf. the 'Dea Syria' of classical antiquity). Anat was the goddess of love, and also of war, a combination of responsibilities similar to that of the Mesopotamian Ishtar. Mut was the god of death, ruling during the season of aridity and infertility, and therefore also an enemy of Baal. Shapash was the sun-goddess, Kusharu (Koshar-wa-hasis) god of handicrafts and fine arts. The last is thought to have derived from Crete or Egypt, perhaps a reflection of the influence of these regions on the Levant.

Baal was the central figure in the myth cycle that formed the heart of the literary tradition at Ugarit. Although the order of the various tablets is not yet established with certainty, the cycle can be reconstructed as follows. Baal, after El honours him, wants a palace of his own, to be built on top of the mountain Zaphon (Hazzi in cuneiform, Mons Cassius in antiquity, the modern Jebel al-Akra). Baal gains the assistance of his sister Anat in this project; the assembly of the gods agrees and El himself confirms the decision – an early 'democratic' procedure projected into the divine world. Kusharu, the architect, comes from Crete, an obvious reference to the impression left by Minoan palaces or to the activities of Minoan master builders in Syria. Baal has to battle with his rival Yam; he is victorious and gains the title of king, the obvious prerequisite for living in a palace. After an agreement with El and his wife Ashirat, the palace construction begins. Anxious because of the wet sea winds sent by the enemy Yam, Baal rejects Kusharu's proposal to make windows. But Baal later changes his mind, because he wants openings through which to send out lightning and thunder. The next episode is Baal's conflict with Mut, death. Baal goes to the netherworld, taking with him his clouds, wind, and rain – the dry season begins. Anat discovers his body, and buries it with immense sacrifices. But at the close of the arid season, Anat succeeds in overcoming Mut. Baal revives and regains rule; the wet season begins, restoring fertility to the land.

Besides additional fragments of the Baal cycle, other myths describe the deeds of other gods, and point out their merits and imperfections. The Ugarit texts also relate epic tales, which contain the same theme of drought and dying vegetation. One such tale is the story of Aqhat. Aqhat, king Danel's son, owns a bow that Anat desires to possess. She kills Aqhat, bringing drought and crop failure. Aqhat's father and sister, Pughat, find his body and mourn, after which time Pughat sets out to revenge her brother's death. The text breaks off at this point, but the remainder of the story doubtless describes Aqhat's revival and the restoration of fertility. Another epic tale concerns the fate of King Keret/Kuritu, whose illness damages the vegetation. The problems of fertility and of life and death clearly prevailed in the literary tradition of Syria, and perhaps also of the 'Canaanite' centres of Palestine.

THE EARLY IRON AGE (1200–800 BC)

According to scholarly consensus, the Late Bronze Age ended in western Asia around 1200 BC. The following period is conventionally named after another metal, iron. This metal was known in earlier times but now came into more common use in the instruments of production, at least toward the end of this period. Iron tools facilitated cultivating difficult soils, digging wells and cutting trees (Snodgrass, 1980). Another important innovation of the period was the use of camels in transportation. The camel's ability to thrive with less frequent watering opened new routes through desert areas, and in particular shortened the trip between Mesopotamian cities and the Mediterranean coast, a contributing factor in the growth of Phoenician trade (Zarins, 1989; Wapnish, 1984).

The transition between the Late Bronze Age and the Iron Age in Syro-Palestine was marked by massive social change. New groups of people moved into the region, while other groups already present formed new ethnic identities. The imperial societies to the north and south collapsed (the Hittites) or withdrew from the Levant (Egypt); although Assyria did exert intermittent pressure in western Syria, the early phase of the Iron Age was one of extreme political fragmentation. In many parts of Syro-Palestine (especially in the south and in upland regions), the Bronze Age urban centres went into decline, and large numbers of people shifted to village life or pastoralism. New kingdoms very quickly emerged, however, and the political history of the Iron Age was one of competition between these petty states, and then efforts to fend off renewed Assyrian imperialism, beginning in the ninth century BC.

Ethnic changes at the beginning of the Iron Age

The 'Canaanite' culture of the second millennium is clearly discernible as the fostering soil for the variants of the ancient West Asian culture that emerged and flourished during the Early Iron Age. The ethnic changes did not interrupt the basic development of political and cultural life, but added new facets and contributed to the 'unity in diversity' which already characterized Syro-Palestinian culture during the Late Bronze Age.

The period around 1200 BC is often called that of the 'Sea Peoples', after a collective designation in Egyptian inscriptions; individually named groups within the wider designation include the Peleset, Tjekker, Sheklesh, Denen and Weshesh (Helck, 1976; Schachermeyr, 1982; Sandars, 1985). The Egyptian sources represented these groups as raiders from across the sea, often in alliance with land-based groups, during the time of Merenptah and Ramesses III. Considerable controversy attends the issue of the geographical origin and the social identity of the Sea Peoples, and the nature and causes of their movements in the eastern Mediterranean. Traditional views regard the Sea Peoples as groups migrating southward from south-eastern Europe, or as marauders displaced from their homelands by other migratory groups (for example, the 'Dorian invasion' of Greece). More recent interpretations, confronting the historical ambiguities of the period, combine external invasions, flight and social revolution as factors that created a new political landscape, but did not mark a complete cultural rupture with the past (Bienkowski, 1982; Muhly, 1984).

Ramesses III stopped the Peleset in the Egyptian zone of Syria, where this group then settled along the southern coast, becoming the Philistines of the Biblical tradition, and giving their name to the region (Palestine). In this new location, the Peleset influenced the local Canaanite culture, but also quickly assimilated. During the twelfth/eleventh centuries, the Peleset penetrated farther into inland Palestine, and there clashed both with local Canaanite rulers and with the Israelites. The Peleset left no documents of their own, and information about their history derives from archaeological observations (Dothan, 1982) and from the records of their enemies, including the Egyptian texts already mentioned and the Biblical tradition.

The Israelites first appear in historical sources at the end of the thirteenth century (c. 1207 BC), when the so-called 'Israel stela' of Merenptah lists them among other places and people of the southern Levant (Stager, 1985a). The Biblical tradition of Israelite origins describes invasion from the desert and conquest of existing communities. Recent scholarship casts considerable doubt on this account, preferring to see a social transformation during the thirteenth-eleventh centuries of groups already in the area. The two main interpretations consider infiltration and sedentarization of herders who had previously existed on the fringes of farming communities, or peasant revolts against Bronze Age urban élites. Both views regard the dispersed village communities in the hill country of the southern Levant at the beginning of the Iron Age as a response to the political upheavals at the end of the Late Bronze Age (Freedman and Graf, 1983; Coote and Whitelam, 1987, Finkelstein, 1988). The conflict between the Philistines and Israelites probably accelerated the development of ethnic identity and complex political organization among the Israelite tribes (Thiel, 1980).

Several other groups also came into existence in the southern Levant, including the Edomites, Moabites and Ammonites. These tribal peoples were related to the Israelites, but living east of the Jordan river. Farther north, in Syria, other movements of people also established new identities. The Aramaeans had existed on the fringe of the Syrian desert during the Late Bronze Age; these people now infiltrated the greater part of Syria. Luwian elements, originating in south-eastern Anatolia and speaking an Indo-European language, had been present in northernmost Syria during the Late Bronze Age. This population increased in number after the collapse of the Hittite empire. Both Aramaeans and Luwians mixed with the indigenous population to develop a culture often called 'Syro-Hittite'.

Political developments in the Iron Age

The end of the Hittite empire and the decline of Egyptian influence brought about a political vacuum in Syria and Palestine, favourable to the political ambitions of those who now ruled the country without an overlord. An Egyptian text, a tale about the adventures of Wenamon (Unamun) in his travel to Syria (placed around 1077 BC)(Blumenthal, 1982), illuminates the situation at the time. The ruler of Gubla/Byblos left unacknowledged Egypt's traditional claim to deliveries of cedarwood. At about the same time, the Assyrian Tiglath-Pileser I (1114–1076 BC) campaigned in Syria, seeking timber for a temple of Ashur and control over caravan routes to the Mediterranean. He reached the coast and received tribute from Gubla/Byblos, Sidon and Armada/Arwad. No political power in Syria was able to resist the Assyrian raid.

The first political entities to gain some importance in Early Iron Age Syro-Palestine were these same coastal cities, especially Tyre, Sidon and Gubla/Byblos. The inroads of the Sea Peoples did not seriously affect trade at these centres, although some partners suffered from the political and ethnic changes of the time, and Ugarit in the north disappeared. Phoenicia was not one state, but rather a loose association of cities and adjacent territories, ruled by local princes and a mercantile aristocracy. But the Phoenician centres had a common historical and religious tradition, a common culture and a special system of writing; their Greek trading partners perceived them as a nation, and gave them a collective name, Phoenicia. Tyre was the predominant city until around 700 BC; Sidon assumed the political lead in the sixth century. Historically information about these cities derives from two sources. The Biblical tradition mentions relations with Phoenician cities, and notably Tyre under Hiram, Solomon's contemporary (c. 950 BC) (Katzenstein, 1973, pp. 77 ff; Donner, 1982). Assyrian military pressure on the Syrian coast renewed in the ninth century, and beginning with the inscriptions of Ashurnasirpal II and Shalmaneser III the Assyrian sources provide details about the Phoenician cities.

The expansion of Phoenician trade had already begun during the eleventh century, marked by the establishment of trading posts, or colonies. Phoenician colonization occurred in Cyprus, Anatolia, Rhodes, Greece, Egypt, Malta, Sicily and even Sardinia. Greek pottery of the tenth century discovered at Tyre and Bassit (in Syria) marks the earliest Iron Age contacts between these two worlds (Courbin, 1990). The Phoenicians founded the colony at Carthage by the end of the ninth century; Carthage in turn established its own colonies in the western Mediterranean and the African Atlantic coast. In other directions, Phoenician trading contacts reached far into the Asiatic hinterland, and Hiram of Tyre is said to have undertaken, in concert with Solomon of Israel, commercial ventures into the Red Sea. The Phoenician improvements in maritime architecture that allowed shipping to cross the open sea were certainly connected to this long-distance trade (Klengel, 1979, pp. 195 ff).

The Phoenician cities engaged not only in a carrying trade, as middlemen between producers and consumers, but also themselves produced commodities for export. The most prominent industries in this respect were purple dyeing, glass making, metal working, and wood and ivory carving. The region also produced some specialized agricultural goods suitable for export, including wine, olives and figs.

These economic activities were the background for a decisive step forward in the development of writing. Based on the experiments already accomplished in the Late Bronze Age, the Phoenicians introduced an alphabetic linear script with twenty-two consonantal signs and written from right to left. Papyrus and parchment became the favoured media for this script — the fragility of these materials relative to the stone and other durable media of earlier writing doubtless accounts for the paucity of surviving textual evidence from Phoenicia itself (Donner and Rollig, 1966–9) (Plate 79). The new Phoenician script spread through western Asia, and the Aramaean variant provided the foundation for other scripts as far away as India, central Asia and Indonesia. The Greeks adapted the linear writing to their own language; the Phoenician system thus became the source of the Latin alphabet now used in most parts of the world. The 'invention' of linear alphabetic writing is one of the most important achievements we owe to ancient west Asia (Rollig, 1985).

Aramaean states

The principalities of the hinterland were in close contact with the coastal cities. A series of new political entities, ruled by Aramaean or 'Hittite' (Luwian) princes arose in Syria. Some of them appear in the written tradition with the name of the legendary ancestor of the dynasty and the term for 'house': (bit PN). Aram-Damascus and Hamath were the most important of these principalities, at the head of Syrian resistance to Assyrian attack in the ninth century. Other polities included Bit Rehob on the upper Jordan, Zoba on the upper Orontes, Bit Agusi around Aleppo, and Carchemish on the Euphrates. The political history of these states is poorly known from the Aramaic or Luwian, Biblical and Assyrian texts (Grayson, 1991); their permanent rivalries and shifting coalitions render a historical evaluation of the Syrian states all the more difficult (Sader, 1987).

Zoba was the first important state in southern Syria, around 1000 BC. This principality extended as far as Damascus and regions east of the Jordan, coming into unsuccessful conflict with Israel. The princes of Damascus then assumed the leading role, taking political advantage of the partition of Israel and Judah after Solomon's death.

During the ninth century, Assyria mounted a series of campaigns in Syria and Palestine, beginning with the raid of Ashurnasirpal II (883–859 BC) that reached the Mediterranean Sea. In 853 BC, Adad-'idri of Damascus and Irkhuleni of Hamath headed a coalition against the Assyrian Shalmaneser III (858–824 BC); the coalition counted Israel, Musri, Irqanata, Arwad, Ammon and camel-riding Arabs (Eph'al, 1982) among its twelve members. Although Shalmaneser defeated this coalition near Qarqar on the Orontes, Damascus and Hamath afterward remained the core of Syrian resistance, and for a time prevented the Assyrians from gaining decisive success in Syria. The Assyrian king Adad-nirari III (810–783 BC) also campaigned extensively in Syria and Palestine, reaching Damascus and extorting tribute from most principalities and peoples of the Levant as far south as Israel. The alliances in the face of the common external danger did not prevent local conflicts between the various Syrian rulers. The Tell Afis stela records an example of such a conflict, in this case the war between Barhadad III of Damascus and Zakir of Hamath, in c. 800 BC (Donner and Rollig, 1966–9, pp. 204 ff).

Assyrian power went into a brief decline during the first part of the eighth century, due to internal political disorder. Various northern Syrian cities went into revolt, and some northern princes tried to form alliances with the king of Urartu, who at the time was extending his influence toward the Mediterranean Sea. This unstable situation illuminates the circumstances of a treaty between the Assyrian Ashurnirari V (753–745 BC) and Mati'el of Bit Agusi; Mati'el also entered into treaties with other principalities (the Sfire stelae). The accession of Tiglath-Pileser III (744–727 BC) to the Assyrian throne marked the renewal of successful Assyrian aggression westward. This king gained victory over the Syrian and Palestinian states, reducing them to provinces of the Assyrian empire (Kessler, 1975; Oded, 1974).

Israel

The process is much discussed by which an urban state organization grew out of the village tribal social structure of the initial Israelite settlement. Recent accounts emphasize technological factors (iron agricultural tools, terracing, lime-lined cisterns), expanded agricultural production, growing population numbers, social competition for wealth, renewal of regional trading relations, political clientage that cut across family groups and the emergence of regional cult centres (Stager, 1985b). In the Biblical account, Saul's election as the (military) king was still a 'democratic' act, under the pressure of Philistine expansion. David, offspring of the 'house of Judah', united Israel and Judah under his rule, around 1000 BC, and then expanded his kingdom into southern Syria and the Transjordan (Malamat, 1983). Jerusalem, a former Jebusite fortress, became the capital and, with the transfer of the 'ark of the covenant', the state religious centre.

Solomon, David's successor, focused his efforts on administrative reform and military reorganization. He divided the kingdom into districts whose boundaries followed those of the old tribal divisions and the formerly independent Canaanite city-states. The incorporation of these city-states, already begun under David, brought an increased prosperity to the ruling class in Israel, and improved the material standard of living. On the other hand, the mass of people were subjected to growing economic exploitation, and had to bear the burden of military expansion and border defence. Solomon was active in foreign trade, partly in partnership with Hiram of Tyre, and had commercial contacts with southern Arabia along the 'incense road' (thus the Biblical story of the queen of Sheba).

After Solomon's death, the united kingdom split into two political entities: Israel and Judah. Each warred with its Aramaean neighbours to the north; and the Assyrian imperial expansion threatened both. Israel became part of the Assyrian empire in 721, when Sargon II took Samaria, and deported many people, replacing them with natives of Babylonia and Hamath. Judah became a client after Sennacherib defeated Hezekiah in 701 BC.

Cultural development during the Early Iron Age

Political and economic polycentrism was the most obvious characteristic of Syro-Palestine during the Early Iron Age, just as in earlier times. Rivalry, temporary opportunistic coalitions, and personal ambitions of local rulers decided political events, and at the same time ensured a regional disunity that encouraged foreign intervention. Social tensions between nomadic tribal groups, villagers and urban dwellers played an important role, sometimes in combination with socio-economic differentiation and its political consequences, in maintaining this regional disunity. The ethnic movements and formation of new ethnic identities during the late second millennium did not seriously affect the long-lasting trade connections and handicraft traditions of the region.

Despite the differences and variants in political structure and orientation, economic development, and language across Syro-Palestine, the region presented a certain 'unity in diversity' in religion and culture. Most of the gods already venerated during the Bronze Age figured also in Early Iron Age beliefs. However, new local panthea and religious practices emerged, reflecting the political and economic polycentrism of the region. Numerous variants of Baal, or Hadad in north-

ern Syria, the weather-god and 'lord', appeared; epithets sometimes differentiate these Baals. The Phoenician colonization spread worship of Baal and other Syrian gods to other regions, thus extending the influence of Oriental religion far beyond its core area. Melqart, the patron deity of Tyre, was now widely venerated in the Mediterranean basin. Eshmun, originally a typical god of Gubla/Bylos, became famous as a god of medicine, and later was equated with Asclepios. The west knew Ashtarte as Tanit. On the other hand, the Egyptian Bes was very popular in Syria, as shown by the many amulets and small figurines discovered in Syrian sites. Baal's role as a vegetation-god received a special protagonist in Adon ('master'), the Greek Adonis, whose death and revival marked the seasons (Rollig, 1973).

The cult of Yahweh, the tribal god of Israel, had to compete with the traditional Canaanite gods, and with the influence of these gods on the settled Israelites. The prophetic tradition interpreted the increasing social tensions of monarchy as an indication of divine anger for the veneration of other gods, especially Baal and Ashtarte. The prophets made their appearance in the ninth century in Israel, and in the eighth century in Judah. Their demand for the restoration of earlier (tribal) social and religious conditions was a programmatic solution to the crisis that centred on the abolition of foreign cults. The cultic reform of Josiah at the end of the seventh century only partially fulfilled these demands. At the same time, the difficult political and social situation gave rise to the first written traditions, including historiography, later to be inserted into the Old Testament. Hebrew literature closely followed Canaanite models of syntax, style and metre.

Archaeological evidence reflects cultural progress in Syria and Palestine. Both areas, and especially Syria, continued to function as a bridge and meeting place for foreign cultural achievements and techniques. Phoenicia and the Philistines, Aramaeans, Syro-Hittites and Israelites created variants of the ancient west Asian culture which were often hardly distinguishable. The reliefs on orthostats and the monumental sculptures from palaces, temples and gates of Syro-Palestinian cities express the peculiarity of artistic development in the region. These monuments point to local variants of imagination and art, but also to different receptions of foreign influence. Besides commerce, the foundations of wealth in Syro-Palestinian centres continued to rest in specialized agriculture (olives, wine) and in craft production; the latter included ivory and wood carving, metallurgy, glass and dyed textiles (especially purple). The period around 700 BC witnessed the loss of political independence, but did not fundamentally change the basic patterns of life in this region of western Asia.

BIBLIOGRAPHY

AHITUV, S. 1984. *Canaanite Toponyms in Ancient Egyptian Documents.* Jerusalem.

ASTOUR, M. 1978. Les Hourrites en Syrie du Nord: rapport sommaire. *Rev. Hittite Asianique* (Paris), Vol. 36, pp. 1–22.

BARRELET, M. T. et al. 1977. *Methodologique et critiques, I: Problèmes concernant les Hurrites.* Paris.

BASS, G. 1986. A Bronze Age Shipwreck at Ulu Burun (Kas): 1984 Campaign. *Am. J. Archaeol.* (Boston, Mass.), Vol. 90, pp. 269–96.

BIENKOWSKI, P. 1982. Some Remarks on the Practice of Cremation in the Levant. *Levant* (London), Vol. 14, pp. 80–9.

BLUMENTHAL, E. 1982. *Altägyptische Reiseerzählungen.* Leipzig.

BORDREUIL, P. 1979. L'inscription phenicienne de Sarafand en cuneiformes alphabetiques. *Ugarit-Forsch.* (Neukirchen-Vluyn), Vol. 11, p. 63.

CADOGAN, G. 1973. Patterns in the Distribution of Mycenaean Pottery in the Eastern Mediterranean. In: International Symposium 'The Mycenaeans in the Eastern Mediterranean', Nicosia, 1972. *Acts.* Nicosia.

COOTE, R.; WHITELAM, K. 1987. *The Emergence of Early Israel in Historical Perspective.* Sheffield.

COURBIN, C. 1990. Fragments d'amphore protogéometriques. In: MATTHIAE, P.; LOONS, M. VAN; WEISS, H. (eds), *Resurrecting the Past.* Leiden. pp. 49–64.

COURTOIS, J. C. 1979. Ras Shamra: Archéologie du site. In: *Supplément au Dictionnaire de la Bible.* Paris. Vol. 9, pp. 1222–94.

DIETRICH, M.; LORETZ, O. 1966–9. Die soziale Struktur von Alalakh und Ugarit I–II. *Welt Orients* (Göttingen), Vol. 3, pp. 188–205, Vol. 5, pp. 57–93.

—— 1981. Die Inschrift der Statue des Königs Idrimi von Alalah. *Ugarit-Forsch.* (Neukirchen-Vluyn), Vol. 13, pp. 201–69.

DONNER, H. 1982. Israel und Tyrus im Zeitalter Davids und Salomons. *J. Northwest semit. Lang.* (Leiden), Vol. 10, pp. 44 ff.

DONNER, H.; ROLLIG, W. 1966–9. *Kanaanaische und aramäische Inschriften, I–III.* Wiesbaden.

DOTHAN, T. 1982. *The Philistines and Their Material Culture.* New Haven, Conn.

EDZARD, D. O. 1985. Amarna und die Archive seiner Korrespondenten zwischen Ugarit und Gaza. In: International Congress on Biblical Archaeology, Jerusalem, April 1984. *Biblical Archaeology Today.* (Jerusalem), pp. 248–59.

EPH'AL, I. 1982. *The Ancient Arabs: Nomads on the Borders of the Fertile Crescent, 9th–5th Centuries BC.* Jerusalem.

FINKELSTEIN, I. 1988. *The Archaeology of the Israelite Settlement.* Jerusalem.

FREEDMAN, D. N.; GRAF, D. (eds) 1983. *Palestine in Transition: The Emergence of Ancient Israel.* Sheffield.

FRITZ, V. 1987. Conquest or Settlement, the Early Iron Age of Palestine. *Biblic. Archaeol.* (Cambridge, Mass.), Vol. 50, pp. 84–100.

GRAYSON, A. K. 1991. *Assyrian Rulers of the Early First Millennium BC.* Toronto.

HANKEY, V. 1967. Mycenaean Pottery in the Middle East. *Annu. Br. Sch. Athens* (London), Vol. 62, pp. 107–47.

HELCK, W. 1962. *Die Beziehungen Ägyptens zu Vorderasien im 3. und 2. Jahrtausend v. Chr.* Wiesbaden.

—— 1979. Die Seevölker in ägyptischen Quellen. In: MÜLLER-KARPE, H. (ed.), *Jahresbericht des Instituts für Vorgeschichte der Universität Frankfurt a.M., 1976: Geschichte des 13. und 12. Jahrhunderts v. Chr.* Darmstadt. pp. 132 ff.

HROUDA, B. 1985. Zum Problem der Hurriter. *Mari, Ann. Rech. interdiscip.* (Paris), Vol. 4, pp. 595–613.

KADRY, A. 1981. Some Comments on the Qadesh Battle. *Bull. Centen.* (Cairo), Vol. 81, pp. 47–55.

KATZENSTEIN, H. J. 1973. *The History of Tyre.* Jerusalem.

KESSLER, K. 1975. Die Anzahl der assyrischen Provinzen des Jahres 738 v. Chr. in Nordsyrien. *Welt Orients* (Göttingen), Vol. 8, pp. 49–63.

KITCHEN, K. A. 1982. *Pharaoh Triumphant: The Life and Times of Ramesses II, King of Egypt.* Warminster.

KLENGEL, H. 1965–70. *Geschichte Syriens im 2. Jahrtausend v.u. Z.* Berlin.

—— 1978a. Mitanni: Probleme seiner Expansion und politischen Struktur. *Rev. Hittite Asianique* (Paris), Vol. 36, pp. 91–115.

—— 1978b. Vorderasien und Ägäis. Ein Überlick über den bronzezeitlichen Handel. In: COBLENZ, W.; HORST, F., *Mitteleuropäische Bronzezeit. Beiträge zur Archaeologie und Geschichte.* Berlin. pp. 5–25.

—— 1979. *Handel und Händler im alten Orient.* Wien.

—— 1982. Zur Rolle des Eisens im vorhellenistischen Vorderasien. In: HERRMANN, J.; SELLNOW, I., *Produktivkräfte und Gesselschaftsformationen in vorkapitalistischer Zeit.* Berlin. pp. 179–89.

KRAUSS, R. 1985. *Sothis- und Monddaten. Studien zur astronomischen und technischen Chronologie Altägyptens.* Hildesheim.

KUSCHKE, A. 1979. Das Terrain der Schlacht bei Qades die Anmarschwege Ramses' II. *Z. dtsch. Paläst. Ver.* (Stuttgart), Vol. 95, pp. 7–35.

LIVERANI, M. 1974. La royauté syrienne de l'âge du bronze récent. In: GARELLI, P. (ed.), *Le palais et la royauté.* Paris. pp. 329–33.

LUCKENBILL, D. D. 1926–7. *Ancient Records of Assyria and Babylonia,* I–II. Chicago, Ill.

MALAMAT, A. 1983. *Das davidische und salomonische Königreich und seine Beziehungen zu Ägypten und Syrien: Zur Entstehung eines Grossreichs.* Wien.

MUHLY, J. D. 1984; The Role of the Sea People in Cyprus during the LCIII Period. In: KARAGEORGHIS, V.; MUHLY, J. D., *Cyprus at the Close of the Late Bronze Age.* Nicosia. pp. 39–55.

MURNANE, W. J. 1985. *The Road to Kadesh. A Historical Interpretation of the Battle Reliefs of King Sety I at Karnak.* Chicago, Ill.

ODED, B. 1974. The Phoenician Cities and the Assyrian Empire in the Time of Tiglath-pileser III. *Z. dtsch. Paläst. Ver.* (Stuttgart), Vol. 90, pp. 38–49.

RAINEY, A. F. 1978. *El Amarna Tablets 359–379.* Neukirchen-Vuyn. (Alter Orient Altes Testam., 8.)

ROLLIG, W. 1973. Die Religion Altsyriens. In: MANN, U. (ed.), *Theologie und Religionswissenschaft.* Darmstadt. pp. 86–105.

—— (ed.) 1978. *Neues Handbuch der Literaturwissenschaft. Altorientalische Literaturen.* Wiesbaden.

—— 1985 Über die Anfääge unsere Alphabets. *Altertum* (Berlin), Vol. 31, pp. 83–91.

SADER, H. 1987. *Les états araméens de Syrie depuis leur fondation jusqu'à leur transformation en provinces assyriennes.* Wiesbaden.

SANDARS, N. K. 1985. *The Sea Peoples, Warriors of the Ancient Mediterranean.* London.

SCHACHERMEYR, F. 1982. *Die Levante im Zeitalter der Wanderugen.* Wien.

SNODGRASS, A. 1980. Iron and Early Metallurgy in the Mediterranean. In: WERTIME, T.; MUHLY, J. D. (eds), *The Coming of the Age of Iron.* New Haven, Conn.

SPALINGER, A. 1981. Considerations on the Hittite Treaty between Egypt and Hatti. *Stud. altägypt. Kult.* (Hamburg), Vol. 9, pp. 299–348.

STAGER, L. E. 1985a. Merenptah, Israel and Sea Peoples, New Light on an Old Relief. *Eretz-Israel* (Jerusalem), Vol. 18, pp. 56–64.

—— 1985b. The Archaeology of the Family in Ancient Israel. *Bull. am. Sch. Orient. res.* (Cambridge, Mass.), Vol. 260, pp. 1–35.

STECH-WHEELER, T. et al. 1981. Iron at Taanach and Early Iron Metallurgy in the Eastern Mediterranean. *Am. J. Archaeol.* (Princeton, N.J.), Vol. 85, pp. 245–68.

THIEL, W. 1980. *Die soziale Entwicklung Israels in vorstaatlicher Zeit.* Neukirchen-Vluyn.

WAPNISH, P. 1984. The Dromedary and Bactrian Camel in Levantine Historical Settings: The Evidence from Tell Jemmeh. In: CLUTTON-BROCK, J.; GRIGSON, C. (eds), *Animals and Archaeology.* London. Vol. 3, pp. 171–87.

WILHELM, G. 1982. *Grundzüge der Geschichte und Kultur der Hurriter.* Darmstadt.

ZARINS, J. 1989. Pastoralism in Southwest Asia: The Second Millennium BC. In: CLUTTON-BROCK, J. (ed.), *The Walking Larder: Patterns of Domestication, Pastoralism, and Predation.* London. pp. 127–55.

12.3
ANATOLIA

Ekrem Akurgal

This account of Anatolian civilizations is based on the classification used by prehistorians, since only in central Anatolia is there evidence of a proto-historic period with the Hattian people (2500–1800 BC) and a historical period with the Hittites (1800–1200 BC), all the other regions of the Anatolian Peninsula being still at a prehistoric stage in their cultural development. Our chronological classification is therefore as follows:

1 The Early Bronze Age (3000–2500 BC)
2 The Middle Bronze Age: the Hattian civilization (2500–1800 BC)
3 The Late Bronze Age: the Hittites and Hurrians (1800–1200 BC)
4 The Iron Age: the Neo-Hittite, Urartian, Phrygian, Lydian, Carian, Lycian and Greek (Aeolian, Ionian and Dorian) civilizations (1180–750 BC).

THE EARLY BRONZE AGE (3000–2500 BC)

After playing a paramount role in the seventh, sixth and even fifth millennia BC, Anatolia found itself considerably behindhand culturally speaking during the fourth millennium BC and particularly during the first part of the third millennium. While writing was being invented in Egypt and Mesopotamia about 3000 BC and the peoples in those regions were attaining a very high level of culture, Anatolia as a whole was still given over to a primitive form of social life similar to that of prehistoric settlements. An advanced and noteworthy civilization did not emerge in the Anatolian peninsula until after the mid-point of the third millennium BC.

Excavations conducted in recent decades show us that social life in Anatolian population centres dating from the first half of the third millennium BC was just beginning to develop. At that period, we find settlements surrounded by a wall and very probably ruled by a local potentate. They were small city-states in which various trades, including metal working, were able to flourish. No doubt the peninsula's abundance of copper, lead, nickel and arsenic played a considerable part in this advance, which constituted one of the most remarkable stages in the development of the productive economy. Bronze objects recently excavated in Anatolia dating from the first and especially the second half of the third millennium BC contain 10 per cent and more of tin. This proves that a metallurgical industry capable of producing high-quality bronze existed in Anatolia in the third millennium BC. Knowing as we do that tin was a substance imported from Mesopotamia to Kültepe even during the

nineteenth and eighteenth centuries BC, we may assume that the inhabitants of Anatolia had established commercial relations with Mesopotamia as early as the Early Bronze Age in order to obtain the tin essential for the production of high-quality bronze.

A large number of systematically excavated sites, of which excellent descriptions have been published, have yielded remarkable finds providing us with a fairly clear view of Early Bronze Age culture in Anatolia. The information comes from the levels and layers of the following sites: Troy I, Demircihöyük (layers D-P), Yortan (part of class A), Beycesultan (layers XIX-XVII), Karatas (layers BA I), Tarsus (layers BA1–BA2), Arslantepe, Malatya (BA), Gedikli and Pulur.

The civilization of the Early Bronze Age in Anatolia shows signs of parallel developments and something of a common character. Nevertheless, we can point to at least four regions which differ somewhat from each other in artistic terms. These are: (1) western Anatolia; (2) south-west Anatolia; (3) central Anatolia; (4) eastern Anatolia (including the east and south-east).

Western Anatolia – Troy I (3000–2500 BC)

The most important and best known civilization in Anatolia during the Early Bronze Age was the first city of Troy (Fig. 32). This first occupation of the site, consisting of ten superimposed strata of habitation, covered a very small area. At the time of stratum 1j, when Troy I was at the peak of its development, the city measured only 90 m in diameter. The plan shows a reconstruction of the ruins made in the light of the discoveries of the German and American expeditions. Troy I-IX was excavated by Schliemann, Dörpfeld and Blegen, and this important site is again the subject of major excavations directed by Manfred Korfmann.

The walls of Troy I (squares EF 5/6 on the plan) are still today in a very good state of preservation. The city gate was 2.97 m wide and was flanked by two towers. The one to the east was found to be in very good condition once the earth covering it had been removed. It was 3.5 m high. Its base was made of quite large stones but those at the top of the tower were smaller and markedly narrower, resembling mudbricks or tiles. The American archaeologists report that the wall, which had a sharply inclined outer face, had been topped by a mudbrick parapet. Any enemies trying to force the entrance, which took the form of a long corridor, would have been repulsed from the flanking towers. The American expedition made a succession of sondages which showed that the wall extended for 115 m.

House 102, situated in squares CD 2/3 on the plan, was

205

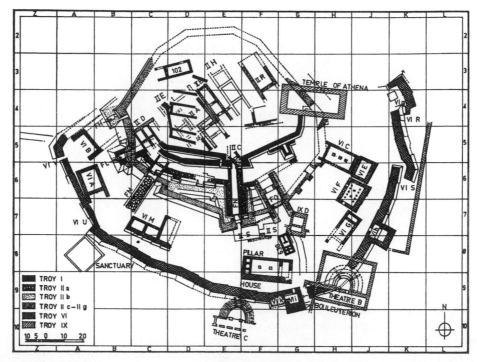

Figure 32 Troy I–IX. Restored plan (adapted from W. Dörpfeld and USA excavations).

uncovered by the American team and is the finest relic of Troy I. It was built in phase Ib. The apse-like structure visible beneath it belongs to phase Ia. The outside measurements of the walls of House 102 were 18.75 m by 7 m. The walls were made of stones arranged in a herring-bone pattern. In the main room were two hearths, one in the middle and the other near the east wall. A few fragments of the centre hearth are still there but none of the other. The same room also contained two benches, which could have been used as beds or divans. The one against the north and east walls and of which no trace remains today was 2 m long, 90 cm wide and 30 cm high. The one that can still be seen near the north-west corner of the room is 2.35 m long, 1.7 m wide and 50 cm high. It was occupied by a double bed. The bothros, which was discovered during the excavations but no longer exists, was a pit in which dough was left to rise. A small platform at the back, against the wall, served as a table for various objects but no longer exists. The animal bones and mollusc shells found there show that it was a place for cooking and eating. Under the stone floor of the main room two children's graves were found, one near the south wall, the other near the north wall. They contained six skeletons of children that had been stillborn or who had lived one or two weeks at most. Infant mortality at that time was high.

No necropolis has yet been discovered in Troy inside the fortress in the residential zone. The graves were probably outside the walls. In the upper part of the walls were long, narrow openings for light and ventilation. These were just under the flat roof, which was made of wood and mudbrick. House 102, long, narrow and detached, with a room in front and a hearth in the centre of the main room, is a typical megaron, one of the most ancient examples so far discovered. South of the house, five parallel walls can be seen. Although no precise ground plan can be discerned, it would seem that these are the remains of megaron dwellings. The south wall of the building (square 4D) is bonded in herringbone fashion. Mention must also be made of a stela bearing the image of a human head. This is the oldest example in

Anatolia of a 'monument' decorated with a figurative motif.

Pottery was fashioned by hand. Trojan ware decorated with human faces appears for the first time in the city at this level. Troy I was linked culturally with the neighbouring Aegean area. The city disappeared as the result of a fire.

Another important Early Bronze Age centre in western Anatolia is the site of Demircihöyük near Eskişehir. A large amount of pottery dating from the first half of the third millennium BC was brought to light in the excavations conducted by Manfred Korfmann and his team (Jürgen Seeher and Tufan Efe), the published account of which is excellent (Korfmann, 1980). A group of terraced houses, like those of Troy I and Troy II, which had been frequently repaired during the first half of the third millennium BC, was uncovered at the same level.

Two other remarkable sites in western Anatolia were discovered at Aphrodisias and Iasos. The results of the excavations on those sites were published respectively by Martha Sharp Joukowsky (1986) and Paolo Emilio Pecorella (1984). There is no doubt that some of the objects found in the course of these excavations date from the Early Bronze Age.

The necropolises located in the central regions of western Anatolia have yielded ceramic ware known as Yortan, decorated with whitened incisions. Part of the class A ceramic identified by T. Kamil (1982) very probably dates from the first half of the third millennium BC.

Lastly, a very well conserved wall, similar to the one at Troy I, has been uncovered at the site of Urla (Klazomenai) which was excavated by Hayat Erkanal.

South-west Anatolia

At Karahöyük near Konya, which was excavated by Sedat Alp, first-rate *objets d'art* not only of the Middle Bronze but also of the Early Bronze Age were discovered in a walled town. Interestingly, this site has yielded pottery displaying a strong affinity with that of Troy I and II.

The excavations at Karataş-Semayük in Lycia, directed

by Machteld Mellink, have uncovered important layers dating from the Early Bronze Age. The centre of the excavated site is occupied by a rectangular house with an oval courtyard and an outside fence. A village consisting of dwellings with a ground plan inspired by the megaron was built with this house as its centre. In the burial ground excavated 200 m away from the fortified site, graves were found with the bodies placed in a crouched position in *pithoi*, the mouths of which were pointed eastwards.

At Beycesultan to the north of Lake Acigöl, which was excavated by Seton Lloyd and James Melleart, layers XIX-XIII have been identified as belonging to the Early Bronze Age. Nevertheless, in our opinion, only a part of the pottery at Beycesultan may belong to the Early Bronze Age as most of the forms have features characteristic of the style of Middle Bronze Age I. The archaeologists who excavated the site consider that the town was fortified from the very beginning. The buildings, with mudbrick walls on stone foundations, were of the megaron type.

The site of Kuruçay near Burdur, which was excavated by Refik Duru, has also yielded *objets d'art*, some of which are in the style of the Early Bronze Age.

Central Anatolia

Some two dozen sites have been excavated in this region, the most important of which are Alişar, Alaca Hüyük, Karaoglan, Etiyokuşu, Ahlatlibel and Polatli. The culture described as 'recent Chalcolithic' by the archaeologists who excavated the sites of central Anatolia actually corresponds to the Early Bronze Age (3000–2500 BC), and the culture which they referred to as the 'Copper Age' should be designated Middle Bronze Age (2500–1800 BC).

The Early Bronze Age is rather poor in central Anatolia as in other parts of Anatolia. The pottery was shaped by hand and fired in the open. Metal objects are extremely rare.

The site of Alişar, excavated by von der Osten, with its partially uncovered wall, appears to have been a fortified town, probably governed by a local potentate. The burial places were located within the town. Bodies were placed in *pithoi* in stone cists, or else simply laid in the ground.

Alaca Hüyük, excavated by R. O. Arik and H. Koşay, offers parallels with Alişar and would seem to have been the residency of a principality already of some importance in the Early Bronze Age.

Eastern Anatolia (including eastern, southern and south-eastern areas)

One of the oldest city-states in Anatolia, surrounded by a wall with a monumental gateway, has been discovered during the excavations at Arslantepe, initially directed by S.M. Puglisi and now by Alba Palmieri. It was probably the seat of a highly influential local monarchy. Some 200 seal and cylinder impressions on clay seals demonstrate that the principality was an important trading centre as early as the beginning of the third millennium BC. Among the finds, particular mention should be made of the copper spearheads and daggers containing 2.7 per cent to 4 per cent of an arsenic alloy, which were made at the beginning of the third millennium BC. The moulds for the production of metal objects which were found at Arslantepe date from the end of that millennium.

Objets d'art of the Early Bronze Age, similar to those at Arslantepe and Malatya, were found at Imamoğluhüyük near Malatya, which was excavated by Edibe Uzunoglu. The important site of Norsuntepe, excavated by H. Hauptmann in the region of Keban, is a noteworthy example of the Early Bronze Age in Anatolia.

The centre of Gedikli located near Sakçegözü, which was excavated by Bahadir Alkim, was a city-state surrounded by a wall 3 m thick. The excavations at Gedikli provide us with information about burial customs during the Early and Middle Bronze Age in Anatolia: there is evidence for cremation and inhumation side by side.

The site of Pulur near Elâziğ, which was excavated by Hamit Koşay, has yielded large vases of the type known as 'Karaz', dating from the end of the fourth and the beginning of the third millennium BC.

Mention should also be made of the site of Ikiztepe near Samsun, excavated by B. Alkim, where layers from the Early and Middle Bronze Ages have been uncovered. It is interesting to note that the pottery from this site is very similar to that of south-east Anatolia. The wooden architecture at Ikiztepe is related to the wooden structures at Karataş-Semayük and in the Balkans.

At Tarsus, an Early Bronze Age centre has been discovered at the Gözlükule excavations being directed by Hetty Goldman. It was fortified by a wall and apparently governed by a minor local king. Among the pottery finds, there were several vases from northern Mesopotamia and Cyprus as well as samples of a type of reddish-orange ceramic ware which also occurs in quantity in south-east regions of the Anatolian peninsula. The pottery at Tarsus was shaped on the wheel as early as the first half of the third millennium BC.

At Yükütepe near Mersin, excavated by John Garstang, an Early Bronze Age culture was discovered similar to the one found at the town of Gözlükule.

Conclusion

The Early Bronze Age in Anatolia was in a state of development. The peninsula had a relatively dense population living in small settlements protected by walls and governed by local potentates. The people generally gained their living from agriculture and hunting and those living in settlements on the sea coast engaged in fishing. There were city-states, especially in the south-west and on the coast, which maintained commercial links with Mesopotamia and the Aegean world. Communication in the interior of the peninsula was undoubtedly by way of caravans of donkeys and mules as was the case one thousand years later at the beginning of the Hittite period.

Metal working was not widespread. It should be noted that only small numbers of simple tools and weapons have been found in the settlements of the Early Bronze Age. Vases made of bronze and precious metal did not appear in Anatolia before the Middle Bronze Age and perhaps not before the last third of the third millennium BC.

When we consider that there were statuettes, large anthropomorphic vases and, above all, extraordinary wall-paintings and large reliefs decorating the walls of bedrooms in Anatolia during the late Neolithic in the sixth and fifth millennia BC, it is clear that the Anatolian mode of life in the first half of the third millennium BC was quite primitive. Even in comparison with the art of the late Chalcolithic, which featured remarkable pottery including large vases known as 'fruit bowls', the level of the Early Bronze Age culture was very low.

With the exception of the ware produced at Tarsus, the pottery was hand-made and fired in the open. Most of the forms originated in the Chalcolithic. However, the squat pitcher with the slightly tapered lip appears to be without precedent in the Chalcolithic period. It was transformed over time into an elegant and sophisticated jug with a long lip, which became the dominant form throughout the period.

THE MIDDLE BRONZE AGE (2500–1800 BC)

During the Middle Bronze Age, the Anatolian peninsula experienced a period of prosperity and an extremely high level of culture, based primarily on the production of a metal-working industry.

The birth of the Hatti civilization in the centre of the peninsula and the foundation of Troy II-V on the Dardanelles established two cultural centres of prime importance. We shall consider the architecture, pottery and decorative art produced during the two successive stages of the Middle Bronze Age established by Carl Blegen for: Middle Bronze I: Troy II and its contemporaries (2500–2200 BC); Middle Bronze II: Troy III-V and its contemporaries (2200–1800 BC).

Middle Bronze Age I (2500–2200 BC)

In order to obtain a clear image of the Middle Bronze Age, we must consider in detail the culture of Troy II-V and that of the cities of central Anatolia.

Troy II (2500–2200 BC)

The history of the culture of Middle Bronze Age I in Anatolia can be seen in the ruins of the second city of Troy. Troy II represents a development of the previous city. The essential features of this new period are of the ancient Cycladic and Aegean type, as in Troy I. The early Helladic Urfirnis pottery, already found in the upper strata of Troy I, was again imported and was also made in local workshops. Furthermore, links with the cultural centres of central Anatolia and those further east are easily recognizable. The rulers of Troy were obviously no mere peasant kings. They knew how to exploit their position on the international trade routes in order to maintain their domination and extend their territory. All the metals – gold, silver, copper and tin – had to be imported from central and eastern Anatolia and from the Orient. Several metal-working techniques used by Trojan artists came from Oriental goldsmiths, among them the sophisticated technique of granulation which had been known in the Orient for 500 years. Their tubular ear-rings, for example, were inspired by an ancient Oriental model. The most refined specimens of the goldsmith's art in Troy were found in the treasure discovered by Schliemann. In addition to bronze vessels and weapons, the treasure included solid gold and silver goblets, gold jewellery and silver bars. The bars must have been ordered for use in barter. A gold dish in the treasure, known as the 'sauce boat', 7.5 cm tall and weighing 600 g, is in the Aegean style. The elegant handles strongly resemble in shape those of the type of vase known as *depas*, a typical Trojan vessel. The two spouts are identical with those of the elegant Helladic spouted bowls of the same period, which were made of clay and decorated with an 'Urfirnis' slip.

The potters of Troy were quite familiar with the two great technical innovations of the time, the potter's kiln and the potter's wheel. In Troy I, vases were hand-thrown and fired in the open. In Troy I and Troy II, the links with the interior of Anatolia are clear to see. The second fortified city of Troy suffered a terrible catastrophe between 2200 and 2100 BC. Its destruction may have been due to the incursions of the Indo-European tribes into Anatolia which began precisely at that time. However, in the succeeding periods from Troy III to Troy V, there is no trace of a new population. No cultural change seems to have taken place before the foundation of Troy VI, about 1800 BC.

Phases II a-g, consisting of seven layers of construction, played an important role in the history of Troy, even though in 2200 BC the diameter of the city was only 110 m. Although Troy I was destroyed by a catastrophe, there is no time gap and not the least change in culture between the two cities. On the contrary, the Troy I culture continued to develop in Troy II.

The second city showed very great progress in town planning. To judge from the megara and the layout of the propylaea in phases II c-g, Troy II was the first city in the world to have a system of planned construction (Fig. 33). With its regular and well-executed ground plan it compares favourably with other cities of the same period in western Asia. The method used, which consisted of placing the megara side by side to form a continuous façade and placing megaron-shaped propylaea at the entrances of the blocks thus formed, was faithfully followed seven or eight centuries later in the citadel of Tiryns in Greece, where it was necessary to pass through a larger propylaeon before entering a set of buildings consisting of megara built against each other. The Acropolis at Athens is a remarkable example of the same type of planning.

As in the case of Troy I, the main gate of Troy II was in the centre of the south wall (FN). In the second city, however, there were other gates. Among them, the remains of the south-west gate (FM, square 6c), and particularly a well-paved ramp 21 m long and 7.5 m wide, are in a good state of preservation. The stone part of the wall, still visible today, leans inwards at the top. A mudbrick perpendicular section crowned the wall.

The paved ramp led up to the propylaeum FM. The entrance was 5.25 m wide and possessed a double door. This propylaeum, like a megaron in design, belonged to phases c-g of Troy II, that is, to its last stage. A little to the rear of this can be seen the remains of walls belonging to Troy IIb in front and IIa behind (to the north). Further to the north, the ruins of a wall (in black on the plan), more or less on the same axis as the propylaeum FM, belong to Troy I. The gate FN in square E7 was the main point of entry into Troy IIa. The large propylaeum FO was the main gate of the city in the last period of Troy II, when it was at the height of its prosperity. This structure, like propylaeum FM, had the ground plan of a megaron, with its two short sides open. This splendid entrance led to an inner courtyard which was built at a time corresponding to phases c-g of Troy II, 2200–2100 BC. To create this courtyard, the top of the phase II a-b walls was levelled and covered with a stone pavement. To enter the royal palace, people had to go through a small propylaeum, also with the ground plan of a megaron. To judge from the stone block forming the threshold, which is

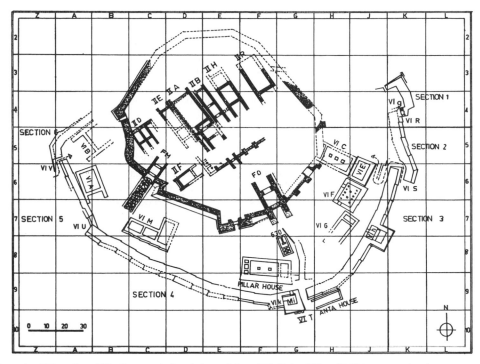

Figure 33 Troy II c-g (and Troy Late VI). Restored plan (adapted from W. Dörpfeld and USA excavations).

on the ground, this propylaeum was 1.82 m wide. There was also a paved courtyard between the phase IIc propylaeum and the great megaron, which had walls 2 m thick on its south and west sides. A stone footing found in the south corner shows that the building had a colonnade. Coming from the megaron, therefore, people had in front of them a fine example of architectural decoration. On days when the sun made the megaron hot, the colonnade offered welcome shade. The regular ground plan of the Troy II citadel has already been mentioned. All the buildings are arranged in accordance with a clear-cut plan. In particular, the situation of the great megaron (IIA) on the crown of the hill, dominating its surroundings, produced a powerful effect. This house, with walls 1.5 m thick, must have been a tall building, standing in the middle of the citadel and attracting the eye. Although the greater part of the megaron was destroyed by Schliemann's north-south trench, it has been possible, on the basis of the present ruins, to determine roughly the plan of the building. As will be seen from the plan, only part of it has been uncovered and part of the east wall is buried under the material from the German excavations. The width of the building, including the walls, is 13 m. It is not certain how long it was, but the length must have been at least 35–40 m. The internal measurements of the large room were 20 m by 10.2 m. In the middle of the room, Dörpfeld discovered the ruins of a platform 4 m in diameter. He deduced that there must have been a hearth in the middle of the room, as in all megara. No place to sit down and no traces of throne-like furniture were found but there were doubtless all sorts of benches, tables and seats in this splendid building, which was long used by the kings belonging to phases c-g. The remains of two other megara of the same type but of smaller size appear on either side of megaron IIA. The one to the east (IIB) was also destroyed by Schliemann's north-south trench but may be taken to have resembled the well-preserved megaron on the western side (IIE). It is believed that these two megara were resting or meeting places for the royal family. Megara IIA, IIR and IIF, identified by Dörpfeld, must have consisted of a number of small rooms and prob-

ably served as a barracks or storehouse.

The American archaeologists established once and for all that the treasure discovered by Schliemann belonged to phase IIg of Troy. Several other objects made of gold and silver, like that treasure, which were discovered in the excavations, indicate that Troy IIg fell suddenly to invading forces. The destruction layer that marks the end of Troy II is on average 1 m thick and bears the signs of a very violent fire, caused by an enemy from outside, probably a horde of Indo-European invaders. This enemy, however, did not occupy Troy, since no trace of a change of culture can be detected in Troy III, IV and V. For the sake of continuity, these are included here, though they belong properly to Middle Bronze Age II (see below). The arrival of a new people will be discussed under Troy VI in Volume III.

Troy III to Troy V (2200–1800 BC)

During the period of Troy III, IV and V, which doubtless lasted a long time, the progressive decline of the kingdom of Troy and the erosion of its prosperity can be seen. Ruins of the buildings of Troy III lie to the north-west of the ramp in square C5. The buildings were houses constructed of small irregular stones. The excavations carried out by the Germans showed that Troy IV no longer even possessed a protective wall. The remains of the original buildings of this period were discovered to the east of House IVA (square B6). It is thought that the city was surrounded by a makeshift fortification. The little wall in square 5A belongs to this period.

The Hatti culture (2500–2000 BC)

It is clear from the *objets d'art* that there was a quite obvious stylistic unity in the various branches of the fine arts during the Middle Bronze Age in western, central, southern and eastern Anatolia. Ceramic forms such as long-spouted jugs, goblets known as *depas amphikypellon*, vases in the shape of human heads, broad-based vases, and statuettes and idols in terracotta, bronze and precious metals, are represented in nearly all the cities of the Anatolian peninsula. The long-spouted jugs and goblets of the *depas amphikypellon* type are widespread even in Greece, Macedonia and the Aegean world. Anatolian art as a whole, however, displays a remarkable degree of stylistic unity. In particular, the decoration of the vases in baked clay, bronze and precious metals presents a style which is specific to the central and southern regions of Anatolia. The decoration is ribbed and is composed of fluted geometric motifs such as triangles, spirals, zigzags and swastikas. This type of decoration is found especially at Beycesultan and the surrounding district as well as at Alaca Hüyük and the other centres in the bend of the River Halys (Plates 80–6). This leads us to ask whether this style was created by the Hattian people who inhabited the central, southern and south-eastern regions of Anatolia before the invasion of the Indo-Europeans whom we know by the name of Hittites. To answer this question, we must consider what we know about this proto-historic people.

During the third millennium BC, there lived in central Anatolia a people, the Hattians, whose name has come down to us through Hittite sources. In the fourteenth and thirteenth centuries BC, when the priests of Hattusas conducted the ceremonies associated with their religion, they sometimes recited verses whose meaning was not entirely known to them. These verses, inserted between the lines in the cuneiform texts, were accompanied by a translation. Wherever these verses occurred, they were always preceded by a note to the effect that the priest would speak Hattic at that point, that is to say the Hattian language.

Hattic is different from all other Asian languages. It is easily recognizable by its abundant use of prefixes. For example, the plural is indicated by various prefixes: god = *shapu*, gods = *washapu*; child = *binu*, children = *lebinu*.

The spread of their religion demonstrates that the Hattians lived in central and eastern Anatolia. We know that the greatest Hittite deity, the sun-goddess Arinna, was called Wurusemu in Hattic. Her husband Taru, the weather-god, her sons, the weather-gods Nerik and Zippalanda, her daughter Mazullas and her niece Zentuhis, were Hattian deities with names of Hattian origin. Likewise Telepinu, one of the most popular Hittite gods, his wife Hatepinus, the goddess Inaras and the group of goddesses Zithariyas, Kaizis and Hapantalliyas, go back to the Hattian period.

The influence of the Hattian civilization is also apparent in Hittite mythology: the myths of Illuyanka and Telepinu are based on Hattian models. Nevertheless, as both these myths have only come down to us in a Hittite version, we are unable to identify their Hattian features. However, we possess fragments of myths in Hattic which were transcribed and in many cases translated by the Hittites themselves. One of the tales, included in a magic ritual of the weather god, begins:

The moon fell from the sky. It fell on the portal. No one noticed. The weather-god left the rain behind him. He left the showers behind him. Fear seized him, anguish seized him.

He went, Hapantali, he went down towards her, beseeching her again and again. From the sky, Kamrusepa noticed that she had fallen. She spoke in these terms: from the sky the moon has fallen, it has fallen on the portal. The weather-god has seen it; he has left the rain behind him, he has left the showers behind him. Fear has seized

him. Anguish has seized him. (E. Laroche)

The name Hattusilis, which was borne by three Hittite kings, means he who is from Hattus. The Hittite suffixes -ili, -ala, and -ula are derived from the Hattic suffixes -il, -al and -ul. The names of the Hittite kings Tudhaliyas, Arnuwandas and Ammunas were derived from the names of mountains in Hattic.

The art of a people which exercised such great influence on the Hittites must also have been of extremely high quality. That is why we believe that the *objets d'art* uncovered in central Anatolia and demonstrating a remarkable level of stylistic unity were created by the Hattians. The finest examples of the Hattian style come from Alaca Hüyük, Mahmatlar, Horoztepe and Beycesultan.

The objects belonging to this civilization (Plates 87, 88) have a distinctly homogeneous appearance. With their carefully polished surfaces and characteristic fluting, the long-spouted earthenware jugs with their graceful proportions found at Alaca, Ahlatlibel, Alişar and Beycesultan represent remarkable transpositions into another material of the metal objects found at Alaca, Mahmatlar and Horoztepe.

The golden bowls from the Alaca tombs give us an Anatolian version of the elegant cups found later, in the Hittite period proper. The same type, decorated in the same style, were found in the princely tomb at Horoztepe, which was contemporaneous. It also exists in the Alaca pottery. The fluted motif, already used by Chalcolithic potters to decorate vases, is derived from the decoration of metal objects. The Bronze Age goldsmiths of Anatolia knew how to produce the most felicitous effects by varying the fluting (Plate 85).

Mention has often been made of the relationship between the objects produced by the Alaca metal workers and the products of neighbouring civilizations. They nevertheless bear witness to the same style being used, a style whose features are purely Anatolian. It is doubtless possible to compare the Cycladic 'frying-pans', made of baked clay, with the bronze mirrors found at Alaca and Horoztepe, the deepest part of which originally contained a silver disc in which the Hattian princesses could admire their faces.

The silver statuette found at Hasanoğlan near Ankara (Plate 86) is a masterpiece of Hattian art. However, as it was found by chance and probably came from a tomb, there is no stratigraphic evidence to date it by, though the style is undoubtedly Hattian. The striated design of the hair arranged round the top of the skull can be seen almost identically on the golden cups taken from the royal tombs of Alaca Hüyük (Plate 84). Similarly, the way the neck is covered with a thin plate of beaten gold is a feature of Hattian goldsmiths' work. (The neck and body of a bronze statuette of a bull from Alaca Hüyük (Plate 80) are similarly covered in silver.) The small spherical gold-covered breasts and the navel in the form of a gold-encrusted button also recall the idols and figurines from the Alaca Hüyük tombs (Plate 83). The stippled pubic triangle, the straps crossed over the breasts and shoulders, and above all the long neck, all represent stylistic elements that make it possible to establish an affinity between the Hasanoğlan statuette and the idols from the late period of the Early Bronze Age in Anatolia. The Hasanoğlan statuette has a large hooked nose (Plate 86): representing faithfully as it does the ethnic type that predominated at the time, a Hattian princess could have been the model for the statuette. This same face will be found again in Hittite art, for a large proportion of the population of central and eastern Anatolia would certainly still have shown a strong resemblance to the Hattians in the thirteenth century BC.

The respectful gesture of the hands suggests that this statuette represents a dead Hattian princess in an attitude of worship or adoration. The information given by the peasants on the circumstances of its discovery and the objects found in the immediate vicinity indicate that this valuable find had been deposited in a tomb. The sureness of touch with which the artist, even at this time, is able to depict to the life the curves of the body, suggests that the statuette belongs to a more recent period than that of the Alaca Hüyük tombs. It could date from about 2000 BC.

Taking the form of discs or animals, the 'standards' of the priest-kings of central Anatolia (Plates 80, 81) also show a unity of style with its roots in the Anatolian heartland. The motifs used to embellish them, trellis-work patterns, concentric circles, crosses, swastikas, series of dots – are also found on vases (Plate 85), on idols (Plate 83) and on other objects of the same period (Plate 82). This consistency in design can be incontrovertibly detected in other details, such as the semicircular shape given to the heads of two statuettes (which are idols), found again not only in idols covered in gold leaf but also on two disc standards found at Alaca, whose star-shaped ornamentation is stylized on the same principle. Several terracotta idols, also from Alaca, have heads of the same shape.

The standards in the shape of bulls or stags probably fitted into some sort of throne (Plate 80). Those in the shape of solar discs were fixed to staves. Their lower portions still have tenons which fitted into slots in the wood of the staves where they were doubtless held in place with cords or straps. These strange, even mysterious objects, shaped like arcs or full circles, are probably nothing more than symbols of the universe, whereas the animal figures are theriomorphic representations of certain divinities.

The significance of the standards

Indeed, most of the objects that were found in the graves were ritual implements. The rattle, the sistrum-shaped bull-roarer and other objects shaped like standards from Horoztepe indicate their religious character. Similar implements are used today in the rites of the Orthodox churches. The priests of Hatti carried sistra and used them during religious ceremonies as an accompaniment to their liturgic chants.

The ritual character of these impressive and mysterious works of art is particularly striking in the disc or arch-shaped standards. The great bull's horns which serve as a base, the halo and the spherical standards indicative of the celestial vault, can hardly be interpreted as purely ornamental compositions. The bull's horns are affixed to a frame so as to raise and support the standards. On some standards the disc's edge is adorned with stars which, as it were, encircle the heavenly sphere like satellites. They are small models of the standards to whose periphery they have been added. The birds in flight which sometimes decorate the edge of the standards may be an indication of their celestial significance. Flowers similarly attached could be a symbolic representation of plant-life growing, reaching towards the sky. We cannot be sure whether the swastikas on a lozenge-shaped standard, revolving partly to the right and partly to the left, should be interpreted as the rising and setting sun; but the total aspect of these standards permits us to assume that it somehow represents the universe. The bull's horns which support this cosmic symbol recall a Turkish fairy-tale which relates that the world rests on the horns of an ox. 'Every time the ox shakes his head', the tale goes, 'the earth trembles'. The precious implements of Hattian priestly rulers may be the oldest figurative representation of this concept. We find the same notion, that of a bull supporting the universe, later on in the various forms of Hittite symbolism. Nor is it accidental that the swift, lithe stag emerges from the solar disc, or that his antlers, which resemble a halo and the celestial vault, should reach to the limit of the heavenly sphere. On a relief of Jupiter Dolichenus, dating from the Roman period but representing an old Hittite motif, the spouse of the weather-god stands, as has been pointed out by Hancar, on the back of a stag. The Hattians called this goddess Wurusemu, and her epithet of 'the sun-goddess of Arinna' defines her as the ruler of heaven and the universe. Considering that the bull is definitely to be understood as the attribute of the weather-god, we may endeavour to interpret the stag appearing in this context as a symbol of his spouse who invariably accompanies him. Certainly in the later Anatolian-Hittite period, the lion and the panther came to be the symbol of the great goddess, while the stag became the sacred animal of male tutelary divinities. But it may be that the Hattian symbol of the great goddess was altered by the Hittites. On a standard from Alaca two panthers occur beside a stag. Perhaps the panther was the sacred animal of the chief goddess and became an object of worship as early as the third millennium BC. The fact that all the animal standards without exception represented either a bull or a stag compels us to interpret the bull as the attribute of the deity identical with the weather-god.

The tombs of Alaca Hüyük belong to the Hattian period, which extends from about 2500 BC to about 1800 BC, and are thus believed to date roughly from between 2100 and 1900 BC. The less extensive sites of Ahlatlibel and Etiyokuşu (near Ankara) must also belong to the last phase – approximately 2100–2000 BC – of this period. The finding of seals at these sites supports this late dating. The last years of the prehistoric era in Anatolia mark the time when the Hatti civilization, coming into contact with the Mesopotamian world, made a great leap forward. The Hattian people were illiterate but their petty kings doubtless had scribes to conduct their correspondence with neighbouring rulers. The advent of seals at this time represents the first step towards the adoption of writing.

The idol found in the royal tombs at Alaca and the statuettes of naturalistic design bear witness to the advanced level of Hattian minor sculpture. A tendency towards realism was already manifest in the Alaca idols. The twin figures of the 'violin' type (Plate 83), covered in gold leaf, were still completely schematic. They were found in the same tomb as the naturalistic copper statuettes, but since they were intended to be sewn on to the robes of the priest-kings, their decorative and ritual role made it essential for them to be in the old style. Although the breasts were still stylized as buttons and the pubis as a triangle (Plate 86), the bronze statuette of a mother suckling her baby – a remarkable work found in a tomb at Horoztepe – shows real progress in the naturalistic rendering of the body's curves. The eyes and ears, which are too large, still exemplify primitive modes of representation, but the asymmetrical pose of the hands and arms and the almost natural shaping of the shoulders and facial features foreshadow the advent of the new trend towards realism. This statuette is the oldest naturalistic representation of mother and child found among the contemporary idols of

Kültepe. This same concept will be found among the lead idols at the beginning of the historical period.

The adoption of Hattian style by the Hittites

Although the style of the objects uncovered in the tombs of Alaca Hüyük, Horoztepe and Mahmatlar is specifically Anatolian, their mode of burial is foreign and of Indo-European origin. At Alaca Hüyük the tombs consist of rectangular pits between 3 and 8 m long and 2 to 5 m wide. These pits, containing the corpse and the burial offerings, were surrounded on all four sides by irregular stonework and roofed with horizontally laid thick wooden beams, themselves covered with a layer of earth, on top of which were found the skulls and hooves of cattle, traces of a funeral feast. This mode of burial is unknown in Anatolia before that date. It is reminiscent of the burial rites of the Mycenaeans and greatly resembles what is found later at Gordion and Ankara among the Phrygians, who were of Indo-European origin. In the same way, the standards in the form of stylized bulls and stags, whose hooves rest on a very small four-part base, recall very similar standards discovered at Maikop. It is also noteworthy that the objects found at Alaca Hüyük, Horoztepe and Mahmatlar represent theriomorphic divinities, whereas the Hattians worshipped anthropomorphic gods. For that reason it appears that these tombs are those of Hittite princes who established themselves in the land of Hatti. These Hittite petty kings therefore kept up their use of sun-discs and standards in the shape of animals as well as their burial rites and their religion with its theriomorphic divinities. However, the style of the objects in question, which is Anatolian *par excellence*, shows that they were made by Hattian workmen. On the basis of the above observations we may say that the Indo-European invasion had already started by the year 2200 and the first of the European tribes had moved into the great bend of the River Halys (Kizilirmak). It is quite probable that the destruction marking the end of Troy IIg and the Middle Bronze Age is related to this Indo-European immigration. It would appear that the occupation of Anatolia by the Hittites came about as a gradual infiltration over several centuries. Indeed, a Hittite state did not take shape until the middle of the seventeenth century BC.

Conclusion

In comparison with the previous period of the Early Bronze Age, Middle Bronze Age I represents a very high level of culture. Metal working reached its high point during this phase. The *objets d'art* made of precious metals, which were discovered in the royal tombs of Alaca Hüyük, Mahmatlar and Horoztepe, constitute the richest and most magnificent treasure dating from the Bronze Age. The works of art in gold and silver from Troy II provide further excellent examples of Bronze Age work after the finds in the Hattian cities.

The city-states of Middle Bronze Age I were quite small, like those of the previous period, surrounded by a wall and governed by a local king. Potentates dominating several cities simultaneously had apparently not yet emerged. It is perhaps for that reason that the architects who built the large buildings known as megara did not build palaces and temples in the monumental style which we shall see during Middle Bronze Age II.

Middle Bronze Age I is the proto-historic period in Anatolia. It provides information which helps us towards a better understanding of the ethnic problem of the Bronze Age in Anatolia. As we have seen, the art of the northern and southern cities was a creation of the Hattian people, several fragments of whose language, religion and mythology and other features have come down to us through the written sources of the Hittite empire.

Another people whose name is known to us through the written sources as early as Middle Bronze Age I are the hurrians. A stone tablet, written in the Hurrian language and guarded by a bronze lion, today in the Louvre Museum, and one other written source, bear witness to the fact that the city of Urkis near Mardin was already inhabited by the Hurrians around the year 2300 BC.

We have no evidence enabling us to form an idea about the ethnic origin of the population of Troy I-V. Nevertheless, we may accept the hypothesis that the Trojans, whose art greatly resembles that of the islands and of Greece, belonged to the same Indo-European ethnic group which lived in the Aegean world at that period. If that is the case then Troy VI represented a new wave of Indo-European invasion. This is not a hypothesis which can be rejected categorically. It is a well-attested fact that the city of Troy was invaded during phase VIIb2 by another Indo-European people of Balkan origin.

As for the Pelasgians and the Leleges who undoubtedly lived in western Anatolia before the arrival of the Hellenes, we have no clear evidence of their history. We know only that a people lived in Greece, the Aegean and Anatolia, whose cities had names ending in -nthos and -assos. In addition, several other peoples were certainly living in Anatolia during the Bronze Age as in the second and first millennia BC.

As we have seen, there is evidence for inhumation and cremation side by side in Anatolia. Cemeteries were located inside and outside the city walls. Only the tombs at Alaca Hüyük represented a different mode of burial, which is why we have attributed them to the Hittite kings rather than to Hattian potentates.

The shapes found in Anatolian pottery and especially in pottery of Troy I and II also occur in Greece, Macedonia and the Aegean world, as Winfried Orthmann (1963), Christian Podzuweit (1979) and M. S. Joukowsky (1986) have clearly demonstrated. This shows that trade by sea was extremely active. The presence of goblets of the *depas amphikypellon* in practically every Anatolian village indicates that trade in the interior of Anatolia, carried on by caravans of donkeys and mules, was also well organized.

Middle Bronze Age II (2000–1800 BC)

Hattian, Hurrian and Hittite principalities

The period corresponding to Middle Bronze Age II is, in fact, the first historical age in Anatolia, since it was at the beginning of the second millennium BC, a thousand years after Egypt and Mesopotamia, that central Anatolia witnessed the invention of writing and made its entry into history in the strict sense of the word. The western part of the peninsula, however, continued to live in prehistoric conditions until the Greek period, around the eighth or even ninth century BC.

In the first quarter of the second millennium BC, central Anatolia was ruled by the same Hattian and Hittite principalities that had co-existed there since the last two centuries of the third millennium (see above). As we shall see, however, towards the end of the first third of the second millennium BC, Anatolia came under Hittite rule. Meanwhile, Assyrian merchants, who in all likelihood had already been plying their trade in Anatolia in the last two centuries of the third millennium BC, set up trading-posts of outstanding importance in the first quarter of the second millennium BC.

Assyrian trading posts

We know from inscriptions on clay tablets found in the excavations at Kültepe, Alişar and Boghazköy that there were Assyrian trading-posts during the nineteenth and eighteenth centuries BC in central and south-eastern Anatolia. They included both major establishments (*karum*) and trading-stations (*wabartum*). The Kanesh *karum* situated at Kültepe, 20 km north-west of Kayseri, exercised a controlling influence over all the other trading-posts established in Anatolia and was itself under the authority of Ashur on the Tigris. Using the Ashur-Diyarbakir-Malatya-Kayseri route or the Ashur-Urfa-Adana and Gülek-Kayseri pass route, the Assyrian merchants would import tin, clothing and textiles by caravans of 200 to 250 donkeys, and sell their wares to the local population in exchange for gold and silver, and also copper, which was cheaper in Anatolia than elsewhere. A metal called amuntum was worth forty times more than silver, and was most probably iron.

The Assyrians exercised no power or influence, either political or administrative. The *karum* at Kültepe was a construction 1,000 m wide by 1,500 m long and was built on the north-eastern, eastern and south-eastern slopes of the hillock inhabited by the citizens and princes of Nesa (Kanesh). In exchange for a pledge of safety, Assyrian merchants had to pay taxes to the local princes. Most of the thousands of extant documents are commercial, economic or legal in character, although there are some that are historical or literary.

The Assyrian settlers used Kültepe level II, contemporary with the Sarrum-Kin (Sargon) and Shamshi-Adad kings, from about 1900 to 1800 BC, leaving 15,000 clay tablets. Following the destruction of level II by a terrible fire, this site was abandoned for forty to fifty years. Subsequently, in about 1750 BC, the Assyrian merchants built city Ib on the ruins of level II. This new settlement, where clay tablets have also been found, was contemporary with Zimri-Lim of Mari and Hammurabi, the king of Babylon (about the second half of the eighteenth century BC). The Assyrian trading-posts of Alişar and Boghazköy, attested by merchants' tablets, also date from the period of city Ib of Kültepe.

The co-existence of indigenous and Hittite settlements: the period of principalities

Following the example of the Assyrian trading-posts, the Anatolian princes also began to employ Assyrian scribes. Hence we have come to be informed about the cities over which the Hittites ruled.

Anittas was no doubt one of the foremost potentates of the eighteenth century BC. We have some information about his city from two tablets in Assyrian from Alişar, another Assyrian text from Kültepe now in the Louvre Museum and, in particular, a Hittite text discovered at Boghazköy. Its name is also on a bronze dagger found among the ruins of a great palace on the Nesa (Kültepe) hill inhabited by the indigenous population and bearing the inscription *egal Anittas rubaim* (palace of King Anittas). According to the Hittite text, Anittas, who was initially king of the city of Kussara, had founded a small kingdom of which Nesa (Kanesh) was the capital. In the text he says that he built the walls of the city and the temples of the storm-god and of Siusummi. He must have reigned at the time of city Ib of Kültepe. The fact that the city is called Nesa is adequate proof that it was inhabited by the Nesians, in other words the Hittites who spoke Nesian (see below).

The cities mentioned repeatedly in the written documents are Kussara, Nesa, Hattusas, Zalpa, Purushanda, Mama, Taisama and Sibuha. Some of them, like Hattusas and Purushanda, were of Hattian origin; Mama was a Hurrian principality. Most of them, however, like Hattusas and Nesa, became pre-eminently Hittite centres during the city Ib phase of Kültepe, contemporaneous with Hammurabi. Undoubtedly the other Anatolian urban centres were also gradually transformed into Hittite cities. The Indo-European invasion of Anatolia, which had already begun in the last quarter of the third millennium BC, continued in successive waves for several centuries. Meanwhile, however, we can be sure that most of the population continued to be Hattian in the centre and Hurrian in the south-east of the peninsula. Moreover, the Hittite princes sometimes took Hattian or Hurrian names to win the good will of the citizens over whom they reigned. For this reason it is often difficult to ascertain the ethnic origin of a potentate. If, however, we bear in mind that the Hittite Old Kingdom was founded towards the beginning of the seventeenth century BC, it is clear that the military operations in the first quarter of the second millennium BC were battles between the Indo-European princes and the indigenous rulers of Anatolia.

THE LATE BRONZE AGE (1800–1200 BC)

The Hittites (Map 13)

The period of the principalities saw a growth in the size of cities as compared with that of the previous urban settlements. The ground plan at Kültepe, Karahöyük, Acemhöyük and Alişar was more or less oval or circular, with a diameter of 400 to 700 m. Examples of fortified walls are to be found at Alişar, Karahöyük and Kültepe. The underground passage at Alişar is the oldest example of the Hittite posterns used at Boghazköy to attack the enemy on the flank.

The palaces and temples from this period discovered at Kültepe, Acemhöyük and Karahöyük similarly attained monumental proportions. Part of the remains of two palaces which, according to the inscriptions, were dedicated to kings Warsama and Anittas respectively, have been discovered on the Kültepe acropolis. The more recent of the two has an almost square central courtyard flanked on all four sides by halls and corridors, strikingly similar in design to the architecture of the Hittite empire.

The best evidence we have of the originality and creativeness of the art of the period of the principalities is to be found in numerous specimens of pottery. Three kinds of vessels can be distinguished: (1) hand-thrown vases painted with polychrome geometric designs, still partly bearing the imprint of the third millennium BC; (2) wheel-thrown vases representing animal and human figures and narrative scenes; and (3) monochrome vases. They are characteristic of a new style which can be termed Hittite since it spread and remained in common use throughout Anatolia until the last centuries of the second millennium BC. The monochrome pottery is

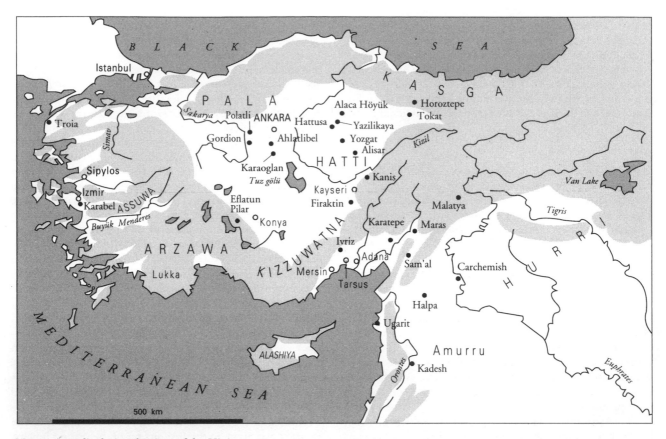

Map 13 Anatolia during the time of the Hittites.

coated with a red-brown slip designed to look like metal. A characteristic long-spouted jug, in particular, represents the culmination of a long process of evolution that has attained its classical form (Plates 87, 88).

Works of art in terracotta, bronze, silver, lead and ivory excavated at Kültepe, Acemhöyük and Karahöyük bear witness to a figurative art of great beauty and extraordinary originality. The influence of Babylonian art is discernible in the iconography of human and animal figures, but the Anatolian artists succeeded in creating a new style, which may be termed a Hittite style, with designs borrowed from Mesopotamia.

Excavations at Kültepe (Nesa-Kanesh), Acemhöyük and Karahöyük were led by Tahsin Özgüç, Nimet Özgüç and Sedat Alp respectively. The valuable finds are on display in the museums of Ankara and Konya.

From written documents and works of art we can draw the following conclusions: the city of Nesa, situated at Kültepe, was inhabited by the Nesians, who spoke the Hittite language. The style of architecture, pottery and all the figurative arts uncovered at the three sites display features and designs that are encountered later during the period of the Hittite empire. This points clearly to the emergence of Hittite civilization in the eighteenth century BC in the cities under the rule of the Hittite potentates. If we bear in mind the fact that, according to a Hittite text from Boghazköy, Anittas was initially prince of Kussara (a city somewhere in the centre of the peninsula) and subsequently conquered the cities of Hattusas, Zalpa (on the shores of the Black Sea) and Purushanda (in the central part of the peninsula), it can be deduced that the whole of central Anatolia was ruled by a single sovereign for some length of time during the eighteenth century BC.

This initial small kingdom, made up of several cities, was, however, short-lived. The account of Hittite history given by the Hittite king Telipinus (1535–1510 BC) reveals that Hattusilis I (1660–1630 BC), who dwelt at Hattusas, had succeeded, towards the middle of the seventeenth century BC, in founding a substantial, firmly established kingdom whose frontiers stretched as far as the sea. The new state was in fact so powerful that a few decades later his son Mursilis I (1630–1600 BC) succeeded in conquering first Aleppo and then Babylon, thus causing the downfall of the Hammurabi dynasty.

Despite this initial, very rapid expansion, the Hittite state saw its conquests wrested from it and was confined to its homeland in the bend of the Halys river several times between the sixteenth and fourteenth centuries BC. During the reign of Suppiluliumas (1380–1345 BC), however, with the submission of the kingdom of Mitanni, the Hittite state became a mighty empire, on a par with Egypt, to the extent that in the fourteenth and thirteenth centuries BC these two powers shared hegemony over the eastern world. Mursilis II (1345–1315 BC), the son of Suppiluliumas, was also one of the great sovereigns of the Hittite empire. His son Muwatallis (1315–1282 BC) waged the celebrated battle of Qadesh (1285 BC) against Ramesses II. Muwatallis had mustered all the available forces of Anatolia and Syria, with 3,500 war chariots, each mounted by two combatants and a charioteer. The outcome of the battle was inconclusive. It was, however, the Hittites who derived benefit from it, for after this date there was no longer any question of Egyptian influence in Syria and Mesopotamia. It was not until 1269 BC that a peace treaty was signed between Hattusilis III (1275–1250 BC) and Ramesses II. It is the oldest known treaty concluded between major powers in world history. Tudhaliyas IV (1250–1220 BC), son of Hattusilis III, and the very influential Queen Puduhepa belong to the period in which the great Hittite empire was still flourishing. During their reign, the fine arts reached their zenith. The reign of Arnuwandas III

(1220–1200 BC), however, saw the beginning of the decline of the empire. According to the new Boghazköy documents, the last king was Suppiluliumas, who reigned only briefly (1200–1190 BC).

Language and writing

As we have shown, the name of the Hittite capital, Hattusas, and the name of Hattusilis, founder of the Hittite empire, are derived from *hattus*, which was the name of the same site during the previous Hattian period. The names of other Hittite kings, such as Mursilis, Ammunas, Huzziyas and Telipinus are also of Hattian origin. This shows that the Hittite rulers attached great importance to winning over the Hattian population, which was no doubt in the majority. Furthermore, in various documents, the Hittite kings always referred to the country which they had brought under their sway by its old name, the 'Hattian land'. This diplomatic approach adopted by the newcomers towards the Hattian people was not only dictated by reason, however, but was also the natural outcome of centuries of co-existence between two peoples. The Indo-Europeans, composed of tribes that were vigorous but not highly civilized, were, as we shall see, strongly influenced by the indigenous peoples in all aspects of social, political and cultural life.

The new Hittite civilization, based largely on that of the Hattians, had its origins in the Indo-European tribes who called themselves Nesians and spoke Nesian, but are mistakenly termed Hittites today. As the only clue found by the philologists who deciphered the language of the tablets excavated at Boghazköy at the beginning of this century was the term 'the Hattian land', they thought that it was the name of the Indo-European people which had immigrated to Anatolia. This, together with the Old Testament references to 'Heth' and 'Hittim', gave rise to the designation 'Hittites'.

So far, four branches of the family of Indo-European languages have been identified in Anatolia during the Hittite period – Nesian, hieroglyphic Hittite, Luwian and Palaic. The first two branches were used by the royal family. Luwian was in use in the countries of Arzawa and Kizzuwatna in the south of the peninsula and Palaic in northern Cappadocia between Kayseri and Sivas or, more probably, in Paphlagonia.

The Hittite kings used Hittite (Nesian) and Akkadian in their official documents. The only other language used by the royal court, albeit rarely, was Hurrian.

The Hittites used cuneiform writing of Old Babylonian origin, dating from a period prior to that of the cuneiform writing used by the Assyrian merchants at Nesa. It is quite possible, therefore, that the Hittite princes who already ruled in central-southern Anatolia, that is to say at Alaca Hüyük, Mahmatlar and Horoztepe in the last quarter of the third millennium BC used (or might have used) this Assyrian cuneiform script; these potentates, who employed outstanding craftsworkers, must have had scribes who could maintain their correspondence with foreign countries. The Hittites also had a hieroglyphic script used mainly for public monuments and royal seals because it was composed of figurative signs that were also comprehensible to the illiterate Hittite populace.

Literature

The literature produced by the Hittites was highly original and quite unlike the written works of their neighbours. It is to the Hittites that we owe the oldest and most beautiful written sources of the Eastern world. The political testament of Hattusilis I (1660–1630 BC), the decree of Telepinus (1535–1510 BC), the personal annals of Mursilis II (1345–1315 BC), the autobiography of Hattusilis III (1275–1250 BC) and the letters from the Hittite kings to the sovereigns of neighbouring countries are the finest literary works of oriental antiquity.

The king, queen and government

The Hittite king was the commander-in-chief of the army and the supreme judicial and religious authority. Responsibility for political negotiations with foreign powers was also his preserve. He was, however, far from being an absolute monarch in the Oriental tradition. No Hittite king was ever deified during his lifetime. On his death, it was said: 'he has become a god'.

Although the monarchy was hereditary, the sovereign was but *primus inter pares*. The concepts of Eastern absolutism and divine right remained alien to the Hittite empire. The testament of Hattusilis I stipulated that the high-ranking nobility was not subject to royal justice. Disputes between nobles had to be brought before the Pankus (assembly of nobles). Similarly, in the rules governing the succession to the throne promulgated by Telipinus, the rights of the nobility were much respected.

The nobles possessed lands granted as fiefdoms by the local lords. They were obliged to provide the royal army with war chariots, which were the main component of Hittite military strength.

A distinctive feature of the Hittite monarchy was the highly independent position of the queen. She kept the title of sovereignty, *tawannana*, which is in fact of Hattian origin, throughout her life-time, even if her husband was no longer on the throne. The wife of a new king could acquire the title *tawannana* only after the death of the previous queen. The *tawannana* accompanied the king during ceremonies and made libations together with the king, as we can see from a relief at Alaca Hüyük (Plate 90). Queen Puduhepa, wife of Hattusilis III, played an important part in the political affairs of the state. She kept up a personal correspondence with the queen of Egypt. She is represented on the rock relief at Fraktin, to the south of Kayseri, making libation to the great goddess. The Hittite text of the treaty with Egypt on a silver tablet informs us that she even had an official seal on which she was represented, naturally in the embrace of the sungoddess of Arinna.

The highly respected social position of women was another characteristic feature differentiating the Hittites from the other countries of western Asia. Only the court had a harem. Polygamy did not seem to be a common practice among the people. The family was organized on a patriarchal basis.

Law

A feature specific to Hittite society, also setting it apart from its Oriental neighbours, was the humanitarian character of its laws. The Hittites held human life and the value of the individual in greater esteem than did their neighbours. They never inflicted any such degrading punishment as mutilation, which was a penalty under Assyrian law. They indulged in none of the acts of cruelty commonly practised by the Assyrians, such as impaling and flaying prisoners, massacring their enemies, burning them alive, or erecting pyramids of heads. Even slaves were treated humanely and were protected by state law.

Administration

The Hittite kings exercised direct control over the territories of the empire. The administration of the provinces was in the hands of their sons and other princes of the royal family. Their duties included keeping the roads, palaces and temples in good repair. Leading cities such as Aleppo, Carchemish and Datassa were governed by vassals chosen from among the royal princes. States under the domination of the empire were usually governed by local vassals but on behalf of the Hittites. These minor potentates did not have the right to engage in negotiations with foreign countries. Their main duty was to pay tribute to the royal household and provide the necessary resources for the imperial army.

Crafts and trade

Written documents reveal that the Hittite empire was populated mainly by rural peoples living off the land. The texts inform us that all kinds of trades were practised. The royal household did of course have its own highly skilled staff. In the great temple at Hattusas, half of a tablet in cuneiform script refers to 'altogether 208 persons of whom 18 are priests, 29 musicians, 19 scribes using wooden tablets, 35 soothsayer priests, 10 singers in Hurrian'. In all, 144 persons are listed, the remainder being on the other half of the tablet which has not survived.

As we have seen, the Assyrian merchants sold tin, clothing and textiles to the Anatolians in exchange for gold, silver and copper. According to a letter from Hattusilis III, the Hittites were familiar with the mining of iron ore and the forging of iron for tools, weapons and furniture. We know from the same text, however, that the manufacture of iron implements was a very lengthy process. Silver was used as the currency for transactions.

There were probably roads that could take war chariots and the four-wheeled vehicles which transported the supplies needed for the royal army. According to the texts, the princes and vassals who governed the provinces and the small dependent states of the empire were responsible for maintenance of the roads. Donkey caravans were probably used for domestic and international transport, as they had been during the previous period of the principalities.

Funeral customs

The Hittite tablets found at Boghazköy (Hattusas) speak of a 'house of stone' (E.NA) in which bones were deposited after cremation. Only the underground chamber at Gâvurkale near Ankara can be identified as a Hittite burial chamber. Significantly, the Gâvurkale chamber represents a tomb of the Isopata type from the early period and the mode of burial is very like the one referred to in the Homeric epic. This means that the Hittite kings, like the Hittite princes of Alaca Hüyük in the last quarter of the third millennium BC (see above), were interred according to the funeral rites of the Indo-European peoples.

In the Osman Kayasi necropolis near Yazilikaya at Hattusas, which the Hittites used for centuries, evidence of 72 burials has been found in clay receptacles of various kinds and sizes, 50 of them containing ashes and 22 containing bones, indicating that both funeral customs – cremation and interment – were in use among the citizens of Hattusas.

Religion

The religion of the Alaca Hüyük principalities, which were probably ruled by Hittite potentates in the last quarter of the third millennium BC, was theriomorphic in character (see above). These primitive beliefs prevalent among the Indo-European immigrants in Anatolia gave way to an anthropomorphic religion under the influence of the indigenous Hattian population. The great Hittite prince Anittas who reigned in the second half of the eighteenth century BC speaks of a storm temple and of another temple, named Siusummi, of *deus* (Zeus), both of which he erected himself (see above). It was at Hattusas, however, that the religion of the royal house was formed, this time under Hurrian influence.

'The thousand gods of the Hattian land' referred to in the texts found at Boghazköy are represented on the walls of an open-air rock sanctuary situated 2 km north-west of Hattusas (Fig. 34). The sixty-three male and female deities portrayed in ceremonial guise form the Hittite pantheon. In the centre is the storm-god and his spouse, the sun-goddess Arinna with their son the god Sarruma. This group of three deities is the oldest representation of the concept of a trinity.

At Hattusas, seven large temples and several dozen small temples have been discovered. The largest of them is dedicated to the storm-god Taru and his wife, the sun-goddess Arinna, who were the principal deities of the empire and of the Anatolian population during the Hittite period, although each city worshipped its own storm-god. Arinna, in her avatar as Ishtar, represented the goddess of war and fertility. The other deities – the sun-god of the heavens and the god of the moon, for example – were of lesser importance. Hittite mythology was profoundly influenced by Hurrian and Babylonian mythology and there are no original features of note in the texts relating to myths and legends.

Architecture

The principalities which flourished during the last quarter of the third millennium BC within the Halys River bend, and which were probably governed by Hittite potentates, had no art of their own (see above). The birth of Hittite art can be traced to the period of the principalities of the eighteenth and seventeenth centuries BC in the cities of Nesa, Acemhöyük, Karahöyük and Alişar. We have seen that a palace at Nesa has affinities with the monumental architecture of Boghazköy and that the Alişar underground passage is the oldest example of a Hittite vaulted passageway. We have also noted that the ceramic and figurative arts of these centres provide evidence of a style that may be termed Hittite. As we shall see later, certain shapes, designs and features of the art of the imperial period are derived from this previous time.

Excavations began at Hattusas in 1906 under the leadership of Hugo Winckler and Theodore Makridi. They revealed that the most significant achievements of the Hittites can be seen in their architecture. Some features were entirely new in terms of both technique and form. An example is the appearance of the system of cyclopean walls, previously unknown in Anatolia.

The city of Hattusas (Boghazköy)

The Hittites were the most remarkable fortress-builders of western Asia. The mighty walls of Hattusas were ingeniously designed, and strategic use was made of even the most rocky terrain. Two narrow, steep staircases leading down from the rampart enabled those inside the besieged citadel to attack the enemy from behind. Sorties could also be made through a 70 m long vaulted underground passage built of cyclopean masonry.

The acropolis, known as Büyükkale or Great Citadel, was occupied in the fourteenth and thirteenth centuries BC by the non-military buildings belonging to the royal family. Building D is the largest monument on the acropolis; it dates from the thirteenth century BC and its spacious hall (39 m by 48 m) on the first floor was probably used as an audience chamber, with a sweeping view over the surrounding countryside, including the temple. Building E, also constructed in the thirteenth century BC, was a small reception chamber. Built to an almost symmetrical plan, this building is quite different from the other edifices at Hattusas and is reminiscent of the *bit hilani* type of structure encountered in the plan of the Niqumepa Palace (fifteenth or fourteenth century BC) at Tell Açana, near Antalya. Building F, constructed in the twelfth century BC in the north-west corner of the citadel, is thought to have been one of the private dwellings of the

royal family. With its strategic position overlooking the great road leading to the capital and the magnificent view it commands in three directions, it must have been a residence ideally suited to the purposes of the great kings of the Hittite empire. The royal palace, of which very little remains, was situated on the eastern promontory in the most protected part of the acropolis. Building M was no doubt reserved for administrative and official purposes. Building C, in which votive offerings have been discovered, is identifiable as a small shrine. Building K housed the archives of the Hittite empire in the thirteenth century BC. It is the oldest building in the history of humanity known to have been built as a library.

Seven monumental temples have been uncovered at Hattusas which, by virtue of their size and architectural style, are among the finest monuments of the second millennium BC (Fig. 34). The largest of these temples (I), dedicated to the storm god and his wife, the sun-goddess Arinna, leaves a vivid impression on the visitor even today. Altogether, including the storehouses surrounding it, the temple measures 160 m in length by 135 m in width. The temple itself consists of a rectangular building with an inner courtyard and a wing facing north-west in which the nine chambers set aside for worship were located. The two largest chambers contained the statues of the storm-god and the sun-goddess Arinna.

Figure 34 Boghazköy (Hattusas). Restored plan (adapted from Kurt Bittel and Peter Neve).

Temples II-V, situated in the north of the city, were roughly similar in type to temple I. Peter Neve has recently excavated temples VI and VII, as well as about twenty small religious buildings to the south of Sarikale and to the east of Yenice Kale, that is to the north of temples II-V. As we know from the texts that each city had its own storm-god, it is highly likely that each of these small shrines belonged to one of the major cities of the empire.

Hittite architecture is characterized by its asymmetrical design. The Hittites used neither columns nor capitals; their buildings rested on square pillars. Typically, the large windows reaching almost down to ground level were not set into the walls surrounding the sanctuary but into the walls of the façade of the temple itself. Since the portions of the two rooms with the statues of the storm-god and the sun-goddess projected forward, the idols were lit from three sides. This need for light and brightness suggests that Hittite religious ceremonies were originally held in the open air, as can be seen at the rock sanctuary at Yazilikaya.

Figurative art

Hittite figurative art dating from the beginning of the Empire (seventeenth and sixteenth centuries BC), is closely related to that of the principalities, but the latter gradually gave way to a remarkable new style. The proportions of the seventeenth- and sixteenth-century BC vessels from Alişar and Alaca Hüyük are more slender and more refined (Plate 88) than the long-spouted jugs from Kültepe and Boghazköy dating from the eighteenth century BC and representing a classical style. In contrast to the fine eighteenth-century vases decorated with single figures in relief found at Kültepe, the remarkable sixteenth-century BC vessels from Inandik and Bitik are entirely covered with narrative scenes in relief on religious themes. The date of the Inandik vase is attested by a document from the same sanctuary dating to the reign of Hattusilis I (1660–1630 BC). Together with the pair of yoked oxen from Boghazköy (Plate 89), also dating from the sixteenth century BC, these two large, very beautiful and stylistically highly original vases are masterpieces of Hittite ceramic art.

By the sixteenth century BC, the Hittites were producing outstanding examples of glyptic art, as represented by the Tyszkiewicz cylinder-seal and similar specimens found in the excavations at Karahöyük. Since Alluwamnas (1510–1500 BC), the Hittite kings had used seals for signing official documents.

The written documents repeatedly refer to monumental sculpture in the temples. The statues of the deities had a very special function in Hittite religious beliefs. They were regarded as the patrons of the cities. If they were removed by the enemy, the city was considered to be deprived of its identity. This is why Muwatallis, who moved the capital of Hattusus to Datassa near Adana, took with him all the statues of the deities to his temporary residence whence he was better able to organize preparations for his Egyptian campaign.

It is unfortunate that no religious statue belonging to a temple has survived. All we have are most of the statues of lions and sphinxes which flanked the gateways to the cities of Hattusas and Alaca Hüyük. Mention may also be made of the monument of Eflatun-Pinar and the colossal stela of Fasillar, both near Konya and both open-air monuments, as is the portal sculpture of Hattusas and Alaca Hüyük (Fig. 35; Plates 91, 92). A large number of magnificent rock reliefs and orthostatic reliefs – the two main types of monumental

sculpture characteristic of the Hittites – have survived. The most remarkable of these reliefs are carved on a rock face at Yazilikaya, where even today one can admire the images of the sixty-three deities of the Hittite pantheon. Other important rock reliefs have been preserved at Sirkeli near Adana (relief of Muwatallis), at Fraktin in Cappadocia (relief depicting Hattusilis III and his wife Puduhepa, both offering libations to the deities), at Manisa (a goddess seated on a throne) and at Karabel near Izmir (a king armed with a bow and a spear with a Hittite hieroglyphic inscription). The only examples of orthostats are from Alaca Hüyük (Plate 90). They represent religious subjects, the king and queen making a sacrifice before an altar, and scenes from everyday life, acrobats, lion-hunting and so on. The relief representing a warrior-god which once adorned the eastern gateway of Hattusas, and now in the Museum of Ankara, is one of the finest examples of Hittite sculpture preserved to this day.

The iconographic details of the reliefs dating from the Hittite imperial period show that the Hittite sculptors followed fixed conventions. Not only the different parts of the head-dress, hair and clothes, but also the parts of the body were rendered according to very strict canons. The facial features, the shape of the eyes, eyebrows, mouth and ears are invariably the same. Male figures always wear a wide bracelet. The Hittites were bearded or unbearded, but never wore a moustache. The position of the arms is invariably the same, whether the figures are holding anything or not; the arm closest to the onlooker is folded and held tightly against the body, while the 'inside' arm extends slightly outward in front of the body. On the other hand, the female figures, always represented in profile as are the male figures, hold both arms out before them, slightly bent, in a pose of veneration which suggests they are making an offering.

From the sixteenth century BC onwards, there were small statuettes in silver and gold which also bear witness to the same specifically Hittite style as can be observed in monumental plastic art. A silver rhyton in the form of a crouching stag, and a bronze ritual axe decorated with reliefs of quite outstanding quality are both on display at the Metropolitan Museum of Art in New York (Plate 92). They are among the finest specimens of the exclusively Hittite conventional style which was common not only in central

Figure 35 Tuthalia IV (1250–1220 BC) in the embrace of the god Sharruma. Relief on the west wall of rock chamber B in Yazilikaya, Boghazköy.

Anatolia but also throughout the Anatolian peninsula, from Antioch in the south-east to Izmir in the west, during the imperial period.

The Hurrians

During the Hittite period there were other states in Anatolia. To the east and south-east was the kingdom of Mitanni, the most powerful of the Hurrian countries, which was of major importance towards the middle of the second millennium (c. 1650–1450 BC). Hurrian is one of the most curious languages of the East. Of the agglutinative type, it resembles neither the Semitic nor the Indo-European languages, nor is it like Hattian with its abundance of prefixes. In religion and literature, Hurrian civilization had a profound influence on the Hittites. At the time of the empire, the Hittites adopted the Hurrian concept of the deities. The reliefs of the Yazilikaya sanctuary reflect that concept. The epic of Gilgamesh, the myth of Kumarbi and the Kikkuli treatise on the breaking-in of horses are of Hurrian origin. Indo-Aryan and Luwian influences can be detected in Hurrian culture.

All the Mitanni sovereigns bear Indian names, showing that the Hurrians were dominated by an aristocracy of Indo-Aryan origin. The members of this noble lineage, apparently a very small minority, were charioteers and horsemen. They were called Marianni and it was undoubtedly through them that the breaking-in of horses and the use of war chariots spread to western Asia. In the present state of research, Hurrian art is known only from glyptics and pottery. The most characteristic motifs of their seals are hybrid animals, the pillars of heaven and the sacred tree. Cretan and Mycenaean influences can be discerned in some of their seals, for example in the representation of chariots and the rendering of the flying gallop. The large cups with decorative patterns on a black background are more typically Hurrian. This type of pottery appeared during the reign of Shaustatar in the middle of the fifteenth century BC and also occurs in more refined form in the Alalakh specimens. The mural paintings of Nuzi may also be considered Mitannian art, showing the heads of cows depicted full-face and women's heads with cows' ears.

Other groups in Anatolia

In the south of the Anatolian peninsula lived the Luwians, an Indo-European race whose existence can be ascertained only from their linguistic legacy. This is equally true of the Palaites, also Indo-European, who lived in Paphlagonia. The countries of Arzawa and Kizzuwatna were situated in the south of Anatolia. Ahhiyawa, mentioned in the Hittite texts, was none other than Hellas, the country of the Achaeans (Achaioi) who had once founded trading colonies in western Anatolia. It would seem that the Achaeans (the Mycenaeans) had noteworthy settlements at Miletus in Caria (Muskebi) and at Panaztepe near Kyme in the Aeolian region in the fourteenth and thirteenth centuries BC. The existence of a powerful kingdom called Ahhiyawa in Aegean Anatolia would not, however, have been tolerated by the Hittite empire. When the Hittites spoke of the country of Ahhiyawa, they were undoubtedly referring to the Achaeans of Hellas and the Aegean islands.

Troy VI (1800–1275 BC)

The founding of Troy VI in the Late Bronze Age, which followed the Trojan civilization of the Middle Bronze Age, occurred at roughly the same time as the founding of the first city-states by the tribes of Indo-European immigrants. It is probably no accident that the Early Helladic Period ended and the Middle Helladic Period began in Greece at exactly the same time. The rise of these new civilizations, contemporary with one another in three neighbouring zones of the Ancient World, must be linked with the great Indo-European immigrations which began towards the end of the third millennium BC and probably continued up until the start of the second. Blegen has shown the kinship between the populations of Troy VI and the Middle Helladic states of continental Greece. A similar but less obvious affinity, having the same origin, can be discerned between the Hittite and Troy VI civilizations. Although the Hittites had always been subject to a strong influence from further east, their civilization has various basic features in common with Mycenae and Troy VI, notably in architecture and town planning. However, it would seem that there was very little direct contact between Troy and Hattusas. Not the least fragment of Hittite pottery has been found at Troy. The similarities that can be seen between the architecture and pottery of the two cultures does not imply direct contact. They can more probably be attributed to local Anatolian influences which reached Troy by various indirect pathways. Overland communications were not safe and Troy by tradition and because of its geographical position turned towards the west.

Pottery with a matt surface, of Helladic and Cycladic origin, and Mycenaean objects predominate among the imported wares. Furthermore, Cretan wares and fragments of Cypriot pottery have been found, proving that Troy VI had indeed established maritime links with the outside world. The local pottery of Troy VI is monochrome, unpretentious and lacking in appeal. The most beautiful pieces are the Minyan ware found in large quantities in the earliest occupation layer of Troy VI.

The inhabitants of Troy VI were illiterate, but their kings undoubtedly had official secretaries to conduct correspondence with neighbouring states. The Trojans attained a high standard of culture. The architectural successes in this brilliant period, the period sung in Homer's *Iliad*, are situated in levels VI f-h. This is the city of the *Iliad*, the city which could not be conquered even after a ten-year siege. Priam and his sons, Paris and Hector, in other words the king and the princes whose names we know from mythology, must have lived in the most glorious age, that of period VIh. The destruction of Ilion, related in the Odyssey, occurred in the following period, VIIa. Blegen rightly attributed the end of Troy VI to a catastrophic earthquake. The debris of phase VIh found under Troy VIIa is clearly the result of an earthquake, as the photographs taken during the excavations show. The traces of this upheaval are still discernible in the area of squares G9 and J-K6.

Troy VIIa (1275–1240 BC)

Apparently the earthquake did not occur unexpectedly, since no remains of human skeletons have been discovered in the debris and the houses do not seem to have been abandoned in a hurry. The American archaeologists assert that there was no interruption in the cultural tradition. Indeed, just as much Grey Minyan ware was found in level VIIa as in level VIh.

Furthermore, they emphasize that the pottery known as Tan ware was also produced at the time of the preceding occupation level. It appears that level VIIa did not last for much longer than one generation.

According to the American expedition, Troy VIIa is the city of Priam, and the Ilion of Homer's *Iliad* dates from this period. However, the present author's observations on the architecture of level VIIa do not allow him to share that opinion. The inhabitants of VIIa repaired the walls of the city and the ruined houses, but they built houses of inferior quality. More important still, the character of the city completely changed from the housing point of view. There is no evidence of any work displaying the high artistic quality or the well-thought-out town planning that can be admired in level VI f-h. In the place of the magnificent buildings of Troy VI are houses that indicate a segregation of social classes, huddled closely together and in complete contrast to the residences of the megaron style.

These houses are well preserved; they can be seen between gates VIT and VIS in the zone situated behind the city wall. There is no comparison whatsoever between these and the houses VIG, VIF, VIE and VIC which form a row on the west side. What can have been the reason for such a striking change in Trojan architecture and town planning? Could an earthquake have caused such a radical break? It could be surmised that this natural catastrophe led to a transformation in the state administration and that the king and royal family, accompanied by the nobles, were driven out of the city and that the humbler classes living outside the citadel moved in to settle in their place. For it is inconceivable that the people who built the megarons and the ramparts of phase VIh set to work to construct houses so different and so mediocre solely as a result of an earthquake. The change could be explained by the disappearance of the king and the aristocracy. Perhaps the people, profoundly weary of more than five centuries of oppression by kings and nobles, were able to cast off their domination, under the leadership of a group of rebels who seized the chance afforded by the catastrophe to seize power. Thus the people may be considered to have risen up against the monarch and his entourage.

As we have tried to establish above, the Ilion of Priam, the glory of which is sung in Homer's *Iliad*, is in reality Troy VIh. The archaeological situation corresponds with the epic, confirming the narrative in the *Odyssey* of the destruction of Troy (VIa) by the Achaeans after the fruitless war, as told in the *Iliad*. Seen from this angle, the stratagem of the wooden horse takes on a new meaning. The Achaeans, unable to capture the city of Ilion despite ten years of effort, gained victory only after the city had been destroyed by an earthquake and the citadel had passed into the hands of an usurper, the leader of the poor and inexperienced 'lower' classes. As the Achaeans knew that they owed their victory to Poseidon, the maker of earthquakes, they erected a statue of a wooden horse to him as a sign of their gratitude for his effective help. It was from this event that poetic imagination created the stratagem of the wooden horse.

Troy VIIb1 (1240–1190 BC)

The thickness of the burnt layer VIIa varies from 0.50 to 1 m. In spite of the terrible catastrophe, the inhabitants of Troy returned to their city and repaired their houses and city walls. As the uninterrupted production of Grey Minyan ware and Tan ware proves, the indigenous culture persisted. The ruins of this period can be seen in squares E-F 8–9. The style of

construction of level VIh and VIIa persists.

Blegen is right to date the catastrophe of Troy VIIa on the basis of the style of Mycenaean pottery. Furthermore, as will be seen later, the year 1240 fits in with other historical events.

Troy VIIb2 (1190–1100 BC)

A change can be seen, for the first time since the establishment of Troy VII, in occupation level Troy VIIb2. At that level, knobbed ware and other similar objects appear for the first time. This type of pottery, hitherto found only in the Balkans, is distinguished by its greyish colouring, its decorative protuberances in the shape of horns and its angular handles. There are also differences in the technique of wall construction: the lower part is reinforced by orthostats, that is, by large, wide, vertically placed blocks of stone. A house built in this style can be seen to the west of gate VIU in square A7; there are also the remains of an orthostatic wall in squares J-K5 and K7.

The people of Balkan origin who settled in Troy VIIb2 probably entered it without any great difficulty, since no traces of a fire or other catastrophe between this layer and that of Troy VIIb1 have been found. It may be concluded from this that, among the tribes who must have played an important role in the destruction of Hattusas around 1180 BC, there were nomads from the Balkans who lived in Troy VIIb2. It was these same tribes who fought under the name of Mushki against Tiglath-Pileser I around 1165 BC, while the 'Sea Peoples' fought Ramesses III (1198–1176 BC). It seems that the Aegean immigration made its first halt at Troy. It is possible that the destruction of Troy VIIa by the Achaeans opened the way for this first wave of immigration. The acropolis of Troy, which acted as a rampart for Anatolia for centuries against the European tribes, lost its traditional power and served as a base for the great migrations of this age.

Troy VIII

The oldest traces of the Hellenic civilization of Troy VIII, consisting of late geometric Greek pottery, date from the eighth or even ninth century BC.

THE IRON AGE (1180–750 BC)

The presence of the Thracians in Troy VIIb2 is proven by the large quantity of knobbed ware found at this level. It is a type of pottery peculiar to the peoples of Eastern Europe. At Hattusas, the written sources come to an end *c.* 1180 BC, a date which also fits in well with the hypothesis that Hattusas succumbed to the attacks of the Thracians. The annals of the Assyrian king Tiglath-Pileser I, who ruled from 1112 to 1074 BC, constitute an important document concerning the immigration of the tribes from Eastern Europe into Anatolia. They state that he waged war against the Mushkis, who had made their first appearance fifty years before the start of his reign on the northern frontier of Assyria in the area of the upper Tigris. Thus it was that the Mushkis (probably the Moesians of south-east Europe) and several other Balkan tribes had gathered at the Assyrian borders around 1170 BC after invading Troy and Hattusas. The Egyptian sources confirm these dates. It is true that Ramesses III (1200–1166 BC) uses the expression 'Peoples of the Sea' or 'Peoples of the Islands' for the tribes who crossed the frontiers and coasts of his realm. None the less, since he said that they destroyed

Arzawa and Carchemish, among other places, we can take this as a confirmation of the Assyrian annals, for Carchemish is situated precisely in the region of the upper Euphrates, not far from the frontiers of the Assyrian empire. The written sources show us that not only the Thracians and the tribes from south-eastern Europe, but also the Peoples of the Sea and the Islands took part in this enormous migration. Another element of this immense human tidal wave is formed by the Dorian migration to mainland Greece.

The consequences of this warlike migration were catastrophic. The invaders destroyed the civilizations of Anatolia with such cruelty and violence that a period of darkness ensued. It lasted two centuries in western Anatolia and for at least four centuries in the rest of the peninsula. Between 1180 and 775 BC, central Anatolia was very sparsely inhabited by nomad tribes who probably left no material traces in their barrows. The upheaval was so great that even the Hittite tradition disappeared entirely from central Anatolia. It is certain that there were no urban centres in this region until the birth of the Phrygian state. Thus, none of the present names of cities in central Anatolia, such as Gordion, Ankara, Yozgat, Gorum, Tokat, Boghazköy or Kırşehir are of Hittite origin. In contrast, the centres south of the bend of the Halys river and the southern Anatolian cities, such as Niğde, Adana, Malatya and Maras all have names of Hittite origin and date from at least the Hittite epoch.

Neo-Hittite art (1200–700 BC)

In south-east Anatolia and northern Syria, neither of which seems to have had a dark age, the Hittite principalities of the later age became remarkably active after the fall of the empire. Late Hittite art can be divided into three distinct styles, early, middle and late.

The early Neo-Hittite style (1050–850 BC) is a continuation of the art of the empire and is found only at Malatya. The great relief of Malatya (Museum of Ankara) is a typical example. Two consecutive scenes are depicted; on the left, the weather-god is seen in a chariot drawn by two bulls called Séri and Hurri; on the right, we see him receive a libation offered by King Sulumeli, after the god has descended from his chariot. In his right hand the god is holding a boomerang and in his left hand a streak of lightning. In the background, level with his head, there are two hieroglyphs representing the deity and the symbol of the weather-god, both of which indicate his identity. The reliefs of Malatya, from a stylistic and iconographic point of view, are late works of the Yazilikaya and Alaca schools which produced splendid sculptures under the empire (Plates 90–2).

The middle Neo-Hittite style (900–750 BC), unlike the early Neo-Hittite, is not a direct continuation of the Hittite Anatolian tradition. Although the artistic forms of the time of the empire are still in evidence, the middle Neo-Hittite style evolved its own particular characteristics. The best examples were found at Carchemish and at Zincirli.

The late Neo-Hittite style (750–700 BC) draws together four distinct artistic currents: the traditional Hittite style, the Assyro-Hittite style, the Hittite Assyro-Aramaean style and the Phoenico-Hittite style. The first includes the reliefs of Carchemish (Plates 93, 94); the second, the reliefs of Araras from Kargamis, sculptures of Zincirli and of Sakçegözü; the third, the majority of the sculptures of Ivriz and Karatepe (Plate 96) and the fourth, the reliefs from Maraş and its surrounding area (Plate 95). Active schools of sculpture produced

remarkable works of art in the second half of the eighth century BC, particularly at Zincirli and at Sakçegözü. These works exerted a strong influence on Greek and Etruscan art. The lions and griffins of Greek sculpture are faithful imitations of the models created in these centres. Greek art was influenced in several other ways by late Neo-Hittite art. This is due first and foremost to the key position of these principalities as gates to western Asia but also to the favourable historical circumstances of the eighth century BC. Thus the common culture of the Hittites, the Luwians and the Aramaeans, which developed in the course of their long and peaceful co-existence, made these peoples worthy representatives of western Asia.

The Urartians (900–600 BC)

In the extreme east of Anatolia, on the plateau surrounding Lake Van, lived the Urartians, descendants of the Hurrians. They built up an empire and a civilization that bore a strong Assyrian imprint. Their works of art were very popular in their time. In particular, the bronze cauldrons decorated with human or animal heads were exported as far as Phrygia, Greece and Etruria. Marvellous examples of Urartian art, bronze cauldrons from the end of the eighth century BC, decorated with human or bulls' heads, are on display at the Museums of Ankara and Istanbul (Plate 97).

The Phrygians (c. 725 BC)

In central Anatolia, the Phrygians created a great civilization, essentially part of the Greek sphere but with strong Neo-Hittite and Urartian influences. The Phrygians were of Thracian origin and probably took part in the destruction of Troy VIIa and Hattusas. The first archaeological traces that they left, however, date from the middle of the eighth century BC. Midas founded the Phrygian empire, but it was short-lived (725–675 BC) and was sacked by the Cimmerian invasion in the first quarter of the seventh century BC.

The most important discoveries were made at Gordion, the Phrygian capital, and in other centres of Phrygian civilization, such as Alişar, Boghazköy, Alaca, Pazarli and Ankara. The works of art found in the course of the German excavations at Gordion at the beginning of the century are today in the Istanbul Museum. The discoveries made by the American expedition led by Rodney S. Young in recent decades are in the Ankara Museum and the Istanbul Museum. The objets d'art recently discovered by Sevim Buluç in a burial mound at Ankara are on display in the Museum of the Middle East Technical University, Ankara (Plates 98–100).

The Phrygian language was akin to Thracian. Phrygian script closely resembled that of the Greeks and was already in use before the end of the eighth century BC. The splendid Phrygian metal objects and Phrygian textiles were greatly treasured in the Greek world.

The Lydians, Lycians and Carians

The same period witnessed the rise of the Lydian, Lycian and Carian civilizations in the centre-west of Anatolia. The Lydian and Lycian languages, like that of the Hittites, belong to the Anatolian Indo-European group. However, Lycian and Lydian have many pre-Indo-European features. These peoples can be considered, at least in part, as representing the old pre-Hittite civilization. Their descendants probably survived until the first half of the first millennium BC, but no archaeological traces of them have yet been found.

Carian has not yet been deciphered, although its script is similar to the Lydian, Phrygian, Lycian and Greek scripts. It is thus not possible to determine to which family of languages it belongs. Herodotus wrote that, according to Cretan legend, the Carians were called Lelegs and inhabited the islands in the Minoan epoch. However, the Carians themselves were not of the same mind and maintained that they were natives of Anatolia and cousins of the Lydians and the Mysians.

The age of the Greco-Anatolian civilization

Recent excavations at Izmir (Smyrna), Miletus and Ephesus have clearly shown that the Aeolian and Ionian cities on the western coast of Anatolia were founded around 1050 BC. With these new facts to hand, it is possible to arrive at a greater understanding of the importance of eastern Greek art in the Hellenic world.

The excavations in ancient Smyrna (Bayrakli) have revealed that the Greeks of Anatolia had already founded cities protected by remarkable fortifications in the ninth century BC, in other words a century before Greece. Smyrna was probably the birthplace of Homer's *Iliad*, the oldest and most important literary work in the Western world, created in the second part of the eighth century (750–700 BC). The Ionians' contribution to the shaping of the universal culture of humankind was even more significant. It is in the Ionian city-states that we find the earliest evidence anywhere in the world of free thought and scientific research. At Miletus and in other Greek cities in Anatolia, the philosophers of nature created an entirely new world which was to become the cradle of Western civilization.

BIBLIOGRAPHY

AKURGAL, E. *Phrygische Kunst*. Ankara.
—— 1961. *Die Kunst Anatoliens*. Berlin. pp. 23–69.
—— 1993. *Ancient Civilizations and Ruins of Turkey*, 8th ed. Istanbul.
ALKIM, U. B. 1966. Excavations at Gedikli (Karahüyük): First Preliminary Report. *Bellet.* (Ankara), Vol. 30 pp. 27–57.
—— 1968a. *Anatolia I. From the Beginnings to the End of the 2nd Millennium BC*. New York.
—— 1968b. *Anatolia I*, Genève.
ALP, S. 1983. *Beiträge zur Erforschang des hethitischen Tempels*. Ankara.
AMIET, P. 1976. *Les antiquités du Luristan*, Paris (Collect. David-Weill).
AMIET, P.; ÖZGÜC, N.; BOARDMAN, J. 1980. *Ancient Art in Seals: Essays*, Princeton, N.J.
AMIRAN, R. B. K. 1952. Connections between Anatolia and Palestine in the Early Bronze Age. *Israel explor. J.*, (Jerusalem), Vol. 2 pp. 89–103.
ARIK, R. O. 1935. *Alaca Höyük*. Ankara.
—— 1937. *Alaca Hüyük (hafriyatinin) ilk Neticeleri*. Istanbul.
AVILA, R. A. J. 1983. *Lanzen- und Pfeilspitzen in Griechenland*. München. (Prähist. Bronzefunde, V, 1.)
AZARPAY, G. 1968. *Urartian Art and Artifacts*. Berkeley, Calif.
BASS, G. F.; PULAK, C. 1989. The Bronze Age Shipwreck at Ulu Burun. *Am. J. Archaeol.* (Boston, Mass.), Vol. 93, pp. 1–29.
BERAN, T. 1967. Die hethitische Glyptik von Boğazköy I, Boğazköy-Hattuşa V. Berlin.
BILGI, Ö. 1945. *Grundzüge der Vor- und Frühgeschichte Kleinasiens*. 2nd ed. Tübingen.

—— 1985. Metal Objects from Ikiztepe-Turkey. Beiträge zur Allgemeinen und Vergleichenden Archäologie, Vol. 6. Bonn. pp. 31–96.
BITTEL, K. 1975. *Das hethitische Felsheiligtum, Yazilikaya*. Berlin.
—— 1976. *Les Hittites: L'Univers des formes*. Paris.
BLEGEN, C. W. 1950. *Troy I: General Introduction. The First and Second Settlements*. Princeton. N.J.
—— 1951. *Troy, the Third, Fourth and Fifth Settlements*. Princeton, N.J.
BOEHMER, B. M. 1976. *Beiträge zur Kenntnis hethitischer Bildkunst*. Heidelberg.
—— 1987. *Glyptik aus dem Stadtgebiet von Boğazköy*. Berlin.
ÇILINGIROĞLU, A. 1984. *Urartu ve Kuzey Suriye*. Izmir.
DANMANVILLE, J. 1955. La libation en Mésopotamie. *Rev. Assyrio.* (Paris), Vol. 49.
DAYTON, J. E. 1971. The Problem of Tin in the Ancient World. *World Archaeol.* (London), Vol. 3, No. 1, pp. 49–70.
DEIGHTON, H. J. 1982. The Weather-God in Hittite Anatolia. Oxford. (Bar Int. Ser., 143.)
DEMIRCIOGLU. 1939. *Der Gott auf dem Stier*. Berlin.
DIAKONOFF, I. M. 1971. *Hurrisch und Urartäisch*. München.
DUPONT-SOMMER, A. 1949. *Les Araméens*. Paris.
DURU, R. 1980. *Kurucay Höyügü Kazilari: 1978/79 Calisma Raporu, Anadolu Arastirmalari, Ek Yayin 2*. Istanbul.
—— 1986. Kurucay Höyügü Kazilari. 1984 Calisma Raporu. *Bellet. L.*, Vol. 50 (Ankara). pp. 247–56.
EATON, E. R.; MCKERREL, H. 1976. Near Eastern Alloying and Some Textual Evidence for the Early Use of Arsenical Copper. *World Archaeol.* (London), Vol. 8, No. 2, pp. 169–91.
EFE, T. 1988. Demircihühük: di Ergebnisse der Ausgrabungene 1974–1973. Vol. 3. *Die Keramik* (2 vols). Mainz am Rhein.
ERKANAL, H. 1977. *Die Äxte und Beile des 2. Jahrtausends in Zentralanatolien*. München. (Prähist. Bronzefunde, IX, 8.)
FISCHER, F. 1963. *Die hethitische Keramik aus Boğazköy*. Berlin.
FRANKEL, D. 1979. *The Ancient Kingdom of Urartu*. London.
FRIEDRICH, J. 1963. *Aus dem hethitischen Schrifttum*. Berlin.
GARELLI, P. 1963. *Les Assyriens en Cappadoce*. Paris.
GARSTANG, J.; GURNEY, O. R. 1953. *Prehistoric Mersin: Yümük Tepe in Southern Turkey*. Oxford.
—— 1959. *The Geography af the Hittite Empire*. London.
GELB, I. J. 1939. *Hittite Hieroglyphic Monuments*. OIP (Chicago, Ill.), Vol. 43.
GOETZE, A. 1957. *Kleinasien, Handbuch der Altertumswissenschaft III*. 2nd ed. München.
GOLDMAN, H. 1956. *Excavations at Gözlü Kule, Tarsus*. Princeton, N.J. Vol. 2.
GONNET, H. 1975. *Catalogue des documents royaux hittites du IIe millénaire avant Jésus Christ*. Paris.
GURNEY, O. R. 1977. *Some Aspects of Hittite Religion*. Oxford.
GÜTERBOCK, H. G. 1982. *Les Hieroglyphes de Yazilikaya*. Paris.
HAAS, V. 1982. *Hethitische Berggötter und hurritische Steindämonen*. Berlin.
HAWKINS, J. D. 1980. *Late Hittite Funerary Monuments*. Copenhagen. (Mesopotamia 8.)
HUOT, J. L. 1982. *Les céramiques monochromes lissées en Anatolia à l'époque du Bronze Ancien*. Paris. 2 Vol. (Inst. Francais d'Archéol. Proche Orient, Bibl. archéol. hist., 111.)
JOUKOWSKY, M. S. 1986. *Prehistoric Aphrodisias*. Vols 1–2. Louvain-La-Neuve.
KAMIL, T. 1982. *Yortan Cemetery in the Early Bronze Age of Western Anatolia*. Oxford. (BAR Int. Ser., 145.)
KAPTAN, E. 1983. The Significance of Tin in Turkish Mining History and Its Origins. *Bull. Miner. Res. ExPl. Inst. Turkey* (Ankara), No. 95/96, pp. 106–14.
KLENGEL, E.; KLENGEL, H. 1970. *Die Hethiter und ihre Nachbarn*. Leipzig.
KOŞAY, H. Z.; AKOK, M. 1960. *Alaca Höyük 1940–1948*. Ankara.
—— 1973. *Alaca Höyük 1963–1967*. Ankara.
KORFMANN, M. 1980. Dermircihüyük. Eine vorgeschichtliche Siedlung an der phrygisch-bithynischen Grenze. Vorbericht über die Ergebnisse der Grabung von 1978. *Inst. Mitt.*, Vol. 30, pp. 5–21.

LAROCHE, E. 1980. *Glossaire de la langue hourrite*. Paris.

LOON, M. N. V. 1966. *Urartian Art*. Istanbul.

MATTHIAE, P. 1963. *Studi sui relievi di Karatepe*. Roma.

MELLAART, J. B. 1957. Anatolian Chronology in the Early and Middle Bronze Age. *Anatol. Stud.* (London), Vol. 7, pp. 55–88.

MERIGGI, P. 1975. *Manuale di eteo geroglyphico*. Roma.

NAUMANN, R. 1955. *Architektur Kleinasiens*. Tübingen.

ORTHMANN, W. 1963. *Die Keramik der frühen Bronzezeit aus Inneranatolien*. Berlin, Gebr. ann. (Ist. Forsch., 24.)

OTTEN, H. 1969. *Die hethitischer historischen Quellen und die Orientalische Chronologie*. Wiesbaden.

—— 1993. *Neufunde hethitischen Königssiegel*. Mainz.

ÖZGÜÇ, T. 1975. *Die Hethiter, Museum für anatolische Zivilisationnen*. Ankara.

ÖZGÜÇ, T.; AKOK, M. 1958. Horoztepe, Ankara. An Early Bronze Age Settlement and Cemetery. *TTKY*, Vol. 5, 18.

PARROT, A. 1961. *Assur*. München.

PECCHIOLI DADDI, F. 1982. *Mestieri Professioni e Dignita nell'Anatolia Ittita*. Roma.

PECORELLA, P. E. 1984. *La Cultura Preistorica di Iassos in Caria*. Roma.

PIOTROVSKI, B. B. 1969. *The Ancient Civilisation of Urartu*. Paris.

PODZUWEIT, C. 1979. *Trojanische Gefässformen der Frühbronzezeit in Anatolia, der Ägäis und angrenzenden Gebieten. Ein Beitrag zur vergleichenden Stratigraphie*. Mainz.

POETTO, M. 1981. *La Collezione Anatolica di E. Borowski*. Pavia.

SPYCKET, A. 1981. *La Statuaire du Proche-Orient Ancien*. Leiden.

STRONACH, D. B. 1957. The Development and Diffusion of Metal Types in Early Bronze Age Anatolia. *Antol. Stud.* (London), Vol. 7, pp. 89–125.

VERMEULE, E. 1964. The Early Bronze Age in Caria. *Archaeol.* (Boston, Mass.), Vol. 17, No. 4, pp. 244–9.

—— 1972. *Greece in the Bronze Age*. 5th ed. Chicago, Ill.

WEGNER, I. 1981. *Gestalt und Kult der Istar-Sawuska in Kleinasien*. Kevelaer. Neukirchen-Vuyn. (Alter Orient Altes Testam. 36.)

WILHELM, G.; BOESE, J. 1987. *Absolute Chronologie und die hethitische Geschichte des 15. und 14. Jahrhunderts v. Chr*. Göteborg.

YAKAR, J. 1974. The Twin Shrines of Beycesultan. *Anatol. Stud.* (London), Vol. 24, pp. 151–61.

12.4
IRAN

Reinhard Dittmann

To write a 'cultural history' of Iran from the third to the middle of the first millennium BC in this limited space is quite an impossible task since, unlike Mesopotamia, the cultural development of Iran is in no respect heterogeneous, due to the geographical situation of the country and the unequal extent of archaeological exploration in the different regions. For a long period the archaeology of the west and south-west dominated the scene. North Iran has up to now been only poorly explored, and large parts of the south and east are virtually *terra incognita*, having been investigated only from the mid–1960s onwards. For Iran as a whole, most of our information comes from early excavations, which neglected the stratigraphy of the sites. More recent work was either mainly on a limited scale, and/or was published in preliminary reports only. But despite these shortcomings, some general trends of Iran's cultural development can be traced.

THE PERIOD OF STATE FORMATION (*c.* 3700–3000 BC)

The roots of primary state development correspond roughly to the final phase of the late Ubaid period in Mesopotamia (*c.* 4000 BC), but only within the so-called Uruk period, at least in Khuzistan in the Susiana (Susa, period II) can a three-level hierarchy in the settlements be traced, as a sign of a primary state. A stratification of society and of the levels of decision-making at that time is suggested by the obvious division of labour, hand in hand with a standardization of various modes of production, which are revealed not only in the products themselves but also in the representation of several manufactures in the glyptic material from Susa. At this time, an early system of effective administration control (using calculi/tokens, clay tablets with inscribed numerals and cylinder-seals) was established. The calculi/tokens and clay tablets served for the control of quantities, while the cylinder-seals, especially on jar covers, door-locks and bullae, assured that the sealed items were untouched by unauthorized persons, and claimed ownership. Such tablets, exclusively bearing numerical signs, occur in Khuzistan at Susa and Chogha Mish, in the Ram Hormuz area at Tall-i Ghazir, in the Zagros at Godin Tepe and, at the very end of this period, at Tepe Sialk in the Kashan oasis.

It is probable that this early state formation did not take place without external influence from Babylonia (to which the Susiana clearly belongs geomorphologically), even reaching sites on the Euphrates as far as Syria (Habuba Kabira South, Jebel Aruda, Tell Sheikh Hasan) and south-east Ana-

tolia (Hassek Höyük, Arslantepe/Malatya). In Iran, this lowland culture infiltrated not only the highlands of the Zagros (Godin Tepe) up to the Qazvin Plain (Tepe Qabristan) and the Kashan Oasis (Tepe Sialk) but also to the south, up to the Marv Dasht (Tall-i Malyan, earlier Banesh Horizon) and the Kerman region (Tall-i Iblis/Aliabad phase).

The reasons for the spread of the lowland culture to the highlands is not entirely known. For some authors, it is a phenomenon of acculturation, while others would prefer a kind of colonialization process or see such development encouraged by the need for raw materials (assumed to be copper from the Iranian plateau). In the Persian Gulf, evidence of a horizon contemporaneous with the Uruk period is scarce. Direct contacts between Babylonia and Iran to the Gulf, based on evidence of the material culture, are not attested. Nevertheless, ancient Dilmun (modern Bahrain) is mentioned at least once in the archaic texts from level IVa at Uruk (end of Uruk culture), where a Dilmun tax-collector(?) is mentioned. One hypothesis is that after the collapse of the lowland Uruk commercial system in the north in Syria and Anatolia, which occurred before the end of the Uruk culture, Babylonia shifted its interest for resource access towards the Gulf, to the Omani copper mines, an orientation which was maintained in the following periods. In any case, the Uruk state appears not to be a regional/territorial state system, but an accumulation of city-states in direct, commercially oriented contact.

THE EARLY STATES (*c.* 3000–2150 BC)

The lowland aspect of the Uruk culture initially had some influence on local polities in the Zagros and in the highland regions of south-west/south Iran. This fast developed into the (early) Proto-Elamite complex (Susa, period IIIA-B), which retained some of the old, indigenous roots of the period before the Uruk influence; or, as is seen in the northern Zagros, at Godin Tepe for example, Uruk is replaced by a completely different complex, the so-called Yanik culture, with strong affinities with the Early Bronze Age I aspect of the Caucasus and eastern Anatolia. In north-east Iran, the local early Hissar culture, with its painted pottery, shows direct connections with the painted-pottery tradition in the Zagros of the Uruk period, with the Kashan oasis, and with Turkmenia in south Russia (in what is called there the Namazga III complex).

In the Proto-Elamite period a new grey pottery, co-existent for some time with and partly reproducing the shapes of the older painted ware (while other forms are clearly inspired from metal vessels), gradually replaces the older painted wares at Tepe Hissar. In the central Zagros developments in this period are still poorly understood. Further to the south, in Khuzistan, in the Susiana, the early Proto-Elamite complex marks a clean break in the development, as seen especially in the pottery inventory and in the glyptic material at Susa (period III), when compared to the material culture of the earlier Uruk period. This can also be recognized in the distribution of settlements: in the Proto-Elamite period in the Susiana there is a drastic decrease in the number of settlement sites, whereas in the adjacent Izeh-Malamir plains to the north there is a prominent increase. North-west of the Susiana, in the Deh Luran region, a completely different picture emerges, showing stronger connections to the former horizon in the modes of production. To the east of the Susiana, in the Marv Dasht and Kerman region, the development from the lowland, Uruk-oriented, so-called Early Banesh and Aliabad complexes to the Proto-Elamite horizon (Tall-i Malyan, Middle Banesh; Tepe Yahya) is a gradual one, even though, south of the Marv Dasht, a local system devoid of any Uruk or Proto-Elamite influence can be traced, the so-called early Vakilabad horizon.

The shift from the Uruk to the Proto-Elamite period is a phenomenon which must be viewed separately from region to region. It is only within this early Proto-Elamite period that a purely Elamite, and up to now undeciphered, script developed, the 'Proto-Elamite A' script which was already out of use at the end of the same period (Susa, period IIIB). The late Uruk and early Proto-Elamite clay tablets are concerned purely with local administration; so far no literary or historical texts have been found. Tablets with this script are found in almost all regions: in Khuzistan at Susa, at Tepe Sialk in the Kashan oasis; perhaps at Tepe Hissar in the Damghan region of north-east Iran; at Tall-i Malyan in the Marv Dasht and at Tepe Yahya in the Kerman region. Even in Seistan, in the Hilmand delta, some Proto-Elamite artefacts, such as one clay tablet with Proto-Elamite signs, and glyptic material of this horizon, have been found at Shahr-i Sokhta (period I). These finds are incorporated in an otherwise local cultural milieu which shows direct connections with the Kandahar region of Afghanistan, especially with the sites of Mundigak and Said Qala Tepe; with Makran and Baluchistan (Early Nal and Quetta-ware horizon at the sites of Nindowari, Niai Buthi, Damb Sadaat and Mehrgarh); as well as with Turkmenia (Namazga III/Geoyksjur phase). Material combining the north-east Iranian Hissar II Grey ware, the Baluchi Quetta and the Turkmenian Namazga III aspects have been found in south Russia in a locality as remote as Sarazm, not too far away from the west Chinese border.

Even though it is impossible to give any consistent interpretation of these pan-regional connections, it becomes clear that the Proto-Elamite universe was in no way less complex than the diffusion of the Uruk cultural complex; it is only more concentrated on Iran as a whole and culturally more diversified. On the level of political control, this period seems to be characterized by regional centres, overseeing economically dependent sub-centres and connected villages. Administrative control can by no means have had the same complexity as the contemporaneous systems in Babylonia, since the Proto-Elamite tablets went out of use at the end of this initial period. Other devices of administrative control, such as the use of cylinder-seals, continued nevertheless in the following middle and late Proto-Elamite periods (Susa, period IIIC-IVB1), contemporaneous with Early Dynastic II-III and the Akkadian dynasty of Babylonia (Susa, period IVB2). This kind of cylinder-seal is also to be found in contemporary graves in Luristan and in settlements of west Iran, as well as in the Marv Dasht and in the Kerman region. Further to the north, in Tepe Hissar (early period III), as well as in Turkmenia (Namazga IV horizon), in Seistan (Shahr-i Sokhta, periods II-III), in the Kandahar (Mundigak IV1-2) and Baluchi region (Damb Sadaat III, Mehrgarh VII), stamp seals are characteristic for the middle to late Proto-Elamite horizon; they have clearly been used as a means of administrative control, as can be shown by the evidence at Shahr-i Sokhta and the Namazga IV sites, suggesting a similar system for the Baluchi sites. What is missing in the eastern site inventories are items that attest to literacy.

In the middle and late Proto-Elamite period further contacts between Early Dynastic Babylonia and Khuzistan can be observed: in some graves at Susa chariots accompany the dead, recalling some of the wealthy graves in the so-called Royal Cemetery of Ur and at Kish in Babylonia. The painted pottery of this period in Khuzistan, called Susa II in the older literature, shows direct connections with the Zagros of west Iran, such as that from necropolises in Luristan, Tepe Giyan and the settlement of Godin Tepe III in the Kangavar valley, settlements which controlled the important interface between Babylonia and the Hamadan region of the Iranian plateau, the so-called Khorasan Road, towards the Hamrin and Diyala regions of Babylonia. Some vessels of this kind of Iranian pottery have been found in southern Babylonia, in late Early Dynastic III contexts: in ancient Lagash (modern al-Hibba), Girsu (modern Tello) and possibly in Ur. Other artefacts at Susa, such as sculptures of the 'worshipper-type' and 'votive plaquettes', manifest ideological beliefs similar to those of the élite in Babylonia, but the style also has local, non-Babylonian features. Statues of the so-called 'worshipper-type' have been found as far east as the cemetery of the south Iranian centre Shahdad.

Furthermore, in this horizon there was also a group of chlorite vessels which either show a so-called 'intercultural-style', found as far west as Syria and Babylonia, or a purely Iranian style. Other chlorite vessels, the so-called 'série récente' exist only from the end of the Proto-Elamite period, from the time of the Akkadian ruler Manishtushu. It is this middle to late Proto-Elamite horizon which shows a process of consolidation in the regional centres, perhaps not unlike the situation in Babylonia, which can best be described as a 'period of concurrent city-states'. But unlike the Babylonian sphere, here we have no direct written evidence for the struggle for domination of one Iranian centre over another, or of coalitions of centres. What is known from Babylonian sources, mainly from the Sumerian King List, is evidence of conflicts between Elam or Elamite powers, such as the dynasty of Awan (which cannot have been located far from Susa), and various Babylonian Early Dynastic rulers.

Another difference is that the regional centres of greater Iran in this period are not directly connected by rivers, which are the basis for the irrigation systems of the city-states in Babylonia, the control of which was one of the major sources of conflict. Furthermore, based on the hydraulic situation in Babylonia, large independent coterminous city-states were in competition for influence on the spheres they would indirectly control. In Iran, on the whole, the situation is completely different, since settlement clusters with urban centres are separated from each other by large, almost uninhabited regions. That this period in Iran was surely not as peaceful as one might think is shown, on the other hand, by the city walls of Tall-i Malyan (ancient Anshan) at the beginning of the middle Proto-Elamite period and at the large centre of Mundigak in the Kandahar region. Surely even Shahr-i Sokhta in Seistan and the large, up to now only poorly excavated centre Shahdad, had some kind of defence structures? Despite the often cited legends of a mythical city on the Iranian plateau, called Aratta (Shahdad? Shahr-i Sokhta? Mundigak?), besieged by the Babylonian hero Lugalbanda, these systems of defence do not seem so much to reflect a need for shelter against inner-Irianian conflicts but more likely they provide resistance to nomadic raids, which have to be included in the political scene of the Iranian plateau at any historical period. The horizon in question is furthermore characterized by large industrial units, producing objects of prestige for the local authorities and upper hierarchical levels of the society, as can be seen at Tepe Yahya, Shahr-i Sokhta, Mundigak and Tepe Hissar.

The centres of this horizon, especially in north-east and south-east Iran and in the Kandahar region, show that urban organization had numerous similarities, especially as between the twin cities of what has been called the Helmand civilization, that is, Shahr-i Sokhta (period II-III) and Mundigak (period IV 1–3A). This urban culture, which is contemporaneous with the Early Harappan period in Pakistan, and which, with the exception of Mehrgarh and Nausharo in the Kachi plain is almost *terra incognita*, could have had some influence on the urbanization of the later Mature Harappan period. That there is an unbroken tradition from the sites of the Helmand civilization via the Baluchi Early Harappan to the Mature Harappan in Sind does seem likely because of the architecture. Examples are: enclosures; city walls; platforms at Mundigak, Mehrgarh, Damb Sadaat and Rahman Dheri; and even the 'acropolis'/lower town principle of the Mature Harappan period which has a forerunner at Mundigak. Similar, too, are the modes of pottery production (mass-produced and standardized), and there are strong correspondences in the different wares and their shapes. The evolution of anthropomorphic terracotta figurines can be seen at Mehrgarh and Nausharo.

In the Persian Gulf, evidence of a horizon contemporaneous to the early Proto-Elamite period in Iran and the Gamdat-Nasr/Early Dynastic I(-II) period in Babylonia is stronger than before. Dilmun is mentioned on several occasions in contemporary Urukian texts. In the Gulf, this horizon is called the Hafit period and its material, for instance from the site of Hili 8 (Phase I) in Oman, can be linked directly with those of Babylonia and Iran. As said before, Mesopotamia's and the south-west Iranian centres' interests in Oman were the copper mines. The later Proto-Elamite horizon is represented in the Gulf by the Umm an-Nor culture, which shows only a few correspondences with the Babylonian Early Dynastic, but which has strong connections to the south Iranian coast, to the modern province of Makran (sites like Bampur and Damin), forming perhaps that cultural unity which is known as Makan in the written sources of Babylonia. The Umm an-Nor cultural complex is best represented, besides a few excavated settlements of this horizon, by innumerable collective graves which have been traced from Bahrain up to Oman.

Besides the already mentioned dynasty of Awan, there was another political entity called Marhashi/Parahshi/Warahshi which was defeated, as was Elam, by the first ruler of Akkad, Sargon. Recent studies do not exclude an east Iranian location for this complex. Conflicts between Babylonia and the Iranian polities continued throughout the Akka-

dian period, and Susa at least seems to have been under Akkadian sovereignty for a certain period of time. Sargon, the first ruler of the dynasty, claims that ships of Meluhha reached the port of Akkad. His second successor, Manishtushu, is supposed to have defeated a large portion of the Iranian plateau, *inter alia* Anshan and Sherihum which, in a later copy of the same account, is replaced by Meluhha. This is thought to represent the Harappan or Indus culture of Pakistan. Contacts with the latter can be found in archaeological records as early as the Early Dynastic III period in the Royal Cemetery of Ur in Babylonia, for instance, deduced from the presence of etched carnelian beads. In the Indus Valley, such beads are to be found exclusively from the initial Mature Harappan period onwards, never in an Early Harappan context. If such beads are a sign of direct contact between the west and the east, then the beginning of the Mature Harappan period, the Amri IIIA horizon in Sind, must date around the Early Dynastic III period of Babylonia. Also Naram-Sin, the fourth king of the Akkadian dynasty, claims victory over the whole of Elam, Marhashi and Meluhha. If the last is to be identified with the Harappan civilization, no direct evidence in the archaeological record of these sites shows any signs of a military conflict. Any claim of a direct supremacy over Meluhha by the rulers of Akkad has therefore to be viewed with scepticism.

THE SHIMASHKI AND SUKKALMAH DYNASTIES (*c.* 2150–1500 BC)

About the reign of the last ruler of the dynasty of Awan, Puzur-Kutik-Inshushinak, contemporaneous with the first ruler of the Ur III dynasty in Babylonia, Ur-Nammu, Elam developed, parallel to the Babylonian cuneiform script, a local writing system known as 'Proto-Elamite B' or 'Linear Proto-Elamite'. This script was in use for a short period only, and is known only from south-western Iran, the Marv Dasht and from the cemetery of Shahdad. Puzur-Kutik-Inshushinak seems to have briefly held a hegemony over large parts of Iran. It is in his inscriptions that for the first time a political entity called Shimashki is mentioned. But this Iranian hegemony soon came to an end, since from the middle of the rule of Shulgi, the second Babylonian ruler of the 3rd dynasty of Ur, Susa was included in the Ur III empire, and Marhashi and Anshan became allies, based on a marriage policy by the Ur III rulers Shulgi and Shuh-Sin. At the time of the last ruler in Ur III, Ibbi-Sin, Elamite forces struck back and took possession of Ur, possibly under Kindattu, the sixth ruler of the Shimashki dynasty, or his son Idadu I. Kindattu claimed supremacy over large parts of Elam, reaching as far as Marhashi. A large number of Elamite rulers of Susa, Anshan and Shimaski are known for this period, though a correct correlation between them and the Babylonian rulers, as well as their chronological order, raises some questions. During the reign of the late Shimashki ruler Ebarti II (Ebarat), a double monarchy of Anshan and Susa was introduced which combined the lowland and highland regions of Elam; the Anshanite god Napirisha was worshipped at Susa from this period on. Both cities, Susa and Anshan, were enlarged, Anshan reaching its maximum extension during this time and in the following Sukkalmah period, locally known as the Kaftari horizon. Relations to the east are suggested by a seal ascribed to a wife of Ebarat which shows direct stylistic and iconographic parallels to a group of composite figurines from Bactria and from the Quetta hoard of the Mehrgarh VIII horizon in Baluchistan. The Shimashki period is a time of continuing conflicts between Elam and the several rulers of the Isin-Larsa period in Babylonia struggling for supremacy after the collapse of the Ur III empire.

The Shimashki dynasty is succeeded by the Sukkalmah dynasty (c. 1900–1500 BC), named after the title *sukkalmah* (grand regent) used by Elamite rulers. This period is one of the best documented in Elamite history, due to a large amount of cuneiform texts and building inscriptions, mostly from Susa. The sovereignty in Elam, at least at Susa, was divided and handed to a kind of triumvirate (which had its roots in the Shimashki period), with the *sukkalmah* at the top, followed by the '*sukkal* of Elam and Shimashki' (usually the brother of the first) and a '*sukkal* of Susa' (in most cases a son or nephew of the *sukkalmah*). The succession to the throne also followed this principle, obviously to secure dynastic stability. Synchronisms with some of the *sukkalmah* and Old Assyrian and Old Babylonian rulers can be established, but real correspondences for the beginning and the end of the Sukkalmah period are still hard to detect. In any event, the period ended before the bulk of the texts of the archives of Haft Tepe were written which, according to new studies on the chronology of the Middle Elamite kings, can be placed, with some certainty, around the beginning of the fifteenth century BC. The Sukkalmah dynasty was not only involved in conflicts with the Babylonian world, sometimes in alliance with the kingdom of Eshnunna in the Diyala region of northern Babylonia, but it also engaged in commercial activities, *inter alia* in the Old Babylonian tin trade, as is proved by the Old Babylonian cuneiform sources of the Syrian centre Mari.

Attempts to locate known political units from textual evidence are problematic. Shimashki, the most important political unit at the beginning of this horizon, has been located either in the western Zagros (Godin III) or as remote as 'Outer Elam' (east/south-east Iran); Marhashi has recently been identified with the Kerman region. If the rulers of Shimaski were as important as is reflected in the extant written sources and in the titulature of Elamite rulers, then any location east of the line from Shahdad to Tepe Yahya becomes almost impossible, based on the simple fact that, archaeologically, roughly around 2000 BC, in east Iran the large urban centres of the Helmand civilization, Shahr-i Sokhta and Mundigak, collapsed and can in no way be linked with this strong dynasty. Aside from Tepe Yahya and Shahdad in the Kerman region, and the cemetery of Khinaman, north-west of Kerman, no important political units farther east of Iran are known, so far, with the exception of the Kulli complex in Makran and the beginning of the mature, urban phase of the Harappan civilization in the Indus Valley. Tepe Yahya, as well as Shahdad, shows some connections to the Mature Harappan, and this influence can be traced as far west as Susa and Babylonia (Ur, Kish, Nippur); even one seal from Hama, in Syria, shows an 'Indian' influence.

In the Shimashki period, trade with the Persian Gulf (Wadi Suq horizon) continued, as seen by the appearance of Persian Gulf seals at Susa, as well as at Umma and Ur in Babylonia. Very quickly this trade seems to have been controlled by Dilmun, because at the end of this and early in the following Sukkalmah period the so-called Dilmun seals became most popular in the Gulf, best known from Failaka; examples can be cited from Susa and from Lothal in west India. As a recent study has shown, this seal group had some influence even on the stamp seals of the Old Assyrian colonies of the Karum period in Anatolia, Turkey.

Turning to north/north-east Iran, the grey-ware horizon

of the late Hissar III complex also reached sites in the north-west, such as Hasanlu, Dinkha and Godin Tepe, roughly contemporaneous to the Khabur-ware horizon of Assyria which can be dated roughly about the time of Shamshi Adad I of Assyria and Hammurabi of Babylonia, in the early eighteenth century BC. This Hissar III horizon had connections with both the west and the east, most prominently with Turkmenia (Namazga V/VI horizon) and the south Russian Bactrian and Tadjikian complex, which was thought to be a local variation of Namazga VI in Turkmenia, but which is probably partly contemporaneous to Namazga V. This Hissar IIIC/Bactrian complex can be traced in a number of sites on the Iranian plateau and further to the east. In east Iran, in Seistan, there is direct evidence of this material; it has also been traced at Yahya, Shahdad and even Susa in Khuzistan, and possibly even Luristan, where a stamp seal of this horizon is said to come from; similar finds are also present in Makran at the sites of Khurab, Kulli, Mehi and Nindowari. Some objects from this horizon are found as far east as China (Ordos seals), then in the Indus Valley at Harappa, Mohenjo-daro and Chanhu-daro and most prominently in the Kachi plain at Mehrgarh (period VIII), Sibri, and in a recently discovered hoard in Quetta town, controlling the Bolan Pass which connects the Kandahar region via the Quetta Valley and the Kachi plain with the Indus Valley. Recent research, especially in the Kachi plain at Mehrgarh/Sibri and at the site of Nausharo, has shown that this horizon has to be equated with the late urban phase in the Indus Valley, with a period represented at the Indus site of Amri in period IIIC (parallel to Wheeler's complex C-D at Mohenjo-daro). What has formerly been seen as a post-Mature Harappan phenomenon, often connected with the Indo-Aryan or 'barbarian' invaders into the Indus system which provoked the collapse of the Harappan culture, clearly appears today as complementary material equipment and an indicator of complex interregional relations in the later part of Harappa's Mature, urban phase. The sites mentioned indicate routes of communication between the regions which recall the several routes of the late historic 'Silk Road'. But even if there is evidence for the existence of silk in the Namazga VI horizon in Turkmenia, there is no other hint to prove that silk was traded on a wide scale at this time. What becomes clear is that inter-city communication existed at least from the early Proto-Elamite period, and probably even before that time. But this phenomenon must not be overemphasized, since there were almost no other possibilities for contact and trade due to the deserts of central Iran which, at any given prehistoric time, made direct contact across very difficult.

THE PERIOD OF TRANSFORMATION (c. 1650–1450 BC)

The end of the Hissar III cultural complex in the north and north-east in the eighteenth century BC marks the beginning of a kind of 'Dark Age' in the archaeological and historical knowledge of Iran. Only at Tureng Tepe, in the Gurgan plain of north-east Iran (period IIIC2), has material of a younger phase been found, showing connections to the following Iron Age I horizon of the north-west. In the north-east, this Tureng Tepe IIIC2 period is thought to end around the middle of the seventeenth century BC or somewhat later. The beginning of the Iron Age I period in the north-west has been conventionally dated not before the middle of the fifteenth century BC, perhaps even somewhat later. Up to now, there has been no real archaeologically excavated site which can bridge the gap between the end of the Tureng Tepe IIIC2 complex in the north-east and the beginning of the Iron Age I culture in the north-west. The 'Dark Age' therefore persisted for about a hundred years. Any evidence that emerges from this 'Dark Age' is mostly based on radiocarbon dates for Tureng Tepe IIIC2 and Hasanlu (period V), and Dinkha Tepe (period III) in the Urmia Sea region of north-west Iran, and on a very problematic typological comparison of pottery and metallurgical artefacts. At least at Dinkha Tepe there are vague hints that a certain period separates the Old Assyrian, Khabur ware related levels from the Iron Age I levels. These possible intermediate levels show affinities to the Urmia ware of Haftavan Tepe which also has strong connections with the Trialeti culture of the Caucasus (Middle Bronze period). Another hint of a close relationship between the Iron Age I period and the Old Assyrian/Old Babylonian period is a cylinder-seal found in an Iron Age I grave at Tepe Sialk, Necropolis A (period V) which, if not considered an heirloom, should date to no later than the middle of the seventeenth century BC. In the western Zagros, the Holmes Expedition of the University of Chicago to Luristan excavated several sites, such as Chigha Sabz, Kamtarlan II, Mir Vali and Surkh Dum-i Luri, and the Belgian archaeologist Vanden Berghe added the sites of Sarab Bagh and Tawarsa, all of which had Late Bronze Age material with vague connections to finds from Susa, dated to between the sixteenth and fourteenth centuries BC. Unfortunately here, too, there is no well recorded stratigraphic overlap between this so-called Late Bronze Age and Iron Age I material.

In south Iran, in the Marv Dasht Plain, following the Kaftari horizon, the complexes of the Qal'eh, Shuga and Taimuran pottery are to be found. Not much about these is known, with the exception that at Tall-i Malyan, incorporated in the local Qal'eh horizon, a Middle Elamite administrative complex has been excavated, dating from the thirteenth century onwards. Older remains have been excavated at Tall-i Malyan, but await publication. Other scarce information has come from a small village site called Darvazeh Tepe. Further to the east, evidence for an equivalent to the Iron Age I horizon is completely missing. Tepe Yahya, period III, apparently belongs to the Iron Age II/III period, but seems also to have had connections with the Archaic Dahistan complex of north-east Iran and south Russia, which might start earlier. In the Kandahar region, Mundigak, period V, shows some correlation with the Chust culture of the Ferghana Valley and to the Jaz Tepe I complex of the Murghab Delta and adjacent regions of south Russia. The date of the beginning of these complexes is under discussion, but based on present evidence it cannot be much earlier than 1600 BC. Most Russian scientists would favour a much younger date. In the Kachi plain, the site of Pirak (period I-II) is clearly later than the Mature phase of the Harappan civilization and is surely partially contemporaneous with the Jhukar complex in the lower Indus (Sind) and the Cemetery H phase in the Punjab (both culturally almost unknown complexes of the Late Harappan period), as well as to Mundigak V in the Kandahar region. Pirak-related material has also been found at a couple of sites in Baluchistan and there are even some connections down to the Gulf, as seen at Tell Abraq in the United Arab Emirates. In Baluchistan, the Early Iron Age remains a mystery which can only be solved by new excavations.

Some historians, as well as some archaeologists, have interpreted the changes, observed at the end of this fourth historical unit where former larger cultural complexes split into smaller, local units, as evidence of a period of movement of new tribes, often connected with the historically reconstructed migration of people speaking an Indo-Aryan and/or Iranian language. Some have even tried to connect the coming into use of the grey pottery in north/north-east Iran at Tepe Hissar and in the Gurgan plain at Tureng and Shah Tepe with these tribes, as well as the grey burnished pottery of the Swat IV phase in the mountainous regions of northern Pakistan. Others see these tribes connected with the painted pottery of the Jhukar and Cemetery H phase of the Late Harappan culture in the Indus Valley. It should be emphasized that up to now there is no direct link between any linguistic group and a specific pottery type. The old concept of 'pots = people' has proved to be invalid, and any historical connection of obvious changes in the material culture with a specific linguistic and – on a more primitive line of reasoning – with a specific ethnic group should be avoided. This is perfectly illustrated by the Old Assyrian Karum period, where native Assyrian tradesmen were present in Anatolia in a linguistically non-Assyrian and an archaeologically purely Anatolian milieu. If the Old Assyrian tablets had not been found, no suggestion of the presence of native Assyrians in Anatolia at this time could have been made. That tribes speaking an Iranian language moved to or infiltrated the Iranian plateau is beyond doubt. But how and when is a matter of debate. At the latest in the first millennium BC Iranians, to judge by their personal names, are present in the cuneiform records of Assyria and Babylonia. Before that time they remain an unknown factor in historical reconstruction, but should, in all likelihood, be included as one group in the multitude of autochthonous, local groups.

THE IRON AGE I PERIOD (c. 1450–1100 BC)

After the period of transformation, which partly overlaps the beginning of the Iron Age I period, large parts of Iran are virtually *terra incognita*. In Elam the old capital Susa was replaced for a short period in the fifteenth century BC in the reign of Tepti-ahar, by a new centre called Kabanak (modern Haft Tepe), located about 20 km to the south of Susa. The administrative tablets excavated in the context of the monumental funeral complex and workshops at Kabanak show that the 'Malamir texts' purchased on the antiquity market and used as a source for the reconstruction of the latest Sukkalmah period in east Khuzistan originate from here and reflect the events of central Khuzistan. What is interesting is the claim of Tepti-ahar to be 'King of Susa and Anshan', since up to now no contemporary structures have been excavated at Anshan. In the second half of the fourteenth century BC the Elamite king Untash-Napirisha founded a new cult centre called Dur-Untash, 40 km to the south-east of Susa. Here a central ziggurat, surrounded by various temple complexes, was erected. In an early building stage an open court was surrounded by several rooms and the complex was dedicated to the 'Lord of Susa', the god Inshushinak. The court was then, in a slightly later phase, used as the base for the erection of a ziggurat with a temple on top, dedicated to the gods Inshushinak and Napirisha, obviously combining the most important deities of the lowlands (Elam, represented by Inshushinak) and the highlands (Anshan, represented by Napirisha). The whole complex was decorated with glazed tiles, baked bricks and gypsum plaster and was extremely rich in finds of bronze weapons, seals and glass beads. Untash-Napirisha was, according to P. Amiet, the first Elamite ruler for centuries to establish an Elamite court art which, besides the architecture at Dur-Untash, is also represented in a stela and a monumental fragmentary bronze statue of his wife Napir-Asu. Building inscriptions from Untash-Napirisha have been found at several sites in Susiana but also in eastern Khuzistan, next to the city of Ram Hormuz in Tepe Bormi. Of the further history of Elam little is known.

The situation changes for the twelfth century BC with the Shutruk dynasty, whose rulers took advantage of the political vacuum in Assyria and Babylonia following the violent death of the Middle Assyrian king Tukulti-Ninurta I. The Elamite king Shutruk-Nakhkhunte I (c. 1165 BC) attacked Babylonia. The aim of this raid was obviously not the enlargement of Elamite territory. Shutruk-Nakhkhunte's army looted most of the Babylonian towns, carrying a vast amount of booty back to Susa, including the victory stela of Naram-Su'en from Sippar and a statue of Manishtushu from Eshnunna. In fact most art objects, considered as the highlights of ancient Mesopotamian art, were 'collected' by Shutruk-Nakhkhunte I and are only known to the scientific community thanks to French excavations at Susa. The political influence of Shutruk-Nakhkhunte I extended as far as Anshan in the east and he also restored a temple at Liyan (built by the predecessor of Untash-Napirisha, Humban-numena). He was followed by his son Kutir-Nakhkhunte I, who dealt the final blow to the Kassite dynasty of Babylonia, deported its king Enlil-nadinahi to Elam, and took the cult statue of the Babylonian national god Marduk to Susa. In spite of his aggressive policy against Babylonia, this king continously embellished the temples at Susa and Liyan. With his successor and brother Shilak-Inshushinak the Shutruk dynasty was at its height, since he extended his raids not only to Babylonia but far to the north, beyond the Diyala River, into the Kirkuk region and the heartland of Assyria. He took care of the temples in Susa and Liyan and building inscriptions attest activities in the mountainous areas towards Anshan as well. His successor Huteludush-Inshushinak is mainly known through building inscriptions from various sites in Elam, and a large administrative complex, excavated at Anshan, possibly dates to his reign. At Anshan he erected temples for the main gods of the Elamite pantheon: Napirisha, Kiririsha, Inshushinak and Shimut. Similar administrative enclaves in other parts of the highlands during the Shutruk dynasty can be traced by surface finds of building inscriptions. The Shutruk dynasty came to an abrupt end after the Elamite war of Nebuchadnezzar I (1125–1104 BC), who finally did not only defeat Huteludush-Inshushinak, but also brought back the statue of the god Marduk to Babylon and thus restored Babylonian power. Due to the general lack of written sources, virtually nothing is known about the following rulers of Elam up to the eighth century BC.

The kings of the Shutruk dynasty had been engaged in the embellishment of the rock sanctuary at Kurangun and upon stylistic considerations the reliefs of Shikaft-i Salman I, II and IV, near Izeh-Malamir can be connected with their reigns. Further reliefs at Kul-i Farah might date, according to a recent study by Amiet, to the period immediately after the fall of the Shutruk dynasty, around the turn of the millennium. So, despite the silence of written sources, Elamite power may not have completely collapsed after Nebuchadnezzar's war, especially since no long-term supremacy of

Babylonia over Elam is known from Babylonian contexts.

The situation between the fifteenth and eleventh centuries BC in other parts of Iran has already been partially described. To the east, in Fars, deurbanization and the decimation of the sedentary population can be traced, which also affected – on a much smaller scale – the Susiana. Outside the city of Anshan, with its administrative complex, no Susian-style artefacts have been found, only locally produced Shogha-Taimuran pottery. Further to the south and to the east of Iran no permanent settlements have been discovered.

To the west a few settlement sites have been found in the Zagros, for example the temple(?) of Surkh Dum-i Luri, perhaps a foundation of the mid-fourteenth century BC, situated at one of the main transhumance routes and 'Construction I' at Tepe Giyan of twelfth-century BC(?) origin. Most artefacts, which can be dated to the Iron Age I period, were found by the Belgian mission under the leadership of L. Vanden Berghe in Luristan, in stone graves. Iron Age I levels are also present at Hasanlu V in the Urmia region of north-western Iran, with its typical Early Western Gray ware. Mid-second millennium BC grave contents are also known from Gilian and Marlik-Tepe. More precise dating of the latter graves is still a matter of debate; for the Gilian graves in general a chronological scheme has been proposed by Haerinck. The material of these graves points to connections with the Caucasus, to the Artik I-II complex investigated by H. Kossack. Iron Age I material in north-east Iran is extremely rare, but shows connections to the Yaz I horizon of Turkmenia, an influence which can be traced further south to the Mundigak V horizon in the Kandahar region of Afghanistan and even to the Pirak aspect of the Kachi plain in Pakistan, which shows some links with a few sites of the Early Ghul complex in Baluchistan. Terracotta figurines from Pirak give evidence of the increasing use of the camel, at that time surely employed in long-distance trade. In the Kachi plain, as well as in regions of the Persian Gulf, sorghum became the most prominent staple food. In northern Pakistan, the Swat IV complex has to be dated to this period. Its architecture and archaeological material show connections to the Neolithic in Kashmir (Burzahom/Gufkral). It is noteworthy that in the Swat IV complex some sherds of Late Harappan/Cemetery H type have been found, showing connections with the Punjab.

THE IRON AGE II PERIOD (c. 1100–800 BC)

For Elam, almost no written sources mention historical events. Archaeologically this is part of the Miroschedjis Neo-Elamite I period, based on the stratigraphy at Susa and dated from 1000–725/700 BC. But due to the limited scale of the excavations at Susa, other than a refined typology of pottery, not much is known. Evidence for some activities in the old cult centre Dur-Untash can be traced but hardly further substantiated. It seems that some time around the eleventh century BC most of the Middle Elamite settlements in the Susiana were abandoned. What was left, and newly founded, was of small to medium size.

In Fars almost no settlements can be found after the tenth century BC. Even the important centre of Anshan had been given up. What was left of the political entity Susa and Anshan was an almost completely deserted highland region, with a concentration of peoples in the lowlands. Dessication occurred in the first half of the second millennium BC in north-east Iran at the end of Hissar IIIC, in Turkmenia (Post-Namazga V/VI), and in Pakistan. This is most clearly seen in the Kachi plain and led to desertion of the Harappan centres in the south and east, and the concentration of Pirak and Iron Age I settlements at the run-off of the mountains. It is not impossible that this desiccation finally had its influence on the highland regions further to the south-west and forced the highlanders of the Iranian plateau to increasing nomadism. What is clear, furthermore, is that the small Elamite enclaves, which had been implanted in the highlands in the Middle Elamite period in order to be under effective royal control, had been given up by this time. So a breakdown on the level of political control of the former structures can be observed as well. In Luristan, graves, dated by Vanden Berghe to Iron Age II, are typical for this period; some must belong to a small kingdom, known from cuneiform sources as Ellipi. Further to the north, south of Lake Urmia, lay the kingdom of Mannea. Midway between these two, along the Great Khorasan Road, several tribes were located, east of which the tribes may be summarized under the collective name of Medes. For the Lake Urmia region the most important settlement of this period is Hasanlu IVB. The date of the destruction of this important site is still under discussion. The excavators R. H. Dyson and O. W. Muscarella have an impressive series of "C dates to around 800 BC; I. N. Medvedskaya, on the other hand, basing his opinion on typologic observations, mainly of some horse trappings with parallels in the Hallstatt C culture in Europe, proposes 714 BC. The problem is that the dating of the European sequence was also based on early views of the chronology of western Asia. Furthermore, the most important sources for interregional cross-dating of horse trappings, the Neo-Assyrian reliefs, are missing between the reigns of Ashurnasirpal II (884–858 BC) and Tiglath-Pileser III (745–727 BC). We have only a little iconographic information from the period in between: the bronze gate of Balawat (which is rich in detail, but surely only part of what was known), some scanty reliefs from the reign of Shalmaneser III (858–824 BC) and a stela from Adad-nirari III (810–783 BC). The amount of the reliefs of Tiglath-Pileser III is unimpressive. Therefore any arguments based on the presence and absence of certain horse bits and the like on Neo-Assyrian reliefs should be made with great caution and the basis of the dating of some chronological prehistoric schemes in Europe should be kept in mind. Accordingly, the dating of Dyson and Muscarella is accepted here, since it seems to be well founded. If one agrees that the destruction of Hasanlu IVB took place at the end of the ninth century BC, then the famous necropolis of Sialk VI/Sialk B at the Kashan oasis may date from this century, as may also the site of Baba Jan III in Luristan. That such a date is not unlikely is shown by the site of Mauyilbak/Delfan, since here pottery of the Baba Jan III type was found together with cylinder-seals which can be dated just after Shalmaneser III, to the end of the ninth century BC. It is this Neo-Assyrian king who was engaged in campaigns against Mannea and the tribes along the Great Khorasan Road, but without gaining any long-lasting Assyrian control in these regions. North Iran is, with the exception of grave groups in Gilian referred to above, furthermore archaeologically undefined. In the Gurgan plain the initial date of Tureng Tepe IVA, which shows affiliations to the Archaic Dahistan complex further to the east, is still a matter of debate. It may start in the ninth century BC or even earlier. Vague connections to Tepe Yahya III may give a hint as to the date of this site in the Kerman area. A sequence for this period in east Iran cannot be established for the moment. In the Kandahar region at Mundigak, the material of late period V and early VI shows good connections to the Yaz I horizon in Turkmenia and to the end of the Pirak sequence in the Kachi plain of Pakistan. The mountainous region of northern Pakistan is archaeologically defined by the Swat or Gandhāra Grave culture, which shows possible connections to surface finds in the Punjab. In the beginning this complex was thought to originate directly in the late Hissar complex of north-east Iran. Typological similarities to the Sumbar and Parkhai necropolises are also recognizable. Nevertheless, no direct link between the Swat complex and the north-east Iranian assemblages can be established for the moment, due to the long chronological interval between them.

THE IRON AGE III PERIOD (c. 800–550 BC)

Elam enters the political scene again around the middle of the eighth century BC. According to the Miroschedji, Elam was less centralized at that time than in the Middle Elamite period, and had three royal seats at once, at Susa, Madaktu and Hidalu, suggesting a three-part division of royal titles as in the Sukkalmah period, Susa functioning as the traditional capital and cult centre, Madaktu as the seat of the king of Elam, and Hidalu, in the Behbehan area, as a refuge in times of trouble and perhaps as the site where the traditions of Elam survived in the Neo-Assyrian I period. Historical information comes mostly from Babylonian chronicles and Assyrian royal inscriptions. Humban-nikash I (743–717 BC) was an ally of Merodakh-Baladan II of Babylon and was in conflict with the Assyrian king Sargon II around the city of Der, the northernmost point reached by this Elamite king. He was succeeded by his sister's son Shutruk-Nakhkhunte II (716–699 BC), who is also known as the builder of a small temple at the acropolis of Susa, decorated with glazed tiles. His epithets 'King of Anshan and Susa' and 'Enlarger of the Realm' seem to be exaggerated, since he lost parts of the Elamite territories east of Der and in western Elam in a counter-attack by Sargon II and retired to the highlands, leaving the Babylonian king Merodakh-Baladan II to Sargon's mercy. As a result Sargon II took possession of the Babylonian throne. The northern shield Elam against Assyria, Ellipi, was lost at this period when, after the death of its king in 708 BC, the Assyrians took advantage of the rivalry of the princes. The Great Khorasan Road was now under Assyrian control. The conflict continued in the reign of the new Assyrian king Sennacherib (704–681 BC), but Sennacherib also fought successfully against the Elamite-Babylonian coalition. In 691 BC an Elamite force, including troops from Babylonia, Ellipi, Parsuash and Anshan, fought at Halule against the Assyrian army. The victory, claimed by Sennacherib, contrary to Babylonian sources, led to the siege and destruction of Babylon in 689 BC. The two following Elamite kings, Humban-haltash I (688–681 BC) and Humban-haltash II (680–675 BC) continued their cordial relations with Babylonian local rulers. But when the Babylonians tried to win over Humban-haltash II against the new Assyrian king Esarhaddon (680–669 BC) they failed. Under the reign of Humban-haltash II's brother Urtak (674–664? BC), relations between Assyria and Elam became quite friendly. This *entente cordiale* lasted only into the first years of the new Assyrian king Ashurbanipal's reign (668–627 BC), when in 665 BC the Elamite king attacked Babylonia by surprise, but was persuaded to withdraw by the Assyrians. The policy of Tepti-humban, following Urtak on the Elamite throne, provoked the emigration of the three sons of Urtak to Assyria. When the Assyrians then attacked and defeated Elam, these three sons were installed as clients of Ashurbanipal: Humban-nikash II at Madaktu (and Susa?) and Tammaritu at Hidalu. In the civil war between Ashurbanipal and his brother shamash-shuma-ukin, installed on the Babylonian throne, Humban-nikash II joined the Babylonian side.

In 647 BC, after the Assyrians had re-established military control over Babylonia, the troops of Ashurbanipal turned towards Elam, and in the following year overran Elam and destroyed Susa. The report of this event parallels the reports on the destruction of the Urartian centre Musasir by Sargon II and of Babylon by Sennacherib. Even if the written sources speak of the complete destruction of the Elamite capital, in the archaeological record this event was without any significant influence on the further development of material culture in Elam and Susa; and Humban-haltash III, who survived the Assyrian attack, reinstalled his residence at Madaktu. In the century between the destruction of Susa in 646 BC and the establishment of the Achaemenid dynasty under Cyrus II (559–530 BC), Elam existed as an ephemeral state. Outside the Susiana, Neo-Elamite reliefs have been found near Izeh-Malamir at Shikaft-i Salman and Kul-i Farah, Kurangun and Naqsh-i Rustam in Fars. Scanty remains are also known from Tall-i Ghazir, near Ram Hormuz. Further to the east, contemporaneous material is completely lacking.

To the west, in the Zagros, at the time of the Assyrian ruler Tiglath-Pileser III (755–727 BC), a province named Harhar, somewhere in the Kermanshah region, was incorporated into the Assyrian provincial system as a buffer against the Medes further to the east, who were driven southward by the Cimmerian invasion to Urartu at the end of Sargon II's or beginning of Sennacherib's reign. Thus control of the Great Khorasan Road seems to have lasted at least up to Esarhaddon's reign. The Assyrian presence is also illustrated by two Neo-Assyrian stelae, dated to Tiglath-Pileser III and Sargon II, found in Luristan(?) and in the Kangavar Valley, near Godin Tepe. The Lake Urmia region, Hasanlu (period IIIB) and Agrab-Tepe, formerly Mannaean territory, were incorporated into the Urartian empire early in the eighth century BC, but nothing substantial of these sites has been published.

In north-east Iran, the situation remained as it had been in the previous period. Further to the east, the Yaz II assemblage, with its links to the Kandahar region of Afghanistan (Mundigak VI), continued. The earliest pottery, found at Nadi Ali in Seistan, may belong to this horizon as well. In Baluchistan unidentified pottery groups of the early Ghul ware seem to continue, along with unpainted wares which have been found in the upper layers at Rana Ghandai and are possibly connected with Iron Age material from the upper levels at Pirak and the early Dur Khan assemblages in the Kachi plain.

In northern Pakistan, the Swat complex continues. Settlements of this period are not only found in the mountainous regions (such as Aligrama and Bir-Kot-Ghundai), but also in the Punjab (Charsadda and at the Hathial mound at Taxila) and at Gumla, period V, in the Gomal Valley of Waziristan.

Further fieldwork in north-east, east and south Iran is necessary in order to elucidate the roots and the formation of the Achaemenid empire. There are enormous gaps in our knowledge of those parts of Iran thought to be the homeland of the Achaemenids, like ancient Parsuash, which archaeologically is not defined for the centuries before and in the early phase of the Achaemenid empire.

BIBLIOGRAPHY

ALLCHIN, F.; HAMMOND, N. 1978. *The Archaeology of Afghanistan from Earliest Times to the Timurid Period*. London.

AMIET, P. 1966. *Elam*. Auvers-sur-Oise.

—— 1986. *L'âge des échanges inter-Iraniens, 3500–1700 avant J.-C.* Paris.

—— 1992. Sur l'histoire élamite. *Iran Antiqua*, Vol. 27, pp. 75–94.

ASTHANA, S. 1985. *Pre-Harappan Cultures of India and the Borderlands*. New Delhi.

BRIANT, P. 1984. *L'Asie centrale et les Royaumes Proche-orientaux du premier millénaire (c. VIIIè-VIè siècles avant notre ère)*. Paris.

CARTER, E.; STOLPER, M. W. 1984. *Elam: Surveys of Political History and Archaeology*. London. (Near East. Stud., 25.)

DITTMANN, R. 1990. Eisenzeit I und II in West- und Nordwest-Iran. Zeitgleich zur Karum-Zeit Anatoliens? *Archaol. Mitt. Iran*, Vol. 23, pp. 105–38.

DYSON, R. H.; MUSCARELLA, O. W. 1989. Constructing the Chronology and Historical Implications of Hasanlu IV. *Iran* (London), Vol. 27, pp. 1–15.

HAERINCK, E. 1988. The Iron-Age in Guilan: Proposal for a Chronology. In: CURTIS, J. (ed.), *Bronze Working Centers of Western Asia c. 1000–539 BC*. London/New York. pp. 63–78.

HOLE, F. 1987. *The Archaeology of Western Iran. Settlement and Society from Prehistory to the Islamic Conquest*. Washington, D.C. (Smithson. Ser. Archaeol. Inq.)

KOHL, P. 1984. *Central Asia. Palaeolithic Beginnings to the Iron Age*. Paris.

KOSSACK, G. 1983. Tli Grab 85. Bemerkungen zum Beginn des skythenzeitlichen Formkreises im Kaukasus. *Beitr. allg. Vergl. Archäol.*, Vol. 5, pp. 89–186.

LEVINE, L. D. 1972. *Two Neo-Assyrian Stelae from Iran*. Ontario, Art and Archaeology. (Occas. Pap., 23.)

MEDVEDSKAYA, I. N. 1991. Once more on the Destruction of Hasanlu IV: Problems of Dating. *Iran Antiqua*, Vol. 26, pp. 149–61.

MIROSCHEDJI, P. de. 1990. La fin de l'Elam: Essai d'analyse et d'interprétation. *Iran Antiqua*, Vol. 25, pp. 47–95.

NEGHABAN, E. O. 1991. *Excavations at Haft Tepe, Iran*. Philadelphia, Pen. (Univ. Mus. Monogr., 70.)

POTTS, D. T. 1990. *The Arabian Gulf in Antiquity. From Prehistory to the Fall of the Achaemenid Empire*. Oxford. Vol. 1.

SCHMIDT, E. F.; VAN LOON, M. N.; CURVERS, H. H. 1989. *The Holmes Expeditions to Luristan*. Chicago, Ill. (Orient. Inst. Publ., 108.1–2).

STEIN, A. 1940. *Old Routes of Western Iran*. London.

VANDEN BERGHE, L. 1979. *Bibliographie analytique de l'archéologie de l'Iran ancien*. Leiden.

—— 1983. *Luristan een verdwenen bronskunst uit West-Iran*. Gent, N.V.

VOGELSANG, W. 1988. A Period of Acculturation in Ancient Gandhara. *South Asian Stud.* (London), Vol. 4, pp. 103–13.

12.5
AFGHANISTAN

Victor I. Sarianidi

Afghanistan is a land of extremely variable landscape. High mountain ranges (in places over 4,000 m), the Hindu Kush, dominate the central portion of the country. Rivers drain these rugged mountains in a radiating pattern, like spokes from a wheel: the Kabul river flows eastward into the Indus; the Helmand, Khash Rud and Farah Rud flow south-west into the Seistan lowlands where they terminate in deltas and lakes; the Har-i Rud and Murghab flow west and north into the Tejen and Murghab deltas of Turkmenistan; and various streams flow northward into the Bactrian plain as part of the Amu Darya drainage. For the most part, the Hindu Kush contains only limited agricultural lands, in narrow river valleys, but does offer seasonal pasture for animal herders. Nevertheless, the upland regions of Afghanistan do contain a wealth of other resources, including copper, silver and various precious stones; Badakhshan, in north-east Afghanistan, contains one of the few sources of lapis lazuli, which during the Bronze Age was traded across western Asia as far as the Mediterranean. Moreover, the rivers form routes, sometimes through narrow mountain passes (such as the Khyber Pass), that allow communication between central Asia and the Indus Valley. The prehistory of the mountain areas is not well known; most likely, the prehistoric communities of these parts of Afghanistan were mostly pastoralist and small village farmers in valleys.

As the Hindu Kush drops in altitude to the north, west and south, the valleys widen out and the rivers eventually flow through flatter lowlands. Two lowland areas have particular importance to the prehistory of Afghanistan, Bactria to the north and Seistan to the south-west of the Hindu Kush. Bactria lies along both banks of the Amu Darya and its tributaries, in modern Afghanistan and Tajikistan. Various streams cross the Bactrian plain within Afghanistan. While the streams (for example, the Surkhab and Kokcha) in eastern Bactria flow into the Amu Darya, those in western Bactria form deltas without connecting with the major river (for example, the Balkhab, Tashkurgan). Surrounded on three sides by mountains (the Hindu Kush to the south, the Pamirs to the east, and the Hissar to the north), Bactria opens towards the west and north-west, a geographical circumstance that encouraged close connections with Turkmenia during prehistoric times. The setting for a satrapy of the Achemenid empire and for an independent Hellenistic kingdom later in the first millennium BC, Bactria was also home to a spectacular Bronze Age culture.

Seistan is a broadly flat region in south-western Afghanistan and neighbouring Iran, bound by the Hindu Kush to the north, the highlands of Baluchistan (in Iran and Pakistan) to the south and east, and by Iranian uplands to the west. The Helmand and other rivers flow out of the Hindu Kush through relatively wide and fertile alluvial valleys into lowland deltas and terminal lakes or marshes. Both the wide mountain valleys in the middle reaches of the Helmand drainage, and the Seistan plain in its lower reaches, offer considerable potential for irrigation agriculture. Seistan falls along a series of routes that skirt the southern Hindu Kush, connecting central Asia, the Iranian plateau, and the Indus Valley (especially via Quetta in Pakistani Baluchistan).

Afghanistan has long beckoned scholars with its ancient and enigmatic remains, but for many years was a country forbidden to foreigners. French archaeologists were the first Europeans to obtain permission to excavate, at the beginning of the twentieth century. The French maintained a near monopoly over archaeological work until after the Second World War, when teams from other countries began working in Afghanistan. Most of the work done in the 1950s through the 1960s comprised exploratory surface surveys and small soundings in Seistan (Dupree, 1963; Fairservis, 1952, 1961; Hammond, 1970; Dales, 1972; Fischer, 1973; Shaffer, 1971). At the same time, however, J. -M. Casal's extensive excavations at Mundigak during the 1950s established a long prehistoric cultural sequence that remains unrivalled (Casal, 1961); the Istituto Italiano per il Medio e l'Estremo Oriente excavation of Shahr-i Sokhta in Iranian Seistan during the 1960s and 1970s produced results that directly bear on the prehistory of Afghanistan. The 1960s also marked the French excavation of the Hellenistic city at Ai Khanum in Bactria, the work which eventually led to the discovery of the Harappan settlement at Shortugai and the systematic study of ancient irrigation systems in Bactria during the 1970s (Francfort, 1989; Gentelle, 1989). In 1969, the joint Soviet-Afghan archaeological expedition began its important work in northern Afghanistan (Sarianidi, 1972, 1975, 1986). When the war during the 1980s halted archaeological research in Afghanistan, the prehistory of Bactria and Seistan were known in broad outline, while that of the other parts of the country remained little understood.

BRONZE AGE ANTECEDENTS

While early agricultural Neolithic villages have been found in Turkmenistan and Iran, no trace of comparable settlements has been detected in the valleys of the Hindu Kush foothills in northern Afghanistan. However, the cave sites at Ghar-i Mar and Ghar-i Asp, in the Balkhab Valley in the

Hindu Kush foothills, contain cultural levels that date to the fifth and fourth millennia BC (Dupree, 1972). These archaeological deposits contain evidence of groups using roughly made pottery and bronze artefacts, and herding sheep, goat, and possibly cattle. A similar pattern, dated to the late third millennium BC, appears in the cave site of Dara-i Kur (the so-called goat-cult Neolithic; Dupree, 1972), in a valley within the Badakhshan foothills. These sites, which seem to represent stations used seasonally by early pastoral nomads in northern Afghanistan, are most remarkable for the early appearance of tin-copper alloying, represented by several objects at Ghar-i Mar.

Settled life in northern Afghanistan is difficult to detect before the beginning of the third millennium BC, nearly 3,000 years after the foundation of farming villages elsewhere in central Asia. Some surface sites in the Balkhab and Tashkurgan deltas represent the local communities of the upper Amu Darya plain during the fifth and fourth millennia BC. The surface finds from these sites are predominantly microlithic chipped stone tools, similar to those of the Kelteminar culture of the Kyzyl Kum desert further down the Amu Darya. The subsistence base of these groups in the upper Amu Darya remains undetermined, but probably involved collecting wild plants, hunting, and perhaps some farming.

A longer history of settled life is apparent in the Helmand drainage. Mundigak, near the modern town of Kandahar, provides the clearest and most significant evidence for early life. The site lies in a tributary valley of the Helmand River drainage; the streams that run down from the foothills provide the best possible conditions for ancient agriculture. In addition, the hills around contained abundant sources of copper, which were a stimulus to progress in ancient metal working. Not coincidentally, the first settlers of Mundigak, in the fourth millennium BC, were acquainted both with agriculture and with metal tools.

Casal's excavation of the site defined seven periods, each of which contained sub-phases. The earliest levels, Mundigak I-II, reveal the initial semi-nomadic settlement of the location, and the emergence of a settled village during the first half of the fourth millennium BC. This village consisted of rectangular structures of mudbrick, with interspersed open areas that occasionally contained special features such as ovens. In the subsequent period, Mundigak III (late fourth millennium BC), the settlement consisted of blocks of rooms, occasionally equipped with benches and pillars; by the end of the period, some larger, multi-room houses appeared. The people of this time buried their dead in ossuaries (brick cists), in which several individuals were interred, often with their skulls detached and arranged at one side of the cist.

From its beginning, the Mundigak community was working copper into tools, weapons and ornaments, and a variety of stones (like alabaster and steatite) into vessels and compartmented seals. Metal working gradually became more complex, and tin-copper alloys (5 per cent tin) were being created by period III. The animal and plant remains from these levels indicate that wheat cultivation and animal herding (sheep, goat and cattle) formed the basis of life. And even in these early levels, the pottery was diverse and indicates some interaction with people in Baluchistan to the east. The painted pottery in Mundigak III levels includes a significant proportion of geometric decoration that is broadly similar to styles found in Baluchistan (Quetta ware) to the east and in Turkmenistan (Geoksyr pottery) to the north-west. A variety of other decorative styles at home in Baluchistan also

occur in smaller amounts. The appearance of exotic raw materials, especially during Period III, reinforces this impression of far-flung relations; imported lapis lazuli (Badakhshan) and turquoise (Kyzyl Kum) were worked into beads, while a piece of ivory from Period III implies connections with India (Jarrige and Tosi, 1981).

THE EARLY BRONZE AGE (c. 3000–1800 BC)

The third millennium BC saw a florescence of Bronze Age societies in Afghanistan, particularly in northern (Bactria) and south-western (Seistan) Afghanistan. These two areas contained very distinctive cultures that developed at different tempos and in different ways. Despite these disparities, however, the two areas did share a common central feature: their intense connections with neighbouring regions.

Northern Afghanistan

By the end of the fourth millennium BC and the beginning of the third, settled life based on irrigation agriculture had developed in Bactria. The best evidence for this development comes from the Taluqan basin in eastern Bactria, where the French team identified simple canal irrigation systems; the pottery found with the associated settlements is similar to that of the contemporaneous occupations in the Helmand drainage to the south-west. By the second half of the third millennium, these irrigation systems were up to 10 km long (Gentelle, 1989). Among the sites found in eastern Bactria at this time is Shortugai, the lower levels of which contain an assemblage of artefacts that belong to the Indus civilization, including painted pottery, seals, inscribed objects, and Harappan-style ornaments (Francfort, 1989). The Shortugai site, located along the Amu Darya near the confluence of the Kokcha, is often supposed to represent a Harappan trading colony or station, since its position gives access to the lapis lazuli of Badakhshan and to the other metal and mineral resources of central Asia.

By the end of the third millennium BC, dozens of ancient settlements appeared in the middle reaches of the Amu Darya, forming separate irrigation oases that stretch from Meymaneh in the west, through Sheberghan, to the oases north of Balkh. These settlements were strung out among the deltas of the streams that ran down from the Hindu Kush foothills into the Bactrian plain. Each settlement consisted of a few dozen houses, built of uniformly sized mudbrick, the walls and floors coated with clay. The rooms of individual residences were grouped around internal courtyards, and probably housed large extended families. The local notables, who stood apart from the general citizenry, built individual fortified strongholds for themselves that stood apart from the ordinary residential places.

Tradesmen, merchants and the local administrative officials lived in larger settlements. Social differentiation is evident in monumental buildings of a public nature. For example, a whole complex of monumental buildings existed at Dashly-3, including the so-called round temple (Fig. 36). The centre of this complex was a round building with rectangular towers, the rooms of which included sanctuaries with raised platforms and fire altars on brick foundations. Residential rooms radiated from the central tower, providing the living spaces for the people serving the temple. A

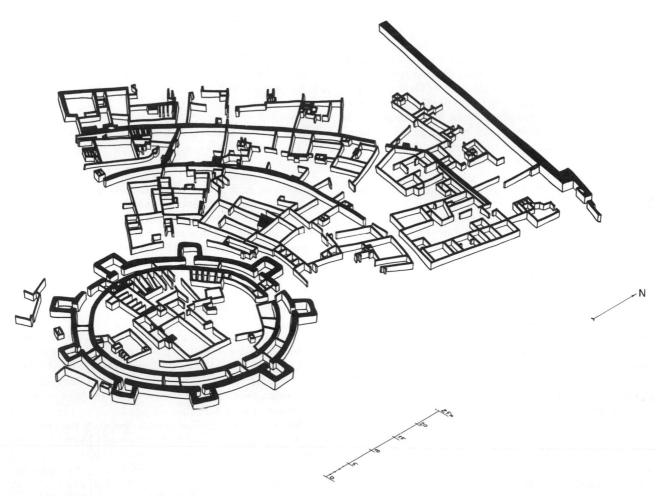

Figure 36 Axonometric projection of the round temple in Dashli-3, north Afghanistan.

second monumental building alongside the first was rectangular, consisting of a spacious interior court in which were scattered small sanctuaries and presumed residences. The four façades framing the internal courtyard all had a similar plan, with T-shaped corridors separating large rooms. The exterior façade of the building was decorated with pilasters, while a broad, water-filled moat encircled the walls. In effect, the building was cut off from the outside world, and probably represents a religious-cum-secular structure, a kind of Bactrian religious and administrative centre of the Bronze Age.

The ancient Bactrians buried their dead in cemeteries near the settlements, and much more rarely in the ruins of deserted settlements. The dead were laid out on their sides, mostly with their heads to the north and with arms and legs bent. The funerary offerings, when present, consisted chiefly of a large number of pottery vessels and smaller amounts of weapons and ornaments, artefacts indicative of prestige. In the rarer instances of élite graves, gold and silver artefacts, mostly vessels, accompanied the body. During the past two decades, local villagers have looted many of these cemeteries to sell the burial gifts in Kabul and elsewhere; many of these objects subsequently made their way into the collections of major museums and of private individuals (Pottier, 1984).

The material culture of the Bactrian Bronze Age contained a number of features peculiar to the region (Fig. 37). The pottery was of high quality, made on a potter's wheel, and fired in sophisticated two-tiered kilns. As a rule, the kilns were set at the edge of settlements, and several kilns were often grouped together to form a kind of potters' quarters.

These factors indicate that the potter's trade formed an independent and specialized branch of the Bactrian economy. These potters made elegant and sometimes fanciful shapes, among which the vases and bowls on tall, slender stems are particularly remarkable. Although finely finished, most of the pottery was undecorated, though a few examples of incised zigzags or circles do occur.

While tools of chipped flint, and particularly arrowheads and drills, continued to be used in the Bactrian communities, metal tools were increasingly common. The skilled hands of the ancient smiths and craftsmen turned out masterpieces of metal work, the variety of which was considerable. Ceremonial axes were decorated with beasts of prey, wild boars, or fantastic animals; the head of one such axe, in silver, is cast in the shape of a man with two eagles' heads, struggling with a wild boar and a winged dragon. Toiletry bottles would be decorated with animal heads, and other vessels were theriomorphic, all rendered with considerable artistry. The heads of pins were sometimes compositions of birds, people and animals. Open-work seals, often described as compartmented, include representations of birds, animals, people, reptiles and imaginary dragon-like creatures; some seals present the winged, anthropomorphic deities with bird-like characteristics that constituted the Bactrian pantheon (Plate 101). A variety of weapons – massive battle spears, javelin heads, daggers and swords – were made of metal, while toothed sickles, razors, knives and pitchforks were used in daily life. In general, ornaments were made of copper whereas tools and weapons were made of arsenic or tin bronze. Although the direct archaeological evidence is scant, the common use of

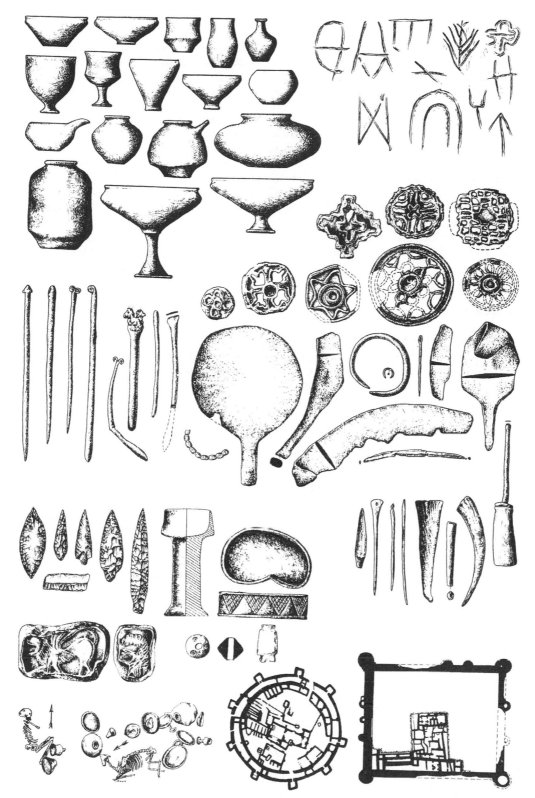

Figure 37 General table of the Bactrian culture.

casting presupposed heat-proof crucibles, equipment for pouring metal, moulds, and furnaces that could achieve temperatures of over 1100°C. The metallurgical technology was so complicated that some experts suggest that Bactrian metal workers were narrowly specialized within the craft.

Stone working also reached an artistic peak in the Bactrian Bronze Age. In addition to a variety of stone unguent bottles, bowls and other vessels, stone amulets formed a striking component of Bactrian art. The amulets, often engraved on both faces, presented both single figures and more com-

plicated thematic representations. The latter permit a glimpse of the ancient Bactrian spiritual world, which seems to have been permeated with a dualistic concept of the struggle of good and evil forces. And stone was also used to create cylinder-seals of the Mesopotamian type, with finely engraved compositions of complex representations in the Bactrian style (Plate 102).

The Bactrian Bronze Age displays extremely strong similarities with the contemporary culture of Margiana, in the extreme south-east of Turkmenia. This common culture is now recognized as the Bactrian-Margiana culture complex (BMAC). The date of the BMAC is hotly debated: many archaeologists of the former Soviet Union argue for a date late in the second millennium BC, while the growing consensus among Western European and North American specialists places the BMAC at the end of the third millennium BC and the beginning of the second (Sarianidi, 1986; Amiet, 1986). At stake in this debate is the nature of the relationship to surrounding areas, since Sarianidi and others want to derive the BMAC from earlier Iranian sources, while many non-Soviet authorities argue that BMAC groups spread southward at the end of the third and beginning of the second millennium BC. The linguistic identity of the BMAC people(s) is one aspect of the debate, and some scholars have suggested that the spread of the BMAC southward to the edges of the Indus Valley reflects the introduction of an Indo-Iranian language group to the region (Hiebert and Lamberg-Karlovsky, 1992).

The Helmand drainage

In the Helmand drainage and in Seistan, the first part of the third millennium BC witnessed the development of large towns or cities that contained monumental public architecture. At Shahr-i Sokhta, in Iranian Seistan, a city perhaps 100 ha in size emerged during the course of the third millennium BC, before abruptly collapsing at the end of that millennium. In the Helmand drainage, in Afghanistan, the settlement at Mundigak expanded to cover perhaps 15 ha during period IV–1. The architecture of this period included monumental buildings on all the high points of the site. One of the monumental buildings, called the palace, presented a massive half-colonnaded wall made of baked brick, broken by doorways into a complex of rooms within the structure. This structure underwent a series of modifications that culminated in the creation of a solid brick platform (equipped with a staircase) inside the original colonnaded façade and the erection of a second colonnaded wall, giving a staged terrace appearance to the building. This building may have been the residence of the local ruler. Another monumental building, identified as a temple, lay east of the palace. The building presented a double casemate wall, decorated with acute-angled pilasters. The space inside these walls contained both courtyard and a regularly laid-out block of interconnecting rooms. In addition, a massive double wall equipped with regularly spaced buttresses and bastions enclosed a large section of the site, including the palace and perhaps also the temple, as well as densely packed residential architecture. Both the palace and temple fell into disuse after period IV–1, while the town wall and its associated residential architecture continued in use through the rest of period IV.

The monumental buildings at Mundigak point to a high level of social development, and to a distinct administrative function. The artefacts of the period display strong continuities with the preceding period III materials, though many classes of artefacts (such as stone vessels, beads, stamp seals) are much more varied in form during period IV than before. The technological skill of the Mundigak artisans retained the high level already achieved during period III, and they added the manufacture of small objects from iron ore to their repertoire. Found also in the neighbouring sites of Said Qala Tepe and Deh Morasi Ghundai, these artefacts are among the earliest known iron objects (Shaffer, 1984).

Mundigak stayed in regular contact with surrounding regions. The styles of artefacts, and especially of pottery, are very similar to those found at Shahr-i Sokhta, and these two sites together define a single cultural, though probably not political, province. The same semi-precious stones and other raw materials as found in period III continue to be imported, while finished artefacts (especially painted pottery) still reflect active connections with Baluchistan. A recent analytic study demonstrates that certain classes of fine pottery (Faiz Mohammad grey ware in Baluchistan, Emir grey ware in southern Iran) were made by skilled specialist potters, whose products could be distributed over long distances. Faiz Mohammad grey ware, for example, travelled from production centres in Kachi (Baluchistan) to Shahr-i Sokhta (Wright, 1989), and also appeared in Mundigak. Other objects also indicate an eastern origin, including several clay figurines modelled after the Zhob style of Baluchistan, and a life-sized human head in limestone that is strongly reminiscent of the Indus civilization style.

THE SECOND MILLENNIUM BC

The early second millennium witnessed major changes across central Asia, Iran and the Indus. Many sites in these regions were abandoned and others greatly reduced in size. At the same time, interregional connections broke down or changed dramatically in character. The period was marked by movements into Afghanistan of peoples with distinct cultural traditions.

In Bactria, the BMAC disappeared after the first quarter of the second millennium, and a new culture appeared. This new culture, characterized by handmade, sometimes decorated, pottery, and dated to the second half of the second millennium BC, is best represented at Tillya Tepe, near the town of Sheberghan. Excavations at Tillya Tepe have brought to light a large temple-like building erected on top of a high brick platform. The temple consisted of large halls whose roofs were supported by rectangular columns. A stepped altar, in which fire burned, sat in the centre of the main hall. The settlement itself, only partly excavated, lay around the temple. The second settlement, inhabited by tribes that made painted pottery, lies between the towns of Mazar-e Sharif and Tashkurgan, at the village of Naibabad; this settlement marks the last stage of the existence of these groups in Bactria. Dwelling side by side with the local tribes, the painted-pottery folk were gradually assimilated, and by the middle of the first millennium BC we find a unity in the general appearance of the local culture.

In the Helmand and Seistan area, many settlements ceased to exist; Mundigak seems temporarily to have been abandoned. In the subsequent occupation at Mundigak, period V, a monumental platform with associated small rooms was erected over the period IV palace; the function of this monument remains unclear. The following period VI is one of gradual abandonment, but also of the more common appearance of iron technology. The pottery and many other artefacts of these periods are distinctly dissimilar from those that characterized the earlier occupations at Mundigak. The pottery of period V, which in general is rough, handmade, and rudely decorated, bears some similarities with the pottery of the Chust culture in the Ferghana Valley in Uzbekistan, while the Period VI pottery resembles in some respects the Yaz I ceramics of the Turkmenistan Iron Age. Mundigak remains the sole excavated site in the region, however, and the society of this time remains largely unknown. This general absence of settlements seems to have continued into the first millennium, when pre-Achemenid occupation at places like Kandahar and Nadi Ali (Whitehouse, 1978; Dales, 1977) appeared. These new settlements presaged the more vigorous renewal of town life during the subsequent historic periods.

SUMMARY

The Bronze Age of Afghanistan was not a culturally or socially unified phenomenon, but rather was localized in areas of greatest agricultural potential, Bactria and the Helmand-Seistan regions. The Bronze Age cultures of these two areas were distinctive from each other in their basic features, and in their chronologies of development. At the same time, the two regions do share a number of fundamental qualities. The Bronze Age cultures were closely allied with those of neighbouring regions, with Turkmenia and other parts of central Asia in the case of Bactria, and with eastern Iran and Baluchistan in the case of the Helmand. These relationships reflect Afghanistan's geographical position between centres of social development in the ancient world, notably the Indus Valley, Turkmenistan, and eastern Iran. Moreover, Afghanistan contains a number of precious and semi-precious raw materials that the ancient world highly prized, including lapis lazuli and silver, as well as copper, tin, and a variety of semi-precious stones. The Bronze Age societies of Afghanistan thus controlled the routes of trade and communication that connected civilizations of western, central, and southern Asia. The archaeological record of Bronze Age Afghanistan reflects the resulting intense interactions across long distances, seen both in exotic styles and raw materials of some artefacts, and in the development of complex, internally differentiated societies.

But just as these Bronze Age cultures profited by their interregional dealings, so eventually did they suffer. The urban societies of Iran, central Asia, and the Indus Valley began to unravel by the early second millennium BC, and the intensity of trade and communication between these regions sharply declined. The Bronze Age societies of Afghanistan, deprived of their advantaged geographical position, also went into a long decline. The archaeological record, though scant for this 'dark age', indicates that the second millennium was a period of large-scale migrations, especially of Indo-Aryan speaking peoples, in central and south Asia. When these ethnic movements slowed, by the end of the second millennium BC, the centres of civilization re-emerged, and the interregional flow of goods intensified again. In this setting, towns began to flourish again in Afghanistan, for the same reasons that they had done in the Bronze Age. These Iron Age developments in and around Afghanistan created the world that the Persians and then the Greeks encountered during their imperial expansions eastward, later in the first millennium BC.

BIBLIOGRAPHY

AMIET, P. 1986. *L'Age des échanges inter-iraniens*. Paris.

CASAL, J. -M. 1961. *Fouilles de Mundigak*. Paris.

DALES, G. 1972. Prehistoric Research in Southern Afghan Seistan. *Afghanistan* (Kabul), Vol. 25, No. 4, pp. 14–40.

—— 1977. *New Excavations at Nad-i Ali (Sorkh Dagh), Afghanistan*. Berkeley, Calif.

DUPREE, L. 1963. Deh Morasi Ghundai: A Chalcolithic Site in South-Central Afghanistan. *Anthropol. Pap. am. Mus. nat. Hist.* (New York), Vol. 50, No. 2.

—— 1972. Prehistoric Research in Afghanistan (1959–1966). *Trans. am. philos. Soc.* (Philadelphia, Pa.), Vol. 62, No. 4.

FAIRSERVIS, W. 1952. *Preliminary Report on the Prehistoric Archaeology of the Afghan-Baluchistan Areas*. New York. (Am. Mus. Novit., 1587.)

—— 1961. Archaeological Surveys in the Seistan Basin of South-western Afghanistan and Eastern Iran. *Anthropol. Pap. am. Mus. nat. Hist.* (New York), Vol. 48, No. 1.

FISCHER, K. 1973. Archaeological Field Surveys in Afghan Seistan, 1960–1970. In: HAMMOND, N. (ed.), *South Asian Archaeology 1971*. Park Ridge, N.J. pp. 131–55.

FRANCFORT, H.-P. 1989. *Fouilles de Shortugai*. Paris.

GENTELLE, P. 1989. *Données paléogéographiques et fondements de l'irrigation. Prospections archéologiques en Bactriane orientale (1974–1978)*. Paris.

HAMMOND, N. 1970. An Archaeological Reconnaissance in the Helmand Valley, South Afghanistan. *East West* (Roma), Vol. 20, pp. 437–59.

HIEBERT, F. T.; LAMBERG-KARLOVSKY, C. C. 1992. Central Asia and the Indo-Iranian Borderlands. *Iran* (London), Vol. 30, pp. 1–15.

JARRIGE, C.; TOSI, M. 1981. The Natural Resources of Mundigak. In: HARTEL, H. (ed.), *South Asian Archaeology 1979*. Berlin. pp. 115–42.

POTTIER, M.-H. 1984. *Matériel funéraire de la Bactriane méridionale de l'âge de bronze*. Paris.

SARIANIDI, V. 1972. *Raskopki Tillja-tepe v severnom Afganistane* [Excavations at Tillja Tepe in Northern Afghanistan]. Moskva.

—— 1975. *Afganistan v epokhu bronzii i rannevo zheleza [Afghanistan in the Bronze and Early Ice Age]*. Moskva.

—— 1986. *Die Kunst des Alten Afghanistan*. Leipzig.

SHAFFER, J. 1971. Preliminary Field Report on Excavations at Said Qala Tepe. *Afghanistan* (Kabul), Vol. 24, No. 2–3, pp. 89–127.

—— 1984. Bronze Age Iron from Afghanistan: Its Implications for South Asian Protohistory. In: KENNEDY, K.; POSSEHL, G. (eds), *Studies in the Archaeology and Palaeoanthropology of South Asia*. New Delhi. pp. 41–62.

WHITEHOUSE, D. 1978. Excavations at Kandahar, 1974. *Afghan Stud.* (London), Vol. 1, pp. 1–35.

WRIGHT, R. 1989. New Perspectives on Third Millennium Painted Grey Wares. In: FRIFELT, K.; SORENSEN, P. (eds), *South Asian Archaeology 1985*. London. pp. 137–47.

12.6

THE ARABIAN PENINSULA

Abdul Rahman Al-Ansary

Although entirely a sandy desert in the popular imagination, the Arabian peninsula contains considerable environmental diversity. At the most general level, this diversity may be classified into four kinds of landscapes, each with different potential implications for its human inhabitants. Mountains form an upland zone, more or less continuous, along the western (the Hejaz and Asir uplands) and southern (Yemen, Jabal Qarra', Jebel Akhdar) coasts. These uplands exceed 1,000 m above sea-level, and reach 3,000 m above sea-level in many places (especially in the Yemen). The mountains are often better watered than other parts of Arabia, and encourage agriculture in mountain and piedmont wadis. The south-western part of the peninsula falls within the monsoon summer rainfall regime.

The Persian Gulf, Indian Ocean and Red Sea border the peninsula on three sides. These coastlines offer both varied marine environments and maritime routes to other lands. However, the mountains bordering the Arabian coast often make difficult access to the coast, and leave only a relatively narrow littoral plain, for example the Tihama in the southern Red Sea, and the Batinah in the Gulf of Oman. The Persian Gulf coast, on the other hand, is broadly low and flat. Although the Gulf receives only a little winter rainfall, areas such as Hofuf and Bahrain are well endowed with artesian sources of water, which support fairly intensive agriculture.

The Arabian interior contains both sandy deserts and rocky plains. The sandy deserts include the Rub al Khali and the Wahiba Sands to the south, the Nafud in the north, and smaller zones of dunes elsewhere. In general, the topography slopes from the mountains in the west to the low coast in the east. Several major escarpments, notably the Jebel Tuwaiq south of Riyadh, along with numerous smaller buttes interrupt this slope, which also contains shallow basins that hold oasis towns. The long wadi beds that cross the interior also contain oasis towns, and link the interior with the surrounding world (for example, the Wadi Batin-Wadi or Rumah system that runs from Khaibar in the southern Hejaz to Kuwait; the Wadi Sirhan that runs from Jawf to Palestine).

Some of these environments encourage settled life based on agriculture and trade; others are far more suitable to animal herding and to hunting. Since the beginnings of agriculture in the peninsula, human communities at any one time in Arabia have practised different ways of life, according to divergent combinations of historical and environmental circumstances. During the periods under review here, roughly 3000 to 700 BC, the combination of more abundant water and greater access to the surrounding world allowed the emergence of town life and political complexity in some areas, while other parts of Arabia, lacking these advantages, remained less advanced.

'NEOLITHIC' FOUNDATIONS

The Arabian peninsula now enjoys very little rainfall, excepting only the mountainous south-west (Yemen and southern Asir), which falls within the monsoonal system. Environments in the past have not always been so forbidding. Over the period 9000/8000 to about 4000 BC, the summer monsoon shifted northward, and the Mediterranean winter storm system intensified somewhat, resulting in more precipitation than today. This climatic amelioration produced semi-permanent (playa) lakes and grasslands even in deep desert settings (McClure, 1976; Hotzl et al., 1984). The denser vegetation in turn supported relatively large bovid herds (wild cattle, gazelle, oryx), and the human populations that consumed both animals and plants. Traces of these human populations, characterized principally by the stone tools they left behind, occur throughout the peninsula. The stone tools form two well-documented traditions, the earlier characterized by a blade industry and the later by bifacial tools.

Blade industries are known for several areas of the peninsula. North-western Saudi Arabia contains many sites with a chipped stone industry comparable in technique and formal typology to that of the Levantine PPNB (Zarins, 1992) while in Qatar a similar industry (Group B) appears (Kapel, 1967). Less well-documented traces of blade industries occur along the southern end of the Jebel Tuwaiq and in the Dhofar and Oman peninsula. Based on comparisons with the Levantine sequence, these industries probably date to the eighth and seventh millennia BC. The scant evidence for economic orientation indicates that these Arabian groups were mobile hunters and gatherers, in contrast to the more sedentary contemporary agriculturalists to the north.

The Arabian bifacial tradition is distributed across most of the Arabian peninsula, in a variety of environmental settings (coasts, deep deserts, mountain fringes). The tradition encompasses a number of regional variants, the details of which are not fully worked out, but which are all dated to the sixth, fifth and probably fourth millennia BC. The traditional industry is perhaps best known from the Rub al Khali, the so-called Rub al Khali Neolithic, where large collections of lithic from playa lake margins are reported (Edens, 1982). Despite its name and the presence of grinding stones, however, the economic orientation seems still to have been a mobile desert adaptation to hunting animals (gazelle and wild equids) and the gathering of wild plants. Domesticated animals appeared only in the fourth millennium BC at several sites, notably Al Markh on Bahrain (Roaf, 1976). Sites of the bifacial tradition occasionally contain permanent stone structures.

The Arabian bifacial tradition on the southern coast of the Persian Gulf is notable for its association with Ubaid pottery. Found on sites dated to the later sixth and fifth millennia BC in the Eastern Province of Saudi Arabia, Bahrain, Qatar, and into the Emirates (Masry, 1974; Oates et al., 1977), this pottery in Arabia marks an intensive interaction with the increasingly complex societies of Mesopotamia. A number of these sites contain sheep/goat and cattle that are probably, though not definitely, domesticates (Masry, 1974). While the nature of this interaction remains debated, at the very least it introduced far-flung exchange connections, evident in the occasional piece of Anatolian obsidian found in the Gulf. At the same time, exchange relations connected other parts of Arabia with the adjacent regions: obsidian from Yemen and Indo-Pacific sea-shells circulated in the Rub al Khali and the Nedj. These interactions with the surrounding world helped to introduce domesticates to Arabia, and laid the foundation for the subsequent trade of the Bronze Age.

Essentially non-bifacial lithic industries, though less well known, also appeared in Arabia during this period. In many mountainous zones, particularly in south-west Arabia and the Oman peninsula, a non-bifacial industry appeared. This 'upland Neolithic tradition', the proposed date of which is 6000–3000 BC, probably reflects responses to the different environmental opportunities of the Arabian mountains. One site of this tradition in northern Yemen contained a dozen elliptical huts built on stone footings (Fedele, 1988). Similar small circular stone dwellings are documented at other sites of the same tradition in the Asir and in Oman. Although hunting continued to be an important source of food, cattle herding is also evident at several fourth millennium BC sites in upland Yemen.

The southern Arabian coastline also hosted different cultural adaptations that are reflected in the equipment of these people. Recent investigations in the Oman peninsula and the Tihama have documented many Middle Holocene shell-middens, the material repertoire of which distinguish them from sites elsewhere in Arabia. Radiocarbon dating place these middens mainly in the later sixth to fourth millennia BC, though many also extend into the third millennium. These adaptations were geared to local opportunities, so that communities in the Emirates were specialized sea-mammal hunters, those in Oman mixed near-shore and off-shore fishing with shellfish collection middens, those of the Tihama looked to mangrove swamps, and so forth.

The middens at Qurum (Ras al Hamra), near Musqat in Oman, are the most extensively researched of these sites (Biagi et al., 1984, 1989). The Italian excavations define a sequence of habitations composed of insubstantial structures, more durable storage pits, and several cemeteries. In addition to a robust flake industry, the toolkits in these middens included various forms of fishhooks and stone net weights, implying a strong maritime orientation. According to the fauna, the sea provided a variety of fish, turtles, marine mammals (porpoise and dolphin) and shellfish. At the same time, terrestrial resources were not lacking. In addition to wild plants (especially zizyphus) and animals, the Qurum shell-middens contain remains of domesticated sheep/goat, cattle and sorghum by the late fifth millennium BC. Although

still a minor component of the diet, the domesticated plants and animals combined with the more abundant maritime foods to promote a more sedentary existence as the local antecedent to farming communities at the beginning of the Bronze Age. Domesticated animals are evident in other littoral settings, notably on the southern Red Sea.

During the fourth millennium BC, north-western Arabia belonged to the desertic Syro-Palestinian region. Small scattered settlements characterized by circular stone architecture appear along the northern fringe of the Nafud sand desert. The associated ceramic and chipped-stone equipment is comparable to that of the Chalcolithic further north. Many stone hunting traps ('kites') appear across the entire region, similar to structures found in Jordan and elsewhere; individual traps sometimes cover several kilometres in length. At Rajajil, in the Jawf basin, are clusters of sandstone orthostats set in rubble platforms; the same pottery and chipped stone appears around these monuments (Zarins, 1979). The latter megalithic monuments may have staged ritual performances, perhaps as expressions of a growing political complexity in the region.

Although the pre-Bronze Age cultures of the Arabian peninsula rarely left behind impressive monuments or other artefacts, they did lay the foundations for the Bronze Age florescence. The majority of these groups remained hunters and gatherers throughout their existence, relatively isolated in the Arabian interior. Several changes did foreshadow later developments, however. The introduction of cultivated cereals and herded animals established, however tentatively, the economic foundation for settled life in the peninsula, while the refinement of fishing techniques ensured basic dietary resources on the coast. The requirements of off-shore fishing promoted boating; although not empirically evident, improvements in boat construction doubtless also aided the coastwise movements of people and goods. These movements are evident in the spread of sorghum through southern coastal regions and the Ubaid penetration of the Gulf. Other evidence for long-distance connections include the appearance of Gulf shells in Neolithic sites of Mesopotamia, the occasional piece of Anatolian obsidian in the Gulf and the circulation of Yemeni obsidian, and the thin flow of marine shell into the interior.

THE EMERGING BRONZE AGE (3000–2400 BC)

Until the late fourth millennium BC, the various cultures of the Arabian peninsula were broadly similar in their economic and social orientations, constrained by the resources naturally available in the landscape, and moving about in small groups to take advantage of seasonal opportunities. Around 3000 BC permanent farming communities began to appear in several places around the peninsula, soon followed by important social changes and more intense connections with the rest of western Asia. These Bronze Age societies first developed in south-eastern and eastern Arabia, and then (by the third quarter of the third millennium BC) in south Arabia.

Elsewhere, the existing hunting and herding adaptations persisted for thousands of years. These communities left few perceptible archaeological traces, with the exception of rock art (Plate 103). Several decades of study have identified regional styles and produced a tentative chronological sequence (Anati, 1968–72). For the most part, this rock art seems to reflect hunting societies that focused on cattle in upland zones, but were also concerned with camel, oryx, onager, fat-tailed sheep and ibex. Although some of the depicted cattle have been identified as domesticated (Anati, 1968–74), the available archaeological information indicates hunting of the wild form. Fat-tailed sheep may have been domesticated during the second millennium BC (Anati, 1968–72), though this claim is controversial. Hunting remained a focal activity for some Arabian groups into recent times.

South-eastern Arabia

The French excavations at Hili 8 in Al Ain/Buraimi oasis (the interior of Abu Dhabi) revealed an early farming community established by the end of the fourth millennium BC. The settlement contained domestic architecture around a square mudbrick tower enclosed by a circular ditch; a deep well sits in the centre of the tower. Crops included cereals (barley, wheat and sorghum), melons and dates; animal herding concentrated on cattle (some of whose bones bear evidence of traction), and also included sheep and goat. The scant pottery of the settlement includes one vessel of probable Mesopotamian origin. Copper working on a small scale occurred at the site, apparently for local consumption. The initial settlement at Hili 8 remains unparalleled in south-eastern Arabia, though contemporary shell-middens are known; a midden at Ras al Hamra also contains a little pottery, this apparently of Baluchistan affiliation (Cleuziou, 1982; Cleuziou and Tosi, 1989).

Burials belonging to the late fourth millennium BC have been excavated on the nearby Jebel Hafit and elsewhere in the Oman peninsula (Frifelt, 1975). These tombs are single-chamber cairns with thick stone walls; access to the small chamber was gained through a side passage. Although most tombs contained only one or two buried individuals, others contained more (perhaps half a dozen). The associated grave goods include pottery whose forms and painted decoration closely resemble Mesopotamian wares of the Jamdat Nasr and Early Dynastic I periods (Potts, 1986).

Documentation of the middle of the third millennium BC is somewhat better, when Early Dynastic II-III period Mesopotamian pottery appeared in some settlements of the area (for example, Umm an-Nar, Ghanadha: Frifelt, 1975; Tikriti, 1985). Around 2500 BC, an indigenous form of black-painted pottery, the Umm an-Nar style, emerged, and continued in use through the remainder of the third millennium. This style betrays stylistic similarities with pottery in south-eastern Iran, and marked the first widespread appearance of pottery in south-eastern Arabia. A tomb form of a slightly later date than the Hafit type is the beehive grave, characterized by multiple concentric walling on a low platform. First identified at Bat (Frifelt, 1975), these tombs appear in many parts of the Oman peninsula, and again contain a Mesopotamian-derived pottery.

Eastern Arabia

Knowledge of this period in eastern Arabia remains scattered. While many sites have been identified by surface evidence or looted remains, very few have been excavated; the latter include the lowest levels at the Qala' and Barbar on Bahrain, the Ramad and Umm an Nussi settlements in Saudi Arabia, and burials on Bahrain and at Abqaiq (Saudi Arabia). In the absence of adequate contextual control, discussion must proceed largely on the basis of stylistic comparisons.

Many sites on the Gulf littoral, including several of the Ubaid sites, contain pottery that bears comparison with Mesopotamian wares of the Late Uruk through Early Dynastic periods (c. 3400–2400 BC). While most of these materials must be dated toward the end of this time range, some older material does appear in eastern Arabia, including a sealed bulla of Late Uruk date, several Jamdat Nasr style seals and painted sherds, and pottery types with a generalized Jamdat Nasr to ED II range. Materials related to the ED III period are more abundant, and include pottery, stone vessels carved in the interregional style, and some statuary (Zarins, 1989; Potts, 1992). Some of these sites also contain Umm an-Nar period pottery (not earlier than about 2500 BC), notably the 'pre-City I' levels at the Qala'at al Bahrain, and burial remains at Abqaiq and on Tarut. The bulk of these materials appear on the mainland and near-shore island of Tarut.

Relatively little is known of the economy of this culture in the Gulf. The excavations at Umm an Nussi and Umm ar Ramadh produced small faunal samples composed predominantly of sheep/goat and lesser amounts of cattle and pig; the first two of these are definitely domesticated. The lithic industries of these sites included frequent sickle blades, some of which have sickle sheen indicative of probable cultivated cereals. The increasing number of foreign artefacts in the Gulf during the mid-third millennium BC reveals a widening connection with surrounding regions. Nevertheless, settlement and population remained fairly thin and dispersed.

South Arabia

Until the 1980s, the origins of the South Arabian civilization remained entirely unknown. Archaeological explorations in the Yemen have since begun to define a South Arabian Bronze Age. Discovery of this Bronze Age culture was first made in the mountain wadis south-east of Sana'a, where over thirty sites of the third millennium BC have been found. Subsequently similar sites have been found elsewhere in the Yemeni highlands. Excavations at several of the sites near Sana'a reveal small settlements composed of multi-room compounds set around courtyards. While most of these structures are similarly sized, in several cases one is larger than the others, and presents a somewhat different internal arrangement; these exceptional structures may be community ritual centres, or the residences of high-status individuals. These communities kept sheep and goats, along with a fewer number of cattle, pigs and donkeys. According to seed impressions in pottery, agriculture emphasized barley over wheat, but also included sorghum and millet, as well as oats and cumin (de Maigret, 1990).

The dating of the South Arabian Bronze Age rests on a relatively small number of radiocarbon determinations. The earliest of these dates belong to the third quarter of the third millennium, and the culture complex may have formed as early as 2900 BC. The same cultural characteristics endured throughout the rest of the third millennium and into the early centuries of the second millennium BC. The South Arabian Bronze Age probably arose from the indigenous Neolithic traditions, representatives of which continued to inhabit the Tihama coast. Some ceramic parallels have been drawn with Syro-Palestine of the EBA IV (de Maigret, 1990); the radiocarbon dates make these parallels irrelevant to the origins of the south Arabian Bronze Age.

BRONZE AGE FLORESCENCE (2400–1800 BC)

During the Bronze Age, eastern and south-eastern Arabia enjoyed direct commercial ties with Mesopotamia and the Indus, and indirect links with more distant lands. While archaeological evidence reflects this trade, the cuneiform texts of Mesopotamia provide important details (Leemans, 1960; Pettinato, 1972; Heimpel, 1987). Many texts refer to trade and other relations with Dilmun, Magan and Meluhha. Dilmun corresponds to Bahrain and the neighbouring mainland, Magan probably to the lands on each side of the Straits of Hormuz (including the Oman peninsula), and Meluhha perhaps to the Indus region. While these regions exchanged a great many exotic products, the trade focused on copper produced in Magan and on textiles and cereals produced in Mesopotamia. Dilmun, on the other hand, usually functioned as way-station and middleman in this trade. In addition to forging commercial links with the surrounding world, the exchange system also exposed the Gulf societies to outside cultural influences, the impact of which is evident in the arts.

Elsewhere in Arabia, the pace of change quickened in some but not all places. The South Arabian Bronze Age culture seems to have altered very little during this period. Across broad stretches of the Arabian interior, moreover, the mobile existence of pastoralists and hunter-gatherers continued largely unchanged from the previous periods.

South-eastern Arabia

This period encompasses most of the Umm an-Nar (c. 2500–2000 BC) and the first part of the Wadi Suq (c. 2000–1300 BC) periods. Late Umm an-Nar period settlements are common throughout the Oman peninsula, especially along the interior foothills. The settlements of the interior usually form multiple residential enclaves within a district, each enclave focused on one or more circular towers. The settlements also typically have cemeteries (often on higher ground) and water-control devices nearby, all related aspects of oasis settlements (Tosi, 1975; Cleuziou, 1980). Coastal sites are also common, including the type-site at Umm an-Nar; these settlements display most of the same characteristics, including towers, cemeteries and water-control devices. Special activity sites are also documented, including isolated towers, shell-middens, transient pastoralist encampments, copper-mining sites, and coastal trading stations. The latter site-type, exemplified by the Ras al Junayez site, reflects intensive commercial interaction with the Indus and other neighbouring regions.

Being obvious features of the landscape and easily accessible, the Bronze Age tombs have attracted much archaeological attention. The Umm an-Nar tombs are circular stone cairns with internal chambers, faced with ashlar or other dressed stone, and constructed on low stone platforms. In several instances, depictions of animals appear in low relief on tomb exteriors. The tombs were used repeatedly, and typically contain the remains of fifty to several hundred people. The burial goods include pottery in various styles, carved stone vessels, jewellery, and some metal work. Among the pottery appear forms and decorative styles that reflect connections with the Indo-Iranian borderlands. Tombs of the Wadi Suq period, though also built of stone, were generally less elaborate than those of the Umm an-Nar period, and often took the form of a long chamber with rounded ends and side entrance, sometimes surrounded by a second ring wall (Donaldson, 1985; Vogt and Franke-Vogt, 1987).

As the typical locations and arrangement of settlements suggests, oasis farming lay at the heart of the Umm an-Nar subsistence economy. Farming depended on a variety of devices, including bunds, ditches and wells, designed both to bring water to fields and to divert floodwaters from fields. Cultivated plants included cereals (wheat, barley, sorghum) and tree crops (dates, zizyphus); the presence of sorghum suggests relatively intensive agricultural production (double cropping). These communities also herded animals, including sheep and goat, donkey and cattle, the latter two species also providing traction. Camels were also present, evident in a few bone samples (especially at Umm an-Nar), and in reliefs on tombs. Considerable debate attends the question of domestication or otherwise in managing camels in late third millennium Arabia. Because of the domesticated camel's enormous consequences for pastoralism, trade and warfare throughout western Asia, the issue has global importance.

Several sites provide evidence for metallurgical production of two kinds. Copper working occurred in many habitation sites such as Hili 8, where the presence of slag and occasionally moulds indicates a small-scale production of copper objects for local community consumption. Copper extraction and production of ingots, on the other hand, occurred at fewer places. One of these is Maysar 1, where the German investigations have documented the relatively simple technology of acquiring and smelting copper ores to form the small bun-shaped ingots that then could either circulate within Oman or enter the long-distance trade of the time (Hauptmann, 1985). In addition to pottery and copper, these communities produced other distinctive goods, notably carved chlorite vessels of a style that achieved a wide distribution in the Gulf and surrounding areas.

Eastern Arabia

During this period, the focus of occupation shifted from the Saudi mainland to the adjacent islands, notably Bahrain and Failaka. The Danish excavations at the Qala'at al Bahrain provide the basic stratigraphic sequence for the region (Bibby, 1970). First occupied in the mid-third millennium BC (pre-City I), the late third millennium settlement (City I) grew to cover nearly 20 ha by 2000 BC. At this time, construction of a stone wall encircled the town (City II); a formal gateway and associated administrative architecture controlled access to the harbour. Excavations at Barbar (Bahrain) uncovered a contemporary sequence of temples built in stone; the small initial temple developed into a stepped temple platform. Work on Failaka revealed residential architecture in several settlements. The ribbed red ware pottery (Hojlund, 1986a) and distinctive stamp seals (Kjaerum, 1983) define the Barbar culture, which dates predominantly to the first quarter of the second millennium (Plate 104). Another characteristic feature of the culture are the tumulus fields on Bahrain and the Saudi mainland, which collectively contain several hundreds of thousands of burial mounds (Mughal, 1983, Ibrahim, 1983).

The Barbar culture marks the first appearance in Arabia of town living. Although perhaps the largest, the Qala'at was not the only large and densely occupied settlement in the area, and villages also existed. This settlement hierarchy implies a social complexity that is also evident in the functional differentiation of architecture and in variable tomb sizes. While not comparable to the state organization of Mesopotamia, the political arrangement of the Barbar culture was certainly more centralized and hierarchical than that elsewhere in Arabia at the time. Intensive agriculture, based on the abundant artesian water of the Gulf, certainly facilitated the growth of political complexity here; unfortunately, little evidence for subsistence practices has been found. More important than local agriculture, however, was commerce. The Mesopotamian cuneiform texts spell out the importance of Dilmun as an entrepôt, through which flowed copper, textiles, exotic stones and woods, and other goods. This commerce is evident in the archaeological record of Dilmun: pottery, some metal work, artistic influences and the occasional use of cuneiform from Mesopotamia; pottery, stone vessels, and other objects from south-eastern Arabia; some pottery, ivory, and a system of stone weights from the Indus; and a few objects from the Iranian side of the Gulf all appear.

THE LATER BRONZE AGE (1800–1200 BC)

The later Bronze Age of Arabia was a period of relative decline, marked by an apparent major emphasis on pastoralism, and a weakening of foreign contacts. Despite these trends, the period did continue some patterns established earlier in the Bronze Age, and heralded important changes in some parts of the peninsula.

In south-east Arabia, the Wadi Suq culture spanned most of the second millennium BC. In its original definition, the Wadi Suq culture was thought to end around 1700 BC, after which time the regional economy was supposed to have been fully pastoralist (Cleuziou, 1981). Recent excavations in the Emirates, particularly at Shimal in Ras al Khaymah (Vogt and Franke-Vogt, 1987) and at Tell Abraq in Umm al Quwain (Potts, 1990), indicate that Wadi Suq patterns must be extended to the beginning of the local Iron Age, around 1200 BC. Tell Abraq in particular provides a settlement sequence through the second millennium, and demonstrates a continued contact with the Indus and with Mesopotamia during the late second millennium BC. Despite this advance, knowledge of the Wadi Suq period as a whole remains rudimentary, and a major shift away from settled agricultural life in the interior seems to have occurred.

In eastern Arabia, the Danish excavations on Failaka and at the Qala'at al Bahrain establish a chronological sequence for the second millennium BC, the details of which are still debated. Although the initial results on Bahrain indicated a gap between City II and III, occupation on Failaka was continuous through the second millennium, and subsequent analysis at the Qala'at indicates a comparable continuity there as well (Hojlund, 1986a; 1986b). In both cases, the connections with Babylonia appear to have strengthened through time: the regionally distinctive pottery of the early second millennium BC was largely replaced by Babylonian forms by the late second millennium. This shift in material culture may reflect a Babylonian control of the region in the fourteenth and thirteenth centuries BC (during the Kassite period). Archaeological evidence for the period is comparatively scant. At the Qala'at al Bahrain (City III), the city walls were rebuilt, and a large architectural complex was constructed in the middle of the settlement; judging by its layout and by the few cuneiform documents recovered from its interior, the latter was probably an administrative centre. Pottery and seals of this period have been recovered from tombs, on both Bahrain and the Saudi mainland; in almost all cases, these second millennium BC burials represent re-use of existing Barbar-period tombs. By the last few centuries of the second millennium, however, the Qala'at was again largely depopulated, and the Failaka settlements abandoned.

Knowledge of the south Arabian situation during the second millennium remains rudimentary. The settlement and economic patterns established late in the third millennium BC evidently continued largely unchanged. By the late second millennium, however, a significant change was occurring – the establishment of the settlement location characteristic of the later south Arabian civilization. The initial occupation at Hajjar bin Humaid may date to the end of the second millennium, while the basal level at Hajar at-Tamrah (in the Wadi Jubah) is radiocarbon dated to the fourteenth century BC (Van Beek, 1969; Sauer and Blakely, 1988). The shift in settlement location probably reflects the initial development of the water-control systems for which the South Arabian civilization was so famous.

THE IRON AGE (1200–400 BC)

With the Iron Age, communities throughout the peninsula established many patterns that endured into recent times, and provided the social milieu in which Mohammad lived. These new patterns rested on three momentous developments. Methods of water control became more sophisticated, thus permitting both increased agricultural production and higher population densities. Full domestication of the camel allowed pastoralism in the deep desert, supplied a new weapon in warfare, and gave new means of long-distance transportation. The latter capacity in turn encouraged the entry of Arabian incense and other goods into the interregional market, which was expanding as the demands of Iron Age and later empires increased. The combination of these factors supported the emergence throughout the peninsula of Arabian states and civilizations that were fully engaged economically and politically with lands from the Mediterranean to India and beyond.

South-east Arabia

During the Iron Age of the Oman peninsula, settlements tended to be less tied to the foothills than during the Bronze Age, and appeared farther onto wide wadi beds and open plains than before. The settlements contained large multiroom complexes of mudbrick architecture, best seen at Rumeilah in Abu Dhabi (Boucharlat and Lombard, 1985). Cemeteries of small single-chamber cairns usually lay near the settlements; these burials contained a characteristic suite of painted pottery, metal weapons and jewellery, and other goods. The maritime orientation of coastal regions continued, evident in the formation of large middens.

The subtle change in settlement location from the Bronze Age pattern was perhaps a consequence of the *falaj* (the Iranian qanat) system of water control by underground tunnels that tap into an upslope water table. Dating the origins of the qanat technique, and its introduction to south-east Arabia, is debated, and no conclusive evidence is yet available. Nonetheless, the German work in the Maysar area of Oman does trace settlement location moving downslope with time, a possible consequence of a falaj system tapping into a progressively low water table (Weisgerber, 1981). Despite this possible fundamental technological change, however, the subsistence effort seems to have involved much the same crops and herded animals as during the Bronze Age.

Production of copper continued during the early Iron Age. A technological innovation of the period was the appearance of tin bronzes, often in the form of heavy bracelets and weapons; the tin in these objects was all imported, implying fairly intense foreign connections. Despite the conventional name for the period, copper and bronze supplied the utilitarian metal of the Iron Age; iron was not common until late in the first millennium BC. Stone vessels decorated with incised geometric motifs were a typical product of the Iron Age; as during the Bronze Age, these local products circulated through neighbouring regions.

Eastern Arabia

As before, the Danish excavations in the area provide the best evidence for affairs in the Pesian Gulf during the Iron Age. At the Qala'at al Bahrain, City IV witnessed a significant renewal of the town after several centuries of neglect but not abandonment. This period of construction is notable for its well-built public architecture in the centre of the site. Although originally identified as Neo-Assyrian period palaces, neither the date nor the function of these structures is certain (Lombard, 1986; Oates, 1986). The buildings are remarkable for the series of snake burials, placed in bowls beneath the floor.

Elsewhere in the Gulf, relatively little archaeological evidence pertains to the first half of the first millennium BC. One locality in coastal Saudi Arabia, named the 'Salt Mine' site, belongs mainly to the late first millennium, but also provides a surface collection of cylinder-seals and pottery that belongs to the first half of the millennium (Lombard, 1988). The later re-use of tombs at Dhahran also belong to this period. Although not extensive, this evidence indicates a population with extensive links with neighbouring regions, as implied by Neo-Assyrian, South Arabian and Egyptian glyptic elements, and by pottery parallel to Babylonian forms. According to the Neo-Assyrian records, Dilmun was a kingdom during the eighth-seventh centuries; one king, Uperi, sent gifts to Sargon. Later in the first millennium BC, marked by City V on Bahrain, Thaj in Saudi Arabia, and reoccupation of Failaka, the Gulf entered the Hellenistic world and was fully caught up in the wide trade network that connected the Indian Ocean with the Mediterranean Sea.

South Arabia

South Arabia entered the world stage during the Iron Age, when intensive agriculture based on sophisticated techniques of water control combined with the growing interregional commerce in incense to stimulate the formation of a high civilization. Dating the inception of the south Arabian cultural tradition, and of the south Arabian script, remains a debated subject, with some urging a low chronology (for example, Pirenne, 1956, who argued a sixth-century beginning) and others a high chronology (for example, W. Albright, 1950, who argued a late second millennium BC beginning). The low chronology is unable adequately to accommodate the accumulated archaeological, historical and epigraphical data; most scholars accept some version of the high chronology, placing the beginning of the South Arabian tradition in the late second millennium, and the oldest texts to the first centuries of the first millennium BC (von Wissmann, 1975).

The history of the south Arabian states is known from their own monumental records. The Sabaean state emerged around the beginning of the first millennium, at first under a system of ritual rule (the *mukarrib*), and then under kingship (*malik*) after the fifth century. The oldest textual sources at Marib, dated perhaps to the eighth century BC, refer to construction of the town wall and a dam. While perhaps not the first to be erected here (tradition ascribes the first dam at Marib to the early second millennium BC), the eighth-century structure served as the core of the massive hydrological system that later developed. Another noteworthy building at Marib was the temple of 'Awwam, dedicated to the moon god 'Ilumquh. Perhaps founded in the eighth century if not earlier, and elaborated through time, the temple formed part of a large oval walled precinct (F. Albright, 1958).

According to Biblical tradition, Saba' was the home of Sheba (Bilqis), who initiated commercial contacts with Solomon in the tenth century BC. The Neo-Assyrian records also refer to It'amara and Karibilu of Saba', who delivered to Assyria tribute that included incense. The Assyrian texts list Saba' among North Arabian groups, perhaps a reflection of Sabaean trading colonies in northern Arabia during the eighth and seventh centuries BC; while Sabaean colonies have not been confirmed, the Minaeans did establish a wide network of commercial colonies later in the first millennium. Sabaean expansion into eastern Africa occurred during the sixth century, when south Arabian texts and architectural styles appeared in the Tigre province of Ethiopia. The Sabaean presence in Africa laid one of the foundations of the later Aksum civilization.

Frankincense grew principally in the Dhofar region (in modern Oman), while myrrh grew more widely in the South Arabian highlands; both incense plants also grew in East Africa. These goods could move either by water (via such ports as Khor Rori or Qana) or overland; the inland routes moved up the Wadi Hadramaut, and then skirted the Ramlet Sabatein sand sea. Numerous important towns lay along the southern and western margins of the Ramlet Sabatein, including Shabwa, Timna' and Marib. From this last point, the route passed along the eastern edge of the 'Asir highlands, through the Hejaz and ultimately to Palestine; towns along the route, such as Najran, Qaryat al Fau (Al-Ansary, 1981), Madina, al-Ula and Tayma', controlled its important bottlenecks or branching points. The growth of Marib and the Sabaean state formation early in south Arabia reflects their strategic location on this route.

Saba' was not the only state in south Arabia by the middle of the first millennium BC. Qataban, with its centre at Timna' in the Wadi Baihan, was a nearby rival; 'Ausan lay south of Qataban and encompassed much of the south Arabian coastal region. Both these states had access to the incense trade, whether on the overland routes (Qataban) or by water ('Ausan). Saba' gained a virtual monopoly of the trade in the fifth century, when it defeated both Qataban and 'Ausan, subordinating them as client states. 'Ausan joined with Qataban to overthrow Sabaean supremacy in the fourth century, but remained a client of the Qataban state, permitting the latter to replace the Sabaean control of trade.

The earliest recorded *mukarrib* of Qataban perhaps belong

to the fifth century BC, to which time the earliest monumental architecture and tombs at Timna' belong. The monuments at Timna' include the impressive city wall with multiple gates (enclosing about 20 ha), the massive 'Ashtar temple complex, and several large residences. At Ha'id bin Aqil, near the town, is a rock-cut tomb complex. Elsewhere in the Wadi Baihan, an extensive run-off control system, supplemented with wells, watered agricultural fields, among which were interspersed villages (including the excavated settlement at Hajjar bin Humaid). The formally constructed route across the Mablaqah pass gave access to the Wadi Harib to the west, and marked an important control point on the incense trade route.

The Minaeans and Himyarites gained importance later in the first millennium. Lying north of Saba', Ma'in had its capital at Qarnawu, and also counted Najran as an important centre on the incense route. The earliest recorded ruler of Ma'in dates to around 400 BC. The Minaeans created a series of trade colonies and representatives farther north in Arabia, Egypt, Syro-Palestine and the Greek Mediterranean during the Hellenistic period. The Himyarites, whose homeland was in Abyan (north-east of Aden), expanded at the end of the first millennium, and soon controlled much of South Arabia.

The early history of the Hadramaut remains poorly known. As earlier mentioned, the settlement at Shabwa began during the Bronze Age, and later grew to a large size. Shabwa controls the western exit of the Wadi Hadramaut, a strategic location on the incense route. The site of Huraida, in the Wadi 'Amd, was the scene of the first scientific excavation in South Arabia in 1937 (Caton-Thompson, 1944). This pioneering work exposed the temple of the moon-god Sin, a rock-cut tomb complex, and a farmstead; the earliest materials at these localities belong to the middle of the first millennium BC.

Taken as a whole, the South Arabian civilization was founded on two developments. The first was mastery of the agricultural possibilities of the south-western Arabian highlands. This mastery involved controlling water run-off with extensive systems of barrages, tanks and channels within wide wadi beds; well irrigation provided an important supplement to this system. The sa'il system supplied agricultural fields with both water and silt, the latter maintaining soil fertility. Terraced hill-slopes made available additional cultivable land for dry-farming. The crops in these fields included wheat, barley, broom millet, teff and oats, along with dates, zizyphus, grapes, cumin and flax.

The second development was the growth of the interregional incense trade, stimulated by the increasing demand for incense and other exotic commodities in the Iron Age empires to the north. Incense allowed south Arabia to enter the far-flung trading network of the first millennium; by the last centuries BC, south Arabia enjoyed connections with India, the Persian Gulf and Mesopotamia, northern Arabia and Syro-Palestine, Egypt, and the Eastern Mediterranean. The trade permitted south Arabia to accumulate a legendary wealth, and exposed the region to alien influences (notably of the Greek world) in the arts.

North-west Arabia

Up to the end of the Bronze Age, the inhabitants of north-west Arabia are scarcely visible, and seem to have been pastoralists and/or hunters-gatherers. This situation changed dramatically at the end of the second millennium BC, when oasis towns appeared and then developed into cities. The history of these north-west Arabian towns was a reflection of the history of the incense trade coming northward from south Arabia, and of the regional competition between towns for control over that trade (summarized in Edens and Bawden, 1989).

The first town to emerge in the Hejaz was at Qurayyah, with which is associated a style of painted pottery called 'Midianite'. The decoration of this pottery had affinities with the Late Bronze Age styles of the southern Levant, and appeared in other parts of the northern Hejaz and in the Negev. Qurayyah, still poorly understood, was encircled by a massive stone wall, and contained a craft quarter devoted to pottery making; an extensive system of channels and walled fields lay next to the settlement (Parr et al., 1970; Ingraham et al., 1981). Although Qurayyah was abandoned early in the first millennium BC, other large places arose in north-west Arabia, including Jawf, al-Ula, Tayma' and Medina. Best known for their importance later in the first millennium occupation, both archaeological and textual evidence indicate persistent settlement from early in the first millennium.

The Assyrian annals describe hostile relations with Jawf (Adummatu), which was often ruled by a queen, during the eighth and seventh centuries BC; no local archaeological information illuminates this period at Jawf. Nabonidus, the last king of an independent Babylonia, invaded and occupied the Hejaz as far south as Medina, and moved his court to Tayma' for ten years in the mid-sixth century. The town achieved its greatest prominence in the middle centuries of the first millennium BC, when it contained a series of massive walled compounds, an extensive irrigation system, and associated residential districts. A cult centre belonging to the fifth century BC contained a ritual iconography that borrowed from south Arabian, Achaemenid, and possibly Egyptian art (Abu Duruk, 1986). Al-Ula, on the other hand, seems to have experienced its greatest growth later in the first millennium, and may be associated with the kingdom of Dedan, and then with that of Lihyan.

During the first millennium BC, peoples in north-west Arabia developed several alphabetic scripts, and left innumerable casual inscriptions (graffiti) (Plate 105). The oldest of these scripts dates to the eighth or seventh centuries BC, and is especially associated with Tayma' (Winnett and Reed, 1970). The later variants, generally known as Thamudic, continued in use at least a millennium. The Thamudic inscriptions are usually short personal messages, and only occasionally contain useful historical information. The inscriptions do, however, refer to various divinities with astral or planetary significance; some graffiti (especially near Tayma') represent these gods with bucrania and stars.

The Iron Age archaeology of north-western Arabia reveals the origins of the world into which Mohammad was born. The interplay between the camel, trading towns and world markets increasingly cemented this part of Arabia to the neighbouring civilizations, and induced a growing cosmopolitan atmosphere in Arabian towns. The evidence of the epigraphy and art reveals an exposure to, and amalgamation of, various religious ideas that form part of Islam's background, while the trade itself created wealth in towns. These forces of change unfolded within the region's tribal societies, and helped create a new community.

BIBLIOGRAPHY

ABU DURUK, H. I. 1986. *Introduction to the Archaeology of Tayma'.* Riyadh, Department of Antiquities and Museums, Kingdom of Saudi Arabia.

AL-ANSARY, A. R. 1981. *Qaryat al Fau – A Portrait of Pre-Islamic Civilization in Arabia.* New York.

ALBRIGHT, F. 1958. Excavations at Marib in Yemen. In: BOWEN, R.; ALBRIGHT, F. (eds), *Archaeological Discoveries in South Arabia.* Baltimore, Md. pp. 215–68.

ALBRIGHT, W. 1950. The Chronology of South Arabia in the Light of the First Campaign of the Expedition to Qataban. *Bull. am. Sch. orient. Res.* (New Haven, Conn.), Vol. 119, pp. 5–15.

ANATI, E. 1968–72. *Rock-Art in Central Arabia.* Louvain.

BIAGI, P. et al. 1984. Qurum: A Case Study of Coastal Archaeology in Northern Oman. *World Archaeol.* (London), Vol. 16, pp. 43–61.

BIAGI, P.; MAGGI, R.; NISBET, R. 1989. Excavations at the Aceramic Coastal Settlement of RH5 (Muscat, Sultanate of Oman) 1983–5. In: FRIFELT, K.; SORENSEN, P. (eds), *South Asian Archaeology. 1985.* London. pp. 1–8.

BIBBY, T. G. 1970. *Looking for Dilmun.* New York.

BOUCHARLAT, R.; LOMBARD, P. 1985. The Oasis of Al Ain in the Iron Age: Excavations at Rumeilah 1981–1983. *Archaeol. United Arab Emirates* (Al-Ain), Vol. 4, pp. 44–73.

CATON-THOMPSON, G. 1944. *The Tombs and Moon Temple of Hureidha (Hadhramaut).* Oxford.

CLEUZIOU, S. 1980. Economie et société dans la péninsule d'Oman au IIIe millénaire: Le rôle de l'analogie avec les sociétés actuelles. In: BARRELET, M.-T. (ed.), *L'Archéologie de l'Iraq.* Paris. pp. 343–59.

—— 1981. Oman Peninsula in the Early Second Millennium BC. In: HARTEL, H. (ed.), *South Asian Archaeology, 1979.* Berlin. pp. 279–93.

—— 1982. Hili and the Beginning of Oasis Life in Eastern Arabia. *Proc. Semin. arab. Stud.* (London), Vol. 12, pp. 15–22.

CLEUZIOU, S.; TOSI, M. 1989. The South-Eastern Frontier of the Ancient Near East. In: FRIFELT, K.; SORENSEN, P. (eds), *South Asian Archaeology, 1985.* London. pp. 14–47.

DONALDSON, P. 1985. Prehistoric Tombs of Ras al-Khaimah. *Oriens Antiq.* (Roma), Vol. 23, pp. 191–312; Vol. 24, pp. 85–142.

EDENS, C. 1982. Towards a Definition of the Rub al-Khali 'Neolithic'. *Atlal* (Riyadh), Vol. 6, pp. 109–24.

EDENS, C.; BAWDEN, G. 1989. History of Tayma' and Hejazi Trade during the First Millennium BC. *J. econ. soc. Hist. Orient* (Leiden), Vol. 32, pp. 48–103.

FEDELE, F. 1988. North Yemen: The Neolithic. In: DAUM, W. (ed.) *Yemen, 3000 Years of Art and Civilization in Arabia Felix.* Innsbruck. pp. 34–7.

FRIFELT, K. 1975. On Prehistoric Settlements and Chronology of the Oman Peninsula. *East West* (Roma), Vol. 25, pp. 329–424.

HAUPTMANN, A. 1985. *Die Entwicklung der Kupfermetallurgie vom 3. Jahrtausend bis zum Neuzeit, 5000 Jahre Kupfer in Oman.* Bochum.

HEIMPEL, W. 1987. Das untere Meer. *Z. Assyriol.* (Berlin), Vol. 77, pp. 22–91.

HOJLUND, F. 1986a. *Failaka/Dilmun, The Second Millennium Settlements, Volume 2: The Bronze Age Pottery.* Åhrus.

—— 1986b. The Chronology of City II and III at Qala'at al Bahrain. In: AL-KHALIFA, H. A.; RICE, M. (eds), *Bahrain Through the Ages.* London. pp. 217–24.

HOTZL, H. et al. 1984. Climatic Fluctuations in the Holocene. In: JADO, A.; ZOTL, J. (eds) *Quaternary Period in Saudi Arabia.* Wien. Vol. 2, pp. 301–14.

IBRAHIM, M. 1983. *Excavations of the Arab Expedition at Sar el Jisr, Bahrain.* Manama.

INGRAHAM, M. et al. 1981. Preliminary Report on a Reconnaissance Survey of the Northwestern Province. *Atlal* (Riyadh), Vol. 5, pp. 59–84.

KAPEL, H. 1967. *Atlas of the Stone-Age Cultures of Qatar.* Åhrus.

KJAERUM, P. 1983. *Failaka/Dilmun, The Second Millennium Settlements, Volume 1/1: The Stamp and Cylinder Seals.* Åhrus.

LEEMANS, W. 1960. *Foreign Trade in the Old Babylonian Period.* Leiden.

LOMBARD, P. 1986. Iron Age Dilmun, A Reconsideration of City IV at Qala'at al Bahrain. In: AL-KHALIFA, H. A.; RICE, M. (eds), *Bahrain Through the Ages.* London. pp. 225–32.

—— 1988. The Salt Mine Site and the 'Hasaean' Period in Northeastern Arabia. In: POTTS, D. (ed.), *Araby the Blest.* København. pp. 116–35.

MCCLURE, H. 1976. Radiocarbon Chronology of Late Quaternary Lakes in the Arabian Desert. *Nature* (London), Vol. 263, pp. 744–56.

MAIGRET, A. de. 1990. A Bronze Age for Southern Arabia. *East West* (Roma), Vol. 34, pp. 5–36.

MASRY, A. 1974. *Prehistory in Northeastern Arabia: The Problem of Interregional Interaction.* Miami, Fla.

MUGHAL, R. 1983. *The Dilmun Burial Complex at Sar, The 1980–82 Excavations in Bahrain.* Manama.

OATES, D. 1986. Dilmun and the Late Assyrian Empire. In: AL-KHALIFA, H. A.; RICE, M. (eds), *Bahrain Through the Ages.* London. pp. 428–34.

OATES, J. et al. 1977. Seafaring Merchants of Ur? *Antiquity* (Cambridge), Vol. 51, pp. 221–34.

PARR, P.; HARDING, G.; DAYTON, J. 1970. Preliminary Survey in N. W. Arabia, 1968. *Bull. Inst. Archaeol.* (London), Vol. 8–9, pp. 193–242.

PETTINATO, G. 1972. Il commercio con l'estero della Mesopotamia meridionale 3. millannio av. Cr. alla luce delle fonti litterati e lessicale. *Mesopotamia* (Torino), Vol. 7, pp. 43–166.

PIRENNE, J. 1956. *Paléographie des inscriptions sud-arabes: contribution à la chronologie et à l'histoire de l'Arabie du Sud antique.* Bruxelles.

POTTS, D. 1986. Eastern Arabia and the Oman Peninsula during the Late Fourth Millennnium. In: ROLLIG, W.; NISSEN, H.; FINKBEINER, U. (eds), *Gamdat Nasr: Period or Regional Style?* Wiesbaden. pp. 121–70.

—— 1990. *A Prehistoric Mound in the Emirate of Umm al-Qaiwain, U.A.E., Excavations at Tell Abraq in 1989.* København.

—— 1992. The Chronology of the Archaeological Assemblages from the Head of the Arabian Gulf to the Arabian Sea (8000–1750 BC). In: EHRICH, R. (ed.), *Chronologies in Old World Archaeology.* Chicago, Ill.

ROAF, M. 1976. Excavations at al-Markh, Bahrain. *Proc. Semin. arab. Stud.* (London), Vol. 2, pp. 144–60.

SAUER, J.; BLAKELY, J 1988. Archaeology Along the Spice Route of Yemen. In: POTTS, D. (ed.), *Araby the Blest.* København. pp. 91–115.

TIKRITI, W. 1985. The Archaeological Investigations on Ghanadha Island 1982–1984: Further Evidence for the Coastal Umm an-Nar Culture. *Archaeol. United Arab Emirates* (Al-Ain), Vol. 4, pp. 9–19.

TOSI, M. 1975. Notes on the Distribution and Exploitation of Natural Resources in Ancient Oman. *J. Oman Stud.* (Muscat), Vol. 1, pp. 187–206.

VAN BEEK, G. 1969. *Hajar Bin Humeid: Investigations at a Pre-Islamic Site in South Arabia.* Baltimore, Md.

VOGT, B.; FRANKE-VOGT, U. (eds). 1987. *Shimal 1985/6. Excavations of the German Archaeological Mission in Ras al-Khaimah, U.A.E.: A Preliminary Report.* Berlin.

WEISGERBER, G. 1981. Mehr als Kupfer in Oman, Ergebnisse der Expedition 1981. *Anschnitt* (Bochum), Vol. 33, pp. 174–263.

WINNETT, F.; REED, W. 1970. *Ancient Records from North Arabia.* Toronto.

WISSMANN, H. VON. 1975. *Über die frühe Geschichte Arabiens und das Entstehen des Sabaerreiches.* Wien.

ZARINS, J. 1979. Rajajil, A Unique Arabian Site in the Fourth Millennium BC. *Atlal* (Riyadh), Vol. 3, pp. 73–8.

—— 1989. Eastern Saudi Arabia and External Relations: Selected Ceramic, Steatite and Textual Evidence: 3500–1900 BC. In: FRIFELT, K.; SORENSEN, P. (eds), *South Asian Archaeology, 1985.* London. pp. 74–103.

—— 1992. Archaeological and Chronological Problems within the Greater Southwest Asian Arid Zone: 3000–1850 BC. In: EHRICH, R. (ed.), *Chronologies in Old World Archaeology.* Chicago, Ill.

12.7

THE INDUS VALLEY

(3000–1500 BC)

B. K. Thapar and M. Rafique Mughal

GENERAL BACKGROUND

The Indus civilization,[1] which ranks geographically as the largest among the four widely known civilizations of the Old World, is known to represent the earliest manifestation of urbanization in South Asia. For a proper understanding of the process of urbanism in this region, however, it would perhaps be relevant to study contemporary development in the neighbouring areas, which seem to constitute a very large sphere of cultural interaction.

The ecological and environmental aspects leading to urbanization have often been emphasized in the development process in southern Mesopotamia and the Iranian plateau. Between the two areas, highland and lowland, a dichotomy seems to have developed that influenced the historical and social organization of both societies. The lowland communities situated on the alluvial plains of Mesopotamia depended upon agriculture to produce surplus foodstuffs, and as such established settlements with nucleated centres along major waterways. In contrast, the highland communities existed in areas of dry-farming with a lower agricultural productivity, a lower population density and a comparative autonomy and isolation. But the needs of one area complemented those of the other. In fact, the interrelationship between the two was forged by their complementarity: the highland communities were rich in resources like copper, turquoise, chlorite, wood and so on, while the lowland centres had a surplus of food-stuffs and manufactured goods, including textiles, for export.

The geographical factors governing settlements in the Indus Valley are somewhat similar to those obtaining in the Mesopotamian lowlands and the Iranian highlands. In the Indus Valley, the whole area can be divided into two principal divisions: the western highlands represented by the Sind Kohistan, Kirthar and Sulaiman ranges; and the lower Indus Valley, divided into western and eastern sectors and the deltaic area. The rugged and desolate character of these mountain ranges is accentuated by the extreme sparseness of their vegetation. Nevertheless, they afforded excellent grazing for sheep and goats and for wild ibex and urial. There are several transverse lines of drainage in these mountain ranges which also serve the purpose of communication from the valley to the Iranian plateau, Seistan, Afghanistan and Turkmenia. A noteworthy feature of the western highlands was the development of steep slopes at the base of the hills, forming a piedmont zone between the western highlands and the alluvium in the east. The ancient settlements were

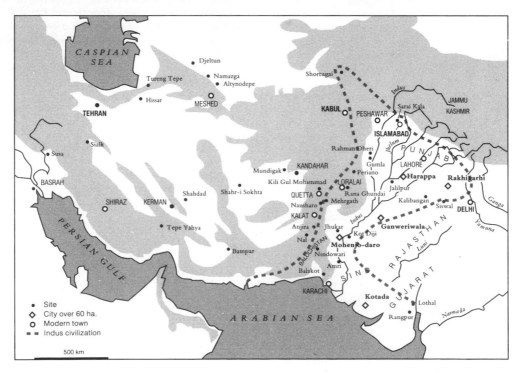

Map 14 Distribution of Indus civilization during the mature and later periods, c. 2500–1500 BC.

246

clustered in the valleys of the Zhob, Loralai, Queta, Pishin and Kej, and in the alluvium plains of Las Bela and Sibi-Kachi and, in their level of cultural manifestation, created the potential for the evolution of cities along the Indus. The scantily habitable dry plateau of Iran and Baluchistan drove the highlanders into the fertile Indus Valley. This movement was possible because the lower slopes of the Kirthar and Sulaiman ranges fall gently into the plains below.

Baluchistan thus was neither a backwater nor a border-land but an area of distinctive physical environment connected with surrounding regions and nearby centres of civilization through easily accessible routes. It was also the most important cultural region, where shifts from hunting and gathering to sedentarism led to primary urbanism. Recent discoveries at Mehrgarh give substance to the hypothesis that Baluchistan played a dominant role in the shaping of urban civilization in South Asia. The Mehrgarh area is the proluvial-alluvial basin of the Nari and Bolan rivers, extending into the plains of Kachi. It is a natural area of transition from true plateau to alluvial plain of the Indus and as such most favourable to the development of the transitional Neolithic and primary urban economies. Excavations at Mehrgarh (Jarrige, 1982; Jarrige and Lechevallier, 1979; Jarrige and Meadow, 1980) have revealed a continuing sequence of cultures from the aceramic Neolithic (eighth millennium BC) through ceramic Neolithic (sixth–fifth millennium BC) to the Bronze Age (fifth–third millennium BC), contemporaneous with Kili Gul Muhammad, Rana Ghundai, Damb Sadaat, Shahr-i Sokhta, Mundigak and Kot Diji. Eight kilometres to the south at Nausharo lies a mature Harappan site, indicating that the Kachi plain was definitely a part of Harappan territory. The last phase of occupation at Mehrgarh, labelled the South Cemetery or Sibi phase, yielded some stone and bronze objects including pottery forms showing analogies with Central Asian sites (Bactria, Margiana, southern Turkmania, and so on), belonging to the close of the third millennium BC, as also with Harappan elements, signifying that the cemetery is contemporary, at least in part,

with the Indus civilization. Excavation at Pirak in the same area links the sequence to the Iron Age, ascribable to the close of the second millennium BC. Baluchistan should, therefore, be considered an area which functioned not only as a cultural conduit linking Iranian plateau developments with those in the Indus Valley, but also as an area which itself had significant cultural development.

DISTRIBUTION (Map 14)

The discovery of the Indus civilization in 1921–2 had, according to Marshall (1931), at a single bound taken our knowledge of India back some 3,000 years. Explorations and excavations, conducted during the twenty-five years following its discovery, indicate that its area of spread lay principally in the Sind plains, with significant cultural contacts to sites in the secluded valleys of Baluchistan, such as Dabar-kot, Sutkagen-dor, Dasht Kaur on the Makran coast close to the Iranian border. Harappa and Chak Purhane Syal on the Ravi, Kotla Nihang Khan near Rupar, on the left bank of the Sutlej in the foothills of the Himalayas, a few sites along the Hakra in the erstwhile Bahawalpur state and Rangpur on the Sukha Bhadar in Kathiawad, Gujarat, were the only recorded sites of this civilization lying outside the Sind region. In 1947, therefore, after the creation of the two independent republics of India and Pakistan, most of the known area of spread of this civilization fell within the borders of Pakistan, leaving only Kotla Nihang Khan and Rangpur, the two seeming outposts, within the territory of India. Sustained fieldwork during the last four decades or so in regions contiguous to the Pakistan frontier, particularly along the ancient beds of Sarasvati-Ghaggar and the palaeochannels of the Sutlej and the Yamuna in Rajasthan, Haryana and Punjab, and the flat alluvial plains and coastal lowlands of Gujarat, has extended the limits of the civilization well within the present-day frontiers of India: in the east, up to Alamgirpur on the Hindou, a tributary of the Yamuna, across the Indo-Gangetic divide, some 45 km north of Delhi; in the north, up to Manda, on the right bank of the Chenab, some 28 km north-west of Jammu, in the foothills of the Pir Panjal range; and in the south up to Daimabad on the left bank of the Pravara, a tributary of the Godavari, some 230 km east-north-east of Bombay. Likewise, during the same period, within Pakistan itself, explorations, particularly in the regions of Gomal, Bannu, Cholistan, Bolan and along the Makran coast extended the distribution both within and outside the Indus Valley. Thus amplified, its total area of spread, falling within both India and Pakistan, covers over 1.2 million km² with about a 1,900–km-long seaboard, much larger than that of the widely known contemporary Bronze Age civilization of either Egypt or Sumer.

SETTLEMENT PATTERN

The core or nuclear area lies in Pakistan, principally within the valley of the Indus and its tributaries, and that of the parallel river system of the ancient Sarasvati (the present-day dry beds of Hakra and Nara). Only one site in interior Baluchistan, Dabar-kot, has evidence of a major Harappan-phase occupation, and even there it is limited to a particular area of the site. All the other known Harappan sites, Nausharo, Pathani Damb and Balakot, Sontakakoh and Sutkagen-dor along the coast, are located along Baluchistan's eastern and southern fringes.

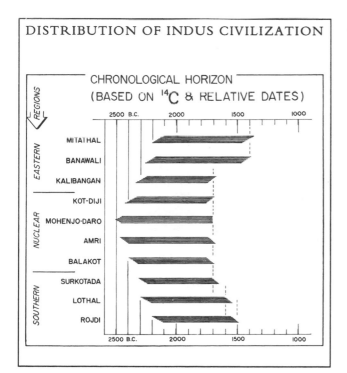

DISTRIBUTION OF INDUS CIVILIZATION

CHRONOLOGICAL HORIZON
(BASED ON ¹⁴C & RELATIVE DATES)

REGIONS

EASTERN
MITATHAL
BANAWALI
KALIBANGAN

NUCLEAR
KOT-DIJI
MOHENJO-DARO
AMRI
BALAKOT

SOUTHERN
SURKOTADA
LOTHAL
ROJDI

Map 14 (Continued)

The Indus does not flow north-south directly but takes a deep S-shaped curve, thus adding more to the cultivable land. Being fed by both snow and monsoon and having a gradient of 4.8 cm per km in the Sind region, periodic flooding has been an important phenomenon of its regimen. The distribution of Harappan sites in the Sind corridor follows the active floodplain of the river or the *dhands* which depend on the summer floods. On the west of the Indus flows a stream known as the Western Nara, whose water sources are the streams of the Kirthar range and the floods of the Indus. Eventually these waters empty into Lake Manchar which, with its periodically changing level of filling and emptying, provided excellent arable land for cultivation and as such witnessed the rise of some early Harappan settlements such as Pandiwahi, Damb Buthi and Ali Murad. Another distinct ecological region from which Harappan sites have been reported is the Kachi plain, a flat expanse of alluvial outwash, located at the foot of the Bolan Pass. On the eastern flank of the Indus is the Eastern Nara of the Ghaggar-Hakra-Sarasvati system, which showed a concentration of sites in Cholistan. Along the Kirthar and Sulaiman ranges and in the Indus Kohistan area in the south-west, the settlements were near spring water. Sutkagen-dor, Sotka-koh, Balakot were essentially sea-ports, controlling coastal traffic and trade. Each of these sites is located at the outlet of an important valley through which the Makran coast is approached from the Baluchi hinterland. Closer to Punjab the tributaries of the Indus have broad alluvial plains largely unaffected by the flood. The reported Indus sites are Harappa, Chak Purhane Syal and Jalilpur on the Ravi.

The classification of Harappan sites into cities, towns and villages is imprecise. The cities, such as Mohenjo-daro, Harappa and Lothal, are generally distinguished by their size and the presence of monumental architecture, including a citadel. Nevertheless one can distinguish industrial centres, such as those in Cholistan which were production centres of specific crafts; camp sites of pastoralists who utilized desert or marginal areas of the valley; port towns like Sutkagen-dor and Sotka-koh, which carried on maritime trade and were at the same time connected with the resource regions of the hinterland; and multifunctional sites. Coastal sites like Allahdino and Balakot exploited the marine resources. In the western fringes of the Thar desert, where between 1974 and 1977 extensive explorations were carried out, the location of sites shows a different distribution. Among high-density sites is the metropolitan city site of Ganweriwala, covering 81.5 hectares in area, and equidistant from both Mohenjo-daro and Harappa. It is reasonable to assume that originally Harappa and Mohenjo-daro were also located in high-density areas, which at present it is not possible to reconstruct due to intensive cultivation and other landform changes resulting from human intervention. The area enclosed by these three cities (Mohenjo-daro, Harappa and Ganweriwala) seems to mark the core or nuclear area of the Indus civilization. It was almost the same area which was under occupation during the Early Harappan period, prior to the maturity of the Indus civilization.

Access to raw material was secured by a chain of sites along the lines of communication. Settlements were established at resource points, such as at Shortugai on the Oxus, for obtaining lapis lazuli from the Badakhshan region. The sites in the hills were intended to guard the passes and to keep the lines of communication open between the Indus Valley and Baluchistan for internal trade and accessibility to sources of raw materials. The sites located in the desert on the eastern

fringes of the valley are marked by limited cultural materials, indicating temporary occupation.

As far as India is concerned, the area of spread of this civilization falls broadly into two separate geographical regions, forked essentially by the Thar desert: (1) the eastern region, covering Rajasthan, Haryana, Punjab, some parts of Jammu and Kashmir and Uttar Pradesh, the river systems being the Ghaggar-Sarasvati, Chautang, Sutlej, Beas, Ravi, Chenab and Yamuna; (2) the southern region, covering Kutch, Kathiawad, the coastal flats of Gujarat and some areas of the hinterland of Maharashtra, the river systems being the Luni, Banas, Sabarmati, Narmada, Mahi, Kim, Tapti and Godavari.

The eastern region, which was a multi-river system, in sharp contrast to the one-river system of Sind, was marked by wide foodplains with a vast surface for the annual flood-silt. Landform studies have shown that Sutlej was at one time the main tributary of the Ghaggar-Saraswati and so was the Yamuna, making Ghaggar-Saraswati a mighty river which probably debouched into the Rann of Kutch through Hakra and Nara. The Ghaggar-Hakra had a well-cut bed in the alluvium but no large delta, which a river of this size is expected to form. Some time towards the first quarter of the second millennium BC, tectonic movements had forced both the Sutlej and Yamuna to take up their present courses, as demonstrated by a multitude of small channels into which they coursed, leaving the non-perennial Ghaggar-Sarawati dry, with the result that its diminished water supply failed to sustain the settlements downstream. This phenomenon is reflected in the distribution pattern of the sites. A large number of the pre-Harappan[2] and Harappan sites are found principally along the now dry bed of the Ghaggar-Saraswati, and along the braided channels of the Sutlej, such as the Naiwals and the Wah, but there are none on the present channels except Rupar. The drying of the river systems resulted in pre-Harappan sites in the Chautang Valley becoming isolated, and developing along their own lines. On present showing, the densest distribution of sites, both pre-Harappan and Harappan, is noticed paradoxically not on the Indus river and its tributaries with which the name of the civilization is associated, but on the now dry Hakra-Ghaggar-Saraswati and its equally extinct tributaries.

In the southern region, the spread was not uniform in scale as in Sind, Punjab and Rajasthan. The drainage networks of Kutch, Kathiawad and the rest of Gujarat are unrelated to each other. This explains the diverse ramifications of the Indus civilization in this region. Surkotada, Dholavira (Kotadi) and Bhatatrav show divergent traits. Significantly, no pre-Harappan sites have so far been located in this region.

As far as the coastal areas are concerned, the indented coastline from the Gulf of Cambay southwards affords suitable sites for ports, as evidenced by the location of Prabhas Patan on the banks of the Hiranya, Lothal on the Bhogavo, Mehgam on the estuary of the Narmada and Bhagatrav on the estuary of the Kim. In the north-eastern coastal zone of the Little Rann, the rivers Banas, Saraswati and Rupen have, by their coalescing silt, formed an estuarine plain which provided a favourable ecological zone for the Harappan communities to settle and there are many sites in that area. The Gujarat plains, located between the marshy coastal zone and the plateau and mountains in the interior, are remarkably flat, with sluggish meandering streams, and as such afforded suitable settlement sites.

The plateau of Kathiawad is marked by a radial drainage pattern. Among the notable sites located in the valleys of these rivers are Rojdi on the Bhadar and Rangpur on the

Sukha Bhadar. An interesting feature of the plateau of Kathi-awad, however, is the occurrence of numerous dikes, some-times as wide as 60 m, which provided raw material for many objects, including beads.

The Kutch plateau is drained by rivers flowing into the Gulf of Kutch in the south and Rann of Kutch in the north. None of these rivers has a course longer than 60 km. Notable Harappan sites include Surkotada, Desalpur, Dholavira and Pabumath. Being located on the margin of the Rann, Dholavira could possibly have functioned as a port station.

The settlement pattern is conditioned by ecological fac-tors; subsistence and techno-economies; perhaps a sloping horizon, indicated by a directional movement from the nuclear area to both the eastern and southern regions; and climate. The ecological factors have already been described, and climate is dealt with in a section of its own below.

Alamgirpur and Hulor, located across the divide of the Indus and Yamuna systems, mark the eastern limit of the ecological zone, beyond which lay the real Indian monsoon-fed jungle which the Indus people found it difficult to bring under cultivation with the tools at their disposal. The upper Ganga-Yamuna, being transitional between the arid Indus and the monsoon Ganga plains, forms the eastern limit of winter farming, which was the basis of the subsistence econ-omy of the Harappans. They depended largely on perennial rivers, which afforded extensive floodplains annually inun-dated by monsoon floods, depositing fresh silt for cereal cul-tivation. The other consideration was the navigability of the river, permitting transport for internal trade, and accessibil-ity to natural resources. The densest distribution of sites is in close proximity to the source of copper, represented by the Khetri belt in Rajasthan and Amba Mata in Kutch. Tin ore deposits are also known to occur in the Aravalli hills, in Bhilwara and Udaipur in Rajasthan and Banas Kantha in Gujarat. This is particularly significant because of the occur-rences of chalcopyrite deposits in the Aravallis. Steatite, yel-low fine-grained stone and dark grey slate were readily available in Rajasthan, while carnelian, agate and other chal-cedonic semi-precious stones could be obtained from Gujarat near Rajpipla. The latter region also offered red ochre, shell and ivory, which were items of long-distance trade. The sources of construction timber, such as pine, deodar and elm, were the lower Himalayan Panchmahals and western ghats. Harappan expansion into the Gujarat seems to have been largely in quest of ports and raw materials. Chert, flint, jade, lapis lazuli, silver, gold and so on, which were not available in these regions, involved long-distance trade through either simple or complex exchange systems, which in turn led to interregional interaction.

CLIMATE

The ancient climate of South Asia has been a subject of con-siderable debate and the available evidence has been inter-preted variously. Both Stein (1931) and Marshall (1931) postulated appreciably wetter conditions during pre-Harap-pan and Harappan times (third millennium BC). Their infer-ence was largely based on five factors: (1) the presence of gabarbands for the control of water; (2) a larger number of ancient mounds in contrast to the present-day settlements, along with their respective depth of occupation; (3) the use of baked brick at Mohenjo-daro, Chanhu-daro and Harappa, requiring a plentiful supply of fuel; (4) the presence at both Mohenjo-daro and Harappa of an elaborate drainage system

to dispose of storm waters; and (5) the occurrence of marsh or jungle animals (tiger, rhinoceros, buffalo, elephant) on seals and the absence or extreme scarcity of camels. The environs of Mohenjo-daro were thought to be covered with dense jungle, being a natural habitat for such animals. At the same time, Marshall was also aware of the weakness of the argument, especially when applied to the contemporary civ-ilizations of Egypt and Mesopotamia and had, therefore, reservations about this pluvial theory. Wheeler (1968), too, felt that the argument of the wet climate would not stand up.

In 1971, Gurdip Singh (1971, 1974) carried out pollen analytical studies of salt-lake deposits (at Sambhar, Didwana and Lunkaransar) and fresh-water lake deposits (Pushkar) in the area centering on the Rajasthan desert. The environ-mental sequence built up from pollen analysis has been grouped into six phases, of which phase IV, ascribable to c. 3000–1000 BC, covers the period of the Indus civilization, including its antecedent and subsequent phases. This phase IV is subdivided into IVA (3000–1800), IVB (1800–1500) and IVC (1500–1000 BC). Of these, IVA shows wet condi-tions, IVB drier conditions and IVC a reversal to relatively weak wet conditions. The palaeoecological picture of sub-phase IVA suggests an annual rainfall of at least 50 cm in excess of the present-day average in the arid belt of Rajasthan. The hypothesis of a wetter climate during Harappan times is supported by meteorological studies (Ramaswamy, 1968), oxygen isotope ratios from the Arabian Sea cores, climatic modelling of monsoon intensities (Meadow, 1989) and eco-logical factors (Agrawal and Sood, 1982).

The wetter-climate theory has, however, been questioned by various scholars (Raikes and Dyson, 1961; Raikes, 1967; Chowdhury; Ghosh, 1951; Thapar, 1977, 1984; Vishnu Mit-tre, 1978, 1982; and Mishra, 1984), who feel that there has been no appreciable change in the climate during the past 9,000 years or so and that the arguments for a wetter climate lack conviction. Vishnu Mittre, in his analysis of the Rajasthan pollen diagram, postulated an arid climate during the period 3000–2000 BC. As for the growth of cities, it was averred that most of the sites were in a floodplain environment where rainfall was of minimal importance, and as such could have prospered on zero rainfall with or even without artificial irri-gation, and that the floodplains of the Indus still support gallery forests which provide a habitat for wild animals. Fur-thermore, it is pointed out that the carrying capacity of the drains found at Mohenjo-daro does not equate with a greater rainfall. Their homely function clearly was that of disposal of domestic waste. The gabarbands again were a device for conserving the silt content of short-lived seasonal floods beside torrent beds that are normally dry. Furthermore, the evidence obtained from pollen studies in Rajasthan cannot justifiably be extrapolated for the entire area of the civiliza-tion without circumspection, especially as the palynological evidence obtained from Balakot in Sind does not seem to suggest a decidedly wetter climate during the fourth-third millennium BC (Dales, 1986). At the same time one need not deny varying environmental contexts, both biotic and abiotic, having short-term fluctuations in different parts of the area.

ORIGIN AND GROWTH

Ever since the discovery of the Indus civilization, various views have been expressed about its origin and subsequent growth into full maturity. Based largely on the occurrence of certain Indus-related material on Mesopotamian sites it was initially suggested that it was an offshoot of the Sumerian civilization which had preceded it and was likewise a riverine one. A closer analysis of the Indus and Mesopotamian cultures would indicate that the basic differences (town planning, scripts, weights and measures) bar the possibility of any direct 'colonization' of the former by the latter. At the same time it must be admitted that the dissimilarities are in the detailed performance of basic concurrences, such as the attributes of the city itself, widespread trade, well-organized agriculture, fertile river valleys, specialist craft and ceremonial centres. Considering the nature of the lands in between the two regions – barren mountains with scattered settlements – it is reasonable to argue that any Mesopotamian-generated influence is unlikely – or to have become radically altered – before it could reach the Indus plain. Whatever influences moved from west to east, and some certainly did, they enhanced an already existing situation.

Another view is that the civilization arose independently in north-western India out of the mosaic of Indo-Iranian borderland and Baluchi village-farming cultures, mostly antedating the Harappan culture and some even contemporary with it (Fairservis, 1971). The plethora of cultures covering the entire food-producing cultural succession has been classified into six phases or five stages, each culturally and technologically more advanced than the preceding one, with the last phase representing the civilization itself. This view would postulate prosperous peasant village economies in the highlands leading to rich urban ones after their inhabitants became sufficiently skilled to exploit the potentials of the floodplains, with the whole empirical tradition of food production, derived from an Iranian ancestry, for a successful adaptation to the new environment. By implication this means that the Indus civilization was the natural culmination of a long process. The genesis of the civilization and its ethos remains, however, unexplained. A close study of the Baluchi hill cultures would no doubt reveal a pattern of a somewhat uniform development level of material culture, but we still lack knowledge of the catalytic agent or motivating factor necessary for the next vital step.

It is well known that on each of the excavated sites where Harappan occupation has been found to be overlying that of the pre-Harappan (Kalibangan, Harappa, Kot Diji, Gumla, Balakot), the Harappan settlement seems to have started suddenly in all its maturity. Amri, however, provides a continuous occupation with a transition from the pre-Harappan to the Harappan phase.

Field research oriented towards early cultural development in the greater Indus Valley (Mughal, 1970) has provided evidence which indicates that cultural processes leading to full urbanization were already under way in this region from the middle of the fourth millennium BC. Detailed analysis of the material excavated from the sites of the antecedent cultures in the greater Indus Valley, including those from Kot Diji, Rahman Dheri, Jalilpur, Amri, Balakot, Kalibangan and so on, have shown the presence of many elements, namely fortifications, ceramic forms (including terracotta cakes, bangles, toy-cart wheels, bulls) and metal technology, which later characterize the Indus civilization. This phenomenon lends some sense of unity in certain cultural traits, styles and techniques antecedent to the emergence of cities. But the idea of the grid-patterned city with the centralization of a variety of interdependent activities, monumental architecture, an elaborate system of

weights and measures, extensive copper-bronze metallurgy and the art of writing, the hallmark of the civilization, was conspicuously absent in these cultural manifestations although it has been argued that the beginnings of writing can be seen in the graffiti and potters' marks occurring on the pottery of cultures which are designated as Early Harappan or formative stages of the Indus civilization. For the origin of the Harappan city, it has been speculated that the increase of agricultural produce in the villages forced the need for markets and hence a merchant class (Agrawal, 1972–3). The merchants not only planned Harappan cities, but also deliberately standardized their cultural traits. The Harappan abruptness was thus argued as deliberate and not a process of natural growth.

There is yet another view which, based on recent archaeological evidence (obtained from excavations at Tepe Yahya and Shahr-i Sokhta), demonstrating the full-scale development of partly literate and economically demanding complex societies on the Indo-Iranian borderlands at the end of the fourth millennium BC, points towards eastern Iran as the homeland of the formative influence on the Indus civilization. It is reasonable to argue that the fairly advanced village communities of Baluchistan, such as Kulli, with possibilities of synoecism, were in contact with the Iranian highlands and southern Mesopotamia, Khuzistan, Turkmenia, Seistan and southern Afghanistan and the native development of village-town complexes, as represented by these cultures, seems to have been spurred on by the diffusion of the idea of civilization from this early urban interaction sphere. The possibilities seem to have been exploited at many sites with varying measures of success. Recent excavations at Tepe Yahya and Shahr-i Sokhta have provided a synchronism between such features as proto-Elamite tablets, Nal ware, or terracotta bulls, the former site also yielding a Persian Gulf seal, a seal-impression with unmistakable Indus script on a potsherd, and Mesopotamian ceramics. The presence of a late fourth- and early third-millennium proto-literate community in the area may in turn have provided the stimulus for the system of writing in the Indus civilization. Furthermore, findings at Bahrain, Failaka, Bampur, Altyn-depe, Shortugai, Sarai Kala and Gumla indicate a pattern of communication between Mesopotamia, Seistan, Turkmenia, Afghanistan, Baluchistan and Sind which would support the movement of ideas.

The role of the idea and stimulus diffusion from Mesopotamia, Iran and Seistan, combined with the genius loci, has to be duly recognized. Wheeler long ago stated that ideas have wings and in the third millennium BC the idea of urbanism was in the air in western Asia. A model of civilization, however abstract, was present in the minds of the Indus founders and the setting was socio-culturally mature enough to assimilate it. One could argue for a catalytic influence of a selective, qualified and transient character which spurred on the synoecism that was to happen. The role of the genius loci was emphasized by Ghosh (1965), who felt that the origin of the civilization should be looked for within the earlier pre-Harappan culture itself and not from outside. He visualized that the local people, without any outside colonizers or conquerors, woke up to new ideas and reacted accordingly, perhaps led by a few genius dictators, trade with west Asia making them realize the need for standardization. But where this explosive phenomenon took place still remains to be established. Do the unfathomed levels of Mohenjo-daro or the unexcavated site of Judeirjo-daro hold the key?

THE PROTO-URBAN AND PRE-LITERATE CULTURES

Baluchistan

By about 5000 BC permanent settlements had come into existence in the Greater Indus Valley and Baluchistan near the sources of water or the moisture-retentive soil of the mountain valleys, where cereal crops were cultivated and goat, sheep and cattle were already fully domesticated. A degree of craft specialization, long-distance trade, complexity in dwelling houses and public buildings that had appeared during the Neolithic period at Mehrgarh and Kili Gul Muhammad were further developed into more complex socio-economic religious and political institutions, which formed the basis of urbanism in the Indus Valley.

The early cultural manifestations, both in Baluchistan and the Indus Valley, are distinguished by the material assemblages of common cultural traits and are usually known after their area of concentration or the principal site names. These cultures present a continuous development from c. 5000 to 2500 BC.

The middle of the fifth millennium BC marks the beginning of the Chalcolithic period in Baluchistan and is represented in the Quetta Valley at Kili Gul Muhammad levels II–III and at Mehrgarh period III. Comparable materials are found in the Kalat plateau designated there as Surab I–II and at Sur Jangal I–II in the Loralai Valley of northern Baluchistan (Fairservis, 1959). Fast wheels for making pottery were introduced and new pottery vessels and decorative designs emerged. An intensification of other crafts is noticeable by the discovery at Mehrgarh of crucibles with copper pieces and of lapidary and shell-working areas. Buildings included compartmented granaries, implying the availability of a surplus and the intensive cultivation of cereals, mostly barley. The evidence ties in well with Mundigak I and II and Namazga period III.

During the second half of the fourth millennium BC further changes and elaborations took place, though there was no cultural discontinuity at Kili Gul Muhammad, Surab or Mehrgarh. New ceramic styles consisted of bichrome and polychrome painted motifs, the 'wet' and grey wares, along with those of earlier traditions. Female figurines as cult objects became more stylized in representation, indicating an increased importance of religion. The houses continued to be built with mud or mudbrick on stone foundations.

The beginning of the third millennium BC in Baluchistan demonstrates increasing complexity in architecture and a profusion of pottery for which the Kachi plain and the Quetta Valley provide the best information. Public or monumental architecture in the form of platforms appeared at Damb Sadaat and Mehrgarh. The form of the 'Mother Goddess' with bejewelled breasts became standardized. Special areas for craft activities were demarcated. The presence of marine shells, lapis lazuli and turquoise suggest that Baluchistan had already established wide-ranging contacts. The distribution of ceramic forms and painted motifs over a wide area shows an extensive communication network both within the Indus Valley and with other regions. The Quetta painted style occurs on the pottery of Mundigak III in Afghanistan, Shahr-i Sokhta in Seistan and even beyond the Early Bronze Age sites in Turkmenistan or Namazga IV. This type of associated ware also extended southward to Nal in southern Kalat and on the piedmont plain of the western part of the Indus Valley.

One of the significant culture areas in southern Kalat is represented by the site of Sohr Damb, which produced a very distinctive wheel-made pottery both in form and decoration and a variety of bronze tools in the burials (Hargreaves, 1929). Canisters with ring bases and other vessels, including cups and bowls, depict a great variety of geometric and floral motifs, including zoomorphic ones. The Nal pottery is also widely distributed and thus provides a good chronological horizon around 3300–2500 BC.

The Loralai-Zhob archaeological sequence is known from Rana Ghandai (Ross, 1946), Sur Jangal and Periano Ghondai. Structures of mudbrick and mud on stone foundations, flint tools, leaf-shaped arrowheads, copper objects, alabaster vessels and terracotta female figurines occur with red wares painted in black in a variety of designs. Contacts with the Bannu basin and Gomal Valley are indicated, especially during the early third millennium BC. At the same time, the lower Indus Valley demonstrates interaction with central and southern Baluchistan.

Sind

In contrast to the regional cultural pattern of Baluchistan, the vast plains of the Greater Indus Valley show great uniformity in materials approaching cultural integration, with the exception of peripheral areas such as south-western Sind and north-east Rajasthan. The Early Bronze Age cultures in the Greater Indus Valley with fortifications, long-distance trade or exchange, craft specialization and the local production of standardized tools, ceramics and other items, an agriculture-based economy, a formalized religion, the beginnings of writing in the form of graffiti and potters' marks, and a large settlement size with complexity of architecture, represent the Early Harappan stage. The appearance of large sites such as Mohenjo-daro and Harappa during the middle of the third millennium BC, in fact, marks the climax of cultural processes which were already under way at least from the middle of the fourth millennium BC (Mughal, 1970, 1988).

Before the appearance of urban centres in about 2500 BC, the lower Indus region was dotted with permanent settlements having varying degrees of complexity in their social organization, architecture, tools technology, and exchange systems, with an economy based on agriculture and animal husbandry. These early settlements, numbering over thirty, were contemporary in date with the Bronze Age cultures of Baluchistan, roughly belonging to the middle of the fourth and early third millennium BC. The most significant sites are Kot Diji and Amri, which in turn form the basic frame of reference for the Early Bronze Age of the lower Indus Valley.

Kot Diji, covering an area of at least 2.6, hectares is located on the east bank of the Indus, opposite Mohenjo-daro (F. A. Khan, 1965). The earliest occupation at the site, termed 'Kot Dijian', was enclosed by a fortification of mudbricks and was represented by levels 4 to 16, which are dated by radiocarbon (calibrated) between 3300 and 2500/2200 BC. The use of bronze, though restricted to household and personal ornaments, is attested. Other objects include chert blades, leaf-shaped arrowheads, stone pestles, grinding stones, beads of carnelian and lapis lazuli, and a variety of terracotta objects, such as cones, toy-cart frames and wheels. The most distinctive element of this culture is the wheel-made pottery, often painted on the neck with a simple black or brown band, and represented in globular vessels on stands, flanged vessels with lids, pans and bowls. The ceramic types in particular are related to those found in early third-millennium contexts at sites of the central and northern Indus Valley. The Kot Dijian levels yielded materials which anticipated some elements of the mature Harappan culture. Kot Dijian materials, therefore, are now considered to represent the early formative or proto-urban stage of the Indus civilization.

The other site meriting attention is Amri, located in the south-western part of the lower Indus Valley, on the right bank of the river. The earliest occupation of the site, termed 'Amrian', goes back to the middle of the fourth millennium BC. Because of its proximity to the river, subsistence at this settlement included fishing in addition to agriculture and pastoralism. A degree of complexity in domestic and other architecture is noticeable in the presence of compartmented structures. Finds of semi-precious stones, alabaster and certain ceramic types, originating from Baluchistan and east of the Indus, shows that Amri and related sites in the Indus Kohistan and Kirthar regions were involved in a large interaction system. Amrian ceramics are distinguished by their vessel shapes and richly painted designs in black or brown and bichrome. Over 80 per cent of the pottery in the early levels was hand-made, but decreased progressively till replaced by the wheel-made pottery in later periods. Amrian painted pottery displays a wide range of geometric animal and plant designs. The polychrome pottery in particular has links with the Kechi Beg painted pottery of the Quetta Valley. There is a great concentration of Amrian sites in the Sind Kohistan area and on the piedmont plain of the Kirthar mountains, where twenty-seven sites have so far been discovered. Another site in the lower Indus Valley showing an antecedent culture below the Harappan occupation is Balakot.

The contiguous region of the upper Indus Valley was densely populated during this period, as indicated by nearly one hundred sites, with as many as forty occurring in the Cholistan area. Their heavy concentration in the upper and central Indus Valley seems to point to this being the core area, which later led to full urbanization. The sites most pertinent to the early development are Sarai Kala in the Taxila Valley, Harappa and Jalilpur in the central Indus Valley.

Frontier regions of Pakistan and the Punjab

Sarai Kala represents two major cultural periods (Halim, 1970–1, 1972). Beginning with the late Neolithic horizon in period I, the occupation was followed by people who used wheel-made pottery and made extensive use of stone and bone tools, bronze and copper and a variety of terracotta objects. No permanent structures were found but the presence of post-holes suggests the use of perishable materials in the construction of dwelling houses in addition to mud walls on stone foundations. The settlement was a permanent one, indicating that sufficient economic resources were available to support growing populations. The pottery is comparable with the known Kot Dijian ceramics of the early third millennium BC. Two other sites in the same valley, at Jhang (Mughal, 1989) and Hathial (G. M. Khan, 1983) repeated the cultural pattern of Sarai Kala II in terms of material equipment.

Jalilpur, near the banks of the Ravi, represents another settlement of the early third millennium BC preceded by an occupation which is related to an earlier 'Hakra' phase known

extensively from Cholistan (Mughal, 1972, 1974). Much lapis lazuli and some buff wares from contemporary sites indicate a large interaction involving inter-settlement and inter-regional trade or exchange. The pottery from Jalilpur is Kot Dijian but also contains bichrome ware, which is otherwise absent from the type-site of Kot Diji but occurs frequently at the upper Indus Valley sites. Harappa, located 70 km north of Jalilpur, was the first site to produce ceramics which are now characteristically Kot Dijian. Recent excavations have uncovered a large area of the Early Harappan occupation.

In the core area of the Early Harappan culture, where at least forty settlements have been discovered in Cholistan and many more on the Indian side, there appears to be maximum concentration of populations. It is possible that they practised agriculture on the floodplain of the Hakra River and its tributaries and also raised cattle, sheep and goat utilizing the desert environment, because camp sites indicating temporary occupation have also been found containing characteristic Early Harappan pottery and other materials. The presence of kilns at some of these sites is suggestive of specialized craft activities in addition to the production of wheel-made pottery (Mughal, 1982, 1989).

The north-western part of the Greater Indus Valley, from the Sulaiman piedmont to the Indus river, including the Gomal plain and the Bannu basin, was also a flourishing centre of early cultures from the middle of the fifth to the third millennium BC. In the Gomal plain two sites have been excavated, Gumla and Rahman Dheri. Of these, Gumla (Dani, 1970–1) showed a twofold sequence of cultures with the earlier occupation showing a Neolithic subsistence economy and the latter a Bronze Age Early Harappan assemblage dated to the second-third millennium BC. During that period, bronze tools were used in addition to microliths and parallel-sided chert blades. Pottery was made on the fast wheel, fired to a red colour and generally painted with either black or brown or in two colours, producing a number of linear and geometric designs. Significantly, the assemblage contained six mature Harappan ceramic types, indicating contacts with the urban centres of the Harappan civilization.

Rahman Dheri, covering an area of 22 hectares, is the largest known site in the Gomal Valley (Durrani, 1988). Excavations revealed three periods of occupation. The site seems to have been fortified from the very beginning. The occupation of period IA showed mud structures, some with circular grain silos, one of which also contained charred wheat grains. The subsistence economy of the people depended on agriculture, with cattle, goat and sheep. In the following period, II, the grain silos were replaced by large pottery storage vessels fixed in the ground. Otherwise, the earlier traits, including the use of packed mud structures, continued through this occupation. In the last period, III, the city wall fell into disuse but the mud platform, after being repaved, continued to be used. Specialized crafts such as lapidary are attested by the occurrence of beads in all stages of manufacture and numerous stone drills. Bronze tools, chert blades and micro-blades, terracotta figurines of animals and females, a large number of household and ornamental objects speak of a flourishing community. The pottery contains all the principal Early Harappan wares, some comparing with those of north Baluchistan ceramics of contemporary date, especially of the Zhob and Loralai valleys. One of two other sites in the region, Hathala, was excavated to a limited extent, the evidence of which repeated that of the Gumla sequence.

The Bannu basin in the north-western frontier province

of Pakistan has recently emerged as an archaeologically important region with early cultural developments. It is watered by three rivers, the Kurram, the Tochi and the Gambila. Intensive exploration has revealed settlement sites of various periods. Of the Early Harappan or Early Bronze Age period, nine sites have so far been discovered, including Tarakai Qila, Islam Chowki, Mirzali Khan Dheri or Seer Dheri, Lak Largai, Takhit Khel, Zabta Khan Dheri and Barrai Khurarra; the first three sites have been excavated to varying extents. The earliest known radiocarbon date, of the mid-fifth millennium BC, comes from the first occupation at Sheri Khan Tarakai, an extensive site about 0.2 km² in area (F. Khan et al., 1986), showing a 2 m thick occupation. Implements of stone such as flakes, cores, polished axes, ring stones, querns and large milling vessels dominate the artefact assemblage. Of considerable interest is the discovery of coarse red ware, occurring at the earliest levels. The painted designs include representations of caprids, usually in pairs, a Maltese cross and geometric designs. Vessels treated on the external surface with mud appliqué resemble those from Hakra and Amri. The characteristic Early Harappan wares of the Greater Indus Valley occur together with those of northern Baluchistan.

The two other sites in the Bannu basin, Lewan or Dar Dariz and Tarakai Qila, represent a single cultural group of early third-millennium settlements which in content and date compare with the Early Harappan Kot Dijian ceramics and other related materials. The structures at Tarakai Qila were made of mudbrick or mud over stone foundations. There is an indication of a fortification wall on the eastern side of the site. Lewan, on the other hand, had no regular structures but showed occupational debris in pits of varying depths. The site produced a large number of special tools, such as ground stone axes, ring stones, querns and hammers, including burins, points, scrapers, blades of different shapes and leaf-shaped arrowheads; and micro-drills for making beads locally of turquoise and lapis lazuli.

India, Punjab, Haryana and Rajasthan

In the contiguous Indian territory, pre-Harappan settlements have been located on the Ghaggar (ancient Saraswati) and Chautang (ancient Drishadvati), being an extension of the pattern obtaining in Cholistan across the border in Pakistan (Mughal, 1981). Noteworthy sites on this river system are Kalibangan, Banawali, Siswal, Sothi, Rakhigarhi, Balu and Rohira. Besides these, another site, Mitathal, was located on the dried-up old course of the river Yamuna, which at one time is reported to have contributed to the Ghaggar system. Except for Sothi, at each site a stratified or cultural relationship between the pre-Harappan and Harappan cultures has been revealed. Among these, Kalibangan, Banawali, Siswal and Mitathal provide the main evidence.

Kalibangan (B. K. Thapar, 1975) is situated 310 km north-west of Delhi, along the left bank of the now dry river Ghaggar in the northern part of Rajasthan. The excavation revealed two periods of occupation, of which the upper belonged to the Indus civilization or the Harappan period and the lower to the previous phase termed, albeit loosely, pre-Harappan.

The settlement was found to have been fortified from the very beginning of the occupation. The fortification wall was made of mudbricks (in size 30 × 20 × 10 cm, ratio 3:2:1), plastered both externally and internally with mud. Within the walled area houses were built of mudbricks of the same size as those used in the fortification wall, the masonry being

in 'English' bonding. The use of the baked brick was attested by a drain, the size of the bricks being the same as that of the mudbricks. Interesting evidence of cooking practices was revealed by the presence within the houses of ovens, both of the underground and over-ground variety, closely resembling the present-day tandoors used in the region.

The distinctive trait of the period, however, was the pottery, which was characterized by six fabrics, labelled for convenience fabric A to F. One of these was marked by a finer textured paste and all-over smooth-slipped surface in shades of red or purple-red and painted in black, and was found to be closely related to Kot Dijian. Similarities in other fabrics with Amri and Baluchistan sites were also noticed. Among other finds of this period, the more noteworthy were small-sized blades of chalcedony and agate, sometimes serrated or backed; beads, variously of steatite (disc), shell, carnelian, terracotta and copper; shell bangles; terracotta objects, comprising a fragmentary bull, toy-cart wheel, bangles; quern stones with mullers; a bone point; and copper objects, comprising a celt, a bangle and a nondescript cutting tool.

Belonging to the same period was also found a ploughed field, showing a grid of furrows, permitting the cultivation of two cereals at a time. This is possibly the earliest ploughed field excavated so far (Lal, 1970–1).

Banawali (Bisht, 1984) lies on the right bank of the now dry Saraswati, some 220 km north-west of Delhi in District Hissar, Haryana. The excavation revealed a threefold sequence of cultures, of which the earliest belongs to the pre-Harappan, followed by the Harappan and Late Harappan.

The 3 m deposit of the pre-Harappan occupation revealed an assemblage strikingly similar to that of Kalibangan, being characterized by the occurrence of all six pottery fabrics and other finds recorded at the latter site. The settlement seems to have been fortified, though not from the earliest occupation. The structures were built of mudbricks (of sizes 30 × 20 × 10 or 36 × 26 × 13 cm, all in the ratio 3:2:1). In addition square 30 × 30 × 10 or 27 × 27 × 9 or 24 × 24 × 12 cm bricks were also used. The use of kilnburnt bricks was also recorded. Noteworthy structures exposed by the excavation include a 2 m wide brick-on-edge pavement, a partially excavated house showing several hearths and fire-pits, with the floor area turned red, pointing perhaps to its use as a metalsmith's workshop. Another interesting find was the existence of circular pits, neatly dug into house floors and containing a fine bluish ash mixed with charred grains, perhaps used as silos or bins. Among other finds obtained from the deposits of this occupation are points and awls of bone; chalcedony micro-blades; shell bangles; faience, copper and terracotta; beads of gold, semi-precious stone, steatite (disc), faience, bone and clay; a stone weight (not conforming to the binary system of Indus weights); and a terracotta animal figurine. A noteworthy find is a sherd depicting a canopied cart having spoked wheels. The upper levels of this occupation showed evidence of the presence of Harappan ware, though without its classical forms, as also of terracotta cakes, and the use of bricks of both pre-Harappan and Harappan size in the same house. The full nature and import of this seemingly transitional phase still remains to be ascertained. Suffice it to mention that such a phase, though absent at Kalibangan despite the continuance of pre-Harappan pottery up to the middle levels of the succeeding Harappan occupation in the lower city, has already been identified at Amri (Casal, 1964), Siswal and Mitathal (Suraj Bhan, 1975).

The other two sites where comparable material has been found are Siswal, situated 26 km west of Hissar on the left bank of the now dry Chautang, and Mitathal, 118 km north-west of Delhi along the dried-up course of the Yamuna (Suraj Bhan, 1975).

In Pakistan many sites besides those in Irani Seistan (Amri, Balakot, Gumla, Hathial, Harappa, Jalilpur, Kot Diji, Lewan Dhari, Mehrgarh, Rahman Dheri, Sarai Kala and Tarakai Qila) have yielded comparable pre-Harappan or Early Harappan assemblages, falling within a time-range of 3400–2200 BC. On the basis of radiocarbon dating the pre-Harappan period at Kalibangan is ascribed to *c.* 2500–2300 BC (uncalibrated). On the other Indian sites it seems to have continued still later, developing on its own lines within the lifetime of the mature Harappan period itself. The pre-Harappan communities appear to have arrived in Rajasthan somewhat later than in Sind.

THE MATURE HARAPPAN CULTURE: FORM AND CONTENT

The mature phase's uniqueness in both form and content stands out conspicuously among contemporary civilizations. A remarkable feature is the general uniformity of city planning throughout its area of spread. The same uniformity is also reflected in the standardized materials of diverse kinds and the representational art. No formal temple buildings comparable to those of Egypt and Mesopotamia have been found at the major urban centres, except for platforms for the fire altars at Kalibangan. Again, no tombs of an upper or rich class have so far been encountered to signify hierarchic burial customs.

The layout of the major cities and towns was rigidly followed with the concept of an acropolis (citadel) raised artificially with mudbrick and mud within a defensive wall and the lower city sprawling at its side. At Mohenjo-daro, Harappa and Kalibangan, the citadels were located to the west of the lower city while at Lothal, Banawali and Surkotada these were parts of the city complex itself, though separately demarcated. The high citadel appears to have been an administrative centre of the city, and perhaps of the area around which the major public buildings were located.

In city planning, the Indus civilization surpassed many of the known Oriental civilizations. Its gridiron pattern, with streets running north-south and east-west, divided the city into roughly rectangular blocks. The social and economic status of the residents was quite pronounced judging by the size of houses and also by their location. The largest houses, which measured up to 26 × 18 m, were enclosed by a thick high wall, having a large courtyard, a series of rooms including a bathroom, a well and a staircase leading up to the second storey. The smaller units had two to four rooms and a courtyard. Within the city, areas were demarcated for specialized craft or labour activities such as pottery (evidenced by kilns), shell and lapidary working and grain husking. An elaborate brick-lined drainage system that still works efficiently after the rains is an unparalleled feat of engineering skill.

A high degree of standardization is seen in brick size, weights and measures, pottery forms and painted designs, chert blades, metal objects and seals. Such evidence leads us to infer that the Harappan administrative system was highly efficient in enforcing standards. The system of government or administration is not yet known, although a hierarchy is implied with provincial or regional branches. Whatever the definition of central authority may be, the maintenance of

an efficient network of communication within the entire area, and the standardization of material remains, indicating a thorough cultural integration, is unparalleled in the history of Oriental civilization.

Although many sites of the Indus civilization have been excavated both in Pakistan and in India, in the present context it suffices to talk about Mohenjo-daro, Harappa, Kalibangan, Lothal and Surkotada which, being horizontally excavated on an appreciable scale, have provided the bulk of the evidence for the form and content of the civilization.

Mohenjo-daro is situated on the right bank of the Indus in District Larkana of Sind. Excavations, though carried out on an extensive scale, have not so far reached the bottom of the occupation owing to a nearly 10 m rise in the level of the plain as a result of the alluvial deposition of centuries, and correspondingly also of the water table. The settlement consisted of two ports with a citadel and a sprawling lower city (Fig. 38).

The citadel, located to the west of the lower city, is built on an artificial platform of mud and mudbricks, atop which were the main buildings. Except for the occurrence of rectangular bastions at the south-eastern corner, two of them flanking a postern gate, no definitive defensive wall has been revealed. Of the excavated buildings within the citadel, the most famous is the Great Bath, measuring 12 m from north to south, 7 m broad and 2.5 m deep. The floor of the bath is approached from north and south by flights of steps. The

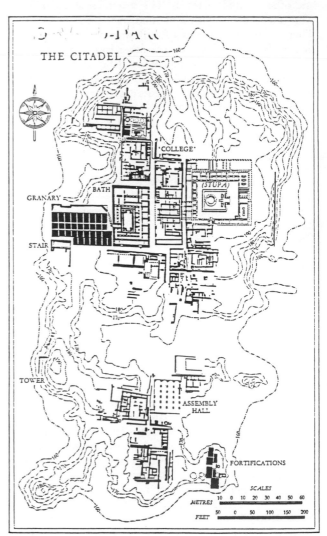

Figure 38 Principal buildings at the citadel mound of Mohenjo-daro (after Wheeler, 1968).

bath was adequately made watertight by the use of gypsum and bitumen. This bath had probably a ritualistic use. Immediately to the west of the Great Bath was a granary consisting of twenty-seven blocks of bricks of varying but regulated size. Other noteworthy structures within the citadel were an unusually long building identified by the excavator as the residence of a high official (or perhaps a college of priests), and an assembly hall.

To the east of the citadel lay the lower city. The basic layout was that of a gridiron of main streets running north-south and east-west, dividing the area into blocks. Six and probably seven such blocks have been identified during excavations. The houses, built exclusively of baked bricks, opened not onto the main streets but onto the lanes. The focus of activity was the courtyard. The streets were unpaved but were provided with brick drains with manholes at intervals.

Harappa, the type-site, lies along the left bank of the Ravi. Nowadays the river flows about 9 km further north. The general layout consisted of a citadel towards the west and a more extensive lower city to the east. The site was very badly wrecked in the middle of the nineteenth century by the extraction of bricks as ballast for the Lahore-Multan railway. Owing to the degradations by brick robbers, very few remains of monumental architecture or signs of a street plan are visible.

The citadel was a rough parallelogram on plan with the longer axis on the north-south. The buildings in the interior stood on an artificial platform of mud and mudbricks which was contained on all sides by a defensive system, show-

ing at regular intervals rectangular bastions. The main entrance seems to have been on the north. On the western side, however, was a curved re-entrant controlled by bastions and supervised from guardrooms. At the southern end of this system, a series of steps or a ramp led up to the citadel.

Overlooked by the citadel towards the north, barrack-like dwellings and circular working platforms were found. Beyond that lay a double range of granaries on a revetted platform. The approach to the granaries was on the north, from the river bank, suggesting the use of water transport for incoming and outgoing supplies of grain. The cemeteries R-37 and H are discussed below (Burials).

The Harappan metropolis at *Kalibangan* consisted of two principal parts, the citadel on the west, represented by a smaller mound (KLB-1) and the lower city on the east, represented by a bigger mound (KLB-2), recalling the identical disposition of the mounds at Mohenjo-daro and Harappa. The citadel was located on top of the remains of the preceding occupation, thus gaining an eminence over the lower city, which was laid out towards the east on the natural plain, leaving a gap of over 40 m between the two parts of the settlement (Fig. 39).

The citadel complex is roughly a parallelogram some 240 m from east to west and consists of two almost equal but separately patterned parts with a bipartite wall in between. Both these parts were contained by a fortification wall, built throughout of mudbricks (size 40 × 20 × 10 cm and 30 × 15 × 7.5 cm; ratio 4:2:1). The southern half of the citadel, which was more heavily fortified, contained some five to six massive platforms,

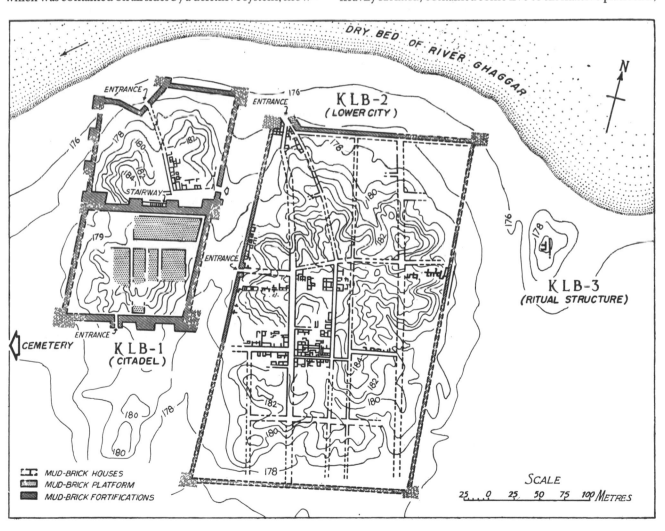

Figure 39 Harappan metropolis Kalibangan; period II.

255

some of which may have been used for religious or ritual purposes as attested by the occurrence of 'fire altars', a brick-lined pit containing bovine bone and antlers, beside wells and elaborate drainage running through the passages. The northern half of the citadel contained residential buildings, perhaps of the élite or the ruling minority. Both these parts had separate entrances besides an intercommunicating one. The lower city was also fortified, being a parallelogram measuring some 360 m from north to south and 240 m from east to west, showing a gridiron or irregular net plan of streets running north–south and east–west, dividing the area into blocks. In the excavated area, the streets do not seem to lead into any important building nor open out into well-defined public squares (Plate 106). The houses were made of mudbricks of the size 30 × 15 × 7.5 cm. No street drains were encountered in the city. House drains were found to discharge themselves into soakage jars buried under the street floors. Two entrances, one on the west and the other on the north, were exposed. Besides the two principal parts of the metropolis, there was also a third one situated about 80 m further east of the lower city, which perhaps was used for ritual purposes.

The finds obtained from the occupation strata are all characteristic of the Indus civilization, for example chert blades, chert weights, terracotta animal figurines, seals, copper objects, and pottery both plain and painted (Plate 107). The following deserve special mention: a cylinder-seal; a terracotta cake incised on the obverse with a horned human figure and on the reverse with a human figure pulling an obscure animal (perhaps a sacrificial animal); a copper bull; a terracotta graduated scale; and an ivory comb.

Lothal is situated on the coastal flats at the head of the Gulf of Cambay, 80 km south-west of Ahmedabad (Rao, 1973, 1979–85). The excavation revealed five phases of continuous occupation, of which the first four labelled Lothal A are Harappan and the fifth, labelled Lothal B, is a variant or sub-Indus representing a later degenerate phase. While the ceramics belonging to Lothal A show all the essential elements of the Indus civilization in the substantive sense, there are two which are not met with in the nuclear region of Sind or in the eastern region: the micaceous red ware and the black-and-red ware both showing painted decoration. Among other noteworthy ceramics of Lothal A is the 'reversed slip' ware which indicates a connection with sites in Sind and Baluchistan. Apart from these specialities, both the pottery and other finds obtained from the excavation are typically Indus. Some of the painted designs, however, do signify a provincial style.

The settlement was found to be fortified with a mud and mudbrick wall measuring some 300 m from north to south and 225 m from east to west, a trapezoidal south-eastern part of which was intended to serve as a citadel or acropolis, being separated from the remaining part of the city by a 7 m high podium made of mud and mudbrick. The prominent structures located on the citadel included what the excavator calls the ruler's residence, a regimented series of rooms each with a brick-paved bath and a warehouse or granary, built of twelve cubicle blocks with air ducts or passages running in between. On the eastern flank of the city was an oblong basin, measuring on an average 214 m in length (north–south) and some 37 m in width (east–west) and perhaps 4.5 m in depth (the extant height of the embankment in the north-west corner being 3.2 m). Adjoining the western embankment was a mud-brick platform, intended perhaps for handling cargo. The basin is claimed to have been a dockyard for shipping, an interpretation which some scholars dispute (Shah, 1960; Leshnik, 1968; Pandya, 1977; Ratnagar, 1981). Notwithstanding

these differing views, both the dock and the warehouse, coupled with the discovery at this site of a Persian Gulf-style seal are indicative of the maritime trade of this coastal site.

Lothal B phase was marked by certain changes in ceramics: the perforated jars and beakers became scarce; the dish-on-stand became squatter; the complicated geometrical designs were replaced by free-style linear patterns, including stylized peacocks and birds drawn on a limited surface of the pot; and terracotta bangles were completely replaced by those of conch shell, cubic chert weights by spherical shaped ones of schist and long ribbon flakes by short blades. A significant change in the seals was the absence of the animal motif and other pictographic elements. The dockyard too became unserviceable. An inclusive time-bracket of c. 2300–1600 BC is indicated for the occupation of both periods A and B at Lothal.

Surkotada, situated some 160 km north-east of Bhuj, provides tangible evidence of the diffusion of the Indus civilization from the lower Indus Valley to Gujarat by the land route (Joshi, 1979). The excavation brought to light a sequence of three cultural phases of the Harappan culture, labelled sub-periods IA, IB and IC. From the very beginning of the occupation (sub-period IA) the settlement was fortified on a rectangular plan (approximately 120 × 60 m with east-west as the longer axis) and was divided into two parts of which the western half was used as a citadel and the eastern half as a residential annexe. The citadel part, built on an artificial podium, was higher than the residential annexe. The fortification wall was built of mud with a veneer of rubble masonry at the base. While the main entrance to the citadel seems to have been on the south, an intercommunicating passage between the two parts of the settlement was provided on the east by a ramp. The objects obtained from the deposits of this sub-period were largely Harappan, and included a typical steatite seal, sherds bearing painted Indus characters, and long chert blades. Besides the characteristic Harappan pottery, a cream-slipped bichrome ware, showing painted designs in brown and purplish-red or black, and the 'reserved slip' ware were also found. The inhabitants practised pot-burial as one of the methods of disposal of the dead. In sub-period IB, Indus elements became less pronounced with the appearance of the new ceramic tradition of coarse red ware. The upper levels yielded sherds of the white-painted black-and-red ware. In sub-period IC, the Indus pottery tradition had further waned, the dominant ceramic being the white-painted black-and-red ware. The fortifications were reconstructed in rubble and partly dressed stone masonry with revetments and corner bastions. An elaborate gateway complex was provided on the southern side of the citadel. Noteworthy finds from this sub-period include a terracotta seal bearing Indus script and chert weights. The existence of a horse is indicated by the discovery of bones of this animal in the deposits of this sub-period, thus supporting the artefactual evidence obtained at Rangpur. An inclusive time-bracket of 2300–1700 BC is proposed for the three sub-periods of occupation at Surkotada.

THE ECONOMY

The economy was largely based on agriculture and animal husbandry, with trade or exchange networks for the procurement and distribution of raw materials and manufactured items within and outside the Indus Valley. The recent recovery and analysis of faunal remains from the Early Harappan (Jalilpur, Mehrgarh IV-VII and Balakot) and mature

Harappan sites (Allahdino and Harappa) demonstrate the dominant use of cattle. By the beginning of the second millennium BC, however, the domestic camel, horse and donkey were also present, while the onager, wild boar, gazelle and rhinoceros were hunted. Other animals known to the Harappan people include the dog, water buffalo and the cat besides fish, river turtle and birds.

The subsistence was based on winter-sown and spring/summer harvested (rabi) crops. Long before the beginning of the Indus civilization, people were already growing winter-sown (rabi) crops once a year. These consisted of five kinds of wheat (einkorn, emmer, hard wheat, bread/club wheat and short wheat), three kinds of six-row barley and also field peas, chickpeas, lentils, flax/linseed, jujube and mustard. Dates and cotton were harvested in summer/autumn from at least the sixth millennium and grapes by the beginning of the fourth millennium BC. In addition, melon seeds and sesame were consumed. Towards the end of the Indus civilization, in the second millennium BC, the Harappans diversified their agriculture by growing autumn harvest (kharif) crops in marginal areas to the east and south of the Indus Valley, especially in Gujarat and even in the Kachi plain in the west-central Indus Valley. Evidence of rice cultivation was found at Lothal and Rangpur in Gujarat and at Pirak (Constantini, 1979; Vishnu Mittre and Savithri, 1982). Sorghum (jowar), finger millet (ragi), bulrush millet (bajra) of African origin and two Asian millets, proso and foxtail, were cultivated. Terracotta models of ploughs closely resembling those used today are reported from Cholistan and Banawali.

TRADE

It is widely known that Sind and the alluvial plains of Punjab are devoid of useful minerals with the result that subsistence related materials had to be imported. These substances include copper, tin, gold, silver, limestone, alabaster, basalt, granite, marble, slate, steatite, gypsum, bitumen, lapis lazuli, carnelian and other semi-precious stones such as jade, turquoise and amazonite (Marshall, 1931; Wheeler, 1968). The sources of some of these materials were far distant. Trade links have been indicated with Afghanistan, Baluchistan, central Asia, north-eastern Iran, Rajasthan, Gujarat, Punjab and south India. The invention of writing, the use of seals and sealings and standardized weights and measures all point to a flourishing trade and commerce. The discovery at Altyndepe of three seals, one with two Indus characters, the other with a swastika, and the third portraying a three-headed griffin along with various items of ivory such as sticks and gaming pieces, decidedly of Indian origin, and of the ithyphallic terracotta type from Namazga, paralleled at Mohenjo-daro, indicate a northern overland route passing through Mundigak to southern Turkanistan (Masson, 1981).

Recent excavation at Shortugai in the Oxus basin has revealed the existence of an Harappan colony that was carrying on trade in lapis lazuli. Apart from typical Harappan painted pottery, a square seal, bearing the Indus script with the figure of a rhinoceros, and the occurrence of graffiti on the rims of jars and on beakers, barrel-shaped agate beads, long tubular and etched carnelian beads, shell bangles, toy cart-frames, terracotta cakes, zebu figurines, and the use of mudbricks of Harappan size (32 × 16 × 8 cm) also confirm the trading character of the colony (Francfort, 1984).

Artefactual evidence of trade contacts with contemporary Mesopotamia and Elam has been adduced by the occurrence of many and varied finds. These include: seals of Indus style; etched carnelian beads; kidney-shaped pieces of inlay made of bone; various objects of ivory; cubed dice; gold discs; beads with tubular perforation, depictions of the Indus trefoil pattern; the Indus bull with manger at various sites in Mesopotamia and Elam, and of pottery bearing knobs on barbotine, pyxis of greenish-grey stone (chlorite); metal pins with spiral or animal heads; leaf-shaped knives and bun-shaped copper ingots; shaft-hole axes, ring kernoi, theriomorphic vases, and barrel-shaped weights. The discovery at Mehrgarh's south cemetery and at Sibri of some objects showing Murgabo Bactrian parallels and of etched carnelian beads on the Iranian sites of Hissar, Marlik, Shahdad and Bakum and at Mundigak in south Afghanistan further reinforces the evidence of contacts between the Indus civilization and neighbouring regions. It is evident that the region was an integral part of the interregional network of exchange or trade of specific items emanating from their respective production centres.

The number of objects of Indus style found in West Asia admittedly does not imply a sizeable scale of trade. Of the Mesopotamian or Mesopotamian-inspired objects found on the Indus sites, the examples are still fewer. Lamberg-Karlovsky (1972), however, argues that such material may have resulted from indirect contact-trade and as such emphasizes the role of sites such as Tepe Yahya in Iran in the Indus-Mesopotamian land-route trade.

In 1954, the decipherment of certain Sumerian and Akkadian documents which refer to lands called Dilmun, Magan and Meluhha added further dimensions to the trade between Mesopotamia and the Indus Valley (Oppenheim, 1954). Sargon of Akkad (c. 2370–2280 BC) mentions that ships from Dilmun, Magan and Meluhha were docked at his capital. Textual evidence shows that the Indus-Mesopotamian contact started with the Early Dynastic III period and continued through the Larsa period, thus covering both the pre-Harappan and Harappan periods. The Mesopotamia texts show a trade contact through both Dilmun and Magan. Among these Dilmun was more a trade entrepôt than a producer of items of trade mentioned in the texts. During the period when the trade via Dilmun was at its peak, another series of seals called the Persian Gulf seals was used. They depict themes mostly influenced from Mesopotamia, though a few still show the Indus script with the bull. These seals are button-shaped and circular in plan; a seal of this distinctive type has been obtained from Lothal.

The land of Dilmun has been identified with the Bahrain archipelago, Failaka and Tarul islands and a part of the adjacent Arabian mainland, and has a unique position in Sumerian mythology (Cornwall, 1946; Bibby, 1969; Ratnagar, 1981). Cuneiform inscriptions from both Failaka and Bahrain support this identification. It is favourably positioned, both geographically and strategically, on the well-frequented maritime trade route, connecting Mesopotamia with the Indus Valley. It was important as a watering station, being blessed with sweet water. The occurrence in Bahrain (Ras al-Qala) and Failaka of gaming pieces of lapis lazuli together with lapis pendants, worked ivory pieces, polished stone weights and Persian Gulf seals, including a few bearing Indus pictographs closely resembling those found at Lothal and Mohenjo-daro, amply demonstrates the role of Dilmun as an entrepôt in this trade. On the Bahrain islands the type-site Barbar provides a chronological sequence from 2900 to 1800 BC.

Magan or Makan has been identified with Oman and

Umm an-Nar near Abu Dhabi (Weisgerber, 1984). It is called a land of mines. Texts mention the following materials coming from Magan: timber, reeds, wood, diorite, onions, stone vases, carnelians, red ochre, copper, ivory, gold dust and goats. Of these, at least two, ivory and carnelian, could have originated from the Indus: Magan only transshipped them. Recent archaeological findings in Oman, particularly at Mayasar I, Ras al Junayez and Hili, have furnished supportive evidence (triangular prismatic and pear-shaped seals, Indus-type decorative patterns on pottery, ivory combs, and sources of copper and chlorite) of a link between the Indus Valley and Oman (Magan) in the chain of maritime trade through the Persian Gulf.

Meluhha is identified with regions in the east of Mesopotamia, including the northern shore of the Persian Gulf and the Arabian Sea and the Indus Valley. Meluhha is reported to have supplied to Mesopotamia timber, a variety of woods, copper, gold dust, lapis lazuli, carnelian, wooden furniture, ivory figurines of birds, peacocks and red dogs, all of which, except lapis lazuli, must have originated in India. In the latter part of the second millennium BC, however, both Magan and Meluhha were thought to be Egypt and Nubia or Ethiopia.

The items of trade reportedly travelling from Mesopotamia eastwards were principally foodgrains, oils, wools and textiles. How much of it reached India is a matter of conjecture, as most of these goods are perishable.

The archaeological evidence of trade with the Elamites, who were political rivals of Sumer and Akkad, is patchy. Alleged connections are indicated by a fragmentary sealing on a potsherd recalling the Harappan seal and two etched carnelian beads (Lamberg-Karlovsky and Tosi, 1973; Lamberg-Karlovsky, 1976) found at Tepe Yahya in stratum IVA. The presence of Harappan sites such as Balakot, Sotka-koh and Sutkagen-dor on the Makran coast indicates the likelihood of an ocean trade route.

WEIGHTS AND MEASURES

The level of standardization and uniformity in weights and measures achieved and maintained during Harappan times was remarkable. The system was so efficient for the economy and for trade that it was also adopted in ancient Dilmun (Bahrain), where a number of weights were found along with Indus seals bearing the script.

The weights were made of chert, limestone, steatite, chalcedony and other stones in different sizes. The most common shape was cubical but some spherical, cylindrical and barrel-shaped weights were also used. Some pottery scale-pans also indicate the use of weighing scales; singularly interesting was one bronze or copper bar with a pair of pans confirming their use.

The Harappan weights are unmatched in the contemporary ancient world because they fall strictly within a system which is binary as well as decimal. The lower denominations are binary: 1,2,1/3 × 8,4,16... to 12,800 with a unit ratio of 16 equal to 13.625 g. The higher denominations are in the decimal system with fractions in thirds.

The system of measures is revealed by a graduated piece of shell from Mohenjo-daro, a fragmentary bronze rod from Harappa and a terracotta rod from Kalibangan. The shell scale has nine subdivisions of 0.670 cm units. Five of these sub-divisions make the Harappan 'inch' equal to 3.352 cm, thus making a Harappan foot equal to 33.52 cm. In addition to linear measurements there was the cubic system. The

bronze rod is marked with lengths of 6.012 cm. It is clear that both the linear and cubic systems were used. The measurements of the buildings at Harappa and Mohenjo-daro conform to both these systems of measurement. The Harappan foot varied between 33.02 and 33.52 cm.

ARTS AND CRAFTS

The arts and crafts of the Harappans are demonstrated by a great variety of material objects. Certain categories of objects, however, stand out to illustrate technological and artistic skills and a high level of craft specialization.

Ceramics are among the most abundant finds at Harappan sites and include a wide range of pottery vessels, human and animal figurines, bangles and other objects of daily use. The pottery was manufactured on a fast wheel and was made of finely levigated clay which was well and evenly fired to different shades of red. The vessels range from large storage jars to bowls, dishes, offering stands, cylindrical and perforated jars. Not only the forms but also the painted designs in black over bright red slip were standardized, reflecting craft specialization. The painted designs are both geometric and floral, the recurrent ones being 'pipal' leaf, fish-scale and intersecting circles (Fig. 40).

The human figurines, both male and female, and mostly hand-modelled in terracotta, are quite expressive, some appearing to be of a cultic nature. The male figurines are depicted with a long or pinched nose, a slit mouth, oblique

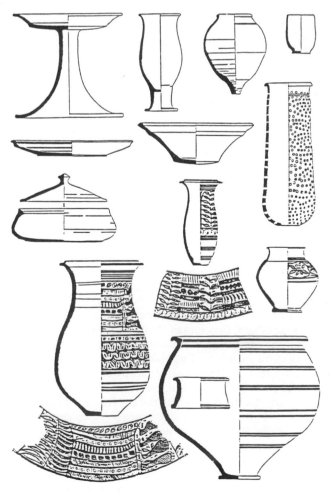

Figure 40 Typical mature Harappan pottery (after Wheeler, 1968).

eyes and a largely flat body. Most of the female figurines are shown in a standing position; each half was vertically moulded, and the two halves were then joined together. In finished form, the terracotta female figurines are depicted wearing a short loin cloth and wide girdle, necklaces and an elaborate fan-shaped head-dress and a cup-shaped pannier on each side, perhaps for an oil lamp or incense.

Among the animal figurines, which again were hand-modelled, the humped bull dominates, other animals represented being the buffalo, elephant, dog, sheep, rhinoceros, pig, monkey, turtle and horse. In addition, terracotta models of carts with solid wheels and toys such as whistles, rattles and cones, thought to be used as styli for inscribing on clay, and cubical dice are also found.

Metallurgy is represented by household vessels, weapons, implements and small objects of gold, silver and lead. Copper was obtained from various sources, including the Chagai hills in Baluchistan, the Kreti-Ganeshwar area of Rajasthan and perhaps Oman and southern Iran (the legendary Magan). The Harappans were familiar with various manufacturing techniques of hammering and the use of simple and complex moulds. Among sculptures, the bronze statuette of a dancing girl, 11.2 cm in height, is a remarkable piece of casting and skilful execution. It depicts an easy standing posture, the right hand on the hip and the left arm adorned with bangles. The animals such as a buffalo with long swept-back horns, a charging bull and ram or goat are rendered in a naturalistic and expressive manner. Apart from this a variety of vessels such as bowls, dishes, cups and weapons, and implements such as spears, arrowheads, knives, axes and pins were also made (Figs. 41, 42).

Of the stone objects, the best specimens of representational art are sculptures of limestone and alabaster from Mohenjo-daro and Harappa, and hundreds of steatite seals. The sculptures portray human heads and seated figures with expressive details of hairstyle. One bust of a male found at Mohenjo-daro is an outstanding example of the sculptural art of the civilization, and is thought to represent the 'king-priest'. The rendering of the beard and shaven upper lip, a fillet on the forehead and ear like a cross-section of a shell resemble the other human sculptures. A cloak across the left shoulder has distinctive trefoil motifs which were originally filled in with red paste. Two small statuettes from Harappa

Figure 41 The Indus bronze and copper vessels (after Wheeler, 1968)

are remarkable examples of realistic modelling in exhibiting naturalistic poses and movement of limbs. In addition to these works of art, large quantities of lithic materials, including chert flakes and blades, were used as tools for a variety of activities.

The steatite seals bear eloquent testimony to the superior craftsmanship and technical achievements of the Indus artisans. Measuring usually 1.8–3 m long and having a perforated boss at the back, the intaglio designs show a great number of animals and other figures with pictographic script or linear designs. The frequently represented animal, the unicorn, or the ox-like animal with a single horn, is invariably shown with the sacred manger or incense-holder, consisting of a bowl-shaped cage on the top of a post. Short-horned bulls are most naturalistically represented, suggesting religious veneration, especially seen in the terracotta bull figurines. In addition, rhinoceros, elephant and tiger are shown with a manger in front. Despite the small size of the finished article, the engravers managed to carve tiny details with great skill including, for example, composite figurines showing three to six heads of different animals radiating from one ring. One such elaborate representation has the face of a human being, crowned with the horns of a bull, the forepart of a ram, the hindpart of a tiger and a tusk of an elephant. The depiction of human figures and those combined with tree and animal motifs were perhaps intended to portray divine figures.

The carnelian beads with etched designs were produced at the lapidary workshops of Chanhu-daro, Lothal and elsewhere. They were in great demand even outside the core area of the Indus civilization. Their occurrence in other regions not only provides relative dating but also demonstrates the degree of interaction. The common shape was a long barrel. Beads were also made of other semi-precious stones, as also of steatite, faience, shell and even terracotta.

THE INDUS SCRIPT

The Indus script, which is essentially pictographic, is found to be unrelated to any contemporary script. It contains over 400 distinctive symbols or characters, and is found chiefly on seals but also on pottery, ivory sticks, copper objects and tablets. The number of characters represented in an inscription may vary from one to twenty-six, the average length of a text being five characters. No long inscriptions with significant recurrent features have so far been reported. Continuing research on the decipherment of this script has so far shown no difference in the script from one site to another nor any definitive evidence of its evolution, notwithstanding certain professed claims of development from syllabic to phonetic with signs reduced to a bare 20 odd (Rao, 1982). Distribution analysis of these seals has failed to yield any coherent pattern. The only aspect on which there seems to be a consensus is the direction of writing, namely from right to left, which is supported principally by four instances of evidence: (a) a seal from Harappa with writing in three planes along three of its sides – top, left side and bottom; (b) a potsherd from Kalibangan with sharply scratched superimposed strokes with a flourish on the left end; (c) a tendency towards slight compression of the signs on the right side – that is on the left side of the impression; and (d) signs carried over to a second line, or overruns. Instances of a boustrophedon sequence of signs is also recorded where there is a second line.

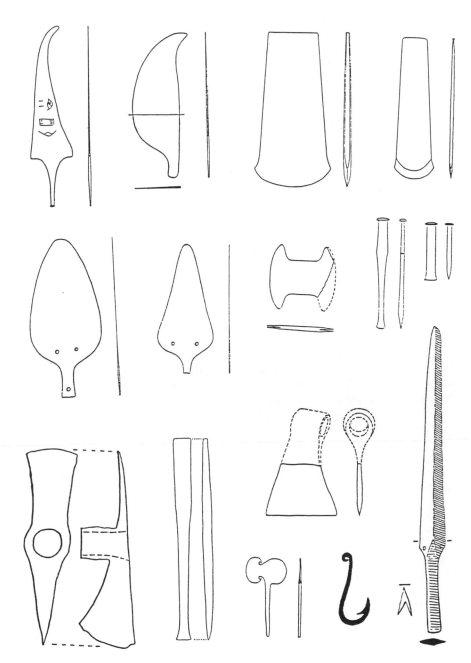

Figure 42 The bronze and copper tools from Harappa and Mohenjo-daro (after Mackay, 1938 and Vats, 1940).

Many claims have been made for the decipherment of the script, but none of them has received universal acceptance. As far as language is concerned, there are two main approaches to the problem, one advocating the proto-Dravidian affinity, and emphasizing the agglutinative aspect of the language (Asko Parpola, 1984), and the other the Indo-Aryan related to Vedic Sanskrit, focusing on the language's inflexional nature and compound signs (Rao, 1982). These lines of argument clash with one another. However, as a useful tool for further investigation a concordance of the texts has been published (Mahadevan, 1977; Koskenniemi et al., 1973; Koskenniemi and Parpola, 1979, 1980). Meanwhile, it could be reasonably argued that writing had a limited use, perhaps by a privileged literati. Whether the seals indicate proper names relevant to trade we do not know but one could conjecture, with due reservations, that unlike the cuneiform texts the Indus seals were not used as a means of more complex communication.

RELIGION

Evidence of this complex aspect of the civilization is inconsistent and, in the absence of any textual records, has to be reconstructed from the surviving material artefacts, noteworthy amongst which are: (a) the seals, the scenes on some of which may be interpreted as religious (including the well-known Pasupati seal from Mohenjo-daro); (b) aniconic and polished phallic objects and ring-stones; (c) a few stone images, particularly the nude ithyphallic torso from Harappa; (d) seminude female terracotta figurines with elaborate head-dresses, and associated with the mother-goddess cult from Mohenjo-daro and Harappa; (e) a terracotta cake from Kalibangan (citadel part), showing a horned deity on one side and a man pulling an animal (goat or ox, perhaps sacrificial) on the other. The occurrence of a brick-lined pit atop one of the platforms in the citadel area at Kalibangan, containing bovine and antler bones, does point to animal sacrifice.

It is surprising that no female terracotta figurines of mother-goddesses have so far been recorded at any of the excavated sites located within the present-day borders of India (Kaliban-gan, Lothal, Surkotada), except for a few examples from Banawali that are not in the style of the characteristic pan-nier-shaped head-dress. Even among the seals found at Kalibangan none depicts a deity except perhaps the com-posite man-faced animal figure on a cylinder-seal. On the other hand, a row of 'fire altars' has been found on top of one platform in the citadel area. Similar 'fire altars' or ritual pits have also been attested individually in many houses in the lower city. Apart from these, an exclusive structure con-taining a group of two such 'fire altars' was found to the east of the lower city outside the fortification wall. The absence of normal occupation debris on this site suggests that the structure was intended for some religious or ritualistic pur-pose. It would appear, therefore, that the ritual connected with these 'fire altars' played a dominant role in the religious life of the Harappans at Kalibangan. The recurrent features of the altars show that a shallow pit, oval or rectangular on plan, was dug out; a fire was lit and put out on site, as shown by the fragments of charcoal in the basal part of the pit; a cylindrical, occasionally faceted or rectangular block of clay, sun-dried or sometimes pre-fired was fixed in the centre, and flat triangular or circular terracotta cakes were placed around the block, perhaps as symbolic offerings. The import-ance of water in connection with these rituals, though not necessarily with deification, is indicated by the almost extrav-agant provision of wells and drainage in the citadel area. At Lothal, too, several fire altars are reported, though with dif-ferent features (Rao, 1979–85). No such altars have so far been reported from Mohenjo-daro and Harappa, though the Great Bath at Mohenjo-daro does point to the association of water with ritualistic and religious purposes. The observ-ance of whatever ritual is associated with the fire altars, there-fore, seems to be peculiar to the region of Kalibangan and perhaps Lothal.

Concrete evidence about the religion of the Indus civi-lization continues to elude us, although from the available evidence it would appear that religious beliefs and practices varied from region to region. It seems to have been a mélange of many contemporary religions or ritualistic observances.

BURIALS

Among the excavated sites, cemeteries have been located at Harappa, Rupar, Chandigarh, Kalibangan, Lothal and Surko-tada, but no royal grave or burial of any other special cate-gory has so far been encountered. At Mohenjo-daro, no orderly burials of the Harappan period have as yet been found. At Harappa, the cemetery (labelled R-37) was located to the south-south-west of the citadel and contained extended articulated inhumations (with the head towards the north) with pottery and other grave goods, including items of per-sonal jewellery, placed in a rectangular or oval grave-pit, which in one singular case contained a coffin of rosewood covered with a lid of deodar, and in another case was lined internally with mudbricks. Within the citadel area were also found some post-cremation burials, containing a mélange of odds and ends, the exact significance of which cannot be assessed (Wheeler, 1968). At Rupar the cemetery was located to the west of the habitation area and contained extended articulated inhumations (generally with the head towards the north-west) in rectangular grave-pits, containing pottery and

grave goods as at Harappa. At Chandigarh, the remains of the cemetery, exposed as a part of the rescue operations con-ducted in one of the shopping areas (sector 17C), shows sim-ilar features of extended articulated inhumations with north-south axis.

At Kalibangan, the cemetery of the Harappan period was located to the west-south-west of the citadel on the present active floodplain of the river; formerly it must have been beyond the reach of the annual floods. Excavation revealed three types of burial: (1) extended articulated inhumations in rectangular or oval graves (with the head towards the north, except for one aberrant example) containing, besides the skeleton, pottery and personal ornaments and toilet objects (Plate 108); one of the graves was found to be internally lined with mudbricks; (2) a pot or urn burial in a circular pit, con-taining, besides the main urn, other pots along with such grave goods as beads, shell bangles and steatite objects; and (3) pottery deposits and personal ornaments such as shell ban-gles and beads in a rectangular or oval grave with the longer axis running north-south. The last two modes of burial were not associated with any skeletal remains. In the case of the third category, the striking feature was the filling, which showed two stages. The occurrence of three varieties of bur-ial practice has posed sociological problems. Meanwhile, it may be affirmed that the grave goods obtained from each of these sites are characteristically Indus.

At Surkotada, the cemetery was located to the north-west of the settlement. The burial practice so far encountered consists of a pot burial in a circular pit, covered by a cap-stone and low cairn.

At Lothal, on the other hand, the cemetery was located to the west of the settlement and showed two types of buri-al practice, both being extended articulated inhumations in rectangular graves with pottery and other grave goods; but while one type of grave contained one skeleton, the other contained two. In two of the three joint burials, skeletons of two individuals of the same sex (male) were found buried together (Rao, 1985).

At Harappa, 'Cemetery H' was found stratigraphically overlying Cemetery R-37. This cemetery, which belongs to a later cultural complex, contains two strata, each repres-enting different modes of burial. Of these, the lower stra-tum (II) contained extended articulated inhumations, with accompanying pottery and grave goods in rectangular graves with the head towards the east of north-east, as distinct from the usual Harappan practice of placing the head towards the north. The upper stratum (I) consisted of fragmentary buri-als in large urns covered with lids. Babies were buried in an embryonic position in these urns (Fig. 43).

While extended inhumation with the necessary grave goods seems to have been the normal burial practice during the Harappan period, simultaneous inhumation of two bod-ies has not been discovered at any other Harappan site except Damb Buthi. Equally divergent is the evidence from Kaliban-gan in respect of pot burials and graves without skeletal remains. Furthermore, there does not seem to be any uni-formity in the location of the cemetery vis-à-vis the city or the citadel. The size of the cemeteries encountered appears to be relatively small in comparison with the corresponding settlements, which would suggest other modes of disposal of the dead.

Studies of the skeletal remains from Harappa indicate two broad categories of ethnic types, proto-Australoid, Caucasian or Eurafrican and Mediterranean Indo-European or Caspian. Similar studies of the Lothal burials show two categories, one

Figure 43 The cemetery H pottery and painted designs from Harappa (after Vats, 1940).

having a dolicho-cranial head while the other a brachy-cranial, which in turn reveal a close relationship with those at Sialk. It is evident that the population of the Indus civilization was a mixed one. The study of thirteen skulls from stratum II and eighteen from stratum I of Cemetery H at Harappa indicated a new group of the round-headed type which was completely absent from the mature Harappan cemetery R-37.

DATING

The problem of chronology is an involved one, especially since there is a time-lag between the origin and growth of this civilization in the nuclear area and the areas to the east, and the possibility of error or disparity in radiocarbon dating.

The lowest levels of Mohenjo-daro have not so far been reached because of the high level of the water table. Marshall, whose excavations at Mohenjo-daro (1921–7) constitute the substantive work, suggested that the occupation of Mohenjo-daro fell approximately between 3250 and 2750 BC. He acknowledged that the short period of 500 years must not of course be taken to cover the whole rise and fall of the Indus civilization, and postulated a thousand years for a period of antecedent growth.

Mackay (1938), who undertook further excavations at Mohenjo-daro from 1927 to 1931, assigned the lowest attainable levels to about 2800 BC and the uppermost to 2500, allowing some three hundred years. Vats (1940), who exca-

vated Harappa from 1921 to 1931, felt that the lowest levels were earlier than those attainable at Mohenjo-daro and suggested a time-bracket of c. 3500–2500 BC, basing his argument primarily on the occurrence of tiny seals and sealings of an archaic type below stratum IV in mounds F and AB. The inclusive time-bracket for the Indus civilization was thus fixed at 3500–2500 BC. This dating was based on a comparative study of objects of Indian origin and type found in the then datable contexts in Iraq and Iran.

This position continued till 1946 when Wheeler undertook further excavations at Harappa and critically examined the chronological evidence. His careful analysis revealed that the fixed point in the estimation of the time-spread of this civilization was its contact with Sumer in and about the time of Sargon of Akkad, whose date is now placed around 2370–2344 BC. Documentary evidence vouches for vigorous commercial activity in the Sargonid and Larsa periods. For the collapse of the Indus civilization, Wheeler held Aryan invaders responsible. Suggesting a plausible explanation for the massacre of men, women and children in a late period strata at Mohenjo-daro, he stated, albeit dramatically, that Indra stands accused. In this computation, the terminal date was conditioned largely subjectively, for 1500 BC is the conventional date for the Aryan incursions into India. Wheeler thus postulated that the millennium, 2500–1500 BC, was a possible inclusive date for the civilization, without prejudice to the unplumbed depths of Mohenjo-daro. He supported his argument by the occurrence of a seal in the Kassite levels at Ur, without discounting the possibility of its later survival, especially when the bulk of the evidence relating to the seals ascribed to a dated context pointed to the Sargonid and Larsa periods. He corrected himself later and proposed 1700 BC as the terminal date of the civilization.

Subsequent to the development of radiocarbon dating, excavations at Rangpur, Lothal, Kalibangan, Surkotada, Gumla, Amri, Balakot and Kot Diji, and renewed investigations at Mohenjo-daro and Harappa have provided fresh evidence for cross-checking or modifying the traditional chronology. A sufficient number of samples obtained from the various levels of these sites has now been radiocarbon dated.

By an objective analysis of the large number of ^{14}C determinations from these sites and two other allied sites, Damb Sadaat and Niai Buthi, Agrawal (1974) proposed a maximum date-bracket of 2300–1750 BC for the total time-spread of the mature Harappan culture (Agrawal and Kusumgar, 1974). We may agree with the upper end of the bracket, but must reconsider the soundness of 2300 BC for the lower end. In view of the unexcavated lower strata of Mohenjo-daro, coupled with seven ^{14}C dates from the upper levels of that site with a mean date of about 1970 BC, there is a good case for ascribing the lower end of the time-spread to 2500, if not earlier. Conversely, at Mohenjo-daro, in the lower attainable levels, we have almost securely dated evidence in the occurrence of a carved steatite vessel which is assigned to the Mesopotamian Early Dynastic period or even earlier, and as such should provide a rough chronological horizon to these levels of Mohenjo-daro.

The 'sloping horizon' depends on the amount of time required for the spread of the elements used as horizon-markers. The Indus civilization has an overall duration of about 800 years and covers an area of not less than one million km². Within such a vast area, environmental differences must have played a significant role in its diffusion, as also in moulding cultural adaptations: manifestations in Gujarat, Haryana, Punjab, Jammu and Kashmir bear ample testimony to this. In

Haryana, many sites of the pre-Harappan complex, which were not affected by the initial spread of the Indus civilization, are found to have continued almost up to the collapse of the latter. Similarly, both the beginning and the end of the civilization in Rajasthan, Haryana, Punjab, Jammu and Kashmir are obviously later than those in the central zone or core area, as is amply demonstrated in the cultural remains.

Coming to the applicability of the radiocarbon dates, it has been found that the method is not without disparities, which become serious in the earlier part of the second millennium BC and increase steadily backwards to the fourth millennium. To overcome these disparities, a calibration curve was decided upon at a conference in New Zealand in October 1972. Since the period during which these disparities are more pronounced corresponds to the time-spread of the civilization and its antecedent phases, it is necessary for us to consider the applicability of the calibration curve *vis-à-vis* historical dates and archaeological material. Although it is admitted that the correction graph is not yet fully adequate, it cannot at the same time be denied that the present time-spread based on ¹⁴C dates without calibration is late. With the suggested MASCA calibration, the bracket would be around 2700–1900 BC; this would justifiably explain the pre-Sargonid contacts.

DECLINE AND AFTERMATH

Environmental factors, including the behaviour of the river, climate and accessibility of natural resources, were largely responsible for the growth into maturity and the expansion of the Indus civilization. Paradoxically, it is these very factors, in a multi-causal framework, which became responsible for its weakening. The occurrence of skeletons lying scattered in the upper levels of houses and lanes at Mohenjo-daro was cited as evidence of attack by the Aryans. The evidence of the late Cemetery H at Harappa was considered to represent the invading group of Aryan-speaking people (Wheeler, 1968). But the postulation of an Aryan invasion as a determining factor for the end of the civilization does not seem to be tenable if 1750 BC is its terminal date.

Long-distance and internal trade in resource materials was badly disturbed towards the first quarter of the second millennium BC affecting the distribution of raw materials and luxury goods, with the result that remote settlements became impoverished. As trade seems to have been a *leitmotiv* of the civilization, its cessation would have adversely affected the prosperity of the cities, leading to de-urbanization and the dispersal of population (Ghosh, 1982). During the same period, shifts in the drainage pattern seem to have occurred; the Ghaggar-Hakra-Wahinda system disappeared, due largely to the capture of the Yamuna by the Gangetic system and the Sutlej by the Indus. It has also been argued that the Harappan cities, under growing population pressure, were destroying their environment by overgrazing, overcultivation and over-consumption of vegetation and thus were wearing out their landscape. Continuing demand for wood during the mature phase resulted in deforestation in the Himalayas, which in turn led to erosion and the displacement of channels due to the raising of their beds through the deposition of detritus. The Greater Indus Valley falls within an active seismic zone. Tectonic disturbances, of which there is tangible evidence, had made the Indus prone to flooding, resulting in ponding and the consequent rise of the water table in the area; and the disruption of the Ghaggar-Nara flow channel,

as evidenced by the reverse gradient of the river near Manot, which resulted in a reduction in the supply of water further downstream. The reduction and ultimate complete termination of this water supply must have adversely affected vital agriculture and forced the population to relocate their settlements, as is abundantly evident by the settlement pattern in Cholistan and further east in Rajasthan. There is evidence to indicate a dam-like extrusion across the Indus as a result of tectonic movements some 120 km downstream of Mohenjo-daro which ponded back the river, making Mohenjo-daro an island. The results of such a phenomenon, which was repeated, must have been disastrous to the morale and organization of the city. Coupled with these factors, towards the close of the second millennium BC eustatic phenomena (tectonic coastal uplifts or marine regressions) took place along the northern margin of the Arabian Sea with consequent rapid morphological changes. As a result some of the old ports, both on the Makran and Kutch-Kathiawad coasts, were left several kilometres inland and lost their trading role; and as the water table receded on inland sites, civic standards declined. Above all one must not underrate the factor of the natural fatigue of an overgrown civilization.

Eustasy, pluvials and aridity produced different reactions in different physiographic regions, which would perhaps explain the survival and variability of the Indus civilization in regions like Gujarat, Haryana and Punjab and the contiguous area of Uttar Pradesh during the first half of the second millennium BC. In both the southern and eastern regions many new small-sized settlements were established in new locations. The Late Harappan settlements in the eastern regions were shifted to those tributaries and braided river courses which had an assured water supply and a higher water table for sustaining their economy, or to peripheral, less arid areas within the monsoon zone of the Ganga-Yamuna doab, thus avoiding the desiccated lower valleys. Similarly (Possehl, 1980), one notices a spread of sites into the interior of Kathiawad, where the number of settlements of smaller size increases appreciably.

In Kathiawad, Prabhas and lustrous red wares are the two distinct ceramic industries which outlived the mature period of the Indus civilization. In Kutch, it is the white-painted black-and-red ware of the Banas Valley, and at other sites in Gujarat it is the sturdy red ware, painted with elementary designs. As compared to this, the Late Harappan phase in the eastern region is represented by an amalgam of an effete culture, consisting of remnant traditions of pre-Harappan, Harappan, Bara and even to a limited extent Cemetery H cultures. The pottery shows a general decadence in fabric, potting and surface treatment, with monotonous geometric designs. The long ribbon-flakes of chert were replaced by small-sized blades of locally available material. Standard weights were no longer in use. As a general rule, the Late Harappan occupations show decadence or loss of civic standards and absence of urban discipline. While typical Harappan seals or characters incised on pottery do occur at some sites (Bhagwanpura, Lothal, Rangpur, Daimabad) they seem to be more a survival of the past than objects of effective use. In the southern region it was a case of transmutation while in the eastern it was of cultural fragmentation.

NOTES

1 Normally cultures are named after the site of their first discovery. This culture therefore should more appropriately

be named the Harappan culture. But since it is an expression of a highly evolved civilization and since its distribution was initially found to be in the Indus Valley, it is here also called the Indus civilization. The terms Harappan culture and Indus civilization are interchangeable.

2 The term pre-Harappan is interchangeable with Early Harappan or proto-urban.

BIBLIOGRAPHY

AGRAWAL, D. P. 1972–3. *Puratattva* (New Delhi), Vol. 6.

AGRAWAL, D. P.; KUSUMGAR, S. 1974. *Prehistoric Chronology and Carbon Dating in India.* New Delhi.

AGRAWAL, D. P.; SOOD, R. K. 1982. Ecological Factors and the Harappan Civilization. In: POSSEHL, G. L. (ed.), *Harappan Civilization: A Contemporary Perspective.* New Delhi. pp. 223–32.

ALLCHIN, F. R. 1981. The Bannu Basin Project (1977–79): A Preliminary Report. In: HARTEL, H. (ed.), *South Asian Archaeology, 1979.* Berlin. pp. 217–50.

ASKO PARPOLA. 1984. Interpreting the Indus Script. In: LAL, B. B.; GUPTA, S. P. (eds), *Frontiers of the Indus Civilization, Sir Mortimer Wheeler Commemoration Volume.* New Delhi. pp. 179–92.

BIBBY, T. G. 1969. *Looking for Dilmun.* New York.

BISHT, R. S. 1982. Excavations at Banawali: 1974–77. In: POSSEHL, G. L. (ed.), *Harappan Civilization: A Contemporary Perspective.* New Delhi. pp. 113–24.

—— 1984. Structural Remains and Town-planning of Banawali. In: LAL, B. B.; GUPTA, S. P. (eds), *Frontiers of the Indus Civilization, Sir Mortimer Wheeler Commemoration Volume.* New Delhi. pp. 89–98.

CASAL, J. M. 1961. *Fouilles de Mundigak.* Paris. (Publ. Deleg., Archaeol. Fr. Afghanistan, 17.)

—— 1964. *Fouilles d'Amri.* Paris.

CHAKRABARTI, D. K. 1990. *The External Trade of the Indus Civilization.* New Delhi.

CHITALWALA, Y. M. 1982. Harappan Settlements in the Kutch Saurashtra Region: Patterns of Distribution and Routes of Communication. In: POSSHEL, G. L. (ed.), *Harappan Civilization: A Contemporary Perspective.* New Delhi. pp. 197–204.

CHOWDHURY, K. A.; GHOSH, S. S. 1951. Plant Remains from Harappa 1946. *Anc. India* (New Delhi), Vol. 7, pp. 3–19.

CORNWALL, P. B. 1946. On the Location of Dilmun. *Bull. am. Sch. Orient. Res.* (New Haven, Conn.), No. 102, pp. 3–11.

COSTANTINI, L. 1979. Plant Remains at Pirak, Pakistan. In: JARRIGE, J. et al. (eds), *Fouilles de Pirak.* Paris. pp. 326–33.

DALES, G. F. 1986. Some Fresh Approaches to Old Problems in Harappan Archaeology. In: JACOBSON, J. (ed.), *Studies in the Archaeology of India and Pakistan.* New Delhi. pp. 117–36.

DANI, A. H. 1970–1. Excavations in the Gomal Valley. *Anc. Pakistan* (Peshwar), Vol. 5 (special number), pp. 1–177.

DURRANI, F. A. 1968. Excavations in the Gomal Valley: Rehman Dheri Excavations Report No. 1. *Anc. Pakistan* (Peshwar), Vol. 6.

FAIRSERVIS, W. A. 1956. *Excavations in the Quetta Valley, West Pakistan.* New York. (Anthr. Pap. Am. Mus. Nat. Hist., 47.)

—— 1959. *Archaeological Surveys in the Zhob and Loralai Districts, West Pakistan.* New York. (Anthr. Pap. Am. Mus. Nat. Hist., 47.)

—— 1971. *The Roots of the Indian Civilization.* New York.

FRANCFORT, H.-P. 1984. The Early Periods of Shortugai (Harappan) and the Western Bactrian Culture of Dashly. In: ALLCHIN, B. (ed.), *South Asian Archaeology, 1981.* Cambridge. pp. 170–5.

GELB, I. J. 1970. Makan and Meluhha. *Rev. Assyriol. Archaeol. Orient.*, Vol. 65, pp. 1–8.

GHOSH, A. 1965. The Indus Civilization: Its Origins, Authors, Extent and Chronology. In: MISHRA, V. N.; MATE, M. S. (eds), *Indian Prehistory.* Poona. pp. 113–24.

—— 1982. Deurbanization of the Harappan Civilization. In: POSSEHL, G. L. (ed.), *Harappan Civilization: A Contemporary Perspective.* New Delhi. pp. 321–4.

HALIM, M. A. 1970–1. Excavations at Sarai Khola, Part I. *Pak. Archaeol.*, Vol. 7, pp. 23–89.

—— 1972. Excavations at Sarai Kala, Part II. *Pak. Archaeol.*, Vol. 8, pp. 1–112.

HARGREAVES, H. 1929. *Excavations in Baluchistan, 1925: Sompur Mound, Mastung and Sohr Damb, Nal.* Calcutta. (Mem. Archaeol. Surv. India, 35.)

JARRIGE, J. F. 1982. Excavations at Mehrgarh: Their Significance for Understanding the Background of the Harappan Civilization. In: POSSEHL, G. L. (ed.), *Harappan Civilization: A Contemporary Perspective.* New Delhi. pp. 79–84.

JARRIGE, J. F.; LECHEVALLIER, M. 1979. Excavations at Mehrgarh, Baluchistan: Their Significance in the Prehistorical Context of the Indo-Pakistani Borderlands. In: TADDEI, M. (ed.), *South Asian Archaeology, 1977.* Napoli. pp. 463–535.

JARRIGE, J. F.; MEADOW, R. H. 1980. The Antecedents of Civilization in the Indus Valley. *Sci. Am.* (New York), Vol. 243, No. 2, pp. 122–33.

JOSHI, J. P. 1979. The Nature of Settlement of Surkotada. In: AGRAWAL, D. P.; CHAKRABARTI, D. P. (eds), *Essays in Indian Protohistory.* New Delhi. pp. 59–64.

KHAN, F. A. 1965. Excavations at Kot Diji. *Pak. Archaeol.*, Vol. 2, pp. 11–85.

KHAN, F. A.; KNOX, J. R.; THOMAS, K. D. 1986. Sheri Khan Terakai: A New Site in the North-west Frontier Province of Pakistan. *J. Cent. Asia* (Islamabad), Vol. 9, No. 1, pp. 13–34.

KHAN, G. M. 1983. Hathial Excavation (A Preliminary Account). *J. Cent. Asia* (Islamabad), Vol. 6, No. 2, pp. 35–44.

KNOROZOV, Y. V.; ALBEDIL, M. F.; VOLCHOK, B. Y. 1981. *Proto Indica 1979.* Moskva. (Report on the Investigation of the Proto-Indian Texts.)

KNOROZOV, Y. V.; VOLCHOK, B. Y.; GURUV, N. 1984. Some Groups of Proto-religious Inscriptions of the Harappan. In: LAL, B. B.; GUPTA, S. P. (eds), *Frontiers of the Indus Civilization, Sir Mortimer Wheeler Commemoration Volume.* New Delhi. pp. 169–72.

KOSKENNIEMI, K.; PARPOLA, A. 1979. *Corpus of Texts in the Indus Script.* Helsinki.

—— 1980. *Documentation and Duplicates of the Texts in the Indus Script.* Helsinki.

KOSKENNIEMI, K.; PARPOLA, A.; PARPOLA, S. 1973. *Materials for the Study of the Indus Script.* A Concordance to the Indus Inscriptions.

KRAMER, S. N. 1963. Dilmun: Quest for Paradise. *Antiq.* (Cambridge), Vol. 37, pp. 111–15.

—— 1964. The Indus Civilization and Dilmun, the Sumerian Paradise Land. *Expedition* (Philadelphia, Pa.), Vol. 6, No. 3, pp. 44–52.

LAL, B. B. 1970–1. Perhaps the Earliest Ploughed Field So Far Excavated Anywhere in the World. *Puratattva* (Varanasi), Vol. 4, pp. 1–3.

LAMBERG-KARLOVSKY, C. C. 1970. *Excavations at Tepe Yahya, Iran, 1967–69.* Cambridge, Mass. (Am. Sch. Prehist. Res. Bull., 27.)

—— 1972. Trade Mechanism in Indus-Mesopotamian Inter-relations. *J. Am. Orien. Soc.* (New Haven, Conn.), Vol. 92, No. 1, pp. 222–9.

—— 1976. Foreign Relations in the Third Millennium at Tepe Yahya. In: DESHAYES, J. (ed.), *Le Plateau Iranien et l'Asie Centrale des Origines à la Conquête Islamique.* Paris, CNRS. pp. 33–43.

LAMBERG-KARLOVSKY, C. C.; TOSI, M. 1973. Shahr-i-Sokhta and Tepe Yahya. Tracks on the Earliest History of the Iranian Plateau. *East West* (Roma), Vol. 23, No. 1–2, pp. 21–57.

LESHNIK, L. 1968. The Harappan Port at Lothal: Another View. *Am. Anthropol.* (Washington, D.C.), Vol. 70, No. 5, pp. 911–22.

MACKAY, E. J. H. 1938. *Further Excavations at Mohenjo-daro.* New Delhi.

MAHADEVAN IRAVATHAN 1977. *The Indus Script, Texts Concordance and Tables.* New Delhi. (Mem. Archeaol. Surv. India, 77.)

MARSHALL, J. 1924. Fresh Light on the Long Forgotten Civilization. *Ill. London News* (London), 20 Sept.

—— 1926. *Annual Report of the Archaeological Survey of India 1923–24.*

—— 1931. *Mohenjo-daro and the Indus Civilization.* London.

MASSON, V. M. 1981. Seals of Proto-Indian Type from Altyn-depe. In: KOHL, P. H. (ed.), *The Bronze Age Civilization of Central Asia*. New York. pp. 149–62.

—— 1988. *Altyn-depe*. Philadelphia, Pa..

MEADOW, R. H. 1989. Continuity and Change in the Agriculture of the Greater Indus Valley: The Palaeo-ethnobotanical and 300 Archaeological Evidence. *Wis. Archaeol. Rev.*, pp. 1–12.

MISHRA, V. N. 1984. Climate, a Factor in the Rise and Fall of the Indus Civilization – Evidence from Rajasthan and Beyond. In: LAL, B. B.; GUPTA, S. P. (eds), *Frontiers of the Indus Civilization, Sir Mortimer Wheeler Commemoration Volume*. New Delhi. pp. 461–90.

MUGHAL, M. R. 1970. The Early Harappan Period in the Greater Indus Valley and Northern Baluchistan (*c.* 3000–2400 BC). (PhD Dissertation, University of Pennsylvania.)

—— 1972. Excavations at Jalilpur. *Pak. Archaeol.*, Vol. 8, pp. 117–24.

—— 1974. New Evidence of the Early Harappan Culture from Jalilpur. *Archaeol.* (New York), Vol. 27, No. 2, pp. 106–13.

—— 1981. New Archaeological Evidence from Bahawalpur. In DANI, A. H. (ed.), *Indus Civilization: New Perspectives*. Islamabad. pp. 33–42.

—— 1982. Recent Archaeological Research in the Cholistan Desert. In: POSSEHL, G. L. (ed.), *Harappan Civilization: A Contemporary Perspective*. New Delhi.

—— 1988. La naissance de la civilisation de l'Indus: Les cités oubliées de l' Indus. In: *Archéologie du Pakistan*. Paris. pp. 71–4.

—— 1989. *Archaeological Explorations in Cholistan, Islamabad*. Islamabad.

OPPENHEIM, A. I. 1954. Seafaring Merchants of Ur? *J. am. Orient. Soc.* (New Haven, Conn.), Vol. 74, pp. 6–17.

PANDYA, S. 1977. Lothal Dockyard Hypothesis and Sea Level Changes. In: AGRAWAL, D. P.; PANDE, B. M. (eds), *Ecology and Archaeology of Western India*. New Delhi. pp. 99–103.

POSSEHL, G. L. 1980. *Indus Civilization in Saurashtra*. New Delhi.

RAIKES, R. L. 1964. The End of the Ancient Cities of the Indus. *Am. Anthropol.* (Washington, D.C.), Vol. 66, No. 2.

—— 1967. The Mohenjo-daro Floods: Further Notes. *Antiq.* (Cambridge), Vol. 41, pp. 64–6.

—— 1968. Kalibangan: Death from Natural Causes. *Antiq.* (Cambridge), Vol. 42, No. 168, pp. 286–91.

RAIKES, R. L.; DYSON, R. 1961. The Prehistoric Climate of Baluchistan and the Indus Valley. *Am. Anthropol.* (Washington, D.C.), Vol. 63, pp. 265–81.

RAMASWAMY, C. 1968. Monsoon over the Indus Valley During the Harappan Period. *Nature* (London), Vol. 217, No. 5129, pp. 628–9.

RAO, S. R. 1973. *Lothal and the Indus Civilization*. Bombay.

—— 1979–85. *Lothal – An Harappan Port Town (1955–62)*. New Delhi. (Mem. Archaeol. Surv. India, 78.)

—— 1982. *The Department of the Indus Script*. New Delhi.

RATNAGAR, S. 1981. *Encounters: The Westerly Trade of the Harappan Civilization*. New Delhi.

ROSS, E. J. 1946. A Chalcolithic Site in Northern Baluchistan. *J. Near East. Stud.* (Chicago, Ill.), Vol. 5, No. 4, pp. 291–315.

SHAH, U. P. 1960. Lothal – A Port. *J. Orient. Inst.* (Baroda), Vol. 9, No. 3, pp. 310–20.

SINGH, G. 1971. The Indus Valley Cultures. *Archaeol. Phys. Anthropol. Ocean.* (Sydney), Vol. 6, No. 2, pp. 77–89.

SINGH, G. R. et al. 1974. Late Quaternary History of Vegetation and Climate of the Rajasthan Desert. *Philos. Trans. R. Soc.*, Vol. 267, No. 889, pp. 467–501.

STEIN, A. 1931. *An Archaeological Tour in Gedrosia*. Calcutta. (Mem. Archaeol. Surv. India, 43.)

—— 1942. A Survey of Ancient Sites Along the Lost Sarasvati. *Geogr. J.* (London), Vol. 99, No. 4, pp. 179–82.

SURAJ, BHAN 1975. *Excavations at Mitathal (1968) and Other Explorations in the Sutlej-Yamuna Divide*. Kurukshetra.

THAPAR, B. K. 1975. Kalibangan: An Harappan Metropolis Beyond the Indus Valley. *Expedition* (Philadelphia, Pa.), Vol. 17, No. 2, pp. 19–32.

—— 1977. Climate During the Period of the Indus Civilization: Evidence from Kalibangan. In: AGRAWAL, D. P.; PANDE, B. M. (eds), *Ecology and Archaeology of Western India*. New Delhi. pp. 67–73.

—— 1984. Six Decades of Harappan Studies. In: LAL, B.B.; GUPTA, S.P.(eds), *Frontiers of the Indus Civilization, Sir Mortimer Wheeler Commemoration Volume*. New Delhi. pp. 1–25.

—— 1985. *Recent Archaeological Discoveries in India*. Tokyo/Paris, UNESCO.

THAPAR, R. 1975. A Probable Identification of Meluhha, Dilmun and Makan. *J. Econ. Soc. Hist. Orient* (Leiden), Vol. 18, No. 1, pp. 1–42.

VATS, M. S. 1940. *Excavations at Harappa*. New Delhi.

VISHNU MITTRE. 1978. Palaeoecology of the Rajasthan Desert During the Last 10,000 Years. *Paleobot.*, Vol. 25, pp. 549–58.

—— 1982. The Harappan Civilization and the Need for a New Approach. In: POSSEHL, G. L. (ed.), *Harappan Civilization: A Contemporary Perspective*. New Delhi. pp. 31–40.

VISHNU MITTRE; SAVITHRI, R. 1982. Food Economy of the Harappans. In: POSSEHL, G. L. (ed.), *Harappan Civilization: A Contemporary Perspective*. New Delhi. pp. 205–21.

WEISGERBER, G. 1984. Makan and Meluhha – Third Millennium BC. Copper Production in Oman and the Evidence of Contact with the Indus Valley. In: ALLCHIN, B. (ed.), *South Asian Archaeology, 1981*. Cambridge. pp. 196–201.

WHEELER, M. 1968. *The Indus Civilization*. 3rd ed. Cambridge.

YASH PAL et al. 1984. Remote Sensing of the Sarasvati River. In: LAL, B. B.; GUPTA, S. P. (eds), *Frontiers of the Indus Civilization, Sir Mortimer Wheeler Commemoration Volume*. New Delhi. pp. 491–8.

12.8

THE POST-INDUS CULTURES
(1500–700 BC)

B. K. Thapar and Abdul Rahman

The eventual collapse of the Harappan civilization in the middle of the eighteenth century BC marked the end of centuries-old human experience of urban life. With it disappeared the idea of town planning and municipal organization, the use of uniform weights and measures, the construction of monumental buildings and writing. Although the dissolution of a civilization does not necessarily presuppose the total extinction of its bearers, yet a considerable proportion of the population in this case also seems to have changed, giving place to newcomers who had their own distinctive pattern of life in which urbanism had no place. The newcomers settled in the conquered territories in the form of scattered peasant communities, fighting among themselves and also against the local population until they had a complete upper hand. These farming communities gradually established nuclei here and there which, with the lapse of time, grew into villages and towns. But these towns were very different from those of the Indus civilization in that there was no rigid planning behind them. In fact the idea of town planning died in the place where it had originated and had to be re-introduced after about two thousand years. Who were these newcomers? At what period did they enter the basin of the River Indus and in what form? What material culture did they themselves possess? These are the kinds of questions which exercise the minds of those who focus attention on the aftermath of the Indus civilization. Two kinds of evidence, each having its own limitations, are available: archaeological and literary.

ARCHAEOLOGICAL EVIDENCE

Noteworthy sites where the stage of decline or change has been identified through excavation are Jhukar (Majumdar, 1934), Chanhu-daro (Mackay, 1943) and Amri (Casal, 1964) in Sind, the South Cemetery at Mehrgarh and Sibri in the Kachi plain (Santoni, 1984), the Kulli complex sites in southern Baluchistan, and the type-site Harappa (Vats, 1940), all in Pakistan, and Rangpur, Lothal, Surkotada in Gujarat, Banawali and Bhagwanpura in Haryana and Bara in Punjab, all in India. At Jhukar, Chanhu-daro and Amri it has been labelled the Jhukar culture, distinguished essentially by a ceramic style – a buff ware, painted in black showing certain designs and shapes which are different from those of the characteristic mature Harappan culture. The commonest designs are groups of connected semicircular lines or loops, rows of elongated lozenges, circles with red dots, squares, and so on (Mughal, 1992). At Amri, a progressive transformation of the classic Harappan pottery is seen in period III which becomes a forerunner of the Jhukar ware

in period IIID. Recent researches have clearly demonstrated that this pottery style existed in association with the continuing but diminishing Harappan ceramic tradition without any break. Notable changes in the cultural equipment were, however: the virtual disuse of the squarish stamp seal and the appearance of the circular ones (button seals with different designs); the restricted use of cubical weights and the stylized female figurines, the occurrence of the Indus script only on pottery; and the increase in the production of beads and of faience objects. Likewise Kulli-complex sites with some distinctive pottery forms appear to have lasted longer to become contemporaneous with Jhukar and Mehrgarh VIII.

At Harappa, the stage of decline is recognized as the Cemetery 'H' culture, marked by two modes of burials in separate strata. The associated pottery handsomely painted with motifs that include human beings, stylized plants, frequent representations of cattle, goat, peacocks and fish, stars, and so on was quite unlike either the Harappan or the Jhukar or the Kulli pottery. Most abundant, however, are the continuous scenes in panels or in roundels and so on. These scenes are a subject of unusual interest, having been attributed by the excavator to the Aryans. The corresponding habitation stratum was marked by shoddy jerry-built structures. However, this type of pottery has been reported from several sites in Cholistan which have both regular settlements and industrial features such as kilns. It is thus no longer an isolated phenomenon. In these sites Cemetery H-related ceramics existed in association with a waning Harappan cultural tradition until the latter retained only a few forms which were ultimately lost.

On the Indian sites, a significant feature of the decline is the increase in the number of settlements in the eastern region, including Cholistan, and the southern region, oriented to different de-urbanized subsistence patterns, including pastoralism. The settlements were essentially smaller in size and located away from the floodplain. These cultures subsequently give way to the various Chalcolithic cultures of central India and Deccan.

During the second millennium BC within the area of the Indus civilization, and also in the adjoining areas, many Chalcolithic settlements sprang up. These settlements represent different regional culture groups and are remarkable in their demonstration of hybrid backgrounds and enduring traditions. In time range they were either contemporary with or later than the Indus civilization.

In Pakistan, clear evidence of post-Harappan occupation is reported from Pirak near Sibi on the fringes of the Indus plains, Jhangar in Sind and the Gomar and Swat valleys, including the Gandhāra plain.

Baluchistan-Sibi

More clear evidence of a post-Harappan occupation on the fringes of the Indus plains comes from Pirak, near Sibi. Archaeological excavations at this site have clearly shown that, after an initial Harappan occupation which was followed by a break of unknown duration, the site was re-occupied in the beginning of the second quarter of the second millennium BC. Three successive phases of this unbroken occupation have been recorded. In the first phase structures of unburnt brick were found in association with pottery which combined its coarse clay and hand manufacture with a painting tradition clearly related to that of earlier periods in this area. A major proportion of the pottery, however, was a coarse ware decorated with appliqué bands and fingertip impressions. Of the animal remains both the horse and the camel were not only represented by their bones but also by terracotta and unburnt clay figurines. Common among the terracotta objects were button seals of circular, square or curved forms. Bronze or copper objects have also been found along with a stone-blade industry which included many serrated edges meant perhaps for working on bone or ivory. A more or less similar assemblage with numerous terracotta and clay figurines of Bactrian camels, horses and human beings including riders was found in the second phase. Along with a large number of copper and bronze tools at this level came to light the first piece of iron. The third phase also shows a continuation of all the elements of the earlier phase, except that iron is now represented by a larger number of examples. Radiocarbon dates indicate for phase III a span of c. 1000 to 800 BC, and an earlier date c. 1370 to 1340 BC perhaps represents the second phase.

The cereal remains at Pirak during period I are wheat, barley, rice, millet and oats. These are fairly well documented in the two sectors where soil samples were taken. Sorghum on the other hand is very scarce and its identification remains dubious on account of the small number of finds and their poor state of preservation (Jarrige, 1979, p. 331).

The material culture of Pirak does not seem to be a purely local phenomenon: it is reasonable to assume that it extended all over the northern part of the Kachi plain. Alongside marked differences, some features of the Pirak culture relate it to a local tradition brought to light at Mehrgarh. At the same time it shows evidence of contact with Central Asia. The Pirak culture, in the words of the excavator, is 'an original synthesis of regional elements and outside contributions from various sources'.

Sind

The assemblages that follow the Late Harappan Jhukar horizon in Sind are known as Jhangar. Stratigraphically it occurs after the Jhukar-period occupation at Chanhu-daro and Amri and is distinguished by a distinctive black and grey burnished pottery, either plain or decorated with incised geometric and linear designs. This ceramic is a complete departure from the Jhukar pottery tradition. A kind of grey incised ware apparently different in fabric from that of Jhangar also occurs at Pirak IIIB in association with iron and is dated to 915–790 and 890–770 BC (calibrated). The occupation of Jhangar may thus reasonably be placed in the beginning of the first millennium BC (Mughal, 1992).

Gomal Valley

In the Gomal Valley, particularly at Hathala, Gumla and Marha Sharif, different types of graves have been termed the Gomas Grave culture. Across the Indus, graves of Sarai Kala period III show a close resemblance to these graves. Stratigraphically, they fall into two periods. The earlier of these was a burial-cum-funeral type wherein besides the human body and a few objects, a sacrificed animal was also interred, which in addition shows evidence of fire. The upper and later burials contain human skeletons generally without any funerary objects. The Sarai Kala graves across the Indus also fall into two types distinguished largely by the method of construction, both of which contain no funerary accompaniments to the skeleton, except for two iron finger-rings and fragments of paste bracelets. The mode of burial, however, resembles the later period graves of the Gumla region which may also be ascribed to the Iron Age. The recognition of the Goma Grave culture thus presents a new cultural complex in the post-Indus civilization period.

Swat Valley

The cultural sequence of the Swat Valley (Stacul, 1984) is based on that of the Ghaligai site where seven periods (I-VII), extending from the third millennium BC into historical times, have been identified. We are concerned with periods IV and V of this sequence.

Period IV of the Ghaligai sequence, belonging to around the seventeenth century BC, is recorded at several sites and seems to be connected with population growth and new forms of stable agricultural settlements. It is marked by a new tradition in pottery, stone and bone tools, and a settlement pattern with evidence of long-distance trade. The sites are situated near rivers on top of or on the slopes of hills not far from valley floors. During this period, around the middle of the second millennium BC, pit-dwellings were replaced by stone-walled houses, built of irregular stones and pebbles. Another technological feature was the introduction of copper. A graveyard belonging to this period was also located at Kherai on the mountain slopes of the Gorband Valley. The graves are rectangular in plan and are covered over by stone slabs. While some of the graves contained inhumations others were without any skeletal material. The grave furnishings, apart from pottery, include in some cases gold ear-rings.

The pottery is represented by a black-grey and buff ware, generally burnished, showing a mottled surface and turned on a slow wheel with frequent basket impressions on its base. Alongside this was a red ware of medium to fine texture, turned on a fast wheel, having painted designs in black, including vegetal representations. While the former recalls the widespread stylistic horizon of the northern Iranian region, the latter seems to have developed from Harappan urban and post-urban cultures. Jade and shell objects testify wide interregional trade. Terracotta figurines, both human and animal, were found mostly around the fireplaces, indicating probably their cultic context. The animal figurines always represent the humped bull. Copper objects included a leaf-shaped spearhead. The faunal remains, with a high frequency of zebu, clearly suggest husbandry rather than hunting as the main activity. The horse is also known. The vegetal remains indicate the existence of wheat, barley and rice and suggest specialized farming in the large areas of fertile and well-watered land.

Between periods IV and V, a transitional phase has been noticed in the occupational layers at Aligrama, marked essentially by a change in pottery and some other associated objects. period IV can be considered the formative phase of the so-called Gandhāra Grave culture, represented by period V. A new stylistic horizon in ceramics, showing close connections with northern Iranian cultures, marks the beginning of period V. The period also witnessed an increase in settlement life. The pottery is characterized by the presence of three classes, grey-black, fine red and coarse red, which remain constant throughout the occupation period of the Grave culture. There is, however, a gradual refinement of the paste and the use of the fast wheel, facilitating the production of vases with thinner sides that take on a distinctly grey colour. The period also witnessed a shrinking of contacts with areas outside the valley. As well as direct relations with the adjoining Dir Valley, remains of the Gandhāra Grave culture have been identified at Zarif Karuna near Michni in the Peshawar Valley and at Hathial near Taxila. It would seem, therefore, that this proto-historic culture does not represent an isolated episode but is part of a much wider culture, spreading into two different regions, the sub-Himalayan zone of the Pakistan-Afghan border in the west and the alluvial plains of Peshawar.

Gandahāra Grave culture

The Gandhāra Grave culture, corresponding to period V of the Swat-Ghaligai sequence, represents the material remains of the cemeteries excavated at Butkara II, Katelai I and Loebar I, all of which share the same characteristics.

Recent excavations carried out by the Italians in Swat have produced remains which suggest to the excavators that the material of Swat has points of contact with Iranian production, and especially with that of north-eastern Iran; it seems particularly close to the ceramic production of the locality of Tepe Hissar IIB. Since Hissar IIB can be dated at least as early as the first quarter of the second millennium BC, it is obvious that some of the Swat sites have great importance in a discussion of the problem of the post-Harappan occupation of the Gandhāra plain.

The burial tombs consist of two small chambers one above the other. The upper chamber (about 2 to 2.5 m² by 2 m deep) was filled with soil and charcoal after the burial and surrounded generally by a rough stone circle. The lower chamber, separated from the upper by stone slabs, was smaller and contained the human remains with accompanying funerary furniture. The great majority of the burials contained either inhumations, in which case the corpse was placed on its side (N.-S.) in a flexed position, or cremation, probably after fractionalizing. At Katelai, not only was a portion of the cemetery devoted to child burials but in the midst of the necropolis two complete skeletons of horses were recovered. A smaller number of the graves contained cremated ashes, sometimes gathered in a pottery cist or 'box-urn' with flat lid, a large urn with a face decoration consisting of appliqué and cut-out features.

The grave goods included large quantities of a distinctive plain pottery, either buff red or grey, and of a distinctive range of forms. These comprised tall 'champagne goblets', pedestal cups, beakers with large flared mouths, bottles with tall narrow necks, an occasional jug with a raised lip, spouted pots – some with small handles and one curious triple pot on three stems rising from a base. There are also sometimes terracotta figurines of a distinctive type – generally flat tablets with rough human forms, appliqué breasts and highly stylized heads, some with incised necklaces and eyes. Metal objects include those of copper or bronze, most commonly pins with decorated tops and, much more rarely, objects of iron.

A. H. Dani's (1967) excavations at Timargarha and Thana have further extended the range of these grave people first identified in Swat. He has found evidence of them in Thana, Dir, Bajaur (Inayat Qila) and Mardan (Panjpir). He has termed this complex the 'Gandhāra Grave culture'.

'As the culture belongs to a people or peoples whose names have not been revealed to us in our excavations', Dani explains, 'we have preferred to derive the archaeological terminology for two main factors; first, the culture is known to us mainly from the grave goods and, secondly, it was first discovered in this region, "Gandhāra".' (Dani, 1967, p. 25). Similar graves have more recently been exposed in Zarif Kuruna in the Peshawar Valley.

Based on both typology and a limited stratigraphy, Dani has divided his material into three periods:

Period   I – Complete burial with copper
Period II – Cremation and burial with copper
Period III – Fractional and multiple burial with copper and iron

The people of these periods apparently placed their settlements on the alluvium and near to the foothills of the river valleys. They also had the horse and practised some agriculture, circular and rectangular storage rooms having been found. In general, the grave furniture is similar to that found in Swat though there are distinct period differences, especially in ceramics. The whole is dominated by grey and red wares. According to Stacul's classification, the graves may be divided into four groups of which only the last, associated with the thin-sided grey and red ware, produced iron tools. Thus there seems good reason to think that a fair proportion of the graves predate the arrival of iron in this area.

The broad chronology of the graves, derived both from cross-dating parallels with sites outside India and Pakistan, and from the dozen or more radiocarbon dates so far published, appears to cover a wide range. Katelai I produced five samples dated between 1500 and 200 BC, from Timargarha two samples give dates of 1710 and 1020 BC while from Barama two samples were dated between 800 and 430 BC. K. Jettmar (1967, pp. 203–9) has produced evidence that Dani's period III may well be of the seventh to sixth century BC. This is based on a comparison of a three-holed cheek piece of iron found in Timargarha with a similar one found in central Asia. Another synchronism of late occurrence may be found in the grey-ware sherds from Hathial (near Taxila Museum) with Kharoshti letters scratched on them. Thus continuity of occupation is attested for agricultural people who had horses and cattle and who lived in and about the Gandhāra plain for almost a thousand years. Their connections to central Asia and Iran are definite, though of what character is still not known.

Cairn burials and Londo ware

Towards the beginning of the first millennium BC iron seems to have been brought to the borders of Baluchistan by a people who buried their dead in cairns, were horse riders and used pottery with a characteristic decoration and a distinctive pot form. Several such cairn burial sites were located by Stein (1937) in Baluchi Makran as far as Kulli and hence north up the Mashkai Valley into central Jhalawan, notable among these being Gatti, Jiwanri and Zangian. The cairn burial pottery is a coarse red ware, painted with continuous bands of large volutes or pot-hook spirals. The typical pot form was a spouted flask with lugs pierced for a carrying cord. Almost contemporary with these burials was another class of pottery designated Londo ware by De Cardi (1951), which occurs at several sites extending from Shami Damb to Kullu Kalat. It is a grog-tempered red ware, probably handmade and painted in black with pot-hook spirals. These Londo ware spirals seem to be copies of the bolder volutes of the cairn burial pottery. That users of Londo ware were also horse riders is attested by horse motifs on their pottery.

Central, western and eastern India (Map. 15)

Within India, during the second millennium BC the following Chalcolithic cultures flourished, some of which were part contemporary with the closing phase of the Indus civilization.

1 The Sawalda culture in the Tapti, Pravara and Godavari (c. 2000–1700 BC)
2 The Kayatha culture in the central Malwa region of the Chambal Valley (c. 2100–1800 BC)

3 The Ahar culture, sometimes also referred to as the Banas culture from its distribution in the Banas Valley in southeastern Rajasthan (c. 2100–1400 BC)
4 The Malwa culture in central and western India (c. 1700–1400 BC)
5 The Jorwe culture in northern Deccan (c. 1400–900 BC)
6 The Eastern Chalcolithic culture in the middle and lower Ganga basin, including the Vindhyan region and West Bengal (c. 1300–1000 BC)

Excepting the last one, the main focus of these cultures was the great central Indian plateau which is characterized by black cotton soil and scanty rainfall (500 to 1000 mm). In the second half of the second millennium BC, the Chalcolithic elements of the northern Deccan also intruded into the Neolithic phase of the Krishna, Godavari and Tungabhadra valleys, by moving down the Bhima River. All these cultures shared a common level of subsistence economy and technology but were distinguished from each other by a distinctive painted ceramic industry. The mixed economy of these Chalcolithic communities was based on agriculture, stock-raising and hunting-fishing. Their equipment included blades and microliths of siliceous material such as chalcedony. They used copper, albeit on a restricted scale, except at Ahar. These cultures were represented by essentially peasant, agricultural settlements, which did not develop into an urban status because of inadequate technology for exploiting the environment.

The salient features of each of these cultures, based on the excavation conducted at some principal sites, are as follows:

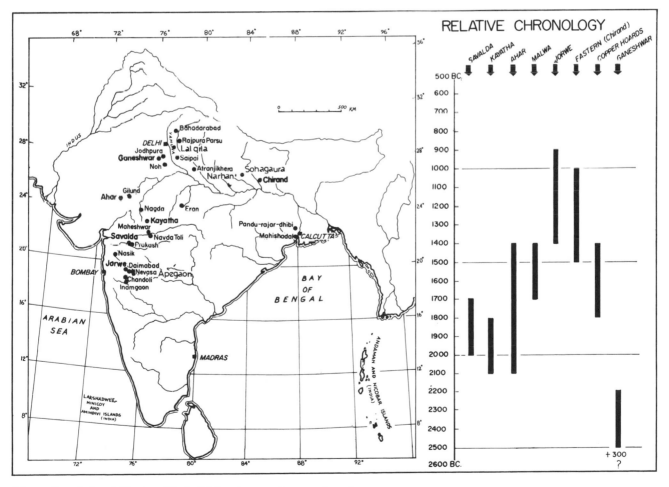

Map 15 Post-Indus civilization: Chalcolithic cultures and copper hoards.

The Sawalda culture

The type-site lies on the southern bank of the Tapti River in District West Khandesh, Dhule, Maharashtra (IAR, 1960). The culture is known to occur principally in the Tapti and Godavari valleys (Deo et al., 1979) but has also been reported from some sites in the Krishna and Kaveri valleys (Sali, 1986). The culture's distinctive trait, however, is pottery, characterized by a medium to coarse fabric, with a thick slip as a surface treatment, in varying shades of brown, chocolate, pink, orange and red which during firing developed crackles. It is painted over in black or purplish red or in both and sometimes also in ochre-red, with geometrical and other designs, depicting plants, animals, stylized human figures, and antennae-ended arrows, double-barbed fishhooks, harpoons, and so on. The types represented comprise high-necked jars, basins, platters, dishes-on-stands and knobbed lids. Associated with this characteristic ware were also found burnished grey and thick coarse red wares (Sali, 1986). The associated finds consist of microliths, beads of semi-precious stone, stone objects such as saddle querns and mullers, and bone arrowheads, harpoons and a few objects of copper. The people lived in mud houses and cultivated wheat, barley, lentil, common pea, green-gram, black-gram, hyacinth bean and *ber* (Indian jujube).

The Kayatha culture

The type-site is situated 25 km east of Ujjain in Madhya Pradesh on the right bank of the Choti Kali Sind, one of the feeder tributaries of the Chambal (Ansari and Dhavalikar, 1975). The culture is known to occur in the Chambal Valley and is characterized by three principal ceramic industries: (1) sturdy violet-painted pinkish-red ware used for big jars and decorated with bold strokes; (2) red-painted buff ware represented by spheroid vases and dishes with linear designs. This ware seems to have been a de luxe ware as attested by the deposit of two necklaces of 175 and 160 beads of semi-precious stones and 27 copper bangles in the pots of the ware; and (3) combed ware used for bowls and dishes occasionally decorated with multiple zigzag or wavy horizontal lines executed by a comb-like instrument.

Other associated finds of the Kayatha culture include: copper objects such as axes, bangles, chisels; blades of chalcedony and agate; a stone mace head; beads of semi-precious stone including micro-beads of steatite. The people lived in houses of mud or wattle and daub with floors made of hard compact silt.

The Ahar culture

The type-site which gives the culture its name lies on the left bank of the river of the same name, about 3 km east of Udaipur in Rajasthan (Sankalia et al., 1969). The principal sites where remains of this culture have been exposed are Kayatha, Ahar and Gilund (IAR, 1960b). The Ahar culture is distinguished principally by a plain ceramic as well as white-painted black-and-red ware, available unburnished, burnished, brown-slipped and coarse, and has a limited range of shapes such as bowls, bowls-on-stands, elongated vases and globular vases. The bowl, however, is the recurrent type.

Among the other cultural remains of the Ahar culture, particularly noteworthy is the occurrence of the short bicone terracotta beads bearing punctured designs, and the terracotta bull figurines. While the bulls show a striking resem-blance to west Asian specimens from Troy and other sites in Anatolia, including Anau in Turkmenia, the stylized form of the bulls is unique. Their occurrence in large numbers would perhaps indicate their use for votive purposes. Depending upon the availability of resource material, the houses were built of mudbricks or kiln-burnt bricks or wattle and daub, sometimes reinforced with quartz nodules.

The Malwa culture

The culture takes its name from the nuclear area of its distribution, namely Malwa, a geographico-cultural unit denoting the region lying between the Chambal in the north and the Narmada in the south. Its eastern boundary may extend to the Betwa River while the western is delimited by the Aravallis. The principal sites where remains of this culture have been exposed are: Maheshwar and Navda Toli on the Narmada (Sankalia et al., 1958); Nagda on the Chambal (Banerjee, 1986); Prakash on the Tapti (Thapar, 1967); Daimabad on the Pravara (Sali, 1986); Kayatha on the Choti Kali Sind (Ansari and Dhavalikar, 1975); Earn on the Betwa (U. V. Singh, 1976) and Inamgaon on the Ghod (Sankalia et al., 1971).

The Malwa culture is distinguished essentially by a ceramic: the Malwa ware. The ware was made on a wheel and was invariably dressed with an orange slip mostly on the outside or, in the case of the dishes, both on the outside and the inside. On the slipped surface were painted linear designs in a thin purplish to brown-black pigment, though the red background predominates. In addition to the geometric, representational motifs, displaying animals such as the stylized peacock, spotted deer and crane, used as fillers, are also employed. The commonest shapes represented in this ware comprise vases, bowls (including spouted), chalices, dishes and dishes-on-stands, saucers, lids and so on.

Associated with this principal ware was another distinctive cream or buff-slipped ware. The ware is made on a wheel and is dressed with a slip ranging from yellowish through reddish to buff cream in colour. On the slipped surface are painted linear designs in black or purple, the designs being largely geometric. Representations of human figurines and antelopes also occur in this ware. The shapes met with include goblets, bowls, including the stemmed variety, dishes-on-stands and globular vases. As evidence of the interrelationship with contemporary cultures, the white-painted black-and-red ware of the Ahar culture and its variant, the white-painted pale grey and black-and-grey ware of Prakash, also occurred at some sites.

The subsistence economy of the Malwa culture was based on farming, hunting and fishing. The people grew wheat, barley, rice, lentil and green-gram. They lived in houses made of mud and occasionally also of mudbrick.

The Jorwe culture

The distribution of this culture extends principally to the semi-arid zones of the northern Deccan plateau with Pravara, in the Godavari basin, as the nuclear area. Noteworthy sites where deposits of this culture have been exposed are Nasik (Sankalia and Deo, 1955), Navase (Sankalia et al., 1960), Chandoli (Deo and Ansari, 1965), Prakash (Thapar, 1967), Navdatoli (Sankalia et al., 1958), Daimabad (Sali, 1986) and Inamgaon (Shankalia et al., 1971; Dhavalikar, Sankalia and Ansari, 1988).

The culture is distinguished by Jorwe ware, which is made on a fast wheel with uniformly built thin walls. The surface colour ranges from drab through light orange to shades of red. It is comparatively more hard-fired than the Malwa ware. On the slipped surface are painted linear designs, singularly monotonous. The decoration is confined to the portion above the girth and in some cases to the inner bases as well. The characteristic shapes in this ware are very few indeed, consisting of a concave-sided bowl, a tubular-spouted vase and a plain high-necked jar. Besides this ware, a burnished grey ware (occasionally red-ochre painted on rim portions) and a coarse red ware were also current during this period.

A distinctive feature of the Jorwe culture was its mode of disposal of the dead. Usually, adults were buried in an extended position, while children were put in two coarse red-grey ware urns, placed horizontally mouth-to-mouth in a grave-pit. In both cases the grave-pits were dug within the houses. At Inamgaon, a departure from the usual practice was shown by a four-legged burial urn of unbaked clay, modelled to resemble the abdomen of a female, which contained the skeleton of a male in a sitting posture.

The Jorwe people subsisted on farming, hunting and fishing. They cultivated a number of crops such as barley, wheat, lentil, kulith, pea and very rarely rice. They also collected fruits such as *ber* (Indian jujube). Barley seems to have been the principal cereal, for it could be cultivated without difficulty in a semi-arid environment.

The houses of the Jorwe people were built of wattle and daub with perhaps conical roofs. The settlements at Inamgaon and Daimabad were found to have embankments against floods.

Two phases of the Jorwe culture have been identified, the earlier of which came to an end around 1000 BC as a result of increasing aridity in the area, which perhaps led to a large scale migration southwards to the Krishna Valley, while the late phase lingered on till 700 BC, reflected by impoverished equipment. The migration of the Jorwe culture people towards the south led to the introduction of Chalcolithic elements in the late phases of the Neolithic cultures of Krishna, Godavari region. There is reason to believe that as a result of this migration in the southern Deccan, the population and the economy therein underwent a concomitant expansion during the period 1500–1000 BC. Some degree of sedentarization seems to have been introduced.

The Eastern Chalcolithic culture

The manifestations of this culture are to be seen in eastern parts of Uttar Pradesh, Bihar and West Bengal including the Vindhyan regions, the principal excavated sites being Koldihawa, Narhan (P. Singh and M. Lal, 1985) and Sohagaura (Chaturvedi, 1985), both in District Gorakhpur and Kheradih (IAR, 1985) in District Ballia, Uttar Pradesh; Chirand in District Saran, Bihar (IAR, 1967–78); and Pandurajardhibi (Dasgupta, 1964) and Mahisdal (IAR, 1967b) respectively in districts Burdwan and Birbhun, West Bengal.

The distinctive ceramics of this culture are: plain and white-painted black-and-red ware; black-slipped ware with occasional paintings in white; grey ware with impressions of paddy husk; red ware painted in black; and a chocolate or buffish ware painted with cream-coloured designs. Amongst these, the grey ware alone is hand-made, the rest being wheel-made. The noteworthy shapes represented were bowls, including channel-spouted basins, tulip-shaped vases, bowls-on-stands, lids and so on.

The subsistence economy of the people continued to be based on farming, hunting and fishing. Among cultivated cereals, wheat, barley and rice were known.

The copper hoards and related cultures

In the mid-Ganga Valley and the *doab* an enigmatic culture, represented by copper hoards, flourished during the post-Indus period. In time range it was largely contemporary with the Chalcolithic cultures of central India, Deccan and the lower Ganga regions.

Since the early part of the nineteenth century copper hoards (consisting of harpoons, anthropomorphic figures, antennae-hilted swords, flat and shouldered axes, bar celts, trunion axes, socketed axes, bangles and rings) have been reported, mostly as caches, from various parts of south Asia (B. B. Lal, 1951). The hard core of the hoards was found in the mid-Ganga *doab*. Their authorship has been variously ascribed to the refugee Harappans, Vedic Aryans, Mundas or the original Mundari-speaking people, and eastern Austronesian tribes, but the other component of their culture has not been clearly defined (M. Lal, 1983).

On the basis of circumstantial evidence, notably at Bahadarabad and Rajpur Parsu where copper hoards had been reported earlier, a ceramic labelled ochre-coloured pottery (OCP), first identified at Hastinapura in Uttar Pradesh (B. B. Lal, 1955), was claimed to be associated with the hoards although they had till then not been found in stratigraphical association with each other. This hypothesis was confirmed in 1970 when excavation at Saipai in District Etawah, Uttar Pradesh, for the first time established the association of OCP with copper hoard objects, notably a hooked spearhead and a harpoon. The epithet ochre-coloured pottery, however, is a misnomer, for the pottery appears to have been a normal red ware, some of which seems to have been also painted in black designs. The ochreous colour of the pottery, which rubs off easily, may have resulted from the humid conditions of the deposit in which the pottery lay buried. Corroborative evidence has also been obtained from the excavation at Lal Qila in District Bulandshahr, Uttar Pradesh (Gaur, 1973). Here, for the first time, copper objects, particularly a fragmentary celt and arrowheads not covered by the hard core of copper hoards were found along with the OCP. The significance of these finds is further underlined by the discovery at Kiratpur (3 km from Lal Qila) of Copper Hoards containing an anthropomorphic figure, two celts and a few bangles.

The culture represented by the copper hoards had earlier been dated to the second half of the second millennium BC (B. B. Lal, 1951). Thereafter, on the basis of the thermoluminescence method (Huxtable et al., 1972) a time-range extending from 2650 to 1180 BC was obtained through potsherds from four sites. Keeping in view the margin of error in these determinations, a central date of 2000–1500 BC seems to provide the workable time bracket. This brings us to another assemblage with which OCP has been reported to be associated.

In Rajasthan, OCP was found at Noh in District Bharatpur (IAR, 1967a; Kumar, 1971–2) and at Jodhpura in District Jaipur, from deposits underlying those yielding the plain black-and-red ware. Recent fieldwork in District Sikar (Agrawal and Kumar, 1982) has revealed another site where OCP has been found in association with a large number of copper objects and microliths. This site, known as Ganeshwar, is located close to the rich copper mines of the Sikar-

Jhunjhunu area of the Khetri copper belt, which in addition contains quite a number of hot and cold water springs favouring the manufacture of tools. The copper objects recovered from the excavation in the Ganeshwar region include arrowheads, spearheads, fishhooks, spiral-headed pins, celts, bangles, chisels, and so on. Some of these shapes closely resemble those discovered at Indus sites. A noteworthy find is a terracotta cake simulating the Indus type. Meanwhile, it must be stressed that the use of the appellation ochre-coloured pottery in the context of Ganeshwar is both misleading and inappropriate. Here OCP is a red-slipped ware often painted in black and decorated with incised designs, and seems to belong to an indigenous regional ceramic industry. Its relation or similarity with OCP associated with copper hoards of the mid-Ganga region remains as yet undefined. According to radiocarbon determinations the deposits at Ganeshwar are ascribed to 2800–2200 BC (Agrawal and Kumar, 1982). This evidence leads us to surmise that this region supplied the copper objects found at the Harappan sites located in Punjab, Haryana and Rajasthan, if not further west.

Notwithstanding these observations, some scholars postulate two categories of OCP, the one associated with the Late Harappan phase in Punjab, Haryana and the Upper Ganga-Yamuna *doab* and the other with the copper hoards of the mid-Ganga *doab* (Suraj Bhan, 1971–2). The Ganeshwar assemblage in time range falls outside these categories.

Peninsular India

The Iron Age

An event of greatest economic consequence was the arrival of iron in South Asia. Among the Iron Age cultures which fall within the first half of the first millennium BC, mention has already been made of those flourishing in Pakistan. From India, the Megalithic cultures and the Painted Grey Ware culture deserve our attention.

Megalithic cultures (Map 16)

Peninsular India has long been known to contain a large number of megalithic structures (burials) of various types belonging to the early Iron Age. Often such burials are grouped in small clusters but occasionally they extend over quite large areas. They also include plain burials such as urns deposited in pits without any significant lithic appendage. Despite structural or regional disparities, they share a common cultural equipment, indicating the widespread influence of a single technological tradition. Outside the peninsula, they have been reported from Baluchistan and Baluchi and Persian Makran Waghador, Shah Billawal and Murud Memom, the last three within a radius of 32 km of Karachi and Asota, 27 km north-east of Mardan, all in Pakistan; and the Leh Valley of Ladakh, Burzahom and Gufkral, within a

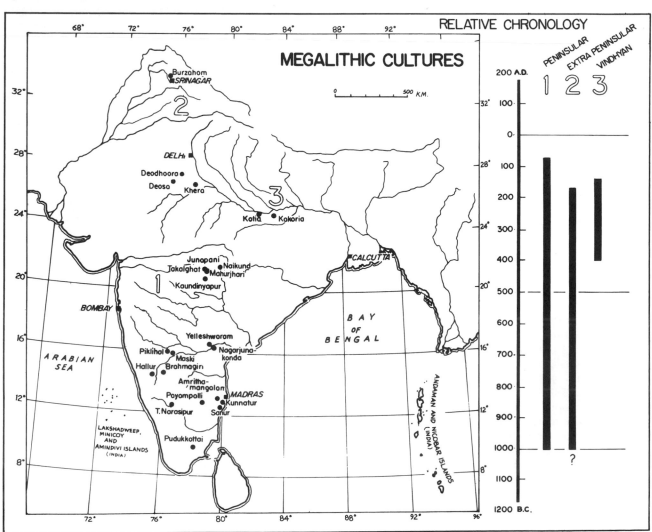

Map 16 Post-Indus civilization: Megalithic cultures.

272

radius of 40 km of Srinagar; Deosa, 52 km from Jaipur; Khera, 6 km from Fatehpur Sikri; Deodhoora and Ladyuna in Almora; and the outcrops of the Vindhyas in Districts Allahabad, Banda, Mirzapur, Varanasi and Singhbhum. An interrelationship of the megalithic practices of these diverse regions has not so far been established, but speculative as it may be, it does stir the imagination (Lesknik, 1974). To this formidable list may be added the megalithic structures of north-east India, introduced by the Austroasiatic immigrants into this region, where they are known to be more or less a living tradition of the aborigines and are mostly commemorative rather than sepulchral. A noteworthy feature of these megaliths is the paucity of habitation sites of a related culture.

As already stated above, the megalithic burials are densely concentrated in peninsular India, falling roughly between 8° and 21° N. While in some regions they are found near large tanks, in others they are located in dry areas where the rock bench is high and in yet others they were erected in the monsoon-fed laterite area. Apart from these topographical considerations, their distribution seems to have also been conditioned by the availability or access to resource material such as iron, gold and so on. For example, the concentration in Vidarbha and Hospet can be easily explained by the availability of iron ore. Similarly, the megaliths of Maski are close to the gold mines.

The subsistence economy which characterizes the megalithic culture of peninsular India is indicated by cereal grains and artefacts found at the excavated burials and habitation sites. The available evidence is admittedly slender but shows a pattern whereby rice seems to be the principal cereal crop of the southern region as against wheat and barley of the Vidarbha and northern Decca. Among the iron objects obtained from the various megalithic burials and related habitation sites, the number of agricultural tools such as sickles and hoes was rather small. Weapons such as daggers and swords far outnumber the agricultural equipment in the burials, but this may be due to their ritualistic significance. The presence of a horse skull with skeletal remains, horse-bits and stirrups among the miscellany of metal objects deposited in some of the megalithic burials, particularly of the Vidarbha region, would suggest that some of the megalithic people were horse nomads. At the same time the evidence of cultivated species (wheat, barley, lentil, common pea, rice, common bean, horse gram) obtained from excavated megalithic sites all over India suggests that the Megalithic people, at least some of them, were regular agriculturists and probably farmed in both summer and winter seasons, producing enough food for the rest of the community (Kajale, 1989).

As regards typology, it is proposed to exclude from discussion the living traditions among the aboriginals of northeastern India, who erect menhirs or build dolmens or flat stone seats essentially as memorials. Ever since the first reported find of the megalithic burials in India, different names, derived from European analogues, have been given to these burials. It was only in 1949 that a scientific attempt was made by Krishnaswami to classify them, largely on surface indications. But this classification is again fraught with difficulties because of the variation between the surface indication and the plan actually revealed by the excavations. Thus what appears as a stone circle or a cairn circle on the surface may, on excavation, reveal a pit, a sarcophagus, or an urn. Again, a cist circle may have a cist with or without a porthole, contain a transept or a passage chamber. Broadly speaking cairn circles are found in Vidarbha, while in lower Deccan and the rest of peninsular India there is a bewildering variety of such tombs: cairn circles, cist circles including the transepted variety and the passage chambers, pit circles, menhirs and alignments, urn burials, dolmenoid cists, hat stones or mushroom-shaped umbrella stones, hood stones and rock-cut underground caves with single or multiple chambers (catacomb tombs). Of these, the last three types were peculiar to Kerala, the passage-chamber tombs are mostly confined to northern Karnataka (Sundara, 1975) and the cists of the transepted variety to the Pudukkottai region in Tamil Nadu. In the extra-peninsular region are found cists, stone circles, cairns and menhirs.

Megaliths have a widespread distribution both in Europe and in Asia. The striking similarities in structural form, and the use of large stones, particularly for tombs, in disparate regions, may possibly argue for a common source at least of the concept. However, the associated cultural remains, including the age of the megalithic burials in Europe, India and East and South-East Asia, are different. The European megaliths belong to the Neolithic and Chalcolithic assemblages, falling between c. 5000 and 2000 BC, while those of India belong to the Iron Age, within the first millennium BC, and those of east and south Asia began essentially with the Bronze Age and continued till the beginning of the Iron Age, covering a period of c. eighth to third century BC.

The first diagnostic trait of the Megalithic culture of South India is a widely familiar dual-tone ceramic, known as the black-and-red ware, and plentiful use of iron. There are in addition four other associated ceramics, all-black ware, red ware, micaceous red ware, and the russet-coated white-painted ware. Among these, the micaceous ware, occasionally painted in black with linear designs, is mostly found in the megalithic burials of the Vidarbha region, while the russet-coated ware decorated with rectilinear or slightly curvilinear patterns in kaoline is known principally in the Coimbatore region with limited occurrence in other areas as well. The remaining two, the black-and-red ware and the all-black ware, are found throughout the peninsula. A related ceramic, however, is the black-and-red ware with white paintings associated with megalithic monuments in the southern parts of the peninsula in the Madural and Tirunelveli Districts. On some pots graffiti, including potter's marks, occur. Various theories have been propounded about their meaning but their real purpose still eludes us. At the same time studies have shown that a large number of such symbols are common on the pottery of the Harappan, Chalcolithic and Megalithic cultures (B. B. Lal, 1962).

The other distinctive trait of this culture is the use of iron. The range of objects included swords, daggers, barbed and tanged arrowheads, lances, flanged spears, axes with cross bands, chisels, saucers, frying pans, lamps, nails, sickles, hoes and so on. One of the excavated burials in Vidarbha (Mahurjhari) yielded a complete horse head made of copper sheet with iron-rivetted knobs stitched over leather. Copper, bronze, gold and silver were also used for ornaments and other less essential objects. Among personal ornaments are beads of semi-precious stones, including the etched variety in carnelian.

It is a curious paradox that a people with such an advanced knowledge of sepulchral architecture should have left very little trace of their domestic architecture, which is reflected only by floors occasionally with postholes, which suggest modest timber constructions.

Of the extra-peninsular megaliths and those of the Vindhyan region, excavations at Burzahom and Gufkral have indicated the association of iron (without the distinctive black-and-red ware) with the menhirs, which were found to be non-sepulchral. Similarly, excavations of some of the megalithic tombs in District Allahabad have established the presence of iron. In the same Vindhyan region (Districts Mirzapur and Varanasi), however, iron was not recorded in the megalithic burials, which nevertheless show a typological likeness to those of District Allahabad and of the peninsula, being cists and cairns. On the other hand microliths and pottery, comparable with the Chalcolithic culture of central India (Mandal, 1972) have been obtained from this group. The excavated cist burials in District Almora have also established the presence of iron.

The megalithic builders have often been recognized as the primary speakers of the Dravidian language, based largely upon the concentration of their occurrence in the peninsula (Heimendorf, 1945), though some scholars postulate an Aryan origin for the south Indian megalithic (Parpola, 1973), basing their arguments on the horse-centred Early Iron Age graves of Caucasus and Luristan, including Necropolis B (c. 1000–800 BC) and those of south India, particularly the portholed tombs (Leshnik, 1974). The cairn burials of Baluchistan seem to provide a link in this chain, thus suggesting an overland diffusion. At the same time other scholars hold, with Sundara, that 'Indian megalithism was derived from the Mediterranean region via the coastal route' (Sundara, 1975), or agree with Leshnik (1974) that the ancestry of Indian megaliths seems to lie in Persia, linked to Caucasian influence.

Studies of the human remains obtained from some of the excavated burials (Zuckerman, 1930; Sarkar, 1960, 1972; Guptr and Dutta, 1962), indicate besides an autochthonous Australoid type, a brachy-mesocephalic people, similar to the Scythio-Iranian stock as encountered in Necropolis B and in the deposits of period III of Tepe Hissar. It is postulated that the great migration of these Scythio-Iranians took place between 2000 and 1000 BC from the Ukraine region. Studies of the head forms from the different types of megaliths have shown on the other hand that the jar burial people, like the one at Adichanallur in the extreme south, appear to possess head forms falling within the dolichocranial range verging towards the hyperdolichocephalic. The megalithic builders seem to be a hybrid population.

As regards chronology, the Megalithic culture of peninsular India overlaps in the initial stage with the Chalcolithic-Neolithic and in the terminal stage with the deposits ascribable to the beginning of the Christian era, yielding inter alia securely dated Roman denarii and rouletted ware. The overlap phase of the Neolithic-Megalithic culture has, at one of the excavated sites in Karnataka (Hallur), been dated, on the basis of ¹⁴C determinations, to c. 1000 BC, which is also supported by six thermoluminescense dates from another site in the same region (Komaranhalli) with a time-range of 1400–900 BC. The Megalithic culture in south India, therefore, endured for nearly a thousand years – the first millennium BC. Within this time-span, two main phases (1100–500 and 500–100 BC) have been postulated (McIntosh, 1985). For the Vindhyan megaliths, ¹⁴C determinations indicate a range 270 ± 150 BC. The menhirs of the Kashmir Valley (both at Burzahom and Gufkral) are also assignable to the first millennium BC, as they succeed the Neolithic occupation of the site.

During the last four decades or so, megalithic burials have been excavated in all parts of India, particularly in the south. Typologically, they consisted of cairn circles (some containing terracotta sarcophagi), burial urns, stone circles, kodaikal, pit circles and cist circles with portholes, passage-chamber tombs and menhirs (Thapar, 1985). Among these, the burials of south India invariably indicated the use of black-and-red ware besides other wares and iron. The associated human skeletal material in a few cases showed extended articulated skeletons, but generally consisted of secondary burials of more than one individual, bundled together in the same grave representing something like a family ossuary or vault. The presence of iron is attested in the stone circles excavated in the Allahabad District of the Vindhyan region, but not in the graves in the same region. In the extra-peninsular region iron was found in the associated deposits of the menhirs of Burzahom and Gufkral, which incidentally did not contain any sepulchral remains.

The Painted Grey Ware Culture (Map 17)

In north India, particularly in the Indo-Gangetic divide and the upper Gangetic basin, painted grey ware appears in the first half of the first millennium BC, when the use of iron was introduced. The present-day distribution of this ware covers the dried-up valley of Sarasvati, including the Bahawalpur area in Pakistan, Punjab, Haryana, western Uttar Pradesh and the adjoining areas of Rajasthan, corresponding to the areas occupied by the Kuru-Pancalas, Surasenas and Matsyas, mentioned in the later Vedic texts and the Mahabharata (Sharma, 1985) and as far south as Ujjain in Madhya Pradesh. The occurrence of some sites has also been reported from as far west as Lakhio Pir in Sind and Harappa in southern Punjab, both in Pakistan (B. B. Lal, 1992). However, most interesting is the discovery of this ware at Thapli on the bank of Alaknanda in District Tehri, Uttar Pradesh, which takes the Painted Grey Ware culture right into the Himalayas. The sites of this culture are located along river banks. The distinctive features of the ware are the superior quality of the paste formed of well-levigated clay and the fine thin well-burnt fabric. On the grey surface of the body are painted linear and dotted patterns in black. Instances of red-on-grey and black-on-black and bichrome painted designs are also attested. The types represented are straight-sided bowls, cups and dishes with incurved sides and saggar bases and occasionally smaller vases. Amongst unusual shapes, special mention may be made of corrugated stems from Hastinapura and Atranjikhera which may have formed part of a dish-on-stand, and a strap handle from Sardargarh. The distribution of the painted grey ware as well as its stratigraphical position in the cultural history of India has given it considerable significance, being one of the dominant ceramic industries of the interregnum following the end of the Indus civilization. Notwithstanding its standardized table-ware character, no urban connotation is discernible in the material culture associated with it. In this context it is important to note that the ware formed 10 to 15 per cent of the ceramic assemblage of any excavated site. The majority of the associated ceramic was of red ware. The material equipment of the people using this ware was none too rich. The houses were generally made of adobe in the wattle-and-daub technique. But sometimes mudbricks have also been reported, but not their size. At Bhagwanpura a house plan has been identified with as many as thirteen rooms. The use of kiln-burnt bricks is also attested at a few sites, the recovered pieces being too fragmentary to indicate the complete size. The impact of iron does not appear to have brought any catalytic change in the economy of the people nor contributed sub-

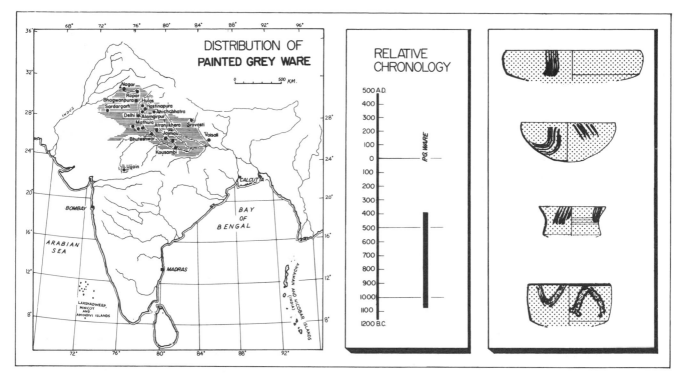

Map 17 Post-Indus civilization: distribution of Painted Grey Ware.

stantially to the specialization of handicrafts. Most of the iron artefacts found from the Painted Grey Ware levels comprise arrowheads, spearheads, sickles, supplemented by nails, pins, hooks, knives, chisels and so on. The social and economic pattern remained rural. It is reasonable to argue, therefore, that though the use of iron may have started around 1000 BC, its industrial use came only around the seventh-sixth century BC leading to urbanization in northern India. Although iron had come into use during the Painted Grey Ware period, copper was still an indispensable material.

The credit for bringing the upper Ganga-Jamuna Valley under large-scale cultivation goes to the Painted Grey Ware people. The subsistence economy was based on agriculture and cattle breeding. Rice seems to have been one of the staple cereals, although evidence of wheat and barley has also been attested, which would indicate that people had begun to grow two crops a year. The horse was known to them, from which one might infer the use of chariots. For their subsistence they depended on domesticated animals such as cattle, buffalo, pig, goat and dog. Besides the introduction of iron, the Painted Grey Ware people were also responsible for bringing in glass technology, as attested by the occurrence of glass bangles and beads. Other associated finds of this period consisted of bone objects, terracotta human and animal figurines and dice and gamesmen.

As to the date of this ware, ^{14}C determinations from different levels of occupation are available from eleven sites, and range between 1025 and 350 BC. On a closer analysis of these determinations, discounting the untenable ones, it is observed that most of them are concentrated between 900 and 400 BC. Notwithstanding this, the excavator of Hastinapura has assigned the beginning of this ware to *c.* 1100 BC (B. B. Lal, 1955) and that of Atranjikhera (Gaur, 1983*b*) to *c.* 1200 BC. Accordingly the Painted Grey Ware levels in the iron-using sites of the upper Ganga-Jamuna basin may broadly be dated between 1100 and 700 BC. The ware has recently been found to overlap with an amalgam of the late Harappan phase on some sites in Haryana and Punjab (such as

Bhagwanpura, Dadheri and Sanghol) in non-iron contexts, which may perhaps support the early dates proposed above whereby the pre-iron phase, which has yet to be firmly established, may well antedate 1100 BC (B. B. Lal, 1992).

Primarily on the basis of its distribution in the area coterminous with the land of Brahmavarta or Brahmarshi-desha, held holy in Aryan literature, postulations have been made linking the ware with the coming of the Aryans (B. B. Lal, 1955) into India. To which wave of the movement of the Indo-Aryans the painted grey ware belongs still requires to be established. In this context the date of the pottery is important. The material equipment which included the painted grey ware, particularly the iron phase, is comparable on many counts to the material culture of the later Vedic texts (Brahmanic-cum-Upanishadic period), which included the beginnings of territorial state formation, the advent of social stratification, the emergence of administrative machinery and so on. There seems to be an overall concordance between the later Vedic-cum-early Brahmanic period on the one hand and the upper Ganga-Jamuna Valley stage of the Painted Grey Ware culture on the other (B. B. Lal, 1992). The Rigvedic people were mostly pastoral and did not know the use of either iron or glass as opposed to the Painted Grey Ware people who used both and were a fully-fledged agrarian society. Furthermore, the painted grey ware had a distinct influence on the later ceramic industries of northern India, such as the northern black polished ware, and more importantly perhaps brought northern India to the threshold of what is known as the second urbanization.

Seen in the present context painted grey ware seems to be unconnected with the relics of any previous culture known in India. It is reasonable to argue that its authors did not spring out of Indian soil. As regards its links further west, the painted grey ware can be compared with the assemblage of the Gandhāra Grave culture of the Swat Valley in Pakistan, which indicated two waves of movement of the people using the grey ware, the first being associated with copper and bronze, and the second with iron. No specific resemblances have, however, been noticed in the shapes represented in the two respective wares: the distinctive type of the Gandhāran Grave culture is the tall pedestalled vase while that of the painted grey ware is the dish or thali, although flat-bottomed vases occurred during the period of the second wave of people, who used fractional burials.

Comparing the two assemblages, that is the painted grey ware of the Ganga-Yamuna *doab* and that of the Gandhāra Grave culture of the Swat Valley, Dani (1967) postulated that it might not be improper to seek the origin of the former in the development of the grey ware of the Gandhāra Grave culture in the as yet unexplored intervening plains between the Indus and the Beas. According to him, 'a definite answer to this question will be provided only when our investigations are extended into Punjab, east of the River Indus' (Dani, 1967, p. 55).

In this context it is worthwhile to record the up-to-date evidence. On the Indian side, the occurrence of this ware has been traced up to Gharinda in Punjab near the Indo-Pakistan border. Persistent explorations in the Pakistani part of Punjab, east of the River Indus, have now resulted in the discovery of sites at Dhok Gangal and Dheri Qila near Chaklala airport, adjacent to the Islamabad highway, 'yielding grey ware associated with red ware with impressed designs which can be related with the Painted Grey Ware of the Hakra River in Punjab' (Salim, 1992, pp. 37, 48). At the present stage the evidence seems to be indicative rather than proven since the classical painted grey ware with characteristic paintings has still not been found. Since, however, the above-mentioned sites lie in the area of spread of the Gandhāra Grave culture, what is needed is a more intensive survey followed by excavation to establish the correlation between the two cultures.

LITERARY EVIDENCE

Another valuable source which can be profitably tapped for information regarding the post-Harappan period is ancient Indian literature. This literature was composed by a people who called themselves 'Arya' (noble) as opposed to the local *dasa* or *dasyu* (slave) and passed it on for many centuries in an oral form. It goes back to the oldest surviving text, the *samhita* or compilation of the hymns of the *Rigveda*. A reasonable estimate of the antiquity of many of the individual hymns is that they extended over several previous centuries. The *samhitas* of the other Vedas, the *Yajur, Soma* and *Atharva*, and the subsequent literature generally classified as late Vedic may be taken to belong to the subsequent seven centuries or so. Thus there are well over a thousand years for which there is textual evidence, though of a limited sort.

The *Rigveda* is a curious document. In length it is approximately equal to the *Iliad* and *Odyssey* together, and consists of over a thousand poems or 'hymns'. These vary from more or less epic chants, hymns of praise and prayers to the gods, to magic spells and fragments of popular songs, all of varying standards – 'sometimes true, genuine and even sublime, but frequently childish, vulgar and obscure', as Max Müller remarks (quoted: Piggott, 1950, pp. 256–7; cf. Müller, 1956, p. 26). The language is elaborate and self-consciously literary and the metrical composition, based on syllabic verse forms, is often extremely complicated. By far the greater part of the *Rigveda* consists of invocations of the many gods of the Vedic pantheon and scarcely more than forty hymns are found which are not directly addressed to these deities. From these materials, it is obvious that conclusions can be drawn

only with much caution.

Although it is difficult to arrive at any definite conclusion regarding the original home of these 'Aryas', generally referred to as Indo-Aryans, we are in a somewhat better position in respect of their early settlements in northern India and Pakistan and their gradual expansion over the whole of this area. For this the evidence of the Vedic literature comes to our aid. Fortunately, the *Rigveda* contains abundant geographical data which can be tied up here and there with current geographical names. Rivers, for instance, have all along played an important part in the lives of the Hindus, and even in the *Rigvedic* age they were esteemed as deities, presumably on account of the immense benefits they conferred on humanity. Out of the thirty-one rivers mentioned in the Vedic texts, about twenty-five names occur in the hymns of the *Rigveda* alone. In the celebrated *Nadistuti* the *Rigveda* enumerates several streams most of which belong to the Indus system.

Of the five streams, that is the Sutudri, Vipas, Parushni, Asikni and Vitasta, which gave Punjab its name and united together flowed into the Indus, the *Nadistuti* omits the Vipas and inserts the Marudvridha. The Sutudri is the most easterly river of the Punjab, identified with the modern Sutlej. Parushni, the modern Ravi, was an important stream which played a decisive part in the *Dasarajña* (battle of ten kings), by rising and drowning the enemies of Sudas. Asikni, known later as the Chandrabhaga, is the modern Chenab in the Punjab. Finally comes Vitasta, the most westerly of these rivers, known today as the Jhelum. Of the western tributaries of the Indus, the *Rigveda* mentions the Kubha (Kabul), Krumu (Kurrum), Gomati (Gomal), Suvastu (Swat) and Gauri (Panjkhora). The word *suvastu* signifying 'fair dwellings' seems to indicate that there were Aryan settlements along its banks. The River Rasa has been identified with the Jaxartes, a stream in the extreme north-west of the Vedic territory. Outside the Indus basin are mentioned the Rivers Ganga, Yamuna and Sarasvati. The Ganga does not appear to be a well-known or even important stream in the period of the *Rigveda*. The Yamuna was mentioned only thrice but the Sarasvati is the river *par excellence*, frequently mentioned in the Vedic texts. As the names of the rivers in the *Rigveda* show, the Vedic people knew the whole of the Punjab and occupied the best part of it. It was probably there that most of the Vedic hymns were composed.

The whole territory known to Vedic settlers was divided into a number of tribal principalities ruled by kings. The one great historical event which reveals itself in the fragmentary allusions of the *Samhits* is the contest known as 'the battle of the ten kings', referred to above. The most probable version of that conflict is that it was a contest between the Bharatas, settled in the country later known as Brahmavarta, and the tribes of the north-west. The Bharata king was Sudas, of the Tritsu family, and his domestic priest, who celebrates according to tradition the victory in three hymns, was Vasishtha. The sage had superseded in that high office his predecessor Visvamitra under whose guidance the Bharatas had earlier fought successfully against their enemies on the Vipas and Sutudri – whereupon a long and bitter rivalry ensued between the two priests, and in revenge Visvamitra led a tribal confederacy of ten kings against the Bharatas, only to meet with utter disaster in the waters of the Parushni.

Of the ten tribes five are of little note. These were the Alinas, perhaps from the north-east of Kafiristan, the Pakthas, whose name recalls the modern Pakhtun, the Bhalanas, possibly connected with Bolan Pass, the Sivas from near the Indus and the Vishanins. Better known in the *Rigveda* are the other five, the Anus who dwelt on the Parushni, the Druhyas who were closely associated with them, the Turvasa and Yadus, two allied tribes, and the Purus, dwellers on either side of the Sarasvati, and therefore probably close neighbours of the Bharatas. As a result of the battle the Anu and Druhya kings were drowned and Purukutsa of the Purus met his death. There was another war that Sudas had to fight in which three non-Aryan tribes, the Ajas, Sigrus and Yakshus, united under King Bheda but suffered defeat with great slaughter on the Yamuna.

The king was pre-eminently the war lord and the *Rigveda* gives some idea of the mode of warfare. The king and his nobles fought from chariots, and the common people on foot. As in later days, we hear of martial music and banners in connection with battle. The principal weapon was the bow and arrow. The arrows were tipped with points of metal or poisoned horn. Other weapons were lances, spears, axes, swords and sling stones. The king was assisted by two assemblies called *sabha* and *samita*. Great importance was attached not only to concord between the king and the Assembly but also to a spirit of harmony among the members of the Assembly. A hymn of the *Rigveda* invokes such a unity: 'Assemble, speak together, let your minds, be all of one Accord.'

The royal authority was to some extent curbed by the power and prestige of the priest (*Purohita*) who accompanied the king to battle and helped him with prayers and spells. The Aryans did not have an advanced economic system and relied for their unit of value and means of barter on the unwieldy cow. The *nishka*, a term later used for a gold coin, is also mentioned as a sort of currency, but at that time it was probably a gold ornament of some kind. There is no evidence of a regular class of merchants or money-lenders, though indebtedness is sometimes referred to.

The immigrant Aryans had to wage bitter and prolonged fights with the indigenous people. But there was no attempt at the extermination of the conquered foes. Theft, burglary, highway robbery and cheating (chiefly at gambling) are among the crimes recorded, cattle lifting at night being a frequent one. Marriage of brother and sister was looked upon as incest. Tying the criminal to a stake was a common form of punishment. The Aryans were in fact a wild, turbulent people and had few of the taboos of later India. They were much addicted to inebriating drinks of which they had at least two, *soma* and *sura*. *Soma* was drunk at sacrifices and its use was sanctioned by religion. *Sura* was purely secular, and was evidently very potent: in some passages it is mentioned with disapproval by the priestly poets.

Among their chief gods was Dyaus, a personification of the sky and identical with the Greek Zeus. Varuna is the upholder of the physical and moral order symbolized in nature (*rita*). He is also called the *Asura*. This aspect of Varuna goes back at least to the Indo-Iranian period since Ahura Mazdah (the wise spirit of the *Avesta*) agrees with Asura-Varuna in character. Surya is the most concrete of the solar deities. As the all-seeing god, he is often called the eyes of Mitra, Varuna, Agni and other gods. The dawn produces Surya and he is said to be the son of the goddess Aditi and Dyaus. Savitra is pre-eminently a golden deity. His eyes, arms, hands and tongue are golden. Pushan is a god with a very vague personality. The greatest god of the *Rigveda* is Indra to whom about one quarter of the hymns are addressed. He is the apotheosis of the Aryan battle leader, strong-armed, colossal, tawny-bearded and pot-bellied from drinking. He wields the thunderbolt and fights like a hero with bow and arrows from his chariot. He is a cattle raider, a destroyer of

enemy strongholds and a victorious leader of the Aryans in their conquest of the hated aboriginal population of the Punjab. With him fight the young warrior bands, the Maruts, who seem to be commanded by Rudra, rival to Indra and yet in some ways his counterpart.

The despicable enemies who dare deny Indra's supremacy are referred to as *dasa* or *dasyu*. They have a black complexion, flat noses and they are indifferent to the gods. They do not perform the Aryan sacrifices and probably worship the phallus. But they are wealthy with great stores of gold and live in fortified strongholds. One such stronghold is Hariyupiya, identified with modern Harappa.

As in all simple pastoral societies, the Aryan vocabulary is rich in names for every aspect of the herds of cattle. Milk evidently formed an important item of diet. The cows were milked three times a day and castration was practised. Beef was freely eaten as the main meal dish; slaying cows for guests was an attribute of highest praise and Indra was champion beef eater. Mutton and goat flesh were also eaten. Leather was used for many purposes such as strings, bow-strings, chariot traces, reins and whips. The grain grown seems likely to have been barley. The ripe ears of barley were cut with a knife or sickle, bound into sheaves, strewn on a threshing floor, and eventually winnowed or sifted to separate the grain from the chaff.

Some form of container or measure was used for which the word *urdara* is used. Fields were tilled by an ox-drawn plough, though the yoke is nowhere mentioned in the *Rigveda* in this connection. Dogs were used for guarding houses and for boar hunting. The horse was the characteristic domesticated animal of the Aryans. The Aryan horses seem to have been used essentially as chariot animals, whether in warfare or for chariot racing, which was a favourite sport.

Practically nothing can be gleaned from the *Rigveda* about the appearance or layout of an Aryan settlement or of the houses, mainly because such mundane affairs did not lend themselves to metaphors in hymns to the war-gods. All the Aryan buildings, however, appear to have been of wood, and the house seems to have been rectangular, with a thatched roof, divided into more than one room or compartment. The central hearth in an Aryan house had a position of special importance, and was the focus of the household religious rite. Little again can be gathered of clothing, except that it was mainly of woollen cloth. Clothes that were either embroidered or woven in ornamental patterns were worn by women, and a cloak or mantle was worn probably by both sexes. Specialized crafts within the community include that of the metalsmith and the carpenter working with an axe or adze and making fine carved woodwork for chariots. No direct mention of a potter occurs. Bronze seems to have been the only metal worked; it follows that copper must also have been used. Household utensils such as kettles were made of metal (*ayas*). What metal the *ayas* was is uncertain, though the word is cognate with the German *eisen* and the English *iron* and is also akin to the Latin *aes* meaning bronze. Its colour is to be inferred from the epithets used, such as reddish, which seems to be a reference to bronze.

It is unfortunate that no written records have come to light from excavations to supply names for different cultural materials. Nor is there anything in the Vedic literature to show that the Indo-Aryan peoples possessed a specific material culture, special pottery, or particular figurines or objects, which being discovered in the field would enable us to establish some kind of identification marks for their migration. As for the sacrificial rites that are the very subject of these ancient texts, they do not imply the building of special monuments, which would be useful as a landmark for archaeologists. And yet there is enough in the *Rigveda* to show that no relationship existed between the mature Harappan cultural milieu and the habitation pattern of the Aryans as described in it. The *Rigveda*, for instance, attests that the horse was a favourite animal of the Aryans, but this is precisely the animal which has not been reported from the mature Harappan levels. In the Late or post-Harappan contexts, however, the horse is abundantly evidenced and this seems to be the period which roughly marks the advent of the Aryans in the Indus basin. It follows therefore that many of the mature Harappan cultural traits, such as town planning and writing, had already been forgotten before the Aryans made the Indus basin their permanent home. Being a pastoral people they were not in need of them, hence they never tried to revive them.

BIBLIOGRAPHY

AGRAWAL, R. C.; KUMAR, V. 1982. Ganeshwar-Jodhpura Culture: New Traits in Indian Archaeology. In: POSSEHL, G. L. (ed.), *Harappan Civilization: A Contemporary Perspective.* New Delhi. pp. 125–34.

ALLCHIN, B; ALLCHIN, R. 1982. *The Rise of Civilization in India and Pakistan.* Cambridge.

ANSARI, Z. D.; DHAVALIKAR, M. K. 1975. *Excavations at Kayatha.* Poona.

ANTONINI, C. S.; STACUL, G. 1972. *The Protohistoric Graveyards of Swat.* Roma.

BANERJEE, N. R. 1965. The Iron Age in India. In: MISHRA, V. N.; MATE, M. S. (eds), *Indian Prehistory: 1964.* Poona.

—— 1986. *Nagda 1955–57.* New Delhi. (Mem. Archaeol. Surv. India, 85.)

CASAL, J. M. 1961. *Fouilles de Mundigak.* Paris.

—— 1964. *Fouilles d'Amri.* Paris.

CHAKRABARTI, D. K. 1976. The Beginning of Iron in India. *Antiq.* (Cambridge), No. 50, pp. 114–24.

—— 1981–3. Study of the Iron Age in India. *Archaeol. perspect. India Indep.*, No. 13–14, pp. 81–96.

CHATTOPADHYAYA, B. D. 1975–6. Indian Archaeology and the Indian Tradition. *Puratattva* (New Delhi), No. 8, pp. 67–72.

CHATURVEDI, S. N. 1985. Advances of Vindhyan Neolithic and Chalcolithic Cultures to the Himalayan Tarai: Excavation and Exploration in the Sarayyapara Region of Uttar Pradesh. *Man Environ.* (Ahmedabad), No. 9, pp. 101–8.

COMPAGNONI, B. 1979. Preliminary Report on the Faunal Remains from Protohistoric Settlements of Swat. In: TADDEI, M. (ed.), *South Asian Archaeology, 1977.* Napoli. pp. 697 ff.

CONSTANTINI, L. 1979. Notes on the Palaeoethnobotany of Protohistorical Swat. In: TADDEI, M. (ed.), *South Asian Archaeology, 1977.* Napoli. Vol. 2, pp. 703 ff.

DANI, A. H. 1967. Timargarh and Gandhāra Grave Culture. *Anc. Pakistan* (Peshwar), No. 3, pp. 1–407.

—— 1992. Pastoral-Agricultural Tribes of Pakistan in the Post-Indus Period. In: DANI, A. H.; MASSON, V. M. (eds), *History of Civilizations of Central Asia.* Paris. Vol. 1, pp. 395–420.

DASGUPTA, P. C. 1964. *The Excavations at Pandu Rajar Dhibi.* Calcutta.

DE CARDI, B. 1951. A New Prehistoric Ware from Baluchistan. *Iraq* (London), Vol. 13, pt 2.

DEO, S. B.; ANSARI, Z. D. 1965. *Chalcolithic Chandoli.* Poona.

DEO, S. B.; DHAVALIKAR, M. K.; ANSARI, Z. D. 1979. *Apegon Excavations, 1976.* Poona.

DHAVALIKAR, M. K.; SANKALIA, H. D.; ANSARI, Z. D. 1988. *Excavations at Inamgaon.* Poona.

FRANK-FORT, H. P.; POTTIER, M. N. 1978. Sondage préliminaire sur l'établissement proto-historique Harappéen et post-Harappéen

de Shortugai. *Arts asiat.* (Paris), No. 34, pp. 29–86.

GAUR, R. C. 1973. Lal Qila Excavation and OCP Problem. In: AGRAWAL, O. P.; GOSH, A. (eds), *Radiocarbon and Indian Archaeology.* Bombay. pp. 154–62.

—— 1983a. The Aryans – A Fresh Appraisal. *Puratattva* (New Delhi), No. 12.

—— 1983b. *Excavations at Atranjikhera.* New Delhi.

GUPTA, P. C.; DUTTA, P. C. 1962. Human Remains Excavated from Megaliths at Yelleshwaram (Andhra Pradesh). *Man India*, Vol. 42, No. 1, pp. 19–34.

HEGDE, K. T. M. 1973. A Model for Understanding Ancient Indian Metallurgy. *Man* (London), No. 8, pp. 416–21.

HEIMENDORF, C. von F. 1945. The Problem of Megalithic Cultures in Middle India. *Man India*, Vol. 25, pp. 73–86.

HUXTABLE, F. et al. 1972. Thermoluminescent Dates for Ochre Coloured Pottery from India. *Antiq.* (Cambridge), Vol. 46, No. 181, pp. 62–3.

INDIAN ARCHAEOLOGY, A Review/(IAR) 1960a. *Excavation at Bahurupa and Savalda, District West Khandesh.* New Delhi. pp. 34–7.

—— 1960b. *Excavation at Gilund, District Udaipur.* New Delhi. pp. 41–6.

—— 1967a. *Excavation at Noh, District Bharatpur.* New Delhi. pp. 28–9.

—— 1967b. *Excavation at Mahisdal, District Birbhum.* New Delhi. pp. 59–60.

—— 1967–78. *Excavation at Chirand, District Saran.* New Delhi.

—— 1985. *Excavation at Kheradih, District Ballia.* New Delhi. pp. 92–4.

JARRIGE, J. H. 1979. *Fouilles de Pirak.* Paris.

JETTMAR, K. 1967. Iron Cheek Piece of a Snaffle Found at Timargarh. *Anc. Pakistan* (Peshwar), Vol. 3, pp. 203–9.

JOSHI, M. C. 1975–6. Archaeology and Indian Tradition: Some Observations. *Puratattva* (New Delhi), No. 8, pp. 98–102.

KAJALE, M. D. 1989. Archaeological Investigation on Megalithic Bhagimohari, and its Significance for Ancient Indian Agricultural Systems. *Man Environ.* (Ahmedabad), Vol. 13, pp. 87–100.

KEITH, A. B. 1912. *Vedic Index of Names and Subjects.* Cambridge.

KHAZANCHI, T. N.; DIKSHIT, K. N. 1977–8. The Grey Ware Culture of Northern Pakistan, Jammu and Kashmir and Panjab. *Puratattva* (New Delhi), No. 9, pp. 47–51.

KIM, BYUNG-MO (ed.). 1982. *Megalithic Cultures in Asia.* Seoul.

KRISHNASWAMI, V. D. 1949. Megalithic Types of South India. *Anc. India* (New Delhi), No. 5, pp. 35–45.

KUMAR, V. 1971–2. The Discovery of Ochre Coloured Pottery from Noh, District Bharatpur. *Puratattva* (New Delhi), No. 5, pp. 43–4.

LAL, B. B. 1951. Further Copper Hoards from the Gangetic Basin and a Review of the Problem. *Anc. India* (New Delhi), No. 7, pp. 20–39.

—— 1955. Excavation at Hastinapura and other Explorations in the Upper Ganga and Sutlet Basins 1950–52. *Anc. India* (New Delhi), Nos. 10–11, pp. 4–151.

—— 1962. From the Megalithic to the Harappan: Tracing Back the Graffiti on the Pottery. *Anc. India* (New Delhi), No. 16, pp. 4–24.

—— 1971–2. A Note on the Excavation at Saipai. *Puratattva* (New Delhi), No. 5, pp. 46–9.

—— 1972. The Copper Hoard Culture of the Ganga Valley. *Antiq.* (Cambridge), Vol. 46, No. 184, pp. 282–7.

—— 1977–8. Chronology and Painted Grey Ware. *Puratattva* (New Delhi), No. 9, pp. 64–83.

—— 1992. The Painted Grey Ware Culture of the Iron Age. In: DANI, A. H.; MASSON, V. M. (eds), *History of Civilizations of Central Asia.* Paris. Vol. 1, pp. 421–40.

LAL, M. 1983. Copper Hoard Culture of India: A Reassessment. *Puratattva* (New Delhi), No. 12, pp. 65–77.

LESHNIK, L. 1974. *South Indian 'Megalithic' Burials: The Padunkal Complex.* Wiesbaden.

MCINTOSH, J. R. 1985. Dating the South Indian Megaliths. In: *South Asian Archaeology, 1983.* Napoli. pp. 487–93.

MACKAY, E. J. H. 1943. *Chanhu-daro Excavations, 1935–36.* New Haven, Conn. (Am. Orient. Ser., 20.)

MAJUMDAR, N. G. 1934. *Explorations in Sind.* Calcutta. (Mem. Archaeol. Surv. India, 48.)

MAJUMDAR, R. C. (ed.) 1951. *The History and Culture of the Indian People: Vedic Age.* London.

MANDAL, D. 1972. *Radiocarbon Dates and Indian Archaeology.* Allahabad.

MUGHAL, M. R. 1992. Jhukar and the Late Harappan Cultural Mosaic of the Greater Indus Valley. In: JARRIGE, C. (ed.), *South Asian Archaeology, 1991.* Madison, Wis. pp. 213–21.

MÜLLER, M. 1956. *The Vedas,* ed. U. N. GHOSHAL. Calcutta.

PARPOLA, A. 1973. *Arguments for an Aryan Origin of the South Indian Megaliths.* Madras.

PIGGOTT, S. 1950. *Prehistoric India.* Harmondsworth.

POSSEHL, G. I. 1961. *Ancient Cities of the Indus.* New Delhi.

RAPSON, E. J. (ed.) 1955. *The Cambridge History of India.* Cambridge. Vol. 1.

SALI, S. A. 1986. *Daimabad, 1976–79.* New Delhi. (Mem. Archaeol. Surv. India, 83.)

SALIM, M. 1992. Archaeological Exploration in Punjab NWFP, Pakistan. *J. cent. Asia* (Islamabad), Vol. 15, No. 1, pp. 34–77.

SANKALIA, H. D. 1972–73. The Cemetery H Culture. *Puratattva* (New Delhi), No. 6, pp. 12–19.

—— 1975–6. Prehistoric Colonization in India: Archaeological and Literary Evidence. *Puratattva* (New Delhi), No. 8, pp. 72–86.

SANKALIA, H. D.; ANSARI, Z. D.; DHAVALIKAR, M. K. 1971. Inamgaon: Chalcolithic Settlements in Western India. *Asian Perspect.* (Honolulu, HI), Vol. 14, pp. 139–46.

SANKALIA, H. D.; DEO, S. B. 1955. *Report on the Excavations at Nasik and Jorwe.* Poona.

SANKALIA, H. D.; DEO, S. B.; ANSARI, Z. D. 1969. *Excavation at Ahar (Tambavati).* Poona.

SANKALIA, H. D.; SUBBRAO, B.; DEO, S. B. 1958. *The Excavations at Maheswar and Navdatoli, 1952–53.* Poona.

SANKALIA, H. D. et al. 1960. *From History to Pre-History at Nevasa (1954–56).* Poona.

SANTONI, M. 1984. Sibri and the South Cemetery of Mehrgarh: Third Millennium Connections between the Northern Kachi Plain (Pakistan) and Central Asia. In: ALLCHIN, B. (ed.), *South Asian Archaeology, 1981.* Cambridge. pp. 52–60.

SARKAR, S. S. 1960. Human Skeletal Remains from Brahmagiri. *Bull. Dep. Anthropol.* (Calcutta), No. 1, pp. 5–25.

—— 1972. *Ancient Races of the Deccan.* New Delhi.

SHARMA, R. S. 1975–6. The Later Vedic Phase and the Painted Grey Ware Culture. *Puratattva* (New Delhi), No. 8, pp. 63–7.

—— 1985. *Material Culture and Social Formation in Ancient India.* New Delhi.

SINGH, P.; LAL, M. 1985. Narhan, 1983–5: A Preliminary Report of the Archaeological Excavations. *Bharati* (Varanasi), N.S., Vol. 3, pp. 113–44.

SINGH, U. V. 1976. Extension of the Chalcolithic Culture in the Betwa Valley. In:—— (ed.), *Archaeological Congress and Seminar: 1972.* Kurukshetra. pp. 63–8.

STACUL, G. 1966. Preliminary Report on the Pre-Buddhist Necropolises in Swat. *East West* (Roma), No. 16, pp. 37–79.

—— 1979. The Black-Burnished Ware Period in the Swat Valley (c. 1700–1500 BC). In: TADDEI, M. (ed.), *South Asian Archaeology, 1977.* Napoli. Vol. 2, p. 661.

—— 1984. Cultural Change in the Swat Valley and Beyond c. 3000–1400 BC. In: *South Asian Archaeology.* Napoli. pp. 205–12.

STEIN, A. 1937. *Archaeological Reconnaissance in North-West India and South-East Iran.* London.

SUNDARA, A. 1975. *The Early Chamber Tombs of South India: A Study of the Iron Age Megalithic Monuments of North Karnataka.* New Delhi.

SURAJ, B. 1971–2. Comments in the Seminar on OCP and NBP. *Puratattva* (New Delhi), No. 5, pp. 16–21.

THAPAR, B. K. 1967. Prakash 1955: A Chalcolithic Site in the Tapti Valley. *Anc. India* (New Delhi), Nos. 20–21, pp. 5–167.

—— 1981. The Archaeological Remains of the Aryans in North-Western India. In: ASINOV, M. S. et al. (eds), *Ethnic Problems of the History of Central Asia in the Early Period.* Moskva. pp. 295–300.

—— 1985. *Recent Archaeological Discoveries in India.* Paris, Tokyo, UNESCO, Centre for East Asian Cultural Studies.

THAPAR, R. 1975–6. Puranic Lineages and Archaeological Cultures. *Puratattva* (New Delhi), No. 8, pp. 86–98.

TUCC, G. 1977. On Swat. The Daids and Connected Problems. *East West* (Roma), Vol. 27, pp. 9–103.

TUSA, S. 1979. The Swat Valley in the 2nd and 1st Millennia BC: A Question of Marginality. In: TADDEI, M. (ed.), *South Asian Archaeology, 1977.* Napoli. Vol. 2, pp. 675 ff.

VATS, M. S. 1940. *Excavations at Harappa.* New Delhi.

WHEELER, R. E. M. 1968. *The Indus Civilization.* 3rd ed. Cambridge.

ZUCKERMAN, S. 1930. The Adichanallur Skulls. *Bull. Madras Gov. Mus.,* No. 2, pp. 1–24.

12.9
CHINA

12.9.1
CHINA (3000–1600 BC)

An Zhimin

THE HUANGHE VALLEY

The Huanghe Valley was the cradle of ancient Chinese civilization. Extending into north China, it covers an area of about 750,000 km², including the Loess Plateau in the west, the alluvial plain in the east, and the hilly land in the Shandong peninsula. As a region enjoying a markedly important position in the history of humanity, it emerged as remotely as the early Palaeolithic age and, as time went on, it displayed more and more obvious cultural continuity. Before about 6000 BC there had been well-developed farming and animal husbandry, and the early agricultural communities represented by the Peiligang, Cishan and Dadiwan cultures had appeared. Later on, the Yangshao and Longshan cultures rose one after another in one continuous line. The Late Neolithic Longshan culture witnessed the transition from a primitive community to the formation of a state, and the emergence of the Erlitou culture marked that final establishment of the Shang-Zhou civilization. Thereafter, during a long period reaching into historical times, the middle reaches of the Huanghe and other parts of the Central Plains constituted the political, economic and cultural centre of ancient China, and thus the Huanghe had an indissoluble connection with the birth of ancient Chinese civilization.

Taking the Huanghe Valley as the main centre of distribution, the Late Neolithic Longshan culture played an important role in cultural evolution and exchange. The Longshan culture developed with considerable regional diversity and its various manifestations should not be lumped together. On the other hand, although during this period in China's vast land there appeared numerous cultural complexes, which had their own characteristics and variations in social development, still, mutual influence and exchanges between them brought about a tendency to fusion and unification. The present chapter will give an introduction to China's Late Neolithic and Early Bronze Ages with stress on the cultural complexes of the Huanghe Valley, at the same time making references to those in the Changjiang middle and lower reaches, the south-eastern coastal region, the northern steppes and the south-western plateaus.

The middle reaches of the Huanghe

After the development and florescence of the Yangshao culture, lasting as long as over 2,000 years, the middle reaches of the Huanghe fostered an entirely new complex, the Longshan culture at about 3000 BC. From then on, great changes took place there not only in cultural aspects and economic development, but also in the social structure, which resulted in the disintegration of the long-prospering primitive communities. The Erlitou culture which followed, with its state organization, ushered in the early Shang civilization.

The Miaodigou II culture

The Miaodigou II culture was first identified at Miaodigou in Shaanxian County, Henan Province, in 1956; it was given the new name because of its transitional character from the Yangshao to the Longshan, and has generally been considered as an early Longshan complex. The culture is spread primarily over the borderland between Henan, Shanxi and Shaanxi Provinces, where the previous Yangshao culture makes the densest distribution. Stratigraphically, its layers have often been sandwiched between the lower Yangshao strata and the upper ones which belong to the Longshan culture, and thus their sequence has been clearly revealed. Radiocarbon analysis dates the Miaodigou culture to c. 3000–2700 BC, roughly between the radiocarbon dates of the Yangshao and Longshan.

Owing to the limitations of archaeological investigation, at present little is known about the layout of settlements of the culture, and the available data are mainly obtained from Miaodigou. Judging from the type-site, the house is round, semi-subterranean, with a flight of steps at the entrance, the floor filled with straw-tempered clay and then smoothly plastered with a limey substance, and with a semi-spherically concave fireplace in the western wall. In the centre of the floor there is the remains of a posthole which, together with some dozen others surrounding the house, indicates that the roof was presumably conical. Near the house are scattered a number of pocket-shaped storage pits, and a vertical pottery-making kiln in rather good condition. In the vicinity of the settlement there is a common cemetery, where 145 shaft graves of single burials have been uncovered in a regular arrangement, the dead being buried with the head pointing in the same direction and in general without any funerary objects, except for two graves each furnished with a small pottery cup of red clay ware. This picture is entirely different from that of Yangshao cemeteries which often yield multiple burials and fairly rich grave goods, and thus represents a change in funeral custom and probably reflects an alteration in social structure.

Farming was still the main economic practice but reached a higher level by comparison with the Yangshao culture. The implements of production consisted largely of ground-stone tools, with some new types coming into being. For example, among the cutting tools emerged a sort of thick axe, very useful for exploiting forests. For digging, apart from the stone spade, there was introduced the double-pronged wooden lei, which raised working efficiency in the sponge loess area; its traces have repeatedly been seen on the walls of ditches; in the historical period, it continued to be used for a long time. For harvesting, besides the chipped stone knife with a notch in both sides and the perforated rectangular stone knife, such as those used in the previous Yangshao culture, there was the perforated semi-lunar stone knife; stone and shell sickles were used more commonly than before. Domestic animals, too, began to increase both in species and in number; in addition to numerous pigs and dogs, goats made their appearance, marking the earliest recorded incidence so far in China. The improvement of farm tools and the increase of domestic animals indicate that the agricultural economy made greater progress at that time than in the Yangshao period.

In pottery making, changes are mainly represented by the emergence of grey-ware vessels in great quantities and the existence of red and black wares in small amounts. They are still handmade, but touched up along the rim on the turntable. Basket-marks are the commonest decorations on the surface, though cord impressions and appliquéd patterns can often be seen as well, while painted designs are rare and simple as a survived element of the Yangshao culture. The pottery shows great variety in form. There are the ding (tripod with solid feet), jia (tripod with thin hollow legs), fu (cauldron), stove, bowl, basin, pot, cup, dou (high-stemmed vessel), pointed-bottomed bottle and so on; a number of the types followed the shapes of Yangshao ones, particularly the cup, dou, pot and pointed-bottomed bottle. The hollow-legged tripod jia was an innovation; it was quite a convenient cooking vessel as it had a broader base in contact with the cooking fire, and was doubtless the prototype of the li (tripod with swollen hollow legs) prevalent in the Longshan culture. In sum, the pottery clearly shows its transitional character, building on the ceramics of the Yangshao culture, and heralding those of the Longshan culture. The Miaodigou II culture was undoubtedly one of the bases on which the more advanced Longshan culture made its appearance.

The Longshan culture

The Longshan culture derives its name from the remains found at Longshan town in Zhangqiu County, Shandong Province, in 1928; it is spread over a vast area, covering almost the entire middle and lower reaches of the Huanghe. As it has different regions of distribution and even various origins, it shows a striking disparity in its cultural aspects. Basically it can be divided into two complexes: the Central

Plains Longshan and the Shandong I Longshan. The former occurs in the middle reaches of the Huanghe and derives from the Miaodigou II culture, while the latter is spread over the lower reaches of the Huanghe and directly succeeds the Dawenkou culture. The present discussion is limited to the complex in the middle reaches of the Huanghe. Stratigraphical evidence obtained at Hougang near Anyang city, Henan Province, in 1931, led archaeologists for the first time to establish the chronological sequence that the Longshan followed the Yangshao and preceded the Shang civilization. According to ^{14}C dating, it goes back to c. 2600–2100 BC, approximately on the eve of the emergence of the state.

The remains of settlements are generally situated on terraces along small or medium rivers and often cover Yangshao or Miadigou layers, though some of them are away from rivers, perhaps due to the fact that the invention of well-sinking techniques ensured water supply. The sites are large in size, usually measuring over 100,000 m².

The largest Taosi site, in Xiangfen County, Shanxi Province, covers an area of 3 million m². The layout of the settlements, however, is not clear at present, though at the Baiying site in Tangyin County, Henan Province, within a space of 1,000 m² stand 46 houses, generally in rows from west to east and in lines from north to south. The building foundations are superimposed layer upon layer. The periodically accumulating deposit has made the whole site look like a raised platform. The houses of the Longshan culture vary in shape and can be roughly divided into three types: (1) a circular dwelling built above ground with walls of straw-tempered clay or adobe, inside or along the walls of which are often seen holes left by posts intended for reinforcing walls or supporting the roof. The interior floor is rammed and plastered with a thin layer of lime to prevent dampness. In the centre of the floor is a fireplace for cooking and warming; (2) the round or square semi-subterranean dwelling of which the floor is covered with a lime layer and has a fireplace in the centre. The postholes are, however, not clear. Instances of double-roomed houses are also available showing the northern wall higher than the others and with a row of postholes along the wall line; (3) the cave dwelling, round or square in plan, dug into the side of the loess terraces, with the upper part of the walls gently curving inward, forming a dome. In close vicinity to all the houses are arranged pits, usually for storage use. At Taosi a patch of lime plaster was found, showing geometric patterns, representing perhaps the remains of the wall plaster of a large house. A noteworthy structural feature was the occurrence of wells over 10 m deep, mostly with square protective timber walls. The introduction of well-sinking techniques provided an effective means of improving living conditions. It is no less significant that pottery kilns were rather common in settlements. At the Wangchenggang site in Dengfeng County and the Pingliangdui site in Huaiyang County, Henan Province, remains of castles measuring 10,000 to 50,000 m² enclosed by rammed-earth walls have also been brought to light, indicating that fortifications such as the castle and the like had already come into being.

The Longshan people in the middle reaches of the Huanghe buried some of their dead within the settlement itself. Children's burials, whether in pits or in urns, are often found near the house, even under the house foundations or in the wall foundations, indicating a special funeral custom. Common cemeteries are generally located near settlements, of which the largest was discovered at Taosi, situated to the south-east of the living quarters. Here, within a space of

5,000 m² have been excavated more than 1,300 rectangular graves of the pit-burial type. According to (a) the size of the pits, (b) the presence or absence of coffins, and (c) the quantity and quality of grave goods, the graves can be divided into three categories. The first type consists of large-sized graves about 3 m long and 2 m wide (Plate 109) containing coffins and a large quantity of grave goods consisting of pottery, including those painted after firing, painted wooden objects such as drums, stone chimes and jade objects. Complete skeletons of pigs are often deposited as mortuary offerings. Such graves have been uncovered in only nine cases, making up about 0.7 per cent of the total. Judging from the osteological data unearthed, the occupants are male. The second type includes medium-sized graves about 2 m long and 1 m wide, containing coffins but fewer grave goods including, as in the earlier case, pottery vessels painted after firing, painted wooden objects and lapidary ornaments. Here, complete skeletons of pigs are replaced by pigs' mandibles, varying from several to dozens of pieces. Graves of this kind total nearly 100, accounting for about 7 per cent of the whole. The occupants are mostly male, the small number of females being buried on one or both sides of large-sized graves. The third type relates to small-sized narrow graves about 2 m long and 0.5 m wide, mostly without coffins, and no grave goods. Such excavated graves number about 1,200, making up about 92 per cent of the total. On the whole, the grave goods unearthed from the cemetery are characterized by pottery painted after firing and painted wooden articles. The former consists of black ware decorated with geometric designs painted in red, yellow and white, generally on the exterior, except for some plates which are painted on the inner wall surface with a scaled dragon coiling the body and extending the tongue, which are the earliest representations of the dragon known so far. The wooden drums have a body hollowed out of part of a tree trunk painted on the surface, with the drumhead made of crocodile skin, which has entirely disintegrated in most cases. Such drums are often found in association with the stone chime, forming a set of musical instruments, the earliest known so far. The findings from the Taosi cemetery seem to indicate a patriarchical society, with a distinction between the rich and the poor.

Agricultural production developed further, millet being still the main crop. Among the farm tools, besides the wooden *lei* and the stone spade, hoes of bone and shell were introduced as implements for intertillage and weeding. For harvesting, apart from the perforated rectangular or semi-lunar stone knives, stone and shell sickles were used to meet the requirements of increased produce. With the advance of agriculture, animal husbandry reached a new level: pigs, dogs, cattle, buffalo, goats, sheep, chickens and perhaps horses began to be raised, among which the pig was the most prolific. Since then the 'six domestic animals' (pigs, cattle, sheep, horses, chickens and dogs), so-called in Chinese antiquity, have all been in existence. Simultaneously, hunting-gathering and fishing continued to be practised to provide a supplementary diet.

The stone implements of the culture consisted mainly of polished ones which showed a distinct increase both in quantity and in typology. In addition, a small number of pecked stone tools such as arrowheads, scrapers and so on were also found. Jade objects for ritual or decorative use, such as the *cong* (hollow tube, square outside and round inside in cross-section), *bi* (disc) and so-called *xuanji* (trilobate *bi*-disc), appeared in large numbers as prototypes of Shang jades. It is interesting to note that some remains of a copper indus-

try have been discovered from the culture: the Meishan site in Linru County, Henan Province, yielded a crucible for copper smelting. From a tomb at Taosi a bell cast of copper was obtained which amounts to 97.8 per cent of the total contents. These finds indicate that it was at least in the late Longshan culture that ancient China's metallurgical and casting technology came into being and heralded the splendid bronze Shang artefacts.

Pottery making also made striking progress. The pottery continued to be grey ware for the most part, with an increasing amount of black ware, and a low percentage of red ware. It was still mainly handmade, touched up perhaps on the turntable. A distinct innovation of the period was the introduction of the fast rotating wheel, which made it possible to produce a thinner walled vessel like those of the 'eggshell ware' with the body as thin as 0.2 cm. In decoration, the commonest patterns are cord-marks, basket and checkerboard impressions, and painted designs executed after firing occur in some cases. The prevalent types include the cup, plate, bowl, basin, *ding* (tripod with solid feet), *jia* (tripod with thin hollow legs), *zeng* (colander-like steamer) and lid, along with new forms: *li* (tripod with swollen hollow legs, Plate 110, right), *yan* (tripod-steamer), *gui* (tripod with a lip-spout, Plate 110, left) and *he* (tripod with a pipe-spout), all taking their rise from the *jia* and becoming characteristic types from the Longshan culture to the Shang-Zhou period. Pottery kilns are found in large numbers. In shape they basically follow those of the Miaodigou II culture. Some kilns are discovered inside houses, which together with the emergence of the potter's wheel indicates that pottery making became an independent industry.

Scapulimancy came into being in the Longshan culture. It was practised with sheep shoulder blades dotted by burning to omen good or bad luck. Such scapulae remain at some sites of the culture. Later, the Shang dynasty developed the art of divination, using numbers of oracle bones.

With the development of agricultural production and division of labour, corresponding changes took place in the social structure, as reflected by the findings of the Taosi cemetery. The graves which contain the wooden drum, stone chime and the pottery plate with a dragon design, all important ritual articles, must have belonged to chiefs of the tribe who wielded ceremony-holding authority and military power. The fact that the human skeletons unearthed from large-sized graves are identified as those of males and that the graves of this kind are mostly found in company with accessory burials of females on one or both sides can be taken as an eloquent argument that patriarchy was completely established at that time. On the other hand, the numerous small graves are so narrow as to contain only the corpse and generally without any mortuary objects, which again vividly mirrors disparity between rich and poor and division of ranks. Nevertheless, the fact that all kinds of graves are built together in one place seems to indicate that the society followed rites that were halfway between those of the primitive community and those of the more sophisticated.

The Erlitou culture

The Erlitou culture derives its name from the discovery at Erlitou in Yanshi County, Henan Province, in 1957. It is largely distributed in western Henan, southern Shanxi and eastern Shaanxi, with the Erlitou site revealing the most important remains. Its cultural layers are often superimposed on Longshan ones, and ¹⁴C dating shows that it flourished about 1900–1600 BC.

The Erlitou site covers an area of about 370,000 m². Its cultural deposits are 2–4 m thick and can be divided into four phases, representing different stages of one and the same culture. It is interesting to note that in the third and fourth phases large-sized palace foundations came into being. Palace foundation 1 is built of rammed earth, 108 m long from west to east, 100 m wide from north to south. In its centre, a little to the north, a hall foundation has been found with neatly arranged pillar-holes, from which the hall can be reconstructed as a wooden building eight bays across and three deep, covered by a hip roof with eaves overhangs. The palace foundation is surrounded by the remains of an enclosure, inside which or on both sides of which are regularly arranged postholes, perhaps left from corridors or wing rooms. The portal is in the southern section of the enclosure and spans eight bays as well, indicating the grandeur of the whole building. Palace foundation 2 is also of beaten earth, 72.8 m long from north to south and 58 m wide from west to east, with a square courtyard surrounded by walls on four sides. In the centre of the northern part, a hall foundation, in an area of nine bays across and three deep, is outlined by pillar-holes containing stone bases and remains of wood-and-earth walls separating the hall into three rooms, measuring about 400 m² in total. Along the eastern and western sections of the enclosure are found remains of corridors. The gate spans three bays across and faces the south. The floor of the courtyard is somewhat lower than that of the hall and has terracotta drainage pipes running underneath. The scale and layout of the construction doubtless indicate that the remains belong to a palace complex – the earliest discovered up to now. Beyond the palace area, a bronze foundry and pottery-making and other workshops were built, indicating a general architectural plan in the city's construction. The small-sized houses are mostly semi-subterranean dwellings of simple structure, little different from those of the Neolithic age. Their simplicity constitutes a sharp contrast to the magnificence of the palace complex, and reflects the depth of class differentiation.

The graves of the period excavated so far are mainly medium- and small-sized pits. The former, which probably belonged to the nobles, yield traces of coffins and such grave goods as a bronze *jue* (wine vessel), *ge* (dagger-axe), *qi* (battle axe) and plaque, and a jade *ge*, *yue* (battleaxe) and handle-shaped ornament. The latter graves, which occur in larger numbers, generally contain no grave goods, except pottery wine vessels such as the *he*, *jue*, *gu* (cup), and so on, reflecting the same funeral custom as is shown in graves at Yin ruins near Anyang city.

In the third phase of the culture, bronze vessels made their appearance. Excavations yielded ten bronze *jue*, three-legged, flat-bottomed, narrow-waisted wine vessels with a long groove-shaped spout, two vertical rods near the mouth and a handle in one side, along with a flat-bottomed bronze *jia*. They anticipated Shang bronze vessels. Although they are simple in shape and have no decoration, a series of comparatively complex techniques was necessary for their casting. Bronze tools such as the adze, chisel, knife, awl and fishhook, and weapons such as the *ge*, *qi* and arrowhead, along with a small bell and a sort of musical instrument, were also recovered. The bronze plaques are inlaid with turquoise in animal masks or geometrical patterns, showing exquisite craftmanship. It is clear from these discoveries that the Erlitou culture had already entered the advanced Bronze Age.

Lapidary made great advances as well, as evidenced by the discovery of a jade ornament, like a square bar in shape, measuring 17.1 cm in length. It is divided into six parts carved alternately with strings, petal motifs and animal masks, with great skill. The other jade finds are of widely ranging types, including the *ge*, *yue*, arrowhead, knife, *cong* and so on; being exquisite in workmanship, they might have been used as a part of the equipment of honour guards or ornaments for daily use, or perhaps as symbols of power and wealth. It can be concluded that Erlitou lapidary provided the prototypes of the jades represented by the Yin finds both in shape and decoration.

The ceramics followed the style of the Longshan culture, continuity being displayed to a certain degree in paste, technique, shape and decoration. Nevertheless, distinctive features can also be noted. For example, the *jia*, *he*, *jue* and *gu* are imitations of bronze counterparts. Some vessels are incised with fish designs, *kui* (dragon-like animal) motifs and double-bodied dragon patterns and impressed with 'cloud-and-thunder' scrolls, having a close correspondence to the decorations of Shang bronzes. A few vessels are engraved with signs, some of which are similar to the scripts on oracle bones of a later time. Further study may show whether they represent a writing system, but all of them occur as single and isolated symbols.

It is clear that the Erlitou culture was not at the same stage of social development as was the Longshan culture. The magnificent palace buildings, excellent bronzes and jades and the existence of pottery and bronze workshops and, possibly, a writing system all indicate that the state had already made its appearance. There has been argument about the relation of the Erlitou culture to the historical Xia and Shang dynasties; to judge by its cultural characteristics it appears close to the generally recognized Shang culture and its time-span might have included the years when the Shang king Chengtang established his dynasty. The middle Shang culture represented by the Erligang complex at Zhengzhou and the late Shang culture represented by the Xiaotun complex at Anyang show a distinct continuation of the Erlitou culture. Even the societies flourishing at that time in the middle and lower Changjiang Valley and in the territory of Inner Mongolia present a number of indications that they were under the cultural influence of the Erlitou.

According to ancient Chinese tradition, the Xia dynasty was the first one in China, going back roughly to 2000–1500 BC, though legendary versions differ much on this issue. It has not been possible to assign with any amount of certainty any complexes to the Xia culture. Various scholars identify respectively the Longshan, the Erlitou and part of the two with the Xia culture. There has so far been no conclusive evidence to link any of them with the legendary Xia dynasty.

The lower reaches of the Huanghe

The Dawenkou culture

The Dawenkou culture was identified in 1959 at Dawenkou in Taian County, Shandong Province. It extends to the north of the Huai River, in the lower reaches of the Huanghe, including Shandong Province as its centre, and also part of Jiangsu, Anhui and Henan Provinces. Being characterized by red ware and having painted pottery as a marker, the early complex of the culture is a variation of the Yangshao. In the middle and late phases, grey ware became its main distinctive feature, with regional differences. In the end, it transformed itself into the Shang Longshan culture. Chronologically, it lasted more than 2,000 years. On the basis of ¹⁴C determinations its middle and lower phases are dated to c. 3500–2400 BC.

The remains of the culture so far identified consist mainly of graves, which total up to over 2,000 at some dozen sites. Houses, storage pits and pottery kilns have been found in haphazard locations with the result that the layout of settlements is debatable. The graves are generally located near settlements, densely arranged in common cemeteries. Mostly these consist of single burials, though some multiple burials are also present. From the middle phase, joint burials of a man and a woman were also reported, occasionally with children buried together. The graves vary both in size and in the quantity of grave goods, which may be a sign of distinction between rich and poor. The large-sized graves are furnished with outer and inner wooden coffins, their grave goods including a large number of pottery, stone and bone articles and fine jade and ivory objects, amounting to over a hundred pieces in each of the richest burials; sometimes ten or more pigs' skulls or mandibles are found as remains of mortuary offerings. The small graves generally contain no coffins, with funerary objects either poor or absent. The human skeletons unearthed indicate that there was a custom of deforming heads and extracting front teeth, but their physical features resemble those of the Yangshao people.

The plentiful funerary objects reflect the florescence of handicrafts, with a distinct social division of labour. In the middle and late phases, the ceramic industry was characterized by the prevalence of grey ware and the use of the potter's wheel, with fine black, white and thin 'eggshell' wares being made as well, and painted pottery existing as a survival of previous times. The pottery has a wide typological range, including the *ding*, *gui* (tripod), *he*, *gu*, pot, *dou*, hanging bottle and so on; some *gui* are made in the shape of a pig or a dog, showing a unique style. The stone tools are mostly polished, consisting mainly of the axe, adze, chisel, knife and some other implements of production, with a few fine jade *yue* unearthed as well. In addition, there are a lot of exquisite ornaments, such as jade rings, *xianji* and pendants, and openwork ivory combs and tubes with a four-petal design, some of the tubes being cleverly inlaid with turquoise beads. All these finds display brilliant workmanship.

Like the Neolithic inhabitants in the middle reaches of the Huanghe, the Dawenkou people mainly engaged in agriculture, as is shown by the carbonized millet seeds and the stone knives, bone and shell sickles, antler hoes and other farm tools unearthed from excavations. The numerous discoveries of pigs' skulls or mandibles from graves can be taken as another sign of flourishing agriculture. The difference in size and in the quantity of grave furniture between the large and small graves obviously represents the development of distinction between rich and poor. This social change can be detected also in the transformation of burial rites: in the joint burials of a man and a woman, most of the grave goods concentrate on the side of the man, which perhaps marks the completion of the transition from matriarchy to patriarchy.

The Shandong Longshan culture

The Shandong Longshan culture developed from the Dawenkou culture and was distributed roughly in the same region. According to ¹⁴C dating, it goes back to c. 2400–2000 BC, being contemporary with the Central Plains Longshan culture. Through mutual exchanges and influence, they shared a lot of cultural elements with each other, which is particularly perceptible in their adjoining areas.

The settlement sites of the culture generally cover an area of about 100,000 m², the largest, Liangchengzhen site in Rizhao County, Shandong Province, being 360,000 m², and a number of sites are superimposed on layers of the Dawenkou culture. The layout of settlements is not yet clear. Most of the houses are round or square semi-subterranean dwellings; their walls are of beaten earth with wooden posts enclosed inside and wall-foundations laid down in ditches. The inner floor is hard rammed, with the remains of a fireplace and postholes left on the surface. Some houses are constructed on rectangular tamped-earth platforms with the sides made into gently sloping aprons. At rare sites, there are the remains of beaten-earth enclosures, perhaps a sign of the existence of castles.

More than 200 graves have been discovered, all of which are single burials in earth pits, and no children's urn burials have been found. The graves vary distinctly in size and in the number of grave goods. The largest are furnished with wooden coffins, while the small ones contain no coffins. In the Chengzi cemetery in Zhucheng County, for example, of the 78 graves excavated the large ones account for 5.7 per cent, yielding rich, fine funerary objects, including thin-bodied high-stemmed pottery cups and pigs' mandibles, both numbering some dozen in each burial. Smaller graves, comprising 20 per cent of the total, contain three or four pottery vessels each; the remainder contain no grave furniture. Such a picture indicates a striking distinction between rich and poor.

The stone tools unearthed are mainly polished, and include the axe, adze, chisel, *yue* (battleaxe), arrowhead, and so on; the double-perforated semi-lunar knife is commonly found as well. A small number of stone implements, such as the arrowhead and scraper, are pecked. In addition, the shell knife and sickle are found. As for copper objects, there has yet been no clear evidence for their presence, but the animal mask engraved on a jade axe from Liangchengzhen and the 'cloud-and-thunder' scrolls incised on black potsherds from the same site bear some similarities with patterns on Shang bronzes and thus possibly imply the introduction of copper articles at that time.

Pottery making was greatly advanced by the widespread application of the potter's wheel and the prevalence of the lustrous black clay ware typical of the culture. It is especially noteworthy that the high-stemmed cup is elaborated in shape and as thin as 0.2–0.1 cm in the body, reaching a peak of ceramic manufacture, without doubt the product of specialized potters. The pottery has a wide typological variety and is characterized by the common existence of flat-bottomed vessels, with large numbers of three-footed and ring-footed vessels. The main types consist of the *ding*, *gui*, *yan*, stubby pot and high-stemmed cup, while the *li* is completely absent. Judging from the paste, the new techniques and the shapes of the pottery, it obviously succeeded that of the Dawenkou culture.

The Shandong Longshan culture was contemporary with the Central Plains Longshan culture and their social structures must have been roughly the same. Pottery-making technology characterized by wheel-made black ware achieved the greatest advance in the Shandong Longshan culture; in the Central Plains Longshan culture, this ware is found mostly in the east, while towards the west it shows a tendency to become less in number and different in shape. This phenomenon provides important evidence for those researching into the regional characteristics of the two cultures and the mutual relation between them.

The Yueshi culture

The Yueshi culture derived from the Shandong Longshan culture and is represented by the Yueshi site in Pingdu County, excavated in 1960. It is distributed basically in the same region as the Dawenkou and Shandong Longshan cultures, and follows on in one continuous line. Radiocarbon analysis dates it to *c.* 1900–1700 BC.

Certain changes took place in ceramics. The black clay ware assumes this colour only in the thin outside and inside layers, which sandwich a thick, red inner part of the body. The pottery is usually decorated with parallel ribs and sometimes made lustrous or painted with red designs on the surface. The main types include the *gui* (basin-shaped container), *zun*, pot, *dou* and lid, while the *ding*, *gui* (tripod) and the like are lacking. As regards implements, stone, bone, antler and shell tools are still used, and the bronze awl makes its appearance, showing that the culture had already entered the Bronze Age.

The Yueshi culture developed roughly contemporaneously with the Erlitou culture in the middle reaches of the Huanghe, but seems not to have entered the state stage. It was replaced by the Shang civilization.

The upper reaches of the Huanghe

The Majiayao culture

The Majiayao culture was formerly called the Gansu Yangshao culture. Its remains are distributed mainly in Gansu, Qinghai and Ningxia in the upper reaches of the Huanghe. It is a local variation of the Yangshao culture; the present name is derived from the site discovered at Majiayao in Lintao County, Gansu Province, in 1923. According to the numerous findings obtained so far, the culture can be divided into four phases: the Shilingxia, Majiayao, Banshan and Machang, forming a chronological sequence. The earliest Shilingxia type has many elements of the Yangshao culture and may be a transitional stage, while the rest constitutes the typical Majiayao culture, going back to *c.* 3200–2300 BC according to ¹⁴C dating, though they vary considerably in cultural aspects.

The sites of the culture are generally situated on second terraces in valleys. They bear a strong resemblance to those of the Yangshao culture in the size of settlements, the shape of buildings and the dominance of agriculture in economic life. At a site of the Machang type, pottery kilns are found grouped together, totalling as many as a dozen, indicating the flourishing pottery industry and the distinct division of labour in the society.

Graves are mostly located near settlements, though some form separate cemeteries further away from living quarters. More than 1,600 have been found, most of which belong to the Banshan and Machang types. These graves are mainly shaft pits, though there are also oval catacombs each with a passage, the entrance being closed with standing wooden bars or stone slabs. Adults are usually buried in wooden coffins and occasionally in stone ones, while children are buried in urns. Single burials constitute an overwhelming

majority, though multiple ones exist. The number of grave goods varies: Tom 564 at Liuwan in Ledu County, Qinghai Province, contains 95 funerary objects, of which pottery vessels number 91 pieces, while in other graves pottery artefacts range from some dozen to one or two pieces. Grave furniture for men commonly includes farm stone tools while that of women, stone or pottery spindles.

The implements of production consist mainly of the polished stone axe, adze, chisel, knife, quern, and so on, with the chipped stone spade, knife and disc present in large numbers; and the discovery of microblades and their bone bases reflects the survival of a microlithic industry. Other tools include the bone spade, awl, arrowhead and needle and the pottery knife and spindle, and so on. As for metallurgy, apart from rare finds of bronze knives, there are no traces of copper or bronze objects at the sites excavated, which perhaps indicates that the copper or bronze industry had not yet appeared in the Majiayao culture.

Pottery included a coarse sandy ware with cord-marks, but the most typical type is a painted pottery of fine clay, well made, richly decorated, distinctly differing between various types in shape and pattern, and showing a tendency to decline over the years. The pottery of the Majiayao type is characterized by richly painted black designs consisting of smooth and gentle lines, with motifs, including frog, fish and bird figures. One basin displays a scene in which five persons dance hand in hand. Jars, bottles and pots are usually covered with paintings on the surface and are sometimes painted only on the upper half of the body, while bowls and basins commonly bear painted decorations on the inside. In the Banshan type, pottery is painted in red and black, with stripes, serrations and circles forming neat, symmetrical designs; the main vessel types are the narrow-necked jar, two-eared pot and curved-belly basin. The pottery of the Machang type is generally red- and black-painted as well, but a little rough, lacking brightness on the surface, and the decoration tending to simplicity, consisting usually of four large circles and geometrized human figures. A nude female figure, combining relief and painting techniques, has been found on a pottery jar from the Liuwan site; being true to life, it can be rated as a significant work of art. The main types of earthenware include the jar, pot, basin and *dou*, with the *li* occurring in rare cases. A number of painted vessels bear various signs, perhaps the marks of their makers.

The graves of the Majiayao culture may to a certain degree reflect changes in social structure. The Majiayao and Banshan types do not show much difference in the type and number of funerary objects, but in the Machang type, distinction between rich and poor is shown quite clearly in grave furniture. This seems to indicate that the Majiayao culture went through the flourishing, declining and collapsing stages of the matriarch clan, which in the end led to its replacement by the patriarchal Qijia culture.

The Qijia culture

The Qijia culture derives its name from the Qijiaping site in Guanghe County, Gansu Province, discovered in 1924. It is distributed basically in the same area as and even broader than the Majiayao culture. Radiocarbon analysis dates it to *c.* 2200–1900 BC, but its terminal date may correspond to that of the Erlitou culture or even later.

The settlement sites of the Qijia culture are situated on second terraces by rivers and often superimposed on those of the Majiayao culture. The houses are roughly the same in shape as those of Longshan culture, with the limey floor present as well.

Over 800 graves have been discovered, located within or near settlements and arranged more or less regularly in cemeteries of various size. In shape they resemble those of the Majiayao culture. Plank and single-log coffins and plank pads for corpses are present. The dead are usually buried singly, but joint burials of a man and a woman have been uncovered as well, generally with the former in an extended supine position and the latter lying flexed sideways and facing the former. In three graves of joint burials, a man lies in the middle, flanked on either side by a woman lying facing him in a flexed position. These women seem to be buried alive by force with deceased men, which indicates that women were subject to their menfolk. The Qijia graves vary in the number of grave goods. For example, at the Huangniangniang-tai cemetery in Wuwei County, Gansu Province, pottery vessels range from 1 to 37 pieces and stone *bi* (discs) from 1 to 68 pieces. At the Qinweijia cemetery in Yongjing County, Gansu Province, pigs' mandibles are found, ranging from 4 to 68 pieces. This may reflect a distinction in wealth.

Agriculture and animal husbandry progressed markedly. Farm tools and carbonized millet seeds are unearthed in much larger numbers and domestic animals unprecedentedly increase both in species and quantity. The stone and bone implements are basically the same as those of the Majiayao culture, yet small bronze objects, such as the knife, awl, axe, chisel, mirror, ring and other ornaments, make their appearance, numbering more than 50 pieces. Examination reveals that most of them, about 64 per cent of the total, are made of copper, and the rest of bronze. They are cast in single moulds. The bronze mirror excavated at the Gamatai site in Guinan County, Qinghai Province, very much resembles those from the Yin ruins near Anyang city and therefore can be taken as an approximate contemporary of the latter.

The Qijia pottery consists of handmade red ware for the most part, lacking traces of the potter's wheel. Its surface is often plain and sometimes decorated with basket, cord-marks and comb-impressions and appliqués. Painted patterns occur very rarely. Being simple designs consisting of lines and trellises, they are an obvious survival of the Majiayao tradition. The main vessel types include the basin, bowl, cup, *dou*, two-eared pot, with the *li* and *he* present in small numbers and rather similar to those of the Central Plains Longshan culture.

The Qijia culture succeeded the Majiayao culture and was influenced by the Central Plains Longshan culture, and can be considered as a regional variation of the Longshan culture. The society was going through the disintegrating stage of the primitive community, before the emergence of the state. Most of the Bronze Age cultures in Gansu and Qinghai Provinces and their vicinity, such as the Siba culture in the Gansu Corridor, the Kayao culture in the Huanghe Valley, and the Xindian culture in the Tao River Valley, all have close connections with the Qijia culture.

CONTEMPORARY CULTURES IN OTHER PARTS OF CHINA

Archaeological discoveries and researches reveal that, during the transition from the primitive community to the state, cultural continuity and succession in ancient China are demonstrated most distinctly in the valley of the Huanghe. There the Shang and Zhou state organizations developed and flourished one after the other. The hypothesis that the Huanghe Valley was the original centre of ancient Chinese civilization has been accepted as an historical fact. In the surrounding regions of the Huanghe Valley, a great number of cultural complexes developed in parallel with those in the valley of the river, and between the centre and the periphery cultural exchanges and mutual influences frequently occurred in various degrees. In social evolution, the peripheral cultures were generally more backward than those of the Central Plains, and they were gradually unified by the Shang-Zhou civilization, thus the foundation of China's historical development. Economically, these cultures were based on agriculture for the most part, with distinct differences between them due to their disparity in geographical environment. From the Changjiang middle and lower reaches, adjoining the Huanghe Valley, with the Qinling Mountains and the Huai River as the boundary between them, to south China, the prevailing productive activity was rice cultivation, while in the highlands, such as the northern steppes and Tibet, millet growing was paramount, with hunting and animal husbandry playing an active part.

The middle reaches of the Changjiang

Contemporary societies are represented by the Qujialing and Qinglongquan III cultures. The Qujialing culture takes the western Hubei Province as its centre and occurs also in the adjoining areas in Henan, Sichuan and Hunan Provinces. Radiocarbon analysis dates it to c. 3000–2600 BC. The pottery consists mainly of black ware in its early period and grey ware in its late period, all handmade. The prevalent shapes are tripods and ring-footed vessels, including the *ding*, *dou*, cup, pot and so on, with painted eggshell ware and pottery spindles as typical objects. Judging from its characteristic features, the earthenware succeeded that of the Daxi culture and has some relation with that of the Miaodigou II culture. The Qinglongquan III culture occupies approximately the same geographical distribution as the Qujialing culture and goes back to c. 2400 BC according to ¹⁴C dating. The pottery is also handmade and consists largely of grey ware decorated with basket-impressions, with red and black wares prevalent, and painted vessels existing in small numbers. In shape there are the *ding*, *jia*, *gui* (tripod with a lip-spout), cup, *dou*, pot and so on (without the *li* and *yan*), showing a strong regional flavour and distinguishing the culture as a local variation of the Longshan culture.

The lower reaches of the Changjiang

In the Changjiang lower reaches, the Liangzhu culture is the main contemporary representative. It is spread over Zhejiang and Jiangsu Provinces and is radiocarbon-dated to c. 3100–2200 BC, though its terminal date may be later. The settlement sites are generally situated on mounds above the surrounding ground, with surface buildings and pile-dwellings. The graves differ in size as well as in the number of grave goods. Some large graves contain abundant jade objects, such as the *cong*, *bi* and other types. For example, Tomb 3 at Sidun in Wujin County, Jiangsu Province, has yielded 33 pieces of *bi* surrounding the skeleton and 57 pieces covering it in one or more layers, along with jade knives, *yue* (axes) and pottery vessels, totalling over a hundred; all this distinguishes the occupant from more lowly members of the community. Stone working was considerably advanced, with the products well polished in workmanship and widely varying in type. Jade working is still more remarkable, the most notable example being the animal mask engraved on some *cong*, which might have been the prototype of the *tao-te* monster mask on Shang bronzes. Ceramics made great progress, the potter's wheel being commonly used. The pottery consists mainly of a grey-bodied clay ware covered by a black layer on the surface, which is easy to peel off, with thin-bodied eggshell ware present as well and rare vessels painted in several colours or single red. The common types include the *ding*, *gui* (tripod with a lip-spout), *he*, *dou*, cup, jar and so on. The culture's roots lie in the Majiabang culture and have the closest relationship with the Shandong Longshan culture. The primitive community was then tending to disintegrate, the society being on the eve of state formation. Later on, the Liangzhu culture developed the use of bronze, was represented by stamped pottery, and chronologically corresponded roughly to the Erlitou culture of the early Shang period.

South China

In the south-eastern coastal region, including Fujian, Taiwan, Guangdong, Guangxi and Jiangxi Provinces, many contemporary cultural complexes existed, of which the Shanbei, Shixia and Tanshishan cultures go back to *c*. 3000–2000 BC according to ¹⁴C dating; the Tanshishan lasted even longer. This culture, with the Fengpitou culture in Taiwan, belongs to one and the same cultural system, which indicates that people had crossed the Taiwan Strait and maintained frequent communications with the continent. All the cultures are characterized by the abundance of polished stone tools with the stepped adze and shouldered axe as the most representative types. The pottery is still handmade and falls, for the most part, into the *fu* (cauldron), *ding*, *gui* (tripod), *gui* (basin), *dou* cup and jar shapes, with painted ware occurring at some sites, and stamped pottery beginning to appear. On the whole, this region culturally was close to the middle and lower reaches of the Changjiang and shared some elements with the Longshan culture.

The Northern steppes

Throughout the northern steppes approximately from northeast China via Inner Mongolia to Xinjiang, there are distributed numerous cultural complexes characterized by the microlithic tradition, which can roughly be divided into two categories. One of them belongs to nomadic groups engaged in cattle-raising and hunting, whose living sites are little known and whose finds consist largely of microliths. The other belongs to settled inhabitants living on agriculture, with the eastern part of Inner Mongolia better known archaeologically. In this area, the Fuhe culture has been distinguished as the Neolithic complex following the Xinle and Hongshan cultures, distributed in the Sirangren Valley and its vicinity. It is radiocarbon-dated to *c*. 3300 BC but may have lasted for a comparatively long time. The settlement sites of the culture have yielded square or round houses of the semi-subterranean type. The stone tools consist mainly of chipped artefacts, with polished ones and microliths existing in significant numbers. The pottery is coarse and includes only the pot, bowl and the like. Agriculture was then the

primary economic activity, but hunting still played a considerable role.

The most remarkable early Bronze Age complex is the Lower Xiajiadian culture, distributed in south-eastern Inner Mongolia, western Liaoning and north-eastern Hebei and radiocarbon-dated to *c*. 1700 BC. Its settlement sites have yielded densely arranged houses of the semi-subterranean type, with remains of stone castles. The productive implements are largely made of stone, with microliths existing as survivals from the previous period, and small bronzes making their appearance. The pottery includes mainly the *li*, *yan*, *ding*, *zun*, pot and *dou*. Some of the vessels are painted with red and white designs like the 'cloud-and-thunder' scroll. The colours are easy to peel off and the objects may have been used just for funerary purposes. In addition, there are the *gui* (tripod) and *jue* similar to those of the Erlitou culture, showing a close connection between the two.

South-west China

In the south-western highlands, including Guizhou, Yunnan and Tibet, only a few findings belong to the late Neolithic Age. Among the remains reported so far the important sites are those of Baiyang and Karuo. The Baiyang site is located near Lake Erhai in western Yunnan and radiocarbon-dated to *c*. 2100–2000 BC. The Karuo site is situated on the Lancang River in eastern Tibet and goes back to *c*. 3000–2000 BC according to ¹⁴C data. Both sites were inhabited by agricultural groups, the former being rice farmers while the latter were millet growers, and hunting was much practised in both cases. The sites are quite different from each other in their cultural aspects. The chipped stone tools and microliths found at Karuo have no analogues at Baiyang, and pottery differs between the two places. Yet the perforated harvesting knives unearthed from both sites and the painted pottery uncovered at Karuo show that both settlements had certain relations to the Neolithic Huanghe.

SUMMARY

As we have seen, between 3000 BC and 1600 BC, China was going through the transition from primitive communities to the formation of the state, which embraces the late Neolithic Age and the emergence of civilization in ancient China centred on the Huanghe Valley. China's ancient cultures, because of the vastness of her territory and the variety of their origins, represent quite an intricate complexion and at the same time exhibit continuity, conglomeration and unevenness in the process of development.

The valley of the Huanghe was one of the centres of ancient world civilization, and its middle reaches and the adjoining areas especially, embracing the Central Plains, played an extremely significant role in the history of China. Here Neolithic agriculture went through an age-long evolution and florescence and the Longshan culture, itself deriving from the Yangshao culture, laid the foundation of the Shang and Zhou states. This succeeding sequence has been strikingly demonstrated. There were constant exchanges and mutual influence between it and the development of the periphery, which of course brought many new cultural elements into the Central Plains during the forming process of Chinese civilization.

Taking a bird's-eye view of the whole country, the cultures of this period display the same development trends. The Longshan culture, widespread in the Huanghe Valley, despite the differences of its variations, has a characteristic uniformity. Similar traits exist not only within the Longshan culture but also between it and the Dawenkou culture in the lower reaches of the Huanghe, the Qujialing and Liangzhu cultures in the middle and lower reaches of the Changjiang, and even the Shanbei, Shixia and Tanshishan cultures in south China. Taking their pottery as an example, although the *ding, gui* (tripod), *he, dou,* cup, jar and so on vary to a certain degree between the cultures, the general style is common to all. These signs reflect the exchanges and mutual influence between the late Neolithic cultures in China as well as the tendency of their development towards fusion and unification, and with the expansion of the territory of the Shang and Zhou states, this tendency made still more rapid and vigorous progress.

The unevenness of development is manifest. For example, ceramics in the Longshan culture changed, while in the Majiayao culture in the Huanghe's upper reaches, the tradition of Yangshao painted pottery was maintained, with handmade earthenware continuing, while at the same time painted vessels were being made even in the Changjiang middle and lower reaches, as well as in south and south-west China. Again, when the Erlitou culture in the middle reaches of the Huanghe first entered the age of civilization, the overwhelming majority of the surrounding areas were still at the stage of the primitive community.

In short, the ancient culture having the Huanghe Valley as its centre exerted influence upon and gave impetus to the peripheral regions throughout its existence. After the region's transformation into a nascent state, it played a still more prominent part as the core of conglomerate societies and thus made an outstanding contribution to the unification of China.

BIBLIOGRAPHY

AN ZHIMIN. 1982. [*Essays on Neolithic China*]. Beijing.

CHANG, KWANG-CHIH (ed.). 1977. *The Archaeology of Ancient China*. 3rd ed. New Haven, Conn.

KEIGHTLEY, D. N. (ed.). 1963. *The Origins of Chinese Civilization*. London.

XIA, NAI (ed.). 1984. [*Archaeological Discoveries and Researches in New China.*] Beijing.

—— 1984. [*Recent Archaeological Discoveries in the People's Republic of China.*] Paris.

12.9.2
CHINA (1600–700 BC)

Zhang Changshou

THE SHANG DYNASTY (1600–1027 BC)

As early as 1600 BC, China entered the Bronze Age, with her oldest civilization coming into being. This civilization founded the earliest state organization, built fortified cities, created a writing system, developed bronze metallurgy and casting, and other cultural innovations. All this happened in the Shang period in China's history.

In about 1600 BC, the king of the Shang state Chengtang defeated the legendary Xia dynasty, which made Xibo (in modern Yanshi County, Henan Province) its capital and held sway in part of the Huanghe middle and lower reaches. Over a long period the Shang dynasty repeatedly moved its capital from place to place and in the end to Yin (near modern Anyang city, Henan Province), and thus it has also been called the Yin dynasty. In 1027 BC, the Shang dynasty was defeated and destroyed by the Zhou people who came from the Wei River Valley.

Regarding the history and culture of the Shang period, there is little information in traditional Chinese records.

Today, our knowledge of the period is obtained mainly from archaeological excavations. Chinese archaeologists have excavated the Yin ruins near Anyang since 1928; in the early 1950s, a capital city of the middle Shang was found in modern Zhengzhou city, Henan Province; and recent explorations have discovered the early Shang capital of Xibo. All these excavations and other relevant work have cast much light upon the cultural aspects of the Shang period.

Capital cities and architecture

The Shang city in Yanshi was a walled capital. Its walls were made from beaten earth and measured about 1,700 m in length from north to south and 1,200 m in maximum width from west to east, with seven city gates and roads between them uncovered. Within the city walls, in the centre, there is a palace city, measuring 200 × 200 m, surrounded by tamped-earth walls as well. Among the palace complexes in this area, so far a set of buildings has been excavated, of which

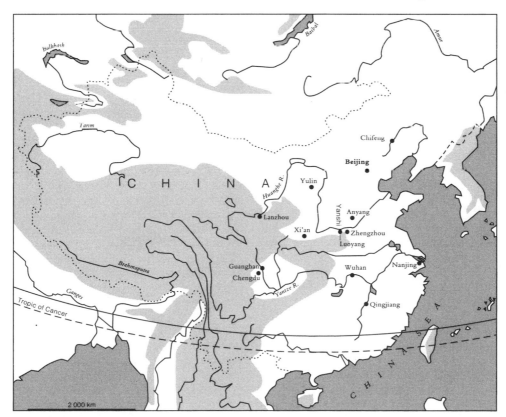

Map 18 China (1600–700 BC).

289

the main hall is 36.5 m long and 11.8 m wide in its foundations, with a courtyard enclosed by the hall itself from the north, two wings from the west and east, and two front auxiliary houses from the south with the portal between them (Plate 111). There are also underground drains in the palace city. All the findings indicate that the early Shang city was a highly developed capital with a strong defensive system, well-planned palace complexes and elaborate drainage works.

The Yin ruins (Plate 112) near Anyang city are even greater in scale. The palace area is situated at Xiaotun village on the southern bank of the Huan River. Here, more than fifty house foundations have been found in three groups, of which the most southerly includes seventeen tamped-earth foundations, arranged regularly and symmetrically, showing that the principle of axiality and symmetry was then developed in architectural design. In the periphery of this area are scattered bronze foundries, pottery kilns, and bone and lapidary workshops. About 2.5 km west of the palace area, on the northern bank of the Huan River, there is a royal burial area, named Xibeigang. Excavations here brought to light more than ten large-sized graves, along with over 1,000 small ones and sacrificial pits. The Yin ruins, therefore, provide an example for understanding the arrangement of palaces and cemeteries in the capital cities of ancient China. However, capital though it was, the site has not yielded any remains of city walls; only to the west of the palace area was a moat which, perhaps, together with the natural defence provided by the Huan River, constituted the fortified boundaries of the palace area.

The houses of the Shang period were all earth and wood constructions. Foundations were first prepared of beaten earth, and then houses were constructed on them by setting stone bases, erecting pillars, fixing beams and thatching roofs; walls were made of tamped earth as well. Such earth and wood buildings are usually preserved in bad condition and their structure can only be inferred according to the pillar bases or holes left in their foundations. It is generally believed that the houses had straw-thatched gable roofs.

Another sort of house was semi-subterranean, with a square or round shallow pit dug into the earth, the floor and walls baked with fire, and the roof, conical or gable, thatched with straw. Semi-subterranean dwellings like these had been traditional in China since the Neolithic Age.

Economic life

Shang society was characterized by settled agricultural life, cereal cultivation being the principal economic practice. The crops were mainly millet, with wheat and rice coming next. The farm implements chiefly consisted of stone tools such as the spade, sickle, knife and so on, along with wooden tools, two-pronged or spade-shaped (lei and si); bronze ones were rare. The Shang people's common fondness for drinking implies that agricultural production at that time must have been progressive enough to provide much grain for wine brewing.

Animal husbandry, too, was well developed in the Shang period. Pigs, dogs, cattle, horses, goats, sheep and so on were bred freely. The fact that the Shang royal family butchered sacrificial animals usually in dozens or even as many as over a hundred in frequent ceremonies may be said to be a sign that cattle-raising was flourishing. Horse-rearing was even more significant. The application of carts drawn by horses improved communications and transportation to a high degree and, moreover, the introduction of chariots changed

the form of fighting. All kinds of vehicles in ancient China were equipped with a single pole and two wheels, and pulled by two or four horses (Fig. 44). Judging from unique characteristic features, it is most probable that they were independently invented by the Chinese themselves.

In technology, the most important achievement was the development of bronze metallurgy and casting. It was during Shang times, especially their late period, that ancient China saw the greatest prosperity of her bronze culture. Among the Shang bronzes the most significant objects are ritual articles, including food containers such as the ding (tripod) and gui (bowl) and wine vessels such as the gu (beaker), jue (three-legged drinking cup), zun (jar) and you (oval pot with a swing handle), all used in offering ceremonies and for banquets. Such bronze ritual vessels represent an extremely high level of bronze industry both in technological and artistic attainment (Plate 113). In the Yin ruins, a large-sized bronze foundry has been excavated, with fragments of pottery moulds (Plate 114), and crucibles were collected in great quantities. The Shang bronzes are all cast with composite moulds. Usually, for casting a single vessel relatively complex in shape, a mould composed of dozens of pieces was used. To illustrate Shang metallurgists' and founders' skill and ability, it seems enough to cite that they were already able to make such heavy bronze containers as the square si-mu-wu ding – a tetrapod weighing 875 kg. The Shang people did not know iron metallurgy yet, but on two bronze weapons dug out from Shang remains badly rusted and eroded edges made of iron have been found, which have been identified as meteoric iron. The edges were first forged out and then inlaid onto the bodies in the process of casting the latter. Objects cast of smelt iron, as known so far, did not appear in China until the sixth century BC.

Pottery making has been a traditional Chinese industry since the Neolithic Age. Shang pottery mainly consists of grey ware, which is made for the most part on the wheel and occasionally in the mould, with cord-marks as the commonest decorations though impressed and incised patterns

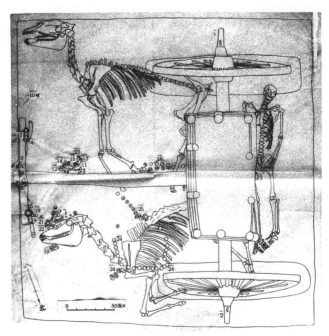

Figure 44 Chariot-and-horse pit in the Yin ruins near Anyang city (Courtesy Institute of Archaeology, Chinese Academy of Social Sciences, Beijing).

can be seen as well. The evenness of its colour indicates that the reductive atmosphere in baking kilns was controlled properly. In the Shang period, the lustrous thin-bodied black ware typical of the Longshan culture was made no longer, but a white ware and a glazed ware appeared as innovations. The former is made of kaolin, in pure white, often with carved designs imitating decorations on bronzes. It was manufactured mainly in the late Shang period and exclusively for the nobility. The glazed ware is painted on the surface with a greenish-grey or yellowish-green glaze and baked at a temperature of 1,200°C. It is generally considered that such glazed pottery was produced in south China as the forerunner of Chinese porcelain.

One of the characteristic features of the Shang civilization was its lapidary. A large number of jades have been unearthed from the Yin ruins. All of them are made of nephrite which came chiefly from the territory of modern Xinjiang. There are various ritual objects, pendants, as well as human and animal figurines in sculpture or relief (Plates 115, 116). These jades display a high technical and artistic skill. Among the finds from the Yin ruins are also many bone and ivory carvings, bearing a number of similarities to bronzes in decoration. An ivory cup is full-carved with fine patterns and inlaid with turquoise (Plate 117); it may be rated as an exquisite and unprecedented artistic masterpiece.

China was the earliest country in the world to raise the domestic silkworm and produce silk textiles. For the Shang period, a few pieces of silk fabric have been unearthed from graves, including plain silk, warp-patterned monochrome damask in lozenge designs, along with some smart embroideries. All this reflects that the spinning and weaving techniques of Shang silk production reached quite a high level.

Among the finds from the Yin ruins there are products coming from distant areas after passing through intermediate places, such as nephrite from Xinjiang, and cowrie and divining turtle shells from the seaside. They must have been obtained through trade or exchange. Cowrie shells were often used as coins.

The social system

The Shang dynasty ruled a slave-owning state. As the largest slave owner, the Shang king was always launching wars upon other tribes in order to seize as many captives as possible. Being their owners' tools and property, slaves had to engage in all sorts of productive and domestic work and, moreover, they were often given away as awards and gifts, and even sacrificed as human victims to be buried with their dead owner or offered to gods and spirits in religious ceremonies. In the royal burial area of the Yin ruins, numerous sacrificial pits arranged regularly have been uncovered, each containing about a dozen headless skeletons, the remains of human victims in successive memorial ceremonies to the departed Shang kings. According to statistical data, the Yin ruins have yielded human victims totalling over 2,300. The large- and medium-sized Shang graves so far excavated all have accessory burials of human immolations, including men, women and children, amounting in some cases to nearly a hundred people. Such large-scale slaughter reflects the slave-owning nature of Shang society.

The Shang state was a monarchy, with the king holding sovereign power and governing the aristocracy, consisting of the chiefs of numerous tribes. The succession of kingship was practised in accordance with the principle of passing on from the elder brother to the younger one, then through the sons of the elder brother. This system, however, often led to struggles for the throne among brothers, which repeatedly weakened the dynastic rule. Therefore, at the end of the dynasty, it was finally abolished and substituted by hereditary succession from father to son.

In Shang society there were a few institutions left from the previous clan system. For example, people inhabited different territories as various clans; each had its own clan emblem and name and a certain occupation. One of the proofs of this comes from written records stating that whole Shang clans were made slaves after the destruction of the Shang dynasty. Nevertheless, the family was still the core and basic unit of society. Monogamy was the rule, and even a departed Shang king was imagined as being accompanied only by the spirit of one legal wife when a sacrificial ceremony was held for him. But in practice, concubinage was a common phenomenon. Men held the dominant position in the family, though women enjoyed a few social rights as well; some of the female members of the royal family were even allowed to take part in military expeditions as commanders of troops. In the appellation of relatives, the father and the uncle were called father, while the mother and the aunt were called mother, which again suggests the survival of the clan system.

Culture and religion

One of the principal signs of a civilization is the emergence of a writing system. Complete written records were made during the late Shang period. There is no doubt about the statements in Chinese historical texts that the Yin ancestors had books and documents. Shang characters have been discovered on pottery, bronze and lapidary objects, and especially on tortoise-shell and animal bones. Inscriptions on bones and tortoise-shell were used by the late Shang royal house for recording and divination (Plate 118). So far, about 160,000 pieces have been unearthed in total, almost all from the palace area of the Yin ruins. The vocabulary used consists of about 4,000 characters, half of which have been deciphered. Analysis of the character-making rules led philologists of the Han dynasty to divide the Chinese characters into six categories: (1) self-explanatory; (2) pictographic; (3) pictophonetic; (4) associative compounds; (5) mutually explanatory; (6) phonetic loan characters. In fact, in the inscriptions on tortoise-shell and animal bones there are only pictographic, ideographic and pictophonetic characters, with the first ones as the basic. The shell-and-bone inscription still displays some primitive characteristics. For example, one and the same pictograph can be written in slightly different forms. The appearance of pictophonetic characters, however, marks a new stage in character creating. The fact that the Shang writing system was mature enough to record spoken languages and human activities indicates that the Shang dynasty indeed came into historical times. As regards the origin of Chinese writing, perhaps it may be traced to an even earlier period.

In the sphere of natural sciences, astronomy was among the first to be developed in China. In Shang oracle inscriptions there are records on the observation of celestial phenomena. One of the applications of astronomical knowledge was the elaboration of a calendar, which had much concern with agricultural production. The Shang calendar was of the lunisolar type, with the circle of the moon's phase-changes as a lunar month ('moon') and with the year consisting of twelve 'moons'. The length of the lunar month varied between 29 and 30 days. Every two or three years it was necessary to add an intercalary month, called the thirteenth moon, so as to make up the days short of the full solar year.

Regarding art and technology, Shang bronzes, jades and ivory objects are incomparable both in shape and decoration; the casting of bronze ritual vessels especially reached its height in the late Shang period. These vessels are grave and majestic for the most part. Their shapes often imitate forms of animals, and the decorations are mainly *tao-te* monster masks, *kui* dragon designs and bird patterns, with the ground full of 'thunder' scrolls, thus displaying richness and splendour (Plate 119).

Shang religious beliefs centred on the worship of gods and spirits. It was conceived that lands, mountains, the sun, the moon, wind, rain and other natural phenomena were all represented by their spirits. Ancestor-worship enjoyed an extremely important position in religious activities. Divination was believed to be the means of communication between human beings and spirits. Therefore, no matter what was about to take place, it was preceded by divining so as to learn the instructions of gods and spirits. Various sacrificial rites were often held to pray for blessings from spirits, and memorial ceremonies to ancestors were especially frequent and solemn. The large number of immolations discovered in the Yin ruins provide distinct evidence of Shang worship.

THE WESTERN ZHOU DYNASTY (1027–771 BC)

The Zhou people, the founders of the Western Zhou dynasty, originated as a group of tribes who lived in the valley of the Wei River and who were relatively backward in culture. Roughly in the middle of the thirteenth century BC, the Zhou came into contact with the Shang dynasty, and were often invaded and pillaged by Shang troops, which caused them sometimes to rebel, sometimes to submit. In the long course of contact with the Shang, the Zhou gradually adopted elements of Shang culture and finally became a subject state under the Shang dynasty. At the end of the twelfth century BC, the Zhou people moved to Zhou-yuan, modern Qishan, Shaanxi, where they built a city, developed agricultural production and thus strengthened their culture. In the mid-eleventh century BC, their leader Wen Wang was invested with the title 'Count of the West' as well as the power of expedition; afterwards, he conquered successively adjacent petty states, expanded actively his influence eastwards, and built Fengyi as a new capital on the western bank of the Fenghe River near modern Xi'an. After the death of Wen Wang, his successor Wu Wang carried on his unfinished life's work by further building up strength and weakening the Shang dynasty. In 1027 BC, Wu Wang entered into alliance with the Yong, Shu, Qiang, Mao, Wei, Lu, Peng and Pu tribes to fight the Shang, and on the *jiaozi* day, second month, fought a decisive battle with Shang king Zhou at Muye. Although the Shang forces were several times larger than the allied army under Wu Wang, they were destined to be defeated for their forward troops turned renegade, and King Zhou committed suicide in a fire. Wu Wang captured the Shang capital at one fell swoop, overthrew the Shang dynasty and established the Zhou dynasty.

After its founding, the new dynasty was faced with the mighty remaining forces of the Shang dynasty and its eastern allies. To consolidate newly-achieved victories, Wu Wang pursued a tolerant policy: he enfeoffed Zhou's son Lu Fu in previously held Shang territory and left him a modicum of power, such as managing Shang sacrificial ceremonies; at the same time, he appointed his younger brothers Guan Shu, Cai Shu and Huo Shu to guard and supervise the periphery of the Shang region, hence the name 'Three Supervisors'. Wu Wang felt deeply that his capitals Feng and Hao, lying in the west of his domain, were inconvenient for ruling the newly conquered regions and intended to build a new capital between the Huanghe and Luohe Rivers. However, before he implemented his plan, he died of an illness in the year after he defeated the Shang. His death soon gave rise to a political crisis.

Wu Wang's son Cheng Wang came to the throne; but he was too young, and Zhou Gong, a younger brother of Wu Wang, was appointed regent. Guan Shu and Cai Shu resented this, and King Zhou's son Lu Fu, taking advantage of the occasion, entered into alliance with the brothers to rise in rebellion against the Zhou, and the eastern states of Xu, Yan and Bogu. The eastern allies of the Shang dynasty responded one after another to their call, and thus the Zhou dynasty was confronted with a dangerous situation. By order of Cheng Wang, Zhou Gong launched eastward expeditions, which lasted for three years; he killed Lu Fu and Guan Shu, banished Cai Shu, and finally put down the rebellion of Xu, Yan, Bogu and other eastern states. Thereafter, Cheng Wang, according to Wu Wang's intention, built a new capital called Luoyi in modern Luoyang city, Henan, making it the centre for pacifying the east, and moved there the old Shang noblemen, putting them under the control of massive garrisons. On the other hand, he enfeoffed meritorious officials of his dynasty and princes and other relatives of the Zhou family to the newly conquered territories, where vassal states of various sizes were established as strong frontier defences. All Shang survivors were sent with their clans to these states. For example, Zhou Gong's son was enfeoffed to Lu and invested with six clans of Shang survivors; Wu Wang's younger brother Kang Shu to the former Shang region, with seven clans; Shi Shang Fu to Qi, Shao Gong Shi to Yan and so forth. This enfeoffment on a large scale much consolidated the rule of the Zhou dynasty, brought about a peaceful situation without punishments for several decades, and laid the foundation of the dynasty's southern exploitation. From the middle Western Zhou on, however, the Zhou dynasty gradually declined; and in 771 BC, it was invaded by the Quanrong tribes and was compelled to move eastwards. Traditionally, the Zhou dynasty is divided into the Western and Eastern dynasties with the move eastward as the demarcation between them.

There are many more documents of the Western Zhou than there are of the Shang in Confucian classics, and a large number of material sources of the period have been revealed through archaeological work over the past thirty years, including especially many bronze ritual vessels with long inscriptions of great importance unearthed from graves and hoards. Therefore, both historical texts and archaeological data available for the study of the Western Zhou are richer in comparison with those of the preceding period.

Capital cities and architecture

The capital of the Western Zhou dynasty in point of fact embraced two cities: one called Feng, built by Wu Wang's father Wen Wang; the other, Hao, by Wu Wang himself.

The two cities were separated by the Feng River and both of them were allegedly enclosed by city walls, though to date no remains of city walls have been found and nothing which can be firmly taken as beaten-earth palace foundations. The eastern capital newly built in the Western Zhou period included two cities as well, for one of which remains of tamped-earth city walls were identified during archaeological exploration, but they date from the Eastern Zhou period, perhaps left from the city rebuilt at that time.

The architecture of the Western Zhou period was roughly the same as that of the Shang. The large-sized buildings were still earth-and-wood constructions with beaten-earth foundations and walls, and wooden pillars and beams. A residence of a noble-rank family, its remains well preserved, has a doorway, an anterior hall and posterior rooms situated along the axis and with wings on both of their sides; thus the rooms, facing south, are arranged symmetrically and enclose a front and a rear courtyard (Fig. 45). It is the earliest example of the most prevalent traditional type in Chinese architecture. Another innovation marking the further development of architecture was the introduction of the tile. Approximately in the middle or late Western Zhou, part of the nobles' houses began to be no longer thatched with straw but roofed with tiles instead. The commonest dwellings, as formerly, were still of the semi-subterranean type. In south China, pile-dwellings constructed of wooden posts and planks, perhaps due to moisture, continued to be built as houses of the local traditional type from the Neolithic Age.

Economic life

According to legend, the ancestor of the Zhou people was an expert in agricultural work in remote antiquity and was called Hou Ji (literally, the master of millet farming), which implies that the Zhou people originally came from a group of agricultural tribes engaging in millet cultivation. The farm tools of the Western Zhou period were still mainly made of stone, wood, bone and shell, and bronze implements remained small in number. Tillage in couples was practised, with one farmer turning up the soil ahead while the other levelled it behind. It seems that cattle were used for ploughing, and the method of crop rotation and fallow was adopted so as to recover soil fertility; while manure began to be applied to the fields. All this considerably promoted agricultural production.

All the land of Western Zhou China nominally belonged

to the king. It was granted to vassals and officials and, of course, cultivated by the peasants. According to Confucian classics, the land was divided into *jings*, which subdivided into square *tian*-fields, each measuring one hundred *mu*. Each *jing* consisted of nine *tians*, of which eight were cultivated by eight peasant households individually and thus called the private field, while the ninth one, in the centre, was tilled by them collectively and called the communal field; the products of the latter had to be handed over to the feudal lord. That is the so-called '*jing-tian* system'. Of course, it is a system modified and idealized by later Confucians.

The Western Zhou period also witnessed great advances in animal husbandry, especially in horse-raising. According to historical documents, ancestors of the Qin people once bred horses under the Western Zhou dynasty and brought about considerable developments in the science. Inscriptions on bronzes repeatedly record that Zhou kings often in person attended ceremonies where adult foals were parted from their mothers and sent into draught herds (Plate 120), which indicates the importance of animal husbandry at that time.

In handicrafts, the Zhou people were relatively backward before destroying the Shang dynasty. However, during the conquering expedition, they captured a large number of Shang craftsmen skilled in various techniques, and the Zhou dynasty carried out a lenient policy towards the captured craftsmen, thus the traditions of the Shang handicrafts were almost entirely retained. The Western Zhou period still belonged to the Bronze Age, and bronze metallurgy and casting remained the main branch of handicraft industry. The bronzes of the early Western Zhou, especially the ritual vessels, are hardly distinguished from those manufactured at the end of the Shang period both in shape and decoration and therefore can be thought of as products made by captured Shang craftsmen or on their technical principles. It was only in the middle Western Zhou that changes began to take place and the new style characteristic of the Western Zhou first came into being. Thereafter, typical Shang wine vessels diminished in number and several new types made their appearance. Meanwhile, the decoration on bronzes departed from its previous richness and mystery and tended towards simplicity and soberness. Technologically, composite moulds were still used for casting, but smelting furnaces of relatively large size were introduced and they were equipped with air-blowers, of which some samples have been found in the remains of a foundry. Lapidary (Plate 121) and ivory carving, too, retained Shang traditional techniques.

The pottery of the Western Zhou period still consists for the most part of grey ware. The sandy ware is commonly decorated with cord-marks, while the clay one is plain or with incised horizontal parallels. As various people have their own traditions in pottery making, the Western Zhou pottery is not exactly the same in shape as the Shang, and Shang white-ware making seems not to have survived. On the other hand, glazed-pottery production made considerable advances, particularly in south China, in the lower reaches of the Changjiang, where vessels of this ware have been discovered, greater in number and richer in shape (Plate 122).

Lacquer making in the Western Zhou period reached a new level. The lacquer has a wooden body for the most part and is not easy to preserve. From Western Zhou graves have been unearthed a number of rotten lacquer objects, among which *gu* (cups), *dou* (high-stemmed plates), *lei* (broad-shouldered, ring-footed vessels) and *zu* (oblong tables) have been restored (Plate 123); they are all lacquered in red on a black ground, sometimes additionally inlaid with fragmental shells

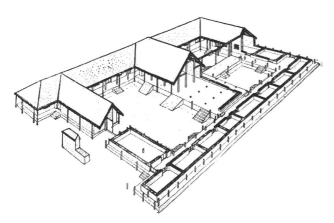

Figure 45 Reconstruction of a large-sized house of the Western Zhou period (Courtesy Institute of Archaeology, Chinese Academy of Social Sciences, Beijing).

in various designs, and even appliquéd with gold. Such fine articles, of course, were enjoyed only by nobles.

The social system

The Western Zhou period saw the further development of the slave-owning system, with a series of reforms carried out in the socio-political sphere, the first being the enfeoffment system. Already at the beginning of the period, a large-scale enfeoffment of vassals was conducted in order to consolidate and strengthen the rule of the dynasty. Under this system, the capital city and its environs were directly ruled by the king, while the vast newly conquered territories were bestowed on members and relatives-in-law of the royal family, to be built into states loyal to the dynasty. It is alleged that there were more than seventy vassals, including over fifty of the same surname as the king's. They came to be divided into five ranks: *gong* (duke), *hou* (marquess), *bo* (earl), *zi* (viscount) and *nan* (baron), all the titles being hereditary. Their obligations to the king were to obey his orders, regularly pay tribute to and have audiences with him, and lead their troops in military expeditions at his call and so on, while their internal affairs were almost completely in their own hands. A bronze *gui* (container) unearthed near Nanjing city bears the inscription which in detail records the feoff bestowed on Marquess Yi by the king. By means of feoffing vassals, the Zhou dynasty consolidated its dominance, expanded its influence and made the country an even stronger slave-owning kingdom.

After destroying the Shang dynasty, Wu Wang, following its example, made all the conquered tribesmen slaves of the nobility, but retained their original clan system. Feoffing vassals, the king invested them with slaves in whole clans. As we have seen, six Yin clans were allotted to the Lu state and seven to the Wei state, which reveals the characteristic clan slave-owning system in Western Zhou China. Slaves were often awarded by upper nobles to lesser ones, as is mentioned in numerous inscriptions on Western Zhou bronzes. Gifts of slaves were either as individuals or whole families. It is thus clear that slaves too could get married and bring up children, but all members of slaves' families were necessarily slaves. Purchase and sale of slaves are occasionally reflected in bronze inscriptions as well, and they were sold so cheaply that five slaves cost only a horse and a bunch of silk. Another difference from the Shang period was that large-scale immolations of slaves seem to have been much rarer in the Western Zhou which, perhaps, may be interpreted as a change in the institution of slavery; though it should be added that none of the Zhou kings' tombs and sacrificial sites has yet been discovered.

In inheritance of kingship and titles of nobility, the Western Zhou dynasty recognized only primogeniture as legal. The king allotted part of his territories and slaves to princes and titled them vassals of various ranks; the vassals similarly enfeoffed their brothers and younger sons – thus a strictly ranked ruling group was formed on the basis of the patriarchal clan system, with the king at the top as the sovereign ruler. The king and vassals controlled a whole set of bureaucratic apparatus, which managed daily governing affairs according to the wills of the rulers. Among the ruled there was the plebeian class who cultivated the 'private field' under the *jing-tian* system and had to work in the 'communal field' for the feudal lord; still they managed to keep their freeman status. At the bottom of society were slaves who had lost their personal liberty.

Culture and religion

The writing system of the Western Zhou was basically the same as that of the Shang period, though being more regular in structure of characters. It was used more widely. The main writings from the Shang are inscriptions on bones and tortoise-shells, while those from the Western Zhou are inscriptions on bronzes. For the last years, shell-and-bone inscriptions have been found. The characters are written in a smaller form, which is one of the most distinct differences from the Shang ones. Western Zhou bronze ritual vessels often bear lengthy inscriptions (Plate 124), the longest of which consists of nearly 500 characters. They are quite comprehensive in content, sometimes recording important historical events. A bronze *gui* (container) bears the date of Wu Wang's conquering of the Shang (Plate 125), which completely corresponds to the record in historical texts. On a bronze *zun* (vase), the construction of the new capital is inscribed. In addition, there are inscriptions of combats with other tribes, kings' orders, investments and gifts to aristocrats, arguments about the ownership of plots and so on. These inscriptions not only show the evolution of and changes in the Chinese writing system in the Western Zhou, but also provide historical information of great importance.

The Western Zhou calendar remained lunisolar, but is a little different from that of the Shang period. In the Shang calendar, the 'moon' was divided into three ten-day periods, while the Western Zhou, to conform with the changes of the moon's phases, divided the 'moon' into four sections. The beginning of the year was adjusted a 'moon' earlier than that of the Shang calendar.

The Western Zhou religion was roughly the same as the Shang one, being still predominately ancestor-worship and nature-worship. The Zhou people observed certain institutions in sacrificial ceremonies to their ancestors and the gods of the sun, the moon, stars, mountains, rivers and land. Some new religious ideas, for instance, the concept of the Supreme God (Shang-Ti), came into existence. The Supreme God was believed to be the sovereign dominating all other gods, and it was he who granted the 'mandate of the heaven' to the kings and entrusted them with the power of ruling the world. Such use of religious ideas for maintaining the dynasty's domination was a new development.

Divination remained prevalent during the Western Zhou period. Apart from scalpulimancy, there was popular magic. It was practised like this: from fifty stalks, repeatedly taking away a certain number of stalks, the final remainder would be an even or odd number, which was figured as a broken or unbroken line respectively and called a *yao*; three *yao* made a single-hexagram, while six *yao* accumulated to a double-hexagram (the two kinds of hexagrams totalling 8 and 64 respectively), and all hexagrams had their own titles and interpretations, by means of which wizards were allegedly able to transmit the gods' instructions. All aspects of the magic was stated in the *I Jing* (*Book of Changes*), a divination manual, which is held to be the most important of the Confucian classics.

Apart from the *I Jing*, the *Shi Jing* (*Book of Odes*) and *Shu Jing* (*Book of Documents*) occupy an important place among the Confucian classics. These books, containing numerous Western Zhou and even Shang documents, legends, poems and so on, were compiled a little later than the Western Zhou period. They exerted great influence upon the formation of later Confucian ideology.

PERIPHERAL BRONZE CULTURES IN THE SHANG AND WESTERN ZHOU PERIOD

The dominion of the Shang and Western Zhou dynasties mainly covered the middle and lower reaches of the Huanghe, including part of modern Henan, Shaanxi, Shanxi, Shandong and Hebei Provinces. Beyond that area, the other territories of China were then inhabited by various tribes, most of them having a Bronze Age technology. The northerners among them were chiefly nomads or semi-nomads, while the southerners primarily engaged in rice cultivation, and all of them were in different degrees distinct from the Shang and Western Zhou peoples in cultural aspects. The relationship of these tribes to the Shang and Western Zhou dynasties was alternately subject and hostile, and often wars broke out between them. According to historical texts, the Shang king Wu Ding made war upon the Guifang tribes which lasted three years. The Zhou king Zho Wang went on a southward military expedition to the Chu tribes and was drowned in the Han River. However, the mutual cultural influence and ethnical fusion between the Shang and Western Zhou peoples and the peripheral tribes were doubtless of great significance in the formation of the Han nationality.

In the north, within eastern Inner Mongolia and western Liaoning, it was the Lower and Upper Xiajiadian cultures that developed in parallel with the Shang and Western Zhou bronze cultures. The Lower Xiajiadian culture has settlements commonly surrounded by walls and other defensive works, within which have been found several dozens or even over a hundred round houses of the semi-subterranean type of surface adobe construction. Near settlements are located cemeteries, from which pottery with patterns painted after baking (Plate 126) has been unearthed as common funerary objects and small-size bronzes as occasional finds. In rare cases, grave furniture includes pottery *gui* (spouted tripods) and *jue* (cups), which resemble vessels of the same types from the Erlitou culture in the Huanghe Valley and therefore must indicate certain cultural connections of the two peoples. Both cultures date from the period corresponding to the early Shang. The following culture is the Upper Xiajiadian. Its pottery is made rough, undecorated on the surface and baked at a low temperature. The bronzes dug up include axes, knives, daggers, spears and other weapons and tools. Western Zhou bronze ritual vessels have been uncovered in association with local bronze cooking vessels, multi-protuberant ornaments and so on, as usual funerary objects of the large-sized graves, which provide evidence for understanding the relation of this culture with that of the Western Zhou.

The Ordos region of Inner Mongolia and its adjoining northern Shanxi and Shaanxi Provinces, too, have yielded bronzes, of which the ritual vessels are identical with late Shang ones of the same type, while the associated objects bear characteristic features of the northern steppe culture, such as daggers with bell-shaped heads and other bronze weapons, along with various gold ornaments. The remains of this bronze culture show that, on the one hand, it borrowed some elements from the Shang culture, on the other, it followed a number of traditions inherent in its own nomadic world. The territory is roughly identified as the domain of the Guifang tribes.

Among the north-west bronze cultures of Shang-Zhou China were the Xindian and Siwa cultures, distributed in part of modern Gansu and Qinghai Provinces. The former is characterized by the high-necked, hollow-legged *li* (tripod), resembling, and probably related to, the early Zhou one in shape; and has yielded some painted pottery vessels and bronze implements, such as the knife, awl, chisel and so on. The Siwa culture has the saddleback-mouthed, two-eared jar as the typical pottery and such bronze weapons as the *ge* (dagger-axe), spear and so on. It goes back to the times corresponding roughly to the early Western Zhou and belonged to the Qiangrong tribes. During the Western Zhou period, the Rong and Di tribes in the north-west often invaded the Central Plains, intruding deeply into the vicinity of the capital and endangering it. It is highly likely that they were the descendants of the Xindian or Siwa people.

The bronze culture in the Western Sichuan Plain of southwest China may have belonged to the ancient Shu people, one of Wu Wang's eight allies during his military expedition against the Shang dynasty. The culture is represented by buildings of wooden construction, pottery with pointed-bottomed vessels as the most characteristic type, bronze weapons and tools such as the *ge* (dagger-axe), *yue* (battleaxe), axe and knife, as well as huge bronze human figures (Plate 127), along with ritual vessels identical with late Shang and early Zhou ones. There are also various jade objects and divining tortoise-shells. It can be concluded that the culture shared many elements with the Shang-Zhou and was roughly contemporary with the late Shang and early Zhou. The earliest bronzes from Yunnan Province are found at Jianchuan County and date to the period corresponding to the late Shang.

Among the bronze cultural complexes of the Changjiang-Han River region in Shang-Zhou times, the most important are Panlongcheng in Huangpi County, Hubei Province, and Wucheng in Qingjiang County, Jiangxi Province. At the Panlongcheng site, a small ruined town has been brought to light, measuring 70,000 m², enclosed by rammed-earth walls, within which large-sized house foundations have been discovered. In the suburbs a cemetery has been excavated, with the large graves all yielding bronze ritual vessels identical with middle Shang ones both in shape and decoration. Here there might have been a local chiefdom of the late Shang period. The Wucheng site contains the remains of semi-subterranean dwellings. The pottery unearthed largely consists of hard ware with stamped geometrical designs, and glazed ware. Among the bronzes there are objects cast with stone moulds. Some pottery vessels and stone moulds bear glyphs and incised signs. The large-sized grave discovered in Xingan, Jiangxi Province, having many ritual bronzes, jades, pottery vessels, and so on as funerary objects, may belong to the head of the tribes who created the culture represented by the Wucheng site. Chronologically, the site goes back to late Shang times. After the Western Zhou period, the Changjiang-Han region gradually became part of the dominion of the Zhou dynasty and was allotted to members of the royal family; thus there appeared a number of small states, all of which were later on conquered by the Chu state.

The Bronze Age of south-east China is represented by the Hushu culture distributed in the Changjiang Valley within Jiangsu and Anhui Provinces. Its sites are mostly situated on mounds above the surrounding ground, with houses characterized by the fire-baked floor. The productive implements mainly consist of stone tools, but small-sized bronzes have been unearthed as usual finds. The pottery is similar in shape to that of the late Shang and early Zhou, and tortoise-shells and animal bones for divination are present as well.

The culture must have been an aboriginal one with a number of elements assimilated from the Shang-Zhou culture. As for the region of modern Fujian and Guangdong Provinces, its bronze culture was developed later; during the Shang-Zhou period it still remained at the Neolithic level.

BIBLIOGRAPHY

CHANG, KWANG-CHIH (ed.) 1979. *The Archaeology of Ancient China.* 3rd ed. New Haven, Conn.

—— 1980. *Shang Civilization.* New Haven, Conn.

CHENG, TE-KUN. 1960. *Archaeology in China*, vol. 2: *Shang China.* Cambridge.

—— 1963. *Archaeology in China*, vol. 3: *Chou China.* Cambridge/Toronto.

KEIGHTLEY, D. N. 1978. *Source of Shang History.* Berkeley/Los Angeles, Calif.

LI, CHI. 1977. *Anyang.* Seattle, Wash.

PARETI, L. 1965. *History of Mankind.* London. Vol. 2, pt 1.

XIA, NAI (ed.) 1984. *Recent Archaeological Discoveries in the People's Republic of China.* Paris.

—— 1984. [*Archaeological Discoveries and Researches in New China*]. Beijing.

II Regions for which only archaeological and anthropological sources are available

EDITOR'S NOTE

Archaeological research is proliferating in Africa, and discrepancies are to be observed from one major region to another in the findings obtained. In order to provide readers with a coherent overall view of the cultural evolution of this vast continent with its complex history, the Reading Committee asked Professor D. W. Phillipson to produce a composite version based on the contributions of the various authors, L. M. Diop-Maes, A. M. Lam, Massamba Lam, T. Obenga and B. Sall, and the text here presented is the outcome of this reworking.

13

AFRICA, EXCLUDING THE NILE VALLEY

Louise M. Diop-Maes (Senegal)
Aboubacry M. Lam (Senegal)
Massamba Lam (Senegal)
Théophile Obenga (Congo)
David W. Phillipson (United Kingdom)
Babacar Sall (Senegal)

In most of Africa the period from the beginning of the third millennium until the mid-first millennium BC may be characterized as that which saw the last major florescence of societies whose technology was dominated by the production and use of stone tools. By the end of this period, the working of metal was probably beginning in several areas but had not yet developed its full impact on African society. In many regions north of the equator the development of local farming systems involving both the cultivation of indigenous crops and, where environmentally feasible, the herding of domestic animals, continued and expanded throughout this period, following the patterns established in previous millennia, as has been outlined by D. W. Phillipson in Volume I of this *History*. There remains considerable uncertainty about the date at which food-producing adaptations were initiated in the equatorial forests of Central Africa. In the sub-equatorial savannahs to the south and south-east of the forest, however, most if not all of the inhabitants appear to have continued their hunter-gatherer lifestyle almost until the end of the first millennium BC. It is with the social processes involved with these economic changes and developments, as well as with the technological advances which accompanied them, that this chapter is primarily concerned. Since the chronological periodization set for this volume has little direct relevance to sub-Saharan Africa, the chapter should be read in conjunction with Chapter 33 of Volume I.

In this volume, the history of the Egyptian and Nubian Nile Valley is considered separately from that of the rest of the African continent. This arrangement is convenient from the point of view of authors' specialisms and because of the nature and quantity of the available evidence. It does, however, serve to perpetuate a historiographical separation which is now increasingly viewed as unreal and which hampers understanding of past developments both in the Nile Valley and in other parts of Africa.

In comparison with the corresponding period in many other parts of the world and, indeed, with other periods of African prehistory, the primary data on which this chapter can draw are extremely sparse. What follows should be regarded, therefore, as an interim, often speculative, statement. In some areas of the continent, as in West-Central Africa, the pace of archaeological research is currently quickening; elsewhere it is at a virtual standstill; in yet other countries it has, to all intents and purposes, never begun. It is hoped that this chapter will help to indicate some of the more glaring lacunae in our knowledge and to act as a pointer for future research needs. Reference to data which strictly belong outside our period of primary concern will, on occasion, be necessary in order to provide a coherent narrative.

This *History* is mainly concerned with scientific and cultural achievements. In non-industrial societies these are generally dependent to a considerable extent upon natural environmental factors. It must not be thought that environment has determined the course of human development, although it has frequently provided stimuli or constraints. It is useful nevertheless to begin the chapter with a brief consideration of the extent to which environmental conditions in different parts of Africa during the last three millennia BC differed from those which have prevailed in earlier and more recent times.

In several regions of the continent this was a period of progressive desiccation. In what is now the Sahara, areas of desert became more extensive, with significant rainfall largely restricted to a few highland zones and surface water to the places fed by the resultant run-off. This process of desiccation was by no means uniform, and recent research has detected significant regional variation from the general pattern. Overall, however, there was, over many generations, an expansion of the desert, particularly to the south, with a concomitant shift and narrowing of the sahelian and sudanic zones. By the early second millennium BC many parts of the Sahara and sahel were probably at least as arid as they are today. In at least some areas there was a temporary climatic amelioration during the centuries around 1000 BC, at the end of the period with which this volume is concerned.

The overall picture of this period in the Sahara and West Africa is one of significant climatic change. Two points should be stressed in this connection. The first is that the effects of such change are cumulative. For example, Lake Chad at its maximum extent was a body of open water large enough to support its own rainfall system, much as Lake Victoria does at the present time. As the lake's area decreased, it ceased to have this effect, thus causing major change in vegetation over a very wide area. The Lake Turkana basin in northern Kenya may have seen similar developments. The second point concerns the extent to which human activities may have contributed to the rapidity of vegetational degradation and thus, indirectly, to climatic change. The period around 3000 BC, as will be shown below, was one when domestic animals were extensively herded in what is now the Sahara and sahel. Over-grazing in a fragile environment can have a calamitous effect upon vegetational cover, often resulting in erosion which precludes renewal. Pending detailed regional studies it may be concluded that the activities of herders have magnified or contributed to the destruction of vegetation. Loss of transpiration and acceleration of run-off would in turn reduce precipitation even further.

In present circumstances, one of the clearest insights on climatic change between the modern Sahara and the northern edge of the equatorial forest is provided by the study of former lake levels. Since the lake waters have rarely been significantly lower than they are today, the high strand-lines of earlier times are clearly preserved. Although regional differences may be detected, falling water-levels may be detected through the third and second millennia BC from Chad to the lakes of the East African Rift Valley. Further confirmation of this general picture is provided by study of pollens and of faunal remains preserved in the lake deposits themselves.

In more southerly latitudes, changes generally seem to have been less marked. In contrast with earlier times, there were no significant fluctuations in sea-level. There was some contraction of the equatorial forest but this was minor in comparison with the vegetational shifts which took place further to the north. The main periods of forest-edge clearance associated with the expansion of horticulture were yet to come. Likewise, in southern Africa, the arid regions of the centre and west did not mirror the increasing desiccation which was so devastating to the north of the equatorial forest.

What emerges from this brief consideration of environmental change is the conclusion that the diversity of African biomes during the last three millennia BC was not in itself significantly different from that which has prevailed more recently. A major contrast was, however, presented in the distribution of these biomes, particularly in the northern half of the continent. It is essential to view human cultural developments in this context. Environments vary not only in the density of human population which they can sustain but also in the economic practices best suited to their exploitation. It is therefore almost impossible to make meaningful estimates of ancient levels of human population on other than an extremely local basis.[1]

As environmental zones have shifted their distributions, so have the animal species that depended upon them. There is often no reason to believe that human populations will have behaved otherwise. Before the establishment of international frontiers there were few barriers to such movement. This fact, combined with the natural richness of many African environments, may on occasion have provided a disincentive to radical economic change, particularly in sub-Saharan Africa.

A further factor which has affected human cultural development but which may itself be largely dependent upon the environment is insect-borne disease, both of people and of domestic stock. This is not the place for a detailed discussion, but the examples of malaria and trypanosomiasis may be cited. In the short term, the presence of such diseases may deter expansion; eventually immunities may be developed. The zones where such diseases prevail will themselves have changed, often radically, for largely environmental reasons.

The factors enumerated above are ones that should be borne in mind whilst reading the regional and thematic surveys which follow.

REGIONAL SURVEY

Northern Africa and the Sahara

Through the greater part of this region, the practice of herding domestic animals had begun long before 3000 BC, as described in Volume I of this *History*. The same may also be true of plant cultivation, but the evidence for this remains largely inconclusive. The fourth millennium BC had been a time when, as noted above, many highland areas of what is now the Sahara had experienced relatively well-watered conditions with concomitant vegetation and fauna. Through run-off, some more low-lying country was also the scene of open water and rivers with regular periods of flow. One such place was at Adrar Bous, in the Ténéré desert of northern Niger, near the eastern slope of the Air highlands. A lakeshore settlement was inhabited by 'Neolithic' people who exploited fish and other aquatic foods and who also herded short-horned cattle. Their use of vegetable foods, including possibly sorghum, is not adequately illustrated by the available evidence, although the presence of numerous grindstones hints at its probable importance. Material culture included backed microliths as well as bifacially flaked knives and projectile points; comparable specimens have been found as far to the east as Borkou in Chad. The pottery and groundstone axe/hoes are of types that were widely distributed in the Sahara and Sudanese Nile Valley during this period.

Early in the third millennium, increasing desiccation led to the progressive shrinking of the Adrar Bous lake and the eventual abandonment of the settlement on its shore. A similar picture prevailed in most other lowland areas of the Sahara. In the central uplands (Plate 128), comprising Tibesti, Hoggar and Acacus, regular human settlement probably survived for rather longer. The evidence, however, comes mainly from rockshelters, use of which may have become increasingly transitory. Much evidence for social and economic practices at this time comes from the rock art, particularly that of the later stages of the so-called bovidean style, generally attributed to the third and, perhaps, second millennia BC. In the later examples of this style, horses are also depicted. The earliest representations of camels may also fall near the end of the period with which this chapter is concerned.

Before discussing the Saharan rock art as a source of information about cultural development, it must be emphasized that its dating remains extremely imprecise, being based largely upon circumstantial evidence. A. Muzzolini has pointed out how the tentative chronologies proposed several decades ago by F. Mori and H. Lhote have been uncritically accepted, despite the great advances that have meanwhile been made in obtaining radiocarbon estimates of the ages of the associated settlement sites. There has been a tendency to try and fit the rock art into an over-simplified sequence based both upon subject-matter and upon stylistic criteria. There has also been an unfortunate emphasis on attempting to ascertain the 'racial' affinities of the people portrayed, with inadequate recognition of the stylistic conventions which must have been observed by the artists. Despite these difficulties, and shortcomings of some of the research that has so far been undertaken, the rock art does nevertheless offer valuable insights into many aspects of the life-styles that were followed in the Saharan highlands during the general period with which this chapter is concerned.

The subjects most frequently depicted are people and cattle (Plates 129, 130). Representations of wild animals, although not unusual, are rarely associated and are more often engraved than painted. It is generally believed (on, it must be admitted, somewhat uncertain grounds) that they are on the whole earlier in date than the cattle paintings. The cattle are often shown in substantial herds. Features emphasized include horn-shape, individual coat markings, and udders. It may plausibly be concluded that importance was attached to the physical characteristics of individual beasts (as is frequently the case among recent African herding peoples) and that, again as today, artificial deformation of the horns was sometimes practised. The detailed portrayal of udders may suggest that milk production was a major focus of herd management strategies. Cattle are also sometimes shown wearing artificial decoration, including a disc between the horns which strongly resembles the conventional headgear of the Egyptian goddess Hathor. Here is a further reminder that it is a mistake to underestimate the cultural links between the Saharan regions and the Egyptian Nile Valley at this time.

It is not unreasonable to suppose that the clothing and other accoutrements such as weapons, with which human figures were depicted by the Saharan artists, may provide some indication of those that were in contemporary use. It must be emphasized, however, that we have as yet no sound evidence as to the original social function of the Saharan art. Without an idea of the meaning which the art had for the societies responsible for its creation (analogous, for example, to that now demonstrated for many South African paintings), it would be imprudent to place too much weight upon the detailed interpretation of its subject-matter.

The chronology of the Saharan rock art remains poorly understood. There are very few instances where it can be tied to a dated archaeological occurrence or sequence on other than circumstantial grounds, but one such situation, at Uan Muhuggiag in the Acacus massif of south-western Libya, is doubly informative. A block of stone fell from the wall after one series of paintings had been executed but before those of a second style were added; the fall took place onto an archaeological deposit from which has been obtained a radiocarbon date around the end of the fourth millennium BC. Both series of paintings depict domestic cattle; it follows that the earlier such art falls outside the period with which this chapter is concerned. Muzzolini has suggested that the later, so-called 'Ti-n-Anneuin' herder paintings at Uan Muhuggiag and other Acacus sites are contemporary with the earliest representations of horses, probably early in the first millennium BC.

Widely distributed in the Sahara are paintings of light, two-wheeled, horse-drawn chariots (Fig. 46). They are assumed to date from around 1000 BC or shortly afterwards. Attempts to plot the distribution of these paintings and thus to recognize 'chariot-routes' across the desert are now largely discredited: the strange new vehicles would have made a profound impression upon Saharan peoples and may have been depicted far from the areas where they were seen. No

Figure 46 Saharan rock painting of horse-drawn chariot (after *Sahara*, Vol. I, 1988, front cover).

physical remains of these chariots have been found. They are assumed to have come from North Africa.

In the easternmost sahel, between the middle Nile Valley and the Ethiopian highlands, the dry plains bisected by the Atbara and Gash rivers saw marked continuity of prehistoric occupation throughout this period. This tradition, named Atbai, was established by at least the fourth millennium BC: its pottery styles may share an earlier common origin with those of the middle Nile. Sorghum was cultivated in this area by at least the mid-second millennium BC and probably earlier. Large villages, some 4–12 hectares in extent, were located in the main river valleys and saw prolonged occupation. Riverine foods were exploited, and there is some evidence for the herding of domestic animals. Away from the rivers, smaller more temporary settlements were the norm, and there is here rather more evidence for herding. As in the middle Nile Valley during earlier times, a complex settlement pattern is indicated, with permanent establishments near the rivers and more temporary or seasonally occupied herding camps in the hinterland.

Developments at this time in the Sudanese Nile Valley to the south of Nubia remain poorly understood. It appears likely that this, too, was an area which witnessed strong cultural continuity with earlier times, with only slight influence from contemporary Nubia. Certainly, as late as the last few centuries BC, the large sites at Jebel Moya and Jebel et Tomat between the Blue and White Niles near Sennar retained a material culture with ceramic styles and flaked stone artefacts which suggest long stability of tradition from Kadero and Esh Shaheinab over 3,000 years previously. The domestic economy was based on the herding of cattle, sheep and goats, together with hunting, fowling and fishing. The sorghum that was grown shows significant morphological development from wild types, indicating that it had been selectively cultivated for a long time previously. It is puzzling that virtually no archaeological sites of the third and second millennia BC have yet been discovered in the central Sudanese Nile Valley. It seems unlikely that the valley was uninhabited at this time; perhaps settlements were so small and transitory that their remains have not yet been discovered, or were located so close to the main river-channel that they have been obliterated by subsequent floods.

Several areas of the eastern desert, between the Nile and the Red Sea, were exploited for minerals that were valued in the Egyptian Nile Valley. The area was also traversed by trade routes whereby goods emanating from the Red Sea coasts and, on occasion, beyond were brought to Egypt. These activities are recorded in the numerous rock engravings of the region, most notable being those along the Wadi el Barramiya (Plate 131). These engravings represent a tradition that was widespread in the Nile Valley and neighbouring regions during pre-dynastic times. In the surrounding deserts it continued into later periods, the earliest representations of the Red Sea trade being probably contemporary with the Egyptian Old Kingdom of the mid-third millennium BC.

Most famous of the Egyptian long-distance trade ventures were those to the 'Land of Punt', the precise location of which has long been a matter of controversy. Most authorities agree on its situation on the Red Sea coast either in what is now northern Somalia or, possibly, in the area between Suakin and Massawa. A case has, however, also been made for a more inland location in the modern Ethiopia/Sudan borderlands. The 'Land of Punt' was apparently known to the Egyptians from the Old Kingdom period onwards, but the most detailed information derives from the mid-second millennium BC when relief carvings (Fig. 47) in the mortuary temple of Queen Hatshepsut at Deir el Bahari depicted boats being laden with local products, listed as including ebony, ivory, gold, resin and leopard skins. Apes and monkeys were also taken, whilst the carvings also show that the inhabitants of Punt lived in dome-shaped houses, cultivated cereals and herded small stock as well as two distinct types of cattle.

The 'Land of Punt' was but one, albeit the best documented, of the African regions beyond the Nile Valley with which the ancient Egyptians had regular contact. The nature both of this contact, and of the available archaeological and documentary evidence, means that we learn more about it from Egyptian sources than from elsewhere, but the geographical referents are almost invariably vague. It is known, for example, that pygmoid people were occasionally brought to Egypt, presumably from the Central African regions to the west of the Nile headwaters. Saharan connections, as illustrated in the rock art of that region, have been noted above.

For the first few centuries of the period under review, the cave of Haua Fteah in Cyrenaican Libya continued to be occupied by Libyco-Capsian herders of small stock, as described in Volume I of this History.[2] Their pottery shared several distinctive features with contemporary wares in the Maghreb. Although no rock art as such is preserved at the Haua Fteah itself, the presence of stone fragments and ostrich eggshells bearing both painted and engraved decoration shows that these techniques were practised. Later developments at the site, from the mid-third millennium onwards, are poorly known.

To the west, in the Maghreb, there is strong evidence for continuity with earlier periods in the so-called 'Neolithic of Caprian tradition', as well as for contact with other circum-Mediterranean regions. The well-established tradition of transhumant herding continued, with modification due to increased desertification of inland areas. Cattle became progressively more important, in place of small stock. Except in a few favoured areas, the population mainly comprised small, mobile groups.

Particular importance attaches to archaeological remains at Dhar Tichitt, near the southern edge of the desert in southern Mauritania, because this is one of very few Saharan areas which have yielded clear evidence for prehistoric use of cereals. The primary evidence comprises potsherds bearing grain-impressions, notably of bulrush millet (*Pennisetum*). It should be noted that Tichitt lies within the area of natural distribution for wild forms of both bulrush millet and sorghum. The main period of prehistoric occupation extended from the mid-third to the early first millennium BC, throughout which time conditions became progressively more arid and several small lakes gradually disappeared. The principal sites represent the remains of stone-walled compounds (Plate 132) concentrated above a cliff over a distance of 40 km, but there are also traces of other, perhaps more ephemeral, occupa-

Figure 47 An Egyptian trading expedition to the 'Land of Punt' as depicted in a relief carving in the mortuary temple of the 18th dynasty Queen Hatshepsut at Deir el Bahari (drawn by D. W. Phillipson).

tion elsewhere in the vicinity. Pioneering investigations in the late 1960s and early 1970s suggested that, during the second half of the third millennium, the local economy was based upon hunting and gathering; and that millet cultivation did not begin on any significant scale until the middle of the second millennium, when cattle and goats were also herded, becoming progressively more important during the succeeding centuries. More recently, it has been proposed that this apparent sequence may, at least in part, reflect changing foci of settlement with seasonally varying economic emphases. The apparent late date for the intensive reliance upon cereal cultivation should, therefore, be regarded as unproven. It may be noted, however, that the earliest radiocarbon date obtained directly on a sherd bearing impressions of cultivated *Pennisetum* is *c.* 1000 BC. Of several thousand cereal impressions that have now been examined (Plate 133), none has been identified as sorghum. The implication is that cereal cultivation in this particular area was a late development, but it must not necessarily be assumed that this was also the case in other parts of the sahel.

Despite the numerous and widespread representations of domestic cattle in Saharan rock art, there is disappointingly little information relating to their chronology, or that of the herding practices which they depict. It has been argued above that, during the mid-Holocene, optimum conditions for human settlement prevailed in the central Saharan highland areas where the painting sites are also concentrated. With subsequent desiccation, these regions became progressively less suited to long-term settlement. The resultant dispersal of herds and herders may be seen in the Tilemsi Valley which rises in Air and extends southwards for a distance of some 400 km to its confluence with the Niger near Gao (Map 19). At Asselar, in the northern part of the valley, there is evidence for the presence of cattle herders in the late fourth millennium BC. Further south, however, there is no sign of them until 1,500 years later, when the inhabitants of the Karkarichinkat sites depended upon domestic cattle as well as hunting, fowling and fishing: there are no data relating to their use of vegetable foods. It is tempting to view the Tilemsi Valley succession as illustrating the gradual expansion of herders southwards towards West Africa.

West Africa

In West Africa, archaeological research relating to this period has been very unevenly distributed. So far as Ghana and Nigeria are concerned there are about half-a-dozen key sequences which, fortunately, provide a general picture of some aspects of local prehistory in the coastal zone, in the forest, and in the savannah which lies to its north. It must be emphasized, however, that virtually all our information comes from the investigation of single sites and that there has so far been little attempt to undertake detailed regional studies of the type which, in other areas, have greatly illuminated the complexity of ancient landscape-exploitation strategies.

In some regions of West Africa the manufacture of pottery and the production of stone tools by grinding began before 3000 BC. Information about the economic basis of the societies responsible for these artefacts is not yet available for periods prior to the second millennium BC, but it is possible that, in the forest and its margins, such societies may have depended heavily upon the care, and subsequently, the cultivation of indigenous yam species. Certainly, the use of pottery implies a certain stability of settlement; and ground-

stone axes/hoes may have been used in cultivation and for clearance of woodland. T. Shaw has noted that, in West Africa as a whole, distinctive variant industries may be recognized at this time beside the lakes and rivers of the present sahel, in the savannah, in the forest zone and along the Atlantic coast. The term 'Guinea Neolithic', by which these industries were formerly distinguished from their aceramic predecessors, is now regarded with disfavour, at least by anglophone prehistorians, as carrying implications of food production which, as noted above, generally remains to be satisfactorily demonstrated.

One of the very few dated sequences in West Africa that cover the period of the beginnings of pottery manufacture is at the rock shelter of Iwo Eleru, just inside the present forest margin in western Nigeria. Here the main innovations – ground-stone tools as well as pottery – are first attested in levels dated as early as the fourth millennium BC. The associated chipped-stone tools are predominantly microlithic. At Afikpo, east of the Niger, an apparently parallel sequence displays a high proportion of non-microlithic artefacts, including chipped axes/hoes such as are typical of densely forested environments elsewhere in West Africa. In Ghana, one of the best documented occurrences of a pottery-associated microlithic industry is still that from Bosumpra Cave near Abetifi. During the site's occupation, which lasted for most of the last four millennia BC, pottery and ground stone artefacts became progressively more common. All these sites have so far been studied effectively in isolation, and virtually no evidence has yet been recovered which relates to their economic base.

Further to the west, the few sites of this period that have been excavated in Côte d'Ivoire, Sierra Leone, Guinea and Senegal do not provide detailed information. It may be tentatively suggested, however, that the appearance of pottery and ground-stone artefacts in these sequences may have been later, by as much as a thousand years, than the corresponding developments in Ghana and Nigeria. If this hypothesis is supported by the results of future research, far-reaching conclusions may be drawn. For the eastern part of the West African forest, unlike that to the west of central Côte d'Ivoire, is the area where yam cultivation has developed to the extent of supporting extremely high population densities. The economic implications of the presence of pottery and of ground-stone axes/hoes have not yet been conclusively demonstrated, but it is not unreasonable to suppose that they imply some degree of sedentism together with activities involving clearance of woodland and/or cultivation of the soil. If these were features of life in the eastern, yam-growing part of the West African forest belt considerably earlier than was the case further to the west, then the propagation of yams may be seen as the first stage in the development of West African food production. Yams are plants indigenous to this area, unknown in the drier lands to the north, and there can be no doubt that their artificial propagation was a truly local development.

If yams were being cultivated in this area at least as early as the fourth millennium BC, it should be emphasized that no other form of food production, involving either plants or animals, is attested anywhere in West Africa until a significantly later period. As usual, the evidence for domestic animals is somewhat more readily recovered, albeit so far extremely scanty. As noted above, by the end of the fourth millennium BC, increasing desiccation in what is now the Sahara had resulted in southward shift of herders and herds to areas south of 19°N latitude, such as the Tichitt and Agadez basins, the plains surrounding Lake Chad and the valley of

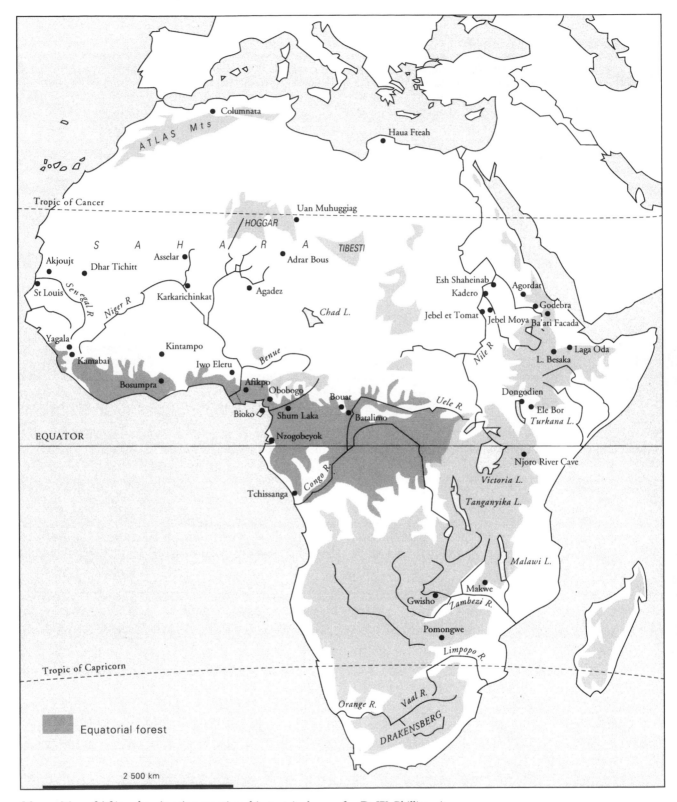

Map 19 Map of Africa, showing sites mentioned in text (redrawn after D. W. Phillipson).

the Tilemsi. In the latter area, extending southwards from Air to the Niger bend, herders' settlements, as noted above, have been dated before 3000 BC in the north at Asselar, but only after 2000 BC at Karkarichinkat near the Niger confluence.[3] Both cattle and small stock were herded. It may be that tsetse-fly infestation at that time extended far to the north of its present limit and delayed the further spread of herds into West Africa.

It is from two groups of sites belonging to the second millennium BC that more comprehensive and informative data

are available. The first is located in central Ghana, west of the Volta and near the present northern margin of the forest. Here, a cluster of rock shelters and open sites near Kintampo permits the reconstruction of a composite sequence in which considerable local continuity is apparent, although with some traits of probable northern affinities – both in pottery decoration and in stone tool typology – accompanying the first appearance of domestic animals around the middle of the second millennium BC. Kintampo assemblages (Fig. 48) are also characterized by stone grater-like objects

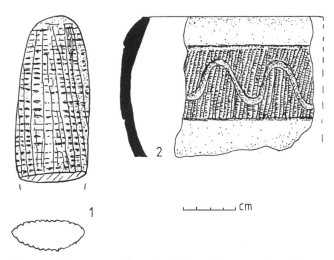

Figure 48 Stone rasp and potsherd from Kintampo sites, Ghana (drawn by D. W. Phillipson).

of uncertain function: it has been suggested, on no very firm basis, that they may have been utilized either in the preparation of yams or in the manufacture of pottery.

The second area lies in a very different setting, in the Bornu plains of north-eastern Nigeria, bordering on Lake Chad. Here, from late in the second millennium BC, if not before, settlements of permanent houses were established with clay floors and wooden walls, the inhabitants of which made standardized pottery and bone tools, there being no locally accessible sources of stone. Hunting and fishing were practised alongside the herding of domestic cattle and goats; probably cereals were also cultivated, although there is as yet no conclusive proof of this.

In more westerly regions the picture remains even more fragmentary and difficult to understand. Pottery and ground-stone artefacts are known from Côte d'Ivoire, where they occur both in rock shelters inland and on coastal shell-middens: in neither context can they be shown to be earlier than the late third millennium BC. A similar situation is indicated in Sierra Leone at Yagala and Kamabai rock shelters. In Senegambia, most of our information comes from coastal shell-midden sites near St Louis and beside the Casamance estuary, where pottery was in use from the fourth millennium BC. Presumably the rich marine/estuarine environment permitted some degree of sedentism, analogous to that of Saharan and East African lakeshore sites, but there is no indication that any form of food production was practised.

There has been considerable controversy over the extent to which metal working in West Africa may have developed during the period, prior to 700 BC, with which this chapter is concerned. As will be shown in Volume III of this *History*, there can be little doubt that the making and use of iron became widespread in the region during the middle and/or later centuries of the first millennium BC. However, during the 1970s evidence was recovered from around Agadez in Niger which was interpreted as indicating the smelting of copper during the period 2500–1500 BC. Further investigations by D. Grébenart and others have shown that there is no clear evidence for metallurgy at this time: what were originally thought to be the remains of furnaces are probably the charred trunks of trees. The earliest confirmed metal-working at Agadez thus belongs to the mid-first millennium BC, and relates to both iron and copper. The latter metal was also being worked at this time around Akjoujt in Mauritania. In both simple low furnaces were in use and hammered

blades produced. Although future research may provide a different picture, the data currently available do not support the view that metallurgy in West Africa extends significantly into the period with which this chapter is concerned.[4]

Rock art, which in other parts of the continent has thrown significant light on the economy and society of early food-producing peoples, is extremely rare in West Africa, and most of what has been recorded appears to be of relatively recent date. A possible exception is provided by two sites on the northern slopes of the Jos plateau in central Nigeria, where there are paintings of long-horned humpless cattle of a breed no longer present in the vicinity.

If one may tentatively propose, from the very sparse data that are available, a reconstruction of some general trends in the prehistory of Ghana and Nigeria during the period 3000–700 BC, the emphasis would undoubtedly be on continuity and local development. Here there is apparent no sharp discontinuity in the archaeological record such as that which accompanied the beginnings of farming south of the equator. The beginning of yam-based horticulture on the forest fringes of West Africa's more easterly regions may well have been an indigenous development: this tentative conclusion deserves to be a prime focus of future archaeological research. During the late third and second millennia increasing aridity in what is now the Sahara stimulated a southward expansion of peoples who practised herding and/or cereal agriculture, evidence for both of which activities first appears in the West African archaeological record at this time. Their impact was, however, largely restricted to the savannah regions and their effect on the indigenous societies appears to have been gradual. Together, these changes in primary food sources were intimately linked, not necessarily causatively, with processes of population growth and increased nucleation of settlement. It is in these latter trends that the roots of subsequent West African cultural development properly lie.

Central Africa

To the east, the forest zone of West Africa is contiguous with the Central African equatorial forest which extends through much of the Congo basin as far as the mountains beside the western branch of the Rift Valley. Until very recently the archaeology of this vast region remained totally unknown. We now know that in the forest fringes of Cameroon, as at Shum Laka near Bamenda, pottery manufacture and the production of stone axes/hoes were at least as early as in West Africa. It thus appears likely that the area of early yam propagation, proposed above, extended into what is now southern Cameroon. For much, if not all, of the period under discussion, the forest was probably significantly more extensive than it is today.

Subsequent developments are illustrated at the complex site of Obobogo near Yaoundé, in a forest location to the south of the Grassfields. Here, it appears that use of pottery and ground-stone tools began rather later than was the case further to the north. By the middle of the first millennium BC, if not before, there is evidence for a village at Obobogo extending over an area of about two hectares. A series of deep pits contained, in addition to sherds of flat-based pots and stone axes/hoes, grindstones and shells of two types of edible nut: oil palm (*Elaeis guineensis*) and atili (*Canarium schweinfurthii*). A few fragments of slag show that iron working was also beginning at this time.

It is to the last millennium BC, too, that current research would attribute the megalithic funerary monuments located around Bouar, in the westernmost Central African Republic, bordering on Cameroon. Well over one hundred of these sites are now known, each consisting of a rubble mound incorporating undressed megalithic walls and cists. Individual stones can reach 2 tonnes in weight but are generally much smaller. Flaked and ground-stone tools, pottery and grindstones are associated with the construction levels of these *tazunu* monuments. It may be implied that the contemporary environment was similar to that of today, with some of the dry woodland perhaps cleared for cultivation.

Recent fieldwork in Gabon has demonstrated that the makers of backed microliths around the Gabon estuary near Libreville began to use pottery that shares some typological features with broadly contemporary wares from Cameroon, perhaps as early as 3000 BC. The date of this innovation remains uncertain pending further research: so far only two sites, River Denis and Nzogobeyok, one on each side of the estuary, have yielded age-determinations prior to the first millennium BC, and their stratigraphic distribution is a cause for caution. To some time in the first millennium BC belong the first village sites in both Estuaire and Ogooué provinces. These sites cover areas of up to 2,000 m², and preliminary explorations have yielded grindstones and oil-palm nuts alongside pottery and flaked stone artefacts. It was probably at this same general period that ground-stone axes/hoes began to be made in this region (Fig. 49). Taken together, these observations indicate that the inhabitants of these coastal regions adopted, at some time during the last three millennia BC, features of settled life and intensive exploitation of forest vegetable foods, notably yams, such as had evolved in earlier times to the north and north-west. The evidence that

this took place significantly before the beginning of metal working must be regarded as inconclusive.

Similar settlements were established further to the south, in the coastal areas of Congo, as in the lower levels at the Tchissanga site near Pointe Noire, by the sixth century BC. It appears, however, that pottery and other indications of sedentism remained unknown in the forested regions inland until significantly later times. Immediately south of the forest, in Bas Zaire ground-stone tools and the characteristic pottery of the Ngovo Group occur on several sites now securely dated to the last two centuries BC. There is no evidence that domestic animals were herded, but nuts of oil palm and *Canarium* probably indicate the practice of non-cereal agriculture. These occurrences pre-date by several centuries the local inception of iron working.

Although convincing chronological indicators are lacking, it is likely that the period considered in this chapter was that of one stage in the interesting archaeological sequence on the island of Bioko, Equatorial Guinea. A flaked-stone industry, lacking pottery, has been considered to be of 'Neolithic' age, although there is some possibility that it is significantly older. All that can confidently be said, on the basis of a stratified succession at Banapa near Malabo, is that this industry predates a pottery-bearing horizon of about the seventh century AD. Bioko's volcanic rocks were extensively used for making ground-stone axes/hoes, some of which may have been traded to the adjacent mainland. Because iron ore does not occur on Bioko, these stone tools continued in use on the island until comparatively recent times.

Data relating to the archaeology of the equatorial forest zone itself remain extremely sparse. Occurrences of flaked stone artefacts that apparently precede the development of pottery are known from several areas but remain undated. Research along the principal river valleys has shown that, contrary to earlier beliefs, much of the area was penetrated by pottery-using people, probably around the first millennium AD. Generalized affinities have been noted between the earliest pottery in this region and that from Batalimo in the Central African Republic to the north and the Ngovo Group wares (see above) in Bas Zaire to the south-west.

Despite the extreme sparsity of the available data it is thus possible to discern that farming, village life and pottery manufacture began – not necessarily concurrently – to the north-west of the equatorial forest, in what is now Cameroon, as early as the fourth or third millennium BC. During the third and second millennia comparable developments are apparent in Gabon, suggesting that they took place earlier in these coastal regions than in the depths of the forest further inland. By late in the last millennium BC these innovations had been established south of the forest, in Bas Zaire. Such evidence as we have suggests that parallel processes affected the inland forest areas significantly later and may, at least initially, have been restricted to the river valleys.

Ethiopia and the Horn

Although there is good botanical evidence that Ethiopia was the scene of important innovations in the development of African agriculture, disappointingly little archaeological field-work has been devoted to illustrating the cultural contexts in which these innovations took place. Likewise in Somalia, the prehistory of the pastoral practices depicted in the region's undated rock art is only now beginning to be investigated. The chronological and social framework for the

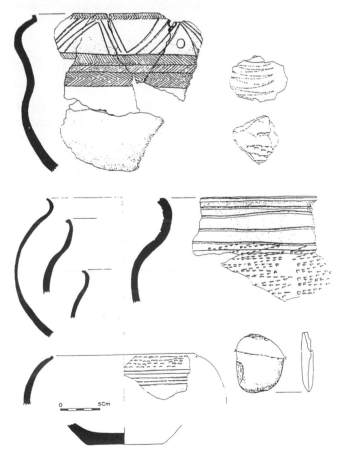

Figure 49 Neolithic pottery from Okala, Gabon (after Clist, 1989).

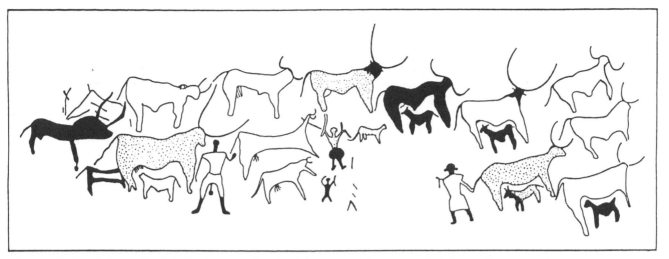

Figure 50 Rock painting at Genda Biftu, Ethiopia, showing herdsmen and domestic cattle (after Phillipson, 1985).

development of food production in this key area thus remains effectively unknown. Although it is likely that aspects of the region's recent history have led some authorities to exaggerate its former isolation, the nature and extent of its contacts with adjacent parts of Africa (and Asia) have still to be demonstrated. When the time comes for thorough investigations of the local later prehistory, these will have to be undertaken with full reference to contemporary events both in the Nile Valley and in Arabia.

Only two isolated sequences have yet been investigated which relate to the period of Ethiopian prehistory with which this chapter is concerned. At Gobedra rock shelter near Aksum, pottery appeared in a microlithic sequence in about the third or fourth millennium BC. It is possible, but cannot be regarded as in any way proven, that domestic animals and/or agricultural practices adopted at about the same time. Concerning the settlement patterns of this period in northern Ethiopia, however, we remain in complete ignorance. In the Lake Besaka area of the Rift Valley, east of Addis Ababa, the data are a little more informative. Around 1500 BC, a shift in settlement location away from the lake-shore seems to have accompanied the adoption of domestic cattle and the resultant decreased emphasis on hunting and fishing. These shifts in economic activity were also reflected in the composition of the associated stone-tool industry. However, the only archaeological project yet conducted in Ethiopia specifically addressed to illustrating the history of food production revealed only material of a later period than that with which this chapter is concerned.

Rock art provides a substantial part of the data currently available concerning early herds and herding practices in both Ethiopia and Somalia (Fig. 50). In the whole of this region there are very few representatives of wild animals and it therefore appears that virtually all the extant art belongs to the period after the advent of domestic herds. There are as yet no clear indications as to when this development took place, but the general concensus would place it during the arid phase *c.* 3000–1000 BC. Since there have been in this area no possible wild prototypes for domestic cattle, sheep or goats, these animals must have been introduced from elsewhere. Increasing desiccation *c.* 3000 BC may have provided a stimulus for this.

Throughout the region, the earliest rock art, whether painted or engraved, is fairly homogeneous in style. The majority of representations are of cattle, probably all of humpless, long-horned type. The later, more schematized, art

shows humped cattle as well as the first local representations of camels. There is some indication from Aksumite sites in northern Ethiopia that humped cattle were not common in that area until well into the first millennium AD although, as will be noted below, the evidence relating to camels is particularly hard to interpret.

The Ethiopian highlands are the southernmost part of Africa where the ox-drawn plough was used prior to European colonization. A single rock painting from Ba'ati Facada near Adigrat shows a plough being pulled by a pair of humpless cattle (Fig. 51); the degree of schematization permits the tentative suggestion that this painting may be of relatively late date.

The area that now comprises northern Ethiopia may have seen cultural developments akin to those of the Nubian Nile Valley as early as the third millennium BC. This is indicated by surface finds made several decades ago at a series of village sites near Agordat in Eritrea. Pottery was in use at this time, and small-scale excavations at Gobedra near Aksum suggest that its local beginning may have been significantly earlier.

Some further clues may be obtained from linguistic studies. In much of the region, Cushitic languages have been spoken for several millennia: they are a branch of the Afro-Asiatic language family. C. Ehret has argued that the distribution of vocabulary roots indicates that food-production (both herding and cultivation) has been practised by speakers of Afro-Asiatic languages in Ethiopia for as long as 7,000

Figure 51 Rock painting of ox-drawn plough, Ba'ati Facada near Adigrat (drawn by D. W. Phillipson).

years. This, it will be noted, is significantly longer than the duration currently suggested by the available archaeological evidence. Semitic languages (another branch of Afro-Asiatic) are not attested in Ethiopia prior to the first millennium BC. Significantly, the Semitic speakers seem to have borrowed words relating to the growing of cereals and the use of the plough from their Cushitic-speaking neighbours. This suggests that cereals were being cultivated by means of the plough at least 3,000 years ago in northern Ethiopia.

In central Ethiopia, two sites provide clear evidence for the presence of domestic cattle during the second millennium BC. At Laga Oda rock shelter, west of Harar, horizons of this age contained cattle bones, pottery and flaked-stone tools whose edge-wear suggests use to harvest grasses, although there is no way of telling whether these were cultivated. Sites near Lake Besaka in the Rift Valley were inhabited by cattle herders who made pottery and whose stone industry, unlike that of earlier times, included numerous scrapers which may have been used for working leather.

East Africa

By contrast with the more northerly parts of the Nile Valley, the southern region of the Sudan Republic has seen only small-scale and intermittent archaeological research; and no more than the tentative bare outline of the local prehistoric sequence can yet be discerned. Although historical linguistic studies appear to suggest that farming practices may have been established here at an early period, this is not confirmed by the available archaeological data. Pottery seems to have been adopted by the stone-tool-making peoples in several parts of Equatoria by at least the second millennium BC. West of the Nile, domestic cattle were also herded at this time both in the Bahr el Ghazal plains and in the hilly country around Amadi near the present northern forest margin. In the more arid country east of the Nile, on the other hand, cattle are not attested until much more recent times. This preliminary archaeological picture contrasts markedly with that now well established in more northern parts of the Sudan and serves, as will be shown below, to link later prehistoric developments in that country's southern region with those of East Africa.

In Kenya and northern Tanzania recent and ongoing research provides a much more coherent picture. In the low-lying regions of northern Kenya the shores of Lake Turkana continued to support fishing peoples, some of whom may have occupied semi-permanent settlements such as had been established in the region a long time previously. During the third and second millennia BC there is evidence for some degree of increased sedentism also amongst the sparse population in the relatively arid country east of the lake and south of the Ethiopian escarpment. Excavations at Ele Bor indicate that people who were previously hunter-gatherers adopted at this time the herding of small stock, the use of (probably wild) cereal foods and the manufacture of pottery (Plate 134). This development seems to have been broadly contemporary with the establishment of herders' settlements near the lake-shore also, as at Dongodien near Ileret, dated c. 2000 BC, where pottery – including the finely decorated internally scored Nderit ware (Plate 135) – was produced by people who herded domestic cattle and small stock. By the late third millennium desiccation led to a steady fall in Lake Turkana water levels and, eventually, to the onset of environmental conditions elsewhere that were suited only to the practice of nomadic pastoralism.

There is thus evidence, in northern Kenya, for a sequence of socio-economic development analogous to that described above for parts of the Sahara and sahel. Sedentism was originally focused on lake-shore situations where it was supported by rich predominantly aquatic food resources. Subsequently, domestic animals became available and were herded over a wide area so that, at least seasonally, areas away from surface water were also exploited. A wider range of plant foods may consequently have been consumed. With subsequent desiccation sedentism ceased to be a viable settlement strategy in many areas and was replaced by nomadic pastoralism which has continued in some areas into recent times.

In more southerly parts of East Africa the archaeology of this period has been relatively intensively investigated. There are some indications that pottery, including Nderit ware (see above), may have been produced here from c. 2000 BC or even earlier,[5] but the major change appears to have occurred very late in the second millennium BC. From this time there is excellent and varied evidence for the exploitation of different environments by means of several economic adaptations, including herding.

Despite, or perhaps because of, the quantity of data available, there remains considerable uncertainty concerning the range and significance of the economic and technological innovation that took place in East Africa at this time. The claim has been made that domestic animals were herded in southern Kenya and northern Tanzania in mid-Holocene times or even before, long anterior, that is, to the period with which this chapter is concerned. These claims, which appear to have been based upon poorly differentiated stratigraphy, doubtful identifications of faunal remains and/or uncertain radiocarbon dating, are now largely discounted. It is generally agreed that domestic animals did not begin to be adopted by the hunter-gatherer peoples of highland East Africa significantly before the mid-second millennium BC.

The extent to which this development was accompanied by any significant shift in population remains a matter for controversy. One point is, however, well established and that is the northerly origin of the actual stock that was herded. Domestic cattle, sheep and goats have no possible wild prototypes in East Africa, and the presence of herds is demonstrated at a significantly earlier date in the regions to the north – about a thousand years earlier in northern Kenya and several millennia earlier still in the middle Nile Valley and the Sahara. Some aspects of material culture – the flaked stone tools and some of the pottery styles – show little affinity with their more northerly counterparts. Others, such as Nderit ware and the stone bowls, may be paralleled in northern Kenya and, in the latter case, in southern Ethiopia also, as has been shown above. It seems safe to conclude that there was at this time some movement of human population into East Africa from one or more regions to the north. Domestic herds do not, after all, move on their own, without herders. This is not, however, to argue for large-scale human migration. Such movement as did take place may have involved only a small proportion of the total population, and have been extended over several centuries. The basic picture that emerges from the archaeological record is one of continuity. Despite the undoubted introduction from the north of the domestic animals on which its economy was based, the East African 'Neolithic' should probably be regarded as an essentially indigenous development.

Study of this period's archaeology in East Africa has been focused to an excessive extent on the associated pottery. Several 'wares' have been recognized, almost exclusively on the basis of a simplistic consideration of techniques of decoration. A more comprehensive view is required, but the account given here must perforce be based on the research that has so far been undertaken.

In highland East Africa, one discrete grouping is represented by the Elmenteitan industry, restricted to a group of sites in a high-altitude, high-rainfall area centred on the Mau Escarpment on the western side of the Rift Valley. Dated between the late second millennium BC and the early centuries AD, Elmenteitan occurrences are characterized by large double-sided obsidian blades and generally undecorated pottery. An unusual feature was the practice of cremating the dead. Multiple cremations were interred at Njoro River Cave c. 1000 BC: each burial was accompanied by a stone bowl, pestle and mortar. Large numbers of stone beads were also recovered from this site, as were charred remains of a gourd and of an elaborately carved wooden vessel of a type that may have been used for the storage of milk (Fig. 52). Bones of domestic and wild animals at Elmenteitan sites show

that their inhabitants practised both hunting and herding in their narrowly defined territory.

Elsewhere in highland East Africa there is very considerable diversity among the different early herders' sites, but discrete groupings are much less readily apparent. Stone-tool industries, pottery, stone bowls and herd composition all vary independently. Considerable confusion has arisen through the naming of pottery 'wares' based on broad categories of decoration. One common feature of all these communities, and one which serves to distinguish them from the Elmenteitan, is the disposal of the dead not by cremation but by inhumation, often under a stone cairn. These burials are often accompanied by stone bowls or platters, which also sometimes occur on settlement sites: their function remains unknown. Faunal assemblages almost always include remains of domestic animals, but these are of very variable frequency relative to those of wild animals. Within the domestic herds, cattle and small stock were present in very variable proportions. No conclusive evidence has been recovered for the exploitation of plant

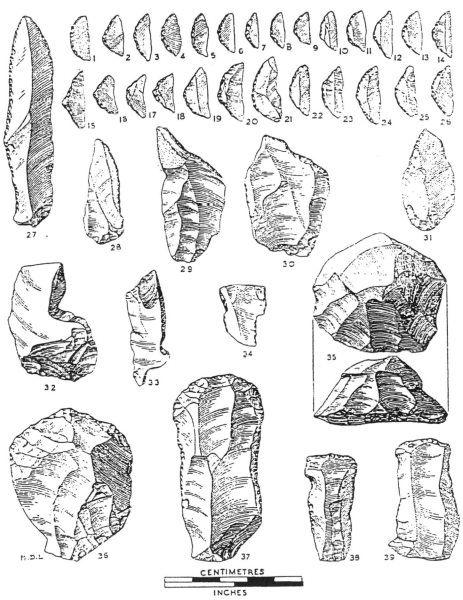

Nos. 1–26 inc. Crescents.   Nos. 32–4 inc. Angle burins.
Nos. 27–31 inc. Backed blades.   No. 35. Core.
Nos. 36–9 inc. End scrapers.

Figure 52 Artefacts from Njoro River Cave, Kenya (after Leakey and Leakey, 1950).

foods, whether wild or cultivated. Considerable mobility is suggested by the wide dispersal of obsidian from its geological sources, particularly those in the Naivasha area. It seems probable that this archaeological heterogeneity reflects a situation in which sections of a society or societies lived in different circumstances emphasizing distinct economic pursuits, perhaps on a seasonal basis. Whether this hypothesis is adequate to account for all the variation apparent in the archaeological record remains to be demonstrated. This complex, sometimes designated the East African 'Savannah Pastoral Neolithic', is dated from the late second millennium BC onwards, being effectively contemporary with the Elmenteitan. In the coastal lowlands mobile stone-tool-using hunter-gatherers continued throughout this period. The situation in the Lake Victoria basin remains unclear, but pottery manufacture and, perhaps, herding appear to have begun there during the first half of the last millennium BC, if not before.

The Lake Victoria basin, at least on its south-western side, was one of sub-Saharan Africa's earliest centres of iron-working. There is good evidence that metallurgy was practised there by the middle centuries of the last millennium BC. It seems likely that it did not extend significantly, if at all, back into the period with which this chapter is concerned, and detailed consideration is therefore postponed to a later volume of this *History*.

We have as yet no clear indication of the types of cattle that were herded by East African Neolithic people. Undated rock paintings on Mount Elgon depict humpless long-horned beasts akin to those shown in the earlier rock paintings of the Horn noted above. F. Marshall has described osteological evidence for humped cattle (*Bos* cf. *indicus*) in south-western Kenya, probably as early as the last centuries BC.

It is constructive to compare the archaeological picture outlined above with the historical conclusions that have been drawn from linguistic studies. Study of recent language forms, distributions and relationships suggests that speakers of both Nilotic and Cushitic languages have been farming in East Africa for some thousands of years. It is tempting to attempt to identify these peoples with those represented in the archaeological record, but the evidence on which such attempts can at present be based is, at best, circumstantial. So far as the antiquity of livestock herding in East Africa is concerned, there is broad agreement between the evidence of archaeology and linguistics. However, the latter studies suggest that crop cultivation has been practised over a similar time-span. This last point serves to emphasize once again the incomplete and unsatisfactory nature of the available archaeological evidence even in East Africa which, of all the regions here considered, has seen by far the largest volume of research. The available data, as in most archaeological contexts, stress meat to the virtual exclusion of plant foods, yet this does not necessarily mean that the latter were of subsidiary importance to the prehistoric peoples concerned.

Despite the not inconsiderable quantity of research that has been undertaken, there are several very basic questions about the East African 'Neolithic' that remain unanswered. To what extent were the region's inhabitants *c*. 1000 BC pastoralists (as has often been claimed) rather than mixed farmers whose agricultural activities remain to be demonstrated archaeologically? Do the entities such as the Elmenteitan, which archaeologists recognize, represent distinct prehistoric populations or particular economic adaptations by people who at other times lived elsewhere in different circumstances? Is there any way of weaving the apparently complementary evidence of archaeology and historical

linguistic studies into a single coherent reconstruction of the past? These are all questions that must be answered before the East African 'Neolithic' can adequately be understood.

Southern Africa

By contrast with the areas discussed above, the southern savannah appears to have seen very little innovative development during the period under consideration. Microlithic technology had been practised through most if not all of this region since at least the early/mid-Holocene, and in some places for very considerably longer. Pottery seems to have been unknown until near the end of the last millennium BC. Prior to that date there is also no evidence whatsoever, from the not inconsiderable detailed archaeological investigations that have been conducted, for the practice of any form of food production. Except in parts of South Africa, most research has so far been carried out on an individual-site basis, but it is nevertheless possible to propose a reasonably comprehensive reconstruction of the hunter-gatherer lifestyle that was practised in some other regions. The discussion that follows is based on four sample areas.

In the savannah regions of the southern Congo basin, best known from the diamond-mining areas around Dundo in northern Angola, the distinctive local technological tradition known as the Tshitolian appears to have continued throughout the Holocene into the early centuries AD. Here, virtually no archaeological material other than lithic artefacts has been recovered, and settlement patterns have barely begun to be investigated. It is generally assumed, largely by extrapolation from better known adjacent areas, that the pre-pottery stone-tool-using peoples of this region during the last three millennia BC were mobile hunter-gatherers who generally lacked nucleated or permanent settlements. There are no serious contra-indications to such a view in the exceedingly sparse archaeological data currently available, but the point cannot be regarded as incontrovertibly proven.

Beside the seasonally inundated Kafue Flats in southern Zambia, the Gwisho Hotsprings were frequented by hunter-gatherer peoples over a prolonged period in the third and early second millennia BC, resulting in the accumulation of mounds whose largely waterlogged deposits have ensured the preservation of much organic material. This unusual circumstance provides a far broader and more comprehensive view of material culture than is generally available on sites of this period. Wooden link-shafts and bows, for example, accompanied the microlithic arrow-points. Digging sticks were represented, probably used in the recovery of burrowing animals and in the excavation of edible roots or tubers as well as in the clearance of waterholes (Fig. 53). Bones of land and water creatures as well as nut and fruit remains indicate the range of foodstuffs that were exploited, although even here the representation of vegetable matter was almost certainly incomplete. Some 35 human skeletons were interred in shallow graves in the spring-side mounds; most individuals had been buried in a contracted position, with few identifiable grave goods. The nature of occupation of Gwisho remains incompletely understood. Discrete periods of occupation were not clearly differentiated; and we do not know to what extent settlement was seasonal, of what scale or duration, or whether the inhabitants' range-territory extended over part of the plateau country to the south of the Kafue Flats.

The research so far undertaken on this period of the prehistory of Zimbabwe and adjacent areas of Zambia and

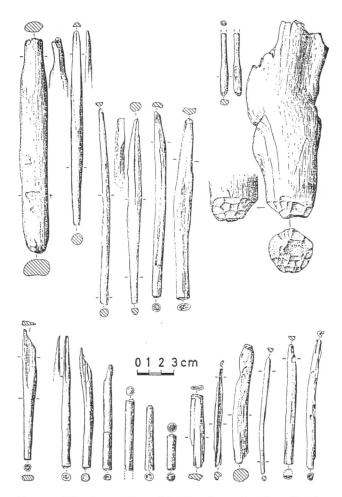

Figure 53 Wooden artefacts of the Late Stone Age from Gwisho Hotsprings, Zambia (after Fagan and Van Noten, 1971).

Malawi has been concentrated on individual rock-shelter excavations, as at Makwe and Pomongwe. All show that a microlithic technology and hunter-gatherer economy continued throughout this period. While such sites often preserve a long succession of occupation horizons, it is often difficult to separate single phases. Their value is thus in providing an overview of general technological and economic trends and their chronology. There is great potential, as yet rarely realized, for interpreting such sites in terms of overall landscape-exploitation patterns rather than as single foci.

In the Cape Province of South Africa, the third millennium BC saw gradual expansion and florescence of the population responsible for the aceramic microlithic industry generally known as Wilton. After a prolonged hiatus, human settlement in the arid interior regions was resumed following climatic amelioration. Most archaeological information relating to this period comes from caves and coastal shell-middens. The excellent preservation of organic materials in some cave sites provides insights not only on aspects of technology rarely illustrated elsewhere (even at waterlogged open sites such as Gwisho), but also on hunting and gathering practices and the seasonal exploitation of different food resources. For example, there appears to have been seasonal transhumance between the Drakensberg highlands in summer and the Indian Ocean coastlands in winter. Such studies are facilitated by extant records relating to the territories and movements of the last hunter-gatherer populations to have inhabited these regions in the nineteenth century AD.

The abundant rock art of southern Africa, although often not precisely datable, is also a potentially valuable source of information about this period. Its study has been transformed in recent years by the recognition that it reflects many aspects of the belief systems of the southern San-speaking peoples. Previously inexplicable paintings may now be interpreted in terms of San trance-experiences. Although many of the extant paintings probably date from the last two millennia, some are of far greater antiquity and provide the important facility to recognize at this time-depth, facets of prehistoric life and belief that often cannot otherwise be discerned by the archaeologist.

Southern African rock paintings and engravings have been studied for many years, initially with emphasis on their perceived artistic naturalism and on a simplistic recognition of their subject matter. Depictions of animals were seen as representing the fauna with which hunter-gatherer peoples were familiar and on which they were economically dependent. Human figures were of particular interest, providing information about clothing, weapons and other artefacts, as well as activities such as hunting, dancing or, in the case of some more recent examples, stock-raiding. It was recognized, however, that there were many representations, particularly among the paintings, which could not be explained in these simplistic terms, examples being often described as 'mythical' or 'imaginary'.

A more sophisticated interpretation became possible following the realization that the types of wild animals shown in the paintings often bore little resemblance to the species that were represented in the faunal assemblages excavated from the painted sites themselves. The commonest antelope, which food debris indicated were often hunted and eaten, were rarely depicted. One of the most frequently painted creatures, often shown with considerable care and naturalism, was the eland; but this was rare in the faunal assemblages (Plate 136). The eland did, however, occupy a very important place in the belief-system of some recent San populations. It seemed that many of the paintings might be better explained by reference to the beliefs of San artists than by comparison with more mundane aspects of their life-style and surroundings.

As a result and largely through the research of J. D. Lewis-Williams, it has proved possible in recent years to build up a far more satisfactory understanding of much of the rock art in areas of Africa south of the Limpopo River. Early records of southern San ethnography have proved particularly relevant and suggest, when compared with recent San practices and traditional beliefs, that the belief systems reflected in the rock art were of wide, relatively uniform distribution. Trance is clearly shown to have had a central and important position, and it seems that the artists were often shamans, who had direct experience of trance. The crouching posture, accompanied by nose-bleeding, is characteristic of San in trance, and is often depicted in rock paintings (Fig. 54). Other features of the art may be shown to represent hallucinations or other features of the trance experience. In their enthusiasm for this new area of understanding, it may be that some students of rock art have erred in believing that all aspects of southern African rock art may be explained by reference to trance, or in extending its application beyond its main geographical area. Be that as it may, we now have (as will be further argued below) a new insight into the meaning of at least one school of ancient African rock art, and thus into the belief-system of the artists.

Recent rock-art studies thus serve to shift the emphasis of archaeology away from technology and domestic economy to subjects which offer a more comprehensive view of peo-

Figure 54 Rock painting showing people in trance, Barkly East, Cape Province, South Africa (after Lewis-Williams, 1983).

ple's lives. What, however, were the social situations in which the shamans underwent trance and/or in which the paintings were executed? A possible insight is provided by the recognition of certain major rock-shelter sites as places of social aggregation where, at a certain season of the year, there came together a population which was at other times scattered over the landscape in smaller groups. Such aggregations have served a vital function in recent San societies, provided a place for the settling of disputes, exchange of information, making of alliances and for certain religious practices. Comprehensive archaeological research, on a landscape rather than a site basis, permits the recognition of such places of aggregation; and thus a far more complete picture of prehistory may be obtained. Such research is in its very early stages in Africa and is, at present, virtually restricted to the southernmost part of the continent. It provides, however, a clear pointer as to the direction to be taken by future investigations.

THEMATIC DISCUSSION

Economy

Our appreciation of ancient economic practices, in Africa as elsewhere, is heavily dependent upon the vagaries both of archaeological preservation and of research emphases. For example, bones of animals are more readily recovered from archaeological sites than are the remains of vegetable foods. Only recently, and still infrequently, have excavators in Africa employed the special techniques such as flotation that are generally necessary to obtain plant remains. As a result, many reconstructions place excessive emphasis on the meat component of the diet, and tend to ignore the vegetable element. It must be admitted that this prejudice probably mirrors that of many ancient African peoples. Perhaps not unconnected with the traditional division of tasks between the genders, whereby the provision of meat and other animal products was seen as a male task and the obtaining of plant foods as

that of women, meat has been regarded as the most important foodstuff. Thus, in the past, animals (whether wild or domestic) were favourite subjects for rock art, but plants were hardly ever represented. So, in more recent times, foraging peoples have regarded themselves, and represented themselves to others, primarily as hunters, even though plant foods may account for the greater part of their diet. Likewise, people who own herds may designate themselves as pastoralists and belittle, or even deny, their dependence upon plant foods. There is thus a prejudice in favour of animal foods both in much of the archaeologist's primary data and in the superficial ethnography on which he or she may, perhaps unconsciously, depend.

A further confusion may arise from an unfortunate tendency on the part of many writers to use the term 'pastoralist' to refer to any society possessing domestic animals, irrespective of the importance which those animals may have had in the overall life-style of the people concerned. Used correctly, the term applies only to those who rely upon their herds for a very large part of their subsistence, and whose activities are based upon the need to care for the herds. Coupled with the bias in the archaeological record noted above, this misleading terminology can impart to the unwary reader a markedly skewed view of early African economic practices.

The period of African prehistory with which this chapter is concerned was primarily one of consolidation rather than innovation. Throughout this time, most of the continent's inhabitants relied for their subsistence to at least some extent upon hunting and gathering, following patterns of resource exploitation, often seasonal, that had been established many thousands of years previously. To the south of the equator, this remained the sole source of food. In the northern half of the continent the range and intensity of food production was gradually increasing, although the roots of these practices can almost invariably be traced back to earlier periods.

It is important to recognize that animal domestication and plant cultivation, despite their conceptual connections, are – in practice – very different. The cultivation of cereals on the one hand, and of vegetatively propagated plants on the other, are likewise clearly distinct. It is important to bear these contrasts in mind and not to over-generalize.

By 3000 BC the herding of both small stock and cattle had been established for many centuries in much of what is now the Sahara, as well as in North Africa and in the Nile Valley from the central Sudan northwards. We are not therefore here concerned with the way in which these practices began on the African continent. Of prime importance for this volume of the *History* is that, during the last three millennia BC, there was a considerable expansion of herding into other areas, primarily southwards. By 1000 BC herding was widely practised in much of West Africa, throughout the savannahs to the north of the equatorial forest, in Ethiopia and the Horn, and in East Africa as far to the south as the Serengeti Plains.

In none of these new territories is there any evidence whatsoever for the presence, at this time or earlier, of any wild animals from which domestic forms of cattle or of small stock could have been derived. It follows from this observation that the initial herds in these territories were not locally domesticated but were introduced from those neighbouring areas, to the north or west, where herding had been practised in earlier times. Since herds do not move on their own, it must be imagined that some movement of human populations also took place. These generalizations must not be misunderstood. Clearly domestic animals adapted, and were selected by their owners, to the various conditions and requirements of their new circumstances. Thus there developed, for example, the dwarf cattle of some West African forest regions, with some immunity to trypanosomiasis, or the drought-resistant varieties of the Horn. Likewise, one should not imagine series of large-scale migrations of herders and herds into more southerly latitudes. In many areas there seems to have been remarkable stability of human population over the period which saw the beginning of herding. The overall effect was that a new subsistence practice was adopted by a pre-existing and stable population. But it would be wrong to deny that some degree of human population movement, probably on a small scale and spread over several generations, contributed to the dispersal of the herds.

There can be little doubt that one important factor, of several which may have contributed to herd-dispersal at this time, was the progressive desiccation of the Sahara.[6] As noted above, this process was accompanied by a general southward shift in the location of sahelian and savannah vegetation belts. Spread as it was over scores of human generations, this shift could have inspired a corresponding movement in the foci of settlement. There was at this same time a similar concentration of population in the Nile Valley of Egypt and, perhaps also, Nubia, which contributed – as argued elsewhere – to the development of complex societies in this rich but tightly circumscribed region.

Although the general picture of herd expansion now appears reasonably clear, that of crop cultivation is altogether more complex and problematic, compounded by the scarcity of primary data, as noted above. The crops that were (prior to the relatively recent introduction of American and Asian species) traditionally grown south of the Sahara were plants indigenous to Africa. Cultivation in the central Saharan highlands, although poorly illustrated by the available archaeological data, was probably concentrated on wheat and barley, crops of ultimately West Asian origin, whose use at this time is very clearly attested in the Egyptian Nile Valley. These are, however, winter-rainfall crops which will not flourish under the conditions which prevail in most regions of Africa further to the south.

There is a significant contrast in the crops traditionally cultivated south of the Sahara. In the savannahs these are predominantly cereals, while in the forest areas vegetatively propagated plants, notably yams, provide the subsistence base. Both groups have been shown through botanical research to be locally derived; in other words, their initial cultivation must have taken place in some sub-Saharan regions. Yams (*Dioscorea* spp.) and other crops, including oil palm (*Elaeis guineensis*), are indigenous to the forest fringes where they were presumably first brought under cultivation. In the case of the dry cereals, notably bulrush millet (*Pennisetum*) and sorghum, botanical and archaeological evidence combines to show that the primary focus was probably in the modern sahel: bulrush millet in the west, and sorghum perhaps in the east. African rice (*Oryza glaberrima*), although also a cereal, is grown under much wetter conditions and appears to have been centred around the Inland Niger Delta. A distinctive suite of crops was brought under cultivation in the unique environment of the Ethiopian highlands.

Much attention has been given by some writers to enquiring whether these African agricultural developments took place completely independently of inspiration from other areas. This is a matter which cannot be resolved from the data currently available if, indeed, it is a valid question. It is not simply that chronological precision is inadequate, but the beginnings of cultivation are almost impossible to define or, indeed, to recognize in the archaeological record. These are serious problems with regard to cereals; for crops such as yams they appear insurmountable with the study techniques currently available. Lastly, the presence or absence of inspiration between contemporaneous populations cannot be assessed. We shall simply never know whether the people who initiated the cultivation of millet south of the Sahara were aware that wheat and barley were being similarly propagated further to the north.

With one important exception, the pattern which emerges from recent research on the beginning of plant cultivation south of the Sahara parallels that described above for the herding of domestic animals. The exception relates to the propagation of yams in the forest-edge areas of what is now southern Cameroon and south-eastern Nigeria. As argued elsewhere in this chapter, there are indications that this may have been a completely independent development, which significantly preceded the beginning of cereal cultivation in neighbouring savannah areas.

Before leaving the topic of plant cultivation it is necessary to emphasize once again the extremely inadequate nature of the archaeological evidence that is currently available. The fact that most of the physical remains of African cultivated plants so far recovered are of relatively recent date does not mean that significantly older examples will not in due course come to light. Furthermore, incipient cultivation may have been practised for many centuries before it resulted in recognizable morphological change to those hard parts of the plant that are likely to be preserved in the archaeological record. Some important crops have no such hard parts and thus remain effectively unknown archaeologically.

Although the emphasis of much that is written here concerns the development of African food production, whether by herding or by cultivation, it must not be forgotten that probably all the societies concerned continued to obtain greater or lesser amounts of food by foraging. Despite the importance which prehistorians rightly attach to food production, there was no sharp break from the hunting, fishing, fowling and gathering subsistence mode of earlier times. Both continued alongside one another and, to some extent, incipient control of wild species allowed old foraging strategies to continue or to be intensified in circumstances of increased demand due to concentration of population and/or environmental change.

The whole of this section has been concerned with the part of the African continent which lies to the north of the equator. By *c.* 700 BC knowledge of herding and/or cultivation extended through most of these northern regions. To the south, however, there is no evidence for such knowledge at this early date. The wild foods of the rich African biomes were sufficient to meet people's needs. Archaeological evidence is steadily accumulating to show how, through diversification, seasonal mobility and flexibility of settlement strategies, people were able to exploit this natural richness to the full. Both this adaptability, and innate conservatism, may be cited as contributory explanations to the delayed adoption of food production in the southern half of Africa. How and when this adoption did finally take place will be discussed in Volume III of this *History*.

Discussion of economy cannot be restricted to means of obtaining food. All the activities considered in the previous section were of wider significance. Animals, whether herded, scavenged or obtained by hunting, yield non-comestible materials such as skins, bone, shell and ivory which may be used for a wide variety of purposes. Domestic animals have, in recent African societies, often been valuable commodities in their own right, renewable through breeding and transferable between owners in many social and political situations not directly related to subsistence: there are indications in Saharan rock art that such practices may have an antiquity extending back through the period with which this chapter is concerned. Plants, too, both wild and cultivated, are sources of fibres, narcotics, aromatics, dyes and other substances which serve a wide variety of purposes. These, together with their animal-derived counterparts, are discussed elsewhere for their technological implications.

Here, it is necessary to consider the transfer and exchange of commodities between individuals and groups. The terms 'transfer' and 'exchange' are here preferred to the word 'trade' which is often employed in this context, because of the latter's implication of formalized organization, regularity and – for some authors – operation over a long distance. Trade in this implied sense undoubtedly did occur during the last millennia BC, as will be shown below; but it represented only a small part of the commodity exchange that took place.

Inter-group transfer and exchange presumably played a large part in the spread of herding and cultivation discussed above. Domestic animals, being both mobile and potentially valuable, are particularly susceptible to such use. Recent African societies provide excellent examples which may be cited as models for the practices of earlier times. Domestic stock may both facilitate and emphasize relationships of interdependance (but not necessarily of equal status) between herd-owning groups and their neighbours, as seen today in Rwanda or in the Kalahari fringe-lands. These situations also serve to emphasize the high status that accompanies ownership of herds; and this may in turn help to explain the rapidity of their spread. Similarly, numerous instances have been recorded in recent times of the transfer of stock in order to cement alliances whether social (matrimonial) or political. Through such usages stock may come to serve as an embodiment of wealth, kept and accumulated for (literally) pecuniary purposes rather than for those of subsistence. This is not the place to discuss such practices in detail, for we have no conclusive

evidence for their employment during the last millennia BC, but it is important to bear them in mind.

The produce of the various subsistence strategies here discussed will also have been transferred between neighbouring individuals or groups. In recent times it has been not uncommon for particular strategies to be recognized as the prerogatives of certain groups. Thus, pygmies in easternmost Zaire are predominantly or exclusively foragers who exchange their produce for that of neighbouring groups who rely primarily upon cultivation or the management of herds.

The products of particular environments may be accorded a scarcity value and be transferred over long distances. This will be particularly true of wild species and their derivatives, such as the skins of lions or leopards, aromatic gums, kola nuts and other narcotics, or sea-shells. Only the last named are likely to survive in the archaeological record – as is the case, for example, in East Africa. Additional evidence, however, comes from written records and artistic representations in Egypt, which show that such items were obtained over a wide area, as from the 'Land of Punt'.

A similar pattern is evident for minerals. Salt is of particular importance to herders and has been obtained in Africa in a variety of ways: quarried in its natural crystalline form, evaporated from marine or inland brine deposits, or produced by more complex means involving concentration of salt which occurs in soils or in certain plants. All these methods are restricted to certain narrowly defined localities, yet the need for salt is widespread. It has thus been transferred or exchanged over long distances; and it is highly likely that such practices are as ancient as the herding of domestic stock.

Stone for tool making and for ornament was also a widely needed commodity of restricted availability. Some inhabited areas, such as the Inland Niger Delta, totally lack usable stone, all of which had perforce to be brought from elsewhere. In other regions, such as East Africa, low-grade material was ubiquitous, but obsidian, with excellent flaking properties, could be obtained only in certain outcrops, whose products were widely dispersed both as raw material and as finished tools. Since obsidian from particular localities may readily be identified, it has been possible for archaeologists to trace in some detail the changing patterns of its distribution, particularly in Kenya. Fine stone for the making of beads, being valued in very small quantities and also enduring in use, was sometimes transported over exceptionally long distances, as from the central Saharan highlands to the Nile Valley.

Much attention has been paid to tracing the distribution of pottery styles. However, most pottery is by nature bulky, heavy, fragile and of low inherent value, being made from material that is readily available in most areas. In many circumstances it thus appears likely that the dispersal of particular pottery styles will have been brought about either by the movement of individual potters or by the transmission of styles between individuals. Most vessels were probably used close to their place of manufacture. Indeed, many people whose life-style involves near-constant mobility do not use pottery, preferring lighter and more readily transportable receptacles of wood, skin or basketry; and there are instances known when people who adopted increased mobility discontinued the use of pottery. More reliable indications of the movement of pottery vessels may be obtained through fabric analysis, as has recently been undertaken for certain Nubian fine wares, the sources of whose clay it has been possible to identify. Trade or exchange of pottery over any significant distance appears generally to have been restricted to fine wares that were regarded as luxuries or prestige items, or to receptacles containing a valuable commodity such as perfume or wine.

For most of Africa, metal was not a significant material during the period here considered. However, in the Egyptian Nile Valley, gold, copper and its alloys were used in large quantities from late pre-dynastic times onwards. Much of the supply of these metals, particularly gold, emanated from far beyond the Nile Valley, particularly in what is now southern Egypt and northern Sudan. It was won both by local people preparing for a known market and by prospectors and traders from the Nile Valley. Many other commodities, such as fine stone, ivory, skins and human captives, were thus imported into pharaonic Egypt, establishing a pattern of exploiting Africa's raw materials, for processing in areas technologically more advanced, which has continued and increased into recent times.

A final point needs to be emphasized, which arises from the frequent uncritical use of the word 'trade'. The usual form of commodity transfer took place on a small scale over short distances. It did not involve special long journeys and was not in the hands of specialist traders. In many instances where an item may be shown to have travelled a long distance from its place of origin, it may be assumed to have done so by repeatedly passing from hand to hand through localized exchange networks of this type. Only rarely, as in the case of the Egyptian prospectors and true traders noted above, do long and special journeys appear to have been made.[7]

Technology

Metal being effectively unknown in the greater part of Africa during this period, our survey of technology is concerned primarily with the use of stone, clay and organic materials. For reasons both of original use and of preservation, the most ubiquitous items are those of stone.

During the last three millennia BC virtually all the African societies of which we have any knowledge made and used tools that were flaked from stone. (It is possible that some inhabitants of the central Zaire basin, an area which remains virtually unexplored archaeologically and where natural occurrences of any form of stone are exceedingly rare, may have been an exception to this generalization.) Throughout the continent, although many regional traditions of stone-tool making may be recognized, the emphasis was on the production of backed microliths such as had originated many millennia previously. The type of raw material that was locally available had a profound – but sometimes underestimated – effect on the size and style of the tools that were produced. For example, the plentiful fine-grained obsidian of the East African highlands permitted the production of large, regularly flaked implements such as those which characterize the Elmenteitan industry c. 1000 BC. On the other hand, in many more southerly regions only small pieces of coarse-grained quartz were available, from which even a skilled person could make only crude and irregular artefacts.

The majority of these microlithic tools must have been used hafted, but only very rarely have specimens been preserved which show precisely how this was done. Other than in Egypt, the notable discoveries are of a sickle from Columnata in Algeria and of some scrapers from caves in the Cape Province of South Africa. Several microliths from Makwe in eastern Zambia preserve the mastic with which they were fixed to grooved hafts, often to form points or barbs for projectiles. We thus have disappointingly little information about the uses to which these stone tools were originally put. Study of edge-damage, which may in due course throw much light on this matter, has only rarely been attempted on material of this period.

For the present, therefore, most interpretations of these stone tools must depend upon conventional labels such as 'arrowhead' or 'scraper', which are based on subjective evaluations of function based on their general morphology. Where the local raw material has permitted both elaboration and standardization, as in parts of the Sahara, such designations are at least plausible, if not demonstrably correct. On occasion, changes in artefact type may accompany other developments which provide an indication of their possible use. An example is at Lake Besaka in Ethiopia where the first appearance of domestic cattle is accompanied by proliferation of 'scraper'-type stone tools which may have been used in the processing of hides: the comparative scarcity of microliths of this time may indicate decreased reliance upon hunting.

Similar problems face us when considering ground-stone tools. The type most frequently encountered in many parts of the continent is elongated and has a fairly sharp edge across one of its narrow ends. Although they have often been conventionally designated as 'axes', it now seems equally, if not more, probable that they often served as digging tools or 'hoes', whether hafted or unhafted. Particularly in the Sahara they have often been regarded as a defining characteristic of a 'Neolithic' industry and thus, indirectly, of the practice of some form of food production. There is, however, no reason why this should necessarily have been the case. Indeed, morphologically indistinguishable ground-stone tools were produced in the savannah country of what is now Zambia many thousands of years before any type of food production is locally indicated.

Another ground-stone artefact, most common in the southern part of Africa, is the bored stone. This may have served a variety of purposes one of which, as shown in South African rock art and recorded in recent times, was as a weight for wooden digging sticks.

Ground stone was also the material for a range of rubbers, grinders and pounders which resemble those used in more recent times in the processing of cereals and, on occasion, other plant foods. During the time-span here considered, such objects were widely distributed through most regions of the continent not covered with dense equatorial forest, but were particularly numerous and widely used in areas north of the equator. Within this group may be considered also the various stone bowls, platters, mortars and pestles of East Africa. The processing of cultivated cereals is often cited as the most probable function served by this class of artefact, but one must remember that wild grains, if collected in significant quantities, could have been treated in precisely the same way. Some of the grinders could also have been used to process completely different materials, such as pigment or temper for pottery manufacture.

Pottery, as noted above, was essentially a local product. By the mid-first millennium BC it was virtually ubiquitous in Africa north of the equator, but had not yet been adopted in more southerly latitudes. It was hand-made, the potter's wheel being unknown outside the Nile Valley. In most areas, vessels had round or pointed bases, being balanced upright between stones, on ring-stands, or in holes in the ground. Only in the first millennium BC, in the area between Cameroon and the mouth of the Congo River, were flat-based vessels in general use. Decoration, generally done before firing, was by a variety of incisions or impressions.

Mica or other additives to the clay also, on occasion, produced a decorative effect. Burnishing, with or without the addition of a slip or graphite, was a common practice, but true glazes were unknown.

For most, if not all, of this period it appears that the only metal objects used in Africa beyond the Egyptian/Nubian Nile Valley were imported either from the latter region or from outside the continent. There is no evidence that a smelting or smithing technology was used in the rest of Africa until around the sixth century BC, and these developments are thus most appropriately considered in Volume III of this *History*. Evidence for imported metal work is sparse and restricted to North Africa and parts of the Sahara. Rock engravings in the Atlas Mountains show bronze weapons that are very similar to European types of the second millennium BC. Paintings, for which the date most generally accepted is *c.* 1000 BC, in the Saharan highlands show light horse-drawn chariots. No physical remains of these vehicles have ever been found but it appears unlikely that they would have been serviceable if metal were not used in their construction, particularly the wheels. We must conclude that, outside the Nile Valley, metal played only a very minor role in African technology at this period.

The use of organic materials may be assumed to have been far more extensive than archaeological discoveries would, at first sight, suggest. Bone tools and shell beads were generally simple, and their frequent preservation suggests that they were widely used in most parts of the continent. Animal skin and vegetable fibre are very rarely preserved, but rock-art representations provide some indications of the uses to which such materials were put for clothing, bags and water buckets, for example. The excellent preservation of ancient organic materials on the desert fringes of the Egyptian Nile Valley shows what a wide range of artefacts may have been lost in other parts of the continent. This is especially true of wooden items, representing not only many objects in everyday use, but artistic representations also. Elsewhere in Africa it is only very exceptionally that wooden objects have survived in the archaeological record. Ironically, it is in the equatorial forest regions where, stone being not always available, people may have been particularly dependent upon wood, that conditions of preservation are poorest. One of the most informative sites to have yielded wooden objects of this period is Gwisho Hotsprings in southern Zambia, where arrows, bows, digging sticks, bark trays and numerous other items were preserved. Attention should also be drawn to a carved wooden receptacle of *c.* 1000 BC from Njoro River Cave in Kenya: it is remarkably similar to items used by more recent pastoralist peoples for the storage of milk.

Finally, it is appropriate to consider the architectural technology of the period. This may be divided into the settlement structures of the living, structures used for the interment of the dead, and those made in connection with subsistence activities. In Africa outside the Egyptian/Nubian Nile Valley there are no architectural remains of this period to which a purely religious or non-funerary ceremonial function may plausibly be attributed.

Domestic structures vary according to the life-style of their inhabitants and it is generally only where a reasonable degree of sedentism may be achieved that durable structures will be erected. The mobile foraging populations of the southern half of Africa made frequent use of natural rock shelters. At open-air settlements, even those which – like Gwisho Hotsprings – saw prolonged or repeated occupation, any shelters that were erected were so flimsy and temporary that no

archaeological trace of them has been recovered. It may be that they resembled the dome-shaped structures of twigs and grass that have continued to be made into recent times at temporary forager camps, or as fishers' or field shelters. A similar situation probably prevailed in more northerly regions, with temporary shelters being the preferred accommodation of many herding groups. It was mainly where agriculture imposed a degree of sedentism and stability of population that substantial settlements were constructed. Those in the Egyptian/Nubian Nile Valley are discussed elsewhere in this volume; of their counterparts in other regions the most noteworthy and informative are at Dhar Tichitt in southern Mauritania, most of which date to the second or early first millennium BC. A large number of drystone compounds are clustered at intervals along the escarpment: examples are illustrated in Figure 10. In higher-rainfall areas further south there are indications that pole-and-mud structures were erected at this time, as at Ntereso in Ghana.

In many areas the dead were buried in simple pit-graves, but funerary monuments are known from several areas. Cairns of piled stone were erected over interments by the most early herding populations in eastern Africa and examples have been excavated both in Tanzania and in Kenya. Megalithic tombs were built in Senegambia, Bioko Island, Ethiopia and what is now the Central African Republic. Only in the last-named area has clear evidence yet been obtained that the monuments date back before the beginning of metallurgy.

Lastly it is necessary to consider those large-scale features, not strictly architectural, which were made in connection with subsistence activities. Several examples may be cited, although in most cases they may be attributed only tentatively to the period here considered. Linear stone settings, whether demarcating cleared fields or providing terracing for hill-slopes, have long been an accompaniment of agriculture. It is likely that some of the field systems of the Maghreb are of pre-Phoenician date, and certain Ethiopian terracing may be of similar antiquity. Deep wells have been dug in arid regions to facilitate the watering of livestock. Most are still in use and their origins are particularly hard to demonstrate. Some Saharan rock art, however, appears to depict water being passed up in hide buckets from hand to hand out of deep wells, in a manner which has continued among many African herding peoples to the present day.

Religion and socio-political organization

Among societies which did not develop prominent monumental architecture under the auspices of a powerful élite, archaeological evidence for socio-political organization must generally be sought by means of comprehensive site survey. The prime data will often relate to disparity in access to resources although it will be recognized that enhancement in this regard is not necessarily linked with political authority. In many parts of Africa the coverage of archaeological investigation has not been adequate to reveal such disparities on other than an interregional basis. On the contrary, the picture that emerges is one of generally similar prosperity in most areas. One of the very few places where a comparative analysis is possible is at Dhar Tichitt in Mauritania, where the stone-walled compounds are grouped in clusters of between 200 and less than 20 compounds. It is possible, but by no means proven, that these uneven distributions reflect differential prosperity.

In more southerly regions, archaeologists are beginning to recognize large sites, often prominent rock shelters which probably served as places of regular seasonal social aggregation, the population dispersing at other times of the year to smaller temporary abodes. This implies a pattern of socio-political organization similar to that which has prevailed among African foraging peoples into recent times, in which groups are small and essentially egalitarian.

In such societies, as in many others, prestige and status are not restricted to persons holding socio-political authority. In southern Africa the rock art, as now interpreted, serves to emphasize the important role played by shamans. It has not yet proved possible to obtain such an insight into the significance of rock art in the Sahara or in the Horn of Africa. Whilst it is tempting to interpret the portrayal of large herds as indicating unequal accumulation of this form of wealth, we have in fact no means of knowing whether what was depicted was actual or desired.

In traditional African society the modern western distinction between political and religious authority is rarely made. The two areas were also intimately connected in pharaonic Egypt. Despite the greater institutionalization of religion in Egypt, and our greatly enhanced knowledge of it due both to the intensity of research that has been conducted and to the availability of written records, it appears that the basic roots of Egyptian religion were common to a wide area, at least in North and North-East Africa. Some hint of this can be discerned in the Saharan rock art, but our understanding of this material is hampered by a research approach that has not attempted to view the art as an integrated whole. Not only does it reveal certain stylistic conventions, such as twisted perspective, which are characteristic of Egyptian painting, but also detailed parallels in head-dresses, ornament and other attire, posture, and treatment of multiple figures which point to a common background. Other representations, as of masks or elaborately costumed dancers, have closer parallels in the recent traditions of more southerly areas. Until a more comprehensive view is taken of the Saharan paintings, and a clearer chronology demonstrated, it will not be possible to ascertain the extent to which these features occur together or successively.

Research into southern African rock art, as noted above, has shown that much of it is intimately connected with shamanism and trance which has continued into recent times to play an important role in the socio-religious life of San-speaking peoples. Contrary to certain claims, it has not been proved that all southern African rock art falls into this category, nor that a similar interpretation can necessarily be applied to East African naturalistic rock painting. However, it may safely be concluded that many of the basic shamanistic beliefs and practices which characterize recent San religion have an antiquity extending over several thousands of years.

Cutting across the areas described above and, indeed, apparently extending over the greater part of the continent, is a tradition of respect for the dead. This should be regarded as one aspect, most readily apparent in the archaeological record, of the ubiquitous animism which underlies African religious beliefs and practices. The possibility that cannibalism may on occasion have been practised, as in more recent times, in no way reduces the validity of this generalization. Grave goods varied according to the emphases of society, examples being painted stones in South Africa's Cape Province, and horns of large animals among hunting peoples of Zambia and Somalia. They should be viewed as evidence for respect rather than for belief in a literal form of after-life in the western sense.

Art

Although art has often been discussed separately from other archaeological materials, an attempt has been made here to provide an integrated overview. This is because we believe that the interpretation of art's historical or archaeological significance can only be meaningful if it is viewed in the detailed context of the society responsible for its execution. To separate art from the rest of a society's material culture is to encourage its consideration simply as art, which is virtually impossible to achieve objectively, other than in the cultural context not of the artist but of the beholder. Whilst such a view may be personally inspiring, it has no historical validity. At this place in the narrative it is thus only appropriate first to enumerate the main classes of African art which survive from the period 3000–700 BC, many of which have been described and evaluated elsewhere in this chapter, and secondly to draw attention to what may have been lost.

The general distribution of rock art, both engraved and painted, in Africa is shown in Map 20. Although precise indications of date are rarely available, there can be little doubt that many examples throughout this distribution belong to the period here considered – in the Sahara, in East Africa and the Horn, and in southern Africa. However, it is only comparatively rarely that artistic representations occur as or on portable objects from archaeological contexts. As examples may be cited the painted 'grave-slabs' from South Africa, clay figurines, rare stone sculptures and engraved ostrich eggshells from the Maghreb. It is conventional not to classify as art such items as decorated pottery or finely made stone tools whose quality surely exceeds purely functional dictates: such omissions merely serve to emphasize the meaninglessness of 'art' as a classificationary concept in archaeology.

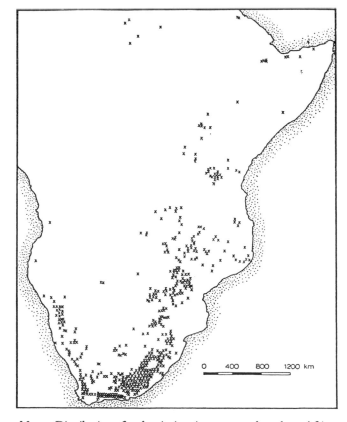

Map 20 Distribution of rock paintings in eastern and southern Africa (drawn by D.W. Phillipson).

Notably absent from the above list is any mention of wooden sculpture. Although the lack of metal tools will have restrained the elaboration of wood-carving, it is almost inconceivable that the practice was unknown prior to the advent of such tools. Wooden sculpture has, in more recent times, accounted for a high proportion of African artistic endeavour and expression, study of which can – as Jan Vansina has shown – provide the historian with many insights. That such material has not been preserved from the period here considered is a major shortcoming in our evidence and a measure of the inadequacy of the historical reconstructions here offered.

CONCLUSION

Contrary to previously held opinion, the period from c. 3000 to c. 700 BC may be seen as one of general stability in most of Africa. As the previous pages have indicated, the coverage of archaeological research has been so incomplete that the recognition of widespread trends is greatly hampered by our inability to differentiate the particular from the general. There is also a danger that the greater archaeological visibility of more recent remains may lead us to regard as this period's innovations, socio-economic complexities that actually originated in significantly earlier times. Recent research in the Sudanese Nile Valley and in East Africa has served to emphasize this point. Nevertheless, it does appear that the basic economic, socio-political and economic trends of this period were essentially continuations and intensifications of processes already discernible in previous millennia. North of the equator these trends were frequently associated with the continued development and intensification of farming. Towards the end of the period here considered a farming life-style began in parts of the Congo basin and in the East African highlands, dominated respectively by non-cereal agriculture and by herding. South of the equator foraging continued to provide the economic mainstay of the population. Here, too, technological developments were essentially continuations of trends begun in earlier times. The major innovations and transformations that accompanied the development of metallurgy had not yet begun.

EDITOR'S NOTES

From comments made by L. M. Diop-Maes on certain points we have selected the following:

1 It is very difficult to make a demographical evaluation of prehistoric populations. We can, however, draw attention, as does A. Muzzolini (1989), to the burgeoning of Neolithic sites throughout Africa south of the Sahara. L. M. Diop-Maes advances a figure of between 1 to 3 inhabitants per km² c. 1000–700 BC. P. Vidal also records an increase in sites in Central Africa between 1500 and 500 BC. (1 inhabitant per km² in *Recherches Centrafricaines*, No. 18, 1984, Aix-en-Provence, p. 20).

2 J. Desanges notes in *The General History of Africa* (Vol. II, Ch. 17), that the Libyans, called Tehenou by the Egyptians, were depicted in Egyptian iconography at the beginning of the third millennium BC as tall, dark, thick-lipped men. Towards 2300 BC a new group of Libyans 'with paler skins and blue eyes, including a considerable proportion of fair-haired individuals' made their appearance. These became very numerous under Ramesses III who, like his predeces-

sors, steered the white 'Peoples of the Sea' away in the direction of Libya at the beginning of the twelfth century BC.

3 According to the earliest datings obtained at Karkarichinkat (Mali), Kintampo and Ntereso (Ghana), there is now firm evidence for the domestication of animals between 2500 and 2000 BC. L. M. Diop-Maes thinks that earlier dates are possible at certain sites, such as 4000 BC indicated by H. Lhote at Arlit (Aïr). (cf. R. Vernet, *Vallées du Niger*, Paris, 1993, p. 70).

4 Nothing very certain is yet known about the beginnings of African metallurgy. A number of discoveries associated with radiocarbon dating of samples would seem to confirm the hypothesis of an early working of local iron. In the *Journal des Africanistes* (Vol. 52, Nos.1/2, Paris, 1982, p. 54), N. C. Van Grunderbeek, E. Roche and H. Doutrelepont mentioned the use of iron in Rwanda/Burundi around 1470 BC, and more certainly between 1250 and 700 BC. It is attested c. 700 BC in northern Cameroon (A. Marliac, *L'âge du fer au Cameroun Septentrional*, Paris, 1988). In Taruga, an area belonging to the Nok culture (Nigeria), the early Iron Age dates back to approximately 850 BC (M. Cornevin, *Archéologie africaine*, Paris, 1993, p. 121; A. Close, *Journ. A. Hist.*, 1988). The evidence is less firm for other earlier dates concerning Nok. Iron is present in the Massif de Termit (Niger), where it is associated with remains dated 1350 BC (G. Quéchon, 'La fin du Néolithique et les débuts de la métallurgie', Communication to the Maghnia Colloquium, December 1988).

5 Pottery, dated 6000 BC, has been found at the lower level of Gamble's Cave at Elmenteita, east of Lake Victoria-Nyanza (J. W. G. Sutton in *The General History of Africa*, Vol. I, Ch. 19, Paris, 1980, p. 482). Pottery dating back to the end of the fourth millennium BC and the beginning of the third millennium BC has been found at two sites to the south-east of this lake (D. P. Collet and P. T. Robertshaw, *Azania*, XV, 1980, pp. 135–45). In Central Africa, a megalithic civilization existed from 1100 to 700 BC (P. Vidal in 'L'Archéologie du Cameroun', Paris, 1992, p. 139, and Nicholas David, 1982).

6 Account must be taken of the likely effects of a very dry phase that lasted several centuries around 5000 BC. Furthermore, around 3000 BC, the northern Sahara was already arid, whereas the southern Sahara, which was still humid, formed a single unit with the Sudan. From 3000 to 700 BC it should not, therefore, be regarded as part of North Africa.

7 We know in particular of the four expeditions by the Egyptian caravan leader Herkhuf to the land of 'Yam' during the reign of Merenre and Pepi II in the twenty-third century BC. The first and second expeditions lasted for seven and eight months respectively. P. Kalck has identified the land of Yam as the north-eastern region of the present Central African Republic (*L'histoire de la République centrafricaine*, Paris, 1974, p. 33). P. L. Shinnie considers that Wadi el Melek was a probable way through to Darfur and Kordofan (in 'Egypt and Africa' ed. by W. V. Davies, London, 2nd ed., 1993, pp. 49–53).

BIBLIOGRAPHY

AMBLARD, S.; PERNÈS, J. 1989. The Identification of Cultivated Pearl Millet (*Pennisetum*) amongst Pottery from Oued Chebbi (Dhar Oualata, Mauritania). *African Archaeological Review*, Vol. 7, pp. 117–26.

BARTHELME, J. W. 1985. *Fisher-Hunters and Neolithic Pastoralists in East Turkana, Kenya*. Oxford, (BAR Int. Ser., 254.)

BOWER, J. 1991. The Pastoral Neolithic of East Africa. *Journal of World Prehistory*, Vol. 5, pp. 49–82.

BRANDT, S. A.; CARDER, N. 1987. Pastoral Rock Art in the Horn of Africa: Making Sense of Udder Chaos. *World Archaeology*, Vol. 19, pp. 194–213.

CABLE, C. 1984. *Economy and Technology in the Late Stone Age in Southern Natal.* Oxford, (BAR Int. Ser., 201).

CAMPS, G. 1974. *Les civilisations préhistoriques de l'Afrique du nord et du Sahara.* Paris.

CARTER, P. L. 1970. Late Stone Age Exploitation Patterns in Southern Natal. *South African Archaeological Bulletin*, Vol. 25, pp. 55–8.

CLARK, J. D. 1954. *Prehistoric Cultures in the Horn of Africa.* Cambridge.

—— 1963. *Prehistoric Cultures of Northeast Angola and their Significance in Tropical Africa.* Lisboa.

—— (ed.). 1982. *Cambridge History of Africa*, Vol. I. Cambridge.

——; BRANDT, S. A. (eds) 1984. *From Hunters to Farmers.* Berkeley, Calif.

——; WILLIAMS, M. A. J. 1978. Recent Archaeological Research in South-Eastern Ethiopia, 1974–5. *Annales d'Ethiopie*, Vol. 11, pp. 19–42.

CLIST, B. 1986. Le néolithique en Afrique centrale: état de la question et perspective d'avenir. *L'Anthropologie*, Vol. 90, pp. 217–31.

—— 1989. Archaeology in Gabon, 1886–1988. *The African Archaeological Review*, Vol. 7, p.59–95.

CONNAH, G. 1981. *Three Thousand Years in Africa.* Cambridge.

DAVID, N. 1982. Tazunu: Megalithic Monuments of Central Africa. *Azania*, Vol. 17, pp. 43–77.

DEACON, J. 1984. Later Stone Age People and their Descendants in Southern Africa. In: KLEIN, R. G. (ed.), *Southern African Prehistory and Palaeoenvironments*, pp. 221–328. Rotterdam.

EGGERT, M. K. H. 1987. Imbonga and Batalimo: Ceramic Evidence for Early Settlement of the Equatorial Rain Forest. *African Archaeological Review*, Vol. 5, pp. 129–45.

EHRET, C. 1980. On the Antiquity of Agriculture in Ethiopia. *Journal of African History*, Vol. 20, pp. 161–77.

——; POSNANSKY, M. (eds) 1982. *The Archaeological and Linguistic Reconstruction of African History.* Berkeley, Calif.

FAGAN, B. M.; VAN NOTEN, F. 1971. *The Hunter Gatherers of Gwisho.* Tervuren, Musée Royal de l'Afrique Centrale.

FATTOVICH, R.; MARKS, A. E.; MOHAMMED-ALI, A. 1984. The Archaeology of the Eastern Sahel, Sudan: Preliminary Results. *African Archaeological Review*, Vol. 2, pp. 173–88.

FUCHS, G. 1989. Rock Engravings in the Wadi el-Barramiya, Eastern Desert of Egypt. *African Archaeological Review*, Vol. 7, pp. 127–53.

GRÉBENART, D. 1988. *Les premiers métallurgistes en Afrique occidentale.* Paris.

HAALAND, R. 1987. *Socio-Economic Differentiation in the Neolithic Sudan.* Oxford, (BAR Int. Ser., 350).

HOLL, A. 1989. Habitat et sociétés préhistoriques du Dhar Tichitt (Mauritanie). *Sahara*, Vol. 2, pp. 49–60.

LANFRANCHI, R.; SCHWARTZ, D. 1990. *Paysages quaternaires de l'Afrique centrale atlantique.* Paris.

LEAKEY, M. D.; LEAKEY L. S. B. 1950. *Excavations at Njoro River Cave.* Oxford.

LEWIS-WILLIAMS, J. D. 1981. *Believing and Seeing.* London.

—— 1983. *The Rock Art of Southern Africa.* Cambridge.

——; DOWSON, T. 1990. *Images of Power.* Johannesburg.

MCINTOSH, S. K.; MCINTOSH R. J. 1988. From Stone to Metal: New Perspectives on the Later Prehistory of West Africa. *Journal of World Prehistory*, Vol. 2, pp. 89–133.

MACK, J.; ROBERTSHAW, P. (eds) 1982. *Culture History in the Southern Sudan.* Nairobi.

MARET, P. DE. 1986. The Ngovo Group: An Industry with Polished Stone Tools and Pottery in Lower Zaire. *African Archaeological Review*, Vol. 4, pp. 103–33.

——; CLIST, B.; VAN NEER, W. 1987. Résultats des premières fouilles dans les abris de Shum Laka et Abéké. *L'Anthropologie*, Vol. 91, pp. 559–84.

MARSHALL, F. 1989. Rethinking the Role of *Bos indicus* in Africa. *Current Anthropology*, Vol. 30, pp. 235–40.

MERRICK, H. V.; BROWN, F. H. 1984. Obsidian Sources and Patterns of Source Utilisation in Kenya and Northern Tanzania: Some initial findings. *African Archaeological Review*, Vol. 2, pp. 129–52.

MOKHTAR, G. (ed.) 1981. *UNESCO General History of Africa*, Vol. II. London.

MUZZOLINI, A. 1986. *L'art rupestre préhistorique des massifs centraux Sahariennes.* Oxford, British Archaeological Reports (International Series 318).

—— 1991. Proposals for Updating the Rock-drawing Sequence of the Acacus. *Libyan Studies*, Vol. 22, pp. 7–30.

PHILLIPSON, D. W. 1976. *The Prehistory of Eastern Zambia.* Nairobi, British Institute in Eastern Africa.

—— 1977. *The Later Prehistory of Eastern and Southern Africa.* London.

—— 1984. Aspects of Early Food Production in Northern Kenya. In: KRYZANIAK, L.; KOBUSIEWICZ, M. (eds), *Origin and Early Development of Food-Producing Cultures in North-East Africa*, pp. 489–95. Poznań.

—— 1985. *African Archaeology.* Cambridge.

—— 1994. Chapter 40. *History of Humanity*, Vol. I. Paris.

SHAW, T. 1978. *Nigeria.* London.

—— 1981. The Late Stone Age in West Africa and the Beginnings of African Food Production. In: ROUBET et al. (eds), *Préhistoire Africaine*, pp. 213–35. Paris.

——; DANIELS, S. G. H. 1984. Excavations at Iwo Eleru, Ondo State, Nigeria. *West African Journal of Archaeology*, Vol. 14, pp. 1–269.

STAHL, A. B. 1985. Reinvestigation of Rintampo 6 Rock Shelter, Ghana: Implications for the Nature of Culture Change. *African Archaeological* Review, pp. 117–50.

STEHLI, P. (ed.). 1978. *Sahara.* Köln.

VAN NOTEN, F. 1982. *The Archaeology of Central Africa.* Graz.

VANSINA, J. 1984. *Art History in Africa: An Introduction to Method.* London.

VINNICOMBE, P. 1976. *People of the Eland.* Pietermaritzburg.

WILLCOX, A. R. 1984. *The Rock Art of Africa.* London.

WILLIAMS, M. A. J.; FAURE, H. (eds) 1980. *The Sahara and the Nile.* Rotterdam.

14

EUROPE

EDITOR'S NOTE

Vast amounts of archaeological literature have been produced on the metal ages in the various countries of Europe, but at the same time there has been a proliferation of different typological and chronological reference systems.

The texts relating to Europe have needed to be harmonized so as to achieve a balance between region-by-region analyses and overall views within a framework of homogeneous references. The aim throughout has been to allow readers to acquaint themselves, chapter by chapter, with the cultural specificities of each part of Europe while at the same time learning about the broad general features of the evolution of the continent during this period.

14.1
INTRODUCTION

Jean-Pierre Mohen

The period from 3000 to 700 BC in Europe corresponds to an important new stage of evolution in society which encompasses the Chalcolithic and the Bronze Age. The Neolithic innovations progressively altered the way of life of men among whose activities production at that time played a predominant role. From 3000 BC onwards, communities of peasants and shepherds colonized as much land as they could, extending to the mountains and to Northern Europe. Their ascendancy over nature was such that the natural environment was affected by it for the first time. The development of societies of a markedly Neolithic type was accompanied by population growth, fairly extensive social structuring, the appearance of a greater number of specialized crafts and in particular the emergence of metal working, first using copper and gold, then bronze and finally, at the beginning of the first millennium BC, iron. The considerably extended trade networks were often indispensable to these activities and a fact to which some authors have drawn attention – the wide distribution of various objects showing links between Greece and the British Isles, between Scandinavia and northern Italy and between the regions bordering the Black Sea and the Iberian peninsula – has led some to speak of the Europeanization of cultures. This evolution did not come about smoothly; several types of more or less violent crisis occurred: climatic, demographic, economic, military and social. Their study, conducted by using the methods of the physical, chemical, natural, human and mathematical sciences to observe and interpret archaeological remains, makes it possible to sketch an historical outline of these societies, which had no written records and to try to understand the processes of adaptation and change among these proto-historic human groups (Map 21).

ENVIRONMENT

In its general features, the physical geography of proto-historic Europe was not very different from that of today, in the sense that four major landscape types can be used to classify the variety of natural surroundings seen. The arctic and sub-arctic landscape was limited to the extreme north of Scandinavia and of what is now the Russian Federation; it was also found in high mountain regions, such as the Alps and the Pyrenees; its vegetation contained no trees; it was of the tundra or the alpine type.

The northern landscape with conifers was found in Scandinavia and the Russian Federation above latitude 60°N, and also in countries with high mountains. The common trees were pine, spruce, silver fir, birch and willow. The landscape of the sub-oceanic temperate zone with aestival deciduous forest contained oak, elm, lime, alder and beech. The Mediterranean landscape with its evergreen forest featured the cork, oak, cypress and the olive tree. In parts it was scaled down to maquis with box, myrtle, juniper, broom, arbutus, oleander and wild vine or to garrigues with lavender, thyme, sage and so on.

The evolution of landscapes between 3000 and 700 BC

Several natural and human factors came to modify these landscapes to some extent, occasionally creating real crises of adaptation for human societies.

Coastal landscapes changed but little, since the shoreline remained very much the same, rising by about a metre in western Europe and falling slightly in northern Europe. At the end of this period the present level was reached. There were of course particular local situations where alluviation (Poitou marsh, France) or subsidence (Venice, Italy) took place.

The general evolution of vegetation in northern Europe in the post-glacial has been established on the basis of the abundant pollen of the peat-bogs (Blytt and Sernander zonation). It has been confirmed and reconstituted in more detail as a result of analyses carried out by palynologists from other countries. The beginning of our period corresponds to the end of the Atlantic period, which we date between 5500 and 3000–2500 BC.

The mildness of the climate (greater than it is today), combined with quite high humidity, brought about an extension of the forest, in the temperate zones especially of the mixed oak forest with a high proportion of limes. The following period, known as the Sub-Boreal, lasted from 3000–2500 until 700 BC. It was characterized by a general cooling down, sometimes dry, sometimes humid. The mixed oak forest retreated from the higher ground, giving way to beech, fir and spruce. At the end of this period, between 1100 and 700 BC, a higher degree of humidity seems to have had dramatic consequences for the farming populations, whose crops no longer ripened, and on the villagers on the shores of the circum-Alpine lakes, who had to abandon their dwellings precipitately, probably owing to an abrupt rise in the water level (the sites at Lake Neuchâtel in Switzerland were abandoned about 850 BC according to several dendrochronological datings). After 700 BC the Sub-Atlantic period experienced a milder climate and a humidity which encouraged a new expansion of the beech and hornbeam forests and which corresponds to the present situation.

Map 21 Europe (after Millotee; Thévenin, 1988).

This picture underwent subtle changes and adaptations in the Mediterranean region, for example, where holm-oak developed at the time of the transition from the Atlantic period to the Sub-Boreal period, during which the Aleppo pine also appeared, or in the Paris basin, where in the Sub-Boreal period elm and lime declined in irregular fashion, alder became more common and beech appeared in Normandy (France). However, palaeobotanic studies have demonstrated above all the impact of human activity on natural vegetation over vast areas. Forest clearances and human influence on the natural landscape became so important that the phenomenon can be detected for the first time in pollen diagrams. Furthermore, human influence sometimes combines with natural evolution; and the retreat of the oak forest in the Sub-Boreal in Mediterranean countries, to be replaced by maquis, seemed to result from this new situation. The effect of human agency was twofold: it influenced natural vegetation as a result of the growing number of domestic animals, especially goats; because of the transhumance of the flocks both the plains and the mountain regions were affected. Secondly, it acted through the clearance of forests, often by burning, from fertile land, which was turned into fields and pasture. The temperate forest zone often suffered as a result of land being brought into cultivation. We can detect traces of intensive deforestation and the appearance of pollen from ruderal and cultivated plants not only in the Gironde, the Massif Central and Brittany (France) but also in the United Kingdom, the Netherlands and central and eastern Europe. The northern limit of human influence on the natural vegetation is the line beyond which cereals would not ripen, which passed through northern England and southern Scandinavia. In regions situated to the north of that line, in high mountain areas or again in certain inhospitable mountain massifs unsuited to agriculture, as in Hungary during the Bronze Age, this effect was due to shepherds and their flocks. The cultivation of land by extensive methods quickly exhausted the soil. For example, in the Rhine Valley the rural settlements of the Early Neolithic on the most fertile soils, in particular the loess deposits, were abandoned in favour of land that was more difficult to till. The search for new lands to cultivate, made still more necessary by an increase in population, explains why inhospitable terrain like the Cheviot Hills in England were colonized, an event that took place at the end of the third millennium BC and in the first half of the second. This undertaking was carried through successfully because climatic conditions were at their best at that time, but archaeologists suppose that when temperatures cooled down and humidity increased at the end of the Sub-Boreal period those upland settlements whose economy had become precarious were abandoned. In the more temperate regions the problem of soil exhaustion was overcome in part by the introduction of new farming techniques during the third millennium BC, such as the use of the ard (scratch plough) and manuring or the cultivation of new, hardier plants. In other regions it seems that pastoral activities, which were practised then over wider areas and especially on windy plateaus, developed at the end of the second millennium BC: this has been shown to have occurred in the United Kingdom and in the Jura in France. These pastoral communities are thought to have furthered the spread of the Iron Age culture.

In southern Europe, and especially in the Iberian peninsula and the Caucasus, arable land was taken into cultivation or brought back into cultivation from the third millennium BC onwards by the development of carefully designed irrigation canals.

Physical and demographic anthropology

Very little is known about human activity in the third and second millennia BC. Physical anthropology teaches that almost all present-day morphological features were already in existence at that time. Some new features did emerge, however: at the end of the third millennium, brachycephalization became common and is evident specifically in the bell-beaker burials. The study of bones and their pathology together with estimations of life expectancy indicate that life was generally hard and full of such dangers as hazardous childbirth, disease, famine and sometimes deliberate slaughter. However, killings do not seem to have been as frequent as might have been expected. The study of unenclosed or even fortified rural settlements tends to show instead a peaceful people whose clothes were made of wool, linen, hide or leather. Some indications of what they wore can be gleaned from the baked-clay statuettes of central and eastern Europe, the bronze statuettes found in Scandinavia and in Mediterranean Europe, in Sardinia (Italy), and especially from the mummified corpses found in peat-bogs in Denmark and north Germany, which were sometimes preserved in humid conditions in marshland or under a tumulus for about 3,300 years. One example is the mummy of Similaun Man, preserved in a Tyrolean glacier for almost 6,000 years (Figs 55–7). Dress varied according to sex, age and season. The girl of Egtved (Denmark), buried in summer, wore a short one-piece bodice, a belt and a short skirt which ended above the knees. A statuette of two young women performing acrobatic dances shows them wearing the same short skirts. This type of summer clothing is also found on a small statuette decorating the handle of a bronze knife found at Kaiserberg in Holstein. Another quite young woman found at Skrydstrup wore a belt; her loose-fitting bodice was made of two pleated sections attached at the shoulder. The old woman of Borum Eshøj also wore a bodice and a wide skirt held at the waist with a belt and reaching down to her feet (Fig. 58). The man from Trindhøj wore a tunic down to his knees which was fastened at the shoulders by leather straps and open at the sides. The flaps, pinned together on the chest, were held in at the waist by a belt. He had a cape thrown over his shoulders and wore a felt cap on his head. In the same way other details are known to us regarding moccasins and the hairnets which kept women's hair in place. What is known of dress in northern Europe is repeated in southern Europe (statuettes in Sardinia). It is difficult to make precise demographic estimates. The notion of territory, as defined by British archaeologists, indicates a certain geographical unit comprising farms, hamlets and one or more fortified settlements. These territories, such as those which existed around Stonehenge, each had between 3,000 and 8,000 inhabitants. According to such calculations, the population of the British Isles, for example, is thought to have been one million people around 3000 BC, to have increased to a maximum of two million around 1300 BC, and finally to have dropped back to one million again around 700 BC. There is evidence from other regions indicating a continuous rise in population, based on the counting of graves in northern Europe.

Techno-economic features

Fishing and hunting centres

Certain northern and eastern European sites give some idea of the development of fishing and hunting, especially in areas where agriculture could not become established for climatic

Figure 55 Similaun Man: reconstruction of his leather garment and shoes (after Egg et al., 1993).

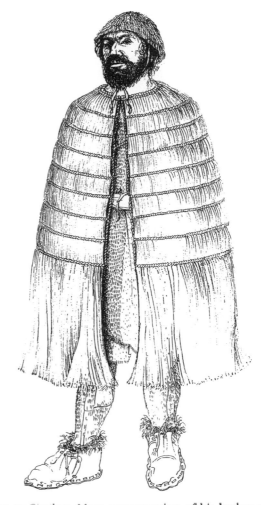

Figure 57 Similaun Man: reconstruction of his leather cap and raffia cape (after Egg et al., 1993).

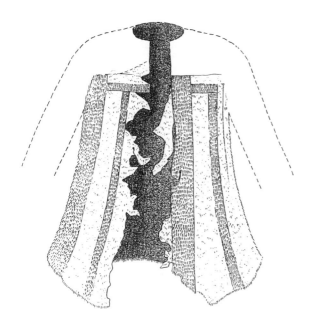

Figure 56 Similaun Man: reconstruction of the jacket made of different coloured leather strips. The top part is missing (after Egg et al., 1993).

Figure 58 Man's and woman's costumes. Bronze Age, Denmark (after Mohen; Baillond, 1987).

or cultural reasons. However, in northern Europe, fishing, hunting and food-gathering played an important role in nourishment. Innumerable Scandinavian stippled figures on rock faces at Himmelstalund (Sweden) and Fossum (Norway), and at Zalavruga near the White Sea in the Russian Federation depict hunting and fishing scenes: skiing hunters, armed with bows, chasing and killing reindeer and large birds, perhaps swans; men in boats encircling a harpooned cetacean, lone fishermen in their boats catching large fish on their lines. Ordinary and hoop nets and snares made large catches possible. A few hooks and especially pronged harpoons used to catch pike were found at the site of Svaerdborg (Denmark), where the abundance of fish heads suggests that they were specifically prepared for preservation, either by drying or smoking. Indeed, new techniques for preserving and storing fish (brine, salting and ceramic jars) seem to have been developed in order to prepare products which were consumed in the winter or bartered for such things as meat, fat, hides and furs, eagle feathers for fletching arrows, down and so on. Some writers think that by means of such bartering the southern Scandinavian countries were able to acquire copper and tin ingots, raw material for an original local metal-working industry. Hunting and fishing also remained the basis of economic activity in the forest societies of eastern Europe, at Usviaty, south of St Petersburg and at Chigir in the Urals, for example. In the rest of Europe, these activities were still a supplementary resource during periods of prosperity for aristocrats and priests (deer hunting: the bronze wagon at Strettweg in Austria; boar hunting: the chariot at Merida in Spain); they were a necessary source of food at less exalted levels during periods of famine (apparently around 1800 and 800 BC).

Agro-pastoral practices and rural settlements

Traces of an agro-pastoral economy in a large part of protohistoric Europe can be seen, with slight geographical variations on account of the climate. The rich soils of the temperate zone were used for both purposes but with intensive agricultural activity, whereas the arid lands of the south and the cold northern plateaus lent themselves to stock-rearing. From 3000 BC onwards a need for new land made itself felt as a result of the exhaustion of the original ground which had been brought into cultivation by the slash-and-burn techniques or laid waste by goats, and especially because of an increase in population. It is found that inhospitable regions such as the mountains of the Spanish Meseta, Brittany, the Alps, the French Massif Central and even Scotland were cleared for cultivation and colonized, while new farming techniques became necessary: manuring for revitalizing the soil, the development of irrigation canal systems in southern Europe (the Iberian peninsula and the Caucasus) and, above all, it would seem, the gradual replacement of the digging stick and the hoe by the ox-drawn ard. The scenes of men ploughing stippled on rocks in northern and southern Europe indicate the existence of two types of plough: the spade-plough (Tustrup in Jutland, Denmark) and the more clearly depicted hoe-plough (Litsleby in Sweden, Sejbaek and Vebbestrup in Denmark, Mont Bégo in southern France and Val Camonica in Italy) (Plate 139). Once the plough was in use the peasant progressed from hortus to ager; the furrow served as a small canal which retained water while aerating the soil. Wheats were always present among cultivated seeds which seem to have become more varied during the third millennium BC, with barley present in the British Isles and millet in northern France, Switzerland and Germany; oats and rye seem to have appeared quite late in temperate Europe. Pod plants then became widely grown (broad beans, lentils, flax) and fruit trees attracted special attention (apple, grape and olive). Large bovines now appeared among the domestic animals, probably as a result

of the local domestication of the aurochs, and also the horse, at the outset, at the end of the third millennium BC, bred from steppe stock but later possibly from local types, especially in Western Europe. These two animals introduced the power of traction and possibilities of travel, both of which were widely exploited.

Rural settlements reflected various aspects of agricultural life. In Europe they were most often dispersed and consisted of isolated farms, hamlets and villages, sometimes fortified, sometimes not. The variety of building materials used, such as stone, earth, wood and thatch, and the range of architectural designs adopted helped to give several regions of Europe their specific character. In the Mediterranean region, round houses were built of stone at Filicudi in the Aeolian Islands and at Porto Perone and Leporana near Taranto in Italy around 2000 BC. Round houses made of decorative stone also appeared at Gruting in the Shetland Islands. Other circular-plan houses consisted of posts driven into the ground and supporting a framework covered with thatch; the walls were made of wattle and daub. Towards 1000 BC, at Gwithian in Cornwall some of these houses were grouped together in the middle of fields with banks and drainage ditches round their edges. Further north, in the Cheviots, others were found with traces of field boundaries. In temperate and continental Europe a rectangular ground plan was most often adopted. Posts driven into the ground formed the framework for wattle-and-daub walls and supported a skilfully built roof structure which was covered in thatch. The methods used for assembling these parts are known from the remains found at lakeside sites, such as those of Lake Neuchâtel (Switzerland), where halvings, potsherds, mortises and dovetails have been found. Some houses were built entirely out of wood by the Blockbau method, in which walls made of horizontal beams met at the corners. An example of this type of house, characteristic of Alpine regions, was found at Hallstatt in Austria (dating from the beginning of the first millennium BC). The interior of these houses was furnished with shelves and beds. In the third millennium carpenters' and joiners' tools included wooden wedges, axes, adzes and chisels made of polished stone. In the second millennium BC these tools were gradually replaced by their bronze equivalents, and gouges and planes can be added to the list. Houses could be locked, as was the case at Morges in Switzerland.

The long rectangular houses at Elp (Drenthe), on their own in the Belgian and Netherlands plain, and even in Scandinavia, were similar to contemporary Friesian farms. Other more humble rectangular houses were grouped together in the plains in hamlets or small villages; at Dampierre on the Doubs in France the houses were arranged in a circle around two central houses with projecting roofs. Houses built on piles could also be found huddled together on the banks of certain lakes. These were the famous lake villages, which were usually built on damp ground and not on the water itself. Some of these lake villages were surrounded by a fence, such as the sites at Fiave in Italy (middle of the second millennium), at Cortaillod on Lake Neuchâtel in Switzerland and at Biskupin in Poland (beginning of the first millennium BC). At the Wasserburg site, near Buchau in Germany, or at Unteruhldingen on the banks of Lake Constance (Switzerland), several stages of development can be discerned. Domestic crafts evolved in these areas of concentrated settlement and were also to be found in the hill-fort settlements, testifying to collective work imposed by a hierarchically organized society.

Domestic and specialized crafts

Domestic crafts were traditional in the sense that the techniques used had appeared during the preceding millennia, particularly the fourth which witnessed the general spread of Neolithic innovations largely connected with rural pursuits. Some prestige objects connected with religion, hunting or war suggest more specialized types of production. However, many details characterize the domestic crafts of the period concerned. As regards stone cutting, the famous transverse arrowheads appeared during the course of the third millennium BC. The most sophisticated of these were the Armorican arrowheads, cut in a translucent white flint at the beginning of the second millennium BC. At the same time, flint factories in Scandinavia and at Grand-Pressigny in France were making daggers whose quality has been compared to that of pre-dynastic Egyptian knives. In these cases, domestic crafts had no doubt already been transformed into specialized crafts. However, the basic domestic stone industry (scrapers, backed knives, sickle blades, points, picks, chisels, axes, which were sometimes polished, and so on) was most certainly operating in many areas of Europe throughout the entire period, at least until the start of the Iron Age. Pottery continued on the whole to be part of domestic production and included food vessels and storage jars. Potters' kilns were still usually in the form of simple pits, but there are a few examples from the second millennium BC of improved kilns comprising a hearth separated from the heating chamber by a baked-clay grid; the Sévrier kiln (Haute-Savoie, France), dating from around 1000 BC, is of this type. It made for even heating, which explains the quality of the vessels made which were diffused all over Europe at that time. The quality was all the more remarkable in that in certain areas the potter's wheel was beginning to be used for the shaping of vases. There is evidence of the device having been used in Crete at the beginning of the Middle Minoan and it later spread to Greek, Etruscan and Phoenician colonies all over the Mediterranean basin; it was only towards the end of the Iron Age that the wheel was adopted by potters in temperate Europe, whereas in Scandinavia it was adopted only in the Middle Ages.

A similar mechanical system (bow drill) allowed other objects to be produced, such as stone bracelets, amber and shale cups from Wessex in the United Kingdom dating from the start of the second millennium BC, and containers, wooden wheels and hubs; a dish made of cypress wood found in a Mycenaean tomb was perhaps already the result of using a wheel and it was certainly used for making a container found in the Etruscan Tomb of the Warrior at Corneto (Italy).

Woodworking is known from the evidence of remarkable sites such as the cart burials north of the Black Sea (Tri Brata), the Danish burial mounds (Egtved), or, above all, the discoveries made beneath the circum-Alpine lakes (Zurich, Neuchâtel in Switzerland, Le Bourget in France) and marshes in Denmark (Ordrup) and the Russian Federation (Usviaty). Here, in addition to the wherewithal for building houses, such as posts, joists, planks, and so on, are found a whole range of objects: tool handles, ladles, combs, wedges, bows, yokes, wheels, caskets, tubs, platters, bowls, canoes and so on. Most of these objects had been cut and polished with stone tools. Towards 1000 BC the use of bronze gouges and chisels enabled finer grooves to be cut that made more precise fitting possible (boxes and buckets). In the north, skis and sleighs have also been found. Bark, particularly birch bark, could be sewn and used to make mats or containers. Birch pitch was often used as glue to repair broken vases or

to attach sickle blades. Wickerwork was also common (different types of baskets) and recent excavations at Auvernier on Lake Neuchâtel (Switzerland) have brought to light a fine selection. Plaiting techniques can also be seen in nets (hairnets and fisherman's nets), in leather fittings (a knapsack from Hallstatt in Austria) and especially in the many textiles found. Textiles were made of vegetable fibres from nettles or flax, or of animal fibres such as wool. The grave clothes from the Danish Bronze Age are good examples of the quality of crafts that were probably domestic, as is proved by the discovery of numerous spindle whorls and loom weights dating from the third millennium BC onwards on settlement sites.

One of the great innovations of the third millennium BC was the emergence of a very specialized stone-working craft, which can be traced from the Russian Federation right across to the United Kingdom. The stone worked in this way varied from particularly hard rock to high-quality flint. The hunter-fishermen of Nostvet (Norway) cut jade in the little island of Hespriholmen, and brought the raw material together on the larger island of Bömlo, whence it was distributed. The factory which produced dolerite at Plussulien (Côte d'Armor, France) was used at two different times to manufacture polished axes. Towards 3000 BC, the outcropping rock was extracted by percussion; the distribution of the first axes had been limited to the coast of Brittany (France). About 2000 BC, following a period during which the quarry had probably been abandoned, production became considerable. Great fires lit at the foot of the rock face to be cut caused the rock to split and all that had to be done was shape it. Petrographic studies have made it possible to trace the distribution of this second series of polished axes, rough-out axes, knobbed axes, axe-hammers and double-headed axes, to the south of England, the Paris basin, the lower Rhine, western and central-western France and to the region around Toulouse. The production of dolerite from Plussulien has thus been estimated to be several tens of tonnes.

Another interesting example is that of hornblendite from Kerlevot in the Quimper area (Finistère, France), which was exploited during the second half of the third millennium BC. This relatively soft rock lent itself to the making of perforated polished axes. Some of these, the plain double-headed axes or boat-axes, were parade weapons. The distribution of these was equally extensive stretching from the Rhine in the north (the double-headed axe of Nijmegen in Holland) to the Lot in the south (the double-headed axe from Castelnau-Montratier, France). These axes are most commonly found in Brittany and in the Paris basin.

Flint mines represented another form of the specialized exploitation of raw materials. They appeared in the fourth millennium BC but became more common in the third. Most of them produced flint nodules for polished axes, but some of them, such as the mines at Collorgnes and Salinelles (Gard, France) belonging to the Ferrières culture, provided tabular flint. The bifacial flaking of this flint made it suitable for making a variety of objects such as scrapers, knives, sickles, daggers and arrowheads. In the Cretaceous period limestone regions in the United Kingdom, northern France, Belgium, Poland, northern Jutland (Denmark) and the Russian Federation, the digging of flint mine shafts went in parallel with the systematic use of polished axes, which were more useful and effective when made of flint than when made of stone, stone axes being mostly restricted to ceremonial use. The site at Krzemionski Opatowskie near Opatow in Poland was contemporary with the funnel beaker and globular

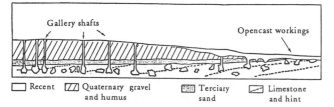

Figure 59 Diagrammatic section of the flint-mining area of Spiennes, Hainaut, Belgium (after Clark, 1955).

amphora cultures. It comprised almost 3,000 shafts up to 11 m deep, which were sometimes linked together by horizontal galleries. The vast deposit at Spiennes in Belgium extended over 100 hectares (Fig. 59). Here studies have been carried out of the remains of dwellings belonging to the Michelsberg culture, a ditch-enclosure, flint-knapping floors and mine shafts, funnel-shaped in their upper part. Some of these are as deep as 25 m and miners' antler picks have been found there. Near Liège (Belgium), at Obourg, a miner with his pick was trapped under a mass of fallen rocks from one of the galleries. In France, the mines of Nointel and Hardivilliers (Oise) and those of Novéant-sur-Moselle near Saint-Mihiel (Meuse) are of this same type (Fig. 60). The best-studied site in England is that of Grimes Graves. Antler picks are abundant here (244 have been found in two shafts): they could be used at the same time to remove blocks of chalk. Other tools can also be recognized: two-pronged rakes, antler wedges, spades made from the shoulder-blades of deer and oxen, flint picks, and so on. Lamps hollowed into the blocks of chalk provided lighting. We can also picture ropes, baskets, leather sacks, ladders and other such objects. The archaeological remains, and in particular the potsherds found at Grime's Graves, testify to a lengthy mining operation which must have lasted throughout the whole of the third millennium BC and the beginning of the second (Windmill Hill, Peterborough and Beaker cultures) (Figs 61–2). Other more modest examples of flint mines show how widespread they were in Europe: Kvarnby and Tullströp near Malmö in southern Sweden, Rocio near Lisbon in Portugal, Monte Tabuto in Sicily. At Mur-de-Barrez (Aveyron, France), fire was used in the mine shafts and galleries to extract the rock more easily.

The deposits of honey-coloured flint in the Grand-Pressigny region (Indre-et-Loire) in France were also intensively

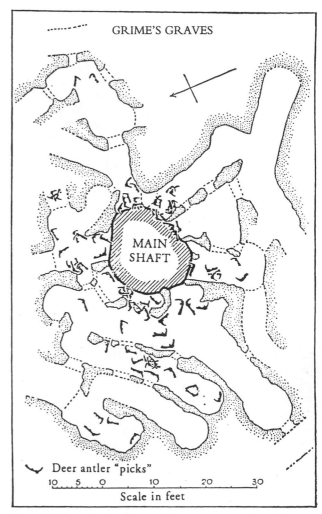

Figure 61 Flint mine galleries radiating outwards from the main shaft, Grime's Graves, Norfolk, United Kingdom (after Clark, 1955).

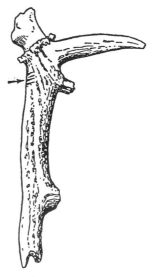

Figure 62 Deer-antler 'pick', Grime's Graves, Norfolk, United Kingdom. The arrow indicates scratchmarks and grooves. (after Clark, 1955).

exploited in the second half of the third millennium BC. The exceptional quality of this flint, which was mined in the open air, made it possible for blades 20 to 30 cm long to be obtained from large blocks (known in French as *livres de beurre*). They were then trimmed to make dagger or knife blades (Fig. 63).

Figure 60 Flint extraction: mines and quarries at Saint-Mihiel, Meuse, France (after Ch. Guillaume).

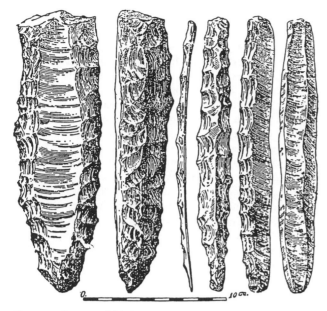

Figure 63 Cores and blades: flints from Grand-Pressigny, France (after Clark, 1955).

Thousands of blocks have been found in the valley factories which produced semi-finished products, roughed-out blades, packed together in clay containers and ready to be exported. Precise petrographic studies have confirmed the wide distribution of flint blades from Grand-Pressigny, which were sometimes copied in local flint, as in the factories at Pleumartin (Vienne, Isère) or Vassieux-en-Vercors (Drôme) in France, 500 km from Grand-Pressigny. The authentic Grand-Pressigny flint is attested in fairly large quantities in Seine–Oise–Marne tombs found widely in Normandy, Belgium and the Paris basin, where hoards of blades have been reported. Such hoards are also found in Brittany and Saône-et-Loire (France). Daggers from Pressigny were found in Holland in tombs with old-type beakers (2300–2000 BC). In the east of France they have been found in two clearly dated contexts: at Charavines (Isère, France), where the ¹⁴C datings are from 2350 to 1290 BC, and at Clairvoux (Jura, France), where the level is dated to 2120 BC. At Ouroux-sur-Saône (Saône-et-Loire, France) the examples from the Saône–Rhône culture have been dated to 2180 BC, which is perhaps too late. In Switzerland, in the region of Fribourg alone, more than 150 daggers from Pressigny have been discovered. At the site of Auvernier-Saunerie they were found at a level dated to about 2000 BC, but other assemblages indicate a context of corded ware from a quarter of a century prior to that time. The discovery of daggers in the primary tombs of the megalithic monument M V I of the Little Hunter at Sion in the Valais (Switzerland) confirms this. The construction of that monument, between 2240 and 2220 BC, was antecedent to the use of bell-beakers.

It is still not clear under what conditions these flint daggers from Grand-Pressigny were produced or to what culture the workers and those who ordered the daggers belonged. A few Artenancian potsherds found in the Grand-Pressigny area provide very little information on this subject. Who were the distributors? It is known for certain that their users belonged to varied cultures in a not insignificant portion of Europe and had no direct connection with the contemporary cultures in Touraine. Although the great period of the wide distribution of these daggers only lasted for a few centuries before 2000 BC, their prestige was such that on certain sites like Fort-Harrouard at Sorel-Moussel (Eure-et-Loire, France), Grand-Pressigny daggers were still in use at the start of the second millennium BC and when they were broken, scrapers, arrowheads and retouching tools were cut from their fragments. These reworked pieces have also been found in Switzerland.

Another industry, the production of salt, made its appearance in the course of the second millennium BC and played an important part in the first. At Sallis-de-Béarn (Pyrénées-Atlantiques, France) in the middle of the second millennium BC, salt water from a spring was heated in small dishes and evaporated, leaving salt. The large amount of ash mixed with the remnants of these dishes suggests a fairly extensive activity. The rock-salt mines at Hallstatt in Austria were controlled by princes, whose rich tombs were built at the very gates of the mine galleries during the first half of the first millennium BC. The grave contents show the relationships which existed between these princes and northern Italy, in which salt doubtless played a major role. It was indeed necessary for certain types of intensive animal husbandry and was also used in new techniques of meat preservation.

All these specialized crafts had certain features in common. They provided high-quality products as a result of the excellent raw material and efficient technology used. There was often only one type of product. The surpluses stocked and distributed indicate a volume of production exceeding the needs of the cultural group that produced them. Bartering systems served to balance supply and demand, in ways which are unknown to us. These features of the specialized crafts indicate the context necessary for the development of metal working.

Metal working: the advent of the metal ages

From the beginning of the third millennium BC (perhaps a little earlier in the Balkans) knowledge of metal was gradually obtained and modified the relations between human groups. The unique qualities of the new raw materials – copper, gold, silver, bronze and iron – together with the possibility of reusing them, which made them a stockable commodity, and their often distant geographic origins must have fascinated proto-historic man and both caused and reflected social divisions that became more and more pronounced. The flourishing of a specialized metal-working industry in regions which were often quite far from the areas where the ores were dressed and the ingots made encouraged in certains areas, such as southern Scandinavia, Normandy or south Germany, the establishment of centres where innovative designs for objects and even innovative techniques were developed.

The first traces of metal working in Europe date from a period a little later than the first traces found in western Asia (Iran and Anatolia). Archaeologists debate the extent of the relations which linked Troy and the northern Balkans and which some say favoured the development of copper-ore mining and smelting centres like that at Rudna Glava in Serbia. Others seek evidence of earlier indigenous activity and others again postulate influences originating from the steppes north of the Black Sea to explain the introduction of metallurgical knowledge. Before 3000 BC miners' copper implements – sledgehammers and picks – were found in Romania in the old copper-rich mountain massifs of Transylvania. Further to the south, at Aibunar in Bulgaria, copper mining was no doubt an opportunity for the princes whose remains lie in the neighbouring cemetery at Varna to increase their wealth and power. Much gold was found in the graves:

an appliqué in the shape of a bull, a very stylized female idol, beads for necklaces or bracelets and rings together with other prestigious belongings all assert the power of the princes, also demonstrated by the baked-clay masks decorated with gold jewels found in a few cenotaph tombs.

The eminent person buried a little later under the *kurgan* at Maïkop in the northern Caucasus is surrounded by similar riches: seventeen gold and silver dishes were laid out beside a baldaquin whose cloth was ornamented with stamped gold appliqué work depicting 70 bulls, 23 lions and 40 rings. The four tubular uprights made of gold and silver are decorated at their base with two statuettes of a bull in gold and two in silver. Two gold diadems, one necklace made of gold, lapis lazuli, turquoise and cornelian beads, and a few copper and dressed-flint tools and weapons are all remarkable pieces.

About 3000 BC, copper slag was produced at Diana on one of the islands of Lipari (Italy). During the following centuries, metal working spread in western Europe. In the Alesia region of Corsica the first evidence is seen at levels dated at 2800 to 2600 BC. In continental France on the southern edge of the Massif Central, copper mines have been found at Cabrières (Hérault) and at Aven de Bouche Payrol (Aveyron) which date from the middle of the third millennium BC. Ores from the Alps were also used at a fairly early date. Objects made of copper at that time included beads, awls, flat axes and dagger blades; articles of adornment in gold consisted of beads and small pieces of appliqué work. All these types of objects also occurred in the Iberian peninsula, where the copper mines of Mola Alta de Serelles (Spain) were in use at this time, as the discovery of moulds for casting flat axes confirms. In Portugal, forts like that at Zambujal were perhaps designed to keep watch on the activity of the nearby copper mines. In the Atlantic zone, copper mines were also found at Mount Gabriel in Ireland, where the same grooved polished stone mauls were used to crush the ore before smelting. From these mining centres, ingots were distributed, thus enabling metal-working factories to be established in areas lacking mined ores, such as Scandinavia. The first great cultures of the metal ages appeared; those of Tiszapoglar and Únětice in central Europe, of Remedello, Rinaldone and Gaudo in Italy, of the Montagne Noire in France and of El Argar and the Tagus in the Iberian peninsula. Factories in the British Isles and the west of France also took part in the onset of the metal civilization. Copper, gold, silver and lead objects were more abundant and varied; they took the form of jewellery (beads, pins, diadems), parade weapons (battleaxes, daggers) and tools (awls, axes). Some authors have argued that the bell-shaped vases, whose maritime style was widespread from Prague (Czech Republic) to Lisbon (Portugal), were produced by peoples with a knowledge of metal working, which they are thought to have introduced into the whole of western Europe. It is now known that the bell-shape phenomenon was one of the manifestations of European relationships at that time, that it was not the only one and that it corresponded around 2000 BC to a relatively advanced stage of metal working. Analyses show in fact that at that time prehistoric man sought for more or less natural alloys of copper and arsenic so as to have the benefit of a harder metal. Thus, the use of arsenical copper corresponds in Europe to a stage in the evolution of metal working that can be recognized from the Caucasus to Brittany (Carnoët blades had a surface enriched with 23 per cent arsenic and date from around 1700 BC) and the British Isles. In Cornwall and in Brittany the deposits of tin known as cassiterite (from the Scilly Isles) were worked from 1800

BC onwards. Tin-bronzes had appeared a millennium earlier in western Asia, in the royal tombs of Ur, for example, but despite a few possibilities of exploiting tin from Bohemia and to a lesser extent from Italy, it was only with the opening of the western tin route, largely maritime, that the true European Bronze Age, whose largest centres were in Greece and Italy, central and northern Europe and western Europe, began to flourish. The great period of tin-bronze (tin formed 15 to 20 per cent of the alloy, which it made more fluid during casting and harder when it solidified) is the Middle Bronze Age (1500 to 1200 BC). Numerous items were produced in the Atlantic area (palstaves, swords, spearheads, bracelets and so on) and rivalled those of central Europe (palstaves, swords, pins, bracelets and greaves) and northern Europe, which also developed original items in the precious metals (plate and jewels). Greece and the Minoan and Mycenaean Aegean were accumulating their treasures at the same time, among them masterpieces of the metal worker's art (Mycenaean daggers and masks).

With the late Bronze Age (1200 to 700 BC) antimony in central Europe and lead in western Europe were introduced into the alloy and partly took the place of tin. The quantity produced was considerable: various technical *tours de force* made it possible to produce Scandinavian cast lurer, breastplates, helmets, shields and cauldron-like vessels. It was a period of very rich stocks of bronze for recasting which numbered several thousand fragments: the hoards of Bologna in Italy, of Larnaud (Jura), of Vénat (Charente) in France and of Isleham (Cambridgeshire) in England. Wrecked ships loaded with bronze mark out the western trade route for tin: Dover in England Huelva in Spain, Rochelongue near Sète in France. Large metal-working centres such as Velem-Saint-Veidt in Hungary and Fort-Harrouard at Sorel-Moussel (Eure-et-Loire) in France prospered and were probably the equivalent of Mycenaean centres such as Pylos, as shown by the abundant traces of metallurgy; remains of furnaces, tuyères, crucibles, moulds and a whole series of tools: hammers, cleavers, anvils, chisels and so on. The quality of the bronzes seems to have declined at this time in favour of almost industrial quantity production. The addition of lead in particular made casting easier but it prevented the formation of a homogeneous alloy and made the metal soft. Towards the end of this period, hundreds of Armorican socketed axes, sometimes made of almost pure lead, could not have been used as tools; they were perhaps ingots and as they were in various standard sizes, they suggest an early form of currency. Some have seen in this uncontrolled increase in production one of the causes of the crisis which led to the advent of iron working. Meteoric iron had only been sporadically worked during the Bronze Age in Europe; one example is the dagger found at Ganovce in the Slovak Republic and belonging to the Otomani culture (fifteenth century BC). The reduction of iron ore of terrestrial origin and the hammering of the new metal into shape required much more delicate techniques than those used for copper. The more or less carburized iron displayed unique properties of suppleness and strength which were not fully exploited until the Iron Age, which began in Europe between 1100 and 700 BC, depending on the region. The technological innovations probably originated from Anatolia and were diffused both by the Eastern Mediterranean settlers who were moving westward and by semi-nomad populations of horsemen whose harness equipment has been found in tombs from the Black Sea to the Iberian peninsula. The first iron objects appeared in the Late Bronze Age in the form of decorative inlays on certain bronze sword hilts in Switzerland, a few sword blades (Velluire, Vendée, France) and other weapons like the arrowheads imitated from bronze specimens found in the Quéroy cave at Chazelles (Charente, France). Regions rich in iron ore such as the Pyrenees, Lorraine and Bohemia adopted iron more rapidly than others. The cemetery at Hallstatt near Salzburg in Austria provides evidence of an early advent of the Iron Age. It was a place where rock salt was extracted and must have been an important trading centre. Iron was found there mainly in the form of weapons, such as a long horseman's sword, spearheads and large knives, bronze being restricted to jewellery (bracelets and buckles) and articles such as situlae, dishes and so on. Little is known about the first forges; there is only one significant assemblage at Byči-Skala in the Czech Republic, which provided stake anvils, hammers and a large pair of tongs. The iron obtained towards 700 BC still lacked the great qualities that it was to have two centuries later in Greece and five centuries later in Gaul. Bog-ore iron, however, was used as well in northern Europe and in some parts of western Europe. Sophisticated techniques such as quenching and welding were only to be fully mastered during those later periods.

COMMUNICATIONS AND TRADE

The broadening of the economic horizon was favoured by the development of specialized crafts and means of communication. The use of animal power for transport and traction altered the conditions of trade. The horse, domesticated at the end of the fourth millennium BC in the Ukraine, Iran and Anatolia, appeared at the same time as harness equipment – cheek-straps made first of antler (Dereivka, Ukraine) and then of copper (Bamut, Caucasus) – that proved that the animal was led. As a riding and pack animal, the horse became an ideal means of transport in the plains of eastern and central Europe. The horseman quickly became an integral part of the society of proto-historic Europe. The ox rather than the horse seems to have been the traction animal: rock art shows it attached to the yoke of a plough. First bovines and then certain members of the horse family pulled the earliest wheeled vehicles, the royal chariots of Ur in Mesopotamia or of Susa in Iran, towards 3000 BC. Use of the wheel spread in the third millennium from the plain north of the Caucasus (Tri Brata) to Switzerland (Zurich) and Italy (Mercurago). Wheels were sometimes attached to funerary or war chariots and sometimes to wagons. Their use implies the development of roads. In the Nordic countries, skis and sleighs were also in use.

Navigation effectively supplemented terrestrial means of transport: islands thus became favoured places for stocking goods and for trade (Cyprus, Sicily, Sardinia, the Scilly Isles, and so on). Scandinavian and Iberian rock art shows large vessels, worthy of Ulysses' ships, able to withstand the waves of the high seas. The remains of a few boats found in Denmark give us an idea of the clever techniques used: sewn planks, bracing, masts and so on. The contents of some wrecks (bronze at Dover, Huelva and Agde) confirm the economic role of navigation.

The means now afforded for easier travel favoured trade and probably affected its volume. The term 'commerce', of Etruscan wine exported in amphoras to the Western Mediterranean and the Celtic countries from the eighth century BC onwards, has been used too often. In other cases, exchanges seem to have been more or less irregular depending on the nature of the items involved: the tin and copper indispensable for bronze metallurgy certainly circulated along relatively organized trade routes but pieces of jewellery or houseware of more symbolic significance could be given away or bartered depending on where their travels took the pedlars. Moreover, systems of money do not seem to have yet been in use, and only a few examples of possible premonetary objects can be quoted, such as the Armorican socketed axes. Two examples are characteristic of this proto-historic exchange – amber and glass beads.

Yellow amber was diffused throughout Europe from the third millennium BC onwards in the form of beads or decorative tablets. Chemical analysis of these objects shows that in most cases they were made of a fossilized resin containing 3 to 8 per cent of succinic acid, characteristic of the deposits from north Germany (Schleswig-Holstein), Denmark (Jutland) and the southern shores of the Baltic (west Russia, Lithuania, Poland). Other less significant deposits were to be found almost everywhere in Europe, but the proportion of succinic acid in the amber was smaller and their exploitation seemed quite secondary in importance. At the end of the third millennium BC, thousands of amber beads and pendants were to be found in the Danish megalithic monuments and they have also been found in France in the Marne hypogea and in the settlements of Charavines (Isère). Small animal statuettes were carved in amber in Denmark and Poland. Amber from the beginning of the second millennium BC has been reported from the lake site of Modlona in the north of the Russian Federation and was also abundant in the burials at Saktych further south in the central part of the Russian Federation. It was also found at this time at Los Millares in the Iberian peninsula as well as in Brittany in France and in Wessex in England. In particular amber discs set in gold mounts found at Manton, Amesbury and Normanton (Wiltshire) have been compared with a jewel of the Minoan epoch found at Isopata in Crete. The discovery of a large quantity of amber granules in Greece at one end of what Pliny calls 'the Adriatic amber route' poses the problem of trade around the middle of the second millennium BC in the Mycenaean epoch; 500 beads were found in a single tomb at Kakovatos. A type of perforated amber tablet known as the 'Kakovatos' type shows similarities with others from central Europe that have been found as far afield as Alsace (France). Thus, the raw material would have been distributed for the making of products locally which subsequently entered established trade channels. This hypothesis would also account for the discovery of unworked blocks of amber in certain sites such as Fort-Harrouard at Sorel-Moussel (Eure-et-Loire, France).

Another product – glass beads – was diffused from the third millennium BC onwards in a large part of Europe, from the Eastern Mediterranean as far as the United Kingdom, where 121 examples have been found in thirty-six tombs from the first half of the second millennium BC. They consist, depending on the proportions of the elements used, of faience made up of a nucleus of fine grains of quartz cemented by melting with a small quantity of lime or alkaline flux and soda-lime-quartz glaze mixed with blue or green copper colorants or of cullet with a glaze as just described or of frit which contained more lime silicate and copper. The Egyptians of the 18th and 19th dynasties knew the secret of this process, which was later imitated in the workshops of central and probably western Europe. One particular variety, the segmented bead, elongated and characterized by a series of globules, is proof of a certain unity in the diffusion of skill in this technique. The phenomenon of exchange is still complex here: it seems to correspond to an acculturation within a very limited field. Many other examples from the typology of ceramic or metal objects and study of the style of certain decorative features could be cited in order to support the idea of very varied north-south or east-south exchanges which sometimes linked very distant regions in Europe. Some authors have interpreted these exchange relationships from a historical standpoint. Some have spoken of an Indo-European unity that took shape from the moment when corded ware was diffused in central Europe and as far as the Atlantic area at the start of the third millennium BC. Others have seen in similarities between archaeological grave goods evidence of the movement of the Dorians from central Europe to Greece. These hypotheses are not unanimously accepted and must often be modified according to the areas and domains under discussion (material culture of the aristocracy or that of the lower classes, anthropology, linguistics, and so on).

SOCIO-POLITICAL FEATURES

Some deductions concerning society are based on spatial analysis and especially on the study of cemeteries and settlements. The pre-industrial stage of specialized crafts implies the existence of surpluses, a division of labour and a structured society. It would seem significant that some so-called 'princely' tombs contained rich offerings as soon as metal working appeared on a significant scale: at Varna in Bulgaria, 'rich' tombs with extended inhumations and cenotaphs with baked clay masks are grouped together in a specific area inside the cemetery. The other tombs were simple and contained flexed burials. The tomb of Maïkop in the north Caucasus, already mentioned, also illustrates the practice of putting prestigious offerings in the tomb of an important person, and perhaps other people were sacrificed, as in the royal tombs at Ur. Princely tombs from the first half of the second millennium BC have been recorded in Germany, for example at Leubingen, in France in certain Armorican barrows, at Carnoët near Quimperlé (Finistère) or at Saint-Adrien (Côte d'Armor), and in England, for example in the Bush Barrow group in Wessex. The Bush Barrow region, over 100 km long and 80 km wide, contains the famous monument of Stonehenge which was built in stages between 2500 and 1500 BC. A systematic study of the monuments, long barrows, round barrows, circles of standing stones and causewayed camps, shows four or five concentrations of remains in the most fertile zones, each concentration defining a territory. A territory was some 20 km in diameter and included one or more camps and some barrows. The natural resources were essentially agricultural: the 3,000 to 8,000 individuals in each territory were divided into families linked to each other and governed by one ruling family which built the most imposing burial monuments. Was there any special link between the ruling families in each territory? It would seem so: the Stonehenge territory with its central position and its monument which required a considerable amount of labour was without doubt ruled by a figure with higher status than that of the rulers of the other territories which he seems to have dominated. The Bush Barrow near Stonehenge, with its individual burial and particularly rich offerings representing the attributes of power (polished stone war mace, copper dagger and axe, gold pectoral and overlay and so on) might well belong to one of these great princes. Their power was political and military, as is shown by the regular placing of weapons in their tombs. Was this power also religious? In four out of the five territories, large standing stone circles (such as the Stonehenge monument) indicate the primordial role of religion in the society of this period; to this must be added the numerous barrows, relics of funerary rites which formed an integral part of their religious practices. It may be surmised that religious authority was restricted to priests, ancestors of the Celtic Druids and possessors of astronomical, medical and other knowledge. This is at least what is suggested by the isolation of the religious monuments from the settlements and their specific astronomical features.

As already stated, the specialized crafts, particularly metal working, required a highly stratified settled society which would allow the working of raw materials and often their transformation into finished products and diffusion, even though this last was likely to be uncertain. The example of the princely tombs of Varna in Bulgaria, near the Aibunar copper mines, could again be cited here. The discovery of hill forts associated with metal-working activity confirms this impression; the Vučedol site in the Serbian Republic of Kraina and the hill fort of Zambujal in Portugal date from the third millennium BC. The camps of Velem-Saint-Veidt in Hungary and Fort-Harrouard in France are reminiscent of the contemporary site of Pylos in Greece, of which it is known from Linear B tablets that the king kept 300 bronze-smiths to make tools and weapons. It thus seems that in certain regions at least the considerable development of metal-working activities was made possible by powerful princes or kings who guaranteed orders and protection. This social context is also confirmed by traces left by military conflicts, the gradual increase in the number of weapons and the sometimes impressive entrenchments of upland sites.

The study of skeletons from burials shows few signs of violent blows having caused death; the most frequent cases date from around 2000 BC. The most famous example is that of the war stratum of the underground tomb at Roaix (Vaucluse, France), where bodies of men, women and children were thrown in pell-mell: numerous flint arrows were found transfixing their bones. A woman was found embracing two young children, with a third lying between her knees. It is not rare to find other skeletons from this period in France; about fifteen in all have been found with arrows piercing their bones which caused their death. In the second millennium BC, evidence of violent conflict has so far been much less common. Only one example has been found – a human pelvis pierced through by a bronze spearhead, discovered at Queensford Mill, Dorchester, England. And yet bronze weapons were becoming more abundant and varied at that period: arrowheads, spearheads, daggers, swords and battle-axes. Defensive gear such as helmets, breastplates, shields and greaves seem to have played more a social than a really warlike role towards 1000 BC. All of these objects were contemporary with the Homeric narratives, which give us a good idea of how they were used. The fortified camps which were spreading all over Europe at that time were perhaps the equivalent of the Mycenaean citadels.

BIBLIOGRAPHY

CLARK, J. G. D. 1955. *L'Europe préhistorique, les fondements de son économie.* Paris.

COLES, J. M.; HARDING, A. F. 1979. *The Bronze Age in Europe*. London.

EGG, M. et al. 1993. *Die Gletschermumie vom Ende der Steinzeit aus den Ötztaler Alpen*. Mainz.

ELUERE, C. 1982. *Les ors préhistoriques*. Paris. (*L'âge du bronze en France*, Vol. 2.)

FORBES, R. J. 1964–9. *Studies in Ancient Technology*. Leiden. 9 vols.

GIMBUTAS, M. 1965. *Bronze Age Cultures in Central and Eastern Europe*. Paris/The Hague/London.

GUILLAUME, C. 1980. Saint-Mihiel, Côte de Bar, Meuse. In: *5000 jahre Feuersteinbergbau*. Bochum, pp. 479–506.

LICHARDUS, J. et al. 1985. *La proto-histoire de l'Europe, le néolithique et le chalcolithique*. Paris.

MILLOTTE, J.P.; THÉVENIN, A. 1988. *Les racines des Européens des racines aux Celts*. Horvarth. Le Coteau. France.

MOHEN, J.- P. 1992. *Métallurgie préhistorique*. Paris.

—— ; BAILLOUD, G. 1987. *La vie quotidienne à l'âge du Bronze: les fouilles du Fort-Harrouard*. Paris. (Vol. 4.)

MUHLY, J. D. 1973. *Copper and Tin, Transactions*. New Haven, Conn.

MULLER KARPE, H. 1974, 1980. *Handbuch der Vor- und Frühgeschichte*. München. Vols 3, 4.

PIGOTT, S. 1983. *The Earliest Wheeled Transport*. London.

RENFREW, C. 1979. *Les origines de l'Europe*. Paris.

RENFREW, C.; SHENNAN, S. (eds) 1982. *Ranking, Resource and Exchange*. Cambridge.

TYLECOTE, R. F. 1986. *The Prehistory of Metallurgy in the British Isles*. London.

WHITTLE, A. 1985. *Neolithic Europe, A Survey*. Cambridge.

14.2
SOUTHERN EUROPE

Renato Peroni

THE THIRD MILLENNIUM BC

The pattern to be found in southern Europe is not unlike that in northern and western Europe during the same period; in other words, megalithic architecture, namely the construction of monuments, mostly tombs and cult objects, hewn from large stone slabs, often of great size, was undoubtedly the most significant cultural phenomenon in southern Europe, while at the same time it provides us with a valuable source of information on the development of science and technology, economic and social structures and political and religious practices throughout the third millennium BC.

With regard to scientific and technological development, megalithic monuments (as in the case of other structures), although belonging to completely different cultural and architectural traditions, including the Egyptian pyramids, some of which were built during the same period, testify indirectly to the way in which small communities, scattered throughout Europe and around the shores of the Mediterranean during the third millennium BC, possessed the necessary skills to carry out extremely difficult and complicated technical procedures. These skills imply a knowledge of various laws of physics, including statics, and involve techniques which ranged from the hewing and subsequent excavation of stone slabs in open quarries to their transportation and installation. Transportation was probably undertaken by means of cylindrical or spherical rollers – the use of the latter being confirmed by data found in the temples of Malta – often over long distances; the installation process must have certainly involved the use of the lever on many occasions. All these were based on sophisticated principles of statics, such as the false vault.

The economic and social aspects raise a series of virtually insoluble problems. Archaeological evidence would seem to suggest that during the third millennium BC the human communities of southern Europe were generally rather small in size, comprising not more than a few dozen people, probably as families or kinship groups of several generations. Moreover, it would be reasonable to suppose that they were neither complex nor stratified communities. The pre-eminence within such groups of a warrior class – widespread evidence of which is found in figures, grave goods and the first metallurgical artefacts – was apparently not yet linked to forms of hereditary transmission of power, still less to forms of concentration of wealth in the hands of individuals and the corresponding inheritance of that wealth. However, all the theories concerning the construction of megalithic monuments agree that the inhabitants must have required a quite outstanding use of the labour force, particularly in relation to the supposedly small size of the community. It must therefore be assumed that a very large proportion of the available work-force had to be withdrawn, over a prolonged period of time, from other areas of economic activity, and particularly from food production, a conclusion which remains valid despite the authoritatively documented theory to the effect that the construction of megalithic monuments came about as the result of mutual co-operation among several communities with close geographical and cultural ties, bound together in a relationship of reciprocal obligation. While this theory appears all the more plausible in that it enables us to reduce significantly the estimated time spent on building each individual monument, it does not answer the question of the relatively high proportion of the work-force engaged in a field of activity not directly concerned with subsistence. On the other hand, the absence in these communities of any form of clearly defined social structure seems to exclude the possibility that specific tasks could have been forcibly imposed from above on the lower levels of the community, to the extent of pushing the threshold of their subsistence level well below the norm, as must have undoubtedly occurred in the contemporary, proto-urban societies of western Asia. It must therefore be concluded, on the one hand, that the communities of southern Europe in the third millennium BC had somewhat greater margins of production than we have supposed and, on the other, that the motivation to build megalithic monuments was particularly strong.

Now let us consider the political and religious aspects. Megalithic tombs were collective burial sites and, as such, were basically similar to underground burial chambers hollowed out of rock. The difference lies in the impact of the megalithic tomb on the surrounding countryside and its generally awe-inspiring massiveness. However, if the burial were collective and therefore communal, it may be assumed that its imposing dimensions were intended to commemorate the prosperity and power of the community itself, as the choice of site for such monuments would seem to confirm. Most of them were constructed on high ground but were also situated near the land used for the cultivation of crops, grazing, and so on, which provided the community with its most vital resources. For this reason they were also frequently used as points of strategic control. Apart from their 'political' significance, megalithic burials clearly emphasize the growing importance of the worship of the dead and, more particularly, of ancestor worship (as indicated by the fact that they were used for several generations). It is not easy to grasp the meanings and religious beliefs inherent in such a cult, but, nevertheless, the occurrence in funerary contexts of symbols and anthropomorphic figures, often surrounded by sacred objects, suggests that certain images of the dead were transformed into god-like heroes through some form of divine assimilation; whereupon the question arises whether and to what extent some form of personification and anthropomorphism of divinities already existed in the third millennium BC among the communities of southern Europe.

The temples of Malta

Apart from their beauty and grandeur, the outstanding interest of these monuments resides in the fact that they are the only known constructions in southern Europe at this time intended for a form of religious expression other than the worship of the dead. The complete absence in these temples of funerary artefacts, the lack of any kind of symbolism connected with funerary practices, the existence of sculptures, veritable statues, representing a female figure of more than ample proportions, often nude, some of which are so massive that there is no alternative but to consider them as objects of religious worship, the figures depicted on the bas-reliefs, combined with the evidence relating to sacrificial rituals, 'hearths', large receptacles, possibly used for libation purposes, 'sacrifical slabs', 'altars', niches for the preservation of offerings, stone caskets in which were placed the bones of sacrificial animals, the presence of figurines and other obviously votive objects, all combine to support the theory that these monuments were sanctuaries dedicated to the worship of divinities. Although the only possible points of comparison constantly emphasize similarities with western Asia, both in terms of the very existence of temples in such ancient times and the recurrence of various forms of symbolism and facilities for worship, the lack of any major Oriental influence on other aspects of their cultural heritage would seem to invalidate the transfer or direct derivation of religious beliefs characteristic of those regions.

However, there seem to be grounds to support the theory that, both architecturally and perhaps also as a representation of religious belief, the Maltese temples were derived from local funerary monuments. The connecting link seems to be the burial vault of Hal Saflieni, a rock-hewn burial complex on three levels, composed of a series of chambers varying considerably in their ground plan. Some of the smaller chambers are reminiscent in shape of the rock-hewn underground cave-tombs which date back to the earlier period of Aeneolithic Malta. Some of the larger chambers, which must have been used, at least initially, for religious ceremonies and in which there is clear evidence of structural partitions, with pillars, niches, ceilings and so on, reveal obvious similarities to megalithic architecture. Archaeological finds also confirm that the period of construction and utilization of Hal Saflieni as a burial site and place of worship spanned both the earlier Aeneolithic period in Malta, preceding, apparently, the erection of megalithic temples, and the later period which saw the construction of such temples. It would seem, therefore, that their interior architecture was inspired by hypogea such as those at Hal Saflieni. It is interesting to note, as an indirect confirmation of this theory, that whereas the interiors of the megalithic complexes in Malta are rich in inter-connections, with two or even three oblong double-apsed chambers running parallel to the main axis which leads from the entrance to the central apse at the rear end (a pattern which is repeated in two or three adjacent

'temples'), their exterior, on the other hand, is rugged and ill-defined, almost barrow-like (as demonstrated by the various ground plans, the elevation of the best preserved complex at Ggantija and the models of temples discovered among the votive objects).

With regard to the form of religious outlook expressed in the Maltese monuments, it is worthy of note that many statuettes representing the characteristic female figure of exaggerated proportions, identical to those found in megalithic temples, have also come to light at Hal Saflieni. The images, which appear to have been objects of worship, seem to have represented some kind of divinity, probably personified. There has been much reference to a goddess of fertility, a mother goddess; however, the evidence found at Hal Saflieni not only indicates that the cave-tombs themselves were used as sanctuaries both for funerary rites and for some form of religious cult, probably at an even earlier period than the megalithic monuments, but also confirms at the same time that this was a chthonic divinity, a goddess of the dead, and that there must have been a profound link between these two aspects.

Megaliths in Italy, the Spanish Levant and in the south of France

Evidence of the megalithic phenomenon in the Italian peninsula during the third millennium BC is either of little significance, as in the case of the few examples among the dolmens to be found in Puglia which may date from the same period, or else it consists of geographically peripheral monuments. One example of the latter is the funerary complex at St Martin-de-Corléans, in the area of Aosta, close to the French border, which is particularly renowned for its extremely fine carved stelae. Similarly, in the south of France, anthropomorphous stelae provide the most impressive and perhaps the most important examples of megalithic architecture. In these monuments, the face is always represented, even if, at times, it is highly stylized; frequently, other parts of the male or female body are also portrayed (sometimes accompanied by additional embellishments, such as head-dresses, items of clothing, ornamental decoration, weapons and other objects). Several characteristics displayed by these figures would seem to establish them as the figurative representations of dead heroes, while also reinforcing the tendency towards a process of deification.

Besides megalithic burials, and small dolmens (underground tombs) between barrows with rectangular chambers and long entrance corridors (Ferrières-les-Verreries), excavations in the south of France have revealed several other monuments of outstanding interest, in the form of extremely elongated chamber tombs with entrance corridors hewn out of the rock but, in this instance, with a covering of megalithic slabs, enclosed by a barrow. These monuments represent a real transition between the megalithic burials and hypogeum-type, single-chamber cave-tombs cut from the rock, and the complexes of one or more chambers found in central-southern Italy, in Sardinia (often noteworthy for their architectural and decorative features, either in relief or painted), in Sicily and in Malta.

The megalithic burials of the eastern region of the Iberian peninsula are of great significance, particularly those on the south-east versant, most of which belong to the Almerian culture, with its main centre at Los Millares, a large fortified settlement with a vast complex of burial sites. The fortifications of Los Millares are particularly impressive, with their stone ramparts, 275 m long, crenellated by a series of semicircular bastions (which would have been surmounted by towers) enclosed by the spur of the plateau where the settlement proper is situated; within this area, on four circular hillocks occupying a commanding position, there is a further series of stone-built circular strongholds, which also feature semicircular bastions. Several similar characteristics (stonework, series of towers) recur in the fortified sites of Lébous and of Boussargues in the south of France. The megalithic burials of south-eastern Spain may be divided into two basic types: the passage or gallery grave, with its elongated rectangular or trapezoidal form, often scarcely wider than the entrance tunnel but usually of great length; and the circular chamber tomb, also with its entrance passage, most of which are relatively long. The latter, in turn, has several variations: the corridor and chamber walls may be made of large upright slabs or, alternatively, may consist of corbelling, or small blocks which gradually jut out towards the top, thus forming a 'false vault' (covered by large stone slabs at the highest point), reminiscent of the Minoan tholoi or beehive domes of Mesarà in Crete, which date from the same period. This feature and other, admittedly rather general, similarities with the civilizations of the Eastern Mediterranean, while emphasizing the 'evolved' nature of the culture of Almeria in comparison with those of neighbouring regions, are nevertheless not sufficient to confirm theories of 'colonization' from the east or even the possibility of strong, direct cultural influences.

The very ancient megalithic tradition in western Europe (see Volume I) was still flourishing at the beginning of the third millennium BC in the Iberian peninsula and southern France, where it came into contact with another collective phenomenon, metallurgy. It is reflected particularly in the hundreds of collective tombs constructed according to a simple rectangular plan in Portugal, southern Spain, Catalonia, the Pyrenees and the Causses. The distinctive set of artificial grottoes in Palmela in the Tagus estuary imitating 'false vault' tombs is contemporary with rather late bell-beakers known as 'ciempozuelos' and copper objects such as tanged arrowheads, awls and flat axes.

The beginning of copper metallurgy

Besides megalithic architecture, another highly significant factor in the cultural pattern of southern Europe in the third millennium BC, particularly in the field of science and technology but also from the economic and social viewpoint, was the widespread development of copper metallurgy. (This was already observed in the fourth millennium BC, but was only sporadically undertaken according to present archaeological evidence, which includes the copper slags found at Diana in the island of Lipari, radiocarbon-dated 3050 BC).

The extraordinary and momentous discovery in September 1991 of a man's remains in the Similaun glacier, on the Austrian-Italian border, throws light on life in the Early Metal Age around 3300 BC. The man, imprisoned in the ice, was completely preserved, as were his clothing, weapons and a variety of other objects. He is the oldest known mummified human being to date. He was short (1.58 m) with wavy brown hair and has some tattoo marks on his back, wrists and knees. He was wearing a cloak made of leather squares sewn together, and boots stuffed with grass (see Chapter 14.1, Figs 55–7). He had a flint dagger in an ash-wood sheath

on his belt. A leather quiver, 80 cm long, was lying a few metres away from the body in a cleft in the rock. It contained fourteen viburnum shafts, only two of which had been made into arrows, fletched with eagle feathers and tipped with flint heads. The bow of yew was 1.8 m long and fixed to the man's belt was the bowstring, carefully rolled up in a little leather pouch which also contained four bone and flint arrowheads, birch-wood tar for sticking the arrowheads on, flint stones and a ripe plum, which indicates that the man died in September, no doubt caught by the first snows and the first cold spells. The pouch also still contained two hallucinogenic mushrooms well known to pharmacologists in the last century. The prehistoric man had on his back a wicker basket containing a hammering tool made from an antler, snares to trap small animals, an animal skin, and maple leaves mixed with charcoal. He was holding an axe made of a copper blade fixed to a yew handle. Several possible ideas to account for his being at an altitude of 3210 m have been put forward. Was he out hunting? Was he prospecting for copper ore? Was he going to meet some genie or divinity? Numerous studies are being carried out at the Institute of Prehistory of Innsbruck University (Austria) and they will tell us much more about this surprising specimen straight from the Early Metal Age.

It would seem reasonable therefore to take the metallurgical production of continental Italy, rather than that of the other regions of southern Europe, as being a typical example of this process, not for reasons of richness or importance, but because it has been more carefully observed, documented and studied. Metal production seems to have been considerable, either because there were local mineral deposits to exploit (as evidence would seem to confirm), such as those found in the metalliferous hills of Tuscany, or because of its versatility: in addition to the manufacture of copper, certainly extracted from oxides as well as from sulphates, there is also evidence of the manufacture of silver, lead (data available only for neighbouring Sardinia) and antimony, together with the use of arsenic in a copper alloy. Of particular technological interest is the early use of two-piece moulds for casting copper objects, a technique which is reminiscent of the metallurgy of the Eastern Mediterranean. The mould fragment found at Terrina, Corsica, is typical.

From the economic and social viewpoint, it is worthy of note that most of the goods produced were weapons (axes, halberds, daggers and so forth) of types whose area of distribution was so widespread that it covered territories including several cultural nuclei. It would therefore seem reasonable to posit the existence during this period of itinerant metal workers or, at any event, craftsmen who were not tied to their home communities, and to conclude that this may have encouraged the emergence of a real transcultural lingua franca of metallic forms.

A number of Italian sites gave their name to regional cultures of the third millennium BC. The characteristics of the Gaudo culture were defined in Campania, the Rinaldone culture in Latium, Umbria and Tuscany, and the Remedello culture spread through the Po Valley. Daggers and halberds typical of this culture served as models for the rock engravings at Mont Bégo near Tende on the French-Italian border and those of Val Camonica in the Brecia region. These rock-art sites were inhabited from the Late Neolithic, through the Early Bronze Age and, in Val Camonica, until the beginning of the Iron Age. The stylized depiction of cattle is also typical of the decorated rocks of the third millennium BC. Mont Bégo was inhabited not only by shepherds but also by

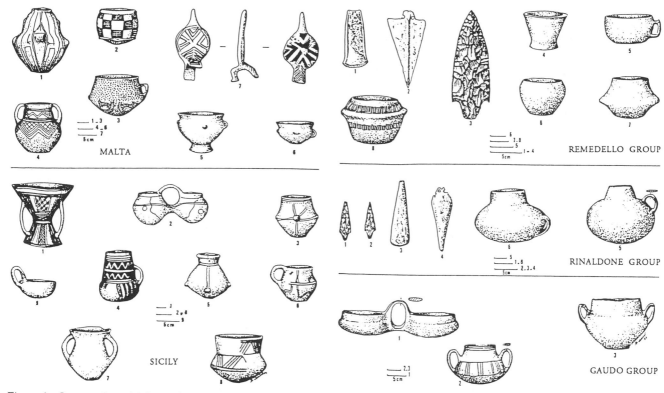

Figure 64 Copper Age: Malta and Sicily (after Millotte and Thévenin, 1988).

Figure 65 Copper Age: Italian peninsula and Sicily (after Millotte and Thévenin, 1988).

those prospecting for mineral ores which are abundant in this region of the southern Alps. There is evidence of copper mining at this period in Cabrières in the Hérault and in Rio Tinto in southern Spain. It was thought that the new wealth represented by copper had led to the emergence of an aristocracy which built fortresses such as Vila Nova de São Pedro or Zambujal in Portugal. In point of fact, traces of metal working are few and far between in the archaeological levels of these sites and do not point to such a social situation. Another acculturation of Atlantic origin is to be found in the upper levels, those of the bell-beakers associated with certain metallic forms such as daggers, awls and arrowheads, which are to be found towards 2000 BC. These beakers are widespread throughout the Iberian peninsula and in southern France, and more scattered in Italy, as far as Sicily (Figs 64–6).

The second millennium BC

The Rhône culture is a fine example of the formation of a homogeneous group linking Europe together. It has been identified in the Jura and in the Valais region in Switzerland, in particular at Sion, and has been traced down the river valley as far as the Mediterranean coast. This cultural group, which developed during the Early and Middle Bronze Age, seems to have originated from the bell-beaker culture. The most characteristic types of bronze objects are flanged axes with splayed cutting edges (hatchets, spatulas, the Neyruz and Roseaux type of axes, and so on), metal-hilted daggers and perforated globe-headed, ring-headed or hammered, trefoil-headed pins. Vases decorated with finger-indented cordons are also found throughout this cultural milieu.

The most important change in southern Europe during this period, as in most other regions of the continent, was the

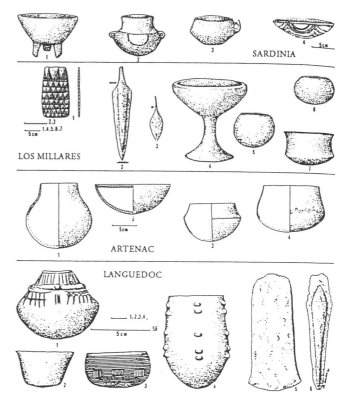

Figure 66 Copper Age: Sardinia, Spain, southern France (after Millotte and Thévenin, 1988)

emergence of the earliest forms of diverse stable socio-economic structures within communities. This development may be identified from various archaeological data. First, individual grave goods, characterizing outward signs of prosperity and power in accordance with established customs, show the regular recurrence of certain characteristics, such as a standard combination of grave goods. Secondly, the emergence of important modifications in the housing pattern of individual settlements, where large houses incorporate features used in the construction of monuments. Thirdly, there is a gradual stabilization, selection and concentration of settlements, together with an increasing awareness of military requirements as to the choice of site, which is usually in an isolated area, on high ground surrounded by natural barriers, for the purpose of ensuring strategic control of the territory.

One of the most far-reaching consequences of these new sites was that, for the first time, conditions existed which favoured the establishment of lasting relations, both intense and broad-based (even if, obviously, they were only to a minor extent direct) between the more sophisticated town-dwelling communities of the Eastern Mediterranean and the communities of less-developed Europe, relations which would eventually lead to a full-scale process of acculturation.

Italy and Sicily as a link between the Aegean and continental Europe

This relationship benefited from two intermediaries in particular; on the one hand there was the Balkan peninsula, which had already played a similar role several millennia before, albeit so indirectly and indistinctly as to be barely perceptible, and which it continued to play at a later date in much the same way; on the other hand, there was the Italian peninsula together with Sicily.

It seems highly significant that the first, direct and enduring contacts between the Aegean and southern Italy occurred as early as the sixteenth century BC and were made by seafaring Mycenaeans; the initial phase of the relationship with the west was therefore contemporaneous with the rise of the Mycenaean civilization in the Argolis, a fact which may perhaps explain, in part at least, the reasons underlying the phenomenon. In the earliest period, the only archaeological evidence which could be used to confirm contact between the indigenous population and Aegean seafarers is confined almost entirely to fragments of imported Mycenaean pottery, excavated locally. From the sixteenth and fifteenth centuries BC, sporadic finds of a similar kind have been made in various parts of southern Italy (although not in Sicily); surprisingly, however, most of these finds were made not, as might be expected, in the south-eastern regions of the peninsula on the Ionian and southern Adriatic versant, and therefore closer to the Aegean and Greece, but much further west, on some of the islands of the South Tyrrhenian Sea, in the archipelago of the Aeolian Islands and the island of Vivara opposite the Bay of Naples. These data seem to indicate that, during this earlier period, the aim of Aegean seafarers was not so much to establish trading contacts with the populations of southern Italy, but rather to create a trade route across western Europe to link up with the 'tin road' which followed the Atlantic coasts of Europe as far as Cornwall. The Tyrrhenian islands probably represented one of the most important stages on this route and almost certainly provided a meeting point for Mycenaean seafarers and their local counterparts.

It seems reasonable to suppose, therefore, that the rising power of Mycenae was greatly interested in establishing a trade route for the supply of metals, particularly tin, as an alternative to the route via the coasts of Anatolia which were under the maritime control of a still Minoan Crete.

From the fourteenth century BC onwards there is evidence, on the one hand, of the reinforcement and development of Mycenaean contacts with southern Italy – on a scale and in ways which suggest that they undoubtedly came about as a result of a radical change in the motivation behind such contacts – and of their extension, albeit to a lesser extent, to areas of central Italy; on the other hand, there is also evidence of the establishment of closer and stronger ties with Sicily. The thirteenth century BC saw Mycenaean influence spread as far as Sardinia. There is no doubt that, particularly in the case of southern Italy and even more so for Sicily, this new phase led to a full-scale process of acculturation (even if limited in scope) and that it brought about significant changes in technological procedures and in economic and social structures.

Archaeological evidence emphasizes the spread of Mycenaean influence in various areas situated along the coasts of southern Italy and south-eastern Sicily. It testifies to the volume and duration of the trading that must have taken place in these ports of call, and suggests that the Aegean mariners were henceforth primarily interested in trading with local populations. These southern coastal settlements must have been dependent on a more widespread trading network, linking them to the inhabited inland areas of southern Italy as well as to those of central Italy and, to some extent, northern Italy. The paucity of Mycenaean finds in central Italy, in sharp contrast to their prevalence in southern areas, seems to lend weight to the theory that they are attributable to secondary trends in local, indigenous trade, rather than to direct contact with Aegean mariners. This premise is even more valid for northern Italy, where limited finds of Mycenaean pottery along the banks of the River Adige nevertheless suggest a direct link with the trade route which crossed the Alps through the Brenner Pass into central Europe.

This trading network seems to have set in motion two main tendencies. First, various maritime centres, acting as ports of call or as nodes in the network, seem to have grown in size and influence, assuming a position of potential supremacy over neighbouring communities, thus contributing to the reinforcement and acceleration of the process of selection, concentration and stabilization of settlements and to the increased emphasis on defence requirements. Secondly, as the direct result of the higher status conferred on them by their new role as trading partners with the Aegean seafarers and with other local communities, as well as by the increasingly military role they played, the higher-ranking levels of society tended to assume a correspondingly exclusive and authoritative socio-economic function. This tendency can be observed in their vast, impressively built residences, contrasting with the homes of the ordinary people; in their monument tombs which stand out from other burial sites; and in their selection of grave goods, featuring a considerable quantity of imported Mycenaean vases.

Among the technological innovations introduced into Sicily and the southernmost regions of Italy through contact with seafaring Mycenaeans, the most significant – being also the most indicative of the profound changes in the general economic and social conditions of the local populations – concern the manufacture of pottery, often in faithful imitation of Mycenaean models, made from refined clay, thrown on the wheel, covered with painted decorations and baked in kilns at a very high temperature.

These technical processes were introduced in such an elaborate and precise form that they can be accounted for only by their transmission by resident Aegean craft workers, who would have taught local apprentices directly, thus throwing an interesting light on the nature of the relationship that developed between local people and Mycenaean seafarers, and indicating that these need not have been confined to the mere exchange of goods. This presupposes that, first, these communities – or their ruling classes – took it upon themselves to subsidize specialists engaged in the production of high-class luxury goods, and secondly, that there was a lively demand for and trade in such goods, phenomena confirmed by extensive archaeological data.

These processes have been observed in Sicily in the context of the Thapsos cultures (fourteenth–thirteenth centuries BC) and Pantalica (twelfth-eleventh centuries BC); in central- southern Italy in the Apennine culture (fourteenth century BC), sub-Apennine (thirteenth–twelfth centuries BC) and Proto–Villanovan (twelfth–tenth centuries BC). These in turn greatly influenced the contemporaneous cultures of northern Italy, particularly the complex known as the Terremare and those of Peschiera.

Terremare dwelling sites are covered with rich dark earth formed by the decomposition of organic matter. They are characteristic of Middle and Late Bronze Age cultures in western Emilia between the Po, the Apennines and the Panaro. Riverbank and lakeside villages such as Gorzano and Castione dei Merchesi were built on piles to protect the floors from damp. Biconical ceramic forms were decorated with fluting, ribs and gadroons. Abundant metal artefacts such as pins, bracelets, pendants, winged axes and daggers attest to the influence of Central Europe but also display an undeniable local originality. In the late phase, there were also razors and fibulas. The ashes of the dead were placed in urns at the burial sites. These sites were abandoned in the twelfth century BC, but we do not know precisely why this occurred.

As already mentioned, the process of acculturation, albeit partial, seems to have occurred at an earlier date and to a more noticeable extent in Sicily. In the Thapsos complex there is evidence of grandiose collective tombs with magnificent grave goods, including a large quantity of imported Mycenaean pottery, and bronze weapons, which were made locally but inspired to a large extent by Aegean models; excavations of the eponymous settlement of Thapsos, situated on the coast, have revealed the remains of brickwork buildings, with a complicated ground plan, laid out in a series of chambers which, although reminiscent of Eastern Mediterranean models only in very general terms, seem to be in no way attributable to local architecture. However, in the absence of conclusive evidence, it seems unwise to rule out completely the theory that these structures are all that remain of a sort of trading-post used by Aegean mariners.

In the Pantalica culture, the quantity of imported Mycenaean pottery was much less significant but, on the other hand, various Aegean and Cypriot designs were adopted as part of traditional local pottery which now involved the use of the potter's wheel and the other technical procedures already mentioned. The eponymous settlement of Pantalica must have housed a community estimated to be of the order of several hundred inhabitants, judging by the area covered by the habitation site and the number of chamber tombs – more than 5,000 – which the surrounding burial sites contained. It can therefore be considered to bear the stamp of an authentic proto-urban centre. The existence within this community of a ruling aristocracy is confirmed by the prince's residence (*anaktoron*), of articulated design, excavated at the

centre of the site. It was built of massive square blocks, a structure of isodomic tendency clearly Aegean in influence, which included a foundry for casting bronze items. On the Italian peninsula, the technological and social changes brought about by Mycenaean influence, less identifiable in the Apennine culture, are clearly demonstrable in the subsequent sub-Apennine culture with centres such as Scoglio del Torino, Torre Castelluccia, Porto Perone and Coppa Nevigata in Apulia and Torre del Mordillo and Broglio di Trebisacce in Calabria, which already display definite proto-urban characteristics, albeit to a lesser extent than at Pantalica; there is no evidence of such characteristics further north.

These varying degrees in the pattern of acculturation generated by the civilizations of the Eastern Mediterranean regions among the various cultures of Sicily and Italy, from south to north as far as the Alps, may perhaps explain the role of intermediary between the Aegean regions and central Europe that the Italian and Balkan peninsulas played during this period, a function which was all the more important in that it did not involve the one-way transmission of cultural influences but helped instead to foster mutual relations.

The establishment of a metallurgical lingua franca, or a common approach to the designs and techniques involved in the manufacture of weapons, decorations, plate and bronze objects throughout a large part of Europe and the areas around the shores of the Mediterranean during the thirteenth and twelfth centuries BC, was undoubtedly one of the most important processes of cultural unification in the prehistory of these regions, and one which certainly involved other aspects of their cultures, especially with regard to ideology and symbolism. However, it has been rightly pointed out that such 'common languages' resulted from the merging and fusion of two different metallurgical traditions, the Aegean tradition and that of central Europe. This phenomenon must have occurred as a result of a full-scale process of osmosis, involving a broad exchange of experience and models which only the widespread movement of artisans could achieve. Mention has already been made of the presence of Aegean craft workers in Sicily and Italy: this is certainly true in the case of the ceramists and more than probable in the case of metal workers. There is, however, no lack of evidence to confirm the presence in Greece and the Aegean regions of workers in bronze who had arrived there from Italy. Finds have been made in these areas, in thirteenth- and twelfth-century sites, which can be attributed to the Mycenaeans, including various bronze objects, in particular swords, daggers, knives and fibulae, of a type which is definitely characteristic of continental Europe, and which has been accepted by experts as proof of the immigration of ethnic groups from the north, linked with the well-known legend of the Dorian invasion. Other artefacts have definite similarities with the metal goods made in Italy during the same period. However, some of their characteristics indicate that they were not imported but produced locally in Greece and in the Aegean region, an observation which seems confirmed by an important find, namely, a casting mould for axes of a specifically Italian type discovered in the so-called House of the Oil Merchant at Mycenae.

From the twelfth century BC onwards, and certainly following the destruction and abandonment of the Mycenaean palace complexes, relations between the Eastern Mediterranean and Sicily and Italy gradually declined, and there was a growing tendency for the latter to gravitate culturally towards continental Europe.

The larger islands of the western Mediterranean: Nuraghi, Talayots and Torre

During the same period and also during the early centuries of the first millennium BC, Sardinia and the Balearic Islands underwent a completely different pattern of cultural development. It found expression in particularly impressive architectural achievements which gave their names to the respective local cultures, namely the 'nuraghi' in Sardinia and the 'talayots' in the Balearic Islands. They take the form of truncated conical towers, sometimes with more than one floor, built of large blocks and featuring internal corbelled rooms and stairs which are also internal. These towers may be either free-standing or part of a village, in which case, arranged in line and linked by walls, they may form the main outer boundary walls (Balearic Islands) or, alternatively, when grouped together to form complex tri-lobed or poly-lobed structures, surmounted by a central keep, they constitute the main citadel, the layout of which seems similar to that of a medieval castle (Sardinia). Besides the nuraghi and talayots, there are also collective megalithic burials, elongated in structure, which bear a faint resemblance to those of the gallery graves (known as giants' tombs in Sardinia and navetas in the Balearic Islands). Another common feature of the nuraghi and talayot cultures, not found in the contemporary cultures of Sicily and Italy, was the existence of recognizable places of worship (where votive offerings, often of great value, were made), including sacred monuments, as exemplified by the 'well temples' of Sardinia. The building methods used in the construction of all these monuments is somewhat varied, with structures ranging from a very approximate polygonal design to an extremely precise isodomic type. The theory that the architecture of the nuraghi and that of the talayots were derived from Oriental and Aegean models is unfounded, although in some specific characteristics very definite similarities do exist which, in some instances, may imply specific influences. There is also evidence that the earliest Mycenaean presence in Sardinia occurred at a time when nuraghi architecture was at its height. On the other hand, the theoretical premises concerning many technical and structural aspects of the architecture of nuraghi and talayots, such as the false vault, circular rooms and so on, were already present as features of megalithic architecture in the third millennium BC in the Western Mediterranean.

During the centuries spanning the second and third millennia BC, the nuraghi cultures of Sardinia enjoyed an outstanding florescence of bronze metallurgy, in both quantity and quality, a particular feature of which was the exceptional increase in the production of small sculpted figurines. However, contemporary with the early stages of this phenomenon but at a period subsequent, in part at least, to that of the Mycenaean influence, there is widespread evidence of the presence in Sardinia of metal craft workers of Eastern origin, who introduced tendencies which were derived from the Cypriot and Syro-Palestinian environment and which seem to some extent to anticipate those which came into being at the beginning of the eighth century BC with the Phoenician colonization of the West.

Sardinia developed during the eighth to seventh centuries BC as a result of commercial links between the eastern and western parts of the Mediterranean. The tradition of the great stone towers, or nuraghi, and of copper metallurgy are characteristic of a Sardinian civilization that produced bronze statuettes, tripods, figurines of warriors, wrestlers, shepherds, women with children, and animals, especially deer.

The Corsican 'torres' are another variety of these enigmatic monuments found on the Western Mediterranean islands. One tower at Filitosa is associated with large carved standing-stone statues representing warriors with their swords and sometimes their helmets.

THE BRONZE AGE IN SOUTH-WEST EUROPE

During the Bronze Age, unlike the main islands of the western Mediterranean, south-west Europe experienced a pattern of cultural development similar to that which characterized the rest of the continent, particularly the Italian peninsula. However, the scarcity of specific similarities in metallurgy and architecture points to a cultural development of a quite different kind, featuring a high degree of isolation. This is particularly true of the earliest periods which, in the south of the Iberian peninsula, saw the emergence of the El Argar culture (with which two similar groups are associated, that of Valencia further to the south and the earliest period of the Atalaia culture in southern Portugal). Various identifiable features of these sites are reminiscent of several other European and Italian cultures – from the hilltop villages with impressive brickwork fortifications to the widespread development of metallurgy, particularly weapons and ornaments (the latter also existed in silver and gold), from stone-slabbed individual tombs and huge urns rather than collective burials to the grave goods varying widely from one tomb to another, proving beyond doubt the existence of considerable social differences (Fig. 67). However, there is no apparent connection between any of these cultures and the design of the bronze artefacts and ceramic ware, even less the custom of burying the dead underneath their dwellings instead of in burial vaults separate from the settlement.

On the other hand, the cultures of the Late Bronze Age

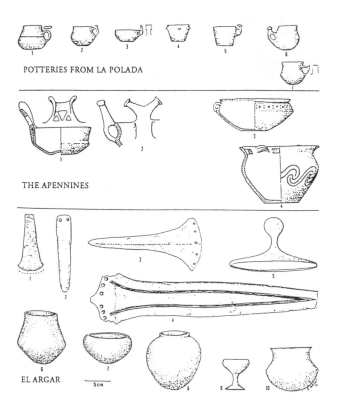

Figure 67 Early Bronze Age: Italy and Spain (after Millotte and Thévenin, 1988).

which flourished in the Languedoc (Mailhac) and Catalonia (Agullana), during the centuries spanning the second and first millennia BC, seem to demonstrate closer ties with the rest of Europe and in particular with central Europe. They were particularly noted for their crematory necropolises, which were similar to the 'urnfields' in the area to the north of the Alps, in terms of the design and decoration of the ossuaries and other ware, and particularly with regard to their bronze artefacts.

Mediterranean and Atlantic connections are also perceptible: the cargo of bronzes found at Rochelongue near Agde in the Hérault (France) was perhaps intended for the Italian foundries, like the other bronzes found offshore from Huelva in southern Spain. These show undeniable Atlantic affinities which are to be found as far away as Sardinia and Sicily (the Sard deposit of Monte Sa Idda) and reveal the penetration in the Mediterranean of Western models as brought together in the Vénat deposit (Charente, France) which, with its 3,000 pieces, represents the peak of the Atlantic Bronze Age.

The explanation that has been put forward several times is that the Italic and Greek bronzesmiths needed tin. Cassiterite, tin oxide from Cornwall in England or from Brittany in France, doubtless circulated at the same time as the resmelted bronzes, as was confirmed several centuries later by the earliest historians such as Herodotus.

Society in south-west Europe was marked by a fairly rigid hierarchical structure at that period. This encouraged a tendency to regard warriors as heroes, depicted on decorated stelae in the south-west of the Iberian peninsula. One example of the same style comes from Substantion in the Hérault in France. The weapons represented are shields, sometimes helmets, swords and spears; fibulae and round clasps often also form part of this panoply, in the form of a man carved in outline. It is not uncommon in the Iberian peninsula to recognize also the chariot pulled by two horses. This seems to confirm that the aristocracy of the period, at least in this part of Europe, resembled that described by Homer.

THE EARLY IRON AGE

The origins of the Italo-Etruscan civilization and the birth of Rome

There is a widely held belief that it was in central-southern Italy that the age of recorded history began, towards the end of the eighth century BC and throughout the seventh, during a period which saw, on the one hand, the impressive phenomenon of Greek colonization in the south and in Sicily and, on the other, the emergence in Etruria and neighbouring regions of the first indigenous urban centres and the earliest city states. The contemporaneity of both processes – although the Greek colonization occurred, in the main, slightly earlier than the first stages of urban Italo-Etruscan civilization – led many scholars to conclude that the latter was brought into being by the former, through the transmission of social and cultural models which originated in the Eastern Mediterranean. Strictly speaking, this theory is not inaccurate, but it leaves other, equally significant aspects out of account.

As mentioned above, the emergence, in Sicily and southern Italy, of centres which displayed clearly defined proto-urban characteristics dates back to at least the thirteenth century BC. This phenomenon must have implied a certain familiarity with social and cultural models typical of the most advanced civilizations of the Eastern Mediterranean. On the other hand, as will be shown later, the development in several areas of central and southern Italy of authentic urban centres was preceded by a prolonged formative phase, characterized by the widespread expansion of proto-urban tendencies. The earliest stages of this process date back to the beginning of the ninth century BC, a period which was considerably earlier than the first Greek colonial settlements in the west and also prior to that brief period which preceded it, known as 'precolonial', when initial contacts, admittedly of a purely commercial nature, were made.

There are, therefore, good reasons to suppose that, across the centuries before and after 1000 BC, an unbroken line of local continuity linked the formative proto-urban phase of the Early Iron Age to those distant Bronze Age antecedents.

The beginning of the ninth century BC saw the development in Etruria of two parallel phenomena. There was the sudden abandonment of a large number of hilltop settlements, which had been surrounded by the natural barriers of very steep slopes or sheer cliff-faces, and were often situated in a commanding position covering several hectares, governing a region of not less than 100 km² and with an estimated population of several hundred. At the same time, there sprang up a limited number of large centres, situated on upland plains and similarly difficult of access, but far larger in size, covering as a rule more than 100 hectares (which suggests an estimated population of the order of several thousand), forming a territorial area of approximately 1,000 km², thus closely resembling what has been referred to as the 'territorial module of the earliest state'. These Early Iron Age settlements were situated, for the most part, in the area in which the great Etruscan city-states sprang up: for example, Tarquinia, Veio, Cerveteri and Vulci. These Early Iron Age settlements had no brick or stone buildings, but consisted instead of wooden shacks, and there is no evidence of urban infrastructure or any form of monumental architecture (temples, public buildings and so on). However, they undoubtedly represent the expression of a form of social organization which explicitly foreshadows that of an urban structure, and therefore can only be described as proto-urban.

On the other hand, the very contemporaneity of the two phenomena, the relatively spontaneous, widespread abandonment of earlier settlements and the emergence of new centres suggests a definite underlying purpose, namely, the establishment of much larger communities, bona fide proto-state units.

At the beginning of the formative phase, to judge by their burial vaults (which were crematory, and show evidence of funerary rites now known as 'Villanovan'), the new communities were probably free of any marked forms of socio-economic structure, but in the space of a few generations the process of diversification led to the emergence of a ruling class which controlled much of the community's power and wealth. There is clearly no continuity between this ruling class, as it appears at its peak during the second half of the eighth century BC, and the urban aristocracy which flourished from the beginning of the seventh century BC, coinciding with the early stages of Etruscan civilization, known as the 'Orientalizing' period.

This process was accompanied by a whole series of phenomena which are of considerable significance as clues. In the first place, since the earliest decades of the eighth century BC, and in some cases even earlier, the burial chambers of the nobility contained objects of value, especially metal artefacts and ceramic ware, of Syro-Phoenician (or, at any rate, Oriental) and Greek manufacture; secondly, there is evidence of the occurrence, at the same time and in the same context, of indigenous imitations of these luxury objects, which entailed the adoption of major technological innovations, some of which were the same as those which, albeit on a lesser scale, had been introduced several centuries earlier in Sicily and the southernmost regions of the Italian peninsula, such as the wheel for manufacturing pottery, the purification of clay, painted decorations and the use of high-temperature kilns; finally, funeral customs once again provide evidence of the assimilation of new practices concerning different aspects of the life-style of such a society, from battle tactics to banqueting etiquette.

Archaeological clues therefore provide information about the beginnings of Etruscan culture at the time of the Villanovan culture (ninth, eighth centuries BC) in a region between Fiesole not far from Florence to the north, and Rome to the south. This region was rich in copper, argentiferous lead and iron ores and presumably attracted industrialists, craftsmen, merchants and navigators with connections in southern Italy and the Eastern Mediterranean shores. Etruria experienced a remarkable effervescence in the seventh century BC. Its population soared, its cities and necropolises grew in number and its activity developed as a result of precious commodities, such as ivory and gold, imported from Asia, Egypt and Greece. It adopted, in its way, the 'Orientalizing' style. Caere (Cervetri) was then a flourishing coastal city, shipping its products to the West. The necropolis of Tarquinia contained, from that time on, the burial mounds of an aristocracy which took the Greek city-states as a model. We can therefore recognize the habits of city life, religious and public architecture, divinities, iconographical motifs, weapons and many other small objects used in daily life like fibulae, pins and razors. The first Etruscan texts were written using the Greek alphabet. These intense contacts, discernible in the ornamentation of the gold items found in the Regolini-Galassi tomb (675–650 BC), are today being put forward as an explanation for the rapid development of Etruscan civilization.

The sudden emergence of proto-urban centres seems to have been a phenomenon confined to Etruria and some areas of Campania. Further south, particularly in southern Apulia and Calabria, it seems to have been the outcome of a more gradual and gentle process which, on the one hand, originated, as already indicated, in much earlier manifestations, or else succeeded at a very early stage in assuming a relatively clearly defined identity (for example, patterns of social structures similar to those which occurred in Etruria in the eighth century BC were already in place here as early as the ninth century BC); on the other hand, the proto-urban centres seemed reluctant to take advantage of their own natural outlets in central Italy, outlets which were exploited in these regions only after the Hellenic colonization.

The indigenous, proto-urban centres of the Early Iron Age in Calabria and Apulia never attained the proportions of the Etruscan cities, whereas centres of the same size as the latter occurred in the colonial settlements of Magna Graecia.

The case of Latium Vetus, the region which corresponds to modern Lazio, differs from that of Etruria and also from the southernmost regions of the peninsula. It lies south of the Tiber, which marked the boundary between Latium Vetus and Etruria. In this region, the rise of proto-urban centres was not a sudden process as it was in Etruria. As a rule, the settlements in existence at the end of the Bronze Age were not abandoned and, initially, they do not seem to have changed in character or size. There seems to have been a substantial, if gradual, increase in the size of several centres from the mid-ninth century BC onwards. Nevertheless, these cities remained very much smaller than those in Etruria: the surface area comes close to 50 hectares but never exceeds it, and the region covered between 200 and 300 km² but was rarely much larger.

The only exception was Rome. Unlike the pattern of events in most other comparable cases, the date, recorded by ancient tradition, of the founding of the city (753 BC) is much later than its true beginning; the most ancient part of the settlement, the Capitoline Hill and its slopes, dates back to the Bronze Age; to be more precise, to at least the fourteenth century BC. Between the end of the Bronze Age and the beginning of the Iron Age, the settlement grew to include the Palatine Hill. From the mid-ninth century BC, it expanded rapidly as far as the Esquiline and Quirinal hills. During this period, Rome was a city which covered an area between 150 and 200 hectares, and its importance was certainly as great as that of the major Etruscan proto-urban centres, even if, compared with their situation on one single elevated plain ensuring natural protection, the topography of Rome was much more irregular and fragmented.

Long before it became a proper city, Rome was destined, as a result of its special situation, to acquire the hegemony of Lazio, which would otherwise have occurred several centuries later and which was an essential prerequisite to the subsequent expansion of Roman power throughout the whole of central-southern Italy.

The earliest period of Phoenician and Greek colonization in the central-western Mediterranean

The process of acculturation, for which the ground had been prepared by Aegean mariners half-way through the second millennium BC, during their contacts with southern Italy, Sicily and Sardinia, revived considerably during the Early Iron Age, following the establishment of several colonies in the Central and Western Mediterranean by another wave of mariners from the east – the Phoenicians and the Greeks.

Although the dates that have come down to us from classical literary sources concerning the earliest Phoenician colonial settlements in the west go back as far as the end of the twelfth and eleventh centuries BC, particularly those in Iberia (Cadiz) and North Africa (where, it is claimed, Utica was founded almost three centuries earlier than Carthage), and which would seem to have been followed only somewhat later by those in Malta, Sicily (Mozia) and Sardinia (Nora, Sulcis, Tharros), there is no archaeological evidence whatsoever of their respective settlement before the early part of the eighth century BC. It is also difficult to establish how many years previously Phoenician seafarers had begun to use that particular route. Small decorative objects of Oriental origin, such as scarabs and other similar pieces, which have been found in a number of Early Iron Age burial vaults in southern Italy from the first half of the ninth century BC, could certainly be considered as indicative of trading activity of this kind. However, their occurrence seems limited.

The Hellenic colonization began at a slightly later date. The respective patterns and forms of Greek and Phoenician territorial expansion have often been compared and contrasted. Thus, the choice of site for settlement seemed highly significant: the Phoenicians placed their centres on small islands or peninsular promontories, whereas the Greeks chose their sites on the coast but in less extreme positions and sometimes even slightly inland. These different approaches served two quite separate purposes: in the former case, the site was considered purely as a commercial port of call; in the latter, it was a means towards territorial domination and expansion. Indeed, the Greek colonies undoubtedly generated much stronger forms of acculturation within the indigenous population than did the Phoenician ones. However, it would be unwise to exaggerate these differences. On the one hand, as will become clear, the earliest Greek settlements in Italy and Sicily had essentially commercial aims at the outset, as is confirmed by their topographical position, which was no less marginal than that of many Phoenician sites; on the other hand, there are areas, in the south-east of the Iberian peninsula, for example, in which it is evident that Phoenician settlements and farms very rapidly succeeded in exercising real territorial control, albeit confined to the coastal belt, thereby also giving rise to the formation of local mixed cultures.

However, the obvious antagonism between Phoenician and Greek colonizers did not prevent a limited exchange of roles: for example, there is evidence of Phoenician artefacts in the earliest Greek settlements (where there are also indications of the physical presence of the Phoenicians), and vice versa, and there is reason to believe that each occasionally traded in the goods of the other, especially during the 'pre-colonial' phase. This period must have been relatively limited if we consider the fact that its earliest stage seems to date back no further than the years spanning the ninth and eighth centuries BC, and that the very first Greek colonies were founded before the mid-eighth century BC.

The earliest of these centres, as unanimously confirmed by ancient literary sources and also by archaeological discoveries, is Pitecusa, on the island of Ischia, facing the Bay of Naples and founded by settlers from Chalcis, a city on the island of Eubea. A few years later, these inhabitants of Chalcis settled on the Italian peninsula, where they founded Cumae on the site of an earlier indigenous settlement.

It is a curious but significant fact that, disregarding more accessible regions at an early stage, the Greeks immediately advanced to a point which would always remain the outermost north-west boundary of their expansion in Italy, a decision which emphasizes the priority given to strategic and trading objectives. The fortunate discoveries made in the course of excavations at Pithecusa revealed an iron-smelting centre which used raw material from the island of Elba, situated off the coast of northern Etruria. It is worthy of note that although the earliest Greek settlers apparently attached great importance to trading with Etruria, they decided against settling on the Etruscan coast, choosing instead to keep their distance. The Etruscan city-states were clearly already in a strong position and their sway over the mid and northern Tyrrhenian Sea was sufficiently secure to prompt a certain degree of caution.

It was only several years later, but still prior to the mid-eighth century BC, that the Greeks of Cumae felt the need to gain control of their own maritime trading routes, and founded Zancle on the site of the modern city of Messina, on the Sicilian shore of the straits of the same name. Some time later, on the opposite Calabrian shore, Reggio was to be founded by settlers from Chalcis.

During the two generations which followed these early colonial settlements, Hellenic expansion changed character completely: from the establishment of isolated trading and military outposts, there was a shift towards the systematic occupation of vast areas of land. First, in less than ten years (734–727 BC), Greeks of various origins, mainly Chalcidians

and Dorians, colonized the whole east coast of Sicily, founding Nasso, Syracuse, Lentini, Catania and Megara Hyblae, followed, ten years or so later, by Milazzo on the north-east coast. Equally rapid was the occupation, towards the end of the eighth century BC, by settlers from the Peloponnese of the whole Ionian coast of southern Italy, with the founding of Crotonia, Sybaris, Metapontuna and Taranto and the subjugation of the local populations. The Hellenic colonization of Sicily and Magna Graecia was gradually completed in the course of the seventh century BC, but around 700 BC it had already acquired the features of a territorial possession and was not dissimilar to what it would become in its final form.

Between the classicial and the barbarian worlds: Venetics, Ligurians and Iberians

During the Early Iron Age, the north of Italy, the Mediterranean regions of present-day France and the Iberian peninsula experienced neither the formative proto-urban phase which prevailed in Etruria, nor territorial expansion comparable to the Hellenic colonization of Sicily and Magna Graecia. In northern Italy, a formative proto-urban period occurred as late as the sixth century BC. The large proto-historic settlement founded in Bologna in the ninth and eighth centuries cannot be regarded as a fully developed proto-urban entity, although it has frequently been compared with Etruscan centres on the basis of the 'Villanovan' funerary rites carried out in its crematory necropolises. It was only in the second half of the seventh century BC that Greek mariners ventured along the coasts of Provence and the eastern Spanish seaboard and began to establish their first colonies in the early sixth century BC, with the foundation of Marseilles. These observations do not alter the fact that, even in the Early Iron Age, the regions mentioned above were already acting to some extent as intermediaries between the classical Mediterranean universe and the barbarian world of continental Europe.

One of the most characteristic features of the cultural development peculiar to Europe over the centuries was the formation of large ethnic groups (Illyrians, Celts and so on) at the same time as, although not exactly parallel to, the development of extensive cultural groupings (cultures of Hallstatt, La Tène and so on). The regions in question anticipated, by several centuries, phenomena which were already present in the Early Iron Age, thus providing a model of development and undoubtedly having a catalytic effect on the less-civilized regions of Europe.

In the north-eastern part of the Po Valley, there is evidence of a culture, known as Este, whose zone of influence coincided approximately with the area that would be settled in the centuries to come by the Venetics, as is conclusively confirmed by epigraphic finds and literary sources. This culture greatly influenced the range of territories beyond the eastern central Alps. Undoubtedly the pattern of civilized society which emerges from the evidence of the eighth century BC burial chambers of Este represents an essential model for the emergent Hallstatt civilization of the seventh century BC, with examples ranging from weaponry to style of dress, and from customs concerning banqueting etiquette to funerary rites.

The region to the north-west of the Alps was probably influenced similarly, if less obviously, by the culture known as Golasecca, which had sprung up in north-west Italy. Reasons similar to those put forward for the area of Venetia, settled by the Venetics, indicate that these cultural developments were of Ligurian origin. During this period, the regions occupied by the Ligurians must have been considerably more widespread and probably included the Mediterranean seaboard of modern France and the Iberian peninsula, at least as far as the Ebro. At this time, the so-called 'urnfield cultures' in the Languedoc and Catalonia, dating back to the Late Bronze Age, continued their development.

In the south of present-day Spain, however, there is still work to be done on the original areas settled by the Iberians within whose range, beyond the Pillars of Hercules, was situated the mythical kingdom of Tartessos (Tarshish) – renowned for its fabulous wealth. From an archaeological viewpoint, this area seems to have been characterized during this period by its outstanding development of bronze metallurgy and the extraordinary variety of its cultural exchanges, ranging from those established with the various regions of the central-west Mediterranean, particularly with Sardinia and Sicily, and, indirectly through the latter, with the Eastern Mediterranean, to those with the Atlantic seaboard as far north as the British Isles.

BIBLIOGRAPHY

ALMAGRO-GORBEA, M. 1977. *El bronze final y el período orientalizante en Extramadura*. Madrid.

ANATI, E. 1976. *Evolution and Style in Camunian Rock Art*. Capo di Ponte.

BARFIELD, L. 1971. *Northern Italy before Rome*. London.

BARKER, G. W. W. 1975. Prehistoric Territories and Economics in Central Italy. In: HIGGS, E. S. (ed.), *Palaeoeconomy*. Cambridge. Vol. 3, p. 75.

BERNABO BREA, L. 1966. *Sicily before the Greeks*. 2nd ed. London.

BIETTI SESTIERI, A. M. 1973. The Metal Industry of Continental Italy, 13th to the 11th century BC, and its Connection with the Aegean. *PPS*, Vol. 39, pp. 383–424.

BLANCE, B. 1971. *Die Anfänge der Metallurgie auf der iberischen Halbinsel*. Berlin.

CAMPS, G. 1988. *Terrina et le Terrinien, Recherches sur le chalcolithique de la Corse*. Roma.

CIVILTA NURAGICA. 1985. Milano.

COFFYN, A.; GOMEZ, J.; MOHEN, J. P. 1980. *L'apogée du bronze atlantique, le dépot de Vénat (Charente)*. Paris.

COLES, J. M.; HARDING, A. F. 1979. *The Bronze Age in Europe: An Introduction to the Prehistory of Europe, c. 2000–700 BC*. Beccles/London.

EVANS, J. D. 1971. *The Prehistoric Antiquities of the Maltese Islands: A Survey*. London.

GUILAINE, J. 1972. *L'âge du bronze en Languedoc occidental, Roussillon, Ariège*. Paris.

—— 1994. *La mer partagée, la Méditerranée avant l'écriture, 7000–2000 avant J.C.* Paris.

LUMLEY, H. de 1994. *La montagne sacrée*. Aix-en-Provence.

MILLOTTE, J.P.; THÉVENIN, A. 1988. *Les racines des Européens des racines aux Celtes*. Horvarth. Le Coteau. France.

PERONI, R. 1963. L'età del bronzo media e recente tra d'Adige e il Mincio. *Memoria del Museo civico di Storia naturale di Verona*, Vol. 2, pp. 49–104.

—— 1971. L'età del bronzo nella penisola italiana. In: *L'antica età del bronzo*, Firenze. Vol. 1.

PHILLIP, P. 1975. *Early Farmers of West Mediterranean Europe*. London.

ROUDIL, J. L. 1972. *L'âge du bronze en Languedoc oriental*. Paris.

SCHUBART, H. 1975. *Die Kultur der Bronzezeit im südwesten der iberischen Halbinsel*. Madrid.

TRUMP, D. H. 1966. *Central and Southern Italy before Rome*. London.

I4.3
SOUTH-EASTERN EUROPE

Roumen Katincharov and Nikola Tasić

The end of the Chalcolithic cultures was, to some extent, a consequence of the fairly extensive inroads made by the steppe tribes, bearers of the pit-grave and later the catacomb-grave culture, as they advanced towards the Yugoslav Danube basin and the Balkans. They exerted an influence on the Vučedol culture (tumulus burials at Batajnica, Vojka and Moldova Veche) which they then completely supplanted. In spite of the importance of these migrations, the principal factors in the historical changes were the organic developments and cultural interactions and assimilations.

Until the beginning of the Bronze Age, cultural exchanges with the Aegean world and especially with western Anatolia were insignificant. Considerable expansion in this area occurred during the Early Bronze Age. The archaeological material discovered shows that at that period the cultures of the regions to the south of Stara Planina were related to the cultures of the Aegean and Anatolia. The area, including the Chalcidice peninsula, was a nerve centre where cultural influences from north and south came together.

On the strength of the near-total correspondence between the clay vessels at the prehistoric site of Thermi (IV-V) on the island of Lesbos and those dating from the first and the beginning of the second phases of the early Bronze Age in south-eastern Bulgaria, as well as a considerable proportion of the vessels at Troy, we may conclude that the same culture developed in south-eastern Bulgaria, north-western Anatolia and certain islands of the Aegean.

THE EARLY BRONZE AGE
(3200–2000/1900 BC)

The tells so far investigated in Bulgaria contain layers corresponding to the Chalcolithic and the Early Bronze Age, between which there is a stratigraphic gap. At present it is difficult to assert categorically that this break is present in all of them. It is highly probable that the tells were temporarily abandoned shortly before the arrival of new peoples. Archaeologists have noted that most of the sites in south-eastern Bulgaria were built on the ruins of Chalcolithic sites (the tells of Karanovo, Ezero, Burgas Province; Kapitan Dimitrievo, Yunatzite, Plovdiv Province; Kirilovo, Khaskovo Province, and so on) and only an insignificant number on the ruins of Neolithic sites (the tell of Veselinovo, Burgas Province). Sites may be found, however, which were populated only from the Bronze Age onwards (the tell of Nova Zagora, Burgas Province, and so on). This constitutes indirect evidence of the expanding population in the area in question during the Bronze Age.

Beside the sites built on tells during the Early Bronze Age, others have been found on naturally fortified hills surrounded by steep slopes. Representative of this type is the site of Mikhalich (Khaskovo), which was fortified by a wall incorporating stones of varying sizes, probably held together by clay. At its base the wall is about 1.6 m thick.

The upper layer of the tell at Ezero, which belongs to the Early and Middle Bronze Age, is approximately 4 m thick. Thirteen levels of construction have been identified. The first Bronze Age site is surrounded by a stone wall whose base is 1.5 m thick. It was faced with large, uncut dry stones. The cavity was filled with stones of varying sizes mixed with clay. With the increase in population, the space enclosed by the wall became too small. For the safety of the inhabitants living outside the wall, a new and even stronger one was built around the base of the tell. The construction of the outer wall turned the site into a fortress similar to the one on the tell of Kazanlak. The Ezero tell shows signs of preliminary planning, albeit of a rather primitive sort. The dwellings at the various levels were arranged in straight lines or else in clusters, all facing the same way. The centre of the site, which remained unoccupied, was the meeting-point for the alleys which led to the entrances in the stone wall.

The sites in northern Bulgaria, unlike those in the south-east of the country, were not occupied for long periods. This was probably due to the instability of a form of economic activity in which pastoralism predominated and also to the incursions of isolated groups of steppe tribes.

During the Early Bronze Age, the sites in north-west Bulgaria were situated on naturally fortified hills (the prehistoric sites of Gradets, Tsar Petrovo, Mikhaylovgrad Province, and so on). As well as occupying sites of this kind, people in northern Bulgaria also continued to live in caves, which provided more reliable protection (Magurata near Rabichae, Mikhaylovgrad Province, the Devetachka cave, Lovech Province, and so on).

Most of the lake sites on Lake Varna and other locations along the Black Sea coast also belong to the Early Bronze Age (the town of Sozopol, the village of Kiten, Burgas Province, and so on). They contain many well-preserved objects from everyday life, including items carved in wood, as well as a large quantity of bones of wild and domestic animals.

The Magura culture in north-western Bulgaria was a part of the large Magura Coţofeni cultural group which was widespread in north-western Bulgaria and the area bounded to the north by Transylvania and to the south by central Serbia. The archaeological material discovered in western Romania provides a fuller picture of the transition from the classical

Chalcolithic cultures to the culture of Coțofeni. Archaeologists have proved that the culture contains certain features which are typical of the Cernavoda III culture, and by the same token that the latter partly precedes the Coțofeni culture and that there is a stage in the development of the Cernavoda III culture between the Sălcuța IV and Coțofeni cultures whose duration has not yet been established. The Cernavoda III culture is also widespread throughout the area of present-day Dobruja, where features of the Ezero culture have also been discovered. On the whole, analysis of the material discovered in the Ezero tell confirms this conclusion but also gives some indication that the Cernavoda and Coțofeni cultures developed in parallel, since fragments of clay pots, typical of both, have been discovered in the oldest levels of construction of the Ezero tell.

The Early Bronze Age in the area of the southern Carpathians is distinguished chiefly by the appearance of the Schneckenberg-Glina III culture. The settlements are located in the plain: they are often to be found in tells of the Chalcolithic Gumelnița culture, on islands in rivers and, more rarely, inside caves. The pottery is inspired to a great extent by the tradition of the Coțofeni culture. That culture is also related to the rather sparse decor of the containers which, such as it is, amounts to no more than digital imprints below the rim. Certain forms, notably pots with one or two handles, were very widespread during the Early Bronze Age in the Carpatho-Danubian region. The rare metallic objects from the Glina III phase were deposited in the burials. In northern Muntenia, apart from a container and a triangular dagger, other objects have been discovered in the cists: a bracelet, a flat axe and so on.

The Otomani culture was formed at the same period or a little later between the Tisza and Transylvania. The concentration of archaeological sites is particularly marked on the upper reaches of the River Crișul, the middle reaches of the Mureș and the upper reaches of the Tisza; it may also be traced northwards as far as Slovakia. The settlements are mainly to be found in the foothills of the Carpathians, especially near the mountainous regions of Transylvania. They are fortified even when they are island sites. The Otomani culture began to develop in the second half of the Early Bronze Age; it continued until the incursion of the bearers of the Carpathian version of the Tumulus complex.

The Mureș or Pecica (Mokrin-Perjamos) culture lay outside the area of the southern Carpathians, but it is important because it was in direct contact with many contemporaneous cultures and formed, in a sense, a bridge between the Early Bronze Age in Pannonia and in the Carpathians. It lasted through the Early Bronze Age until the beginning of the Middle Bronze Age and was a rich culture: there have been numerous finds of copper, bronze and gold objects. The most thoroughly explored necropolises are situated in the vicinity of Mokrin (312 tombs), Dezsk, Pitvaros and Szoreg (229 tombs). They consist mainly of crouched burials containing large numbers of objects: metallic ornaments and containers. Urn burials were much less common: at Mokrin, for example, there are four burial urns out of a total of 312 graves.

It is difficult to establish clearly and precisely when the Bronze Age began in the area of the Danube basin. The Vučedol culture may be placed at the junction of the two periods and, in the view of certain researchers, the end of that culture occurred during the Early Bronze Age. The Vinkovci or Vinkovci-Somogyvár culture took shape in that substratum, preserving the old forms of the pottery but completely abandoning the Vučedol style of ceramic decoration (engraving, incision or impression). Typical forms are vases with a handle, rather large amphorae with handles on the rim or body and a somewhat unusual form of cylindrical (bottle-shaped) container. Besides the pottery, the gold ornaments are of major significance, especially the hoard of concave applied ornaments from Gradina/Bosut and the fairly large circular plaques from Orolik. In the Yugoslav Danube basin, the Vatin culture appeared towards the end of the Early Bronze Age. It also stretched southward from the Danube in Serbia. The classical phase on its own is sometimes referred to as the 'Vatin culture', with its baroque shapes for containers, its lids, amphorae, urns, stands and zoomorphic figures, its gold ornaments, bronze axes and, above all, remarkable objects made of bone. The running spiral or simple spiral decoration and certain gold objects would appear to prove that direct contacts existed with Mycenae.

The most important archaeological sites of the Vatin culture in the Banat are Vatin, Zidovar and Pančevo, then Feudvar and Popov Salas to the north of Novi Sad (Bačka), Gomolava in the Srem district, Vinča near Belgrade and Ljuljaci in Šumadija. The houses were spacious and well built; they had two or three rooms (Zidovar, Popov Salas, Feudvar, Ljuljaci) and were semi-subterranean (Vinča, Gomolava).

The Vatin culture did not last as long in the Yugoslav Danube basin as some believe. In round figures, it would have covered the period from 1700 to 1500 BC, which, in our opinion, places a question mark over the thesis of the influence exerted by the Mycenaean population at the time of the pit-graves or the migration of that population towards the Yugoslav Danube basin.

In the Early Bronze Age, the region to the south of the Sava and the Danube – the central area of the Balkans – was a little-known transitional area. Danubian cultures developed in the northern parts of the region. The pastoral component was more in evidence there than in the agricultural districts of the Danube basin.

Very little research has been done on the central Balkans, Macedonia and Kosovo during the Early Bronze Age. The only indications which we have are derived from the dwellings of an insufficiently differentiated culture in the vicinity of Niš, Aleksinac and also in Kosovo, called by the excavator, M. Garašanin (1971), the Bubanj-Hum III Group.

THE MIDDLE BRONZE AGE
(2000/1900–1600/1500 BC)

Certain tells inhabited during the Early Bronze Age were also occupied in the Middle Bronze. Some tells which had their origin in the Middle Bronze Age continued to be occupied during the Late Bronze (the tell at Manole in the province of Plovdiv).

The upper levels of the Ezero tell contain pottery shapes which are new or else rare or unidentified in the earlier layers of construction corresponding to the Early Bronze Age. The new features are present in developed form in the tell at Nova Zagora. The excavations organized on the site made a particularly important contribution to the store of knowledge about the Middle Bronze Age. The role of bronze tools and weapons was on the increase. Among the tools, pride of place goes to the heavy axes with shaft-holes. The end of the Bronze Age witnessed the appearance of a new weapon, the lancehead.

Characteristic of this period were elegant cups and jugs with slanting spouts and high handles. The cups with a pointed or rounded base, which have two vertical handles with triangular lugs projecting above the level of the rim, deserve special attention because of their unusual shape. Their surfaces are brown or a glossy black and some of them have an engraved or impressed decoration, inlaid with white material. From the point of view of typology, these vases may represent a development of Trojan-style cups. They are also the predecessors of the Late Greek form known as the *kantharos*. These typical vases are found in both southern and northern Bulgaria.

The pottery of Troy V and VI contains only isolated examples of ware similar to that of the Balkans during the Middle Bronze Age.

THE LATE BRONZE AGE
(1600/1500–1200/1150 BC)

There are considerable changes in the structure of the sites during the Late Bronze Age. With only a few exceptions (the tells of Ruse and Manole), life had disappeared from the tells at that period.

The sites established at new locations in south-eastern Bulgaria (Pchenichevo, Khaskovo Province; Assenovetz, Burgas Province) and in north-western Bulgaria (Baley, Novo Selo, Vrav, Archar, Mikhaylovgrad Province; Varbitsa and Valchitran, Lovech Province, and so on) are of a different nature. They are scattered over a great flat plain or valley, close to rivers and springs. Their remains, especially in northern Bulgaria, confirm that, whereas sites in the Early and Middle Bronze Age were between 3 and 10 km apart, the distance between sites increased during the Late Bronze Age. They were no longer compact as in earlier times. In addition to sites of this type, sites on remote hilltops were also established during the Late Bronze Age. Apsidal mudbrick dwellings built on high stone foundations which date from the Late Bronze Age have been discovered on the large island of Durankulak in the Province of Varna.

Metal working made further great strides in the course of the Late Bronze Age. Evidence of this is provided by the large numbers of moulds for casting a variety of metal objects. A large collection of moulds was discovered in the neighbourhood of the village of Pobit Kamak in Razgrad Province for the casting of axes with shaft-holes, socketed axes, swords, lanceheads, axes for use in religious rites, and ingots (Plate 138). The find at Sokol in Burgas Province contains nine moulds for casting socketed axes, lanceheads and awls.

The gold hoard from Valchitran in Lovech Province, which is unique, provides evidence of the development of the goldsmith's art during the Late Bronze Age. It consists of thirteen objects in near 22-carat gold, and its total weight is 12.5 kg. It dates from some time between the fifteenth and thirteenth centuries BC.

A sudden and radical change in practically all types of tools and weapons occurred during the Late Bronze Age. New types of metal objects appeared: socketed axes with or without ring, sickles of varying sizes, daggers, swords, lanceheads and arrowheads: 'Mycenae-type' rapiers have also been found on Bulgarian soil (Dono Levski, Perushtitsa, Plovdiv Province; Doktor Yossifovo, Galatin, Mikhaylovgrad Province; and Sokol). After a detailed analysis, B. Hänsel has concluded that these objects were produced locally under southern influence. The end of the Bronze Age saw the appearance of another type of sword – with a solid hilt – which was intended for cut and thrust. These swords are different in shape from the Mycenae type. They are more numerous to the north of Stara Planina, especially in the Carpatho-Danubian region. Double axes are also typical of this period.

Most of the clay pots typical of the Middle Bronze Age continued to be produced in the Late Bronze. Many new forms of vessel also appeared. Vessels with two high handles are typical of the period. During the Late Bronze Age a specific culture, distinguished by pottery found particularly in necropolises for cremation burials, developed over a wide area along both banks of the Danube, from the Tisza and the Sava rivers to the Oltul and the Iskŭr. The clay pots, which had a fine smooth surface and were often polished, were dark grey, grey-brown or black. Four cone-shaped studs sometimes appear on the body. Most are decorated on the outside with highly varied geometrical motifs, bands, triangles, circles, spirals and interlinking shapes, inlaid with a white substance.

The Late Bronze Age had two phases in the Carpatho-Danubian area and the central Balkans: the earlier phase was marked by the dominance of inlaid pottery in the Danube basin and the continuing development of several cultures of the previous period (Wietenberg III, Monteoru II, Otomani II) in the mountainous region of the southern Carpathians; the later phase saw the appearance of the Tumulus culture and the beginning of the cultures of the Belegis and the Belegis-Cruceni in the large area of the Carpathian basin and the central Danubian basin. In a sense, the first phase represents the continuing development of the cultures of the Early and Middle Bronze Age, whereas the second phase marks their final dissolution. A greater degree of conservatism is discernible in the cultures encompassing the mountainous regions of the southern Carpathians.

With the appearance and propagation of inlaid pottery, a major integration of cultures and styles was effected in the region stretching northwards from southern Hungary and then crossing the Yugoslav Danube basin to the Romanian and Bulgarian Danube basin further south. This shared cultural development appears under the names of different cultures, such as Dubovac, Dubovac-Zuto Brdo, Dubovac-Cirna, Zuto Brdo-Girla Mare, Dubovac-Cirna-Vratsa. V. Dumitrescu (1961) uses the broader concept of a 'Danubian basin urnfield culture'. It is clear that the different designations are due primarily to the vague definition of the cultural affiliation of certain archaeological sites, to regional conceptions and to uncertain dating of the development, which in fact continued for some time in the Danube basin. Recent Yugoslav research refers to the Dubovac-Zuto Brdo culture, whereas Romanian studies speak of the Zuto Brdo-Grila Mare culture. At all events, the sites containing inlaid pottery, including the finds in north-western Bulgaria, belong to the same cultural complex. It should be noted that its duration was not the same throughout the area. In the region where it was not supplanted by the Belegis-Cruceni culture, as was the case in the limited area of Serbia to the south of the Danube and in the Djerdap/Iron Gate gorge (Klicevac, Usje, Zuto, Brdo, Livade, Vajuga and so on), this culture continued for some considerable time until the appearance of the Gáva group, or, in other words, practically until the end of the Bronze Age. Excavations have concentrated on the necropolises, because of the interesting material and the very rewarding sites. Almost 1,000 tombs have been excavated, primarily in the necropolises of Oltenia (Girla Mare,

Gogosu, Cirna, Balta Verde and Ostrovul Corbului), the Serbian Danube basin (Pesak and Glamija near Korbovo, Dupljaya, Dubovac, Oresac, Vajuga, and so on) and north-eastern Bulgaria and the vicinity of Vidin and Vratsa Balej, Orsoja, Archar, Makres, Dolno Linevo and so on). The funeral furniture from these necropolises is rich and varied, and is also highly decorated: urns, dishes used as lids, pots and anthropomorphic and zoomorphic figures. In terms of the method of ornamentation and techniques employed, the white inlay and elaborate system of motifs, the pottery of the Dubovac-Zuto Brdo culture achieved the highest quality decoration of containers known in prehistoric cultures up to that time. The imagination of the potters also found expression in the anthropomorphic and zoomorphic figures discovered in the tombs and dwellings. First-class examples of the art of this culture are well known: the 'Dupljaya chariot', the idols from Vršac and Klicevac as well as large numbers of figures from necropolises in the Banat, Oltenia and north-western Bulgaria (Orsoja) (Plates 139, 140).

There is every reason to believe that the culture of Dubovac-Zuto Brdo-Girla Mare-Cirna-Vratsa was of extended duration. We incline to the view of V. Dumitrescu (1961), for whom the entire complex of the 'Danube basin urnfield culture' lasted from 1600 to 1100 BC and the Cirna necropolis from 1500 to 1200 BC.

The Belegis or Belegis-Cruceni culture took shape in the Srem region and the Serbian Danube basin during the second half of the Late Bronze Age, towards the end of the 'Banat inlaid pottery' phase. It coincided with, and was influenced by, the arrival of the bearers of the Tumulus culture between the Danube and the Tisza. There were local variations in the inlaid pottery. Evidence of the chronological relationship is provided by the presence of inlaid pottery in the necropolises of the early phase of the Belegis culture (for example, at Ilnadza or Belegis). Territorially, it occupied much of the area in which the Dubovac phase of inlaid pottery had previously developed.

The urnfield cremation cemeteries cover several hectares in some places. The necropolis at Karaburma near Belgrade contains 230 graves and Belegis has 178 graves. As regards dwellings, only the site of Gomolava near Hrtkivci in the Srem is representative.

The Belegis culture is characterized by pear-shaped urns, generally with a high cylindrical or elongated neck, decorated with incised lines or by means of the technique known as cord ornament. In addition to the urns, two-handled vessels are common. In certain cemeteries (Belegis and Karaburma), fairly large vessels were used as urns for the burial of children. The dishes represent the other form common in the Belegis culture. They were used as lids for the urns in the necropolises. Metal objects were placed in the urns with the ashes and remains and were often warped by fire. These are usually bronze ornaments: hair ornaments, pendants, pins, diadems and bracelets. Their typological features indicate that these finds belong chiefly to the Br B2–Br C horizon in the Central European system of dating. The last phase of the Belegis culture – graves containing urns with a fluted decoration – belongs to a slightly later period. The earliest phase may be situated in the period following Br B2 and before the end of Br C, which, in real terms, would be from 1400 to 1200 BC. That was followed by the durable emergence of the Gáva-Belegis II complex.

It is only in the last few decades that a little more light has been shed on the development of Late Bronze Age cultures in the central Balkans. The discovery and excavation of dwellings and necropolises belonging to the Paraćin culture, the Medijana culture and archaeological sites in western Serbia provide a relatively clear picture of the cultures of that period. The Paraćin culture is an important feature of the Late Bronze Age, establishing a link between the cultures of the Danube basin and those of the Balkans and the Aegean. It extends through the region traversed by the main route followed by the movements of prehistoric cultures, the valley of the Morava, and stretches towards Kosovo in one direction and towards the valley of the Vardar in the other. Necropolises containing cremation graves and urn burials have been attributed to this culture, as have centres of population, including Stalac (Gologlava), which has been particularly well excavated. At this site on the hill rising above the great plain of the Morava, at the confluence of the southern Morava and the western Morava, well-constructed houses have been discovered with floors paved with pebbles from the river. They contain many traces of the material culture: pottery, stone and bone objects, and a few metal objects, including a characteristic lancehead.

The cremation urns are quite crude, as are the objects which they contain or which are deposited alongside. Stone slabs, rather large fragments of pottery containers and slightly biconical dishes are used as lids for the urns. Conical and biconical beakers with raised handles figure most prominently among the rest of the pottery.

The handles are decorated with a protuberance in the shape of a button or horn, an important stylistic feature in this culture. Ornamentation is sparse: it consists of a moulded strip with incisions, shallow, roughly modelled flutings or incised motifs derived from the spiral. Two fairly small, two-handled pots (kantharos) from Paraćin and Obrezs, decorated with spirals and other symbols, are a reflection of the communication between the Carpathians to the north and the Aegean cultures to the south in the Late Bronze Age.

The Paraćin culture lasted for a considerable period of time: throughout the Late Bronze Age and into the first half of the final phase of the Bronze Age. The forms of certain pottery urns (decorated with fluting), the bronze objects discovered at Stalac (lancehead) and other data indicate that the end of this culture should be placed between 1200 and 1100 BC.

The regions of Kosovo and northern Macedonia have not been thoroughly explored. Mention can be made of the metal objects from Rogovo and Iglarevo, where the burials were covered by tumuli. The Mycenaean sword from Iglarevo and the findings of recent excavations at that site suggest that a chronological parallel may be established with the shaft graves (Schachtgräber) of Circle A at Mycenae, which would correspond to Late Helladic IIIA or the middle of the fourteenth century BC. In terms of Central European dating, that would be stage Br C. The objects discovered at Rogovo are thought to be of approximately the same period, as is the pottery from the layer occupied by dwellings at the site of Dnja Brnjica, where there is also an urnfield of a later date.

THE END OF THE BRONZE AGE
(1200/1500–950/900 BC)

The final stages of the Bronze Age in the Carpatho-Danubian-Balkan region are characterized by two important phenomena: the fluted pottery of the Gava-Belegis II type and the presence of a great many hoards of bronze objects, especially in western Romania, in the Serbian Danube basin

(Djerdap/Iron Gate and Vrsacko Gorje), and especially in the Srem and in Slavonia. These two phenomena are to some extent interdependent.

The Gáva culture is found in the eastern part of the Carpathian basin. Its pottery is distinguished by its very fine, often black and glossy, surface which is decorated with fluting. The bosses accompanied by arched flutings, also mentioned in the context of the 'Aegean migrations', are also typical. The largest group of objects discovered are those from cremation cemeteries (Vajuga-Pesak, Banatska Palanka). Among these discoveries, the Susana tumulus near Lugoj in south-western Romania is a special case: it contained hundreds of whole vessels, urns and amphorae, cups of various shapes with ribbon-shaped handles protruding high above the rim and dishes. The Gáva site in the Danubian region of the Carpathians may be dated on the basis of the bronze objects from the tombs, which are comparable to those from the hoards of the type associated with Ha A period, that is, the end of the second millennium and the beginning of the first millennium BC: approximately the period from 1100 to 900 BC. To the west of the Gáva culture, in the Srem, the Banat and the Serbian Danube basin (around Belgrade), the Belegis culture continued to develop in the final period of the Bronze Age (Belegis II).

The necropolises, large and small, also contain, as a rule, burials from the early phase of this culture: Karaburma, Surcin, Belegis, Ilnadza, Vojlovica near Pančevo; in the Romanian Banat, the same is true of the necropolises of Cruceni, Bodba and Tolvadija. The dwellings have been less fully explored and look as if they were intended to be occupied for short periods, that is, that they were virtually temporary: pits and caves, without any durable structures for habitation. The sites of Jakov (Ekonomija Sava), Gomolava near Hrtkivci and Belegis (Gradets) have produced metal/bronze objects belonging to the same horizon as the hoards of the Ha A period. The transition from the end of the early phase to the late phase occurred gradually from 1250 to 1150 BC and its end may be linked to the presence of large numbers of hoards of the Ha A1 and A2 periods at the transition from the second to the first millennium, up to approximately the year 950 BC.

Glossy black pottery also continues to occur at the sites to the south of the Sava and the Danube, in the valley of the Morava, the Nišava, the vicinity of Kruševac and in Kosovo. The discoveries made in the vicinity of Svetozarevo, Kruševac and in Šumadija mark the end of the Bronze Age in the central Balkans.

THE EARLY IRON AGE (950/900–700 BC)

The archaeological research carried out in recent years in Bulgaria has proved that there is a clear line of continuity in the material culture between the Late Bronze Age and the Early Iron Age. It is important to note the conclusions of the research on the famous site of Troy. The archaeological evidence proves that Troy VIIa was burned and pillaged. In all probability, many of its inhabitants, who fled at the time of the attacks, returned after the departure of the attackers. The rebuilding of Troy VIIb on the basis of the plans

of its predecessor was apparently the work of the Thracians of Bulgaria, newcomers who maintained close relations with the natives of Troy, with whom, we may assume, they shared common origins.

The construction of solidly built fortresses on peaks difficult of access in mountainous regions also began during the Early Iron Age. Their walls were built of uncut dry stone without mortar. These fortresses were probably intended to protect people and livestock in times of danger. Traces of life during the Early Iron Age have also been discovered in certain caves: Magura and Devetachka.

The oldest tools and weapons at first copied the shape of the bronze objects. For example, some swords dating from the tenth century BC have the same form as the older bronze swords of the Carpatho-Danubian type. Flat axes with side handles and other tools and various weapons also appeared during the Early Iron Age. The introduction of iron ploughs, and especially their manufacture, brought about a sharp increase in agricultural yields. The beginning of the Early Iron Age features the formation of a so-called 'megalithic' culture in south-eastern Thrace.

The Greek colonies established on the Thracian shore of the Aegean and the Black Sea contributed much to the growth of relations between Thrace and Greece.

BIBLIOGRAPHY

BLEGEN, C. W. 1963. *Troy and the Trojans*. London.

BONA, I. 1975. *Die Mittlere Bronzezeit Ungarns und ihre südöstlichen Beziehungen*. Budapest.

CHILDE, V. G. 1929. *The Danube in Prehistory*. Oxford.

DUMITRESCU, V. 1961. *Necropola incineratie din epoca bronzului de la Cîrna* [Bronze Age Crematoria in Cîrna]. Bucareşti.

FOLTINY, S. 1955. *Zur Chronologie der Bronzezeit der Karpatenbeckens*. Bonn.

GARAŠANIN, M. et al. 1971. Praistorijski kulturi vo Makedonija [Prehistoric Culture in Macedonia]. Stip.

GEORGIEV, G. I. 1961. Kulturgruppen der Jungstein- und der Kupferzeit in der Ebene von Thrazian (Südbulgarien); Symposium, 'L'Europe à la fin de l'âge de la pierre'. Praha. pp. 45–100.

—— 1967. Beiträge zur Erforschung des Neolithikums und der Bronzezeit in Südbulgarien. *Arch. austr.*, Vol. 42, pp. 126 et seq.

GIMBUTAS, M. 1965. *Bronze Age Cultures in Central and Eastern Europe*. Den Haag.

HÄNSEL, B. 1970. Bronzene Griffzungenschwerter aus Bulgarien. *Prähist. Z.* (Berlin), Vol. 45, pp. 26–41.

—— 1976. *Beiträge zur Regionalen und chronologischen Gliederung der älteren Hallstattzeit an der unteren Donau*. Bonn.

KATINČAROV, R. 1974. Division en périodes et caractéristique de la civilisation à l'âge du bronze en Bulgarie du sud. *Archeologuia*, Vol. 16, No. 1, pp. 1–22.

—— 1981. Etat des recherches sur l'âge du bronze en Bulgarie du Sud-Est. *Bull. Inst. Archéol.* (Sofia), Vol. 36, pp. 118–26.

—— 1982. Sur la synchronisation de civilisations de l'âge du bronze ancien en Thrace et dans la région d'Egée et d'Anatolie. *Thracia Prehist.* (Sofia), Vol. 3, Suppl. Pulpudeva, pp. 132–49.

MOZSOLICS, A. 1967. *Bronzefunde des Karpatenbeckens*. Budapest.

MÜLLER-KARPE, H. 1980. *Bronzezeit I–III*. München. (Handb. Vorgesch., Vol. 4.)

TASIĆ, N. (ed.) 1984. *Kulturen der Frühbronzezeit des Karpatenbeckens und Nordbalkans*. Revised. Beograd.

14.4
CENTRAL EUROPE[1]

Istvan Ecsedy and Tibor Kovács

The Copper and Early Bronze Age history of central Europe is by no means securely dated owing to the unclarified contradiction of radiocarbon samples and the traditional chronology. This insecurity makes any general survey extremely difficult and a broad enquiry into the periods in question has rarely been attempted. It is rather the examination of details, the tendencies of 'micro-regional development' that are in focus and the ever-recurring polemics mostly concern the often divergent systems of chronology and terminology. Thus our review of the two millennia of central Europe's cultural history can be no more than an inadequate attempt to examine the regional characteristics and the most important facts.

The Copper Age populations living in the vast territory from the Rhine to the Vistula and from the north Balkans to the north European plain at about 3000 BC can be regarded as the late descendants of the Early Neolithic linear pottery culture. In the course of previous development clearly discernible cultural units had been formed within different geographical areas. It is the description of the main characteristics of these units which enables us to reconstruct the cultural history following the Late Neolithic period.

The inhabitants of central Europe, enjoying a continental climate, assimilated gradually and transmitted to northern and western Europe primary cultural influences which had originated in the eastern Mediterranean, Anatolia and the eastern European steppes. The transmission started with the distribution of agricultural communities, whose food production was well adapted to local circumstances. This self-sustaining development on a wide ethnic basis made continuous cultural assimilation possible. The first, archaeologically well observable, phase of this development was the formation of the linear pottery culture, and it seems reasonable for C. Renfrew (1987) to assume that the groups belonging to this Early Neolithic culture may well have formed a population speaking one of the most ancient Indo-European languages. The whole territory can be separated into two main parts: the first is north of the Alps and the Carpathians with rivers mainly of south-north direction (the northern region), while the second consists of the areas inside the Carpathians and east of the Alps (the southern region). The central Danube, with Bohemia, the Moravian basin and upper Austria display transitional characteristics geographically, and play an important role in cultural transmission between the two main regions.

No significant ethnic movements can be detected in the period around 3000 BC in central Europe, neither between the two regions nor within the regions themselves. The finds, however, seem to prove the intensification of cultural con-

tacts, and some kind of acceleration of cultural diffusion and integration, which, in some cases may have resulted in the formation of new features of material culture. South-eastern connections had already been very important in the earlier, Neolithic development of the southern region, which is geographically open towards the Balkans and is connected with the Black Sea region through the Danube.

The autochthonous population of the Carpathian basin in the Early Copper Age developed the most owing to the influence of southern and south-eastern neighbouring cultures: the gradual integration of the late Lenguel (Brodzany-Nitra, Tiszapolgár, Salcuţa, Vinča-Plocnik) resulted in the formation of the Bodrogkeresztur, Ludanice, Laznany, Balaton-Lasinja, early Mondsee and Retz-Gajary cultures. The Early Copper Age groups of the Carpathian basin gradually shifted from their basic grain-growing economy to animal keeping. In the area of the earlier Neolithic villages only poor remains of temporary dwellings can be found. The grave groups of the pastoralists indicate, however, that the Copper Age population was the descendant of the local Late Neolithic. The dead were buried in contracted positions on their sides, similar to earlier period burials, and the pottery forms found in the graves can be traced back to the Neolithic. The growing enhancement of leading personages, the chieftains indicated by characteristic copper weapons and gold pendants in the graves, is due partly to the change in the economic system.

The changes in the Carpathian basin had significant influence on the cultural development of the Moravian basin and that of some areas in Poland (Jordanów, Zlotniki, Brzesc Kujawski and so on). Many scholars suppose that the continuous dispersal from the southern region is responsible for the cultural change north of the Alps and for the new forms in the Late Neolithic material of the northern region as well.

The Funnel-beaker culture appeared in the North European zone after the Neolithic and its influence can be detected as far south as the Moravian basin in the Copper Age. The new cultures of the northern region (Michelsberg, Baalberg, Wiorek, Altheim and so on) were an amalgamation of the traditions of the indigenous Late Neolithic populations, south-eastern cultural traits and those of groups of northern origin. Although these cultures can be defined by typologically characteristic differences as their pottery varies according to their local traditions, nevertheless, some common trends of their development are not to be neglected: evidence indicates the general disintegration of the stability of Late Neolithic settlements and the emergence of more mobile, mainly pastoral groups. The prestige and power of the leaders of these communities became more explicitly demonstrated; the graves and cemeteries of the Bodrogk-eresztur culture present clear and significant evidence of this. Generally speaking, the changes in life-style, the more intensive cultural interaction and small, archaeologically hardly detectable migrations resulted in a change in burial rites, namely in the distribution of the cremation burials and the appearance of barrow graves with smaller or larger mounds. As for the latter, barrows appear in various cultures in the whole Eurasian territory, and these *kurgans* themselves do not prove ethnic movements or migrations.

We have already mentioned the significance of the early copper metallurgy of undoubtedly south-eastern origin, which was an extremely important development not only in the southern region but in the whole of central Europe. Finds prove the intercultural character of the spread of technological innovations. It seems indisputable that this metal industry was the result of autochthonous development in the north Balkans and the Carpathian basin, since the Late Neolithic cultures display products of a technologically initial phase. So we find beads made of copper ore (malachite, azurite) together with bracelets and rings, proving the successful smelting of these ores. This does not, however, exclude the possibility that the knowledge and experience leading to the discovery and exploitation of the local copper-ore deposits arrived by way of cultural diffusion from Anatolia and the Eastern Mediterranean. These importations are even more probable if the analogous features of cultural development are considered. The Neolithic smelting technology could produce enough metal for small objects, mostly ornaments. Compared with this, the Copper Age production of heavy flat axes, axes and axe-adzes implies a revolutionary technological change (Tiszapolgár and Bodrogkeresztur cultures) and a relatively large-scale exploitation of the simple copper ores found near to the surface, and naturally that of the native copper.

The products of this first flourishing period of central European metallurgy can be found to a certain degree in the material culture of the whole territory. Thus the characteristic copper axe-adzes were found in central Germany, in Silesia, and the fashion for copper jewellery was carried as far as Kujavia in Poland (Plauen, Jordanów, Hlinsko, Stollhof and Brzesc Kujawski).

The emergence of copper metallurgy in the Balkans and the Carpathian basin initiated the exploitation of copper-ore deposits in the Alps and its vicinity, as attested by the crucibles of the Michelsberg, Pfyn and Mondsee cultures. It is also clear that the copper metallurgy of the Funnel-beaker culture developed within the framework of the same interregional diffusion.

Although there are relatively many copper weapons (axe-adzes, simple leaf-bladed daggers) and tools (flat axes and chisels), most of the implements were still made of stone. The general spread of obsidian and silex blades, polished axes and flat axes, the intensive exploitation of the flint mines in Little Poland and in Hungary indicate that copper objects together with gold ornaments were primarily signs of social status. Metal tools and weapons became generally used only in the second upswing of the metal industry during the Bronze Age.

A population movement from the Black Sea region resulted in ethnic change and cultural rearrangement in the southern region in the first half of the third millennium BC (for the first though not by far the last time in the history of central Europe). The first small groups of the earliest nomadic pastoralists appeared in Transylvania and in the eastern part of the great Hungarian plain as early as the period of the copper axe-adzes, after they had successfully domesticated the horse in the formative phase of their characteristic economy, most suitable for the steppe region. These early steppe nomads probably belonged to an early group speaking an Indo-Iranian language, and perhaps they contributed to the destruction of the Gumelniţa culture which had produced the outstandingly rich finds of Varna. The next wave of the steppe people, the population giving rise to the pit-grave *kurgans* (labelled generally the 'Ochre-grave culture' or 'Kurgan culture') appeared on territory very favourable for a nomadic economy in the Late Copper Age. Mounds, similar to their characteristic *kurgan* burials, can be found nearly everywhere in Europe from the Late Neolithic till the Middle Ages, but the distribution of pit-grave *kurgans* that are really characteristic of the culture does not reach as far as the Budapest-Belgrade line. No general European significance of the groups coming from the steppe can be proved concerning the spread of the Indo-European languages or the formation of new cultural complexes in the Early Bronze Age. Their penetration into the south-eastern areas of central Europe, however, brought about important changes. It had a part in the cessation of the material culture connected with copper metallurgy. A cultural vacuum, even if not an ethnic one, appeared in a large part of the lower Danube area and the Carpathian basin. After the destruction of the indigenous cultural development the effect of this vacuum was the adoption of a material culture of Aegean origin, which was transmitted by Balkan groups. This must have been the main factor leading to the emergence and distribution of the Baden culture within a relatively short time, the material culture of the initial phase of which is strikingly homogeneous. The differentiation of the various groups started later, according to the ethno-cultural reorganization of the area.

The settlements of the Baden culture consist mostly of pits, storage pits and semi-subterranean huts. Fortified settlements and carefully built large houses are rarely seen (Vučedol, Nitrianski Hradok). In the cemeteries the distinguished position of the leaders is indicated by the sacrifice of cattle. Copper objects are rare and probably indicate the minimal survival of the metallurgy of the earlier phase. The copper torques found in Austrian graves near the western border of the culture's distribution area represent a very significant exception, as they are proof of the healthy survival of early Alpine metallurgy which started before the formation of the Baden culture. (The development of the territories left intact by 'Badenization' shows a peculiar asynchrony; the cultural continuity radically changed on Baden territory, while some older cultures of the neighbourhood continued. On the southern and south-western border of the Baden territory the population attached to the Retz-Gajary-Mondsee sites can be regarded as one of the important components of the later Vučedol culture, thus one of the direct predecessors of the Early Bronze Age.)

The direct contact between the steppe and the central European region in the Baden period probably led to a very important change in animal husbandry. The domestication of the horse and the appearance of wheeled vehicles are signs pointing towards the later development of chariotry. These wagons, judging by the models and depictions available, were heavy and could be drawn only by oxen; their initial distribution can be followed in the Baden area as well as in the neighbouring cultures and on the steppe. The products of the secondary exploitation of animal domestication were woollen tapestry and dairy products as well as traction. The factors leading to the cultural transformation of the third millennium BC seem to have accumulated in the Late Copper Age: pastoralism became more and more important in the life of the communities and produced a more mobile life-style with a more overtly expressed social differentiation. These changes acted as catalysts for cultural contacts which may have been trading activities as well as raids. Following the long period of the Neolithic, a new type of economy developed due to the interregional relations of the Copper Age. It can be characterized by the growing demands of the chieftains, the development of new production methods and the spread of new techniques.

Some areas of the southern region (river valleys in Transylvania, the eastern part of the Hungarian plain) were occupied in the Late Copper Age by the Pit-grave culture of steppe origin, while in the eastern and southern part of the Baden complex the related Coţofeni and Kostolac cultures developed. The Baden culture itself ranged as far as Little Poland beyond the Carpathians towards north and lower Austria on the west. Its influence can be detected in Moravia, Silesia and in almost all the northern region.

New cultural complexes were formed north of the Alps on the sites of the earlier Baalberg, Altheim and Michelsberg cultures in the late phase of the Funnel-beaker development, integrating Baden influences. These new cultures established hillforts, and sometimes megalithic grave structures were built due to western and north-western influences (the Salzmünde, Bernburg and Walternienburg cultures, megaliths in Hessen).

The burial structures of the period, the grave chambers sometimes decorated with engraved and carved ornament, the stone-cist burials and the mounds show many varieties. It seems probable that the majority of the cultures regarded the grave as 'the house of the dead' and this general idea played an important role in the burial rite. The careful construction of the resting-place of the dead, resembling a house, a tent or a hut can be observed among the steppe cultures, in the Balkans and in Central Europe as well, in the form of stone constructions and in carefully executed wooden buildings. Among the pit-grave burials of eastern Hungary we also find the remains of the yurt-like matting tent erected above the grave and even the protecting roof made of split tree-trunks. The stone-cist burial was practised by quite different cultures, and catacomb graves are observed in the steppe area, in south Poland and in the Balkans. The sometimes striking monumentality of grave constructions can probably be ascribed to social differences in the occupants.

The large-scale cultural integration of the northern region started in the last third of the third millennium BC. This was actually independent of southern influence and also that from the east. The spread of the Globular Amphora culture east of the Elbe towards the Dnieper was the first step, followed by the appearance of the Corded-ware culture superimposed on the whole territory previously occupied by the Funnel-beaker culture. The general distribution of corded ware with the same significant characteristics in the northern half of Europe was explained for a long time by postulating different migrations, and it was also supposed to have originated from the steppe region. It seems more probable, however, that during the Funnel-beaker period in the northern territories of central Europe extensive cultivation and exploitation exhausted the larger part of the arable land, resulting in the formation of steppe-like areas which favoured the change of economy, now consisting mostly of animal husbandry.

The pastoral groups, due to their common ethnical basis (Funnel-beaker culture) and their compact community, produced a poor, still unified material culture and burial rite, which became standardized over the vast territory relatively quickly (all-European horizon: single graves under barrows, 'A' axes, amphorae and beakers).

Two new factors play an important role in the development of the new cultural units of the territory from the Alps and Carpathians to Scandinavia at the end of the third millennium BC: one is the appearance of the Bell-beaker culture, the other is the influence of the Early Bronze Age cultures of the northern Balkans, transmitting some of the achievements of the Early Hellenic civilizations towards central Europe.

The series of archaeologically observable changes in the southern region starts by the gradual 'melting away', disappearing of the Baden culture. As before, in the time of the formation of the Baden culture, these changes took place over a wide area and the formation of new cultures started by the adaptation of new, mainly southern elements. The new metallurgy was the most important, or at least the most characteristic among them. New techniques of smelting and casting made their appearance in the Balkans and in the Carpathian basin. New types of ores, and new implements for casting them appeared, as bivalve moulds came into use. The material of the shaft-hole axes, flat axes and chisels is copper with an arsenic content (arsenic bronze). This material is almost exclusively used in the first phase of Bronze Age technology. The integrating influence of cultural contacts is reflected by the identical metallurgy and the analogous features of the pottery of the new cultures in the Carpathian basin (Somogyvár, Makó, Caka, Nyírség, Jidogin, Glina III-Schneckenberg and early Nagyrév). The relatively quick change of material culture suggests a dynamic period, though the settlements, consisting of huts and pits, are mostly similar to the earlier ones. Thus the way of life in the Late Copper Age must have been carried over into the first period of the Early Bronze Age (Plate 141).

The cultural diffusion of the Early Bronze Age and the appearance of the Bell-beaker culture together gave rise to a change in the Corded-ware cultural groups. The Bell-beaker population, named after its characteristic vessels, found its way to the Vistula and the Carpathian basin. Sooner or later it became integrated with the local populations, resulting in a specific material culture containing bell-beakers and local, central European pottery which can be found around Budapest just as in Little Poland. The appearance of a new variety of domestic horse can also be linked with the settlements of the Bell-beaker population (Plate 142).

It was around the early eighteenth century BC that the period of new cultural influences and ethnic movements of various degrees and origins ended and a new status quo was achieved in central Europe. A certain ethnic continuity can be generally observed in the several sub-regions of the territory during the next period of nearly one millennium, although small migrations and local rearrangements undoubtedly occurred. The various groups were of heterogeneous ethnic origin and composition, but their development reached differing levels even in the same periods, according to their different habitats and the diversity of their culture contacts. The Bronze Age inhabitants of central Europe not only absorbed the culture and technical innovations of other regions (Caucasus, Pontus area and the Balkans), leading to the acceleration of their development, but they also acted as a spur to socio-economic relations and changes of political power in the continent, especially in the second half of the millennium. This outstanding span of European prehistory is sketched here in three phases: the Otomani/Füzesabony-Únětice period (eighteenth–fourteenth century BC), the Tumulus period (fourteenth–thirteenth century BC) and the Urnfield period (thirteenth–eighth century BC).

THE OTOMANI/FÜZESABONY-ÚNĚTICE PERIOD

The development of the Bronze Age in the Carpathian basin is in several respects different from that of other regions in central Europe. As we have seen, Bronze Age development started here earlier due to the direct and indirect contacts with the Balkans and the Pontus area. Full Bronze Age status is shown by the 'standardization' of tribal territories; and the development of 'tell' settlements, attesting long-lasting stability and sometimes even the continuity of settlements established in earlier periods. The most important of all features is that of an economy capable of producing a surplus regularly for exchange and trade, and of sustaining a highly developed metal industry often using imported material and able to produce tools and weapons demanded by a new life-style.

The roots of the process leading to this point go back to the beginning of the second millennium BC, though the first significant stage was the formation of the Pecica, Otomani, Füzesabony and Wietenberg cultures in the eastern half of the Carpathian basin, which here marked the beginning of the middle phase of the Bronze Age (Plates 143–7). The more or less contemporary populations of the western Carpathian basin (Vatya, Incrusted pottery and Madarovce cultures) not only combined the characteristics of the central Danubian and the eastern Carpathian basin but also – especially the last – had an integral role in the circulation of wares and in the transmission of certain manifestations in the spiritual sphere (Plates 148, 149). The majority of Central Europe was occupied by the ethnic conglomerate called the Únětice culture. The population in present west Slovakia, Moravia and Bohemia, south and central Germany and south Poland was by no means homogeneous. As we have seen, the beginnings of the culture's formation go far back to the early second millennium BC, so the ethnic composition of the territorial units was defined first of all by the makers of bell-beakers and corded ware.

The territorial units and especially the chronological phases of the Únětice culture have been distinguished in many ways. It seems probable that the development of the culture was connected mainly with the exploitation of its ore deposits (copper, tin) which provided a basis for the precocious local metallurgy and for the bronze trade which supplied the demands of the north European bronze industry. In the northern zone of the Alps and the adjacent territories the existence of populations settled on plateaus and lake sides or sometimes river banks was also regulated by the ore, first of all copper. The raw material must have been transported, mostly from around Salzburg, along river valleys to distant areas. The population of the sub-region has been split up into various cultural divisions (for example Unterwölbing, Böheimkirchen and Wieselbur in Austria), according to characteristic sites and hoard groups (Straubing, Singen, Adlerberg, Lanquaid, and the later Locham in Germany), or to their topographical position (central land group and Alpine group in Switzerland).

On the upper reaches of the Vistula the widespread Trzciniec culture followed the Mierzanowice culture, related to the north Carpathian basin, while east-central and east-European features combine in the Trzciniec culture due to its geographical situation.

Two correlative factors had a decisive influence on the economic and social development in both the eastern and western parts of central Europe (theoretically divided by the western branches of the Carpathians east of the Moravian basin). One is the control of ore deposits and their exploitation, leading to bronze production and trade, which increased steadily as the technology advanced and the demand grew quantitatively. The growing dependence on metal seems to have determined the interaction of the ore-possessing populations (for example Wietenberg, Únětice) with other cultures. This factor also modified the division of labour in the ethnic units, and influenced the position of individuals and certain families, creating layers in the social hierarchy. The process is rarely indicated by the finds, thus we can only guess how it gathered pace in the different areas. Nevertheless, we can visualize the general outcome. A certain stabilization can be observed from the seventeenth century onwards, indicated by the continuity of the ethnically homogeneous populations which absorbed the earlier groups of different origins, as proved by the anthropological data. It is this continuity that became significant, no matter how some cultural features changed according to the trends of inner development, or influenced by external impulses introduced by traditional contacts.

The other main formative factor was the apparent tension caused by the lack of ores in north Europe and the metal demand of Mycenae, the most developed society of Bronze Age Europe. From the sixteenth century on, however, this tension resulted in the emergence of interregional trade relations in which nearly the whole of the continent was involved. The inhabitants of central Europe had their intermediatory role with its concomitant material profit, enriched by the production of copper and gold in the east Carpathians. The intermediate trade accounts for the cultural influences which reached this area along the lower Danube and via Transylvania (perhaps along the west Balkan route as well) and brought about progressive changes.

The Aegean-Pontic influence affected the whole pattern of everyday life in Europe. It would be hard to exaggerate the importance of developments emerging as consequences of exchange and trade. Even if only a few finds can be regarded as direct imports from Mycenae (for example the Dohnsen bronze cup), it is not difficult to demonstrate that the inhabitants of central, especially east-central, Europe made use of the knowledge acquired through trade contacts and assimilated innovations of Mediterranean origin, sometimes modifying their original content and form. Some of them, such as the pattern of city settlements, carts with spoked wheels, antler cheek-pieces for bridles, long swords and daggers, metal vessels and shrines exercised a decisive influence on the further development of the material and spiritual culture.

Villages very much resembling the tell settlements of the Balkans appeared first in the Tisza-Maros area. Many of them were associated with earthwork enclosures, though in some cases (for example Békés) only the central part was fortified. The huts, often partly sunk in the ground, gradually disappeared and houses with plastered walls painted white and plastered clay floors were built, sometimes with timbers in the bedding trenches supporting the walls (for example,

Tiszafüred). In Békés even remains of log-built houses were found. The roofs were gabled or pitched, rarely flat, and the oblong buildings (3.5 by 6.11 m) had one to three rooms. Settlements and hillforts of similar character were also built in the central part of the region in the second part of this period, at Bánov, Kromeriz-Hradisko and Blucina. Stone and wood were used for houses (Arbon Bleich, Baldegg) and fortifications (Möching, Cesky Krumlov, Ivanovce) on the hilly areas from the early period (Fig. 68). Later, a new, perhaps East Mediterranean structure appeared, the best example being the stone-walled fort of Spissky Stvrtok. Proof of the cultivation of wheat, barley, millet, beans and flax and of animal husbandry (cattle, sheep, goat, pig, horse) can be found nearly everywhere. Their proportion in the economy was determined first of all by geographical constraints: broadly speaking, in the eastern part of the territory, plant cultivation with animal keeping, in the western part mainly pastoralism, dominated.

Two large centres of metallurgy emerged in central Europe: one in the east Carpathian basin, the other in the central Danube area. The former had direct contacts with southeast Europe, and thus it not only prospered earlier but became the initiator of the astonishingly productive metallurgy of west-central Europe. Judging from the remains of moulds and tuyères, foundries were set up in all the most significant sites in east-central Europe, with products being exported to the main centres (for example Pecica, Varsand, Barca). The high standard of metallurgy is shown by finds from the cemeteries – inhumation, cremation burials or those of mixed rite (Füzesabony, Tiszafüred, Dunaujváros) – especially the gold and bronze hoard of Tufalau-Smig and Hajdusámson type. As with the later bronze finds of Koszider type, these show a mixture of local tradition and influence from the central Danube area.

It was in this period that the characteristic equipment of Bronze Age warriors took shape in the Carpathian basin. It consisted of the battleaxe, bronze-hilted sword, long dagger with wooden or bone hilt, spear with socketed head and stone mace.

The metallurgy of the western areas arrived at its peak in the late Únětice-Lanquaid phase, and is known from cemeteries with flat graves at Gemeinlebarn, Statzendorf, Rebisovice, Roggendorf and Grossbrembach; from chieftains' graves at Helmsdorf, Leubingen, Leki Male and Renzendühl and from several hoards (for example at Kozi Hrbetky, Dieskau, Breisinchen, Trassem, Gaubickelheim and Granov). The richly decorated bronze-hilted daggers, the long-shafted halberds, wide-bladed flat axes, solid torques and bracelets, and pins with globular and discoid heads are the most conspicuous items. The exchange of products between the two centres of metallurgy, and the mutual adoption of fashionable types is attested by numerous examples. This seems to have been one of the reasons for a certain uniformity, which is apparent even in the effectiveness of the tools and weapons. A similar phenomenon can be observed in the case of pottery as far as the function, fabric and basic forms are concerned. Although most of the storage vessels, bowls, jugs, cups and urns are of various forms and patterns according to the given culture, others, such as the fish pans, pyrauni, ember covers, loom weights and so on, are nearly uniform everywhere, similar to the antler and stone artefacts.

Social distinction, or at least the existence of a strong élite, is testified by several find groups: the citadel-like parts of larger sites, family hoards, groups of warrior graves lavishly equipped with weapons, and the richly furnished tumulus graves of wooden or stone construction. Division of labour is proved by the special grave furniture with the attributes of goldsmiths or medicine men, and perhaps also the loom weights found in women's graves. Accordingly, at around the middle of the second millennium BC, Central Europe can be characterized by a certain coherence of development resulting from multilateral contacts, by a deepening social differentiation, and by a stability based on the balance of power among equally matched populations in the region. We may add that diffusion from the Carpathian basin towards the north-north-west maintained its effect even in the closing period of the Middle Bronze Age. It is specially well indicated by the Koszider-type hoards and the bronze objects of similar, nearly identical form and decoration from Moravia (Hodonin), south Germany (Ackenbach, Bühl) and south Poland (Grodnica).

THE TUMULUS PERIOD

At this time the centre of decisive change had shifted to the western part of central Europe. A certain cultural transformation, not entirely clarified by research, resulted in the emergence of a cultural cohesion during the nearly two centuries of the 'Tumulus period', named after the characteristic burials. The diverse populations of the period were held together by the cohesive force of economico-political interest, with a more or less similar way of life all over the immense territory from the Rhine to the Tisza River. The population conglomerate of the Tumulus culture has been divided into several territorial units: Alsatian, Swiss (central-land, Alpine), middle Rhine, east Hesse, Lüneburg, Bohemia-Oberpfalz, central Danubian and Carpathian. It seems reasonable to distinguish three chronological phases, although no sharp boundaries can be established between them. The formation area cannot really be determined, though it seems to have been on the earlier Únětice and Madrovce-Veterov territory – at least that which concerns the eastern part of the central Danubian area and the Carpathian basin respectively. It is not clear if the culture was rooted in a central nucleus or – which is more probable – was the result of a convergent transformation, as seems to be supported by the history of Bronze Age development in western central Europe. The reasons for the change in the earlier status quo are not clear. Probably differences in the rhythm of devel-

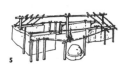

Figure 68 Types of Middle Bronze Age dwellings: 1, Partly underground house with walls of wattle; 2, Frame house – the exact location of the joints was determined during excavation; 3, Houses with saddle-bag roofs and wattle-and-daub walls; 4–5, idem., details of construction (after Kovács, 1977).

opment in the various sub-regions resulted in the deepening of social differentiation in certain communities and in the modification of external power relations. The significance of the climatic change at the beginning of the second half of the millennium can be neither excluded nor proved. The cooler and more humid climate in fact favoured the animal-keeping agriculturalists. Accordingly, this economy became general in the Tumulus period.

Owing to the deficiencies of settlement research, the period is known primarily from the tumulus graves excavated mainly at Hagenau Forest, in Swabish Alb, in Thüringia and in west Bohemia. Though the main features of the burials are nearly identical everywhere, there are minor differences in the different territories in the size and form of the graves, the wooden and especially stone constructions and the number of the burials in the tumulus, which usually contained contracted skeletons, but sometimes cremations. Between other characteristics of the burials and the richness or poverty of the graves hardly any connection can be observed, even in tumulus fields with sometimes hundreds of burials (for example, Dysina). In many cases traces of wooden coffins were observed (Weiningen, Schwarza) and remains of cloth were found (Schwarza, Tápé). The garments, tools and weapons and also the frequency or lack of them varies from place to place.

While the pottery maintains the local tradition (incised and hatched decoration in the west and moulded in the east), the metallurgy produces more common types than earlier. The weapons generally used by the Tumulus culture are short swords with wooden hilts fastened by two or four rivets, flanged or bronze-hilted slashing swords, bronze arrowheads, *Absatzbeile* (palstaves), seal-headed pins, corrugated sheet armlets, armlets with spiral endings and so on. It seems probable that local migrations of various intensity also played some role in the integration resulting in the similarities of material culture and a common tradition.

The population north of the Carpathians preserved its ethnic continuity and developed the pre-Lusatian culture, affected by the influence of the Tumulus culture. Similarly, the Piliny culture emerged in the north of the Carpathian basin, while the cultural development of the more eastern areas was different (Szamos-Tisza area: Siciu de Sus culture, Transylvania-Moldavia: Noa culture – with East European connections).

THE URNFIELD PERIOD

It can be supposed and partly archaeologically proved that events in the East Mediterranean in the last third of the millennium (the decline of the Mycenean civilization, the raids of the Sea Peoples, the collapse of the Hittite empire) and their consequences influenced the trade and politics of Late Bronze Age Europe. Consequently this was the period of the first levelling process, which considerably moderated the discrepancy between the southern and northern part of the continent. This was also the time of the 'technological explosion', leading to the mass production of metals, based on several centuries of metallurgical tradition in 'barbarian' Europe. It affected the whole economy, as the effectiveness of agriculture and craftsmanship was raised by improved implements (sickle, knife, awl, chisel, socketed axe), the discovery of new ones (for example the saw) and by the sudden quantitative growth of both. The helmet, corselet, shield and greaves hammered from bronze plates became widespread, paralleling the lessening importance of the battleaxe. This indicates not only the division of weapons used for attack or defence but also a change in the nature of warfare. Over the majority of the region we can see many related features of material and spiritual culture, and change in the forms and patterns of artefacts became much slower over nearly six centuries. All these, together with the homogeneity of the flat cemeteries with cremation burials (Wölfersheim, Gammertigen, Hart, Acholshausem, Salzburg-Morzg, Knoviz, Milavce, Partizanske, Baierdorf, Vál and so on), attest cultural integration. The usually large, fortified settlements (Bleineskopf, Knetzberg, Seusslitz-Goldkuppe, Bachau-Wasserburg, Niemcza, Lubowice, Velemszentvid and Bükkszentlászló), the hoards of Lazany, Suchol, Uriu-Ópályi, Kurd, Cincu-Suseni and Hajduböszörmény type, and similar ones often consisting of several hundred items, can be understood as signs of increased social differentiation (Plates 150, 151); the total weight of the hoard at Uioare de Sus is *c.* 1,300 kg, that of Spalnaca II *c.* 1,200 kg, and that of Aiud, 752 kg.

There is no agreement so far as to what initiated the Urnfield period, how the Urnfield culture, occupying half of Europe, was formed or even when it took place. Some postulate that the changes heralding the culture were rooted in local developments; others put forward the theory that the Urnfield development was the result of migrations for the acquisition of new ore resources, or territories most suitable for tilling in the twelfth century BC. Nevertheless, it has been proved archaeologically that the material culture of the Urnfield period is connected with that of the late Tumulus period by many common forms and types.

The theory of a Great Expansion from the Urnfield territory to the Mediterranean cannot be accepted by modern research. At the same time several data seem to indicate that sub-regional migrations (such as the infiltration of the Lusatian culture into north Moravia and north-west Slovakia, or the western expansion of the late Urnfield culture) played an important role in the formation of ethnic groups and the monolithic material culture of the period, though its modifications varied in space and time, as did the diffusion of technical innovations (for example hollow-casting or the improvement of plate technique, the production of body armour, bronze vessels, brooches and so on), and of traditions and beliefs. And, to complete the picture, the fortifications, the weapons of impressive quality and quantity, the number of non-sacred hoards and treasures all suggest a world more warlike than peaceful in the following centuries, when the finds testify to a population that grew much faster than before.

Three large cultural conglomerations can be recognized in central Europe in the last period of the Bronze Age: the Urnfield, Lusatian and Gáva cultures (Plates 152–4). They are further divided into territorial groups and chronological phases according to varying systems of terminology and chronology.

As we have seen – if only superficially – the evaluation of the continuity/discontinuity, the existence/non-existence of cultural diffusion connected with the economico-social development, and the role of migrations, are often sources of uncertainty. This makes every assumption as to ethnic-linguistic identification doubious from the outset. Therefore, it remains only a possibility that the population of the western Urnfield territories was the predecessor of the Celtic people, the Lusatian culture preceded that of the western Slavs, or the Gáva culture belonged to the pre-Thracians, however plausible these possibilities may seem.

NOTE

1 This text was completed in the early 1980s. As far as the chronology is concerned, we now know that the period in question commenced much earlier than had been previously assumed. This summary has none the less retained its validity as regards the main trends of prehistoric development.

BIBLIOGRAPHY

BANNER, J.; BÓNA, I. 1974. *Mittelbronze-zeitliche Tell-Siedlung bei Békés.* Budapest.

CHILDE, V. G. 1929. *The Danube in Prehistory.* Oxford.

COLES, J. M.; HARDING, A. F. 1979. *The Bronze Age in Europe.* London.

ECSEDY, I. 1979. *The People of the Pit-Grave Kurgan in Eastern Hungary.* Budapest. (Fontes Archaelogici Hungariae.)

FOLTINY, ST. 1955. *Zur Chronologie der Bronzezeit des Karpatenbeckens.* Bonn.

GIMBUTAS, M. 1965. *Bronze Age Cultures in Central and Eastern Europe.* The Hague.

HACHMANN, R. 1957. *Die frühe Bronzezeit im westlichen Ostseegebiet und ihre mittel- und südost-europäischen Beziehungen.* Hamburg.

HÄNSEL, B. 1958. *Beiträge zur Chronologie der mittleren Bronzeziet im Karpatenbecken.* Bonn.

KALICZ, N. 1968. *Die Frühbronzezeit in Nordost-Ungarn.* Budapest.

KOSSACK, G. 1954. *Studien zum Symbolgut der Urnenfelderkultur und Hallstattzeit Mitteleuropas.* Berlin.

KOVÁCS. T. 1977. *A Bronzkor Magyarországon [L'age du Bronze en Hongrie].* Budapest.

MOZSOLICS, A. 1942. *Der frühbronzezeitliche Urnenfriedhof von Kisapostag. Arch. Hung.* 26.

—— 1973. *Bronze und goldfunde des Karratenbeckens.* Budapest.

—— 1985. *Bronzefunde aus Hungarn, Deptfundhorizonte von Aranyes, Kurd und Gyermely.* Budapest.

PATEK, E. 1968. *Die Urnenfeldkultur in Transdanubien. Arch. Hung.* 44.

PITTIONI, R. 1954. *Urgeschichte des Österreichischen Raumes.* Wien.

POPESCU, B. 1944. *Die frühe und mittlere Bronzezeit in Siebenbürgen.* Bucureşti.

RENFREW, C. 1987. *Archaeology and languages: The Puzzle of Indo-European Origins.* London.

STIG SØRENSEN, M. L.; THOMAS, R. (eds.). 1989 *The Bronze Age – Iron Age Transition in Europe.* Oxford. (BAR Int. Ser., 483.)

14.5

EASTERN EUROPE
(Fourth millennium to seventh century BC)

Nikolai J. Merpert

In Chapter 52 of Volume I of this work, stress has already been laid on the singular variety of both natural and historical conditions in eastern Europe which, even in the Neolithic age, had led to inequality and highly specific features in the development of particular parts of that territory. This related both to the time and pace of the advent of the Neolithic of each of these areas and to their cultural originality, as reflected in archaeological finds. These specific features and the unequal development of individual regions persisted to a considerable extent in the following period as well, which was marked by the appearance and spread of copper and bronze metallurgy and is the special subject of this chapter.

It must be noted straight away that eastern Europe is a vast area containing a wide variety of landscape and climate zones, from the eastern boundaries of central Europe (Hungary, the Czech Republic, Slovakia and Poland) in the west to the Urals in the east and from the Danube region, the northern Black Sea area, the Caucasus and the Caspian area in the south to the subpolar regions in the north. The southern part of this territory includes the mountains, foothills and intermontane plains of the Carpathians, the Crimea and the Caucasus, with their mild, temperate, continental and, in the extreme south, subtropical climate, and also a significant portion of the Eurasian steppe (changing into semi-desert in the east, in the Caspian depression), with an adjacent southern area of forest steppe within the confines of the east European depression. The northern part includes the remaining forest steppe, vast forest regions, and, further to the north, park tundra and pure tundra with a harsh subarctic or arctic climate.

The palaeo-climate of these areas is still a matter for debate, concerning as it does the last three millennia BC. Some palaeographers think that in the third millennium BC there was some aridification of the climate in some parts of the Eurasian steppe but this cannot be said to have been either general or decisive. On the whole, the development of the population of eastern Europe from the end of the fourth to the first quarter of the first millennium BC occurred in a landscape and climate close to those of today. Their variety was no less significant.

The historical conditions in which particular areas developed were just as varied. It should be noted first of all that the southern area was immediately adjacent to advanced cultural centres which already possessed a highly developed productive economy and which, later on, played a decisive role in the development and spread of metallurgy. Where eastern Europe is concerned, two of these centres, the Balkans and the Caucasus, played a special role. Some parts of the southern zone were directly linked with these centres. To the north, they were bounded by the Black Sea Caspian steppes which extended to the east where, already on the confines of Asia, they touched a third highly important centre – the western Asian civilizations. With the widespread settlement of the steppe, brought about by the development there of specific migratory forms of stock-raising, the conditions were created for a unique 'focusing' of the achievements of all three cultural centres and for their effective spread over vast areas. This was a most important factor in the gradual development both of the steppe zone itself and of the forest steppe adjacent to it and, later, of certain parts of the forest regions. Above all, stress should be laid here on the consequent spread of productive types of economy which were many times superior to those of the Neolithic age and now took in a significant part of eastern Europe as well as all the southern and part of the northern zone.

At the same time, the western and north-western (Baltic) areas had direct links with central Europe where, at the beginning of the metal-working age, there were significant movements and consolidation of human groups. Large cultural communities became established and spread. Similar events occurred in the adjacent areas of eastern Europe. Active interplay between these areas played a significant part in the histories of each and determined the specific nature of the cultural development of the western part of the territory.

Only in the northern part of the forest zone, the park tundra and pure tundra, remote from advanced cultural centres and isolated from cultural contact, did reserves of Neolithic life remain for the greater part of the period. Even there, however, certain progressive movements occurred. They were evident both in the improvement of traditional activities such as hunting, fishing and gathering and, in individual penetrations, right to the far northern zones, of the productive economy with the emergence of innovations, according to particular local natural conditions (this concerned stock-raising above all).

Where the rest of eastern Europe is concerned, it should be emphasized that in the period in question there was a sharp increase in population density, in the activity of the population, in the general standard of its economic, social and cultural development and particularly in the pace of cultural development.

Altogether there was a consolidation of contacts, collaboration and cultural integration. Together with the productive economy, an enormous role was played by the appearance of metallurgy and metal working within eastern

Europe. Metal working became one of the decisive factors in technical, economic and cultural development, in the promotion and direction of contacts and in the organization of production and the general structure of society. Metallurgy significantly widened not only productive capabilities but also people's knowledge, leading to the use of vast natural resources which till then had remained only potentially useful. This knowledge extended both to the nature and to the properties of the new materials being used and to the chemical, physical and technological processes associated with them. The establishment of mining and metal-working centres had a marked influence on the general level and pace of development in specific regions and on the relationship between them. On the one hand, this exacerbated inequalities in historical development and, on the other, sharply increased the capabilities and importance of a number of regions, leading to a kind of 'redistribution' of their historical roles.

The changes did not, however, occur all at once. The traditional centres in the Balkans, Danube basin and the Caucasians, which had emerged in the Neolithic era, maintained their characteristic importance in the early stages of the establishment of metallurgy in eastern Europe, where they were the first metallurgical centres. At the same time, the traditional influences and the corresponding systems of communication persisted. Only later were new sources of metal developed and did new centres of metallurgy emerge; metal working spread over vast areas, which led to considerable changes both in the system of communication and in the nature of the interaction between various regions.

It should be stressed that metal and the phenomena associated with it are from then on the clearest indicators of the stages and general level of development of specific areas.

THE EARLY BRONZE AGE

In the second half of the fourth millennium BC, eastern Europe was affected by considerable cultural and ethnic changes. The evidence indicates that these changes took place at the beginning of the early metal age. This was marked by the use of admixtures to form alloys, by a significant increase in the use of metal, and by the transition to the Bronze Age proper and its development. This stage lasted up to the first half of the second millennium BC. Two specific phases can be distinguished within it. The first covers the end of the fourth and a large part of the third millennium BC and can be considered as the Early Bronze Age of eastern Europe. During this period, the Balkan-Carpathian and the Caucasian metallurgical areas retained their importance. In the first, however, there were considerable changes in the siting of the centres, while in the second there was great activity and the general role and influence of metal working on vast adjacent territories increased sharply. The most important trend during this phase was the integration of metallurgical traditions in the vast territory, embracing the Balkans and Carpathians, the south of eastern Europe as far as the Aegean in the west and the Urals in the east, and the Caucasus, Anatolia and western Iran. The circum-Pontinc metallurgical province came into being. With that territory are associated considerable displacements of large ethnic groups and substantial changes in the relationships between the advanced cultural centres of the southern area and the other zones. The contrast between their levels of development was considerable. The Chalcolithic early agricultural

cultures in the southern zone ceased to exist both in the Balkan-Danube region and in the Caucasus. There came into being interconnected cultures taking in the whole of the territory and also the vast steppe and forest steppe regions of central and eastern Europe adjacent to it. This makes it possible to speak not only of a metallurgical province but of a circum-Pontine contact zone, distinguished by particularly active interrelations between a number of cultures and by stronger ties, extremely significant from the general historical point of view and from that of the study of cultures. A considerable role was played by the tribes of the steppe, who had developed migratory forms of stock-raising. They brought about genuine contacts between the various cultural groups, gave vitality and territorial breadth to the processes of interaction and also provided a certain continuity of contact within the new system of cultural communities. At the same time, groups of professional metallurgists and smiths spread out from the main metallurgical centres and fostered the diffusion of metal-working methods and the general promotion of contacts.

In the Caucasus, Anatolia and the Aegean, artefacts of arsenical bronze became widespread, whereas in the districts further north, pure copper predominated. In the technology of casting used to produce the most representative type of artefact, the socketed axe, the characteristic moulds were of the two-leafed variety, which opened fully from the face of the tool.

In the Chalcolithic cultural centres of the southern area, the early agricultural tradition continued into the Early Bronze Age, although the composition of the population and its culture underwent substantial changes. Thus, in the north-west Black Sea area, the late stage of the Tripolje culture belongs to the third millennium BC, although considerably transformed by the influence of central European cultures (funnel-beaker, globular amphora, corded ware) from the west and of the stock-raising cultures of the steppe from the east. Here, the syncretic Usatovo variant is particularly characteristic. In this, groups with permanent fortified settlements were associated with nomads who had moved far to the west, with reminiscences of Tripolje decorated pottery and anthropomorphic sculptures in association with tapering vessels and corded ornamentation and, most important of all, with the appearance of the typical steppe phenomenon of *kurgan* burial.

In the Caucasus at the end of the fourth and beginning of the third millennia BC, two very large metallurgical and general cultural centres came into being – the Kura-Araks in central and eastern Transcaucasia and the Maikop in the northern Caucasus, the Kuban Valley and the upper reaches of the Terek.

The Kura-Araks culture spread into north-west Iran, and parts can be traced as far as the Eastern Mediterranean. It was based on agriculture and stock-raising. Its remains consist chiefly of large, frequently fortified, settlements with round houses. The metallurgy of the Kura-Araks was based on ores from the deposits in the Little Caucasus, both copper and arsenic. As the most important eastern part of the circum-Pontine area, this culture is distinguished by evidence of links with Anatolia right up to its western borders and the Aegean-Balkan region.

The Maikop culture developed at the same time as the Kura-Araks but was based chiefly on stock-raising. It is represented by settlements, some fortified (Meshoko) and by many graves, chiefly of the *kurgan* type, with a striking richness of grave goods in the tombs of the leaders of the tribal unions, beginning with the outstanding Maikop *kurgan* (Munchaev, 1975). The culture did not have a mining base and in this respect depended on the Kura-Araks culture. Metal working nevertheless reached a significant level of development and its products spread over a wide area. This culture had links both with the Eastern Mediterranean and with the Black Sea–Caspian steppes.

In these same steppes, the Early Bronze Age is distinguished by significant integration and the interdependence of cattle-raising groups with the southern agricultural centres. The development of migratory forms of stock-raising led to a considerably more extensive settlement of the steppe. From being something which separated, the steppe became something which united. The rapid growth in population and in numbers of stock and the need for more extensive pastureland, agricultural produce, metal and other vital resources, stimulated the emergence of large and quite powerful, although somewhat unstable, tribal unions. They had active contacts with each other and formed enormous cultural and historical regions. The first of these was the shaft-and-chamber area which, at its height, embraced a vast tract of steppe and forest steppe from the Urals and the Caspian region in the east to the Dniester in the west, with the intrusion of individual groups into the Balkan and the Danube region (Merpert, 1974, 1982). It is chiefly represented by its funerary monuments. Settlements are extremely rare. A number of the Chalcolithic steppe elements went into its formation. Their integration is linked with the spread of large nomadic groups from the eastern part of the area (the Volga, the Don and Ciscaucasia). Within the area, several territorial variants can be distinguished, united by a number of common features, such as the absolute predominance of *kurgan* burials, bodies buried individually in a hunched position and scattered with ochre, the small number of grave goods, the characteristic round-bottomed (and later also flat-bottomed) pottery with incised, stamped and, later, corded ornamentation, the spread of wooden carts with solid wheels and monumental stone anthropomorphic stelae. These cultures developed from the end of the fourth to the first centuries of the second millennium BC. On the territories adjacent to the agricultural cultures (the Dnieper and Don regions), individual tribes using shaft and chamber graves established themselves and created fortified settlements with a complex cattle-raising and agricultural economy (Lagodovska, Shaposhnikova and Makarevich, 1952). In the remainder of the steppe, migratory stock-raising was predominant. There was little metal working in the early stages and it is represented by small artefacts made of pure copper. In the late stages, large axes, celts and daggers became widespread, made of arsenical bronze.

The progress of individual groups of shaft-and-chamber makers in the various stages of their development in the Danube region and the Balkans played a definite role in the cultural and ethnic history of that region (Dimitrescu, 1963; Ecsedy, 1979; Iovanovič, 1979; Gimbutas, 1973; Panajitov and Degračov, 1984). In the forest steppe regions of the Carpathians, Podolia, Volynia, and the middle reaches of the Dnieper, the shaft-and-chamber tribes came into contact with the founders of the corded ware and battleaxe cultures and exercised a definite influence on them (Merpert, 1976). This concerned primarily the culture in the middle and upper reaches of the Dnieper, the sub-Carpathian region on the upper Dniester and Gorodsko-Zdolbitska and Stzhizhovska in Volynia. Further to the east, it is not impossible that the shaft-and-chamber tribes played a part in the formation and subsequent development of the Maikop culture of the northern Caucasus and also of the steppe cultures of the Ural region and southern Siberia.

In the late stages within the shaft-and-chamber cultural and historical area, the differentiation and isolation of individual territorial variants increased considerably. In general, the cultures of this area were the most important foundation for the whole of the subsequent development of the Bronze Age on the steppes and forest steppe of eastern Europe.

THE MIDDLE BRONZE AGE

The Middle Bronze Age included the end of the third and a large part of the first half of the second millennium BC. Typical of this phase was the spread of arsenical bronze to the steppe and forest steppe areas and of bronze made with tin into the Carpathians. The main centre for the production of arsenical bronze was still the Caucasus. The western or Carpathian centre was distinguished by considerable activity. Both centres continued to exercise influence on vast adjacent territories where a number of centres were established in turn. One of them, the Black Sea centre, came into being in the steppe areas round the Black Sea, the Don and the Azov Sea. It was influenced both by the Carpathian and by the Caucasian centres but itself also influenced them (Chernykh, 1978, p. 67). The second centre, Poltavkin, came into being in the middle and lower reaches of the Volga. Towards the end of the Middle Bronze Age, the isolation of the centres increased. Correspondingly, the cultural contacts within the circum-Pontinc zone, which at the beginning of this stage was still fully intact, weakened considerably towards its end, which led to the zone's economic decline.

In the technology of axe-casting, the changeover was finally made from open two-leafed moulds to covered moulds, the metal being poured in through a special pouring gate. Artefacts improved and their variety increased.

The development of the northern Caucasus took on very specific forms (I restrict myself to the features characteristic of the European part of the Caucasian region). In its western part, the Dolmen culture had spread. It is distinguished mainly by megalithic tombs or dolmens (Markovin, 1978). The dead were inhumed in a hunched position, individually to begin with but later in mass graves. Grave goods, in addition to pottery and stoneware, included bronze axes and daggers. The culture developed from the end of the third to the third quarter of the second millennium BC. Its origin is debatable. There is an interesting theory that a Mediterranean population may have migrated here by sea.

Over a considerable territory, from the region round the Kuban to the borders of Dagestan, lay the north Caucasian cultural and historical area which united no less than five related cultures (Markovin, 1960), represented mainly by individual *kurgan* burials with a large array of stone, ceramic and bronze grave goods. The culture went on developing even in the Late Bronze Age and during its development the influence of the steppe cultures increased.

Further east, in Dagestan, a particular culture of the Middle Bronze Age developed from the end of the third to the first half of the second millennium BC. It is represented by settlements with stone houses, both rectangular and round, and by burials in pits covered by a stone and in catacombs, and sometimes by collective graves with grave goods particularly rich in metal artefacts – in some cases up to 1,500 items. The economy of all these cultures was based on stock-raising and agriculture, with stock-raising predominant.

In the steppes of the Black Sea and Caspian areas, the differentiation of the shaft-and-chamber cultural and historical area, the redistribution of the population and the appearance of new groups and of new metallurgical centres and sources of influence led to a considerable cultural transformation. In the steppe and forest steppe regions of the Don area, the Azov Sea and northern Black Sea regions, at the end of the third millennium BC, a number of stock-raising cultures developed with closely related forms of a specific burial structure – catacombs – and some elements of material culture (stone battleaxes and clubs, bronze axes and ornaments). They formed the catacomb cultural and historical area (Popova, 1955), within which no less than five separate cultures have now been identified (Bratchenko, 1976; Bratchenko and Shaposhnikova, 1985). These cultures were distinguished by the shape of the catacombs, the position of the corpses (with bodies hunched or extended) and particularly by the type of vessel. The majority of the vessels are flat-bottomed, frequently with corded ornamentation, but there are also round-bottomed vessels, reminiscent of the shaft-and-chamber culture forms.

The chief influences in the establishment of this system were those of the Caucasus in the east and of the corded-ware cultures in the west, although a number of shaft-and-chamber cultural traditions were retained at the same time.

In their turn, the cultures of the catacomb area exercised a considerable influence on the vast adjacent steppe and forest steppe and further afield in the forest zone. In the east, in the middle and lower reaches of the Volga, this found expression in the establishment of the syncretic Poltavkin culture which combined and transformed shaft-and-chamber culture and catacomb elements. In the west and north-west, the catacomb cultures interacted with the middle Dnieper culture and the corded-ware cultures of Podolia, Volynia and the Carpathian region which, at that period, were in their prime. A very important contact zone was established there, linking the steppe with the main body of the cultures of the Middle Bronze Age of central Europe and the Balkan–Danube region.

In the late Middle Bronze Age (second quarter of the second millennium BC) there was a certain regrouping of the population, the forest steppe groups becoming notably more active. In the Dnieper region and in the area between the Dnieper and the Don, the formation of a stock-raising and agricultural culture with multi-ridged ceramic ware is associated with this, and in the area between the Don and the Volga, with the formation of the Abashevo culture which later spread right up to the southern Ural region, where its population founded its own metallurgical centre, using local ores.

In the Middle Bronze Age, there was a sharp change in the development of the forest zone too, where, until then, Neolithic traditions had persisted. This was brought about both by the cultural progress of the local population and by the arrival there of large groups with a metal-using economy. At the end of the third and the beginning of the second millennia BC, in the Baltic area, corded ware and battleaxe (boat-axe) cultures made their appearance, the members of which were familiar both with stock-raising and with the rudiments of agriculture. Their mutual assimilation with the descendants of the local late Neolithic cultures was a most important factor in the cultural and ethnic history of the region.

At that period, a large population group belonging to the corded-ware culture penetrated eastwards and settled in the Volga Valley, where two extremely similar cultures developed – the Fatyanovo and the Balanovo. The territory of the first took in the upper reaches of the Volga and the area between the Volga and the Oka and the second, the middle reaches of the Volga and the area to the east of the Volga as far as the Vyatka. With the arrival of the Fatyanovo and Balanovo tribes, forest stock-raising developed here and, possibly, slash-and-burn agriculture. The Fatyanovo culture is represented in the main by flat-grave burial grounds with wooden constructions and individual burials in a hunched position with a rich array of grave goods, such as round-bottomed vessels with corded ornamentation, stone battleaxes and celts, copper axes, spears and ornaments. Graves similar to the Fatyanovo have been found in the Balanovo culture, and also settlements, sometimes fortified with earthworks (Bader and Khalikov, 1987). There was possibly also a Balanovo metallurgical centre (Chernykh, 1966).

The Fatyanovo and Balanovo population, having substantially influenced the cultural development of this part of the forest zone, itself was subject to increasingly strong influences from outside until it was completely assimilated by new communities already belonging to the Late Bronze Age.

THE LATE BRONZE AGE

The period of mass migration and of the destruction of cultural systems that marked the end of the Middle Bronze Age in eastern Europe at the conclusion of the second quarter of the second millennium BC was succeeded by a period in which new metallurgical centres and major cultural communities came into being. It marked the beginning of the Late Bronze Age, which lasted here until 900–800 BC and was distinguished by the very great variety and spread of bronze artefacts, by the predominance of tin-based bronze and by the further improvement of technology, which included the wholesale casting of thin-walled implements using the so-called 'blind' core, and of celts and spearheads (Chernykh, 1978). There was a sharp increase in the number of metal-working centres. They were grouped in three newly formed metallurgical provinces: the Eurasian, the Caucasian and the European. The first took in the steppe region from the Dnieper as far as the Yenisey and was brought about by the cultural and economic consolidation of migratory stock-raising groups, which played an important part in general cultural integration in this vast territory. In the west, in the Dnieper region and the north-west Black Sea area, it bounded the European province, which included the Balkan and Danube region, and also exercised an active influence on the steppe. In the Dnieper region, a contact zone was established where the influences of both provinces combined, with increasing activity on the part of the eastern Volga-Urals centres. This led to the active interplay of cultural phenomena which had originally been distinct and to general integrationist processes. The third metallurgical province, the Caucasian, underwent fundamental changes in the Late Bronze Age in the siting and nature of specific centres, in the range of artefacts and in technology. Here, tin-based bronze was widespread. Artistic casting, using a wax model and multi-leafed moulds, reached a very high degree of development. However, the influence of this major centre on the adjoining European territories declined sharply, which ties in with the general trend towards the isolation of the main cultural groupings in the Late Bronze Age.

One of the fundamentally new and most outstanding phenomena of the Late Bronze Age in Eurasia was the spread, in the sixteenth and fifteenth centuries BC, of groups of horse-borne warriors and metal workers who have left, in the forest steppe and forest area, remains of the Seima-Turbino type, represented by a number of necropolises and sanctuaries. Some of the human remains in a number of the burial grounds have been destroyed as a result of ritual acts by hostile communities. A high proportion of the grave goods consists of bronze weapons such as celts, spears and daggers. Analysis of the shapes and materials of the artefacts has shown that one of the main components originated in the mountains and foothills of the Altai with their mineral deposits. The second component is linked with the Siberian lands which lie between the Yenisey and Lake Baikal. As it penetrated westwards, this syncretic culture incorporated new elements, primarily from the Urals. Their rapid and far-reaching spread was made possible by their sophisticated weaponry and well-developed horsemanship. In eastern Europe, they penetrated as far as the Oka in the west and the Pechora in the north; their artefacts are found from Mongolia to Moldavia and their technological discoveries exercised a decisive influence on the whole subsequent development of metallurgy in both the forest and the steppe zones.

Further to the south, in the Black Sea and Caspian steppes and forest steppes, the Late Bronze Age was marked by the emergence and development of gigantic cultural communities, within which settled groups in the forest steppes and river floodplains combined with the nomadic stock-breeders of the open steppe. Chief of these occupied the 'timber-frame' cultural territory from the southern Urals to the right bank of the Dnieper and even as far as the Driester. Its original nucleus was formed in the sixteenth to fifteenth centuries BC in the eastern part of the area and was founded on late shaft-and-chamber culture, with Poltavkin and Abashevo elements. As it spread westwards, the culture combined with the local substrate of the Don region, the northern Donets, the Asov Sea region and the Dnieper region and with the population of the catacomb cultures, the multi-ridged ceramic culture and so on. These developments, together with the natural and historic conditions of each region, led to the formation of a number of specific cultures within the 'timber-frame' area, the material culture of which retained a number of common features, principally burial customs. In the late stage of the development of the timber-frame area, the individuality of the cultures that had emerged within its boundaries increased sharply, bringing an end to this phenomenon in the ninth century BC.

Timber-frame culture remains consist of settlements, graves and hoards of metal artefacts and moulds for casting. The settlements are sometimes fortified. The houses were partly dug into the ground and were of wooden, and more rarely of stone, construction. Burials were in *kurgans* and sometimes in flat graves. The constructions in the pits were frequently of wooden beams (timber-frame chambers). The skeletons were hunched and laid on their sides with their wrists in front of their faces. In isolated instances, the corpses were cremated. In the tombs, animal bones are frequent and include the skulls of bulls and horses. The vessels are flat-bottomed with incised and stamped geometrical ornamentation. Among the bronze artefacts are tools (sickles, axes, celts and knives), weapons (socketed spears and daggers), and decorations (pendants and bracelets). The metal came from various deposits in the Eurasian province. Traces of local metal working are found throughout the region of the timber-frame culture. (Fig. 69)

Within the boundaries of the timber-frame culture region, but in the contact zone on the right bank of the Dnepr, there emerged the Sabatinovka culture in the fourteenth to twelfth centuries BC (Berezanskaya and Sharafutdinova, 1985), in which timber-frame cultural features are combined with strong influences from the Balkan-Danube cultures and the European metallurgical province. Its place was taken by a culture of a syncretic nature – the Belozersk culture of the end of the twelfth to the ninth century BC – which was the final stage of the whole timber-frame cultural and historical area (Otroshchenko, 1985).

The main source of western and south-western influence on the north Black Sea region was the north Balkan Noua culture of the thirteenth to the twelfth centuries BC, which had spread right up to the forest steppe of Moldavia and the right bank of the Dniester.

A number of cultures of the Late Bronze Age in the forest steppe, right up to the southern part of the forest area, were linked with the descendants of the population of the corded-ware cultures and with the transformation of their traditions. These include the Komarovo culture of the middle and upper reaches of the Dniester and the Trzciniec culture of the western regions of the Ukraine and Belarus (Artemenko, 1987), the Belogrudovo culture of the forest steppe on the right bank in the Ukraine (Berezanskaya, 1985b), and the Sosnitsa culture of the middle and upper reaches of the Dnieper (Artemenko, 1987).

Another group of important cultures from the north of the forest steppe and the south of the forest zone was influenced by the timber-frame cultural area and its direct penetration northwards, and with reciprocal assimilation with the local population. These include the Bondarikha culture of the territory between the Dnieper and the Don, the Pozdniakovo culture of the upper reaches of the Volga and the upper and middle Oka (Bader; Popova, 1987), and the Kazan area culture of the middle reaches of the Volga and the middle and lower Kama.

In the eastern Baltic area in the second half of the second millennium BC, there were still a number of Neolithic traditions living on, but by the end of the second and the beginning of the first millennium BC agriculture and stock-raising had become dominant, metal working, which had emerged in the Middle Bronze Age, became widespread, and fortified settlements were established. Flat graves were typical to begin with, the bodies being either inhumed or cremated. *Kurgans* made their appearance later, both types of burial still being found.

In the northern part of the forest region, the persisting predominance of assimilating economies and of Neolithic traditions were associated in the second millennium and the beginning of the first millennium BC with the appearance of metal artefacts and the establishment of local metal-working centres on the White Sea coast, in Karelia, the Onega and Ladoga regions and in the Pechora basin (Oshibkina, 1987).

Finally, at the extreme south-east of eastern Europe, in the northern Caucasus, the local metallurgical centre, despite a number of changes and the weakening of contacts with the steppe, reached the height of its power. General cultural development can be seen both in the continued development of the communities that had emerged earlier, and in the introduction of significant new cultures, primarily that of Koban. This emerged in the twelfth to eleventh centuries

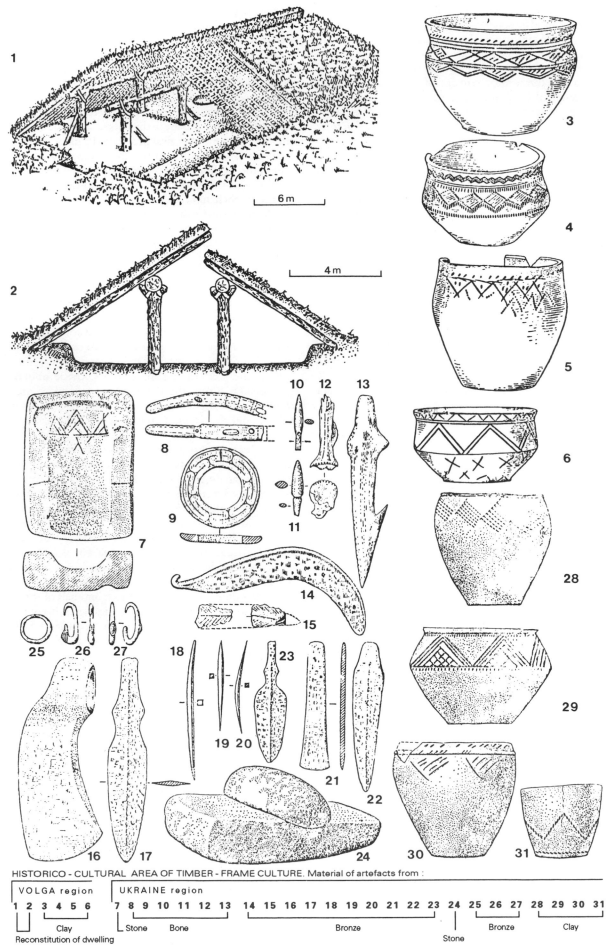

Figure 69 Historico-cultural area of timber-frame culture. Materials of artefacts from Volga region and Ukraine.

BC in the mountain regions of northern Ossetia and spread in the first quarter of the first millennium BC to the whole of the central part of the northern Caucasus, continuing to develop in the Early Iron Age right up to the sixth century BC. It is represented by settlements, tombs and hoards (Krupnov, 1960). The settlements are in places which are difficult of access and are sometimes fortified with ditches. Houses with stone foundations, potteries and bronze foundries, as well as sanctuaries, have been found there. The tombs are of the flat-grave type and, more rarely, under *kurgans*. The dead are buried in stone coffins, singly, on their sides in a hunched position. Skeletons or individual bones of horses have been found next to them. The range of grave goods is very large (including clay and bronze vessels, bronze axes, spears, daggers, belts, tins, bracelets and fibulae). The clay vessels have a black glaze with incised ornamentation. The bronze artefacts are decorated with geometrical, animal and anthropomorphic engraving. The metallurgy was based on local deposits of copper, arsenic, lead and antimony, while tin was brought in from Transcaucasia. Stock-breeding was the mainstay of the economy, although in the mountain foothills an arable agriculture developed, using draught animals for ploughing.

Further east, in Dagestan and the adjacent Checheno-Ingush regions in the thirteenth to the ninth centuries BC, the Kayakent-Khorochaya culture developed, similar in level to the Koban culture and, like it, associated with a definite cultural levelling and with the emergence of its own metal-working centre. It is represented by burials in stone coffins. The skeletons, either in a hunched or sitting position, were accompanied by vessels ornamented in relief and by decorations made of bronze and antimony (Markovin, 1969).

In the second half of the second millennium BC, in the north-western Black Sea area, in the steppe region and in the Caucasus, isolated iron artefacts have been found. Nevertheless, only from the second quarter of the first millennium BC did iron begin to be the main material in human productive activity, thus making it possible to speak of the beginning of the Early Iron Age.

BIBLIOGRAPHY

ARTEMENKO, I. I. 1985. Srednedneprovskaya kultura [The Culture of the Middle Dnieper]. *Arheol. ukr.* (Kiev), Vol. I.

—— 1987. *Kultury pozdnego bronzovogo veka yuzhnoy polosy lesov Evropeyskoy chasti SSSR* [Cultures of the Late Bronze Age in the Southern Forest Zone of the European Part of the USSR]. In: KRAYNOV, D. V., KOSAREV, M. F. (eds.), *Epoha bronzy lesnoy polosy SSR. Arheol. SSSR.* (Moscow).

BADER, O. N.; KHALIKOV, A. C. 1987. Balanovskaya Kultura In: *Epoha bronzy lesnoy polosy SSSR. Arheol. SSSR.* (Moscow).

BADER, O. N.; POPOVA, T. B. 1987. Pozdniacovskaya kultura [The Pozdnyakovo Culture]. In: *Epocha bronzy lesnoy polosi SSSR* [The Bronze Age of the Forest Zone of the USSR]. Moscow.

BRATCHENKO, S. N. 1976. *Nizhnee Podon'e v epohu sredney bronzy* [The Lower Don in the Middle Bronze Age]. Kiev.

BRATCHENKO, S. N.; SHAPOSHNIKOVA, O. G. 1985. Katakombnaya kulturnoistoricheskaya obshchchnost' [The Catacomb Cultural and Historical Community]. *Arheol. ukr.* (Kiev), Vol. I.

CHERNYKH, E. N. 1966. *Istoriya drevneyshey metallurgii Vostochnoy Evropy* [The History of the Earliest Metallurgy in Eastern Europe]. Moscow.

—— 1976. Metallurgische Bereiche der Jüngeren und Späten Bronzezeit in der USSR. *J. Indo-Eur. Stud.* (Washington, D.C.)

—— 1978. Metallurgicheskie provintsii i periodizatsiya epohi rannego metalla na territorii SSR [Metallurgical Provinces and Dating of the Early Metalworking Period on the Territory of the USSR]. *Sov. Arheol.* (Moskva), No. 4.

—— 1980. Metallurgical Provinces of the 5th-2nd Millennia BC in Eastern Europe in Relation to the Process of Indo-Europeanization. *J. Indo-Eur. Stud.* (Washington, D.C.), Vol. 8, No. 3/4.

DIMITRESCU, V. 1973. A propos d'une nouvelle synthèse concernant l'époque néo-énéolithique du Sud-Est et Centre-Est de l'Europe. *Dacia* (Bucharest), N.S., Vol. 17.

ECSEDY, I. 1979. *The People of the Pit-Grave Kurgans in Eastern Hungary*. Budapest.

GIMBUTAS, M. 1973. Old Europe c. 7000–3500 BC: The Earliest European Civilization Before the Infiltration of the Indo-European Peoples. *J. Indo-Eur. Stud.* (Washington, D.C.), Vol. 1, No. 1.

JOVANOVIC, B. 1979. Indoevropljani i eneolitski period Jugoslavije [The Indo-European and Eneolithic Age of Yugoslavia]. In: GARAŠANIN, M. V. (ed.), *Praistorija jugoslavskih zemalja*. Sarajevo. Vol. 3, pp. 27–54.

KÓSKO, A. 1985. Influences of the 'Pre-Yamnaya' ('Pre-Pitgrave') Communities from the Black Sea Steppe Area in Western European Cultures. In: KOZLOWSKI, J. K.; MACHNIK, J. (eds), *L'énéolithique et le début de l'âge du bronze dans certaines régions de l'Europe*. Krakow.

KRUPNOV, E. I. 1960. *Drevnyaya istoriya Severnogo Kavkaza* [The Ancient History of the Northern Caucasus]. Moscow.

MARKOVIN, V. I. 1960. *Kultura plemen Severnogo Kavkaza v epochu bronzy* [The Culture of Tribes of the Northern Caucasus in the Bronze Age]. Moscow. (Mat. issled. arheol. SSSR, 63).

—— 1969. *Dagestan i gornaya Chechnya v drevnosti* [Dagestan and the Mountains of Chechnya in Antiquity]. Moscow.

—— 1978. *Dolmen Zapadnogo Kavkaza* [The Dolmens of the Western Caucasus]. Moscow.

MASSON, V. I.; MERPERT, N. J. (eds) 1982. *Eneolit SSSR* [The Eneolithic Age of the USSR]. Moscow.

MERPERT, N. Y. 1974. *Drevneyshie skotovody Volzhsho-Ural'skogo mezhdurech'ya* [Early Herdsmen of the Volga-Ural Interfluvial Region]. Moscow.

—— 1976. Drevneyamnaya kulturno-istoricheskaya oblast'i voprosy formirovaniya kultur shnurovoy keramiki [The Pit-Grave Cultural and Historical Arca and the Formation of the Corded-Ceramic Culture]. In: *Vostochnaya Evropa v epohu kamnya i bronzy*. Moscow.

MOORA, K. A. 1964. *K voprosu o vozniknovenii Pribaltiyskoy istoriko kulturnoy oblasti* [Origin of the Baltic Historical and Cultural Area]. Moscow.

MUNCHAEV, R. M. 1975. *Kavkaz na zare bronzovogo veka* [The Caucasus at the Dawn of the Bronze Age]. Moscow.

—— 1982. Eneolit Kavkaza [The Eneolithic Age of the Caucasus]. In: MASSON, V. I.; MERPERT, N. J. (eds), *Eneolit SSSR* [The Eneolithic Age of the USSR]. Moscow.

OSHIBKINA, S. V. 1987. Eneolit i bronzovyj vek severa Evropeyskoy casti SSSR [The Eneolithic and Bronze Age in the North of the European Part of the USSR]. In: *Epoha bronzy lesnoy polosy SSSR* [The Bronze Age of the Forest Zone of the USSR]. Moscow.

OSTROSHCHENKO, V. V. 1985. Belozerskaya kultura [The Belozersk Culture]. *Arheol. ukr.* (Kiev), Vol. I.

PANAJOTOV, I.; DERAGČOV, V. 1984. Die Ockergrabkultur in Bulgarien (Darstellung des Problems). *Stud. Praest.* (Sofia), Vol. 7, pp. 99–116.

POPOVA, T. B. 1955. *Plemena katakombnoy kulturi* [The Tribes of the Catacomb Culture]. Moscow.

VASILIEV, I. B. 1980. Eneolit Povolzh'ya. Step'i lesostep' [The Chalcolithic in the Volga Region; Steppe and forest-steppe. In: *Eneolit Vostochnojy Evropy* [The Eneolithic Age of Eastern Europe]. Kuibyshev.

14.6

WESTERN EUROPE

Jacques Briard

THE ATLANTIC BRONZE AGE

Western Europe in the Bronze Age was characterized by a cultural and economic entity that can be called the Atlantic Bronze culture. This does not preclude Mediterranean influences, in the Iberian peninsula in particular, and constant interaction with influences from central Europe. One of the foundations of Atlantic prosperity was the existence of metal ores – copper (Ireland, Cornwall, Asturias), tin (Cornwall, Brittany, Spain), gold (Ireland) and lead, which sometimes contained silver (Spain and Brittany). These metals were bartered all along the coast of the Channel (which was like an inland sea) as were the finished products: axes, swords, ornaments, jewels made from gold or Baltic amber and, in the Late Bronze Age, cauldrons or bronze shields from Ireland. People from the Mediterranean came in search of the tin from the Cassiterides, the 'tin-bearing isles', and gave in exchange precious products such as glass beads, which were soon imitated locally. As witness to the means by which the bartering was done, the remains of a wooden boat have been excavated at North Ferriby in the sands of the Humber and cargoes of bronze which sunk as a result of shipwrecks have been recovered from the sea near Dover and Plymouth in the south of England.

The appearance of metal in Atlantic Europe, which dates back to the end of the third millennium BC, was accompanied by changes in religious and funerary customs. The custom of individual burials was spread by the 'corded-ware' civilizations (pottery decorated with cord ornament), under the influence of groups from northern Europe. Cultural entities such as the bell-beaker culture spread knowledge of the first metals, with small gold jewellery items and copper axes and daggers, although they never produced a very wide range of artefacts. The discovery of bronze, an alloy of copper and tin, marked the real beginning of metal working and of the Bronze Age, a particularly active period in Atlantic Europe.

In the first stage of the Atlantic Bronze Age brilliant princely civilizations developed on both sides of the Channel, succeeded by pastoralists and workers in metals with an intense production that enables us to follow their development. The Atlantic Bronze Age developed between 2000 and 800 BC, the period when it was at its zenith being followed by a crisis caused by the appearance of iron, which shattered the Western economic circuits based on the mining of tin and the distribution of bronze objects.

The Chalcolithic

The period of transition from the Neolithic to the Bronze Age saw the appearance of new groups, some of which, like the Artenacians, have only recently been discovered. In 1962 a burial grotto was explored at Artenac in the commune of Saint-Mary, Charente, in west-central France. Flint daggers and arrowheads were found alongside the skeletons, together with pieces of an unusual style of pottery with turned-up handles, which were referred to as 'nose-shaped'. This facies has been identified in Aquitaine and also in the Paris basin, at the fortified site of Fort-Harrouard. These groups were mainly agricultural, growing wheat and barley and raising cattle, sheep and pigs. They played an important role in trade, particularly exporting flint blades, and metal was only of minor importance in their economy. The chronological position of the Artenacian has been discussed at length. Initially held to be a 'Bronze Age' without bronze, it is now seen as a Chalcolithic civilization which developed between 2400 and 2200 BC, a view which is confirmed by radiocarbon datings (2300–2040 BC).

A variant of the Artenacian in northern France, the Gord group, derives its name from a settlement to the south of Compiègne, on the Oise. The ceramic forms differ slightly from those of the Artenacian although small pots with four lugs are also found there. The Gord group succeeded the Seine–Oise–Marne civilization but predated those groups such as the Beaker groups which were familiar with copper.

In fact, the Beaker groups were crucial in the formation of the European Bronze Age. Inverted bell-shaped pottery of very high quality, often accompanied by small copper objects, was noticed at an early date in burials throughout Europe. Around 1930, G. Childe developed the idea that they were the burials of itinerant groups which spread metal working throughout Europe. Spanish writers thought that the centre of the Iberian peninsula was the point of departure for this phenomenon, migratory groups setting out from there for north-western Europe. E. Sangmeister (1963) developed a more complex theory in 1961, according to which an initial migratory movement northwards was succeeded by a period of intermixing with the groups of northern Europe and then by a reflux which took from the Netherlands to the south of France more recent types of pottery developed as a result of that intermixing. These theories of population movement have now been jettisoned. One now thinks more in terms of cultural or economic influence, of movements of ideas and manufactured objects rather than of itinerant peoples. In any case, more detailed analysis of the groups concerned has revealed great regional variety and several different chronological sequences.

In northern Europe the bell shape derived from the local types of ceramic, the protruding foot-beakers (PFB). These gave rise to several types of beakers, some of which were all-over ornamented (AOO), the others all-over corded (AOC).

Dutch writers place these series well before the second millennium BC on the basis of radiocarbon datings (2190 BC from Anlo in the Netherlands). From the Netherlands the AOO and AOC wares spread into lower Saxony and Westphalia before reaching Belgium and northern and eastern France. They are found in individual burials and re-used dolmens. The influence of these types of ornamentation can be seen as far away as the south of France (La Halliade, Hautes-Pyrénées) (Fig. 70). The Dutch groups persisted up to the beginning of the Old Bronze Age, with squat-looking beakers and 'contracted' ornamentation. These beakers came from Veluwe, a region in central Netherlands, and have been found in burial mounds together with metal instruments and metal-working tools, small hammers and polished stone abraders.

One type of bell-beaker was so widespread that it is referred to as the 'international type'. These elegant beakers with an S profile, decorated by hatched horizontal bands with oblique lines impressed by means of a comb or cord, have been found from the Iberian peninsula to the Netherlands. They were deposited in individual burials, as at Portejoie (Eure), but they have also been found in re-used dolmens and in gallery graves. Certain megoliths even yielded a most unusual series of bell-shaped pots (Kerbors, Brittany). The Beaker peoples disseminated products of copper metallurgy: tanged daggers, copper awls and small gold pearls. Among the late Iberian groups, such as those at Palmela in Portugal, we find small arrowheads which were exported to most parts of the French Atlantic coast (Palmela points). Flat axes also became more common at that period and were often made of arsenical copper of Iberian origin.

The Beaker folk written about by English and Irish specialists played a considerable role in the British Isles, where there are over a thousand reconstituted pots of this type.

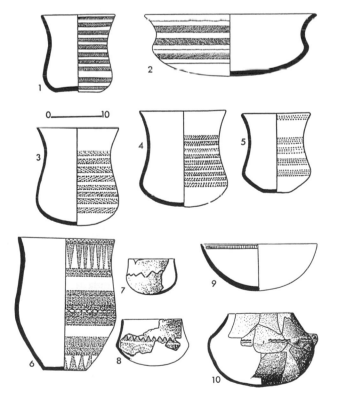

Figure 70 Bell-shaped pottery from France: 1 and 2, Kerbors, Brittany; 3–5, Vendée; 6, pottery with contracted decoration, Wallers, Nord; 7–10, pottery from Artenac, west-central France (drawn by J. Briard).

Alongside the regional types (Wessex, north Britain) we find 'international' and Dutch-style (AOO, AOC) bell-beakers, and a large number of variants developed rapidly and spread widely at the beginning of the Old Bronze Age, the precursor of the Wessex civilization.

The Beaker peoples are connected with individual burials but also with structures in circular ditches. The oldest stage of the famous Stonehenge monument belongs to this category. Beaker settlements are well known in the British Isles, with oval huts such as the one found at Gwithian in Cornwall, which has a double ring of stakes and an entrance with a porch. Some villages indicate the existence of enclosures for animals (Sussex) and the first open-field agricultural systems (Celtic fields). But the wealth of the Beaker folk came from their control of trade, first in flint blades and then in metal goods, leading, even in Britain, to the formation of a ruling caste dominating the agricultural communities descended from the local Neolithic groups.

THE EARLY BRONZE AGE

During the Early Bronze Age, the British Isles witnessed the development of varied civilizations (Burgess, 1980). Some, derived from Neolithic groups, are characterized by pottery with geometrical designs: the food vessels found mainly in Ireland, Scotland and the north of England. These are pastoral populations who buried their dead in cists or cremated them under barrows. Amongst the other pottery groups, those who used a distinctive bell shape form an important element. Copper daggers and gold jewellery are found in the individual tombs of these Beaker people. These groups seem to have played a predominant role in the distribution and control of the first wealth in the form of metals. They were the founders of the Wessex culture, the most important civilization in the Early Bronze Age in the British Isles (Fig. 71). Large tumuli, like Bush Barrow, contain the tombs of petty princes buried with the symbols of their power (sceptres), their swords and daggers made of copper and bronze, sometimes decorated with gold, and their amber and jet jewels. Some types of flanged axes and pins bear witness to contacts with central Europe (Ünětice), while some of the jewels suggest contacts with the Mediterranean. These Wessex princes held sway over other pastoral groups which cremated their dead. At the same period, Ireland was exploiting its copper and gold mines. The most remarkable pieces are the copper daggers and halberds, the axes decorated with geometrical motifs and above all the golden lunulae, diadems or throat-pieces which were exported to the Continent (Brittany, Normandy) and imitated there.

The astronomers' temple at Stonehenge, near Salisbury in Great Britain, consisting of circles and horseshoes of trilithons, shows that sun and moon worship was very important to these populations, who relied for subsistence on agriculture and livestock raising. Metal working was of concern only to the aristocratic part of the population and at the outset metal was reserved exclusively for warlike purposes and for articles of prestige intended to assert the power of the rulers. Objects made of gold, such as the gold cups of Rillaton in Cornwall, Fritzdorf in Germany or Eschenz in Switzerland were exchanged for status reasons. Brittany saw the development of the Armorican Barrow culture, obviously closely akin to that of Wessex: the same type of bronze daggers decorated with gold studs, the same flint arrowheads, the same jewels or precious vessels made of gold or silver

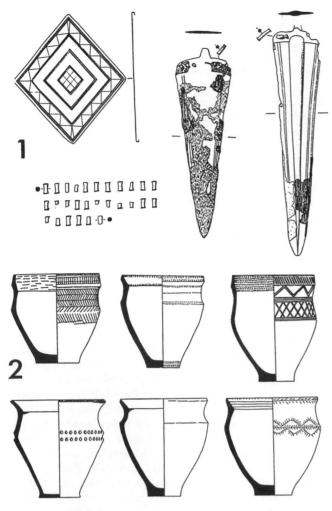

Figure 71 Early Bronze Age in Britain: 1, tumulus at Bush Barrow, Wessex; 2, collared urns, Devizes Museum (after Annable and Simpson, 1964).

(Briard, 1984). The petty lordlings of Armorica were buried under huge barrows in tombs of megalithic stones or, a novelty at that time, wooden coffins. These barrows are fairly spaced out in Armorica, as if they represented the traces of equitable divisions of land. The petty chieftains of the time must have controlled the trade routes, especially those for Baltic amber and locally mined tin. As in Wessex, there was bartering of fine vessels in gold (Ploumilliau) or silver (Saint-Adrien). There is an Iberian component in this early Armorican Bronze Age – the pistil-shaped swords from Carnoët, which are similar to the Argaric type of sword in Spain. Moreover, the presence of silver also confirms the links with the Argaric culture in the south-east of the Iberian peninsula. Side by side with the large barrows, poorer tombs are found, evidence of marked social differences: simple cists or small tombs with very scanty grave goods. An original set of tombs is that containing glass or faience beads. These female tombs on the Isle of Groix in Morbihan, or at Plouhinec in Finistère, contain individual burials. Analysis of the beads, revealing traces of copper and tin, suggests that they were made locally or in Britain on the basis of Mediterranean prototypes. This is the period in which the last big menhirs, which are often dressed to a regular shape, were erected in Brittany. Typical Bronze Age pottery has been found at the foot of some of them (Kerloas, Plouarzel; Finistère). Elements of domestic life are rarer: domesticated animals (sheep

and cattle) have been found in peat-bogs at Plouescat, querns for crushing wheat have been re-utilized in barrows, and pottery with finger-tip decoration has been found. A funerary structure found under the Saint-Jude tumulus at Bourbriac, Côtes d'Armor, shows the existence of wooden-framed houses roofed with thatch and ferns.

The chronology of the Wessex and Armorican cultures has long been a subject of argument. At one time it was thought that the precious vessels found had been imported from western Asia or the eastern Mediterranean and that certain daggers of the Mycenaean type engraved on the stones at Stonehenge were proof that that astronomical monument had been built by architects from the Aegean. Recent radiocarbon datings, particularly in Brittany, have made it possible to assign this stage of princely tumuli to about 2000–1600 BC.

A somewhat meagre Early Bronze Age developed in the Netherlands, derived from the bell-beaker cultures, with decorated beakers (of the Veluwe type) and some objects imported from central Europe, such as the little triangular dagger with the handle decorated with tin studs at Bargeroosterveld (De Laet, 1982). The tumuli are associated with complicated structures with shrines surrounded by post circles. At the end of the Early Bronze Age, large urns were used in which the bones of the cremated dead were deposited (the Hilversum type).

The Iberian peninsula remained under the influence of the bell-beaker culture which marked the end of the third millennium BC (Los Millares). However, the Argaric culture, with Mediterranean affinities, developed in the southeast of the peninsula. The site which gives its name to the culture is a fortified hilltop on the northern bank of the Rio Antas. It contained a cemetery of about a thousand burials, which was studied by L. Siret in 1913. Other sites on high ground have been found over a range of some 300 km from Granada to Murcia (Coles and Harding, 1979): El Oficio, Ifre, Zapata, Bastada de Totana. Excavations have taken place recently at Cerro de la Virgen, revealing circular huts with facings with double posts and wattle. H. Schubart has classified the grave goods found at El Argar into two stages: stage A comprises cists with copper and bronze halberds and daggers, stone wristguards for archers, V-perforated bone buttons and little sagging-based vessels. The B stage sees the appearance, side by side with cist burials, of a majority of a new type of burial in which the remains of the dead are contained in big pottery jars. More sophisticated daggers, with four rivets, axes, and silver diadems with a small frontal plate accompany them. The pottery imitates the shapes of the metal vessels with chalice-shaped cups; the jewellery includes spirals of bronze, gold and silver. The impact of the Mediterranean can be seen in the importation of glass beads (Fuente Alamo). At a more developed stage, the El Argar metal workers produced large swords which were distributed as far away as the north-west of the Iberian peninsula in places like Entrambasaguas and Cuevallusa, Santander. Ornamental blades were even mounted in hilts made of gold (Guadalajara). These blades were distributed as far away as the southeast of France. It is probable that one of the sources of wealth of the Argaric world was the local exploitation of silver-bearing lead, but the agricultural and pastoral activities of these populations should not be underestimated. There are traces of irrigation ditches at La Virgen and water cisterns were constructed on the fortified site of El Oficio. Other regions in the Iberian peninsula were fairly prosperous in the Early Bronze Age. A group in the south-east with burials in circular stone enclosures was recognized by H. Schubart (Atalaia, Beja). Copper mines were exploited early in the Rio Tinto (Rotenberg and Freijero, 1981) in the south-west and then in the north in Galicia and Asturias (De Blas Cortina, 1983), and enabled the production of flat axes and ingots (Gamonedo) which, on analysis, showed arsenical copper in their composition. These Iberian arsenical coppers were distributed in the Early Bronze Age all along the Atlantic coast of France from the Gironde to Normandy.

THE MIDDLE BRONZE AGE

The Middle Bronze Age in western Europe is characterized by a decline in long-distance contacts such as those established with the Mediterranean world. The luxurious princely tombs disappeared and a degree of regionalization set in with, in particular, a growth in the importance of pottery facies. However, metal working was to make enormous progress and the production of series of articles with specific regional features resulted in the setting-up of innovative workshops which were to compete with one other.

In the British Isles the tradition of urn burial continued, some of the urns having their edges reinforced by a sort of decorated flange, which gave them the name of 'overhanging-rim urns'. This fashion of burial urns also developed in the Netherlands with the Drakenstein urns, characterized by a horseshoe decorative motif which served as a handle. It reached north-west France. Thus J. C. Blanchet (1984) defined the Eramecourt type, characterized by cinerary urns with arc-shaped motifs buried under tumuli as at Eramecourt (Somme) or sometimes surrounded by circular ditches as at Pontavert, Aisne (Fig. 72). This last burial contained a metal item in the form of a small socketed tool. The fashion for cinerary urns reached Brittany, where they are to be found where megalithic monuments have been re-used (Colpo, Morbihan) or in the circular ditch structures like that of the Chapelle-de-l'Iff at Languenan, Côtes d'Armor, radiocarbon dated at 3030 ± 70 years BC (Gif-5564).

In Armorica the last tumuli are also elevated, sometimes in considerable concentrations in interior zones like the Monts d'Arrhée and inland Morbihan. The tombs are dry-stone vaults covered with a slab and a small mound protecting an individual dagger grave with an urn, the most characteristic being a biconical ceramic vessel with four handles.

In the centre-west of France, influences from the east had an impact in conjunction with the central European barrow culture. J. Gomez defined this facies on the basis of material collected in the Duffaits cave at La Rochette in Charente, which has been under excavation since 1980 (Gomez, 1980). The pottery includes basins, bowls and jugs, some of which are decorated by means of the chip-carving techniques of the Hügelgraberkultur, with excised motifs in which the geometrical ornamentation is set in relief by removing the surrounding slip (Fig. 73). This influence from the east, penetrating as far as the centre-west of France, may be explained by the search for new ores. Some groups of metals from this period have a considerable proportion of nickel in the copper, which could indicate that it originated in the Alps. However, apart from the purely economic factors, cultural influences which reached France by way of the Rhine, the Rhône, the Seine and the Loire, also begin to take effect.

One of the innovations in research in the last few years has been the recognition of agrarian habitats and structures, an area of study which has been particularly well developed in the British Isles. The studies of A. Fleming in the

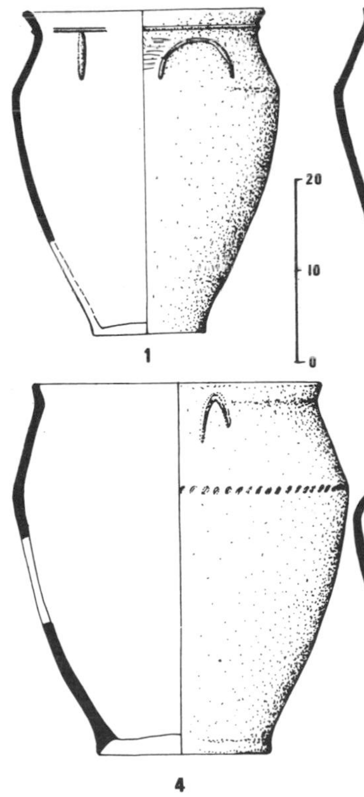

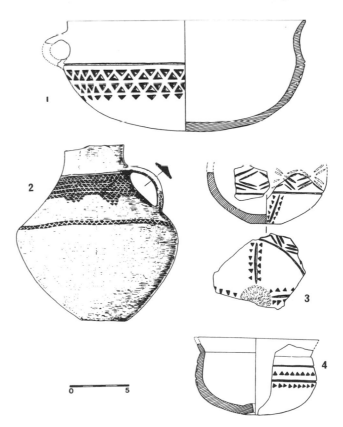

Figure 72 Middle Bronze urns, Eramecourt group, France. 1, Croucy; 2, Bucy-le-Long; 3, Compiègne; 4, Mezières-sur-Seine (drawn by J. Briard).

Figure 73 Middle Bronze excised pottery from west central France. 1, Rancogne; 2, Les Duffaits; 3 and 4, Bois-du-Roc (after Gomez, 1980).

Dartmoor area, and of C. Burgess in the Cheviots and Northumberland afford remarkable examples of the structures known as 'Celtic fields'. Thus, in the Cheviots, terraced agricultural structures, enclosures, field boundaries and round houses in stone enclosures with holes for the posts which supported the wooden roof, have been found. The houses vary from big structures 9–10 m in diameter, sometimes clustered into small villages, to simple, isolated shepherds' huts with cattle enclosures attached. In the region of Dartmoor in south-west England the large boundary banks known as 'reaves' are associated with circular enclosures protecting groups of ten to twenty round houses. Other regions in England (Sussex, Hampshire) and Ireland show the abundance of these systems of fields which are often open, signifying a well-advanced organization of agricultural territory (Fig. 74). Some examples have been noted in Brittany (Brennilis) and in the Netherlands. Agriculture was based essentially on cereals (wheat and barley) and the main domesticated animals were cattle, goats and sheep. It is more difficult to distinguish between the domestic pig and the wild boar. It was from this period on that the horse began to be domesticated in these regions. Hunting made a considerable additional contribution. The search for deer is particularly noteworthy, antlers being valued both for practical applications (mattocks, sleeves for hafting axes) and for ritual uses (amulets for warding off evil). All along the Atlantic and the Channel coasts it has been possible to recognize considerable resources of shells and many provisional hoards of shells or permanent ones (like Le Gurp in Gironde). It was also in the Bronze Age that rational exploitation of sea salt began, as well as attempts to crystallize it in receptacles to facilitate its transport.

In the Netherlands, remarkable finds have been made in the peat-bogs, in Drenthe in particular, such as wooden causeways either in the form of corduroy roads, an arrangement which is found in Somerset in England, or long single-track paths made of planks assembled by various systems. The marshes were used the better to protect the villages but were also places of worship. In Bargeroosterveld a wooden temple has been found and reconstituted. It has been radiocarbon dated to 1295 BC. It included an enclosure of big stones arranged in a circle 6 m in diameter. In the centre, two big pieces of oak served as the base for four pillars which supported lintels in the shape of sacred horns (Bloemers et

al., 1981). This bull or cattle cult was very widespread and a few votive horns made of pottery existed a little later as far away as the east of France (Courtavant). These agrarian cults competed with the sun cults. Golden discs, distant relatives of the celebrated Trundholm sun chariot found in Denmark, have been found in particular in the British Isles (the Lansdown disc in Somerset). In Ireland, these solar discs are sometimes set in pins in the Late Bronze Age, as at Boolybrien, in County Clare (Herity and Eogan, 1977). Other possible sun symbols are golden cones, a sort of sacred betyles, an example of which was found in France at Avanton near Poitiers (Pautreau, 1979). They resemble those found at Schifferstad and Etzelsdorf in Germany, which some authors, such as H. Müller-Karpe, consider to be symbolic flames and which can be dated to the Middle Bronze Age in view of their association with palstaves.

Cave drawings in Ireland, Great Britain, Galicia and Portugal also seem to be related to the sun cult. These are concentric circles, or sometimes spirals, cut in the natural rock and associated with other abstract symbols such as cup-marks and herring-bone patterns; sometimes axes are depicted (Krockmany, County Tyrone; Cairban, Argyll).

The metal industries of the Middle Bronze Age in western Europe began to diversify their production by making new models of flanged axes, followed by palstaves, and big, fairly broad, swords (the Saint-Brandon type in Brittany) or, on the contrary, very narrow ones (the rapiers found in the British Isles). Spearheads were being improved. A special model specific to the British Isles is equipped with two eyelets or two loops on the socket or at the base of the lugs. Different workshops can be distinguished by what they produced. In England there were groups at Arreton Down and then at Acton Park producing looped spearheads, palstaves and rapiers. In Brittany, the Tréboul group produced big swords with a broad base, some gigantic examples being symbolic ceremonial weapons. They were exported to central France (Beaune) and to the Netherlands (Ommerchans).

At the end of the Middle Bronze Age, the production of palstaves intensified and gave rise to multiple exchanges throughout the Atlantic world. In Ireland there were short, stubby models, in Britain and Normandy broad-bladed axes which were often decorated under the stop ridge with trident or shield motifs. In Brittany the axes were narrow and decorated with a raised band down the middle. Solid gold bracelets decorated with geometrical motifs in panels (the Bignan type) were found in association with them. In the centre-west of France, axes with trapezoidal blades were manufactured. In Médoc, long flanged axes were used for a long time, probably until the Middle Bronze Age. In the Iberian peninsula, the Middle Bronze Age long perpetuated the Argaric traditions with swords with pistil-shaped blades but, at the end of the period, the first palstaves, genuinely 'Atlantic' tools, were to appear.

Magnificent objects were also made from gold. Twisted golden torcs come from Ireland (Tara). Examples of these are found on the Continent (Fresné-la-Mer in Normandy; Cesson-Sévigné in Brittany). Solid gold bracelets decorated with geometrical motifs are found in both Brittany and the north-west of the Iberian peninsula. There were developments in this period in the composition of metals. Bronze lost some of its impurities (arsenic), which are replaced by others (nickel). Lead occasionally appeared in these alloys, in Britain in particular. In Brittany, however, it was tin that was used in great quantities at the end of the Middle Bronze Age, lead being then only an unimportant impurity. The

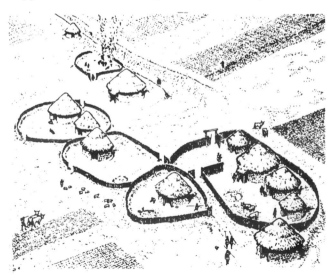

Figure 74 Reconstruction of the settlement at Ilford Hill, Sussex (after Mohen and Baillond, 1987).

alluvial deposits of tin-bearing ores seem to have been exploited to the utmost during this period.

Casting techniques also developed. The first single-valve moulds of the Early Bronze Age were succeeded by two-piece moulds for flanged axes or palstaves, spearheads and so on (Hanvec, Finistère). Copper was stocked in ingots of various shapes: bars, pigs or plano-convex ingots (cakes).

THE LATE BRONZE AGE

Multiple cultural and technical changes were to take place at the beginning of the first millennium BC as a result of the upheavals that occurred in the Mediterranean: the fall of Mycenae and the great classical empires as a result of the invasions of the Sea Peoples. Formerly, from a very 'diffu-sionist' archaeological viewpoint, this was seen as giving rise to an 'urnfield culture' which surged in successive waves from central Europe to the west and south-west. Modern scholarship has somewhat toned down this view, although there is no doubt that a great general movement did affect the Bronze Age cultures. The Atlantic region was not immune to these influences but, in a way, it 'digested' them and adopted some of their features in a process now known as 'acculturation'.

In eastern France, new cultures appeared which often showed traits of the central Europe and barrow cultures. They have often been referred to as 'transitional groups'. Among the best illustrations of this mixed facies are the Colombine burials at Champlay in the Yonne. A hundred tombs were excavated, including a female burial in which a skeleton was found wearing coiled anklets, bronze tubes which must have been dress ornaments, earrings and an elegant piece of jewellery made of a wild boar tusk mounted in a coiled-bronze ornament. Pottery was decorated with wide grooves, a style originating in the German groups of the same period (Riegsee). The transitional groups are characterized by their flanged pins, widespread in eastern France and reaching central France (Chéry, Cher), and poppyhead pins together with new types of sword: the narrow blades found at Rixheim (a site in Alsace) with their distal part consisting of a simple metal tang with rivets. These sword blades were to be imitated by the Atlantic bronzesmiths in the Western group at Rosnoen (the Finistère hoard). The hoards at Rosnoen contained new spearheads with long sockets, massive palstaves and also the first winged axes of the Eastern type. Implements were to become diversified with the first socketed hammers, the first gouges, and chisels with tang and socket. Razors with oval blades and flat tangs appeared, perhaps the sign of a change in fashion, with warriors no longer wearing beards. Similar items were to be found throughout the Atlantic area at the beginning of the Late Bronze Age. In particular, the Iberian peninsula became more closely integrated into the Western community. Occasionally, however, items appear at different times. The finds at La Huerta de Arriba, in the province of Burgos in Spain, include tanged razors and notched-butt swords similar to those at Rosnoen but found in association with two-ring palstaves from a later period.

In the British Isles, changes also occurred, with new ranges of products (the Penard stage), including types of swords inspired by Continental models, new types of ornaments, torcs, ribbed bracelets and socketed tools: hammers and small chisels. The two cargoes of bronze which sank off the south coast of England belong to this period. The Moor Sand wreck, which was brought to the surface near Plymouth in 1977, thus included swords of the Alsatian type from Rixheim, Breton-type palstaves and a sword with a curved hilt of the type found in the east of France (Pépinville). The wreck in Langdon Bay, to the east of Dover, was bigger: there were about 300 bronze pieces with median-flanged axes (another Eastern type), notched swords, spearheads and pins. This is a remarkable example of the export of Continental metal products to the British Isles.

One of the innovations of the Late Bronze Age was to be the manufacture of new swords with broad leaf-shaped blades. The oldest types seem to have been produced in the south of Germany: the swords of Hemigkofen and Erbenheim. But, very rapidly, the craftsmen in Western Europe were to produce original series in the new metal-working groups of Wilburton, England; Saint-Brieucdes-Iffs, Brittany; Saint-Denis-de-Piles, south-west France and those of the Iberian peninsula: the swords of Saint-Juan-del-Rio, Rio Esla, Bella Vista in Spain; Evora in Portugal and so on (Coffyn, 1985). These swords were to display an immense diversity in details making it easier to single out the various regional groups. But soon these models were to lead to a single model at the end of the Late Bronze Age, towards 800 BC. It was known as the 'carp's-tongue sword' because of its tapered tip, a type of sword which has been found in the Iberian peninsula (Ria de Huelva, Rio Guadalimar in Spain, Fieies-de-Deus, Portugal), in south-west France (Saint-Léon-sur-l'Isle), Brittany (Nantes; Gouesnach), the British Isles (Reach Marsh, Beachy Head), the Netherlands (Nijmegen) and Germany (Catlenburg). At one point, it was considered that there was a fairly uniform carp's-tongue sword complex, but recent studies have demonstrated that, apart from the sword, each regional metal-working group had its own specific features. Some, like the Vénat group in centre-west France, show strong Continental influences (Coffyn et al., 1981). The ornaments in particular are inspired by the Alpine regions, with numerous bracelets with incised decoration, and pins and buckles whose original place of production is to be found in the region of the Swiss palafitte and the Rhône valley. In the Parisian basin a balance was struck between these series of Western productions and the Continental types of sword (the Proto-Hallstattian swords). The metal composition of the two groups differed, the Western swords including higher proportions of lead (Mohen, 1977). Lead was to be worked increasingly both in the British Isles and in France (Brittany) and in Spain. Tin deposits were probably being gradually exhausted and increasing amounts of lead were added to the alloys, which even gave rise to low-grade alloys with an excessive proportion of lead. This poor quality was perhaps to be one of the factors that facilitated the replacing of bronze by iron from 700 to 600 BC. The diversity of production made it easy to recognize where exchanges had taken place and numerous maps of the distribution of typical objects bear witness to the wealth of trading relations at the end of the Atlantic Bronze Age. Ireland was the source of magnificent cauldrons, which doubtless served a ritual function during sacred feasts. Roasting spits are amongst other prestigious objects linked to banqueting that are widely distributed and of which there were Continental and Atlantic models, particularly from Iberia. It is curious to note that animal motifs reappear in this instance. The spit in the Chailland hoard in Vendée, France, ends in a small, stylized deer head. This was a novelty because for most of the Bronze Age it was the 'old European geometrical style' which was used to decorate everyday objects, the funerary vessels or weapons.

Religious taboos must have forbidden the reproduction of animals or human figures.

The Iberian peninsula, at the height of its economic expansion, produced series of axes with two rings which could thus be used either as axes or as hoes. The most widespread are massive palstaves, but socketed axes with two rings are also found. Moulds for two-ring palstaves have been found in Galicia (Lugo Museum) and a mould for two-ring socketed axes in the Asturias at Los Oscos (De Blas Cortina, 1983). This trade reached Sardinia in the Mediterranean, but was particularly strong in the Atlantic area: south-east and central France (Angers), Brittany (Le Folgoet), the southwest of the British Isles (Curland, West Buckland and so on), Ireland (Ballycoling, Cork). Rather more doubt is in order as to the authenticity of the two-ring axes reported from north Germany (Wildeshausen) and even in Sweden at Svanhais (Coffyn, 1985). The trade in two-ring palstaves from the Iberian peninsula is only one example amongst others of the spread of workshops in the Late Atlantic Bronze Age. This vitality gave rise to the term 'apogee of the Atlantic Bronze Age'.

Our knowledge of Late Bronze Age burials in the Atlantic cultures is quite patchy. In the British Isles rather coarse urns decorated with linked horseshoe motifs or fingerprints were used to hold or accompany the cremated bones (barrel or bucket urns). In the south of England, a particular facies, that of Deverel-Rimbury, was formerly considered to have been imported from the Continent. In reality, these cordoned urns are examples of the old tradition of burial urns in the Middle Bronze Age in England.

On the Continent, the influence of Urnfield groups was felt over a wide area as far as the Atlantic zone. The Rhine-Switzerland-France group in the east was particularly dynamic and influenced the cultural groups in the Late Bronge Age II, contemporary with the metal-working groups of Saint-Brieucdes-Iffs and Wilburton. Numerous Urnfields have been recognized in the east and centre-west of France, as well as in Champagne (Marais de Saint-Gond). These groups were to diversify in the final stage of the Late Bronze Age. The pottery is varied, extending from the initial grooved decorations of the Late Bronze Age I (Courtavant), to complex series partly of Rhenish origin: bowls shaped like a cardinal's hat, with pedestal bases, plates shaped like a truncated cone, stepped, decorated with curvilinear or herring-bone motifs, grooved bowls, bossed beakers, vessels in the shape of a truncated cone and so on.

All these collections of pottery are associated with cremations, some of which are protected by circular or rectangular systems of funeral enclosures (Champagne), or curious keyhole-shaped ones (Netherlands and Germany). This Urnfield culture extended to the centre-west of France, where there are burials in caves (Rancogne, Charente) and to the north of the Iberian peninsula. In this region, original local facies are associated with fortified sites (Castros de Galice, the fortified dwellings at Cortes de Navarra in the Ebro valley in Portugal).

One of the original features of the Late Iberian Bronze Age is the presence of funerary stelae representing dead warriors with their accoutrements or sometimes with their war chariot. One of the best known, at Solana de Cabanas in the province of Cacerès in Spain, depicts a dead warrior lying on his back on the right of the stela. At the top, there is a spear and a sword with a hilt similar to those found in the Balearic Islands. A mirror and a helmet (or a razor?) are shown near his head. In the centre of the stela is a big shield

with a scalloped edge of a type that is found both in Spain and in Ireland, evidence once again of maritime trade. At the foot of the Solana stela, a two-horse chariot is evidence of knowledge of war chariots. A whole series of similar stelae has been found in Estremadura, Spain, and described by M. Almagro Gorbea (1977). There is considerable development in style: stelae on which there are only weapons shields, swords, spears, war chariots, helmets, mirrors (Torrejon del Rubio, Spain) are replaced by ones on which the warrior is depicted, as at Salana de Cabanas, Portugal, or Zarza de Montanchez, Spain. In the last example, the helmet had little conical buttons on the side like the real bronze helmets found, sometimes as offerings, in rivers, as in the Seine at Paris (Mohen, 1977) (Fig. 75). Stelae with Iberian warriors depicted on them have been found in the south of France at Substantion, near Montpellier, and at Buoux in the Vaucluse.

It was also in the Late Bronze Age that some pottery bore diagrammatic decorations which have been interpreted as

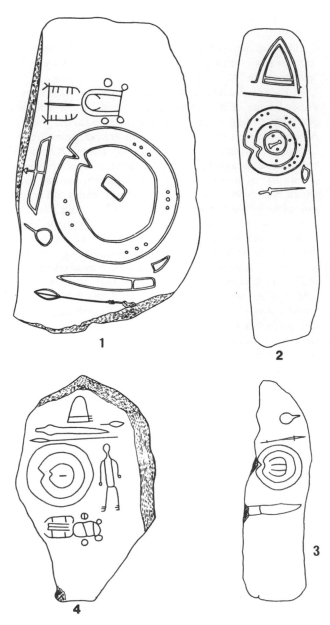

Figure 75 Warrior stelae, Estremadura, Spain. 1, Torrejon del Rubio; 2, Valencia de Alcantara; 3, Arroyos; 4, Zarza de Montanchez (after Coffyn, 1985).

messages or 'pictograms'. At Moras en Valloire in the Drôme, the pottery has friezes of symbolic, abstract, human or animal signs. There are sun signs, rondelles or swastikas, swans and horses above a herring-bone design which may represent the sea of heaven. Human beings are gathered together in circles of little folk holding each other's hands. These representations are also found in the centre-west with the Rancogne and Quéroy vases in Charente. These pictograms are also found in Languedoc in France and beyond the Pyrenees, particularly in Catalonia. They are evidence of the first attempts at symbolic writing in Atlantic Europe.

Among the instruments intended for religious celebration, there are votive chariots that are either large in size with real bronze wheels, or miniatures, often made in pottery. Among recent discoveries is the magnificent bronze wheel with sun motifs inlaid with red copper found in a bog at Coulon, Deux-Sèvres. These parade chariots were to inaugurate a fashion which went on until well into the beginning of the Iron Age. Ritual chariots could carry divinities, representations of the sun but also sacred cauldrons and buckets or 'situlae', which may have been linked to the water cult. Sometimes small clay figurines are found with the small pottery votive chariots, both in the Alpine regions (Lac du Bourget) and in the Atlantic world of southeastern France (Chalucet, Haute-Vienne).

Music played an important role in religious ceremonies in the Bronze Age. In the Alps or northern Europe processions are found depicted on rocks. The Atlantic zone lacks evidence of this nature but there is proof of the existence of musical instruments. In Ireland, a whole series of copper trumpets has been discovered. The trumpets have lateral or central mouthpieces and emit different ranges of tones. It has been assumed that they replaced instruments made from animal horn, from cattle in particular. Among other instruments from Ireland are rattles, large hollow spheres with rings which could be part-filled with bronze granules or little pebbles to make a clinking sound. J. Coles, who has studied these instruments, considers that horn-shaped trumpets and rattles resembling the genitals of a bull may have been used in a bull cult which was very widespread in Europe from the Mediterranean to the north. In France, other rattles are found, tintinnabula and hollow cylinders to which bronze rings and crescents were attached. 'Rattle-pendants' are known from the Baltic, but also from Wales and France; these are discs with clappers which could be attached to ceremonial belts or to horse harnesses. They may also have played a mythical role during the ceremonies and ritual dances. Some of the more fragile musical instruments are missing – bone whistles or reed pan-pipes although some examples of these have been found in Poland. Evidence from several digs suggests that certain types of pottery could have skins stretched over them and serve as drums.

THE END OF THE ATLANTIC BRONZE AGE

The Atlantic culture was in its heyday between 800 and 700 BC. At that period, well-established trade networks, doubtless based on the existence of a real navy of which there is some evidence, brought prosperity to populations which had founded their economy, and in particular their trade, on the spread of bronze. The arrival of iron was to cause an economic crisis in western Europe. Attempts were often made to use the unsold stocks of bronze for other purposes. In

Brittany at that time the phenomenon of Armorican socketed axes developed. Thousands of axes containing a high proportion of lead, and sometimes even made of pure lead, were manufactured to make 'axe-coinage'. They were hollow-socketed axes which were useless because of their poor-quality metal, the depth of the socket and inferior casting. Various models have been distinguished: the big type found in Tréhou, Finistère, Dahouet and Plurien, Côtes d'Armor, and the small axes at Maure and Couville in upper Brittany and in Normandy. These axes were stocked by the thousand in hiding places discovered in modern times in bogs, where they may have been offered in homage to gods. They were exported as far as the north of the British Isles, to Germany, to the Netherlands and to south-west France but not to Spain, where surpluses of bronze must also have existed, with two-ringed palstaves or socketed axes, some models, like the uniface axes, appearing to be means of exchange rather than functional tools.

The Launacian (from the Launac hoard near Montpellier) collection of recycled bronzes, including axes, bracelets and truncated-cone chapes, objects which here again were intended for exchange rather than for practical use, represents a similar phenomenon in the south and south-west of France. The Rochelongue wreck, which was dredged up a few years ago, seems to demonstrate that these Launacian bronzes may have been exported to the Mediterranean. Indeed, while bronze had been replaced by iron for ordinary manufacture, it remained an excellent metal for the trade in ritual or precious objects and the ancient world of the Eastern Mediterranean sought it eagerly in the Cassiterides, those tin-islands scattered over the area from the Iberian peninsula to the British Isles, including Brittany. Trading posts for tin and bronze in conjunction with the Mediterranean merchants are even presumed to have existed not only in Spain (Tartessos) but as far as the estuary of the Loire (Corbilo). These trading posts must have existed from the end of the Bronze Age onwards.

There were to be numerous mutual influences between items produced in Iron Age I and in the traditional Bronze Age. A whole series of well-known swords in the British Isles in particular have sometimes been termed proto-Hallstattian type, given the impossibility of clearly distinguishing between a Continental-type imitation or a prototype of the Late Bronze Age which was then adopted by Iron Age populations. In England, this type of sword is known as the Ewart Park type. Hoards in Britain contain tools that were common in Iron Age I which bear witness to the continuation of Atlantic production at that time. In Belgium, the Iron Age I cemetery at Court-Saint-Etienne, Brabant, includes iron antennae dagger hilts alongside socketed bronze axes which are relics of the Late Bronze Age (Marien, 1952). The extensive French hoards in the centre-west and the centre include fibulae from Iron Age I or other late productions. At Vénat in Charente, the last items produced are Ewart Park swords, belt buckles with claws, knobbed bracelets and an antennaed sword hilt which could have been copied from Continental models. It even appears that a small amount of iron has been found in this hoard.

The same phenomenon is found in the Iberian peninsula. The large hoard at Ria de Huelva (Almagro Basch, 1958) includes an impressive series of carp's-tongue swords of the classic Atlantic type, swords with solid hilts of the Balearic type, notched-butt or riveted daggers but also the double rings found in Iron Age I in Languedoc and the jointed fibulae which are also the ornaments of Iron Age I in the

Mediterranean and can be found in Cyprus or in the French hoards at Notre-Dame d'Or or Vénat. All these collections can be dated from around 700 BC and are evidence of a degree of prolongation of the Atlantic Bronze Age at a time when the first Iron Age cultures were reaching eastern France and the Rhône Valley.

In conclusion, the Atlantic Bronze Age shows considerable development between the Early and the Late stages. The Chalcolithic period had seen a degree of unity develop in Europe around the bell-beaker phenomenon which, while it does not entirely coincide with the migrations of peoples as used to be thought, does at least correspond to trends in the spread of ideas and of technical knowledge. In the Early Bronze Age, the rise of cultures was very irregular. Around the Channel, Wessex and Armorica grew wealthy with princely societies that bear witness to a degree of opulence and a system of economic relations which extended as far as the Mediterranean. North-west Europe remained closer to the bell-beaker tradition and often only received the metal in the form of small imports from the Atlantic coast or from central Europe. The Iberian groups were subject to the influence of El Argar and the groups derived from it, with a tendency to maintain relations with the Mediterranean. However, it has been seen that Argaric sword blades were found as far afield as south-west France and Brittany.

The sources of external prosperity of the Early Bronze Age disappeared in the Middle Bronze Age. Societies became more regional with highly distinct metal-working facies. But they were almost all characterized by a typical tool – the palstave. The Netherlands entered increasingly into barter with the British and Atlantic groups. Original Urnfield cultures took the place of the first barrow cultures and developed throughout north-west Europe. The Iberian peninsula withdrew into itself to some extent, continuing the Argaric tradition and not exchanging very much bronze at that point with the countries to the north. In the Late Bronze Age, an intense thrust from the Eastern urnfield cultures destabilized the Atlantic world but the hoards show that there were doubtless intensified bartering and a process of acculturation rather than real military confrontations. However, the times were not at all settled. Fortified sites were fairly numerous and insecurity shows in the Iberian stelae with their war chariots and homage to the dead warrior. Throughout this period, the inventiveness of the Atlantic bronzesmiths was revealed by their ability to create new ornaments and weapons on the basis of ideas borrowed from the east. The well-known carp's tongue sword is a typical example.

BIBLIOGRAPHY

ALMAGRO BASCH, M. 1958. *Deposito de la Ria de Huelva.* Madrid.

ALMAGRO GORBEA, M. 1977. *El Bronce Final y el Periodo Orientalizante en Extra madura.* Madrid. (Bibl. praehist. hisp., 14.)

ANNABLE, F. K.; SIMPSON, D. D. A. 1964. *Guide Catalogue of the Neolithic and Bronze Age.* Devizes.

BLANCHET, J. C. 1984. Les premiers métallurgistes en Picardie et dans le Nord de la France. (Mém. Soc. préhist. fr., 17.)

BLAS CORTINA, M. A. de. 1983. *La Prehistoria reciente en Asturias.* Oviedo.

BLOEMERS, J. H. F.; LOUWE KOOIJMANS, L. P.; SARFATIJ, H. 1981. *Verleden Land Archeologische opgravingen in Nederland.* Amsterdam.

BRIARD, J. 1984. *Les tumulus d'Armorique.* Paris. (L'âge du Bronze en France, Vol. 3.)

—— 1985. *L'âge du bronze en Europe (2000–800 avant J.C.).* Paris.

—— 1989a. *Poterie et civilisations, I: Néolithique de la France.* Paris.

—— 1989b. *Poterie et civilisations, II: Chalcolithique et l'âge du bronze en France.* Paris.

BURGESS, C. 1980. *The Age of Stonehenge.* London.

CHILDE, G. 1957. *The Dawn of European Civilization.* 6th ed. London.

COFFYN, A. 1985. *Le bronze final atlantique dans la Péninsule ibérique.* Paris.

COFFYN, A.; GOMEZ, J.; MOHEN, J. P. 1981. *L'apogée du Bronze atlantique. Le dépôt de Vénat.* Paris. (L'âge du Bronze en France, Vol. 1.)

COLES, J. M.; HARDING, A. F. 1979. *The Bronze Age in Europe.* London.

ELUERE, C. 1982. *Les ors préhistoriques.* Paris, Picard. (L'âge du Bronze en France, Vol. 2.)

FLEMING, A. 1988. *The Dartmoor Reaves.* London.

GOMEZ, J. 1980. *Les cultures de l'âge du bronze dans le Bassin de la Charente.* Périgueux.

HERITY, M.; EOGAN. G. 1977. *Ireland in Prehistory.* London.

LAET, S. J. DE. 1982. *La Belgique d'avant les Romains.* Wetteren.

MARIEN, M. E. 1952. *Oud Belgie.* Anvers.

MOHEN, J. P. 1977. *L'âge du bronze dans la région de Paris.* Paris.

MOHEN, J. P.; BAILLOUD, G. 1987. *La vie quotidienne.* Paris. (L'âge du Bronze en France, Vol. 4.)

PAUTREAU, J. P. 1979. *Le Chalcolithique et l'âge du Bronze en Poitou.* CAEP, Musée de Poitiers.

ROTENBERG, B.; FREIJEIRO, A. B. 1981. *Studies in Ancient Mining and Metallurgy in South-West Spain.* London.

SANGMEISTER, E. 1963. La civilisation du vase campaniforme. In: COLLOQUE ATLANTIQUE, 1., Rennes, Sept. 1961. *Les civilisations atlantiques du Néolithique à l'Age du Fer: Actes*, pp. 25–55.

SIRET, L. 1913. *Questions de chronologie et d'ethnographie ibérique*, Vol. I. Paris.

SCHUBART, H. 1974. *Zur Gliederung der el Argar-kultur, Studien zur vor- und frühgeschichtlichen Archeologie.*

—— 1974. *Die Kultur der Bronzezeit im Südwesten der Iberischen Halbinsel.* (Madríder Forschungen, 9.)

14.7
NORTHERN EUROPE

Henrik Thrane

The area is not uniform; great variations in relief, climate and soils are reflected in contemporary as in ancient culture. A convenient regional division is: (1) The south-eastern Polish plain characterized by loess soils and by close affinities to the Czech Republic and further south-east; (2) a central region formed by north Germany and south Scandinavia with a rather uniform geography and culture displaying the richest material culture and divisible into many smaller regions or units; (3) central Scandinavia from Kalmar to Gothenburg and from Trondheim to Falun, where the narrow coastal zone with the many islands, along the deeply cut Norwegian fjords and around the Swedish lake district offered suitable soils for agriculture, while inland there was little to offer farming communities and therefore it had more in common with (4) north Scandinavia, which, with the long Norwegian coast and the rivers draining the east remained marginal to the other regions. Nearly half of this region is north of the Polar circle. North of Tromsø agriculture is impossible.

Although Scandinavia and north Germany have a very long tradition and certainly an enormous number of ancient monuments, new discoveries are constantly being made. A chronological division into four stages seems practical, although it does not coincide with the traditional archaeological periodization.

The first, or young Neolithic stage is placed between 2800 and 2200 BC according to present ^{14}C calibrations. This comprises the Neolithic 'corded ware', 'battleaxe' or 'single grave' cultures. Some of the evidence adduced to uphold the old invasion hypothesis has proved wrong or too slender, especially as a series of ^{14}C dates indicates a unilinear development without the dramatic sequence of events proposed earlier. The innovations which caused archaeologists to create the corded-ware/battleaxe cultures are now seen as internal development of the local cultures, assisted or triggered by a moderate external influence. This does not belittle the remarkable super-regionality of the most characteristic new feature, the battleaxes, and does not explain why this feature spread so rapidly or at all.

The second stage, from 2200 to 1500 BC includes the bellbeaker, Únětice and contemporary Bronze Age cultures. The first metal-working groups now appear in the north.

The third stage, from 1500 to 1000 BC, is occupied by the northern equivalents to the central European tumulus cultures and marks the start of the full Bronze Age: the Early Lausitz culture and the apogee of the Nordic Bronze Age.

The fourth stage, from 1000 to 700 BC, is contemporary with the central European urnfield groups and was the heyday of Lausitz culture south of the Baltic, and with a richly diffentiated material from Scandinavia.

A more regionally diversified division is possible, but it suffices to note that while there are marked regional differences in each phase, there is also a long list of features common to most of the area – and even with larger areas outside it. The whole of the area is devoid of natural metal resources exploited in the Bronze Age and thus depended upon the supply of metals from the south.

STAGE 1: 2800–2200 BC

Current views of the history of these centuries differ radically from the traditional interpretation. It is possible to recognize from the battleaxes and pottery a series of local groups and developments, showing that external impulses were quickly transformed by local traditions. How far new population elements contributed must remain an open question for the time being. The new unilinear model does not permit the association of the Indo-European languages with corded-ware cultures any more than with a number of other Neolithic cultures. The slender evidence for the physical anthropology of this stage makes a very heterogeneous impression, much more so than in earlier Neolithic populations. It does not seem possible to distinguish the bearers of the corded-ware cultures anthropologically from other cultures or to name any specific race as the bearer of the corded-ware cultures.

The central region was already bound together by the Megalithic cultures and in this area burials were commonly placed in existing megalithic tombs. While the inhumation burial rite was omnipresent, the disposal of the corpse varied. Small mounds covering the bole or plank coffins were erected in north-west Germany and Jutland. Sometimes one mound contained a dozen graves through succeeding generations, providing us with useful stratigraphic evidence for the evolution of the material culture represented by the grave goods. In north-east Germany, Poland, north Jutland and the Danish isles stone cists were built, while simpler inhumations, such as pit graves, prevailed in the rest of Scandinavia.

Men were accompanied by their weapons in the grave, such as battleaxe, or flint working axe, a flint flake (knife) and an amber disc, while women are best recognized by a string of amber beads or by the absence of weapons. Skeletons are normally too poorly preserved to allow measurements or gender attributions. The east–west oriented graves normally contained one body placed flexed on the right side, men with head towards the west, women the other way round. An extended position became increasingly popular over time. The odd copper trinket in the occasional Swedish grave indicates continued contact with the continent. Flint arrowheads in some graves may indicate the cause of death.

It has been proposed that the colonization of the sandy soils was the primary reason for the rise of the new culture. Population surplus could be one of the causes of this expansion. By interaction with the surrounding older settlement areas the new fashion was then spread all over the area of the Megalithic culture and received its local colouring.

In Sweden and south-eastern Norway the battleaxes and the pottery did not conform with the south Scandinavian and the north German. The local 'boat-shaped axes' display a long sophisticated development which seems to have been initiated in southern Sweden and thence spread towards the north, north-west and north-east. The pottery, however, did not accompany the battleaxes on their way, nor did the grave ritual. There are only 253 graves from Sweden and six from Norway, all without tumuli. Thus the northern regions presumably were not radically transformed by the material or spiritual culture of this period.

The most important single type of axe is the battleaxe made of hard rock; it is preserved by the thousands in Denmark, Schleswig-Holstein (c. 3,500), Sweden (2,450) and there are 160 in Norway. The earliest 'pan-European' type has been compared to metal axes, but no such ones are known from our area. Later types were apparently developed from these primary types, and the tradition persisted over several centuries to the end of the Bronze Age. Although many axes would undoubtedly serve well on an opponent's skull, the shaft holes often allow only a very slender shaft (diameter c. 2 cm). 'Battleaxes' in soft material are also known and may indicate that the primary function of the axes gradually became more symbolic than practical. If battleaxes indicate warrior chiefs or aristocracy, then their power base must have been quite narrow in view of the large number of axes. There can be no doubt about the practical function of the flint axes often found in graves or in hoards. They continued a long tradition and must have been indispensable for everyday work. Arrowheads are rare in the graves, but occur in all groups and their absence must be an example of how cultural habits determined what it was appropriate to place with the dead. Hoards containing flint axes, gouges and spearheads as well as rough-outs are primarily found in northern and eastern Denmark and further north outside the grave region. Single battleaxes or flint axes, club heads and pots were placed in wet areas or by large stones, presumably as offerings.

In north Sweden a striking group of hoards, containing about 260 axes of south Scandinavian (Danish) flint appears around the Bottnian Bay, mainly in Norrland. They are believed to have been distributed by the Swedish boat-axe culture and its contemporary coastal hunter groups (pitted-ware culture) and reflect the deep penetration of south Scandinavian goods northward. How far this involved ideas and a wider range of cultural elements remains to be seen. The change from the use of primarily quartz to quartzite as tool material is placed within the time covered by stages 1 and 2. The inland group along the rivers presumably spent the summers and autumns in the foothills, and winters and springs in the forest, using different types of residential hunting and processing camps for units of one to two huts (families). A similar social system may have existed in northern Norway, where the coast, however, provided for winter settlements, which have left a large number of agglomerated hut sites still recognizable thanks to the good preservation of the rubbish

dumps and turf walls in the cold climate. Here the local slate provided material for spearheads and arrowheads, scrapers and even fish-hooks. Presumably summers were spent inland hunting elk (or reindeer?) in the pine forest along rivers such as the Lule and the Alta, and fishing the rivers for trout and salmon. People may have crossed the mainland seasonally as the Lapps do even today and there certainly was no cultural divide between the hunters on both sides of the Lapmark and Finnmark mountains. Without sufficient ^{14}C dates, it is difficult to date the very gradual development due to the crudeness of most of the lithic types and the absence in the settlements of chronologically sensitive south Scandinavian types.

The corded-ware settlements are little known; they seem to have been small and have left little material beyond flint refuse, scrapers, arrowheads, quernstones and potsherds. Normally the settlements were placed on sites where other Neolithic cultures had lived or came to live, presumably indicating similar subsistence strategies. The small settlements have induced the idea of short-lived occupation as a result of a pastoral life-style.

Few houses are known. One example is the small rectangular house with wall posts and partly sunk floor, 5 × 6 m in area, at Vorbasse where large-scale excavation established the fact that this house was 300 m from its nearest possible neighbour (presumably another single house). Not much is known of the subsistence pattern. Animal bones are rare, but those found do not indicate a preference for sheep, but rather for cattle. Grain is mainly known from impressions in pottery, which indicate a preference for barley, but emmer and millet, apples, prunes and acorns are also known. Some barrows cover ploughed soils, which cannot be much older than the barrows themselves. The character and pattern of the ploughmarks from ards do not differ from those of the Megalithic culture or the Bronze Age, so presumably cultivation was carried out in much the same way, although now also on very light soils. There is no good evidence for the use of horses for riding or as draught animals outside eastern Poland. Solid disc wheels indicate ox-drawn carts.

The pottery mainly consists of handled types presumably used for fluids, but large storage vessels are known. Exceptional preservation conditions have allowed the survival of the odd wooden bowl or birch bark container (for example, in the stone and wood cist from Kobberup in central Jutland).

In the bay of Gdansk a local group (Rzucewo) specialized in marine resources. Seals, small guinea pigs, whales, wild geese, swans and a variety of fish were hunted or caught as well as the aurochs, brown bear, wild cat, various species of deer, wolf and boar. This was not, however, a purely Mesolithic way of life as pig, cattle, horse and dog, emmer and barley were known and eaten. The settlements were placed on terraces along the waterside and the rectangular houses were post constructions. The artefacts reflect specialization. Horn harpoons and various kinds of bone chisels were especially important, while amber beads and pottery with affinities northwards are also characteristic. The dead were sometimes buried inside the houses.

This coastal culture has a Scandinavian equivalent, the 'pitted-ware' culture, which has left many traces on the Danish and Swedish coasts with sometimes quite substantial settlement remains. It is still a riddle whether this culture represents a coastal adaptation of the contemporary inland culture of a different population group, thriving on fishing and 'trading'. Another group comprised most of the Polish interior down to the upper Oder and westwards into the Republic of Germany. Axes made of the special Sobitka serpentine were distributed far away from the source.

STAGE 2: 2200–1500 BC

A brief transitional phase is characterized by the so-called bell-beaker culture with its characteristic decorated beakers, in many ways like the corded-ware beakers. They are now accompanied by metalwork in the graves. Small dagger blades with organic handles and occasional ornaments, including special amber beads are the main types. Bows and arrows now became a widespread part of the equipment of the dead males. Flint remained the preferred arrowhead material even throughout the Bronze Age, apart from the Lausitz culture where bronze arrowheads appear around 1000 BC.

The bell-beaker pottery tradition with its zonar decoration spread as far as south-west Norway (settlement at Ogna). It is characteristic that no proper western or southern bell-beaker has been found in the north. Knowledge of what this style looked like must, however, have been available locally so that versions of it could be made in Jutland and Norway. While the bell-beaker phase in the Netherlands and north-west Germany is associated with local metalwork, it seems doubtful how much the bell-beaker culture was able to contribute in this respect further north. It did, however, introduce the dagger fashion from the west (in Poland from the south, that is, Bohemia). Still, the honour of introducing metallurgy to the north must go to the Únětice culture. The first type of axe to be made locally in south Scandinavia copied Únětice axes, with additional western features. Proper western axes are rarely found in Scandinavia, so the Únětice culture must have the benefit of the doubt. The cultural magnets of this stage are the Únětice culture of the south-east and the tumulus culture of north-west Germany. Both were vital for the development of the Scandinavian metal age.

The centuries 2200 to 1500 BC are characterized by the gradual pervasion of metallurgy and knowledge of the technique of casting simple objects throughout the area. Daggers and copper axes in new shapes, but in principle like the old Neolithic axes, characterize the new era. The dagger has given its name to the period in Scandinavia. It was not the copper dagger, but its local imitation in flint which was ubiquitous in male graves, just as the battleaxe had been previously. The production of the thin broad dagger blades necessitated another flint technique, that of pressure flaking – second to none. This was presumably introduced from the west where similar simple, smaller daggers are known slightly earlier. The technical refinement must have taken place in south Scandinavia, however.

North of the Baltic, pottery and grave rituals continued in the Neolithic tradition. Great tumuli covering wooden chambers were built south of the Baltic over single individuals, with exceptionally rich equipment far exceeding any previously known. They are some of the most striking expressions of the Central European Únětice copper/bronze culture in Poland and Germany (Silesia and Saxony). In our area the great tumulus IV at Leki Male, measuring 5 × 24 m, was constructed over a deep wood-lined chamber covered by a cairn. With the skeleton were pots, a bronze dagger, axe and halberd, arm-rings and two gold earrings. A secondary tomb has male equipment only slightly less rich. Another tumulus at Leki Male contained a series of re-interred skeletons. The great tumuli were not evenly distributed over the area covered by the Únětice culture. They cluster within very narrow limits around present Wroclaw.

The normal flat-grave cemeteries contain flexed skeletons oriented north-south. Large stone or wooden chambers are also known from Silesia. Here the difference between commoners' graves and the gold and bronze rich tumulus burials illustrates another novelty – the development of a dimension to social hierarchy. It presupposes the accumulation of foreign metal and objects in the hands of a privileged group who disposed of these riches out of the reach of the living. Besides the graves there are great bronze hoards with daggers, axes and halberds, arm-rings and neck-rings. The hoards sometimes duplicate the grave equipment. This stage marks the first massive import of metal into the north. Finally south Scandinavia was incorporated into the by now nearly all-European community using metal for practical and symbolic purposes alike.

North of the Baltic graves and hoards are poorer, and it took some generations before the tendency to exorbitant display was able to strike root here. Thus metal does not appear in graves till the very end of this stage; instead it was buried in hoards.

In south Poland and neighbouring parts of Germany the hoard practice continued much longer than in the Únětice area. The idea behind the dominant axe hoards must represent a Neolithic tradition. Only late in this stage do graves with bronze weapons, ornaments and dress fittings appear in large numbers, above all in north-west Germany's 'Sögel-Wohlde' group, which is really an offshoot of the south German Tumulus culture, with a strong local accent which remained for some centuries. This group seems to have been partly responsible for the local colour of the initial south Scandinavian Bronze Age. More eastern currents canalized through the Únětice area and Baltic coastal zone inspired the first native ornament style, a rather dry imitation of south-eastern European curvilinear and geometric decoration.

The first metal production in Scandinavia consisted nearly exclusively of flanged axes combining Únětice features with west-European (British) features. The number of actual imported axes is slight compared to the number of local axes. These were distributed as far north as 68° 40'N. Only very gradually did new types of metalwork appear and begin to accompany the dead instead of the omnipresent flint dagger. For several generations flint daggers and stone battleaxes continued in their traditional role. South of the Baltic it took even longer to leave the old corded-ware traditions, which in parts of Poland (north-east) persisted into the next stage. The Únětice burial ritual follows the corded-ware tradition faithfully, having crouched burials oriented north-south with a different position for men and women. The introduction of tumuli and cremation (in Poland) or extended burial in the west reflect the importance of new ideas spreading from the southern tumulus cultures.

In Scandinavia and Schleswig-Holstein the most characteristic single type of weapon is the flint dagger, spanning nearly a thousand years. The daggers number nearly 20,000. The majority are from southern Sweden and Denmark, but they extend across north Germany to the Netherlands and Poland and as far south as Slovakia; their northern limit is the Polar circle. The largest daggers exceed 40 cm in length. When damaged they were reshaped so thoroughly that not much more than the grip remained. The original, leaf-shaped type presumably had an organic grip like the sheath dagger from Wiepenkathen in north-west Germany. Most of the daggers must have been deposited in graves, but only a minority has been found *in situ*; grave inventories follow a stereotype with only a few items in addition to the daggers. They substitute the shaft-hole axes of the preceding period and indicate the strength of the innovation. The material for the largest daggers was obtained by regular mining in the strata of good flint in north Denmark, but must have been substituted locally by resources from the cliffs of the eastern Danish coasts. All daggers found outside south Scandinavia must have been imported. In Poland a local flint resource was utilized for a special type (Strzyzow) but south of the Baltic bronze daggers were more readily available, at least for the prominent men. The same flint technique was used for sickles, which are less common, but follow the distribution of the daggers. They, too, must have been substitutes for metal sickles. Both daggers and sickles could be used as strike-a-lights besides their original function.

In north Scandinavia asbestos-tempered pottery and slate tools and arrowheads, above all one-edged knives characterize this phase and the rest of the Bronze Age. Textile-impressed pottery is another element testifying to eastern connections with the north. Fish was the dominant food, as much as 96 per cent of the bones coming from the settlements. Sub-square houses with sunk floors and stone-set hearths reflect the cold climate.

The grave ritual and the sordid looking pottery reflect the continued Neolithic tradition. Inhumation was ubiquitous, but the Scandinavians now placed the corpses in an extended position like the chiefs of the great Únětice tumuli. Individual graves continued to be bole coffins, often inserted into Megalithic tombs. Stone cists grew bigger and were given a special entrance facilitating reuse. Barrows were erected over stone cists or oak coffins alike.

Settlements are now known from south Scandinavia, covering the period of the bell-beaker influence onwards. East-west oriented longhouses with a single row of posts along the axis have lately begun to appear in south Scandinavia with or without sunken floors. They have widths of 6.5–8.5 m and lengths up to 44 m, though smaller houses of 5 × 18 m are also known. In Scania houses with the whole floor dug *c*. 40 cm into the ground have been found, both in long and short versions. Settlement in Scandinavia shows a preference for the coastal zone even in Denmark and south Sweden where the interior soils are just as arable as the coastal soils. This trend became pronounced by stage 2 and remained so well on into the Iron Age. The need for access to information, innovation, foreign goods and ideas could be a primary motive behind this trend. Gold daggers from Swiatkowo and Inowroclaw at the Vistula River clearly parallel the gold axe from Dieskau in Saxony, and they are equally useless for practical purposes. The Tumulus groups with their rich burials and neighbouring hoards show that, for reasons unknown, it was now possible to gather more material riches than elsewhere and to bury them in the ground. How far this reflects political and/or economic developments has not been sufficiently explored.

The use of gold not only for armlets and other ornaments but for weapons indicates that these objects had transcended the practical world and had come to be regarded as symbols – of political and/or religious power? This may apply to the bronze versions too.

The metals – bronze and gold – offered a new and unique opportunity to display status and prestige because of their limited availability and the resources needed to extract and work them, as compared to the old flint and stone resources.

Thus the whole aspect of display and symbolic values now became invested in metal, a feature which was to characterize the following Bronze and Early Iron Ages.

A number of skeletons from Danish dagger-period graves were well enough preserved to allow anthropological study. This population was remarkably sound, with long limbs and robust bones. The average male height was 176.7 cm, and the female 162.5 cm, only equalled in the third and fourth centuries AD and much later. Skulls were shorter, higher and rounder than those of the Danish Iron Age population. We have no reason to suppose that the skeletons represent another section of the population.

Social implications must have been the driving force behind the spread of the metal culture through a Scandinavia devoid of mineable metals. The possession of metal immediately divided the world into two. South Scandinavian flint axes and daggers presumably meant as much to those prevented from access to metal as the metal objects did to the more lucky groups in the south.

STAGE 3: 1500–1000 BC

Around 1600 BC metal had become so abundant in south Scandinavia that a full Bronze Age was reached. This does not mean that every individual owned bronze or that every grave contained metal, but it means that the range of metal objects had become so broad that even ordinary tools like needles or sickles, buttons or fishhooks were made in bronze, quite apart from all the ornaments, weaponry and objects with religious/cultic significance like razors and sun symbols which now developed. Nobody knows how much bronze was buried, but the region of Schleswig alone (9,435 km²) has produced more than 2,000 bronze and 250 gold objects from the period 1600–1050 BC. An equal amount, if not more, must have been destroyed before museums were instituted around 180 years ago.

This stage is dominated by the tumulus cultures in their northern variations. In Poland there are marked concentrations in Pomerania oriented towards the west and across the sea towards Scandinavia, with another in Silesia oriented southwards. Native types such as pins up to 63 cm long and spiral-ended armlets are easily distinguished.

It seems that the development of new types and styles did not proceed uniformly over south Scandinavia. At some stage the west developed faster than the east; later it was the reverse. This may be taken as a warning that even within a geographically uniform and small area like Denmark or northwest Germany regional differences have played a prominent part in the development of culture. Local tradition is strongly shown by the continuance of such features as the grave ritual – oak bole coffins, stone cists (in north Jutland) or in the disposal of the corpse. Pottery and flint techniques remain indistinguishable from the preceding period nearly to the end of this stage.

One remarkable trend through this and the following stage is the emergence of the individual in the archaeological record. Of course individual graves are known from various Stone Age cultures, but only the Corded-ware cultures have left them in sufficient number for us to study variations statistically. The equipment accompanying the dead remained stereotyped but diversified with the full Bronze Age. Standard equipment combinations continued, but the number of non-standard graves is now surprisingly large. This is repeated in the grave ritual where nearly every other barrow has its own special features. On a background of uniform pottery, flintwork and architecture these individual deviations cannot but catch the eye.

No other period has left such a corpus of burials, where the position and combination of a wide range of objects, ornaments, weapons and tools has been observed *in situ*. This enables a study of local variations in fighting equipment, dress styles and decoration, whose potential is far from exhausted. The average equipment would be a sword (or dagger) and axe, a razor and belt-hook or double button (for the same purpose) for the men, neck-ring, arm-ring, plus comb and belt-disc (occasionally a dagger, too) for the women. In the Lüneburg area a preference for drole head-gear ruled among the women. The extraordinary preservation conditions of some Jutish turf-built tumuli have left us the first complete European dresses. Apart from children's clothes, a complete range of seemingly well-worn everyday clothes is preserved. Men wore long loincloths and half-length cloaks plus round or cylindrical caps. Women wore blouses with short sleeves and either short string skirts or longer plaid-like skirts. It has been suggested that the short skirt represents the married women's dress, while the unmarried had to wear long skirts. The girl from Egtved (aged 16 or 18) had short hair and a short skirt; the woman from Skrydstrup (aged about 18) had elaborately arranged long hair with a hairnet and wore a long skirt. The deplorable absence of anthropologically suitable skeletal material from this period prevents further study.

Three male graves yielded little pieces of haematite from which powder was rasped, presumably in order to colour the face red. During the last two centuries before 1000 BC men quite regularly were characterized by a solid torsioned gold armlet, which could well be a sign of dignity or of a special position among the sword-bearing population. Other such signs were specially decorated axes, bronze or wooden bowls, wheeled cauldrons, folding stools or gold discs. Such extraordinary male burials are the cauldron graves from Peckatel and Skallerup, gold disc graves, the grave of the sorcerer(?) from Hvidegard, identified from remains of a special long hooded dress and a bag with pieces of amber animal parts, fossils and so on.

The most famous Bronze Age funeral monument is the Kivik cist placed in a huge stone cairn (75 m in diameter). The slabs of the cists are decorated with rock carvings on the inside. They form a northern analogy to the Hagia Triada sarcophagus of Crete and could be an illustration of religious practice in which the deceased had participated (or conducted). Only tiny fragments of a bronze sword and cup have survived earlier despoilation. A famous slab shows a two-wheeled chariot drawn by two horses with a standing charioteer. This is a close parallel to scenes from Mycenaean Greece. The use of the horse as draught animal is first shown here and by the equally famous contemporary Trundholm vehicle, where a single bronze horse pulls a spiral-decorated bronze disc, gold plated on one face. This is the sun chariot, embodying the adoration of the sun as the great power of fertility, presenting a night and a day face. Another scene shows the great cult axes known in pairs from a series of hoards extending through the next stage too.

The number of tumuli rises steeply. This is partly because metal objects abound and enable us to date the graves within much narrower limits than previously. We now see the climax of tumulus construction. The average mound of 2 × 20 m was often enlarged to make room for new burials and sometimes great barrows were heaped over just one individual's grave. Such super-barrows are known on both sides of the Baltic and distinguished burials from these or other mounds must denote the emergence of a new social class displaying its position by monumental mounds and rich equipment alike. These successors of the Únětice super-mounds now appear more widely, indicating a broader acceptance of the new social order.

In Scania there was no enormous distance from top to bottom of the scale, as in Únětice culture. There are more rich graves and they are more evenly distributed, but there is also a very gradual transition from the richest to the average grave. It should, however, be remembered that quite a number of graves without metal exist with or without tumuli. It is still being debated whether the graves now known are representative of the whole population. Children are clearly under-represented and it is most unlikely than even the most liberal multiplication of the number of mounds known (50,000 in Denmark) will produce a population sufficiently large to maintain a society as that indicated by the graves.

The barrows destroyed cultivated land when the grass turf was cut from the surface of 2–4 hectares for the average tumulus. In central and north Scandinavia this problem did not exist. Here the tumuli were heaped by the omnipresent boulders left by the inland ice to form cairns. They lie on the coast of southern Norway and Sweden all the way round the Bottnian Bay and up there are practically the only material evidence of an attempt to emulate the Bronze Age proper of south Scandinavia. The cairns number nearly 3,000 in Sweden, so the attempt was serious enough, but metal to accompany the dead was rarely available. The cairns were so frequently placed on promontories along the coasts that they may well have served as guides for the sailors or as territorial markers.

House plans are now known in sufficient numbers to show more than haphazard variations. There are some curious small oval houses measuring between 3 × 6.5 m and 4 × 8 m with post or turf(?) walls as well as large entirely post-built longhouses from south Jutland. Some still have sunken floors in part of the houses, most do not. These houses measure between 6.2 × 17.5 m and 9.5 × 25.5 m and have two rows of internal posts carrying the roof and walls of wooden planks or basket work (and daub?). They have rounded ends and are oriented east–west. It is hardly accidental that at Trappendal a barrow was placed over such a burnt-down house with a grave in the centre. The three-aisled longhouse (east–west oriented) with different wall constructions but always with wooden post constructions as the fundamental feature was to characterize north-west Germany, the Netherlands and south Scandinavia during the following 3,000 years. In eastern Germany and Poland houses were rectangular, nearly square, also post-built, but with roof constructions.

The rock carvings present us with a unique pictorial record strangely unattached to the burial sector (apart from Kivik, Sagaholm and possibly Rege). The carvings outline objects such as axes, spears and cloaks in proper size or depict scenes such as fighting, marriage, processions and ploughing or they represent individual motifs such as feet or hands, but above all various kinds of circles and ships. The carvings are placed on the smoothed rock surface on level ground but sometimes on steep slopes or in caves. Traces of activities at the carvings are rare and not very informative. Rock paintings are also known mainly from the north-east. At Nämforsen in Norrland the largest agglomeration of rock carvings in all Scandinavia (1,400 single carvings) indicates a religious and social centre where southern motifs combine with the local ones. The rock carvings occur in clusters with cairns, heaped from fire-cracked stones from nearby settlements as substitutes for the northerly rock faces.

Striking parallels to Swedish rock carvings – and Indo-European literature – are the triple ard furrows marking the limits of a cemetery on Bornholm. Ploughing was not only a necessity for the treatment of the soil and for the sowing, but had strong religious/cultic overtones long preserved in popular practices in the north, as well as in India and elsewhere (cf. *Iliad* XIII).

Ordinary ploughing is attested in the buried soils under many Bronze Age barrows. On Sealand small fields of 300 m² up to 1,000 m² surrounded by lynchets are ¹⁴C dated to around 1200 BC and later. Elsewhere less permanent fields with wooden fences would have left no trace on the surface and only become known when they are observed under excavated barrows. So far fields are known from Denmark, Scania and north Germany but there is no reason why they should not be characteristic of the agriculture of the whole area. In northern Scandinavia agriculture is attested between 1800 and 500 BC by pollen analyses and ¹⁴C dates.

In southern and western Norway there is a strong correspondence between the arable soils along the coast and the metal-using Bronze Age and rock-carving areas, but most of the arable lands were already occupied during the preceding stage. Further inland and in the uplands bronzes and moulds attest the connections of the inland population. Never did these hunters and gatherers in the highlands, however, attain the level of a proper Bronze Age culture. It remained a Stone Age culture until the time when iron was able to substitute the various local quartzes and schists as raw material for tools and weapons. This is the great dichotomy of Scandinavian prehistory which only becomes important in the Bronze Age when the stark contrast between the metal-rich south and central Scandinavia and the metal-poor north and east Scandinavia becomes so striking.

Objects from south Scandinavia and even Central Europe were imported into Finland. The occurrence as far north as the extreme northern Lapland illustrates how keenly the shining metal was sought by the hunters of *ultima Thule*. It has been suggested that furs were the products exchanged for metals.

Even the rock carvings and paintings of north Scandinavia differ from the southern ones. They show wild animals – the prey of the hunter – who presumably continued the magical rites responsible for the wonderful cave paintings of Palaeolithic times, while the carvings of our stages 2–3 illustrate the world of the farmers and sailors of the Bronze Age proper. The cast bronze horse of the Trundholm sun vehicle and a similar pair of horses from Scania are not only the biggest pieces of individual sculpture of the northern Bronze Age, they are also the earliest representations of the horse. This is hardly a coincidence, but may be a forceful expression of the impact of the horse on a northern cult. The horse remained an important cult animal during the next stage, as indicated by the use of horseheads on ships' prows, razors and gold bowls.

The flat round surface of dress ornaments was ideal for spiral decorations and this foreign element completely dominates from 1500 to 1300 BC in Scandinavia and north Germany, followed by the simpler concentric circles used in the same way, presumably the result of another foreign inspiration.

Around 1300 BC Mecklenburg became a leading province with strong urnfield traits. The remarkable increase in the number of graves with much metal and great barrows like Friedrichsruhe and Peckatel was coupled with a strange preponderance of female graves, quite contrary to the general trend towards male dominance throughout the Bronze Age. During this stage cremation gradually became dominant all over the area. This innovation was presumably ultimately caused by new ideas from central Europe, which continued to make themselves felt with varying intensity.

Just as the flint dagger was a local reaction to new trends from the south, so renewed innovation now took place spurred on by the metal objects and fashions of the Tumulus – and Urnfield – cultures of central Europe. New sword types, metal vessels, pottery, glass beads and perhaps even chariots of Mycenaean type were imported, but immediately copied, giving rise to local types. Thus local provinces arose in Mecklenburg, western Holstein, Jutland, Sealand and Scania, where the rhythm of evolution varied and each had its own tinge. Now the range of material expressions is so varied that it is possible to describe the cultural state on a very broad basis and to study ideas and renewal on a level previously unknown.

Amber was washed ashore on the Danish coast and the Baltic, mainly along the east Polish coast and on into the Russian Federation. While amber was still prominent in the graves of stage 1, there is only one decent amber hoard (3.3 kg) from stage 3, and amber objects, even beads, are rare in later graves. Still, single beads, rings or little bits of amber were put in the graves throughout the Bronze Age. The magic, apotropeic qualities were probably satisfied by the mere presence of even the smallest fragment. Gold presumably took over the role of amber as the most precious material for ornaments and charms. Conversely amber reached high estimation in central Europe and the Bronze Age Mediterranean during the period, when it became rarer in northern finds.

STAGE 4: 1000–700 BC

The change to the fourth stage around 1050 BC was gradual. The later part of the preceding period is contemporary with the early urnfields of Central Europe. The major change was in the grave ritual. Now urn burial became practically uniform throughout the area. The Polish Lausitz culture exerted a strong influence on its neighbours towards the west and north, best expressed in Late Bronze Age pottery. The urn-burial custom had serious consequences for the archaeological material. No longer were the bronzes placed with the corpse in the way that the living person had worn them. No longer are complete garments available, only the odd textile fragment shows the same technique for making the woollen cloth as before. A few figurines indicate that the same short skirt was worn at least by some women.

Another consequence was that large objects could no longer find room in the graves. This means that swords, belt discs and so on no longer appear. Miniature swords were sometimes made as substitutes, but other objects were not made in miniature, emphasizing the importance of the sword not only as a weapon, but even more as a symbol of power. We know from hoards that there was no discontinuity of these objects, only now they were buried outside the graves. This may have been a direct result of the urn-burial rite. Another result was that a grave no longer needed such a large covering mound. Thus in Scandinavia and along the south coast of the Baltic Sea we find small barrows down to 0.5 × 5 m being heaped over a number of urns – the work of individual families?

Great barrows were now the exception and were only erected over men with swords as well as other signs of wealth and status such as King Björn's tumulus in Uppland and the royal mound at Seddin. The discussion of social and political structures has only just begun. Currently a sort of chieftainship is favoured for societies such as those bordering the western Baltic. In places like Seddin, Banie, Voldtofte or Kivik the archaeological expressions are so strong that an interpretation as petty kingdoms could easily have been accepted for later periods. No doubt local structures varied greatly even within regions such as Denmark or Pomerania but they certainly did so from the Baltic to north Scandinavia. Only recently are sources such as settlements and hoards included in this discussion and convincing reconstructions of local societies have still to be made due to the lack of coherent excavations and studies.

While tumulus burial remained the norm in Scandinavia and north Germany, cremation cemeteries under a flat surface became the typical rite of the Lausitz culture and extend to south Scania, Holstein and north Germany. Tumulus cemeteries are also known from the Lausitz culture. Secondary burials were in vogue throughout the Bronze Age as they had been already in the single-grave stage, but must have been associated with some sort of right of access presumably exerted by the family (or clan). Not only did large objects rarely find their way to the grave, but there was a general tendency to reduce the number of objects placed there. This may indicate an increasing rarity of metal, or a change to a more symbolic use of the metal objects owned by the deceased. Fragments of sickles or razors support the latter interpretation. The number of metal grave goods as well as their character seems to follow rules presumably reflecting the social order of local societies, but was extraordinarily similar in Lausitz and northern cultures. Judging by the grave goods there were few rich people but many were poor in metal. In between there was a modest-sized group (Plate 155).

Religious sites are difficult to define, but the steep hill of Borbjerg on Sealand with its two hoards of gold bowls remains the best guess. Rock-carving localities must have had cultic functions other than just pecking the pictures. On both sides of the Baltic sites with large numbers of regularly spaced earth ovens (up to 300), now registered as pits with fire-cracked stones and charcoal, attest large-scale cooking of meat hardly intended for everyday meals. The cult was presumably practised without special buildings or constructions, focusing on natural features such as hilltops, rivers and lakes, rocks, stones or trees (groves), as witnessed by hoards and rock carving. It has been suggested that the cult was aniconic, using only symbols for the gods. Proper cult figures are unknown, apart from a few bronze figurines.

The deities worshipped appear to have been natural ones – above all the sun. There has been an attempt to interpret axes, spears and so on as symbols of gods known only much later, such as Odin/Wotan. During this stage the duck or swan was introduced from central Europe as a cult animal/symbol associated with the sun. Competition with the horse seems to have ended in a draw as both animals were used with sun symbols or alone. Bulls or goats only feature peripherally, perhaps following a more easterly inspiration?

What Kivik was to the previous stage Seddin is to this one. The greatest tumulus in northern Europe outside England measures 11 × 90 m and contains extraordinarily rich funeral equipment in a stone chamber with plastered and painted walls. This great tumulus near Perleberg in east Germany was surrounded by various others of lower degrees of richness. Similar situations recur in Uppland, south-west Fyn and west Holstein (Dithmarschen), but nowhere equalling Seddin. Gold played an important part in these groupings just as in the Únĕtice culture previously. Only at Voldtofte on Fyn is the funereal richness matched by a settlement of unusual proportions and contents (painted walls and the only evidence of the casting of lurs). The significance and interpretation of these monumental expressions of the use of wealth remain unexplained, but they form the last links in a very loose chain of such centres in central and northern Europe during the Bronze Age and predate Heuneburg by centuries.

The production of bronze was a highly individual affair, apart from stereotype objects such as sickles, knives and certain axes which were produced in moulds suitable for a number of castings. More complicated objects, such as larger tools, ornaments and weapons, were made in wax over a clay core with an outer clay mould. These had to be smashed in order to get at the cast bronze. Thus the Nordic bronze corpus works are characterized by individuality and never reached the mass production of central Europe. Hammered metalwork never became the fashion in Scandinavia, but south of the Baltic even large objects like the Herzsprung shields, bronze vessels and diadems were hammered out in expert fashion.

How far casting was practised at every settlement remains to be seen. For the Lausitz culture it is stated that the fortified settlements have better indications than ordinary settlements, while casting seems present on most Scandinavian ones. Settlements seem as a rule to have contained only a few families. Both excavated settlements and cemeteries indicate population groups of ten to thirty in the Lausitz culture (Tornow) as well as in Scandinavia.

Proper grain hoards stored in clay vessels are known from Voldtofte. As previously noted, barley seems more important than wheat, millet and oats; prunes and apples and south of the Baltic beans and flax were also used and a beverage made with honey sometimes accompanied the dead (beer or mead?). Analyses of charred crusts on the inside of pots have shown them to consist of a variety of amino-acids, indicating a blood-rich food. All bone samples from settlements, whether Swedish, Danish, Polish or north German show a preponderance of cattle with pig or sheep coming second. Horse is present in small quantities, but is only given special attention in the burial rite of the Lausitz area, with separate horse burials. Cattle were needed as draught animals for ploughs and carts, and may at this stage have represented wealth at a lower level than bronze. The importance of agriculture is attested by the field systems and plough systems known mainly under barrows. Ploughs of the primitive ard type are known from the Bronze Age in Denmark and north Germany.

Fortified sites became an integrated feature of the Lusatian culture in Poland and Germany during the ninth to eighth centuries BC, but are primarily an Iron Age phenomenon. They cover quite large areas (Wroclaw 'Swedenschanze': 6.7 ha). Apart from fortified sites and the stone foundations of the central Scandinavian houses, Bronze Age settlements are only recognizable on ploughed land by potsherds and charcoal-coloured patches. Houses continued the tradition outlined above and sometimes had the east end marked as a stable by constructions for the cattle – in order to keep more beasts during the winter? The neatly smoothed and painted plaster or daub fragments from the Voldtofte settlement must indicate a special status for this particular house, whether ritual or secular (chief's residence?). It is unparalleled at the moment – but compare the painted house urn from Stora Hammar in Scania.

During something like 500 years great bronze horns (lurs) were cast in Scandinavia. These lurs were made in pairs, identical apart from the curvature, and deposited in bogs around the western Baltic in up to three pairs. The lurs, if not wonders of musical prowess, were technical masterpieces, some 2.25 m long, constructed in 4–5 tube lengths with a separate sound plate. Rock carvings show them in action on ships or ashore and they must belong to the special ritual equipment which reached its climax during this stage. So music, including metal rattles, formed an important part of the ceremonial, presumably with an apotropeic function, along with other elements such as mock combats, processions, and various sacrifices (cannibalism is only proclaimed from the Lausitz area). Lurs, gold bowls, parade armoury, helmets and shields (a new find from Fröslunda in Västergötland has 16–18 north German shields), great spearheads and swords and impractical axes belong to this stage and may represent communal offerings or deposits by chiefs who controlled the 'clan' ritual equipment.

Other hoards are clearly personal, consisting of one or more person's dress ornaments or equipment and are valuable sources for the reconstruction of local dress and local production areas. Other hoards with scrap metal or large quantities of tools could represent metal-value hoarding. New types continued to be added to the available range, but after a period of great variety a more uniform phase followed with the most developed decoration style outside the Lausitz area, equalling the spiral style of the earlier stage.

Sculpture played a very small part in the bronze-caster's work. Only rare statuettes of naked females with neck-rings or horned men with great axes are known around the western Baltic, but not from the Lausitz culture, where pottery, bulls and birds are integrated features. A Norwegian find of wood carvings gives an idea of what has been lost by the decay of materials like wood, leather, straw and textiles. There can be no doubt of the cultic relevance of these anthropozoomorphic pieces of *Kleinskulptur*.

Foreigners are supposed to have reached the Oder mouth area from the Carpathians and east-central Sweden from Finland, and wholesale renewal of equipment could indicate other such movements or close exchange relationships between Sealand and the mouth of the Oder, central Jutland and the Elbe mouth areas. Pins and other ornaments and pottery are signs of Lausitz influence in the neighbouring areas, indicating movement of women, perhaps as part of a regular bride exchange. Now, as always, such traffic had to go by sea, Jutland being the only part of Scandinavia immediately accessible by land from the culturally leading areas south of the Baltic. No actual ship is known from the Bronze Age apart from hollowed-out oak bole canoes, but ships are extremely important on rock carvings and bronzes, and especially on razors. The reason for these pictures of paddled or unmanned ships is undoubtedly that they were important parts of the cult. This of course reflects the importance of the ship in Scandinavia, where the interior was forbidding while the coastal areas were fertile and littered with

hundred of islands. Bronze Age settlement reflects the importance of the sea by its closeness to the coastal zone. Although farming communities could live happily inland, it was only the sea that gave access to a supply of bronze and enabled the local societies to keep abreast with current ideas and innovations. Whether the ship pictures show plank-built or leather-bound constructions is currently under discussion. In north Scandinavia rock carvings depict a boat very like the Esquimo *umiak*.

By 800 BC iron had been introduced to the north but it took a long time before Scandinavia was able to enter a proper Iron Age. In some ways the final stage of the period described here marks a climax. The social distinction between rich and poor as measured by the ability to accumulate and bury metal and other commodities in the earth was sharper during the last centuries before 700 BC than earlier on. What this signifies for the historical development is not yet understood. For more than a thousand years the Scandinavian peninsula, Denmark and the southern neighbouring areas retained one of the richest and technically most advanced Bronze Age cultures known by European standards, in spite of the absence of any natural copper, tin or gold. This remains the paradox of the northern Bronze Age.

BIBLIOGRAPHY

References in Scandinavian or Polish are not listed. Readers are referred to *Nordic Archaeological Abstracts*, Vol. 72, Viborg, 1975 and following years; and *Polish Archaeological Abstracts* from 1969.

AMBROSIANI, B. (ed.) 1989. *Die Bronzezeit im Ostseegebiet*. Stockholm.

BAUDOU, E. 1990. Stand der Vorgeschichtsforschung in Nordschweden. *Prähistorische Leitschrift*, Vol. 65, pp. 1–45.

BERGLUND, B. G. 1969. Vegetation and Human Influence in South Scandinavia during Prehistoric Times. *OIKOS* (København), Supplement 12, pp. 9–28.

BJÖRHEM, N.; SÄFVESTAD, U. 1989. *Fosie*. Vol. 4. Malmö. (Engish summary)

BRØNDSTED, J. 1961, 1963. *Nordische Vorzeit*, Vol. 1, *Steinzeit*; Vol. 2. *Bronzezeit*. Neumünster.

BURENHULT, G. 1973. *The Rock Carvings of Götaland*. Bonn/Lund.

COBLENZ, W.; HORST, F. (eds) 1978. *Mitteleuropäische Bronzezeit*. Berlin.

GARDAVSKI, A. 1976. Lausitzerkultur oder Lausitzerstil? *Arb.– Forsch. ber. sächs. Bodendenkmalpfl.* (Berlin), Vol. 20/21, pp. 131–49.

GEDIGA, B. 1980. Forschungsprobleme der frühen Bronzeperioden in West-Polen. *Archaeol. Pol.* (Wrocław), Vol. 29, pp. 177–91.

GEDL, M. 1980. *Die Dolche und Stabdolche in Polen*. München (Prähist. Bronzefunde, Vol. 6, 4).

—— 1985. Die Kulturumwandlungen von der Früh– bis in die Mittelbronzezeit in Südwestpolen. In: *L'énéolitique et le début de l'Age du bronze dans certaines régions de l'Europe*. Kraków. pp. 99–114.

HAGEN, A. 1967. *Norway*. London.

HAKANSSON, I. 1985. *Skånes Gravfünd från Aldre Bronsålder som Kjälla til Studiet av Socialstruktur*. Lund. (English summary).

HELSKOG. E .T. 1983. *The Iversfjord Locality*. Tromsø.

HERRMANN, J. (ed.) 1976. *25 Jahre Archaeologische Forschungen der Deutschen Demokratischen Republik, Ausgrabungen und Funde*, Vol. 21. Berlin.

HOPF, M. 1982. *Vor- und Frühgeschichtliche Kulturpflanzen aus dem Nördlichen Deutschland*. Mainz.

HORST, F. 1985. *Zedau, eine Jungbronze– und Eisenzeitliche Siedlung in der Altmark*. Berlin.

—— 1986a. Jungbronzezeitliches Fernhandelzentrum im Gebiet von Brandenburg/Havel. *Veröff. Mus. Ur- Frühgesch. Potsdam* (Berlin), Vol. 20, pp. 267–75.

—— 1986b. Die Jungbronzezeitlichen Steinäxte mit Nachenknauf aus dem Elbe-Oder-Raum. In: *Jahrbuch Bodendenkmalpflege in Mecklenburg 1985*. Berlin. pp. 99–123.

HVASS, S.; STORGAARD, B. (eds) 1993. *Digging into the Past: 25 Years of Danish Archaeology*. København.

IVERSEN, J. 1973. *The Development of Denmark's Nature since the Last Glacial*. København. (Geol. surv. Denmark, Vol. 5, Ser. 7c.)

JAANUSSON, H. 1981. *Hallunda: A Study of Pottery from a Late Bronze Age Settlement in Central Sweden*. Stockholm.

—— 1983. Main Early Bronze Age Pottery Provinces in the Northern Baltic Region. *Stud. balt. stockh.* (Stockholm), Vol. 1, pp. 39–50.

JENSEN, J. 1982. *The Prehistory of Denmark*. London.

—— 1987. Bronze Age Research in Denmark 1975–1985. *J. Dan. Archaeol.* Vol. 6.

KADROW, S. 1991–2. *Iwanovice*. Vols 1–2. Kraków.

KÜHN, H. J. 1979. *Das Spätneolithikum in Schleswig-Holstein*. Neumünster.

KRISTIANSON, K. 1987. From Stone to Bronze: The Evolution of Social Complexity in Northern Europe 2300–1200 BC. In: BRUMFIELD, E. M., EARLE, T. K. (eds), *Specialisation, Exchange and Complex Societies*. Vol. 1, pp. 130–45. Cambridge.

LERSSON, T. B. 1986. *The Bronze Age Metalwork in Southern Sweden*. Lund.

LOMBORG, E. 1973. *Die Flintdolche Dänemarks*. København.

MACHNIK, J. 1977. *Frühbronzezeit Polens*. Wrocław.

MALINOWSKI, T. 1962. Les rites funéraires chez la population de la civilisation lusacienne en Pologne. *Prz. Archeol.* (Wrocław), Vol. 14, pp. 1–140.

MALMER, M. P. 1962. *Jungneolithische Studien*. Bonn/Lund.

—— 1981. *A Chronological Study of North European Rock Art*. Stockholm.

MAZUROWSKI, R. F. 1984. Amber Treatment Workshops in the Rzucewo Culture. *Zelawy. Prz. Archaeol.* (Wrocław), Vol. 32.

SCHWANTES, G. 1958. *Geschichte Schleswig-Holsteins;* Vol. 1: *Urgeschichte.* Neumünster.

STENBERGER, M. 1967. *Sweden*. London.

STRÖMBERG, M. 1974. Untersuchungen zur Bronzezeit in Südostschonen. *Medd. Lunds Univ. Hist. Mus.* (Lund), pp. 101–68.

—— 1975. *Studien zu einem Gräberfeld in Löderup*. Lund.

STRUVE, K. W. 1971. *Geschichte Schleswig-Holsteins*, Vol. 2, Part 1: *Die Bronzezeit, Periode I-III*. Neumünster.

—— 1979. *Geschichte Schleswig-Holsteins*, Vol. 2, Part 2: *Die Jüngere Bronzezeit*. Neumünster.

WIDHOLM, D. 1980. Problems concerning Bronze Age Settlements in Southern Sweden. *Medd. Lunds Univ. Hist. Mus.* Lund, pp. 30–46.

WILLROTH, K. H. 1985. *Die Hortfunde der älteren Bronzezeit in Südschweden und auf den dänischen Inseln*. Neumünster.

WISLANSKI, T. (ed.). 1970. *The Neolithic in Poland*. Wrocław.

WÜSTEMANN, H. 1974. Zur Sozialstruktur im Seddiner Kulturgebiet. *Z. Archäol.* (Berlin), Vol. 8, pp. 67–107.

WYSZOMIRSKI, M. 1974. Scandinavian Flint Daggers. *Medd. Lunds Univ. Hist. Mus.* Lund.

14.8

RELIGION AND ART

Lili L. Kaelas

In this chapter[1] we shall deal with general aspects of those artefacts and other finds which have been interpreted as an expression of religion and art. The geographical area of our concern is Europe 3000–600 BC, with the exception of the Aegean world in the Eastern Mediterranean. To survey such a huge area is an almost impossible task. We have to contend with a richly varied cultural life, differing from area to area. Consequently, we can only give a broad outline of the major characteristics and similarities, ignoring the exceptions, though these are attested in several of the regions in question.

Some discussion of the geographical orientation is in order here. When referring to southern Europe we mean principally Europe south of the Massif Central, the Alpine areas and the Carpathians. Central Europe comprises central Germany to the edge of the Carpathian Mountains and the Vistula, from Berlin and Warsaw to the Austrian and Hungarian borders. For west, east and north Europe we adopt the prescriptive definitions as used by contemporary European newspapers. In none of these vast territories can we expect a uniform cultural pattern. We also emphasize that our archaeological knowledge of European prehistory is not equally good from all parts of the continent. Nevertheless, the information available concerning burial traditions and material finds enables us to draw an outline of Late Neolithic and Bronze Age religious practices and notions in the whole of Europe.

The conclusions reached here are interpretations, based on grave goods, traces of burial ceremonies and symbolic or naturalistic pictures. Hypotheses are legion, not least because religion is a diffuse concept which has a different significance for different peoples over time and space. 'Art' is an equally undefined concept, and in considering prehistoric relics and thought processes, it goes without saying that hypotheses and assumptions are numerous and varied. We consider religion today as a socially active factor, as a uniting, 'conservative' ideology. And art can be understood as a status creating, communicative factor in our society. We in Catholic and Protestant Europe are inclined to see an historical connection between religion and artistic creation. This, perhaps, also is the case in Buddhism. In other religions, however, it may not exist.

Graves and their contents have always constituted an important material upon which our interpretation of prehistoric religion in Europe relies. Burial conventions give signals about existential ideas and changes in them. For scholarly interpretation we need a framework of reference. A basic one is dependent on comparisons with other early religions about which we possess written notions and/or oral tradi-

tions. Anthropologists' reports on the religious practices and ideas of present-day tribes living at a 'Stone Age' level have, however, come to play a greater role as analogies for interpretation.

In our interpretation of burials we have to be cautious. The megalithic stone chambers, discussed in Volume I, Chapter 55, seem to have been built for eternity, and have often been considered as an indication of ideas about the beyond, or as the eternal abode for the ancestral spirits. If those monuments – the great and sophisticated ones in particular – and with them associated ceremonies and offerings only concerned a few individuals, as evidenced by several recent studies, it is not justified to assume that the idea of immortality concerned others than those whose bones were inserted in the tombs. Only those with rank and status in the society warranted such ceremonies. Hence the megalithic monuments give us more precise information about contemporary society than about the religious belief of the entire community. Their social function was to bestow status and a permanent position of power for a family.

BURIAL CUSTOMS

When individual graves under a barrow, and flat graves, were introduced into regions with megalithic tombs, it seems to indicate the emergence of new religious ideas. This can, however, at the same time indicate that these individuals had succeeded in obtaining a more important position in society. This change is already apparent in the third millennium BC. The details of grave layout vary from region to region and sometimes even in the same region. The body for instance can be buried in a contracted or outstretched position in a wooden or stone cist (coffin). Large monuments, especially in the west, followed the Neolithic practice of graves covered with a mound or barrow, or megalithic chamber tombs.

The most radical change of religious belief is, however, expressed by the introduction of cremation. This soon became a common burial custom and replaced inhumation over vast areas in the Early Bronze Age, some time after the beginning of the second millennium BC, above all in central Europe. After the mid-second millennium it was practised more or less all over Europe. Disposals associated with incineration (such as ashes placed either in an urn, a wooden container or a piece of cloth) occurred in many variations.

In the later Bronze Age, from the mid-thirteenth century BC onwards, urn burials below the ground were grouped together in vast fields – the so-called urnfields – in a broad belt across Europe from Romania, Hungary and Russia, towards the west and south, and later northwards as well. In eastern-central Europe an interplay of inhumation and cremation continued throughout the whole Bronze Age, sometimes with both types in the same cemetery. It is most probable that the basic ideology expressed by incineration was the same all over the area. The appearance of vast urnfields raises the question whether the change is related to economy, or rather a step towards social equality. This seems not to be the case. When grave gifts became minimal for the most part and indicated a change of religious traditions, rich hoards of bronzes increased.

The postulation on the other hand that the annihilation of the corpse implies the release of the anima, soul or some other spiritual property – as sometimes proposed as an explanation for cremation – remains a hypothesis and no more.

It is appropriate to recall that the Bronze Age was a great formative period in the history of Europe. Many novelties in the social, economic and technical domains were introduced. The most obvious is the emergence of armed warriors and the rise of the privileged – as evidenced by the graves of the 'rich' and the 'poor'. The difference between the rich and poor had already been noted in the emergence of megalithic tombs, but now it becomes more emphatic. For the few, the growth in wealth marks a social stratification in the society which increased considerably in most developed areas in the Late Bronze Age. The changes which were introduced during that period continued, the differences in later periods showing themselves principally in shifts of emphasis. As the regional chapters on Bronze Age material culture show, the development did not start everywhere at the same time, nor did it end simultaneously. The introduction of novelties was slower in northern Europe compared with central and southern parts of the continent, which were closer to influences from the high cultures of the Mediterranean and the Orient. In the Late Bronze Age a markedly homogeneous culture spread over most of Europe.

ART ON OBJECTS

When pictorial art was first introduced, notably on rocks (rock art), on objects (ornamental pottery, weapons, jewellery) and as sculpture, we have a more sophisticated medium of communication. Art, however, does not consist only of human figures, animals and recognizable objects but comprises abstract symbols as well (common for a large part of Europe). Though conjectures and interpretations about religious symbolism remain manifold, pictorial art opens the door and offers quite a different challenge. Rock-art figures have not always been understood as religious notions. In former times they were believed to be records of contemporary events. Now scholars agree that they express existential ideas, feelings and imagination. Visual art is the epitome of human reaction to a contemporary vision of the universe and the various phenomena in it.

With reference to the word 'art', we reiterate that it is not always meaningful in a prehistoric context. In its restricted sense the word implies a purely aesthetic concept. But the motifs and symbols pecked on rocks in the open air were surely not made for decorating the cliffs but for carrying a message to transcendental powers as well as to the living. On the other hand tools, too, could be decorated, but all such decorative elements are unlikely to carry a message.

It is rather a rule than an exception that objects whose practical use is difficult to comprehend have been interpreted as relics of religious activities: pictures and pictograms have been particularly susceptible. As pictorial art is communicative (like the symbol-language of some religions today), we are inclined to read a profounder religious meaning into rock-art pictures and signs than strictly speaking we are entitled to. For example, a lavishly decorated bronze object – such as an axe – can be explained as intended for cultic use. At the same time, it simultaneously shows the social status of the owner. The alternative interpretation is that symbol and decoration were inseparable for preliterate people.

Costly objects such as bronze cauldrons and gold bowls have been designated as items used in religious ceremonies. Typical examples of this are the many magnificent cauldrons, decorated with embossed ornaments, scenes of feasting with humans and animals, processions or fighting that have been found all over central Europe, in Austria, Hungary and even in Scandinavia. The same can be said about the miniature four-wheeled bronze vehicles carrying a cauldron, sometimes the vehicle being supplied with 'ducks' as draught animals. Another example is the famous Trundholm (Sealand, Denmark) vehicle on six wheels with a richly decorated gold-coated disc upon it, drawn by a horse. Quite a number of wrought bronze cauldrons and bowls are found as containers for the ashes of the distinguished deceased, and probably were expressly made for this purpose.

MUSIC

There are in existence many finds indicating that music played an important role in ceremonies. From western Europe comes a series of copper trumpets that emit different tones. In Scandinavia, especially in Denmark, great bronze 'lurs' (horns), masterpieces of bronze casting, were produced over a period of about 500 years. These lurs are found in bogs, with up to three pairs in the same deposit. Rock art shows them in use: men blowing them on ships or ashore. Also rattles – large hollow rings – which could be filled with bronze granules, coarse gravel or tiny pebbles to make a clinking sound, are quite frequent. All these instruments, not forgetting horns and flutes and other instruments made of perishable materials, may have been used at special ceremonies. It is plausible that the sound produced was implied when depicting figures on rock, and that this also was an essential element.

BRONZE STATUETTES

Finds of female and male statuettes of bronze at, for example, Grevens Vaenge, Sealand and Faardal, Jutland, Denmark, and rock-art designs of dancers turning head over heels above a ship, indicate the role of dance in ceremonies. There were certainly more elements incorporated in these feasts, though we at present have not recognized them.

Among identifiable motifs on bronzes, birds, including water-birds such as swans and ducks were appreciated by central European Bronze Age people. In northern Europe the horse's head was a favourite motif and it occurs also in rock designs. These animals were also made three-dimensional as small sculptures. It is, however, impossible to establish whether all tiny sculptures, including anthropomorphous statuettes, had symbolic meaning and were used on ceremonial occasions. Some may be children's toys. But when we find them for instance on burial urns and cauldrons, and on musical

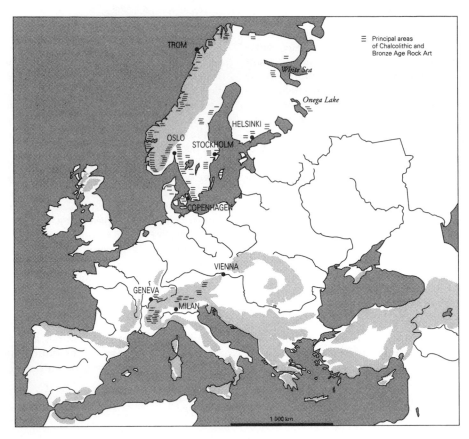

Map 22 Principal areas of Chalcolithic and Bronze Age Rock Art

instruments such as bronze lurs, we may assume that they had a symbolic meaning. A similar assumption is plausible with regard to ornaments and decorations on swords, helmets and shields – the accoutrements of chieftains and warriors.

ROCK ART

Only one category of 'art' – rock art – can without any doubt be characterized as exclusively having a religious purpose. As a phenomenon, rock art in the open air has a world-wide distribution and varies greatly in style, configuration and date. In Europe the richest areas are the Alpine regions, especially the foothills of the Alps along the valleys in northern Italy and the Alpes Maritimes in France; in northern Europe they occur in north Germany, Denmark, Norway, Sweden and the Finnish and Russian Karelia. Further eastward there are no concentrations beyond Lake Onega until east of the Ural Mountains. Further north they are comparatively rare because of unfavourable conditions for preservation. Referring to the general geographical distribution of rock art, it should be emphasized that the phenomenon occurs on the periphery of contemporary culture centres. They are most abundant in Spain, south France, north Italy, Karelia and Scandinavia.

We find rock art also in Late Neolithic/Early Bronze Age gallery graves (dealt with in Volume I, Chapter 55), but the richest rock-art treasures are found on cliffs and loose stone blocks in the open air. A striking feature in the spread is that, apart from some isolated, scattered sites, the Alps and northern Europe have a remarkable concentration of rocks covered by a multitude of motifs, totalling hundreds or thousands of pictures and signs. This phenomenon surely implies that rock art was the vehicle for proclaiming or expressing something – a means of communication. This is valid for art in all civiliza-

tions, including our own, but its communicative role was certainly more dominant and important in prehistoric societies.

Another noticeable feature in Bronze Age rock art is a change of gender in anthropomorphs. In the Neolithic the image of the deity was female, where it is possible to determine the sex. Compared to male representations the symbolism of the female gender is by far the dominant one at that stage. Male representation forms a tiny minority, about 3 per cent out of the known total (Gimbutas, 1991). Even if the percentage increases in the future through new discoveries, the relation of masculine to female images will remain negligible.

It is possible to follow how the female characteristic progressively loses importance. In the Chalcolithic (Copper Age), in south France, for instance, we witness the flourishing of anthropomorphic statue-menhirs (discussed in Volume I, Chapter 55) of both sexes (Plate 15), which gradually gave way to a preponderance of male statues. From the Early Bronze Age onwards we meet a predominantly masculine world.

Rock engravings, as they are often termed, are not engraved but are contour–'drawings', outlined or carved on the surface of the rock with a stone. Often the entire motif is then chiseled and appears as a bas-relief.

However, rock art is not an invention either of the Neolithic or of the Bronze Age. It started in the Palaeolithic and is best preserved in caves. Carvings and paintings are also known from the Mesolithic period, but they are not as frequent except in northern Scandinavia, Karelia and the White Sea area, where the tradition continues into the stage which coincides with the south Scandinavian Bronze Age. Whether the continental rock-art tradition was practised continuously from the Palaeolithic is uncertain. As regards the motifs and style of design, the Bronze Age rock art differs from that of previous periods in that naturalistic representations give way to stereotypes, pictorial signs for humans, ships and so on – an intelligible picture-language – that the initiated could 'read' in the same way as we 'read' and understand international traffic signs.

From the geographical point of view, the difference also lies in the profusion of rock art in new areas where there was none before.

Important rock-art areas

In the Alpine area the occurrence of rock art from Lake Garda to the Swiss border is impressive. The richest regions are the mountain valleys of northern Italy, especially the Camonica Valley. A western prolongation comprises the high valleys of the Alpes Maritimes in France. The rock art of the Alps resembles that of south Scandinavia.

Italy

The best studied area in Italy – the Camonica Valley – is penetrated by, among others, the rivers Oglio, Upper Adige and Lungiana. The highest mountain here is Mount Adamello (more than 3,500 m above sea level), but it is the c. 1,000 m lower peak, Pizzo Badele – visible from every rock-art site – that is important for people coming to Val Camonica sites. The rock-art sites are situated at the foothills of the Alps, on slopes and terraces about 300 to 500 m above the valley bottom. The valleys have been densely inhabited and under cultivation for many hundreds of years. Settlements seem to have vanished without trace. Petroglyphs and statue-menhirs (anthropomorphous sculptures, though occasionally the resemblance to humans is faint indeed) are practically the only prehistoric remains left.

The commonest petroglyph motifs in the Italian Alps are discs with rays (often considered as sun symbols – an interpretation not shared by all scholars), cup-and-ring marks, wheels, foot-soles and so on. Many of these signs are frequently linked with animal symbols (stags in particular), less commonly with humans. Drawings of houses associated with 'sun' symbols have been interpreted as temples, table-like structures together with animals as scenes of sacrifice. Human 'portrayals' of two combatants are common. Other frequent motifs are horses, humans with raised arms (worshippers) and funerals with mourners (also with upraised arms) beside a prostrate corpse. Others comprise a pair of oxen pulling a four-wheeled cart or a crook-ard (primitive plough), scenes with armed men and so forth. Among the humans those in strange plumage or other ritualistic(?) garments are noticeable. Usually motifs vary on one and the same rock, but there are also plenty of rock panels covered partly or entirely by repeated motifs, weapons (such as daggers), house-gables, animals and so on (Plates 156, 157). The cultural attribution and dating of the motifs is based on datable weapon design, particularly that of daggers, the types of which have their affinities within well-dated Chalcolithic communities, and especially the Remedello culture. Scenes with Etruscan warriors (the combatants) are evidence of a long-lasting tradition. It was surely practised until the Roman conquest of Cisalpine Gaul in c. 200 BC.

France

Another vast Alpine rock-art area lies next door to that of northern Italy, in the high valleys of the Alpes Maritimes c. 80 km north-east of Nice, in south-eastern Provence. From the environmental point of view it is a highly remarkable area. In the valleys, above all of Merveilles and Fontanalba (other valleys of interest include Valaurette and Valmasque) at heights of 2,200–2,600 m above sea-level, there is a concentration of petroglyphs. The symbols on rocks or erratic stone blocks surround the highest peak of the area, Mont Bégo (2,872 m) like a belt. The preferred rock for engravings or bas-reliefs, which form the majority, was schist.

Here, in the chaotic tumble of the barren valleys of Merveilles and Fontanelba in particular, littered with stone blocks that were dragged along by glaciers in the last Ice Age, the Quaternary, only small lakes and brooks enliven the moon landscape. It is a wild, hostile environment – at quite a distance from habitable areas. Place names such as the Lake or Valley of Hell, the Devil's Peak and so on bear witness to the fear that Christians probably felt on seeing the great number of heathen signs in this wilderness. No dwelling sites are known in those high valleys. However, we have to bear in mind that in the Bronze Age the climate was warmer and drier and the tree limit probably higher (today it is 2,300 m above sea-level). Nevertheless, it was not a comfortable place to live except during the summer season. Winters were long and cold, often with deep snow. Settlements were on the lower slopes and in the bottom of the valleys, close to the Mediterranean coast. On the other hand, paths over the mountain passes bear witness that shepherds drove their sheep higher up to the grasslands in the dry season. Transhumance, still practised, has deep roots in antiquity, as attested by finds elsewhere in Alpine passes, such as the St Bernard pass between Italy and Switzerland.

The repertoire of motifs in the Alpes Maritimes is limited and more homogeneous than that of northern Italy. The difference between the two areas is, however, more than that, since it includes the geographical landscape. Italian rock art occurs in pastureland in the foothills of the Alps, where people could settle all the year round. Notwithstanding this difference, the inhabitants of the Alpes Maritimes used a similar pictorial language of weapon motifs and abstract symbols. Of identifiable motifs, a bovid is a central symbol. It is a stylized, stereotyped figure – mostly an animal head with overlarge horns, but at times the entire animal, either alone or as a draught animal for the ard (with or without a ploughman). As with drawings that include weapons, here too the human is in miniature compared to the animal and the ard – people were thus not deemed to be important. The bovid is usually interpreted as an ox.

Further frequent symbols are daggers, spears, axes and tools (such as sickles). Anthropomorphic symbols are a tiny fraction of all motifs. They are associated with animals and weapons. The majority of the humans appear sexless, though if the sexual characteristic is given, it is indicated as male (Plate 158). Only a few clearly female figures, indicated by a vulva, are present. Abstract symbols consist of circles, spirals, crosses, star-shaped signs, squares, rectangles with reticulation, parallel lines, dots and so on. Some symbols are interpreted as houses, fields and paths, but this interpretation seems to us unrealistic. They are more likely abstract symbols with an unidentifiable meaning. As in northern Italy, the majority of pictures are in bas-relief. In the course of time the sedimentary schist rocks have acquired a yellow, orange and reddish patina. This makes the motifs appear clearly in different shades of grey against the background of the untouched patinated rock surface.

The cultural attribution of rock art in the Alpes Maritimes is analogous to that in north Italy, based upon weapon designs

– various types of daggers and halberds. Here, too, the size of the weapons is striking. Those in natural size have surely been contoured after the originals in bronze, whereby even the rivet holes were copied exactly. The size of such weapons is even more pronounced when associated with the humans holding them or placed next to them. Many of the weapon designs are reminiscent of bronze weapons known from the Rhône and the Polada cultures of the Early and Middle Bronze Age, c. 2300–1500 BC. The homogeneous character of the rock art in the Alpes Maritimes is an indication that the tradition here was not as long-lived as in northern Italy.

Northern Europe

Compared to Alpine rock art, that of north Europe is far more varied. Here we can distinguish two main groups: Stone Age or hunters' rock art (sometimes referred to as the Arctic group) which is characterized by more or less naturalistic animals. The other group, the south Scandinavian or Bronze Age rock art, has stylized designs in a form of picture-language. There is no clear dividing line between the two groups, and there are many transitions in style, subject and topography.

Rock art of the northern group occurs as far south as the Oslo Fjord area. The motifs belonging to the Bronze Age group appear as far north as the 66th parallel, near the Arctic Circle. Occasionally, motifs and styles characteristic of the two groups appear on the same rock, witnessing the activity of two different ethnic groups in the same area. The contact of the two cultures is evidenced by petroglyphs on rocks in the rapids of the Nämforsen River in the province of Ångermanland in central Sweden. There, the mingling of motifs of the north and the south group attests that the hunter-gatherers' rock art was still performed in the Bronze Age. A Swedish scholar has explained the co-appearance as evidence of a trading place for fur traders from south Scandinavia, furs being one of the items that were exchanged for bronze (Malmer, 1989). The animal style of the south Scandinavian group shows the influence of the north group, as shown by the game on the rock panels at Ausevik in Flora on the Norwegian west coast. The two traditions were thus at least for some time synchronous after the emergence of the Bronze Age group proper.

The northern group occurs over a vast area, penetrated by rivers, from the Atlantic coast in the west to the forests of central Sweden and south-east Finland (Karelia) and to the White Sea district (the only arctic region in the whole area) in the east. The area covers a range of climatic zones. The Scandinavian west coast had and still has a mild climate because of the Gulf stream, while that of the White Sea is more arctic. The petroglyphs of this group are found predominantly near or with direct attachment to water – fjords, rivers and lakes, communication ways where the terrain was passable. The natural conditions of this wide area vary and so does the style of petroglyphs – a result of many scattered groups of hunters on the move. Typical motifs are game: elk, reindeer and red deer (and swan at Lake Onega). The only beast of prey is the bear, hunted for food. Of sea creatures we can identify the seal, whale, salmon, and flat fish. Except for the ubiquitous elk, the frequency of other species varies; birds are more common in the east, fishes in the west, on the Atlantic coast. Anthropomorphic figures are comparatively few and so are the boats associated with humans. The drawings are in a more or less realistic style; but a trend in development towards more conventional forms can be distinguished. Differences probably reflect changes in spiritual concepts. The countour-lined animals and those with a 'life line', heart and other organs, or a skeleton delineated inside the body contour, are perhaps also examples of different concepts.

As much of this type of rock art is found in mountainous and forested areas, on sloping cliffs on the coast and at rapids, it is regarded as 'the hunters' art' of the Stone Age. The cultural setting of this art is clear – it is the world of hunter-gatherers that is mirrored in these petroglyphs, that of people who have followed for centuries their traditional mobile way of life. Though it is commonly thought that their rock art can be dated to the Mesolithic period, beginning approximately in the sixth millennium BC and continuing into the Bronze Age, both its beginning and its end are uncertain. But one thing is clear – their Mesolithic type of culture overlapped with the south Scandinavian Iron Age into the early centuries AD.

Rock art of the Bronze Age proper is encountered not only in south Scandinavia but also in adjacent areas of north Germany. In a broad sense the occurrence of the south group coincides with that of the Nordic Bronze Age culture area. In this part of Europe, Denmark is culturally one of the most developed areas north of the Alps. The petroglyph-rich regions in Norway and Sweden represent the periphery in relation to the Nordic Bronze Age culture centre.

In Denmark/north Germany there was a fashion for abstract motifs, while south Norway/south Sweden (particularly the neighbouring provinces of Östfold/Bohuslän) demonstrate a remarkable proliferation of animated scenes; these rank as the most outstanding rock-art regions in the world (Plate 159). Here we meet humans in action (ships with strokes above the gunwales that represent crew members paddling or rowing, among them often one or more larger figures blowing a lur or trumpet, and sometimes a human or two above the ship performing acrobatics). Some 'ships' are probably sledges. There are figures of unarmed and armed men, the latter equipped with sword or dagger, spear, shield and helmet. They appear singly or in groups, as worshippers with raised arms, alone or in procession, with further scenes of combatants, mourners, ploughmen, couples copulating and parts of the human body (arms, hands, feet and foot-soles). Occasionally, humans are related to animal figures such as pigs or boars, stags, cattle, horses, deer or dogs in hunting scenes. Sometimes animals are alone: domestic animals and game, by far the majority being stags, deer and boars. Bulls' heads and horns also occur, as do fish (such as salmon) and birds (such as the crane) and huge serpents. Even plant or tree motifs occur, though not frequently. Besides the identifiable figures there are a large number of abstract symbols (circles, concentric circles, ring- and wheel-crosses, spirals, wavy lines, labyrinths, grid patterns and so on) and the ubiquitous cup-marks. As in the Alps the profusion of individual motifs is not spread over the whole rock-art area.

As in Alpine areas it is noticeable that some armed men are depicted towering over other figures as if to dominate a particular scene. Their size has led to interpretations that they are representations of the gods. Swords and spears, either singly or in groups, appear in natural size. Ships more than any other motif vary most in size, from several metres to some centimetres from prow to stern. Next to cup-marks, bare feet and foot-soles, the ship symbol is found most frequently in south Scandinavian rock art. The reason for it is probably the role ships played in everyday life as a natural means of communication in this area rich in gulfs, lakes and streams. As north Europe did not have copper mines or tin resources, all metal was transported from mining areas along these waterways. Ships had thus a high status in Scandinavia: the ship symbol so characteristic in Scandinavia does not appear elsewhere. Among the more extraordinary motifs should be mentioned four-wheeled carts with or without oxen, and two-wheeled war-chariots. The latter, more numerous than carts by far, were never used in Scandinavia and must have been copied from the pictures on some imported object: they resemble the chariots on near-contemporary Greek vases. Representations of identifiable women are few. It is, however, worth mentioning that among the animals pregnant ones are present.

As is obvious from the motifs, Alpine and north European rock art have much in common. In both areas the humans are mainly male or male-associated (armed men, weapons, men with erect penises). Miniature figures are more common by far than those of natural size. A single figure is unusual; for the most part there is a multitude, often unstructured, but sometimes two or more figures appear to have an intentional relationship. However, compositions are rare. Though in all areas symbols in miniature dominate, it is striking that many weapons are shown in natural size (daggers, swords, spears), as are feet/foot-soles. When weapons or carts are associated with humans, their size becomes accentuated overall. Further numerous common motifs are abstract.

It is certainly no coincidence that in north Italy, south France and south Scandinavia one and the same motif is repeated over and over again on the same rock panel. In all three areas it may have been an invocation, the deepening of an image, instead of doubling it, probably reinforcing the magic.

This does not, however, mean that the north European motifs are derived from Alpine ones. The explanation for the similarity is that they have a common background through contacts with the Hallstatt culture in central Europe, in Austria and Hungary. The Hallstatt culture of the Alpine regions, rich in metal and salt, had close contacts with the Etruscans in north Italy and the Greek-Oriental Mediterranean culture. The south Scandinavian finds show that even this area had either direct or indirect contacts with these areas. In places without rock art, designs occur on bronze and gold weapons, cauldrons, bowls and belt-plates, and on pottery. Perishable materials were undoubtedly also decorated. Other works of art include small three-dimensional anthropomorphic or zoomorphic bronze statuettes.

An example of the importation of motifs and possibly even ideas occurs in a magnificient tomb at Kivik on the Baltic coast in south-east Sweden. It was covered by a huge cairn (now 70 m in diameter, 3.5 m high, but originally considerably bigger). Its wall-slabs are decorated with stylized figures in a symmetrical arrangement – five exclusively with motifs in pairs (two horses, two ships, two sun(?) wheels, two axes). This calls to mind the hoards with objects in pairs found in bogs and marshes. Two stone slabs have narrative scenes, usually interpreted as processions, sacrificial acts and a two-wheeled war-chariot with a charioteer (a motif typical of the Mediterranean area). The scene on each slab is framed by a line, and the whole resembles a woven tapestry hanging. Whether the unique decoration symbolizes a ceremony in honour of the chieftain – a sea lord – or a ceremony whose meaning is lost, we shall never know. As the tomb was robbed 200 years ago, only tiny bronze fragments with typical Nordic Bronze Age decoration, dated c. 1300

BC, remain. The date agrees fairly well with that of the pictures depicted on the wall-slabs. Such compositions are a testimony to cultural importations, most of which arrived as bronzes, others as textiles, from southern and central Europe. But rock-art motifs were not only transported on bronzes with embossed decorations. The most important foreign influences were carried in the minds of people travelling outside their home district. Subsequently, cultural novelties were easily transported, and spread if accepted as attractive for one reason or another.

The dating of identifiable objects in Bronze Age rock-art designs is often based on real bronze items found in well-dated graves and hoards, and on the rock-art motifs found on stone slabs in datable Bronze Age graves. The dating of style changes and superimposed motifs has proved difficult.

In the very north the repertoire mainly consists of game: land animals, fish and birds. Motifs of datable objects are lacking, and style changes have been practically the only indication of a time-scale. In recent years, however, palaeogeographical research on the White Sea and Lake Onega has made it possible to date changes of water-level in rocks bearing petroglyphs which are below the present-day water-level. According to this, hunter-gatherers' petroglyphs of the north group date from the fourth millennium BC (Savvateev, 1990). The tradition is long-lasting – to the south Scandinavian Early Bronze Age. The south Scandinavian rock art goes back to the Neolithic, but the main period is the second half of the Bronze Age, c. 1000–500 BC, though it was practised even later, a century or two into the Early Iron Age.

The purpose and meaning of rock art

In Europe rock art has been studied for about 150 years. During that time the main endeavour has been to establish a tenable chronology, a study of the content and a reconstruction of myths.

The northern group in particular has been difficult to date. But, as we have said, in recent years studies of shore-line changes in Karelia have made it possible to fix its age to a certain extent. Whether this dating has only local value or can be transferred to north Scandinavia is an open question. However, this geological dating offers a landmark. The dating of Bronze Age rock art began nearly 100 years ago when weapon design began to be compared with dated bronze weapons.

Besides chronology, studies simultanously concentrated on the significance of the symbols. It has been plausibly assumed that these have a message, and that they consequently are a medium of communication.

Today scholars agree that rock art is a religious picture-language, a conclusion that has initiated an endless number of hypotheses and suggestions for the interpretation of the meaning of various petroglyphic symbols.

When we characterize religions of our own time, we consider their mythical content. We make distinctions between the great religions according to their conception of divinity (one god, several gods, a trinity, and so on), their views on the genesis of life and other eschatological problems. It is thus natural that this attitude has marked the aim and direction of rock-art research, efforts being made to explain the content of rock-art figures and signs according to these concepts.

In one of the most influential analyses of south Scandinavian rock art, petroglyphs were interpreted as an expression of a fertility mythology of an agrarian society (Almgren, 1934). Almgren pointed to analogies with Oriental and ancient religions, such as those of Babylon, Egypt and Greece, and characterized Scandinavian Bronze Age rock art as showing ceremonies associated with the fertility cult. Rock-art designs of ships, for instance, were considered equivalent to those of the age-old tradition in Egypt, where models of ships – 'ships of the gods' – were used at religious feasts. Various rock-art scenes with humans were assumed to illustrate the wedding, killing, mourning, resurrection and revenge of a fertility god; the scenes of fighting as ritual games of combat between the fertility god and his opponents; the foot designs, on analogy with Indian folklore, as marking the presence of the god, and so on. Elements of magic or religious cults in pictures of, for example, a human with a bird's head bearing a round symbol (sun?), or a man ploughing while holding a green branch in his hand, were pointed out as strong evidence for Almgren's hypothesis. The meaning of these and other scenes and symbols was considered in this way to maintain the force of yearly ceremonies and to disseminate them further to other parts of the district.

When the fertility-cult hypothesis was launched, it was at the same time an argument against that of a mortuary cult, proposed earlier by other Swedish archaeologists. The concept of a mortuary cult was based on ship designs, feet, round figures and cup-marks on grave-slabs. Cup-marks were interpreted as bowls for offerings, and ship symbols as mortuary ships for the deceased's journey to the hereafter. The fertility cult, however, had an almost charismatic appeal and became predominant for more than fifty years.

A more extreme hypothesis relates to Indo-European myths, while different cultures and sources, near and distant, provide an explanation of carts and war-chariots, wheels, ships, feet/foot-soles and so on as an invisible deity in its various guises (rather than a particular god or goddess) whom it was forbidden to portray.

Görman (1987) studied a set of petroglyph symbols in Swedish rock art – above all humans, snakes and complex round figures – and compared them with similar motifs on various artefacts from Hallstatt and from Celtic cultures. Görman tries to identify these rock-art designs as the Celtic gods Cernunnos, Taranis and Lugh, and opines that this indicates a shift of the old Indo-European myths to the Celtic religion.

It is undeniable that quite a number of rock-art symbols have their prototypes in Celtic culture – and it is not excluded that they are associated with Celtic mythology; there was, after all, a strong cultural influence from the Celtic area to south Scandinavia. About the same time as new decorative elements appeared on Nordic bronzes, new motifs can be seen in rock art. It is plausible that this cultural impact caused Late Bronze Age religion to change, along with other noticeable changes in the cultural profile. Nevertheless, it is not even possible to accept unreservedly the interpretation of the Celtic religion as described by late Roman writers, including the names of the gods, which vary from author to author. Some Roman sources assimilate them with Roman deities.

Today there is a unanimous reaction against the fertility-cult interpretation; that of sun-worship, another favoured explanation of some circular rock-art designs, is also met with scepticism, the reason being that there are no real indications of a sun-cult in the Nordic archaeological material, except for the Trundholm wagon with its gold-coated disc. Statistical studies (Malmer, 1981) have shown that the

motifs with an agricultural connection are marginal compared with other kinds, and with abstract symbols. We should also remember that the neighbouring arable land was cultivated only from historical times, in the richest rock-art regions in Sweden and Norway as late as from the nineteenth century. Livestock most probably had greater importance than cultivation, but this too does not show up very much. More remarkable is that fishing, which was one of the basic food sources in Scandinavia, appears only once as a rock-art motif; nor are fishes a recurrent motif in Bronze Age rock art. Wild animals (game?) occur more often, but hunting scenes are infrequent. Hence, subsistence is not a major theme of south Scandinavian rock art.

When we turn to Alpine rock art, we find a somewhat different but nevertheless parallel situation as regards theories and assumptions. A religious explanation is current, and in this the theories of Georges Dumézil have played their part. Dumézil (1958) postulated the social triple division of Indo-European peoples into rulers, warriors and handicraftsmen, which had their equivalents in the triple deities of heaven, of thunder and of healing. Furthermore, myths had universal applicability and could be recognized in Celtic, Roman and German religions. This theory is strongly questioned today by other scholars, because there is no evidence at all for an Indo-European culture with so distinctive and such specific features.

The agglomeration of petroglyphs in valleys around Mont Bégo in the Alpes Maritimes prompted Henry de Lumley (1984) to consider those parts in the region in which rock art appears as open-air sanctuaries for people living along the Riviera. It is true that high mountains – Ararat, Sinai, Olympus – have played an important role in the myths of Mediterranean peoples. In the same way Mont Bégo may have been a religious locale in the Merveilles Valley proper. It is easy to establish that the rock panel was often chosen so that when facing the symbols, the peak or wall of the mountain chain of Merveilles was in sight.

De Lumley (1984) also addresses the theory of Indo-European religion in its Mediterranean version. According to him, the Bronze Age population of the southern Alps, having an agrarian and pastoral economy, practised the cult of the ox, as the mass of bovid symbols (usually interpreted as oxen) on rocks and stones seems to indicate. Secondly, the cult of the earth-goddess, or the great goddess, is symbolized by geometric figures and some anthropomorphs. Thirdly, the cult of the thunderstorm, or the god who brings rain and fertilizes the earth, is occasionally in disguise as a tauromorph or anthropomorph with a disc-head. In some exceptional cases the two specific anthropomorph designs – the god of thunder and rain and that of earth (receiving rain) – appear together in a scene, according to de Lumley's view.

Emmanuel Anati (1964, 1974), too, is of the opinion that the population of the north Italian valleys represented Indo-European myths by petroglyphs, and that there also a triple set of gods can be traced on the rock or stela where the surface is divided into three parts by three different symbols (not always the same). These symbols represent respectively a celestial, terrestrial and underground deity.

Among other French and Italian scholars it is quite usual for certain symbols – the ox, ard, harrow, scythe and weapons – to be interpreted as elements of Bronze Age daily life. It is presumed that motifs related to field work were made in the spring for assuring a good harvest. Interpretations proliferate; even the Old Testament has been seen as a source for the rock designs.

Our reservations are the same as were expressed when discussing the interpretation of south Scandinavian rock art according to fertility myths. Depictions of objects directly related to agriculture or livestock in the Alpes Maritimes and in north Italy are, compared to the quantity of all other rock art motifs, marginal. The bovine symbols, including the horned head, probably have a double meaning in which the symbol has a central place.

All these interpretations are, and will remain, speculative hypotheses. They lead to a blind alley, for they cannot be tested or proved.

THE ROLE OF RELIGION IN THE SOCIAL SYSTEM

As we cannot identify the mythical content of Bronze Age religions, we will try to come round another way. As we have said, rock art is a special symbolic expression of a phenomenon which we call magico-religious. The petroglyphs may have been a natural medium of communication with transcendental powers, but simultaneously a message to the society where they were produced. Religion as ideology has not only philosophical aspects; it comprises social elements as well. Hence the question, what role did it play in the social system?

The outward and observable forms of religion consist of ceremonies, buildings where ceremonies take place, and institutions, that is, officiants and their relation to the congregation. According to anthropological research, ceremonies are modelled and led by officiants, who may be priests or chieftains. Religion was not a private but a public matter, and may have been a means of conserving the social traditions. Anthropological research has shown that the exercizing of religion can accentuate and secure power and authority for a chieftain's family. With respect to this aspect, it should be possible to illuminate the role of rock art within the social system.

A quite different set of questions now comes to the fore. What is their spatial relation to the settlement area? Were places with rock art intended as local sanctuaries for a family or for an entire settlement area? Taking into account the time-range of thousands of years during which the symbols were developed and used and their message learned generation after generation, is there not evidence of a certain degree of stability in the communication system?

These questions have been studied by Scandinavian scholars since the 1970s, and the new approach has been rewarding. The studies show clearly that in south Scandinavia there is a correlation between habitation and rock-art areas. In some cases it seems to be possible to distinguish a cult centre within a region, as in western Sweden at Tanum.

In order to understand the meaning and purpose of rock art's language, it is important to know what kind of society it was part of. There was certainly a considerable difference between the hunter-gatherers' idea of the world of the north and that of Bronze Age people with a mixed economy (stock-breeding, fishing/hunting, agriculture and specialized handicrafts such as bronze casting) in south Scandinavia. There was a further difference in world-view between the people in the two Alpine areas on the one hand and between the Alpine areas and south Scandinavia on the other.

Taking the northernmost group of rock art, of which only a part belongs to the time-range of our consideration here, we can with reference to socio-anthropological research say that a society of trappers and fishers (or hunter-gatherers) was more or less egalitarian. The goal and meaning of their art equates with that of Palaeolithic art – to gain power over the quarry. The picture was a magical means for hunters to accomplish their desires. This phenomenon is sometimes discussed as though there is a difference between magic and religion. We wish, however, to emphasize that magic does not exist without a religious aspect and vice versa: hunting magic is part of a hunter's religion. Besides their magical message the petroglyphs depicting game were directed towards fellow-hunters as well and may have marked hunting territory or even simple traps, at propitious catching places. They may have become places for annual gatherings and feasts. Rock-art sites with thousands of petroglyphs, for instance at the end of Alta Fjord in northernmost Norway, probably were places to which people came for seasonal gatherings from near and far.

Although totemism is associated with mythological ideas of a type that we understand as religious, totemic interpretations are also sociological phenomena – for totemism is associated with the organization of society. The totemic interpretation is often refuted by Scandinavian scholars on the grounds that neither Scandinavians nor the Samis have preserved traditions which have a bearing on the meaning of the north Scandinavian rock art. Furthermore, they argue, the low population density in the vast northernmost area in prehistoric times is unlikely to have been compatible with totemism. But these arguments do not take into account the fact that the religion of the historical Samis is separated from that of the Stone Age trappers by many thousands of years. It is no wonder that today there are no remnants of totemism preserved in their culture.

A totemic interpretation is emphasized by Russian and Finnish scholars. Among the Balto-Finnish people, a totemic myth tradition extends back to the late medieval period around AD 1400–1500. An argument in favour of totemism is that the trappers/hunters did move in an east-west direction, as for instance is attested by stylistic and other affinities in archaeological finds of the Alta region (Norway) and Zavalruga, Vesovi Sledki and Besovi Nos near the White Sea. Exogamy must have occurred and the totemic phenomenon may have spread. How else could we explain the occurrence of anthropomorphic figures in extraordinary dress and in violent movement if not as shamans or sorcerers?

The themes of Alpine and south Scandinavian Bronze Age rock art are as different from those of the very north as is the character of their societies. One of the characteristics of the Scandinavian Bronze Age is that all bronze had to be imported by long-distance transport, whereas Alpine areas were closer to bronze-producing centres.

Archaeological finds show an abundance of weapons in Bronze Age centres, even in south Scandinavia (above all in Denmark). In central Europe weapon finds indicate the emergence of a new social group in the Early Bronze Age, that of the warriors. This is a sign of a warlike epoch, or one in which copper mines or trade over Alpine passes needed protection. In areas with access to rich copper mines, the new technology and trade promoted the growth of wealth. The economic growth continued and in some areas the upper echelons in what we can characterize as chieftain societies developed a princely luxury, as shown by some remarkable graves and their accoutrements, and decorations on bronzes. A typical feature of the time is that even less wealthy societies were affected by this development. In those areas – for instance in south-western and south-eastern Sweden – access to bronze was not easy and bronze objects were not the average person's property but a luxury for the few and thus status-giving.

When considering the whole of Scandinavia and adjacent parts of north Germany, archaeological finds have given us a picture of societies characterized by inequality between different areas, but even more by unequal distribution of resources between individuals. Besides burials, evidence is provided by offerings of bronze and gold items as hoards or deposits of varying worth. Hoards are abundant in Denmark and the southernmost area of Sweden, but less frequent in the rest of south Scandinavia. Certain hoards were probably a bronzesmith's hidden stock, but those found in marshes surely were a component of the religious system. The deposition of hoards must have been an important act for the society and those with resources, whose wealth became visible to all at ceremonial occasions. But to whom, on what occasion and for what purpose the offerings were made, we do not know. Nevertheless, we can be sure that they, too, were connected with myths, though we cannot trace them.

A hierarchical system is demonstrated by status-giving weapons such as daggers, swords and other equipment, together with the exquisite ornaments with which resource-rich people adorned themselves and showed their taste for luxury. It seems to have been a common habit that symbols of wealth and status became symbols in less prosperous areas. For this, the identifiable figures in the repertoire of rock art offer convincing testimony both in Alpine areas and in south Scandinavia.

Therefore, it is not surprising that many scholars in Nordic countries have interpreted rock designs of weapons, ships, war-chariots and horses as offerings to transcendental powers. A new hypothesis (Malmer, 1989) has gone even further. According to this, the symbols are substitutes for bronzes which people in poorer areas could not afford as offerings; myth interpretations were abandoned. This was a fruitful breakthrough in sociological terms, though we consider that it is not consistent with prehistoric thinking, though typical of the 'economic' mentality of our own time. Nevertheless, if we do not share the idea of rock designs as substitute offerings we agree that certain symbols imply status. According to us their task was to transmit a social message to the society by pictorial language and demonstrate who had the power in this period of changing ideology and social structure.

In the Alps, and the Alpes Maritimes in particular, we find a large complex of symbols – rectangles, squares, stippled plots united by winding line(s) – which are usually considered to be symbols of homesteads with fields, a sort of cadastral map. But prehistoric people did not need maps, being familiar with the landscape from childhood. Nor is the alternative interpretation of these composite figures as settlements plausible – that the difference in size of the 'huts and enclosures' indicates differences in property and power. To this we should like to reply: there was no shortage of ground in the Bronze Age. Hence, wealth was not measured by the amount of land owned but by livestock and hands for cultivating fields. The size and control of labour was the decisive factor for prosperity in prehistoric times. The exploitation of copper mines is an added proof of it.

It comes as no surprise that the privileged began to protect their interests. In order to legitimate and maintain their power, symbols and ceremonies were used to reinforce it and to demonstrate who had rights over resources. The status symbols on rock panels could thus also serve as reminders. It is reasonable to assume that petroglyphs 'addressed' the

myths by means of symbols explaining the world that encompassed the society, and simultaneously made clear the relationship between the upper and lower echelons of the society.

On the other hand, there is a large number of rock-art motifs, such as snakes and various abstract symbols, which can scarcely be interpreted as status markers. It is true that their prototypes are found as decorations on bronze artefacts in the Hallstatt and Celtic culture sphere in central and southern Europe, where it is not unlikely that they were associated with Celtic mythology. Trade over the Alpine passes into north Italy promoted the spread of the Celtic influence, including religious ideas. There it met, and perhaps intermingled with, the older Mycenaean and Etruscan elements. The export of bronzes to Scandinavia brought these novel designs, though it is not possible to say whether they arrived directly from the production centres in north Italy or through middlemen passing them on from one area to the next. Whether the myths and meanings behind the symbols on imported products were understood and retold here, or adjusted to local traditions, is another question for which we have no answer. Imports particularly to Denmark, an important area for Scandinavian trade, both of bronzes and raw materials, must have been considerable. The trade was rewarding, for it initiated a remarkable development in bronzesmithing and in handicrafts; from the artistic point of view, one of the highlights of Bronze Age Europe.

The great quantity of bronze imports must have been matched by exports of equal value. This required a large exploitation area, for example of amber, furs, slaves, flint and dried fish. As a direct or indirect result of this trade less prosperous areas also became influenced by novelties. A part of these ideological and social changes are mirrored by rock art.

Summing up, we emphasize that rock art is a rich source of many-sided information, confirming and strengthening data from archaeological sources, and contributing information that cannot be obtained elsewhere. It reflects the different qualities of the spiritual life, that of abstract thinking in pictures and abstract symbols. The interpretations have to remain unproven hypotheses. Today there is a reaction against the concept that every motif or every scene has its absolute religious significance, wherever and from whatever time zone it is to be found. In order to find patterns whereby we may interpret their 'sayings' or messages, we should, instead of examining the possible meaning of individual symbols, pay more attention to the frequency of symbol combinations. For this, field studies are a must wherever rock art appears, and they should not be carried out as a discipline that is separate from archaeological research. If we wish to find out the role rock art played in the society, studies of the neighbourhood, the art's proximity to settlements, to graves and fairways, and so on – an aspect of study only in its infancy – should be intensified. The economic and social aspects as mirrored by finds and by rock-art symbols should be studied thoroughly in order to draw tenable conclusions; deductions upon which hypotheses about the core of Bronze Age religion are based must have a solid foundation.

In consequence of this new aspect of rock art, we now have further research objectives. It is important to establish the relationship between the geographical position of rock-art areas and the contemporary culture: their proximity to the nearest dwelling site, burial site and communication routes, including waterways. Furthermore, attention must be paid to the frequency of the symbols used and their precise orientation. Although important contributions in this respect have already been made, the research as a whole is still in its infancy.

NOTE

1 Megalithic tombs and other monuments (menhirs, henges, alignments, stone circles, and so on) erected throughout the Early Bronze Age are dealt with in the author's chapter in Volume I (Chapter 55).

BIBLIOGRAPHY

Publications on Scandinavian rock art are mostly in Scandinavian languages. As these languages are usually not read by scholars from other language groups, the bibliography below lists mainly recent publications in English from 1981 onward. References to earlier works in this paper, see Malmer 1981, where works from 1839 to 1980 are listed.

ALMGREN, B. 1967. *Den osynliga gudomen [The Invisible Divinity]*. Stockholm.

—— 1988. *Die Datierung bronzezeitlicher Felszeichnungen in Westschweden*. (Acta mus. antiq. septentr. regiae Univ. upsalaiensis, 6.)

ALMGREN, O. 1934. *Nordische Felszeichnungen als religiöse Urkunden*. Frankfurt am Main.

ANATI, E. 1961. *Camonica Valley*. New York.

—— 1964. *Camonica Valley*. London.

—— 1974. *Methods of Recording and Analysing Rock-Engravings*. Capo di Ponte. (Camunian stud., 7.)

BERTILSSON, U. 1987. *The Rock Carvings of Northern Bohuslän. Spatial Structures and Social Symbols*. Stockholm.

BOSTWICK BJERCK, L. G. 1988. Approaches to Scandinavian Petroglyphs, from Fertility Cults to Graffiti. *Festskrift til Anders Hagen, Arkeologiske Skrifter Historisk Museum*, No. 4, pp. 301–9.

BURGTELLER, E.; LAUTH, L. 1965. Felsgravierungen in den österreichischen Alpenländern. *Jahrb. Oberösterr. mus. ver.*, Vol. 110, pp. 326–78.

COLES, J. M.; HARDING, A. F. 1979. *The Bronze Age in Europe*. London.

DUMÉZIL, G. 1958. *L'Idéologie tripartie des Indo-Européens*. Bruxelles.

GEORGIEV, G. II. 1961. *Kulturgruppen der Jungstein – und der Kupferzeit in der Ebene von Thrazien/Südbulgarien*, Sym-posium 'L'Europe à la fin de l'âge de la pierre'. Prague.

GIMBUTAS, M. 1991. *Civilization of the Goddess*. San Francisco.

GÖRMAN, M. 1987. *Nordiskt och keltiskt. Südskandinavisk religion under yngre bronsålder och keltisk järnålder*. Lund (German summary: Nordisch und Keltisch. Südskandinavische Religion während der jüngeren Bronzezeit und keltischer Eisenzeit).

HULTKRANTZ, Å. 1986. Rock Drawings as Evidence of Religion. In: STEINSLAND, G. (ed.), *Words and Objects. Towards a Dialogue between Archaeology and History of Religion*. Oslo.

KAELAS, L. In Press. Interpretation des gravures rupestres protohistoriques du nord de l'Europe. Une remise en question. In: *Le Mont Bégo*. Laboratoire de Préhistoire du Musée Nationale d'Histoire Naturelle, Institut de Paléontologie Humaine.

LUMLEY, H. DE, 1984. Les gravures rupestres de l'âge du Bronze de la Vallée des Merveilles Mont Bego, Alpes Maritimes. *L'Anthropologie*, Vol. 88, pp. 613–47.

MALMER, M. P. 1981. *A Chronological Study of North European Rock Art*. Stockholm. Kungl. Vitterhets Historie och Antikvitets Akademiens Handlingar. (Antik. Ser., 32.)

—— 1989. North-European Bronze Age Rock Art. In: NORDSTRÖM, H. Å.; KNAPE, A. (eds), *The Bronze Age Studies*. Stockholm. (Mus. nat. Antiq. Stud., 6.)

SAVVATEEV, J. A. 1990. Rock Art from Lake Onega: 4000–2000 BC. Swansoncs.

15

ASIA

15.1
CENTRAL ASIA

Vadim M. Masson

Central Asia may be regarded as the region east of the Caspian Sea and west of the Pamir and Tien Shan mountains, with the northern and southern boundaries more vaguely defined respectively by the Kara Kum and Kyzyl Kum deserts and by the highlands of Iran and Afghanistan. In modern political terms, this territory is divided among the republics of Turkmenistan, Uzbekistan, Tajikistan and Kazakhstan, along with northern Afghanistan and north-eastern Iran. The region as a whole is extremely varied in topography and environment, containing inhospitable deserts, rugged mountain ranges with verdant intermontane valleys, well-watered piedmont zones, and lowland alluvial plains and deltas.

The major drainages include the Amu Darya, flowing north-west from the Pamir toward the Aral Sea. The Zeravshan is the major tributary to the Amu Darya, flowing out of the Hissar range and providing the location for Samarkand and Bukhara; smaller rivers empty into the Amu Darya from the Hissar and Pamirs ranges further upstream. The Syr Darya drains the Tien Shan, and also flows north-west toward the Aral Sea. Further south, the lower mountains of Afghanistan give rise to smaller water courses such as the Balkh that move northward toward the Amu Darya, but which form alluvial deltas before meeting the river. A similar situation occurs further west with the Murghab and Tejen Rivers, both of which flow northward toward the Kara Kum, where they form deltaic fans. In contrast, the Atrek drains westward through the Kopet Dagh range and into the Caspian Sea.

These water courses defined zones of prehistoric settlement. The most important of these for the periods reviewed in this chapter are: the lower section of the Atrek, around which formed Dakhistan and Parthia of antiquity; the minor streams through the piedmont zone along the northern edge of the Kopet Dagh; the Tejen and the Murghab rivers, the latter forming the heart of classical Margiana; the middle section of the Amu Darya and associated tributaries, the centre of classical Bactria; the Zeravshan; and the lower section of the Amu Darya, the later Khorasmia.

Central Asian prehistory witnessed an early appearance of Neolithic communities in the south-western region by the late seventh millennium BC. Given the archaeological name of Djeitun, this farming society provided the foundation for the subsequent emergence of an indigenous Eneolithic/Chalcolithic culture (Namazga I–II) early in the fifth millennium BC. This chapter addresses the final phases of the Central Asian Eneolithic (Namazga III), its Bronze Age evolutions (Namazga IV–VI), and the expanding regional diversity of Bronze Age cultures within Central Asia (especially in Margiana and Bactria). The chapter also examines the steppe areas to the north and its relations with southern Central Asia. While the Bronze Age societies were forming in the south, the Kelteminar culture continued a mixed economy of hunting/gathering and animal herding, but sometimes constructing reed and wood dwellings and working copper and turquoise. The subsequent steppe Bronze Age, expressed in the Andronovo culture complex, played an important role in forming the Central Asian world.

THE LATE ENEOLITHIC (3500–3000 BC)

Toward the end of the fourth and the start of the third millennium BC, early agricultural communities in the southwest of what are now the republics of Central Asia were making ever greater advances in culture and technology. These communities lived along a narrow band of oases on the northern foothills of the Kopet Dagh mountains and in the delta of the Tejen-Gerirud River. While agricultural villages also appeared further east, in the Murghab delta area and even in the upper Zeravshan region, the early focus of intellectual and cultural progress was in the more densely populated regions to the south-west.

The material culture found in the Kopet Dagh oases clearly indicates two territorial groups, which evidently corresponded to two groups of ancient tribes (Masson, 1964; Masson and Sarianidi, 1972). Kara-depe and Namazga-depe were the two principal settlements of the group to the west. Kara-depe at this time covered some 8 hectares, and contained some 700 people. The ceramics of this group are distinctively painted with well-executed geometrical designs and representations of various animals. Altyn-depe and Geoksyr are typical centres of the eastern group. Altyn-depe greatly increased in size during this period, attaining an area of 25 hectares. The ceramics of this group typically bear polychrome painted crosses and half-crosses (Khlopin, 1964; Masson, 1977). A third group is also present, in the highlands of the western Kopet Dagh where grey-ware ceramics characterize the culture.

Despite these developments in south-western Central Asia, Neolithic tribes of hunters, fishers and gatherers continued to occupy large parts of central Asia. The archaic culture and economy of these communities satisfied minimum daily needs (Masson and Sarianidi, 1972). At the same time, these cultures did lay the groundwork for the eventual development of the steppe Bronze Age. Excavations at Sarazm, a settlement on the upper Zeravshan (near Panjikent in Tajikistan), show that the Neolithic hunters were in direct contact with the settled agricultural community at this place: the coarse pottery of these tribes appears in the same level as the brightly painted wares of the settled population (Isakov, 1986). The cultural impact of the early agricultural civilization on their northern neighbours remained negligible, and was confined to certain shapes and decoration of pottery.

The technical and economic basis of the agricultural communities expanded greatly during this period. The introduction of irrigation farming eventually led to the development of integrated irrigation systems. One such system was that near the Geoksyr I settlement, in the Tejen delta (Lisitsina, 1978). The three canals of the system are about 3 km long, and 2.5–5 m wide; water reached the fields through a series of feeder ditches. Similar irrigation works are evident in the foothill zone. The fields themselves supported crops of barley and wheat; the barley was a form that required irrigation. In addition to their crops, these communities also kept animals. Sheep and goats were the most important of these, though cattle and pigs were also tended.

Specialized craft production appeared as an important aspect of the economy. The standardized objects made by potters, smiths and lapidaries display a specialist's skill and advanced control over productive technology. For example, pottery was baked in kilns that fired to a constant temperature, and the potters controlled these kilns with remarkable certainty. The workshops of these craft specialists were probably in full-time operation. But since the workshops were not concentrated in a single quarter of settlements, the craftsmen probably remained connected to a network of kinsmen; craft production served the community through kinship ties, rather than through marketing, a form of specialized production called community craft production in Russian literature.

An additional factor in the formation of the Central Asian world at the beginning of the Bronze Age was the growing intensity of interregional connections. The technological, formal, and decorative characteristics of some pottery at Kara-depe relate to those found in north-eastern Iran; the Geoksyur tradition of painted pottery appeared in significant amounts at Shahr-i Sokhta in the Seistan region of eastern Iran, and the influence of this style is detectable in such sites as Mundigak. Links with the Mesopotamian Elamite world appeared in the influence of this region on some small works of art. These influences may have been related in part to the migration of tribes into southern Central Asia, and from there into other areas. At the same time, trade increasingly linked large parts of western Asia, giving rise to the proto-Elamite presence across the Iranian plateau. Foreign wealth, including carnelian and lapis lazuli, began appearing in Central Asia in increasing amounts.

All these factors led to social differentiation and property inequalities as aspects of a more complex social structure.

Large settlements contained twelve to fifteen multi-roomed dwellings with communal kitchen, grain stores and courtyards. These houses probably belonged to extended family communities to which small families attached themselves by descent ties and by co-ordinated economic activities; the extended family became the basic unit of society. Collective tombs, often holding twelve to twenty bodies, appeared at the same time; these tombs might be regarded as the family vaults of extended families. Individual graves also exist. While most of the single burials contained only one or two pottery vessels, others were far richer in grave goods. One grave at Kara-depe held eight beautifully decorated vessels and a large, carefully made terracotta figurine; another damaged tomb contained fifteen decorated vessels and a terracotta figurine of a standing bearded man. A woman's grave at Altyn-depe held five pottery and two stone vessels in addition to a number of copper artefacts. A woman's grave at Sarazm included a large array of ornaments, including gold, lazurite and carnelian beads. These richly equipped single interments probably contain the leaders of early agricultural society – chieftains, priests and priestesses – whose high social standing required special burial rites. These leaders resided in the major settlements such as Altyn-depe and Kara-depe.

A very important prerequisite for these changes, especially those in the technical and economic spheres, was the accumulation of knowledge. A look at ancient industries gives clear evidence of this knowledge. The agrarian cycle of crop irrigation could not have been regulated without a calendar system based on astronomical observations. The solar symbols on a large female terracotta figurine imply that the annual cycle consisted of fifteen months of twenty-four days, with five additional 'extra' days. The advances in metallurgy involved the accumulation of practical chemical and pyrotechnological knowledge. Judging by discoveries of the appropriate stone tools, metal ores were smelted in the settlements themselves, not at the place of extraction. Metal working involved a variety of techniques, including hot and cold hammering, and casting. Various forms of heat treatment improved the performance of metal tools. Tests show that cold hammering increases the hardness of copper knives and axes (surface hardness up to 137 kg/mm^2, interior hardness only $80–85 \text{ kg/mm}^2$). Annealing after cold hammering was also practised. The purest metals were used for high-quality products, and oxidized mixed ores for the rest. In pottery, too, a correlation existed between the kinds of clay used and the different categories of product. These indications of advancing knowledge, which forms the basic layer of primitive science, all pertaining to production, crafts and agriculture.

The intellectual achievements of early agricultural society in Central Asia were, if anything, more significant than the technical advances. Decorated ceramics are the best represented surviving embodiments of the early agricultural cultures studied by archaeologists. Pottery was an applied art, the products of which were in everyday use. At the same time, the decoration of pottery was not primitive and hastily executed, but instead represents an ornamental world in which can be sensed the hand of master craftsmen, the development of traditions and schools of design. The painted geometrical motifs, like carpet patterns, display rules of symmetry, composition and colour that border on the abstract. The spirit of this art abstractly expressed the ordered rhythm of everyday life, the cycles of agrarian economic production. Representation, especially of animals, also appears in pottery decoration. Images of mountain goats and snow leopards are very common, possibly connected to a system of binary attributes and to totemic concepts. Semantic associations are also evident: for example, depictions of birds and of sun circles are consistently found together, making a link between bird and sky. Some vessels have complex scenes depicting a variety of animals and symbolic figures, which may refer to mythological concepts. The most prominent symbols are the stepped cross and stepped triangle. The large number of everyday objects decorated in a similar way established a definite aesthetic and intellectual atmosphere, and played an important part in the organization and education of the various age groups in society.

Objects clearly connected with religious activity shed additional light on the world-view of this early agricultural society. Sanctuaries with a central ritual hearth and podium are widespread. In Kara-depe, two such sanctuaries adjoin a group of outbuildings, courtyard and granaries to form an integrated architectural complex. This complex represents an early temple that combined ritual observation with vital economic functions, especially the storage of food reserves and seed on behalf of the agricultural commune. In the Geoksyr oasis, domestic sanctuaries are common. These sanctuaries consist of a small room within a multi-roomed residential complex, the room containing a circular altar/hearth in its centre.

The terracottas found in every house, and often in tombs as well, also convey important information about the cultural world. The terracottas include a number of hastily fashioned anthropomorphic figures, which were probably made to be used only once in some specific ritual. Other figurines are carefully made and often massive, most of them representing females with painted or appliqué decoration and elaborately styled hair; these figurines, sometimes executed in stone, were clearly designed for repeated use. These more elaborate figurines were probably placed in shrines – a fragment of a painted vessel at Kara-depe shows a scene in which a seated female statue is flanked by two apparently bowing figures. The figurines are probably images of a female deity, a protectress of fertility, a mother-goddess. Even so, the goddess representation was already complex and polymorphous, and was sometimes combined with a serpent. For example, a figurine discovered in a burial has a serpent crawling up its thigh, the serpent perhaps expressing the hypostasis of a chthonic goddess of the underworld. The presence of twin sanctuaries in the Kara-depe ritual building complex implies the presence of two protectors: the fertility goddess and her husband.

THE EARLY BRONZE AGE (3000–2500 BC)

The coalescence of the Bronze Age patterns of civilization in the Kopet Dagh oases occurred during the first half of the third millennium BC, the Namazga IV period. During this time, various technological innovations induced structural changes and development of the previous late Chalcolithic economic base. The previous regional differences within the Kopet Dagh piedmont continued during this period. Although the settlement of the Tejen delta area largely disappeared, the Geoksyr tradition of painted pottery and small works of art evolved in places like Altyn-depe. In the western piedmont the grey wares became characteristic of sites such as Ak-depe and the Parkhai cemetery, forming a zone between Ashkabad and the Gorgon plain in Iran. By the end of the period, the first agricultural settlement in Margiana seems to have been established (for instance at Kelleli).

The excavations at Altyn-depe provide the clearest picture of the general cultural and social progress of the period. Altyn-depe was a major centre and presents features indicative of an expanding urbanism. A massive sun-dried brick wall enclosed an area of 26 hectares. The central gate, framed by two pilastered towers, was 15 m wide, and divided by two walls into two narrow lanes on each side of a paved central corridor. Excavation in a residential area inside the town wall revealed a gradual cultural development through five building horizons (Altyn 8–4). The houses of the earlier levels consisted usually of a living room and outbuildings, focused on an open square. The largest building of this ensemble apparently also functioned as a place of ritual, evident in the niched walls and the presence of many little terracotta boxes whose sides bear incised decoration. In the later levels, a new house form appeared, characterized by a suite of rooms, one room containing a raised hearth; the largest of these houses covered 50–65 m². Their dimension and layout indicate that these dwellings housed nuclear families; the area as a whole may have contained a corporate group of related families that owned a granary and observed rituals in common.

The graves provide information about contemporary social structure. Some burials were placed beneath the floors or walls of dwellings. Most of these intra-mural burials were of children, though sometimes also of adults. The funerary offerings of these burials were usually minimal: at most several pottery vessels and some stone beads. Some richer burials, usually of young women, do occur, in which were placed copper and stone artefacts, including marble lamps. The latter burials contained people of a particular social category, perhaps associated with some ritual function. Collective graves, placed between houses, account for about one-third of the burials. These extra-mural burials usually held two to five people, but as many as fourteen individuals have been found in a single burial. The collective graves probably were the 'burial vaults' of small families. In addition to everyday objects, the collective tombs contained prestige goods, such as knobs from staffs of office, seals and lamps. The fairly minor difference of wealth contained in both kinds of graves indicates that the social structure of the community in this part of Altyn-depe was relatively undifferentiated by status or class.

Signs of general technological advance are also apparent in this residential quarter of Altyn-depe. The basic means of subsistence seems little changed from the late Chalcolithic condition, and involved the same crops and herd animals, and the same productive equipment. The Bactrian camel seems to have been domesticated; model clay carts imply that these beasts expanded potential efficiency of transportation. Changes are more notable in other production, where increasing craft specialization and skill are apparent. Advances in pottery technology involved both the introduction of the potter's wheel and greater control over the kiln. The adoption of the potter's fast wheel was fairly rapid: already 15 per cent at the beginning of the period, the proportion of thrown vessels quickly rose to 90 per cent. The development of the fast wheel may derive from other applications of a rotary motion, such as the bow drill and thread spinning, both of which had considerable antiquity. The new potting technology led to greater uniformity of vessel form, and the mass production of pottery induced a decline and eventual disappearance of individually painted objects. At the same time, the two-tiered up-draught kiln made its appearance. This technological shift improved control over firing temperatures and atmospheres.

Advances in metallurgical practices also occurred. Various copper alloys came into use, including copper-lead, copper-silver, copper-lead-arsenic, and copper-lead-tin; the last variety of bronze appeared relatively late in the Early Bronze Age. The different alloys were put to different uses. At Altyn-depe, for example, arsenical bronze was used for various kinds of implements, while the copper-lead and copper-silver alloys were used for ornaments and dress items. Cast and wrought metal-work became common, including pins with decorative heads, and seals with loop-handles. At Altyn-depe, at least, the metallurgical kiln, together with the stone tools used in metal working, were scattered through the town, next to the dwellings and workshops, in contrast to the creation of craft districts in the following period; an area of smelting furnaces did exist at the edge of the Khapuz-depe settlement. Similar specialization occurred in other crafts. Trace-wear analysis of the tools used in weaving, leather working, stone cutting, and bone working reveal an increased sophistication in these industries. The new technological and economic power considerably expanded the potential cultural developments, which climaxed in the following period of the Bronze Age. This progress laid the cultural foundation for an urban way of life.

In the applied arts, best represented in the painted ceramics, a trend toward brightly-coloured rug patterns is evident. The motifs in the geometrical patterns form uniform and rhythmic structures in which the individual elements are not readily distinguishable. More naturalistic figures also occur, notably goats, trees and coiling snakes. Trees are depicted either singly or in groups, occasionally also with a goat. These representations are probably of the Tree of Life, a motif common to many cultures around the world. The cross and half- or quarter-stepped pyramid indisputably carried a special semantic content. These motifs were incised on the sides of small terracotta boxes, often with four feet; these boxes had a probable ritual use. The Parkhai cemetery contained four-legged rectangular vessels of similar function; these mortuary vessels were decorated with small lamp-cups set on the corners, rams' or bulls' heads along the rim between, and coiling snakes along the vessels' sides. This complex semantic grouping perhaps represents a three-part hierarchical model of the universe, with fire for the sun above, hoofed animals for the firmament, and serpents for the underworld below. The cross motif also appeared on seals and sealings; the seals probably had a dual significance, as ritual talisman and as symbols of ownership.

The changing terracotta figurines illustrate additional transformation of the cultural system. Seated women modelled in the round initially were common, a continuation of the Geoksyr style. These figures, and the painted decoration on pottery also, gradually coarsened. At the same time, the figures flattened, and details appeared more commonly in clay than paint; appliqué ornamentation was particularly frequent on the grey-ware figurines in the western part of the Kopet Dagh piedmont. Moreover, various symbols appeared on figurines. For example, incised zigzags covered the massive female figurine from Khapuz-depe, perhaps a representation of the goddess as patron of the waters, that vital agricultural requirement. An appliqué figure at the breast of another female figurine emphasizes the traditional function of guardian of fertility. In general terms, the settled oases of Central Asia experienced a gradual cultural evolution and accumulation of considerable technical potential, thus paving the way for the broad cultural and intellectual developments of the Middle Bronze Age.

THE MIDDLE BRONZE AGE (2500–2000 BC)

The culmination of the Bronze Age civilization is marked by three basic features: the growth of the local urban civilization in the foothill zone; expansion of settled life into new oases of the Murghab delta; and a consolidation of links with neighbouring regions, including Afghanistan, Iran, Baluchistan, the Indus Valley and Mesopotamia.

The Kopet Dagh piedmont provided the setting for an urban civilization during the third quarter of the third millennium BC. While Altyn-depe is the most extensively studied of these cities, others also existed. Namazga-depe, for example, reached about 50 hectares in size, and possessed a large hinterland dotted with smaller settlements such as Taichanak-depe, Shor-depe and Kosha-depe. Although smaller settlements have not yet been discovered around Altyn-depe, villages probably did exist there, but now are buried under deltaic sediments up to 2 m thick. Very likely, Altyn-depe and Namazga-depe formed city-states in control of the Kopet Dagh oases. Even at the height of the Bronze Age, however, the process of state formation could not have progressed very far: neither royal tombs nor palace-like architecture has been found at either town.

The work at Altyn-depe reveals an urban layout in multiple districts or quarters. A pottery quarter, covering about 2 hectares and containing some fifty kilns, lay in the northern part of town. Metal-workers, identified by the high concentration of their tools, occupied another quarter. In these two quarters, and also in other ordinary residential districts, multi-roomed houses along narrow winding lanes composed the town fabric. Such residential districts were distinct from the 'upper-class' districts, where the streets were laid out regularly at right angles, and where the dwellings were more spacious and better made. All these residential areas were in turn separate from the ritual centre, focused on a stepped tower-like structure (12 m high), the ritual centre also encompassed vast storehouses, workshops, and a cemetery for the priesthood.

Judging by its complex internal structure, its evident social differentiation, and the multiplicity of its economic functions, the town was clearly more than simply a large agricultural centre. The architectural centrality of the temple complex may reflect a theocratic constraint on civil authority. Altyn-depe at this time contained between 6,000 and 7,500 people, who were divided into social groups that were distinctive in their standards of living and way of life. The social distinctions probably corresponded in turn to particular positions in the system of production and distribution.

The artisan district of potters, for example, contained multi-roomed houses similar to those of the extended family communities characteristic of the late Chalcolithic settlements. Collective graves in the district contained only a few clay vessels, and the interred bodies were wrapped in simple reed matting. These material attributes characterized the lowest social ranks. The middle social rank contained wealthier families, who lived as separate families in 'flats' of five or six rooms and a kitchen. These people buried their dead around their houses; the burials typically included not just pottery, but also many bronze rings, stone bead necklaces, terracotta figurines and metal seals. Those in the upper social ranks inhabited large and spacious residences. The collective graves near these houses contained a rich assortment of seals, figurines, bracelets and stone bead necklaces and belts; the bodies placed in these graves were wrapped in fine woollen cloth. Individual tombs in the same district sometimes contained unusual grave goods. In one case, a man was interred with a massive 'column' of white marble and a long stone staff in addition to the more usual beads and vessels. In another case, the tomb of a young woman contained a rich array of toilet articles, including ceramic and marble vessels, copper objects, a silver mirror and a decorated ivory rod of clear Indian origin. These extraordinary grave goods doubtless marked the special social status of the deceased, who belonged to the secular and priestly aristocracy.

The ivory staff from the previously mentioned burial at Altyn-depe is not the only indication of connections with India. Other ivory objects have also been found, as have several square stamp seals with a general Harappan character. Many of these objects at Altyn-depe may be dated to early Namazga V contexts, to the century or two just after 2500 BC. Not coincidentally, the urban, or mature, phase of the Harappan civilization began around 2500 BC. The mature Harappan peoples very soon established at least one outpost in Central Asia, at Shortugai on the upper Amu Darya in eastern Bactria (Francfort, 1989), perhaps as a colony to control the long-distance circulation of lapis lazuli from Badakhshan to the east. The presence of Indian objects at Altyn-depe reflects this wide-flung exchange network. At the same time, Central Asia enjoyed connections westward with the Iranian plateau, Elam and Mesopotamia. The Mesopotamian ziggurat may have inspired the stepped tower in the Altyn-depe ritual centre. Various art forms also betray a stylistic influence from the west.

The various developments in Central Asia at the height of the Bronze Age reflect a tremendous growth in organized knowledge, keeping pace with the increasing social differentiation, economic complexity and technical skill. While the nature and range of this knowledge can today be understood only indirectly, the archaeological evidence does bear mute testimony to some of its facets.

Irrigation agriculture everywhere remained the central productive activity. This reality naturally presupposed a fixed calendar system linked to the agrarian cycle. The corresponding development of astronomical observations and knowledge seems to have given rise to astral symbolism, which is particularly well represented at the Altyn-depe ritual centre. A stone tablet found in this ritual centre bore the images of a cross and a crescent moon; the grave of a priest contained a golden bull's head adorned with an inlaid moon. The sign of a shining star decorates a group of terracottas, representing one of the hypostases of a female deity, the sky-goddess.

The cultivation of new types of crops and the raising of new types of animals demanded the accumulation of empirical biological information as the basis for selective breeding. For example, a special breed of dog appeared at Altyn-depe. These dogs were large and thickset with square chests, short muzzles and powerful jaws. Terracotta figurines represent the breed with trimmed ears and docked tails, practices which emphasized their resemblance to the modern Central Asian sheepdog. The breed was evidently developed as a sheepdog-cum-wolfhound.

The potter's craft was enhanced by the common use of a sophisticated two-tiered kiln, providing for controllable high temperatures. These structures provided the technical basis for mass production of high-quality, standardized vessels. A more judicious selection of raw materials (clays, temper) is also apparent. Metal working shows a comparable refinement, with the appearance of specialized techniques. For example, the lost-wax technique was used to produced a silver seal, on which the three-headed dragon motif was then engraved.

The urban phase of the Central Asian civilization did not long endure in the Kopet Dagh piedmont. Around 2200 BC, the occupied area at Altyn-depe shrank and Namazga-depe may have been largely abandoned; few other sites of the period have been identified in the Kopet Dagh piedmont. At the same time, small towns appeared in the Kelleli, Gonur and Togolok oases of the Murghab delta to the east. The material culture of these Kelleli phase occupations is virtually identical to that found in the late Middle Bronze Age occupation at Altyn-depe. This cultural correspondence with the Namazga civilization indicates that communities from the west colonized the Murghab, bringing with them their traditional pottery, female terracotta statuettes, and metal compartmented seals. The new settlements in the Murghab delta set the stage for the subsequent spectacular developments in Margiana and Bactria.

THE LATE BRONZE AGE (2000–1500 BC)

Around the middle of the second millennium BC, fundamental historical and social changes occurred in Central Asia as they did in neighbouring regions. In the Kopet Dagh piedmont, small settlements (not more than several hectares in size) replaced the urban centres, sometimes springing up on the ruins of the former cities (for example, the 'tower' of Namazga-depe, the southern hill of Anau, Ulug-depe), or emerging in new locations (such as Tekkem-depe, Elken-depe). Isolated burial grounds also appeared (Yangi-Kala). These settlements contained houses solidly built of unfired brick, as in earlier times. However, a decline occurred in other realms of material culture: ceramic forms coarsened somewhat, production of female terracotta figurines sharply declined, and few seals appeared.

Yet, as the former heartland of the Central Asian civilization declined, vibrant new centres formed in the Murghab valley (ancient Margiana) and in the middle reaches of the Amu-Darya (ancient Bactria) to the east. At the same time, especially in the second half of the second millennium BC, the Bronze Age tribes of the steppes spread vigorously, and penetrated as far as northern Afghanistan. The resulting contact of cultures involved mutual influence and symbiosis, and initiated a cultural synthesis.

The Bactrian-Margiana archaeological complex (BMAC)

The Late Bronze Age in both Margiana and Bactria may be divided into two periods, the earlier (the Gonur phase in Margiana, the Sapalli phase and Dashly complex in Bactria) dated to 2000–1750 BC., and the later (the Togolok phase in Margiana, the Djarkutan phase in Bactria) dated to 1750–1500 BC (Masson, 1959; Sarianidi, 1977, 1990; Masimov, 1979; Askarov, 1973, 1977; Askarov and Abdullaev, 1981). The first of these periods evinces a striking uniformity in material culture, and has recently received the name Bactrian-Margiana Archaeological Complex (BMAC).

Settlement formed oasis clusters of towns and villages in the Murghab delta; a similar settlement clustering along the small tributaries of the Amu Darya occurred in Bactria. Irrigation agriculture supported the population in both areas;

the water drawn from the Murghab channels and the Amu Darya flowed into fields of cereals, chick-peas and grapes. Animal herds provided another important aspect to subsistence production. The herds consisted mainly of sheep and goats, but cattle, pigs, horses, camels and donkeys were also kept; the appearance of the domesticated horse marks the introduction of this species from the steppes of Kazakhstan. The relatively frequent appearance of pig bones indicates that the water supply was steady.

In both areas, the settlement clusters contained several larger sites, typically more than 5 hectares in area. Examples of these towns include Taip I (12 hectares) and Gonur (28 hectares) in Margiana, and Sapalli-depe in Bactria. The larger settlements usually consisted of a fortress adjoining amorphous settlement mounds. The fortresses were roughly square, equipped with round towers set in the corners of the wall; the fortress walls encompassed as much as 1.5 hectares. Towns contained separate craft quarters, in which kilns were located, and where pottery and metal-work were produced. Some towns, such as Togolok 21 and Djarkutan, also included a walled rectangular cult centre. The Djarkutan cult centre held an altar between four pillars standing on a paved surface, and also household and storage facilities. In contrast, the more numerous villages usually lacked both fortresses and specialized craft-production quarters, and covered only 0.5 to 3 hectares. The towns should be seen as settlements of an urban type, to which the surrounding villages were attached. This configuration laid the foundation for the emergence of the city-state, though no evidence yet firmly indicates this level of political organization during the Late Bronze Age.

The burial evidence implies a comparatively high level of prosperity in the BMAC societies. The cemetery at Djarkutan held about 700 graves, while over 100 burials have been recovered at Sapalli-depe; looters have pillaged innumerable tombs in Bactria to supply the illicit world art market (Pottier, 1984). The graves generally contain a significant number of different materials, including as many as thirty ceramic vessels and a dozen bronze and copper artefacts. In the Sapalli-depe graves, women were interred with significantly more wealth than were men, and such administrative objects as seals occurred only with women; this pattern implies that women, at least those of élite rank, enjoyed a status equal to that of men. The discovery of a battleaxe is noteworthy, since it points to the increasing importance of weapons. The frequency of cenotaphs probably reflects the increase of military conflict. A bronze axe and spear in a cenotaph at Sapalli-tepe implies that the cenotaph was constructed in memory of a warrior who died elsewhere. The cenotaphs, significantly, often included a larger inventory of goods than did the single graves.

While the material culture of the initial settlements in Margiana (the Kelleli phase) was closely related to the Namazga civilization, this culture spontaneously transformed to produce the distinctive material culture of the BMAC. In contrast to the higgledy-piggledy construction of residential districts in the older towns such as Altyn-depe, clearly laid out rectilinear house plans became common in the BMAC settlements: A characteristic lay-plan was a roughly square structure enclosed by a wall and, sometimes, also a passage. The fortresses were essentially larger versions of the same plan, and the same concept is evident in structures that may be cult centres. In Sarianidi's view, Togolok 21 contained a cultic structure of this type (Sarianidi, 1986b). This structure possessed four round towers at the corners of an outer rectangular wall that measured 50 × 60 m and was 4

m thick. The rooms inside these walls were often plastered; narrow storerooms and large storage vessels formed part of the interior accoutrements. The artefacts associated with this architecture include spouted vessels suitable for libations, numerous small stone columns, the head of a bull statue in stone, and a massive bronze battleaxe.

The number of female statuettes declined sharply, and changed in style; crude human forms were also widespread. Figures of humans, snakes and four-legged animals were sometimes set around the rims of cult vessels. Remarkable changes also occurred in the glyptic arts (Sarianidi, 1976; Masimov, 1981). The Margiana Bronze Age produced three kinds of seals. The first sort is a flat bronze seal with a loop-handle similar to those found in the Kelleli phase in Margiana. The form and the decoration with geometric and zoomorphic motifs of these seals continue the Altyn tradition; the large open-work seals, on which the decoration is more varied, are obvious typological developments from the earlier tradition. The second sort of seal is a flat stone amulet pierced horizontally for suspension on a string. The Central Asian tradition is detectable in the seal's shape, which sometimes was a stepped cross. The style and subject of decoration, on the other hand, was largely new; including an eagle with outstretched wings, bulls fighting dragons (horned serpents) and a hero holding two defeated animals, the iconography betrays Mesopotamian-Elamite and Harappan influence. The third kind of glyptic is the cylinder-seal, with complex subjects and scenes often arranged in two registers. This seal form derived from the Mesopotamian-Elamite tradition, and its presence in Central Asia, reveals a complex cultural synthesis.

Casting of alloys continued from the previous period, and the alloys varied according to the technological requirements of the product. Of the 220 metal objects recovered from Sapalli-depe, 90 per cent are made of alloys, and 19 per cent are made of tin bronzes. Tin bronze appeared with much lower frequency in the Kopet Dagh foothill zone, a region fairly distant from tin sources. The range of metal artefacts dramatically increased, especially in Bactria. Among the most remarkable are the artistic bronzes: ceremonial axes, mirrors with anthropomorphic handles, pins with carved heads and embossed vessels decorated with small sculptures.

One of the most fascinating aspects to this new Central Asian culture is its appearance in distant places. Pottery, seals, stone vessels, metal-work and other objects characteristic of the BMAC have been found, usually in tombs, in many places in southern Iran and western Pakistan. The evidence from Mehrgarh VIII, Sibri and other sites on the Kachi plain, just west of the Indus Valley, is particularly striking (Santoni, 1984; Jarrige and Hassan, 1989). Considerable debate attends this wide dispersion of BMAC objects and (probably) people. The linguistic identity of the BMAC people(s) is one aspect of this debate, and some scholars have suggested that the spread of the BMAC southward to the edges of the Indus Valley reflects the introduction of an Indo-Iranian language group to the region (Hiebert and Lamberg-Karlovsky, 1992).

In the later phases of the Late Bronze Age (1750–1500 BC), the cultures in Margiana and Bactria changed in many details. Settlement in the Murghab delta shifted southward as the river started to dry; sites in Bactria may have shifted eastward. Most settlements were small, though a few sites such as Takhirbai in Margiana were larger (roughly 20 hectares). Many characteristic BMAC features continued at first, especially in the pottery and seals; pottery and other artefacts of the Steppe Bronze Age appear in greater numbers. At the same time, important discontinuities are evident. For example, excavations at Kuchuk-depe in southern Uzbekistan reveal a pottery and other aspects of material culture that are very different from the BMAC. At this same site fortifications set on thick mudbrick platforms appear, an architectural feature not present in the BMAC.

Contemporary with these changes to the east, the Kopet Dagh piedmont region was again occupied, evidenced at sites like Namazga-depe (the 'tower'), Anau (the south mound) and Ekin-depe. Most of these settlements were small, with only a few towns (such as Ekin-depe, perhaps 20 hectares in size) appearing. The Sumbar cemetery dates to the end of the Late Bronze Age; ceramic parallels with Sialk A and Khurvin in Iran has sparked a debate about the westward movement of Iranian speakers and the origins of the Medes and Persians.

The Steppe Bronze Age and the spread of Indo-Iranian languages

At the same time as the urban cultures of southern Central Asia were developing so vigorously, momentous changes were also occurring to the north. In the steppes, primitive hunting groups were giving way to Bronze Age communities, who lived by cattle herding and by agriculture. These northern peoples led a more nomadic life than did their southern neighbours. Study of the northern Bronze Age groups has been uneven.

The Andronovo culture complex spread over wide areas of Kazakhstan and southern Siberia during the second millennium BC. These steppic cultures engaged in agriculture or in a mixed agricultural-pastoralist economy. Cattle herding was important in the steppes and steppe-forest areas, while sheep and goats were the animals more suitable to the semi-desert areas and foothills. Other aspects of these cultures included bronze metallurgy, square fortified settlements and the use of horse-drawn chariots.

The Eurasian steppes were the setting for the domestication of the horse and invention of the light two-wheeled chariot, developments of fundamental historical importance. While initial horse domestication seems to have occurred in the North Pontic area during the fourth millennium BC (Anthony, 1986), their application to chariotry occurred later. The burial mounds (kurgans) at Sintashta in the southern Urals, which date to the seventeenth-sixteenth centuries BC (Gening, 1977), reflect the latter development. The earthen mounds cover wood-lined pits in which were placed cha-riots with ten-spoked wheels. Horses occurred in the actual burial pits and also in the earthen mounds, where they seemingly were placed as sacrifices. The spread southward of horses, chariotry and, apparently, steppe peoples themselves played an important role in the history of Central Asia and the surrounding regions (Masson and Sarianidi, 1972).

While the main centres of the steppe-dwellers lay outside Central Asia, some groups did penetrate southward, assimilating or forcing out the local populations. In Khorasmia, on the lower reaches of the Amu Darya, a distinctive group of monuments identify the Tazabagyab culture (Itina, 1977), which belongs to the Andronovo culture complex. The roughly fifty known Tazabagyab settlements are small, consisting of two or three large rectangular log cabins slightly sunk into the ground. These settlements contained up to a hundred people, including some metal-workers. The Tazabagyab people developed an irrigation agriculture in the Amu Darya delta, by running small ditches from the diminishing delta channels to the fields.

A similar culture extended along the lower reaches of the Zeravshan, and steppe-dwellers also moved into the mountainous zones of Transoxiana. The work at Zaman-baba revealed a settlement and cemetery on the lower reaches of the Zeravshan. This community lived in semi-subterranean huts and produced a rude, often round-bottomed pottery. Yet these people also worked bronze, and traded with the more settled communities to the south. The cemetery at Dashti-Kozy, on the upper Zeravshan some 60 km east of Panjikent, contained pottery and metal work typical of the Andronova culture. Settlements with similar materials also existed in the mountainous regions of south-west Tajikistan.

In zones of interaction with the settled agricultural areas to the south, features of both the steppic and agricultural cultures appear together. At the Dashti-Kozy cemetery, the basic material culture, the use of red ochre in burial rites, and the presence of small pieces of charcoal at the base of graves are all characteristic Andronovo features; the mortuary architecture, on the other hand, follows the Sapalli tradition of catacomb tombs (Potemkina, 1987; Isakov and Potemkina, 1989). The pottery found at Dashti-Kozy was thrown on a wheel, and clearly was a product of the settled oases. The Beshkent and Vakhsh cultures of southern Tajikistan (P'iankova, 1981) are examples of this cultural mixing, in which settlements and agriculture were added to animal herding; many of the ceramics in the Beshkent tombs are similar to those of late phases of the Late Bronze Age (Molali phase) in southern Uzbekistan. Judging by recent discoveries, pottery vessels of the southern agricultural communities were exported as exotic commodities as far as northern Kazakhstan, where they appear in Andronovo contexts.

Evidence for contact also appears in the settled agricultural communities of Margiana and Bactria. Numerous permanent settlements in Margiana contain fragments of crude earthenware vessels with simple incised patterns that differ sharply from the usual ceramics of the region (Sarianidi, 1975). This pottery type is typical of a group of cultures in the steppes during the Bronze Age; its presence in Margiana demonstrates the southward movement of steppe-dwellers, and possible integration with the populations of fortified towns. Cremation, a pattern characteristic of the steppes, also appears in the south; the cemetery at Djarkutan includes cremations in stone boxes, a pattern entirely uncharacteristic of local tradition but quite at home in an Andronovo cemetery.

The archaeological evidence allows several broad conclusions to be drawn about cultural genesis and ethnogenesis during this period of movements and migrations. Steppe-dwellers with pastoralist traditions extensively penetrated Central Asia. These peoples were mainly concerned with cattle-raising, and were led by a military aristocracy that made wide use of chariots and bronze weapons. Some of these immigrants seem to have integrated gradually with the established populations of the settled oases, a process that led to their cultural assimilation. At the same time, the Central Asian settled tradition influenced the neighbouring steppic peoples; the Andronovo culture differed from contemporary groups in Kazakhstan and southern Siberia precisely in this respect.

The archaeological patterns of the Late Bronze Age are explicable by the second millennium BC dispersal of Indo-

Iranian tribes following the collapse of Indo-Iranian linguistic and historical unity (Zaehner, 1961; Boyce, 1975). Linguistic analysis convincingly demonstrates that these tribes generally engaged in intensive animal herding, with ownership of cattle serving as the measure of wealth and prosperity. War chariots (Iranian *rata*, Indian *ratkha*) were highly important, and warriors (*rataishatry*, 'standing on chariots') played a central social role. Scholars long ago connected the southward spread of Andronovo groups with the movement from the north-east of Indic speakers into India. The nature of the evidence does not permit the precise identification of individual archaeological cultures with specific ethnic groups of the second millennium BC. Most probably, two parallel processes were at work in the oases of Bactria and Margiana: the linguistic assimilation of the local population, and the cultural transformation of the newcomers. The varying intensity of interactions between peoples created a complex archaeological picture; nonetheless no reasonable doubt exists that an Indo-Iranian *ethnos* was forming in Central Asia during this turbulent period of migrations, military conflict and mutual assimilation. The distribution of BMAC materials to the edge of the Indus Valley early in the second millennium BC offers a possible archaeological witness to the spread of this *ethnos*.

The Central Asia synthesis stimulated cultural and intellectual development through a process of mutual enrichment and a sharing of experience. The existing system of practical knowledge provided a solid basis for further progress. Significant progress was made especially in metallurgy, which expanded greatly in scale and in specialization. Possession of the ore sources in central Kazakhstan provided the Andronovo communities with a source of power and wealth; these mines provided such essential Bronze Age metals as copper and tin. The main metallurgical centres were the Atasu and Myrzhik regions. Alloying of copper and tin was increasing steadily, the resulting bronzes characteristically also containing arsenic, antimony or lead (Kuznetsova, 1987). The proportions of metals reflected the intended uses of weapons and tools: striking implements contained 4 per cent tin, cutting tools 5–9 per cent tin, and piercing and construction tools 9–12 per cent tin. Local metal-working centres gradually developed specific techniques and often special types of products. For example, a special centre in Semirechiya (Kuzmina, 1970) made extensive use of tin-lead alloys during the Late Bronze Age; judging by the rarity of admixtures, the centre relied on local ores. Contacts with the north also contributed to the technological progress of the southern oases, which received ores and technological expertise from increasingly distant regions. The metal artefacts at Sapalli-tepe include arsenical bronze, tin bronze, arsenical bronze with lead, and arsenical-tin bronze (Askarov, 1977). The nature of some of these alloys may reflect use of polymetallic ore deposits.

Changing architecture also reflects a merging of traditions. The regular square architecture of Margiana and Bactria may have originated in the steppes. A rectangular settlement plan enclosed by ramparts and ditch, covering 60 × 95 and 70 × 120 m, appeared in the Andronovo culture area. The layout of the so-called circular temple at Dashly 3 in northern Afghanistan has attracted considerable attention. Oval huts and semi-subterranean frame-and-post structures are typical in the zones outside settled oases. An Andronovo settlement at Arkanm in the southern Urals follows the same design, down to the smallest detail. Northern canons of religious architecture may have influenced the southern oases, despite the greater suitability of mudbrick to rectilinear layout.

Significant changes also occurred in intellectual life. The production of female terracottas ceased in the southern oases. Previously found in nearly every house and often placed in collective burials, their disappearance reflects important changes in popular rites and cults. Fire altars appear in temples everywhere in Margiana and Bactria, but the divine forces in whose honour the sacred flame burned remain unidentified. Pouring vessels clearly used in libation achieved wide distribution, and some scholars connect these vessels with the well-known sacred drink *soma-haoma* of Indo-Iranian mythology; the Togolok 21 religious site contained a set of these vessels. However, the drink once contained in the vessels could simply have been wine.

The iconography of seals provides another insight into these cultures, and some scholars have attempted to identify a Bactrian pantheon on the basis of the glyptic iconography (for example, Sarianidi, 1986a). The introduction of a new, strikingly dynamic, artistic style on the square amulet seals is itself significant. The representations of snake-like winged dragons attacking bulls and other animals may express the struggle of opposing forces. Images of birds are also important elements of the glyptic iconography in Margiana and Bactria; these motifs include two birds sitting on a tree, flying birds and a procession of birds. The bird and bird-like figures are important to Indo-Iranian mythology.

THE IRON AGE (1500–600 BC)

The cultural changes in the first half of the second millennium BC were only forerunners of more fundamental changes in Central Asia. In south-western Turkmenia, the ancient Dakhistan, cities re-emerged on a massive scale in the area of the lower Atrek; places such as Madau, Izat Kuli and Tangsikildzha each covered more than 100 hectares. A large and integrated irrigation system supported the livelihood of these cities (Lisitsina, 1978).

The Yaz culture covered the oasis areas to the east, from the upper Atrek across the Kopet Dagh piedmont and Margiana, perhaps reaching as far east as the Ferghana valley. Yaz settlements in these regions tended to be smaller than before, but still impressively dominated by citadels built on solid platforms several metres high. Extensive irrigation networks provided water for fields of wheat, several species of barley, rye, chick-peas and grapes; qanats, a system of underground tunnels and shafts bringing water from distant hill-slopes, appeared during the first millennium BC at places such as Ulug-depe in the Kopet Dagh piedmont (P'iankova, 1981). These advances in settlement type and some aspects of technology were accompanied by some contrasting changes. For example, use of the potter's wheel declined, and hand-modelled wares became common; some of this new pottery was decorated with simple painted geometric patterns in an apparent revival of earlier Bronze Age traditions.

Some efforts have been made to explain these phenomena by reference to migrations of people. However, convincing sources have not been discovered for the new cultural tradition, either in Central Asia itself or in neighbouring regions. A more likely explanation is the transformation of indigenous cultures by the formation of an early class society, when the processes of cultural integration contributed to the constant spread of cultural patterns over a wide area (Masson, 1985). Under this interpretation, the Iron Age culture of Central Asia, and particularly the complexes of the Yaz type, may be regarded as representing the peoples of the

Eastern Iranian language group; this period was the culmination of a long episode of ethnogenesis which began with the first Indo-Iranian penetration of Central Asia. The southern oases, including the valley of the Zeravshan, indeed became the hub of socio-economic progress in the Iron Age. These societies provided the basis for the kingdoms in Parthia, Bactria, Sogdia and elsewhere that formed part of the Achaemenid empire after the sixth century BC.

In regions further north, the local Bronze Age cultures of steppic origin underwent a transformation in which southern influence played some part. The Amiraba culture of Chorasmia was one outcome of this process; this culture retained such archaic features as frame dwellings and hand-modelled pottery. In contrast, the Chust culture in Ferghana revived the tradition of painted pottery, but now with different forms, floral motifs and, at times, decorative patterns. Judging by a number of features, the Chust culture was part of a wider culture area that extended across eastern Turkistan. The tombs at Tagisken, east of the Aral Sea, provide evidence both for the emergence of an aristocratic élite among the steppe tribes and for close links with the settled southern oases. These tombs, dated to the ninth-eighth centuries BC, are monumental mausoleums constructed of unbaked brick, a southern feature, whereas the funeral rites and furniture exhibit characteristics of the steppe tradition (for instance, cremation, felt lining on the tomb walls). These changes established the conditions for the lasting and historically momentous division of Central Asia into two large interacting zones: urban civilization and nomadic tribes.

BIBLIOGRAPHY

ANTHONY, D. 1986. The 'Kurgan Culture', Indo-European Origins, and the Domestication of the Horse: A Reconsideration. *Curr. Anthropol.* (Chicago) Vol. 27, pp. 291–313.

ASKAROV, A. A. 1973. *Sappalitepe.* Tashkent.

—— 1977. *Drevnezemledel'cheskaya Kultura Yuga Uzbekistana* [The Ancient Agricultural Culture of southern Uzbekistan]. Tashkent.

ASKAROV, A. A.; ABDULLAEV, B. I. 1981. *Dzharkutan.* Tashkent.

BOYCE, M. A. 1975. *History of Zoroastrianism.* Leiden.

FRANCFORT, H.-P. 1989. *Fouilles de Shortugai.* Paris.

GENING, V. F. 1977. Mogilniki Sintashta i Problema Rannykh Infirenskikh Plemen [The Burial Grounds of Sintasta and the Problem of the Early Infirensky Tribes]. *Sov. Arheol.* (Moskva), No. 4, pp. 53–73.

HIEBERT, F. T.; LAMBERG-KARLOVSKY, C. C. 1992. Central Asia and the Indo-Iranian Borderlands. *Iran* (London), Vol. 30, pp. 1–15.

ISAKOV, A. I. 1986. Sarazm – Novii Rannezemledel'cheskii Pamiatnik Srednei Azii. *Sov. Arheol.* (Moskva), No. 1, pp. 152–67.

ISAKOV, A. I.; POTEMKINA, T. M. 1989. Mogil'nik Plemen Epokhi Bronzy v Tadjikistane [A Burial Ground of a Steppe Tribe of the Bronze Age in Tadjikistan]. *Sov. Arkheol.* (Moskva), No. 1, pp. 145–67.

ITINA, M. A. 1977. *Istoria Stepnykh Plemen Yuzhnogo Priaralya (II-Nachalo I Tys. do N.E.)* [The History of the Steppe Tribes on the Southern Shores of the Aral Sea (2nd-Beginning 1st Mill. BC)]. Moskva.

JARRIGE, J.-F.; HASSAN, H. U. 1989. Funerary Complexes in Baluchistan at the End of the Third Millennium in the Light of Recent Discoveries at Mehrgahr and Quetta. In: FRIFELT, K.; SORENSEN, P. (eds), *South Asian Archaeology 1985.* London. pp. 150–66.

KHLOPIN, I. N. 1964. *Geoksiurskaia Gruppa Poselenii Epokhi Eneolita.* Moskva.

—— 1981. The Early Bronze Age Cemetery at Parkhai II: The First Two Seasons of Excavations: 1977–1978. In: KOHL, P. (ed.), *The Bronze Age Civilization of Central Asia.* New York. pp. 3–34.

KUZMINA, E. E. 1970. *Semirechensky Variant Kultury Epokhi Pozdnei Bronzy* [The Semirechiye variant of the Late Bronze Age Culture]. Moskva. (Kratk. Soobšč. Inst. Arheol., 122.)

KUZNETSOVA, E. F. 1989. Proizvodstvo tsvetykh i blagorodnykh metalof v tsentralnom Kazakhstane v epokhu bronzy i ranykh kotsevnikov [Production of Noble and Coloured Metals in Central Kazakhstan in the Bronze Age and Early Nomads]. In: MASSON, V. M. (ed.), *Vzaimodeistvie kochevykh kultur i drevnikh tsivilizatsii.* Alma-Ata, pp. 118–21.

LISITSINA, G. N. 1978. *Stanovlenie i Razvitie Oroshaemogo Zemeledeliia v Juzhnoi Turkmenii.* Moskva.

MASIMOV, I. S. 1979. Izuchenie Pamiatnikov Epokhi Bronzy Nizov'ev Murgaba. *Sov. Arheol.* (Moskva), No. 1, pp. 111–31. [Translated as: 1981. The Study of Bronze Age Sites in the Lower Mughab. In: KOHL, P. (ed.), *The Bronze Age Civilization of Central Asia.* New York, pp. 194–220].

—— 1981. Novye Nakhodki Pechatei Epokhi Bronzy s Nizovy Murgaba [Recently Discovered Bronze Age Seals from the Lower Murghab]. *Sov. Arheol.* (Moskva), No. 2, pp. 132–50.

MASSON, V. M. 1959. *Drevnezemledelcheskaya Kultura Margiana* [The Ancient Agricultural Culture of Margiana]. Moskva.

—— 1964. *Sredniaia Asiia i Drevnie Vostok.* Moskva.

—— 1977. Altyn-depe v Epokhu Eneolita. *Sov. Arheol.* (Moskva), No. 1, pp. 164–88. [Translated as: 1981. The Study of Bronze Age Sites in the Lower Mughab. In: KOHL, P. (ed.), *The Bronze Age Civilization of Central Asia.* New York. pp. 63–95.]

—— 1981. *Altyn-depe.* Leningrad. [Translated as: 1988. *Altyn-depe.* Philadelphia, University Museum.]

—— 1985. La dialectique des traditions et des innovations dans le développement culturel de la Bactriane. In: GARDIN, J. C. (ed.), *L'archéologie de la Bactriane ancienne.* Paris. pp. 31–8.

MASSON, V. M.; SARIANIDI, V. I. 1972. *Central Asia: Turkmenia Before the Achaemenids.* London.

PIANKOVA, L. T. 1981. Bronze Age Settlements of Southern Tajikistan. In: KOHL, P. (ed.), *The Bronze Age Civilization of Central Asia.* New York. pp. 287–310.

POTEMKINA, T. M. 1987. K Voprosu o Migratsii na Yug Stepnykh Plemen Epokhi Bronzy [The Southward Migration of the Steppe Tribes in the Bronze Age]. In: MASSON, V. M. (ed.), *Vzaimodeistvie kochevkykh kultur i drevnie tsivilizatii.* Alma-Ata. pp. 76–8.

POTTIER, M.-H. 1984. *Matériel funéraire de la Bactriane méridionale de l'âge de bronze.* Paris.

SANTONI, M. 1984. Sibri and the South Cemetery at Mehrgahr: 3rd Millennium Connections Between the Northern Kachi Plain (Pakistan) and Central Asia. In: ALLCHIN, B. (ed.), *South Asian Archaeology 1981.* Cambridge. pp. 52–60.

SARIANIDI, V. I. 1975. Stepnye Plemena Epokhi Bronzy v Margiane [Bronze Age Steppe Tribes in Margiana]. *Sov. Arheol.* (Moskva), No. 2, pp. 20–9.

—— 1976. Pechati-Amulety Murgabskogo Stilya. *Sov. Arheol.* (Moskva), No. 1, pp. 42–68. [Translated as: 1981. Seal-Amulets of the Murghab Style. In: KOHL, P. (ed.), *The Bronze Age Civilization of Central Asia.* New York. pp. 221–55.]

—— 1977. *Drevnie zemledel'tsi Afganistana* [Ancient Agriculturalists in Afghanistan]. Moskva.

—— 1981. Margiana in the Bronze Age. In: KOHL, P. (ed.), *The Bronze Age Civilization of Central Asia.* New York. pp. 165–93.

—— 1986a. The Bactrian Pantheon. *Int. Assoc. Stud. Cult. Cent. Asia, Inf. Bull.* (Moskva), No. 10, pp. 5–20.

—— 1986b. Le complex culturel de Togolok 21 en margiane. *Ars asiat.* (Paris), Vol. 41, pp. 5–21.

—— 1990. *Drevnosti Strani Margush.* Aščabad.

ZAEHNER, R. C. 1961. *The Dawn and Twilight of Zoroastrianism.* London.

15.2
SOUTH-EAST ASIA
AND THE PACIFIC

Charles F. W. Higham and Wilhelm G. Solheim II

The areas covered here are Mainland and Island South-East Asia (the latter including Taiwan), Melanesia and Micronesia. Polynesia was not inhabited except for Tonga and Samoa (Map 23).

The data available for reconstructing the scientific and cultural development of the people are extremely variable. There has been little archaeological research done in major portions of Mainland and Island South-East Asia and much of what has been done is neither well dated nor published for this time period. Archaeological research in Micronesia has only got under way during the last fifteen years and only a few reports have been published. Island Melanesia is better known. Most of the archaeological research, until the last few years, has been artefact oriented.

There are three major sources for the data used in this reconstruction: biological anthropological, archaeological and linguistic. Co-operation between archaeologists and linguists in reconstructing the movements and dating of these movements in Melanesia and Polynesia began about twenty years ago (Pawley and Green, 1973). Linguists and social anthropologists using linguistic evidence have reconstructed prehistoric social organization for early Austronesian speakers and Island Oceania (Marshall, 1984). Their results have been controversial but the methods look promising.

Of the three language families predominant in South-East Asia today only Sino-Tibetan was probably not in the approximate areas where found at this time. The Tibeto-Myanmar languages have been spoken in the north-western border areas of Myanmar (Burma) but there is no indication that the Myanmar language was present in Myanmar. Austroasiatic languages were probably predominant in Mainland South-East Asia at the beginning of this period but Austronesian would have been spoken in some areas along the coast of south China and Vietnam. From some time during the second millennium BC Chinese languages started to penetrate northern south China but to what degree they were in place by the end of the period is not known.

The Austronesian languages were spreading in Island South-East Asia and out into the Pacific during this time. It is likely that Austroasiatic languages were spoken in Sumatra and possibly western Java. If so, these would have been gradually replaced by Austronesian languages except for some areas in Sumatra. At some time during this period the Austronesian language ancestral to Cham, and other Austronesian languages present today in interior central Vietnam and eastern Cambodia, would have started moving inland from the coast, quite possibly before 1000 BC Austronesian languages would also have penetrated inland from the east coast of west Malaysia.

During our period, as today, there were three major varieties of *Homo sapiens* in this area: Melanesians, Negritos and Southern Mongoloids. It is likely that all three populations had, to a considerable degree, a common ancestry, in Mainland South-East Asia. The earlier hypothesis was that each of these evolved on the South-East Asia mainland and entered Island South-East Asia and the Pacific by separate migrations, at different times, from the mainland.

Negritos are found today in several Philippine islands, in the northern half of the Malay Peninsula, and north into Myanmar and Thailand. New data and new methods of analysis have led to new interpretations. The Negritos are the least in number and most widely scattered of the three. It was held that they were the earliest inhabitants of both Island and Mainland South-East Asia but this is no longer believed. Analysis of genetic data indicates that the Philippine Negritos 'possess the Asian-Pacific genetic pattern and are wholly unrelated to the African pygmies. Intergroup analysis suggests that Negritos are a relatively recent Sundaland adaptation, evolving within the last 20,000 to 30,000 years, after the initial occupation of Australia' (Turner, 1985, p. 9). It has further been suggested that they evolved locally in the different areas where they have been found in South-East Asia, during the early Holocene. Melanesians, who at one time probably inhabited all of Indonesia and probably some of the southern portions of Mainland South-East Asia, continued to lose ground to the southern Mongoloids, remaining only in the eastern Indonesian islands, New Guinea and Melanesia.

MAINLAND SOUTH-EAST ASIA

Charles F.W. Higham

This consideration of South-East Asian prehistory from 3000 until 700 BC will follow three themes. The first concerns the survival of long-established mobile bands of hunter-gatherers adapted to upland evergreen forests. Secondly, we will review the evidence for complex, sedentary coastal communities which were probably heirs to a long maritime tradition now lost to the rising sea. Finally, there is the major expansion of human settlement along the interior river systems, the communities involved becoming familiar with bronze working.

Five thousand years ago, this part of the world had just undergone a physical transformation when, as a result of the end of the Pleistocene ice age, the sea-level rose by between

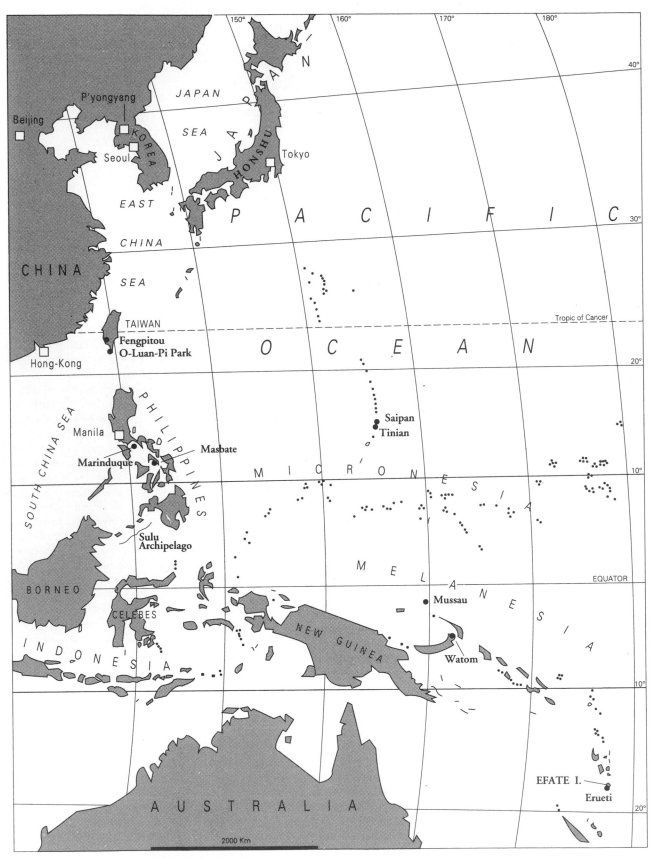

Map 23 Island South-East Asia

40 and 60 m over a period of only five millennia. While this change was world-wide, it was particularly severe in South-East Asia, because of the immense tract of low-lying land which was inundated. Three major rivers drain away the torrential rains which fall during the five-month rainy season, and if we were to identify a unifying physical theme for the mainland of South-East Asia, it would lie best in the regular beat of the pulse of these waterways. For the Mekong and the Yuanjiang (Red) rivers, the huge increase in water volume induced by the monsoon is further increased by the spring melt of snow into their headwaters in the eastern Himalayas. The Chao Phraya is fed by the numerous trib-

utaries issuing from the Phetchabun range and the uplands of western Thailand. All three had their courses truncated with the advancing coastline, which reached its highest point about 5,000 years ago. Geomorphological studies in the marine clay deposits behind Bangkok and in the lower reaches of the Yuangjiang River disclose raised beach lines now many tens of kilometres from the coast.

Human settlement in South-East Asia over the millennia has been greatly influenced by water flows and, in characterizing the region, it would be logical to follow this theme ourselves. As a very general rule, this mainland area receives dry and relatively cool north-east winds between December and April. In the Yuangjiang River delta and coasts of Vietnam down to the region of Hue, any residual moisture descends as a persistent coastal drizzle, and once over the Truong Son cordillera they are christened the 'Lao' winds, hot and dry for months on end. Sometime during April and May, the timing is unpredictable, the wind pattern shifts to the south-west. Thunderclouds bank up and after so many arid months the populace embarks on festivals of great antiquity to encourage and welcome the rain. During the Bang Fai festival in north-east Thailand, huge phallic rockets are despatched to fertilize the clouds and bring down rain. Now the rice is transplanted and the landscape, so recently parched to a uniform dun colour, is suddenly green. The Mekong, which during the month of February 1949 carried only 1,700 m³ of water a second, increases its water flow twenty-fold. Without the excavation of drainage canals or the construction of retaining bunds, these rivers burst their banks and floodwaters encroach over extensive areas. In the case of the Mekong, the volume of water is so great that it reverses back up the Tonle Sap River at Phnom Penh to fill the great lake of Cambodia, the Tonle Sap itself. In effect, the lake is a gigantic natural flood-control system.

The contrast between wet and dry seasons in the lowlands beneath about 400 m encourages what is known as a dry deciduous forest cover. Behind the moist gallery vegetation along the watercourses, many trees lose their leaves during the dry season, the open and light conditions at ground level encouraging herbaceous growth which sustains herds of wild cattle and deer. As one ascends the surrounding uplands, however, the shortening of the dry season with altitude, a lowering of the temperature and sharply changing soil conditions promote a quite different forest cover. This is known as the wet evergreen forest, the trees providing a permanent screening canopy which protects the ground from the full glare of the sun and the impact of torrential rains. The dominant fauna no longer lives at ground level, but is found among the sustaining leaves and fruits of the forest trees. Here, the full impact of the changing monsoon is dulled and seasonal shifts in human responses are less of an imperative. The same reduction in the importance of the seasons is also felt in one further environmental zone: the coast. In the past, too little emphasis has been put on prehistoric coastal adaptation, probably because the rising sea-level would have destroyed the evidence. Yet, with access to the rich resources of estuarine habitats, it is hard to imagine a problem with food supplies at any time in the past.

UPLANDS AND LOWLANDS IN PREHISTORY

It is often said that the major contrast in terms of human settlement in South-East Asia is that between the plains and the surrounding hills. This contrast, manifested today between the sophisticated and bustling metropolis of Bangkok and the hunters of northern Thailand, is a pattern easily recognized during the prehistoric period. Most of the early research was undertaken by French scholars during colonial times, and this involved a concentration of effort in the general area of the official capital of Hanoi. From the 1920s Madeleine Colani and Henri Mansuy identified numerous rockshelters in the rugged limestone uplands of Hoa Binh and Bac Son provinces (Colani, 1927; Mansuy, 1924). Usually set at the junction of the escarpments and tributary stream valleys, these sites disclose a pattern of collecting shellfish and fish on the one hand and hunting local mammals on the other. Since excavation techniques were less delicate then, the recovery of the plant component of the diet was unusual. The surviving material culture of the occupants of these rockshelters, who are often described as 'Hoabinhian' after the province where they were first identified, comprises a range of flaked stone tools. The commonest comprises a fist-sized river pebble flaked to a working edge on one side only. With time, increasing attention was given to grinding the surfaces of some stone artefacts to the shape of an adze, a procedure which provides for a sharp and more effective cutting implement.

Vietnamese archaeologists have devoted much time to the pattern of settlement in these small rockshelter sites. They have recovered plant remains from some sites, including rice from Xom Trai. This same site has also yielded what look like stone hoes. According to Hoang Xuan Chinh (1984), the micro-wear on the working edges of these large and heavy implements is consistent with breaking the soil. There are, however, two issues which have yet to be resolved before we can conclude that the inhabitants of these Vietnamese rockshelters were cultivating rice. The first is the biological status of the rice remains themselves. So far, only Xom Trai has provided a sample. The second is that hoes can be used in obtaining wild plants for consumption just as well as for cultivating a domestic plant.

There is a further problem which surrounds these sites in Vietnam. While there are radiocarbon determinations which indicate the development of this tradition between 12,000 and 6000 BC, the terminal dates are not defined. In northern Thailand, however, Chester Gorman has excavated three rockshelters, one of which, Banyan Valley Cave, has provided radiocarbon dates which indicate a vigorous hunting and gathering tradition, employing a material culture closely akin to that from Hoa Binh, still flourishing between 3000 BC and about AD 900. Again, we encounter a cultural stratigraphy at Banyan Valley Cave comprising numerous ash lenses and hearths which might reflect intermittent occupation of a large and airy cavern adjacent to a swiftly flowing stream. The prehistoric inhabitants exploited the stream for crabs, shellfish and fish, and clearly hunted and trapped in the forest. Plant remains included cucumber and gourd fragments, canarium seeds and 110 rice husks. In his analysis of these, Yen (1977) concluded that they probably derive from a wild variety of rice, and that the rice grains had been expressed from the husks using some sort of grinding stone. Like many other such sites, the uppermost layers of Banyan Valley Cave contained a small sample of pottery sherds, and edge-ground stone adzeheads. It is not yet possible to determine whether pottery vessels were actually made by members of the hunter-gatherer community, or were obtained by exchange from other communities within their exchange orbit. Generally, pottery is of little use to mobile people because of its tendency to fracture.

These same features, that is a long continuation of occupation of small rockshelters, a hunting and gathering subsistence and familiarity with pottery and ground stone tools, have been found by Pookajorn (1981) during his excavations at Khao Talu and related sites on the western margins of the Chao Phraya plains. His radiocarbon determinations show occupation from the tenth millennium BC down to at least 1500 BC. As one skirts the Cardamon range to the valley of the small stream known as the Stung Sangker in western Cambodia, the same basic pattern has been identified at Laang Spean, or 'Bridge Cave'.

If the pattern identified in such upland areas is one of conservatism among small, mobile bands of hunter-gatherers, that now recognized in coastal and lowland valley situations is in stark contrast. Although many coastal sites will have been drowned by the rising sea, some settlements have survived along the raised beaches formed when the sea-level was higher than it is today. Such sites have been identified along the raised beaches of northern Vietnam, particularly in Thanh Hoa and the islands of the Gulf of Bac Bo, and inland from the present shore of the Gulf of Thailand. In 1985, a particularly revealing insight into the wealth and ritual of such coastal groups was provided by the excavation of Khok Phanom Di. This 5-hectare settlement, which rises 12 m above the surrounding rice fields, was once located on the edge of the estuary of the Bang Pakong River. Excavations covered an area of 10 x 10 m and reached the natural substrate at a depth of 6.8 m. During the excavation, Bernard Maloney took several cores from the surrounding sediments, from which he extracted the fossil pollen and charcoal fragments. His results are most revealing. The pollen rain for most of the sedimentary sequence was dominated by mangrove trees, with only a small count of microscopic fragments of charcoal. At a depth of 2 m below the present ground surface, however, there was a dramatic change. The charcoal count increased remarkably, and the mangrove pollen showed a decline. Grass pollen became more abundant. It is hard to explain these changes other than through the impact of human settlement at Khok Phanom Di (Fig. 76).

When we consider the contents of the lowest horizon at the site, there is confirmation for these events from a cultural source. We find caches of polished stone adzeheads which had been used in such heavy work as forest clearance. The layers are rich in ash, and we encounter much evidence for rice. It is not yet clear whether this rice was actively cultivated. The inhabitants could, for example, have collected wild rice heads by boat, as remained the practice along the margins of the Tonle Sap within living memory. Over 400 small shell knives have been found at the site, and these have all the appearances of the South-East Asian hand-held harvesting knife. While we must await the results of the analysis of the rice remains from the site, there is no doubt that the people of Khok Phanom Di enjoyed an abundance of food from the estuary, mangrove swamps, open beaches and the sea. We encounter numerous remains of fish, shellfish, turtle and crab. It is very hard to envisage a food shortage when such rich and annually replenished maritime resources were available.

Mortuary remains are an important source of information on the social organization of prehistoric societies. The area of Khok Phanom Di excavated in 1985 incorporated a cemetery with particularly clear evidence for a changing pattern of social relationships and status within the community. Just over 150 individual interments were found, nearly all the people being buried with the heads pointing to the rising

Figure 76 Red Corded-ware culture pottery, principal shapes of vessels: 1, fine red ware; 2, sandy red ware; 3, sandy gray ware (after Chang, 1969).

sun. Among the earlier burials, the range of grave offerings placed with the corpse was not great. There may have been one or two pottery vessels, items of personal shell jewellery and, occasionally, an adzehead, perhaps a fishhook or the remains of a fish. The body was then dusted with powdered red ochre, wrapped in a bark-cloth shroud and placed on a wooden bier within the prepared grave. On two occasions, the stomach contents of the dead survived to reveal the person's last meal: fish, including the bones and scales.

It is particularly interesting to note how the dead were buried in discrete clusters. According to our radiocarbon dates, the site was first occupied about 2000 BC, with the first interments taking place soon after initial settlement. The clustering of burials, side by side and one on top of the other, continued while about 4 m of cultural material accumulated and about three centuries passed. When we look at the structure of these clusters, we find some intriguing leads. First, the members of each cluster included men, women and infants. In terms of the sequence of burials, we find clear evidence for specific stages whereby what look like family groups were buried over preceding families over about ten generations. When we examine the birth-scarring on the women's pelvic bones we find that, in most cases, women would have borne at least the number of infants buried alongside them. There are hints, too, that a number of genetic abnormalities were inherited through the successive generations.

In terms of mortuary ritual, the clusters of interments were usually surrounded by thick deposits of food and occupation material. The distribution of postholes is consistent with a series of wooden structures over and round the collected graves, which protected them from being covered by the remains of everyday living. The disposition of circular pits near the graves also suggests that some food was placed in the ground near the tombs, perhaps as part of the burial rite, perhaps as food for the ancestors.

If it is assumed that each of the mortuary clusters represents a social grouping, perhaps related as in a family, over ten generations, then is there, on the basis of material goods, any evidence for one being richer and more influential than the other? During the first three mortuary phases, the answer is no. But with the fourth phase, dated to about 1600 BC, there are hints of a change in the air. People were buried in deeper, more individual graves. Males alone were now interred with highly ornamented turtleshell ornaments, which had been broken and placed with the body. When reconstructed, these splendid objects fit over the chest rather like ornamental breastplates. One has holes for suspension. With Mortuary Phase 5, all changed dramatically. The centuries-old tradition of interring the dead in neat clusters was set aside. The entire excavated area contained the remains of only one person, a woman who died in her late thirties. Her grave (burial 51) was particularly large, measuring 3 m in length and nearly 1 m in depth. The woman's body lay under a raised pyramidal heap of clay cylinders representing an early stage in the shaping of a pot. On top of this were balanced three fractured cooking vessels. Removal of the cylinders revealed the remains of the woman covered in red ochre and accompanied by an outstanding array of grave goods: over 120,000 shell beads over and under the chest, a shell head-dress, two shell horned discs on each shoulder, a shell bracelet, and beside the right ankle a shell containing two pebbles used for burnishing pots and a potter's anvil.

It is clear that the woman had very high status within her community. So, too, had her family. She had given birth to two or three children, one of which seems to have been interred alongside her after her death. The grave in question contained the remains of an 18-month-old infant interred with an identical ritual and similar set of grave goods even down to a miniature potter's anvil. A second rich infant's grave was found one metre to the south of the woman's burial.

There was a further modification in burial behaviour during the ensuing mortuary phase. Gone was the extreme wealth associated with burial 15, but the high status of women continued. Two adult women were found interred beside each other and under an almost square structure. This mortuary edifice was made up of over twenty individual layers of levelled fill, and was surmounted by clay wall foundations. A six-year-old child had been interred in the same grave as one of the women, but after the construction of the chamber, since the grave was cut through its foundations. These burials were relatively wealthy. The child was buried with 18,000 shell beads and a heavy shell disc. Each of the women was interred with a clay anvil and thousands of shell beads. In front of the chamber, however, was a row of contemporary graves with far fewer grave goods. The adult

female had borne five or more children, and at least four infants or children were interred alongside her. Only nine shell beads were found in the eight burials which make up this row.

What were the technological skills of these people, whose way of life came to an abrupt end when, about 1500 BC, the sea-level fell and the rich coastal resources receded? They commanded an excellent source of potting clay, and developed outstanding skills in the shaping and decorating of ceramic vessels. Some of those in the burials have been described as masterpieces. They also manufactured a range of shell jewellery items from the beautiful nacreous shells to which they had access. They obtained, through exchange, all their stone. We find stone adze beads worn down to small stubs through constant sharpening. They also obtained sandstone, so useful for sharpening and shaping objects of stone, bone and shell. They fashioned shell knives, bone fishhooks and harpoons and clay net sinkers.

The inclusion of artefacts in graves opens an important insight into the attitudes and beliefs of this extinct society. It is beyond reasonable doubt that they increasingly measured a person's rank and status through the bodily display of ornamental jewellery. During the early phases of the occupation of the site, there seems to have been little differentiation between the rank of individuals or groups. But after about ten generations, they became intimately involved in recognizing status differences. We find that, quite apart from the great wealth of burial 15, more attention was given to puberty rites involving the removal of certain teeth, and masculinity was advertised through the wearing of turtleshell ornaments. Khok Phanom Di, with its strategic coastal location commanding a major river estuary, was clearly a focus for the exchange of prestige goods. It is not hard to imagine that high status might accrue to those who had particular skills in making quality ceramic vessels, or who increasingly controlled access to the prestige goods within a community growing in number.

THE SETTLEMENT OF THE LOWLANDS

Little is known of the spread of human occupation into the interior lowlands of South-East Asia. Perhaps the densest concentration of sites is to be found in the Middle Country, that tract above the junction of the Yuanjiang and Lixianjiang rivers. Here, Vietnamese archaeologists have examined over fifty prehistoric settlements which they ascribe to the Phung Nguyen culture. Phung Nguyen is a 3-hectare settlement of which a massive 3,960 m² have been excavated. Sadly, no mortuary data matching that from Khok Phanom Di was encountered, but the numerous polished stone adzes and finely decorated ceramics reveal similar aspects for the material pursuits. Set inland, nephrite rather than shell was the preferred material for the manufacture of bangles. At the site of Lung Hoa twelve human burials have been found in an excavated area of 365 m². Two were associated with stone bracelets, beads and earrings as well as pottery vessels and stone adzes, a level of wealth which was not found with the other ten burials, and which encouraged the excavators to feel they had found further evidence for social ranking. Unfortunately, only three radiocarbon dates are referred to these Phung Nguyen sites. All come from late contexts, and suggest that the terminal phases belong to the middle of the second millennium BC. Early sites could, therefore, well have been contemporaries of Khok Phanom Di.

While there also remains a paucity of information bearing on the subsistence activities of these people, it is probable that they already cultivated rice and maintained domestic cattle and pigs in addition to the ubiquitous interest in fishing and collecting which so characterizes such small-scale agricultural societies down to the present day in South-East Asia.

We have rather better information on the date of the initial settlement of the interior river valleys of north-east Thailand due to excavations at three important sites, Non Nok Tha, Ban Chiang, and Ban Phak Top. The first two have revealed an early cultural context in which human graves were found with a range of grave goods, which included complete pottery vessels and shell beads. These graves overlay a natural substrate in which charcoal was identified. At Non Nok Tha, a radiocarbon date on such a piece of charcoal found 11 cm deep in the otherwise sterile soil underlying the site has provided a date of 3510–2865 BC. At Ban Phak Top, a date from an equivalent context is 2635–2085 BC, while at Ban Chiang, a sample from sterile has been dated to 3885–3045 BC. These three dates tell us only that initial settlement was later, but how much later is not disclosed. Dating the basal cultural contexts in all three sites is not straightforward, quite simply because if the excavators could identify charcoal in the natural soil under their sites, so too could the prehistoric people who cut graves down into the same natural material. Relocated and then collected by archaeologists, such samples might well provide spuriously early determinations. This simple fact underlines the importance of collecting charcoal for dating from such contexts as hearths and culturally formed burning layers. Sadly, none of these three sites has produced much, if any, charcoal from such *in situ* context.

Nevertheless, it is still possible to conclude that at some time later than about 3000 BC there was an expansionary movement of human settlement up the tributary stream valleys of north-east Thailand as well as central Cambodia, the Chao Phraya plains and the lower Mekong Valley. At the best-documented sites of Non Nok Tha and Ban Chiang, men, women and children were interred in association with a range of grave goods which demonstrate skills in pottery making, exchange in stone jewellery and adzes and an interest in exotic shell bracelets and beads. At Non Nok Tha, people were interred with the limbs of cattle and pigs which came from domestic animals. We can imagine that the graveside ritual involved feasting, and inclusion of part of the sacrificed animal with the departed. To judge from the fragments of rice chaff used to temper potting clay, the inhabitants were also familiar with rice. Yen has not been able to be definitive on whether the rice was cultivated or collected as a wild harvest along the naturally flooded waterways near which the pioneer settlers chose to live.

We simply have insufficient information to offer a detailed description of the social organization. Bayard (1984) has suggested that there was a weakly ranked system on the basis of the early burials from Non Nok Tha, and he may well be right. Certainly, none of the burials approaches the wealth of those described from later Khok Phanom Di.

THE COMING OF BRONZE

The smelting of metal ores and casting of metal artefacts is one of the major technological advances in the development of our species. In many parts of the world, skill in bronze working preceded that of iron, and South-East Asia is no exception. It is also stressed that the uplands of South-East Asia are particularly well endowed with both copper and tin deposits. We are aware that at such sites as Khok Phanom Di, Phung Nguyen and Non Nok Tha there was an exchange network linking upland and the adjacent plains settlements which supplied stone resources. While we are still largely ignorant of the means whereby tin was smelted and exchanged, research in Thailand has greatly illuminated our understanding of the extractive processes for copper. Pigott (1984) and Natapinto have been active in identifying copper sources used in prehistory, and at Phu Lon, on the southern bank of the Mekong, they have investigated a large copper mine and associated processing area used, it seems, from the end of the second millennium BC for about a thousand years. Having extracted the ore by mining, it was crushed using stone cobbles and anvils. The debris of this activity accumulated to a depth of 10 m. One piece of stone mould was found during excavations, but as yet no evidence for smelting furnaces has been isolated.

In a sense, a much more complete set of evidence for the extraction of copper has been found more recently in the Khao Wong Phra Chan Valley of central Thailand. Non Pa Wai, a 5-hectare mound, contains the residue of smelting activity to a depth of 3 m. There are smelting crucibles, the remains of tuyères, fragments of copper ore and cup moulds for the casting of ingots. At Nil Kam Haeng, there are many lenses of copper ore which has been crushed using stone pounders, as well as slag and crucible fragments which have built up to a depth of 5.25 m. Even the copper ingots have been recovered. Just as the people of Khok Phanom Di, who controlled access to the coast and its marine shell, grew wealthy, so those who oversaw the extraction and distribution of copper could be expected to prosper. Just such a person has been found in his grave at Non Pa Wai, for under the deep layer of accumulated mining and smelting debris, Pigott and Natapinto identified a cemetery in which one man was interred with a pair of double stone moulds for casting an axe.

At Ban Na Di, a small settlement in north-eastern Thailand excavated in 1981, we are able to pick up the thread of bronze working away from the mines. The original settlers of this site were aware of bronze at the initial settlement, though it was clearly a very rare commodity. Excavations there encountered a series of small clay-lined furnaces which contained an abundance of charcoal. Each was surrounded by concentrations of bronze fragments, broken crucibles and charcoal spreads. It seems that ingots of copper and tin were mixed in small crucibles, which were then placed within the furnaces charged with charcoal. To realize sufficient heat to melt the alloy, tuyères were probably used. When the ore was in a molten state, a bivalve sandstone mound was readied and the metal poured into it. To avoid fracture of the stone due to thermal shock, the mould may itself have been pre-heated. Such stone moulds were used for casting axes, spearheads and arrows. For the intricately decorated bangles, the lost-wax method was employed. This involved the preparation of a form of the bracelet in wax, which was then coated in clay. Once the wax was melted out of its clay casing through a vent hole, it could be replaced with molten bronze.

The same technique of casting using bivalve stone moulds is widespread. It was first recognized over a century ago at Samrong Sen in Cambodia (Noulet, 1877; Mansuy, 1902). More recently, excavations at Dong Dau in the lower valley of the Yuanjiang River during 1965 and 1967–86, which covered an area of 550 m², uncovered a stratigraphic sequence between 5 and 6 m deep. This revealed a Phung Nguyen context at the base of the mound, developing into the so-called Dong Dau phase, with bronze working. Three radiocarbon determinations from Thanh Den, a nearby site where Ha Van Tan recovered sandstone moulds virtually identical with those from north-east Thailand, suggest that bronze casting was under way from about 1500 BC. This dating context is in agreement with a date of 1885–1415 BC for a late Phung Nguyen layer at Dong Dau. In the lower Mekong area, two dates of 1735 to 1105 and 800 to 415 BC have come from the important site of Doc Chua where, once again, stone moulds were recovered. With the exception of three charcoal samples taken from contexts the excavator described as insecure, the four thermoluminescence dates run on pottery, the radioactive determinations from bronze contexts at Non Nok Tha are quite consistent with a beginning of metal used between 1500 and 100 BC. Graves including bronze at Ban Chiang allow the same conclusion, while at Ban Na Di, initial occupation took place, it seems, within the same period. The radiocarbon dates from Non Pa Wai and Phu Lon leave no doubt that mining and smelting took place during the second half of the second millennium BC. One interesting determination from the former site also hints at a much earlier beginning, perhaps by 2200 BC. We must await a series of dates from basal Non Pa Wai before this possibility can be investigated further. Higham (1988, p. 126) has elsewhere suggested for Non Nok Tha: 'Thus, the bronze-bearing levels probably fall within the time span 2000–1000 BC, though greater precision is still not possible.' During the Circum-Pacific Prehistory Conference, held in Seattle in August 1989, Vincent Pigott reported two dates for copper working from Non Pa Wai in the middle to late third millennium BC. In excavations at Nong Nor, near Khok Phanom Di south-east of Bangkok, in early 1991, Higham discovered a burial with bronze bracelets, the site and burial securely dated to mid-third millennium BC (Solheim, 1968). While this does not confirm the early dates for bronze working at Non Nok Tha previous to the mid-third millennium BC it at least indicates that they are not unreasonable.

It therefore seems that the knowledge entailed in smelting and casting objects from a copper and tin alloy spread fairly rapidly along the established exchange networks of South-East Asia. To judge from the distribution of bronze, rivers and coasts were the natural highways in such an exchange of prestige goods and information. The evidence from Khok Phanom Di and, to a lesser extent, Phung Nguyen, reveals that bronze working was adopted by sophisticated, sedentary communities already given to the use of the rare and beautiful to indicate rank.

It is within this social context that we can perhaps best appreciate the role of this metal in the cultural development in South-East Asia from 1500–1000 until 700 BC. Again, it is necessary to turn to mortuary information for the clearest insight into the life of the communities which adopted metallurgy. While several sites are now known in which people were interred together with bronze artefacts, only at Ban Na Di and Non Nok Tha do we, as yet, have sufficient information to be able to infer aspects of social patterning. Both sites sustain the same basic conclusion: that bronze was very rare in mortuary contexts. At Non Nok Tha only 14 out of 217 graves or mortuary features included bronze artefacts or implements used in the casting process, such as moulds and crucibles. At Ban Na Di, only 11.5 per cent of the 60

graves contained bronzes. What was the metal used for? It seems that quite the most popular artefact, at least in mortuary contexts, was the bangle. There were also some beads at Ban Na Di, while at nearby Ban Chiang a spearhead was found in one grave and an axehead in another. Axes, too, were identified at Non Nok Tha. Small arrowheads were found at Ban Na Di, but none in a definite mortuary context. A further application of the metal at the latter site was to repair broken stone bracelets by casting a wire-like rod through two holes bored in the adjacent sections of the bracelet. It seems likely that bronze joined stone, shell and pottery vessels as exotic items interred with the dead.

It was particularly fortunate that at Ban Na Di the excavators encountered two contemporary clusters of graves in different parts of the site, separated by a distance of about 30 m. In each case, the cluster of burials had clearly defined edges, and corpses had been interred next to and over each other in a manner recalling that described at Khok Phanom Di. When the distribution of exotic goods in each cluster was considered, it was apparent that one had significantly more than the other. Thus, over 90 per cent of the shell beads were found in the more favoured group, as well as all the marine-shell bangles. Members of this group were the only people buried with elaborate cattle figurines and exotic stone bangles, while the earliest iron, right at the end of this mortuary phase, was found in these graves. This information led the excavators to suggest that, while the village was small and in all probability quite independent in political terms, the inhabitants recognized that one group of people, perhaps related to each other by blood or marriage ties, was consistently of higher wealth and, by inference, rank. As more sites are excavated, it will be interesting to see if this pattern recurs.

At Non Nok Tha, there was also a pattern in the distribution of graves of the bronze period. We find that men, women and children were disposed in linear rows. Each row contains some unusually rich graves measured in terms of the actual number of artefacts found in each burial, and these richer interments were male. Bayard (1984) has suggested that the cemetery was used by two different affiliated groups, one richer than the other. He has suggested that one factor which provided for different wealth involved corporate ownership of the best land for rice cultivation. Another contributory factor could be preferred access to the distribution of metal.

Further insight into the nature of social organization during the period when bronze joined other prestige goods in exchange circuits will turn on the identification of where people lived, how large their settlements were, how many people lived in these communities and the degree to which they were autonomous or influenced by leaders of a differentially large and powerful group in their orbit. During a series of site surveys in north-east Thailand, emphasis has been given to the location and the sizes of sites to identify where and when political changes involving the imposition of authority over a web of communities from chiefly centres occurred. Wilen has worked in the Huay Sai Kao basin, Higham and Kijngam in the middle Chi Valley and the area round Lake Kumphawapi and Welch has undertaken fieldwork in the upper Mun Valley. To the west of the Phetchabun range, Ho has applied the same questions in the Lopburi region (Ho, 1984; Higham and Kijngam, 1984; Welch, 1984). There is a consistent thread to the results of these programmes: there is no evidence that any site in the survey areas grew differentially larger than others by 700 BC. This situation suggests that we encounter what are termed segmentary communities, linked to each other through exchange of goods and perhaps marriage partners. These communities probably incorporated only a few hundred inhabitants at most, and were probably divided into differently ranked groups. Within such a system, the provision, exchange and ownership of prestige objects could have been the critical means to obtaining, displaying and enhancing the relative status of individuals and communities (Dalton, 1977). Under such conditions, a key position fell to those who controlled sources. At Khok Phanom Di, we have seen how ranking occurred rapidly, within the span of a few centuries. Bronze was subsequently added to the list of prestige goods, but among end-users of the metal at Non Nok Tha and Ban Na Di there was not the same intensity of ranking behaviour as one suspects occurred among those who controlled the mining and smelting. Trends to centralized chiefdoms did occur on the mainland of South-East Asia, but at a later date than the period encompassed in this volume.

ISLAND SOUTH-EAST ASIA AND THE PACIFIC

Wilhelm G. Solheim II

It is hypothesized that a maritime culture started developing in South-East Asia around 5000 BC. By 3000 BC there were probably several related maritime cultures surrounding the South China Sea and along coastal areas of the Philippine and eastern Indonesian islands in intermittent contact with each other. In eastern Indonesia and the southern and central Philippine islands the land-oriented peoples had a stone flake industry, in some cases including blades or blade-like flakes. In south-western Sulawesi these people had developed true microlithic tools somewhat before 3000 BC. People of one of the maritime cultures of Indonesia probably settled in the New Britain/New Ireland area north of New Guinea soon after 2000 BC.

It is likely that one or more of these South-East Asian maritime cultures was situated along the coast of south China and had intermittent contact with people of coastal southern Korea and western Kyushu in Japan from around 4000 BC or earlier. They did not make a major impact on the cultures in these areas, however, until shortly after 2000 BC, when they introduced rice culture first to Korea and then to Kyushu. They no doubt intermarried to some extent with the Kaya of southern Korea and the Wa of western Japan.

The people of these maritime cultures had some effect physically and linguistically on the coastal Melanesians of New Guinea and those nearby Melanesian islands already inhabited. For much of Oceania, however, the maritime people, formerly from South-East Asia, were the first to arrive.

ISLAND SOUTH-EAST ASIA

Taiwan

The east coast hunting and gathering cultures continue from before with the latest date from the Changpinian Cave sites at between 3275 and 2575 BC (Y–2638; Chang et al., 1969, p. 134), and the earliest from the open site at O-Luan-Pi Park between 2835 and 2735 BC (Beta–6159; Li, 1983*a*, p. 40);

The artefacts from the two sites are not particularly similar. The long continuing industry found in the Changpinian Cave sites includes stone, bone and antler tools. The stone tools have been divided into a fine and a coarse series. The coarse series comprised primarily flake and a few pebble tools; most of the flakes, struck off from beach pebbles without prepared platforms, were unretouched. The pebble tools were all unifacially flaked choppers. The fine tools were flakes (no blades) struck from beach pebbles, rarely utilizing faceted striking platforms or retouched. 'The tool types that can be recognized include side-scraper, point, knife, combined tools, and notched scraper' (Chang et al., 1969, p. 135), their use probably including the manufacture of the bone and antler tools. These fine tools came later in the sequence but overlap with the coarse tools. The bone and antler tools included 'pointed bone splints ... long bones with a bone joint on one end and a point or a fork on the other ... eyed needles ... double-pointed gouges ... and chisel-edge long implements' (Chang et al., 1969, p. 135). These tools suggest manufacture of basketry and possibly netting.

Above the non-ceramic, hunting and gathering layer at O-Luan-Pi Park is a culture extending from 2200–1800 BC (NTU–244) to 550–350 BC (Y–1577; Chang et al., 1969, pp. 45–56), with red cord-marked pottery in its lowest phase, painted pottery, polished stone and bone, and shell tools starting around 1000 BC in its next phase, and a continuation of this in the last phase. Subsistence was fishing and gathering of shellfish with some agriculture and hunting (Chang et al., 1969, pp. 80–1). A large cemetery at Peinan had stone-slab graves with earthenware pottery unlike any other prehistoric pottery known in Taiwan. With practically every burial there was a jade earring similar to those of northern Vietnam and the Philippines. The beginning of this site was about 3000 BC. To the north, up the east coast, a variety of megaliths of the Chilin cultural tradition (distinct from the Peinan cultural tradition) are later in time but probably beginning before the end of our period.

The western side of Taiwan, from the coast up the major valleys, exhibits a series of probable agricultural cultures, the Corded Ware culture first. With one date of 2540–2430 BC (SI–1229; Chang, 1973, p. 525), no certain evidence of agriculture was found, though rice impressions have been found in pottery of about 2000 BC in a site in the far south (Li, 1983*b*, pp. 105–6). The following cultures, at first considered to originate whole through migrations from the China mainland (Chang et al., 1969; Dewar, 1978), are now felt to result from local evolution with additional elements from the mainland. Both areas share tool types and pottery forms with the mainland but the Taiwan cultures do not show a close resemblance to any mainland culture. Both language and artefact distribution suggest, to this author, trading contacts among Taiwan, mainland China, northern Vietnam, and the northern Philippines, but no major migrations from any of these areas after about 3000 BC. The east coast cultures are distinct from those on the western side of the north-south running mountains except that sites at the southern tip of Taiwan share a few artefact types with the Taipei basin.[1]

The Tapenkeng culture of the western lowland is the first Taiwan culture with pottery. Starting before our period, it continued to around 2500 BC. This pottery is commonly cord-marked. There are notched pebbles that were probably fish-net weights so we know that they made cord and probably fish-nets. The few illustrated, reconstructed pottery vessels have either relatively flat bottoms or low ring feet and have a low centre of gravity, suggesting storage vessels. Stone artefacts include small, polished adzes, quadrangular in cross-section, a few of these in northern sites with a step for hafting, pitted pebbles, possibly for breaking open hard shelled nuts or for use as hammerstones, polished, perforated, triangular slate points with straight base, and possible stone hoes (Chang et al., 1969, pp. 53–9, 164–71, 211). Other than the stone hoes, which could have been used for digging up wild tubers, there is little to suggest that agriculture was of importance, or what might have been grown if it were important.

At least two separate cultures developed out of the Tapenkeng culture, the Yuan-shan in the north, and the Red Corded ware culture in the south. It appears likely that the non-pottery artefacts of the Tapenkeng culture continued, with some additions from the continent, to form the technological basis for the later cultures (Li, 1983a, pp. 103–5): in the north stepped adzes, several varieties of hoes and triangular, perforated slate points become much more common, with the addition of other varieties of points, shouldered adzes and pottery spindle whorls. In the later levels a few jade ornaments were found (Chang et al., 1969, pp. 175–85). In central and south-western Taiwan the following culture continued for 2,000 years with developing complexity and some additions from outside to the technology but with local evolution probably primary (Chang et al., 1969, p. 111; Li, 1983a, pp. 103–5). The additions were rectangular and semi-lunar stone knives, centrally perforated pottery discs, at around 1000 BC, a rather rare pediform adze or knife, a variety of shell ornaments, some shell implements, and at some sites stone-cist graves. Pottery forms and decoration evolved in great variety (Chang et al., 1969, pp. 64–109; Li, 1983b). Clay spindle whorls were probably present at Fengpitou from the beginning, while at O-Luan-Pi Park they appear in different form at around 1000 BC (Li, 1983b; Plate 116).

The Philippines, East Malaysia and Eastern Indonesia

Two areas in the Philippines have a number of sites dating to this period: in the north the Cagayan Valley of northern Luzon and in the west the Palawan cave sites. Certainly all the major islands and many of the smaller ones were occupied but only scattered sites have been excavated.

Agriculture has not been conclusively demonstrated for this period but types and wear of stone tools suggest that there were scattered areas with agriculture or horticulture combined with hunting and gathering. No settlements have been excavated but the bases of shallow, semi-subterranean houses have been found in north-eastern and central Luzon sites.

Unretouched flakes, struck off without prepared striking platforms, are the common artefacts while a few cores are found (Ronquillo, 1981). At some sites flakes with a minimum of retouching have been found and, from widely scattered sites in the central Philippine islands and as far north as central Luzon, a few blades have been recovered, some of them made on prepared cores. The flakes were not ordinarily made to a specific form. What was desired was a specific edge shape and angle. Used edges were straight, concave or convex. One artefact with a concave edge is similar to a spokeshave. Some of the cores were used and these were often with high angles. Edge grinding of flaked adzes started showing up by the beginning of this period. Shell flake tools and edge-ground adzes were found at sites in the southern Philippines and in Palawan. These are similar to the stone flakes and edge-ground adzes. Shell flakes appear to have been struck from *Tridacna* shell but very little study has been done on the manufacture and use of the shell tools. A shell spoon and pendant were recovered in Palawan, and a lime container from a burial there suggests the betel-nut complex was present at this time.

From about 2000 BC ornaments of shell, fired clay and then stone began to appear. Beads of carnelian and jade and earrings of jade, polished and very well made, followed in sites in Palawan and the Cagayan Valley soon after 1000 BC. Several varieties of jade bracelets and armbands made from large shells became common. Stone barkcloth-beaters were present, probably coming into use some time during the second millennium BC, with spindle whorls appearing in the Cagayan Valley not long after. There was an evolution of polished stone tools, particularly with the development of a modified butt for hafting, leading to the typical stepped adze of the Philippines. A moderate number of bone tools, such as needles, awls, tattooing tools, and points have been recovered (Beyer, 1948; Fox, 1970; Solheim, 1964, 1968, 1981).

The earliest known pottery, a little before 3000 BC, is from sites in the Cagayan Valley, and in eastern Indonesia as well. Pottery this early is not yet known from central Luzon south to Mindanao. The first pottery is plain but shortly after this the technique of red slipping appears, as well as typical South-East Asian forms of shallow bowls with or without ring feet, low ring feet on other forms, small globular vessels and carination. Pottery decoration arrives also, with impressed circles and dashed lines, sometimes inlaid with lime, and punctations in simple angular patterns. This style of decoration has been found at sites in the northern end of the Cagayan Valley of Luzon, in the Batungan Cave sites of Masbate (Solheim, 1968) and in Sulawesi, Indonesia. Some time before 1000 BC new styles and patterns of pottery decoration started showing up in both the Tabon and Niah caves, and eastern Indonesia, designs that had been common in northern and southern Vietnam for more than 2,000 years. Metal enters at the end of this period, both rare bronze and, slightly later, iron (Fox, 1970; Solheim, 1964, 1968, 1981). Flexed burials have been found in Niah cave in Sarawak from before this period and around 2500 BC extended burial with associated earthenware pottery started to come into fashion (B. Harrisson, 1967). Some time between 2000 and 1500 BC the idea of primary and possibly secondary burial in large earthenware jars was brought to Palawan, as found also in the Tabon caves. This presumably came from Mainland South-East Asia, where it had been practised in north-eastern Thailand and northern Vietnam for some time.

A maritime trade network, called the Nusantao Maritime Trade Network, has been suggested as developing from before the beginning of the period (Solheim et al., 1979, pp. 196–9). Communication through the trading network may have brought about the addition of blades to the existing generalized flake industry, the technique of making these blades probably being brought up from Sulawesi in Indonesia. These hypothesized maritime traders no doubt developed out of coastal fishing groups and were closely related to them culturally and linguistically. Somewhat before 3000 BC they brought the knowledge of edge-grinding of stone tools into the Philippines from the south. Probably the southern Philippines and north-eastern Indonesia was where they had started to develop tools from shell, the manufacturing techniques for which they brought north into the Philippines. By 3000 BC their network had extended all around the South China Sea bringing the knowledge of pottery manufacture from Mainland South-East Asia over the following thousand years to Taiwan, the Philippines, Borneo and eastern Indonesia.

At about the same time different kinds of polished stone artefacts started to appear in Taiwan, the Philippines, and in the Niah caves, not exactly the same in all areas, but some found in the northern Philippines and Taiwan and others in the Tabon and Niah caves. Around 1000 BC varieties of the new style of pottery that had appeared in Niah and Tabon caves started to appear in the central Philippines, east of Palawan. First reported in the Philippines from the Kalanay Cave site in Masbate (Solheim et al., 1979, pp. 22–78), this pottery was a part of the Sa-huynh-Kalanay pottery tradition. Similar pottery had been reported long before from the site of Sa-huynh, on the coast of southern-central Vietnam. Pottery with this distinctive decoration has been found in much of eastern Island South-East Asia and coastal southern Vietnam, with relationships in western Cambodia and along the coasts of the Gulf of Thailand (Solheim, 1959). Also found in the Kalanay Cave site were rare iron tools and a small bronze bell (Solheim et al., 1979, fig. 23b), the latter similar to bells found in Dongson sites in Vietnam.

In the Tabon caves, beads made of carnelian were found, probably brought from the east coast of India. About 1800 BC jade beads started to show up in the Tabon caves and soon after that a variety of earring, called the *lingling-o*. Exactly the same kinds of jade earring, from the same time period, have been found in the Cagayan Valley of northern Luzon, in south-eastern Taiwan, at Niah Cave in Sarawak, in sites along the coast of central and southern Vietnam, in southern-central Thailand and on the east coast of peninsular Thailand. A much rarer but related type of earring, a double-headed animal., has been found in much the same area and with the same dating. One of these was found as an heirloom piece in Botel Tobago, off the south-east coast of Taiwan, and one was found at Ban Don Ta Phet, Kanchanaburi province, western Thailand, associated with artefacts suggesting a dating of around 1400 BC.

The maritime trading network connecting the east coast of India with coastal eastern Mainland and eastern Island South-East Asia, and north-eastern South-East Asia with Korea and Japan, was probably in place by 1000 BC or before. This network also brought the knowledge of bronze manufacture to the Tabon caves by the end of this period. This was not a single, integrated, trade network but probably many different, intersecting networks, carrying somewhat different trade items in each one. This can be seen by the lack of jade beads and the *lingling-o* in the Visayan Islands and Mindanao of the Philippines, and only one, so far, found in the Niah caves (Fox, 1970; Patanne, 1972; T. Harrisson, 1970, 1971; Solheim, 1964, 1981; Solheim et al., 1979).

There are very little data from much of eastern Indonesia and Irian Jaya (Indonesian New Guinea), and only a very few excavated sites are well dated. Those areas that are known are similar to the central and southern Philippines. There are dated sequences in the Talaud Islands (south of Mindanao), south-western Sulawesi, and in eastern Timor that cover this period. Artefacts from the Great Cave of Niah are similar to those from the Tabon Cave site and nearby sites in Palawan. A noticeable difference in the technology of the two areas is that the variety of ornaments, both of stone and shell, found in the Tabon caves is not present in the Niah caves and the other three areas, except for the single jade earring from the Great Cave. From sites in Sarawak and in south-eastern Mindanao both cord-marked and basket-

marked pottery are found (Chin, 1980; Bellwood, 1976, pp. 255–67; 1985, pp. 227–8; B. Harrisson, 1967; T. Harrisson, 1970, 1971; T. Harrisson and Medway, 1962; Solheim et al., 1979).

Artefacts from sites in western and north-eastern Sulawesi and Timor are generally similar. The earliest pottery is plain, and soon after, red slipped as in the Philippines, with small, impressed circles, hachured triangles and impressed half circles that in some examples look like a running scroll. The south-western Sulawesi sites have primarily plain pottery in the earlier level but include two illustrated sherds from one site with concentric impressed circles in a decoration similar to sherds from one of the Batungan Cave sites in Masbate, Philippines, of about the same dating. Stepped adzes have been found in Sulawesi and stone barkcloth-beaters in Sulawesi and Borneo, similar to some from the Philippines (Bellwood, 1976, 1985; Glover, 1969, 1971, 1977; Solheim, 1968).

The Timor sites are comparable, with pottery coming in around 3000 BC but no polished stone tools. With the pottery are indications of agriculture and domesticated pigs plus marsupials, probably from New Guinea (Glover, 1971). At many of these sites pottery similar to the Sa-huynh-Kalanay pottery of the Philippines appears at about the end of this period or somewhat later.

Western Indonesia and West Malaysia

There is no reliable indication of agriculture or Neolithic society in Sumatra, western Java, and west Malaysia until around the end of this period. A Late Hoabinhian style of culture with pebble tools and flakes from unprepared cores seems to be the norm in the northern half of Sumatra. In southern Sumatra and western Java unretouched flakes are found with a few of the typical Hoabinhian tools. The rare pottery from the upper levels of one or more of these sites is undated and is probably late in our period. It is likely that the maritime traders of eastern South-East Asia made contact along the coasts in the first millennium BC trade with India.

West Malaysia is more like Sumatra, prehistorically, than it is like the rest of Mainland South-East Asia so it is here included with Island South-East Asia. There are four sites with dates in our period but for one the date is not associated with a level. Two of the other sites have Hoabinhian industries in their lower levels. Gua Cha has a distinct boundary between its lower Hoabinhian levels and the upper 'Malayan Neolithic' level. There was no pottery in the Hoabinhian levels. The charcoal date for the interface between the two is 1280–750 BC (ANU–2217). It appears likely that the 'Malayan Neolithic' people were ancestors of the Orang Asli (Negrito) in varying combinations with southern Mongoloids, resulting in the different appearing groups of today. The 'Neolithic' levels suggest a culture at least partly dependent on agriculture, with polished stone adzes and very nice pottery, related at least to some extent with the Sa-huynh-Kalanay pottery tradition (Peacock, 1959).

The second site is Gua Kechil. Here there is simple cord-marked pottery in lower layers, a modified cord-marked pottery in intermediate layers, and 'Malayan Neolithic' pottery in the upper layers but with cord-marking continuing. It appears that the original Hoabinhian people came into contact with the newly arrived 'Neolithic' people on the coast and as a result of the contact modified their pottery forms in due time all the way to the 'Neolithic'-style pottery. Most Hoabinhian sites contain marine shell, indicating trade with coastal people or excursions to the coast. This continued in the 'Neolithic' levels with the inland people trading forest products for lowland and coastal products (Dunn, 1975, pp. 132, 136–7). Lowland and coastal sites are not yet known. The site of Jenderan Hilir, with a date of 3600–2000 BC (I–10758) found in alluvial tin-bearing deposits, has tripod pottery like that of 'Malayan Neolithic' pottery (Peacock, 1959, Fig. 12a).

Oceania

The primary activity in most of Oceania during this period was the expansion of the Austronesian-speaking peoples. This was a continuation of the maritime trading/expansion of Austronesian-speakers in South-East Asia. The earliest archaeologically indicated expansion out of Island South-East Asia was into north-western Melanesia and, probably separately, into Micronesia. Archaeological excavations suggest the possibility of pre-ceramic Austronesian settlement in the Bismark Island area. With pottery manufacture in eastern Island South-East Asia shortly before 3000 BC it is likely that this first settlement in Melanesia would have come about the same time. It has been suggested that these first arrivals from Island South-East Asia had a stratified society with an incipient form of chiefdoms. This would seem questionable but difficult to test at this time.

Melanesia

Melanesia can be divided into two parts, Mainland and Island Melanesia, the former being New Guinea. New Guinea and the closest major islands of New Britain and New Ireland, with their small offshore islands, were occupied in the late Pleistocene and so at least some of the cultures present were a continuation of the earlier cultures while others were brought into the area by newly arrived peoples. There is no indication of a large population of Melanesians at the time of first contact by the maritime peoples from South-East Asia but these new people probably stayed primarily on small islands off the shore of larger islands or on the coast of the larger islands without mixing much with the Melanesians. There must have been a fair amount of contact over time, however, as soon after 1500 BC Melanesians had learned some of the maritime practices of the new arrivals and were moving south into New Caledonia and other previously uninhabited islands of Melanesia. Some of the Melanesians also took over the language of the new arrivals, as their descendants today speak Austronesian languages. Agriculture in the interior of New Guinea continued.

Archaeological research in New Guinea is primarily restricted to Papua New Guinea and here large areas are still unknown with the known areas not contiguous. Most research has been in the interior highlands with less done in the lowlands.

Found throughout much of Papua New Guinea, mostly below 2,000 m altitude, and in the Bismarck archipelago, are stone mortars, pestles, figurines and club-heads. These form a complex sharing design elements such as birds' heads, and their method of manufacture (pecking, grinding and polishing). While their dating is usually unknown, fragments of mortars have been recovered from Waniek dated between 3000 and 1000 BC and from a site in the eastern highlands with dates from 1500 to 1000 BC. Continuing from earlier

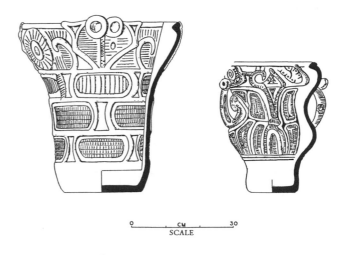

Figure 77 Central Honshu Middle Jomon elaborately decorated pottery (after Kamikawanha, 1968).

times, used flakes, without preconceived forms (except for edges), are common in many sites, as are polished axes/adzes, lenticular in cross-section. Also continuing, and often associated with the lenticular adzes/axes, were large, flaked, wasted blades. Around 500 BC there was a change from the widely found lenticular adzes to polished adzes with a rectangular cross-section, knowledge of this type being brought in from South-East Asia.

Pottery appears to have come into Papua New Guinea after our period but a few sherds have been recovered from Waniek dating to 3000–4000 years ago. The pottery forms are simple, with rounded or pointed bottoms, and were made by coiling. This Northern Papuan pottery tradition later spread along the northern coast for over 1,000 km. Most sites are not directly on the coast but inland in the hills.

The best known sites of this period do not contain artefacts. These are agricultural sites in Kuk Swamp of the central highlands. Originating as early as 9000 years ago, phase 3 of this extensive site is made up of channels made to drain water and forming many small islands on which plants were grown. From more recent levels wooden spades and digging sticks were recovered. It is likely that these types of tools were used earlier as agricultural tools and to dig and keep in repair the water control channels. Occasional house-posts have been recovered indicating pile dwellings, probably built over the water. These people brought with them domesticated plants and animals from South-East Asia (such as taro, yams, breadfruit, pigs, chickens and dogs) and New Guinea (such as bananas and sugarcane) (Bellwood, 1979, pp. 233–79; S. Bulmer, 1985; R. Bulmer and S. Bulmer, 1962; Burton, 1984; Garanger, 1972; Golsonk 1972; Green, 1979; Swadling, 1981; White and O'Connell, 1982, pp. 171–97).

In much of Island Melanesia the Lapita cultural complex is the earliest and best known culture, known primarily for its distinctive pottery. Around 1500 BC pottery manufacture was brought in from Island South-East Asia and the Lapita pottery tradition developed from this and spread out to Fiji. Slab-building was the common method of manufacture with paddle-and-anvil finishing. The range and the common forms are much like those of the Sa-huynh-Kalanay pottery tradition of Island South-East Asia with rounded and flat bottoms or ring-stands, a variety of shallow bowls, rounded pots with low, out-turned rims, and with carination common. Sites with this pottery first appear shortly after 2000 BC in north-western Island Melanesia, and are present out to Tonga and Samoa in the east and New Caledonia in the south around 1000 BC. The fine dentate-stamped decoration (Fig. 78) suggests tattooing both in patterns and in technique, and probable tattooing tools have been found. The rapid spread of this pottery points to ocean-going sailing boats, most likely with outriggers, but these have not been found. Within the area of the Lapita pottery tradition long-distance trade quickly developed in obsidian and other materials.

Unretouched obsidian flakes and cores are found at most sites. Polished shell and stone adzes with lenticular, circular, rectangular, trapezoidal and other cross-sections, and some with modified butts for hafting are found. Shell scrapers, peelers and fishhooks are common as are a variety of shell and bone ornaments such as bracelets, beads and pendants. Coral and volcanic rock files and sharpening stones are common. Probable oven-stones have been found at some sites.

Other cultures with distinctly different pottery traditions are known from Mangassi and other sites in Vanuatu (New Hebrides) and sites in New Caledonia. A few Lapita sherds were found at the site of Erueti on Efate. Much of the pottery of these cultures is built up by coiling rather than slab-building. Artefacts of stone and shell are, in general, more similar to those of the Lapita culture than is the pottery (Bellwood, 1979, pp. 244–62; Garanger, 1972; Kirch, 1987; Poulsen, 1987; Spriggs, 1984).

Micronesia

Intensive and extensive archaeological research did not begin in Micronesia until about 1977 and only preliminary reports are in print. The field is changing rapidly. The western Micronesian islands, as far east as the Marianas chain, are thought to be the first inhabited. The only early site yet known in eastern Micronesia is on Bikini Atoll, in the Marshall Islands, where a date of about 1800 BC has been reported from a test-pit with no artefacts at the level from which the charcoal sample came. A fragment of a shell adze, similar to those from pre-ceramic sites in the northern Melanesian islands, and an artefact made of coral, have been recovered from a level dating just before the end of this period (Strecht, 1987). The next earliest dates for eastern Micronesia are at the end of our period.

The earliest published sites in western Micronesia are from Guam in the Marianas, at about 2000 BC. The first reported early pottery was called Marianas Red, a red-slipped pottery, some of it with a simple, incised and impressed decoration, at times inlaid with lime. Associated with this pottery were an edge-ground basalt flake and adze and shell beads, bracelets, adze fragments and pendants. This early pottery is now called Calcareous Sand-Tempered ware (CST) to distinguish it from the later Volcanic Sand-Tempered ware (VST). It is now recognized, at least for Guam, that the lime inlaid pottery did not appear until about the end of our period.

The earliest trustworthy dates for pottery are from the Tarague site on Guam, from about 1500–1000 BC. This pottery is red-slipped and at times decorated with impressed circles, similar to that of the Batungan, Philippines, and south-western Sulawesi sites in Indonesia. Two shell adzes have been recovered from the Tarague site, one from the bottom layer, and both are made of *Tridacna gigas*, a shell not known to occur in the Marianas during the Holocene (Spoehr, 1957; Spoehr and Sinoto, 1981).[2]

The present suggested sequence for Guam names four stages: the first, called Early Pre-Latte, dates from prior to 1485 to about 500 BC. Little is known about the non-pottery artefacts of this first stage but there were *Tridacna* shell adzes, shell fishhooks and probably shell gorges. The known forms of the early CST were shallow bowls, often carinated (Moore, 1983).

The most recent research on northern Guam reports an earlier date of about 2000 BC from charcoal. From this level a number of thick, poorly fired sherds were recovered from very large vessels, without decoration. Though not yet analysed they do not look like the Marianas Red pottery. From the same layer a coral file was recovered. From a level dating about 1000 BC came thinner pottery, probably the CST pottery, a shell adze blank and a basalt fragment. From a level dating between 1000 to 500 BC in another site, pottery and a coral file were found. Finally, from a third site, from a level dating around 2300 BC, post-mold evidence for four houses, potsherds, one shell ornament, one fishhook blank and a piece of red pumice were recovered. A layer dating around 1400 BC yielded sherds, one fishhook, coral files or abraders (including one drill tip), one basalt pestle, two sling-stones, and two shell beads.

While considerable archaeological research has been done on Palau, there are only two dates from the hypothesized period of early occupation which perhaps started around 1800 BC. Simple pottery with sherd temper is present in this period. The only illustrated form is not at all like the shallow bowls of Guam during this period. The only non-

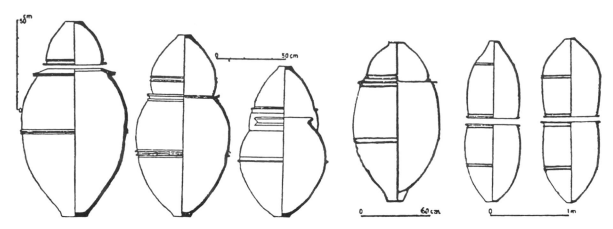

Figure 78 Early Yayoi burial types, varieties of double jars (after Kaneko, 1964).

pottery artefact that appears to be from this early period is a *Tridacna* shell adze.

Polynesia

Tonga and then Samoa were the first islands to be settled in Polynesia, Tonga by Austronesian-speakers from Fiji, both of them around 1000 BC. They brought with them the Lapita pottery tradition and the domesticated plants and animals that they had in Fiji. The people in these three island groups stayed in contact through long-distance voyaging for practically a thousand years, developing here the typical Polynesian culture. Their spread from Samoa east into the rest of Polynesia came after the end of our period (Bellwood, 1979, pp. 253–4).

NOTES

1 I should like to thank Erika Kaneko for information on Taiwan prehistory. She is not responsible for my interpretation, though in most cases I have followed her suggestions.
2 I should like to thank Charles Strecht for unpublished information on Micronesian archaeology.

BIBLIOGRAPHY

ALLEN, J.; GOSDEN, C. (eds) 1991. *Report on the Lapita Project*. Department of Prehistory, Research School of Pacific and Asian Studies, Australian National University.

AYRES, W. S.; HAUN, A. E. 1985. Archaeological Perspectives on Food Production in Eastern Micronesia. In: FARRINGTON, I. S. (ed.), *Prehistoric Intensive Agriculture in the Tropics*. Oxford. pp. 455–73. (BAR Int. Ser.)

BAYARD, D. T. 1984. A Regional Phase Chronology for Northeast Thailand. In: —— (ed.), *Southeast Asian Archaeology at the XV Pacific Science Congress*. University of Otago Studies in Prehistoric Anthropology, Vol. 16. Dunedin, New Zealand. pp. 161–8.

BELLWOOD, P. 1976. Archaeological Research in Minahasa and the Talaud Islands, Northeastern Indonesia. *Asian Perspect.* (Honolulu), Vol. 19, No. 2, pp. 240–88.

—— 1979. *Man's Conquest of the Pacific*. New York.

—— 1985. *Prehistory of the Indo-Malaysian Archipelago*. Sydney.

BEYER, H. O. 1948. *Philippine and East Asian Archaeology, and its Relation to the Origin of the Pacific Island Population*. Quezon City, National Research Council of the Philippines. (Bull., 29.)

BULMER, R.; BULMER, S. 1962. Figurines and other Stones of Power among the Kyaka of Central New Guinea. *J. polyn. Soc.* (Wellington), Vol. 71, No. 2, pp. 192–208.

BULMER, S. 1985. Papuan Pottery: An Archaeological Consideration. *Bull. Indo-Pac. prehist. Assoc.* (Canberra), Vol. 6, pp. 123–32.

BURTON, J. 1984. Field Research at the Stone Axe Quarries of Western Highlands and Simbu Provinces, Papua New Guinea. *Bull. Indo-Pac. prehist. Assoc.* (Canberra), Vol. 5, pp. 83–92.

CHANG, KWANG-CHIH et al. 1969. *Fengpitou, Tapenkeng, and the Prehistory of Taiwan*. New Haven, Conn. (Yale Univ. Publ. Anthropol., 73.)

CHIN, L. 1980. *Cultural Heritage of Sarawak*. Kuching.

COLANI, M. 1927. L'Age de la pierre dans la province de Hoa Binh. *Mém. Serv. geol. Indoch.* Vol. 14, No. 1.

DALTON, G. 1977. Aboriginal Economics in Stateless Societies. In: EARLE, T. K.; ERICSON, J. E. (eds), *Exchange Systems in Prehistory*. London. pp. 191–212.

DEWAR, R. 1978. Ecological Context and the Prehistory of the West Central Taiwan Coast. *Asian Perspect.* (Honolulu), Vol. 21, No. 2, pp. 207–41.

DUNN, F. L. 1975. *Rain-Forest Collectors and Traders: A Study of Resource Utilization in Modern and Ancient Malaya*. Kuala Lumpur. (Monogr. Malays. Branch r. asiat. Soc., 5.)

EGLI, H. 1972. Neusteinzeitliche Typenkreise an der Ostkuste van Taiwan. *Anthropos*, Vol. 67, pp. 229–67.

FOX, R. B. 1970. *The Tabon Caves: Archaeological Explorations and Excavations on Palawan Island, Philippines*. Manila, National Museum. (Monogr., 1.)

GARANGER, J. 1972. *Archéologie des Nouvelles-Hébrides*. Paris.

GLOVER, I. C. 1969. Radiocarbon Dates from Portuguese Timor. *Archeol. phys. Anthropol. Ocean.* (Sydney), Vol. 4, No. 2, pp. 107–12.

—— 1971. Prehistoric Research in Timor. In: MULVANEY, D. J.;

GOLSON, J. (eds), *Aboriginal Man and Environment in Australia*. Canberra. pp. 158–81.

—— 1977. The Late Stone Age in Eastern Indonesia. *World Archaeol.* (London), Vol. 9, No. 1, pp. 42–61.

GOLSON, J. 1972. Both Sides of Wallace Line: New Guinea, Australia, Island Melanesia and Asian Prehistory. In: BARNARD, N. (ed.), *Early Chinese Art and its Possible Influence in the Pacific Basin*. New York.

GREEN, R. C. 1979. Lapita. In: JENNINGS, J. D. (ed.), *The Prehistory of Polynesia*. Cambridge, Mass.

HARRISSON, B. 1967. A Classification of Stone Age Burials from Niah Great Cave, Sarawak. *Sarawak Mus. J.* (Kuching), Vol. 15, No. 30/1, pp. 126–200.

HARRISSON, T. 1970. The Prehistory of Borneo. *Asian Perspect.* (Honolulu), Vol. 13, pp. 17–45.

—— 1971. Prehistoric Double-spouted Vessels Excavated at Niah Caves, Borneo. *J. Malays. Branch r. asiat. Soc.* (Kuala Lumpur), Vol. 44, No. 2, pp. 35–78.

HARRISSON, T.; MEDWAY, L. 1962. A First Classification of Prehistoric Bone and Tooth Artefacts. *Sarawak Mus. J.* (Kuching), Vol. 10, No. 19–20, pp. 335–62.

HIGHAM, C. F. W. 1983. The Ban Chiang Culture in Wider Perspective. *Proc. br. Acad.* (London), Vol. 69, pp. 229–61.

—— 1988. *The Archaeology of Mainland Southeast Asia*. Cambridge.

HIGHAM, C. F. W.; KIJNGAM, A. 1984. Prehistoric Investigations in Northeast Thailand. Oxford. (BAR Int. Ser., 231.)

HO, C. M. 1984. *The Pottery of Kok Charoen and its Further Context*. London. (PhD thesis.)

HOANG XUAN CHINH. 1984. The Hoabinhian Culture and the Birth of Botanical Domestication in '. In: BAYARD, D. (ed.), *Southeast Asian Archaeology at the XV Pacific Science Congress*. University of Otago Studies in Prehistoric Anthropology, Vol. 16. Dunedin, New Zealand. pp. 169–72.

KIRCH, P. V. 1987. Lapita and Oceanic Cultural Origins: Excavations in the Mussau Islands, Bismarck Archipelago, 1985. *J. Field Archaeol.* (Boston, Mass.), Vol. 14, pp. 163–80.

LI, KUANG-CHOU. 1983a. Problems Raised by the Klen-ting Excavation of 1977. *Bull. Dept. Archaeol. Anthropol.* (Taipei), No. 43, pp. 86–116.

—— 1983b. *Report of Archaeological Investigations in the O-Luan-Pi Park at Southern Tip of Taiwan*. Taipei.

MAJID, Z. 1982. The West Mouth, Niah, in the Prehistory of Southeast Asia. *Sarawak Mus. J.* (Kuching), Vol. 31, No. 52, pp. 1–200.

MANSUY, H. 1902. *Stations préhistoriques de Samrong-Seng et de Longprao (Cambodge)*. Hanoi.

—— 1924. Stations préhistoriques dans les cavernes du massifcalcaire de Bac-Son. *Mém. Serv. géol. Indoch*, Vol. 11, No. 2.

MARSHALL, M. 1984. Structural Patterns of Sibling Classification in Island Oceania: Implications for Culture History. *Curr. Anthropol.* (Chicago), Vol. 25, No. 5, pp. 597–637.

MOORE, D. 1983. *Measuring Change in Marianas Pottery: The Sequence of Pottery Production at Taraque*. Guam. Agana, University of Guam. (MA thesis.)

NOULET, J. B. 1877. *L'âge de la pierre dans l'Indo-Chine*. Paris. (Matériaux pour l'Histoire primitive et naturelle de l'Homme, Ser. 2B).

PATANNE, E. P. *The Philippines in the World of Southeast Asia: A Culture History*. Quezon City, Philippines.

PAWLEY, A.; GREEN, R. C. 1973. Dating the Dispersal of the Oceanic Languages. *Ocean. Linguist.* (Honolulu), Vol. 12, pp. 1–68.

PEACOCK, B. A. V. 1959. A Short Description of Malayan Prehistoric Pottery. *Asian Perspect.* (Honolulu), Vol. 3, No. 2, pp. 121–56.

PIGOTT, V. C. 1984. The Thailand Archaeometallurgy Project 1984: Survey of Base Metal Resource Exploitation in Loei Province, Northeast Thailand. *Southeast Asian Stud. Newsl.* (Bangkok), Vol. 17, pp. 1–3.

POOKAJORN, S. 1981. *The Hoabinhian of Mainland Southeast Asia: New Data from the Recent Thai Excavations in the Ban Kao Area.* Pennsylvania. (unpublished MA thesis on deposit with the Department of Anthropology, University of Pennsylvania.)

POULSEN, J. 1987. *Early Tongan Prehistory.* Canberra, Australian National University. Vol. 2. (Terra Australis, 12.)

RONQUILLO, W. P. 1981. *The Technological and Functional Analysis of the Lithic Flake Tools from Rabel Cave, Northern Luzon, Philippines.* Manila. (Antropol. Pap., 13.)

SOLHEIM II, W. G. 1964. *The Archaeology of Central Philippines.* Manila. (Mogr. natl. Inst. Sc. Technol., 10.)

—— 1968. The Batungan Cave Sites, Masbate, Philippines. In: —— (ed.), *Anthropology at the Eighth Pacific Science Congress.* Honolulu, HI. pp. 20–62. (Asian Pac. Archaeol. Ser., 2.)

—— 1981. Philippine Prehistory. In: FATHER, G. C. et al. *The People and Art of the Philippines.* Los Angeles. pp. 16–83.

—— (ed.) 1959. Sa-huynh Pottery Relationships in Southeast Asia. *Asian Perspect.* (Honolulu), Vol. 3, No. 2, pp. 97–188.

SOLHEIM II, W. G; LEGASPI, A. M.; NERI, J. S. 1979. *Archaeological Survey in Southeastern Mindanao.* Manila. (Monog., 8.)

SPOEHR, A. 1957. *Marianes Prehistory Archaeological Survey and Excavations on Saipan, Tinian and Rota.* Chicago. (Fieldiana, Antropol., 48.)

SPOEHR, A.; SINOTO, Y. H. (eds). 1981. Micronesian Prehistory. *Asian Perspect.* (Honolulu), Vol. 24, No. 1 (special issue), pp. 1–138.

SPRIGGS, M. 1984. The Lapita Cultural Complex: Origins, Distribution, Contemporaries and Successors. *J. Pac. Hist.* (New York), pp. 202–3.

STRECHT, C. 1987. *Archaeological Reconnaissance Site Survey of the Islands of Bikini Atoll, Republic of the Marshall Islands, Micronesia.* Honolulu, Berkeley, Bikini Atoll Rehabilitation Committee.

SWADLING, P. 1981. *Papua New Guinea's Prehistory: An Introduction.* Port Moresby.

TURNER, C. G. 1985. The Modern Human Dispersal Event: The Eastern Frontier. *Q. Rev. Archaeol.* (Salem, Mass.), Dec., pp. 8–9.

WELCH, D. 1984. *Adaptation to Environmental Unpredictability: Intensive Agriculture and Regional Exchange at Late Prehistoric Centers in the Phimai Region.* Honolulu. (PhD thesis.)

WHITE, J. P.; CROOK, K. A. W.; BUXTON, B. P. 1970. Kosipe: A Late Pleistocene Site in the Papuan Highlands. *Proc. prehist. Soc.* (Cambridge), Vol. 36, pp. 132–70.

WHITE, J. P.; O'CONNELL, J. F. 1982. *A Prehistory of Australia, New Guinea and Sahul.* Sydney.

YEN, D. E. 1977. Hoabingian horticulture: The evidence and the questions from northwest Thailand. In: ALLEN, J. et al. (eds), *Sunda and Sahul.* London. pp. 567–9. .

15.3
KOREA

Tadashi Nishitani

In Korea, the period covering 3000 to 700 BC corresponds to the period from the Middle Chulmun (geometric, comb-pattern) pottery period (Neolithic Age) to the Early Mumun (plain) pottery period (Bronze Age). Accordingly, this chapter surveys the technology and culture of the Chulmun pottery period and the Mumun pottery period (Map 24).

THE CHULMUN (GEOMETRIC) POTTERY PERIOD

Approximately 12,000 years ago, after the last glacial epoch, when the earth entered the climatically warm interglacial period, the rise in sea-levels associated with the melting of glaciers resulted in the coastlines in East Asia, as in other areas of the world, retreating inland. It was during this period that the Korean peninsula appeared in virtually the form we see today. After that, for over 1,000 years, sea-levels rose and fell regionally, slightly changing the coastline topography. Pottery made a sudden appearance during the Palaeolithic, into a world which had existed over hundreds of thousands of years using only crude stone tools. At present the oldest pottery (Yukimun pottery) yet found in Korea, from such sites as Osanni in Kongwon Province, and Tongsam-dong site in Pusan city, is decorated with pinched, raised and appliqué designs, and is mainly composed of flat-based bowls. Yukimun pottery has not yet been discovered in the west coast region.

In the western region deep bowl-type pottery with either round or pointed bases and classical comb-marked designs made a sudden appearance. The origins of this pottery are probably to be found in the north-eastern regions of China, in particular in the vicinity of Liaoning Province. It is thought to have appeared first on the south-eastern tip of the Korean peninsula near Tongsam-dong, and that it has also been found in the area of Tsushima Island. However that may be, Tongsam-dong in Pusan was certainly influenced from early times by both the east coast and subsequently the west coast, and it appears as though both cultural sources intermingle or integrate here.

The Chulmun pottery culture of Korea, according to experts and textbooks of the Democratic People's Republic of Korea and the Republic of Korea, is placed in the Neolithic period and ranked as a Neolithic culture. However, the inception phases of agriculture and animal husbandry, important indices of Neolithic culture in a world-wide context, occur later in Korea. At this period subsistence still relied mainly on the hunting and fishing activities of the Palaeolithic, and thus the author prefers to call this period the Chulmun pottery period rather than the Neolithic period.

Among the lithic tools, remarkably well-developed stone arrowheads were used for hunting, stone harpoons were used for fishing, and other tools are also known. In view of the fact that saddle-querns, dating from at least the second half of the Chulmun pottery period have been found throughout the whole country, and occasionally in association with stone sickles, foxtail millet (*Setaria italica*) and other plant remains, the existence of primitive agriculture is certain. Furthermore, as acorns have been found, we know that the collecting of food plants took place. The majority of sites from this period are located in coastal areas and along the banks of large rivers. In the case of the former, shell mounds frequently remain. These shell mounds are rich archaeological storehouses, containing both natural remains such as animal and fish bones, and shells, along with artefacts such as pottery and stone tools. Bone and antler artefacts are also detected in no small amounts, among which the fishhooks and harpoon points are quite striking.

The people of the Chulman pottery period lived in pit-houses, clustered in village groups. At present, more than ten settlement sites are known on the Korean peninsula as a whole, but excavations have only been carried out on about seventy dwellings, leaving the elucidation of settlement structures as an important problem to be solved in the future. The Chulmun pottery period of Korea, although it tends to possess various elements common to the world-wide Neolithic cultures, forms a culture peculiar to Korea, a prehistoric culture which is also of a similar level to the Jomon culture of Japan.

THE MUMUN (PLAIN) POTTERY PERIOD

In approximately the first half of the first millennium BC, Chulmun pottery disappeared, after which, plain (*mumun*) pottery appears as the main pottery trend, hence the author refers to this period as the Mumun pottery period. However, in the academic worlds of both republics of Korea, great weight is placed on the fact that, during this period superb bronze objects peculiar to the Korean peninsula occur, and thus they generally refer to the period as the Bronze Age. The author has made a detailed examination of period divisions in Korean archaeology in another paper (1982), and so will not discuss this here, except to say that this is a problem which needs to be re-examined in the future.

As a rule, Mumun pottery has no surface decoration or patterns. However, during the early phase, slight decorations, such as rows of punctuates and short incised linear decorations can be seen. Non-decorated pottery is also found in the Chulmun pottery period, but the colour and fabric differ

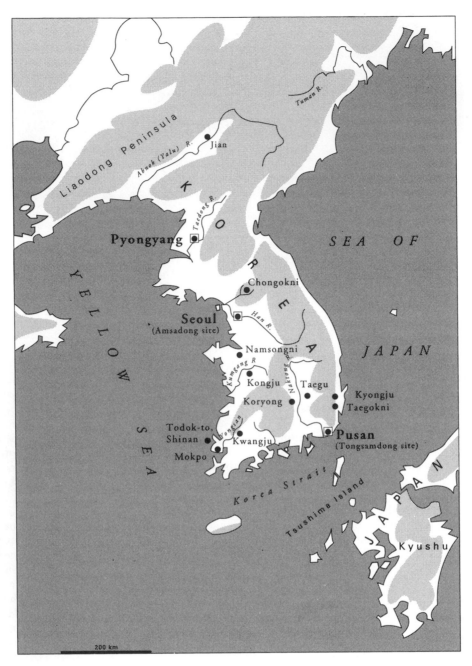

Map 24 Korea

from those of the Mumun and can therefore be distinguished. When compared to Chulmun pottery, the Mumun pottery of this period in general has a relatively refined fabric, was fired at a high temperature and has a bright brownish colour. The morphology and manufacturing techniques, however, show regional and temporal diversity. One thing that is held in common is the richness of the pottery assemblage, containing a wide-mouthed globular vessel, a constricted-neck vessel, a set accompanied by cups and bowls, with the addition of pedestal bowls in later periods. The Taedong basin in the north-east, however, is characterized by vessel shapes resembling Korean top-shape pottery and the doubled-over rim structural technique. In the area extending from the north-eastern region to the southern region, wide-mouthed globular jars of the first half of the period are decorated with rows of punctuates and protrusions, with polished, vermilion-lacquered narrow-necked jars being found occasionally. In the second half of the period, clay coils or bands are attached to the mouth of the same wide-mouthed globular jars, the use of attributes characteristic of Mumun pottery flourishes and long-necked black-polished jars are also found.

In the assemblage of production tools or sharp-edged tools, polished stone tools account for the main body during at least the first half of the period, with only a very small number of bronze objects being detected connected with wood-working tools and body accessories. In the latter half of the period remarkable developments are seen in weaponry, such as bronze daggers, spearheads and halberds. At the beginning of the phase in which the production of bronze implements flourished, bronze mirrors with multiple string attachments and finely ridged line patterns, small bronze bells, various kinds of unusually shaped bronze objects and other, probably magical, products increase. While these kinds of polished stone tools and bronze objects appear simultaneously on the Korean peninsula, the influence of the Longshan – origin Neolithic culture and Liaoning-type bronze dagger culture of north-eastern China can be recognized strongly in the background. These evidently caused the creation of a culture peculiar to Korea, with the thus-formed Korean Mumun pottery period subsequently directly influencing the formation of the Yayoi culture of Japan.

In the latter half of the Mumun period, when bronze objects began to flourish, iron implements also appear. At first they were cast implements, with origins in the Chinese Warring States, but from the time of the Rakran-gun colony built by the Han empire, these begin to be replaced by forged-iron objects. Thus, the few hundred years occupied by the Mumun culture was a period of rapid technological innovation and development in the field of production tools and sharp-edged tools. Furthermore, several new phenomena can also be seen in various aspects of the life-style and society of this period, though pit-dwellings, as of the Chulmun period, continued to be built with basically no major changes. The scale of villages ranged from small, such as at Susuk-ri in Kyonggi, where it is assumed five dwellings existed contemporaneously, to villages usually composed of up to ten dwellings. A previously unseen phenomenon, that of large-scale settlements, also appears. At Suktan-ri in north Huanghe Province, over one hundred dwellings have been identified within an area of 10 km², extending over the three phases of this period. Also, at Songguk-ri in south Ch'ungch'ong Province, what is believed to be an extraordinarily large settlement has been reported to extend over an area of 2 km by 1.5 km, although it is possible that this settlement was subdivided internally into a number of grouped dwellings. Similar temporal tendencies are also apparent in burial styles, where striking burial mounds such as megalithic dolmens and box-shaped stone-cist burials not only make an appearance, but were built in large numbers.

The context bringing about such increased settlement size developments in tumulus construction, and a denser distribution of sites, was probably largely influenced by the establishment of the Mumun economic base. That is, in this period a shift occurred from the Chulmun period's food-gathering economy to an economy centred on agriculture. In the far north-eastern region, hunting was still actively conducted, but even there food plants such as foxtail millet (*Setaria italica* P. Beauv) and broomcorn millet (*Panicum miliaceum* Linne) were cultivated. Cultivation on the Korean peninsula as a whole centres around minor grains, but from the west coast to the south coast of the southern region, in areas affected by the monsoon, from rice (*Oryaza sativa* Linne) remains and grain impressions on pottery we may infer that rice cultivation was quite well developed. Incidentally, the rice cultivation of this area first diffused to northern Kyushu, forming the direct momentum for the formation of Japan's Yayoi culture, and then moved north up the peninsula to the 39th parallel. A representative site of the latter is Namgyong, Honam-ri, in the suburbs of Pyongyang, where in addition to foxtail millet, broomcorn millet, sorghum (*Sorghum bicolor* Moench) and soybean (*Glycine max* Merr.), what is thought to be dry-land rice was also cultivated.

In the north-eastern area hoes and spades made of stone were used for dry-field farming, and although no actual artefacts have yet been found, it is thought that wooden farming implements were used in most areas. One reason for this deduction is that a farming scene depicting the use of what is thought to be a kind of wooden spade has been found cast on a bronze object. The shaft of the spade is set at an angle to the head, enabling it to be thrust into the ground by applying additional pressure with the foot. Secondly, the polished stone-tool assemblage of the Mumun period includes various distinctive tools which are believed to be effective in the manufacture of wooden farming implements. These include a large felling axe, quadrangular stone adze and flat plano-convex adze. Although temporal and regional differences in form have been found, crescent-shaped stone knives used for harvesting various kinds of grain have been found in all areas of the Korean Peninsula as a whole. Threshing implements include the saddle-quern, which remains firmly entrenched from the previous period.

With the beginning of agricultural production, the storage of crops gains importance. Korea's one and only example of a 'bag-shaped' storage pit has been found at Songguk-ri.

The associated artefacts discovered in the stone burial chamber at Kwaejong-dong, Taejon city, south Ch'ungch'ong Province, include several distinctive funerary objects. The Mumun pottery vessels were probably used as receptacles for food and drink offerings to the deceased, with the comma-shaped beads made of amazonite possibly being accessories worn by the deceased. The problem is the bronze objects, which can functionally be divided into two main groups. The first is weaponry, symbolized by polished stone arrowheads and slender bronze daggers. The second is magical ceremonial vessels, and includes the small bronze bells, linear decorated bronze mirrors with multiple string attachments, and unusually shaped bronze objects. Both these assemblages seem to attest to the status of the deceased while alive. In other words, weapons tell us that the deceased was a holder of political, economic and military strength. At the same time, ceremonial vessels may indicate that the buried person performed a priest-like role, possibly a shaman, in agricultural ceremonies. If so, this means that in the Mumun pottery period priest-like leaders had already made an appearance. Moreover, it may be inferred from burial-mound and artefact distributions that agricultural communities consisting of several villages and led by such priest-like chiefs, that is a tribal community, was forming.

BIBLIOGRAPHY

NISHITANI, T. 1982. Period Divisions in Korean Archaeology. In: *Kobayashi Yukio Hakase koki kinen roubunshu.* (A collection of papers to commemorate the 70th birthday of Dr Yukio Kobayashi), pp. 873–92, Heibonsha.

15.4

JAPAN
(3000–700 BC)

Tatsuo Kobayashi

JAPANESE LIFE-STYLES

The Jomon culture developed in a chain of small islands off the eastern extreme of the Asian continent. Radiocarbon dating shows this culture evolved from the preceding Palaeolithic culture about 10,000 BC and was succeeded around 400 BC by the Yayoi farming culture. Through this long period, the Jomon culture was supported on the basis of a hunting, fishing and gathering economy rather than a farming economy. It is important here to keep in mind that this culture did in fact endure for almost 10,000 years. Also important is the fact that the Jomon culture developed in an island region and received extremely little influence from cultural developments on the nearby continent. The Jomon was a comparatively isolated culture that evolved an independent way of life.

The major characteristics of the Jomon cultural complex are: (1) a hunting-fishing-gathering economy, (2) the manufacture and use of pottery, (3) bow-and-arrow hunting, (4) the domestication of dogs, (5) travel on the open sea in dugout canoes, (6) settlement in sedentary villages, and (7) a highly structured social organization. The roughly 10,000 years of the Jomon culture are broken down into six periods according to the pottery chronology: (I) Incipient, (II) Initial, (III) Early, (IV) Middle, (V) Late and (VI) Final Jomon. The Jomon population, as reflected in the numbers of sites, increased from Incipient to Middle Jomon, with minor vicissitudes along the way. All evidence points to the Middle Jomon being the peak of cultural development. This peak was reached about 3000 BC and is the focus of the discussion to follow. The population increase halted in the Late Jomon, and in some regions it dropped dramatically. This trend strongly suggests that the Middle Jomon was the time when the culture attained its best adaptation to the environment of the Japanese islands.

The manufacture and use of pottery is without doubt one of the most important underpinnings of the Jomon culture. Jomon pottery certainly served as containers, but that was by no means the only purpose it served. More importantly, it provided a means of boiling foods. This is evidenced by the discoloration of the pottery from secondary heating and by the carbonized residues on the insides of many vessels. Moreover, the quantity of pottery found in Jomon sites is extremely high and very unusual for foragers anywhere in the world. This suggests that boiling foods had become an everyday way of cooking. This made it possible for the Jomon people to exploit many plant resources that were not edible raw. In other words, boiling made it possible for the people to find sufficient food in a limited area throughout the seasons, eliminating the need to move around in the quest for food. This in turn made sedentary village life possible.

One direct result of this sedentary life-style was the building of sturdy dwellings requiring considerable input of labour. This eventually led to the model Jomon village with dwellings set out in a circle around a central plaza area. Storage pits were also built in the village as the people began to employ all kinds of subsistence strategies. And, unlike most foragers who keep their material possessions to a minimum in order to enhance mobility, the Jomon people became the ultimate prehistoric possessors of 'things': large quantities of pottery, heavy stone-grinding equipment, and all kinds of large and small ritual paraphernalia.

Before the Jomon people could develop this sedentary life-style, however, they first had to develop new and sophisticated ways of interacting with their environment. They had to develop the concept of meeting all of their needs with the resources from a limited area, through all seasons of the year, for years and even for generations. But by settling in one place, they would have acquired a much more intimate knowledge and understanding of their environment, and thus they would have been able to refine their strategy for exploiting it efficiently. Part of this strategy would have been the scheduling of subsistence activities, the 'Jomon calendar'.

Under these conditions the Jomon cultural-environmental relationship intensified. First, the people discovered more and more edible plants and animals which they exploited, greatly increasing the list of available foods to select from. Specifically, in Initial Jomon (period II) the people began to use fish and molluscs, and probably also most kinds of seaweeds, thereby adding greatly to their food resources and improving the stability of their subsistence base. The formation of shell-mounds from this time clearly tells of the changes that were occurring. Middle and Late Jomon (Periods IV and V) saw the formation of large circular and horseshoe-shaped villages more than 100 m across.

Unfortunately, we shall probably never know the complete list of plants and animals used by the Jomon people because of poor preservation in most sites. But the shell-mounds and a few cave sites, and some bog sites, have preserved a partial list for us.

The animals included the deer, boar, bear and serow, medium-sized animals such as the wolf, fox, racoon, dog and hare, and small animals such as rats, the total exceeding sixty different species, or nearly the entire list of mammals in the Japanese islands. Many peoples do not eat monkeys because they resemble humans, but the Jomon people ate these animals too. This wide variety is not because the Jomon people could not find enough of their preferred deer and boar. These two species, to be sure, do show signs of hunting pressure, but this was not enough to decimate the herds. Rather, the Jomon exploitation of a wide variety of animals seems to have been consciously planned. This same wide exploitation of resources is seen in the Jomon use of over 300 species of molluscs, over 70 species of fish and over 35 species of birds.

Plant remains do not preserve well, so our knowledge of the Jomon use of plants is relatively poor. But wet sites have yielded fifty-eight species of edible plants. The Jomon people also certainly used bracken, royal fern, *udo* (*Aralia cordata* Thunb.) and other such plants; if these are considered, then the list of Jomon plant foods cannot have been less than 300 species. Considering also that different parts of the same plant – roots, stems, leaves, flowers, seeds – are edible at different seasons, Kotaro Shirai has estimated the edible resources at 450. (To this figure should probably also be added the more than 100 species of edible mushrooms.)

Without doubt a major characteristic of the Jomon culture was the purposeful exploitation of a wide variety of plants and animals for food. This point is important to understanding the Jomon life-style. The people overcame problems of good and bad taste, easy or difficult obtainability, and consciously spread their diet across nearly the entire spectrum of usable plants and animals. But to use such a variety of food resources requires a high level of knowledge, and the Jomon people must have had the desire to acquire this knowledge. In other words, the Jomon people saw the need for varying their diet and for the knowledge to do so, and then purposefully set about reaching that goal. This was the Jomon strategy for 'sustainable development', and it clearly illustrates their relationship with their environment.

This Jomon strategy was to exploit all possible food resources provided by nature – from the sea, the rivers, the plains and the mountains. And the evidence shows that they did this quite successfully. The Jomon excellence lies here. Of course, in the process of learning which species were edible and which were not, they also learned which could be used medicinally or for poisons. In the end the Jomon people acquired a very thorough and accurate knowledge of the natural world.

There is a further very important aspect to the Jomon exploitation of a wide variety of plants and animals: most could not be properly digested when eaten raw. To overcome this barrier required a whole new way of behaving. This new behaviour was like the production of a stone tool from a natural pebble; it was the 'production' of food through the modification of the plants or animals from their natural state, such as by boiling them in pottery utensils. But this boiling in pots was not simply to make the plants softer and easier to eat; more importantly, it made possible the removal of tannin (tannic acid or lye) and bitterness, and sometimes poison, from the plants.

For example, the acorns of the deciduous forest must be boiled to remove the tannin before they can be eaten. This technique was known already to the Incipient Jomon people. But there are some species of acorns that require much more elaborate processing to remove their tannin. Especially buckeyes require a very elaborate process to make them edible. The Jomon people had discovered this process at least by the beginning of the Middle Jomon, *c.* 3000 BC. In its simplest form this process involved boiling the acorns or buckeyes, grinding the meat to flour, and leaching this flour in cool running water for up to one week. In this way tannins were removed both by heat and by water. Once this process

was discovered, acorns and buckeyes were added to the other major staples in the Jomon diet, chestnuts and walnuts.

Among the fish, some species of blowfish are extremely poisonous. A major delicacy in the modern Japanese diet is the puffer. But this fish is so dangerous that the law requires a special licence for a restaurant to serve it. Still, Jomon shell-mounds yield puffers' lower jaw bones in abundance, clear evidence that the Jomon people knew how to remove the poison from this fish.

Cultivation is a second technique for producing foods. Some Jomon sites have yielded perilla, green gram, gourd and buckwheat remains, suggesting the Jomon people did practise at least some cultivation. Many archaeologists have taken this to mean that they farmed. But this misses the point: even though they did cultivate a few plants, their basic strategy was still to exploit the widest possible variety of plants and animals. There is no need at all to see this cultivation as evidence of a farming way of life. Farming in Japan did not begin until the fourth century BC, when rice cultivation became the main means of ensuring a staple food base. This is an entirely different strategy from that of the Jomon people. A little cultivation in an essentially varied hunting-fishing-gathering economy needs to be clearly distinguished from an economy depending on cultivation.

Raising animals is a third way to produce food. The Jomon had already domesticated the dog by the beginning of the Initial Jomon period, and dog burials are found dating from this period. Most likely they were caring for dogs long before this first archaeological evidence appears. There is no evidence, however, that they domesticated any other species of animal, fish or bird, and the possibility that they did so seems remote. But there are some special conditions related specifically to the wild boar. For example, boar bones are found abundantly in sites on the smaller volcanic islands around the main Japanese islands, places where the boar is not indigenous. Almost certainly, the Jomon people carried young boar to the islands in their dugout canoes so that they could enjoy the meat of this highly preferred animal there too. (They even took boars across the Tsugaru Strait to Hokkaido, where some escaped their pens and reverted to the wild state. These became destructive to later farmers and were destroyed.) There are some burials of young boars, suggesting the Jomon people became fond of them much like pets. These are the only animals other than dogs that were buried by Jomon people.

A technology not unlike the production of food is the modification of plants and animals from the raw state in order to store them for long periods of time. Drying, smoking and fermentation are three of the main ways of preparing foods for long-term storage. These technologies added greatly to the stability of the Jomon food base.

The Jomon subsistence economy was supported by a variety of tools and techniques. Primary tools were the spear, bow and arrow, and pitfalls used in hunting; hooks, harpoons, nets and weirs used in fishing; and digging tools and baskets for gathering plants. Secondary tools included pots for boiling and cooking; and grinding stones, pounders and knives, and hearths for preparing foods and for cooking them. Tertiary tools were those for making and maintaining the primary tools: drills, axes, whetstones and so on. Most of these tools were in the Jomon toolkit from the beginning, and there was very little real change in this toolkit throughout the period. There was considerable regional and temporal variation in the style of the tools, but the overall function of the toolkit remained virtually unchanged. Moreover, this toolkit was not at all unique to the Jomon culture; it is found all over the world. These three groups of tools can together be called Class 1 tools.

Class 2 tools are another category of adaptive tools that were highly developed in the Jomon culture. Tools in this class are often called non-functional, because their functions are not readily determined from their forms and they do not appear to have a direct relationship to the acquisition and consumption of food. The Jomon people, however, invested far more time and care into producing Class 2 tools than into producing Class 1 tools. Thus, the farmer should be seen as serving some important function in the Jomon adaptive system, but a function different from that of Class 1 tools. This different function would lie in the needs of the Jomon world-view. These Class 2 tools became major parts of the material culture from the Middle Jomon on, evidence of the uniqueness of the culture and of its increasing stability. Clay figurines, stone phalluses, stone daggers and swords, and clay and stone plaques were the major forms of Jomon Class 2 tools (Plate 160).

Finally, about 700 BC, at the end of the Late Jomon (period V), rice farming entered north-western Kyushu from the Korean peninsula. Contact with these strange people and their new language and way of life had a tremendous impact on the local Jomon people and their culture. The totally new economy based on farming, and the world-view that went with it, began to affect the Jomon world-view. Until this time, Class 2 tools had been very secondary in the Jomon culture of western Japan, as compared with their importance in the Jomon of eastern Japan. But suddenly, clay figurines now appeared in Jomon sites in Kyushu. This can be seen as a revival movement in opposition to the foreign farming culture. But this revival was short-lived, and within a century or so the Jomon line was drawn at the centre of the islands in Kinki, where again there were attempts to revitalize the culture. This is when the stone daggers and swords and other types of stone Class 2 tools became most prominent in the Jomon regions closest to the intruding farming culture. But 200 years later the Jomon culture was overwhelmed by the new way of life, and around 300 BC the farming-based Yayoi culture had replaced the hunting-fishing-gathering Jomon culture.

List of animals and fishes exploited by the Jomon culture

General name	Species
deer	*Cervus nippon* Temminck: shika deer
bear	*Ursus arctos* Linne: brown bear
	Selenarctos thibetanus (G. Cuvier) *japonicus* (Schlegel): Japanese black bear
serow	*Capricornis crispus* (Temminck): Japanese serow
racoon dog	*Nyctereutes procyonoides* Gray: racoon dog
fox	*Vulpes vulpes* (Linne): common fox, red fox
wolf	*Canis lupus hodophilax* Temminck: Japanese wolf
boar	*Sus scrofa* Linnaeus: wild boar
monkey	*Macaca fuscata* (Blyth): Japanese macaque
rat/mouse	*Rattus* sp.: rat
	Mus sp.: mouse
hare	*Lepus brachyurus* Temminck et Schlegel: Japanese hare
puffer	Tetraodontidae *Takifugu* sp.: puffer, blowfish; tiger puffer

Sources: Okada, 1965; Nihon Gyorui Gakkai, 1981.

List of plants exploited by the Jomon culture

General name	Species
royal fern	*Osmunda japonica* Thunb.: Japanese royal fern
bracken	*Pteridium aquilinum* (L.) Kuhn var. *latiusculum* (Desv.) Underw. ex Heller: eastern bracken, northern bracken
udo	*Aralia cordata* Thunb.: udo
perilla	*Perilla frutescens* (L.) Britton var. *japonica* (Hassk.) Hara: Egoma
buckwheat	*Fagopyrum esculentum* Moench: Soba

Sources: Makino, 1989; Iwatsuki, 1992; Satake et al., 1981, 1982.

List of possible domesticated plants grown by the Joman culture

General name	Species/Japanese name/reference
green gram	*Phaseolus radiatus* L. var. *typicus* Prain. syn. *P. vidissimus* Ten.: Ryokuto (Takashima et al., 1971)
	Vigna radiata (L.) Wilczek: Yaenari (Ryokuto) (Satake et al., 1981)
	Phaseolus radiatus L.: Ryokuto (Torihama, 1979, p. 159)
gourd	*Lagenaria leucantha* Rusby var. *Gourda* Makino: Hyotan (Makino, 1961)
	L. siceraria (Molina) Standley var. *gourda*: (Ser.) Hara; Hyotan (Makino, 1989; Okuyama, 1977)
	L. leucantha Rusby: Hyotan (Torihama 1979, p. 159)

Note: Phaseolus radiatus L. var. *aurea* Prain. syn. *P. angularis* (Willd.) W. F. Wight is the Japanese Azuki, not to be confused with Ryokuto.

BIBLIOGRAPHY

AIKENS, C. M.; HIGUSHI, T. 1982. *Prehistory of Japan*. New York.

IWATSUKI, K. (ed.) 1992. *Nihon no Yasei Shokubutsu: Shida* [Ferns and Fern Allies of Japan]. Tokyo.

KOBAYASHI, T.; KATO, S.; FUJIMOTO, T. (eds) 1981–84. *Jomon Bunka no Kenkyu* [Studies in Jomon Culture]. Tokyo.

MAKINO, T. 1961. (Rev. ed. 1989.) *Shin Nihon Shokubutsu Zukan* [Makino's New Illustrated Flora of Japan]. Tokyo.

NIHON GYORUI GAKKAI [Ichthyological Society of Japan] (eds.) 1981. *Nihonsan Gyomei Daijiten* [Dictionary of Japanese Fish Names and their Foreign Equivalents]. Tokyo.

OKADA, K. (ed.) 1965. *Shin Nihon Dobutsu Zukan* [New Illustrated Encyclopedia of the Fauna of Japan]. Tokyo. Vol. 3.

OKUYAMA, S. (ed.) 1977. *Terasaki Nihon Shokubutsu Zufu* [Terasaki's Illustrated Flora of Japan]. 2nd ed. Tokyo.

SATAKE, Y. et al. (eds) 1981, 1982. *Nihon no Yasei Shokubutsu* [Wild Flowers of Japan]. Tokyo. Vols 2–3.

TAKASHIMA, S.; SOBAJIMA, Y.; MURAKAWA, M. 1971. *Yuyo Shokubutsu* [Common Useful Plants in Colour]. Osaka. (Hyojun Genshoku Zukan Zenshu, 13 [Colour Illustrated Series 13].)

TORIHAMA KAIZUKA KENKYU GURUPU (ed.). 1979. *Torihama Kaizuka* [The Torihama Shellmound Site]. Fukui.

15.5
NORTHERN ASIA AND MONGOLIA
(3000–700 BC)

Anatoly P. Derevyanko

The development of ancient cultures during the Holocene proceeded in a variety of ways in different regions of the Old and New Worlds. In some regions of the globe (including western and eastern Asia), ceramics had appeared and a productive economy had taken shape by the eighth millennium BC, metallurgy developing a little later. In other regions, the Neolithic continued until the first millennium BC. This patchy cultural development may be observed in both northern Asia and Mongolia.

NORTHERN ASIA

Cultures in northern Asia developed at different rates during the third millennium BC: the first metal appeared and there was a gradual transition to livestock rearing in southern Siberia during that period. In the central and northern regions of western and eastern Siberia, in the far east and the north-east the ancient tribes continued to live in the Stone Age and hunting and fishing remained their main occupations.

Geographically, western Siberia is an immense area of lowland with an abundance of lakes, traversed by the valleys of the Ob, the Irtysh and the Yenisey. The most typical Neolithic settlement (third millennium BC) is Uesty-yag (Chernetsov, 1953) on the lower reaches of the River Ob.

The settlement was located on a marshy floodplain terrace on the left bank of the River Lyapin, which flows into the Ob. In the south-western part of the islet, it consisted of seventeen dwellings lying very close to each other. Most of them were rectangular, nearly square-shaped, measuring from 9 × 9 to 20 × 20 m. Some of the dwellings covered more than 600 m². These large, semi-subterranean dwellings were 3 or 4 m deep.

The Neolithic sites on the lower reaches of the River Ob constitute a distinctive culture, clearly based on fishing, with hunting of secondary importance: in Siberian conditions fishing was the only reliable way of obtaining food which could sustain a settled way of life at a single site over a long period of time.

The Upper Ob Neolithic culture occupied southern regions of western Siberia, on the upper reaches of the river. Its sites are to be found both throughout the forest-steppe zone and in part of the forest zone in the Ob basin. All in all, some hundred sites are known: burials, camp sites and places where isolated Neolithic artefacts have been found. The Upper Ob culture dates from the fourth and third millennia BC. The burial grounds at Samus and Tomsk and the

old Muslim cemetery at Tomsk together with the Novokuskovo camp site represent the late stage in this culture.

Members of the tribe were buried by their fellows in collective graves which were evidently covered at first with wooden planks. The most striking feature is the presence of inhumation and cremation in the same burial ground. Funeral feasts were sometimes held after burials and the burial place was purified by fire. Flat-bottomed vessels, work tools and weapons have been found in the graves. The vessels had flat bases and rims delineated only by a horizontal row of pit-marks. The sides of the vessels were usually covered by ornament which most often consisted of lines impressed with the aid of a stick.

A larger number of polished implements has been found in graves of the Samus burial ground. Well-polished knives with concave blades and narrow spearheads with a rhombic section have been discovered in association with large, asymmetrical knives with convex blades and almond-shaped knives made on flakes. The burials have also yielded chopping tools: adzes and axes. Vessels with a round or conical base are decorated with complex patterns of fine comb-impressions.

A highly individual art style, represented by bone and stone sculptures and petroglyphs, is one of the most typical features of the western Siberian Neolithic tribes. The commonest carved figures represent bears and elks (Fig. 79 a, b). A remarkable 'picture gallery' at the village of Pisanaya on

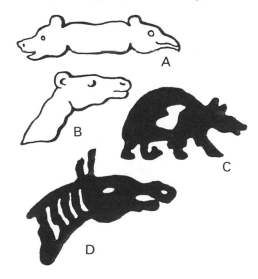

Figure 79 Carved animal figures of the Upper Ob Neolithic culture.

the banks of the Tom offers thought-provoking material for the study of the art of the south Siberian Neolithic tribes (Okladnikov and Martynov, 1972). The oldest drawings, produced by pitting, include figures kneeling with their legs apart, as if squatting in a dance pose. Their arms are outstretched and also bent. But the petroglyphs at the river Tom site mainly depict animals (Fig. 79 c, d). They resemble the petrified fragment of an early animal epic, a poem to wild animals. The most common image among these drawings is that of the elk, the most hunted animal during the Neolithic. They are depicted in motion, with their short heavy bodies, large humps and lean croups. Schematic but nevertheless vivid representations of their muzzles have the depth of work executed in relief. Bears and birds are also depicted in the petroglyphs.

Four Neolithic cultures have been identified in eastern Siberia. Serovo and Kitoi are cultures of the developed and late Neolithic (Okladnikov, 1950). Our knowledge of the Serovo culture (late fourth millennium to first half of third millennium BC) comes from the excavations of camp sites and burial grounds and from rock art. The Neolithic culture of the forest-belt hunters of eastern Siberia began to flourish during the Serovo period. Large numbers of arrowheads, spearheads, daggers, scrapers, racloirs, burins and other stone artefacts, manufactured with very fine retouches, have been found in burials and at camp sites. The graves have also yielded well-preserved composite knives and daggers, the blades worked from both sides and carefully chipped to fit the bone haft.

The Serovo population made significant improvements to their hunting gear and were the first in Siberia to use a stronger type of bow. Many burials contained bow plates made of bone. Judging from extant fragments, the Serovo bows were over 1.5 m in length. The vessels from Serovo have a rounded base and are comb-stamped with a dotted pattern or decorated with zigzag parallel lines.

The Kitoi stage (second half of third millennium to early second millennium BC) was distinguished by the absence of masonry in the burials and the practice of strewing the skeletons liberally with ochre, symbolizing the life-force, the 'blood of the dead'. Distinctive sticks with a toothed edge used as fishhooks were found in the Kitoi burials (Fig. 80 a, b). Common tools included nephrite adzes with a lenticular section, triangular nephrite knife points, flat mudstone knives (the blades flattened further by broad diagonal facets made by pressure flaking sandstone 'arrow-shaft straighteners'/burnishers), composite daggers and knives (Fig. 80 c) and other typical objects. Ornaments included white marble rings.

The most graphic and complete demonstration of Neolithic art is to be found on the River Angara, on the cliffs of the Kamennye Islands. There are hundreds of splendid drawings on all three islands. This amazing Stone Age picture gallery stretches for several dozen metres. Sometimes the drawings are superimposed. Of course these pictures are not the work of a single talented artist or even of a single tribe or people. Dozens of generations succeeded one another and each left new drawings for their descendants.

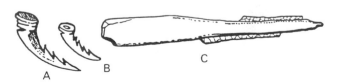

Figure 80 Fishhooks and daggers found in the Kitoi burials.

The Belkachi culture (third to early second millennium BC) represents the developed Neolithic in Yakutia (Mochanov, 1977). Stone implements continued to be made on blades (roughly 65 per cent of all tools). At the same time an increasing number of tools were made on flakes, reaching 60 per cent by the end of the Belkachi culture. The most typical stone artefacts are backed blades, blades with bevelled sides, cutters with a blunted edge, end-scrapers on narrow blades, angle- and side-scrapers on blades, multi-faceted burins with core-like handles, chisel-like implements on flakes, end-scrapers with lugs, pebble net-weights, polished bone needles, awls and cutters for hafted tools.

Belkachi vessels were egg-shaped with rounded bases and straight rims under which a row of holes was pierced. The combination of indented stamped decoration on the rims with cord ornament on the body of the vessels was a novel feature in pottery decoration.

The Ymyyakhtakhskaya culture belongs to the final stage of the Neolithic and the early Bronze Age in Yakutia: 3700–2700 BC (Fedoseeva, 1980). A rough total of 145 sites can be ascribed to this period. They are spread over a vast area: the eastern and northern regions of central Siberia (Taimir and Yakutia to the west of the Verkhoyansky range), north-eastern Siberia and Chukotka.

The cores that have been found are prismatic with one or two planes. Tools were made from blades and flakes. Elongated triangular arrowheads, bifacially worked, with straight or hollowed bases are very common, as are small triangular and trapezoidal end-scrapers with sharply angled blades; multi-faceted burins; elongated triangular spearheads, retouched on two sides; oval knives with an amygdaloid transverse section; and solid, rectangular, retouched backed blades. Small, rectangular adzes and chisels were made from siliceous schist and green nephrite. White nephrite was used to make ornaments in the form of delicate flat rings with small round holes in the middle. The bone inventory largely consisted of spearheads and knives with one or two narrow grooves for the insertion of backed blades, bone awls, needles, flaking implements and retouchers.

The commonest vessels of the Ymyyakhtakhskaya culture were egg-shaped, with a bulging body and outlined rim. Near-spherical vessels with a very clear outline are also encountered. The earthenware was decorated with a chequerboard pattern consisting of rectangular or diamond-shaped impressions.

The first bronze objects, daggers, knives and ornaments, also appeared during the later stage of the Ymyyakhtakhskaya culture (2800–2700 BC). Bronze reached Yakutia from regions further to the south and bronze vessels found there are similar to the Seima-Turbino and Karasuk ware.

Hunting and fishing formed the basis of the economy of the Neolithic tribes in Yakutia. People lived in the type of portable dwellings known as *chums,* in settlements which were sometimes occupied over long periods. They frequently returned to the same site within a comparatively short time, which resulted in the formation of an archaeologically very productive cultural layer. One area in which distinct cultures were formed during the Neolithic was the southern part of the Russian far east. Three regions, the Middle Amur, the Lower Amur and the Maritime region, exhibited distinctive Neolithic features (Okladnikov and Derevyanko, 1973).

The Osinovoe Ozero culture comes under the developed Neolithic in the Middle Amur (late fourth to third millennia BC). The stone industry discovered during the excavation of settlements belonging to this culture is comparatively insignificant. There are no cores of consistently identifiable shapes, but flint and chalcedony nodules bear traces of random flaking unaccompanied by additional shaping. The flakes from such cores were used to manufacture arrowheads, backed blades, scrapers and awls. Agricultural implements were found at the settlements: pestles, mullers, grain-grinders and weights for digging sticks. The tribes led a settled existence, living in semi-subterranean dwellings. At the end of the third millennium BC and the start of the second, the region was penetrated by tribes from the Lower Amur, who were also making the transition to agriculture.

The Kondon culture belongs to the developed Neolithic (late fourth to third millennium BC) on the Lower Amur. Excavations have revealed willow-leaf arrowheads, artefacts on blades and prismatic cores. However, the number of implements on blades is insignificant in comparison with that of bifacially worked tools. The Neolithic settlement of Kondon has been dated to around 2550–2500 BC.

The highly original Voznesenovkoe culture spread in the final stage of the Neolithic on the Lower Amur (late third to mid-second millennium BC). It is characterized by a complete absence of blade industries, their place being taken by bifacial retouch. Arrowheads, backed blades, scrapers, knives and other tools were manufactured from special blanks and carefully retouched on both sides.

The Neolithic tribes of the Amur basin lived in large settlements of semi-subterranean pit houses. Excavations on the lower and middle reaches of the river have demonstrated that the dwellings of all the tribes living in those areas were very similar: semi-subterranean houses entered through the smoke opening.

The settled way of life of the tribes who inhabited the Lower Amur in the early and developed Neolithic was based on fishing. The lakes and the many tributaries of the Amur, both large and small, were extremely rich in fish, and it was in this area that the spoonbait was invented (Fig. 81 a). Extensive use was also made of nets, hooks and harpoons (Fig. 81 b). The migrating hordes of salmon during the spawning period were of particular economic importance for the Neolithic tribes of the Amur.

Several Stone Age 'picture galleries' have been discovered: most interesting among them in terms of the expressiveness and brilliance of the drawing are the petroglyphs at the Nanai village of Sakachi-Alyan and those on the banks of the small rivers Kiya and Ussuri and in other places. Stylized anthropomorphic facial masks occupy a central position among the earliest drawings, of which there are hundreds. There are also images of birds, animals, snakes and hunting scenes (Fig. 81 c), and many drawings of boats. At Sakachi-Alyan boats form part of a large composition chipped out on a single large boulder. A mask is represented at the centre, above which is a spiral, probably depicting a snake. Bow-shaped boats with human figures are seen on the flanks (Fig. 81 d).

The tribes of the Maritime region exhibited many of the cultural features which were held in common. Those belonging to the Zaisanovka culture (third millennium BC) lived in semi-subterranean dwellings, each settlement comprising from ten to twenty such dwellings. Typical features of the culture included polished schist tools, smaller obsidian implements and pottery decorated with parallel rocker patterns made either by comb stamps or incised. Clay figurines of a man, a turtle and other animals are of particular interest. The stone industry comprises chopping tools, arrowheads, knives, scrapers, racloirs and backed blades.

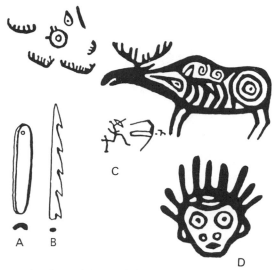

Figure 81 Artefacts of the Neolithic tribes on the Lower Amur: a, spoonbait; b, harpoon; c and d, drawings on stones (hunting scene, mask and bow-shaped boats).

The Kirovskoe culture which emerged in the third millennium BC had many features in common with the Zaisanovka culture, its predecessor. The tribes of the Maritime region in the developed and late Neolithic were hunters, fishers and gatherers, who included sea food in their diet: molluscs, seaweeds, trepangs and crabs. A primitive form of agriculture also made its appearance in the late Neolithic.

In the late fourth and early third millennia BC as Stone Age cultures continued to develop over large areas of northern Asia, major advances were taking place in southern Siberia, the Altai and the Minusinsk Depression: the ancient tribes were moving over to a food-producing stock-breeding economy and the first metal artefacts made their appearance.

The Afanasievo culture was the first metal-age culture in southern Siberia. The Afanasievo tribes lived on the banks of rivers and lakes. Their burials are the best researched aspect of the culture. The dead were buried in *kurgans* which were surrounded by a circular wall of between 5 and 20 m in diameter (Fig. 82 a). The walls, which were up to 1m in height, were made of vertical stone slabs dug into the ground or large stones of varying shapes. In the centre of the enclosure were one or two or, less commonly, three graves, squarish in shape, occupying an area of roughly 10 m² and lying on a south-west/north-east axis. Logs positioned lengthwise, the remains of wooden roofing, are often found at the edges of the graves. The earth mound placed over the grave was sometimes faced with stone slabs. Three to eight people were buried in each grave, lying on their backs with their knees drawn up or else on their sides in a contracted position. Usually ochre was strewn over the bodies.

Many features of the material and spiritual culture of the Afanasievo tribes were linked with Neolithic traditions. They continued to use stone tools extensively in their everyday existence: arrowheads and lances, knives, axes, pestles and scrapers (Fig. 82 b). This may be explained by the fact that the Afanasievo people were not familiar with the technique of casting. Metal was used mainly for ornaments (earrings, bracelets) and for binding, repairing wooden containers and the manufacture of needles, awls and small knives. Metal products were mostly made by welding, and the Afanasievo tribes used copper, gold, silver and even iron for that purpose. The remains of a bracelet made from meteoritic iron

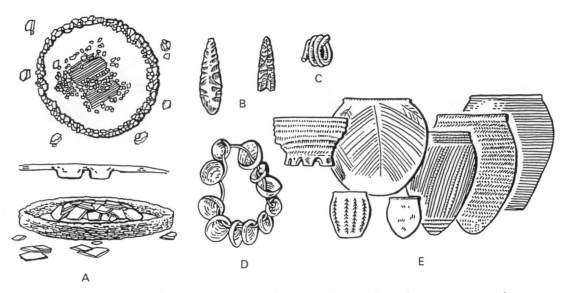

Figure 82 The Afanasievo culture in southern Siberia: a, *kurgans*; b, stone tools; c and d, metal ornaments; e, vessels.

have been found on the arm of an old woman in the burial-ground on the Afanasievo hill in the Minusinsk Depression (Fig. 82 c, d).

Vessels were made from wood and clay (Fig. 82 e). Most of them were egg-shaped with a rounded base but, less commonly, flat-based jugs have also been found. Although these containers are mostly small in size – from 1.5 to 3 litres – some have a capacity of as much as 200 litres. The earthenware was decorated with horizontal and vertical rocker (herring-bone) patterns, wavy lines and various kinds of stamped decoration.

Great economic changes occurred among the Afanasievo tribes, who added stock-breeding to the traditional occupations of hunting, fishing and gathering. Evidence of this development is provided by the remains of meat dishes placed next to the dead. The bones of the domestic livestock include those of sheep, horses and cows. In addition to stock-breeding, the Afanasievo tribes also appear to have taken up agriculture: pestles and grinders for grain testify to this fact.

The Afanasievo people lived in small villages in two types of dwelling: dug-outs and timber-frame huts. Judging by the number of burials in the burial grounds, the villages were small, containing from five to ten families (Okladnikov, 1968). There are no signs of differentiation between individuals on the basis of property or of a relationship of dependence between men and women. Double burials do occur but interments with both men and women are very rare: graves containing men, women and children are found more frequently. Child mortality was very high, judging by the number of children's graves in the burial grounds. Early motherhood was a feature of the tribes: young girls of 13–14 years of age are often found in burials together with a newly born baby, a child of less than one year or a foetus (Vadetskaya, 1986). The upper age-limit of those buried was 40–50 and very few people reached the age of 60.

The origin of the Afanasievo culture is a complex question. The population was of Europoid race (Alekseev and Gokhman, 1984) and differed chiefly from the indigenous Mongoloid population in that they were mostly tall and of large build. Many researchers consider that the Afanasievo tribes came from the west and are genetically linked to the pit-grave culture of the area between the River Volga and the River Ural. In the course of excavations at the multi-layer

site of Toora-Dash on the Yenisey, a link has been found between the Neolithic horizons and the Afanasievo culture (Semenov, 1983). It is highly probable that the culture was formed by the fusion of population groups from the west with the local Late Neolithic tribes. Traces of the Afanasievo culture have also been discovered in western Mongolia and Xinjiang, where the Europoid type was also present.

At the beginning of the second millennium BC, the Afanasievo culture in southern Siberia gave way to the Okunev culture, knowledge of which is based on the excavation of burials, stone sculpture and petroglyphs. The burial grounds consisted of one, or, less commonly, four *kurgans*. Only one burial ground has been found, having fourteen enclosures (Vadetskaya, 1986). The rectangular enclosures are edged with sandstone flags standing on end, or of stones. They can be up to 50 cm in height and measure from 2.5 × 3 to 40 × 40 m. There are between one and twenty-two graves within the enclosures. Okunev graves are small and shallow and contain one or two bodies. The walls and base of the graves are lined with stone slabs, which are also used to cover the graves, over which rise small mounds of earth and stones. Grave coverings made of logs (over which stone slabs were placed) are less frequently encountered. Each grave contained a single person or, less often, a woman and child or a man and woman, sometimes also with a child. The dead person was laid on his or her back with knees drawn up and arms extended, usually with the head pointing westwards. A stone was placed under the head or, sometimes, a slab was found with a depression for the head. The face and body were painted with horizontal stripes. All the dead were buried in their clothes with many religious objects and amulets connected with hunting magic.

Although the Okunev culture developed during the Bronze Age, stone artefacts are still encountered: arrowheads, spears, axes and adzes. Metal objects were made of copper or bronze and the forms of metal working employed were forging and casting. Fishhooks, knives, axes, needle-cases, awls and temple bands were made from metal (Fig. 83 b–d). Awls and knives were inserted in wooden or bone handles. Needle-cases, needles for sewing and net-making and harpoons were made of bone. Needle-cases were also made from hollow bird-bones. Wool threads were discovered in some needles. The needles used for net-making were large,

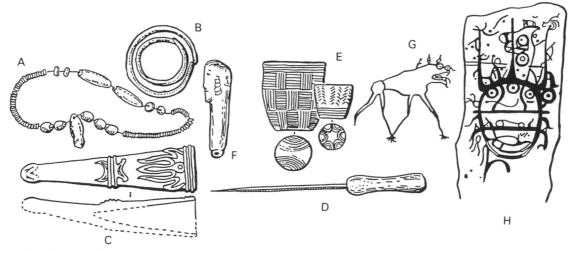

Figure 83 The Okunev culture in southern Siberia: a, necklace; b–d, metal tools; e, vessels; f, female statue; g and h, stone carvings of birds and animals.

elongated oval flakes with rounded ends. Needles of the same type have been found in the Kitoi and Glazkovo burials in the Baikal region.

There were two types of earthenware: broad flat-bottomed jars with straight walls splaying out slightly towards the top and pots with a slightly tapering neck. They were decorated with indented stamped ornament or stick impressions. The design covered the base of the vessels as well as their walls (Fig. 83 e). Incense burners were another distinctive artefact of the Okunev period. The clothes worn by the population have also been successfully reconstructed (Vadetskaya, 1986). Underclothes were made of wool. Collars, sleeves and hems were decorated with stone beads of different colours. Fur chest-warmers, worn over the outer garments, were adorned with fox and marmot teeth, small rings or beads. The remains have been discovered of a fur purse embroidered with forty Siberian deer teeth. Shoes were made of hide and were embroidered with sable teeth (from 70 to 160 teeth), only the third right upper molar being used for the purpose. Beads, the teeth and fangs of wild animals, the ankle bones and phalanxes of roe deer and elk were used for necklaces and amulets (Fig. 83 a).

A remarkable testimony to the Okunev period is provided by original artistic creations of various kinds: stone statues with human faces, small stone heads and bone blades with engravings of female faces, bone and stone carvings of birds and animals, imaginary beasts of prey, engraved or hammered out on stone slabs and real animals – bulls or cows – carved in fine lines on stone slabs (Fig. 83 g, h). All the miniature representations of females clearly convey Mongoloid facial features (Fig. 83 f). The anthropological material also indicates that the Okunev population was more Mongoloid than that of Afanasievo. The Okunev tribes engaged in hunting and fishing but their economy was based on the breeding of sheep, horses and cattle. The images on their stelae indicate that they used one- and two-axled carts to which bulls were harnessed.

The Karakol culture, which was related to the culture of Okunev, existed in the Altai in the first third of the second millennium BC. Its pottery differed in some respects. Monumental sculpture was almost completely absent but the funerary sites feature unique polychrome painting.

Other types of remains discovered to the north-west and west of the Okunev culture on the upper reaches of the Ob belong to the Samus-Seima historico-cultural layer, which

originated in the late Neolithic in the west Siberian Taiga. These tribes were essentially hunters and fishers, whose tools and weapons were made mainly from stone, bone and wood. The first metal artefacts were, however, making their appearance at that time. The life-style of these tribes was semi-settled.

In the middle of the second millennium BC, the Okunev culture and other similar cultures in southern Siberia were superseded by the Andronovo culture, evidence of which has been found in the Ural region and Kazakhstan. It was not a unified culture but a historico-cultural community which developed during the Bronze Age, consisting of a number of related cultures. The Andronovo community is known mainly from its burial grounds and settlements. The burial grounds consist of one or more dozen enclosures. Some of them contain *kurgans*, some have graves with no *kurgans* and some flat graves. The Andronovo tribes first built an enclosure and then dug the grave inside it. The enclosures, which were placed at a considerable distance from each other, were up to one metre in height with a diameter of 5–10 m, and were made of slabs placed vertically in the ground or, less commonly, laid flat. A grave – sometimes two or three – was dug 1–3 m deep within the enclosure. The graves were usually rectangular and their walls were reinforced with wood or stone slabs. After the burial the grave was covered with logs or stone slabs and the *kurgan* mound piled up on top. The Andronovo tribes practised both inhumation and cremation of the dead. In the former case, the body was placed on a litter on one side with knees flexed and hands crossed in front of the face.

There are two main types of Andronovo pottery: bowls and jars (Fig. 84). The surface of the first type of vessel was carefully polished and decorated with meander patterns, wavy and straight lines and hatched triangles. Vessels of the other type were decorated with a herring-bone pattern.

The Andronovo tribes attained a high level of proficiency in bronze casting. Tools and weapons were cast in two-part moulds. Socketed and drop-headed axes; Seima-Turbino-type spears; sickles, daggers, hoes and various kinds of adornment were common. Metal working and smelting were carried out in the settlements.

The main occupation of the Andronovo tribes was stock-breeding. They raised cattle, sheep, goats and horses, living a settled existence. Their villages, located on the banks of rivers and lakes, consisted of long-term dug-out dwellings,

Figure 84 Bowls and jars of the Andronovo culture (Ural region and Kazakhstan).

occupying an area of up to 200 m² or more. Agriculture was also important and wheat and other grains were grown.

The large *kurgans* for single burials and the observance of special funerary rites testify to differentiation among members of the population on the basis of wealth, the setting apart of some families from the rest of the community, and the special position of men in the family. There are no links between the Andronovo culture and the preceding cultures. The Andronovo tribes most probably came to Siberia from Kazakhstan between 3600 and 3500 BC. They were people of a distinctive Europoid anthropological type which has been designated the Andronovo type.

At the close of the second millennium BC, the Andronovo culture in southern Siberia gave way to the Karasuk culture (3100–2600 BC), the final stage and period of maximum development of the Bronze Age cultures of southern Siberia and Mongolia. The Karasuk culture is best known from its burial grounds, which can contain several hundred *kurgans*. They took the form of round or rectangular enclosures made of vertical stone slabs. Stone coffins covered with slabs were assembled within the enclosures and then covered with earth. The enclosures were often built side by side. The dead were placed in the graves on their backs, or sometimes on their side, wearing their clothes and with their heads pointing towards the north-east. They were buried with the objects which they would require in the supposed world beyond the grave: one or two bowls of liquid nourishment were placed at the head and meat at the feet. The bowls were spherical with convex or sometimes flat bases. They were decorated with incised or stamped geometric patterns: hatched triangles, diamonds and meanders (Fig. 85 d).

The most common bronze artefacts are various types of knives and daggers, often with decorated hilts ending in a ring, a mushroom cap or an animal head (Fig. 85 c). Typical features of the Karasuk culture are bronze celts, battleaxes, spears, arrowheads, adzes, various types of ornaments, including pieces for the head, aprons and shoes, and also earrings, necklaces, bracelets and rings (Fig. 85 a, b).

The dwellings, both small and large, were semi-subterranean, the larger occupying up to 200 m². Large houses had

several hearths, often in a row. Plank-beds were placed against the walls. The population lived in the settlements in the winter-time. In the summer, the tribes migrated with their herds and lived in light, portable dwellings. People belonging to the Karasuk culture obtained everything that they needed from stock-breeding: meat, milk, wool and hides. They herded horses, cattle, sheep and goats and hunting and fishing were additional sources of sustenance. It would seem from the rock art that the Karasuk period was marked by the appearance of spoked wheels and two- and four-axled carts. It is quite probable that horses were also used for riding during the final stage of the culture.

Karasuk art is reflected in fine bronze artefacts with decorative patterns and images of animal heads, petroglyphs and stone stelae, most frequently depicting stylized deer.

During the Karasuk period, the burial grounds were clan cemeteries. Kinship on the basis of the male line was increasingly important, and we find *kurgans* of noble families and kinship groups which are distinguished from other burials by their size and the profusion of grave goods.

The origins of the culture pose a very complex problem. Some experts consider it to be indigenous and genetically linked to the Andronovo culture (Okladnikov, 1968). The Andronovo component was undoubtedly a key influence on the formation and development of the culture, but the Karasuk tribes share many anthropological features with 'Europoid' groups which are jointly referred to as the 'Pamir-Ferghana' race. The problem is that, just like the tribes on adjacent territories, the Karasuk tribes were in close socio-economic and cultural contact with others during the final stage of the Bronze Age and it is virtually impossible to give an unequivocal answer to questions about the origin of their culture at this stage. Typical Karasuk bronze ware is found to the east in the Trans-Baikal region, Manchuria and as far away as southern areas of the Russian far east; to the south and south-west in Mongolia, the Ordos and Kazakhstan; and to the north in the forest-steppe belt of western Siberia.

Unlike the tribes in western Siberia, those in eastern Siberia in the second millennium BC continued to practise a food-gathering economy. But important changes nevertheless

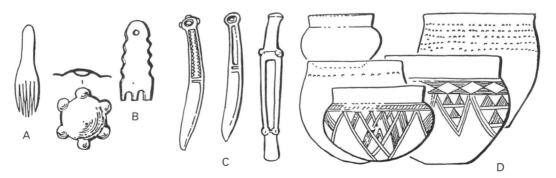

Figure 85 The Karasuk culture in southern Siberia: a and b, bronze ornaments; c, bronze knives and daggers; d, vessels.

occurred, and the dead were now buried with copper and bronze artefacts. This new Glazkovo culture, which represents the beginning of the metal age in the Baikal region, spans the period from 3600 to 3100 BC (Okladnikov, 1955). The version of this culture found in Buryatia is known as the Fofanovo and that in the Trans-Baikal region the Doroninskoe culture.

Traditional Neolithic stone-working techniques continued to be practised to a considerable extent during the Glazkovo period. Arrowheads, spears, scrapers, adzes, axes and many other tools were still made of stone by pressure flaking. However, the precision pressure flaking which was typical of the Serovo and Kitoi cultures is not apparent in the Glazkovo culture. This decline in the technical tradition was, clearly, connected with the appearance of a new material – metal.

The number of metal artefacts found in the burials and settlements of the Glazkovo culture is quite insignificant in comparison with the number of stone and bone objects. Knives, fish-hooks, needles, awls and ornaments made of copper and bronze have been found, the most common find being fine, leaf-shaped copper knives with bone or wooden handles (Fig. 86 a–c). Hunting, fishing and gathering remained the basis of the tribal economy in the Baikal and Trans-Baikal regions. Fishing was of particular importance and fishing tackle was improved during the period: new types of harpoons and hooks appeared as well as new lures (Fig. 86 d–f). Fish were also caught with nets and the fishermen used light boats made of birch-bark.

Important changes also occurred in social relations during the Glazkovo period. Double burials are frequently found in the burial grounds. Men's graves mainly contain fishing and hunting gear. In women's graves, equipment connected with hunting, the processing of fish and animals and food-gathering have been found together with large numbers of ornaments. The clothing of a woman of the Glazkovo culture has been reconstructed on the basis of the material found

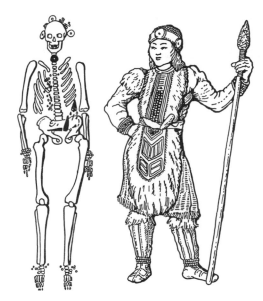

Figure 87 Reconstruction of the clothing of a woman of the Glazkovo culture.

in one burial (Fig. 87). Shamanism was evidently widespread during the period. Unmistakable attributes of shamanistic dress have been discovered for the first time in these burials, and also a tambourine and a mallet.

The Shiversky stage (3000–2600 BC), which seems to be a continuation of the Glazkovo culture, belongs to the final period of the Bronze Age in eastern Siberia. One typical feature of this stage is the appearance of a new kind of ware: the round-bottomed Glazkovo pottery with its stamped decoration is replaced by flat-bottomed vessels decorated with textile-like impressions or chequerboard decoration. Bronze objects of the Karasuk type appeared at this period in the Baikal region and were even more common in the Trans-Baikal region.

Major changes also occurred in the Amur basin and the Maritime region at the end of the second millennium BC, connected with the gradual introduction of metal into these areas. The most detailed studies of the Bronze Age have been conducted in the southernmost part of the Russian far east in the Maritime region, where the Siny Gai culture (3100–2600 BC) has been identified. The tribes belonging to this culture led a settled life in villages consisting of from ten to forty semi-subterranean, rectangular or oval dwellings, each with an area of 25–70 m² and, in the centre, one or two hearths.

The pottery, all of which is flat-bottomed, was made without using the potter's wheel. There is a variety of forms: bowls, wide-necked jars and also vessels with a neatly shaped body and turned rim. They were decorated with applied ridges and with horizontal and vertical rocker patterns. Vessels have been discovered which have a red burnished surface and are painted black. Stone tools have been found in the dwellings: axes, arrowheads, polished daggers, knives, mullers, graters and grain-grinders. Bone was widely used to make armour plates, ornaments and tools. Over twenty bronze artefacts have been discovered at the settlement of Siny Gai on Lake Khanka: knives, awls, hooks. The presence of ladles and moulds makes it clear that bronze objects were actually smelted in the settlements (Fig. 88). The influence of tribes in the west is very marked in the southern region of the Russian far east: the polished daggers, knives and ornaments are simply copies of the bronze Seima-Turbino

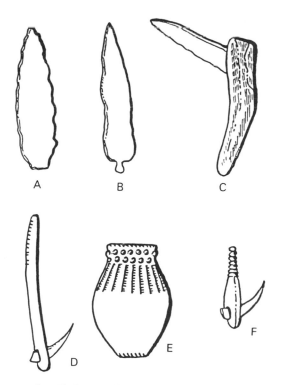

Figure 86 The Glazkovo culture in eastern Siberia: a–c, copper knives; d and f, hooks and harpoons; e, lure.

Figure 88 Bronze artefacts of the Shiversky stage, found at Siny Gai (eastern Siberia).

and Karasuk types. The principal occupations were agriculture, pig-rearing, hunting and fishing. Carbonized grains of foxtail millet have been found at a number of settlements. The tribes living on the coast engaged in sea-fishing and the gathering of sea produce.

MONGOLIA

Neolithic cultures continued to exist in Mongolia during the third millennium BC. Distinctive features developed in two regions, eastern and southern Mongolia. Information about the Late Neolithic in eastern Mongolia has come from the excavation of dozens of temporary camp sites and also a number of settlements with dwellings belonging to the Tamsagbulag culture.

Excavations have uncovered the remains of some semi-subterranean dwellings (with an area of up to 40 m² and more). The framework for the walls of this kind of dwelling consisted of vertical posts positioned 40–60 cm apart. The binding supporting the lower edges of the roof was placed horizontally across the upper ends of these posts. The upper ends of the roof rested on the inner binding which rested, in turn, on the posts erected at the centre of the dwelling. The space at the top through which the smoke escaped most probably served as an exit with a specially notched log inserted. Archaeologists have observed similar entrances in Neolithic and later settlements in northern and eastern Asia, and ethnographers have recorded their presence up to the nineteenth century.

The first point which should be made in relation to Tamsagbulag stone tools is that many traditions associated with earlier stages of the Neolithic and with the Mesolithic may be detected in many of their technical and morphological features. Various shapes of cores were used for blade-flaking at the preliminary stage. Often the used cores were subsequently turned into a variety of tools: striking implements, cutters, adzes and plane-type tools for working bone and wood. Many of the blades are comparatively small and straight edged. A number of flakes, especially those made of tuff, show signs of having been used without any retouching of the cutting edge. Signs of work are less apparent on the flakes made of harder materials. Blades were used to make burins, knives, backed blades, awls and scrapers, in fact to make the majority of the tools found. Most of the tools found in the dwellings were scrapers, racloirs or adze/racloir-like tools. Bone was used on a large scale in the settlement to make arrowheads, knife and dagger hafts and ornaments. Two flints have been found in a bone haft.

Several fragments of tools for grinding grain and an intact boat-shaped grain-grinder have been found in dwellings together with fragments of pestles and mullers. The working surface of the grain-grinders is well polished and has been hammered. The agricultural implements include a stone disc with a biconical hole, used as a digging-stick weight.

The pottery at the settlement was thick-walled, consisting of jars lacking a clearly marked profile. These vessels were decorated with deeply cut parallel lines. The paste contained additions of fine sand and shells, was well mixed and was light yellow or dark grey in section.

Another vast region of Mongolia in which Neolithic cultures developed distinctive features is the dry southern steppes of Mongolia and the Gobi Desert, where human beings were forced to adapt to extreme climatic conditions. The first Neolithic camp sites in southern Mongolia were excavated by the United States expedition to Central Asia led by R. C. Andrews (1926). The dune camp sites at Shabarak-Usu are best known, although the dating of the finds there remains a subject of debate. The Soviet-Mongolian historical and cultural expedition subsequently managed to identify several layers at Shabarak-Usu (Okladnikov, 1962). The earliest horizons (seventh to sixth millennia BC) lie just below the base of the dunes, whereas the later horizons lie within the body of the dune deposits in buried soil (30–40 cm) covered by sand.

Flaking continued to constitute the preliminary stage of working during the Late Neolithic in southern Mongolia (third millennium BC): the cores were either conical or prismatic. Arrowheads, scrapers, backed blades and burins were made on blades but most tools were already bifacially retouched.

The ceramic had a quite different look: the vessels were thin walled with a clear profile and flat bottoms, and were painted for the first time. Their outside surfaces were often painted red, but sherds have also been found with black decorative painting on a red background. In some settlements a dark coloured paint was applied on a yellow background. Painted ceramics are fairly common at the Neolithic sites in the southern Gobi Desert.

This period also saw important changes in economic life: the settlements have yielded large numbers of grain-grinders, mullers and pestles. It is also significant that cultural artefacts of the period are mostly found in buried soil. The tribes engaged in both hunting and agriculture.

Studies of Neolithic sites in Mongolia have made it possible to answer some questions concerning the beliefs and arts of these ancient populations. All the graves found in eastern Mongolia testify to the unity of burial customs over a considerable area, and therefore, to a certain ethnic unity. The Late Neolithic population was of the Mongoloid type. Skeletons were found in a seated position, facing either westward or eastward. The burial pit was small and so narrow that it could contain only one sitting body. The graves for the most part yielded very little and only the grave in dwelling No.1 at Tamsagbulag contained ornaments and bone daggers with inset blades.

The Neolithic tribes of eastern Mongolia left traces of animal worship. Tamsagbulag yielded a cluster consisting of the skull of some small animal, beads of decorated bone and the canines of a maral or Asiatic red deer. Another cluster containing the bones of a large animal gathered and packed into a special shallow pit was probably a burial related to an animal cult. Camp sites in the basin of the River Kerulen have yielded some ritual burials consisting of the bones of wild animals.

Knowledge about the arts practised is still rather meagre. Ornaments found in the eastern areas include maral canine pendants and *unio* shell beads, while sites in southern Mongolia have yielded ostrich eggshell beads, sometimes with geometric ornamentation. Tens or even hundreds of thousands of mainly Bronze and Iron Age drawings have been found in Mongolia. The rock art of the Ulzit *somon* in the central part of the Gobi may be dated to the second half of the third millennium BC. The sand-scoured, 'rusted', flat shale surfaces are covered with dozens of chiseled representations of animal and human figures. Many of the pictures are covered with the same dense patina of 'rust' as the rock surfaces on which they were executed. The most ancient subjects are wild horses with exaggerated genitalia. These images no doubt express the ancient notion of the fertility of the animals which were the chief source of sustenance of hunting tribes in ancient times.

Little work has yet been done on the adoption of metal as a new material for the manufacture of tools by the ancient tribes of Mongolia. The start of this process is put at the end of the third and the first half of the second millennium BC. It was at that period that the climate in Mongolia started to become more arid. Primary and secondary blade tools were almost entirely replaced by bifacially worked tools. Far fewer stone tools are found at camp sites than for the Neolithic. Most of the known sites are located on eroded sand-banks beside small water courses (underground springs) or lakes, where the movement of sand at a later period left many camp sites exposed. The hearths around which finds (mainly stone tools, sherds and animal bones) were concentrated are clearly visible on the surface.

Several complexes in eastern Mongolia dating back to the early metal age have been investigated. Part of one of these camp sites beside the small watercourse of Khuityn-Bulag, 130 km to the north-east of Choibalsan, has been excavated. Several hearths with a diameter of between 0.4 and 1.5 m were uncovered in the course of the excavations. They were lined with large basalt or quartz pebbles. Small fired and cracked pebbles, which may have been heated up and used to cook food, were also found inside the hearths. Horse and camel bones and pottery sherds were found both inside and outside the hearths. The stone inventory assembled around the hearths and in their vicinity contained a large percentage of finished tools. Most of the tools were made of chalcedony, flint being used much less frequently. The most common items were backed end blades for knives and three types of arrowhead: with a straight tang, with asymmetrical barbs and with a rounded base (laurel-leaf arrowheads). All these arrowheads are similar to those of the Glazkovo early metal-age culture in the region of Lake Baikal.

The burial excavated at the locality of Norovlin-uula, 72 km from the town of Choibalsan on the right bank of the River Kerulen, also dates from the Encolithic (Volkov, 1975). Part of the burial had been destroyed and what remained measured 75 × 70 cm. A skeleton was found seated in a contracted position amid sprinkled ochre at a depth of 1.6 m below the present surface. The body had also been sprinkled with ochre. Some 3,000 small cylindrical beads with a diameter of 1.5 to 2 mm and made of white paste were recovered during the excavation of the site. The largest number was found beside the skull. Larger, round hollow beads were found beside the neck vertebrae. These beads are similar in type to those from Afanasievo in southern Siberia. Beside them were two cylindrical rings notched around the edges which were also similar to rings from Afanasievo. Near the face lay a piece of a pendant made from the fang of a wild boar, a few flat beads, one side of which was covered with decorative vertical incisions, and also ten pendants made from the teeth of musk deer. A bone, double-edged dagger 28 cm long was found beneath the arm, near the chest. Grooves had been cut along its edges into which flints had been inserted. The upper part of the handle was pierced by a hole, obviously in order to suspend the dagger. Two large

flakes with no signs of retouching and six miniature flakes with retouching along the edges were discovered not far from the dagger.

Of the other ornaments found, seven small flat plates made of shell are worthy of mention. Two of them are round with holes pierced through the middle and radial notches and two are zoomorphic, in the form of a wild boar or a bear, with two holes towards the top. Of particular interest is an amulet, a well polished stone pestle measuring 22.5 cm in length, with rounded ends. A hole had been drilled through the top of the amulet so that it could be suspended. A human face is carved on one side. The eyebrows are carefully traced by deeply cut lines. Oval depressions represent the eyes, which are framed by a curved ridge. The bulge of the cheeks is slightly in relief, separated by recessed areas from the nose, which is also in relief, long and straight and broadening slightly towards its base. Two vertical ridges below the nose are possibly intended to suggest a moustache. A small hollow represents the mouth. Four rows of symmetrical incisions have been cut into the lower part of the amulet along its sharpened edges.

In spite of the schematic modelling of the facial features, this image from the burial at Norovlin-uula is extremely expressive and clearly conveys the anthropological features of the face, which are more Europoid than Mongoloid, whereas the actual skull found in the burial is of the Mongoloid type.

A number of important features (the contracted position of the skeleton, the bone dagger with inserted stone blades), indicate that the burial at Norovlin-uula is closely related to the Late Neolithic burials at Tamsagbulag, whereas ornaments similar to all those at the site, including the amulet, have been found among the Eneolithic cultures of southern Siberia: Afanasievo and Glazkovo.

Many camp sites have been uncovered in southern Mongolia in areas where the sand has blown away. Some cover tens of thousands of square metres and it is difficult at Ermes to identify within their limits complexes dating from the Neolithic or the Eneolithic. Shabarak-Usu and Tygrigiyn-Shirete in the southern Gobi are sites which fall into this category. The sand dunes have been eroded by wind action, leaving enormous quantities of material at surface level. The hearths may often be located from the concentrations of stone tools and animal bones surrounding them.

Stratigraphically, the Eneolithic camp sites lie in strata of buried soil and above them in layers of sand. During the Eneolithic the climate was becoming dryer and windborne deposits were formed in southern Mongolia. During that period people continued to make considerable use of stone in the manufacture of various tools: however, the techniques for primary and secondary stone working changed considerably during the period. Flaking was gradually replaced by bifacial retouching.

It was during the Eneolithic that painted pottery made its appearance in Mongolia. The decoration, executed in black paint on a grey background, took the form of geometric figures: squares, diamonds, triangles and fine lines running at a variety of angles. Similar decorative motifs have been found on the pottery at Eneolithic settlements in the adjoining territories of Xinjiang and the Ordos as well as at Eneolithic settlements in central Asia.

Burials similar to those of the Afanasievo culture in Siberia have also been discovered and excavated in western and north-western Mongolia. One burial ground has been excavated in the area of Altan-sandal on the upper reaches of the northern Tamir in the Arhangay *aimak*. Three *kurgans* have been examined (Novgorodova, 1989). Flat and covered with a heavy layer of turf, they measure 4 to 4.5 m in diameter. Their small mounds (20–40 cm) consisted of the stones in the covering earth. The actual burial pits are located to the south-west and east of the centre-line and are circular in plan. The burials were at a depth of 1.2–1.5 m. The bottom of the graves and the individuals buried were strewn with ochre. The skeletons were lying on their backs with their knees in a drawn-up position. Very few grave goods were placed with the bodies.

Three similar *kurgans* have been excavated in the locality of Shatar-Chuluu on the River Tuin-Gol in Bayanhongor *aimak*. These *kurgans* are large: the first has a diameter of 10 m and a depth of 0.7 m. Two circular layers of granite slabs were discovered beneath the mound, which mainly consisted of river pebbles and small modulous rocks. In the northern part of the *kurgan*, between the granite slabs, pottery sherds were found with incised decoration.

The quasi-rectangular burial pit (2.8 × 2 m, 1.7 m deep) was located at the centre of the *kurgan*. The body was lying on its back with the knees flexed and head towards the east. The face was covered with a piece of birch-bark. Both the body and the bottom of the pit were sprinkled with ochre.

The second *kurgan*, which measured 6.5 m in diameter and 35–40 cm in height, was situated at a distance of 50 m from the first. The *kurgan* mound consisted of pebbles and small boulders and was surrounded by a circular layer of granite blocks some 30–35 cm high and up to 50 cm wide. Another circle could be traced around the oval burial pit (1.5 × 0.9 m and 0.7 m deep), which was sprinkled with ochre. The body was placed on its back with the knees flexed.

The third *kurgan* was similar in terms of its construction and also the funerary rites. Although the grave goods in all of the excavated *kurgans* were extremely meagre, the material found left the excavators in no doubt that all belonged to the Afanasievo culture: the design of the burial structure, the burial rites, the paleoanthropology, the pottery sherds decorated with typical Afanasievo ornament in the form of a horizontal herring-bone pattern. This kind of pattern is often encountered on vessels of the Afanasievo culture from the Altai and the Minusinsk Depression. These burials in western Mongolia clearly date from the end of the third or the beginning of the second millennium BC.

The Bronze Age in Mongolia has not been studied in sufficient detail. Many artistically worked artefacts made of bronze have been found there, including knives, daggers, axes, celts, awls and ornaments. However, most finds have come from assemblages close to the surface or are poorly documented and are conserved in different museums in Mongolia. On the basis of a chemical analysis of some bronze artefacts from western Mongolia and their typology, it is possible to state that bronzeware similar in appearance to that from Seima and Turbino (Chernykh and Kuz'minykh, 1989) found its way into Mongolia in the middle of the second millennium BC.

The Bronze Age is associated with the Karasuk culture which is known from a large number of bronze artefacts. No settlements from this period have been discovered, and the number of excavated burial grounds is tiny. It will only be possible to reconstruct the economy and social relations on the basis of the research being conducted in southern Siberia.

As noted above, a large number of bronze artefacts of the Karasuk type have been found. The largest and most strik-ing category are the knives which are divided into two main groups, concave and convex (Volkov, 1967). The handles are decorated with vertical rows of triangles along the edges, rows of squares, twisted cord, interrupted at regular intervals by round bulges or a groove, divided by a raised vertical line (Novgorodova, 1989). The Karasuk-type bronzeware includes many daggers, celts, awls and ornaments.

The most striking, well-documented Bronze Age finds were recovered from the excavation of three *kurgans* at Mount Tevsh uul in Övörhangay *aimak* on the eastern slopes of the Gobi Altai (Volkov, 1972). The shape of the *kurgans* was slightly unusual: the long, low mounds with concave sides were a variation of what are known as 'figured slab graves'. The funeral rites were identical in all three cases: burial in a narrow burial pit (up to 1 m deep), face-down, with the head towards the east. Over 560 paste beads, 126 carnelian beads and 24 turquoise beads were found in two of the graves, as well as some 200 hemispherical bronze plates of different sizes, stone grindstones and a painted fragment of pottery.

In addition to beads, the third grave contained two unique, solid gold hairpins lying on either side of the skull. The ends of the hairpins are decorated with the heads of mountain rams, finely executed in the Karasuk style. Small cylinders set with turquoise are cast along the outer edge of the hairpins. They are decorated with horizontal notches, also in typical Karasuk style. In the view of E. A. Novgorodova (1989), these burials of the Karasuk period may be dated to the second half of the second millennium BC.

The art of the age of metal may be judged from the many bronze artefacts decorated with the heads of animals. There was a clear preference for representation of goats, rams and deer. This was a reflection of the ancient herders' cult, the cult of the hoofed animal as totemic ancestor. Bronze and clay objects were also decorated with geometric patterns: rhythmically repeated combinations of triangles, diamonds and squares. Such motifs were widely employed on clay and bronze objects in China where they are interpreted as fertility symbols.

A large number of Eneolithic and Bronze Age petroglyphs have been discovered in Mongolia. The drawings depict animals in repose and in rapid movement: deer, mountain rams, horses, snow leopards and tigers. Many ancient engravings are connected with hunting, battles and complex magical rites. There are pictures of chariots dating from the end of the Bronze Age. The chariots are four-wheeled or two-wheeled and are harnessed to teams of two, three or four horses. The drivers stand with their legs wide apart and some hold bows. Stock-breeding started in the Eneolithic and the Bronze Age and reached its high point during the Karasuk period, when cattle, sheep and goats were herded.

Summarizing briefly the development of the ancient cultures of Central Asia from the third to the beginning of the first millennium BC, we may draw a few general conclusions:

1 Neolithic cultures developed over the greater part of northern Asia and Mongolia in the third millennium BC. The economy was based on hunting, fishing and gathering. There is evidence of primitive agriculture and the use of wild grains only among the tribes of the Amur and in Mongolia.

2 The first metal artefacts made of copper appeared in southern Siberia, in the Minusinsk Depression and the Altai at the end of the .fourth millennium and during the third millennium BC. The tribes began to engage in stock-breeding as well as food gathering.

3 The Bronze Age developed rapidly in northern Asia and Mongolia in the second millennium BC. Stock-breeding was the principal occupation.

4 An Iron Age culture took shape over a vast area of northern Asia and Mongolia from 800 BC.

BIBLIOGRAPHY

ALEKSEEV, V. P.; GOKHMAN, I. I. 1984. *Antropologija aziatskoj casti SSSR [The Anthropology of the Asian USSR]*. Moskva.

ANDREWS, R. C. 1926. *On the Trail of Ancient Man*. New York/London.

CHERNETSOV, V. N. 1953. *Drevnjaja istorija Niznego Priob'ja [The Early History of the Lower Ob]*. Moskva/Leningrad. pp. 25–34.

CHERNYKH, E. N.; KUZ'MINYKH, S. V. 1989. *Drevnjaja metallurgija Severnoj Evrazii [Ancient Metal-Working in Northern Eurasia]*. Moskva.

DEREVYANKO, A. P. 1986. *Drevnjaja Mongolija [Ancient Mongolia]*. In: ASHFAFYAN, K. Z. et al. (eds), *Istorija narodov Vostocnoj i Central'noj Azii s drevnejsih vremen do nasih dnej*. Moskva. pp. 75–81.

DEREVYANKO, A. P.; OKLADNIKOV, A. P. 1969. Drevnie kul'tury vostocnyh rajonov Mongol'skoj Narodnoj Respubliki [*Ancient Cultures of the Eastern Regions of the Mongolian People's Republic*]. *Sov. Arheol.* (Moskva), No. 4, pp. 141–56.

DORZH, D. 1971. *Neolit Vostocnoj Mongolii [The Neolithic in Eastern Mongolia]*. Ulaanbaatar.

FEDOSEEVA, S. A. 1980. *Ymyjahtahskaja kul'tura Severo-Vostocnoj Azii [The Ymyjahtahskaja Culture of North-Eastern Asia]*. Novosibirsk.

MOCHANOV, Y. A. 1977. *Drevnejsie etapy zaselenija celovekom Severo-Vostocnoj Azii [The Earliest Stages in the Settlement of North-East Asia]*. Novosibirsk.

NOVGORODOVA, Ê. A. 1989. *Drevnjaja Mongolija [Ancient Mongolia]*. Moskva.

OKLADNIKOV, A. P. 1950. *Neolit i bronzovyj vek Pribajkal'ja [The Neolithic and Bronze Age in the Baikal Region]*. Moskva/Leningrad.

—— 1955. *Neolit i bronzovyj vek Pribajkal'ja (Glazkovskoe vremja) [The Neolithic and Bronze Age of the Baikal Region – the Glazkovo period]*. Moskva/Leningrad. Vol. 3.

—— 1962. Novoe v izucenii drevnejsih kul'tur Mongolii (po rabotam 1960) [New Material in the Study of the Ancient Cultures of Mongolia (Based on the Research Conducted in 1960)]. *Sov. Etnogr.* (Moskva), No. 2, pp. 33–40.

—— (ed.). 1968. *Istorija Sibiri [The History of Siberia]*. Leningrad. Vol. 1.

OKLADNIKOV, A. P.; DEREVYANKO, A. P. 1970. Tamcag-Bulak – neoliticeskaja kul'tura Vostocnoj Mongolii [Tamsagbulag, A Neolithic Culture of Eastern Mongolia]. *Mater. istor. filol. Cent. Azii* (Ulan-Ude), Vol. 5, pp. 3–22.

—— 1973. *Dalekoe prosloe Primor'ja i Priamur'ja [The Distant Past of the Maritime and Amur Areas]*. Vladivostok.

OKLADNIKOV, A. P.; MARTYNOV, A. I. 1972. *Sokrovisca Tomskih pisanic [Treasures of the Tom Petroglyphs]*. Moskva.

SEMENOV, V. A. 1983. Mnogoslojnaja stojanka Toori-Das na Enisee [The Multi-layered Camp Site of Toori-Dash on the Yenisei]. In: *Drevnie kul'tury evraziatskih stepej*. Leningrad. pp. 20–33.

VADETSKAYA, E. B. 1986. *Arheologiceskie pamjatniki v stepjah Srednego Eniseja [Archaeological Remains on the Steppes of the Upper Yenisei]*. Leningrad.

VOLKOV, V. V. 1967. *Bronzovyj i rannij zeleznyj vek Severnoj Mongolii [The Bronze Age and Early Iron Age in Northern Mongolia]*. Ulaanbaatar.

—— 1972. Raskopki v Mongolii [Excavations in Mongolia]. In: RYBAKOV, B .A. (ed.), *Arheologiceskie otkrytija 1971 goda*. Moskva. pp. 554–6.

—— 1975. Arheologija Severnoj i Central'noj Azii |The Archaeology of Northern and Central Asia]. In: OKLADNIKOV, A. P. (ed.), *Arheologija Severnoj i Central'noj Azii*. Novosibirsk. pp. 76–9.

16

AUSTRALIA

Josephine Flood

Prehistoric Aboriginal society was dynamic; neither the land nor the people were unchanging, and constant adaptation was made to environmental fluctuations. In contrast with other continents, however, there has also been a basic stability and continuity of the hunter-gatherer way of life, from more than 40,000 years ago till the present. Australia was the only inhabited continent where the end of the Pleistocene did not herald major cultural changes, such as the development of farming and urbanization. Australia remained a land of nomadic hunter-gatherers while most people in the rest of the world, including nearby Papua New Guinea, became farmers, horticulturists or herdsmen. Other traits which never developed in the fifth continent were the bow and arrow, pottery or the use of metals.

The basic adaptation to the Australian environment took place when the continent was first occupied, and the environment was to a remarkable degree modified by its prehistoric occupants, particularly by 'fire-stick farming' (Jones, 1969). The hunter-gatherer way of life was ideally suited to Australia, the world's driest continent, and Aboriginal people lived well in a range of harsh environments where European agriculture was later to prove an abysmal failure. Once the nomadic way of life had become well established, with its consequent need to travel light, it was unlikely that agriculture or horticulture, pottery or sedentary life would be adopted, except in response to major environmental or other changes, which did not occur.

ECONOMY AND ENVIRONMENT

The end of the Pleistocene was a period of gradual change in Australia. Unlike the northern hemisphere, there was no sharp boundary or drastic climatic change between the end of the Pleistocene and the beginning of the Holocene period. Consequently no rapid and widespread change was imposed on the existing Aboriginal way of life. The broadly based economic systems of Australian Aborigines which were developed during the Pleistocene era allowed them the flexibility not only to survive but to flourish in reasonable affluence, and to adapt to the post-Pleistocene diminution and desiccation of the Australian continent caused by rising sea-level and temperatures, without major changes in economy or life-style.

The sea apparently rose quite rapidly until about 7,000 years ago, and then more slowly until the present level was reached about 5,000 years ago. This means that the coast of

Australia has been much as it is today for the last 5,000 years. The rising of the seas inundated large tracts of land, but at the same time stabilization of sea-level extended tidal reefs and estuaries, zones of the shore most productive of fish and shellfish reasonably accessible to the Aboriginal foragers. At the mouth of rivers these formed lagoons held back by sandy barriers, which previously had been swept away by the ever-rising sea. Likewise the drowning of river valleys led to development of many food-rich small inlets and bays.

While some regions, particularly those on the coast, became more favourable for human exploitation, others became less well-endowed or even uninhabitable. An example of a habitat which had deteriorated by 5,000 years ago from the human point of view is the Willandra Lakes region in western New South Wales (Map 25). This semi-arid region fringing the continent's desert core contains Lake Mungo, and is on the World Heritage List because of its archaeological and geomorphological significance (Flood, 1994, pp. 39–55). In the Pleistocene the Willandra Lakes were generally full of fresh water and teeming with large fish and mussels, supporting a substantial human population, but about 17,500 years ago climatic change induced increased evaporation and a major drying up of the lakes and by 15,000 years ago most lakes were dry. New food resources were needed, and the hunter-gatherers adapted by moving to large rivers such as the Murray and Darling and changing their staple food to flour made from grass seeds. This extensive collecting, grinding and baking of grass seeds as food was a great technological step forward, taken as early as in western Asia or elsewhere in the world.

Why did this use of grass seed (*Panicum decompositum* or native millet) not lead to farming and a sedentary way of life? Possible reasons which have been put forward to explain why Australian Aborigines did not become farmers, horticulturists or herdsmen have been lack of suitable plants and animals to domesticate, lack of the stimulus of major environmental changes necessitating drastic adaptation, innate cultural conservatism and affluence. Hunter-gatherers have sometimes been characterized as 'the original affluent society', in harmony with their environment (Lee and Devore, 1968). While this view may be more idealistic than realistic for some hunter-gatherer societies, it may be reasonably accurate for the Aborigines of Australia. Hunter-gatherers in Australia may have been so affluent that they had no need to increase the yield of food plants or to store food. This affluence may have been achieved by the development of a balance, in which population was kept below the level the

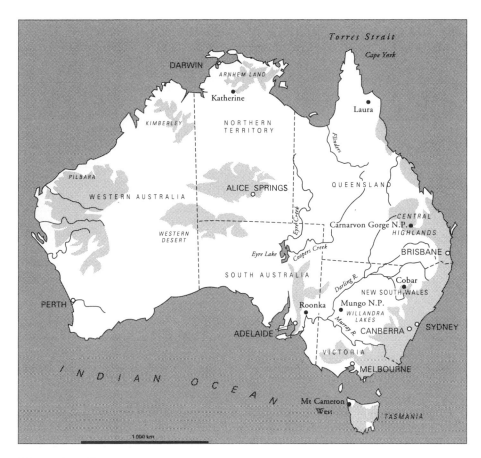

Map 25 Australia

country could support. In other words, the available food could have fed far more mouths than actually had to be fed. There would therefore have been no incentive to increase the food supply by developing agriculture, unless some major environmental or population stress were experienced.

This seems the most plausible explanation of the absence of agriculture from prehistoric Australia. The hunter-gatherers had no need to increase the food supply, because they kept their population in equilibrium with their environment. The return from their highly efficient foraging was so great that expenditure of additional effort on cultivating crops was not worthwhile.

THE QUESTION OF AGRICULTURE

The question of the possible domestication of Australian mammals is easily answered: there were no native marsupials suitable for domestication. None of the animals such as pigs, cows, sheep, goats or chickens that were domesticated in other countries existed in Australia in prehistoric times. However, native birds such as geese, pelicans or scrub turkeys might have been domesticated but were not. This situation contrasts with that in Papua New Guinea (White and O'Connell, 1982, pp. 171–97).

In northern Australia some food plants are gathered by Aborigines which are cultivated in Papua New Guinea. One such food plant occurring along the east coast of Cape York in prehistoric times was the coconut, which probably established itself naturally following dispersal of coconuts across the sea as flotsam. There is no evidence that Aborigines deliberately planted or tended coconut palms before the time of European settlement.

The yam (*Dioscorea* sp.) was a staple in both northern Australia and Papua New Guinea, and also present were other tubers such as taro (*Colocasia* sp.) and 'Polynesian arrowroot' (*Tacca* sp.). It is not just the presence of a food plant that is important, however; its relative abundance and ease or otherwise of cultivation must also be considered. Many food plants which grow wild in Cape York, but which are domesticated in Asia, are adapted to regular rainfall and have a limited distribution in the infertile soils and seasonally dry climate of Cape York (Golson, 1971). The soils most suitable for agriculture in Cape York were occupied by rainforest. Whilst this could have been cleared by would-be farmers with the aid of fire, motivation would have had to be strong to undertake such hard work. Unlike island horticulturists, mainland Aborigines could respond to food shortages by moving elsewhere, so the incentive to cultivate gardens was never likely to be strong.

Prehistoric Australia was not endowed with the corn that formed the basis of agriculture in Mexico and Meso-America, or the wheat and barley of central Asia, but it does have one native cereal grain, which became a major food in parts of arid inland Australia. This is wild millet (*Panicum decompositum*), which is a closely related member of the same plant family which in other parts of the world produced the domesticated common panicum (*Panicum miliaceum*) and Italian millet (*Setaria italica*).

Given that seed collection had been practised since the end of the Pleistocene in Australia, why did the cereal gatherers not become cereal cultivators? They had all the 'pre-adaptations' usually deemed necessary; they ate a broad spectrum of wild foods, they had developed ground-stone technology and storage facilities. The semi-arid river basins of inland New South Wales offer similar environments to

Mexico and Mesopotamia where agriculture did develop, although the last two have more varied topography and probably suffer less severe floods and droughts than did inland Australia.

One of the main problems in gathering wild cereals is the tendency of the seeds to ripen at different times, making it difficult to harvest large quantities of grain at any one time. This problem was overcome by gathering the grass when the seed was full but the grass still green. The grass was then stacked in heaps and the seeds left to dry and ripen, until later they were threshed so that the seed fell to the ground in one place.

The harvesting of grass seed was done on a large scale by pulling up the cereal grasses by the roots, pulling the stalks off or pulling the seed off into a bark dish, the usual method in central Australia. In the Cooper Creek area in south-west Queensland stone knives were used for reaping, important evidence of semi-agricultural practices in inland Australia.

Cereal gathering was predominantly an adaptation to the arid lands of the dry heart of the continent, in areas that received annual average rainfall of 300 mm or less. In better watered areas in tropical and coastal Australia, the fruits, nuts and tubers of plants provided the main vegetable food rather than seeds. In the centre and south of the continent there were virtually no foods that could have been domesticated except the wild millet, which was exploited intensively but not stored on a large scale or planted. The people of these inland riverine plains were really the only people in temperate Australia who could have become cereal farmers. Their exploitation of wild millet has been called 'incipient agriculture' and it provided about 30 per cent of their diet, but they did not take the final steps of tilling the soil, planting seeds, and storing the surplus food produced. No doubt the labour involved in tilling and planting outweighed the possible advantages. Instead they ensured a maximum return of food by hunting and gathering a wide range of foods and by using a sophisticated array of highly specialized techniques.

PROCESSING OF POISONOUS FOODS

The most specialized and sophisticated economic process was the exploitation of toxic *Macrozamia* nuts and other cycads. The technology is claimed to have arrived in Queensland 4,500 years ago in nearly the same form in which it is applied today, the main support for external origin being the considerable expertise required to process the poisonous nuts (Beaton, 1982).

Macrozamia is a species of cycad, a palm or fern-like plant whose history goes back 200 million years. It produces unique, pineapple-like reproductive structures called 'stroboli'. These are large and brightly coloured, but extremely poisonous, as a number of Europeans have found to their cost. They are also toxic to herds of livestock, causing what is described by stockmen in the outback as 'the zamia staggers'. Moreover, it has been discovered that cycads contain one of the most powerful carcinogenic substances in the world.

Removal of the poison from cycad kernels was lengthy and complicated. Slightly different processes were used in different regions. One method was to cut open the kernels and soak the poison out with water. When the kernels were free of toxin, they were ground into a starchy, flour-like substance and baked into 'cycad bread'. Another technique was fermentation, in which the dissected kernels were placed in large containers or pits for several months. The material is safe to eat when the kernels have either frothed or grown mouldy, but there is no such thing as a person who eats cycads and who is only just learning about how to prepare them.

The food value of cycads is remarkably high: about 43 per cent is carbohydrate, and 5 per cent protein. Many species produce huge quantities of kernels, yielding more food per hectare than many cultivated crops. Aborigines even increased the size of the stands of cycads by careful use of fire to clear competing vegetation. Such cycad stands are therefore ecological artefacts. Regular burning could also increase production by seven or eight times and make all the kernels ripen at the same time. This meant that cycads could be used to support large gatherings of people on ceremonial occasions.

Cycads were certainly used in regions such as Arnhem Land to provide an adequate food supply for ceremonies, when hundreds of people were gathered in a camp for weeks or months at a time. Similarly, the main use of *Macrozamia* nuts in the Central Highlands of Queensland was as a 'communion food', supporting large gatherings for ceremonial or ritual purposes (Bowdler, 1981). Whether a staple or a 'communion' food, cycads are a highly nutritious, productive, predictable and easily harvested food, once the way to process them is known. And the whole process is not as time-consuming as one might think. The collecting and processing of cycad bread among the Anbara of Arnhem Land yielded about 1 kg, containing 1,300 calories, per hour of work. This meant that one woman could feed herself adequately on just two hours' work per day (Meehan, 1982).

FIRE-STICK FARMING

While Aborigines did not till the soil, they carried out a number of horticultural techniques, such as replanting the tops of yams and other tubers and encouraging growth of fruit trees round their camps (Flood, 1994, pp. 259–60). They also used fire as an artefact for conserving and increasing their food supply, a process that has been called fire-stick farming (Jones, 1969). Fire is one of the Aborigines' most important artefacts but one that is largely invisible to the archaeologist. Much of the vegetation encountered by early white settlers in Australia was artificial: an Aboriginal artefact created by thousands of years of burning.

Fire was used for signalling and also to make travel easier by clearing undergrowth along the route and killing snakes lurking in the bush. Aboriginal tracks were kept open by regular firing in tropical grasslands, and in the dense scrub and heavily timbered ranges of temperate forests. Throughout the continent burning was used for hunting; animals could be speared or clubbed as they broke cover to escape the flames.

Other reasons for extensive burning were longer-term hunting strategies. After firing, the bush would regenerate, new grass would spring up and attract kangaroos and other herbivores on which the hunters could prey. Likewise fire encouraged the regrowth of eucalyptus trees and of edible plant foods, such as bracken roots, young leaves and shoots. The ashes acted like manure, and sweet, new green shoots would spring up after the first hard rain following the burn (Flood, 1994, pp. 250–2).

Fire-stick farming cannot be equated with slash-and-burn agriculture, but extensive and regular burning had the long-term effect, whether intentional or not, of extending the human habitat and increasing the quantity and diversity of food resources.

POPULATION CONTROL

People such as the Bagundji of the Darling River basin were in some form of balance with their food supply. During bad seasons new-born children were killed, but there is no evidence that droughts caused deaths in the rest of the population. The number of mouths to feed was regulated by bad seasons, and finding enough food during normal or good seasons required little effort (Allen, 1974).

When food was in short supply, the food quest required more time and effort rather than new strategies. There was also no shortage of land available, in strong contrast to Central Asia and the narrow neck of Mexico. When times were hard, people simply moved more frequently and further afield. In the harshest environment of all, the Western Desert, journeys of 400 to 500 km were common, especially during droughts. Indeed, one group in recent times was observed to move nine times in three months, foraging over almost 2,600 km² of the sand desert (Gould, 1980, pp. 6–28, 68–9).

The typical Australian Aboriginal economy is flexible, with a wide range of foods being utilized and advantage being taken of seasonal abundance or chance events, such as the stranding of a whale on the beach. Such a broad-based foraging system minimizes risks and overcomes shortages of any one type of food much better than can an agricultural community relying on more restricted food sources. Aboriginal Australia was never vulnerable to famine due to the failure of one crop.

The population was controlled by the available food, which in turn was related to water resources; areas with the highest rainfall were generally richest in food. The number of mouths that could be fed was regulated by the food available at the leanest time of year, which in temperate regions was usually winter. The summer abundance of food was used, not to feed more people by collecting and storing surplus food, but as a time when there was more leisure for intellectual life. In a rich environment the food quest occupied only an hour or two each day in a good season; in the poorest environment it generally required less than six or seven hours each day. Even during drought in the desert, only two or three hours of collecting by the women could provide a day's food for the whole group (Gould, 1980, p. 64).

DIET AND FOOD STORAGE

Aboriginal people living a traditional life not only had more leisure than is available for the average farmer or office-worker, but they also generally ate better. The diet of groups whose economy has been recorded in detail emerges as more balanced, varied and nutritious than that of many white people. The Anbara of coastal Arnhem Land have an average intake of about 2,400 kilocalories a day, of which 40 to 50 per cent comes from the flesh of fish, shellfish, crustaceans, and about fifty species of land animals and birds (Meehan, 1982).

The production of food surpluses led to development of food storage techniques and facilities in other parts of the world. In Australia, however, long-term preservation of many foods presented serious problems. Indeed, the difficulties of food storage in the Australian climate may be germane in understanding why food surpluses were not produced. The combination of high temperatures and pronounced seasonality of rainfall made food storage difficult in tropical Australia, not only for Aborigines but also for early European settlers. Likewise early European 'explorers', even with the benefit of salting and smoking techniques unknown to Aborigines, often found that the game they killed went bad within a few hours.

In many food-preservation techniques used in other parts of the world boiling was an essential part of the process, but Aborigines had no means of boiling food. On the Torres Strait islands, almost within sight of the tip of Cape York, large shells were used to boil up slices of turtle meat, which were then put on skewers and dried in the sun. Such dried meat provided food for canoe voyages lasting several weeks. In contrast, on Cape York, shells were used as water containers but not for boiling; cooking was done in earth ovens or by roasting or grilling.

Factors operating against food storage were not only the difficulties of preservation from damage by heat, water, animals, birds and insects such as termites and locusts, but also the traditional nomadism of Australian Aborigines. Groups might stay for several months at the same camp in a rich environment but no groups stayed in the same place all the year round. Where less food was available, they would move camp more often. A few items, such as large grindstones, might be left behind, but hunter-gatherers carried all their basic equipment along with them, together with the babies and young children who had to be carried. Comparison of the material culture of different regions has shown that the largest range of material goods is owned by those in rich environments where there is relatively little nomadism.

The main reason that agriculture, with its sedentism and increased material possessions, did not develop in Australia was probably affluence, and lack of the stimulus of major environmental changes on a continent-wide scale. Archaeological evidence has shown that the characteristic Australian economic system of a varied rather than specialized diet obtained by seasonal movement has great antiquity. In spite of the drying up of the inland Pleistocene lakes, the diet of people at Lake Mungo 30,000 years ago is similar to that of the Bagundji last century, except for the addition of grass seeds some time during the first half of the Holocene.

MATERIAL CULTURE

Artefacts

A number of innovations occurred during the mid-Holocene. Between about 5,000 and 4,000 years ago new specialized composite artefacts, known as the 'Small Tool Tradition', were added to the toolkit. Their outstanding characteristics are the symmetry and delicate trimming or pressure-flaking of tiny, slender blades made from fine-grained rock, hafted onto a wooden handle to make a lightweight but highly effective tool. These composite tools, consisting of two or even three parts, included spear-throwers (atlatl) and stone projectile points hafted with resin onto the tips of long wooden spear shafts.

The spear-thrower or woomera (its most common Aboriginal name) seems to have been independently invented in Australia in the mid-Holocene. It increased the distance to which a spear could be thrown to more than 100 m, making the Australian spear a most effective and deadly weapon, used both to hunt large animals and as a weapon of war and personal combat.

Something that has long puzzled culture-historians is why the bow and arrow were never used in Australia. If mainland Australia, like Tasmania, had been completely isolated from the outside world since its invention, its absence would be explicable, but this is less easily explained when other overseas items, such as outrigger canoes, were adopted by Aborigines. The bow and arrow were in use in every inhabited continent except Australia during the post-glacial period. It has usually been assumed to be a more efficient hunting and fighting weapon than the spear, but in the case of Australia this assumption would appear to be wrong. Bows and arrows were used in Papua and in the Torres Strait islands, and they were seen by Captain Cook on small islands immediately off Cape York, but they were not used by Australian Aborigines. It seems that not only Cape York Aborigines but also the islanders regarded the mainland spears and spear-throwers as superior weapons for fighting, hunting and fishing. The main items traded by Cape York Aborigines were spears, which were eagerly sought after in the western Torres Strait islands. Spear-throwers were also traded to the islands and were used in spear fishing for dugong. The two main types of spear traded were the fishing spear with four bone barbs, and fighting spears with a bone lashed on to form both a barb and a point. Spears were probably Australia's first export goods.

A spear, with its range and penetrating power increased by the extra leverage of a spear-thrower, was doubtless more effective than an arrow against the large marsupials found in Australia. Arrows were used to hunt the largest Papuan wallaby, *Macropus agilis*, in the Trans-Fly region, but much larger animals exist in Australia, with rougher hides, against which an arrow would have little effect.

Other new weapons included the 'death spear', which was a long wooden spear with as many as twelve stone barbs set with resin into a groove down each side of the shaft. These stone spear barbs were oriented in such a way that when a spear penetrated flesh it would not easily fall out, and the hunted animal would tend to die from loss of blood if it were not killed outright.

Not all the new artefacts were weapons of war or the chase; some, such as the small steep-edged adze stones often set on the end of the spear-thrower, were specialized tools developed for particular purposes; in this case as chisels to fashion the very hard timber of the arid zone into wooden artefacts, such as boomerangs, carrying dishes or shields. Other artefacts were developed for particular purposes, such as large flat upper and lower 'millstones' for grinding the hard seeds of native grasses in arid Australia into flour to make bread.

Rock art

Most rock paintings and engravings are impossible to date, but there is sufficient circumstantial evidence to indicate that paintings, engravings and stencils were being produced in Australia during this time period, and that a figurative style had developed and in some regions replaced the earlier geometric style of engravings.

Australia's rock art of the late Holocene is distinguished by great regional diversity (Flood, 1990; 1994, pp. 276–9;

Walsh, 1988). These differences do not stem from the different types of rock surface available as 'canvas', but appear to reflect different culture areas. Tasmanian rock art is virtually all engravings (Plate 161), that of Victoria almost all paintings. In New South Wales the most colourful galleries lie in the west in the Cobar region, where small, lively, red and white figures dance across the walls of dozens of shelters. In contrast, on the coast of New South Wales paintings are larger and include more marine subjects, but the outstanding feature of the Sydney region is the engraved art. There are thousands of outline engravings, and the figures usually approximate life size. Subjects range from whales to lyre birds, from ancestral beings to dingoes.

The art of the engravers reaches its height in the Pilbara region of western Australia, where the development of this art medium can be seen in all its richness and variety. Some extinct animals are portrayed, such as the distinctive striped thylacine or 'Tasmanian tiger', which has been extinct outside Tasmania for some 3,000 years. There are also realistic linear drawings of animals, often life-size, and pecked-out human and animal figures, standing out a fresh cream-colour against the brown of the background rock. Although it is impossible to date these engravings, the fresher, lighter coloured ones are obviously younger than those almost obliterated by cracks, heavy weathering and patination.

This younger art is amazingly full of vitality and movement for such a difficult medium as rock engraving, executed with stone hammer and chisel. Elegant figures are shown in bold silhouette and dramatic compositions – running, dancing, fighting, love-making. The many humans include strange anthropomorphs known as *kunungera*. These male figures have forked hands instead of fingers, gigantic genitals, protruding muzzles and long 'antennae' waving from their heads. *Kunungera* and other engravings were not kept secret, for they are often placed on tiers high on pyramidal piles of huge boulders, where they look out, as if from the walls of a gigantic picture gallery, across the featureless sand plains.

Not only could these sites be seen by women and children as well as by men, but they may also have been the work of women, for they are invariably close to a waterhole and usually within a few metres of oval patches of rock worn smooth from seed-grinding. Often the upper millstone is still left on the milling floor, and debris consistent with grass seeds has been found in the cracks of some of the ground surfaces. Grinding of seeds to be mixed with water and made into dough was traditionally women's work in Aboriginal Australia. There is a consistently close association between seed-grinding patches and engravings, and the virile *kunungera* men seem likely to be women's art, in the same way that voluptuous female figures have been painted as 'love magic' by male Aboriginal artists elsewhere.

In visual splendour the rock paintings of the Kimberleys, Northern Territory and Cape York rival those anywhere in the world. The Kimberleys are famous for their huge colourful *wandjina* figures. Equal vigour and artistic excellence appears in the tiny *mimi* figures of early Arnhem Land art. Impressionistic and dynamic, they depict in remarkable detail lively scenes of prehistoric life (Plate 162). Much better known is the later style of Arnhem Land, the elaborate X-ray rock art, in which the skeleton and internal organs of creatures are portrayed as well as external features.

The rock art of Queensland is different again. The Cape York peninsula contains one of the most colourful and prolific bodies of rock art in the world (Plate 16). Huge naturalistic figures of animals, birds, plants, humans and spirit figures adorn the walls of hundreds of rock-shelters. Mythological ancestral beings are finely executed with careful decoration. Other paintings were used in magic or sorcery – showing men and women, upside down with distorted genitals, being struck by a spear or bitten by a snake.

Stencil art is found over most of Australia but is most highly developed as an art form in the Carnarvon National Park in the Central Highlands of southern Queensland, where stencils predominate. The motifs or hands, feet, pendants, axes, clubs, boomerangs and other artefacts are arranged in decorative patterns, and stencilled with red, yellow and black pigment which stands out vividly against the white sandstone walls. Colourful and striking as art, these stencils are also a valuable record of local material culture (Plate 163). There is archaeological evidence that this art style appeared in southern Queensland about 4,000 years ago, at the same time as the Small Tool Tradition and cycad-processing techniques.

Aboriginal art was never 'art for art's sake', but a part of religious life and a vital accompaniment to ceremonies and rituals. The aesthetic value has always been secondary to the religious or practical use of the decorated item. There were no professional artists in traditional Aboriginal society, although some individuals were recognized as particularly gifted. The most significant Aboriginal art is a manifestation of spiritual beliefs. It conveys aspects of myth through symbolic representations of the great spirit beings, linking Aborigines to the Dreamtime, the era of Creation. It is the tangible expression of the relevance and reality of myth and an Aboriginal unity with nature.

Burial practices

A wide variety of burial practices existed in Holocene Australia. In Tasmania cremation was practised but on the mainland inhumation was more common. Important evidence regarding burial practices between 3000 and 700 BC comes from the extensive excavations carried out at Roonka on the Murray River in south Australia over the last decade (Pretty, 1977). More than 150 burials have been discovered there. The remains lie in a sand dune on a flat beside a bend in the river and were exposed by erosion after a flash flood in 1956. The dune probably served as a refuge for hunter-gatherers during the annual inundations of the river, which would have submerged the greater part of the valley floor for long periods. Three sorts of burial were utilized· the bodies were fully extended lying on the back, contracted lying on the side, or in the 'recumbent-contracted' position, lying on the back but with legs folded or drawn up. The last mode of burial is the earliest of the three types in Roonka III (about 4,000 years old), indicating that major change did occur in the method of disposal of the dead. The extended and the contracted style appear to be contemporary, alternative choices of burial.

The Roonka burials contain evidence for status as a factor in mode of burial. It seems that part of the population received elaborate rites, whereas others were disposed of in a cursory manner. Some broken and burnt human bones were found among habitation refuse in the camp site contemporary with the status burials of Roonka III. These may have been the bones of enemies defeated in battle, but it also seems that the remains of the young and very old were disposed of elsewhere, interment in the dune being reserved for adults. These cannot have just been the warriors of the

tribe, for females were represented as well. However, adult males predominated, and some showed evidence of tooth avulsion, the sign of the initiated. This fits the pattern recorded for the Murray region in historic times, in which the old and sick were sometimes left to die in the open, and the remains of the very young were either disposed of immediately or wrapped in bundles and transported around to desiccate, whereupon the bundle was deposited in a rock crevice or a cleft in a tree.

The most elaborate status burials contain numerous grave goods. The most striking tomb yet unearthed in Australia is grave 108 from the earliest phase of Roonka III, dated to around 4,000 years old. The deep cylindrical shaft opens into a small chamber, in which an adult male was buried on his back but with legs folded up. By his side on his left arm lay a small child. Both man and child were splendidly attired. The man had a fillet or band of wallaby teeth in two parallel rows around his head. This was made of matched pairs of incisors which were notched to give greater purchase to the band which must have held them in place. (The band may have been made of human hair spun into thread and plaited, as is still done by Aborigines in central Australia.) A second fillet of wallaby incisors lay extended across the man's left forearm; this may have been an armband or a second headband. Headbands are a sign of an initiated male in present-day Aboriginal Australia, and this Roonka grave strongly suggests that both the customs of wearing headbands and the rite of tooth avulsion during initiation rites goes back at least 4,000 years.

A skin cloak appears to have been wrapped tightly around the body, because his right arm was pulled close against his side, and down the centre of the body lay a series of bone pins such as were used for fastening cloaks in historic times. Behind his left shoulder was a dense mass of foot bones of small animals, suggesting that the cloak was fixed at the shoulder with the paws of animal pelts hanging down over the shoulder. It may well have been a possum skin cloak, some of which were made up of as many as eighty pelts. Bird bones found along the left side of the body probably indicate that the garment was fringed with a decorative band of bird feathers. The child wore a bird skull pendant, a necklace of reptile vertebrae, and had ochre staining on its feet.

This burial implies that both social stratification and ritual infanticide existed several thousand years ago. There are several other similar graves containing an adult, a child and grave goods, so the simultaneous burial of adult and child is not likely to be due to their accidental contemporary death, but rather to the ritual killing of young children. Since adult males were involved, we are not simply seeing evidence of the simultaneous death of mother and infant, nor of the killing of a child because its mother was unable to care for it any longer. The most satisfactory explanation of this infanticide is that it was a ritual connected with social status which was considered more important than the life of a child.

The evidence from Roonka has thrown a new light upon Australian prehistory with its indications of cultural change, evolving social organization and stratification, and the antiquity of characteristic Aboriginal customs, such as primary and secondary burials, grave goods and tooth avulsion.

INTENSIFICATION

Intensification is a term which generally refers to increases in both productivity and production, and there is evidence in prehistoric Australia since about 5,000 years ago of 'increases in the complexity of social relations and economic growth, semi-sedentism, and by inference, population sizes' (Lourandos, 1985). During this period archaeological evidence shows that increases occurred in:

1 intensity of usage and rate of establishment of sites;
2 complexity of site economy (an increase in the range of resources exploited and improvement in harvesting and capturing methods);
3 use of marginal environments, such as arid, montane, rainforest or swampland areas;
4 the quantity of exchange: trade goods, social networks and ceremonial events.

Throughout Australia there is a remarkable upsurge from about 5,000 years ago in the number of sites and the intensity of occupation. There seems to have been an economic expansion in terms of land, food and other resources, increasing sedentism exemplified by a trend towards the establishment of longer-term base camps, and more intensive inter-group relations, reflected in the increase in exchange and ceremonies. These trends were also present in prehistoric Tasmania some 3,000 years ago, although it was completely isolated from the mainland, suggesting that the process of intensification took place there independently and is a natural development among evolving hunter-gatherer societies.

Diffusion is therefore not an acceptable explanation for these late Holocene economic and cultural changes in Australia, although certain elements certainly diffused into the continent, such as the dingo, the Australian wild dog (Canis familiaris), often portrayed in rock paintings (Plate 164). Dingoes seem to have been introduced from Asia, probably deliberately but possibly as castaways, some time between 5,000 and 4,000 years ago. Dingoes held an important place in Aboriginal ritual and mythology, and were taken as pups from the wild, to which they would eventually return. They were largely used as pets and as a 'blanket' on cold nights.

Other elements which may have diffused into Australia were the new specialized small tools such as projectile points, but these may equally well have been independently invented on the mainland. They do not occur in Tasmania, which was cut off from all contact with the rest of the world from about 10,000 years ago, by the formation of the wide and stormy Bass Strait in the post-glacial sea rise.

The dingo's closest relative appears to be the domesticated dog of the Indus civilization city of Harappa, dating from 1500–2000 BC. The appearance of the dog in Australia, but absence of Neolithic elements such as pottery and

agriculture, suggests that diffusion was mainly in pre-Neolithic times from a society of hunter-gatherers rather than cultivators. Diffusion seems to have been minimal, apart from a number of items of material culture such as smoking pipes, skin drums and outrigger canoes, which found their way onto the north coast of Australia but not into temperate regions further south.

Trends towards greater complexity and regional diversity appear to amplify with time throughout the late Holocene. The expansive economic and cultural epoch of the last 5,000–4,000 years coincides with drier conditions, at least in south-eastern Australia and Tasmania, but this climatic change is considered to have played an influential rather than a determining role. The Late Holocene intensification in Australia is similar to cultural processes from other continents, such as the Mesolithic of Europe, and may be considered a natural evolutionary step towards more intensive levels of hunting and gathering and to more complex social relationships.

BIBLIOGRAPHY

ALLEN, H. R. 1974. The Bagundji of the Darling Basin; Cereal Gatherers in an Uncertain Environment. *World Archaeol.* (London), Vol. 5, pp. 309–22.
BEATON, J. M. 1982. Fire and Water: Aspects of Australian Aboriginal Management of Cycads. *Archaeol. Oceania* (Sydney), Vol. 17, No. 1, pp. 51–9.
BOWDLER, S. 1981. Hunters in the Highland: Aboriginal Adaptations in the Eastern Australian Uplands. *Archaeol. Oceania* (Sydney), Vol. 16, pp. 99–111.
FLOOD, J. 1990. *The Riches of Ancient Australia: A Journey into Prehistory.* Brisbane.
—— 1994. *Archaeology of the Dreamtime.* Sydney/London. Rev. ed.
GOLSON, J. 1971. Australian Aboriginal Food Plants. In: MULVANEY, D. J.; GOLSON, J. (eds.), *Aboriginal Man and Environment in Australia.* Canberra. pp. 196–238.
GOULD, R. A. 1980. *Living Archaeology.* New York.
JONES, R. 1969. Fire-stick Farming. *Aust. nat. Hist.*, Vol. 16, pp. 224–8.
LEE, R. B.; DEVORE, I. (eds) 1968. *Man the Hunter.* Chicago, Ill.
LOURANDOS, H. 1985. Intensification and Australian Prehistory. In: PRICE, T. D.; BROWN, J. A. (eds), *Prehistoric Hunter-Gatherers: The Emergence of Cultural Complexity.* Orlando, Fla. pp. 385–423.
MEEHAN, B. 1982. *Shell Bed to Shell Midden.* Canberra.
PRETTY, G. L. 1977. The Cultural Chronology of the Roonka Flat. In: WRIGHT, R. V. S. (ed.), *Stone Tools as Cultural Markers: Change, Evolution, Complexity.* Canberra. pp. 288–331.
WALSH, G. L. 1988. *Australia's Greatest Rock Art.* Bathurst.
WHITE, J. P.; O'CONNELL, J. F. 1982. *A Prehistory of Australia, New Guinea and Sahul.* Sydney/New York/London.

17

THE AMERICAS

EDITOR'S NOTE

While the chronological limits set for this volume are appropriate to part of the Old World, they are only very broadly relevant to the New World. Although this period did indeed witness, in both of them, the beginnings of metal working and an emerging interest in counting and writing systems, and saw certain societies developing into states, traditional approaches to research in the western hemisphere attach less importance than they do in Europe and Asia to cut-off points located precisely at 3000 and 700 BC, whence the difficulty of observing such artificial limits in the writing of the chapters that follow. It has, in particular, been necessary to shorten some of the contributions in order to keep to the volume's chronological framework and avoid digressions.

17.1
AN OVERVIEW OF THE CULTURAL EVOLUTION

Mario Sanoja Obediente

The overall climate began to show an increase in temperature starting from 8000 to 7000 BC, and peaking between 5000 and 3000 BC. This change had a great effect on the lives of the specialized hunters. The Pleistocene megafauna that had survived systematic extermination at their hands (Martin, 1973) had gradually died out with the disappearance of the right climatic conditions for their reproduction. These changes meant that the pattern of life of the general hunter-gatherers came to assume a decisive importance throughout the continent, with different peoples in it beginning to domesticate food plants and plants for producing raw materials. Some hunting peoples also originated ways of domesticating animals, and some coastal peoples diversified the ways in which they harvested marine, riverine and lacustrine resources during periods of changes in sea-level and consequently came to adopt sedentary types of production.

NORTH AMERICA

In about 3000 BC the Archaic cultures of peoples who lived by hunting, fishing and gathering came to occupy practically all the inhabited areas of the North American continent. They developed a highly diversified and 'stratified' strategy for harvesting natural food resources that can be seen in a great variety of regional patterns.

Western Regions

The Desert culture (Heizer and Krieger, 1956; Spencer and Jennings, 1965, pp. 40–2) was a very sophisticated social response to the adverse living conditions prevailing in the arid far western regions of North America. The assemblage of tools of production is evidence of the existence of techniques for the manufacture of baskets, the working of wood and stone, the manufacture and processing of fabrics and wickerwork, the preparation of animal skins, hunting with bows and arrows, the gathering of grasses, seeds, roots and tubers, and the use of sea shells to manufacture body ornaments. The fruit of certain trees was also gathered to make hallucinogenic drugs taken in connection with ceremonial acts.

One of the most characteristic forms of Desert culture is known as the Cochise culture (Sayles and Antevs, 1941), located in the desert region of south-eastern Arizona, where pestles for grinding seeds and fruit with hard outer coverings have been found. The conditions existing in many of the sites associated with the Cochise culture have persevered and enabled us to retrieve woven sandals of vegetable fibres and leather moccasins, bone implements, artefacts for making fire by friction and drills and sticks for sowing, which clearly indicate the characteristics of the initial process of sedentarization Archaic culture represents. The diversity of regional environments both in the far west and south-west of North America led to the development of regional traditions. In the south-west, the introduction of more productive cultigens from Mesoamerica, together with other cultural traits that were disseminated through the exchange networks between communities, helped to accelerate the disintegration of Archaic culture and the establishment of distinctly agricultural societies (Aikens, 1978; Lipe, 1978).

Archaic developed under natural conditions marked by the presence of temperate forests and a wide range of both animal and plant food resources. Manufacturing techniques also influenced similar forms of exploitation and processing of natural resources in the Archaic societies of western North America. The dominant characteristics were the grinding of plant products using pestles or milling stones, the use of axes and stone hoes, and the working of native copper by hammering to make pins and other metal objects (Fowler and Winter, 1956; Fowler, 1959a, b; Spencer and Jennings, 1965; Griffin, 1978).

In some places, such as the Eva site in Tennessee (Lewis and Kneberg, 1959), human groups also practised the gathering of bivalves from rivers and river fishing. The use of bone in the manufacture of implements and the presence of stone artefacts such as spoons and projectile points of various shapes, spear-throwers, perforators and what might be hoes show us that in the period 5200–500 BC the exploitive communities that formed the basis of Archaic society had already reached a high level of diversity and complexity in manufacturing processes; it might even have included the making of clothes and shoes, and the preparation of animal skins.

Eastern Regions

A particular expression of these all-purpose exploitive patterns is found in the Archaic communities in the north-east of what is now the United States and shows an affinity with similar processes that had been in existence since 5000 to 6000 BC in the subarctic and arctic regions of North America. In sites such as Lamoka in New York, the presence of stone implements such as hoes, gouges and semi-lunar spoons are reminiscent of the Boreal Archaic (Byers, 1959). Another very characteristic example is the 'Old Copper culture' – possibly a manufacturing process of certain peoples in the north-east, found in what are now Michigan, Wisconsin and

Minnesota. It already appears to represent the regional development of a specialized type of cold metal working, the products of which are found all along the eastern coast of the United States: pins, fish-hooks, pipes, rattles, harpoon heads, awls, semi-lunar spoons and projectile points, starting from approximately 3000 BC (Griffin, 1978, pp. 234–46).

The Archaic pattern of life, with its enhanced sedentary existence because of the increased capability to exploit all the subsistence resources of the environment, also produced particular features in the northern regions of North America. These are characterized by large cemeteries and a complex set of rituals associated with mortuary customs. A diversification of work techniques is seen in the variety of tools of production used such as scrapers, burins, spoons, hammers, hoes, projectile points and various types of bone implements (Harp, 1978, pp. 102–14).

Generally speaking, the peoples who led the Archaic pattern of existence, characterized by generalized exploitation, seem to have developed a semi-settled life-style in North America. There were camps and villages, or dwellings in caves, and spatial organization according to the type of activity with fireplaces or hearths, places to keep tools, collective burials and rubbish dumps. The apparent existence of organized exchanges of manufactured goods and raw materials over vast areas of territory shows that there were complementary types of economic activity between different communities.

The pace of the socio-historical development of the Amerindian communities of North America was similar to – and possibly in some respects faster than – that of the other Amerindian societies of the American continent up to the first millennium BC, after which time there was a loss of momentum in their capacity for change. Influential factors at work must have included not only natural environmental conditions but also, in particular, the absence of a set of cultigens that would have ushered in productive agriculture and, even more important, the absence of an intense process of interaction and contradiction within and between societies, as there was in Mesoamerica and the Central Andes. As a result, the pattern of work of Archaic society, based on the gathering of plants and river bivalves and hunting and fishing, continued to form the basis of social life in most of North America.

By about 2000 BC the quantity of edible natural resources that could be harvested, using the appropriate techniques, seems to have reached a sufficient level in eastern North America to permit the temporal association of relatively dense human groups and the birth of ruling classes able to plan extensive earthworks, as seen in Poverty Point, in lower Mississippi (Caldwell, 1958; Gibson, 1974; Fowler, 1983; Spencer and Jennings, 1965, pp. 57–60). Exchanges and circulation of raw materials and manufactured goods between distant communities was another part of the terminal forms of the Archaic and the initial phases of what is called Woodland culture. However, the non-reproductive accumulation associated with ritual consumption in burials did not lead to a liberation of the productive forces capable of ensuring the differentiation and contradiction within and between societies that would have brought about the final disintegration of the egalitarian Archaic mode of life.

In about 1000 BC, in eastern North America, there were types of farming involving local species such as sunflowers, amaranths and chenopods and the construction of terracing was intensified. The development of handicrafts such as pottery – particularly funerary urns, pipes and anthropomor-

phic figurines – ornaments made of copper and sea shells, axes of copper and spoons of obsidian was extraordinary. These work techniques constitute what is called the Hopewell culture, whose initial phase dates back to about 350 BC. It typifies the level of development reached by the Amerindian communities of eastern North America during the period in question.

With the beginning of the Archaic, south-western North America also underwent a sustained process of socio-historical development. An outstanding characteristic was the introduction of agriculture in about 2000 BC, much earlier than in the east of the continent which in all likelihood was the result of the influence of the proximity of farming population groups in the north of Mesoamerica. By about 1000 BC the human groups identified with the Mogollon culture had also introduced irrigation, appreciably increasing the area of land under cultivation and the possibility of obtaining many harvests each year.

Within a relatively short space of time, towards the end of the first millennium BC, many of the peoples of the region had adopted a sedentary pattern of life based on irrigation, an example being the Hohokam, who lived in south-western Arizona. The gradual development of types of agricultural production is also seen in an increase in population and the size and structure of the houses and villages, leading in later centuries to the development of densely populated urban areas (Di Peso, 1983).

MESOAMERICA AND NORTHERN CENTRAL AMERICA

Mexico and northern Central America constitute the extension southward of the North American continent, a geographical formation that continues through Guatemala, Honduras, El Salvador and Nicaragua as far as the Nicoya peninsula. It encompasses various environmental zones: wet lowlands covered by savannah, tropical rainforests and deciduous forest borders on mountainous cold lands. Since the earliest times this situation has resulted in the interdependence of the separate regions that developed in different environmental conditions. In about the first millennium BC this led to the establishment of markets for the distribution of manufactured goods in distant regions and intensive forms of agriculture to maintain the communities of artisans and traders that were formed in the nascent towns.

Between 5000 and 3000 BC the human groups that inhabited northern Mesoamerica, in the valley of Tehuacán and Oaxaca, were already carrying out the cultivation and domestication of plants for food, some of which were kidney beans, chili, avocados and maize, or to produce raw materials such as gourds for the manufacture of handicrafts. After a fairly short period of time they created villages with quite dense populations, the inhabitants of which could live stable lives almost throughout the year, supplementing the food derived from farming with hunting, fishing and gathering. A similar process occurred in the valley of Mexico around the lakeside beaches of the basin of Lake Chalco-Xochimilco (Niederberger, 1979). In contrast with the model of sedentarization and agricultural development in semi-arid areas advanced for Mesoamerica in previous works (McNeish, 1971), the evidence derived from Chalco-Xochimilco indicates a process of alternating sedentarization occurring in optimum bioclimatic zones in which there existed side by side plant species such as maize (*Zea*), possibly domesticated between 3000 and 2000 BC, Graminaceae, which included amaranth and physalis, and plants such as capsicum and curcubita. These added to a diet also derived from the hunting of lake birds, tortoises, small rodents and, to a lesser degree, deer.

Generally speaking, between 3000 and 800 BC there was a considerable increase in agricultural production and a development of handicrafts such as pottery, weaving and stone working. In many areas, for example the Tehuacán Valley, the increasing area of land under cultivation seems to have indicated the need to control a water supply that was scarce but necessary for maintaining and increasing agricultural production. By 800 BC there were already irrigation canal systems for diverting water from brooks and streams and storing it in reservoirs for future use. The existence of irrigation systems made it possible to establish farmland in areas far away from watercourses and to grow different crops during the year on the same plot, thereby stimulating population growth and giving the people greater protection against starvation and drought.

By 1000 BC an established pattern of village life already existed in Mesoamerica. In areas like the Valley of Mexico, the Oaxaca Valley and the Gulf coast, towns with a fairly dense population had established themselves as political and administrative centres for a number of lesser, dependent villages. The coast of the Gulf of Mexico witnessed the growth of populated centres such as San Lorenzo and La Venta (Flannery, 1968) in which there was organized communal work. The building of structures such as pyramids and temples that reflect organizational, political and religious needs testify to the process of the disintegration of egalitarian society.

Starting from 1100 BC, Olmec society, with its administrative and ceremonial centre at La Venta, became the motive force behind an extensive network of exchange of raw materials and manufactured goods that reached vast areas of Mesoamerica. In about AD 500 the centre of gravity of Olmec society moved toward the Oaxaca Valley, where the preplanned construction of the city of Monte Alban was begun.

This process began to occur in other parts of Mesoamerica. The growing use of goods made of jade, magnetite, haematite and basalt, together with the prospecting for and exploitation of these raw materials in some places which were very far from the urban centres, led to the social differentiation of labour within urban and rural communities. The need to expand the systems of agricultural production that underpinned the urban organization of Mesoamerica grew from an ever greater concentration of people in the cities in which the workshops for processing raw materials and the structures that controlled their movements to other areas were located.

A process that was basically similar to that of the Valley of Mexico was also set in motion in the south of Mexico and Belize. Beginning in 2500 BC with small villages of horiculturist hunters (Hammond, 1977), the Maya by 1250 BC had achieved farming systems based on the cultivation of fields with ridges along rivers, enabling them to farm throughout the year independent of their seasonal flooding.

SOUTHERN CENTRAL AMERICA, NORTHERN SOUTH AMERICA, THE ANTILLES AND BRAZIL

Between 5000 and 3000 BC southern Central America, northern South America, the Antilles and Brazil were inhabited by human groups that still practised all-purpose exploitive techniques. A large part of the Pacific, Caribbean and Atlantic coasts was inhabited by groups of marine gatherers whose subsistence depended essentially on hunting, sea and riparian fishing and the gathering of molluscs.

Many of these groups of marine gatherers who exploited stable resources co-existed with other groups who lived inland and subsisted by gathering or accidentally cultivating food plants, hunting or fishing. The possibility thus existed for the beginnings of a semi-sedentary pattern of existence in some coastal areas, and this sometimes led to the adoption of an agricultural village life pattern.

From 3000 BC there were great changes in the way food was obtained in the south of Panama. This might have occurred by the use of experimental farming methods begun in the Talamanca phase and the Boquete phase, characterized by a rudimentary assemblage of stone tools, culminating between 950 ± 70 BC and 350 ± 75 BC with the appearance of pottery and diversified types of subsistence that included not only plant cultivation but also that of maize (Linares, 1975; Linares and Ranere, 1971; Ranere, 1972, 1976). Various places on the Pacific coast· also witnessed the parallel development of communities of marine gatherers, which are typified by the Monagrillo phase (Willey and McGimsey, 1954, p. 136), during which, by 2500 BC, we find pottery being manufactured and possibly pestles and stones used for milling, showing that plant foods were processed. The work carried out in this region by Piperno, through the study of lithophytes, has borne out previous work showing the possible use of cereals in the diet of human groups starting from 4900 BC, and proposing possible evidence of slash-and-burn agriculture by 3000 BC in communities without pottery (Piperno, 1989).

By about 3000 BC the settlement sites of hunter-gatherer societies in north-eastern Venezuela were found on the banks of the lagoons and in the estuaries that had formed in river basins inland as a result of the rise in sea-level that took place between 5000 and about 2000 BC. The human groups in these locations could exploit the abundant animal resources of the extensive mangrove swamps bordering the lagoons and estuaries, gather the varied endemic plant species and hunt the abundant terrestrial and riparian fauna around their settlements. Between 3000 and 2600 BC the presence of axes, hoes, pestles for milling and plates of polished stones, net sinkers, bone harpoons and projectile points reveals the possible existence of methods of food production that characterize true village life (Sanoja, 1989a, 1989b).

Starting from very early times, communities practising the gathering pattern spread to the Lesser and Greater Antilles. Evidence can be found in various sites in the Dominican Republic, dating back to about 2000–3000 BC, of a similar context of production tools associated with the gathering and processing of indigenous plants, such as Zania integrifolia, that were used to make flour and bake bread using a set of techniques similar to those employed in the processing of bitter cassava (Veloz Maggiolo, 1976, Vol. I).

Without any doubt, Manihot esculenta Crantz was cultivated in the lower Orinoco, starting about 1000 BC, and in the middle Orinoco, from about 700 BC (Sanoja, 1979, pp. 262–6; Vargas, 1981, pp. 461–9; Sanoja and Vargas, 1983). It was linked with Barrancas and Ronquín pottery traditions whose presence in these regions could signify a process derived from communities living on the eastern slopes of the Peruvian or Ecuadorian Andes, or the lower Magdalena in Colombia (Sanoja, 1979, pp. 321–3).

From quite early times the gathering societies in the northeast of Venezuela, like those on Guyana's Atlantic coast, seem to have found, by accident or through experiment, new methods of cultivation – which did not, however, succeed in changing the basically exploitive character of these societies. Venezuela's gathering societies seem to have led an independent existence until 600 BC, when they began to be influenced by the communities of ceramist horticulturists that had been developing in the Orinoco basin.

By approximately 3000 BC the Brazilian coast, especially the southern coast, was inhabited by long-established groups of marine gatherers. They derived their subsistence essentially from the exploitation of shellfish found in the brackish waters of the estuaries and lagoons. Occasionally, whales beached on the coast, peccaries and the wild fruits that could be gathered in the countryside bordering on the coastal slopes contributed to their subsistence (Hurt, 1974, pp. 20–1).

In the interior of Brazil other groups belonging to what is known as the Brazilian Archaic also lived by hunting, river fishing and the gathering of land and river gastropods. They lived in rocky shelters and open sites and continued a pattern of life that began thousands of years before (Sanoja, 1982a, pp. 25–7; Schmitz, 1987).

Beginning in 1000 BC a substantial change took place with the appearance of groups of agriculturalist ceramists on Brazil's northern coast. They may have remote origins in the Mina phase (Simões, 1981), between 3000 and 1600 BC, in which there was already the coastal gathering of sea shellfish, associated with the production of pottery and the use of stone tools that might indicate the processing of plant foods. This is consistent with the evidence of maize and cassava cultivation in Rio de Janeiro, Espirito Santo and Minas Gerais between 2144 and 1644 BC (Schmitz, 1987).

The region of the lower Amazon contains evidence, dating to about 980 BC, of groups of ceramist potters belonging to what is known as the Ananatuba phase (Meggers and Evans, 1957), which also reveals evidence of plant cultivation and average-sized villages. As in the lower Orinoco, the characteristics of the early pottery found in the Mina and Ananatuba sites seem to indicate the result of a process derived from other societies of early ceramist horticulturists in northeastern Colombia. Such a theory is hardly plausible, however, given the lack of development of the forces of production in those societies, which were redesigning their productive processes and the functioning of their social organization to create a sedentary pattern of life.

Similarly, for the period between 1800 and 1000 BC there is evidence of pottery-making communities belonging to the Tutiscayno phase (Lathrap, 1959; 1970), in the forest of the Peruvian Amazonas. They derived their subsistence from the gathering of land and freshwater gastropods, and although there is no direct or indirect evidence of cultivation it is possible that they practised the cultivation and domestication of Manihot esculenta, already known in north-western Colombia, starting from 4000 BC (Sanoja, 1982a, p. 145).

Perhaps one of the most successfully linked sequences in the transition from exploitive to productive social patterns in the north of South America is to be found in the lower Magdalena, Colombia, where, from 4000 to 3000 BC, the cultivation and processing of Manihot esculenta in the form of cassava flour existed side by side with the making of pottery in a typical context of marine and riparian gathering and terrestrial hunting (Sanoja, 1982a, pp. 46–53; 1982b, pp. 166–72; Reichel-Dolmatoff, 1965, 1985). The processing of Manihot esculenta to produce food with characteristics different from the natural raw material represents genuine technological innovation. It made the daily consumption of food possible without the daily gathering of roots from sown fields and the accumulation of food reserves and surpluses for future consumption. It also made the use of such reserves and surpluses possible for trade with other, non-agricultural, communities.

In northern South America the domestication of the cassava greatly influenced human groups. The sophisticated technical processes used to transform bitter cassava to cassava flour spread with remarkable speed throughout northern America and, in many cases, created the right conditions for the development of sedentary village life patterns. This happened in the lower Magdalena, for example, where in about 1000 BC there appeared communities of agriculturalist ceramists such as Malambo (Angulo Valdez, 1962, 1981), which showed a progressive emphasis on agricultural labour and the gradual abandonment of hunting, fishing and the collecting of shellfish as the basic means of subsistence.

The area of the Pacific coast now occupied by the present-day republics of Ecuador and Peru and the northern part of Chile gives us a clearer vision of the historical process between 3000 and 700 BC that led to the achievement of substantial changes in the lives of the Amerindian communities. These communities changed from egalitarian tribal patterns to the beginnings of the socially stratified state, a unique phenomenon in the South American continent.

In about 2300 BC the pattern of life of the peoples living on the Ecuadorian coast underwent profound change. At about that time there were already densely populated settlements covering vast areas. There were houses with domed roofing arranged in rectangular blocks, monticules – possibly, the foundations of public buildings – arranged around a square, and evidence of an underground chamber for the burial of individuals who held high rank in the community (Patterson, 1981, p. 300). A similar process took place on the desert coast of Peru and northern Chile.

Agriculture may possibly have already reached the Peruvian coast by about 4000 BC as a result of the influence of the highland peoples who, starting from 5720 BC, were already cultivating Phaseolus lunatus, Phaseolus vulgaris, and manufacturing textiles using vegetable fibres (Kaplan et al., 1973). Ayacucho's highland localities contain what may be evidence for this same period of the early domestication of plants and animals during the Jaywa phase (McNeish et al., 1970, p. 3), in association with bone vestiges of Lama glama and Cavia porcellus, which would seem to bear witness to the beginnings of animal domestication. This latter element is probably a significant aspect of the process of sedentarization that may have occurred in the central Andes and northern Chile, where groups of former hunters may have reached the sedentary stage by becoming keepers of llamas, alpacas and vicuña (Nuñez, 1994).

Plant domestication had a profound social and economic influence on the Peruvian coast among societies of gatherers, leading to a process of growing sophistication in social organization. The presence of cultivated cotton and the manufacture of textiles was a milestone in the historical evolution of the coast. Its introduction marked the beginning of a long tradition of excellence that was to characterize both coastal societies and those on the high plateaux of Peru until the sixteenth century AD.

The progression of Peru's coastal and highland regions into the Neolithic period was made possible by intense social interchange between the people of the two regions, a factor which seems to have been absent in Ecuador. Also on the Peruvian coast, dating to around the beginning of the second millennium BC, are found vast sites with monumental buildings, such as Chuquitanta, in which there are dwelling houses, palaces, terraces, platforms, monticules and so on, built of stone and adobe. By the end of the second millennium BC there were already irrigation systems in the coastal valleys, which considerably increased agricultural productive capacity, thus promoting an extraordinary increase in population and the division of society into social hierarchies. This anticipated state forms of political organization to control the production and exchange of manufactured goods and raw materials between the coastal populations and those of the Peruvian highlands (Patterson, 1981, pp. 302–3; Moseley, 1975, pp. 103–19; Lumbreras, 1983, pp. 34–6).

The various communities on the Peruvian coast and highlands lived in close contact with each other, forming a vast network of contacts that paved the way for the establishment of sophisticated integrated socio-political systems which regulated their historical stages of development by ensuring that the individual types of production of the different regions complemented each other. An example of this can be seen in the emergence of Chavín de Huántar in the Mosna Valley, in the north of the Peruvian Andes, with an iconography that reveals the fusion of related concepts and ideas both with the woodland areas of the eastern Andes and the highlands and coastal regions of Peru. Chavín seems to have been a ceremonial centre specializing in the production of information on climatic cycles, which was vital for agricultural production, in exchange for payment in the form of manufactured goods and raw materials obtained from the communities receiving the service (Patterson, 1981, pp. 306–7).

By about 500 BC the central Andes had introduced almost all the technological advances that were to foster the development of the Andean state societies towards the types of supra-regional political unions that characterized the region during the sixteenth century of our era.

BIBLIOGRAPHY

AIKENS, M. C. 1978. The Far West. In: JENNINGS, J. (ed.), *Ancient Americas*. San Francisco. pp. 131–82.

ANGULO VALDEZ, C. 1962. Evidencias de la Serie Barrancoide en el norte de Colombia. *Rev. Colombiana Antropol.* (Bogotá), Vol. 11.

—— 1981. *La tradición Malambo*. Bogotá.

BYERS, D. S. 1959. The Eastern Archaic: Some Problems and Hypotheses. *Am. Antiq.* (Washington, D.C.), Vol. 24, pp. 233–318.

CALDWELL, J. R. 1958. *Trend and Tradition in the Prehistory of the Eastern United States*. American Anthropological Association. (Mem., 88.)

CORREAL, G.; HAMMEN, T. VAN DER. 1977. *Investigaciones arqueológicas en los Agrigos Rocosos de Tequendama*. Bogotá.

DI PESO, C. 1983. Las sociedades nucleares de Norteamérica: La Gran Chichimeca. In: ACADEMIA NACIONAL DE LA HISTORIA, *Historia General de América*. Caracas. Vol. 7.

FLANNERY, K. V. 1968. The Olmec and the Valley of Oaxaca: A Model for Interregional Interaction in Formative Times. In: BENSON, E. (ed.), *Dumbarton Oaks Conference on the Olmec*. Washington, D.C.

FOWLER, M. 1959a. Modoc Rock Shelter: An Early Archaic Site in Southern Illinois. *Am. Antiq.* (Washington, D.C.), Vol. 24, pp. 257–70.

—— 1959b. *Summary Report of Modoc Rock Shelter, 1952, 1953, 1955, 1956*. Illinois.

—— 1983. Las sociedades nucleares de Norteamérica: Llanos, Praderas y el Este. In: ACADEMIA NACIONAL DE LA HISTORIA,

Historia general de América. Caracas.

FOWLER, M.; WINTERS, H. 1956. *Modock Rock Shelter. Preliminary Report*. Illinois State Museum.

GIBSON, J. L. 1974. Proverty Point: The First American Chiefdom. *Archaeol.* (New York), Vol. 27, No. 2, pp. 97–105.

GRIFFIN, J. B. 1978. The Midlands and Northeastern United States. In: JENNINGS, J. (ed.), *Ancient Native Americans*. San Francisco. pp. 221–80.

HAMMOND, N. 1977. The Earliest Maya. *Sci. Am.* (New York), Vol. 236, No. 4, pp. 116–33.

HARP, E. 1978. Pioneer Cultures of the Sub-Arctic and the Arctic. In: JENNINGS, J. (ed.), *Ancient Native Americans*. Calif.

HEIZER, R. F.; KRIEGER, A. D. 1956. *The Archaeology of Humbolt Cave*. University of California. (Pub. am. Archaeol. Ethnol., 47.1.)

HURT, W. 1974. *The Interrelationship between the Natural Environment and Four Sambaquís*. Bloomington, Ind. (Occas. Pap. Monogr., 1.)

HURT, W.; HAMMEN, T. VAN DER; CORREAL, G. 1976. *El Abra Rock Shelter, Sabana de Bogotá, Colombia, South America. The Quaternary of Colombia*. Bloomington, Ind. Vol. 2. (Occas. Pap. Monogr., 2.)

KAPLAN, L.; LYNCH, T.; SMITH, C. 1973. Early Cultivated Beans (*Phaseolus vulgaris*) from an Intermontane Peruvian Valley. *Science* (Washington, D.C.), Vol. 179, No. 4086, pp. 76–7.

LATHRAP, D. 1959. The Cultural Sequence at Yarinacocha, Eastern Peru. *Am. Antiq.* (Washington, D.C.), Vol. 23, No. 4, pp. 379–88.

—— 1970. *The Upper Amazon*. New York.

LEWIS, T. M. N.; KNEBERG, M. 1959. The Archaic Culture in the Middle South. *Am. Antiq.* (Washington, D.C.), Vol. 25, pp. 165–83.

LINARES, O. 1975. De la Recolección a la Agricultura en el Itsmo. *Rev. Panameña Antropol.*, Vol. 1, pp. 9–27.

LINARES, O.; RANERE, A. J. 1971. Human Adaptation to the Tropical Forest of Western Panamá. *Archaeol.* (New York), Vol. 24, No. 4, pp. 346–55.

LIPE, W. 1978. The Southwest. In: JENNINGS, J. D. (ed.) *Ancient Native Americans*. San Francisco. pp. 327–402.

LUMBRERAS, L. 1983. Las sociedades nucleares de Suramérica. In: ACADEMIA NACIONAL DE LA HISTORIA, *Historia General de América*. Caracas.

MARTIN, P. 1973. The Discovery of America. *Science* (Washington, D.C.), Vol. 179, pp. 969–74.

MCNEISH, R. et al. 1970. *Second Annual Report of the Ayacucho Archaeological Botanical Project*. Andover, Mass.

—— 1971. Speculations about How and Why Food Production and Village Life Developed in the Tehuacan Valley, Mexico. *Archaeol.* (New York.), Vol. 24, No. 4, pp. 307–15.

MEGGERS, B. J.; EVANS, C. 1957. *Archeological Investigations at the Mouth of the Amazon*. Washington, D.C. (Bur. am. Ethnol., Bull. 167.)

MOSELEY, M. E. 1975. *The Maritime Foundations of Andean Civilization*. Menlo Park, Calif.

NIEDERBERGER, C. 1979. Early Sedentary Economy in the Basin of Mexico. *Science* (Washington, D.C.), Vol. 203, pp. 131–42.

NUÑEZ, L. 1994. The Western Part of South America (Southern Peru, Bolivia, North-west Argentina and Chile) during the Stone Age. In: DE LAET, S. J. (ed.), *History of Humanity*. Paris/London. Vol. 1, pp. 348–62.

PATTERSON, T. 1981. *Archaeology: The Evolution of Ancient Societies*. Princeton, N.J.

PIPERNO, D. 1989. Non Affluent Foragers: Resource Availability, Seasonal Shortages and the Emergence of Agriculture in Panamanian Tropical Forests. In: HARRIS, D.; HILLMAN, G. (eds) *Foraging and Farming* London. pp. 538–54.

RANERE, A. 1972. Ocupación Precerámica de las Tierras Altas de Chiriquí. In: SIMPOSIO NACIONAL DE ANTROPOLOGIA, ARQUEOLOGIA Y ETNOHISTORIA DE PANAMÁ, 2. *Actas*. Panamá. pp. 197–207.

—— 1976. The Preceramic of Panamá: The View from the Interior. In: ROBINSON, L. (ed.), *Proceedings of the First Puerto Rican Archeology*. San Juan, Fundación Arqueológica, Antroplógica e Histórica de Puerto Rico. (Inf., 1.)

REICHEL-DOLMATOFF, G. 1965. Excavaciones Arqueológicas en Puerto Hormiga (Departamento de Bolivar). Bogotá, Universidad de los Andes. (Antropol., 2.)

—— 1985. *Monsú. Un sitio arqueológico*. Bogotá.

SANOJA, M. 1979. Las Culturas Formativas del Oriente de Venezuela: La Tradición Barrancas del Bajo Orinoco. Academia Nacional de la Historia. Col. Estudios, Monografías y Ensayos, No. 6. Caracas.

—— 1982a. De la Recolección a la Agricultura. *Historia General de América*. Vol. 3. Caracas.

—— 1982b. *Los Hombres de la Yuca y el Maíz*. Caracas.

—— 1989a. From Foragings to Food Production in North-Eastern Venezuela and the Caribbean. In: HARRIS, D.; HILLMAN, G. (eds), *Foraging and Farming*. London. pp. 523–37.

—— 1989b. Origins of Cultivation around the Gulf of Paria, North-Eastern Venezuela. *Research*, Vol. 5. pp. 448–58. Washington D.C.

SANOJA, M.; VARGAS, I. 1983. New Lights on the Prehistory of Eastern Venezuela. In: WENDORF, F.; CLOSE, A. (eds), *Advances in New Archaeology*, Vol. 2, pp. 205–44. New York.

SAYLES, E. B.; ANTEVS, E. 1941. *The Cochise Culture. Medallion Papers*. Vol. 29.

SCHMITZ, P. I. 1987. Prehistoric Hunters and Gatherers of Brazil. *Journal of World Prehistory*. Vol. 1, No. 1.

SIMÕES, M. 1981. Colectores-Pescadores Ceramistas do Litoral do Salgado (Pará). *Boletim do Museu Paranense Smilio*. No. 78, Belem, Pará, Brazil.

SPENCER, R.; JENNINGS, D. 1965. *The Native Americans*. New York.

VARGAS, I. 1981. *Investigaciones Arqueológicas en Parmana: Los sitios de La Gruta y Ronquín, Edo, Guarico. Venezuela*. Academia Nacional de la Historia. Caracas. (Serie Estudios, Monografías y Ensayos 20.)

VELOZ MAGGIOLO, M. 1976. *Medioambiente y Adaptación Humana en la Prehistoria de Santo Domingo*. Vol. I. Editorial de la Universidad Autónoma de Santo Domingo. (Col. Historia y Sociedad 24.)

WILLEY, G.; MCGIMSEY, C. 1954. *The Monagrillo Culture of Panamá*. Cambridge, Mass. (Pap. Peabody Mus. Archaeol. Ethnol., 49, No. 2.)

I7.2
RELIGION AND ART

José Alcina Franch

The chronological period covered by this volume essentially corresponds to the stage called, in the New World, the Formative. For reasons and arguments that have been summarized by North American archaeologist James A. Ford (1969, pp. 1–5), English and Latin American literature on the subject tends to use the term 'Formative', which Ford in turn would divide into two phases: a Colonizing Formative (3000–1200 BC), and a Theocratic Formative (1200–400 BC), beyond which would emerge a Proto-Classic phase itself announcing the full flowering of civilization (Fig. 89).

In the following pages we will be referring to the now abundant evidence gathered in those three areas which correspond to 'Nuclear America': to wit, Mesoamerica, an Intermediate area, and the Andean area. In each of these regions, numerous cultures unearthed over the last few years are yielding rich evidence concerning the birth of the first religious systems, especially in the two civilizations located,

respectively, in Mesoamerica and in the Andes, that is, the Olmec and Chavín civilizations.

MESOAMERICA

The sites of the most important archaeological sequences for this period are concentrated in the Valley of Mexico, in Tlaxcala, in the Valley of Oaxaca, in Chiapas, along the Gulf Coast (southern Veracruz and Tabasco), in western Mexico, and on the highlands of Guatemala. The two most ancient cultural sites in this region are to be found at Tlapacoya-Zohapilco by the lake of Chalco (Niederberger, 1976) and in the Mexican Valley basin, where the sequence includes the following phases: Zohapilco (2500–2000 BC); Nevada (1400–1200 BC); Ayotla (1200–1000 BC); and Manantial (1000–800 BC). The Terremoto-Tlaltengo location confirms

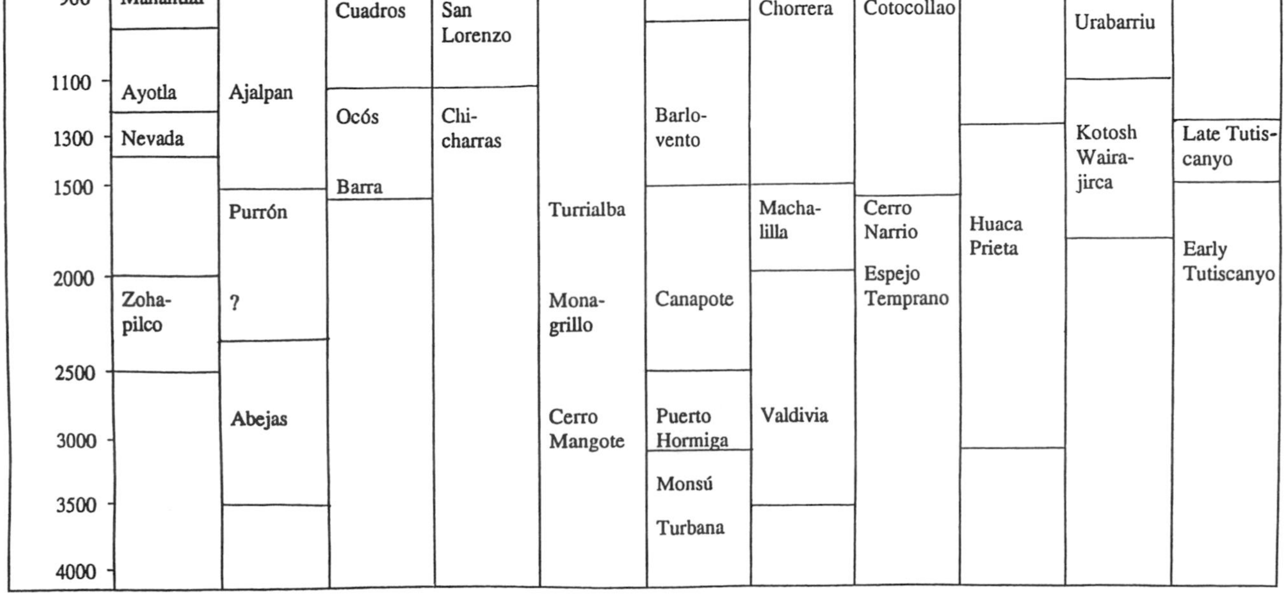

Years	Valley of Mexico	Valley of Tehuacán	Chiapas	Southern Veracruz & Tabasco	Central America	Colombia	Ecuador: coast	Ecuador: highlands	Peru: coast	Peru: highlands	Peru: eastern regions
500		Santa María								Chakinaui	
	Zacatenco		Conchas			Malambo				Ofrendas	
700											
900	Manantial		Cuadros	San Lorenzo		Chorrera		Cotocollao		Urabarriu	
1100	Ayotla	Ajalpan				Barlo-vento					
1300	Nevada		Ocós	Chi-charras						Kotosh Waira-jirca	Late Tutis-canyo
1500			Barra								
		Purrón			Turrialba		Macha-lilla	Cerro Narrio	Huaca Prieta		
2000		?				Canapote		Espejo Temprano			Early Tutiscanyo
	Zoha-pilco				Mona-grillo						
2500											
		Abejas				Puerto Hormiga	Valdivia				
3000					Cerro Mangote						
						Monsú					
3500						Turbana					
4000											

Figure 89 The Formative period.

human occupation in the course of the Ayotla phase, in this case by an agricultural population specifically adapted to a lake-dwelling environment.

In general, one might approximately describe the more ancient phases – down to 1200 BC – in terms of egalitarian or tribal societies, whereas from that date onwards we observe a considerable increase in evidence and data pointing to and confirming an incessant process of social evolution. Here, ever more complex social and political organization is attended by increasing complication in the field of art, which, in turn, obviously implies ever greater complexity in the religious content of such forms of artistic expression. Within the range of what we know as Mesoamerica, we observe an especially significant increase in the particular region which Alfonso Caso would call 'Mesoamerica's Mesopotamia', that is, the southern zone of Veracruz along with neighbouring sectors of Chiapas and Tabasco, forming the heartland of the so-called Olmec civilization. The finds accumulated over the last few years, especially in the region of Guerrero, make it difficult to argue for, or at least render doubtful, a so-called Olmec expansion. What seems rather to have happened is a simultaneous social and political evolution, both in the valleys of Mexico and Oaxaca and in the territory of Guerrero and along the Gulf Coast, all coming to crystallize in the last region where the first ceremonial centres make their appearance at La Venta, San Lorenzo and Tres Zapotes, with their monumental sculpture, altars and stelae.

At the same time, one should stress that, along with the rural way of life which apparently prevailed in Terremoto-Tlaltengo, an urban or semi-urban way of life also seems to have developed around, say, Tlapacoya or Tlatilco, as is the case with the capital, or with the towns and small cities typifying organization into lordships or chieftainships (Alcina, 1991, pp. 32–5).

It is especially in the course of the Ayotla phase that there occur, in the Valley of Mexico, important developments in social hierarchy and in trade between different regions, which again mark 'the crystallization of certain institutionalized forms of administrative authority'. Through such manifestations of political organization in Mesoamerica, there also appears what I have termed – for the Andean region – a 'sanctuary-market-fair' complex (Alcina, 1990), that is to say, a convergence between economic interests, religious cults and multi-faceted fairs, involving such activities as redistribution of goods, popular rejoicing, and religious pilgrimage. Many of the figurines discovered in Tlatilco or Tlapacoya point directly or indirectly to the existence of such fairs. They depict dancers of both sexes, musicians playing the drum and the ocarina (or *omechicahuastli*), contortionists and acrobats, while others represent true shamans or priests embellished with ever more complex trappings – such as head-dresses and other adornments – which specifically distinguish or emphasize the importance of the figures wearing them (Fig. 90).

A very common element, charged with strictly sacred significance, was the mask, which was buried by the side of the body of its owner but never on the body's face. One is tempted to think that a number of these masks were used exclusively by certain brotherhoods, while others served groups of mimers or societies of dancers, reciters or buffoons.

As is characteristic of all Mesoamerican art, but most especially in the tradition of Central Mexico from the time of the Formative period under consideration here, a multitude of symbols and emblems confronts us. These amount

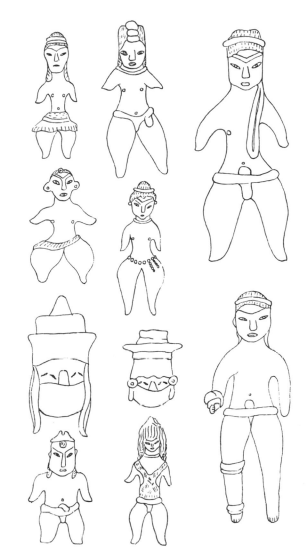

Figure 90 Figurines from Tlatilco, Valley of Mexico (after Pina Chan, 1958).

to a true form of writing, that is, they transmit specific messages concerning a vision of the cosmos and a religious system. From the lengthy series of these symbols studied by Joralemon (1971), one may especially distinguish the following: a sign in the form of a U; a five-pointed motif or 'quintet'; a four-petalled flower; a human hand; and the feathered serpent.

For a number of authors, including Joralemon, such signs and symbols indicate thoroughly formalized divinities, amongst whom Joralemon has managed to distinguish as many as ten. These include a polymorphic dragon, that is, a reptile further endowed with the attributes of feline and bird and also associated with the earth and with agrarian cults; a mythic, winged monster-bird with forked tongue; an anthropomorphic dwarf; a god that is half-man and half-jaguar; a serpent-god with the attributes of a bird; and so forth.

While these signs and symbols have been interpreted differently by other authors, it remains permissible for us to think that here, just as in the case of the México art of the post-Classic phase, we find ourselves in the presence of a complex language with grammatical elements of a metaphorical character which render it exceptionally difficult to interpret (Alcina et al., 1992, pp. 31–7). Such use of metaphor might in turn explain why certain glyphs or graphic signs appear in different contexts, with widely varying associations and thereby with distinct global meanings, although we can attribute to each one of these signs a given, single, specific significance. What all this means is not only that the religious system and cosmic vision of the peoples of the highlands in the Ayotla-Manantial phases (1200–800 BC) had become exceedingly complex, but that their corresponding artistic expression already presented a highly elaborate system which we shall meet again in the Classic and post-Classic phases in this same region.

The most important of the cultures known to us is that of the Olmecs, whose artistic style covered an extensive region but whose chief focus of activity was to be found along the coast of the Gulf of Mexico. Here the first cities or ceremonial centres arose: La Venta, Cerro de las Mesas, Tres Zapotes, San Lorenzo and so on.

Of the various forms of Olmec artistic production, undoubtedly the most outstanding are its works of sculpture and in relief. In turn, the most noteworthy and famous of all Olmec sculptures are the colossal heads, of which as many as fourteen examples are known. Of gigantic proportions – for they range up to 3 m in height and may weigh as much as 10 tons – these depict faces of negroid appearance with flaring nostrils, fleshy lips and bulging eyes, topped by a close-fitting head-dress extending down each side of the head. Since these figures do not represent gods – for they lack the distinguishing characteristics and symbolic signs which might allow such an interpretation – they may rather depict 'lineage leaders' or 'ancestors'. Such representations would be justified in a society which, in all probability, was politically organized into various chieftainships.

Olmec art is characterized by two apparently contradictory styles. On the one hand, it offers us a highly realistic style, as in the case of the colossal heads. On the other, it goes to the extreme of a style so highly abstract as to appear glyphic. Among typical traits of Olmec art, especially where pertaining to anthropomorphic representation, we may distinguish the so-called 'Olmec mouth', and also a V-shaped cleft or 'Olmec groove' which appears on the crania of various mythological beings depicted on different sorts of ceremonial 'axes' (Fig. 91).

In addition to the colossal heads and anthropomorphic images, other 'realistically' carved sculptures include figures generally depicted in a sitting position that occasionally resembles the attitude of Egyptian-style scribes. Others hold upon their laps either the figure of a divine child, or a sceptre, or a cylinder, or again a sacred coffer. The style of these sculptures and that of the colossal heads has been analysed by Mexican scholars; they show a degree of perfection which the arts of other Mesoamerican cultures have only rarely attained. In any event, possibly the supreme masterpiece of this whole series of seated human figures may be the sculpture known as 'The Wrestler' (*El Luchador*), from Santa María Uxpanapa (in Veracruz, Mexico). This depicts a bearded man with his legs and arms folded, but giving the impression, through the straining of his entire body, of immense physical effort.

The altars constitute an absolutely original type of sculpture whose use was to last down the centuries, especially in Mayan cities. These are great blocks of stone, shaped like prisms, on whose sides appear scenes carved in high and low relief. Many altars show a seated figure, similar to those mentioned above, but seen as if emerging from a cave or niche that might be interpreted as the mouth of a dragon which, in turn, could represent the god or goddess of the under-

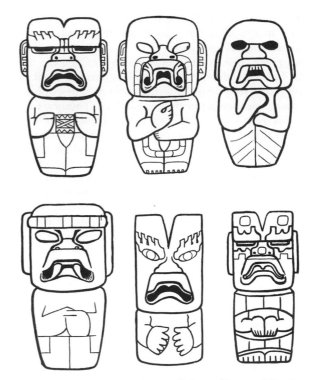

Figure 91 Olmec art: colossal axes and plaque-like axes (after Covarrubias, 1946).

world. In various instances, such anthropomorphic figures bear in their hands a divine child. Indeed many altars display upon their side panels the images of priests cradling in their arms the figure of this divine child, which is of such frequent occurrence in Olmec art.

Still in the field of monumental sculpture, we may finally mention here stelae, which, just as the altars, were thereafter to be used in profusion throughout the Mayan cultural area. Those known to us from Tres Zapotes, Cerro de las Mesas, La Venta, El Baúl, Izapa and other sites represent figures clad in complex garments and series of ornaments which in turn may depict mythological scenes which are extremely difficult for us to interpret, although we cannot entirely rule out the possibility that we may be dealing here with purely realistic representations.

From the iconographical studies of Miguel Covarrubias (1946), Philip Drucker (1952), Michael D. Coe (1972) and P. D. Joralemon (1971), we may infer that the many images populating the world of Olmec sculpture correspond to mythic figures or indeed to true divinities, many of whom were thence to find a place in the pantheon of Mesoamerica, there to develop and take on ever fuller traits in later periods and distinct cultures. In practice, the dragon-style head with its 'Olmec mouth', long jaguar's fangs and 'Olmec groove' and other ornaments over the brow, seems to have been the source for the head of the rain-god, which was to acquire various stylistic characteristics according to the different cultural regions in which it appeared, under the names of Tláloc, Chac, Cocijo or Tajín.

Another mythic form often found in this art is that of a eunuch-like dwarf or divine child, shown nestling in the arms of a priest-king or adult anthropomorphic figure. No less interesting here is the presence of such typical traits as closed eyelids and vertical blindfold, which may bespeak the appearance of a divine predecessor to the god Xipe Totec.

All this, in conjunction with the development of temple-like architectural forms, points sharply to the existence of a solid religious system, one implying a state-like political organization going beyond that of mere chieftainship or headmanship; one, indeed, with a corresponding body of priests, to which the ruler most certainly belonged.

THE INTERMEDIATE AREA

For the purposes of this chapter, we draw upon Irving Rouse's terminology (1972) to designate, as an 'intermediate area', the Central American isthmus and the northernmost reaches of the Andean region, in order to group a mass of extremely ancient clues corresponding to the Formative period examined here. In reality, the area in which these clues are found clustered is reduced to a region stretching from the Bay of Parita, in Panama, down to the immediate surroundings of Cartagena de Indias, in Colombia. Here, the sites and cultures of Cerro Mangote, Monagrillo, Puerto Hormiga, Monsú, Canapote, Barlovento and Malambo pertain to dates corresponding to the period extending from 4000 to 1000 BC, and relate without a doubt to the finds of Valdivia, Kotosh, Yarinacocha and others in the central and northern Andean region (Meggers et al., 1965, pp. 168 ff), as well as to those of the more recent civilizations belonging to the Ronquín, Barrancas and Bocachica traditions (down to 600 BC) in the Venezuelan area, which once also culturally embraced the Antilles down to 200 BC.

The most ancient manifestation of the Formative in Central America occurs around the Bay of Parita, where the site of Cerro Mangote may offer an immediate antecedent to the Monagrillo culture. The chronology of this archaeological site goes back to about 2900 BC, corresponding to a period in which pottery had not yet been introduced, although finds include hand-mills, which could be considered as proof of the existence of an agricultural or agricultural-gathering economy. For the rest, burials were relatively complex, with recourse to two different procedures, the first with the body folded over, and the second with the bones collected and interred so as to form a bundle.

The Monagrillo culture, also to be found along the Bay of Parita and flourishing c. 2140 BC, already offers us an example of a typical ceramic-producing civilization, although its level of technological and artistic development still remained rather low. In fact, Monagrillo pottery is still quite coarse, decorated with incised curvilinear motifs or with painted bands coloured red on an off-white base. Stone-cutting crafts showed progress in terms of elaboration, although they continued to follow basically the same techniques as those of the period of Cerro Mangote where the pottery, decorated with incisions of varying width, displays patterns of parallel lines ending variously in circles, dotted lines, spirals, T-figures and so forth (Willey and McGimsey, 1954). Although agriculture was the main source of food, plants and shellfish were also gathered, while hunting and fishing supplemented the diet.

In connection with these sites, we may mention that of Turrialba (Costa Rica), whose elaborate style of ceramic arts, known as 'La Montaña' (1515 BC), also shows correspondence to the pottery of the Formative period. The links between Turrialba's culture and that of the northern coast of Colombia are confirmed by the presence of baking pans, or large-size platters, typical for the baking of the *yuca* bread known in Spanish as *cazabe* (cassava).

While sites in the region of Cartagena, in Colombia, especially those of Barlovento and Puerto Hormiga, are relatively ancient, the more recent ones at Monsú (Reichel-Dolmatoff, 1985) complete the sequence in this zone and take our knowledge of the use of pottery as far back at least as the fifth millennium BC, all of which makes this area one of the most important for the Early Formative period in the entire continent. The sequence, as established since the finds at Monsú, is as follows: Turbana, Monsú, Puerto Hormiga, Canapote, Barlovento and Malambo (Reichel-Dolmatoff, 1985, pp. 53–81).

The oldest radiocarbon date corresponds to that of the Monsú period, that is, to 3350 BC. However, since the Turbana period goes back even earlier than that of Monsú, the beginnings of pottery found at Turbana could perhaps correspond to the period 3800 or even 4000 BC, which would make this particular cultural site the most ancient in the entire continent so far as the use of pottery was concerned, and hence, probably, even older than the site of Valdivia, in the Guayas basin, whose earliest date goes back only to 3500 BC. Obviously, we are far from having completely clarified the origins of pottery in the Americas, since the number of sites pertaining to the Formative period found in the area between Cartagena de Indias and Guayaquil is still quite limited. In addition, while it is probable that pottery constitutes an independent invention in the Americas, we still cannot yet entirely rule out the possibility of contacts across the Pacific, as defended by Meggers, Evans and Estrada (1965).

As the site's discoverer put it, 'the technological and aesthetic development of pottery is notable' in Monsú. The decoration here is mainly incised and geometric. The next stage, found at Puerto Hormiga, is seen in a site known for years, excavated by Reichel-Dolmatoff (1965), and chronologically belonging to the period between 3100 and 2500 BC. The culture yields us our first artistic depictions of living figures. Thus, on the rim of a large tray is a human face, partly modelled and partly incised, with eyes surrounded by a number of incised concentric circles. Other modelled and incised forms include animal figures. Abundant geometrical pottery decoration was further created by impressing clay with sea-shells or by using other means of incision.

The next stages in the sequence for the Cartagena area belong to the Canapote sites, found in a suburb of Cartagena and dating back to c. 2000 BC, and of Barlovento, set in the swamps to the north-east of Cartagena and whose radiocarbon dates range between 1500 and 1000 BC. At this stage, pottery decoration followed the lines of previous stages, with starkly simple geometric designs, incised or engraved.

The cultural phases to which we have just referred are connected with settlements of extended families in large-dimensioned, 'longhouse'-type dwellings, with an economy based on incipient agriculture. Cultivation of yucca and manioc predominated, along with the collection of mussels and other shellfish, fishing, and the hunting of an abundant and varied wildlife typical of an environment of forest and savannah, whose hot climate tended, however, towards desiccation, a characteristic of the Holocene period from around 7000 BC.

The ultimate stage to be considered in this sequence corresponds to the Malambo culture (1120 BC to AD 70), whose artistic development is extraordinarily rich in representations of anthropomorphic faces as well as in generally female figurines, and also in pottery vessels whose decoration combines modelling with incision, and whose style shows kinship with the deep-grooved ware of Venezuela.

Finally, the site of Zipacón, not far from Bogotá, manifests a transitional society whose agriculture was supplemented by hunting and gathering. The date 1230 BC is for the moment the earliest which we have for the Bogotá savannah region (Correal and Pinto, 1983).

THE ANDEAN AREA

The last of the great areas where we will be dealing with the transformation from a world of magic and myth to one of religious experience and artistic expression – the whole process characteristic of the Formative age in America – is the Andean. This area in turn may be subdivided into two regions or sub-areas: a northern Andean area, including a well-documented sequence along the coast – Valdivia, Machalilla and Chorrera – as well as various highland sites; and a central Andean area with a number of early sites such as Huaca Prieta, Kotosh and others, and also a great pristine civilization: Chavín.

The sequence offered by the Guayas basin, on the coast of Ecuador, begins with the Valdivian culture, the discovery of whose site – Valdivia – yielded at the time the oldest dated pottery on the American continent, 3200 BC (Meggers et al., 1965); today, after the discoveries at Real Alto, an even earlier date, 3545 BC, can be cited (Damp, 1988, pp. 25–32), which accords better with the period of Monsú in Colombia. Valdivian culture in general is more generally known at present than any other Formative culture in South America, as we not only possess dates from Valdivia itself, but also from San Pedro, Real Alto, Loma Alta and El Encanto (on the island of La Puná).

The main focus of Valdivian art is centred on the so-called images of Venus, generally female figurines which appear in profusion in all the sites of this culture. Such figurines of Venus are usually moulded and are only about 10 cm in length; occasionally they may be larger and, if so, they are hollow. In all of them, the breasts and pubic zone are especially emphasized, since these statuettes are generally naked or only scantily clad, so that their modern popular name finds ample justification in their marked sexual character. Among other features, the modelling of their hair is stressed through burnishing or incisions attempting to reproduce the lines of individual hairs, occasionally painted red or green when not left in the natural colour of the pottery. Hands usually meet or cross in repose under the breasts, although they sometimes rise to meet the mouth in a somewhat tentative gesture. Some of the larger, hollow figurines show a swelling of the belly, depicting pregnancy, and include a pebble inside allowing the statuette when shaken to function as a rattle. Other figures have two heads, similar to a number of examples found in the Valley of Mexico and elsewhere.

The main question, still unresolved, concerns the function of these figurines. A number of writers have suggested that they were used for healing by shamans and medicine men. We believe that most of these figurines, as in Mesoamerica, could have been used for propitiatory agricultural rites. Nor can we rule out that they were somehow related to the use of such drugs as the coca leaf or various inhaled hallucinogens.

Several writers have suggested that the geometric decoration of Valdivian I and II pottery, which shows frequently recurring designs of the same type, could be interpreted as highly abstract serpent and feline representations, which would confirm both the relation of this culture to a forest environment and its link to the civilization of Chavín (Damp, 1988).

Later developments following on the Valdivian culture – the phases at Machalilla and Chorrera (1500–500 BC) – both deepen and amplify the characteristics of the earliest pottery culture, and attain, especially in Chorrera, what has been defined as an initial pan-Ecuadoran range. The ceramic art of this culture is without doubt most noteworthy not only from an aesthetic point of view, but also regarding its technique. While the characteristic of vessels of the Machalilla style is the so-called 'stirrup-handle', this is replaced in the Chorrera period by a large tubular spout at the top of the vase along with a generally flattened handle. As for figurines in the maté style, the level of perfection in execution and classical beauty becomes truly exceptional.

Despite the fact that the Formative phase in the highlands of the Andean area is much less well known than along the coast, a number of cultures and sites belonging to this period occur, including the Early Mirror (*Espejo Temprano*) culture (2200 BC) by the lake of San Pablo; the Cotocallo (1700–500 BC) near Quito; and the Cerro Narrio (2000 BC) at Cañar, near Cuenca.

The site of Cotocallo represents a village complex whose organizational characteristics are somewhat simpler than those of Real Alto on the coast. Abundant pottery finds show a geometric-type decoration which may be similarly interpreted as that on other vessels of this kind, given that the general cultural environment appears to have resembled the Valdivian. Otherwise this site has yielded us only a few isolated examples of statuettes, such as one worked into a fragment of pottery and depicting a figure seated cross-legged and wearing a turban.

In the region of the upper Amazon, several writers have discovered and studied a complex of cultures which belong to the Formative period. The most important are Tutiscayno and Kotosh. The Tutiscayno culture was discovered at the site of Tarinacocha in the Ucayali River basin. Two phases can be distinguished: an Early Tutiscayno (around 2000 BC) and a Late Tutiscayno (1500–1300 BC). As in other Formative cultures, artistic expression is found concentrated on the rim decoration of pottery, where one finds stepped edges and also what may possibly be the earliest feline representation, which, as we shall see, becomes a dominant form in the central Andes.

The culture of Kotosh Waira-Jirca (1800–1300 BC), in the Huánuco River basin, a site excavated by a Japanese archaeological mission led by Seichi Izumi (Izumi and Sono, 1963), has yielded us most noteworthy clues concerning the development of religious thought and artistic expression. The famous 'Temple of the Crossed Hands' (*Templo de las Manos Cruzadas*), with its adornments moulded of clay, constitutes without a doubt the oldest known example of the use of sculpture in the decoration of an architectural monument. In addition, the pottery decoration shows major technical and artistic complexity, implying the fusion of different ceramic traditions within this cultural centre in the Huánuco basin in the second millennium BC.

The site of Huaca Prieta, in the Valley of Chicama along the Pacific coast, was excavated by Junius B. Bird in 1946–7. (Bird and Hyslop, 1985). Huaca Prieta is a pre-pottery site (3100–1300 BC), but a considerable quantity of examples of textiles has been discovered here. Aside from geometric-type designs which are difficult to interpret, the weaving displays several representations of forms which were to become widely popular, especially in the art of Chavín, such as the condor (Bird and Hyslop, 1985, p. 165, and Figs 110–11), serpents, anthropomorphic figures and so on.

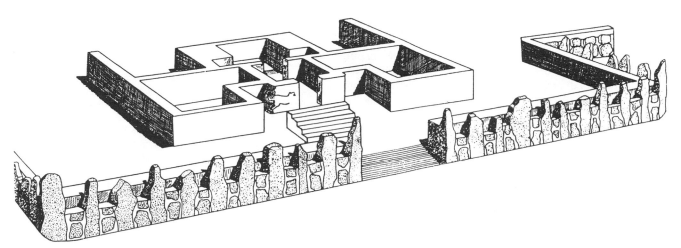

Figure 92 Suggested reconstruction of the Temple of Cerro Sechin; Chavín culture, Peru (after Hauffmann-Doig).

Finally the Chavín civilization represents a phenomenon similar in all ways to that of the Olmec civilization in Mesoamerica. This constitutes the first major area of the cultural sequence of the central Andean area, and represents the most important step in the process of artistic and religious evolution considered here (Fig. 92). From studies by Richard L. Burger (1989), and many others, we are in a position to classify the sequence of Chavín pottery according to four phases: Urabarriu (1200–800 BC); Ofrendas (800–600 BC); Chakinaui (600–400 BC); and Rocas or Janabarriu (400–300 BC). While Chavín's pottery alone – which ranks among the most accomplished artistic productions of Peru – would suffice to bear witness to this civilization's aesthetic development, this can also be verified in its sculpture in the round and in relief, whether in stone or in other materials. Chavín's art, despite the fact that it appears as a consequence of purely autonomous local development, may nevertheless be linked to other cultures, whether belonging to the same region, such as that of Huaca Prieta, or originating in neighbouring areas, such as Chorrera. Links can even be seen with the forest cultures of the eastern slopes of the Andes or the upper valleys of the Marañón. In turn, Chavín's influence makes itself felt in regions much farther to the south, both along the coast and in the Peruvian interior: Chicama, Cupisnique, Ancón, Paracas, Ayacucho and so on.

Chavín de Huántar was probably a shrine or ceremonial centre dedicated to the god Huari, serving purposes equivalent to those of the sanctuaries at La Venta or Tres Zapotes on the coast of Veracruz in Mexico. One of the most important stages in the life of this ceremonial centre is represented by the New Temple (*Templo Nuevo*) (Fig. 93), while to the

north of the site rises a no less important structure, the Temple of the Shepherd's Crook, or Hooked Staff (*Templo del Lanzón*), which actually reproduces an ancient Andean architectural model, U-shaped with a depressed circular plaza in its midst. The *Templo del Lanzón* appears to be the most ancient building in the complex. The entire structure is crisscrossed by numerous subterranean galleries: *Las Ofrendas* (The Offerings), *El Campamento* (The Encampment), *Los Laberintos* (The Labyrinths), *El Lanzón* (The Hooked Staff) and others. Lumbreras's excavations in *Las Ofrendas* suggest that this gallery corresponds to the oldest period of the temple, contemporaneous with the era when the image of *El Lanzón* was being worshipped. To the second period of the temple's construction therefore belong the galleries known as *La Portada* (The Portal), *Las Columnas* (The Pillars) and *Las Vigas Ornamentales* (The Ornamental Beams).

The religious development which created the Chavín de Huántar shrine obviously sparked a corresponding development in the figurative arts – the sculptures in the round or in relief which populate the entire area of the site.[1] Rowe (1962), through careful comparison with the ceramic arts of Paracas pertaining to the Ocucaje period, managed to establish a sequence in the sculpture, which he divides into four phases, AB, C, D and EF. To the earliest of these phases he assigns the Hooked Staff, whereas the Tello Obelisk – one of the most complex works in the Chavín style – he regards as corresponding to phase C, and the Raimond Stela as a relief most representative of the final stage.

From Chavín art there derive for the most part, without any doubt, the later artistic forms of the central Andean area. In Rowe's opinion, Chavín's art constitutes a highly complex linguistic system in which metaphorical expression is analogous to euphemism in a literary context. Rowe considers there to be three levels of increasing complexity: the first consisting of straightforward allusion; the second being indirect, allusive, or metaphorical; and the third utilizing substitution. To establish a proper analogy between literary procedure and the formulations of Chavín's art, Rowe mentions, as the main conventions: symmetry; repetition; the measure of size; and the reduction of motifs.

NOTE

1 The main works to be taken into account when studying this form of artistic expression, as was done by North American archaeologist John H. Rowe, include the following: *La*

Figure 93 Eagle from the New Temple (*Templo Nuevo*) at Chavín de Huántar, Peru (after Rowe, 1962).

Gran Imagen (The Great Image), *El Lanzón* (The Hooked Staff); *El Obelisco Tello* (The Tello Obelisk); *El Estela Raimondi* (The Raimond Stela) preserved in the Lima Museum; the eagle and hawk of *La Portada Blanca y Negra* (the Black and White Portal) of the Great Pyramid; and numerous other pieces scattered throughout the entire area covered by the Chavín site.

BIBLIOGRAPHY

ALCINA FRANCH, J. 1990. El complejo 'santuario-mercado-festival' y el origen de los centros ceremoniales en el Area Andina Septentrional. In: *Homenaje a Richard P. Schaedel*. Austin, Tex.

—— 1991. En torno al urbanismo precolombino de América: el marco teórico. *Anu. Estud. am.* (Sevilla), Vol. 48, pp. 3–47.

ALCINA FRANCH, J.; LEÓN-PORTILLA, M.; MATOS, E. 1992. *Azteca Mexica. Las culturas del México Antiguo*. Madrid. Lunwerg-Quinto Centenario.

BIRD, J. B.; HYSLOP, J. 1985. *The Preceramic Excavations at the Huaca Prieta, Chicama Valley*. Perú. New York. (Anthropol. Pap. am. Mus. nat. Hist., 62.)

BURGER, R. L. 1989. Long before the Incas. *Nat. Hist.* (New York), No. 2, pp. 66–73.

COE, M. D. 1972. Olmec Jaguars and Olmec Kings. In: BENSON, E. (ed.), *The Cult of the Feline*. Washington, D.C. pp. 1–12.

CORREAL, G.; PINTO, M. 1983. *Investigación arqueológica en el municipio de Zipacón. Cundinamarca*. Bogotá.

COVARRUBIAS, M. 1946. El arte 'olmeca' o de La Venta. *Cuad. am.* (México, D.F.), Vol. 4, pp. 153–79.

DAMP, J. 1988. *La primera ocupación Valdivia de Real Alto*. Quito, Corporación Editora Nacional. (Bibl. ecuat. Arqueol., 3.)

FORD, J. A. 1969. *A Comparison of Formative Cultures in the Americas: Diffusion of the Psychic Unity of Man*. Washington D.C.

IZUMI, S.; SONO, T. 1963. *Excavations at Kotosh, Peru. Andes 2*. Tokyo.

JORALEMON, P. D. 1971. *A Study of Olmec Iconography*. Washington D.C. (Stud. Pre-Coloumbian Art Archaeol., 7.)

MEGGERS, B. J.; EVANS, C.; ESTRADA, E. 1965. *Early Formative Period of Coastal Ecuador: The Valdivia and Machalilla Phases*. Washington, D.C. (Smithsonian Contrib. Anthropol., 1.)

NIEDERBERGER, C. 1976. *Zohapilco: Cinco milenios de ocupación humana en un sitio lacustre de la Cuenca de México*. México, D.F., (Colecc. Cient., Arqueol., 30.)

—— 1979. Early Sedentary Economy in the Basin of Mexico. *Science* (Washington, D.C.), Vol. 203, pp. 131–42.

REICHEL-DOLMATOFF, G. 1965. Excavaciones Arqueológicas en Puerto Hormiga (Departamento de Bolivar). Bogotá. (Antropol., 2.)

—— 1985. *Monsú: Un sitio arqueológico*. Bogotá.

ROUSE, I. 1972. *Introduction to Prehistory: A Systematic Apporoach*. New York.

ROWE, J. H. 1962. *Chavin Art: An Inquiry into its Form and Meaning*. New York.

WILLEY, G.; MCGIMSEY, C. 1954. *The Monagrillo Culture of Panamá*. Cambridge, Mass. (Pap. Peabody Mus. Archaeol. Ethnol., 49, No. 2.)

17.3
NORTH AMERICA

Melvin L. Fowler

The Archaic period of prehistory in North America does not belong within the chronological boundaries set for Volume II, as it begins as far back as the start of the fifth millennium BC and ends in the first half of the first millennium BC without any significant event marking a precise date. The weight of the hunting tradition of the Archaic period lies heavily on this long stretch of time, which nevertheless displays, in certain regions, cultural developments which are due to increasingly varied uses of the natural environment, an expanding population and technical innovation.

The discussion will deal with that portion of the North American continent north of Meso-America represented by the following areas: (1) the Arctic and sub-Arctic; (2) western North America; (3) the south-west; (4) eastern North America including the Great Plains. While there was cultural and natural diversity within these areas they represent convenient units within which uniform cultural themes evolved, making them useful for delineating a general picture (Map 26).

THE ARCTIC AND SUB-ARCTIC

The only habitable portion of the Arctic before about 4000 BC was primarily Alaska and the western portions of the Yukon and North-west Territories of Canada. East of this the Arctic was still locked in the grip of the retreating Laurentide ice sheet. This western portion of the Arctic had been occupied by *Homo sapiens* for thousands of years. During the Wisconsinan glacial period it was connected to Asia and was the bulk of the Beringia landmass which had served as the corridor through which *Homo sapiens* had gained a foothold in North America.

The earliest post-glacial cultural traditions in the western Arctic all belong to what Dumond has referred to as the Palaeoarctic tradition. This tradition is defined as one based upon a blade technology of a 'Levallois technique' (Dumond, 1983, p. 74). There are several regional variations of this tradition in the quantity and nature of bifaces included in the assemblages suggesting perhaps local adaptations, but all seem to participate uniformly in this single tradition of a blade technology. The Palaeoarctic tradition may well represent a technology introduced to the area from Asia at the end of the Pleistocene as well as the foundation on which several later traditions were developed.

About 4000 BC there were influxes into the Arctic of Archaic traditions from the interior of the North American continent. This is characterized by side-notched projectile points which have no widespread analogy in Asia (Dumond,

1983, p. 78). Throughout the northern portions of the North American continent there were similar spreads of Archaic life-styles into the northern latitudes as the post-glacial climate warmed and the forests spread northward with the diminution of the glaciers. In the Hudson Bay area this is manifested by the Shield or Boreal Archaic. On the east coast the Maritime Archaic spread northward into Labrador and Newfoundland. These spreads of forest and coastal-adapted hunters and gatherers appear to have coincided with the Hypsithermal climatic episode and were of hunters and gatherers fully adapted to modern flora and fauna.

About 2000 BC there developed, probably in the Bering Sea region of Arctic Alaska, a new tradition referred to as the Arctic Small Tool tradition (AStT). This tradition spread rapidly so that within a relatively short time it reached right across the Arctic rim of the North American continent all the way to north-eastern Greenland (Bielawski, 1988; Maxwell, 1985). In the eastern Arctic it is referred to as the Pre-Dorset culture. The AStT was first discovered at Cape Denbigh on Norton Bay in Alaska (Giddings, 1964, 1967). The complex is made up of distinctive small tools including microblades, well-prepared small cores, burins and tools made from burin flakes, and other artefacts. The subsistence strategy was oriented toward both coastal fishing and exploitation of anadromous fish, and inland hunting.

The origins of the AStT are not clear although Dumond (1983) suggests its derivation from the Palaeoarctic tradition perhaps in Asia. Whatever its origins it represents the first Pan-Arctic culture and may also represent the last population intrusion into North America from Asia. This might be related to the spread of the Inuit or Eskimo who are the most Asiatic of all the pre-European North American populations.

WESTERN NORTH AMERICA

Western North America denotes the area from the Rocky Mountains west to the Pacific coast. Aside from the mountain ranges themselves the area is composed of three very broad physiographic zones. In the areas of British Columbia southward in the states of Washington, Oregon and Idaho are high intermontane plateaus. These are drained by large rivers into the Pacific Ocean. In many of these large rivers salmon came upstream to spawn and provided an abundant seasonal food supply. Confined largely to the state of Utah is a large intermontane basin known as the Great Basin. This is an interior draining basin the centre of which is the Great Salt Lake. The Great Basin is a semi-arid environment. Along

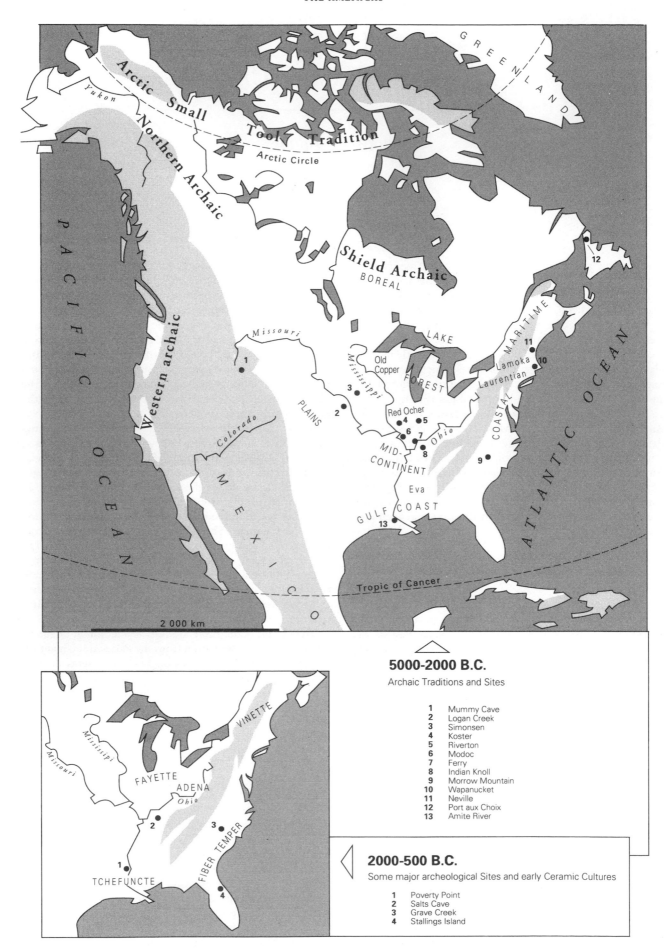

5000-2000 B.C.

Archaic Traditions and Sites

1	Mummy Cave
2	Logan Creek
3	Simonsen
4	Koster
5	Riverton
6	Modoc
7	Ferry
8	Indian Knoll
9	Morrow Mountain
10	Wapanucket
11	Neville
12	Port aux Choix
13	Amite River

2000-500 B.C.

Some major archeological Sites and early Ceramic Cultures

1	Poverty Point
2	Salts Cave
3	Grave Creek
4	Stallings Island

Map 26 Outline map of North America, showing the location of various archaic cultures and traditions.

the Pacific coast of North America, especially in California, is coastal plain. Along this coastal plain are abundant maritime resources including anadromous fish. Large rivers drain interior valleys. In these valleys and the foothills nearby are plentiful acorn-bearing trees.

In all of these areas of western North America long-lived Archaic traditions developed. These adaptations to the different environmental zones had become well established by 5000 BC and in most areas lasted until the incursion of American settlers into those areas, primarily in the nineteenth century. In the plateau area salmon fishing was a significant seasonal resource, as were plants. Aikens (1983, p. 195) points out that 'in the Plateau and Great Basin, local abundances of salmon, root crops, or piñon pine seeds seasonally attracted groups of harvesters from hundreds of square miles around. People travelled to where the desired resource was and carried it away themselves.'

On the Pacific coast, with its more abundant and concentrated resources, more local and permanent settlements developed with larger populations. Resource distribution was through the mechanism of trade 'that used concretely measurable standards of value' (Aikens, 1983, p. 195).

The Archaic cultures of the Pacific coastal region are more similar to the Eastern Archaic of the Mid-continent region than to the basin and plateau cultures of 5000–1000 BC. These comparisons are in terms of level of socio-cultural integration and population size rather than in specific artefact similarities.

THE SOUTH-WEST

During the period from 5000 to about 1000 BC, two Archaic patterns, the Chiricahua phase of the Cochise and the Oshara tradition (Irwin-Williams, 1968, 1973) of the western Archaic, show an increasing intensity of plant-food utilization, population growth, and the typical transhumant or seasonal round pattern. A major artefact category found in these assemblages contains large milling stones. Settlement systems seem to be dominated by relatively large base camps which include storage pits and numerous hearths. Artefactual, floral and faunal analyses of materials recovered from these middle Archaic period sites from the south-west indicate that subsistence was based on extensive seed-food utilization, possibly a simple horticulture, and the hunting of small mammals.

There is some indication that primitive maize may have been utilized before 1000 BC. Evidence for this comes from Bat Cave in New Mexico where some remnants of maize were found, dating possibly as early as 2000 BC (Dick, 1964). Further evidence comes from the Armijo phase of the Oshara tradition (1800–800 BC), where pollen evidence suggests the presence of cultivated maize. Other tropical cultigens such as squash and beans appear in these contexts somewhat later. Full dependence on maize agriculture in the south-west did not take place for another millennium, however.

EASTERN NORTH AMERICA

The evidence in the archaeological record shows that the big game hunters of earlier epochs had faded from the scene. The adaptation of these specialized hunters was no longer viable in the changing post-glacial east. Populations had increased and a localized adaptation using the variety of resources available in restricted areas was effective.

Although the broad Archaic adaptive pattern was spread throughout the east of the North American continent, there were variations within the broad pattern. These variations are based upon both stylistic differences in the way tools were made and the differing adaptive strategies to varied resources. Some recognizable variations are: Maritime Archaic, Coastal Archaic, Boreal Archaic, Lake Forest Archaic, Mid-continent Archaic and Plains Archaic.

Maritime archaic

A cultural adaptation extending along the north-east coast of North America from Maine to Labrador is known as the Maritime Archaic. It is characterized by an adaptation to sea-mammal hunting as indicated by bones found in the coastal sites as well as by bone harpoon heads. Other tools in this assemblage include chipped-stone and ground-slate projectile points of straight to contracting stemmed varieties as well as polished stone adzes and gouges. This tradition is dramatically illustrated by the discovery and excavation of a cemetery at Port aux Choix on the north-west coast of Newfoundland (Tuck, 1970, 1971, 1978). The excavation found evidence of over 100 burials with attendant grave goods. Many of the bodies had been painted or treated with red ochre as part of the processing of the deceased for entering the after-life. This characteristic has been found rather commonly in Archaic burials in the north-east. Associated with these burials was a wide variety of tools, but especially harpoon heads and other tools associated with sea-mammal hunting. Besides the maritime orientation, which probably took place seasonally, the Maritime Archaic peoples exploited the interior where they hunted elk and caribou. Other sites throughout the area document the presence of this special adaptation. It pertains to the period 5000 to 2000 BC.

Coastal archaic

Adaptation to the coastal environment and the immediate inland resources was prevalent from Massachusetts southward to the Carolinas. Although not stylistically uniform throughout this area the basic adaptation was similar. A main feature of this Coastal Archaic was the exploitation of anadromous fish, bivalves and deer. Dincauze (1972, 1976) has excavated several sites pertaining to this adaptation. Two phases are recognized by her for the New England coastal area, Neville and Stark. Most diagnostic of these are large, straight-based projectile points referred to as a narrow-stemmed tradition. Associated with these are various perforators, choppers, axes and adzes. Dincauze sees a similarity of this development with that in North Carolina (Coe, 1952, 1964) in the Stanley to Morrow Mountain sequence. Thus this may be a somewhat uniform tradition throughout the Atlantic coast.

Boreal archaic

The Laurentian Shield area of Canada surrounding Hudson Bay is a region of spruce fir forest with willows and birch near waterways and lakes. This area was essentially the last from which the glaciers retreated and could not have supported human colonization before 5000 BC. The Archaic adaptations to this area have been referred to as the Shield

Archaic by Wright (1972a, b). The earliest representatives of the boreal forest adaptation may have been big-game hunters adjusting to the changing environment. The hunting of the caribou, a herd animal, might not have been that different from hunting other big game. As the forest encroachment became stronger the hunting of other animals, elk and deer, and the exploitation of riverine and seed resources may have added to the subsistence pattern. Chipped-stone projectile points range from large-stemmed forms to smaller side-notched and triangular shapes. Many projectile points were made of ground and polished slate. The seasonal round of Boreal Archaic peoples probably varied from fishing stations near streams and lakes to the hunting of caribou.

Lake forest archaic

Forests of mixed hardwoods and pines dominated the area just south of the Great Lakes from New England to Minnesota. These forests extended southward along the streams feeding into the Great Lakes. The prairie peninsula, or tall grass prairie, marked the southern limits of this zone in Wisconsin, Illinois and Indiana. This zone had a more abundant fauna and plant-food resource base than did the Boreal Forest area north of the Great Lakes. This is one of the better known archaic cultures including Laurentian of New York and the Old Copper of Wisconsin. The tool assemblage of this type of Archaic includes side-notched and straight stemmed projectile points, end-scrapers made from broken points, expanded base drills and bifacial cutting tools. In later periods, ground stone tools such as gouges, axes, adzes, knives, ulus and spear points were added to the complex in the east. Some of these tools made of slate appear very similar to tools characteristic of the Boreal Archaic.

Similar forms of tools were made in the Wisconsin and Lake Superior region out of naturally occurring copper. This industry has been referred to as the Old Copper culture. In fact, the Lake Forest people of the western Great Lakes had discovered a raw material that was much easier to work than the cherts and even slates they were accustomed to using. It was treated as a soft and malleable stone. Most of the techniques used in making chipped stone tools, heat treating, pounding, and so on, were applicable to the raw copper. This material was so useful that the Archaic peoples mined it systematically (Griffin, 1961). It was traded, probably as finished products, over wide areas of the north-east. Essentially though the Archaic cultures of that area were basically the same as those to the east. Common items in the Lake Forest Archaic toolkit were various items for catching fish. These include hooks made either of bone or copper, leisters (spears with two or more prongs) and spears. Nets may well have been used but these have not been preserved.

Mid-continent archaic

Referred to as Riverine Archaic by R. Ford (1974), this variation of the Archaic adaptive strategy is probably one of the most extensively studied of all the patterns. It is distributed throughout the central basin drainage of the Mississippi and its major tributaries. This area is primarily covered with broad-leaf forest with a particular emphasis on oak and other nut-bearing species. The main river valleys provided an abundance of aquatic food sources. Even in the area of the prairie peninsula, the river bottom forests were utilized. This broad

area extending from New York state to Wisconsin and from northern Illinois to the lower Mississippi Valley was undoubtedly one of the most abundant, in terms of natural resources, in the entire continent. Within short distances of the river valleys was a wide variety of biogeographic resource zones. A seasonal round of food-getting activities could take groups from the river bottoms to the forest valley edge, to the prairie upland and provided a surfeit of food. It is in this setting that some of the larger Archaic sites are known. There is evidence that populations may have been greater in this region and that sedentary settlements may have developed in this heartland during the period 5000 to 2000 BC.

In Mid-continent Archaic sites there is evidence of the use of deer, racoon, opossum and other small mammals. Fish was apparently an important food component. Birds, particularly waterfowl, were exploited. Intensive gathering of wild plants, particularly pioneer or disturbed habitat types, has also been demonstrated.

Artefacts utilized by Mid-continent Archaic peoples include projectile points of side-notched and various stemmed types. Side- and end-scrapers, some hafted or made from broken projectile points, manufacturing tools, drills, spokeshaves, and other manufacturing tools are also found. A variety of ornamental objects such as beads, bone pins and pebble pendants appear in the assemblage. Ground and polished stone tools of a variety of forms and functions make up a strong component of the toolkit. Among these are the so-called bannerstones. These are present in a wide variety of forms. A tear-drop shaped object called a plummet was probably a stone used as South Americans used bolas stones, that is, as weights on the ends of cords used to entangle prey. In this area they were probably used in the capture of waterfowl.

Large numbers of grinding stones are common and were probably used in milling the seeds from trees and pioneer plants. Sandstone was also used as an abrading device to sharpen and manufacture other tools.

Stylistic variations existed in the area, so sub-areas of the Mid-continent Archaic can be delineated through the use of projectile point forms and other artefacts. Variations also undoubtedly existed in the toolkits of various smaller areas. The subsistence patterns varied according to the local resource base. For example the riverine to prairie season cycle would be somewhat different from that of the riverine and Ozark hills adaptation.

Archaeological evidence for the Mid-continent Archaic has been found at a number of sites and regions. The Lamoka phase of New York (Ritchie, 1969) is probably the most north-easterly extension known. This phase interacts with the Laurentian segment of the Lake Forest Archaic. Its artefact ties seem to be with the Mid-continent sites. The Koster site in Illinois is a well-documented example of Mid-continent Archaic, while further to the south the Modoc rockshelter provided information of its long-term *in situ* development (Fowler, 1959). In the Tennessee and Cumberland river valleys are some of the largest Mid-continent sites. This may be due to the exceptional quantities of river mussels in this area as well as the rich forest resources.

Studies in the Mid-continent area on Archaic cultures have contributed greatly to our understanding of the seasonal cycle adaptive strategy. Notable among these is the study by Winters (1968) of the Riverton culture in the Wabash Valley, in which he was able to illustrate the seasonal movements of these people within a restricted area of the valley. These annual movements included a summer base camp, transient camps in the spring and autumn and small winter settlements. Augmenting these throughout the year were hunting, gathering, and camping localities.

Plains archaic

Big-game hunters dominated the plains area of North America during the end of the Wisconsin glacial period and for several thousand years thereafter. However, this way of life moved northward with the big-game animals in post-Pleistocene times. Slightly earlier in some areas, but basically during and after the Altithermal, a new adaptive strategy moved into the plains from both the west and the east. This was made up of hunters and gatherers with 'a wide spectrum of interests in food acquisitions, reflected in the extensive use of a large variety of small mammals, seeds and other vegetal products, and occasionally fish, reptiles, amphibians, and the like' (Wedel, 1983, p. 216).

Various Plains Archaic sites demonstrate this broad range of food-getting activities throughout the plains. Many of the earlier sites are characterized by side-notched projectile points and later ones with various forms of stemmed and notched points. Remains of both bison and Virginia deer are found on Plains Archaic sites. Although communal bison hunting was common throughout much of plains prehistory it does not seem to have been an important factor during the Archaic.

All the hypotheses proposed for the origin of the Plains Archaic consider, in one manner or another, the effect the Altithermal had on the plains area. It is probable that, due to the hotter and drier climate of the Altithermal the forage of the short grass prairie was not as abundant. This may have brought about the extinction or movement out of the plains of the large forms of bisons favoured by the big-game hunters, as well as of the big-game hunters themselves. Hurt (1966) suggests, however, that the plains were never completely abandoned by human beings. There probably remained a few favourable areas serving as refuges for people and animals. The human populations that remained may have had to diversify their food hunting habits to survive. It is possible that the development of the smaller modern bison could have been a response to the harsh conditions of the Altithermal.

Much of the data on the earlier Plains Archaic suggests that its development may have been in areas marginal to the high plains. Mummy Cave (Wedel et al., 1968) in Wyoming shows a long intermittent use by western Archaic people over several thousand years. On the eastern margins of the plains early Archaic sites, dating from before 4000 BC, have been found. Following the Altithermal, from about 3500 BC to 1000 BC, Archaic sites are found throughout the Plains and especially along the main river valleys. Plains Archaic is in effect a blending of eastern and western Archaic brought about by peoples moving into and adapting to the plains area after the climatic moderation following the Altithermal.

MAJOR DEVELOPMENTS DURING THE ARCHAIC PERIOD

Several significant changes took place during the evolution of the Archaic way of life in North America. These served as foundations or stepping stones upon which the later cultural elaborations took place.

Population Growth

During the Archaic the maximum population expansion and adaptation took place. Certainly by 1000 BC all areas of North America had been populated following the final freeing of the northern areas from the grip of the great ice sheets. The exception to this was the island of Greenland which remains to this day largely glaciated. However, even there those coastal portions which were ice-free were peopled during Late Archaic times.

These late population expansions comprised peoples already well established, who brought various Archaic adaptations into newly opened environments. The most dramatic of these expansions was that of the Arctic Small Tool tradition which, as it was probably the culture of the pioneer Inuit, is sometimes referred to as the Palaeoeskimo. This culture has its earliest manifestations in the Bering Straits regions of Alaska but within several hundred years had expanded all the way to the north-east coast of Greenland. This may well have represented the first development and expansion of a coastal oriented culture along the north slope of Alaska and the islands and bays of northern Canada (Dumond, 1987; Bielewski, 1988; Maxwell, 1985).

There were several thrusts of Archaic cultures adapted to the woodlands of interior North America into the Arctic, sub-Arctic and other areas. One of these is the Northern Archaic (Dumond, 1987; Anderson, 1968). Further to the east is a better defined Archaic tradition, the Shield Archaic. This represents a northward expansion into the sub-Arctic of peoples from the Great Lakes area. The culture and people moved northward as the boreal forest zone expanded into previously glaciated regions along the margins of Hudson Bay and to the west. On the north Atlantic coast, the Maritime Archaic spread from the New England area northward during Late Archaic times. The development of the Plains Archaic after the Altithermal represents another population expansion into a previously under-inhabited area.

Social differentiation – burial elaboration

Evidence of developing social distinctions within Archaic cultures is found in the treatment of the dead as seen in excavated burials. In much of the Archaic stage the societies seem to have been egalitarian with little social differentiation. Later there was a developing concern with burial ceremonies and distinctions between the burials. Some burials received more, and more specialized, goods than others.

Few skeletons have been unearthed pertaining to the earlier period between 5000 and 2000 BC though many burials have been found after this latter date. Later burials at the Modoc site (the earliest are from c. 6000 BC) contained simple grave goods: in one instance a stone axe, in another a projectile point. One case was particularly interesting in that a cache of bird bones, mostly metacarpals of large birds such as swan, were with the burial. Some of these bones had been made into awls, while about half were maintained in their original form. These offerings tell us little about social differentiation in the community.

At a later period, c. 2000 BC, a large group of over a thousand burials accompanied the Indian Knoll site in Kentucky (W. S. Webb, 1946). This area was probably a cemetery of Mid-continent Archaic peoples as well as a habitation site. There seems to have been some differentiation in these burials in that about one-third of them had grave good accompaniments, suggesting at least two divisions in the society. The people with the grave goods could have been those who achieved fame or status during their lives, thus becoming 'big people'. This form of social distinction is common among egalitarian societies. Another distinction in these burials is that only a small percentage had grave goods that came from a long distance, for example, copper artefacts, probably from the Lake Superior region, and pendants made of conch shell from the Gulf coast. These items represent a great 'investment' by the group for procurement. They, therefore, probably would only be buried with persons of outstanding position.

A third intriguing factor about the Indian Knoll burials is that the grave goods were buried with individuals of both sexes and all ages. It may be that the grave goods therein are an indication of social distinctions within the society that are ascribed and inherited (Binford, 1971). More research needs to be done along these lines.

Across the area of the Lake Forest Archaic there was a burial complex which included the use of red ochre and the presence of gorgets and other artefacts. These burial practices are found from New England to Indiana and Illinois. One facet of this is known as Red Ochre culture in Illinois, and has exotic blades called 'turkey tails' as part of the burial goods. Other artefacts such as ground slate blades and stone axes are more commonly found in the New England area. Most of these burials, however, do not yield any information on social differentiation. They do suggest that, late in the Archaic development, concern about the treatment of the dead had increased.

Burial treatment of the Maritime Archaic is an extension of the Red Ochre ceremonies further south. At Port aux Choix a large cemetery was uncovered with exceptional preservation of both the skeletons and the bone tools (Tuck, 1971). Grave goods were found associated with most of the burials. There was a division based upon sex in terms of the types of tools included. However, both children and adults had grave goods. The tools represent the full range of activities of the Maritime Archaic as well as many items of personal adornment.

In the vicinity of San Francisco Bay a burial site was excavated, although somewhat later than the period we are discussing, which shows the development of social differentiation in the Late Archaic of western North America. There were over forty burials in this site. Of these the eighteen in the centre were accompanied by over 60 per cent of the grave goods and were of individuals who were cremated or interred. On the basis of this differential treatment of individuals a 'hierarchical social structure' was proposed (King, 1974).

In general, then, the data on the later Archaic burial practices indicate a growing concern with the treatment of the dead. Most of the data are consistent with an egalitarian society with some indication of individuals being recognized for achieved status. There are some data which suggest the development of social distinctions, which might have become hereditary, giving the individuals ascribed status.

Exchange networks

In the Archaic cultures there was an elaboration of exchange systems for the procurement of exotic goods, such as copper, excellent types of flint, shells from the Gulf coast and perishable materials. These systems of procurement were probably reciprocal and no specialized traders were required. Goods flowed in both directions, being passed from group to group in exchange for other goods. In this way desirable and needed materials were distributed over large areas. Such exchange systems as these are well known among hunting and gathering peoples. They probably developed as a mechanism for the exchange of food resources to balance out unequal resources or to survive years of scarcity. These exchanges were probably not needed at all times but the network would be kept open by the exchange of exotic goods which often ended up as burial offerings.

Evidence for these exchange systems can best be seen in the distribution of exotic goods from outside the territory of the original resource. Copper, for example, is most plentifully available in the Lake Superior region. In this area the so-called Old Copper culture manufactured many items from copper. These included gouges, socketed axes, crescent-shaped knives similar in form and function to Eskimo ulus, socketed and tanged spear points, and beads and other ornamental objects. Many of these objects in the Lake Forest Archaic are similar to ground and polished stone objects from the Boreal and Maritime Archaic (Plate 165).

Outside the immediate Old Copper area a lesser number of copper artefacts are found. It is assumed that these are objects traded from the Lake Superior region, although some of them could have been made from nuggets found in glacial drift. Copper artefacts are found more commonly in the Lake Forest and Boreal Archaic but are known from the Mid-continent Archaic as well.

One of the more interesting studies of exchange networks in the Archaic was that of exotic goods included with the Indian Knoll burials. A large portion of these were items made of conch shell from the Gulf coast region. Winters (1968) concluded that these items were obtained or exchanged for other items with an actual 'value' in mind. He further concluded that these exchanges were cyclical with a regular interval of influx. Such valuable items were probably only part of the exchange network. They were buried with their owners, having been contributed to the burial ceremony by near kinsmen and indebted individuals. These offerings restated the social position of the deceased. They also effectively took those specific items out of circulation, thus keeping up the demand and reinforcing the need for exchange networks; thus the exotic accompanied the more common items that were passed from hand to hand.

Development of permanent settlements and central communities

In many Archaic sites there are little or no data as to the actual settlement organization of the people. Shelters were flimsy and temporary. The settlement pattern was one of small seasonal camps. The possibility of macro-band, or multiple band, camps developing in an area of an abundant seasonal resource should be considered. In the later Archaic, perhaps by 3000–2000 BC, central bases of year-round villages may have developed.

Evidence for structures is rare although some have been found. One such locality is the Wapanucket No. 6 site in south-eastern Massachusetts (Robbins, 1959). Six circles of postholes were found which were interpreted as belonging to house sites. A part of the circle overlapped, providing an entry. These circles ranged from 9 to 14 m in diameter, with one larger, 20-m diameter, structure. Hearths were found inside the structure area. The larger building may have been a community ceremonial hall.

In the Helton phase at the Koster site a rectangular house area has been found. Other evidence suggests storage structures and roasting pits. This area may have been a developing central base camp.

One site which suggests an autumn meeting camp for Archaic peoples is the Ferry site overlooking the lower Ohio Valley in southern Illinois (Fowler, 1957). Here there was abundant evidence of the processing of nuts, including grinding stones and hammer stones. The larger mortar-like grinding stones were probably left at the site for the people to use each year upon return. The surface scatter of Archaic materials covers several acres, and includes many projectile points, a great number of which were made from chert available in the bluff nearby. A large number of bannerstones, either whole or fragmentary, and in a variety of forms, were found. One hypothesis is that these different forms of bannerstones were emblems of different groups. The site represents a gathering place for several bands in the autumn, when the acorns were ready for harvest. The yearly visit may also have provided an opportunity to collect the local chert and manufacture points.

In the riverine areas tributary to the central Mississippi Valley are many large shell-midden sites. Mussels are plentiful in this area and may have proved a sufficient resource for larger populations to make these riverbank areas central camps (Fowler, 1959). At such sites tools, ornaments and so on are found indicating that the full round of food extracting, manufacturing, and ceremonial activities was carried on. Indian Knoll may be one such site. Another is the Eva site on the Big Sandy River in Tennessee. The Eva site itself is a large shell-midden of long-term and intense occupation. Other sites related to Eva show specialised subsistence activities. Some evidence of structures was indicated by the many postholes. These however, were so dense that it was not possible to extract the pattern of a structure. Eva was possibly the central camp with the others being specialised activity camps.

An elaborate example of early earthwork construction is at the site of Poverty Point in Louisiana. Poverty Point suggests a society sufficiently well organized to command the labour of a large number of persons. The central structure at this site is a large geometric earthwork c. 1,200 m across. In its original form it probably comprised a series of six concentric octagons of earthen ridges. Almost half of this earthwork has been eroded by the nearby river. Between the ridges are ditches: a series of five ditches and six ridges forms each of the eight sections of the earthwork. The sections lead from the central open area to the outside of the octagon. The ditches may be in part the source of the earth for construction of the ridges. Today the ridges are only a couple of feet high but it is thought that they originally might have been as high as 3 or more metres. The inner diameter of the octagon was about 595 m and the outer 1,210 m. The investigators suggest that the ridges were house platforms (Ford and Webb, 1956, p. 128) supporting up to 600 houses.

Associated with the earthen ridges were three mounds, one of which is in the form of a bird. These together with the octagon utilized about 800,000 m³ of earth (C. H. Webb, 1968, p. 318). There was certainly no other construction in all of eastern North America to compare with Poverty Point at the time.

The uniqueness of the earthworks both in size, complexity and context and associated small worked stone objects have suggested to some investigators that this site represents an intrusion of peoples from outside the area. Some have suggested that it was an Olmec outpost in the lower Mississippi Valley. There is no question about the unusual nature of the site, though it may be part of a much more widely-spread cultural phenomenon. A hallmark of this is fired clay objects that seem to have been used for 'stone' boiling. Pottery found at Poverty Point relates to general fibre tempered wares from the south-east. The ridge construction, although more formal in arrangement, is similar to the ring shell-midden communities of the Atlantic coast. It may, therefore, be that Poverty Point represents an unusual flamboyance of community patterns in that area. It seems to have been short-lived, possibly no longer than 200 years, and at any one time may have supported no more than a few hundred people. Satisfactory explanations of its origins and functions must await future investigations.

Ceramics

During the earlier Archaic there is little or no evidence of containers. Baskets and skin vessels for stone boiling were undoubtedly used as were wooden bowls and mortars, but evidence of these is not preserved. There is evidence of the manufacture of stone bowls in late to Archaic contexts in the lower south-east and in the north-east between 2000 and 1000 BC. These bowls were made from soft stone and of generally shallow form with lug handles on the margins. In the north there are some deeper almost conical forms, though the use to which these might have been put is conjectural.

Based upon these same forms, the technique of mixing clay with an aplastic, modelling the shape and firing the product seems to have developed first in the area of the Atlantic coast of Florida and Georgia. In the Savannah River area of Georgia so-called fibre-tempered pottery has been radiocarbon dated to about 2500 BC and consists of plain surfaced bowls. Similar pottery appears a few hundred years later in the St Johns region of Florida (Bullen and Stoltman, 1972). Later (perhaps 2000 BC) vessels with exterior decorated surfaces appear in both areas. This technique of making vessels spread westward into the lower Mississippi Valley area by 1500 BC.

A parallel ceramic development took place in the north-east at a later date. These ceramics were grit-tempered and often textured by cord roughening on both the interior and exterior surfaces. They also were preceded by a stone vessel industry. Somewhat typical of this development are the Vinette ceramics from New York (Ritchie, 1969) and the Fayette materials from Illinois and Indiana.

Although some investigators have proposed the diffusion of this technology from outside the area, Mexico and northern South America for the south-east and the western Arctic and Asia for the north-east, this does not seem to be necessary. The most economic explanation is that they were indigenous developments. Whatever the origins of these innovations, they are the foundations upon which later ceramic manufacturing in eastern North America was based.

In Alaska ceramics are found in the Choris culture at about the beginning of the first millennium BC (Giddings, 1964, 1967; Dumond, 1983, p. 81). They are clearly derived from Asia and are indicative of the continuing interaction of peoples in Asia and North America.

Plant collecting and plant cultivation

The Archaic cultures, except in the Arctic and sub-Arctic regions, are known for their extensive use of plant foods. In many areas these are the seeds of trees, such as acorns, walnuts and pecans, that provide a rich food source. Other seed foods, also, were abundant: they include pioneer, or disturbed habitat plants such as amaranths, chenopods, sumpweed, sunflowers and others. These types of plants, while prolific in nutritious seed production, can survive in the same habitat for only a few years when they are replaced by other plants in the succession towards climax vegetation. If, however, the habitat continues to be disturbed many of them can survive to produce. Although data are scanty, it is assumed that Archaic peoples encouraged the growth of many of these plants and thus took steps toward domestication. This is particularly true of the area of the Mid-continent Archaic.

Sunflower (*Helianthus* sp.) was probably domesticated in the Mid-continent area and spread from there to other areas of North America. There are data for the use of sumpweed (*Iva* sp.) in the Koster site area of the Illinois River valley. Mud-flat horticulture in this area took advantage of the fact that annual flooding produced new disturbed habitats each year (Struever and Vickery, 1973).

There is growing evidence that gourd and squash may have been part of this complex in the Mid-continent Archaic. Rind and seed fragments have been found in archaeological contexts in Missouri, Illinois, Kentucky and Tennessee dating from c. 6000 to 2000 BC (Smith, 1987, p. 11). These may represent the diffusion of tropical domesticates northward. However there is growing evidence to indicate that they are disturbed habitat plants independently domesticated in the east. There is no evidence of maize being utilized in the east during Archaic times.

In general, it appears that Archaic peoples in the Mid-continent area were encouraging the growth of seed-bearing plants. In some cases this may have included burning the area to provide a less competitive habitat for the plants or merely taking advantage of the mud-flats' disturbed habitat. In other cases it appears that more manipulation of the habitat was necessary (R. I. Ford, 1974). This led, during the late Archaic, to a food-plant complex which became increasingly important as part of the subsistence strategy. It was based upon the domestication of pioneer plants and the tropical complex of maize, beans and squash was not involved. A similar pattern was present in the Archaic developments of the south-west with the possibility of the addition of maize to the complex perhaps as early as 1000 BC.

SUMMARY

The period between the fifth millennium BC and the beginning of the first millennium BC on the North American continent was the era of the full development of the Archaic way of life. It was a period of 'settling in' to the vast variety of resource zones which developed in the post-Pleistocene or Holocene epochs. During this period a series of distinct and recognizable traditions developed, tied to the environmental zones to which they were adapted. These traditions varied from region to region in terms of the toolkit, and the types of flora and fauna exploited. They all shared in the basic Archaic strategy of a seasonal round of resource utilization, an increasing dependence on floral resources and an intensive use of a restricted territory.

During the period under consideration Archaic populations spread into, and adapted to, newly opened habitat zones such as the eastern Arctic, the sub-Arctic, and the plains. The most dramatic population expansions was that of the Palaeoeskimo (Inuit?), who rapidly spread from the Bering Straits region as far eastward as Greenland.

In many areas, such as the eastern woodlands and Mid-continent riverine areas and the south-west, horticulture became a major subsistence strategy for Late Archaic peoples. It was based upon the use and domestication of disturbed habitat plants such as sumpweed, chenopods, sunflowers and others. In the Meso-American portions of North America this process started in the Early Archaic and by Late Archaic times, c. 2000 BC, maize had been domesticated and horticulture had given way to agricultural subsistence. Maize was present in the south-west perhaps as early as this, but did not become a major cultigen for a millennium or more. There is no evidence for maize utilization during the Archaic in eastern North America. The horticultural strategy however provided a 'preadaptive' mode which served as a foundation upon which maize agriculture spread in the east after the beginning of the current era.

By Late Archaic times relatively large sedentary communities developed in those areas where food resources were abundant and horticulture was well established. This is particularly true of the Mid-continent region and the south-west. These communities probably served as centres of territorial exploitation with smaller extractive localities in the surrounding and supporting hinterland. Similar communities developed in the coastal areas of western North America where marine resources such as anadromous fish and inland resources such as acorns were particularly abundant. These western Late Archaic developments may have been without horticulture.

In areas such as the Mid-continent, east and coastal California, there are indications of developing social distinctions. These are indicated primarily from the data of differential treatment of the dead. Whether these distinctions are of acquired or ascribed status is a problem remaining to be solved. In both California and the east trade became more extensive. This is manifested particularly in the presence of exotic goods with status burials. However the trade also served as a mechanism for the wider distribution of comestibles and other soft goods.

It is also during the Archaic that the earliest ceramics are found. In the east they date back to about 2000 BC and are probably an indigenous development. In the Arctic, ceramics appear after 1000 BC and probably arrived from Asia. In the south-west ceramics appear much later and probably as a result of the expansion of agricultural people northward from Meso-America.

In sum, the period from the fifth to the beginning of the first millennium BC in North America was the period in which the foundations were laid on which the later more complex developments were able to build.

BIBLIOGRAPHY

AIKENS, C. M. 1983. The Far West. In: JENNINGS, J. D. (ed.), *Ancient Native Americans.* San Francisco. pp. 149–201

ANDERSON, D. D. 1968. A Stone Age Campsite at the Gateway to America. *Sci. Am.* (New York), Vol. 218, No. 6, pp. 24–33.

BIELAWSKI, E. 1988. Paleoeskimo Variability: The Arctic Small-Tool Tradition in the Central Canadian Arctic. *Am. Antiq.* (Washington, D.C.), Vol. 53, No. 1, pp. 52–74.

BINFORD, L. R. 1971. Mortuary Practices: Their Study and their Potential. In: BROWN, J. (ed.), *Approaches to Social Dimensions of Mortuary Practices*. Washington, D.C., Society for American Archaeology. (Mem. 25.)

BULLEN, R. P.; STOLTMAN, J. B. (eds) 1972. *Fiber Tempered Pottery in the Southeastern United and Northern Colombia: Its Origins, Context and Significance*. Florida Anthropological Society.

CHARLES, D. K.; BUIKSTRA, J. E.; KONINGSBERG, L. W. 1986. Behavioral Implications of Terminal Archaic and Early Woodland Mortuary Practises in the Lower Illinois River Valley. In: FARNSWORTH, K. B.; EMERSON, T. E. (eds), *Early Woodland Archaeology*. Kampsville, Ill. pp. 458–74.

COE, J. L. 1952. The Cultural Sequence of the Carolina Piedmont. In: GRIFFIN, J. B. (ed.), *The Archaeology of the Eastern United States*. Chicago. pp. 301–9.

—— 1964. The Formative Cultures of the Carolina Piedmont. *Trans. am. philos. Soc.* (Philadelphia.), New Series, Vol. 54.

DICK, H. 1964. *Bat Cave.* (Monogr. Sch. am. Res., 27.)

DINCAUZE, D. 1972. The Atlantic Phase: A Late Archaic Culture in Massachusetts. *Man Northeast*, Vol. 4, pp. 40–61.

—— 1976. *The Neville Site: 8,000 years at Amoskeag, Manchester, New Hampshire*. Cambridge, Mass. (Peabody Mus. Monogr., 4.)

DUMOND, D. E. 1983. Alaska and the Northwest Coast. In: JENNINGS, J. D. (ed.), *Ancient Native Americans*. San Francisco. pp. 69–113.

—— 1987. A Reexamination of Eskimo-Aleut Prehistory. *Am. Anthropol.* (Washington, D.C.), Vol. 89, pp. 32–56.

FARNSWORTH, K. B.; EMERSON, T. E. (eds) 1986. *Early Woodland Archaeology*. Kampsville, Ill.

FORD, J. A.; WEBB, C. H. 1956. Poverty Point, A Late Archaic Site in Louisiana. *Anthropol. Pap. am. Mus. nat. Hist.* (New York), Vol. 46, No. 1.

FORD, R. I. 1974. Northeastern Archaeology: Past and Future Directions. *Annu. Rev. Archaeol.* (Palo Alto, Calif.), Vol. 3, pp. 385–413.

FOWLER, M. L. 1957. *Ferry Site in Hardin County, Illinois*. Springfield, Ill. (Sci. Pap., 9, 1.)

—— 1959. Modoc Rock Shelter: An Early Archaic Site in Southern Illinois. *Am. Antiq.* (Washington, D.C.), Vol. 24, pp. 257–70.

GIDDINGS, J. L. 1964. *The Archaeology of Cape Denbigh*. Providence, R.I.

—— 1967. *Ancient Men of the Arctic*. New York.

GRIFFIN, J. B. 1961. *Lake Superior Copper and the Indians*. Ann Arbor, Mich. (Misc. Stud. Great Lakes Prehist., 17.)

HARP, E. 1983. Pioneer Cultures of the Sub-Arctic and the Arctic. In: JENNINGS, J. D. (ed.), *Ancient Native Americans*. San Francisco. pp. 114–47.

HURT, W. 1966. The Altithermal and the Prehistory of the Northern Plains. *Quaternaria* (Roma), Vol. 8, pp. 101–13.

IRWIN-WILLIAMS, C. 1968. Archaic Culture History in the Southwestern United States. *Contrib. Anthropol.*, Vol. 1, No. 4, pp. 48–53.

—— 1973. The Oshara Tradition: Origins of the Anasazi Culture. *Contrib. Anthropol.*, Vol. 5, No. 1.

KEEGAN, W. F. (ed.) 1987. *Emergent Horticultural Economies of the Eastern Woodlands*. Carbondale, Ill. (Occas. Pap., 7.)

KING, T. F. 1974. The Evolution of Status Ascription around San Francisco Bay. In: BEAN, L. J.; KINGS, T. F. (eds), *Antap: California Indian Political and Economic Organization*. pp. 35–54. (Anthropol. Pap., 2.)

LIPE, W. D. 1983. The Southwest. In: JENNINGS, J. D. (ed.), *Ancient Native Americans*. San Francisco. pp. 421–93.

MAXWELL, M. 1985. *Eastern Arctic Prehistory*. New York.

MEIGHAN, C. W. 1959. California Cultures and the Concept of an Archaic Stage. *Am. Antiq.* (Washington, D.C.), Vol. 24, No. 3, pp. 289–305.

RITCHIE, W. A. 1969. *The Archaeology of New York State*. Rev. ed. Garden City, NY.

ROBBINS, M. 1959. *Wapanucket No. 6, An Archaic Village in Middleboro, Massachusetts*. Attleboro, Mass.

SMITH, B. D. 1987. The Independent Domestication of Indigenous Seed-Bearing Plants in Eastern North America. In: KEEGAN, W. F. (ed.), *Emergent Horticultural Economies of the Eastern Woodlands*. Carbondale, Ill. pp. 3–48. (Occas. Pap., 7.)

SMITH, B. D.; COWAN, C. W. 1987. Domesticated Chenopodium in Prehistoric Eastern North America: New Accelerator Dates from Eastern Kentucky. *Am. Antiq.* (Washington, D.C.), Vol. 52, No. 2, pp. 355–7.

STARNE, W. A. 1979. The Archaic Concept: Its Development in North American Prehistory. *New York State Archaeol. Assoc. Bull.* (New York), No. 75, pp. 67–77.

STRUEVER, S.; VICKERY, K. D. 1973. The Beginnings of Cultivation in the Midwest Riverine Area of the United States. *Am. Anthropol.* (Washington, D.C.), Vol. 75, No. 5, pp. 1197–220.

STYLES, B.; AHLER, S.; FOWLER, M. L. 1983. Modoc Rockshelter Revisited. In: PHILLIPS, J.; BROWN, J. (eds), *Archaic Hunters and Gatherers in the American Midwest*. New York. pp. 261–98.

TUCK, J. A. 1970. An Archaic Cemetery in Northern New Foundland. *Sci. Am.* (New York), Vol. 222, pp. 112–21.

—— 1971. An Archaic Cemetery at Point aux Choix, New Foundland. *Am. Antiq.* (Washington, D.C.), Vol. 35, No. 3, pp. 343–58.

—— 1978. Regional Cultural Development, 3000 BC to 300 BC. In: TRIGGER, B. (ed.), *Handbook of North American Indians*. Washington, D.C. Vol. 15, pp. 28–43.

WATSON, P. J. (ed.) 1969. *Prehistory of Salts Cave*. Springfield, Ill. (Report of Investigations, 16.)

WEBB, C. H. 1968. The Extent and Content of Poverty Point Culture. *Am. Antiq.* (Washington, D.C.), Vol. 33, No. 3, pp. 297–331.

WEBB, W. S. 1946. *Indian Knoll, Oh 2, Ohio County, Kentucky*. Lexington. (Rep. Anthropol., 4, 1.)

WEDEL, W.R. 1983. The Prehistoric Plains. In: JENNINGS, J. D. (ed.), *Ancient Native Americans*. San Francisco. pp. 183–219.

WEDEL, W. R.; HUSTED, W. M.; MOSS, J. H. 1968. Mummy Cave: A Prehistoric Record from the Rocky Mountains of Wyoming. *Science* (Washington, D.C.), Vol. 160, pp. 184–5.

WILLEY, G. R.; PHILLIPS, P. 1958. *Method and Theory in American Archaeology*. Chicago.

WINTERS, H. D. 1968. Value Systems and Trade Cycles of the Late Archaic in the Midwest. In: BINFORD, S.; BINFORD, L. (eds), *New Perspectives in Archaeology*. Chicago.

WRIGHT, J. V. 1972a. *The Shield Archaic*. Ottawa. (Publ. Archaeol., 3.)

—— 1972b. *Ontario Prehistory*. Ottawa.

17.4
MESOAMERICA:
GENESIS AND FIRST DEVELOPMENTS

Christine Niederberger

The trajectory of Mesoamerica – the first advanced civilization of the New World – begins a little before 1500 BC and spans a period of some 3,000 years.

The term 'Mesoamerica', first used by Kirchhoff in 1943, is primarily a cultural concept. It defines a civilization which occupied a vast geographical continuum in Middle-America, comprising the southern half of present-day Mexico, Guatemala, Belize, El Salvador, part of Honduras and the western regions of Nicaragua and Costa Rica. In 1519, at the time of the first contacts between the Amerindian societies and the European world, Mesoamerica – then under the influence of the Maya civilization and the Aztec power – covered approximately one million square kilometres. More than eighty main languages, each accompanied by a host of dialectal variations, were in use.

Rooted in a very wide variety of ecological and ethnic environments, this civilization, despite certain regional variations, displayed a remarkable degree of cultural homogeneity in the sixteenth century.

The subsistence economy was based on the cultivation of maize, beans and squash, although a myriad of other plants, such as amaranths, tomatoes and chili-peppers, were also cultivated. In addition to avocados and other hot climate fruits, cacao and cotton were grown in the 'lowlands' zones and, together with other commodities, they gave rise to active systems of inter-regional trade.

Agriculture included both extensive systems of cultivation (slash-and-burn cultivation) and specialized techniques of intensive production. The latter took two main forms: 1) the creation of hill-side irrigated terraces, particularly in semi-arid zones; and 2) the construction of raised fields and artificial islands (*chinampas*) in lacustrine and swampy areas, characterized by an excess of water. These artificial islands, linked by networks of fresh-water canals, provided an unrivalled environment for intensive horticultural activities.

The agrarian societies of Mesoamerica had a marked hierarchical structure. A highly centralized political control and the organization of religious life and ceremonialism were in the hands of an hereditary elite. Between this aristocratic group and the class of rural peasantry came the orders of warriors, organized corporations of craftsmen and powerful groups of merchants travelling throughout Mesoamerica to trade such utilitarian products as prismatic blades of obsidian, or luxury goods such as jadeite, cacao or quetzal feathers.

Mesoamerican cities offered formal features of civic and religious architecture. Residential houses – often provided with steam baths – and palaces in cut-stone masonry, generally covered with stucco and polychrome paintings, were built around courtyards and patios. These architectural complexes, as well as consecrated structures for ceremonial ball-games and constructions dedicated to commercial activities, were dominated by high-stepped pyramids surmounted by sanctuaries.

A complex system of specific conceptualization patterns and beliefs subtended both ideology and religion. An examination of various pre-Columbian manuscripts and historical accounts enables us to overcome some Western thought-conditioning and to apprehend more clearly the irreducible 'otherness' of the Mesoamerican world. Chronicles in the Nahuatl language, collected in the sixteenth century by men of universalist beliefs considerably in advance of their times, such as the Franciscan friars Andrés de Olmos and Bernardino Sahagún, as well as the modern exegesis of these texts provided by A. Ma. Garibay and M. León-Portilla, offer us a sort of Ariadne's thread leading to the pre-Hispanic universe. All these texts reveal some important aspects of the Mesoamerican ways of conceiving authority, diplomatic relations, the organization of economic and commercial life, codes of behaviour, family life, as well as typical forms of wit and humour. The transcriptions of the *huehuetlatolli* ('old men's tales') are a record of popular oral traditions. The *icnocuicatl* (elegies of 'deep meditation') is an important collection of philosophical thoughts on the ephemeral nature of all life. Poetic creation includes songs about love, the 'flowering tree of friendship' (*xochicuicatl*) or the verdant rebirth of nature at the advent of the rainy season (*xopancuicatl*). The war songs (*yaocuicatl*) describe the soldier's equipment (thick, cotton-padded 'armour', distinctive head-dresses for each order of warriors, shields decorated with feathers, lances fitted with sharpened blades of obsidian), accounts of battles, codes of honour and the fatal lot of prisoners, who were often sacrificed to the gods. However, it is the *teocuicatl* or sacred hymns, and the *teotlatolli* or divine words about gods, priests or ritual practices, which give us the best insight into cosmovision, time- and space-conception and the existence of complex theogonies, crystallized in the most distant Mesoamerican past.

The organized world, which was regarded as being extremely unstable, was ruled by numerous spirits, both terrestrial and celestial, capable of countless metamorphoses and possessing attributes which varied depending on their position in the different segments of time and space. In the Nahuatl world, at the beginning of the sixteenth century, the major sacred powers included very ancient divine creatures. An example is Quetzalcoatl (literally 'the Feathered Serpent'), a civilizer-hero – associated with writing and the calendar – who was also the incarnation of the planet Venus (*Tlahuizcalpantecutli*), the symbol of death and rebirth, the wind (*Ehecatl*), as well as a dual god endowed with magical skills (*Xolotl*). *Xipe Totec* ('Our Lord the Flayed One') represented the principles of the rebirth of nature, while *Tlaloc* was the spirit of the mountains and the rain. *Tonatiuh* impersonated one of the manifestations of the sun, captured every evening by the nocturnal powers of the West. The cosmic struggle to ensure the rebirth of this star in the East, and, as a corollary, the survival of mankind, was partly sustained by the 'precious water' or blood obtained from human victims or ritual self-sacrifice.

The Mesoamericans possessed a set of writing systems which combined pictograms, signs representing ideas (ideograms) or sounds (phonograms) and determinatives. Numerical calculations were based on a system using multiples of twenty. This vigesimal system of notation was used for recording historical and dynastic events, for geographical data, commercial transactions, divination or ritual practices, mathematical operations (which with the Mayas involved the use of the concept of zero) and for calculating the movements of the stars and other heavenly bodies.

Finally, time was measured by the simultaneous operation of two calendars: the ritual calendar of 260 days (the apparent cycle of Venus of twenty 13-day periods); and the solar calendar consisting of eighteen months of twenty days, to which five days were added. The initial dates of these two calendars coincided every fifty-two years. The beginning of this fifty-two-years cycle – a kind of Mesoamerican 'century' – was marked by ritual public manifestations, such as the great 'New Fire Ceremony' among the Aztecs.

These are, briefly outlined, the main features of the Mesoamerican world, as they appeared at the eve of Spanish conquest, in the final stages of this civilization. Going back in time, it is now possible, through archaeological evidence, to observe the rise of a series of concomitant phenomena which, during the second millennium BC, have laid the socio-political and cultural foundations of Mesoamerica: a civilization which, by the very fact of its isolation, represents one of the most original manifestations in the history of humankind.

The early Holocene techno-economic adaptation and the development of the agrarian village towards 1500 BC

The post-Pleistocene period in Middle America is marked by the development of not only agrarian practices but also of a whole integrated set of phenomena which characterized a 'neolithic' way of life. Closer man/plants relationships were accompanied by changes in patterns of settlement, with the development of a sedentary way of life in certain favourable areas, and by new strategies in systems of food procurement. The first unquestionable evidence of plant's cultivation in Middle America comes from a surprisingly early date for this region with the discovery of cultivated squash (*Cucurbita pepo*), in ancient caves of the Valley of Oaxaca, dated to 8000 BC (Smith, 1986). Intensified manipulation of plants, including protection and selection, led, through early Holocene times, to the domestication and development of major staple foods, particularly of the first Amerindian cereal crop, maize (*Zea mays mays*).

Sedentary settlements

During early Holocene times, complex and asynchronous sedentarization processes had developed in Middle America

following different trajectories in accordance with the widely different types of environments. Although early examples of sedentarism towards 5000 BC have been reported in marine estuaries or in high lacutrine basins, this was, however, the homogeneous distribution of sedentary forms of territorial occupation – towards the middle of the second millennium BC – which, together with agriculture, defined the nascent Mesoamerican cultural area, while nomadism continued to be the rule elsewhere, in particular in the vast spaces of the northern part of Middle America.

The spatial expansion of early Mesoamerican features in the middle of the second millennium BC is better understood today through the archaeological research of these last decades. Numerous permanent agrarian communities occupied towards 1500 BC a wide range of bio-climatic environments and altitude levels. Critical to the understanding of the development of early complex societies are several key zones. One of them – the coastal plains of Southeastern Mesoamerica – has recently yielded a large corpus of new data. First studied by Coe and Flannery (1967) and by Green and Lowe (1967), the southern Pacific coastal region is now more thoroughly understood thanks to recent excavations carried out in the Mazatan region (Clark, 1994), at Paso de la Amada (Blake, 1991), at La Blanca (Love, 1991) or at El Mesak (Pye and Demarest, 1991). Towards 1400 BC, during the Locona/Ocos phase, progressive socio-political changes seem to have occured leading to the *emergence of small independent chiefdoms* and the first appearance of regional centres with elite residential structures. Another key area is the southern lacustrine region of the high temperate Basin of Mexico, where a long sequence of occupations, from *precocious proto-agrarian sedentary settlements* (Playa phases I and II : 5500–3500 BC) to early ranked societies (Nevada phase: 1400–1250 BC) has been studied (Niederberger 1979, 1987). Other sites or regions, with contemporaneous cultural levels have yielded important archaeological data. Among them, El Openo in the state of Michoacan (Oliveros, 1974) and numerous sites scattered over the state of Colima (Kelly, 1980) in Western Mexico; or the semi-arid valley of Tehuacan, where a long archaeo-botanical sequence has documented food procurement systems and plant's domestication processes culminating in the well-established agrarian economy of the early Ajalpan phase, towards 1500 BC (MacNeish, 1967). Finally, the Valley of Oaxaca and the pioneer studies carried out at the Tierras Largas phase's settlements remain a major source of information concerning the rise and development of complex societies (Flannery, 1968, 1976).

The subsistence economy towards 1500 BC

Subsistence economy is based everywhere on the exploitation of a very wide variety of resources. The long history of the domestication of maize, which began in Middle America towards 6000 BC, led to the development of small ears of corn which, according to archaeo-botanical studies carried out at Oaxaca, could produce an average of some 300 kg per hectare towards 1000 BC. The cultivation of maize, a cereal with an extraordinary capacity to adapt to widely differing ecological environments, was accompanied in the village economy by that of beans (*Phaseolus* spp.), squash (*Cucurbita* spp.), amaranths and tomatoes (*Physalis*), and several condiments which are central to the Mesoamerican culinary tradition, such as *epazote* leaves (*Chenopodium*) or chile peppers (*Capsicum annuum*). In addition, many other plants were cultivated in the lowlands, such as avocados (*Persea americana*) and the savoury fruit of the sapodilla (*Casimiroa edulis*). Some researchers, relying on the analysis of the lithic tools found at their sites, believe that, in some regions of southern Mesoamerica, tubers, such as manioc (*Manihot esculenta*), were also cultivated.

One of the remarkable characteristics of Mesoamerica's food-procurement systems is the maintenance of ancestral gathering traditions within a predominantly agrarian economy. In semi-arid regions, and following multi-millennial traditions, exploited wild plants included agave succulent leaves (which were baked in underground ovens), the leaves and fruit of the prickly pear (*Opuntia*), and *pitahaya*, the fruit of the giant candelabra cactus (*Lemaireocereus*). The pods of many leguminous plants (*Prosopis, Leucaena*) and of the wild cotton tree (*Ceiba parvifolia*) were also regularly collected.

Regarding animal food consumption in the period between 1500 and 700 BC, archaeological research has shown that among the mammals, the domestic dog occupied first place. Next came the white-tailed deer, the rabbit, the American antelope and the peccary. Turkeys (*Meleagris gallopavo*) played an important role in the diet in many areas, although it is uncertain whether they were already domesticated at that time. Among the reptiles, the fresh-water turtle (*Kinosternon*) was highly valued everywhere, while the iguana was an important source of food in lowlands regions. Villages situated close to marine estuaries, such as Ocos on the Pacific coast of Guatemala, consumed large amounts of duck, fish, crab, oysters, mussels and small snails. In the temperate regions of the high mountain lakes, deer, antelope, dogs, rabbits and peccaries were also eaten. These sources of food were complemented by an extremely rich and varied selection of lacustrine resources. In the Basin of Mexico, this included species of fresh-water fish belonging to the families of the Atherinidae, Goodeidae and the Cyprinidae, turtles, water snakes, frogs and a neotenic amphibian, the famous *axolotl*, or salamander (*Ambystoma* spp.), which was later considered as a gourmet dish for Aztec princes. An extraordinarily large number of lacustrine birds were also hunted, which included both the resident Anatidae, such as the *Anas diazi*, and a large collection of winter migratory birds (ducks, coots and 'Canadian' geese). Indeed, the Basin of Mexico constituted a major winter ground for a large number of migratory bird species up until historic times when, towards 1900, its main extensions were artificially drained. In 1862, Orozco y Berra noted in special reference to ducks and geese that: 'these palmipeds arrive, in their season, in such prodigious number that they *cover*, in the most rigorous acception of the word, considerable surfaces' of the lakes. In pre-Columbian times, this abundant wildlife helped make the Basin of Mexico – particularly its southern part, which has important freshwater expanses – a highly favourable region for human settlements.

Technology

The earliest known baked-clay figurine found so far in a dated archaeological context comes precisely from a third millennium pre-pottery level of Zohapilco in the south of the Basin of Mexico (Niederberger, 1979). As to the first appearance of pottery in Middle America, our knowledge remains still uncertain, but during the second millennium BC the art of the potter developed throughout Mesoamerica, along with the manufacture of anthropomorphic or zoomorphic terracotta figurines. Domestic pottery, consisting of hemispherical bowls (*jicara*) and typical globular neckless jars (*tecomate*), seems to imitate the different sections of

a gourd (*Lagenaria sicecaria*), long used in Middle America as a container. Carefully shaped and polished, these bay or brown earthenware pots were sometimes decorated with geometrical motifs painted in red. It has been noted that some of the large *tecomate* were used to cook maize with ashes or lime to soften the grains, following a typically Mesoamerican custom. Finely modelled potteries also included highly polished flat-bottomed vessels and finely decorated bottles with squash-like bodies decorated with vertical, oblique or spiral grooves.

Early Mesoamerican tools used in everyday life were made of different materials: wood (digging sticks, traps), bone (awls, needles), shells and various kinds of lithic raw material, used for making hammer-stones, scrapers, knives, drills, burins, sharpeners, abraders or polishing stones (Lorenzo, 1965). At this time occurs an impressive development of the remarkable lithic technique of snapping off thin blades from a specially prepared obsidian core to obtain fine and efficient prismatic blades. Named *ixtete* by the Aztecs, they were highly prized as cutting tools throughout Mesoamerica's sequence.

According to the iconography shown on some terracotta seals, the most widely used weapon appears to have been the *atlatl*, or spear-thrower. Projectile points, generally made of obsidian, were fitted onto the spear's distal end.

From 2000 BC onwards, ground-stone artifacts used for grinding maize and other seeds underwent notable morphological changes. Towards 1500 BC, the grinding surface of *metates* (or passive grinding stones) become considerably larger, and long two-hand *manos* (or active mullers) make their first appearance.

Weaving and basket-making were highly developed activities. The cultivation of cotton (*Gossypium* sp.) is already attested. Pottery shards which have been reworked to form a circular disc, with a central perforation, were used as spindle whorls. Cactus fibres and reed stalks were used to produce rope, nets, baskets and mats.

The early Mesoamerican house and its area of domestic activities

For several decades it has been clear to Mesomerican researchers that the study of an ordinary house and its village context provides fascinating insights for the global understanding of a civilization. As a result of such studies, accurate evidence on Mesoamerican village life between 1500 and 700 BC is now available. The best corpus of archaeological data comes from the Valley of Oaxaca (Mexico) (Winter, 1976; Flannery and Marcus, 1983).

The Oaxaca house was rectangular and covered, on average, an area of 18 to 24 m². Its floor was made of beaten earth, sometimes overlayed with fine sand. The walls, supported by posts made of pine, consisted of branches covered with clay that was often smoothed over to give a polished surface and, more rarely, whitewashed. The internal space of the house seems to have been divided into men's and women's working activities areas. The household unit, which covered about 300 m², consisted of the house itself, together with an external area where most of the family activities took place, such as grinding maize, cooking foods or manufacturing pottery. This outside domestic area contained pottery kilns, bell-shaped storage pits and burial zones. Once abandoned, storage pits were re-used as rubbish dumps and thus provide excellent evidence of the activities of the household. Excavation of these middens has yielded maize husks, avocado seeds, fragments of milling-stones and *manos*, bone needles, bone fragments of deer, rabbits, hares and fresh-water turtles, and also non-utilitarian remains associated with some ritual activity, such as marine fish spines, probably used in personal bloodletting, parrot feathers and fragments of drums made from turtle shells.

Interesting new data from the Pacific coastal plains of Southern Mesoamerica suggest, as mentioned above, that several relevant socio-political changes may have already taken place towards 1400 BC, with the incipient development of small independent chiefdoms and social-ranking (Clark, 1994; Blake, 1991). At Paso de la Amada (Chiapas), Structure 4 of Mound 6 – a large elaborate apsidal house with a total area floor of 122 m² – seems to reflect the wealth and status of an emerging hereditary elite. Burial practices in this region – such as the sepulture of a child with white mica forehead mirror, a high status symbol – is another indicator of an incipient level of social differentiation.

It is towards 1200 BC, however, that a new type of territorial settlement's patterns clearly emerges. Regionally related sites offer signs of differentiation in size and functions. At the beginning of the first millennium BC, the hamlet of Tierras Largas in Oaxaca covered an area of two hectares and contained five households. A short distance away the regional centre of San José Mogote extended over 20 hectares and consisted of 80 to 130 domestic units, together with several public buildings constructed on wide stepped platforms of stone and dried clay chunks. A pit covered with white stucco and containing powdered lime was discovered within the floor of one of these single-room structures. One of the hypotheses advanced to explain this feature states that the building was considered a sacred space in which ritual practices were carried out by a restricted group of the social community. Among the historical Zapotecs of Oaxaca, certain practices associated with specific rituals – which were perhaps already current in San José Mogote – consisted of chewing narcotic substances, such as tobacco, mixed with lime. Whatever the merit of this hypothesis, a new conception of socio-political relationships was beginning to develop. In summary, the crystallization of new spatial and social schemes towards the end of the second millennium BC leads to the clear emergence of this typical Mesoamerican centripetal settlement pattern, in which a constellation of small village communities are linked to a regional capital, centre of political, religious and economic specialized activities.

The Olmec civilization and the development of regional capitals (Map 27)

Towards the end of the second millennium BC, Middle America became the scene of numerous innovations linked not only to the world of beliefs and the conception of the individual and collective spaces, but also to the field of techniques and economic strategies. This intermediate period, of crucial importance for an understanding of the future development (at the beginning of the Christian era) of the first large *urban* centres, such as Tikal in the Maya lowlands, Monte Albán in the Zapotec zone or Teotihuacán in the Basin of Mexico, was for a long time little understood. In the absence of information, or faced with fragmentary or contradictory data, many researchers have argued that most of the 1000 BC communities – except for some sites on the Gulf coast – had the archaic economic and socio-political status of relatively Equalitarian villages.

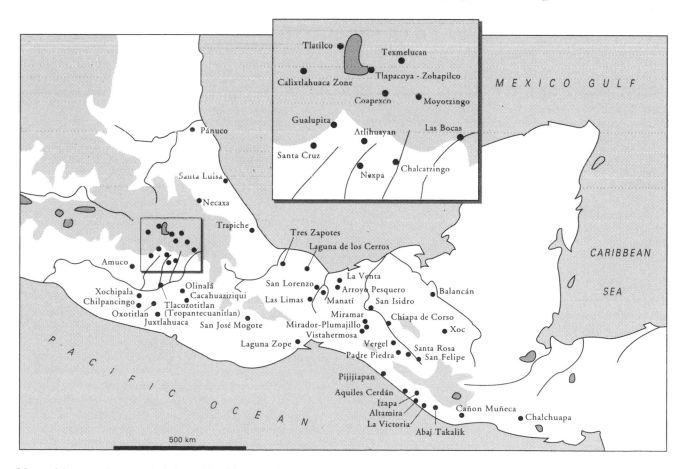

Map 27 Mesoamerica: principal sites of the Olmec civilization (1250–600 BC)

This view has been profoundly modified by recent archaeological discoveries, which have led a growing number of archaeologists to support the hypothesis that cities developed at an early date in Middle America. However, this position implies a clear definition of this specific form of spatial organization.

Certain criteria regarded as necessary to account for the emergence of a city in the archaeology of western Asia (such as a system of writing used in trade, or metal working) do not apply in the case of Mesoamerica. In turn, if we decide that a Mesoamerican site attains the status of a city when there are signs of the concomitant existence of: a) elaborated political and religious institutions; b) clear social ranking; c) planned public architecture; d) a class of highly specialized craftsmen; e) inter-regional trade networks; and f) complex intellectual achievements (such as an integrated system of astronomical observations or an iconographic method for the permanent recording of certain concepts or events), then we must accept that cities (*caput* not *urbs*) were already fully developed there from 1200 BC onwards (Niederberger, 1987, pp. 692–722). From this point of view, there is only a difference of degree, and not of nature, between the regional capital of 1000 BC and the city-state, which was to develop in Mesoamerica at the beginning of the Christian era (Bray, 1979).

The development of regional capitals in Mesoamerica, towards 1200 BC, is linked to the development of an original style and iconography based on a set of specific beliefs. Since the beginning of the 20th century this particular cultural expression has been designated as 'Olmec'. In time, the initial ambiguity of this appellation – already noted by W. Jimenez Moreno in the 1950s – has increased, as I have analysed at length in earlier works. Unfortunately, the term has now been in use for too long to seriously consider the possibility of discarding it. However, we must now examine the misleading postulates involved in its use.

The term 'Olmec': a semantic problem

In the history of research, it is interesting to observe how a series of random events can determine particular currents of thought and patterns of interpretation. In 1925, when the authors of *Tribes and Temples* (1926–7), F. Blom and O. La Farge, and later M. Stirling (1940) discovered, among the marshy plains of the Gulf coast of Mexico, the archaeological sites of La Venta, Tres Zapotes and San Lorenzo – with their monumental sculptures in volcanic rock – it was not possible to ascribe them to any Mesoamerican culture known at that time. This remarkable cultural complex was finally classified, for the sake of convenience, as 'Olmec' – a term which had been suggested towards the end of the 1920s by Beyer and Saville. In fact, the name refers to a proto-historical ethnic group, inhabitants of the Land of Rubber (the Olmecs) who lived on the Gulf coast shortly before the arrival of the Spaniards and who probably had no specific connection with the archaeological complex which had been discovered. Be that as it may, the convention became established and the term 'Olmec' soon began to acquire ambiguous semantic properties. This confused association of an historical ethnic group with a yet undefined archaeological discovery, combined with a kind of linguistic determinism, led to the assumption that in archaeological times the Gulf coast was the geographic centre of a 'promethean' ethnic group, the 'Olmecs', characterized by a remarkable cultural precocity and dynamism and thus predestined to influence, dominate or conquer neighbouring peoples whose very anonymity seemed to place them within a passive and rudimentary stage of development.

Archaeological excavations carried out over the last few decades provide no data which would sustain the hypothesis of early cultural development along the Gulf coast gradually spreading to other areas in Middle America. A much more complex perspective results from last decades research. First, the substantial corpus of radiocarbon datings yielded by field research from numerous sites clearly demonstrates that the 'Olmec' cities of the Gulf coast offer no signs of chronological precedence over the sites which are now studied systematically in other regions of Middle America. It can also be noted that the 'Olmec' archaeological finds outside the Gulf coast area do not show any provincial features. Furthermore, certain theories, such as the one which states that local 'provincial' elites were 'Olmecized' as a result of inter-regional trading relations and the acquisition of rare goods in order to reinforce their status, are no longer regarded as entirely satisfactory. In fact, as we have tried to demonstrate since the early 1970s, ancient Mesoamerica cannot be viewed as an area of coexistence of two qualitatively different levels of evolution. Studies of the inter-regional trade or exchange network also indicate the existence of complex multidirectional movements, implying the existence of a great number of top-level political and administrative centres in Mesoamerica (Niederberger, 1974, 1976, pp. 265-6, 1987, pp. 678–92 and 750–1). Most encouraging is the fact that some researchers are now coming round to the argument for the *'lattice-like model of interregional interaction'* formulated by Demarest (1989, p. 337) for ancient Mesoamerica. Several clear reappraisals also strongly refute today the postulate infering the existence of a culturally more advanced ethnic group on the Gulf coast (Hammond, 1989; Flannery and Marcus, 1994).

In summary, sound anthropological reasoning and recent discoveries call for the formulation of new working hypotheses which will help to explain, in a broader context, the genesis and development of ancient Mesoamerican civilization. With this in mind, the word 'Olmec' will not be used here to refer to a particular people; instead, its use will be strictly limited to two concepts: style and, more broadly, civilization.

The definition of a style and its cultural implications

From a semiotic point of view, and following Saussure, the concept of style includes both the formal aspects (*signifiers*) and the semantic content (*the signified*), which give meaning and value to systems of signs. It is immediately apparent, therefore, that the analysis of Olmec formal expression and the Olmec semantic field is a task that is neither easy nor without risks.

The passionate interest, aroused since the beginning of the 20th century by the power and undeniable beauty of Olmec stylistic expression, has often caused the study of this phenomenon to fall into a poorly structured and reductive history of art, unconcerned by either rigorous analysis or – and this raises very serious problems – *internal chronology*.

The whole range of Olmec 'signifiers' and stylistic repertoire, embedded in a multitude of sculptural and graphic forms of expression, is inspired by several central themes. One of the fundamental themes behind all these figurative variations is rarely the jaguar itself, as it has often been stated, but a hybrid being, a complex amalgam of human and feline characteristics (Plate 166). The human infant, with feline features, is, for example, a recurring subject in stone-carving and pottery arts. Fascinated by this fact, Miguel Covarrubias (1957) – a great pioneer in 'Olmec' studies in the 1940s – wrote that it is not clear whether these are men disguised as jaguars, or jaguars about to change into men.

One of the most striking features of man/feline depictions is the famous 'Olmec mouth' – shaped like an upside-down 'U' and with the lips' commissures turned downwards – which Covarrubias once described as a combination of the mighty wrathful expression of a snarling jaguar and that of a crying child.

Several attempts have been made to decipher the content of these representations. In the religious field, these themes might be linked to the belief, widely held in American pre-history, concerning shamanistic 'man-animal' transformations, during which a man engaged in a sacred or medicinal ritual can absorb the power of a feline. It has also been suggested that the various forms of human/feline representations, together with specific attributes – such as closed eyes – might be prototypes of traditional Mesoamerican deities such as the 'god' of death or the 'god' of maize. It should be pointed out, however, that the concept of Mesoamerican personified deities, as it occurs in Greco-Latin theogonies for example, has been strongly challenged. Some researchers have convincingly argued that Mesoamerican cosmology and systems of beliefs are sustained by a more fluid and *animistic* notion of one or more series of major forces, represented by a combination of different creatures and natural elements (Marcus, 1978; Pohorilenko, 1977).

Finally, these feline/human representations, symbols of domination and force, might have a political significance, as already noted by M. Coe in 1972. As emblems of power, they might be associated with sacred political rulership and the dynastic rituals of an hereditary elite.

Some researchers have cast doubt on the pre-eminent position occupied by the jaguar, the puma or other felines in Olmec iconography and have rightly emphasized the importance of reptiles, such as caymans or snakes. However, one should beware of oversimplified, reductionist or exclusive interpretations which are incompatible with the extraordinary complexity of Olmec styles and symbols.

In a comprehensive approach, Joralemon (1976) has underlined the recurrence in Olmec iconography of biologically aberrant creatures. He points out that these mythological creatures, figments of the human imagination, are derived from real creatures whose characteristics have been dissociated from their biological context and recombined to form unreal composite beings. In this process of reconstruction some natural features retain their original identity. In the composite creature of the 'Olmec dragon', we can recognize a cayman's tooth, a jaguar's muzzle, a bird's wing and a snake's body. In his study, Joralemon gives several examples of hybrid and fantastic mythological creatures which often occur in Olmec iconography, such as the jaguar-man, the jaguar-bird, the snake-bird, the jaguar-cayman-fish, the cayman-jaguar-bird and the snake-mammal-bird.

Certain isolated iconographical features may attain a high level of abstraction or stylization and be used, on the synecdoche principle already noted by G. Kubler, to convey on their own a complete message. These motifs – which might be related to celestial bodies or underworld powers, to mythological beings, to status symbols or to sacralized events of social life, such as the ball-game – include the 'St Andrew's cross', the U, L and reversed E motifs, circles, bars, spirals,

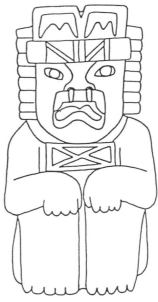

Figure 94 Basalt sculpture from San Lorenzo, Veracrux, representing a recurrent theme of Olmec iconography, the anthropomorphic jaguar; h 0.90 m. (after Coe; Diehl, 1980).

diamonds, five-pointed figures, four-petalled flowers, isolated features representing an eye, a foot, a hand or predator's claw, feathers, small hand shields, burning torches, and V-shaped or cleft head motifs (alone or combined with sprouting plant elements). Some of these elements could already represent an early form of the graphic recording of information, and thus be considered as the first steps of a developing writing system. Coe (1976), for example, has argued that the four-petalled flower motif represents a proto-typical form of the Maya glyph *kin*, which is equivalent to 'sun' in later 'classical' cultures.

Nevertheless, Olmec systems of signs and art are not restricted to surreal or abstract forms. In the case of stone carvings and small terracota statues, human beings may be represented with great realism. In fact, in this field, the Olmec

Figure 95 Reproductions of excised motifs on the body of pottery of the Olmec civilization (Period I, 1200–900 BC (after M. Covarrubias). The various stages in the increasingly abstract rendering of the dominant symbolic motif – that of a mythical, dragon-like, hybrid being at once feline, reptile and bird – can be traced.

period represents a highlight within the pre-Columbian trajectory, with specialized craftmen showing a keen sense of volume and an admirable mastery of three-dimensional representation (Plate 167). The small statuettes of seated figures, in an attitude of serenity and meditation, or the figurines with shaved heads which are found at Las Bocas (Puebla) or Tlapacoya (state of Mexico), as well as the green stone figurines (Offering 4) of La Venta (Tabasco), are excellent examples of this. This mastery is also apparent in the manufacture of other terracota figurines representing fat chubby-cheeked babies modelled in an effortless interplay of curves and counter-curves. Monumental art may also show an acute sense of naturalistic rendering, such as San Lorenzo Monument 34 (Plate 168). Finally, outstanding among Olmec sculptures-in-the-round are the powerful representations of colossal human heads – which vary in height between 1 and 3 m and may weigh up to 25 tons – a category that I shall discuss later.

Chronology

A better control of Olmec-period internal chronology is essential. If we want to understand Olmec civilization – and interconnect processes between sites and regions – more fully, it is necessary to establish a much more reliable and precise chronological framework for architecture and sculpture development. In fact, until recently, Olmec art was regarded by many scholars as a static entity which had sprung *ex nihilo* and remained nearly unchanged until the end of its trajectory. Fortunately, the excavations carried out over recent decades, which have all produced a large number of radiocarbon dates, provide a much clearer idea of the chronological distribution of pottery styles and of their associated archaeological contexts.

The period spanned by Olmec civilization covers some five to seven centuries. On the basis of an analysis of pottery style and iconography, this period may be divided into three main parts, briefly outlined in Table 1.

Table 1: Chronology of 'Olmec' Mesoamerica

Non-calibrated ^{14}C dates	Phases	Definition	Ceramic characteristics
1200–900 BC	I	Ancient Olmec (Plate 169, Fig. 94)	Greatest frequency of excised decoration with isolated abstract motifs
900–700 BC	II	Olmec climax (Fig. 95)	Greatest frequency of 'double line-break' motifs and fluid and fine incised motifs, including cleft head and almond-shape-eyed creatures
700–500 BC	III	Olmec deculturation	Disintegration of style, rigidity in the expression of the old motifs and a shift towards new themes

Phases I and II show synchronous development in all the regions concerned. On the other hand, the 'deculturation' which took place at the beginning of phase III does not seem to have occurred simultaneously in all the regions of Mesoamerica. In some areas this process took place before 600 BC, while in other regions it only began towards 500 BC.

The geographical distribution of a style and of a civilization

Costa Rica could represent the southern boundary of Olmec Mesoamerica. However, it is possible that many artifacts in the pure Olmec style (masks, 'spoons', pendants and anthropomorphic figurines in splendid bluish-green jadeite) from museums or private collections were brought into this region at a later date.

Indisputable evidence of Olmec-style settlements, with an impressive pyramidal mound, was reported in El Salvador, in the region of Chalchuapa (Sharer, 1978). Important archaeological sites are also found in Guatemala, particularly along the Pacific coast (Coe and Flannery, 1967) and inland at Abaj Takalik, where a large corpus of monumental sculptures, including irrefutable 'olmec' sculptures-in-the-round, such as Monument 16/17 or Monument 23 – a colossal head, 1.85 m high, re-worked into the representation of a dignitary seated within a niche – has been reported (Graham, 1981). Little is known about Honduras during these periods, but some evidence of occupation has been detected at Los Naranjos, near Lake Yojoa (Baudez and Becquelin, 1973).

As to Mexico, our knowledge, concerning the emergence of a Mesoamerican way of life, is still uneven. Some states, which are of crucial importance in the birth and growth of 'Olmec' civilization, such as the state of Puebla (as is shown by the evidence found at many sites, such as Las Bocas and all the sites of the Nexapa Valley, Necaxa or Tepatlaxco, or by the all too rare cases where there have been systematic excavations (Aufdermauer, 1973) remain virtually unexplored. The same could be said for the state of Guerrero if it were not for the recent discovery of the major 'Olmec' site of Tlacozoltitlan-Teopantecuanitlan, where excavations were carried out in the 1980s (Donjuan, 1986, 1994; Niederberger, 1986). This state also provided one of the most remarkable collections of 'Olmec' portable stone carvings (Olinala, San Jerónimo, Tlaxmalac or the Amuco Stela – cf. Grove and Pàradis, 1971; Griffin, 1981) and superb specimens of rupestrian paintings (Juxtlahuaca, Oxtotitlan, Cacahuaziziqui).

The early archaeological cities of the states of Veracruz and Tabasco on the Gulf coast were the first to be explored and – among Mesoamerican sites of this period – they remain the most fully studied. The site of San Lorenzo, discovered by M. Stirling, later systematically excavated by Coe and Diehl (1980) and more recently by Cyphers (1994), is an important source of information for Phases I and II, at which time the site of Laguna de los Cerros (Bové, 1978) was also occupied. For Phases II and III, the site of La Venta, tested by Drucker and Stirling in 1942 and 1943, systematically excavated in 1955 by Drucker, Heizer and Squier (1959), and now studied by Gonzalez Lauck (1994), has already yielded a considerable mass of evidence. Tres Zapotes, another important site which was occupied from at least the same time as La Venta, eventually took over and went on into the post-Olmec period. Again in the Gulf coast region, one of the most moving finds of recent years is, perhaps, the discovery made in 1988, in a spring area of Cerro Manatí, of a whole set of *in situ* dedicatory offerings. Exceptionally well preserved and set in their original cultural context, these Olmec-period testimonies of sacred activities include eleven anthropomorphic wooden busts, highly polished stone celts, infants' osseous remains, hematite fragments and the most ancient rubber balls known to date (Ortiz and Rodríguez, 1994).

The state of Chiapas, a source of abundant data documenting the transition from the post-Olmec phases to the

Izapa style, is also remarkably endowed with evidence of phases I and II of the 'Olmec' period (Navarrete, 1974). As noted by Lee (1989), early Olmec occupations have been identified at Río Totopac, San Isidro and Maritano in the Middle Grijalva region, at Chiapa de Corzo, Amatal, Santa Rosa, Vergel, Padre Piedra, San Felipe, Vistahermosa, Mirador/Miramar in the Central Depression, and at Alvaro Obregón, Izapa, Altamira, Alvarez, Aquiles Serdán, Pijijiapan, on the Pacific coast. In several sites, architectural remains have been observed and consist of low terraces, sometimes with volcanic ash or whitish sand floors, and small basalt platforms. However, it is during Phase II – with the development of public space planning – that architectural practices show revolutionary changes. During Phase II, as underlined by Lee (1989, p. 207): 'The general Chiapas architectural arrangement consists of three basic structures: one or more earthen pyramids, a long cruciform platform, and large squarish or rectangular basal "acropolis" platforms with one or more superstructures ... the pyramid and elongated platform and the several structural units are always separated by plazas'. Three of these Phase II sites – Finca Acapulco, Vergel and San Mateo – already possessed architectural structures for the ball-game, which are among the earliest known in Mesoamerica (Lowe 1977).

The excavations carried out in the state of Oaxaca, particularly in the Oaxaca Valley (Flannery and Marcus 1983, 1994) (cf. *supra*) but also in the region of the Isthmus (Zeitlin, 1978) offer data of considerable value concerning food-procurement systems, settlement patterns, rituals and interregional exchange systems, between 1200 and 600 BC.

The state of Morelos has a host of sites, such as Gualupita excavated by Vaillant in 1932 and corresponding to phases I, II and III. Most famous is the site of Chalcatzingo, known since 1934 for its remarkable Olmec-style rupestrian reliefs. Recent archaeological excavations have now yielded a new coherent set of data and a total of 70 slab-stone, bedrock and boulder carvings has been reported to date (Grove, 1987, 1989; Oliveros, 1994). Among them, 31 correspond to elaborate reliefs, stelae, free standing monuments and megalithic sculptures-in-the-round, such as 'altars/thrones', human heads or the conventional 'Olmec' representation of power by a massive seated personage with cape and 'St Andrew's cross' pectoral (Monument 16). As to the chronological repartition of this large corpus of carvings, the major part seems to correspond to pan-Mesoamerican Phases I and II, although some stelae and other carvings indicate clear stylistic links to Phase III or later. Outstanding and exhibiting a meaningful concentration of Phases I and II beliefs and stylistic conventions is the thematically related group formed by Monument 13 (the 'Governor'), Monument 1 (*El Rey*) and Monument 9. All three carvings show a stylization, whether in front or in profile, of an earth monster with a wide-open mouth, a metaphoric image of caves, and underworld entrance from which volutes – as breath, wind or fertility symbols – or plant motifs are emerging. In two instances, a high status dignitary, seated inside the cave, seems to serve as an intermediary between earth, human world and celestial spheres. Other reliefs seem to translate important sequences of mythical cycles into visual messages, including plants (*Cucurbitaceae*), rain symbols, or zoomorphic forms with felines dominating or eating humans. If the *in situ* archaeological levels of occupation corresponding to carvings from Phases II and III are extremely well documented in Chalcatzingo, little or none is known about Phase I settlements (the theoretical *Amate* Phase) at the site. The search and def-

inition of *in situ* early levels is of crucial importance to a more accurate understanding of interaction processes between regions in ancient Mesoamerica.

Present knowledge indicates that the Basin of Mexico also played a pivotal role in the emergence of specific pan-Mesoamerican techno-economic strategies and cultural patterns (Tolstoy and Paradis, 1970; Niederberger, 1970, 1976, 1979, 1987). The fact that this region had strongly contributed to the crystallization of 'Olmec' style and beliefs – in other words, to the birth of ancient Mesoamerica – has long been obscured by a series of unfortunate facts. First, a 'monumental' error in the relative and absolute chronology of the sequence of occupations -untiringly repeated through a dense archaeological literature from 1940 to the late 1960s – has led to the conviction that the relatively recent El Arbolillo-Zacatenco archaeological sites, wrongly dated to 2000/1500 BC, represented the primitive 'first villages' of the Basin. Thus, when Olmec-style artifacts were discovered, in particular at the site of Tlatilco, they were supposed to be the mark of culturally more advanced intruders. In fact, the late Zacatenco-type settlements, evolving from 500 to 200 BC, were contemporaneous with the proto-Teotihuacan 'late Formative' levels, that is to say that they occurred 600 to 1,000 years *after* the first Olmec-style archaeological levels of the Basin of Mexico. Even though the myth concerning the El Arbolillo-Zacatenco early villages – under external influence – has now broken down, the underlying belief in a Basin of Mexico marked by cultural lag and passivity during the pan-Mesoamerican Phases I, II and III, is *still* directly or indirectly implied in many publications. This misjudgement is also due to the fact that few of the early structural surface remains have survived the impact of three successive and powerful urban centres and demographic concentrations of pre-Hispanic and modern times: classical Teotihuacan and satellite settlements, Aztec Tenochtitlan and the twentieth-century megalopis of Mexico City. Among eradication and 'recycling' processes of early archaeological sites and features, a 'coup de grâce' event has been the destruction of the foremost site of 'Olmec' times, Tlapacoya, in great part bulldozed out in 1958 to provide building material for the Mexico-Puebla Highway. A large earthen platform, projecting from the hill towards the ancient lake – of which some basal external limits can still be observed – was then destroyed (Niederberger, 1987, p. 702). Phases I and II ceramic vessels, shell ornaments, jade artifacts and elaborate burial offerings that were associated with this structure are now in the Roch Collection, in nearby private *haciendas* and in Mexican and US museums, such as the Museum of the American Indian in New York. Nevertheless, on the edge of the destroyed area, in the Zohapilco *locus*, a sequence undisturbed for 6,000 years has been excavated (ibid.). This sequence shows the multi-millennial *in situ* evolution from the proto-agrarian sedentary egalitarian village of 5500 BC reported above, to an early ranked community, leading to the emergence of an 'Olmec' major regional centre, towards 1250 BC.

Phases I and II are characterized by elaborate ceramic vessels decorated with stylized motifs such as the St Andrew's cross and paw-wing, flame eyebrows, opposed volutes, diamond shaped or five dots elements. At first deeply carved into the vessel surface during Phase I, these motifs tend to be made with fine and fluid incised lines during Phase II, allowing the representation of very complex inter-twined graphic symbols. Ubiquitous in the Tlapacoya superb repertoire of graphic messages are the human/feline heads, with masterly designed profiles, hand and almond-shaped eye elements, or cleft-headed creatures, sometimes associated with plant motifs. Besides the incised representations of fantastic hybrid creatures, such as the human/amphibian/feline head with closed/death eye, or the remarkable grey clay sculpture of the 'Olmec dragon' (Reilly, 1994, p. 243), naturalistic themes, including fishes and ducks, were depicted. Clay figurines include dignitaries with towering head-dresses and concave mirror pectorals, personages with intentionally deformed heads – partially or totally shaved – hollow baby-face figures, and a notable number of high-status personages and ball-players wearing elaborated ball-game paraphernalia with wrist and ankle bands, tiered head-dress, heavy protective belt or waist yoke, and leather-like hip padding (Niederberger, 1987, pp. 434-9; Bradley and Joralemon, 1993). Rupestrian paintings were discovered in 1992 above the Zohapilco-Tlapacoya site. Several of these – including a chubby-chinned baby-face profile and an oval cartouche with cross-hatched motifs – seem to pertain to Phases I and II. Painted on cliffs or in caves whose entrances have since been dynamited, they are oriented towards the East, the most important Mesoamerican cardinal direction, and towards the mighty snowy summits of Popocatepetl and Iztaccihuatl volcanoes. Receiving the early morning light of sunrise they might have constituted a relevant segment of a sacred space. Finally, a large set of data from these early Mesoamerican horizons now documents the active role of Tlapacoya-Zohapilco within the inter-regional multidirectional exchange networks of goods and ideas.

Syntheses of recent years and new data are opening a more coherent understanding of the socio-political complexity and economic importance, during Phases I, II and III, of the Basin of Mexico's early sites. Now we can fully appreciate the pioneer discoveries of Covarrubias (1957), Piña Chan (1958) and Porter Weaver (1953) and offer a cultural context as well as a firm chronological framework to the elaborate iconography of seals and pottery vessels, miraculously recovered in such sites as Tlapacoya and Tlatilco. In fact, a systematic study of the 'Olmec' graphic repertoire of symbols indicates that these two sites, together with the Las Bocas zone in Puebla, have yielded – as far as ceramic iconography is concerned – one of the most complete and sophisticated records of ancient Mesoamerica.

The city, public architecture and territorial organization

The emergence of Mesoamerican regional capitals, such as San Lorenzo (Veracruz), La Venta (Tabasco), Chalcatzingo (Morelos) or Teopantecuanitlan (Guerrero), is linked to a series of interdependent factors: efficient land-use systems, population growth, an increasingly complex level of polity and a marked development of interregional trade.

San Lorenzo was built on a large *meseta*, rising about 50 m above periodically flooded plains. The major part of public mounds visible today belongs to late Classic times (Villa Alta phase), and Olmec public architecture at the site is still poorly understood. Nevertheless, recent excavations carried out by A. Cyphers (1994) have revealed the existence of deeply buried low platforms, basalt columns perhaps used as roof supports, stepped structures covered with L-shaped stone benches and elite dwellings with local bentonite pavements or red-pigmented clay floors. Elaborate water systems included artificial reservoirs linked to underground drainage channels made of U-shaped trough stones fitted with basalt covers. Among activities areas identified at the site are obsidian tool manufacturing zones, areas for preparation of glue paste from bitumen, and workshops for processing small illmenite artifacts or for carving and recycling large basalt monuments.

Most remarkable among San Lorenzo public-space features are basalt sculptures-in-the-round, stelae and carved columns (Coe and Diehl, 1980) which offer a rich and coherent set of signs for decoding Olmec cultural norms and ideology. Large table-top rectangular 'altars' or 'thrones', such as Monument 20 and Monument 14 (1.83 m high), each with a personage seated within a frontal niche, in some cases holding a child, could be related to ancestors cults, myths of origin or dynastic legitimation rituals. Ten colossal human heads – including the most recent specimen discovered in 1994 by Cyphers – have been found in San Lorenzo. Matthew W. Stirling – who discovered in 1946 the impressive San Lorenzo Colossal Head No. 1, known as 'El Rey' and weighing 25 tons – has suggested that each monolithic head has an individual quality and was probably the portrait of a prominent ruler. It has also been proposed that these heads, with helmet-like decorated head-dresses, head bands and chin straps, may represent sacralized ball-game heroes. Finally, a large corpus of sculptures-in-the-round includes seated anthropomorphic or feline figures. Fitting into this category is the magnificent discovery made in 1992 in Loma Azuzul, south of San Lorenzo. This find consists of a group of three *in situ* east-west aligned sculptures in the round with two masterly carved identical young males – in an attitude of *orantes* – facing a small feline. Nearby, a larger feline was also found. For ethnohistorians and readers of the pre-Conquest Maya manuscript of the *Popol-Vuh*, this scene instantly evokes a pristine vision of the handsome adolescent heroic twins of Maya mythology, caught in a constant struggle between veneration and rebellion with the masters and the fierce creatures (including felines) of the underworld. Whatever the plausibility of this hypothesis may be, this scene offers an extremely rare occasion in Olmec archaeology to study a set of related sculptures in their original context.

The period from 900 BC onwards is best illustrated by the site of La Venta, set on a low *meseta* surrounded by swampy areas, rivers and lagoons. The 1955 excavations have shown that the centre of La Venta consists of three groups of civil and ceremonial structures, known as complexes A, B and C, oriented along a north-south central axis showing a slight deviation of 8°West. Complex C contains the most renowned feature of the site: the Great Mound C1, a large pyramidal structure of clay and sand, about 30 m high, in the form of a fluted cone with a series of ridges and troughs running down the slopes. At the base of the southern face of this large mound and its underlying platform, high stone slabs appear to have been originally set in a row. Each stela-like monument has been decorated with bas-reliefs, some of them representing feline masks. Complex B, about which little is known, consists of several oblong mounds of beaten earth and a large platform known as the Stirling Acropolis. Complex A, which is the area that has been most fully studied, is composed of two courtyards flanked by platforms and mounds of beaten earth, arranged symmetrically, and surrounded by a 'fence' of natural prismatic basalt columns.

Excavations carried out in Complex A show that the floor of the inner courtyards, and the surface of the mounds enclosing them, were carefully maintained and overlaid with specially coloured layers of clay and sand. Stratigraphic studies have revealed sequences of distinctly coloured floors, including pink, olive green, white, yellow, brown, orange or bright red layers. In the area of Complex A, elite burials, in sand-stone-carved cists or under basalt-column structures, have been found. Small dedicatory caches of celts and figurines as well as massive deep-buried offerings of blocks of polished serpentine – sometimes arranged in several layers or laid out in the form of mosaics representing a stylized feline mask – were also uncovered.

More than 90 monolithic sculptures – colossal heads, seated figures, stelae or 'altars' – were distributed within the city's public space. Stela No. 2, an imposing basalt monument 3.5 m high, presents a frontal view of a standing hieratic figure, clearly a high-status dignitary, wearing a cape (of feathers?), holding a curved artifact and wearing a high three-tiered head-dress with elaborate motifs (Fig. 97). Mythical or

historical in nature, Stela No. 3 shows the official encounter of two personages of high rank, specifically identified by distinctive head-dresses and pectorals.

At La Venta as well as at San Lorenzo, the dating and relative chronological distribution – to within Phases I, II and III – of this large corpus of sculptures are still under discussion. This chronological uncertainty has even led, in some cases, to surprisingly impassioned debates. The dating of independent sculptures is indeed a difficult task, and the credibility of the result is proportionate to the amount of prudence involved. Fieldwork still under way at these sites may provide clearer insight in this matter.

Recent excavations and surveys at La Venta and surrounding areas, directed by Gonzalez Lauck, have led to the elaboration of a new topographical map and a better understanding of the global lay-out of architectural surface remains, including six other architectural Complexes, classified from D to I. But much work must still be done in order to understand the constructive stages and chronological position of many architectural features within Phases I, II, III and other later periods, among them for example, the Late Classic/Early Post Classic Complex F. In fact, La Venta was a major site throughout the first millennium BC, as shown by the C14 samples gathered at the site in 1955. During the last span of this period – that is in post-Olmec times – the form of the Great Mound C1, as suggested by some researchers, might have been similar to late pre-Classic structure 'E-VII Sub' of Uaxactun.

That leading sites, with 'Olmec' period architecture and sculptures, remain to be found outside the Gulf coast area is proved by the discovery in 1983 of the site of Tlacozoltitlán (Guerrero). Renamed Teopantecuanitlán, this ancient capital, situated near to the confluence of the rivers Balsas and Amacuzac, is an excellent example, outside the Atlantic watershed zone, of a planned city with both civil and

1

2

Figure 96 Olmec civilization: symbols and styles of Period II (900–700 BC). Flowing linear motifs incised on the body of pottery or jadeite objects are common. Here we see extraordinary, overlapping, frontal representations of an almond and slit-eyed mythical being incised: 1, on pottery from Tlapacoya (Valley of Mexico) and 2, on a polished jadeite axe from Arroyo Pesquero, Veracruz (after Joralemon, 1976).

Figure 97 Monumental art: monumental sculpture was closely linked to the religious rituals and public life of the major regional capitals in the Olmec period. This basalt stele, 3.40 m in height (after M. Covarrubias), found *in situ* to the south-west of the great earth pyramid (Mound C1) of the La Venta site, Tabasco, represents a ruler wearing a cape and a tall, tiered head-dress decorated with special insignia and symbols. This dignitary is escorted by secondary figures carrying, as he does himself, an enigmatic object.

ceremonial architectural complexes. Three architectonic units, called Groups A, B and C, and a residential area have been reported until now.

Group A, in the main valley, dominated by the southern platform, is distributed upon ascending levels, interrupted by a sunken enclosure. Excavated by M. G. Donjuan (1986, 1994), this rectangular closed area or precinct, whose sides measure 14.2 m by 18.60 m, is bounded by four vertical walls made of large well-cut parallelepiped travertine stones, fitted together without mortar. Inside the precinct, four monoliths weighing between 2.5 and 3 tons and shaped like an upside-down T were found. Each one is decorated with deep incisions representing a powerful image of an anthropomorphic feline with almond-shaped eyes, an inverted U-shaped mouth, in some cases covered with red cinnabar, and a frontal band displaying the stylemes of the cleft motif and the 'St Andrew' cross.

Outside the sunken precinct, earthen architectural remains have been uncovered, including steps of staircases with ramps, ending in pillars in the form of stylized feline heads, with flame eyebrows. To the east and west of the enclosure, underground drainage systems with stones carved in a U-shape and with covers, similar to those found at La Venta and San Lorenzo, have been built. North of the precinct, several carved monoliths have been unearthed, including stelae, reptilian-shaped sculptures-in-the-round and large rectangular thrones, like blocks with a protruding human head in a cartouche, carved on the front side, as well as a 1 m high megalithic human head. Outside the ceremonial area, evidence of major hydraulic works linked to intensive agrosystems is provided by the existence of a large-scale aqueduct made of two parallel rows of raised megalithic blocks, covered with slabs. This large irrigation system – the first of its kind reported in Mesoamerica – was used for channelling and controlling the flow of water from a higher storage dam towards the flood plain and the Balsas-Mezcala River below the site. Group B, to the north-east of Group A, consists of a superimposition of structures, the last of which (Structure 3), with V-shaped niches and dots, recalls the building and decorative techniques of the altar and patio area of T-25 in Chalcatzingo. Group C corresponds to a series of later mounds and platforms near the Barranca Seca, including yet undated ball-game structures.

Teopantecuanitlan is broadly contemporaneous with La Venta, although it cannot be ruled out that some earlier occupations might be found in the future, corresponding to the C14 date of 1400 BC obtained from levels underlying the precinct's floor.

On the hill, northwest of Group A, corbelled vaulted stone architecture with looted burials was found. In this respect, it must be noted that 'Olmec' Phase II stone mortuary architecture, with chambers roofed with corbelled vaults, was discovered in 1989 in Chilpancingo (Reyna Robles and Gonzalez Quintero, forthcoming). These recent archaeological discoveries reveal the existence of this specific roofing technique in Guerrero, well before its development in Classic Maya architecture.

Outside the northwest corner of the Teopantecuanitlan precinct, infant burials associated with dog burials, distributed around an altar-like structure, were excavated. Related material included Phase II pottery shards, obsidian and delicately worked marine shell, drilled and shaped into zoomorphic and geometric motifs (Gamez Eternod, personal communication).

Evidence of a Phase II marine shell workshop, from which

some of these ornaments may have originated, was identified in Teopantecuanitlan's Site 6 residential area (Niederberger, 1955). It includes unworked shell specimens or fragments, objects in process and finished products of seven species of imported sea-shells, of which the pearl oyster (*Pinctada mazatlanica*) represents 75.6 per cent of the total. In this residential area – which contains numerous fragments of hollow white-slipped 'baby-face' figurines and pottery shards with cleft-head motifs – an unusual amount of imported obsidian (74 per cent of the total number of lithic artefacts in Site 5) was also gathered. This obsidian – worked *in situ* into prismatic blades – was associated with local chert artifacts, serpentine earspools, lip-plugs and stylets, translucent and amber-coloured onyx ornaments, a fragment of iron-ore mirror and numerous mica sheets. The analysis of household debris has yielded some data on the inhabitants' diet which includes – in addition to maize identified in the pollen record – river cat-fish, crabs, rabbits, red brockets, white-tailed deer and, in a high proportion amounting to more than half of the total animal consumption, dogs.

The development of a systematic *contextual analysis* of Olmec-style features, together with a more precise definition of an internal chronology within its evolutionary sequence, in numerous zones of ancient Mesoamerica, should aid the formulation of more reliable answers to questions concerning the rise, development and inner articulations of this ancient cultural system named, *faute de mieux*, Olmec.

Political power and social ranking

Two main obstacles arise in the attempt to define the political nature of non-writing societies: the unavoidable gaps within the archaeological record and the limits of conceptual tools used in theoretical classifications. Americanists generally lean on the Service and Fried three-fold scheme, which define three levels of socio-political evolution: 1) egalitarian societies; 2) ranked societies or chiefdoms; 3) states with stratified societies. Although this scheme possesses the advantage of getting rid of the ancient traditional dual division into pre-State and State societies, its effectiveness is hindered, in our opinion, by the still too-large and imprecise character of the second category: the chiefdom level. Indeed, it is precisely within this intermediary level – between egalitarian communities and state stratified societies – that the greatest variety of political integration and power configurations can be found.

Concerning the political organization of the Olmec world, different theses have been held proposing the existence of an 'empire' (Caso, 1965; Bernal, 1968; Coe, 1989), of a 'state' (Heizer, 1960) or a 'pristine state' (Drucker, 1981), in all cases based on the southern Veracruz-western Tabasco region, defined as a 'nuclear zone' or a 'metropolitan area'. As an implicit or explicit corollary, the socio-political organization of the communities outside the Gulf coast zone was considered as the expression of a lower degree of cultural complexity. The Olmec socio-political system has also been ascribed to the chiefdom level (Sanders and Price, 1968). But, even in this interpretative context, many non-Gulf societies, in particular in the Highlands, have been described as backward, relatively egalitarian communities. This belief is far from being dead and gone, and it is interesting to note that most articles in the March 1995 issue of *Arqueología Mexicana*, dedicated to the Olmec world, tend to revive these suppositions.

As rightly observed by Drucker (1981, p. 30): 'the

definition of category of organization is far more than nit-picking over labels. It concerns our understanding of Olmec culture'. Since fieldwork in the southern part of the Basin of Mexico, it has been our contention, subsequently sustained in Spanish and French publications, that all ancient Mesoamerican Phase I and II Olmec period societies pertain to a similar level of socio-political evolution. With the continued growth of field data, and for the sake of anthropological consistency, it will no doubt be increasingly difficult to uphold the postulate that one particular ethnic group or region – whether in the Gulf coast, or in Guerrero as suggested by Covarrubias – had directly or indirectly controlled more primitive groups within the ancient Mesoamerican sphere.

As for the nature of Olmec period polity, the placement of the 1200-600 BC communities within the chiefdom intermediary level seems acceptable, but still too vague. 'Olmec' polities have often been reduced to relatively primitive chiefdoms, following Melanesian ethnological models, without taking into account the intellectual achievements and the qualitatively different nature of political integration, prelude to the great Classic Mesoamerican cities. The debate is still open. Nevertheless, it seems now reasonable to assume, without using necessarily the much-debated expression of 'pristine state', that the socio-political organization of ancient Olmec Mesoamerica corresponds to 'ranked societies' of a high degree of complexity. Together with institutionalized political structures and well-defined centralized authority, a strong development of social ranking is indeed confirmed by the archaeological evidence gathered in Chiapas, Oaxaca, Guerrero, Morelos, the Basin of Mexico and the Gulf coast region. The analysis of mortuary practices reveals highly differentiated patterns of internments – from simple direct burials in earth or in refuse pits, to stone delimited graves, elaborate crypts, carved sarcophagi or corbelled arch chambers – as well as a great variety of grave offerings.

At the end of the second millennium BC, the regional capitals of these complex ranked societies have become an essential focus for information treatment, including the production, reception and redistribution of graphic symbols and messages. Among observed intellectual achievements is the set of Phases I and II graphic symbols that have been interpreted (Niederberger, 1987, pp. 716–7) as mythograms – that is, an ideographic notation not yet integrated into oral systems – and, perhaps, related to toponymic emblems, lineages, titular distinctions or celestial or earthly sacred forces. Their role as direct antecedents to true ideograms – with precise meaning, doubled with phonetic reading – seems to be validated by the emergence of ideographic writing systems during Phase III. This phenomenon has been convincingly documented in the study by Flannery and Marcus (1983, p. 57), carried out in San José Mogote (Oaxaca), of a Rosario phase (700-500 BC) glyphic set – part of a ritual calendar – which could be interpreted as the date of 'One Movement'.

The dual nature of inter-regional exchange networks: final comments

At this concluding point, a question arises: how can one explain the relative stylistic unity – expression of a shared system of beliefs – in ancient Mesoamerica, if one cannot draw upon diffusionistic models of direct or indirect influence or control from a single area? It seems that the analysis of economic exchange systems provides relevant information.

Long-distance exchange networks – including obsidian – were established throughout Middle America from early Holocene times. At the end of the second millennium BC, a remarkable intensification, in volume and in variety, of commodities exchanged is observed. As shown by numerous field reports and specialized studies (Hirth, 1984; Pires-Ferreira, 1976; Niederberger, 1976, 1987), circulating goods and products included obsidian, chert, lime, salt, clay, asphalt, porous volcanic rock used in the manufacture of grinding stones as well as cotton, mica, iron-ore for the fabrication of concave mirrors, calcite onyx, amber, amethyst, rock crystal, jadeite and serpentine used in small lapidary art, sharks' teeth, turtles, and Pacific and Atlantic sea-shells.

Since the early 1900s and the pioneering ethnological works of Marcel Mauss, the non-economic dimension of such exchange systems has been well stressed. As for ancient Mesoamerica, we have examined, in earlier works, how the fully structured system of goods exchange at the end of the second millennium BC also involved an equally dense and regular parallel network of information and message circulation. Through this dual communication network, some form of cultural symbiosis is intrinsically associated with economic symbiosis. It is our belief that all the agrarian ranked societies, part of these interregional communication networks, not only manipulated a common set of visual symbols, semantic fields and cognitive systems but also actively contributed to their codification, evolution and transmission.

The development at the end of the second millennium BC of complex ranked societies, regional centres, earthen and stone public architecture, codified graphic symbols and organized interregional exchanges – the base of cultural symbiosis and macro-regional integration – was the result of several millennia of evolution in the southern part of Middle America. This long process of maturation eventually gave birth to an original socio-cultural system – pan-Mesoamerican and multi-ethnic in nature – that can be defined as Mesoamerica 'Time I'.

BIBLIOGRAPHY

AUFDERMAUER, J. 1973. Aspectos de la cronología del preclásico en la Cuenca de Puebla-Tlaxcala. *Comunicaciones.* (Puebla.) Vol. 9, pp. 11-24.

BAUDEZ, C. F.; BECQUELIN, P. 1973. *Archéologie de Los Naranjos, Honduras.* Mission archéologique et ethnologique française au Mexique. Mexico. (Etud. Mesoam., 2).

BERNAL, I. 1968. *El Mundo Olmeca.* Mexico.

BLAKE, M. 1991. An Emerging Early Formative Chiefdom at Paso de la Amada, Chiapas, Mexico. In: FOWLER, W. R. (ed.), *The Formation of Complex Society in Southern Mesoamerica.* Boca Raton/Ann Arbor, Mich. pp. 27–46.

BLOM, F.; LA FARGE, O. 1926-7. *Tribes and Temples.* (Publ. 1.). New Orleans.

BOVÉ, F. J. 1978. Laguna de los Cerros: An Olmec Central Place. *J. New World Archaeol.*, Vol. 2, No. 3.

BRADLEY, D. E.; JORALEMON, P. D. 1993. *The Lords of Life.* Indiana.

BRAY, W. 1979. From Village to City in Mesoamerica. In: MOORLEY, P. R. (ed.), *The Origins of Civilization.* (Oxford.) pp. 78–108.

CASO, A. 1965. Existió un imperio olmeca? *Memoria del Colegio Nacional.* (Mexico.) Vol. 3, pp. 11–60.

CLARK, J. E. 1994. Antecedentes de la cultura olmeca. In: CLARK, J. E. (ed.), *Los Olmecas en Mesoamérica.* Mexico. pp. 31–67.

COE, M. D. 1972. Olmec Jaguars and Olmec Kings. In: BENSON, E., *The Cult of the Feline.* Washington, D.C. pp. 1–18.

—— 1976. Early Steps in the Evolution of Maya Writing. In: NICHOLSON, H. B. (ed.). *The Origins of Religious Art and Iconogra-*

phy in Preclassic Mesoamerica. (Lat. Am. Stud. Ser., 31). Los Angeles. pp. 109–22.

—— 1989. The Olmec Heartland: Evolution of Ideology. In: SHARER, R. J.; GROVE, D. C. (eds), Regional Perspectives on the Olmec. New York. pp. 68–82.

—— ; DIEHL, R. A. 1980. In the Land of the Olmec: The Archaeology of San Lorenzo Tenochtitlan. Vol. 1. Austin, Tex.

—— ; FLANNERY, K. V. 1967. Early Cultures and Human Ecology in South Coastal Guatemala. (Smithsonian Contrib. Anthropol., 3). Washington, D.C.

COVARRUBIAS, M. 1957. Indian Art of Mexico and Central America. New York.

CYPHERS, G. A. 1994. San Lorenzo. In: CLARK, J. E. (ed.), Los Olmecas en Mesoamérica. Mexico. pp. 43-67.

DEMAREST, A. 1989. The Olmec and the Rise of Civilization in Eastern Mesoamerica. In: SHARER, R. J.; GROVE, D. C. (eds), Regional Perspectives on the Olmec. New York. pp. 303–44.

DONJUAN, M. G. 1986. Teopantecuanitlán. In: Arqueología y etnohistoria del Estado de Guerrero. Mexico. pp. 55–80.

—— 1994. Los Olmecas en el estado de Guerrero. In: CLARK, J. E. (ed.), Los Olmecas en Mesoamérica. Mexico. pp. 143–73.

DRUCKER, P. R. 1981. On the Nature of Olmec Polity. In: BENSON E. (ed.), The Olmec and Their Neighbors. Washington, D.C. pp. 29–47.

—— HEIZER, R. F.; SQUIER, R. J. 1959. Excavations et La Venta, Tabasco, 1955. (Bull. 170). Washington, D.C.

FLANNERY, K. V. 1968. Archaeological Systems Theory and Early Mesoamerica. In: MEGGERS, J. (ed.), Anthropological Archaeology in the Americas. Washington, D.C. pp. 67–87.

—— . (ed.). 1976. The Early Mesoamerican Village. New York.

—— . et al. 1967. Farming Systems and Political Growth in Ancient Oaxaca, Mexico. Science. (Washington, D.C.) Vol. 158, pp. 445-54.

—— MARCUS, J. (eds). 1983. The Cloud People: Evolution of the Zapotec and Mixtec Civilizations of Oaxaca, Mexico. New York.

—— 1994. Early Formative Pottery of the Valley of Oaxaca, Mexico. Prehistory and Human Ecology of the Valley of Oaxaca. Vol. 10, Mem. of the Mus. of Anthropology No.27. (Ann Arbor, Mich.)

GONZALEZ LAUCK, R. 1994. La antigua ciudad olmeca en La Venta, Tabasco. In: CLARK, J. E. (ed.), Los Olmecas en Mesoamérica. Mexico. pp. 93–111.

GRAHAM, J. A. 1981. Abaj Takalik. In J. A. GRAHAM (ed.), Ancient Mesoamerica. pp. 163–79.

GREEN, D. F.; LOWE, G. W. 1967. Altamira and Padre Piedra, Early Preclassic Sites in Chiapas, Mexico. (Pap. 20). Provo, Utah.

GRIFFIN, G. G. 1981. Olmec Forms and Material found in central Guerrero. In: BENSON, E. (ED.), The Olmec and their Neighbors. Washington, D.C. pp. 209–22.

GROVE D. C.; PARADIS, L. 1971. An Olmec Stela from San Miguel Amuco, Guerrero. Am. Antiq. (Washington, D.C.) Vol. 36-1, pp. 95–102.

—— ; et al. 1987. Ancient Chalcatzingo. Austin, Tex.

HAMMOND, N. 1989. Cultura hermana: Reappraising the Olmec. Quarterly Review of Archaeology. Vol. 9, No. 4, pp. 1–4.

HEIZER, R. F. 1960. Agriculture and the Theocratic State in Lowland Southeastern Mexico. American Antiquity. Vol. 26, No. 2, pp. 215–22.

HIRTH, K. G. (ed.) 1984. Trade and Exchange in Early Mesoamerica. Albuquerque.

JORALEMON, P. D. 1976. The Olmec Dragon: A Study in Pre-Columbian Iconography. In: NICHOLSON, H. B. (ed.), Origins of Religious Art and Iconography in Preclassic Mesoamerica. (Lat. Am. Stud. Ser. 31). Los Angeles. pp. 27–71.

KELLY, I. 1980. Ceramic Sequence in Colima: Capacha, an Early Phase. (Anthropol. Pap., 37). Tucson, Ariz.

KIRCHHOFF, P. 1943. Mesoamerica. Acta Am. (Mexico.) Vol. 28, pp. 67–77.

LEE, T. A. 1989. Chiapas and the Olmec. In: SHARER, R. J.; GROVE, D. C. (eds), Regional Perspective on the Olmec. New York. pp. 198–226.

LORENZO, J. L. 1965. Tlatilco. Los Artefactos. (Ser.Invest. 7,III). Mexico.

LOVE, M. W. 1991. Style and Social Complexity in Formative Mesoamerica. In: FOWLER, W. R. (ed.), The Formation of Complex Society in Southeastern Mesoamerica. CRC Press. Boca Raton/ Ann Arbor, Mich. pp. 47–76.

LOWE, G. 1977. The Mixe-Zoque as Competing Neighbors of the Lowland Maya. In: ADAMS, R. E. (ed.), The Origin of Maya Civilization. Albuquerque.

MACNEISH, R. S. 1967. A Summary of the Subsistence. In: BYERS, D. S. (ed.), The Prehistory of the Tehuacan Valley, Environment and Subsistence. Austin, Tex. pp. 290–309.

MARCUS, J. 1978. Archaeology and Religion: A Comparison of the Zapotec and Maya. World Archaeol. (London.) Vol. 10, No. 2, pp. 172–91.

NAVARRETE, C. 1974. The Olmec Rock Carvings at Pijijiapan, Chiapas, Mexico, and Other Olmec Pieces from Chiapas and Guatemala. (Pap. 35). Provo, Utah.

NIEDERBERGER, C. 1955. Nacar y 'jade' Guerrero y las rutas de comunicación interregional en la Mesoamérica Antigua (1000-600 BC). Espacio, Cultura y Sociedad en Guerrero. Coloquio Internacional CIESAS/CNRS/INAH. June. Mexico.

—— 1970. Excavations at Tlapacoya, Mexico. Cultural Remains II. XXXV Annual Meeting. Society for American Archaeology. Dpt de Prehistoria. Mexico.

—— 1974. Inicios de la vida sedentaria en America Media. Historia de Mexico, Vol. I. (Barcelona/Mexico). pp. 39–120.

—— 1976. Zohapilco: Cinco milenios de ocupación humana en un sitio lacustre de la Cuenca de México. (Colecc. Cient., Arqueol., 30). Mexico.

—— 1979. Early Sedentary Economy in the Basin of Mexico. Science. (Washington, D.C.) Vol. 203, pp. 131–42.

—— 1986. Excavaciones de una área de habitacíon doméstica en la capital 'olmeca' de Tlacozoltitlan, Guerrero. In: Arqueología y Etnohistoria del Estado de Guerrero. Mexico. pp. 81-103.

—— 1987. Paléopaysages et Archéologie préurbaine du Bassin de Mexico. 2 vols. (Collect. Etud. Mésoam., Sér. 1, 11). Mexico.

OLIVEROS, J. A. 1974. Nuevas exploraciones en El Opeña, Michoacan. In: BELL, B. (ed.), The Archaeology of West Mexico. Jalisco, Sociedad de Estudios Avanzados de México, A. C. Ajijic, Mexico. pp. 182–201.

—— 1994. Imagen precolombina del huracán. Arqueologia Mexicana. (Mexico.) Vol. 2, No. 7. pp. 66–69.

ORTIZ, P.; RODRÍGUEZ, M. C. 1994. Los espacios sagrados olmecas: El Manatí, un caso especial. In: CLARK, J. E. (ed.), Los Olmecas en Mesoamérica. Mexico. pp. 69–91.

PIÑA CHAN, R. 1958. Tlatilco. (Ser. Invest., 1, 2). Mexico.

PIRES-FERREIRA, J. W. 1976. Shell and Iron-Ore Mirror Exchange in Formative Mesoamerica, with Comments on Other Commodities. In: FLANNERY, K. V. (ed.), The Early Mesoamerican Village. New York. pp. 311–26.

POHORILENKO, A. 1977. On the Question of Olmec Deities. Journal of New World Archaeol. (London.) Vol. 2, No. 1, pp. 1-16.

PORTER WEAVER, M. 1953. Tlatilco and the Preclassic Cultures of the New World. Viking Fund Publications in Anthropology (New York.) Vol. 19.

PYE, M. E.; DEMAREST, A. A. 1991. The Evolution of Complex Societies in Southeastern Mesoamerica: New Evidence from El Mesak, Guatemala. In: FOWLER, W. R., The Formation of Complex Society in Southeastern Mesoamerica. Boca Raton/Ann Arbor, Mich. pp. 77–100.

REILLY, F. K. 1994. Cosmología, soberanismo y espacio ritual en la Mesoamérica del Formativo. In: CLARK, J. E. (ed.), Los Olmecas en Mesoamérica. Mexico. pp. 239–59.

REYNA ROBLES, R. M.; GONZALEZ QUINTERO, L., Preface by Niederberger, C. (forthcoming). Rescate arqueológico de unespacio funerario de época olmeca en Chipancingo, Guerrero. Mexico.

SANDERS, W. T.; PRICE, B. 1968. Mesoamerica: the Evolution of a Civilization. New York.

SHARER, J. (ed.). 1978. *The Prehistory of Chalchuapa, El Salvador.* Philadelphia.

SMITH, C. E. 1986. Preceramic Plant remains from Guilá Naquitz. In: FLANNERY, K. (ed.), *Guilá Naquitz. Archaic foraging and Early Agriculture in Oaxaca, Mexico.* New York. pp. 265–274.

STIRLING, M. W. 1940. Great Stone Faces of the Mexican Jungle. *Nat. Geogr. Mag.* (Washington, D.C.) Vol. 78, No. 3, pp. 309-34.

TOLSTOY, P.; PARADIS, L. 1970. Early and Middle Preclassic Culture in the Basin of Mexico. *Science.* (Washington, D.C.) Vol. 167, pp. 344–51.

WINTER, M. 1976. The Archaeological Household Cluster in the Valley of Oaxaca. In: FLANNERY, K. V. (ed.), *The Early Mesoamerican Village.* New York. pp. 25–31.

ZEITLIN, R. N. 1978. Long-distance Exchange and the Growth of a Regional Center on the Southern Isthmus of Tehuantepec. In: STARK, B.; VOORHIES, V. (eds), *Prehistoric Coastal Adaptation.* New York. pp. 183–210.

17.5
SOUTH AMERICA

17.5.1
THE NORTH-EAST AND EASTERN REGION

Mario Sanoja Obediente

THE GATHERING WAY OF LIFE

In the New World the period from 3000 to 2000 BC was a time of optimum climatic conditions, with warm temperatures marking the end of the predominant influence of glaciation in the Pleistocene and the early Holocene. In Colombia, this trend towards a warmer climate characteristic of the Recent Epoch is reflected in the palynological records of different parts of Colombia's eastern cordillera (Correal and van der Hammen, 1977, p. 16) and in some of the north-eastern regions of South America, although less prominently.

From that time on, there is a discernible trend in various parts of the New World towards intensification of plant gathering, and possibly towards experimenting with plants for food production. In the north of South America these changes appear in the hunting-gathering variant that we include in the 'tradition of non-specialized stone artefacts', some of the earliest examples of which are to be found in the sites of El Abra, Tequendama, Sueva, Nemocón and Chía, studied by Hurt, Correal, van der Hammen and Ardila.

As noted in Volume I of this work, the characteristic feature of the non-specialized stone artefacts tradition, and in particular of the *abri* or 'shelter' technique, is the production of flakes and secondary cores chipped from a primary core. The resulting fragments are put to different uses depending on their morphology with, in some cases, deliberate alterations to one edge of the artefact. This complex of stone artefacts exists alongside a bone industry consisting of tools obtained by breaking up and shaping long mammal bones. All the stone and bone artefacts seem to have been used for cutting, scraping, pounding and piercing, though generally there is no fixed relationship between the shape and the function.

This variant on the 'appropriative' mode of production seems to have been associated with a generalized practice of capturing and gathering animal and plant species and an ability to appropriate available subsistence resources in the varied marine, river, forest, savannah and other ecosystems of northern South America, the West Indies and Central America; and later on, with the emergence of early forms of horticulture, possibly plant cultivation, which determined the

basic features of the mode of production of the agricultural tribal society in the region.

Between 5000 and 3000 BC, the people of the Vegas hunting-gathering community seem to have abandoned the Santa Helena peninsula, possibly because of a general desiccation of the environment (Stothern, 1976; Lumbreras, 1983, p. 26). It was precisely in the third millennium (3000–2300 BC) that the so-called Valdivia culture appeared in that region (Meggers et al., 1965; Lathrap et al., 1977), a culture that already showed traces of extremely complex pottery making and perhaps the cultivation of maize of the Koello strain in the Real Alto site, dating from roughly 2400 BC (Zevallos et al., 1977). The people of Valdivia seem to have assimilated the working methods of the early hunting-gathering communities, not only in shellfish collecting and fishing but also work processes aimed at exploiting coastal and inland resources, reflected – in this case – in the existence of pottery-making communities specializing in the gathering of marine bivalves, particularly *Anomalocardia subrugosa* Sby., and gastropods such as *Cerithidea purpurescences* Brod., and of agricultural communities inland. This division of work between components of a single ethnic group was a feature of other ancient societies in the Old and the New Worlds and has been associated *inter alia* with differences in forms of social and religious organization.

According to the data so far available, the gathering communities that lived on the coast of Ecuador between 6000 and 5000 BC had already begun to introduce certain forms of food-production control. They were seemingly in the early stages of pottery making, a process which was crucial to social development, and reflected in the so-called Achalla complex, whose shards are extremely primitive, even compared with the most primitive of Valdivia A or Valdivia I, with which it is contemporary (Stothern, 1976, p. 91; Meggers et al., 1965; Hill, 1966, 1975). Moreover, already in Late Vegas or Achallan we find the idea of a territorial space organized as a permanent village, strategically located for the exploitation of both the marine ecosystem and the river and forest ecosystem of the interior, surrounded by seasonal camp sites located, in many cases, in the coastal area. The site of Real Alto (Lathrap et al., 1977) seems to reproduce a similar form of territorial space organization: on the one hand, a large village in which the domestic living areas are arranged around a central space or structure used for meetings or joint festivities and, on the other, a territorial division into a central village and coastal camps. In the central village, the predominant agricultural work process represents a break with the predatory character of the Vegas or Achallan community in terms of the development of the productive forces. On the coast, gathering, fishing and hunting communities shared with the inland pottery-making farmers the same pottery-making process, with the addition of 'superstructural' features possibly linked with fertility rites, clearly visible in the Valdivian figurines; but their method of work preserves technical, social and ideological relationships characteristic of the hunting-gathering way of life superseded by Valdivian tribal society.

Without entering into a discussion of the substance and form of the dissemination theory of Meggers, Evans and Estrada (whose hypothesis is well supported by facts) or the argument of local evolution put forward by Lumbreras, Bischof, Stothern, Marcos and other researchers, it is clear that the final break in the predatory pattern of the hunting-gathering society on the Guayas coast was brought about by an induced process, on the whole without local precedents. Predatory forms generated by the socio-historical development of local hunting-gathering communities persisted, growing more intense and changing form within a tribal formation based mainly on food production, whose emergence was due to the presence of communities in which the productive forces were more highly developed.

THE ORIGINS OF FOOD PRODUCTION IN COLOMBIA

The origins of food production in the territory of present-day Colombia also seem to be rooted in the socio-historical process beginning with the hunting-gathering societies associated with the cultural tradition of non-specialized production tools.

The spread of the non-specialized tool complex into the valleys and lowlands of Colombia's Atlantic coast has been described by Hurt et al. (1976, pp. 16–17); Correal and van der Hammen (1977, p. 110), and Reichel-Dolmatoff (1965a, pp. 48–9). Although there are no absolute dates to provide a time-frame, Correal and van der Hammen link this possible population movement with a series of climatic and demographic changes occurring on the Colombian high plateau between 4000 and 3000 BC. Around that time there was a decline in the population of the area, coinciding with a rise in the average temperature and a very pronounced process of desiccation. Concurrently with a possible demographic decline in the hunting-gathering communities of the high plateau, the coastal variant of cultural forms and work processes characteristic of hunting and gathering communities was developing on the Caribbean coast of Colombia around 3350 BC.

An inventory of the fauna consumed by the inhabitants of Monsú, a site typical of the early form of that process (Reichel-Dolmatoff, 1985, pp. 169–70), shows for the period around 3350 BC a predominance of land hunting (deer, wild pigs, rodents) over fishing, hunting (turtles) and gathering (crabs, land gastropods), possibly in swamps and shallow water near the coast.

However, in Puerto Hormiga (Reichel-Dolmatoff, 1965b, 1971), situated in the vicinity of Monsú, we find 260 years later that the same populations had virtually given up hunting large mammals, confining themselves to small rodents, while the gathering of bivalves – particularly those of the *Pitar* genus and the *Ostrea* – had replaced the gathering of freshwater gastropods. Moreover, most of the fish caught, together with the turtles and crabs, came from marshes or rivers. The shells of some species of freshwater or estuarine gastropod, for example the melongena, may have been used as a receptacle, with modifications to the lip and the front end of the axis (Reichel-Dolmatoff, 1971, p. 342; 1965b, p. 45). This takes on special importance when one considers that the inventory of fauna hunted or captured by the hunting-gathering community of Tequendama indicates precisely a life-style based on the hunting of large mammals (*Mazama*, *Odocoyleus* sp.) and small rodents such as the agouti and dasyprocta, and the gathering of land gastropods belonging to the *Drymaeus* and *Plekocheilus* genera, most of which were found in the late Tequendama period (Correal and van der Hammen, 1977, p. 56).

If the interpretations of Correal and van der Hammen are correct, they indicate that the hunting-gathering communities that moved towards the Caribbean coast of Colombia changed within about two centuries. From a work process based essentially on the hunting of land mammals, they graduated to a varied selection involving the gathering of marine and estuarine bivalves, fishing, and gathering in rivers and lagoons. The stone production toolkit associated with this kind of work includes unifacial flakes, cutters, what may have been perforators and burins – some with bulbs of percussion – and rounded stones used as pestles, hammers, polishers, anvils or quebracocos (stones with a hollow centre), axes and prismatic cores reminiscent of the implements of early marine gatherers in the north-east of South America.

In Monsú, the stratigraphic record also indicates the presence of awls or punches made of the horn of *Mazama* sp., possible projectile points made from splinters of long mammal bones or the tails of rays (*Dayasatis* sp.), bone and seashell plates and beads. In Puerto Hormiga, on the other hand, sea or freshwater shell artefacts predominate. The presence in Monsú and Puerto Hormiga, and in Rotinet and the Lower Magdalena (Angula, *pers. comm.*), of hoes and axes made from the shell of *Strombus gigas*, and of baking pans or plates for roasting bitter cassava flour as early as 2250 BC, makes it conceivable that the Lower Magdalena region was one of the original centres of plant cultivation in South America (Sanoja, 1979; 1982).

The environmental conditions of the Lower Magdalena seem to have been instrumental in reorienting the economic activity of the hunting-gathering-fishing communities who migrated to the Caribbean coast of Colombia. An important circumstance might have been the concentration of vegetation, particularly toxic and sweet varieties of *Manihot esculenta*, which seem to have existed in that region (Rogers, 1963; Sanoja, 1979; 1982a, b). Such vegetation was included among the edible plant species of the hunting-gathering-fishing communities of the Lower Magdalena, at least from the third millennium BC, not simply as vegetables that could be eaten boiled or roasted but as roots whose pulp had to be processed to convert it into flour and then into cassava.

The toxic varieties of cassava are best suited to making cassava bread. The roots contain more starch and less fibre than the sweet variety and their quality and yield for flour and cassava bread production are higher. However, their preparation involves a series of operations: grating the root, pressing the pulp to extract the hydrocyanic acid, sifting the dry pulp and cooking the flour or manioc in clay dishes or baking pans. Each operation required a knowledge of how to make the wooden graters with inlaid micro-flakes to produce the abrasive surface, the set of baskets for processing the pulp, including the manioc strainer or *tipiti*, and a knowledge of pottery to make the baking pans. In addition, the indigenous cultivator needed to be familiar with the technique of cultivation by making cuttings or slips to separate the different varieties of cassava into clones, avoiding introgression between wild and domesticated species by interrupting the inflorescence and pollination of the plant.

Clearly, the co-ordination of the different work processes involved in producing cassava bread called for an appreciable qualitative and quantitative change in the productive forces of the ancient hunting-gathering-fishing communities of the Lower Magdalena. The change might be interpreted as an early example of the 'Neolithization' process marking the end of the appropriative mode of production of the hunting-gathering society and the beginning of the food-producing tribal society in the north of South America.

Analysing the stylistic aspect of the decorative pottery of Valdivia, Puerto Hormiga, Monsú and Monagrillo, Meggers, *et al.* (1965, p. 168) and Reichel-Dolmatoff (1985, pp. 191–2) have argued either that Valdivia was the precursor of Puerto Hormiga or that, conversely, Monsú and Puerto Hormiga were the precursors of Valdivian pottery. However, while recognizing the formal kinship that clearly exists between pottery decoration in the two cultures, it should be noted that while the socio-historical processes determining the constitution of both tribal communities basically reflect the dissolution of the gathering society and the development of a food-producing tribal society, the rate of change was not the same. In the case of Valdivia, the process was completed rapidly by maize-cultivating village communities who soon reached a certain level of socio-political stratification and organization and, in general, a comparatively high level of development of the productive forces.

In the case of Monsú and Puerto Hormiga, the dissolution of the hunting-gathering society was very slow. Although the hoe was already being used for cultivation before the third millennium BC, the association of plants such as cassava with gathering, hunting or fishing, while initially capable of relatively high productivity, in the long run acted as a curb on the general development of the productive forces of the village tribal community.

Owing to its distinctive characteristics, plant cultivation calls for a minimum investment of labour and social organization for work. Combined with predatory work processes such as hunting, fishing and gathering, it can offer a high – albeit neither continuous nor growing – return in terms of the production of carbohydrates and proteins. But the conservation of the roots underground, or the cassava flour in the dwelling-place, do not require the development of communal storage systems or the improvement of distribution and consumption, except for the provision of fair and equal apportionment of the plots whose yield is directly consumed by the cultivator. Similarly, the fauna hunted, captured or fished is maintained and developed by natural processes without human intervention. The plant-growing variant of village society thus becomes an improved and expanded version of the predatory mode of work. In the tribal village variant producing crops such as maize, agricultural production and the distribution and consumption processes develop as an integrated mode of work, preserving complementary processes surviving from earlier societies. In the Valdivian

culture, for example, the persistence of pottery-producing villages of the marine gathering and fishing communities on the Guayas coast is seen, but they play no intermediary or decisive role in the development of the productive forces of the agricultural communities of the interior, which are of relevance to the socio-historical development of the society as a whole. We thus have confirmation of the dialectical historical argument that social progress does not occur through adaptation to natural economic forms but through sustained withdrawal from them.

In the light of the foregoing considerations, the fact that the village tribal communities of the Lower Magdelena and the Guayas coast share 'superstructural' elements, such as the symbolic codes of formal representation used in pottery, does not imply that one had a culturally determining relationship over another. It may imply that they shared forms of ideological expression denoting a historical condition: that of being tribal societies. This theme has given rise to innumerable theories on the part of archaeologists: the existence of a plastic decorative tradition of a 'modelled-incised-punctate' nature common to potters in the so-called formative societies, the most distant ancestors of the tribal grouping in South America.

Ford (1969), in his monumental comparative work on formative American cultures, objectively demonstrated how 'superstructural' forms are determined by the material basis in tribal society and in some communities in the initial class formation: communities associated with the emergence of the state. But when this determination is reflected in tangible manifestations such as an aesthetic stylistic tradition of pottery decoration, does it imply the spread of human groups, the dissemination of ideas, or independent development? Childe (1981, pp. 239–63) has explained these phenomena in terms of the existence of a historically determined social tradition shared by different peoples. The environment or environments that were exploited by those cultures by means of different agricultural, predatory, or other practices were worlds that had to be explained through group representations. These were realized through plastic decorative techniques whose execution required only a change in the volume of the raw material and surface of the clay objects through the addition or subtraction of material. The decorative style was basically a form of reflection on the natural environment, manifested in zoomorphic, anthropomorphic, topomorphic and other representations which differ according to their vital cause: 'Given that in the egalitarian village way of life the main contradiction spurring the development of society is still closer to the human being–nature relationship than to the human-human relationship, the phenomenal responses, in accordance with the vital cause of the economic social formation in question, especially those connected with the superstructure, tend to reflect the main contradiction' (Vargas, 1985a, pp. 97–8; Delgado, 1985, p. 69).

The egalitarian village way of life, supported by a mixed productive basis of plant cultivation, marine gathering, fishing and land hunting, remained stable for several millennia on the Caribbean coast of Colombia in sites such as Barlovento, Canapote, Bucarelia, Zambrano and Rotinet. The aboriginal communities seem to have moved gradually from the coast to the marshes and lagoons formed by the River Magdalena before flowing into the Caribbean Sea, places where food production could be carried on more effectively in combination with the appropriation of land and aquatic fauna.

An example of this process is the Malambo phase (Angulo,

1962, 1981), dated to 1100 BC, where the abandonment of shellfish gathering and an increase in both land and river hunting and in fishing are discernible. Moreover, Malambo contrasts sharply with the preceding socio-historical process, an early example of the formation of a large stable nuclear village with intensive development of the different modes of work characteristic of the egalitarian village tribal way of life: plant cultivation, pottery, textiles, hunting and fishing. As seems to be the case in all egalitarian village tribal communities, the domestic area was used not only as a dwelling space but also as a burial place. The skeletons were generally associated with offerings reflecting the individual's sex and habitual activity in daily life. There is evidence of possible differentiation in the treatment of the dead: although direct primary burials were universal, a minority were buried in clay urns with offerings of food and production implements.

The continuation of the modelled-incised tradition of pottery originating in Monsú and Puerto Hormiga can be seen in anthropomorphic masks, cylindrical bakers' tools, spindle whorls, necklace beads and a great variety of vessels, in some cases of complex morphology. In general, Malambo seems to prefigure the type of nuclear community that was to be characteristic of the egalitarian village tribal society of the Caribbean coast of Colombia throughout the first millennium BC and the early centuries of the Christian era.

THE ORIGINS OF FOOD PRODUCTION IN PANAMA

As we saw in the first volume, around 4840 BC the gathering way of life was also established on the Pacific coast of Panama, a characteristic site being that of Cerro Mangote at the mouth of the Santa María River (McGimsey, 1956, pp. 151–61). A study of the archaeological remains of Cerro Mangote indicates the presence of human groups organized in small but stable communities, who lived on shellfish, fish, wild plants, and by hunting.

In Panama the first evidence of pottery making was found at the site of Monagrillo, dated c. 2140 BC, in the region of Bahéa de Parita, on the Pacific coast of the isthmus (Willey and McGimsey, 1954). The cultural context of the site indicates that the individuals of the Monagrillo community supported themselves mainly by fishing and by gathering shellfish, particularly Ostrea chiliensis and Tivela gracilor, on the muddy bottom of the mouth of the Parita River. A further substantial portion of their food was obtained through hunting, as attested by the presence of Odocoyleus chiriquensis Allen, Pecari ungulatus, Procyomidae, freshwater tortoises, rabbits and agoutis. There is no evidence of cultivation, although some production implements such as manos and metates indicate that plant foods and palm nuts were also processed.

The settlements of the Monagrillo hunting-gathering community were distributed along an ancient beach in Parita Bay, although conditions seem to have changed during the occupation of the sites. During this time sedementation led to the formation of a coastal lagoon which increased the stocks of fish and bivalves in the area and was therefore conducive to more permanent occupation until the lagoon became a salt pan and the site was abandoned (Linares, 1977, p. 18; Ranere and Hansell, 1978, pp. 47–8).

In general, the Monagrillo hunting-gathering community maintained the predatory mode of work that had existed since Cerro Mangote, so that the presence of incised pottery in Monagrillo might be the result of a process derived from other communities in neighbouring regions. The stylistic features point towards north-eastern Colombia, where other plant-growing, hunting-gathering communities had also been making incised pottery since c. 3300 BC.

Other sites such as the Aguadulce rockshelter provide stratigraphic evidence of the succession of cultural changes that occurred on the Pacific coast of Panama between 5000 and 2000 BC, with a Cerro Mangote component at the base and Monagrillo pottery at a higher level (Linares, 1977; Ranere and Hansell, 1978). The diet of the occupants of the Aguadulce shelter indicates the predominance of hunting of large mammals such as deer (Odocoyleus sp.), rodents, armadillos, iguanas and tortoises. Like the Monagrillo people, they consumed shellfish as well as sea and freshwater fish from the coastal area, which must have been closer then than at present.

This period, in the interior of Panama, known as the Boquete phase, is associated with a gradual stabilization in the trend towards food production, culminating around 940 BC with the appearance of pottery and a diversified form of subsistence including both plant growing and possibly maize cultivation (Ranere, 1972, 1976; Linares and Ranere, 1971; Linares, 1975, 1977; Fonseca, 1985). It is possible that in the transition to forms of food production in Panama the hunting-gathering communities took advantage of he exceptional opportunity of being able to exploit simultaneously the marine ecosystem and the forest-river ecosystem of the interior in such a narrow region as the isthmus, flanked by the Caribbean on the east and the Pacific on the west.

In the mountainous valleys of Chiriquí in northern Panama, sites such as El Hato and Cerro Punta show that there were already village tribal formations around 500 BC, whose productive system was based on the cultivation and processing of maize, possibly a hybrid of the Chapalote, Pollo and Nal-Tel strains, and beans. A prominent feature of these early Panamanian farming cultures is the development of artistic stonework in the form of huge metates, drums and large human figures showing men carrying trophy heads (Linares, 1977, pp. 24–5). But the earliest evidence of village tribal communities, hence of food production in the south of Central America, is to be found in the sites of La Montaña and Chaparrón in the Valley of Turrialba, Costa Rica (Snarkis, 1984, 1976; Fonseca, 1985) and the corresponding sites of Bahía de Culebras (Lange, 1980) in north-eastern Costa Rica.

It may be inferred from the studies hitherto undertaken that there were strong stylistic affinities between the pottery of the ancient inhabitants of La Montaña in the valley of Turrialba and the incised-plastic tradition that was characteristic of the early pottery-making communities of the northeast of South America and the tradition known locally as Bicromo en Zonas. Moreover, the presence of baking pans indicates the cultivation and consumption of bitter cassava, one of whose possible centres of domestication seems to have been the Lower Magdalena region. The lithic production toolkit includes grinding stones, wedges or chisels, scrapers, knives and axes.

In addition to cassava and perhaps other roots and vegetables, the La Montaña settlers also gathered from trees, as attested by finds of Persea sp. (avocado) seeds. The dwelling sites seem to be small and scattered, perhaps indicating a semi-sedentary form of community (Fonseca, 1985).

Alongside La Montaña, whose South American origins seem quite clear, Chaparrón is an example of Meso-American influences beginning to filter through into the south of Central America in the first millennium BC. They were later to dominate the cultural scene throughout Central America.

THE HUNTING-GATHERING WAY OF LIFE IN VENEZUELA

The archaeological evidence presently available indicates that the communities associated with hunting-gathering had already settled on the coast and possibly in the interior of Venezuela by the fifth millennium BC. In the north-east there is radiocarbon evidence of the existence of gathering communities from 3770 to 3400 BC known archaeologically as El Heneal complex, Yaracuy state (Cruxent and Rouse, 1958, p. 76; Rouse and Cruxent, 1963, p. 155), in the region where the Aroa River flows into the Caribbean Sea. Production implement finds included hammers, anvils and grinding stones resembling those of Cerro Mangote and Monagrillo in Panama, the lateral surfaces serving as the active part of the artefacts.

There is no direct evidence of plant gathering, but the presence of grinding artefacts points to the processing and consumption of some type of nuts or grains. These gathering communities, seemingly linked through the characteristics of their implements to those of the Pacific coast of Panama, appear to have settled along the western coast of Venezuela. It is possible to trace their spread as far as the central coast, with the Cabo Blanco complex (Cruxent and Rouse, 1958, pp. 92–3).

To the east of El Heneal, between Zazárida and Capatárida in the state of Falcón, there are shell deposits of species such as *Donax* and *Tivela*, the remains of human consumption. In some there seems to be a complex of bifacial points and scrapers made of quartz, chert and sandstone, associated with the El Jobo culture; and weights for nets and polished axes similar to those found in the West Indies. These associations might signal the co-existence of hunting with marine gathering in the hunting community of El Jobo (Elena Rodríguez, personal communication).

The earliest indications of the presence of hunting-gathering-fishing communities in Venezuela have hitherto been found on the north-eastern coast of Venezuela. Current research, sponsored by the National Geographic Society, has led to the discovery of a series of shell deposits at the foot of the Serranía de Paria range, in the Gulf of Cariaco, on the Araya peninsula and at the foot of the Caripe massif (Sanoja, 1979, 1982a, 1982b, 1984, 1985a, 1986; Sanoja and Vargas, 1978, 1983; Sanoja and Romero, 1986; Rodríguez, 1985; Rondón, 1986). These also contain rough stone production implements manufactured by means of the stone percussion technique or, in later sites, associated with burnt or polished stone and sea-shell and bone artefacts. The earliest sites, Guayana and No Carlos, on the Atlantic coast of the peninsula, have been dated to between 4220 and 4370 BC.

The tradition of hammered stone artefacts characteristic of Guayana and No Carlos is also represented in other shell deposits of the Gulf of Cariaco, such as El Bajo, and is predominant in the lower layers of the Las Varas shell deposit. Both these sites are located on high ground in the vicinity of the Compoma lagoon. These gathering communities supported themselves by combining the gathering of mangrove oysters and gastropods such as *Melongena* sp. and *Cassis* sp. with hunting and fishing. There are also traces of the possible processing of plant food.

The stratigraphy of Las Varas, a site now located in a setting of mangroves and palm groves, reveals, in the early stages of occupation, the presence of hammered stone tools and a small quantity of axes, hatchets and hoes of polished stone, conical grinding stones, bone and shell projectile points and stone vessels, becoming much more numerous in the upper layers of the deposit. The site also contains a very large number of possible ritual objects cut from mica schist and shaped like phalluses or daggers, modified gouges and sea-shell ornaments.

The soil covering the area of the deposit is black and of a sandy texture, similar to that found in the shoals formed by mangroves, creating an area resembling the so-called 'black lands', contrasting with the reddish clayey matrix of the hillock on which the shell deposit was found. This led to the idea that they might be anthropic soils created to facilitate cultivation at the site.

Analysis of the domestic space indicates the possible presence of windbreaks providing shelter for the Las Varas settlers; the concentration of the artefacts in different areas of activity, together with food remains, suggest that each individual or nuclear family carried out all the work processes for the social group. There was an area of collective activity, the hearth, for the processing of food. The dead were buried in the dwelling area. The distribution of the bones suggests secondary burials for which the bones were placed in baskets, sometimes associated with grinding stones and sea-shells.

The range of local variants found in the hunting community of north-eastern Venezuela is enriched by the 'manicuaroid' series (Cruxent and Rouse, 1958; Rouse and Cruxent, 1963), consisting of pre-ceramic complexes – Cubagua, La Aduana, Manicuare, Punta Gorda and Carúpana – located both on the present coastline of Paría and Araya and on the island of Cubagua. The tools characteristic of this gathering community are projectile points and harpoons made of bone or shell, biconical stones possibly used as projectiles for slings, manos and grinding stones possibly used for processing vegetable matter, and gouges and vessels made of the shell of *strombus gigas*.

The radiocarbon dates for the 'manicuaroid' series indicate that this particular hunting community had its origins around 2325 BC on the island of Cubagua, remaining both there and on the northern coast of Araya until 1730 and 1090 BC. From a typological comparison with the sequence at Las Varas, the presence of shell gouges in the Las Varas upper layer suggests a tentative dating at between 2000 BC and the end of the first millennium BC (Sanoja, 1986).

The general characteristics of the hunting-gathering communities of north-eastern Venezuela point to the existence of two major cultural variants: one based on the exploitation of marine, estuarine and river resources and using stone as a raw material, which possibly culminated in the generation of incipient forms of horticulture around the second or first millennium BC; and the other consisting of gathering communities strongly oriented towards fishing and marine gathering, using shells as a basic material for the manufacture of tools.

The first variant, found at Guayana, No Carlos, Remigio, Las Varas and El Bajo, forms part of the South American tradition of the use of non-specialised production implements, including the *sambaquís* of the coast and interior of Brazil. The second appears to be a Caribbean regional development with representative sites both in north-eastern Venezuela and in Cuba and Florida, dating to 2000 BC in Guayabo Blanco and to approximately 5000 to 2000 BC in the St John River sites (Veloz Maggiolo, 1980, pp. 21–2; Sanoja, 1982a, pp. 43–4; Rouse, 1951, pp. 260–1; 1960, pp. 8–24).

In the case of the first variant, sites such as Cueva del Elefante in the south-east of Venezuelan Guayana, with jasper and quartz flakes, grinding stones and possibly metates in a rockshelter on the Caroní River (Sanoja and Vargas, 1970), and the Canaima complex (Rouse and Cruxent, 1963, pp. 43–4) in the same region might provide evidence of inland communities related to the major gathering tradition of the north of South America, with origins traceable to the non-specialized production implement industries of the El Abra and Tequendama type in eastern Colombia or the El Jobo tradition of hunters (Rouse and Cruxent, 1963, pp. 42–3).

Both variants of the gathering way of life became hybrid around the first millennium BC, giving rise to social forms that may have succeeded in mastering certain horticultural practices, as in the case of the Pedro García complex, Anzoátegui state, dated to about 570 BC. The gathering community here was already using axes, conical pestles, metates and flaked implements, together with gouges and vessels made of the shell of *Stromgus gigas*. In the Michelena complex in the basin of Lake Valencia, state of Carabobo, the presence of conical pestles and stone plates indicates the existence of inland gatherers, technically related to those of north-eastern Venezuela, who had perhaps reached a similar level of development of the productive forces.

THE ORIGINS OF FOOD PRODUCTION IN VENEZUELA

In the light of the data hitherto available, two important aspects of early food production in Venezuela seem to be discernible: (a) a self-generated process within the gathering communities of eastern Venezuela; and (b) a derived process generated by the pottery-making village tribal communities, who appear in the Orinoco basin and the basin of Lake Maracaibo in the first millennium BC.

In the first case, the gathering communities seem to have succeeded in developing a set of agricultural implements for deforestation, ploughing the land, wood working and possibly creating anthropic soils for cultivation. There is no indication of the type of cultigens or plants gathered, although it might have been any of the wide variety of native roots and tubers existing in eastern Venezuela: the cassava (*Manihot esculenta*), the 'mapuey' (*Dioscorea triphyda*), the taro (*Xanthosoma saggitifolium*), the 'lairén' grape (*Calathea* sp.), and others. If this interpretation were correct, we might assume the existence of a centre of horticultural development within a mixed economy of hunting, fishing and gathering that came into being with the arrival in north-eastern Venezuela of village tribal communities from the middle and lower Orinoco, known as the Barrancas tradition and the Ronquín tradition.

From 900 BC, these communities had been developing a form of production in the Orinoco very similar to that appearing on the Colombian coast from the third millennium BC, which associated the cultivation of bitter cassava with hunting, fishing and gathering. The pottery of the Barrancas tradition has much in common, as regards the shapes of vessels and decoration, with that of early tribal societies of western South America, such as those of Puerto Hormiga, Kotosh and even Valdivia (Sanoja, 1979, 1982a, b, 1984, 1985a, b, c). The Ronquín tradition includes many shape and decoration features characteristic of the Andean Middle Formative, the Chorrera culture in Ecuador and the Monsú culture in the Lower Magdalena, Colombia (Vargas, 1979, 1981; Sanoja and Vargas, 1978, 1983). In the light of the foregoing, one may view the origins of pottery in eastern Venezuela as part of a process set in motion by the influence of other tribal or primitive class societies of western South America, which were integrated into the food-producing modes of work that had already begun to evolve in the local gathering communities (Sanoja, 1985b, c).

In western Venezuela, the work of Tartusi and Nuñez Regueiro (1984, pp. 67–88) has led to the elimination of Rancho Peludo as an early instance of the domestication of cassava in north-western Venezuela, a theory advanced by Rouse and Cruxent (1963, pp. 48–9). These two authors put the date of the site at 2820 BC, but later excavations have placed it chronologically in the first centuries of the Christian era.

There are traces of bitter cassava cultivation to the south of Lake Maracaibo, Caño Grande phase, around 650 BC in a cultural context related to the tribal societies of the Lower Sinú and the Lower Magdalena (Sanoja and Vargas, 1978, pp. 67–72; Sanoja, 1969, 1982a, pp. 145, 194–5, 1972, 1982b, pp. 184–7, 1985a; Vargas, 1985a, b). A characteristic feature of the pottery of these early tribal societies is the perforated bulbous pedestal base, found in the Malambo tradition in the Lower Magdalena. Various archaeological sites on the north-western coast of Lake Maracaibo also seem to confirm the spread of Malambo cultural influences to this region (Tartusi et al., 1984).

Again, there seem to be early signs of maize cultivation in the Lagunillas phase identified on the north-eastern coast of Lake Maracaibo by Wagner and Tarble (1975) and Wagner (1980), and dated at between 600 and 200 BC; this has also been identified as a process derived from early tribal societies of northern Colombia, a theory which would be confirmed by the shell deposit of La Pitía in the Lower Guajira of Venezuela (Gallagher, 1964; Acosta Saignes, 1953).

THE ORIGINS OF FOOD PRODUCTION IN THE AMAZON REGION OF BRAZIL

The history of food production in the Amazon region of Brazil raises interesting problems for the study of the subject in the north of South America. On the one hand, the region of Lower Amazonas, containing the earliest sites with signs of possible plant cultivation, is separated by enormous distances from the main centres of development of grain or root horticulture in north-western South America and also from those with contemporary traces of pottery making. On the other hand, there are as yet no intermediate sites with dates prior to those of the Lower Amazonas that could be interpreted as evidence of migration of ancient horticultural and pottery-making communities downstream towards the Atlantic coast.

The earliest evidence of pottery-making communities with possible horticultural practices is to be found in the Mina phase, on the Pará coast in an area known as Salgado, washed by brackish waters extending from Marajó Bay to the mouth of the Gurupí River (Simões, 1981). Radiocarbon dating based on plant carbon and shell scourings used in pottery indicate a chronological sequence running from 3000 to 1600 BC.

The production implement complex consists of grinding stones, hammers, scrapers and stone cutters, resembling tool combinations found in the *sambaquís* of the southern coast of Brazil. The general cultural context points to a mode of work based on shellfish gathering, fishing, hunting, the consumption of plant species that were processed by grinding or crushing with stone hammers and pottery making.

The Mina phase pottery used ground shell as antiplastic, and is decorated with red paint, incision and broaching. According to Simões, there seem to be similarities between the Mina pottery and that of sites such as Puerto Hormiga and Machalilla, in north-western South America, suggesting migratory processes whereby early pottery-making groups moved from the Caribbean coast of Colombia or the coast of Ecuador to the Atlantic coast of northern Brazil. The Mina pottery likewise seems to have certain features in common with that of the Alaka phase, also associated with the shellfish gathering, identified in the marshes of the north-western coast of Guyana (Evans and Meggers, 1960).

The clear emergence of food and pottery-producing village tribal communities in the Amazon region is attested in the Ananatuba phase in the Amazon delta (Meggers and Evans, 1957; Evans, 1964; Simões, 1969). The predominant work processes in the Ananatuba community reflect the persistence of those already existing in the initial hunting-gathering society: hunting, fishing and gathering, with some forms of cultivation or processing of grains or other seeds, as indicated by finds of grinding stones and metates. Radiocarbon techniques give a date of 980 BC for the Ananatuba phase. Its villages seem to have consisted of a single communal house, either oval or circular, covering an area of 300 to 700 m², accommodating between 100 and 150 individuals and generally located in a wooded area, near a savannah or a relatively deep waterway.

Associated with the Ananatuba community, the settlement of Jauarí (Hilbert, 1968) indicates the presence of pottery-making horticultural communities, gathering both freshwater shellfish and gastropods. Judging by finds of tubular clay pipes, the Jauarí individuals used tobacco to make cigars, a practice that persists in many present-day aboriginal communities in the Amazonas-Guayana region. This, together with the presence in Jauarí of stone axes and hoes, pestles and metates, provides evidence of techniques for preparing fields for cultivation and for processing and consuming plant resources.

As already noted, the Lower Amazonas stands apart from the major migratory routes of the South American continent, although the exceptionally rich habitat in terms of animal and vegetable food resources created the conditions for a balanced livelihood, even in the absence of cultivated plants (Meggers, 1971, pp. 35–8). As indicated by the characteristics of the Mina phase, there may have been an early process of formation of semi-permanent pottery-making communities based on access to plentiful natural food supplies. But it is also clear that the formal characteristics of the Ananatuba and Jauarí pottery point to the introduction of decorative forms such as incision and cross-hatching divided into zones by incision, which had already been developed many centuries before by pottery-making communities in the eastern foothills of the Andes.

One of the sites in which this decorative element has appeared from early times belongs to the Pastaza phase (Porras, 1980, pp. 113–17). Although there is no specific agricultural context, the existence of spindle whorls makes the use and possible cultivation of cotton seem likely. More-over, in the eastern foothills of the Peruvian Andes we also find the Tutiscayno phase (Lathrap, 1958, 1970). Their pottery is decorated with fine crossed incision, divided into zones by wide incision, in a context of freshwater shellfish gathering. It is similar to that found in the Jauarí phase of Lower Amazonas, although there is no direct or indirect evidence of cultivation indicative of plant-growing or maize cultivation.

There are no radiocarbon dates; however, the typological similarities with Kotosh pottery suggest that Tutiscayno should be dated between 1000 and 1800 BC (Lumbreras, 1974, pp. 51–4).

There are two important aspects of the formation process of the village tribal communities of Lower Amazonas. First there is the existence of a local productive basis assumed to have been generated by the hunting-gathering-fishing communities, and second, the existence of imported developments, particularly evident in improvements in pottery-making that may have originated in other early communities of western Amazonas, in which appropriative, productive forms apparently continued to predominate.

THE ORIGINS OF FOOD PRODUCTION IN THE WEST INDIES

The presence of hunting-gathering communities in the West Indies may be traced back to 5000 BC, a date relatively close to that of the early sites in north-western Venezuela. That of Banwari, Oropouche lagoon on the island of Trinidad, opposite the eastern end of Paría peninsula, shows the existence of a production implement kit that seems to be associated with plant food processing: conical pestles modified by abrasion, rough metates, stone spheres and discs, choppers or cutters made of rounded stones, micro-flakes, possibly rectangular or tapered axes, and bone points and needles (Veloz Maggiolo, 1980, pp. 35–6; 1976, 1982; Harris, 1973, 1976).

The Banwari hunting-gathering-fishing community has generally been interpreted as representing the development of a form of mixed appropriation related to the mangrove ecosystem and including, from a very early stage, modes of work associated with the gathering and processing of plant foods. According to Veloz Maggiolo (1982, pp. 35–7), the Banwari culture spread along the West Indian arc around 2200 BC, reaching Quisqueya or Hispaniola in the same period.

The influence of Banwari is discernible in the deposit of Hoyo del Toro, Macorís Province, Dominican Republic, dated to 1840 BC, and El Porvenir (1200 BC), containing a production toolkit which includes tabular pounders, cylindrical hammers, rough metates and winged axes in an appropriative context characterized by the gathering of *Crassostrea rizophorae* and land snails such as *Polydontes* and *Caracollus* sp. This indicates the existence of a form of exploitation of the mangrove ecosystem resembling those existing in north-western South America from 5000 to 4000 BC.

Almost at the same time, other West Indian communities associated with Banwari began to develop a trend towards the gathering of plant species such as the guáyiga (*Zamia debilis*) and the cupey (*Clusea rosea*), and the use of coral graters, together with sea fishing, the hunting of iguanas and hutias (*Heteropsomys, Isolobodon portoricensis, Nesophontes*) and marine gathering (*Cittarium pica, Geocarcinus lateralis*). The use of the guáyiga as a plant food is interesting, as the process of converting the root into flour and bread for consumption is similar to that for the bitter cassava. From the standpoint of the transfer of technical skills, it might have facilitated the acceptance of the bitter cassava by Dominican hunter-gatherers when it was introduced in later millennia by pottery-making communities from north-eastern Venezuela (Sanoja, 1982a, p. 224).

The trend just described begins to appear in sites such as Cueva Berna, La Altagracia, Dominican Republic (Veloz Maggiolo et al., 1977), dated 1890, 1625 and 1225 BC, reflected in the abandonment of mangrove exploitation and greater emphasis on the gathering of plants and land gastropods and on hunting. The dead were also buried within the domestic space, in the kitchen middens formed by human activity in the cave. The analysis of skeletal remains carried out by Luna Calderón (Veloz Maggiolo et al., 1977, pp. 27–32) indicates that the members of the Berna gathering community suffered from severe malnutrition and infectious diseases, giving an average life expectancy of 12.5 years, evidence of the harshness of their living conditions.

Towards the end of the second and the beginning of the first millennium BC the gathering communities related to that of Banwari Trace had settled in different regions of what is now the Dominican Republic, specifically in archaeological sites such as El Porvenir, Madrigales and La Piedra in San Pedro de Macorís. Concurrently, we find other settlements of gathering communities in the same region of San Pedro de Macorís, such as La Isleta, with a recurrence of the production toolkit made of sea-shell (*Strombus gigas*) characteristic of the Manicuare tradition of north-eastern Venezuela (Veloz Maggiolo, 1980). But it is in Cuba that the sea-shell variant of production implements becomes most evident, in the settlements of Cueva Funche and Guayabo Blanco, with radiocarbon dates running from c. 2050 to c. 120 BC for Cueva Funche and from 2000 to 1500 BC for Guayabo Blanco. There is also evidence in these sites of a continuing industry of laminar implements of flaked flint, dating back to 3190 BC in the site of Levisa, Oriente Province, Cuba (Kozlowky, 1974). In c. 1775 BC these implements are also found associated with Banwari Trace and Manicuare remains on the island of Antigua, Jolly Beach site, indicating an intermingling of the three cultural traditions (Veloz Maggiolo, 1976, p. 64; Davis, 1974).

The tradition of laminar production implements in flint and jasper seems to have had its main centre of development in the Greater Antilles. It is represented in Cuba by the sites of Levisa and Aguas Verdes (Kozlowky, 1972, 1974), Caniman, Matanzas Province (Febles, 1982), and in particular in the Dominican Republic by Barrera-Mordán and Pedernales, dating from 2610 to 2590 BC; El Curro and Las Salinas, 1450 and 2480 BC (Veloz Maggiolo, 1976, p. 111; Pantel, 1975; Ortega and Guerrero, 1981). The typology of laminar implements includes, in particular, plano-convex blades, plano-convex scrapers, razors, punches, points, chisels, notched scrapers, anvils, hammers and so on. Although a number of authors have considered this extensive tradition of plano-convex production implements as a species of Antillean palaeo-Indian, the context in which such implements appear contains evidence of work processes peculiar to the gathering way of life: shellfish gathering, fishing, sea and land hunting, and possibly work processes that include wood processing. The existence of a stone-production toolkit as singular as that described in the Greater Antilles may have been the result of a process introduced from specialized hunting societies in Central America, Meso-America or north-western Venezuela, but their socio-historic character can be explained only in the context of the gathering way of life.

The palaeo-pathological evidence obtained from the study of skeletal remains in the Cueva Roja site, associated with the Barrera-Mordán tradition in the Dominican Republic, indicates that the community's average life expectancy was between 25 and 30, causes of death being accidents, severe fractures, arthritis, degenerative bone disease, anaemia and infections. This again illustrates the harsh living conditions in which these ancient West Indian gathering communities managed to survive. The studies by Luna Calderón have also shown that the poor physical condition of these communities was due to excessive protein consumption and excessive dependence on the environment. Owing to the low level of development of the productive forces, they never succeeded in achieving productive or even appropriative ways of life that would provide a diet more balanced in carbohydrates and proteins (Veloz Maggiolo et al., 1977).

The predatory way of life of the West Indian gathering communities could not evolve towards food production. It was only towards the beginning of the Christian era, with migrations of village tribal groups from north-eastern Venezuela associated with the Barrancas and Ronquín cultural traditions, that the qualitative and quantitative leap could be taken. The new immigrants introduced a mixed form of production, plant cultivation-hunting-marine gathering, which had been developed on the continent and then changed in turn to become the basis of West Indian tribal society (Sanoja, 1979, 1980; Vargas, 1979, 1981; Sanoja and Vargas, 1983).

CONCLUSION

Summing up the historical and cultural information available for the region and the period analysed, we may observe that in the hunting-gathering-social formation the way of life of the ancient hunters had already begun to decline around the sixth millennium BC. The causes of the process were varied: the series of glacial climatic changes that affected a way of life so heavily dependent on environmental resources, the gradual disappearance of the large fauna, changes in sea-level, changes in temperature and general changes in fauna and flora.

The changes in, and characteristics of, the environment also seem to have influenced the structure of the basis of subsistence and organization of the gathering communities. The move away from parasitical forms of existence and the search for increasingly plentiful and stable food resources, seen in particular in the ancient gathering way of life, seem to have led to ever greater territorial stability of human groups and to a greater interest both in seeking and using plant food and in producing or adopting a complex of techniques and artefacts for the specialised gathering and proto-cultivation of specific plants.

The emergence of agriculture and the domestication of plants do not seem to have been sudden inventions, or specific to a particular society. On the contrary, they might be viewed as the logical consequence of the different processes of intensification of the relationship between human beings and plants occurring in various parts of the world.

According to Clark, the origins of pottery are not fortuitous. It is precisely at the time when cultivated plants begin to predominate over wild plants that pottery appears (Clark, 1980, p. 14). It might be added that the introduction of clay vessels as production implements is also due to the development of the productive forces which begins to take place in gathering societies, and to the new view of the land as a medium for human work, calling for a restructuring of social organization in such a way as to intensify the changes underpinning the new agricultural tribal society.

BIBLIOGRAPHY

ACOSTA SAIGNES, M. 1953. Arqueología de la Guajira Venezolana. *Bull. Soc. Suisse Am.* (Genève), No. 7, pp. 6–8.

ANGULO VALDEZ, C. 1962. Evidencias de la Serie Barrancoide en el norte de Colombia. *Rev. Colombiana Antropol.* (Bogotá), Vol. 11, pp. 73–88.

—— 1981. *La tradición Malambo.* Bogotá.

ARDILA, G. 1984. *Chía. Un sitio precerámico de la Saban de Bogotá.* Bogotá.

BATE, F. 1983. Comunidades Primitivas de cazadores Recolectores en Sudamerica. In: ACADEMIA NACIONAL DE HISTORIA. *Historia General de América.* Caracas. Vols 1–2.

BULLEN, R.; SLEIGTH, F. 1963. *The Krum Bay Site. A Preceramic Site on St. Thomas.* Virgin Island. (Am. Stud., rep., 5.)

CHILDE, V. G. 1981. Los Mundos Sociales del Conocimiento. In: PEREZ, J. A. (ed.), *Presencia de Vere Gordon Childe.* México, D.F. pp. 239–63.

CLARK, G. 1980. *Mesolithic Prelude.* Edinburgh.

CORREAL, G.; HAMMEN, T. VAN DER. 1977. *Investigaciones arqueológicas en los Abrigos Rocosos del Tequendama.* Bogotá.

—— 1979. *Investigaciones Arqueológicas en los Abrigos Rocosos de Nemocón y Sueva.* Bogotá.

CRUXENT, J. M.; ROUSE, I. 1958. *Arqueología Cronológica de Venezuela.* Washington, D.C. (Est. monogr., 6.)

—— 1974. Early Man in the West Indies. In: ZUBROW, E. et al. *New World Archeology* (New York), pp. 71–81.

DAVIS, D. 1974. Some Notes Concerning the Archaic Occupation of Antigua. In: CIPECPAN 5. *Actas.*, pp. 65–71.

DELGADO, L. 1985. Bestiario y Animismo en la Afarería del Oriente de Venezuela. *Gens, Bol. Soc. Venez. Arqueól.* (Caracas), Vol. 1, No. 3.

EVANS, C. 1964. Lowland South America. In: WILLIAM RICE UNIVERSITY. *Prehistoric Man in the New World.* Chicago. pp. 419–50.

EVANS, C.; MEGGERS, B. 1960. *Archaeological Investigations in British Guiana.* Washington, D.C. (Bur. am. Ethnol., 177.)

FEBLES DUEÑAS, J. 1982. *Estudio Tipológico y Tecnológico del Material de Piedra Tallada del Sitio Arqueológico Canimar I, Matanzas, Cuba.* La Habana.

FERRERO, L. 1977. *Costa Rica Precolombina.* 2nd ed. San José, Costa Rica.

FONSECA, O. 1985. Historia Antigua del Caribe de Panamá, Costa Rica y Nicaragua. In: SIMPOSIO DE VIEQUES, 2. *Actas.* Fundación Arquiológica del Caribe.

FORD, J. 1969. *A Comparison of Formative Cultures in the Americas: Diffusion of the Psychic Unity of Man.* Washington, D.C. (Contrib. Antropol., 11.)

GALLAGHER, P. 1964. *La Pitía: An Early Site in Northwestern Venezuela.* Ann Arbor, Mich.

HARRIS, P. 1973. Preliminary Report on Banwari Trace. In: CIPECPAN 4. *Actas.*, pp. 115–25.

—— 1976. The Preceramic Period in Trinidad. In: ROBINSON, L. S. (ed.), *Proceedings of the First Puerto Rican Symposium on Archeology.* San Juan, Puerto Rico. pp. 33–64. (Informe, 1.)

HILBERT, P. P. 1968. *Archeologische Untersuchungen am Mittleren Amazonas.* Berlin.

HILL, B. 1966. *A Ceramic Sequence for the Valdivia Complex.* Ecuador.

—— 1975. *A New Chronology of the Valdivia Ceramic Complex.* Ñawpa Pacha. Lima.

HURT, W.; BLASI, O. 1960. *O Sambaquí do Macedo, Paraná, Brasil.* Curitiba, PR (Arqueol., 2.)

HURT, W.; HAMMEN, T. VAN DER; CORREAL, G. 1976. *The El Abra Rock Shelters, Sabana de Bogotá, Colombia, South America.* In: *The*

Quaternary of Colombia. Vol. 2. Bloomington, Ind. (Occas. Pap. Monogr., 2.)

KOZLOWSKY, J. K. 1972. *Industria Lítica de Aguas Verdes. Baracóa, Oriente, Cuba.* La Habana. (Ser. 9, Antropol. Prehist., 1.)

—— 1974. Preceramic Cultures in the Caribbean. Zeszyty Naukowe, Praha, Universitetu Jagiello nskiego 386. Prace Archeologczne, Zeyst No. 2.

LANGE, F. W. 1980. The Formative Zoned Bichrome Period in Northwestern Costa Rica (800 BC to AD 500) based on Excavations at the Vidor Site. Bahía de Culebra. *Vínculos* (San José, Costa Rica), Vol. 6, No. 1/2, pp. 33–42.

LATHRAP, D. 1958. The Cultural Sequence at Yarinococha, Eastern Peru. *Am. Antiq.* (Washington, D.C.), Vol. 23, No. 4, pp. 379–88.

—— 1970. *The Upper Amazon.* New York/Washington, D.C.

LATHRAP, D.; MARCOS, J.; ZEIDLER, J. A. 1977. Real Alto: An Ancient Ceremonial Center. *Archaeol.* (New York), Vol. 30, No. 1.

LINARES DE SAPIR, O. 1975. De la Recolección a la Agricultura en el Istmo de Panamá. *Rev. Panameña Antropol.*, Vol. 1, pp. 9–27.

—— 1976. From the Late Preceramic to the Early Formative in the Intermediate Area: Some Issues and Methodologies. In: ROBINSON, L. S. (ed.), *Proceedings of the First Puerto Rican Symposium on Archeology.* San Juan, Puerto Rico. pp. 65–77. (Informe, 1.)

—— 1977. *Ecology and the Arts in Ancient Panamá.* Washington, D.C. (Stud. Pre-Colombian Art Archaeol., 17.)

LINARES DE SAPIR, O.; RANERE, A. J. 1971. Human Adaptation to the Tropical Forests of Western Panamá. *Archaeol.* (New York), Vol. 24, No. 4, pp. 346–55.

LUMBRERAS, L. 1974. *The Peoples and Cultures of Ancient Peru.* Washington, D.C.

—— 1983. Las sociedades nucleares de Suramérica. In: ACADEMIA NACIONAL DE HISTORIA, *Historia General de América.* Caracas. Vol. 4.

MCGIMSEY, C. R. 1956. Cerro Mangote: A Preceramic Site in Panama. *Am. Antiq.* (Washington, D.C.), Vol. 22, pp. 151–61.

MEGGERS, B. J. 1971. *Man and Culture in a Counterfeit Paradise.* Chicago/New York.

MEGGERS, B. J.; EVANS, C. 1957. *Archaeological Investigations at the Mouth of the Amazon.* Washington, D.C. (Bur. am. Ethnol., Bull., 167.)

MEGGERS, B.; EVANS, C.; ESTRADA, E. 1965. *Early Formative Periods of Coastal Ecuador: The Valdivia and Machalilla Phases.* Washington, D.C. (Smithsonian contrib. Anthropol., 1.)

ORTEGA, E; GUERRERO, J. 1981. *Cuatro nuevos sitios paleoarcaicos en la isla de Santo Domingo.* Santo Domingo.

PANTEL, A. G. 1975. Progress Report and Analysis of the Barrera-Mordan Complex, Azua, Dominican Republic. *Rev. Domin. Anthropol. Hist.* (Santo Domingo), Nos. 5–7.

PATTERSON, T.; LANNING, E. 1974. Early Man in South America. In: ZUBROW, E. et al., *New World Archaeology.* New York. pp. 44–50.

PORRAS, P. 1980. *Arqueología del Ecuador.* Otavalo.

RANERE, A. 1972. Ocupación Precerámica en las Tierras Altas de Chiriquí. In: *Simposio Nacional de Antropologia, Arqueologia y Etnohistoria de Panama, 2,* Panamá. *Actas.* Panamá. pp. 197–207.

—— 1976. The Preceramic of Panama: the View from the Interior. In: ROBINSON, L. (ed.), *Proceedings of the First Puerto Rican Symposium on Archaeology.* San Juan. (Inf. 1, pp. 103–107).

RANERE, A; HANSELL, P. 1978. Early Subsistence Patterns along the Pacific Coast of Central Panama. In: STARK, B. L.; VOORHIES, B. (eds.), *Prehistoric Coastal Adaptations: The Economy and Ecology of Maritime Middle America.* New York. Chap. 3.

REICHEL-DOLMATOFF, G. 1965a. *Colombia.* New York.

—— 1965b. Excavaciones arqueológicas en Puerto Hormiga (Departamento de Bolívar). *Antropol.* (Bogotá), No. 2.

—— 1971. Early Pottery from Colombia. *Archaeol.* (New York), Vol. 24, No. 4, pp. 338–45.

—— 1985. *Monsú. Un sitio arqueológico.* Bogotá.

REICHEL-DOLMATOFF, G.; DUSSAN, A. 1958. Reconocimiento Arqueológico de la Cuenca del Río Sinú. *Rev. Colomb. Antropol.* (Bogotá), Vol. 6, pp. 31–149.

RODRIGUEZ, M. E. 1985. Aproximación al Modo de Vida Recolector del Oriente de Venezuela. *Gens, Bol. Soc. Venez. Arqueol.* (Caracas), Vol. 1, No. 3, pp. 22–40.

ROGERS, D. 1963. Studies in Manihot Esculenta Crantz and Related Species. *Econ. Bot.* (New York), Vol. 90, No. 1, pp. 43–54.

RONDÓN, J. 1986. *Recolectores Múltiples Litorales: Un Modo de Vida.* Caracas, Universidad Central de Venezuela. (MA thesis in Anthropology.)

ROUSE, I. 1951. *A Survey of Indian River Archaeology, Florida.* New Haven, Conn. (Publ. Anthropol., 44–5.)

—— 1960. Entry of Man into the West Indies. In: MINTZ, S. *Papers in Caribbean Anthropology.* New Haven, Conn. (Publ. Anthropol., 61.)

ROUSE, I.; CRUXENT, J. M. 1963. *Venezuelan Archaeology.* New Haven, Conn.

SANOJA, M. 1969. *Investigaciones Arqueológicas en el Lago de Maracaibo: La Fase Zancudo.* Caracas.

—— 1972. La Fase Caño Grande y sus relaciones con el Norte de Colombia. In: *International Congress of the Americanists, 40, Roma.* Vol. 1, pp. 225–60.

—— 1979. *Las Culturas Formativas del Oriente de Venezuela: La Tradición Barrancas del Bajo Orinoco.* Caracas. (Est., Monogr. Ens., 6.)

—— 1980. Los Recolectores Tempranos del Golfo de Paria, Edo. Sucre, Venezuela. In: CIPECPAN, 8. *Actas.* Phoenix, Ariz. (Anthropol. pap., 22.)

—— 1982a. De la Recolección a la Agricultura. In: ACADEMIA NACIONAL DE HISTORIA, *Historia General de América.* Caracas. Vol. 3.

—— 1982b. *Los Hombres de la Yuca y el Maíz.* Caracas.

—— 1984. Problemas de Arqueología del Noreste de Venezuela. In: URSS, ACADEMIA DE CIENCIAS. *Instituto de Arqueología. Los Problemas de la Arqueología de América Latina.* Moskva.

—— 1985a. Arqueología del Noreste del Lago de Maracaibo. *Gens, Bol. soc. venez. Arqueol.* (Caracas), Vol. 1, No. 2, pp. 54–73.

—— 1985b. Preceramic Sites in Eastern Venezuela. *Nat. Geogr. Soc. res. rep.* (Washington, D.C.), Vol. 18, pp. 663–8.

—— 1985c. La Sociedad Tribal del Oriente de Venezuela. *Gens, Bol. soc. venez. Arqueol.* (Caracas), Vol. 1, No. 3, pp. 41–67.

—— 1986. La Formación de Cazadores Recolectores en Venezuela. In: VARGAS, I. (ed.), *Actas de la 2° Reunión de Vieques, P.R.* Fundación de Arqueología del Caribe.

SANOJA, M.; ROMERO, L. A. 1986. *Excavaciones arqueológicas preliminares en los concheros precerámicos de Guayana y Ño Carlos, Edo. Sucre, Venezuela.*

SANOJA, M; ROMERO, L. A.; RONDÓN, J. 1982. Investigaciones Arqueológicas en los Concheros de Guayana, El Bajo y Las Varas, Edo. Sucre, Venezuela. *Acta scient. venez.* (Caracas), Vol. 33, suppl. 1, p. 16.

SANOJA, M.; VARGAS, I. 1970. *Proyecto Orinoco. Informe N° 2: Investigaciones Arqueológicas en el Bajo Orinoco: La Cueva del Elefante.* Caracas.

—— 1978. *Antiguas Formaciones y Modes de Producción Venezolanos.* 2nd. ed. Caracas.

—— 1983. New Lights on the Prehistory of Eastern Venezuela. In: WENDORF, F.; CLOSE, A.(eds), *Advances in New Archaeology.* New York. Vol. 2, pp. 205–44.

SIMÕES, M. 1969. The Castanheira Site: New Evidence on the Antiquity and History of the Ananatuba Phase, Marajó Island, Brazil. *Am. Antiq.* (Washington, D.C.), Vol. 34, pp. 402–10.

—— 1981. Coletores-pescadores ceramistas do litoral do Salgado (Pará). *Bol. Mus. para. Emilio Goeldi* (Belém, Pa.), No. 78, p. 27.

SNARKIS, M. J. 1976. La Vertiente Atlántica de Costa Rica. *Vinculos* (San José, Costa Rica), Vol. 2, No. 1.

—— 1984. Central America: The Lower Caribbean. In: STONE, L.; STONE, D. (eds), *The Archaeology of Lower Central America.* Albuquerque, N.M. Chap. 8.

STOTHERN, K. 1976. The Early Prehistory of the Santa Elena Peninsula, Continuities between the Preceramic and Ceramic Cultures. In: *International Congress of the Americanists, 41, Mexico. Actas.* México, D.F. Vol. 2, pp. 88–9.

—— 1979. La Prehistoria Temprana de la Península de Santa Elena, Ecuador: Una Interpretación Preliminar. *Vinculos* (San José, Costa Rica), Vol. 5, No. 1/2, pp. 73–87.

—— 1985. Los Cazadores y Recolectores Tempranos de la Costa del Ecuador. In: *International Congress of the Americanists, 45, Bogotá. Actas.* Bogotá.

TABÍO, E.; GUARCH, J.; DOMINGUEZ, L. 1976. La Antiguedad del Hombre Pre-agroalfarero en Cuba. In: INTERNATIONAL CONGRESS OF THE AMERICANISTS, *41, Mexico. Actas.* México, D.F. Vol. 3, pp. 725–32.

TARTUSI, M.; NIÑO, A.; NUÑEZ-REGUEIRO, V. 1984. Relaciones entre el área Occidental de la Cuenca del Lago con las áreas vecinas. In: WAGNER, E. (ed.), *Relaciones Prehispánicas de Venezuela.* Caracas. pp. 67–88.

TOLEDO, M. I. 1985. Evidencias Prehispánicas en la Región Oriental del Lago de Maracaibo. *Gens, Bol. soc. venez. Arqueol.* (Caracas), Vol. 1, No. 2, pp. 74–87.

UBELAKER, D. H. 1980. Human Skeletal Remains from Site OGSE-80, a Preceramic Site on the Santa Elena Peninsula, Coastal Ecuador. *J. Wash. Acad. Sci.* (Washington, D.C.), Vol. 70, No. 1, pp. 3–24.

VARGAS, I. 1979. *La Tradición Saladoide del Oriente de Venezuela: La Fase Cuartel.* Caracas.

—— 1981. *Investigaciones Arqueológicas en Parmaná: los Sitios de La Gruta y Ronquín, Edo. Guárico, Venezuela.* Caracas.

—— 1985a. Arqueología de la Zona Sur del Lago de Maracaibo. *Gens, Bol. soc. venez. Arqueol.* (Caracas), Vol. 1, No. 2, pp. 88–102.

—— 1985b. Visión General de la Arquología del Lago de Maracaibo. *Gens, Bol. soc. venez. Arqueol.* (Caracas), Vol. 1, No. 2, pp. 5–37.

VELOZ MAGGIOLO, M. 1976. *Medioambiente y Adaptación Humana en la Prehistoria de Santo Domingo.* Vol. 1. Santo Domingo. (Col. Hist. Soc., 24.)

—— 1980. *Las Sociedades Arcaicas de Santo Domingo.* Santo Domingo.

—— 1982. The Antillean Preceramic: A new Approximation. *New World Archaeol.* (Los Angeles). Vol. 5, No. 2, pp. 33–44.

VELOZ MAGGIOLO, M. et al. 1977. Arqueología de Cueva de Berna. San Pedro de Macorís, R.D. (Ser. Cient., 5.)

WAGNER, E. 1980. *Los Pobladores Palafíticos de la Cuenca del Lago de Maracaibo.* Caracas.

WAGNER, E.; TARBLE, K. 1975. Langunillas: A New Archeological Phase for the Lake Maracaibo Basin. *J. Field Archaeol.* (Boston, Mass.), Vol. 2, pp. 105–18.

WILLEY, G.; MCGIMSEY, C. 1954. *The Monagrillo Culture of Panamá.* Cambridge, Mass. (Pap. Peabody Mus. Archaeol. Ethnol., 49, No. 2.)

ZEVALLOS MENENDEZ, C. 1971. *La Agricultura en el Formativo Temprano del Ecuador (Cultura Valdivia).* Guayaquil.

ZEVALLOS MENENDEZ, C. et al. 1977. The San Pablo Corn Kernel and its Friends. *Science* (Washington, D.C.), Vol. 196, No. 4288.

ZUCCHI, A.; TARBLE, K. 1984. Los Cedeñoides: un nuevo grupo prehispánico del Orinoco Medio. *Acta cient. venez.* (Caracas), Vol. 35, pp. 293–309.

17.5.2
THE EASTERN REGION

Osvaldo R. Heredia

THE SHELLFISH-GATHERERS AND FISHERMEN OF THE BRAZILIAN COAST

In the corresponding chapter of Volume I dealing with the hunters and gatherers of eastern South America we divided the territory of Brazil into two large regions characterized chiefly by their phytogeographical features. These were the caatinga and cerrado region of north-eastern and central Brazil and the forest and grassland region of southern Brazil and north-eastern Argentina. From ancient times both regions were inhabited by peoples with life patterns based on wild fruit gathering and hunting.

From the information available, other areas were occupied around 3000 BC, such as the coastal region including the adjoining areas affected by variations in the sea-level and the mouths and lower stretches of rivers flowing into the sea. We might call this the 'coastal region with its lagoons and river mouths', although it encompasses a wide variety of environments governed by various factors: mainly their degree of exposure to the open sea. The oldest known human occupation dates from 3000 BC, although some suggest an even earlier date, reaching back to a time when the sea was some metres below its present level. This would mean that ample areas of land were available for settlement close to the early coastline.

It is difficult to identify particular characteristics for a sea coast extending over 8,000 km, because its features alternate and recur over its whole length and include more or less enclosed bays (some forming what are virtually inland lakes) interspersed with straight beaches entirely open to the sea winds and curved stretches offering some measure of protection at their extremities. The land fauna and flora associated with these coastal features also vary from one location to the next, although broadly there are two predominant vegetation types: mangrove swamps in the areas with calmer waters, comprising such species as *Rhizophora mangle* and *Avicenia nitida*, which form dense growths with other accompanying species in muddy ground, and typical shoal vegetation in more exposed locations. In the former case, the dominant fauna has a life-cycle determined by the tides and the salinity of the water. It includes oysters and various types of molluscs and the fish which feed on them as well as some species of crabs and birds. On the shoals the fauna is sparser and consists of land animals which also frequent environments somewhat farther from the shore. The lower reaches of rivers flowing into the sea offer scope for a wider range of fauna – fish seeking less salty water for spawning, alligators, capybaras (*Hydrochaeridae* sp.), some shellfish, deer and so on.

Most of the coastline is bordered by mountain ranges which, when close to the water, form a narrow shoreline constricted by the rock face, or, when more distant, provide a large flat or gently sloping area known as a *baixada* or low coastal strip. Over the last 10,000 years or more these coastal lowlands have, from time to time, been occupied by the sea when its level rose by a metre or more, causing it to invade areas sometimes as much as 5 or 6 km from the present shore. Only small rocky outcrops or confined areas of greater elevation escaped the waters and provided sites for human settlement. It is here that the prehistoric camps are now found. The original vegetation of these coastal lowlands varied with the changes in sea-level, sometimes being converted into dense shoal woodlands with abundant land fauna threatened by a mangrove invasion when the sea-level rose or, conversely, by tropical forest of the kind known as *mata atlántica*, which covers the slopes of the coastal sierras.

As mentioned above, some suggest that the first settlements of the Brazilian coastline may date from around 3000 BC. The hypothesis is that areas were settled from the north to the south following the line of the coast; settlement carries the implication of prolonged human specialization in coping with this highly specific environment. It has so far not been possible to establish a sequence of dated settlements in the northern and north-eastern coastal regions of Brazil, because sites of this early type have not yet been studied in depth, but the few available references suggest that these settlements are of a later date than those on the country's southern and central coast.

It is possible that the areas close to the sea were colonized by hunters and gatherers moving out from the interior. For a variety of reasons they may have migrated at different periods and gradually adapted to an environment offering them an abundance and diversity of resources.

About 5000–2000 BC the populations of the interior, and those of the Goiás and Minas Gerais region especially, exhibit an increased emphasis on the gathering of wild fruits and land molluscs. At the same time there is an increase in river fishing, although hunting is confined to a few small land mammals such as armadillos, tortoises, lizards and possibly deer, all of which suggests a relative scarcity of food. A situation of this sort in the caatinga or the cerrado may have exerted pressure on some groups, forcing them to migrate in search of new environments, including the coastline.

The greatest concentration of prehistoric human settlements linked to the marine environment is found on Brazil's southern and central coasts. The earliest of these are 5,000 years old and appear to represent the first encounters of human groups with an environment which was unknown to them a short time previously. If earlier camps had existed, today submerged by the sea, it may be assumed that the technology of these groups of 3000 BC would have belonged to a complex that was already adapted to the exploitation of marine resources, but this is not reflected at the lowest levels of the oldest explored sites. Here the gathering of shellfish and mangrove oysters is found to be particularly important and these could simply be collected by hand without any need for elaborate implements or artefacts.

The mangrove swamp seems to have been the most suitable environment for early human coastal habitation as its recesses provided a site for the development of a rich fauna capable of supplying food to fairly small groups. These resources included shellfish as well as crustaceans and fish which entered the river mouths in search of quieter waters for spawning or in some cases looking for shellfish to feed on. At the earliest sites such as Piaçaguera (c. 2982 BC) and Mar Casado (c. 2450 BC) and on the coast of the state of São Paulo the technological equipment includes stone axes typical of the cultures existing in the dense woodlands and forests of the interior and certainly designed for tree felling.

The stone axes are accompanied by polishing tools and sharpeners for the axes as well as anvils used as a support when chipping quartz cores to produce chips with a very sharp natural edge – a common feature of most of the coastal sites.

The fringes of the bays and inlets seem to have offered security to these hunter-gatherers, who took from the quiet waters most of what they needed for their subsistence, especially bivalve molluscs, which were probably conveyed to the camp in baskets made of plant fibres. Here they were eaten communally after being placed on a bed of embers which was intended rather to open the shell than cook the food. This practice would explain the many superimposed ash beds which sometimes extend over considerable areas within the site. It is significant that cooking hearths in the form of structures specially prepared for that purpose are not found. The food refuse accumulated in the living area itself, which also served for the disposal of the dead and for discarding tools with the passing of the seasons.

At first fish consumption appears to have been secondary and fishing to have been confined to quiet shallow waters where slow-moving, spawning fish could easily be taken with a bone-tipped wooden spear. The bone point had a curved profile so that the end opposite the tip projected considerably when it was tied to the haft. The barb was intended to anchor the fish to the spear after it had been pierced. There are no traces of such devices as fishhooks which would have enabled fishing to be conducted in deep and turbulent water. The vestiges of shark, whale and dolphin bones are probably the remains of dead or dying animals washed ashore, which were retrieved by the coastal dwellers. Their bones and teeth were used to make artefacts, necklaces and bracelets.

Some of the species of shellfish which were consumed lived in the clean sands of beaches open to the sea and indicate that these locations were also frequented by fishers. The strong sea winds, however, would certainly have prevented permanent settlements there.

Although these people were former inland hunters adapted to the marine environment, there was no special emphasis on the hunting of land fauna. In their camps we find only a few traces of small rodents or, occasionally, medium-sized animals like the paca (*Agouti paca*), deer (*Mazama* sp.) and the capybara – the last a dweller of the river bank. Often their bones were used to make points or spatulas.

The inhabitants of these prehistoric shell-mounds (*sambaquís*) lived on top of the refuse generated by the food they consumed. Consequently the ground was continually rising since the valves of the shellfish took a long time to disintegrate. In the state of Santa Catarina there are shell-mounds over 20 m high. Such a mobile floor provided no scope for more solid or permanent structures, and the refuges used by these people were not proper houses but makeshift timber and straw shacks or shelters intended to last a few days or weeks. Some traces in the remains of the camp sites, and mainly visible in the stratigraphic deposits, are interpreted as the post-marks of such structures. They suggest that the inhabitants occupied the site for a short period before moving to another to exploit fresh resources. Some of these sites were perhaps located in the interior of nearby areas, but the greatest probability is that such migrations followed the line of the coast or coastal lagoons. Each group must have occupied a number of shell-mounds according to the cycle of replenishment of the shellfish banks following a period of intensive gathering, thereby establishing a pattern of seasonal exploitation of food resources. The social structure was probably made up of small bands with some flexibility as regards numbers and the relationship of their members. Burial remains do not suggest any difference in the status or role of the individuals in a group.

This way of life extended, during the following millennia, in the coastal area where in some locations shellfish gathering continued to be the main means of subsistence. In these places fishing and more particularly hunting were relegated to a secondary position. There were several different reasons for this, including the beneficial water temperature and the existence of protected beaches and bays with mangrove swamps enabling colonies of shellfish and marine gastropods to continue providing a major food source. Finds from the oldest levels of the settlements indicate that gastropods were not then harvested systematically, as they are relatively infrequent, but in the more recent periods there is a tendency for their use to increase, probably because the settlers were making use of more diverse environments and leaving their mangrove swamps to exploit more open shores. These, offering cleaner water and a gradual increase in depth, are a suitable habitat for most of the gastropods whose shells are found in the camps. Bivalve molluscs of other species inhabiting these shores were also collected at the same time. This considerably widened the range of available resources, as humans were brought into contact with species not frequenting the waters of bays or the rivers discharging into them, such as sea turtles, sea urchins, shore crabs and, perhaps, weakened dolphins and sharks which came into the shallows or approached the shore.

In these more recent periods the occupational layers of the shell-mounds show a notable increase in the proportion of fishbones. There is no doubt that a greater intimacy with the sea enabled these groups to make regular rather than secondary or sporadic use of a resource whose volume was, most beneficially, greater than that of their traditional food source – the mollusc. For instance, a small fish weighing, say, 1,000 g is equal to fifty shellfish with an average unit weight of 20 g, and this also made it easier to transport to the camp, which was not always close to the spot where the food was gathered. It is probable that fish became an important element of the diet from 1000 BC, and a number of artefacts connected with fishing seem to become commoner. These include worked fishbones with an intentionally enlarged joint orifice for attaching a thread, which may have been used as needles in the fabrication of fishing nets. These artefacts are always associated with levels characterized by a large quantity of fish remains. Much of the fishing seems to have been carried out in shallow water using spears or bows and arrows. Fishing with fishhooks does not seem to have been practised as only a few specimens of bone have been found at Forte Marechal (Santa Catarina) dating from around AD 1100 at levels corresponding to pottery-making populations (Bryan, 1977).

Generally speaking, the shell-mounds and coastal camps of southern Brazil share the characteristics just described, but they do exhibit some features which point to a relationship with the inhabitants of the interior. These features include the artefacts known as 'zooliths', although they do not invariably represent animals but may take geometrical or even human forms, and in a few cases the raw material used is whalebone. As a rule they are made of hard stone, and commonly depict fish or birds, most having a cavity in one of the sides or the back. This cavity appears to have been intended to receive some substance of a ceremonial nature as its characteristics preclude any daily domestic function, although no such object has been found in a context implying a specific cultural association. Some writers date them as early as 2500 BC, but they probably originate from the first millennium of our era, as some specimens have been found in camps of that date. About 85 per cent of the zooliths have been discovered in the states of Paraná and Santa Catarina within a linear distance of 420 km, although a few have occurred further to the north on the coast of São Paulo and others have been encountered further south at Rio Grande do Sul and even to the south of the Republic of Uruguay. But what proves the relationship of coastal groups with the interior is the occurrence of zooliths along the Jacuí River and up to the borders of the southern Brazilian planalto. Probably these artefacts represent the earliest available evidence of a link between the shellfish gatherers and fishing populations of the coast and the hunters of the interior, although we do not yet know the degree or the characteristics of this relationship. The hypothesis that the people responsible for the presence of zooliths in the interior were the coastal dwellers themselves who shifted their habitations with the season cannot be discounted. In this area the gathering of araucaria cones provided at various times an important vegetable complement to the diet of many hunting peoples.

The economy based on fishing and mollusc gathering remained active and efficient along the coast until the arrival of the first pottery-making and probably agricultural peoples. Many shell-mounds and camps had apparently already been abandoned, or were relinquished at this juncture, as their upper levels usually show no evidence of the presence of pottery makers. Where the opposite is the case, the occupation was temporary and sporadic. This does not mean that the cultivators totally dispensed with the resources of the sea but only that they settled at some distance from the shore where they built their villages, so that the sea became just one of the exploited environments whose importance was shared with farming, hunting and plant-gathering.

Although most of the information available originates from Brazil's central and southern coasts, we should not fail to mention the existence of prehistoric human settlements on other parts of the coastline, such as the settlements of mollusc-gatherers and fishermen that have been found on the coasts of the north-eastern states of Maranhao and Bahía, whose age is not yet known.

THE HUNTER-GATHERERS OF THE BRAZILIAN INTERIOR

During the two or three millennia preceding the advent of farming towards 2000 BC, the same artefacts as in previous periods continued to be fabricated, although some reduction in size is discernible. This is exemplified by the large elongated scraper with a carinated back typical of the Paranaíba (Itaparica) culture, which is superseded by similar but smaller shapes. However, these scrapers are now accompanied by a wider spectrum of stone implements including side-scrapers and end-scrapers, knives with finely retouched edges and chips and flakes which were used, even without further working, true artefacts for cutting and scraping. As none of these artefacts is strictly a weapon, it must be assumed that they were used for preparing objects made of wood, leather, horn or shell. This fact suggests the practice of a wider and more diversified range of craftwork than in the preceding period, when practically only one type of tool existed.

At the time when people were adapting to marine, lagoon and riparian environments and sometimes also to swampy areas, these hunter-gatherers of the interior were improving their adaptive techniques.

Around 4000 BC the use of stone projectile points started to spread, especially in the areas of open grassland sometimes broken by belts of dense riverside vegetation and in areas of open woodland such as the araucaria woods of southern Brazil. This suggests the existence at that time of groups of hunters developing a life-style different from that of their predecessors. This is also reflected by many groups of relatively varied stone complexes comprising various types of scrapers, knives, brushes and a multitude of unretouched but utilized chips and flakes, which have been detected in areas in the interior of São Paulo, Paraná, Santa Catarina and Rio Grande do Sul. We see repeated here a situation similar to that described for the centre and north-east of Brazil in an area coinciding with the cerrado and caatinga types of vegetation.

These hunter-gatherers of the interior must have learnt to identify edible fruits, roots, buds and the like which had probably not been consumed by their forebears. This is substantiated by the profound knowledge of a multitude of medicinal plants which the medicine men (pajés) of some existing tribes have accumulated over time by dint of prolonged experimentation. The people of this period also learnt to make intensive use of the large land snails (Strophochelidae) which form genuine shell-mounds in some caves of the cerrado region. This is no doubt evidence of an adaptive technique in operation.

It is likely that other similar mechanisms, such as the hunting of the ñandú (Rhea americana), will be detected as research is extended and deepened. The ñandú is one of the few gregarious animals inhabiting Brazilian territory, the hunting of which may possibly have been connected with the bolas found on many southern Brazilian sites. The age of the bolas has not yet been properly established, but generally speaking they appear to have achieved their greatest popularity in more recent periods, although there are references according to which some of these bolas are associated with materials of the Umbú culture of 5000 BC.

Small fishhooks have been found at some sites in the interior which indicate more systematized fishing activity. This artefact is clearly a product of the intention to exploit a resource which had previously been utilized only sporadically, if at all. Fishhooks have been found on the sites at Unaí (Minas Gerais) and Santana do Riacho (Minas Gerais). However, the fish remains found at archeological sites, almost all in caves and shelters, do not occur in sufficient quantity to determine whether this resource formed a major element in the diet. If it did, it is likely that the fish were consumed at once close to where they were caught, leaving no traces at the living sites. Only at the GO–I site, where the Paranaíba and Serranópolis cultures have been identified, is there a significant occurrence of fish remains in the case of the latter culture.

BRAZIL'S FIRST FARMERS

The earliest evidence of cultivated plants on Brazilian soil is still a somewhat hazy aspect of the country's archaeological history. In a context of intensive plant-gatherers and hunters of small animals and deer, maize appears in the Serra do Cipó (MG) with a date of 1950 BC. On this site, the dry cave of Santana do Riacho produced some grains of this age, though others seem to originate from lower, older levels (Prous, 1980). In the same central region of Brazil, to the west of Minas Gerais, there are other signs of cultivated plants. A more varied range of cultivated species has been found in the upper levels of the Gentío cave, which is also associated with a context of plant gatherers and hunters: squashes (Cucurbitacea), peanuts (Arachis hypogaea) and maize (Zea mays). Simple pottery is also associated with this site. This period, known as the Unaí culture, has also been dated to 1950 BC, although the average age is between 1550 and 1150 BC (Dias, 1980a). The lower levels of the same cave were occupied by groups for which the gathering of plants and land snails provided the main means of subsistence in conjunction with the hunting of small animals.

In spite of their proposed age, the use of crops does not appear to have produced fundamental changes in the way these peoples lived. Unlike other parts of the world, where societies assumed more complex socio-economic forms, hunting and gathering continued to be the most effective means of subsistence in this part of Brazil. Plant cultivation always seems to have occupied a secondary place in the diet. No plant was cultivated in such a manner that it could, either in quantity or quality, supersede the great variety of edible fruits, roots, leaves and shoots which peoples had already learnt to exploit and which were furnished by their various environments.

On the other hand, with rare exceptions none of these uncultivated resources was available in large enough quantities to support many individuals living together, and this factor limited the size of human communities. It is also probably the case that none of these plants was suitable for processing with a view to storage, or that a technological process for this purpose was never discovered. Both hunting and the systematic gathering of plants, which continued to be the main activities, demanded movements over large distances taking many days, and this too no doubt contributed to the neglect of farming.

An examination of the archeological records and ethnographic data for the sixteenth and seventeenth centuries yields no evidence that the farmers of these tropical and subtropical areas employed new technologies or means adapted to their specific ecological conditions in order to improve or increase food output. Adverse environmental factors such as the low natural fertility of the soil, the rainfall pattern in some areas, consisting of prolonged droughts followed by excessive precipitation, blights and so forth did not prompt any technological counter-measures. We have no knowledge of the reasons behind this lack of interest and the absence of such improvements as the use of fertilizers, the construction of embankments to prevent erosion, dam building, the

utilization of the flooding areas alongside rivers which retain their moisture for longer periods, or the exploitation of different ecological levels. The generally accepted hypothesis that crop cultivation in this area could not be increased because of the poor soil, that is, for exclusively ecological reasons, does not totally explain the different course followed by these societies with regard to their socio-economic organization. There are no doubt cultural factors which need to be emphasized in an analysis of this kind.

It seems clear that most of the adaptive techniques developed by the peoples living in this central, north-eastern and south-eastern region of Brazil were extremely effective in ensuring a balanced subsistence throughout the year. The fishermen and shellfish-gatherers of the seashore and the riverbanks, the fishermen-hunters of the southern lagoons and swamps and the hunter-gatherers of the central and north-eastern interior took from their environments all the foods necessary to their subsistence.

Consequently, when cultivated plants arrived in the central region of Brazil (Minas Gerais) there was already a very well balanced and stable hunting and gathering culture. The difficulty of adapting these crops to an environment for which technologies capable of overcoming or mitigating the ecological disadvantages had not been developed may have contributed to the fact that the cultivation of maize, peanuts and possibly squashes and manioc involved a 'gathering' rather than a harvesting technique. Although information on the subject is only indicative, there is a suggestion that at later periods the natives of the eastern region of Brazil consumed maize when it was soft, on the point of ripening. There are also indications – again for the historical periods – that some of these groups (such as the Timbira) resumed their hunting and gathering cycle as soon as the output of maize and other cultivated crops had been consumed (Lowie, 1946). As a result, only the grain destined for use as next year's seed was stored, so that a surplus which could be stockpiled was probably never produced. It is suggestive that the archaeological sites never yield artefacts or implements which could have been used for agriculture or for the processing of cultivated crops.

THE NORTH-EASTERN REGION OF ARGENTINA

The north-eastern region of Argentina is dominated by two more or less parallel rivers flowing from north to south – the Uruguay and the Paraná. The history of its indigenous occupation shows great continuity and similarity with that of Brazil. In the northern part of the region, the province of Misiones, the Altoparanaense II culture (flourishing from c. 8000 BC), called the Humaitá culture in Brazil, with its typical boomerang-type stoneware, was succeeded by other cultural traces left by hunter-gatherers using triangular stone projectile points with peduncle and barbs resembling those of Brazil's Umbú culture. To the south of this region other stone projectile points indicate the presence of hunters evidently more concerned with hunting the land animals typical of the flat land alongside the rivers, such as deer and ñandú. This picture is repeated to the east of the River Uruguay, in the country of the same name. On the Paraná River to the south-west of this fluvial region we find, on the other hand, clear traces of fishing people. Around 550 BC the Cululú culture is developing bone working centred on the production of fishing spears.

The presence of farming peoples in this region is indicated only by the appearance of pottery. If this association is valid, the cultivation of various plants was probably introduced around 50 BC and established among peoples who were exploiting the potential of hunting and fishing backed up by fruit-gathering. In the northern area, the first pottery to appear is similar to that of the Taquara culture of Brazil, with its typical decoration of dots and lines incised in the surface and basketware markings made in the fresh clay body. To the south the pottery continues to exhibit the same decorative patterns and vessels of the same shapes, though more detailed analyses reveal slight regional variations such as the use as antiplastic agents of ground pottery, ground shells and sponge spicules (*cauxi*), which are features that may suggest influence from various cultures of Brazil's central and/or Amazonian regions.

THE ARGENTINE PAMPA REGION

The pampa is a region characterized mainly by an almost total lack of relief over most of its area, which consists of an extensive, gently undulating plain. There are admittedly some mountain chains, such as the eastern outliers of the Central Sierras (Córdoba and San Luis), which separate it from the more broken topography of the Andean foothills, and the Sierra del Tandil and the Sierra de la Ventana which interrupt its homogeneous flatness in the south. Although today it consists entirely of cultivated land and pasture, its original vegetation was bunch-grass; it was virtually treeless apart from small stretches of low-growing species and shrubs in the north-west (Córdoba and Santa Fé). Two subregions can be identified: the humid or eastern pampa and the dry or western pampa in which the climatic characteristics and vegetation of the former are gradually superseded by a countryside of sands and dunes in which localized woods of calden trees predominate. The humid pampa is characterized by the presence of lagoons, swamps and many rivers, which must have been strong attractions for humans and animals.

For the period after that of the Trandiliense hunters, who had no stone projectile points and who inhabited the region in about 5000 BC and possibly survived into historical times, we lack information until about 1500 BC, when stone implements with various characteristics made their appearance. This industry involved mainly quartzite as a raw material for the production largely of graters and to a lesser extent of medium and large-sized unifacial scrapers with marginal percussion retouching. The industry, known as Blancagrandense, seems to have been widespread throughout practically the whole of the humid pampa, including the Atlantic coastline, to judge by various finds of stone implements of more or less similar size and features (Piana, 1981). Problems of chronology and stratigraphy have recently emerged which make it difficult to assign a positive date to this culture. In identifying it at the periphery of the Blanca Grande lagoon in the western-central Buenos Aires pampa, Bórmida assigned it to the subarboreal period during which the layer containing the artefacts had been formed, that is, to between 3500 BC and the early years of our era. However, the same layer has revealed the remains of cattle, which certainly date from some time after the Spanish conquest, in the sixteenth century AD. The lack of investigations on sites with undisturbed associations, and bearing in mind that most of our information is derived from surface finds, prevents the establishment of definite dates.

ARGENTINE PATAGONIA

Argentine Patagonia, which extends from the Atlantic Ocean to the Andes, was inhabited from the start of human occupation around 10,000 BC by peoples who derived their main source of subsistence from hunting guanaco. Most of the published investigations, relying heavily on radiocarbon dating, concentrate on the southern-central part of the Patagonian tableland and that is the source of most of the information considered below. The oldest periods, represented by the Toldense and Casapedrense cultures with their characteristic ranges of implements, are described in Volume I. The Toldense culture is characterized by artefacts made from chips with marginal retouching; these include scrapers, knives, medium and large borers and, in particular, unpedunculated triangular projectile points. This culture existed to around 5000 BC. The Casapedrense culture, on the other hand, fabricated its scrapers and knives from flakes and blades with obliquely bevelled retouching at the edges. There are no stone projectile points, their place being taken by the bolas as the only hurled weapon in use. In the Cueva de los Toldos there are remains of the Casapedrense culture with these characteristics dating to at least 3000 BC.

However, guanaco hunters possessing stone implements exhibiting a mixture of the two industries are found further south in the Rio Pinturas area with later dates extending to 1450 BC (Gradin, 1984). According to the sequence established for this area (Gradin et al., 1979), Rio Pinturas II extends between the limiting dates 2950 BC and 1430 BC. The artefacts of this period still conform to some types of the previous period, but there is a noticeable tendency towards the use of long blade flakes for the fabrication of scrapers and knives. There are no stone projectile points. Later (Rio Pinturas III), dated to 190 AD, we can observe a continuation of the same stone technology but with a reduction in the size of the silica flakes used for the range of artefacts, which still does not include projectile points.

Guanaco, and secondarily ñandú, hunting provided the main basis of the diet of these peoples at all times. Ultimately, these resources were supplemented by plant foods (roots), small mammals in the interior and shellfish in specific niches of the coastal interior. Plant cultivation was not practised by these groups. The importance of the guanaco is indicated not only by the presence of guanaco remains at practically every layer of habitation in the cave dwellings but also by the pictorial representation of the guanaco from the moment the area was occupied. The first images, corresponding to the Toldense culture (around 10,000 BC), show groups of guanaco being pursued by hunters armed with bolas. In lesser quantity we can also see the typical painted hands produced on the cave walls with the painter's own hand as model. The hand was applied to the wall and its outline marked with pigment blown through a tube. Later, during the development of the Casapedrense culture, hunting scenes disappear from the paintings, but the representations of the guanaco persist in the form of pregnant females or females accompanied by their young. The hands and anthropomorphous figures complete the motifs. Later, towards the beginning of the Christian era, the pictographs are characterized by abstract and naturalistic geometrical forms, the latter including human and animal figures. The pictorial technique is now supplemented by engraving used to depict human footprints, or the tracks of ñandú, puma and guanaco, or the silhouettes of guanaco, lizards and, less commonly, human beings (Gradin et al., 1979). In one way or another the guanaco is always the predominant element in these representations, which doubtless had a meaning beyond their mere aesthetic value and very likely formed part of a complex system of rituals whose significance is now lost to us.

The sea coast appears to have been occupied by the same guanaco hunters from the interior at a date after 1500 BC. This did not involve a true adaptation to the marine environment as the main if not the sole source of food, as the presence of remains of inland fauna such as the guanaco and various rodents bears witness that the nearby Patagonian plains and gullies continued to be exploited. Furthermore, the stone projectile points found on these coastal sites resemble those of the Patagoniense culture of the interior, which suggests that they were still used for the same purpose. However, having settled on the sea shore, these groups also exploited shellfish, especially *Mytilus* sp. and *Chione* sp., as well as fish, and so introduced a new element into a diet which had for millennia been based on guanaco meat. It seems that no special technology was developed for coping with these aquatic environments. No special fishing appliances have been found, and fishing must have been carried on in the rock pools which were submerged at high tide, as has been suggested by Caviglia and Borrero (1978) in relation to the Bahía Solano (Chubut) site.

BIBLIOGRAPHY

BORRERO, L. A.; CAVIGLIA, S.E. 1978. Estratigrafia de los Concheros de Bahía Solano: Campaña 1976–1977. In: CONGRESO DE ARQUEOLOGIA ARGENTINA, 5, SAN JUAN. *Actas.* San Juan.

BROCHADO, J. J. P. 1977. *A alimentação na floresta tropical.* Porto Alegre, RS. (Inst. Fil. Cienc. hum., cad., 2.)

BRYAN, A. L. 1977. *Resumo de Arqueologia do Sambaquí do Forte de Marechal Luz.* Belo Horizonte, MG, Universidade Federal de Minas Gerais. (Arq. Mus. Hist. nat., 2.)

CAGGIANO, M. A. 1983. Caracterización y antropodinamia en el NE a propósito de los fechados radiocarbonicos para el Delta del Paraná. *Relac. Soc. argent. Antropol.* (Buenos Aires), N.S., Vol. 15.

CALDERÓN, V. 1969. *A Fase Aratú no recôncavo e litoral norte do Estado da Bahia.* Belém, PA.

CAVIGLIA, S. E.; BORRERO, L. A. 1978. Bahia Solano: su interpretación paleoetnozoologica en un marco regional. In: CONGRESO DE ARQUEOLOGIA ARGENTINA, 5, SAN JUAN. *Actas.* San Juan.

DIAS, O. 1978–80a. *Os cultivadores do planalto e do litoral.* Goiânia, GO.

—— 1978–80b. Rio de Janeiro: a tradição Itaipú e os Sambaquís. In: SCHMITZ, P.; BARBOSA, A.; RIBEIRO, M. B. (eds.). *Arcaico do litoral.* Goiânia, GO.

GRADIN, C. 1980. Secuencias Radiocarbónicas del Sur de la Patagonia Argentina. *Relac. Soc. argent. Antropol.* (Buenos Aires), N.S., Vol. 14, No. 1.

—— 1984. Arqueologia y Arte Rupestre de los Cazadores de la Patagonia. In: SEMINARIO SOBRE LA SITUACIÓN DE LA INVESTIGACIÓN DE LAS CULTURAS INDIGENAS DE LA PATAGONIA, MADRID. *Las Culturas de América en la Epoca del Descubrimiento.* Madrid.

GRADIN, C.; ASCHERO, C. A.; AGUERRE, A. M. 1979. Arqueologia del area del Río Pinturas (Provincia de Santa Cruz). *Rel. Soc. argent. Antropol.* (Buenos Aires), Vol. 13.

GUIDON, N. 1978–80. *Os Cultivadores do planato e do litoral.* Goiânia, GO.

HEREDIA, O.; GASPAR, M. D. 1985. Projeto 'Aproveitamento Ambiental das Populações Pré-históricas do Rio de Janeiro': abordagem ecológica. In: REUNIÃO NACIONALE DE ARQUEOLOGIA BRASILEIRA, 3, GOIÂNIA. *Atas.* Goiânia.

HEREDIA, O. et al. 1981/82. *Pesquisas arqueológicas no Sambaquí de Amourins, Magé, RJ.* Belo Horizonte, MG. (Arq. Mus. Hist. nat., 6–7.)

—— 1984. Assentamentos pré-históricos nas ilhas do litoral centro-sul brasileiro: o Sítio Guaíba (Mangaratiba, RJ). *Rev. Arqueol.* (Belém, PA), Vol. 2, No. 1.

—— 1985a. Escavações arqueológicas no sítio Salinas Peroano, Cabo Frio, RJ: nota prévia. In: REUNIÃO NACIONAL DE ARQUOLOGIA BRASILEIRA, 3, GOIÂNIA. *Atas.* Goiânia.

—— 1985b. Resultados preliminares das escavações arqueológicas no sítio Boca da Barra (RJ). In: REUNIÃO NACIONAL DE ARQUOLOGIA BRASILEIRA, 3, GOIÂNIA. *Atas.* Goiânia.

—— 1985c. Pesquisas arqueológicas no sítio Geribá I. In: REUNIÃO NACIONAL DE ARQUOLOGIA BRASILEIRA, 3, GOIÂNIA. *Atas.* Goiânia.

—— 1985d. Pesquisas arquelógicas na Ilha Grande: sítio Ilhote do Leste. Nota prévia. In: REUNIÃO NACIONAL DE ARQUOLOGIA BRASILEIRA, 3, GOIÂNIA. *Atas.* Goiânia.

JACOBUS, A.; SCHMITZ, P. I. 1983. *Restos alimentares do sítio GO-JA–01, Serranópolis, Goiás. Nota prévia.* São Leopoldo, RS.

LOTHROP, S. K. 1946. Indians of the Paraná Delta and La Plata Littoral. In: *Handbook of South American Indians.* Washington, D.C. Vol. 1, pt 1. (Bur. am. Ethnol., Bull., 143.)

LOWIE, R. H. 1946. Eastern Brazil: An Introduction. In: *Handbook of South American Indians.* Washington, D.C. Vol. 1, pt 3. (Bur. am. Ethnol., Bull., 143.)

MADRAZO, G. B. 1973. Síntese de Arqueología Pampeana. *Etnia* (Buenos Aires), No. 17, art. 73.

MENGHIN, O. F. A.; BORMIDA, M. 1950. *Investigaciones Prehistoricas en Cuevas de Tandilia (Provincia de Buenos Aires) Runa III.* Buenos Aires.

METRAUX, A. 1929. *La civilisation materielle des Tupinambá et ses rapports avec celles de outres Tupi-Guarani.* Paris.

MIGLIAZZA, E. C. Linguistic Prehistory and the Refuge Model in Amazonia. In: PRANCE, G. T. (ed.), *Biological Diversification in the Tropics.* New York.

MILLER, E. T. 1967. *Pesquisas arqueologicas efetuadas no Nordeste do Rio Grande do Sul.* Belém, PA.

PIANA, E. L. 1981. *Topominia y Arqueologia del Siglo XIX en La Pampa. Luchas de Frontera con el Indio.* Buenos Aires.

PROUS, A. 1978–80. *Os Cultivadores do planalto e do litoral.* Goiânia, GO.

—— 1980–1. Fouilles du grand Abri de Santana do Riacho (MG), Brésil. *J. Soc. am.* (Paris.)

REX GONZALEZ, A. 1979. Las Exequias de Painé Güor. *Relac. Soc. argent. Antropol.* (Buenos Aires), N.S., Vol. 13.

SCHMITZ, P.I. 1976. *Sítios de Pesca Lacustre em Rio Grande, RS, Brasil.* São Leopoldo, RS.

—— 1978–80. *Os Cultivadores do planalto e do litoral.* Goiânia, GO.

SCHMITZ, P. I.; BARBOSA, A. S. 1985. *Horticultores pré-históricos do Estado de Goiás.* São Leopoldo, RS.

STADEN, H. 1974. *Duas viagens ao Brasil.* Itatiaia, SP, Edusp.

UCHOA, D. 1978–80. *Arcaico do litoral.* Goiânia, GO.

WÜST, I. 1983. Aspectos da ocupação pré-colonial em uma área do Mato Grosso de Goiás. Tentativa de análise espacial. São Paulo, SP. (MA thesis.)

I7.5.3

THE WESTERN REGION

Luís Gillermo Lumbreras

The territory of the Andes comprises those countries of western South America now known as Colombia, Ecuador, Peru, and Chile, as well as western Argentina and Venezuela. These countries are basically associated with the shores of the Pacific Ocean, and share in common the lengthy mountain chain originating in the Caribbean – that huge gulf which separates North and South America – and running longitudinally down the western edge of the southern continent before losing itself in the region of the Antarctic.

All along this enormous territory – except at its southernmost tip where extremely primitive hunters and gatherers survived down to our own times – the discovery and gradual spread of agriculture allowed a generalized process of neolithicization which by 3000 BC prevailed throughout most of the area, except for pockets towards the south where the 'Neolithic chain' reached only later.

The Neolithic peoples of the Andes responded in different ways to the living conditions offered by their agricultural world, even though, generally speaking, they chose various forms of sedentary life with gradual assimilation of the demands of agrarian production. This in turn determined a preference for village-type settlements, or settlements around the edges of alluvial bottoms, even in those areas where herding prevailed which, according to all available data, was always associated with agriculture. But at all events, herding did not predominate in all cases, especially not along the coast, where teeming marine life allowed the concentration of numerous groups of fisher folk and mollusc-gatherers in the coves and on the beaches of the sea shore.

Hence we could outline a general typology of Neolithic Andean settlements as follows:

1   Tropical farming peoples: dwellers in the hot, damp forests, whose basic subsistence depended upon growing cassava (*Manihot utilissima* and *M. esculenta*) and also maize (*Zea maize*) and other plants pertaining to a macrothermic habitat, complemented by plant gathering and the hunting of forest game (notably deer and rodents). The agriculture of these peoples – based on slashing or clearing of the forest – forced them to adopt a semi-nomadic way of life in areas far from the alluvial regions where agriculture was more stable. Such peoples occupied the entire northern ranges of the Andes and the eastern slopes generally, where they came into close contact with the dwellers of the Amazon, who also had a similar productive system, although for the most part they grew cassava at various levels of complexity.

2   Temperate zone farming peoples: these dwelt in valleys and ravines, and their subsistence was mainly based on growing leguminosae (*Phaselus vulgaris*, *Ph. lunatus*,

Canavalia sp.), maize, gourds or squashes (*Cucurbitaceae*, *Lagenaria siceraria*) and various fruits such as the chile pepper (*Capsicum anuum*, *C. pubsecens*) and other products of a temperate climate – including cotton (*Gossypium barbadense*). This subsistence diet was complemented by food fished from the sea (both along the coast and as far as the foothills), and by domestically raised animals such as ducks (*Cairina moschata*) and guinea pigs (*Cavia porcellus*) – even though these seem to have been adopted only after the end of the third millennium BC. These peoples occupied the coastal valleys of the Central Andes and the valleys and ravines of the foothills.

3   Highland farmers and herders: these dwelt in the 'puna' – the cold high Andean steppe – and its surrounding areas; their subsistence was based primarily on growing the potato (*Solanum tuberosum*) and other tubercles pertaining to a cold climate such as the *olluco* (*Ullucus tuberosus*), the *oca* (tuberous sorrel) (*Oxalis tuberosa*), or the *mashwa* (tuber nasturtium) (*Tropaeolum tuberosum*), as well as grains such as the *quinua* and the *caniwa* (various kinds of goosefoot) (*Chenopodium guinoa* and *Ch. pallidicaule*), to which must surely be added the *kiwicha* amaranth (*Amarantus sp.*). These peoples also had the domesticated camelidae of the Andes, the llama (*Lama glama*) and the alpaca (*Lama pacus*) and ate various sorts of game, forest plants, and salt- and freshwater fish.

4   Seashore peoples: these relied mainly on fishing and shell gathering. They were close neighbours to transhumant groups who exploited the plant resources of certain seasonal formations of the desert coast known locally as *lomas* (hills), which flower in winter (from May to September) and revert to desert in the summer.

Each one of these peoples hence enjoyed its own way of life, even though account should be taken of the fact that various forms of exchange did occur, allowing for cross-fertilization of their different kinds of experience.

The tropical village dwellers certainly show the most marked differences in development and also the widest distribution, owing to their climatic environment and not to any cultural uniformity. These were highly mobile peoples, although this need not necessarily imply that they were nomads – such mobility was due to the constant search for ever wider stretches of territory for farming.

The main concern of this chapter is the study of those dwellers of the basin and coastline near the Río Guayas, in Ecuador. These people produced the most ancient pottery in the Andes – although not in South America, since even more ancient pottery is known from Colombia. We are dealing now with the period around 3000 BC,[1] which yields us the most ancient dates for the Valdivia culture with its established farming, since evidence allows us to mark out a Vegas phase – pre-pottery – as the first known to make use of cultivated plants, two to three thousand years earlier. There is also the possibility that this region had a pre-Valdivian form of pottery, such as that known as the Achallan-type (Stothert, 1976). In any event between 3000 and 2500 BC, along the Guayas coast and apparently also in the alluvial region of the great river, the Valdivian peoples enjoyed a well-established Neolithic culture, and farmed maize and even cotton.

The Valdivia is a uniform culture, and one relatively better studied than many other Neolithic formations in South America. Most of the known sites are to be found concentrated along the coast, to the west of the Chongon-Colonche mountain chain, from Manabí to the north, down to the gulf of Guayaquil, the island of Puna and, in later periods, as far as the shore of El Oro province. Recently, late Valdivian sites have come to light farther to the north and east (at San Isidro, to the north of Manabí, and in the Cañar-Azuay highlands). Everything seems to indicate that the development of the first phases was restricted to the Guayas coast and to southern Manabí and that it began to spread with phase 6. Archaeologists recognize eight phases.

In the first two phases, a clearly defined type of village appears with hut-like houses more or less elliptical in shape, measuring some 5 × 3.5 m, built of plant materials. While they were built directly on the ground in the initial stages, by phase 2 there appear dug trenches serving to fix the 'bahareque walls' made of bound reeds plastered with mud. Apparently the villages were themselves also of elliptical shape, made up of undifferentiated houses, which might signify not only an egalitarian social pattern, but also a lack of differentiation between functions within the built-up area. Hence, in phase 2 of the Valdivia culture, changes in the technology of building the walls of the living areas may be observed, but no change in social organization – which remained very similar to that of the preceding pre-pottery Las Vegas phase (Damp, 1985).

As of phase 3, however, and prevailing down to phase 5, important innovations appear (Zeidler, 1984). In construction, houses increased in size up to 12 × 18 m and began to be internally divided with a sort of central 'screen'; in addition, side entrances were made in accordance with the areas into which the house was divided. Concerning the organization of the settlements, a division into halves is to be noted – as at the site of Real Alto – with four mounds, two major and two minor in the centre of the village, which would tend to indicate a segmented organization.

In this period, the site of Real Alto, which has been the most studied, would have reached the height of its development, which was maintained down to phase 5. The village occupies a grid-like space facing south. Available information indicates that the population tended to cluster in major villages, in a compact and ordered pattern. According to Jorge Marcos (personal communication), this would indicate a certain organization into chieftainships.

In phase 6, great changes again made themselves felt, especially regarding the organization of the settlements, apparently as part of a process of the diversification of production. At the site of Real Alto, the size of the settlement is shown to be significantly reduced, while a series of small villages appears, in the manner of settlements in the neighbourhood of the site, developing into a model of increasingly dispersed occupation, apparently following a long drought in Santa Elena peninsula, which reduced the area of agricultural pro-

ductivity to the existing plains. However (again according to Jorge Marcos), the occurrence could be explained as a process of disintegration of the pattern of centralized chieftainship, owing to the lack of surpluses to ensure its continuance; a cycle of search for complementary means of subsistence through trade would also have been initiated, for example through aggressive development of the trade in marine shells like the *Spondylus princeps*.

Precisely as of phase 7 begins a process of expansion which took the Valdivia culture in different directions, reaching as far as the Atacames neighbourhood – in northern Manabí – and southwards at least to the Río Arenillas, in El Oro. An increase in the foreign population in the region brought about a series of innovations which would later form part of the Machalilla culture, as well as part of the highland culture of Cerro Narrio. In the Azuay area evidence appears of pottery of Valdivian aspect, similar to that of phase 8 as it appears in San Isidro (Manabí).

The Valdivian peoples were fishermen, shell-collectors, hunters and gatherers, and farmers, adapted both to the conditions of the tropical rain-forests and to the semi-arid xerophytous-type forests and groves. These social conditions had begun in the Vegas age by at least 5000 BC, according to all available evidence, so that one can infer that pottery appeared when a Neolithic style of life was already flourishing – hence pottery was only an added innovation and not the bearer of Neolithic culture in this region. Indeed, even though Valdivian pottery may have had anterior models, in Colombian pottery or other local or imported productions, examination of its manufacture, forms, and decoration which appear so complex at first sight, betrays an elaborate but most primitive ceramic technique, to the extent that all its elements appear copied from basket-weaving, which may well have been the original vessel-making technique from which it derived. Even today – albeit with no direct tie – baskets are woven in the Santo Domingo de los Colorados area which repeat Valdivian forms from technical patterns that include the geometrical patterns characteristic of Valdivian decoration.

Work was carried out with very rudimentary instruments, formed of shells, stones and wood, simply made by percussion or abrasion; the most complex of the tools was a polished axe in the form of a 'T', which appears as of the Vegas phase and was widely used throughout the Valdivian sequence. Fishing was done with hooks of shell and also with nets. It has been proved that cotton was used very early, and cloth was woven from it (Marcos, 1973) using the loom.

Deborah Pearsall's studies (1978 and personal communications) show that the Valdivian peoples also grew maize and beans (*Phaseolus vulgaris*), *pallares* or butter-beans (*Phaseolus lunatus*) and squashes (*Lageraria siceraria*), combining this diet with proteins provided by seafood and also by game, notably deer.

The evolution of Valdivia in this region is unfortunately not so well documented as this culture. There is a phase known as Machalilla which seems to have played a major role in the spread of pottery as far as the mid-Andes and even towards Central America – but for which we possess only meagre pottery remains and some sparse data. Further on, towards 1500 BC, the Chorrera culture evolved, which extended over a vast region, although here again data are all too few – yet those we have do allow us to suppose that a Neolithic pattern of life was maintained in this area. Nevertheless, it is important to note the advances made in the management of the land, especially regarding use of water.

Apparently, from Valdivian times onwards, earthworks were constructed to hold water. These were artificial dykes to hold the rainwater running down the nearby slopes, permitting the watering of an area suitable for market gardens. These dykes required communal labour, over and beyond the merely domestic level. In this same regard, in the area near the Río Guayas, where constant flooding occurs caused by rain and the swelling river, the Chorrera period saw the development of the culture of 'little camels' (camellones), which consisted in shaping mounds and elevated fields so as to take advantage of the flooding and avoid the inundation of crops.

The highland farming and herding peoples, whose development occurred much farther to the south, especially in the desert environment of the south-central Andes, in southern Peru, Bolivia, and northern Chile, seem to have carried out their most important discoveries in this period but they have not been adequately studied. Our information about them concerns only later periods: a few clues found along the northern coast of Chile indicate a Neolithic way of life strongly related to fishing and hunting activities.

Concerning the farming peoples of the temperate zone and the dwellers of the central Andean coast, we do, however, have considerable information.

In fact, agriculture matured notably in the central Andes during the third millennium BC, and turned into a driving force of the first order, even when filling a role similar to the exploitation of shellfish banks amongst the peoples of the coast.

According to available data, before 3000 BC, the peoples of the coast derived a considerable portion of their subsistence from the exploitation of the coastal hills, by fishing and by gathering shellfish, and lived in scattered and sparsely inhabited villages. For reasons which remain unclear, we note as of this period a lessening in the use of the hills and greater dependence on the resources of the sea, which led to the appearance of quite large villages associated with an intensive consumption of shellfish and with a lesser use of plants from the hills.

In general, there occurred a considerable growth in the population, with profound changes in the organization and productive capacity of the village communities. Thanks to the work carried out by various archaeologists, beginning with initial studies by Junius Bird in 1946, we have considerable information concerning settlements in this period (3000–1500 BC) along the Peruvian coast. More than a hundred sites have been located, to which have been recently added various others in different parts of the highlands. All these sites belong to the northern region of Peru, in a territory known to us as the Andes del Marañón, which includes the highlands as well as the coast, from Lambayeque and Cajamarca in the north down to Lima and Junin in the south.

An important innovation in this period was the appearance of new crops, especially maize and cotton, which until this time had been absent from the area. Some scholars believe that they were imported from the north; others, that they were domesticated independently in the Central Andes. To these were added the many others hitherto known, especially leguminosae such as the bean (Phaseolus vulgaris), the pallar or butter-bean (Phaseolus lunatus), the guava-bean (Canavalia ensiformis) and a series of squashes (Lagenaria siceraria, Cucurbita ficifolia, C. moschata), fruits, and tubercles such as the red pepper (Capsicum sp.), the achira (Canna edulis), and an edible tuber, the jíquima (Pachyrrhizus tuberosus). Plant foods along the coast were hence restricted to those exhibit-

ing mesothermic genetic characteristics, and whose range only spread with the addition of macrothermic type plants domesticated further to the north and east, such as the cassava (Manihot utilissima), the camote (sweet potato) (Ipomoea batatas), peanuts (Arachis hypogaea), and others. In the same way, only towards the end of this age, and coinciding with the appearance of pottery or even later, did the products of domestication from the south likewise make their appearance, such as the llama.

In fact, the peoples of the coast were major consumers of sea foods, which could include sea mammals and the larger aquatic species as well as fish and shellfish. It is interesting to note that there was a gradual drop in the consumption of sea mammals and fish, which were replaced by a diet of ever more shellfish, to be explained, not by lack of technology – on the contrary, this was developing – but by other factors which various archaeologists attribute to the climate.

Along the Peruvian coast, climatic changes, apart from the major ones affecting the whole world, are a relatively frequent occurrence, determined by an unstable correlation between the Humboldt Stream – which flows cold up from the south – and the warm 'El Niño' current from the north. Because of this correlation, very dry and very rainy cycles alternate along this coast, especially along its northern section.

Let us turn now to the new aspects in agriculture. The first problem concerns maize. Recently, based on his studies on the site of Los Gavilanes, in Huarmey, D. Bonavia (1982, pp. 346 ff.) has drawn up a summary of the state of the debate concerning maize. Leaving aside numerous anecdotal references, it would seem that the pattern tends to show an independent Andean domestication of maize, originating in the temperate valleys of the highlands, in the Marañón Andes, developing from a very primitive strain of the plant, known as the 'confite morocho' (sweet maize) (Bonavia, 1982, pp. 369–371). So far, the only evidence supporting such a hypothesis comes from excavations carried out by Thomas Lynch on the site of Guitarrero, by Huaylas in El Callejón, and by R. MacNeish in Ayacucho. In Guitarrero there has been found maize from a pre-pottery context datable to between 5780 BC and the first millennium BC, on the basis of calculations of the oldest maize as going back to about 3000 to 2000 BC (Smith, 1980, p. 122), corresponding to a middle period illustrated by Complex III of the Guitarrero cave. The problem is that the period of time within which the find may be placed is very large. In Ayacucho, in the 'Chihua' phase, situated between 4300 and 3100 BC (MacNeish et al., 1970, p. 38), evidence was found for the cultivation of cotton, maize, and other plants. W. Gainat (MacNeish et al., 1970, p. 38), a specialist in these matters, was then of opinion that the primitive maize from Ayacucho belonged to the confite morocho complex and showed evidence of independent domestication. In point of fact, it is confirmed that by around 3000 BC, before pottery had reached the Peruvian Andes, maize was already being cultivated, as confirmed by such finds along the coast as that of Huarmey referred to above – where, however, its introduction may have been more recent. Indeed, no maize is known in sites close to the third millennium BC such as Huaca Prieta, but it has been located in second-millennium BC sites such as Aspero in Supe and Los Gavilanes in Huarmey (both on the central coast).

Concerning cotton (Gossypium barbadense), which plays an important part in this period, as far as is known only four cultivated species exist, two of them belonging to the New

World (*G. barbadense* and *G. hirsutum*). The origin of these cottons has been a matter of interest for geneticists ever since they discovered that both these species are allopolyploids. That is to say, these are hybrid species that have become different through the sum of a number of chromosomes from one cotton cultivated in Asia, and another, forest cotton from the New World (Towle, 1961, p. 64). The trend seems to be towards considering that there occurred a fusion between a Peruvian forest plant (*G. raimondii*) or a similar ancestor, and a cultivated Asian type, probably *G. arboreum*. On the other hand, *G. hirsutum*, which is Meso-American, enjoys in Mexico an antiquity dating back to around 5800 BC, which would signify hybridization far anterior to possible Asian influences, and indeed independent domestication. This allows one to suppose that the *G. barbadense* which occurs in the Andes could also derive from a process of hybridization independently of any Asian influence. It is interesting to note that in Peru, there also exists a forest variety, or more exactly a non-cultivated variety, of the *barbadense*.

Cotton played a major role in the economic and social development of the coast, permitting the development, among other things, of nets and ropes useful for fishing, thereby notably expanding the possibility of exploiting marine resources.

There is no doubt that the new economy greatly favoured the coastal dwellers, as it enabled them adequately to combine the abundant production of the sea with crops from the hills and the humid zones near the rivers flowing down from the mountain range.

The archaeological sites studied along the coast, although they reflect a general Neolithic pattern with the formation of mounds from the debris of domestic life, also show numerous variations in their organization, building techniques, and so on, which make it impossible for us to speak of a single culture for this age. They consist far more of local developments with certain interregional contacts.

Generally speaking, groups tended to settle near the sea, but also settled near sources of fresh water allowing them to practise horticulture, even though village settlements were always distant from torrents, which has led some archaeologists to suppose the existence of a tendency to choose places for settlements more with a view to fishing and shellfish-gathering than to cultivation. The fact that no sites are found in the valleys is nevertheless no definite indication, since later occupations intensively and extensively used the valleys for cultivation, erasing earlier clues which have existed there. Known sites are generally in desert locations, which has enabled them to be preserved.

The site best studied is that of Huaca Prieta, in the Valley of Chicama, which was examined in 1946 by Junius Bird. Huaca Prieta is a hillock some 12 m high, formed by accumulated strata of refuse and other debris left by successive occupants. It rises on the edge of the old bed of the river Chicama, on the northern coast of Peru, some 4 km from the present bed of the river near a small fishing cove known by the name of El Brujo. A modern beach separates the hillock from the sea. It is a zone apparently difficult to fish in as the beach is full of stones, the sea is somewhat rough and there are no natural harbours affording protection from the winds.

John Hyslop has been editing Bird's posthumous notes on his excavations at Huaca Prieta for many years now (Bird and Hyslop, 1985). Huaca Prieta underwent a lengthy pre-pottery occupation, extending from 3000 to 1200 BC, as radio-chronologically measured (Bird and Hyslop, 1985, p. 53). According to the critical evaluation carried out by Hyslop (Bird and Hyslop, 1985, pp. 245 ff.), while no drastic changes can be discerned throughout the long temporal sequence of the site, some can be seen that are not devoid of significance. In the most ancient phase – No. 6 – are already to be found all the components characteristic of the period. Nevertheless, the houses typical of later periods are lacking and there appear signs of domestic use of only certain areas, as if these were encampments. It appears that fishing was very important, as may be inferred from the abundance of fishing nets, hooks, and fishbones in the debris. In the succeeding phase – 5 in the stratigraphical sequence – appears the first evidence of decoration both on textiles and gourds. The textiles are woven according to the primitive technique known as 'twining' and the patterns are made by working with various threads dyed blue or red or simply left in their natural colours of brown and white. The designs show zoomorphic creatures, usually birds with wings outspread and shown in profile, as well as double-headed snakes and anthopomorphic beings. Gourds are decorated with pokerwork and show anthropomorphic and zoomorphic figures. Textile technology became most important as of phase 4 and especially during this phase itself. The finest examples of textiles decorated with figurative and geometric designs date from this age and at this time new decorative techniques destined for further development also appear. This phase 4 also shows a change in diet, with a clear reduction in the number of stone artefacts and the consumption of fish nd fowl. Phase 3, estimated at around 2000 BC, is a time of major changes in various aspects, especially in textiles. Textile production increased and became technologically more varied, although woven materials (and also the decorated gourds) diminished and became simpler. Phase 2 pursued this trend, although a clear change from the consumption of fish to that of shellfish can be noted. A greater number of artefacts made of shell are also found. The most recent phase is characterized by still further simplification of the decorative textiles, which no longer show figurative designs. Pottery appears later within a similar economic context. In reality, apart from these changes, the history of Huaca Prieta, as Bird pointed out (Bird and Hyslop, 1985, p. 253) in his preliminary notes, reveals a most conservative population.

In his excavations, Bird found an architecture of rounded stones forming walls adhering to the debris, then giving way to small semi-subterranean houses, oval or square in plan. These houses appear to have been related to a great supporting wall, still visible. The houses were distributed in no particular pattern, with small entrances and stairs to communicate with the surface. The houses reached depths of up to 1.6 m. The roofs of most of them seem to have been supported by wooden beams.

These constructions occupied only the higher part of the *huaca*, indicating that building techniques in this zone were slowly developing throughout the third millennium BC. A similar situation occurs farther to the south, in the Valley of Virú, in a place also close to the sea, where W. Strong and C. Evans (1952) excavated another similar-looking mound known as Cerro Prieto de Guañape. Here were found roughly built houses with walls of clay moulded with sea-water, and disposed at random.

Study of these northern sites clearly indicates that social development in the first part of the third millennium BC consisted basically of a form of village life or settlement which tended to be run as an autarchic unit of production and consumption, although there is evidence of contact – probably by sea – with distant populations such as that of Valdivia in the Guayas region, which at this time had a knowledge of pottery. Bird, in Tomb 903, found poker-worked gourds with designs very reminiscent of the style of phase 3 Valdivian pottery (Byrd and Hyslop, 1983, p. 71); nevertheless, not only was there no attempt to make pottery in Peru at this early date, but the technology was not adopted until the first centuries of the second millennium BC.

In various sites, evidence has been emerging over the last few years of the use of raw clay to mould little figures, including imitations of gourd vessels. In the Mito phase at Kotosh (Huasnaco), there are various objects of unfired clay, miniature pieces representing anthropomorphic figures, gourds, and vessels which might be imitations of split gourds or stone mortars. On the coast in Aspero (Valley of Supe) and Bandurría (near Huaral, north of Lima), dolls in the same style have been found. What was not yet known was the process by which to fire clay in order to turn it into pottery. The first evidence of pottery proper in the central Andes appears as late as between 1800 and 1500 BC.

It would appear that the most notable changes in Huaca Prieta were the result of its sporadic contacts with the outside world, occupying an intermediary position between the Neolithic with pottery in the northern Andes, and the complete development which began to occur farther to the south, on the coast of Ancash and Lima. This broke with the dominant village or settlement pattern to establish what became the origin of the Andean urban centres.

To the south, from the Valley of Casma to the valleys of Lima, the final years of the third millennium and the first years of the second were ones of active economic development, although the northern coast did not entirely escape this development. Near the Valley of Moche – between Chicama and Virú – has come to light a site known as Alto Salaverry (Pozorski and Pozorski, 1979), which shows a quite complex village, with a majority of domestic constructions, semi-subterranean like those of Huaca Prieta and Cerro Prieto, simple and arranged in no particular order, together with constructions of an apparently communal nature. There are a number of rectangular complexes which could have had community functions, or at least functions not entirely domestic, combining enclosures with platforms and tombs. They are architecturally more elaborate than the domestic units, and their layout and construction had clearly been planned to some extent. To the side of all this is a precinct, shaped like a sunken patio, circular in plan, which later was constantly associated with multi-purpose ceremonial centres and seemed to have served as a solar observatory and calendar. Only two other pre-pottery sites – amongst those known – have structures of this type: one is Piedra Parada the Valley of Supe, and the other is the Salinas site in the Valley of Chao. The latter is very close to Alto Salaverry, which could mean that this type of structure originated in the north, although this is highly speculative in the present state of knowledge. After the second millennium and especially in relation to sites with early pottery, circular wells would form an important part of the temples, as in the case of Chavín de Huantar, a famous ceremonial centre of the early first millennium BC.

Along the central coast, sites as old as Huaca Prieta are not known, and it is possible that the situation of village life might have been similar here to that of this site during the first half of the third millennium BC. More is known of sites

belonging to the period between the second part of the third millennium BC and the first part of the second.

Before reaching Casma, in the north, there is a place called Los Chinos, in the Valley of Nepeña, where there are various groups of stone houses, most of them subterranean, placed together without any plan in the fold of the hills that make the valley. There are isolated houses and complexes of houses – as in Alto Salaverry – made of irregularly-sized stones, bound with clay, with the stones so arranged that the interior face of the walls is slightly plane. Round, rectangular and square houses are to be found, semi-subterranean, with a depth reaching 1.5 m from the surface and an average size of 1.5 × 1.8 m. In several of the enclosures, a tendency to ornament the walls with geometrical patterns made with the stones themselves can be seen. The problem is that at this site, no adequate examination has been carried out to determine exactly the age and internal sequence of its various components.

In Casma, however, several kilometres to the south of the valley, is to be found one of the most spectacular sites of this age, known as Las Aldas, which contains a vast complex of constructions corresponding to buildings for public functions. This is one of the oldest sites with buildings of a pyramid shape. One of them, the most important, is a central edifice with up to seven platforms, built starting from a natural hill. Houses here were not subterranean but built on the rock, with walls sufficiently strong to stand on their own without support from the debris which covers them now. All the same, the most important construction on this site dates from the age of pottery, in the first half of the second millennium BC, so that the enormous ceremonial complex which took shape here flourished mostly between the years 1800 and 1200 BC.

Another site, near Las Aldas to the south, in the ravine of Las Culebras, is an architectural complex with both dwellings and public buildings. Las Culebras stands on the south side of a bay, near the bed of a river which is now dry. The site is completely buried and various types of structures can be found. Some consist of small square or rectangular units made with irregular field stones, with their flat surfaces on the inside of the walls as at Los Chinos in Huarmey. Another type consists of larger buildings, which also have structural architectural decorations on the walls, with rectangular niches in the internal faces of the enclosures. A third type consists of various kinds of buildings built in terraces bordered with blocks of stone with great stones raised to produce an ornamental effect. The terraces, as at Las Aldas, cling to the folds of a hill, from midway up to the summit. In the central part, several large series of stone steps can be admired, leading from the uppermost terrace down to the very bottom of the lowest. There are also passageways and constructions for unknown purposes. The walls of several houses show signs of having been covered with clay, and several of them had several storeys. Once again archaeological examination of this site has remained insufficient, even though it quite clearly belongs to the period with which we are dealing.

Moving further south, we reach a complex known as Aspero, which has new and very interesting components. We have here a series of public buildings in the form of mounds, associated with living areas, making a township very similar to those that were later characteristic of ceremonial centres, that is, a living area grouped around public buildings. Robert Feldman (1980) has excavated one of the mounds, known as the Huaca de los Ídolos, which is a pyramid whose apex has a series of precincts interpreted as parts of a temple or ceremonial complex. Even so, this pyramid formation is only part of a complex of buildings standing on a hill and its folds, near the Valley of Supe. There are six major mounds, some of them grouped in pairs, the others isolated, which could have been built at different periods and also could have coexisted. Joined to them are 11 other minor mounds and a very vast area with remains of deposits of domestic origin. What is noteworthy is the lack of any single orientation for the supposedly ceremonial buildings. They rather follow the topography of the folds, which were used for the foundations of the structures. The topography seems also to have dictated whether the public buildings were grouped together or stood alone. The 'public' character of such buildings not only refers to their function – apparently either ceremonial or communal – but also to the fact that the construction itself implies more work that would go into a domestic unit.

Several of the mounds in Aspero were constructed using a technique more or less generalized throughout Peru's central region in this period. The mounds were packed with stones in containers made of reeds or tough cane forming a kind of crate, placed side by side and finally kept in place at each end by dressed stone walls. This seems to have been the case for labour on a communal scale and was used for public buildings, generally associated with worship.

According to radiocarbon data[2] (Feldman, 1980, p. 246), Aspero's period should be placed between the beginning and the middle of the third millennium BC, more or less contemporary with Huaca Prieta. There are a few more ancient dates, but isolated and not highly significant.

This complex organization of the coastal settlements in the pre-pottery age continued farther south in a clearer way, including a greater trend towards uniformity. One such site is that at Río Soco, examined by W. E. Wedt (1964), consisting of a group of mounds to the north of the Valley of Chancay almost at the edge of the sea on the southern bank of a dried river bed. Close to remains of dwellings, with residues of cultivated plants and sea products, are up to six large mounds surrounded by minor ones, as at Aspero. Houses here are grouped into isolated units, in no visible order. The largest mound, No. 6, reveals an architecture based on large stone blocks, blocks of coral and whale bones. Mound No. 7 encloses several buildings, being the most complex centre of all.

Unlike the public buildings, domestic units were simple, rectangular in plan, made of low walls of stones bonded with clay, which served as a foundation for a structure of trunks and cane that supported the roof. According to Engel (1958), remains of stores or warehouses were also found.

The study of food stores, built as architectural elements and always associated with settlements, has recently been buttressed by the study of this sort of structure, dug into the sand and especially prepared to serve this function, at the site of Los Gavilanes in Huarmey (Bonavia, 1982), belonging to a date corresponding to the end of the third millennium BC. Food stores, in the Andes, provided the basis for the subsistence and reproduction of the urban system and normally, apart from stores of a purely domestic character, each city had communal and state stores which not only guaranteed food and clothing for the community and its officials, but also represented the means by which the urban centre could sustain the work done on public construction, religious buildings and so on.

Farther south, in the Valley of Chillón to the north of Lima, a complex has been studied corresponding to the first part of the second millennium BC and known as Paraíso.

This site is close to the mouth of the River Chillón, some two kilometres from the sea, and represents the final stage of a process divided into three distinct phases by the archaeologists Moseley and Barret (1969), based on the study of changes in textile technology. According to these scholars, in the most ancient phase called Playa Hermosa (Comely Shore), the dominant textile technique was that of 'twined' threads, whereas in the second phase, called Conchas (Seashells), the weave became more complex with the addition of separate pairs. Finally, in the third phase, the Gaviota (Seagull), separate pairs became the dominant weave. This sequence, which apparently held good along the coast near Lima, did not necessarily observe the same chronological order, nor even show the same components in other localities, where all these various textile techniques have been found but in a different order, or with no particular sequence at all. This is the case at Aspero, Los Gavilanes and Huaca Prieta. According to this chronological pattern, during the first phase, sites were small, covering only a few hundred square metres, whereas by the final phase they grew to cover several thousand square metres. Patterson (1971) states that some 100 individuals dwelt on a given site at the outset of the period, whereas 1,500 lived there by the close of the period, during the Gaviota phase. The initial phases would have concerned the low valley between 2500 and 1900 BC and the Gaviota phase would have corresponded to between 1900 and 1750 BC, the time when pottery reached the central coast. Paraíso belongs to this last period. It is also the largest site of the period and consists of a vast architectural complex, covering between 50 and 60 ha, with close-packed living quarters and several enclosures of a public character. Constructions are of field stones bound with mud and faced with polished stucco. Several walls show a few simple lines cut in the stucco, like graffiti, forming undefined figures.

So far as is known, no similar sites exist farther south, where everything indicates that life was lived within strictly village confines, as may be seen in the few localities examined south of Lima. In the Valley of Asia, it has proved possible to study a village of reed huts which are rectangular in construction (Unit 1), visible as a small mound some 15 m round and one metre high. The buildings which once existed here were made with clay walls, of which only the bases remain, now about 80 cm high, but the original walls were presumably not much higher. These walls surround a rectangular enclosure some 12.5 m long, with inner rooms, and an entrance facing north. Spaces have been hollowed out in the ground beneath, and the date may be ascribed to the late second millennium BC (c. 1314 BC).

If we proceed farther south, as we enter the vast desert regions of Ica, information points to a more clearly identifiable Neolithic village pattern, as at the site of Otuma, near Paracas, a settlement of fisher folk and seashell gatherers at that same period.

It thus becomes clear that along the coast corresponding to the Marañón Andes, Neolithic culture had entered a stage of utter disintegration, basically due to changes in the social order, with the appearance of a sector of the population associated with the temples and the consequent development of ceremonial centres, with public buildings differentiated from domestic dwellings both in shape and size.

What is noteworthy at the same time is that the process occurred within patterns of autarchy allowing for local differentiation in development. This autarchy, however, did not prevent a certain level of contacts, as we may infer from the concurrence of certain building techniques and ideas between the closest centres, allowing us to appreciate a certain familiar resemblance between such sites as Huaca Prieta, Cerro Prieto, Las Culebras, Aspero and so on. Likewise, certain materials found on these sites reflect a distinct level of trade in products and/or raw materials.

Variety, and the trend towards autarchy, yield us different forms. In the highlands, the pointers are towards a more uniform process, as if it were the expansion of a single culture, with formalized patterns of conduct.

To all appearances, the eastern slopes of the Andes, in the neighbourhoods of the great rivers Marañón and Huallaga, enjoyed considerable importance – although its impact was felt in both the central portions and the western reaches of the mountain chain. The region is a temperate one, with constant rain throughout the summer (which lasts nearly six months), and is very favourable for the adaptation of meso- and macrothermic plants. These uplands are also suitable for fruit trees and offer the possibility of game such as deer, rabbits, viscachas (*Sylvilagus sp.* and *Lagostomus crassidens*), and lesser species. The production of maize was also favoured by the pattern of rainfall, without the need for irrigation networks and elaborate preparation of the soil. Cassava (*Manihot utilissima*) could also be grown without major problems, and a great variety of fruit trees. This whole zone had many connections with the nearby Amazonian rain forest, and also with the humid northern Andes.

Here, in this period, in association with villages made stable by the construction of houses built of stone and mud, buildings appeared whose function seems to have been ceremonial, consisting of enclosures which had at the centre a most elaborate hearth, with underground systems for providing a draught. The first site of this kind was found as recently as the early 1960s (Izumi and Sono, 1963), near the city of Huánuco, in Kotosh. The pre-pottery phase, known here as Kotosh Mito, is represented by a series of such buildings, which have been given such names as: North Temple, White Temple, Temple of the Small Niches, Temple of the Crossed Hands and others. These are square precincts delimited by walls made both of field stones bonded with clay, and of cut stone with rounded edges and flat dressed faces. In cases such as that of the Temple of the Crossed Hands, the walls have survived to their full height so that one can see narrow rectangular niches, perpendicular to the floor, in the inner face of the wall of the precincts, inside which have been found remains of bones, as if they were offerings. Below two of these niches have been found depictions of lifesize hands – or rather, arms – modelled in clay, and crossed one over the other. At the centre of these enclosures is a section, generally on two levels, with a sort of bench surrounding a small flat courtyard or patio, in the middle of which is a hearth. The hearth is of special importance since it is carefully dug into the patio and has a subterranean shaft running from the bottom of it horizontally to the outside to bring in air. Examination of a cross-section made in one of these hearths showed that they were probably used over a long period of time, restored, and used again. Perhaps such hearths fulfilled the purpose of preserving a permanent flame – given the difficulty then of kindling one – within a closed and roofed-over space, with some kind of ritual and appointed attendants. At the site of Paraíso on the Lima coast, similar elements have been found, although they are not very common in the coastal settlements.

This system is encountered more and more frequently in the sites of the region, as at Tantamayo (Huánuco), where E. Bonnier and C. Rosenberg found remains of precincts from the pre-pottery period with these characteristics (Bonnier et al., 1985), and at the site of Piruru, in association with underground dwellings. A similar find was made at the site of La Galgada, in the western range, in the province of Pallasca, in Ancash, where a system of buildings of this type was in an excellent state of preservation. The precincts have an oven and central hearth, small niches in the walls, and polished floors. As in the temples at Kotosh, entrance to these precincts is through a central doorway in one of the walls, giving access to a square hall in the middle of which is the circular hearth, the draught for which comes through the stone shaft that has its opening underneath the threshold of the doorway. Surrounding the hearth, again, is a bench. T. Grieder has found something similar at Santiago de Chuco, at a site called Pajillas (Bueno and Grieder, 1979), and R. Burger's digs at El Callejón de Huaylas have brought to light still other precincts of the same type, belonging both to the pre-pottery and early pottery phases.

Obviously, when pottery reached this region, such a system was fully developed and had spread to a much larger area, reaching as far as Cajamara in the North, covering practically the whole chain of the Marañón Andes. The spread of pottery, from the north and east (?), was an event that invigorated the process in the central Andes and reinforced the trends outlined in this chapter, even though it was not a source of major technological innovations.

According to available data, pottery reached the central Andes in the first part of the second millennium BC, spreading throughout the region between the years 1800 and 1200 BC, along the coast and in the uplands. As mentioned above, the use of unfired clay to mould small figures has been encountered in various places, both along the coast and in the highlands, for example, at Aspero (Feldman, 1980), Kotosh-Mito (Izumi and Terada, 1972: plates 51a–b), Bandurría near Huacho (Rosa Fung, personal communication), Paraíso (Engel, 1966, pl. VI-1), and Asia (Engel, 1963, p. 82). It could be thought that we are dealing here with communities just discovering the plastic virtues of clay as part of their own development and so finding their own way towards pottery, but it so happens that almost by coincidence, only a few years later, pottery makes its appearance in these same sites, as a craft already fully formed and obviously reflecting a long previous tradition. We know, at least partially, that this tradition originated with the Valdivia culture of Ecuador. We should not be at all surprised to find that even the almost simultaneous appearance of these objects moulded from unfired clay was the result of the first contacts between the peoples of the Central Andes, still living in a pre-pottery phase, and those dwelling along the coast where the Valdivia culture flourished. Independently of the resemblance, already noted, between the designs on Valdivia 3 pottery and those on the poker-worked gourds of Huaca Prieta, at the site of Los Gavilanes, in the Valley of Huarmey (Bonavia, 1982, p. 143), a bead has been found made from a Spondylus, which is a shell only to be found in the North, and not in the waters of Peru or Chile.

The *Spondylus princeps* or *Mullu* is a mollusc which was greatly appreciated by the ancient Peruvians for use in many of their ceremonies, especially those linked to the cult of water. But to obtain this shell, they necessarily had to turn to the peoples of the coasts of Guayas or Manabí, and, exceptionally, even to those of Tumbes. It seems that demand for the shellfish was associated with its value as an indicator helping to predict the phenomenon known as El Niño. This is the alternation of periods of years of heavy rainfall with periods of drought, caused by the advance and retreat of the warm sea current of El Niño. The *Spondylus* appears to be a mollusc with high sensitivity to temperature and a considerable capacity for movement, causing it to appear or disappear according to the fluctuations of El Niño. The Peruvian priests could therefore predict these climatic phenomena merely by registering the presence, abundance, and latitude, of the 'mullu'. The 'mullu' was also regarded as fine material for necklace beads, body adornments, ritual objects, and so forth, and highly appreciated throughout the region, so that trade in the *Spondylus* was one of the most widespread activities, even over very great distances.

The arrival of pottery certainly did not have an identical effect throughout the central Andes. In each case, the new craft found its niche in each community through adaptation to local needs and conditions, both in shape and function, thus acquiring local and regional characteristics from the very moment of its adoption. Similarly, this process of regional adaptation found expression in the variety both of pottery-making techniques and of the techniques of making parts not easily shaped, which gave a starkly primitive look to some pottery complexes, although others appeared very developed.

In addition and as a result of all this, Rosa Fung (1972) has suggested the alternative hypothesis of the independent invention of pottery along the central coast. If this were the case, then one might also suppose that knowledge of pottery spread throughout Peru from three major centres: one in the northern Andes, one on the central coast, and one in the Amazonian East. In any event, these three 'foci' correspond in fact to three main morphological tendencies in early Peruvian pottery. Thus, pottery along the coast, as defined by Fung, would have introduced both the vessel with a tubular spout and the neckless pot, and is the most differentiated pottery. That of the East would have been responsible for the appearance of vessels with a double spout and bridge-like handle, as well as for painted decoration applied after firing. Such pottery became widespread in the southern regions, especially at Ica and Ayacucho-Andahuaylas. The trend in the North could have been the one that introduced the jars with low, wide necks, the shallow bowls and, a little later, the vessels characterized by stirrup handles. All these shapes, of course, were associated with various shapes common to all and similar manufacturing techniques. Noteworthy among such shapes are the streamlined forms, which existed only at this initial stage and disappeared at the beginning of the first millennium BC.

It is interesting to note that in Peru's central region, coinciding with the pottery which Rosa Fung suggests was of local origin, urban development had already achieved considerable proportions, as pointed out above. This was also the zone where, somewhat later, in the course of the first millennium BC, the Chavín civilization flourished, which was famous for its economic and social refinement. Similarly, 'eastern'-type pottery coincides with the neolithic-type found on the southern fringes of the Chavín area, and the 'northern'-type with the pottery found to the north of this same region.

In the region of Ancash and Lima, urbanization became fully defined, in the sense that areas were established that were differentiated from rural- or village-type settlements, with public constructions and community services as the central element of the groups of buildings. Urbanization has so far been best studied in the coastal valleys, which grew very rich through successful irrigated agriculture. Similarly, the development of urban or proto-urban settlements at this

time must also be associated with the success of their religious functions, amongst which the most important must have been that of predicting the major periods of rainstorms and drought, specialized astronomical observations providing support in this regard. Coastal agriculture basically took advantage of the waters of the rivers of the western ranges of the Andes. These normally run low for most of the year, but in summer – from January to March – the rainfall in the highlands swells the rivers, causing floods of varying magnitude in the coastal valleys, which use this water for extensive irrigation. The valleys to the north have the problem of draining the floodwater which, if not controlled, can become catastrophic. All this required appropriate calendars, careful regard for the weather, and prediction of cosmic events. As already mentioned above, the sea – with its fish and molluscs – certainly played an equally important part in contributing to the region's wealth.

As it happens, one of the sites displaying the most vigorous development at this early pottery stage (1800–1200 BC) was the ceremonial centre of Las Aldas, which became established, as we have seen, in the second half of the preceding millennium, in pre-pottery times. Fung (1972, p. 23) says: 'Construction of the temple at Las Aldas required many labourers to prepare the ground; to quarry, transport and position the stones; to cut, dry and twine the rushes with which to make the network of baskets supporting the stone structures of the platforms. All this was executed with a rudimentary technology which naturally demanded a major investment of human energy. Much of the work-force could have come from the Valley of Casma and the other neighbouring valleys of Culebras and Huarmey. Wherever the labour force came from, it had to be controlled and co-ordinated by a group of men who knew precisely what they were ordering, and who were capable of commanding or empowered to do so. Las Aldas was chosen as the appropriate site to erect a ceremonial centre because, despite its remoteness, it was located within accessible limits for easy and quick communication with the populated centres of the neighbouring valleys, especially the Valley of Casma ... 'The arrangement immediately around the Temple of certain carefully oriented standing stones, and the same fixed orientation of the Temple, features also seen in the case of various other temples in the Valley of Casma as at Sechín Alto, suggest an advanced practice of astronomical observation.'

Las Aldas was obviously only one of the various ceremonial complexes which arose in this period, at the beginning of the second millennium BC. Carlos Williams (1980, p. 401) points out that at least three architectural components became part of established practice in public constructions at this period: the mound or pyramid; the circular wells or sunken circular courtyards; and the temples, whose ground plan took the shape of a 'U'. All these forms derived from precedents in the pre-pottery age of the third millennium BC, and in turn provided the models for the ceremonial centres which came to dominate the landscape of the Marañón Andes in the course of the first millennium BC.

Several of these components, such as the circular sunken wells, seem to have a northern origin, as may be inferred from their appearance in the pre-pottery sites of Alto Salaverry and Salinas de Chao. Other forms, such as the U-shaped structures, may rather derive from the central coast, specifically from the valleys of Chillón, Rimac and Lurín, around Lima. Pyramid-type platforms, however, appear in both zones. To such coastal features should of course be added the upland and eastern features such as the precincts at Kotosh (the Temple of the Crossed Hands, etc.), which also were a legacy from pre-pottery times.

Some valleys, especially Casma, acquired tremendous wealth at this time. There came to be organized here ceremonial centres on a scale comparable only to the urban centres of late classical times. The most important was Sechín Alto, nearly 2 km long and almost 1 km wide, the chief feature of which is an immense main pyramid, which Julio C. Tello (1965) considered to be the greatest architectural work ever to have been carried out on the Peruvian coast. Its base measures 200 × 350 m, and it rises nearly 35 m above the valley floor. In front of the pyramid stretches a wide avenue consisting of courts or patios laid out at different levels, over an area of 400 × 1,400 m. Along the line of the courts are at least two circular wells, while along the great avenue itself are a large number of buildings of lesser size, as well as platforms, all oriented in accordance with the central axis which runs north-east.

In the valleys of Supe, Pativilca, Huaura and those around Lima, as far as Lurín, urban development reached levels which, if not quite equal to this, were at least similar. Ceremonial centres expanded in the highlands, although so far, there are none known to be of the size of those that were established along the coast. The region of Cajamarca and Trujillo did not attain the apotheosis-like climax of the central area of Peru, and the South retained its marginal character, even though the craft of pottery spread in all directions, so that by the beginning of the first millennium BC it had already reached both the area of Lake Titicaca and the oases of the coastal desert.

In point of fact, by the year 1000 BC, a general overview of the Andean area presents us with the spectacle of a process of disintegration of exclusively village life. Urban centres now strongly predominated, and these channelled society's economic activity and organized powerful and centralized taxation systems on a regional scale.

In the central Andes, in what is now Peru, roughly between latitudes 6° and 15°S, historical and archaeological evidence records the existence of important developments in civilization culminating in the formation of powerful, conquering states such as the 'Empire of the Incas'. It was established around the fifteenth century AD, bringing about the political unification of an extensive area stretching more than 5,000 km from the northern or equatorial Andes (to the north of the equator) to the southern Andes (as far as latitude 35° S.).

The formation of the Inca empire was not an isolated event in the Andes and its origins are found in the remote dawn of Andean civilization when, after the end of the Neolithic period, the central Andes saw the rapid development of urban cultures.

The Andean *cordillera* runs longitudinally down the continent of South America from north to south, bordering the Pacific Ocean. It displays a great variety of landscapes which may be divided into four main orological areas: the northern or equatorial zone, the central zone, the central-northern zone and the southern zone. In each area the development of Neolithic culture and the subsequent progress towards civilization took different forms. This may clearly be seen in the period from 1500 to 700 BC, which is the subject of this chapter (Map 28).

THE CHAVÍN CULTURE

As early as the beginning of the third millennium BC, the central Andes had already begun its own separate process of

development, which was most clearly marked in the northern region, also known as the Marañón Andes. When ceramics arrived in this region from the equatorial Andes towards the beginning of the second millennium BC, the pre-ceramic Neolithic culture had already progressed beyond a purely village structure to develop gradually into a society organized around ceremonial centres of various kinds. These obviously channelled a large part of the productive activities into highly specialized tasks, such as large-scale irrigation works and the measurement of time for agricultural purposes. At the same time, the existence of such centres led to the accumulation of surpluses in community stores (larger than individual household stores), which made it possible to feed those dedicated to the service of the temples and allocate resources for the construction of public works, through the use of systems of redistribution which we are not yet able to describe with any degree of accuracy.

In northern Peru, the introduction of pottery was linked to the rapid development of trade. Pottery making became one of the factors in consolidating this process, in that it led to much greater freedom in the choice of settlements (in places some distance away from direct sources of water) and to greater variety in eating habits as a result of new methods of preparing, storing and transporting food.

The process, which lasted from about 1500 to 1000 BC, was extremely successful. The Marañón Andes became a rich and abundant area, while to the north and to the south – in the northern Andes and in southern Peru (the Apurímac Andes) – the village pattern of life continued to exist. The ceremonial centres increased both in size and in number: there were several in each valley, surrounded by highly developed villages and extensive areas of cultivation. The villagers displayed a strong tendency to satisfy their needs not just from local resources, but also through trade over both short and long distances. Their undoubted ability to produce surpluses is shown by the size of the public works projects, by their capacity to absorb expensive luxury articles which had been transported considerable distances and by what appears to have been the far-reaching and effective settlement of the most productive areas in each region and the diverse uses made of local resources. In addition, there is evidence of a considerable increase in population which spread out to occupy practically all the areas which could be put to productive use.

From Cajamarca in the north to the *meseta* of Junín in the south the whole of the sierra was settled by agriculturists, although they preferred to settle in the more temperate zones where water for irrigation was easily accessible. The same was true in the valleys and along the coast, from Lambayeque to Lima, where the abundance of fish and seafood offered a plentiful supply of animal proteins.

The available archaeological evidence reveals that the process of domesticating plants and animals had reached an extremely advanced stage in the Andes. Agriculture and animal husbandry were able to draw upon the whole range of resources known to be of Andean origin, with the exception of a few secondary products. All the evidence seems to indicate that most of the techniques and methods of working the land and using water resources were known, such as the construction of agricultural terraces and systems of irrigation channels of various sizes and the use of calendars and methods of weather forecasting and so on.

The Marañón Andes occupy an intermediate zone, lying between the wet equatorial north and the dry Peruvian south. Here, moorlands and high, bleak plateaus (punas), which are

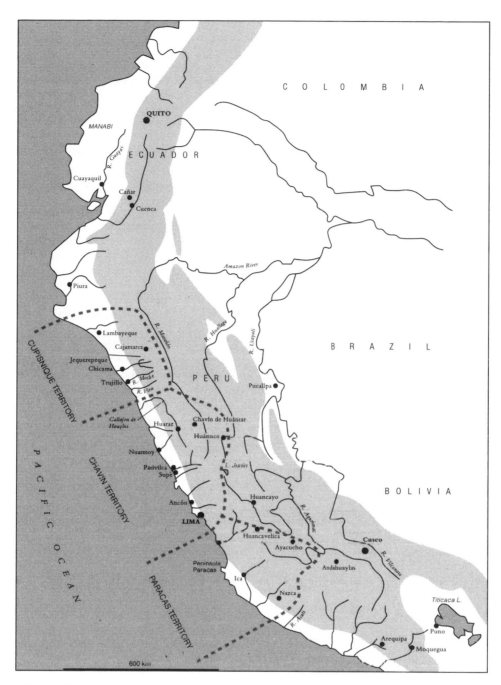

Map 28 The Andean empires

typical features of the high Andean landscape in the north and the south, meet. It is a land of maize, beans, squash, and plentiful fish and seafood. It is a temperate zone with average temperatures whose inhabitants, because of its intermediate position, had access not only to many of the resources of the hot rain forests of the northern Andes and the eastern Amazon, but also to agricultural products from the Neolithic cultures of the cold, dry regions in the south. Thus, between 1500 and 1000 BC, the coastal and mountain areas of northern Peru were extremely well supplied and acted as a kind of laboratory where many different plants and animals were adapted to new environmental conditions. It was in this way that the domestic camelidae (the llama and the alpaca) were introduced into the north from the southern Andes, and probably also the potato, the quinoa and other similar crops.

However, unlike anything that had occurred in previous millennia during the development of the Neolithic culture,

a new phenomenon appeared during this period with the emergence of 'spheres of influence', arising from the formation of homogeneous regional cultures. Archaeologists have given the name 'Chavín' to the most distinctive of these cultures with the widest area of influence. Local names have been given to the other cultures, which include the Cupisnique culture in the north and Kotosh in Huánuco.

As a result of the relations established with the north and the south this 'urban revolution' spread beyond the area of north Peru and, although it had comparatively little effect on the highly developed Neolithic culture of the tropical northern Andes, it had a substantial impact on conditions of life in the south. Thus, the arid regions of Ica and Ayacucho, where Neolithic culture had made only slow progress during the previous two millennia, were overwhelmed by their contacts with the Chavín culture and a vigorous culture grew up around the oasis to which archaeologists have given the name 'Paracas'. This was to act later as a bridge between the peoples of the north and the south, leading to the exchange of goods and techniques in both directions between the northern maize cultures and the southern cultures centering on the cultivation of the potato and on animal herding. It encouraged the emergence of urban life in the Andes of the punas some centuries later (about 500 BC), with the formation of the Pucara culture which developed in the areas drained by Lake Titicaca and the Vilcanota River.

However, at the centre of this whole process was the Chavín culture, which was situated in what are now the departments of Ancash and Lima; to the north was the Cupisnique culture with a series of local variants in Lambayeque, La Liberdad and Cajamarca, while to the south was the Paracas culture, which existed in a marginal and derivative form in Ica, Ayacucho and Huancavelica. To the north and south of these areas, during the period extending from 1500 to 700 BC, Neolithic villages continued to be the predominant life-style.

The Chavín culture is an outstanding example of the urban revolution in the Andean area. It lay within a vast system of irrigated valleys and was based on the cultivation of temperate crops such as maize, kidney beans, cotton and various kinds of cucurbitaceous plants, together with cassava or manioc, peanuts (Arachis hypogaea) and other hot-weather crops. It was also based on the intensive exploitation of marine resources, whose extensive use throughout the whole area is shown by the discovery of the remains of molluscs in the mountains as far from the sea as the site of Chavín itself, hundreds of kilometres from the coast.

However, although we should emphasize the important part played in the Chavín culture by agriculture and the exploitation of marine resources, together with the breeding of a kind of rodent (guinea pigs), and, apparently, of a kind of domestic fowl (Cairina moschata or Muscovy duck), this was not the only distinctive feature. In fact, everything stemmed from the major advances which had occurred during the previous Neolithic period, especially changes in the production of artefacts and in the development of public works.

Part of the work of producing artefacts, previously carried out on a largely domestic basis, was taken over by an élite of specialized craftsmen, associated with the major ceremonial centres and apparently varying in status according to the size and importance of the centre. Pottery and textiles obviously continued to be produced on a domestic, utilitarian basis, but at the same time their range of uses expanded through the creation of new and more varied forms: bowls, drinking vessels, serving dishes, plates, cups and so on. On the other hand, other arts developed well beyond the purely domestic sphere and became the special province of skilled artisans. The clearest example of this is provided by the stone cutters who became sculptors and engravers and were definitely associated with the major temples. They knew the strengths and qualities of the rocks in different quarries and also possessed a knowledge of the complicated patterns of images which had to be carved or engraved on different kinds of stones. Thus, the art of stone-carving and sculpting became a separate activity carried on in the public, nondomestic sector. Similar developments occurred in the production of jewels and luxury articles made from shells, bone, deer horn or semi-precious stones. In the temples of this period archaeologists have found examples of skilfully made works of art in the form of anklets, bracelets, necklaces, medallions and other personal ornaments which are valuable, not only because of their workmanship, but also because of the material chosen in each case, whether exquisite shells from the tropical seas of the north (Spondylus and Strombus), semi-precious stones from the southern desert (malachite, turquoise or sodalite) or rare stones such as obsidian, which apparently came from as far south as Huancavelica. The distance between Huancavelica, which supplied the stones, and Guayas-Manabí where the shells came from, is almost 2,000 km.

Clearly, too, the ceramic dishes and cotton fabrics for the élite were manufactured by specialists in workshops associated with the temples, which provided the artists with models to be copied. Although the technology used in the manufacture of pottery was basically the same whether it was produced domestically or in the ceremonial centres, there was a difference in the quality of the finished articles: sophistication of the designs and other details which made the luxury ceramics outstanding as works of art. The same is true of the decorative textiles, such as tapestries or brocades, which have figures of the Chavín deities.

The second change lies in the construction of public works and it is this which clearly distinguishes the system of urban life from the village structure of the previous Neolithic period. These projects are on a very large scale. In the Cupisnique area there are remains of roads constructed for public purposes (although this does not mean that the whole community had access to them) between places several kilometres apart (Beck, 1979). There were also irrigation works which extended far beyond a single community and required cooperation and agreements between two or more communities: agreed time-tables for the operation of the irrigation channels and a whole series of arrangements which could only be implemented by co-ordinating or, even better, centralized bodies. However, apart from these large-scale projects which must have been carried out on the basis of intercommunal agreements, it is the construction of ceremonial complexes, with large buildings arranged according to a very detailed plan, and their orientation, style and form of construction defined according to formal rules, which really marks the change from the village system.

Prior to this period, although the ceremonial centres had many formal and constructional features in common, they were clearly local in type and, given their individuality, it is not possible to assign them all to a single culture. It appears that the system set up to administer them only covered part of a valley or, at the most, a single valley, uniting communities which already had territorial and/or ethnic links. This localized pattern ended with the emergence of the Chavín culture. It involved the construction of public buildings such as temples, which extended their influence over a whole region and not just over individual valleys or communities. Chavín marked the introduction of a particular style in an extensive area which included at least twenty coastal valleys (from the Santa River to the Ica River) and several mountain valleys. However, this did not merely involve the spread of an artistic style – although that was important enough in itself – but the real significance was that the construction of public works followed standardized models with similar methods of construction, dimensions, orientation and form and, in some cases, even using similar materials. Within this high degree of uniformity in the area, it is possible to distinguish regional variations. Some valleys gave greater emphasis to some features and less to others, which must be evidence of a degree of regional autonomy within an overall framework in which there were clearly centralized methods of organizing the construction of public works and, probably, the whole system of production.

It would be unwise, given the present state of our knowledge, to attempt a detailed description of the political system, although it was obviously something approaching complex policy organization. In support of this hypothesis may be cited the existence of certain forms of tribute which were concentrated in the ceremonial centres. In Chavín de Huántar, the site which has given its name to the culture, temple offerings have been found which came from the coast of the central area, from the Cupisnique region and from the northern sierra. However, there is no evidence of any reciprocal offerings, which leads us to believe that there was an asymmetrical relationship which consisted essentially in the payment of tribute.

Clearly, this did not all happen overnight. There was, rather, a gradual process of development, which began during the second half of the second millennium BC and reached its highest point of development around 700 BC, when all the features we have described could be observed. During an initial period, which may have lasted until around 1000 BC, all these strands of cultural unification and centralization were developing on a regional basis in adjacent valleys or in small mountain valleys. This is what occurred in the valleys in the department of Lima (Ancón-Chillón, Rímac and Lurín) and the valleys of Supe-Huarmey-Pativilca, which apparently formed local centres of cultural development, but at the same time became linked within a similar political and economic system. Between 1000 and 700 BC these local forms came under the authority of the major regional systems, such as Chavín. Subsequently, from about 700 to 500 BC, a third phase seems to have occurred which saw an even greater expansion of Chavín influence, since during this period we encounter a general trend towards uniformity extending over the whole of the Marañón Andes, from Piura and Cajamarca, as far as the Apurímac Andes in Ayacucho and Ica. For the present, the only evidence of this expansion comes from a very similar kind of pottery which is recognized by archaeologists as being Late Chavín. Then a sudden collapse occurred, and after 500 BC – the result, it seems, of the defeat of the unifying power – regional and local cultures began to develop which were very different from one another and eager to preserve their independence.

It was in about 500 BC that the ceremonial centre of Chavín de Huántar was abandoned and this site is seen by some archaeologists, following the theories put forward by Julio C. Tello, as being the 'capital' or centre of what was probably the unifying state of that period.

Chavín de Huántar is clearly the most outstanding example of this stage of cultural development. It is the meeting-place of all the different skills and knowledge acquired over the centuries by the peoples of the coast and the sierra from the north, south and east. It consists of a group of buildings laid out within a triangle formed by the confluence of two rivers and the slopes of a high mountain range which rises several thousand metres up to where the snow lies above 5,000 m. Starting above the snowline the Wacheqsa River flows down on the western side and joins the Mosna on the south, to turn north-eastwards and flow into the broad Marañón River, the source of the Amazon which flows into the Atlantic Ocean on the other side of the continent.

The site of Chavín was not chosen by chance; the reason for the choice of the site where the two rivers meet and where the valley suddenly becomes much narrower is clear when it is seen together with the buildings. The valley or rather the gorge in which Chavín lies is extremely narrow: hardly more than a few hundred metres wide and only a few kilometres long. It is, in fact, a narrow passage bordered on the east and west by high mountains which in little less than two or three kilometres rise to a height of over 4,500 m. Chavín lies at the head of this passage, at a height of 3,180 m, and provides excellent conditions for measuring and observing the movements of the stars within a panorama studded with the sharp peaks of the surrounding mountains. In addition, Chavín lies at the centre of a network of tracks from the coast to the jungle and is a focal point for the whole of the Marañón Andes.

The ceremonial centre of Chavín was not completed as a single project within a short period of time. In fact, it was a continuous process with buildings being superimposed on one another and new features added. In general terms, this process may be divided into two main phases: the first or 'ancient' phase of construction and occupation between 1500–1200 and 1000–700 BC; and the second or 'new' period running from 1000–700 to 500 BC. Clearly, buildings may have been constructed both before and after these two periods, but so far we have no evidence of this.

According to the available archaeological evidence the construction of the 'ancient' temple of Chavín was begun during the last centuries of the second millennium, between 1350 and 1100 BC. This building was repaired, extended and even completely remodelled on more than one occasion, as may be seen from the existing architectural remains. At about the beginning of the first millennium (c. 1000–700 BC), at the same time as major changes were occurring in all aspects of the Chavín culture, much more extensive work was carried out to enlarge and remodel the temple. The old temple ceased to be the focus of the ceremonial centre, and the centre of gravity shifted towards the south, where a larger and more magnificent building took over its role. This 'new' temple, unlike its predecessor, apparently underwent few changes and its subsequent decline, which seems to have been accompanied by some catastrophe, perhaps of seismic origin, marks the beginning of the decline of Chavín's importance.

The ancient temple of Chavín is partially covered by the new temple, so that few of its remains are still visible. The main building was U-shaped with the open side facing east, so that the rays of the morning sun shone directly on to the façade, which was at the bottom of the 'U'. Thus, it had two arms, one to the north and one to the south, and a central section to the west, framing an open space in the centre measuring 40 m each way, so as to form a kind of atrium. Both the arms and the central section are made up of platforms which are some 12 m above the level of the atrium and form the top level of a series of stepped platforms, covering an area of more than 10 ha, sloping down to the Mosna River some 30 m below.

The building was constructed on a series of superimposed terraces lying on foundations of a mixture of rubble and mud contained by thick walls of masonry lying parallel to one another and about a metre apart. Some of the spaces between these walls were left free of rubble, creating underground passages or galleries, which were intended for a wide variety of uses. These galleries form labyrinths inside the foundations. In some cases, the walls have been very carefully constructed so that the flat faces of the stones are on the outside (and in the new temple they are even carved), although this is not common and the evidence is that they were plastered with mud and painted.

The platforms look very solid and compact. On the outside they are protected by a plating of enormous carved stones, some of which weigh several tons. On the parts which were covered with stucco, little effort was made to polish the stones, but on those parts not covered with plaster the finest slabs were chosen and they were very finely carved and then polished. The stones were undoubtedly joined together with mud and, in order to make the join between each block as secure as possible, small wedge-shaped stones were mixed in with the clay. One important feature is that these gigantic slabs were arranged in thick and thin string courses, usually with two thin courses alternating with one thick course, on the section of the wall which was not covered with plaster.

The atrium consists of a quadrangular platform with a sunken, circular court (diameter 21 m) in the centre. The two flights of steps which lead down to the court follow an east-west line forming an equinoctial axis, which makes it possible to determine the position of the sun by using as points of reference the centre of the court and the point where the atrium meets the central platform. The platform is so positioned as to be an exact continuation of the western stairway.

The circular court has a floor of large flat slabs of yellow limestone. Its surrounding wall, which acts as a parapet for the platform or atrium, is one of the most beautiful walls in Chavín. A small plinth course, no more than 10 cm high and about 5 cm deep, runs along the bottom of the wall, separating it from the floor of the court. Above it there is another course, about 36 cm high, consisting of a row of stone slabs with carved reliefs of a line of jaguars, all different, facing towards the western stairway (there are fourteen jaguars going towards the stairway from the north and the same number from the south). They are all in the western half of the court, where the rays of the rising sun fall. In the other half of the court the stone slabs are not carved, except for two of them, lying either side of the eastern stairway.

Above the row of slabs with carvings of jaguars, there are two thin courses of stones supporting another row of quadrangular slabs 80 cm high, which are carved with images of anthropomorphic, elegantly attired figures (the head-dresses are particularly elegant), holding in their hands what appear to be musical instruments, including a trumpet shaped like a snail. Like the jaguars, they are facing towards the centre, where the stairway leads to the central section of the temple. There were probably twenty-eight of them, like the jaguars, but only a few have survived.

As throughout the building, the platform surrounding the circular court is not a completely solid structure, but is crossed by a number of galleries, in which offerings for the temple were placed. The excavation of one of these galleries has brought to light several hundred beautiful objects of very fine ceramic ware, receptacles made of imported stone, small ornaments of bone, horn and decorative shells brought all the way from the sea, together with the remains of food – duck, venison, the meat of llamas and guinea-pigs, and shellfish (Chavín is some 300 km from the nearest point on the coast and separated from it by two very high mountain ranges).

The front of the central part of the old temple has been almost completely destroyed; it collapsed at some point, either as a result of some kind of natural disaster or because it was unable to bear the stresses set up inside the building as a result of changes to its internal structure. The whole of the central part is full of curious passageways, one of which

is clearly the most important, since not only is it in the very centre of the building, along the equinoctial axis mentioned above, but in the centre of the passage, which is in the form of a cross. Here there is the most impressive stone-carved statue known in Peru, which on account of its shape is known as the Lanzón. It is more than 4 m high and represents an anthropomorphic deity, which was almost certainly the main god worshipped at Chavín. It is set into the centre of the crossing, facing towards the east. It faces a long passage (over 12 m long) which is connected with a small duct through which a certain amount of light and air filters from outside. According to calculations, during the equinoxes the sun would shine in through this duct – perhaps for only a few minutes – and the rays then advanced up the long passage to light up the savage face of the Lanzón.

While it is clear that the gallery of the Lanzón acted as the setting for the statue, there are other subterranean galleries about whose function we know little or nothing. Some of them were used for drainage, others contained offerings, while many were probably used as storage places or depositories for valuables. There are also some which, although obviously drainage ducts, had no containers outside to collect the water and we do not know what water they carried. In this connection, we have evolved a hypothesis (Lumbreras et al., 1976), which applies to some of the galleries or ducts whose function was to bring water through passages which were invisible from outside: the water was brought through underground channels from a high point on the Wacheqsa River and was then distributed through a system of invisible ducts with special valves which were used to amplify the sound caused by the falling water, creating a noise of no identifiable origin from within the temple, as part of the liturgical 'apparatus' required by the Chavinese religion. This hypothesis was put to the test with one of the channels or ducts of the old temple and the noise produced was similar to the roaring of a lion or of a crocodile or, more simply, the sound of a waterfall. In addition, the engineer Chacho Gonzales has put forward the broader hypothesis that some of the galleries might have been used to vary the sound of the water and create a 'sound picture' which could be controlled at will. An examination of part of this complex of subterranean passages, which form strange labyrinths, revealed a structure similar to that of an enormous saxophone.

After passing through the underground channels, the water flowed out into the Mosna through a duct which emerged in the bed of the river where it could not be seen. We have also discovered the intake pipe in the Wacheqsa and segments of the underground water ducts supplying water to the temple, and everything seems to indicate that the old temple, with the Lanzón statue inside, was constructed so as to produce a sound like thunder.

All this provides confirmation of the theory that the site was chosen after an extremely detailed examination of the conditions required to build a 'thunder' temple which would also act as a good astronomical observatory and which – if this hypothesis is correct – could provide accurate measurements of the equinoxes by means of a complex system of illuminating the Lanzón on such dates, not to mention the circular court which was a very effective sundial.

As far as the new temple is concerned, it seems to have been the final stage in a long series of extensions and alterations. In its final form, it developed into an enormous complex, several times larger than the old temple. With the same U-shaped structure, its major feature is the main, pyramid-like platform, which gives on to a large square courtyard several metres below. Once again, the central axis is east-west and runs along the stairways, through the centre of the courtyard and through one or two small courts or atriums to the centre of the pyramid where there was an imposing portal giving access to the great temple. This portal consisted of two cylindrical columns decorated with beautiful carvings of imaginary birds, which supported a projecting lintel carved with what appear to be fourteen birds of prey (sparrow-hawks, falcons or eagles), seven facing towards the north and seven towards the south, the former in white stone and the latter in black stone and meeting at a central equinoctial point. The portal was extended outwards on both sides in the form of a long, low wall of huge stone slabs, which are white to the south and black to the north, creating a kind of dichotomy between light and dark.

The portal, which gives on to an atrium, which was covered with flagstones carved with various figures from the Chavinoid pantheon, is in fact a blind entrance. There is no direct access through the portal, as it is only possible to proceed a few metres towards the west and then there are two stairways to the north and to the south which go up to the two entrances to the upper part of the pyramid, along the sides.

The whole construction was surrounded by a kind of cornice consisting of slabs carved with felines and, above all, birds. Below the cornice, acting as a kind of support, there was a line of large monster-like heads carved in stone and set into the wall.

Clearly, one of the most outstanding aspects of Chavín is its complex decoration, which was obviously part of a much more complicated liturgical system. In addition to the carved stones, the lintels and the carved columns and even horizontal stone slabs, it would seem that much of the building was covered with mud plaster and, as in the case of similar temples on the coast, may have had figures modelled and painted on the surface. On the basis of comparisons which have been made, it is clear that the carvings on the stones are from various periods, revealing very substantial differences in both form and content between the figures on the old temple and those from later periods.

The art of the earlier period is more sober and heavy, while the later style is lighter, although heavily overlaid with additional decorative features. The anthropomorphic figure of the Lanzón is basically naturalistic in design, even though it represents a demon with large fangs, hair in the form of snakes, nails like claws and is generally terrifying to look at. An obelisk, which was probably in the centre of the circular court of the old temple, represents two monstrous reptiles (crocodiles) whose bodies are made up of plants, animals and imaginary zooanthropomorphic creatures, but without any additional decoration, despite the complexity of the images. During the later period, the gods or whatever the figures are which are carved on the slabs are subordinated into a complex pattern of spirals, additional fangs and so on, to such an extent that in some cases these features appear to be the main element in the carvings.

Clearly, however, leaving aside these stylistic changes, it is the basic way in which the figures are represented which is the most important feature. These savage-looking gods, when represented anthropomorphically, are given the most frightening and deadly attributes of species which are equally terrifying and, when represented in zoomorphic terms everything which symbolizes destruction is given particular prominence: the curved fangs as of snakes or reptiles, the crossed

fangs and claws of the felines and the claws of birds of prey such as the falcon or the eagle. Everything seems designed to induce fear in the viewer, including the angry expressions on the faces and the repulsive representation of hair and eyebrows as twisting, writhing snakes. The creation of these monsters, in association with a temple reverberating like thunder and a mythology clearly loaded with elements intended to frighten people into submission, were the external expression of an extremely complex power structure (let us call it religious or theocratic) covering many communities on large tracts of the coast, the sierra and the jungle-covered highlands.

However, Chavín's influence, which was particularly strong by about 700 BC, obviously could not have been based solely on its liturgical paraphernalia, however complex that may have been; the whole of this complex ritual was only the framework within which technico-magical functions were performed by the occupants of the temple, who were priests specially trained in the mechanics of time, in hydraulics and in other practical skills. The 'oracle' which Chavín possessed maintained its prestige, albeit it in a vestigial form, right up until the seventeenth century AD: a Spanish visitor in 1616 wrote that 'close to the town of Chavín there is a large and extremely impressive building of stones covered in carvings; it was a "guaca"[3] and one of the most famous pagan sanctuaries, like Rome or Jerusalem for us, where the Indians went to give offerings and make sacrifices, because the demon which lived in this place uttered many prophecies and predictions' (Vásquez de Espinosa, 1948, p. 458). The existence of a similar state of affairs during the period when it was at the height of its power would explain the presence of offerings from different places in the country, hundreds of kilometres away.

However, Chavín was not just an oracle to which pilgrims flocked from thousands of different places to worship and apply for predictions and advice. The presence of its gods and its architects and skilled artisans in other places is also an important factor. Chavín was not the only temple of its kind which existed, although it is the most spectacular of those we know. As has already been stated, in each valley and in each region there was a ceremonial complex of a similar kind and, associated with each, ceramics and an iconographic system which, while not identical with those of Chavín, may be regarded as clearly following the same pattern. This went beyond the mere imitation of stylistic or formal features, involving the same subject matter and the same approach to it. In fact, many of the features which go to make up Chavinoid architecture and art clearly stem from interactions between regions, so that some of the antecedents of Chavinoid technology and art are to be found both on the coast, in Lima and Ancón, Casma and Nepeña, and in the Callejón de Huaylas and probably in the east, as well as in the northern Andes and in the Cupisnique area.

The U-shaped temples, with one side open towards the direction in which the sun's rays were regarded as being of particular significance (in some cases towards the east and in other cases towards the west), became a symbol of the civilization. They were particularly common in the valleys of the Department of Lima: in the Chillón Valley there were two or three; in the Rímac Valley we know of three and in the Lurín Valley there are more than three. They are all very similar, if not virtually identical: the same orientation, the same size, the same form of construction. The best known is the temple of Garagay, situated in a low-lying area at the confluence of the Chillón and Rímac Valleys, in what is now the northern part of the city of Lima. It consists of a series of five small mounds arranged on three sides around a very large open area, 415 m long and 215 m wide, the axis running NNE–SSW. The central mound, which is covered with massive stepped platforms, and lies to the south of the open area, is 385 m long, 155 m wide and 23 m high in the central part which is four-sided. The side arms are lower: the western arm is 260 m long and 115 m wide and only 9 m high, while the eastern arm is 140 m long, 40 m wide and scarcely 6 m high. There are several sunken, circular courtyards in the open area and within the body of the pyramid or central platform there is an atrium similar to the one at Chavín. It is also U-shaped, decorated with beautiful friezes modelled in mud plaster and painted in bright water colours with figures in an obviously Chavinoid style. The figures form a procession facing towards the centre, as at Chavín.

In the eastern arm, where excavations have also been carried out, there are other friezes and mud reliefs which, on account of the presence of marine motifs, would appear to be associated with forms of religion prevalent on the coast. Some of these friezes also provide evidence of contacts with the Cupisnique region in the north.

The presence of Cupisnique elements, both in Chavín itself and in the whole of its area of influence, clearly indicates that Cupisnique culture was very closely linked with Chavín. Indeed, all the evidence indicates that was in fact the case, since Cupisnique objects have been found at many Chavinoid sites. Moreover, the similarity between some of these remains has led to the two cultures being confused, to the extent that up until a few years ago Cupisnique ceramics were described as 'typical' of the classical art of Chavín. In fact, some archaeologists had always distinguished between them, although they referred to Cupisnique as 'coastal Chavín', which is nowadays regarded as wrong. It is wrong not only because Chavín itself also developed on the coast, in the Departments of Lima and Ancash but also because Cupisnique extended its influence inland in Cajamarca and in the Trujillo highlands.

THE CUPISNIQUE AND OTHER CULTURES

Like Chavín, Cupisnique began to develop in the pre-ceramic period during the Neolithic Age and acquired a position of importance by about 1500–1000 BC. However, there appears to be a lesser degree of uniformity in what we might call the Cupisnique area than in the Chavín culture, as a result, it would seem, of the centralizing authority being weaker. Although there are family likenesses in the pottery, the iconography and the other archaeological remains found in this area, archaeologists have been relectant to include them all within one single culture: the Cajamarca area has one variant called Pacopampa and another called Huacaloma; in Lambayeque we can identify one subculture and in the valley of Jequetepeque there is another. The Cupisnique culture of Chicama differs from that found at Virú and even from the form it takes in Moche. It has proved difficult to separate all these groups of the north from their original subjugation to Chavín and we do not know a great deal about them. Perhaps the local variations are less important than the general features. We may not yet have discovered the northern Chavín which will provide a central point of reference for all this evidence, although to the north of Cajamarca the imposing ceremonial centre, Pacopampa, with monolithic

cylindrical columns and large stone carvings in the walls, has sculptured figures and very highly developed ceramics. In the upper part of the valley of Jequetepeque, in the Cajamarca region, there is the temple of La Copa or Kuntur Wasi, which is also pyramidal in form and has stone sculptures. In Trujillo, a team of archaeologists recently excavated a very fine temple, the 'Huaca de los Reyes', which contained several figures modelled in clay, including some colossal feline heads. Obviously, large-scale public building projects, which led to the construction of temples and their dependent buildings, were as important as in Chavín and reflected a similar form of development, but there does not appear to be – or at least it is not readily apparent – any uniformity.

If we attempt to identify uniform features, we find that Cupisnique sculpture is itself a feature which distinguishes it from Chavín, since in Chavín the characteristic feature is the stonework rather than the sculpture as such. Both in Pacopampa and in Kuntur Wasi figures are carved in the round as statues and not merely as decorative architectural elements. This emphasis on sculpture is also found in the pottery, which is not only incised or excised in the style favoured by Chavín artists, but is very often modelled to represent human beings, animals or plants. In fact, this emphasis is fairly general, although the pottery for domestic use mainly employed well-finished designs and was decorated with incisions.

It is in the iconography that uniformity is most apparent. While the creatures represented in Chavinoid art are thorough-going monsters, despotic, terrifying products of the imagination, Cupisnique iconography, with the exception of a few highly stylized though not necessarily ferocious figures, tends to be naturalistic – almost portrait-like – and in no way esoteric. It might almost be asserted that when terrifying features do appear, they are the result of contacts with Chavín. Felines, snakes and, to a lesser extent, perhaps, eagles repeatedly occur as objects of worship, although they are not represented in quite the same way as in Chavinoid art. In fact, the concept of the state – in whatever form it may have existed – was not well defined even though – like Chavín – there is evidence that the same basic conditions appear to have existed. There is evidence of the widespread use of surpluses for the construction of public works (albeit on a smaller scale than in the case of Chavín) with specialized workers in the temples. There is also evidence of long-distance trade in raw materials and luxury articles and of a tendency towards cultural unification, to such an extent that we might be led to posit the existence of a common religion.

Cupisnique serves therefore as a frame of reference for this whole cultural process which is now being studied, and provides some evidence of the development of a complex civilization bordered to the south by Chavín and to the north by the vigorous Neolithic Chorrera culture, on the site of the Valdivia culture which produced the earliest pottery known in the Andes. Chorrera, like Cupisnique with which it had some contact, is distinguished by its very colourful pottery which is essentially sculptural in form, but as far as we know it never developed a social structure which went beyond village life.

The links which Chorrera maintained with Cupisnique and Chavín mainly centred on the trade in 'mullu', the *Spondylus princeps* sea-shells which were much in demand in the central Andes. It seems that they were the main suppliers of these molluscs and distributed them in the south through the Cañar region, spreading the Narrío culture during this period. The two peoples – the Narrío and the Chorrera – carried on an active trade, although neither of them advanced beyond a form of life organized around the village. The same thing could have occurred in the case of the Cupisnique people, but in fact they underwent a more complex process of development, with ceremonial centres occupied by people specializing in particular skills. We have already seen that there was Cupisnique pottery in the Chavín area and although some pieces, like those from Chavín de Huántar, have been found in the middens at Ancón, they may have arrived there simply as the result of trade.

Other peoples, such as the Kotosh in the Sierra de Huanuco to the east of Chavín territory, appear to have been at a similar stage of development, although we do not even know the exact territory they occupied or whether they managed to establish an economic and political system or continued to live within a Neolithic village structure.

The same appears to be true towards the south in the high Andean plateaus (punas) and the large desert areas. However, unlike the Cupisnique region and Kotosh, where some form of autochthonous development appears to have occurred, Neolithic culture only achieved a limited impact in the south and everything seems to indicate that not even the introduction of pottery – which is clearly prior to the arrival of Chavinoid influences – brought about any major changes. On the other hand, the arrival of Chavinoid influence in the regions of Ica and Ayacucho brought about a process of change towards increasingly complex forms, as may be seen in the formation of the Paracas culture.

Paracas, like Cupisnique, is a distinctive culture and, in fact, is so distinctive that archaeologists have found it hard to agree that it developed as a result of Chavín relationships. In the Ica region agriculture centred on the oases and differed greatly from the agriculture of large-scale irrigation in the valleys to the north of Lima. Likewise, the Ayacucho region is an arid zone with little water and far fewer agricultural resources than the whole of the sierra in the Marañón Andes. In such circumstances there was no possibility of agriculture based on maize developing there, as happened in the north, and instead it was the cultivation of potatoes and the raising of livestock which provided *kawsay*[4]. Clearly, the expansion of Chavín influence was not a result of the priestly caste's seeking access to sources of food. On the other hand obsidian could be obtained from Huancavelica and Ayacucho, and wool and good-quality cotton from Ica, and it would seem probable that Chavín's links with these regions were dictated by efforts to find the raw materials used for the manufacture of luxury articles. This is not only possible: in fact, the temples required such contacts. If this was indeed the basis of the contacts, it would also explain the nature and form of the characteristic features of the Paracas culture, which has many Chavinoid iconographic features, while at the same time having its own very distinctive stamp.

We do not know if the Paracas people had many temples and when they started building them. In Chincha we know of several ceremonial centres, but they date from after the sixth century BC. In Ica, the Cerrillos complex, which is of an earlier date, is rather crude in its construction, with some use of mud, and shows signs of having been built by a comparatively small number of unskilled workers. In fact, the construction of the temple of Cerrillos may have been the work of the local community or even the result of co-operation between a few families. In Ayacucho the temple of Wichqana, which appears to have been begun prior to the

spread of Chavín influence, is also not particularly large, while the temple of Chupas, which is also in the high valley of Ayacucho, might have been built as a result of the efforts of a single community at the very most. Chupas, which was built during the period of Chavín influence, is a settlement which probably had more than one temple in the form of a mound or platform, and although the buildings seem to be of different periods, none of them reveals any great degree of technical skill in construction or shows signs of centralized planning, and their construction does not appear to have involved anything more than co-operation among the local community on a household basis. Thus, such cases confront us with societies which were on the fringes of Chavín influence. Paracas was only to attain a degree of importance many centuries later, shortly before it declined and merged into the Nasca culture. The innovations which were introduced, such as polychrome pottery painted after firing and the use of wool in multi-coloured textiles, are not in themselves sufficient to lead us to assume a level of development which it probably never attained. Moreover, it seems that village life remained the most common form of social organization, with people grouped together in small settlements. These only developed later into urban complexes, although of a different character from those influenced by Chavín.

Just as Cupisnique was bordered on the north by Neolithic cultures such as Chorrera or Narrío, Paracas had poorly defined frontiers with Neolithic societies towards the south: Marcavalle and Qaluyu in the departments of Cusco and Puno, Chiripa to the south of Titicaca, Wankarani in the Oruro department of Bolivia and Faldas del Morro in northern Chile.

However, these southern Neolithic cultures, in addition to many other differences, such as their basis in animal husbandry, had one major innovation: the use and production of metals such as gold and copper. Thus, to some extent, they were a kind of Eneolithic. In Chavín, as far as we know, as in Paracas and Cupisnique, metallurgy was unknown until about 1000 BC.

The earliest remains of metal objects are those which have been found at the site of Waywaka, in Andahuaylas, to the south of Ayacucho. They are hammered sheets of gold, involving the use of special tools (Grossman, 1972, p. 270) including a stone anvil and hammer specially chosen and shaped for this purpose. According to the radiocarbon dates, the age of these finds is between 1700 and 1300 BC, or even earlier if we accept Grossman's corrected ^{14}C datings (Grossman, 1983, p. 58) which date the finds to between 2180 and 1115 BC.[5] The culture associated with these finds has been given the name of Muyu Moqo and is definitely non-Chavín (it is in fact pre-Chavín) and developed within a restricted area which includes Andahuaylas and Ayacucho (the Rancha phase) with relations with the south coast (the Hacha phase) in Acarí, to the south of Ica. According to Grossman, Muyu Moqo was a comparatively simple village-based culture, with pottery which, though mainly produced for household use, was well made. There is no evidence of complex forms of social organization, although it is clear that trade relations extended over considerable distances, down to the coast, from which sea-shells were imported (the sea is more than 250 km away), to Ayacucho and Huancavelica for obsidian and to the extreme south (Moquegua or as far as the north Chilean desert, at San Pedro de Atacama) for supplies of lapis lazuli and turquoise. All these stones have been found in the form of beads for necklaces, together with gold.

Further south, around Lake Titicaca and in association with the Wankarani de Oruro culture, there is evidence that by 1000 BC (Ponce Sanginés, 1970), or at least between 1000 and 500 BC, copper was being smelted during an extremely active stage of Neolithic development in the Peruvian-Bolivian Altiplano.

Clearly, copper and gold were not in common use. No specialized industries were developed to work them, and they did not apparently give rise to any special economic structure. The appearance of metallurgy did not bring about an 'age of metals' with consequences similar to those which occurred in the Old World. Indeed, it was only much later that metallurgy was introduced into the advanced cultures of the north, where gold was first to appear, but it produced no significant effects there either. Gold appeared in Chavín and Cupisnique about 1000 BC and copper only around 700 BC.

The Chiripa and Qaluyu cultures, which grew up around the great Lake Titicaca in the southern Altiplano in the high Andean plateaus, at a height of over 3,600 m, were undoubtedly the most highly developed cultures in the region. The other cultures, to the east and to the west of the Altiplano, or to the south, were much less highly developed, comparatively primitive Neolithic cultures. Clearly, they were desert cultures which had to overcome great difficulties in providing food; agriculture was subject to great uncertainty and was, as a matter of course, supplemented by hunting, fishing and food-gathering. However, they were extremely advanced in manufacturing textiles and ceramics and in using and working copper. On the other hand, in Chiripa and Qaluyu there was considerable population growth and there is some evidence that there existed communal constructions going beyond purely domestic needs, such as temples and public buildings. The economy of this area was mainly pastoral, consisting in the herding of llamas and alpacas which provided meat and also wool for textiles and high-quality leather. Animal husbandry could be supplemented by the cultivation of root crops (potatoes, *ollucos*, *ocas* and *mashwa*) and Chenopodiaceae such as quinoa and *cañiwa* or its related species the amaranth (*kiwicha*). Together they provided a basic diet which was well balanced in carbohydrates and animal proteins.

However, the environmental conditions in this area are extremely harsh. Although the seasons are defined in relation to the periods of rain (three months) and of drought (nine months), wide temperature differences occur on a daily rather than on a seasonal basis, so that there is summer heat every midday and winter frost every midnight throughout the year, while the temperature difference between summer and winter does not exceed 1° or 2° C. This makes agriculture very difficult, apart from the altitude and the problems of obtaining water. The annual rainfall varies between 200 and 700 cm and occurs irregularly during a three-month period, with some years of heavy rainfall interspersed with long years of drought. Despite the difficulties involved in overcoming such conditions, the peoples of the Altiplano managed to establish a stable economy as early as the Neolithic period and achieved even greater success after the fifth century BC, when a process of urban organization developed there with the Pucara and, later, the Tiwanaku cultures.

In fact, these harsh conditions were skilfully exploited: the people took advantage of the freezing nights and daily extremes of temperature to convert soft, wet foods into dehydrated forms, which could be conserved for long periods and easily transported (dehydrated potatoes or *chuño*, dehydrated meat or *charki*, etc.).

According to the available evidence, none of these peoples lived in isolation and many trading networks were established between north and south and east and west, extending hundreds of kilometres across deserts and the broad expanses of the cold, dry steppelands. Thus, Paracas was always in contact with Cusco and Puno, that is to say, with Marcavalle and Qaluyu, and also with Chiripa. This explains the exchanges of techniques and knowledge and of products between them.

It is these conditions which also made possible, between about 700 and 500 BC, the great expansion of Chavín, towards the end of the period under discussion. It appears that it developed into a conquering state although in fact we have no specific evidence to show whether this happened. What we do know, from the presence of the same type of pottery and the appearance of particular deities in the local iconographies, is that Chavín's sphere of influence extended over the whole of the Cupisnique region and also to Ayacucho and Ica. During this period it also extended into the northern Andes, as far as the Cañar region in Ecuador. However, it did not extend further south than the Paracas area; its known limits are the valleys of Ayacucho and Ica.

NOTES

1 Bischof (1980, p. 383, note 108): (I-7076) 5010 ± 120 BP; (15GS-142) 5000 ± 190 BP; (I-7075) 4920 ± 120; (15GS-146) 4750 ± 120 BP.

2 ^{14}C at Huaca de los Sacrificios (without correction): (UCR-242) 3950 + 150, (UCR-243) 4060 + 150; (UCR-244) 4150; 150 (GX-3862) 4260 + 150 B.P. These dates, as corrected, would yield: 2533, 2674, 2790 and 2930 BC.

3 *Guaca* is a Quechua expression which means 'holy place'.

4 *Kawsay* is a Quechua word which means food or sustenance; resources ensuring survival.

5 Known ^{14}C dates are (Grossman, 1972):

UCLA – 1808E – Carbon – 3550 ± 100 BP.
UCLA – 1808A – Carbon – 3440 ± 100 BP.
UCLA – 1808J – Carbon – 3185 ± 160 BP.
UCLA – 1808D – Carbon – 2200 ± 430 BP.

BIBLIOGRAPHY

BECK, C. M. 1979. Ancient Roads on the North Coast of Peru. Berkeley, Calif. (PhD thesis.)

BIRD, J. 1948. Preceramic Cultures in Chicama and Virú. *Mem. Soc. am. Archaeol.* (Menasha, Wis.), No. 4, pp. 21–8.

BIRD, J.; HYSLOP, J. 1985. *The Preceramic Excavations at the Huaca Prieta, Chicama Valley, Peru*. New York. (Anthropol. Pap. am. Mus. nat. Hist., 62, pt 1.)

BISCHOF, H. 1980. San Pedro und Valdivia – Frühe keramikkomplexe an der Küste Südwest-Ekuadors. *Beiträge zur allgemeinen und vergleichenden Archäologie*. Vol. 1, Deutches Archëologisches Institut, V. C. H. Beck.

BONAVIA, D. 1982. *Los Gavilanes. Mar, desierto y oasis en la historia del hombre*. Lima.

BONNIER, E.; ZEGARRA, J.; TELLO, J. C. 1985. Un ejemplo de crono-estratigrafía en un sitio con super-posición arquitectónica – Piruru – Unidad I/II. *Bull. Inst. français Étud. andin.* (Lima), Vol. 14, No. 3/4, pp. 80–101.

BUENO, A.; GRIEDER, T. 1979. Arquitectura precerámica en la sierra Norte. *Espacio* (Lima), No. 5.

BURGER, R.; SALAZAR, L. 1985. The Early Ceremonial Center of Huaricoto. *Early Ceremonial Architecture in the Andes*. Washington, D.C.

DAMP, J. 1979. Better Homes and Gardens: The Life and Death of the Early Valdivia Community. Calgary. (PhD thesis.)

—— 1985.

ENGEL, F. 1957. Sites et établissements sans céramique de la côte peruvienne. *J. Soc. Am.* (Paris), N.S., Vol. 46, pp. 67–155.

—— 1958. *Algunos datos con referencia a los sitios precerámicos de la costa peruana.* Lima, (Arqueol., 3.)

—— 1963. A Preceramic Settlement on the Central Coast of Peru: Asia, Unit 1. *Trans. am. philos. Soc.* (Philadelphia, Pa.), N.S., Vol. 53, pt 3.

—— 1966. Le complexe précéramique d'El Paraiso (Perou). *J. Soc. Am.* (Paris), N.S., Vol. 55–1, pp. 43–95.

FELDMAN, R. A. 1980. Aspero, Peru: Architecture, Subsistence Economy and Other Artifacts of a Preceramic Maritime Chiefdom. Cambridge, Mass. (PhD thesis.)

FUNG PINEDA, R. 1969. Las Aldas: su ubicación dentro del proceso histórico del Perú antiguo. *Dédalo, Rev. Arte Arqueol.* (São Paulo), Vol. 5, No. 9–10, pp. 5–208.

—— 1972. El temprano surgimiento en el Perú de los sitemas socio-políticos complejos: Planteamiento de una hipótesis de desarrollo original. *Apunt. Arqueol.* (Lima), Vol. 2, pp. 10–32.

GROSSMAN, J. 1972. An Ancient Gold Worker's Tool Kit. The Earliest Metal Technology in Peru. *Archaeol.* (New York), Vol. 25, No. 4, pp. 270–5.

—— 1983. Demographic Change and Economic Transformation in the South-Central Highlands of Pre-Huari, Peru. *Nawpa Pacha* (Berkeley, Calif.), Vol. 21, pp. 45–126.

IZUMI, S.; SONO, T. 1963. *Excavations at Kotosh, Peru. Andes 2.* Tokyo.

IZUMI, S.; TERADA, K. 1972. *Excavations at Kotosh, Peru, 1963 and 1966. Andes 4.* Tokyo.

LANNING, E. P. 1960. Chronological and Cultural Relationships of Early Pottery Styles in Ancient Peru. Berkeley, Calif. (PhD thesis.)

—— 1967. *Peru Before the Incas.* Newark, N.J.

LATHRAP, D. W. 1974. The Moist Tropics, the Arid Lands, and the Appearance of Great Art Styles in the New World. In: KING, M.; TRAYLER, J. (eds), *Art and Environment in Native America.* Austin, Tex. pp. 115–58.

LATHRAP, D. W.; COLLIER, D. 1976. *Ancient Ecuador, Culture, Clay and Creativity, 3000–300 B.C.* Chicago.

LUMBRERAS, L. G. 1971. Towards a Revaluation of Chavín. In: CONFERENCE ON CHAVÍN, Washington, D.C. *Acts.* Washington, D.C. pp. 1–28.

—— 1974. *The Peoples and Cultures of Ancient Peru.* Washington, D.C.

LUMBRERAS, L. G.; GONZALEZ, C; LIETAER, B. 1976. *Acerca de la función del sistema hidráulico de Chavín.* Lima.

MACNEISH, R.; NELKEN-TERNER, A.; GARCIA COOK, A. 1970. *Second Annual Report of the Ayacucho Archaeological-Botanical Project.* Andover, Mass.

MACNEISH, R. S. et al. 1981. *Prehistory of the Ayacucho Basin, Peru.* Vol. II: *Excavation and Chronology.* Ann Arbor, Mich.

MACNEISH, R. S.; PATTERSON, T. C.; BROWMAN, D. L. 1975. *The Central Peruvian Prehistoric Interaction Sphere.* Andover, Mass. (Pap. Peabody Fond. Archaeol., 7.)

MARCOS, J. 1973. Tejidos hechos en telar en un contexto Valdivia Tardío. *Cuad. Hist. Arqueol.* (Guayaquil), Vol. 40, pp. 163–76.

MEGGERS, B. J.; EVANS, C.; ESTRADA, E. 1965. *Early Formative Periods of Coastal Ecuador: The Valdivia and Machalilla Phases.* Washington, D.C. (Smithsonian Contrib. Anthropol., 1.)

MENZEL, D.; ROWE, J. H.; DAWSON, L. 1964. *The Paracas Pottery of Ica: A Study in Style and Time.* Berkeley/Los Angeles.

MOSELEY, M. E. 1975. *The Maritime Foundations of Andean Civilization.* Menlo Park, Calif.

MOSELEY, M. E.; BARRET, L. K. 1969. Change in Preceramic Twined from the Central Peruvian Coast. *Am. Antiq.* (Washington, D.C.), Vol. 34, No. 2, pp. 162–5.

PATTERSON, T. 1971. The Emergence of Food Production in Central Peru. In: STUEVER, S. (ed.), *Prehistoric Agriculture.* New York. pp. 181–207.

PATTERSON, T.; MOSELEY, M. E. 1978. Phytolith Analysis of Archeological Soils: Evidence for Maize Cultivation in Formative Ecuador. *Science* (Washington, D.C.), Vol. 199, No. 4325, pp. 177–8.

PONCE SANGINÉS, C. 1970. *Las culturas Wankarani y Chiripa y su relación con Tiwanaku.* La Paz. (Publ., 25.)

POZORSKI, S.; POZORSKI, T. 1979. Alto Salaverry: A Peruvian Coastal Preceramic Site. *Ann. Carnegie Mus.* (Pittsburgh, Pa.), Vol. 48, Art. 19, pp. 337–75.

RAVINES, R.; ISBELL, W. H. 1976. Garagay: sitio temprano en el valle de Lima. *Rev. Mus. nac.* (Lima), Vol. 41, pp. 253–72.

ROSAS LANOIRE, H. 1970. La secuencia cultural del período formativo de Ancón. Lima. (BA thesis.)

ROSAS LANOIRE, H.; SHADY, R. 1970. Pacopampa, un centro formativo en la sierra nor-peruana. *Seminario de Historia Rural Andina, Lima. Actas.* Lima.

ROWE, J. H. 1967. Form and Meaning in Chavín Art. In: HOWE, J. H.; MENZEL, D. (eds), *Peruvian Archaeology: Early Selected Readings.* Los Angeles. pp. 72–103.

SMITH, E. 1980. Vegetation and Land Use Near Guitarrero Cave. In: LYNCH, T. (ed.), *Guitarrero Cave, Early Man in the Andes.* New York. pp. 65–83

STOTHERT, K. 1976. The Early Prehistory of the Santa Elena Peninsula, Ecuador. In: CONGRESO INTERNACIONAL DE AMERICANISTAS, 41., MÉXICO, 1974. *Actas.* Mexico, D.F. Vol. 2, pp. 88–98.

STRONG, W. D.; EVANS, C. 1952. *Cultural Stratigraphy in the Virú Valley, Northern Peru.* New York. (Stud. Archeol. Ethnol., 4.)

TELLO, J. C. 1942. Origen y desarrollo de las civilizaciones prehistóricas andinas. In: CONGRESO INTERNACIONAL DE AMERICANISTAS, 27, LIMA, 1939. *Actas.* Lima.

—— 1956. *Arqueología del valle de Casma.* Lima.

—— 1960. *Chavín: Cultura matriz de la civilización andina.* Lima.

TERADA, K.; ONUKI, Y. 1982. *Excavations at Huacaloma in the Cajamarca Valley, Peru, 1979.* Tokyo.

—— 1985. *The Formative Period in the Cajamarca Basin, Peru: Excavations at Huacaloma and Layzon, 1982.* Tokyo.

VASQUEZ DE ESPINOZA, A. 1948 (1629). *Compendio y descripción de las Indias Occidentales.* Washington, D.C.

WENDT, W. E. 1964. Die präkeramische siedlung am Rio Seco, Peru. *Baessler Arch.* (Berlin). Vol. 9, No. 36, pp. 225–75.

WILLIAMS, C. 1980. Arquitectura y Urbanismo en el Antiguo Perú. In: *Historia del Perú.* Lima. Vol. 8, pp. 367–585.

WING, E. 1977. Animal domestication in the Andes. In: REED, C. (ed.), *Origins of Agriculture.* The Hague/Paris. pp. 837–59.

ZEIDLER, J. A. 1984. Social Space in Valdivia Society: Community Patterning and Domestic Structure at Real Alto, 3000–2000 B.C. Urbana, Ill. (PhD thesis.)

17.5.4

THE SOUTH-WEST REGION

Lautaro Núñez

The vast Andean region can be divided roughly into four: central southern, southern (western valleys sub-area), extreme south, and the Patagonia archipelago. They correspond to southern Peru, Bolivia, north-western Argentina and Chile. From the desert to the sub-Antarctic steppe, a wide variety of resources were to be found throughout the Andean and Pacific areas, and these gave rise to singular cultural processes.

The hunting and gathering society in the central-south highlands adopted the twofold activity of llama-breeding and highland agriculture. Semi-tropical agriculture predominated in the valleys running eastwards and westwards down from the summits, while fishing and specialized gathering were the typical activities of the Pacific area.

The repercussions of these advances in civilization extended towards the southern area and in part towards the extreme south, where hunting and specialized gathering survived, owing to the abundance of wild plants and animals. This transitional activity was quite different further south in the Patagonia archipelago region, where scarcity of plant resources and abundance of herbivores made hunting the dominant activity right up to historical times, along with greater reliance on coastal resources.

The Neolithic revolution had a greater impact in the arid and semi-arid habitats of the north, where the Andean slopes were used for grazing, while valleys and oases lent themselves to the earliest known horticulture and agriculture, and resulted in the emergence of new, more sedentary, ways of life. Nevertheless, the resources of the Pacific, both in the deltas and the interfluvial areas, encouraged semi-sedentary occupations, which in turn led to population growth, with the establishment of a distinct complementary movement of goods, resources and people along the contours of the coast, the Andes and the tropical forest zones.

Although Neolithic changes predominated in the central-southern and southern areas, there were veritable 'ethnic islands' of hunting-gathering-fishing communities that survived the process and stayed put in pockets where there was a high concentration of wild resources, such as in the Pacific delta areas, the Andean lakes, the archipelagos and the Patagonian pampa. As a result, there was no need in these areas to farm for food, and dense populations exposed to extremes of climate were able to survive quite adequately, cut off from Andean civilization. Nevertheless, a number of these 'contemporaneous primitive peoples' and their ancestors (Uros, Changos, Pehuenches, Fueguinos and Onas) developed highly complex ideological and technological values, separately from the advances made in herding and agriculture (Map 29).

LATE HUNTING AND GATHERING COMMUNITIES AND FOOD PRODUCTION (THIRD TO FIRST MILLENNIUM BC) (FIG. 98)

During this period the Pacific coast was populated by semi-sedentary settlements grouped together at the mouths of rivers and, to a lesser extent, along the interfluvial shores, with the bulk of the population occupying the coast of the Patagonia archipelago region. A few well-organized and stable settlements, with circular dwellings and cemented stone walls, were scattered between Taltal and the mouth of the Loa (site Huelén 42), while others with flimsy huts (simple dwellings supported on posts) were found along a large expanse of the shore next to compact kitchen middens (Fig. 99).

The coastal resources were more reliable because of the variety of choice in the event of a food crisis, so that mobility on the shore was on a fairly small scale compared to the greater amount of energy expended by the hunters of the interior. This tendency towards the stability of coastal occupations was found throughout the territory. In fact, the Pacific encouraged fairly permanent residential activities, but this semi-sedentary life is characteristic of communities prior to the first millennium BC.

During this period there was a system of base or primary and secondary settlements, varying in their degree of stability and the distances between them, which oscillated between a spasmodic and mobile-type subsistence and a more local or fixed subsistence, in relation to each habitat's capacity for self-reliance. A particular sector would become impoverished or rich as a result of various natural causes which had nothing to do with human intervention: effects of the El Niño current, red tides, rise in the level of the beaches' sandbanks, an abundance of fish shoals, concentration of bird life, spawning phases, mammal reproduction and so forth.

In normal conditions, the shoreline bordering the base camps provided the community with a wide variety of foodstuffs, ensuring self-reliance for those groups which, because of their age and sex, carried out local tasks. Since the communities were dense and semi-sedentary, other groups of adults specialized in tapping the potential of those places where large reserves of resources were temporarily to be found.

The fact that certain groups moved about made it possible for foods acquired far away to be brought back to the base camps. With regard to labour-intensive activities, it must be remembered that there are only two seasons in the coastal area: summer (October to March) and winter (April to September). Summer is the period of greatest activity,

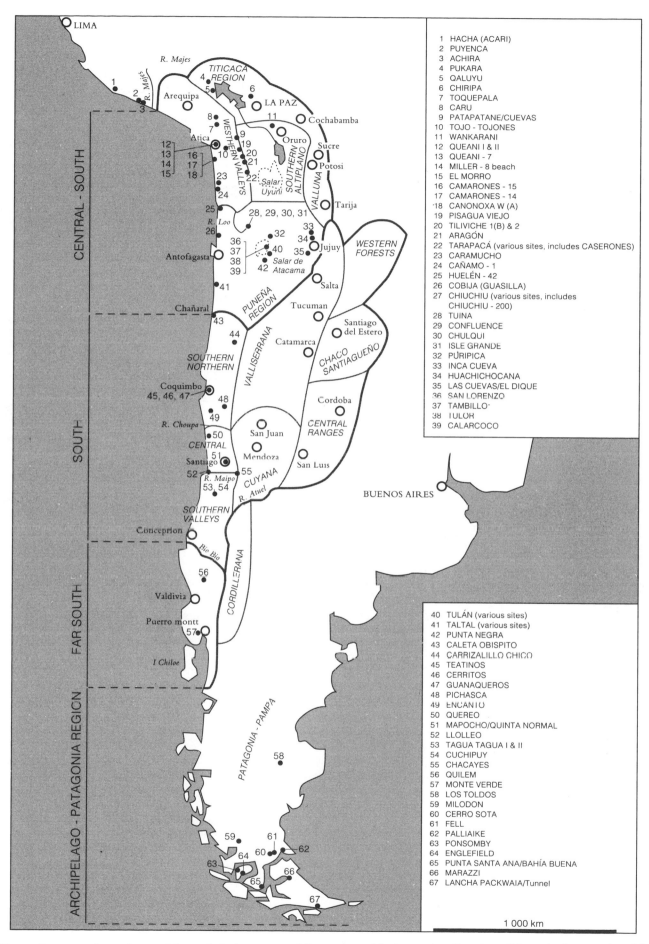

LIMA

R. Majes

TITICACA REGION

R. Majes

Arequipa

LA PAZ

Cochabamba

Atica

Oruro

Sucre

Potosi

Salar Uyuni

Tarija

R. Loo

Jujuy

WESTERN VALLEYS

SOUTHERN ALTIPLANO

VALLUNA

WESTERN FORESTS

Antofagasta

Salar de Atacama

Salta

PUNEÑA REGION

Chañaral

Tucuman

VALLISERRANA

Catamarca

Santiago del Estero

CHACO SANTIAGUEÑO

SOUTHERN NORTHERN

Coquimbo

45, 46, 47

R. Choupa

Cordoba

CENTRAL RANGES

San Juan

CENTRAL

Santiago

Mendoza

San Luis

R. Maipo

CUYANA

R. Atuel

BUENOS AIRES

SOUTHERN VALLEYS

Conception

Bío Bío

CORDILLERANA

Valdivia

Puerro montt

I Chiloe

PATAGONIA - PAMPA

CENTRAL - SOUTH

SOUTH

FAR SOUTH

ARCHIPELAGO - PATAGONIA REGION

1 HACHA (ACARI)
2 PUYENCA
3 ACHIRA
4 PUKARA
5 QALUYU
6 CHIRIPA
7 TOQUEPALA
8 CARU
9 PATAPATANE/CUEVAS
10 TOJO - TOJONES
11 WANKARANI
12 QUEANI I & II
13 QUEANI - 7
14 MILLER - 8 beach
15 EL MORRO
16 CAMARONES - 15
17 CAMARONES - 14
18 CANONOXA W (A)
19 PISAGUA VIEJO
20 TILIVICHE 1(B) & 2
21 ARAGÓN
22 TARAPACÁ (various sites, includes CASERONES)
23 CARAMUCHO
24 CAÑAMO - 1
25 HUELÉN - 42
26 COBIJA (GUASILLA)
27 CHIUCHIU (various sites, includes CHIUCHIU - 200)
28 TUINA
29 CONFLUENCE
30 CHULQUI
31 ISLE GRANDE
32 PÚRIPICA
33 INCA CUEVA
34 HUACHICHOCANA
35 LAS CUEVAS/EL DIQUE
36 SAN LORENZO
37 TAMBILLO
38 TULOR
39 CALARCOCO

40 TULÁN (various sites)
41 TALTAL (various sites)
42 PUNTA NEGRA
43 CALETA OBISPITO
44 CARRIZALILLO CHICO
45 TEATINOS
46 CERRITOS
47 GUANAQUEROS
48 PICHASCA
49 ENCANTO
50 QUERERO
51 MAPOCHO/QUINTA NORMAL
52 LLOLLEO
53 TAGUA TAGUA I & II
54 CUCHIPUY
55 CHACAYES
56 QUILEM
57 MONTE VERDE
58 LOS TOLDOS
59 MILODON
60 CERRO SOTA
61 FELL
62 PALLIAIKE
63 PONSOMBY
64 ENGLEFIELD
65 PUNTA SANTA ANA/BAHÍA BUENA
66 MARAZZI
67 LANCHA PACKWAIA/Tunnel

1 000 km

Map 29 Centre-south, southern and far south Andean areas and Patagonian archipelago region. Location of the main sites mentioned in text.

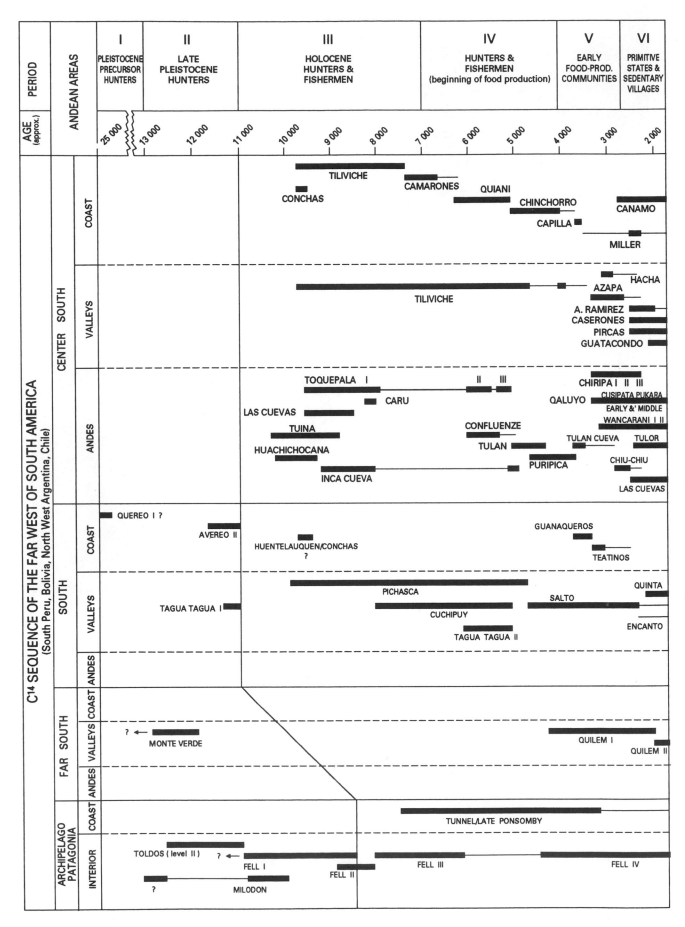

Figure 98 Chronological table with radiocarbon datings from the westernmost parts of South America (southern Peru, Bolivia, north-western Argentina and Chile).

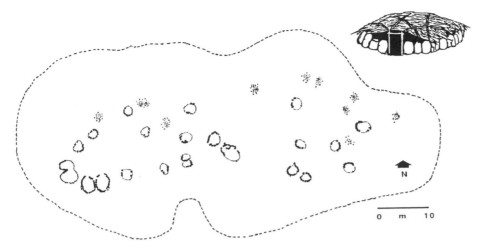

Figure 99 Semi-sedentary encampment of hollowed-out circular dwellings with cemented stone walls. Fishing-gathering communities at the mouth of the River Loa; third to second millennium BC. Shows model reconstruction of a dwelling (Huelén-42, Chile; Núñez et al., 1974).

whereas resources are in shorter supply in winter. In accordance with the seasonal use of resources, the base camps were more active in summer, employing less complex appropriation technologies and leading more semi-sedentary lives. Conversely, the secondary or remote camps became active in the winter season, the emphasis being on mobility, effort and the use of more complex technologies (such as the use of fishing lines and hooks). The inhabitants also hunted an alternative range of species such as birds that never migrated from the coast. These movements occurred throughout the year but were more or less intensive according to the season. Itineraries were both horizontal along the coast and vertical in search of subsistence goods and raw materials in the interior. This activity resulted in self-sufficiency in one of the most fertile coastal regions in the world, so that much less biological damage was caused on the coast by fishers and hunters who lived there than by the exploitation of resources practised by the hunters of the interior (Allison, 1985).

During this period the transhumant hunters and gatherers stationed further in from the coast intensively exploited Andean camelids and increased their gathering activities in the valleys and oases. In the southern Peruvian mountains occupation of territory continued in Toquepala during the third millennium BC, with movements of transhumance between the sierra and the coast (Ravines, 1972). At that time, as can be seen at the San Nicolas site on the Peruvian south coast, the mountain hunters moved there, bringing with them obsidian tools from the highland mines.

Further south, hunters and gatherers from Tiliviche, Aragón, Conanoxa and Tarapacá stepped up their activities, alternating between the coast and the oases of the interior. Others, mountain dwellers, occupied the outskirts of the Atacameña puna on the eastern slope near Jujuy. Here, the descendants of the Huachichocana hunters and others that were more advanced, such as the people from Inca Cueva, took shelter in caves at the beginning of the second millennium BC (Aguerre et al., 1975). These groups show a high degree of cultural complexity, hunting a larger number of species and focusing on gathering and cultivation. They moved through circuits of seasonal migration that brought them into contact with subtropical eastern territories (attested by the presence of macaw feathers). It has even been suggested that they reached the Pacific coast, since their treatment of fibres and textiles is very similar to that of the Chinchorro fisherpeople.

Early in the second millennium BC many enclaves of hunters and gatherers on the western slope of the Atacama puna developed a high degree of specialization in the hunting of camelids and rodents (for instance, at Tulan-52). They had a flourishing and diversified lithic industry, grinding implements and camps clustered together with circular stone enclosures. From here they exploited all the resources between the puna and the Atacama basin (Fig. 100).

One of these communities, established on the Puripica River, managed to broaden its food base by the domestication of camelids during the third and second millennia BC. It is associated with a few hunting tools, grinding implements (mortars with a conical cavity) and microliths with triangular sections, also characteristic of the ChiuChiu hunters and domesticators who settled on the Loa Medio River, and who are contemporaneous (Druss, 1977). These phenomena of renewal combined hunting, gathering and llama domestication during the closing years of this period, when they came into contact with more complex ceramic-making groups.

On the coast of the central-southern Andean area the development of Chinchorro communities succeeded in establishing more stable settlements at the mouths of rivers up to the second millennium BC. The hunters and gatherers of the interior made contact with them, as is substantiated by the presence of vicuña and of quinoa, a typical Andean cereal.

There were movements towards the coast of the southern area via the Cáñamo, Abtao and Taltal camps between the third and second millennia BC. The use of large thin bifacial stone blades and, later, shell hooks suggests coastal migrations at this time towards the semi-arid Chilean coast.

Subsequently, other coastal camps such as Arica (Queani-7 and Camarones-15), dated at 1660 and 1160 BC respectively, show that despite a continuity in tradition, radical changes were now beginning to take place: gourd cultivation, poker-work, domestic camelids, baby-slings, turbans, individual tombs, forest seeds and feathers of forest birds, tropical manioc and so on. In other words, groups arrived from the part of the Altiplano adjoining the east and transformed the local life-style. The significant and persistent practice of artificial human mummification engaged in by the Chinchorros ceased to appear as a dominant funerary rite.

In the valleys and foothills of the southern Andean region, the hunters and gatherers of Pichasca, Morrillos, Atuel and

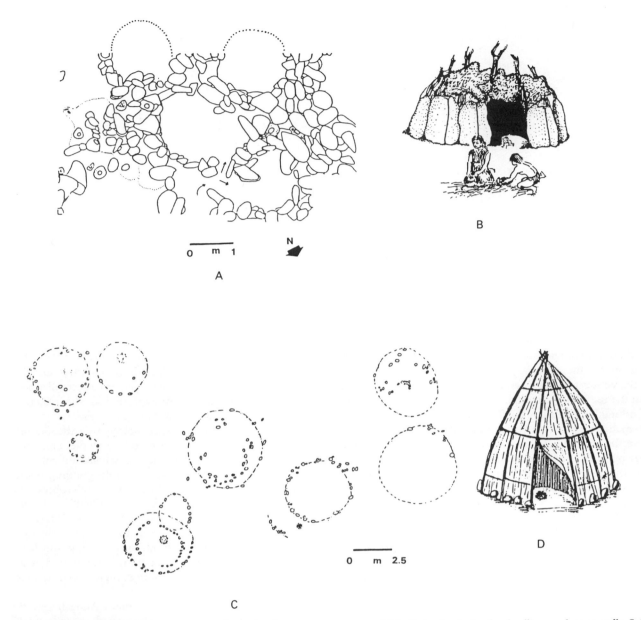

Figure 100 Sequence of settlements: a, part of a semi-sedentary encampment with hollowed-out circular dwellings and stone walls. Sub-Andean hunters and gathers of the third millennium BC (Tulan-52, Chile; Núñez, 1983); b, model reconstruction of a Tulan dwelling; c, embryonic village composed of circular dwellings with pillars and central hearths, and with evidence of early pottery. Fishing-farming communities of the River San José de Arica, second to first millennium BC (Acha-2, Chile; Muñoz, 1982); d, model reconstruction of an Acha dwelling (Muñoz, 1982).

thereabouts exploited camelids and perhaps even domesticated them. Moreover, they were already acquainted with certain crops which they carried with them on their seasonal migrations, although they had seasonal encampments on the Andean tablelands. Fishing communities from the Guanaqueros and Teatinos stages at this time maintained highly populated semi-sedentary settlements which were located alongside the adjacent valleys in which beans (*Phaseolus vulgaris*) were cultivated and probably incorporated into the coastal diet.

Although current evidence to this effect is not yet very plentiful, it is possible to claim that during this period llama domestication expanded, to judge from finds at Puripica, Huachichocana and Inca Cueva in the region around the puna, and that a distinctive proto-pastoral society without ceramics spread throughout the highlands of the central-southern area, reaching its apogee in the second millennium BC (see Volume I). However, there is evidence of other

domestication and food production activities in the coastal part of the central-southern area. Consumption of rodents such as the guinea-pig (*Cavia* sp.) increased between the fifth and second millennia BC in the Tiliviche oasis. The flesh of these mammals is extremely rich in proteins, only slightly less so than llama flesh; they can be kept in captivity in small pens or batteries for human consumption; indeed, they were bred more intensively for this purpose in later periods (Hesse, 1982; Núñez et al., 1986).

A similar development occurred in the upper valleys, where these animals also appear in pre-ceramic contexts close to the Loa Medio River, when the ChiuChiu hunters bred llamas and guinea-pigs. As a rule, they were reared by communities of hunters and domesticators from the fifth to second millennia BC and greatly increased in numbers when the farming and herding communities expanded between the second millennium BC and the beginning of our era, becoming a diet staple from the Altiplano to the coast throughout the Andes. This doubtless made a considerable contribution to the production of alternative forms of meat in such places as the lowlands and mid-level areas where mammals were scarce and even camelids did not abound.

The hunters and gatherers of the Tiliviche Valley, close to the Pacific, cultivated small plots of maize (*Zea mays*), as did the inhabitants of the central Andes (Fig. 101). These appear in Guitarreros, Ayacucho and the Peruvian coast of Huarmey between the fifth and second millennia BC, always in pre-ceramic contexts (Lynch, 1973; McNeish et al., 1975; Grobman et al., 1977).

Further south, in the puna region, the hunters that inhabited one of the caves of Huachichocana, near Jujuy in Argentina, apparently cultivated maize between the eighth and sixth millennia BC (Fernández Distel, 1974), although the great antiquity of this practice has not yet been corroborated. Be that as it may, there is no doubt that horticultural practices existed among hunters and gatherers prior to the third and second millennia BC in the densely populated Andean regions, as well as in areas further south.

The association of guinea-pigs with maize in Tiliviche, in a predominantly hunting and gathering environment, confirms that these activities of domestication and the relocation of crops from higher areas boosted the importance of oases close to the Pacific. This occurred through the migratory flow between the highlands and the coast, as evidenced by the presence of vicuñas in Camarones and obsidian in Tiliviche. Such movements were compatible with the establishment of base camps grouped together in coastal centres with more stable resources.

In this way, a more permanent life-style gradually developed, both on the coast and in the oases, as can be seen from settlements with concentrated dwelling areas, the use of posts supporting roofs, kitchen middens, lithic workshops and burials. These activities tended to be specialized and associated with more reliable resources and more robust health. However, demographic imbalances did occur, as shown by the high infant-mortality rate, evidence of which may be found in a burial of this era (Tiliviche), so that there were reasons for speeding up food production.

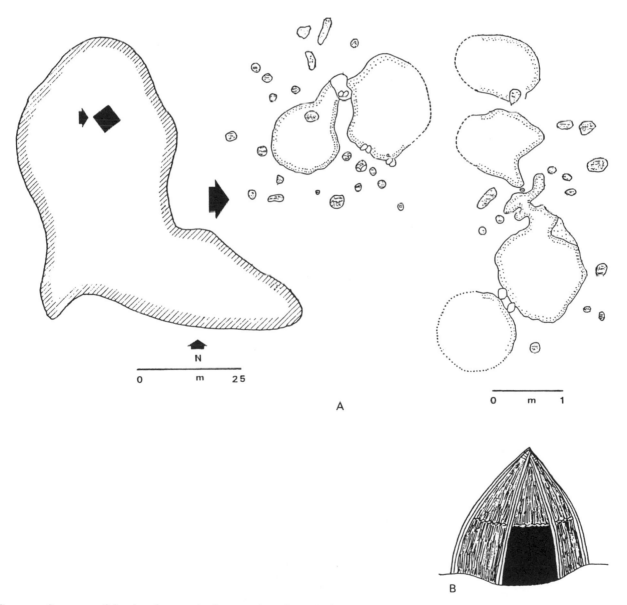

N

0   m   25

A

0   m   1

B

Figure 101 Sequence of dated settlements in the central-southern Andean region: a, semi-sedentary encampment and stone workshop with hollowed-out circular dwellings and pillars. Hunting-gathering communities engaged in maize (*Zea mays*) and guinea-pig (*Cavia* sp.) breeding, between the eighth and third millennium BC (Tiliviche (B), Chile; Núñez, 1983); b, model reconstruction of a Tiliviche dwelling.

The need to cope with a series of critical food situations stimulated extensive diversification of subsistence activities: hunting, fishing and gathering, as well as cultivation and animal husbandry. Thus, between the fifth and second millennia BC the horticultural advances and the initial breeding of guinea-pigs speak for themselves and were stepping-stones to new and better levels of life expectancy in the lowlands. In fact, maize crops show that subsistence activities were graded according to the selection and use of non-coastal products that compensated for carbohydrate deficiency, in parallel with an increase in animal protein in the diet.

It has been suggested that the eastern slopes of the Altiplano and north-eastern Argentina contained concentrations of ancestral wild plants which were successfully cultivated and transferred to hollows where they were more productive (Núñez, 1974). It has also been suggested that the Altiplano guinea-pig was bred in captivity at an early date (Lumbreras, 1981). What is certain, however, is that these transhumant hunters practised horticulture in an ancient cultural context featuring leaf-shaped projectile points, plant-fibre baskets, thick gouges, hooks, mats made from bulrushes and pestles and mortars for grinding, during the fifth to second millennia BC (Núñez, 1986).

Other fishing communities established in Arica, Camarones and at the mouth of the Loa apparently cultivated maize in the adjacent areas or brought it from the valleys in the interior, but this has not yet been reliably recorded (Bird, 1943; Schiappacasse and Niemeyer, 1984; Zlatar, 1983). Nevertheless, in the Terapacá Valley near Tiliviche, hunters and gatherers settled in smaller open-air encampments where they also exploited guanacos, mesquite forests and the roots and fibres of aquatic plants, together with fish and shellfish which they brought back from the coast. It has been discovered that they cultivated maize and quinoa (*Chenopodium quinua*) during the fourth and third millennia BC, within the context of their strongly predominant range of gathering activities. They used the edible fibres and roots of the cat's-tail (*Typha angustifolia*) and ate the pods and crushed seeds of the mesquite (*Prosopis juliflora*), which they ground to the consistency of flour. To a lesser extent, they ate amaranth, a widely used Andean cereal with an even higher protein and fat content than maize, and virtually identical in calorie and carbohydrate content. Maize and quinoa continued to appear in the soil in Tarapacá until the arrival of new, totally sedentary population groups from the middle of the first millennium BC, through the agrarian settlements of Caserones and Pircas, where these crops are also found.

Maize was subsequently grown by farmers from the Azapa Valley (Arica) from 1350 BC onwards, and there is evidence of changes in the type of food waste in the coastal desert of Cáñamo around 850 BC. It is conceivable that both maize and quinoa from the Initial and Formative periods, associated in this instance with pottery, were derived from the old horticultural experiments conducted within the hunting and gathering traditions of the central-southern Andean area.

There is evidence of experimental cultivation in both Tiliviche and Tarapacá in the context of intensive gathering and milling activities in carob and cat's-tail patches. As occurred in the territories further south, grinding tools eventually became characteristic of these communities. From the coast and sierra of the central Andes to central Chile, seeds, pods, bones, dried meat, fish and so on were crushed in stone and wooden mortars with deep conical hollows, or grains were ground in shallower mortars to obtain carob, maize and quinoa flour. These foods were dispersed throughout the western valleys and those adjacent to the puna during the first millennium BC.

Maize spread from Canada right down to Chile, thus becoming the world's third most important crop. Although it contains less protein and fat than wheat, it is richer in calories and carbohydrates, and is therefore an extremely nutritious high-yield food that can be adapted to different environments. While it may be cultivated at an altitude of around 4,000 m, it is not a typical Altiplano product but more characteristic of the mesothermal valleys to the east and west of the Andean range. The abundance of varieties to be found in the valleys of eastern Bolivia suggests that it came from across the Andes and even from north-eastern Argentina.

Another cereal, quinoa, is typical of the Peru/Bolivia highlands. It has been adapted to grow in lower mesothermal valleys where it is associated with maize cultivation, but it was grown at even lower altitudes of approximately 1,200 m on the western slopes. Here it also co-existed with maize plantations, at least from evidence found in Tarapacá, and it spread to lower altitudes and latitudes, as occurred in central Argentina and central-southern Chile (Núñez, 1974).

Both guinea-pig breeding and maize and quinoa cultivation tended to impose a somewhat sedentary way of life in the oases further inland. Although neither of these activities altered the dominant hunting and gathering structure, they led the way to the gradual development of farming in the oases, starting with typically coastal foods. The abundance of circular settlements of tents or huts built on posts and kitchen middens, as well as other sequentially arranged encampments nearby, suggests high levels of semi-sedentary organization among the groups that settled in Tiliviche.

If the establishment of a rather crowded burial dated 1880 BC is anything to go by, some groups lived more permanently in this oasis at the end of the period. Since these groups came to the oasis from the coast, we may assume that they gradually perfected a pattern of dual residence in which both the shore and the valleys of the interior formed part of a continuum of complementary natural and dietary resources.

The fact that on the Arica coast, likewise groups of fisher people travelled up to the Acha pampa, along the San José River, proves that access to the oases was common in the central-southern area. In this instance, they established a temporary camp of flimsy circular dwellings and concentrated on gathering wild cereals and hunting smaller animals. They also introduced certain village practices geared to gourd and squash cultivation, alongside craftwork involving rustic ceramics and the use of seafood detritus between the second and first millennia BC (Muñoz, 1982).

It is almost certain that at the end of the ancient hunting period between the fourth and second millennia BC a variety of domestic crops farmed on the Amazonian slope of the Andes became rife throughout the valleys and shores of the Andes: achira (*Canna edulis*), peanuts (*Arachis hypogaea*), cassava (*Manihot seculenta*), sweet potato (*Ipomoea batata*), gourds (*Cucurbita ficifolia*) and squash (*Cucurbita moschata* and *maxima*), all of which grew together along the valleys on the Pacific side. It is unclear whether maize and beans were domesticated or readapted to the upper valleys, but both *Phaseolus lunatus* and *Phaseolus vulgaris* were grown domestically in hunting contexts in the valleys of the central, central-southern and southern Andes before the fourth millennium BC.

At the same time, potatoes (*Solanum* sp.) and quinoa (*Chenopodium quinua*) originating in the Altiplano were first introduced into valleys such as the Ayacucho basin during the third millennium BC, whereas the amaranth was cultivated there between the fifth and fourth millennia BC and gradually spread to the south of the Altiplano heartland and on to southern Chile. This movement of llamas, potatoes and quinoa away from the upper Andean nucleus down to the southern and even coastal regions was due to the fact that the new herding pattern was very quick to expand. This involved a high degree of mobility between areas, which transferred early farming and livestock-rearing advances to regions as remote as central-southern Chile.

In the southern Andes, in the semi-arid valleys of Chile, the Pichasca hunters occupied a tributary of the Hurtado River during the eighth millennium BC in an environment suited to intensive hunting and plant-gathering, as shown by triangular, narrow, leaf-shaped points found in conjunction with grinding implements (Ampuero and Hidalgo, 1975). A few cultural techniques such as basketry, twined textiles and fire-lighting sticks, suggest a mature occupational development which even had contacts with regions as remote as the coast 80 km away.

The floor of this vast cavern is located at an intermediate level dating from the fifth millennium BC, and it was there that the first harvested beans (*Phaseolus vulgaris*) were deposited through horticultural activities that supplemented local hunting and gathering. Some time later, during the third millennium BC, experimental cultivation increased with the arrival of gourds and maize. The latter was domestically grown, possibly transported from the slopes of eastern Argentina during the seasonal migration circuits. There is evidence that in these semi-arid valleys the hunters also lived on leguminous plants well suited to that environment, such as the beans found in great quantities in the El Salto cave.

It is not known whether these crops eventually disrupted the pattern of life in natural shelters by encouraging settlement in encampments with a more semi-sedentary life-style. It is assumed that these early specialized farmers and gatherers worked in groups of regular density. However, their successors in the second and first millennia BC probably established more stable settlements in valleys suited to the trend towards agriculture, well before the civilizing expansion of the Molle peoples who reoccupied the Pichasca cave in approximately 475 BC.

Fishing communities identified as Huentelauquén lived on the coast from perhaps as early as the eighth millennium BC and relied heavily on marine resources, for which they established large semi-sedentary encampments. It has not been determined whether they spread across the adjacent valleys in search of supplementary resources when the sea became rough, especially in winter.

These developments are followed by a gap in the available information until a later period called the Guanaqueros. Here, semi-sedentary coastal communities, largely dependent on the sea, continued to exist from the second millennium BC, but we may assume that the adjacent valleys played some role in furnishing dietery supplements. This, at any rate, occurred in the next period – the Teatinos – around the beginning of the first millennium BC, since there is evidence that the sea did not supply all the proteins required. This led to greater exploitation of the plant resources in the valleys, through specialized gathering and greater use of grinding implements. Since the Pichasca hunters and gatherers travelled as far as the coast, it is probable that communities like the Teatinos assimilated in the lower valleys more than a few of the crops such as those which had existed for so long inland.

Nevertheless, where the shore adjoined farming valleys and grazing lands the civilizing changes were more significant, since the continental hunters and gatherers who lived there before the first millennium BC had succeeded in domesticating and/or adapting wild animals and plants, preparing the ground for society's transition to the Neolithic, the repercussions of which transcended territorial borders.

EMERGENCE OF AGRICULTURAL AND LIVESTOCK-REARING SEDENTARY VILLAGES (FIRST MILLENNIUM BC) (FIG. 102)

Evidence from the central-southern Andean area

This analysis will cover the area stretching from the highlands to the coastal valleys, and will end with the towering peaks located around Lake Titicaca.

In ancient times, shepherds occupied the Tulan gorge on the Chilean slope of the puna region from the second to the first millennia BC, near San Pedro de Atacama. They also harvested and collected wild plants and fruit. The presence of llama, rough pottery, maize and quinoa suggest that flocks and small-scale farmers migrated in the direction of this stream.

Nevertheless, from the first millennium BC, pastoral and agricultural life began to be concentrated in small villages linked with the presence of vegas (fertile valleys) or permanent grazing land irrigated by underground water sources. A herding community built a very simple village for temporary use. It has a great many semicircular areas with excavated floors, dating from the beginning of the first millennium BC (Benavente, 1981). In ChiuChiu-200 the predominant activity was llama-breeding in the vegas of the Loa, associated with quite sophisticated craftwork: woven textiles, knotted fabrics, woven mats, looms, corrugated, modelled, incised or burnished ceramics and so on. Here there was greater meat production within a rather large scale pastoral pattern with long-distance contacts, as evidenced by tropical bird feathers and shells from the Pacific. The settlers travelled in caravans, using llamas as beasts of burden, in search of more suitable places for breeding and cultivation.

The channels of communication between the ChiuChiu-200 shepherds and the western mountains and valleys of Argentina passed through the Atacama oases, so that very early on a network of ancient agricultural-pastoral villages was established and initiated the regular use of fodder above 2,000 m, alongside more highly developed pottery. The inhabitants maintained settlements in the low-lying vegas of the Loa and in the more fertile upper meadows at Turi in a broad area of occupation, or among the groves of carob, chañares (a tree with an edible fruit) and grasslands of the Poconche and Tchapuchayna oases in San Pedro de Atacama, including the vegas and forests of Calama. Henceforward pastoral movements were concentrated in territories that provided forage and where sedentary and village life was combined with the movement of livestock.

These shepherd-farmers of the first millennium BC had maintained their hunting habits, as they were probably descendants of the hunters and domesticators of the Puripica/ChiuChiu period. The fact that peoples like those of ChiuChiu-200 used hollow-based arrowheads similar to those of the Wankarani shepherds of the Altiplano, together

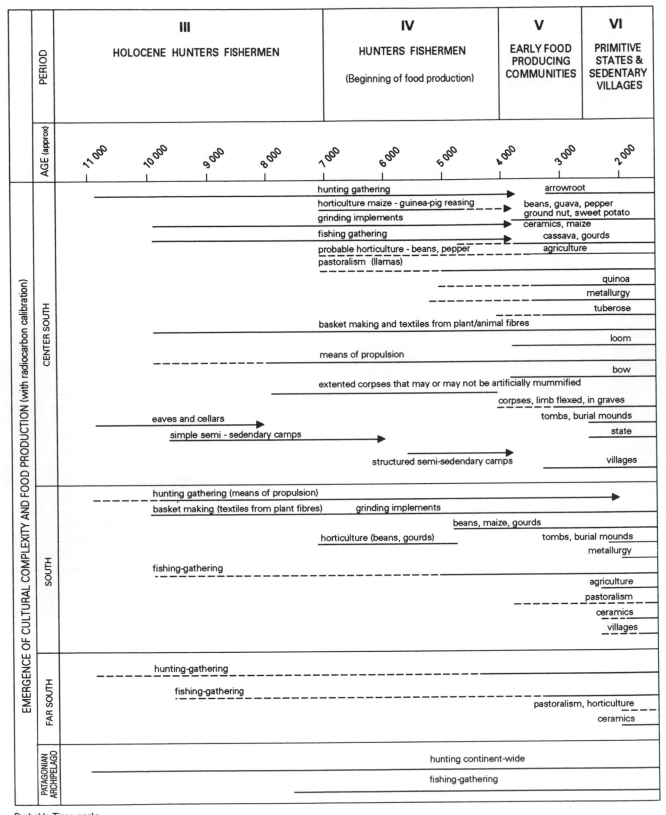

Figure 102 The emergence of cultural complexity and food production in Chile, in the context of the Andean region. Centre-south, south, far south and Patagonian archipelago.

with microliths and borers with triangular sections similar to those used by the domesticators of Puripica, suggest that this population was descended from the area's most ancient inhabitants.

The agricultural and livestock-raising activities that took place during half of the first millennium BC expanded and, in conjunction with further sedentary advantages, succeeded in providing more food for the growing population and resulted in settlements on a larger scale. In the western area around the puna, llama breeding, cultivation of maize and other as yet unidentified crops, alongside fruit gathering from the chañar and carob trees, centred on settlements such as

Tulor (Fig. 103). Here, dug-out circular dwellings were built with adobe walls and conical roofs and were surrounded by a protecting wall. This coincided with the settlement of Caserones in the Tarapaqueño Valley; here they chose to dam the mouth of the San Pedro River and the resulting floods provided alluvium and forests that boosted the first fully sedentary activities (Llagostera et al., MS.; Núñez, 1974).

In the village of Tulor the massive use of burnished grey ceramics and copper metalwork and, in particular, the tendency to build large storehouses backing on to the dwelling areas, point to the existence of substantial surpluses that could be transported over a wide area. Indeed, the presence of shells from the Pacific and some pottery sherds from the Salta region and the western forests of Argentina suggest caravan trade to the lower areas and to enclaves across the Andes. These links were established with the smaller villages bordering the eastern fringe of the puna, such as Potrero Grande and Campo Colorado. A similar pattern occurred in the case of the populations that came from Wankarani in the southern Altiplano.

In other nearby oases such as Toconao-Oriente, some villages had attained a high degree of cultural complexity by 630 BC (Le Paige, 1971), more or less at the same time as the village settlements of San Francisco in the trans-Andean lowlands.

In the specific case of the El Toro gorge, around 650 BC llama breeding was effectively accompanied by pumpkin, quinoa, peanut, bean, maize, achira and potato cultivation. There is no doubt that the renovating changes were well consolidated around llama breeding and agriculture and that the number of villages – some of them extremely elaborate with protecting walls – increased gradually. In conjunction with the use of grazing land, caves were once more occupied on a temporary basis, but as a means towards livestock-raising outside the more sedentary settlements, to which they

Figure 103 South American members of the Camelidae family: a, Guanaco (*Lama guanicoe*), wild species; b, vicuna (*Vicugna vicugna*), wild species; c, llama (*Lama glama*), domestic species; d, alpaca (*Lama pacos*), domestic species (Núñez et al., 1986).

returned every so often. These advances are apparent in the emergence of more complex craftwork, since the use of metal and semi-precious stones suggests the establishment of status symbols that increased family and communal wealth (Raffino, 1977; Tarragó, MS.).

It has been suggested that the villages of the El Toro gorge are characteristic of the uplands of the western foot of the puna. They were the result of mutual influence and contacts with the peoples of the region around Titicaca and connections with the shepherds of the district around Lake Poopo in Bolivia.

From the experiments in domestication of camelids in the western puna, we can conclude that similar episodes occurred in the western Altiplano, thereby giving rise to the early villages of Wankarani. These altiplano groups probably spread through their search for new grazing land and places suitable for agriculture, fanning out through the highlands of the southern altiplano towards the oases and valleys around the Atacama puna and the heads of the western valleys.

It is certain, however, that communities of farmers like that of San Francisco were diffused throughout the lowlands of north-eastern Argentina between 650 and 450 BC, and developed independently of the Altiplano cultural process. They seem to have generated a movement of surpluses that reached as far as the oasis of San Pedro de Atacama, where incised ceramic fragments belonging to this culture have been identified.

The village settlement of Acha, dated between 1060 and 1050 BC, near Acari (Arequipa region), is an example of highly significant early agriculture: Cucurbitaceae, beans, peanuts, guavas, peppers and cotton fibres. This pattern extended throughout various lowland valleys of southern Peru.

Further south, in the western valleys of Arica, there is evidence that agrarian and sedentary activities began in approximately 1350 BC, although few specific settlements are known (Santoro, 1980). The sequence of earlier coastal activities was tied exclusively to the acquisition of maritime produce. It is likely that cultivation and guinea-pig breeding were assimilated prior to the second millennium BC, as occurred among the settlers of Tiliviche. Nevertheless, the semi-sedentary fisher people of this coast began to receive new cultivated foods in 1690 and 1160 BC in Queani 7 and Camarones 15 respectively. Their diet consisted partly of pumpkins (*Cucurbita maxima*) and cassava (*Manihot esculenta*), the latter having arrived via the Altiplano from the eastern Amazon, together with tropical bird feathers and ornamental seeds. Llama remains found on the coast suggest that during this period they had access to surpluses from Andean pastoralism. Other vestiges of cultivation found in the coastal cave of La Capilla de Arica confirm that between 1820 and 890 BC sweet potato, gourds and manioc introduced substantial dietary changes, since in the later Chinchorro fishing communities only a little cotton and quinoa are found (Muñoz, 1982).

In the Arica valleys adjacent to the shore there were episodes of hunting and gathering similar to those in Tiliviche and Tarapaca. The diet on the coast and in the uncultivated valleys was enriched with maize, quinoa and guinea-pigs. It is also clear that the food crops which reached the coastal populations were harvested in the adjacent valleys, using horticultural techniques, and the seeds were transferred from the Altiplano to the eastern Amazon. Nevertheless, in approximately 1350 BC the agricultural change in this region assumed definitive importance through the development of communities of cultivators who lived in the valleys and are buried there in large graves, near the early kitchen gardens and the huts of lightweight material characteristic of the early sedentary villages. The peoples of the so-called Azapa phase cultivated beans, gourds, sweet potato, manioc, maize and peppers (*Capsicum* sp.), and engaged in sophisticated craftwork including metal objects and woven wool fabrics that probably originated in some local herd bred in captivity (Santoro, 1980).

Somewhat later, around the middle of the first millennium BC, these valleys were populated by a larger number of agrarian villages, simply built, such as Alto Ramírez. Judging by the large fields of funerary tumuli, the group continued to live there successfully, using semi-tropical cultivation techniques, with intensive harvesting of maize.

In these villages lived Altiplano emigrants or settlers who were involved with the circum-Titicaca region, since their textiles display an unmistakeable style that links them to the beginnings of the ceremonial centre of Pucara (Mujica, 1985). These settlers mingled with the inhabitants that preceded them in the valleys and on the coast, developing a social matrix geared to the exploitation of marine surpluses as a sideline to the new, fully sedentary agrarian labour.

The predominance of maize alongside gourds, pumpkins, sieva beans, sweet potatoes, achira and quinoa suggest that the agrarian change in Alto Ramírez had developed in parallel with small-scale breeding of llamas in captivity, unless the wool for their flourishing textile industry was brought in from the highlands.

These advances, which were civilizing because of their formative character, spread over a broad region covering the lower valleys and the shore, reaching intermediate points in the Camarones valley, and the mouths of the Loa and the Cobija, in the last years of the first millennium BC. The fact that ceramics, llama wool, elaborately worked textiles, metallurgy, maize and quinoa were found between the mouths of the Loa and the Cobija confirms the fact that these changes were introduced on the desert coast. They brought great benefits to a peripheral region where the sea was the only source of sustenance (Santoro, 1980; Moragas, 1982; Núñez, 1971).

During this same period, around the middle of the first millennium BC, the settlement of Caserones became established in the Tarapaca Valley, and its village installations were so complex as to assume semi-urban proportions. It has rectangular areas with walls of chalk blocks and pointed roofs made from branches, with stout carob posts (Núñez, 1982). Architectural advances are to be observed in the layout of the residential conglomeration consisting of a few collective circular storehouses and internal courtyards, the whole surrounded by a double wall for protection and fortification. The floors of the dwelling areas, also excavated, have pits for cooking hearths and deposits of earthenware jars where grain was kept, and the typical holes in which the posts were inserted, as in Tulor (San Pedro de Atacama). The presence of side and corner storehouses within the precincts confirms the existence of a high production of surpluses, basically of maize and carob, used intensively for grinding into transportable flour.

The progress made in craftwork can be seen in the large-scale use of domestic ceramics, with special emphasis on black-burnished pottery similar to that associated with the emergence and climax of the culture of San Pedro de Atacama. So the links between these settlements of the puna area and the Tarapaqueños were evident at a time when various waves of shepherd-farmers were staking their claim to carob-bearing areas with streams in order to engage in their first fully sedentary experiments.

Metal objects, complex textiles, very fine basketware, all furnish evidence that the population had perfected its means of production. The fact that the population had expanded is borne out not only by the size of the settlement, probably three times as large as Tulor, but also by the greater number of burials and middens.

Agricultural activity here was paramount, with the predominance of maize over the sieva bean, gourd and capsicum and the predominance of carob-gathering over that of the pepper tree and pacay (*Inga pacae*). Finds of flour made from maize, quinoa and carob associated with emphasis on grinding activities suggest specialization in the transport of flour and grain by caravan. Since remains of fish, shellfish, wool used in many different ways and tropical bird feathers from the east (via the Altiplano) are common, it may be assumed that this settlement was familiar with goods from the whole regional cross-section, supported by a network of long-distance trade. It has been proved that llamas were bred in captivity and that they were used as pack animals specialized in moving complementary goods between the shore and the Andes, where Caserones was a crucial centre.

Evidence from the southern and extreme south areas

In the semi-arid and fertile regions of the western valleys that descend to the Pacific to the south of the Copiapo River, communities of hunters had achieved some degree of success with certain horticultural products and more specialized plant-gathering before the arrival of the peoples from across the mountains, who brought agricultural, livestock-breeding and ceramic skills.

At the beginning of the first millennium BC there were dense semi-sedentary coastal settlements in this area. Nevertheless, there is evidence that the sea did not yield any high protein potential: as a result, more intensive specialized plant-gathering developed during the Teatinos period in the surrounding valleys, with greater emphasis on grinding activities. It is probable that more than one crop was derived from those brought by the Pichasca hunters, since they reached the coast at an early stage. These innovations and the intermingling of productive systems also occurred further south. To the south of the Santiago basin, dense semi-sedentary hunting and gathering communities of the late Cuchipuy stage were organized in encampments situated on the shores of rivers and lakes, with access to the coast. There could have been no difficulty here in channelling specialized plant-gathering into horticultural practices, but, at the same time, it seems unlikely that llama-breeding, as practised by the early shepherds, would have been successful.

In the Patagonia archipelago region the abundance of wild camelids led to a diminution in livestock-raising, since hunting resources here were the most plentiful in the territory. Nevertheless, it would seem that some attempt was made at semi-domestication of guanacos, tamed and tethered near the slopes as decoys. Moreover, it is still not clear whether the few camelids used as beasts of burden and found in the region during the period of Spanish influence were tamed guanacos or llamas (*chilihueques*), fully domesticated and used by the Araucans, which may have spread further south

(Latcham, 1922). But hunting activities here were predominant, following the long tradition of hunters of the Fell stage in its later phases, in parallel with the predominance of the sea nomads; both patterns of exploitation survived until contact with the first Europeans.

EMERGENCE OF EARLY CIVILIZATION IN THE CENTRAL-SOUTHERN ANDEAN AREA AND ITS REGIONAL REPERCUSSIONS

At the end of the sequence that can be traced up to the first millennium BC, agrarian sedentary villages were constructed without any significant religious architecture on the banks of the rivers that flowed down to the Pacific, or on the slopes of the western Andes around the upper regions of the central-southern area. Nevertheless, in the Altiplano nucleus of the circum-Titicaca region, quinoa and potatoes (*Solanum tuberosa*) were cultivated in villages by shepherd-farmers who also bred large flocks of llamas, a state of affairs resulting in the emergence of more complex communities such as Qaluyu, Chiripa and Cusipata.

The Chiripa culture entered its pre-classic phases between 1350 and 650 BC in a marshy area of Titicaca, with the cultivation of potatoes (*chuño*) supplemented by fishing and llama-raising. Dwellings were rectangular in shape and built around a central courtyard. The elaborate stone stelae suggest a liturgical emphasis, alongside selective trading in gold and copper objects (Browman, 1977). The Classical period between 650 and 250 BC involved movements towards the western slope, and perhaps towards the circum-puna region, as evidenced by the presence of copper alien to the Altiplano.

At the same time, around 650–550 BC, another culture emerged in the vicinity of Lake Titicaca whose civilizing repercussions were pronounced. Indeed, a complex ceremonial centre was built in Pucara with a central pyramid and stone stela portraying an anthropomorphous deity whose face represents a feline. The presence of an axe and amputated head in its hands suggests that it was the sacrificer or executioner, this cult being shared by the villagers of the district (Mujica, 1985).

The emergence of this sanctuary acted as a political bond for a dense rural population through an early socio-political organization whose influence spread throughout the area. For example, the influence of this ceremonial centre extended as far as the villages of the western valleys of Azapa and Tarapacá, near the Pacific, where caravans brought shepherd-farmers from Pucara, accustomed to a semi-tropical climate. Here, fabrics with symbols of the Initial and Middle periods were produced by farmers of the Alto Ramírez and Pircas stages respectively.

Further south, in the southern Altiplano, llama-breeding and potato and quinoa cultivation were practised among the early villages of Wankarani in the first millennium BC. All these civilizing changes had an impact on the eastern and western slopes of the Chilean-Argentine Andes in the puna area: circular dwellings made of adobe, protection walls, copperwork, stone sculptures of llama heads, zoomorphous and anthropomorphous clay statuettes, pipes, ceramic whistles and pottery skilfully put together.

It is beyond doubt that caravan trade brought down considerable contributions from the Altiplano to enrich the farming and livestock-breeding activities, even establishing them in some western valleys where they had not been found before. Thus, in various enclaves in the foothills of the Atacama puna and in the western valleys sloping down towards the Pacific, a village life-style began to spread, and, in its turn assimilated the achievements of pre-existing populations of ancient ancestry (Ponce, 1970; González and Pérez, 1966; Núñez, 1974; Mujica, 1985).

Simultaneously with the development of Pucara, in the Altiplano area of Tiahuanaco, a village settlement with clustered rectangular dwellings had been growing since 1550 BC. These dwellings were associated with agriculture, livestock-raising, ceramics and gold and copper working (Ponce, 1970).

CONCLUSIONS

In the course of the forth millennium BC the hunters and gatherers of the Andean central-southern territory exhausted their resources under the pressure of environmental changes. In pan-Andean terms, the beginning of food production, whether agricultural or in the form of livestock-raising, was a significant change because it supported a larger population and diversified the production of goods, creating longer life expectancy in comparison with that of earlier populations.

The communities that were able to take advantage of plants and domestic animals had previously experienced a certain level of semi-sedentary life, which had enabled them to increase their capacity to practise new productive activities. In the relatively arid areas, as occurred in Chile, the fluctuations in rainfall altered the terrain used for hunting and gathering, through changes in the migratory itineraries of the hunters. This insecurity encouraged the transfer of crops and animals to places with more reliable resources, with suitable climates and soil, sufficient forage and water, leading to more sedentary villages and/or encampments (Lynch, 1973; Núñez, 1974).

At the same time, in the lowlands, the Andean episodes of domestication and the early breeding of llamas expanded between the second and the first millennia BC, as is apparent from the evident links between the coast and the Andes. The fact that the coastal dwellers did not participate directly in this process did not exclude them from its benefits, since their diet improved. What is more, they shared their resources with the first cultivators of the adjacent valleys, supporting the process of food production on the irrigated land near the Pacific.

So far there is no evidence that cultivated semi-tropical plants had local ancestors apart from those found in the mountain ranges. On the contrary, the majority seem to have been domesticated outside the limits of this study, in the area reached by the hunters and gatherers. The latter apparently readapted them to the various territorial situations found between the Andes and the Pacific, creating greater awareness of the need for food production. These movements were more significant when other settlers and immigrants from across the Andes arrived during the first millennium BC, with more advanced techniques (such as ceramics, llama caravans, textile making and metallurgy), improving the conditions for expanding and consolidating more sophisticated agricultural and livestock-raising practices.

The need to store foodstuffs against periods of food shortage encouraged the establishment of the first village settlements. The resources available from the sea and the use of irrigation by flooding and terracing made it possible for the first small farms to be set up in the mouths of the lower valleys. The carob woods and the mouths of the Andean rivers in the highlands encouraged agriculture and cattle-raising. The fertile lowlands of the Andes, which could rely on ground water, and the tola groves of the mountains provided stable and seasonal fodder for the first wide-scale pasturage of llamas, backed up by hunting activities.

The gradual establishment of agricultural and breeding successes spread during the first millennium BC, causing people to converge on places where the soil and grazing facilities encouraged community life without the need to rely exclusively on natural refuges, thereby establishing an initial domestic architecture in an atmosphere of greater security and work stability.

Nevertheless, such advances leading to the development of sedentary village life were not universal. Some shepherds continued to lead a semi-nomadic existence, living in caves in hostile climatic conditions, while others bred llamas without the support of cultivation, and there were even those who persisted with the old hunting and gathering activities.

As agrarian and livestock-raising changes developed, so human relations became more those of a community, and conflicts became less tense, since before the first millennium BC agricultural land and pasture was not densely populated and settlements were possible without territorial disputes. Ideological and productive achievements were passed down from generation to generation, giving rise to cultural traditions in ecological zones isolated among vast uninhabited areas. Gradually there emerged a new ideology of distribution of goods based on each community's self-sufficiency, and resources from elsewhere were procured through seasonal migrations and journeys to other neighbouring regions.

This new progressive thinking encouraged greater recourse to more varied resources, compared with the limited demands of the hunting and gathering communities. Exploitation of woods was intensified and the sturdiest crops were selected for immediate consumption and for storage, and this was facilitated by dry climates and dehydration by freezing. In short, activities took on a more lasting character, whether in terms of residence, stores, tools, kitchen gardens or farmyards, while material culture was enriched through more elaborate craftwork.

The consequences of these changes made themselves felt through the emergence of more sedentary villages over a large area. Production expanded, as did the use of resources to meet new needs: the use of adobes, irrigation, metallurgy, textiles, ceramic kilns and so on. The productive forces extended across the land and to livestock breeding, increasing food reserves and affording greater access to new raw materials to meet the new demands of communal ownership. In this context, an attempt was made to take advantage of the more energy-producing resources of each region by improving technology and the organization of human energy: shovels, hoes, flat mortars for grinding, earthenware storage jars, canals.

While the resources of the sea were already sustaining a more hierarchical form of production in semi-sedentary encampments, the agrarian villages on the banks of rivers and in the higher pastoral settlements discovered a new source of wealth that combined with the coastal resources through the incipient llama-caravan trade. At this time, luxury articles began to appear, such as feathers of tropical birds, semi-precious stones and shells from the Pacific, transported from remote areas. These settlers kept on the move in search of more suitable places in which to expand and complement the new production of foodstuffs and goods that tended to symbolize status.

This extension brought with it greater concern about ideological matters, such as rites of passage between life and death, as evidenced by the presence of large burials. Moreover, various everyday activities were ranked in order of priority under the guidance of ethnic leaders who provided more comprehensive civil and religious protection.

A few groups gradually distinguished themselves by their various activities: those that set more store by village organization drew apart from those that concentrated on cattle-raising, cultivation, mining or trade. Thus, the craft workers of the more complex villages came to form an increasingly important subgroup.

Part-time craft workers improved the old forms of manufacture such as basket making, rope making and cloth weaving, but now the wool derived from llama breeding was used in a more sophisticated fashion. Cast metal objects became status symbols, and ceramics came into more widespread use.

Generally speaking, the concept of Andean civilization applies to those communities that succeeded in assimilating the religious, political, architectural, scientific and technological and artistic benefits, derived from agriculture, livestock raising and coastal activities, which ease the struggle for survival as life comes to be lived increasingly in an urban context.

Nevertheless, in the light of the episodes observed, several of these benefits were incidental to the dominant urban life-style. Outside the nuclear cultures of the cirum-Titicaca region, a large part of the territory analysed developed on the village pattern, evolving from the simple to the complex, held in equilibrium by a network of caravan routes that led to a flow of ideas and resources, set apart from centralized management and excessive concentration of power.

On the other hand, the hunting and gathering encampments survived even longer in the south, bringing some of the advantages of renewal. The advances in agriculture, cultivation and cattle-rearing in the course of the first millennium BC showed that it was possible to live without travelling to find resources; rather those resources multiplied wherever people decided to settle. This occurred over a large expanse of the territory under consideration, and presages the early civilized patterns of its cultural history, on the southern periphery of the Andean nucleus, even at the dawn of our era.

BIBLIOGRAPHY

AGUERRE, A. M.; FERNANDEZ DISTEL, A.; ASCHERO, C. 1975. Comentarios sobre nuevas fechas en la cronología arqueológicas precerá mica de la provincia de Jujuy. *Relac. Soc. argent. Antropol.* (Buenos Aires), N.S., Vol. 9.

ALLISON, M. 1985. La salud de las poblaciones arcaicas. In: CONGRESO NACIONAL DE ARQUEOLOGÍA CHILENA, Arica. *Resúmenes de Ponencias.* Arica.

AMPUERO, G.; HIDALGO, J. 1975. Estructura y proceso en la pre y protohistoria del norte chico de Chile. *Chungará* (Arica), No. 5, pp. 87–124.

AMPUERO, G.; RIVERA, M. 1971. Secuencia arqueológica del alero de San Pedro Viejo-Pichasca. *Bol. Mus. Arqueol. Serena* (La Serena), No. 14, pp. 45–69.

BENAVENTE, M. A. 1981. Chiu-Chiu-200: Un campamento de pastores. Santiago de Chile. (BA thesis.)

BIRD, J. 1943. *Excavations in Northern Chile.* New York. (Anthropol. pap. am. Mus. nat. Hist., 38.)

BROWMAN, D. 1977. Tiwanaku Expansion and Altiplano Economic Pattern. In: CONGRESO DE ARQUEOLOGÍA CHILENA, 7, Talca. *Ponencia.* Talca.

CASTILLO, G. 1974. Fortaleza Molle en el flanco sur del Valle de Elqui. *Creces* (Santiago de Chile), No. 6, pp. 12–15.

CHILDE, G. 1946. *Orígenes de la civilización.* México, D.F.

DRUSS, M. 1977. Environment, Subsistence Economy, and Settlement Patterns of the Chiu Chiu Complex (ca. 2,700 to 1,600 BC) of the Atacama Desert, Northern Chile. New York. (PhD thesis.)

FALLABELLA, F.; PLANELLA, M. T. 1982. Nuevas perspectivas en torno al periodo alfarero temprano en Chile Central. In: CONGRESO NACIONAL DE ARQUEOLOGÍA, 9, LA SERENA. *Resúmenes de Ponencias.* La Serena.

FERNÁNDEZ DISTEL, A. A. 1974. Excavaciones arqueológicas en las cuevas de Huachichocana. Dep. de Tumbaya, prov. de Jujuy, Argentina. *Relac. Soc. argent. Antropol.* (Buenos Aires), N.S., Vol. 7, pp. 101–27.

GAMBIER, M.; SACCHERO, P. 1970. Secuencias culturales y cronologías para el Sudoeste de la provincia de San Juan. *Hunuc Huar*, No. 1, San Juan, Argentina.

GONZÁLEZ, A. R.; PÉREZ, J. 1966. El área andina meridional. In: INTERNATIONAL CONGRESS OF AMERICANISTS, 36, SEVILLA. *Actas.* Sevilla. Vol. 1.

GROBMAN, A. et al. 1977. Study of Preceramic Maize from Huarmey (North Central Coast of Peru). *Bot. Mus. Leafl.* (Cambridge, Mass.), Vol. 25, No. 8, pp. 221–42.

HESSE, B. 1982. Animal Domestication and Oscillating Climates. *J. Ethnobiol*, Vol. 2, No. 1, pp. 1–15.

LAGIGLIA, H. 1962–8. Secuencias culturales del centro-oeste Argentino; Valles de Atuel y Diamante. *Rev. Cient. Invest. Mus. Hist. nat. San Rafael* (Mendoza), Vol. 1, No. 4.

LATCHAM, R. 1922. Los animales domésticos de la América precolombina. *Publ. Mus. Etnol. Antropol.* (Santiago de Chile), Vol. 3, No. 1, pp. 1–199.

LE PAIGE, G. 1964. Los cementerios de la época agro-alfarera en San Pedro de Atacama. *An. Univ. Norte* (Antofagasta), No. 3, pp. 51–91.

—— 1971. Paleolítico en el sureste del Salar de Atacama, Tulán. In: CONGRESO DE ARQUEOLOGÍA CHILENA, 6, SANTIAGO DE CHILE. *Actas.* Santiago de Chile. pp. 151–61.

LLAGOSTERA, A.; BARON, A. M.; BRAVO, L. Investigaciones arqueológicas en Tulor-1. In: SIMPOSIO DE ARQUEOLOGÍA ATACAMEÑA, 1., ANTOFAGASTA. *Actas.* Antofagasta.

LUMBRERAS, L. G. 1970. *La evidencia etnobotánica en el análisis del tránsito de la economía recolectora a la economía productora de alimentos.* Lima. (Arqueol. Soc., 1.)

—— 1981. *Arqueología de la América Andina,* Lima.

LYNCH, T. 1973. Harvest Timing, Transhumance and the Process of Domestication. *Am. Anthropol.* (Washington, D.C.), No. 75, pp. 1254–9.

MACNEISH, R. S.; PATTERSON, F. C. BROWMAN; D. L. 1975. *The Central Peruvian Interaction Sphera.* Andover, Mass. (Pap. Peabody Found. Archaeol., 7.)

MEIGHAN, C. W. 1979. Archaeology of Guatacondo, Chile. In: MEIGHAN, C. W.; TRUE, D. L. (eds), *Prehistoric Trails of Atacama: Archaeology of Northern Chile.* Los Angeles. pp. 99–126. (Monum. archaeol., 7.)

MORAGAS, C. 1982. Túmulos funerarios en la costa de Tocopilla (Cobija) – II Región. *Chungará* (Arica), No. 9, pp. 152–73.

MUJICA, E. 1985. Altiplano-Coast Relationships in the South-Central Andes: from Indirect to Direct Complementary. In: MASUDA, S.; SHIMADA, I., MORRIS, C. (eds), *Andean Ecology and Civilization.* Tokyo. pp. 103–40.

MUÑOZ, I. 1982. La Capilla No. 4: Un asentamiento poblacional tardío en la costa de Arica. *Doc. Trab.* (Arica), No. 2, pp. 98–112.

MUÑOZ, I.; CHACAMA, J. 1982. Investigaciones arqueológicas en las poblaciones precerámicas de la costa de Arica. *Doc. Trab.* (Arica), No. 2, pp. 3–97.

ÑEZ RIGUEIRO, V. 1974. Conceptos instrumentales y marco teórico en relación al análisis del desarrollo cultural del Noroeste Argentino. *Rev. Inst. Antropol.* (Córdoba), No. 4, pp. 69–190.

NIEMEYER, H. 1985. Descubrimiento de la primera aldea Molle. *Creces* (Santiago de Chile), No. 6, pp. 3–7.

NÚÑEZ, L. 1971. Secuencia y cambio en los asentamientos humanos de la desembocadura del río Loa, en el norte de Chile. *Bol. Univ. Chile* (Santiago de Chile), No. 112, pp. 3–25.

—— 1974. *La agricultura prehistórica en los andes meridionales.* Santiago de Chile.

—— 1980. Asentamientos de cazadores-recolectores tardíos en la Puna de Atacama: hacia el sedentarismo. *Chungará* (Arica), No. 8, pp. 137–68.

—— 1982. Temprana emergencia de sedentarismo en el desierto chileno: Proyecto Caserones. *Chungará* (Arica), No. 9, pp. 80–122.

—— 1983. *Paleoindio y arcaico en Chile: diversidad, secuencia y procesos.* México, D.F.

—— 1986. Evidencias arcaicas de maíces y cuyes en Tiliviche: hacia el sedentarismo en el litoral fértil y quebradas del Norte de Chile. In: CONGRESO NACIONAL DE ARQUEOLOGÍA, ARICA. *Actas.* Arica.

NÚÑEZ, L.; GARCES, H.; LLAGOSTERA, A. 1986. *Guía del Museo Arqueológico.* San Pedro de Atacama.

POLLARD, G. C. 1971. Cultural Change and Adaptation in the Central Atacama Desert of Northern Chile. *Nawpa Pacha* (Berkeley, Calif.), No. 9, pp. 41–64.

PONCE, C. 1970. *Las culturas Wankarani y Chiripa y su relación con Tiwanaku.* La Paz.

—— 1978. *El Instituto Nacional de Arqueología de Bolivia: su organización y proyecciones.* La Paz. (Doc. Internos, 3178.)

RAFFINO, R. 1977. Las aldeas del formativo inferior en la quebrada del Toro (Salta, Argentina). *Estud. Atacameños* (Antofagasta), No. 5, pp. 64–108.

RAVINES, R. 1972. Secuencia y cambios en los artefactos líticos del sur del Perú. *Rev. Mus. Nac.* (Lima), pp. 133–84.

RAVINES, R.; ALVAREZ, J. 1972. *Fechas radiocarbónicas para el Perú.* Lima. (Arqueol., 11.)

SÁNCHEZ, M.; VALDES, C. 1982. Excavaciones arqueológicas en Cautín: alero Quillem I. In: CONGRESO NACIONAL DE ARQUEOLOGÍA, 9. La Serena. *Resumen.* La Serena.

SANTORO, C. 1980. Estratigrafía y secuencia cultural funeraria: fases Azapa, Alto Ramírez y Tiwanaku (Arica, Chile). *Chungará* (Arica), No. 6, pp. 24–5.

SCHIAPPACASSE, V.; NIEMEYER, H. El arcaico en el norte semiárido de Chile. Un comentario. (Unpublished MS.)

—— 1984. *Descripción y análisis interpretativo de un sitio arcaico temprano en la quebrada de Camarones.* Santiago de Chile. (Publ. Ocas., 41.)

STEHBERG, R. 1984. Arqueología de Chile Central. *Gac. Arqueol. Andina* (Lima), No. 12, pp. 4–5–15.

TARRAGÓ, M. (Ms.) La historia de los pueblos circum puneños en relación con el altiplano y los andes meridionales. In: SIMPOSIO DE ARQUEOLOGÍA ATACAMEÑA, 1, SAN PEDRO DE ATACAMA. *Actas.* San Pedro de Atacama.

UHLE, M. 1919. *La arqueología de Arica y Tacna.* Quito,.

ZLATAR, V. 1983. Replanteamiento sobre el problema Caleta Huelén. *Chungará* (Arica), No. 10, pp. 21–8.

AFTERWORD

Jean-Pierre Mohen

If we cast our minds back over the 3,000 years covered in the second volume of the *History of Humanity: Scientific and Cultural Development*, we are left with a number of impressions which lend a degree of unity to this volume.

The first of these concerns the acceleration of time. In the first volume, prehistoric time shifts from a geological pace to one determined by climate: the basic unit of calculation is 1,000 years, but by the end of the volume, references to the 100-year unit begin to occur, although it is as yet not clearly defined. From 3000 BC onwards, a few historic dates emerge, even though their authenticity may be somewhat doubtful and open to discussion. Political, legal and historical landmarks start to take shape, thanks to large countries and to the advent of writing which leaves clear records on tablets, stelae and monuments. The memory of these events is thus preserved and used for both moral and political ends: the names of princes are revealed along with those of the gods.

Two remarkable features combine to give us this impression of time speeding up. The first is the spectacular increase in exchanges, as means of transport develop and a separate merchant class emerges. As a result, innovations spread rapidly and are adapted for local use, giving the impression of ever faster technical advances.

The second factor is related to written sources, the very roots of historical science, through which official or private information is preserved for posterity. As the techniques of writing spread more and more rapidly, historical memory as it expands convinces us that with the passage of time we have more history, or in other words that history is moving more quickly. This illusion of events moving at higher speed gives rise to the notion of progress, which is central to our thinking on historical developments in this period. The successive metal ages as they are traditionally presented provide a good example of this: after the Copper Age, in which the working of basic metals (copper and gold) developed, along with the reduction of simple ores such as carbonates or oxides (copper ores), came the Bronze Age – the age of copper alloys, using arsenic, tin and then pewter, which, though technically complex, was more functional (more fusible and more resistant). The last metal age was the Iron Age, which demanded competence and skill in order to obtain the best steel, metal of incomparable quality, first used in the manufacture of weapons. The pattern of technical progress cannot be questioned, but some subtle qualifications may be made according to the geographical and cultural context, which prompts certain choices (gold, symbolizing eternity for the pharaohs), or alternatively rejection (unwillingness to use metals in the forest regions of Russia and Siberia). In fact, we can no longer take this single model of technical evolution as the sole point of reference for the evolution of societies. We can understand why it has been so used until recently, because the successive links in the development of technical objects are often spectacular. However, as interest shifts to different types of society, new demographic and ecological balances emerge which reveal a wealth of ingenuity in the way in which groups adapt to their environment, rather than clear proof of social progress. Thus in the debate on the relationship between nomadic and sedentary populations, it is now obvious that the former do not represent an archaic stage of the latter, but rather a form of society linked to a certain type of geographical surroundings, to traditions and immediate circumstances. We have seen how the introduction of the dromedary into the deserts of Arabia led to the enrichment of the nomad-merchants of that region, who became one branch of a vast Achaemenid system. We have also seen the example of the hunter-fishers of the forest areas of northern Europe and Asia, whose outstanding civilization easily rivalled the rural societies further south.

We have also emphasized several times the relative autonomy of the urban system and the state system. As one of the first settlements to resemble a city, Jericho in the eighth millennium emerges far earlier than the formation of any state, which only appears for the first time shortly after 3000 BC. And although the state is often focused on an urban settlement as its capital, it may also, as in America, develop around a religious, rather than a strictly urban, centre.

Thus the course of history no longer follows a linear pattern. We can no longer accept the simple explanation of a succession of hunters, farmers, merchants and city-dwellers.

If the evolution of societies can no longer be regarded as linear, we must now see it as a branching structure. We are more sensitive to the wide variety of cultures, which seem to correspond to a diachronic development of populations. Thus the great phases of human history, such as the Neolithic age and the age of metal, which concern this volume, are represented in such a way as to bring out the distinctive local features of each cultural adaptation – which on a world scale has the effect of weakening the force of the concept of such great evolutionary phases. We have moved past the stage of being surprised to discover that stock-rearing and agriculture were practised simultaneously in Eurasia, Africa and America, or that copper was worked at the same time on all these continents. Interest now focuses on why and how these forms of production occurred within societies. Archaeology is no longer a matter of revelation but one of interrogation. From being an area of discovery it has become a human science.

The third characteristic of the enquiry conducted in this second volume is precisely the difficulty of defining, in the present state of the art, the relationship between the various fields covered by the subject. There are, for example, incompatibilities between the different historical and physical-chemical approaches with a view to determining a definitive, unanimously agreed chronology. Another example is the fact that historians, linguists and archaeologists do not always agree upon what is called the Indo-European phenomenon. In addition to these very specific points of view, specialists in this period tend to place emphasis on economics or politics, or even religion or other fields (such as the history of art, linguistics, or archaeology).

We have decided to leave these debates open whenever the authors have set out their arguments clearly. The reader can thus read each presentation and form an opinion on problems which are all of undeniable interest. We have endeavoured to bring together here the most representative accounts.

CHRONOLOGICAL TABLE

	EUROPE			AFRICA			ASIA		
	North/West Europe	East/Central Europe	South Europe	Egypt/Nubia	Africa: North Sahara	Other African countries	Anatolia	Syria/Palestine	Mesopotamia
	Final Neolithic	Eneolithic	Eneolithic	Beginnings of history (3300–3100)					Uruk Jamdat Nasr period (3100–2900)
				Thinites (3100–1700)					
−3000	Chalcolithic (3000–2000)	Early Bronze (3000–2000/1900)	Early Bronze (3000–2000)		Bovidian Tenerean	Pastoralism	Early Bronze (3000–2500)	Early Bronze (3000–2500)	
									Early Dynastic I (2900–2750)
				Old Kingdom (2700–2200)					Early Dynastic II (2750–2600)
									Early Dynastic III (2600–2375)
−2500							Middle Bronze (2500–1800)		
									Akkadians (2375–2230)
			Minoan Middle Bronze (2100–1600)						Ur III (2113–2006)
−2000	Early Bronze (2000–1600)	Middle Bronze (2000–1600/1500)		First intermediate period				Middle Bronze (2000–1600)	
							Late Bronze (1800–1200)		
				Middle Kingdom (1785)		Agriculture			
	Middle Bronze (1600–1300)	Late Bronze (1600–950)	Late Bronze (1600–1100)	Second intermediate period (1785–1570)				Late Bronze (1600–1200)	
−1500				New Kingdom (1570–1070)			Hittites (1500–700)		Kassites (1500–700)
	Late Bronze (1300–800)		Mycenaeans Trojan War				Trojan War (1300)		
					'Equidian'			Iron Age I (1200–800)	
			Iron Age I (1100–700)				Iron Age I (1180–750)	Israel (1100)	
−1000				Third intermediate period (1070–656)		Appearance of the Bantus (c. 1000)			
		Iron Age I (800–500)			Copper	Iron Age		Assyrians (911–609)	
	Iron Age I (800–500)								
−700			Rome (753)		Carthaginians			Phoenicians	
−600									
−500								Hurrians	

ASIA					AUSTRALIA OCEANIA	AMERICA			
Iran	*Central Asia*	*Arabia*	*Pakistan/ India*	*China/ Japan*		*North*	*Central*	*South*	
Formation of states					Pottery				
First states (3000–2150)	Early Bronze (3000–2500)	Early Bronze (3000–2400)	Indus (3000–1500)			Old copper			−3000
	Middle Bronze (2500–2000)							Hunters and first cultivators	−2500
		Middle Bronze (2400–1800)							
Shimaskhi and Sukkalmah (2150–1500)					Naturalist art Pottery				
	Late Bronze (2000–1500)			Hia			First village: *Cuello*		−2000
		Late Bronze (1800–1200)							
				Shang (1600–1027)					
	Iron Age I (1500 600)		Post-Indus (1500–700)				Early pre-classic		−1500
Iron Age I (1450–1100)									
		Iron Age I (1200–400)							
Iron Age II (1100–800)									
			Aryans (1000–800)	*Chou* (1027–771)	Horticulture Stock-raising		*Olmecs*		−1000
								First villages of cultivators	
Iron Age III (800–550)								*Chavín*	
									−700
									−600
									−500

INDEX

Bold page numbers refer to figures and maps, plate numbers prefixed by **Pl.**, are also in **bold**

A-Group culture (Nubia) **Pl.26**
Abdu-Ashirta and Aziru of Amurru 199
Abdullaev, B. I. 396
Abikhil, seated alabaster statuette **Pl.20**
Abraham 99, 102, 105
Abu Duruk, H. I. 244
Abu Simbal (Egypt) 130
Abu Simbel (Egypt) **Pl.33**, 108, 142
Abusir Papyri 122
Abydos (Egypt)
    necropolis 118, 119, 126, 127
    royal tombs 120–1
    temple 135
acculturation
    Early Iron Age 342
    Europe 338, 369
    Sicily 339
aceramic Neolithic (eighth millennium BC) 247
Achaean religion 104
Achaeans (Anatolia) 219
Achaemenid dynasty (Iran) 60, 231–2
Achallan community (South America) 477, 493
Achilles 93
Adad-nirari III, King of Assyria 202, 230
Adams, D. Q. 84
Adams, R. 173, 176, 178, 180
Adams, R. M. C. 183, 189
adaptation, environmental and cultural 524
administration
    Hittite 216
    Iran 224–5
Adrar Bous (Niger Africa) 300–1
Aegean **152**, 153
    culture 155–6
    Cyprus relations 168
    decline 159–64
    Early Bronze Age 143–7, 154–5, 345, 358
    European links 41, 338–9, 345, 358
    Geometric period 159
    maritime activity 21
    mineral exploitation 16
    wheel invention 20

Aegean-Pontic influence, Europe 353
Aeneolithic period (Malta) 335
Aeschylus 17–18
Afanasievo culture (Siberia) 423–4
Afghanistan
    Bactria 232–7, **235**, 392
    cemeteries 234
    Egypt 133
    languages 236
    lapis lazuli 20
    seals **Pl.101, Pl. 102**
    temple **234**
Afikpo (West Africa) 303
Africa 299–319, **304**
    agriculture 38, 303, 309, 313–14, 316
    art 301, 317–18
    cairns 316
    cannibalism 317
    climate 300
    economy 312–15
    equatorial forest zone 307
    food production 305, 310, 314
    hunters and foragers 38
    iron technology 20
    languages **70**, 71, 73, **74**, 307–8, 309
    Nile Valley 118–32
    pottery 301, 303–10, 315–16
    religion 317
    Rift Valley 300
    rock art 301, 303, 305, 307–8, 312, 316–17
Afroasiatic languages 71
Afrosian 73
Agadez (Nigeria) 305
Agamemnon, citadel 110
Agordat village sites (Eritrea) 308
agrarian societies, Meso-American civilization 462, 463
Agrawal, D. P. 249, 262
Agrawal, R. C. 271–2
agriculturalist ceramists, Brazil 443
agriculture
    Aboriginal Australia 433
    Africa 38, 303, 308, 309, 313–14, 316

Americas 440–4, 449
Andes 92, 492, 493, 494, 516, 517–20, 522
Andronovo culture (Siberia) 426
Arabian Peninsula 240, 519
Argentina 490, 519
Australia 432, 434–5
bell-beaker culture 365
Brazil 489
British Isles 368
Central America 38
Central Asia 392–3, 396, 398
Central Old World 42
Chavín culture 500–2
China 38, 281–2
cults (Netherlands) 368
Cyclades and Crete 156
development 4, 5
discoveries 5
Ethiopia 307
Europe 38, 40, 41, 324, 326
evolution 37
fire-stick, Australia 432, 434–5
first 37, 489
Greece 155
Harappan 257
India 273
Jomon culture (Japan) 419, 420
Kerma (Nubia) 140, 141
Longshan culture 282
Mamun pottery period, Korea 417
Meso-America 462, 463
Mesopotamia 176–7
Northern Europe 374, 378, 379
Palestine 193, 199
Philippines 409
Post-Indus Cultures 269
proto-Indo-European 85
Qijia culture 286
rock engraving, Val Camonica (Italy) **Pl.137**
sedentary populations 37–42
slash and burn 360, 442, 462
South Africa 313
South America 492
South East Asia 403
spread 38
Syria 199
Venezuela 481
Western Asia 38
Western Old World 40
Zhou dynasty 293
agriculturists, Indo-European 90
agro-pastoral practices, Europe 326–9
Aguadulce rock shelter (Panama) 479
Aguerre, A. M. 513, 522
Ahar culture 269–70
Ahituv, S. 199
Ahlberg, G. 162
Ahmose, King of Egypt 134, 141
Ahura Mazda (Iran) 103
Aikens, C. M. 455
Aikens, M. C. 440
Akhenaten (Amenhotep IV), King of Egypt 102, 134–5, 141
Akkadian civilization
    alphabets 75–7
    Babylonia 225–6

cylinder seal **Pl.68**
    rites 100
Akkadian Empire (Syria) 172, 174, 193
Akrotiri trading centre (Cyclades) 156
Akurgal, E. 205–22
Al-Ansary, A. R 170, 238–44
Alaca Hüyük (Central Anatolia) **Pl.90**, 207, 210, 211, 212, 216, 218
Alalakh (Orontes River) 196, 199
Alambra dagger 16
Alamgirpur (Indus) 249
Alara, King of Kush 142
Alashiya, copper production 168
Alaska (North America) 453
Albright, F. 243
Albright, W. 243
Alcina Franch, J. 447
alcohol, emergence 38
Las Aldas site (Peru) 496, 499
Alekseev, V. P. 424, 431
Aleppo (Syria) 194
Alexiou, S. 157–8
Algeria
    Alhaggar highlands **Pl.128**
    rock painting, Arakoukam **Pl.130**
Alhaggar highlands, Algeria **Pl.128**
Alisar Huyuk (Anatolia), copper metallurgy 16
Alkim, B. 207
Allahab, megalithic tombs 274
Allahdino, Harappan site 257
Allen, H. R. 435, 438
Allison, M. 513, 522
alloys
    Bactrian-Margiana archaeological complex 397
    Eastern Europe 358
Almagro Basch, M. 371, 372
Almagro Gorbea, M. 370
Almgren, B. 388
alphabets
    see also writing
    Aegean 163–4
    Arabian Peninsula 244
    Armaic 77
    Greek 67, 77, 93
    Hebrew 77
    Latin 67–8
    Phoenicians 67, 73–4, 77–8, **Pl.79**, 202
    Syria and Palestine 200, 202
Alps (Central Europe) 350–2
Altithermal, Plains Archaic sites 457
Alto Salaverry site (Peru) 496, 499
Altoparanaense II culture (Argentina) 489
Altyn-depe (Central Asia) 257, 392–4, 394–5
amalgam, Olmec 467
Amarna Age, Syria and Palestine 199
Amazon cultures 450, 492
amber 331, 378
Amélineau, E. 120, 132
Amenemhat I, King of Egypt 127
Amenemhat III, King of Egypt **Pl.18**, 127
Amenemhat IV, King of Egypt 133
Amenhotep, scribe and architect **Pl.30**
Amenhotep I, King of Egypt 134
Amenhotep III, King of Egypt 134, 141
Amenhotep IV (Akhenaten), King of Egypt 102, 134–5, 141

Amenirdis I, Queen of Kush 143
Amenophis I, King of Egypt 198
Amenophis II, King of Egypt 134, 198
Amenophis III, King of Egypt 183
Amenophis IV, King of Egypt 72, 183, 198
Americas 439–60
    cultural evolution 440–4
    farming development 38
    formative period 446–52, **446**
    intermediate area 449–50
    monumental art 111
    myths 11
Amerindian communities (North America) 441
Amiet, P. 236
Amiraba culture (Central Asia) 400
Amon's musician playing harp, stela of
    Djedkhonouioufankh **Pl.21**
Amorica (Brittany) 365, 366, 367
Amorite palace, Mari dynasty **196**
Amorites (Syria) 182, 193
Amosis, King of Egypt 197
Amphictyonic Council (Aegean) 164
Ampuero, G. 517, 522
Amri (Indus Valley) 251–2, 266
Amu Darya watercourse (Central Asia) 392
amulets, Okunev culture 425
Ananatuba phase (Amazon) 443, 482
Anati, E. 239–40, 388, 391
Anatolia
    Achaeans (Mycenaeans) 219
    Aegean 152
    agriculture 88
    architecture 110
    art 82, 210, 213–14
    Assyrian settlements 213
    Carian civilization 221–2
    Chalcolithic 167
    city-states 205, 207, 213
    civilizations 205–22
    destruction 221
    Early Bronze Age 205–8, 345, 358
    Greco-Anatolian civilization 222
    Hattian art 210
    Hittite occupation 212, 213–19, **214**
    immigration 220–1
    Indo-Europeans 212, 213, 219
    Iron Age 220–2
    kingship 99
    languages **70–9**, 81–3, 87–9
    Lycian civilization 221–2
    Lydian civilization 221–2
    metallurgy 16, 205
    Middle Bronze Age 208–13
    Phrygian civilization 221
    religion 99
    royal standards 211, 212
    Urartians 221
Anatolia–Armenia, Indo-Europeans 87
Anderson, D. D. 457
Andes 450–2, 492–508, 510–22, **511**
    civilization 521–2
    empires **501**
    religion and art 46
    settlements 520
Andrae, W. 184, 189

Andreev, N. 87
Andrews, R. C. 428, 431
Andronovo culture (Southern Siberia) 392, 398, 425, **426**
Angola, Dundo 310
Angulo Valdez, C. 443, 479
animal figures, Upper Orb Neolithic culture **421**
animal husbandry
    see also livestock; stock-breeding
    Andes 514–15, 522
    British Isles 368
    Bronze Age Europe 41
    central Old World 42
    Chavín period (Andes) 500, 502, 506
    China 286, 290, 293
    development 4, 10
    Europe 326
    Kerma (Nubia) 140, 141
    Mesopotamia 176–7
    Western Old World 40, 41
animal species, rock art, Europe 386–7
animal worship
    neolithic, Mongolia 428
    religion 428
Ankara Museum 221
Ansari, Z. D. 270
Anshan (Iran) 226, 229
Antevs, E. 440
Anthony, D. 90, 398
Antilles, Americas 442–4
Aqhat, King Danel's son, Syria 200
Arabia
    alphabet 77
    Bronze Age 240–2
    Ethiopia and the Horn 307
    gold mining 16
    Iron Age 242–4
Arabian Peninsula 238–44
Arad (Palestine) 193
Aramaeans 50, 58, 202
Aramaic writing 67, 77
Archaeans 153
Archaemenian Empire 35
archer on skis, Russia **53**
Archipelago Patagonia **511**
architecture 107–11
    Aegean 154–8, 162
    Las Aldas 499
    Caserones (Andes) 520
    Central Asia 399
    China 111, 289–90, 292–3
    Egypt 108–9, 118, 119, 122–3, 126
    Europe 326, 334, 340
    Hittite 216–18
    India 273
    Indus Valley 110–11
    Karnak (Egypt) 126
    Mediterranean 110
    Meso-America 462, 470–2
    Mesopotamia 109, 173–5
    Peru 495–7, 499
    proto-Indo-European culture 85
    stone-built, pharaonic Egypt 122–3
    Syria, Bronze age 192–5
Arctic small tool tradition 453
Argaric culture, Iberian Peninsula 366, 372

Argentina 486, 489–91, 492, 510
Argos (Aegean) 162
arid phase, Ethiopia and the Horn 307
Arik, R. O. 207, 222
arithmetic 23, 121–2
Ark of the Covenant 99, 102, 113
Armaic alphabet 77
Armenian, language 81, 84
armour, bronze, Marmesse (France) **Pl.13**
Aroa River, food production 480
arrowheads
    Amorocan 327
    Scandinavia 374
arsenical bronze, Europe Bronze Age 358–60
art
    see also rock art
    Aegean 154–8
    Africa 301, 317–18
    Americas 446–52
    Argentine Patagonia 490
    Australia 165, **Pl.162**, **Pl.163**, **Pl.164**, 436
    Bronze Age 98, 105
    cave 98, 105
    Central Asia 395
    Chavín 504, 505
    China, Xia dynasty 111
    Cupisnique (Andes) 506
    Egypt 109, 120, 126, 127–8
    emergence 4
    Harappan culture 258–9
    Hattian 210–11
    Hittites, Anatolia 213–14, 218
    Hurrian 219
    Indus Valley 111
    Karasuk culture (Siberia) 426
    Mexico 111, **Pl.166**, **Pl.167**, **Pl.168**, **Pl.169**, 467–8
    Middle Kingdom, Egypt 127–8
    Mongolia 428–9
    mythical figures 107
    Neo-Hittite 221
    Neolithic, Siberia 421–2, 423
    Northern Europe 377–8, 382–91
    Okunev culture 425
    oral traditions and literature 92–3
    pharaonic 120–1, 124
    religion 98–105
    Shang dynasty 292
    Siberia 421–2, 423, 426
artefacts
    see also bronze artefacts; stone artefacts; wooden
      artefacts
    Anatolia, Early Bronze Age 207–8
    Australia 435
    Brazil 488
    Chilean-Argentine Andes 521
    earliest analysed **19**
    flint, Europe 329
    horn disk (Hungary) **Pl.144**
    iron **17**, 417
    Karasuk culture (Siberia) **426**
    Mid-Continent Archaic 456
    Nimrud (Iran) 18
    Njoro River Cave, Kenya **310**
    Okunev culture 424
    Old Copper Culture (USA) **Pl.165**

    shellfish-gatherers, Brazil 487–8
    Siberia 422, **423**, **424**, **426**
Artemenko, I. I. 359, 361
Artenacians, Charente (France) 364
artisans, Mesopotamia 177
Aryans 87, 263, 275–7
Aschero, C. 513, 522
Ashtar temple complex (Arabian Peninsula) 244
Ashur (Assyria) 49, 59
Ashur-Uballit I, King of Assyria 183
Ashurbanipal, King of Assyria 230
Ashurhaddon, King of Assyria 144
Ashurnasirpal II, King of Assyria 59, 62
Asia 392–413
    archaeological research 170
    farming economies 37
    homelands 87
    Iron Age 399
    iron making 18
    proto-Indo-European 88
Asiatic hypothesis, Renfrew, C. 89
Askarov, A. A. 396, 399
Asko Parpola, 260
Aspero complex, Peru 496–7, 498
Assurnasirpal II, King of Assyria 202
Assyria
    Aramaen states 202
    army 5, 60
    Babylonian influence 182
    bilingual dictionaries 189
    culture 184–5, 188–9
    dance 113
    decline and collapse 185, 186, 187
    early Iron Age 34
    empire 47, 186–9
    government 186–7
    imperial expansion 34, 58
    Iran 227–31
    iron use 60
    laws 184
    levies 63
    literature 189
    medicine 189
    military campaigns 58, 60–1, 186
    monarchy 46
    resurgence 183
    royal inscriptions 230
    science 189
    trade 63–4
Assyrians
    Anatolia 213
    Cyprus 169
    horse breeds 60
Astour, M. 198
astral cults 98
astronomy
    Babylonian 27
    Central Asia 393
    Chavín culture (Andes) 504
    China 291–2
    mathematical methodology 25
Aswan high dam 130
Atasu metallurgical centre (Central Asian steppes) 399
Atbai tradition (Africa) 301
Athens 62, 92–3, 161–2

athletic contests, Aegean 164
Atlantic Bronze Age 364, 370–2
Atlas Mountains, rock engravings 316
Atrek, watercourse (Central Asia) 392
Aufdermauer, J. 468
Australia 432–8, **433**
    rock paintings, Magnificent Gallery **Pl.16**, 108
Austria 329
Austroasiatic languages (Central Asia) 401
Austrocratic immigrants (Peninsular India) 273, 440
Austronesian languages 401, 411, 413
autarchy, Andes 497–8
autobiographies, Egypt 128
autocracy, Egypt 44
Avaris (Egypt) 133
Awan dynasty (Iran) 226
axes
    bronze (China) **Pl.119**
    Caucasus 358
    Europe 359, 374
    Iberian Peninsula 370
    Unetice 375
Axonometric projection, round temple (Afghanistan) **234**
ayas, metal (Peninsular India) 277
Ayotla phase (Meso-America) 447–8

Baal 200
Baalat Gebal temple (Syrian coast) 193
Babylon
    demography 15
    dynasty 49
    fall 28
    numerology 22, 24
    uprising 50
Babylon chronicles 230
Babylonia
    Bronze Age 242
    culture 184
    cylinder seals 184
    Iran 224, 229
    Iron Age 34
    Kassite dynasty 182, 185
    literature 184
    social and economic conditions 183–4
Babylonian King List 182
Babylonian language 75
Bactria (Afghanistan) 232–7, **235**, 386, 392, 398
Bactrian-Margiana archaeological complex (BMAC) 236–7, 396–8
Badakhshan (Afghanistan) 232
Baden culture (Central Europe) 351–2
Bader, O. N. 360–1
Bahia de Culebras (Costa Rica) 479
Bahrain Island 241–2
Baiyang site (China) 287
Balakot, Early Harappan 257
Balanovo culture 360
Balearic Islands, Talayots culture 340
Balkans 152, 338, 352, 354–9
ball game, Meso-American religion 409, 462, 470
Baltic region, homeland 84
Baluchistan (Indus) 228, 247, 250–1
Baluchistan-sibi, Post-Indus cultures 267

Balwat (Iran) 230
Ban Chiang excavation 406
Ban Na Di (South East Asia) 407–8
Ban Phak Top excavation (South East Asia) 406
Banawali (India) 253
Banerjee, N. R. 270
Bannu basin (Pakistan) 253
Bantu language spread 20
Banwari (Trinidad) 482–3
Banyan Valley cave excavation (South East Asia) 403
Barbar culture (Arabian Peninsula) 241
Barber, E. J. W. 144
Barlovento site, Intermediate Area (Americas) 449
Barnett, R. D. 189
Baron, N. S. 65, 68, 96
Barrancas tradition (Venezuela) 481
Barrelet, M. T. 198
Barret, L. K. 497, 509
barter, Europe 326, 329, 331, 364, 366, 372
Barth, F. 37, 42
Barthes, R. 95, 96
Bas Zaire ground stone tools 306–7
Basch, L. 145, 147
Bass, G. 200
Baudez, C. F. 468
Bawden, G. 244
Bayard, D. T. 406–7
Beaker groups, European Bronze Age 364, 365
beaker jug, Hittite style (Turkey) **Pl.88**
Beaton, J. M. 434, 438
Beck, C. M. 502, 508
Becquelin, P. 468
Behistun rock (Persia) 75
Beit Mirsim, destruction of 197
Belgis-Cruceni culture (Europe) 348
Belgium 328
Belize 442
Belkachi culture (Siberia) 422
bell-beaker culture 375–6
    Atlantic Bronze 365
    Bronze Age Europe 41
    Central Europe 352
    Europe 329, 336
    Iberian Peninsula 366
    Western Europe 364, 365, 372
bell-shaped pottery, France **365**
Bellwood, P. 410–13
Belogrudovo culture (Eastern Europe) 361
Belozersk culture (Eastern Europe) 361
Benevente, M. A. 517, 522
Beran, T. 184, 189
Berberic language 73
Bergstrasser, G. 75, 77, 79
Beringia landmass (North America) 453
Bernabo Brea, L. 144–5, 147
Bernal, I. 472
Beshkent culture (Central Asia) 398
Betancourt, P. P. 146, 147
Beyer, D. 170, 191–7
Beyer, H. O. 409
Bhagwanpura, painted grey ware culture 274
Biagi, P. 239
Bibby, T. G. 241, 257
Bible
    logos doctrine 143

prophecies 92, 93
texts 6
vernacular 66
Bicromo en Zonas tradition (Panama) 479
Bielawski, E. 453, 457
Bienkowski, P. 201
bifacial tradition, Arabian Peninsula 238–9
Bikini Atoll (Micronesia) 412
Binford, L. R. 6, 458
Bioko Island (Equatorial Guinea) 306
bipedalism 3
Bird, J. B. 450, 494–6, 516, 522
Bisht, R. S. 253
Bismarck Archipelago (Melanesia) 411
bivale stone moulds (South East Asia) 406
black lands, Venezuela 480
black and red ware, Peninsular India 273
Black Sea 17, 83, 359–60
blade industries, Arabian Peninsula 238
Blake, M. 465
Blakely, J. 242
Blancagrandense industry (Argentine) 490
Blanchet, J. C. 367, 372
Blas Cortina, M. A. de 366, 372
Blegen, C. W. 145, 147, 154, 155, 219, 222
Bloemers, J. H. F. 368, 372
Blumenthal, E. 201
Boardman, J. 162, 163
boat-axe culture, Swedish 374
boats
    rock engraving, Wadi el-Barramiya (Egypt) Pl.131
    Yorkshire 53
Bocachica traditions (Venezuela) 449
Bodrogkeresztur culture (Europe) 351
Boeotia (Aegean) 153
Bolivia 494, 510
Bonavia, D. 494, 498, 508
Bondarikha culture (Eastern Europe) 361
bone artefacts (South America) 476
Bonnet, C. 131, 132
Bonnet, Professor G. 139
Bonnier, E. 498
Book of the Dead Pl.14, Pl.23, 93, 99, 101
Boquete phase (Americas) 442, 479
Bordreuil, P. 200
Boreal Archaic (North America) 441, 455–6
bored stone, South Africa 315
Bornu plains (Nigeria) 305
Borrero, L. A. 491
Bosch-Gimpera, P. 89
Bottero, J. 189
Boucharlat, R. 242
Boussard, M. 72
Bove, F. J. 468
Bowdler, S. 434, 438
Boyce, M. A. 399
bracelets
    gold and silver Pl.146
    Late Bronze Age (Hungary) Pl.150
brachycephalization 324
Bradley, D. E. 470
Brandenstein, W. 90
Branigan, K. 144, 145, 146, 147
Bray, W. 466
Brazil 442–4, 481–2, 486–9

Breuil, Abbé 6
Briard, J. 364–72
Brinkman, J. A. 182, 183–4, 185, 186, 189
British Isles *see* United Kingdom
British Museum 121, 126
bronze
    Andronovo culture 425
    Atlantic Bronze Age 372
    Eastern Europe 357–8
    emergence 8
    Erlitou culture 283
    Harappan culture 252
    Indus civilization 251–2
    Karasuk culture 426
    Shang dynasty 290
    Siberia 426
    smelting 16
    South East Asia 406–8
    Zhou dynasty 293–4
Bronze Age
    see also Early Bronze Age; Late Bronze Age; Middle
        Bronze Age
    Afghanistan 233
    animal husbandry and farming 41
    Arabian Peninsula 239–42
    art 105
    astral cults 98
    Balkans 345–9
    burial practices 99
    China 40, 289, 295–6
    death beliefs 41, 99
    economic developments 30–3
    foundations of science 23
    horse use 41
    Indo-European languages 81
    medical sciences 25
    metallurgy uses 18
    Mongolia 430–1
    priesthood 98
    proto-Indo-European 82
    religions 99, 100, 105
    ships, rock paintings Pl.12
    socio-political developments 30–3
    South-West Europe 340–1
    states 30
    warriors 61
    Western Europe 364–72
    wheeled vehicles 41
Bronze Age Florescence (2400–1800 BC) 241–2
bronze artefacts
    armour (France) Pl.13
    figure (China) Pl.127
    Karasuk culture (Siberia) 426
    Late Bronze Age (Slovakia) Pl.154
    Mongolia 430
    Mumun pottery period, Korea 417
    statue of armed god (Cyprus) Pl.61
    statuette (Qatna) Pl.77
    surpluses 371
    tools (Harappa and Mohenjo-Daro) 260
    vessel, Western Zhou (China) Pl.125
bronze casting mould, Late Bronze Age Pl.138
bronze foundry debris, Fort-Harrouard (France) Pl.3
Browman, D. 521, 522
Bryan, A. L. 488, 491

Buddha, India 35
Bueno, A. 498, 508
Buhen Fortress (Nubia) **Pl.27**
buildings
    Andean neolithic 496–7
    Chavín culture 502–3
    Egypt and Mesopotamia 20
Bulgaria 332, 345
bull palette (Egypt) 120
bull wall-painting (Greece) **Pl.49**
Bullen, R. P. 459
Bulmer, R. 411
bureaucracy, Incas 46
Burger, R. L. 451
Burgess, C. 365, 367, 372
burial practices
    see also cremations
    Afanasievo culture (Southern Siberia) 423, 424
    Amorica 366
    Anatolia 207
    Andronovo culture 425
    Archaic period 457–8
    Atlantic Bronze culture 364
    Australia 437
    Crete 147, 157
    Cyclades 157
    Eurasian steppes 42
    Europe 41, 382–3
    Hittite 212
    Karasuk culture (Siberia) 426
    Korea 417
    Mongolia 429–30
    Neolithic, Siberia 421
    Northern Europe 373, 375–9
    Okunev culture, Siberia 424
    post-Indus cultures 268–9, 274
    Scandinavia 376
    Siberia 423–4, 426
    Western Europe, Late Bronze Age 370
burials
    see also cemeteries; graves; tombs
    Arabian Peninsula Bronze Age 240
    Bactrian-Margiana archaeological complex 397
    Central Asia Late Eneolithic 393
    Central Europe 351–2
    China 281
    Harappan culture 261–2
    Longshan culture 281–2
    megalithic 273–4, 334–6, 340
    Meso-American 465
    Palestine 193, 195–6
    Philippines 409
    South East Asia 404–5, 407
    Southern Europe 334–6, 340
    tumuli 354
    urn, Europe 382–3
    Urnfield period 355
    Venezuela 480·
    West Indies 483
Burnaburiash II, King of the Kassites 183
Burton, J. 411
Bush Barrow, Wessex 332
Byblos 17, **Pl.76**, 136, 193, **195**
Byci-Skala (Moravia), ironsmith's tools 18
Byers, D. S. 441

Cabo Blanco complex (Venezuela) 480
Cadogan, G. 157
Cagayan Valley (Philippines) 409
cairns
    Africa 316
    Post-Indus Cultures 268–9, 274
Cairo Museum 121, 124
Calcareous Sand-Tempered ware (Micronesia) 412
Calderon, L. 483
Caldwell, J. R. 441
calendars
    Central Asia 393
    China 291–2, 294
    Egypt 122
    establishment 23, 27–9
    Meso-American Civilization 463
    Peru 499
    Shang dynasty 291–2
    Zhou dynasty 294
calligraphy, development 65
Camelidae species, South America 513–14, 519, **519**
camels 42, 55–6, 201
Cameroon (Africa) 306–7
Canaan
    culture 201
    gods 203
    relations with Egypt 63
    script 77
Canada (North America) 453
Canaima complex (Venezuela) 481
canals *see* irrigation
Canapote sites, Cartagena area (Americas) 449
Canciani, F. 162
cannibalism, Africa 317
Caño Grande phase (Venezuela) 481
Cape Gelidonya wreck 52
Cape Province (South Africa) 311
caravans
    Andes 519, 521
    Syria and Palestine 202
carbon-dating techniques 28
carburization, iron 59
Carchemish (Euphrates) 199
Cardascia, G. 184, 189
Carian civilization (Anatolia) 221–2
Carnarvon, Lord 6
Carnarvon Tablet 134
carnelian beads, Harappan arts 258–9
Carolingian script 68
Carpathians 346, 350–4, 359–60
Carpatho-Danubian-Balkan region 348–9
cart from Dupljaya (Federal Republic of Yugoslavia) **Pl.139**
Cartagena area, Intermediate area (Americas) 449
Carter, E. 183, 189
Carter, Howard 6
Carthage, metallurgy 20
Casal, J. M. 232, 253, 266
Casapedrense culture (Argentine Patagonia) 490
Caserones settlement (Andes) 519–20
Caskey, J. L. 144, 147, 154–5
Caso, A. 472
Caspian sea 73, 83
cassava, South America 443, 478–9, 481, 483
catacomb culture, Eastern Europe 360

Catalonia culture, Late Bronze Age 341
Caton-Thompson, G. 244
cattle
    Andes 522
    Central Asia 398
    East Africa 309
    Ethiopia and the Horn 307
Caucasian language 73, 87, 89
Caucasus
    Bronze Age, metallurgical centre 363
    Eastern Europe Bronze Age 357–60
Cauvin, J. 15
cavalry, Assyrian Army 60
cave art 105, 368
cave drawings, Western Europe 368
Caviglia, S. E. 491
Celtic culture 355, 367–8, 388, 390
cemeteries
    see also burials; necropolises; tombs
    Afghanistan 234
    Arabian Peninsula 239
    Bodrogkeresztur culture 351
    Bronze Age 349
    Central Europe 354
    China 281–2, 286
    Cyprus 167–8
    Dashti-Kozy (Central Asia) 398
    Greece 155–6
    Harappan culture 255
    Iran 226, 228
    North America 441
    Parkhai (Central Asia) 395
    Peinan Island 408
    Port aux Choix 455, 458
    Taosi (China) 282
    Urnfield period 355
cemetery, Ur Babylonia 225–6
cemetery 'H' culture, Post-Indus Cultures 266
censuses, Egypt 28
Central America 442–4
    northern 441–2
Central Asia and the Pacific 401–13
Central Europe, Late Neolithic culture 350–1
centre of gravity 83–4, **83**, 87–9
centres of domestication, Panama 479
ceramics
    Archaic period 459
    Central Asia Late Eneolithic 393
    Erlitou culture 283
    Harappan arts and crafts 258
    industrial production beginnings 20
    Tulor (Andes) 519
cereals
    Andes 516
    diet (Americas) 442
    impressions (Africa) 303
    seed impressions, Neolithic (Mauritania) **Pl.133**
ceremonial centres, Americas 447
ceremonial vessels, Mamun pottery period (Korea) 417
Cernavoda culture, Dobruja 346
Cerny, J. 134, 137
Cerro Mangote site (Panama) 449, 479
Cerro Narrio culture (Americas) 450
Cerro Punta cultivation (Panama) 479
Cerro Sechin temple (Peru) **451**

Chadwick, J. 153–6
chain, gold, Late Bronze Age (Romania) **Pl.151**
Chalcide Peninsula (Balkans) 345
Chalcolithic period
    Baluchistan 251
    Central Asia 394
    Cyprus 167
    Eastern Europe 355, 358
    Post-Indus Cultures 266, 269
Chalconithic Gumelnita culture 346
Champollion, J. F. 28, 72, 139
Chandigarh, Harappan burials 261
Chang, K. C. 408–9
Changjiang, lower reaches 286–7
Changjiang (China) 286–7
Changjiang-Han region (China) 295
Changpinian Cave sites (South East Asia) 408
Changshou, Z. 289–96
Chaparron food production (Costa Rica) 479
chapel, Tutankhamen treasuries (Egypt) **Pl.31**
chariots
    Bronze Age, Mongolia 430
    Central Asia 399
    central Old World 42
    design 54–5
    military function 60
    rock painting (Sahara) **301**
    Sumarian period 60
    Western Europe, Late Bronze Age 371
    Yin ruins (China) **290**
Charlemagne 68
Chaturvedi, S. N. 271
Chavín culture (Peru) 450, 466, 500–6, 508
    art 111, 450–1
    chronological science 28
Chavín de Huántar (Andes) 444, 451, **451**, 496, 503–5
Chengtang, King of Shang 289
Chengzi cemetery (Zhucheng country) 284
Cheops, King of Egypt 129
Chernetsov, V. N. 421, 431
Chernykh, E. N. 41, 359–61, 430
Cherry, J. F. 145, 147
Cheviot Hills (England) 324
Chiapas (Meso-America) 468–9
child mortality, Afansievo tribes 424
Childe, G. 364, 372
Childe, V. G. 7, 23, 26, 30, 89, 478
Chile 492, 494, **518**
chimaira, orthostat relief, Neo-Hittite art (Turkey) **Pl.94**
Chin, L. 410
China 280–96, **289**
    architecture 292–3
    Baiyang site 287
    calendars 291–2, 294
    confederations 45
    dance 113
    farming development 38
    Han emperors, chronology 28
    Iron Age 34
    iron-working 17, 19
    languages 74, 77–9
    Late Neolithic Age 280
    monarchy 11
    religions 104–5
    scientific development 24

script 24, **78**, 93
Shang dynasty 31, 32, 40
    architecture 111, 289–90
    calendars 291–2
    music 113
    spoke-wheeled vehicles 42
Shou dynasty 35
state structures 35
Xia dynasty 111
Zhou dynasty 33, 40, 292–4
Chinchorro culture (Andes) 513
Chinese Warring States 417
Chinh, H. X. 403
Los Chinos site, Peru 496
Chiricahua phase, Americas 455
Chiripa culture (Andes) 521
Choris culture (Alaska) 459
Chorrera culture 450, 481, 493
Chowdhurry, K. A. 249
chronology
    Olmec civilization 468
    science 28
    table **527–8**
Chubinishvili, - 358
Chulmun pottery period (Korea) 415
Chuquitana monumental building (Peru) 444
Chust culture (Central Asia) 400
circum-Pontine metallurgical province (Eastern Europe)
    358
Cirna necropolis 348
citadel, Harappan culture 254–6
citadel mound, Mohenjo-daro **254**
cities
    Anatolia 213
    development 9
    emergence 30, 38
    Indus civilization 254
    Meso-America 465–6, 470–2
    Shang dynasty 289–90
    Zhou dynasty 292–3
city-states 7, 9–10
    Aegean 161
    Anatolia 207, 212, 219
    birth 4, 5
    Mesopotamia 172, 173, 175
    Syria 135
Clark, G. 463, 465, 483
Clark, J. G. D. 328, 329, 332
clasp, Hattian style (Turkey) **Pl.82**
clay container, Early Cycladic (Greece) **Pl.40**
clay figures, Middle Bronze Age **Pl.60**
Clay, J. S. 163
clay tablets
    Linear A script (Greece) **Pl.42**
    Mesopotamia 10
Clerc, G. 139, 140, 144
Cleuziou, S. 240–2
climate
    Africa 300
    Americas 440
    Eastern Europe 357
    Europe 321, 324
    Indus civilization 249
    proto-Indo-European 85
    South America 476

Clist, B. 306
clothing
    Africa 301
    Bronze Age Denmark **325**
    Egtved girl 377
    Glazkovo culture, Siberia 427, **427**
    Northern Europe 377, 378, 380
    Okunev culture 425
    ornaments, Northern Europe 378
    Similaun Man **325**, 336
Clytemnestra, tomb 110
Coastal Archaic culture (Eastern North America) 455
Cochise culture (North America) 440
Code of Hammurabi 179
codex 95
Coe, J. L. 455
Coe, M. D. 448, 463, 467–8, 470, 472
Coffyn, A. 369, 370, 372
Colani, M. 403
Coldstream, J. W. 162, 163
Coles, J. M. 366, 372
collar, Middle Kingdom (Egypt) **Pl.24**
Collier, D., Incas 46
Colombia 492
colossi of Memnon, Thebes (Egypt) 20, 134
communications
    see also travel
    Europe 331–2
Confucians
    China 35
    Zhou dynasty 293–4
Congo basin (Africa) 306
Constantini, L. 257
Cook, Captain J. 436
Cooper, J. 172, 180
Coote, R. 201
copper
    Arabian Peninsula 240–1, 243
    Central Asia 395
    Cyprus 167–8
    Eastern Europe 357–8
    Iran 226
    painted grey ware culture 275
    South East Asia 406
    Southern Europe 336–7
Copper Age
    beginnings 15–16
    Europe 337, 350–1
    Italian peninsula and Sicily **337**
    Malta and Sicily **337**
    medical science 25
    Sardinia, Spain, Southern France **337**
copper mines
    Persian Gulf 224
    Phu Lon 406
copper tools (Harappa and Mohenjo-Daro) **260**
copperwork, Tulor (Andes) 519
Coptic Christian Church (Egypt) 72
Corded ware culture
    Europe 41, 332, 352, 359–61, 364, 373–4, 376
    Taiwan 408
cords, use in antiquity **21**
Corinth (Aegean) 162
Cornwall, P. B. 257
Correal, G. 450, 476–7

Corsica, torre culture 340
Côte d'Ivoire (West Africa) 304
Cotocallo culture 450
Cotofeni culture (Bulgaria) 346
cotton, Andean cultivation 494–5
Coulmas, F. 65, 68
counting *see* mathematics
Courbin, C. 202
Courtes, J. 67, 68
Courtois, J. C. 200
Covarrubias, M. 448, 467, 470
crafts
    Andes 522
    Caserones (Andes) 520
    Chavín period (Andes) 502
    ChiuChiu-200 (Andes) 517
    Egypt 20
    El Toro gorge (Andes) 519
    Europe 327–9, 332
    Hittites 216
    Hyaca Prieta (Peru) 495
    Kerma (Nubia) 140, 141
    Late Bronze Age 32
    Liangzhu culture 287
    Longshan culture 282
    Middle Kerma (Nubia) 139–40
    Palestine 199–200
    proto-Indo-European 85
    Syria 199–200
    Valdivian (Andes) 493
    Zhou period 293
Crawford, - 171
cremation
    Central Asia steppes 398
    East Africa 309
    Europe 348–9, 382, 382–3
Cretan-Mycenaean religion 104
Crete 153, 156–8
    art 110
    burial practices 147
    dance 113
    Early Bronze Age 146
    proto-Palatial period 157
    regional divisions 154
    script development 24
crops
    see also agriculture; maize cultivation
    Andes 493–4, 502, 509, 515–16, 518, 519, 520–1
    Brazil 489
    cereals **Pl.133**, 303, 442, 516
    Chavín period (Andes) 502
    China, Bronze Age 40
    city needs 37
    Europe 326
    Valdivian (Andes) 493, 509
Crossland, R. A 84
Cruxent, J. M. 480–1
Cuba 483
cubit (525 mm), Egyptian measurement **Pl.7**
Cueva del Elefante (Venezuela) 481
Cueva Roja site (West Indies) 483
Las Culebras site (Peru) 496, 498
cults
    see also religions
    Aryan 103

    astral 98
    Netherlands 368
    Scandinavian rock art 387–8
    Western Semites 100–1
cultural development 4, 11
    adaptation 524
    Americas 440–4
    Andes 522
    China 45
    diffusion 7–8
    Holocene 38
    South-west Europe 340–1
    Southern Europe 343–4
    Syria and Palestine, Early Iron Age 203
Cululú culture, Argentina 489
cuneiform 71, 74–6, 79
    Arabian Peninsula 241–2
    Harappan 257
    Iran 226–7, 230
    Late Bronze Age 198
    Mesopotamia 171
    origin **75**
    Syrian texts 192, 194
    tables 199
    Ugantic 77
Cupisnique culture (Andes) 506–7
cups
    gold, Vaphio (Greece) **Pl.45**
    ivory, Yin ruins (China) **Pl.117**
cursive script 72–3
Cyclades (Aegean) 143, 145–6, 156–8
cylinder seals
    Akkadia **Pl.68**
    Babylonia 184
    Bactria (Afghanistan) **Pl.102**
    Kalibangan **Pl.107**
    Mesopotamia 109
    Sumirapa, King of Tuba **Pl.73**
    Syria **Pl.72**, **Pl.74**, **Pl.75**, 194
Cyphers, G. A. 468, 470
Cyprus 167–9
    bronze statue of Enkomi **Pl.61**
    prehistoric civilization 167
    Salamis Royal Tomb **Pl.62**
    tabular idol **Pl.59**
Cyrillic alphabet 67, 68
Cyrus II, King of Persia 231

Dales, G. 232, 236
Dales, G. F. 249
Dalton, G. 408
Damascus princes, Aramaen states 202
Damb Buthi, Harappan burials 261
damos, Greek commune 154
Damp, J. 450, 493, 509
dams
    Aswan 130
    Caserones (Andes) 519
dance, *see also* music
dance 112–13, 383–4
Dandamaev, M. A. 44
Dani, A. H. 6–12, 252, 268, 276
Daniels, T. 75, 77, 79
Danish dagger-period 376
Danube

Bronze Age 346–8, 353, 359
culture 16, 152
neolithic 89
Dar Dariz, Bannu basin 253
Darai-i Kur cave site (Afghanistan) 233
Dark Age
Aegean World 159, 168
Iran 227–8
dasa people, Peninsular India 277
Dasgupta, P. C. 271
Dashti-Kozy cemetery (Central Asia) 398
dating
Bronze Age rock art 387
Harappan culture 262–3
Longshan culture 281
physico-chemical 6, 28
prehistory 7
David, King of Israel 102, 203
Dawenkou culture (Huanghe Valley) 281, 283–5
De Cardi, B. 269
De Laet, S. J. 3–5
de-urbanization, Late Bronze Age 31
Deccan plateau, Jorwe culture 270
deer antler 'pick', Grime's Graves (United Kingdom) **328**
Deger-Jakoltzy, S. 161
Degracov, V. 359
Deir el Bahari (Egypt) 134
deities *see* gods and goddesses
Delgado, L. 478
Delphic oracle 161–2
Demarest, A. 463, 466
democracy 47–8, 92–3, 154
demographic evolution, prehistory to history transition 15
demotic script 72
Denmark 324, 325, 376
costumes **325**
model boats **53**
Trunholm 107, 377, 383, 388
Deo, S. B. 270
Der, Elamite 230
Derevyanko, A. P. 421–31
Desert culture, North America 440
deserts
Central Asia 392
transport 56
Deshayes, J. 155
Devore, I. 432, 438
Devoto, G. 88
Dewar, R. 408
Dhar Tichitt (Mauritania) **Pl.132**, 303, 317
Dhavalikar, M. K. 270
Di Peso, C. 441
Diakonoff, I. M. 172, 173, 174, 179, 180
Diakonov, I. 83, 88
diamond mining, Dundo 310
Dias, O. 489, 491
Dick, H. 455
dictionaries, Assyria 189
Diebold, D. 85
Diehl, R. 468, 470
diet
see also food
Andes 492, 514, 516, 519
Argentine Patagonia 491
Australia 435

Brazil 487, 488–9
hunter-gatherers 488, 516
innovations 40
Northern Europe 379
Peruvian coast 494
shellfish-gatherers 487
South Africa 312–13
Dietrich, B. C. 163
Dietrich, M. 185, 189, 199
Dilmun (Arabian Penisula)
Bronze Age 241–2
Harappan trade 257
Iran 226–7
Iron Age 242–3
Dincauze, D. 455
dingos, rock paintings **Pl.164**, 438
Diodorus of Sicily 138, 144
Diop-Maes, L. M. 299
diplomacy, Egypt 63
Diringer, D. 67, 76, 78
Dittmann, R. 224–31
divination, Zhou dynasty 294
Djarkutan, Bactrian-Margiana archaeological complex 396–7
Djeitun farming society (Central Asia) 392
Djoser, King of Egypt 122–3, 129
Dnepr culture (Eastern Europe) 360
dog, domestication, Japan 419
Dolgopolsky, A. 87–8
Dolukhanov, P. 89
domestic animals, *see also* animal husbandry; livestock
domestic animals 6, 10
Central Europe 352
China 281
East Africa 308–9
proto-Indo-European 85
South Africa 313–15
Dominican republic 442, 483
Donaldson, P. 240
Dongodien (Ileret) 308
Donjuan, M. G. 468–9, 472
Donner, H. 202
Dothan, T. 201
Doumas, C. 143–7, 158
Dra Abu el-Naga, Thebes 134
drainage systems
Central Asia 392
Helmand civilization 236
Indus civilization 248–9
Dravidian language (Peninsular India) 274
Drews, R. 87–8, 152, 161
Drucker, P. 448
Drucker, P. R. 472
druids, Celtic 332
Druss, M. 513, 520, 523
Dubovac-Cirna-Vrasta culture (Europe) 347
Duhoux, Y. 153
Dumézil, G. 99, 103, 105, 388, 391
Dumitrescu, V. 347–8, 359
Dumond, D. E. 453, 457–9
Dunand, M. 193
Dundo (Angola) 310
Dunn, F. L. 410–11
Dupree, L. 232–3
Dur-Kurigalzu (Babylonia) 49

Dur-Untash, Susa 228–9
Durrrani, F. A. 252
Dutta, P. C. 274
dwellings
    see also houses
    Americas 449
    Andes 493, 495, 497, **513**, 520, 521
    Caserones (Andes) 520
    China 281, 290
    Jomon culture (Japan) 418
    Middle Bronze Age, Europe **354**
    Mumun pottery period, Korea 417
    Peru 497
    Siberia 423, 426
Dyaus, god of the sky (Peninsular India) 277
Dynastic period
    Arabian Peninsula 240
    Iran 225
    Mesopotamia 47
    nome states, Euphrates 47
Dyson, R. 249, 265
Dyson, R. H. 230, 231

Early Bronze Age
    Anatolia 167, 207–8
    Central Asia 394
    China 280
    Cyprus 167–8
    Eastern Europe 358–9
    Europe 345–6, 349
    Indus civilization 251
    Italy and Spain 340
    objets d'art 207
    Palestine 193–4
    Syria 191–3
    vessels (Hungary) **Pl.141**, **Pl.142**
Early Cycladic
    clay container (Greece) **Pl.40**
    culture 145
    female figure (Greece) **Pl.38**
    harp player figurine (Greece) **Pl.37**
    marble vase (Greece) **Pl.39**
Early Dynastic III, Harappan trade 257
Early Egyptian language 72
Early Hebrew alphabet 77
Early Helladic culture 144
Early Mirror Culture (Americas) 450
Early Neolithic linear pottery culture, Europe 350
earthquake, Troy VI 219
East Africa 300, 308–10
Eastern Europe 357–63
    Early Bronze Age 358–9
    fishing and hunting 324–6
    Late Bronze Age 360–3
    Middle Bronze Age 359–60
Eastern Iranian language group 400
Ebarti, Shimaski ruler 226
Ebers papyrus 129
Ebla (Syria) 192–4
economies
    Africa 312–15
    Andes 495
    Arabian Peninsula 240
    Atlantic Bronze Age 371
    Australia 432–3, 438
    Babylonia 183–4
    Central Asia 393
    Central Europe 353
    development 33–5
    Greece 155
    Harappan culture 256–7
    Huanghe Valley 286
    India, Post-Indus Cultures 269
    megalithic cultures 273
    Meso-America 462–4
    New World 39
    proto-Indo-European 82
    Shang dynasty 290–1
    shellfish-gatherers, Brazil 488
    Southern Europe 334
    Syria and Palestine 203
    Zhou dynasty 293–4
Ecsedy, I. 350–5, 359
Ecuador 443–4, 492, 493, 498
Edens, C. 170, 238, 244
Edwin Smith papyrus 129
Edzard, D. O. 171, 178, 180, 183, 189, 199
egg-shell-ware, China 282, 284
Egtved girl (Denmark) 324, **325**, 377
Egypt **119**
    administration 119, 120
    architecture 108–9, 118, 119, 122–3
    art 20, 108–9, 113, 120–1
    autobiographies 128
    autocracy 44
    bronze metallurgy 16
    calendars 23, 25, 27–8, 122
    Canaan 63
    classical age 125
    collar found at Illahun **Pl.24**
    crafts 20
    cubit (525mm) **Pl.7**
    culture 118, 168–9
    Cyprus 168–9
    dance 113
    dynasties 28, 133–4, 137
    embalming 101
    expansionism 58
    feudalism 133
    First Intermediate Period 125, 125–32, 128
    funeral rites and beliefs 124
    geography 118
    geometry development 121–2
    glazing and glass-making 20
    hieroglyphics 73
        aesthetics 67
        decipherment 79, 139
        determinatives 26
        invention 120
        numbering system **Pl.6**
        Phaistos Disk **Pl.41**
        script 71–2, **72**
    Hyksos conquests 133–4
    intellectual life 22, 128–9
    Iron Age 34–5
    iron technology 19–20
    King Hor, 13th dynasty **Pl.28**
    kings 118–19
    language 71–3
    literature 128–9

mathematics 24–5, 129
medicine 25, 26, 129
Middle Kingdom 125–32, 133
models 128, 195
musical instruments 112
Narmar palette **Pl.22**
necropolises 127–8
New Kingdom 134–5
Nile Valley, Africa 302, 313
Nubia 141–2
Old Kingdom 121–5, 128
pharaonic state 44, 119–20
political unity 118–19
private sepulchres 124, 127
pyramids 15, **Pl.17**, 108, 123–4
Ramesside period 135–6
religion 98, 99, 101, 124, 125–6, 128
royal tombs 108
scientific observations 23
scribes **Pl.8**, **Pl.19**
sculpture 108–9, 121
shrines 125
society 118
states development 44
statuary 121
Syria and Palestine 58, 198
Thinite period 119–21
tomb models 128
trade 63
urbanization 118
wealth 118
Egyptians, physiological characteristics 138–9
Egypto-Nubian Nile Valley 138–9
Egyptology, chronology 28
Egypty, hieroglyphics, tombs 109
Eickhoff, T. 184, 189
El, Syrian god 200
El Agar culture (Iberian Peninsula) 340
El Bajo (Venezuela) 480
El Hato cultivation (Panama) 479
Elam
    Babylonian coalition 230
    Harappan trade 257, 258
    Iran 226–30
    political history 183
Elba
    hematite ore 18
    stone ritual basin **Pl.71**
Ele Bor excavations (East Africa) 308
Elmenteitan pottery (East Africa) 309–10
Emar (Meskene) harbour (Syria and Palestine) 199
embalming, Egypt 101
Emir grey ware (Afghanistan) 236
Eneolithic culture (Central Asia) 392–4
Eneolithic sites, Mongolia 429–30
Engel, F. 497, 509
England see United Kingdom
English language 88
engravings, Vallée des Merveilles (France) **Pl.158**
Enkomi, Late Bronze Age 169
entrepreneurs, Mesopotamia 178, 179
enumeration, invention 8
environment
    adaptation 524
    Africa 300

Australia 432–3
Brazilian coast 486
Central Asia 392
Indus decline 263
proto-historic Europe 321
proto-Indo-European 84, 85
environmental zones (Americas) 441
Eogan, G. 368, 372
epic poetry 92, 93
Epipalaeolithic Age 4
Erbse, H. 163
Erlitou culture (Huanghe Valley) 280, 282–3, 285
Esarhaddon, King of Assyria 230
Esarhaddon treaty, Tyre 64
Esh Shaheinab, Africa 302
Eshnunna
    code 22
    gypsum statuette **Pl.67**
Espinsoa, Vásquez de 505
Estrada, E. 449–50, 477–8
Ethiopia 307–8
ethnic groups
    Aegean World 159
    formation, Europe 343
    Syria and Palestine 201
    warfare 47
Etruscan civilization 93, 341–2
Euphrates River (Syria) 47, 49, 191–2, 195
Euphrates and Tigris Valley 171–80
Eurasia
    Indo-European family 80
    Late Bronze Age 360
    nomadic pastoralism 38
    steppes 42
Euro-Asiatic steppes, horse domestication 60
Europe 320–91, **322–3**
    Aegean links 338–9
    agro-pastoral practices 324, 326–9
    architecture 326, 340
    Beaker groups 364, 365
    climate 321, 324
    communications 321, 331–2, 338
    crafts 327–9, 332
    Early Iron Age 341–4
    farming 37, 40, 324
    iron working 330–1
    landscape evolution 321–4
    Late Bronze Age 369–71
    metal working 329–31, 332
    Middle Bronze Age 330, 367–9
    pottery 327
    proto-historic, environment 321
    religion 332
    rock art 386, 387
    socio-political features 332
    South-West, Bronze Age 340–1
    trade 321, 331–2, 338
    vegetation evolution 321–4
    weaponry 327, 331, 332
    Western Bronze Age 364–72
    wood working 327
Europoid populations, Eurasian steppes 42
Eusebius (Manethon), Egypt 28
Eva site (Tennessee) 440, 459
Evans, C. 443, 449, 477–8, 482, 495

Evans, Sir Arthur 6, 143
evolution
    demographic 15
    human 44
    societies 524
    Western Asia 32–3
Evret, C. 82
exchange networks
    Archaic period 458
    inter regional 473
Execration texts, Egypt 133
Exodus, Hebrews 28

Fagerstrom, K. 162
Failaka (Arabian Peninsula) 227, 241
fairs, Andes 447
Fairservis, W. 232, 237
Fairservis, W. A. 250, 264
Falcon state shell deposits (Venezuela) 480
farming see agriculture; crops
Fars (Iran) 229
Fatyanovo culture (Eastern Europe) 360
faunal assemblages, South Africa 312
Febles Dueñas, J. 483
Fedele, F. 239
Fedoseeva, S. A. 422, 431
Feist, S. 89
Feldman, R. 496, 497, 498, 509
felines, Olmec iconography 467
Felten, F. 144, 148
Feng, Zhou dynasty 292–3
Fengbitou culture (China) 287
Fengyi (China) 292
Fernández Distel, A. A. 513, 515, 522, 523
Ferry site (Illinois) 459
fertility cult, rock art 387–8
feudalism, Egypt 133
field systems, Africa 316
figure, Early Cycladic (Greece) **Pl.38**
figurines, Tlatilco, Valley of Mexico **447**
Finkelstein, I. 201
fire
    mastery 3
    use 7
fire-stick farming, Australia 432, 434–5
Fischer, H. G. 120, 132
Fischer, K. 232
fishing
    Andes 492, 493, 494, 516, 517
    Argentina 489
    Brazil 486–8, 488–9
    Europe 324–6
    North America 453–5
    Siberia 423
    Valdivian (Andes) 493
flagon, Hattian style (Turkey) **Pl.84**
flake industry, Central Asia 409
flaked pottery, Africa 307
Flannery, K. V. 442, 463–4, 468, 473
Fleming, A. 367, 372
flint cores and blades, Grand-Pressigny (France) **329**
flint mining
    Europe 327–8, 328, 329
    Grime's Graves (United Kingdom) **328**
    Saint-Mihiel (France) **328**

Spiennes (Belgium) **328**
Flon, - 37
Flood, J. 432–8, 434, 436, 438
Flood, The 100, 172
floods, Nile 118, 121, 122
Florence Museum 138
flotilla, wall-painting, Thera (Greece) **Pl.46**
foal-shape zun vessel (China) **Pl.120**
Fonseca, O. 479
food
    see also crops; diet
    Africa 305, 310, 314
    Australia 433–4, 434, 435
    Banwari tool kit 482
    Brazil 481–2
    Brazilian coast 487
    Central-Southern Andes 521
    Chile **518**
    Columbia 477–9
    Jomon culture (Japan) 418–19, 420
    Late Bronze Age 32
    Panama 479–80
    potatoes 516–17, 521
    principal sources c.1500 BC **39**
    production 4, 9
        Andes 510
        Scandinavia 376
        Siberia 426–7
        storage 435
        surpluses 5
        Venezuela 481
        West Indies 482–3
Ford, J. 478, 484
Ford, J. A. 446, 452
Ford, R. I. 456, 459–60
forest belt, West Africa 304
forest zone, Europe 360
Forman, - 187
Fort-Harrouard (France), bronze foundry debris **Pl.3**
fortifications
    Crete, Aegean 154
    Hittite Empire **Pl.10**
fortified settlements
    Bulgaria 345
    Europe 332
    urnfield period 355
Fortress of Buhen (Nubia) **Pl.27**
fortresses
    Bactrian-Margiana archaeological complex 397
    Bronze Age, Europe 349
fossil fields, United Kingdom 41
Fossum (Norway), rock face figures 325
foundry debris, Fort-Harrouard (France) **Pl.3**
Fowler, M. L. 440–1, 453–60
Fox, R. B. 409–10
France 321, 324, 337
    megalithic monuments 335–6
    new cultures, Late Bronze Age 369
    rock art 385
Francfort, H.-P. 232–3, 237, 257, 264, 396
Franch, J. A. 446–52
Franke-Vogt, U. 241–2, 245
Frankfort, H. 188, 189
frankincense, Dhofar 243
Freedman, D. N. 201

Friedrich, P. 85
Frifelt, K. 240
Fuhe culture, Northern steppes 287
funeral furniture 348
funeral rites 93
   see also burial customs; cemeteries
   Bronze Age 99
   Egypt, Old Kingdom 124–5
   gold, Mycenae (Greece) **Pl.44**
   Northern Europe 376–7
   funerary monuments
   Bouar 306
   South Africa 316
Fung, R. 498, 499
Funnel beaker culture (Central Europe) 350, 352
Furumark, A. 155

Gabon (Africa) 306–7
Gadd, C. J. 189
games, development 23
gaming board, Ur 180
Gamkrelidze, T. 83, 87
Gandhara Grave Culture 230, 268–9, 275–6
Ganeshwar, copper hoards 271
Ganga, Indus civilization 249
Ganga-Jamuna Valley, cultivation 275
Ganga-Yamuna doab, painted grey ware culture 276
Gansu Yangshao culture (China) 285
Garanger, J. 411–12
Garasanin, M. 346
Gardiner, A. H. 136, 137
Garelli, P. 184, 188, 189
Garstang, J. 207, 222
Gaur, R. C. 271, 275
Gava culture (Carpathian basin) 349
Gelb, I. J. 66, 68, 96, 173, 174, 180
gender representations, European rock art 384
genealogical records, ancient Egypt 28
Genesis, Book of 102, 112
genetic relations, linguistic approaches 82–3
Gening, V. F. 398
Gentelle, P. 232–3
Geoksyr (Central Asia) 392–44
Geometric period, Aegean 159
geometry, development, Egypt 121–2
Germany 373, 375
Ghaggar (India) 253
Ghaligai site, Post-Indus Cultures 267
Ghana (Africa) 303–5
Ghar-i Asp cave sites (Afghanistan) 232
Ghar-i Mar cave sites (Afghanistan) 232
Ghosch, A. 249–50, 263
Gibson, J. L. 441
Giddings, J. L. 459
Gilgamesh epic poem 47, 100
Gimbutas, M. 90, 359
Gironde, France 324
Giza (Egypt) 15, **Pl.17**, 20
glass beads, Europe 331
glass technology, painted grey ware culture 275
glass-making, Egypt, 18th-19th dynasties 20
Glassner, J.-J. 172, 180
Glazkovo culture, Siberia 427
Glob, P. V. 41, 42
glottochronology, proto-Indo-European 82

Glover, I. C. 410
glyptic arts, Bactrian-Margiana archaeological complex 397
Gobedra rock shelter (Askum) 307
Gobi desert, neolithic cultures 428, 429
gods and goddesses
   bronze statue from Enkomi (Cyprus) **Pl.61**
   Chavín (Andes) 502, 504, 505
   Elamite pantheon 229
   Huari 451
   Indo-European 103
   Kassite 182
   Kupaba, Neo-Hittite relief (Turkey) **Pl.93**
   Memphis (Egypt) 143
   Meso-American Civilization 462–3
   Neolithic 98
   Northern Europe 379, 388
   Pantheon of Ugarit 200
   Peninsular India 277
   rock art, Europe 388
   Semites 99
   Shamash **Pl.70**
   Syria and Palestine 200, 203
   Ugarit, goddess from **Pl.78**
   Zhou dynasty 294
Gokhman, I. I. 424, 431
gold artefacts, Europe 329–30
gold working, beginnings 16–17
Goldman, H. 207
goldsmiths art, Aegean World 162
Golson, J. 411, 433, 438
Goma Grave culture (Post-Indus Cultures) 267
Gomal (Indus Valley) 44, 267
Gomez, J. 367, 369, 372
Gonur, Bactrian-Margiana archaeological complex 396–7
Gonzales, C. 504
González, A. R. 521, 523
Gord group, Compiègne (France) 364
Gordion (Phrygia) 18
Gorman, C. 40, 42
Görman, M. 388, 391
Gornung, B. 88
Gorodstov, 359, 361
Gossman, P. 186, 189
Gothic script 68
Goudea seated, statue **Pl.11**
Gould, R. A. 435, 438
government bureaucracy, Incas 46
Grace, W. 95, 96
Gradin, C. 490, 491
Graf, D. 201
Graham, J. A. 468
Gratien, B. 131, 132, 139, 144
grave goods
   Archaic period 457–8
   Australia 437
   Europe 382
   Iberian Peninsula 366
   Northern Europe 376
grave slabs
   Africa 317
   Spain **55**
graves
   Aegean World 152–3

Africa 316
Central Asia 394–5
China 283–7
Eastern Europe 359–61, 363
Iran 225, 229
Iron Age 229–30
Kalibangan **Pl.108**
Tumulus period 355
Grayson, A. K. 202
Great Basin (North America) 453
Great Bath, Mohenjo-daro 254–5
Great Salt Lake (North America) 453
Great Temple, Abu Simbel **Pl.33**
Greater Indus Valley 252
Greco-Anatolian civilization 222
Greece 152–5, 159–64, **160**
    alphabet 67, 77, 93, 154
    bronze horse **Pl.56**
    bronze male statuettes **Pl.57, Pl.58**
    bull wall-painting **Pl.49**
    cemeteries 155–6
    city-states 35
    clay container **Pl.40**
    crater **Pl.48**
    culture 155–6
    female figures **Pl.38, Pl.54**
    funeral mask **Pl.44**
    gold cups **Pl.45**
    harp player figurine **Pl.37**
    kraters **Pl.53, Pl.55**
    language 88, 168
    Linear A script **Pl.42**
    logos doctrine 143
    marble vase **Pl.39**
    mathematics 24
    musical instruments 112
    mythology 184
    Phaistos Disk **Pl.41**
    ritual vessels **Pl.51, Pl.52**
    sculpture 112
    sea powers 56
    'Snake Goddess' statuette **Pl.50**
    theatrical tradition 93
    urbanization 104, 144
    wall-paintings **Pl.43, Pl.46, Pl.49**
Green, D. F. 463
Green, R. C. 401, 411
Greimas, A. J. 67, 68
grey-ware culture
    China 281–2
    Iran 224–5, 227, 229
    Peninsular India 274–6
Grieder, T. 498, 508
Griffin, J. B. 440–1, 456
Grimes Graves site (United Kingdom) 328
grinding artefacts
    Brazil 482
    Meso America 480, 482
Grobman, A. 515, 523
Grossman, J. 507, 509
ground-stone tools, South Africa 315–16
Gua Kechil site (West Malaysia) 410
Guatemala 70, 73
Guayana site (Venezuela) 480
Guerro, J. 483

guinea-pig breeding, Andes 516, 519
Guitarrero cave, Andes 494
Gulf of Mexico 442, 468
Gumelnita culture, Central Europe 351
Gumla sequence, Indus civilization 252
Gupta, P. C. 274
Gusdorf, G. 143, 144
Gwisho Hotsprings (Africa) 311, 316

Hadramaut (South Arabia) 244
Hafit period (Iran) 226
Haft Tepe archives, Sukkalmah dynasty 227
Hagg, P. 157
Hahrah, Kermanshah region 231
Hakra River (Indus) 44, 276
Hal Saflieni burial vault (Malta) 335
Halim, M. A. 252
Hallstat culture, rock art 387, 388, 390
Hammen, T. van der 476–7
Hammond, N. 232, 237, 442
Hammond, N. G. L. 159, 165
Hammurabi, King of Babylon **Pl.69**
    calendar 27
    code 179
    cuneiform script 75
    dynastic fall 182, 214
    justice 179
    laws 49, **Pl.69**
    politics 178
    religion 176
Hamp, E. 84
Hankey, V. 200
Hansell, P. 479
Hao, Zhou dynasty 292–3
Harappa (Indus civilization) 45, 67, 226, 249–63, **255**, **258**, 266
Harding, A. F. 366, 372
Harp, E. 441
harps
    Amon's musician **Pl.21**
    Early Cycladic (Greece) **Pl.37**
    Ur 112
Harris, A. 83
Harris, P. 482
Harrisson, B. 409–10
Haryana (Indus) 253–4, 263
Hassanlu (Iran), weapon discoveries 18, 228, 230
Hathial (Indus) 252
Hathor, Egyptian goddess 301
Hatshepsut, Queen of Egypt 134, 302
Hattians
    Anatolia 209–11
    art **Pls 80–6**, 210–11
Hattic language 210
Hattusas (Anatolia)
    city 215, 217–18
    restored plan **217**
    tablets 100
Hattusili III, King of the Hittites 62, 63, 199
Hauptmann, A. 241
Hauptmann, H. 207
Hauta Fteah cave (Libya) 303
Haworth, K. A. 65, 68
Hayes, J. L. 74
Hazor, Upper Galale 196

head rest, Tutankhamen treasuries (Egypt) **Pl.32**
Hebrew alphabet 77
Hebrew prophets 35
Hecataeus of Miletus 18
heilotes (Sparta) 162
Heimendorf, C. 274
Heimpel, W. 241
Heizer, R. F. 440, 472
Helck, W. 198–9, 201
Helladic culture 143, 144
    Hellenic culture
    see also Greece
    Afghanistan 232
    colonization 342–3
    iron use 18
Helmand civilization 226, 227, 236
Helton phase, Koster site (Americas) 459
Henan (China) 77
Heraclitus 93
herding 10
    Andes 492, 494, 516, 517, 522
    East Africa 309
    South Africa 313–14, 316
Heredia, O. R. 486–91
Herity, M. 368, 372
Hermann, G. 178, 180
Herodotus 18, 19–20, 109, 138, 144, 341
Hesiod 92, 93
Hesse, B. 514, 523
Hidalgo, 517, 522
Hiebert, T. 236
hierarchies
    China 45
    Egypt 118
    Europe 390
    Harappan culture 254
    Meso-America 462
hieratic languages 72
hieroglyphics 73
    aesthetics 67
    decipherment 79, 139
    determinatives 26
    invention 120
    numbering system **Pl.6**
    Phaistos Disk **Pl.41**
    script 71–2, **72**
    tombs 109
Higham, C. F. W. 401–13, 407
Hilbert, P. P. 482
Hill, B. 476
hill forts, Europe 354
Himmelstalund (Sweden), rock face figures 325
Himyarites, Arabian Peninsula 244
Hindu Kush (Afghanistan) 232, 268
Hissar (Iran) 227, 230
history, acceleration 3
Hittite Empire
    administration 216
    Anatolia 212, 213–19
    architecture 216–18
    art 213–14, 218
    crafts 216
    destruction 58, 183, 185
    Egypt 135
    empire 58, 214–15
    fortifications **Pl.10**
    funeral practices 216
    Hattian influence 212
    iron industry 17, 18, 59, 98
    kingship and government 215
    languages 81, 215
    law 215–16
    literature 215
    military activities 62
    queenship 215
    religions 100, 216
    Syria 135, 198–9
    trade 216
    Troy VI 155
    writing 215
Hjelmslev, L. 66, 68
Ho, C. M. 407
Hoabinhian style culture (Sumatra) 410
Hojilund, F. 241–2
Holocene Age 4, 38
Homer
    aristocracy 341
    burial customs 169
    dance 113
    funeral ceremony 93
    hymns 163
    Iliad 110, 219, 220
    iron-making 18
    poems 93, 161–2
Homo erectus 3
Homo habilis 3
Homo Sapiens 3–4
Homo Sapiens sapiens 4
Hongshan culture, Northern steppes 287
Honshu Middle Joman pottery **411**
Hood, S. 144, 145, 146, 148, 155, 157–8
Hooked Staff Temple (Americas) 451
Hooker, J. 154
Hor, King of Egypt **Pl.28**
Horemheb, King of Egypt 135
horn, carved, Middle Bronze Age **Pl.148**
Horn of Africa 307–8
horn disk, Middle Bronze Age (Hungary) **Pl.144**
horses
    Assyrian breeds 60
    bronze, Olympia (Greece) **Pl.56**
    Bronze Age 41
    Central Asia 398
    chariots 42, 54–5, **55**, **301**
    domestication 60, 331
    Europe 351–2, 377, 378
    hunting 31
    importance 10
    introduction 58
    Karasuk tribes 426
    Kikkuli's treatise 60
    military use 60–1
    Peninsular India 277–8
    proto-Indo-European culture 85
    saddle 54–5
    trade 64
    training 60
    war use 31, 32, 58
Horus 141
Hotzl, H. 238

Hou Ji, Zhou dynasty 293
houses
    see also dwellings
    Andean neolithic 493, 496, 498
    China **293**
    development 4
    Dhar Tichitt (Mauritania) **Pl.132**
    Meso-America 464–5
    Northern Europe 374, 377, 380
Hrouda, B. 198
Huaca Prieta site (Peru) 450, 494–8
Huanco basin, Americas 450
Huanghe Valley (China) 45, 280–6
Huangniangniangtai cemetery, China 286
Huari 451
Huld, M. 84
Hulor (Indus) 249
Humaitá culture (Brazil) 489
human development 46
human evolutionary process, states 44
Humban-Haltash I, King of Elam 230–1
Humban-Haltash II, King of Elam 230, 231
Humban-Haltash III, King of Elam 230, 231
Hungary
    bell-shaped vessel **Pl.142**
    bracelet **Pl.150**
    bronze pendant **Pl.152**
    clay urn **Pl.153**
    footed vessel **Pl.147**
    hanging vessel **Pl.141**
    horn disk **Pl.144**
Hunter, G. R. 67, 69
hunter-gatherers 4
    Andes 492–3, 510, 513–14, 515, 516, 519, 522
    Argentina 486, 489
    Australia 432–4, 438
    Brazil 486, 488–9
    central-Southern Andes 521
    rock art 386, 387, 389
    South East Asia 403–4, 408
    sub-Saharan Africa 38
    Valdivian (Andes) 493
    Venezuela 480
hunters
    Andes 520, 521, 522
    Argentine 490–1
    culture 4
    Europe 324–6
    Korea 417
    Neolithic Siberia 422
    South Africa 311, 313
hunting-fishing-gathering, Japan 418
Hurrians
    art 219
    emergence 182
    language 212, 219
    Late Bronze Age 198
Hurt, W. 443, 457, 477
Hushu culture (China) 295
Hutchinson, R. W. 146, 148
Huteludush-Inshushinak, Shutruck dynasty (Iran) 229
Huxtable, F. 271
hydrological dislocation, Indus 45
Hyksos
    Egypt 133–4, 141, 168

Palestine 195–7
hymns
    Meso-American Civilization 462
    Mesopotamia 100
    Rigveda (Indus) 276
Hyslop, J. 450, 495, 496

Iakovidis, S. E. 155
Iamhad, Syria (2000-1600 BC) 194
Iberian Peninsula 324, 330
    cultures 366
    El Agar culture 340
    megalithic monuments 335–6
Ibrahim, M. 241
iconography
    dance depiction 113
    Olmec 467
ideograms, China 78
idols
    Cyprus **Pl.59**
    Korbovo (Federal Republic of Yugoslavia) **Pl.140**
    sheet gold, Hattian style (Turkey) **Pl.83**
Idrimi, King of Alalkh 198
Ilford Hill, Sussex settlement **368**
Iliad 104, 110, 163–4, 219, 220
ilku, Neo-Assyrian Empire 62
Imhotep, architect, Egypt 122
Immerwahr, S. A. 158
Incas empire 46, 500
India
    black and red ware 273
    Brahmanic ritualism 99
    Indus civilization 247–8, 253–4
    knoll site, Archaic period 457–8
    literature 276
    Pauranic history 11
    Post-Indus Cultures 266, 269–72, 272–6, 276
    pre-Vedic religion 101
    Upanishadic thought 99
Indic writing 67
Indo-Aryans
    languages 81, 84, 260
    Peninsular India 276
    script 260
Indo-Europeans
    Anatolia 212–13, 219
    arrival 6
    classes 103
    Hellas 104
    languages 67, 70, 80–1, 82–90
    population spread 42
    priesthood 99
    religions 102–4
    rock art 388
    sacrifice 103
    subgroups 84
Indo-Iranian borderland, Indus civilization 250
Indo-Iranian languages 90
    Afghanistan 236
    Central Asia steppes 398–9
    Central Europe 351
    Iran 228
Indonesia 409, 410–11
Indus, maritime activity 21
Indus Valley

architecture 110–11
art 111
bronze and copper vessels **259**
civilization 31, 246–64
crops 40
culture regionalism 45
dance 113
decline 263
development 44–5
growth 30
industry 248
Iron Age 34
scientific knowledge 24
script 259–60, 266
script development 24
industry
    beginnings 23
    Indus civilization 248
Ingraham, M. 244
inscriptions 244
    languages 78
    Shang Royal House 291
    Western Zhou (China) **Pl.124**
Inshushinak, Iranian god 228
Intermediate Area, Americas 449–50
International Phonetic Alphabet (IPA) 67
Inuit culture 37
Ionians of Athens 164
Iovanovič, - 359
Iran 224–31
    Awan dynasty 226
    Indus civilization 250
    Period of Transformation 227–8
    tribes 81
    urbanization 246
iron
    Asia 18
    development 17–20
    earliest artefacts **17**
    Europe 18, 330–1
    Hittites 98
    India 273–4
    painted grey ware culture 274–5
    spread 60
    weaponry development 18–20
    Western Asia 58
    working 58–64
Iron Age
    Arabian Peninsula 242–4
    beginning 58–64
    Central Asia 399
    emergence 6
    Europe 341–4
    graves, Peninsular India 274
    Hittite military activities 62
    Indo-European languages 81
    Iran 227–30
    new technologies 58
    Northern Asia and Mongolia 431
    Peninsular India 272–3
    Scandinavia 380
    socio-economics 33
    socio-political developments 33–5
    Syria and Palestine 201–3
    transport 53
    warriors **61**
    weaponry 18
iron carburization 59
iron tablets, Ashur 59
irrigation
    Afghanistan 233
    Andes 493–4, 500, 502, 504, 508, 521
    Central Asia 393, 396–9
    China 45
    development 37
    Eastern Old World 40
    Iran 225
    Mesopotamia 48, 177
    North America 441–4
Irwin-Williams, C. 455
Isakov, A. I. 393, 398
Isin-Larsa period, Babylonia 227
Israel
    creation 105
    divine kingship 99
    Early Iron Age 203
    monarchy 102
    monotheism 99, 102, 105
    staging posts 56
Israelites, Syria and Palestine 201
Italy 321, 337, 338
    Etruscan civilization 341–2
    megalithic monuments 335–6
    rock art 385
Itaparica culture (Brazil) 488, 489
Itina, M. A. 398
Ivanov, I. 87
ivory 291, 396
Iwo Eleru rock shelter (Africa) 303
Izumi, S. 450, 498, 509

Jacobsen, T. 172, 174, 175, 179, 180
jade
    elephants (China) **Pl.116**
    figurine (China) **Pl.115**
Jakobson, V. R. states 44
Jalilpur (Indus) 252, 257
Japan 418–20
Jarrige, J. F. 247
Jarrige, J. H. 267
Jauari settlement (Brazil) 482
Jawf (Adummatu), Arabian Peninsula 244
Jaywa phase, South America 443
Jazirah (Syria) 191–2
Jebel Barkal, Temple of Amon 143
Jeffery, L. H. 163
Jennings, D. 440–1
Jericho 15, 197, 524
Jerusalem, sacking of temple 137
Jettmar, K. 268
jewellery
    Late Bronze Age **Pl.2**
    Okunev culture 425
Jhang (Indus) 252
Jomon culture (Japan) **Pl.160**, 418–19
Jones, R. 432, 434, 438
Joralemon, D. 467, 470
Joralemon, P. D. 447–8
Jorwe culture (Indus) 269–71
Joshi, J. P. 256

Joukowsky, M. S. 206, 212
Judah 203
jugs
    clay
        Hittite style (Turkey) **Pl.87**
        Middle Cycladic (Greece) **Pl.47**
    gold, Hattian style (Turkey) **Pl.85**
justice, Mesopotamia 179–80

Kabanak (Iran) 228
Kabul (Afghanistan) 234
Kacachi (Indus) 44
Kadashman-Enlil I, King of the Kassites 183
Kadero (Africa) 302
Kadmos (Aegean) 163
Kadry, A. 199
Kaelas, L. 382–91
Kaftari horizon, Sukkalmakh period 226
Kafue Flats settlements (Zambia) 311
Kahlikov, A. C. 360
Kajale, M. D. 273
Kalanay cave site (Central Asia) 410
Kalavassos-Ayios Dimitrios **168**
Kalibangan 253, 254
    cylinder seal with impression **Pl.107**
    grave **Pl.108**
    Harappan religion 260–1
    lower city, excavated thoroughfare **Pl.106**
Kamil, T. 206, 222
Kamose, King of Egypt 134, 141
Kandahar region (Iran) 225–6, 228–9
Kapel, H. 238
Kaplan, L. 443
Kara-depe (Central Asia) 392
Karageorghis, V. 167–9
Karakol culture 425
Karasuk culture (Siberia) 426
Karnak (Egypt) 134, 143
    architecture 126, 127
    temple 108, 109
Kartvelian language group 83
Karum period (Iran) 227–8
Karuo site (China) 287
Kashta, King of Kush 142
Kassite Babylonia, trade 184
Kassite dynasty
    Babylonia, expansionism 58
    destruction 185
    Iran 229
    Mesopotamia 182–9
    political history 182
Kassite language 182
Kassite period, Arabian Peninsula 241–2
Katincharov, R. 345–9
Katzenstein, H. J. 202
Kayakent-Khorochaya culture (Eastern Europe) 363
Kayatha culture 269–70
Kazan area culture, Late Bronze Age 361
Kelly, I. 463
Kelteminar culture (Central Asia) 392
Kemp, B. J. 133, 137
Kenya 308–9
Kenyapithecus 3
Kerma, Kingdom of (Nubia) 131–2, 139–41, 140, 141–2, 144

Kerut (Kuritu), King of Syria 200
Kessler, K. 202
Khabur ware (Assyria) 227–8
Khalidov, 361
Khan, F. A. 251
Khan, G. M. 252
Khanzadian, 358
Khao Talu excavation (South East Asia) 404
Khao Wong Phra Chan Valley 406
Khartoum 142, 144
Khazanov, A. M. 42
Khender, King of Thebes 133
Khetri copper belt 272
Khlopin, I. N. 393
Khoi-San language family 73
Khok Phanom Di (South East Asia) 408
Khorasmia watercourse (Central Asia) 392
Khorassan road (Babylonia) 225
Khuityn-Bulag site (Mongolia) 429
Khuzistan, Sukkalmah dynasty 224–5, 228
Khyan, King of the Hyksos 134
Kijngam, A. 407
Kikkuli, horse training treatise 60
King Lear 96
King, T. F. 458
kingships
    see also royalty
    Aegean 154
    China 11
    Hittites 215
    Mesopotamia 48
    sacral 98–9
    Shan dynasty (China) 291
    states 46
    Sumer and Akkad 49
Kintampo assemblages (West Africa) 305
Kiratpur copper hoards 271
Kirch, P. V. 412
Kirchhoff, P. 462
Kirovskoe culture (Northern Asia) 423
Kirthar ranges, Indus civilization 248
Kish, Kingdom of 48, 172, 174, 175, **175**
Kissonerga-Mosphilia (Cyprus) 167
Kitchen, K. A. 142, 144
Kitoi culture (Siberia) 422
Kivik cist 377, 387
Kjarum, P. 241
Klengel, H. 170, 198–203
kleros land tenure, Aegean World 161–2
Kneberg, M. 440
Knossos (Crete) 110
knowledge, empirical to scientific transition 23–6
Koban cultures (Eastern Europe) 363
Kobayashi, T. 418–20
Kocher, F. 189
Komarovo culture (Eastern Europe) 361
Kondon culture (Siberia) 423
Konsola, D. 144, 148
Kopet Dagh (Central Asia) 394, 398
Koran 143
Korea **416**
    Chulmun pottery period 415
    Mumun pottery period 415–17
Korean script 68
Korfmann, M. 206, 223

Koşay, H. 207
Koskenniemi, K. 260
Kossina, G. 88
Koster site 456, 459–60
Kot-Dijian (Indus) 251–3
Kotosh pottery (Brazil) 482
Kotosh Waira-Jirca, Huanco River Basin 450
Kovacs, T. 350–5
Kowolsky, J. K. 483
Kozenkova, - 363
Krainov, - 360
kraters
    Late Geometric, Dipylon (Greece) **Pl.55**
    Middle Geometric from Kerameikos (Greece) **Pl.53**
Krauss, R. 198
Krieger, A. D. 440
Krivtsova-Grakova, 361
Krupnov, E. I. 363
Kubler, - 467
Kuffit, - 358
Kulli cairn burial sites 269
Kullu Kalat londo ware 269
Kumar, V. 271–2
Kupaba **Pl.93**
Kupper, J.-R. 171, 181
Kura-Araks, Early Bronze Age 358–9
kurgan burials
    Central Asia steppes 398
    Eastern Europe 358, 359, 361
Kurgan culture 90, 152, 351
Kurgan theory 89–90
Kuritu, King of Syria 200
Kurram River (Indus) 253
Kuschke, A. 199
Kush, Kingdom of 19–20, 142–4
Kushnavera, - 358
Kusumgar, S. 262
Kutir-Nakhkhunte I, King of Elam 229
Kuzmina, E. E. 399
Kuz'minykh, S. V. 361, 430
Kuznetsova, E. F. 399

Labat, R. 188, 189
labour
    Central Europe 354
    Mesopotamia 47
lacquer, Zhou dynasty 293
Laet, S. J. de 366, 372
Lahore Multan railway 255
Lake Besaka (Ethiopia) 307–8, 315
Lake Chad (Africa) 300, 305
Lake Chalco-Xochimilco (Mexico) 442
Lake Forest Archaic (North America) 456, 458
Lake Manchar (Indus) 248
Lake Mungo (Australia) 432
Lake Neuchâtel (Switzerland) 321, 326, 327
Lake Turkana (Africa) 300, 308
Lake Varna (Balkans) 345
Lake Victoria basin (East Africa) 309
Lal, B. B. 271–5
Lal, M. 271
Lam, A. M. 299
Lam, M. 299
Lamb, W. 144, 145, 148
Lamberg-Karlovsky, C. C. 170, 171–80, 236, 257–8

Lambert, M. 172, 177, 180
Lambert, W. G. 184, 186, 189
laminar implements, Cuba 483
Lamoka (New York) 441, 456
lancehead, Bronze Age Balkans, Europe 346
land ownerships 8–9
Land of Punt (Africa) 302, 314
land tenure, Aegean 161
Landsberger, B. 73
Lange, F. W. 479
languages
    acquisition 4
    Africa 20, 70, 71, 73, **74**, 307–8, 309
    Afroasiatic 71
    Americas 447–8
    Anatolia **70–9**, 81–3, 87–9
    Aramic 50
    Armenian 81, 84
    Austroasiatic 401
    Austronesian 401, 411, 413
    Babylonian 75
    Berberic 73
    Beringia landmass 453
    bilingual 73
    Caucasian 73, 87, 89
    China 74, 77–9
    determinants 74
    dialectal links 84
    dictionaries 189
    Dravidian 274
    Egypt 71–3, 72
    English 84, 88
    families 65–8
    Greek 88, 168
    Hattic 210
    hieratic 72
    Hittite 81, 215
    Hurrian 212, 219
    Indo-Aryans 81, 84, 260
    Indo-European 67, 70, 80–1, **80**, 82–90
    Indo-Iranian 90, 228, 236, 351, 398–9
    Iranian 228, 400
    Kartvelian 83
    Kassite 182
    Khoi-San family 73
    Mayan 70–1, 73
    Meroitic 73, 139
    Meso-America 462
    Mesopotamia 71, 73, 172
    Miao-Yao 77
    Myanmar 401
    Nilosaharan 73
    Nubia 73
    Old English 84
    Old Prussian 80
    origins 67
    Persian 75–6
    pictographs 53, **54**, 66, 74, 78, 490–1
    pictorial, rock art 385
    pronounciation 75
    proto-Dravidian 67
    proto-Elamite 67
    proto-Indo-European 67, 70, 80–1, 82–90, 86
    rock art 385
    Romance 76

Sanskrit 70, 79
Semitic 70, 73–7, 83
Sumerian 70, 71, 73, 75
Tocharian 84
Vietnemese 78
writing 70–9
Languedoc culture 341
Lanzón statue (Andes) 504
lapidary
Erlitou culture 283
Shang dynasty 291
lapis lazuli 20, 257
Lapita Cultural Complex (Melanesia) 411
Laroche, E. 210
Larsa period, Harappan trade 257
Larsen, M. 179, 180
Lascaux caves 7
Latcham, R. 521, 523
Late Bronze Age
bracelet (Hungary) **Pl.150**
bronze object (Slovakia) **Pl.154**
bronze pendant (Hungary) **Pl.152**
Catalonia 341
Central Asia 396–8
clay urn (Hungary) **Pl.153**
craftsmen 32
Cyprus 168–9
de-urbanization 31
Eastern Europe 360–3
empires 182
Europe 347–9
evolutionary trends, Western Asia 32–3
food production 32
gold chain (Romania) **Pl.151**
Hittites, Anatolia 213–19
Languedoc 341
merchants 32
peasants 32
priests 31–2
Syria & Palestine 198–201
tool and jewellery hoard **Pl.2**
Troy VI 219
warrior class 31
wealth centralization 31
Western Europe 369–71
Late Geometric
bronze male statuettes, Olympia (Greece) **Pl.57**,
Pl.58
krater from Dipylon (Greece) **Pl.55**
Late Harappan phase (Punjab) 272
Late Helladic periods (Greece) 156
Lathrap, D. 443, 476, 482
Latin alphabet 67–8
Latium Vetus, proto-urban centres 342
Launacian bronzes 371
Laurentian Shield area (Canada) 455–6
Laurentide ice sheet (North America) 453
Lausitz culture (Poland) 378, 379
Le Paige, G. 519, 523
Lechevallier, M. 247
Leclant, J. 27–9, 139, 140, 144
Lee, R. B. 432, 438
Lee, T. A. 469
Leemans, W. F. 177, 179, 180, 241
legends, Mesopotamia 10–11

Leshnik, L. 256, 273–4
Levallois technique, Palaeoarctic tradition 453
Levant
farming 38
groups 201
levies, Assyrian Empire 63
Lewan, Bannu basin 253
Lewis, T. M. N. 440
Lewis Williams, J. D. 312
lexico-cultural analysis 84, 90
Lhote, H. 301
Li, K. C. 409
Liangchengzhen site (Shandong Province) 284
Liangzhu culture (Changjiang) 286–7
Libby, Willard 6
Libya 303
Libyco-Caspian herders (Africa) 303
Lihyanite inscription, Hereibh (Saudi Arabia) **Pl.105**
Limet, H. 177, 180
Linares De Sapir, O. 479
Lindgren, M. 153–4
Linear A script **Pl.42**, 67, 155–6
linear B script 155–6
Linearbandkeramik culture 88–9
Ling, Wang 24
linguistics 80–90
Lipe, W. 440
Lisitsina, G. N. 393, 399
literacy, implications 7
literature
Assyria 189
Babylonia 184
Egypt 128–9
Hittite 215
Mesopotamia 180
oral traditions 92–3
Syria and Palestine 200–1
writing 95–6
lithic industries Arabian Peninsula 239
Liverani, M. 30–5, 199
livestock
see also stock-breeding
Afansievo tribes 424
Andes 517–22
Central Old World 42
Europe, Early Bronze Age 365
Middle Kerma (Nubia) 139
rock art, Scandinavia 388
techniques 38
Llagostera, A. 519, 523
llamas
breeding 517–19, 520, 521, 522
caravan trade 522
domestication 513, 514
Lloyd, S. 207
logographic scripts 66
logos doctrine, Memphite philosophy 143
Lombard, P. 242–3
londo ware, Post-Indus Cultures 268–9
longhouse dwellings (Americas) 449
Longshan culture, Huanghe Valley 280–2, 281, 284
Loralai-Zhob archaeological sequence 251
Lorenzo, J. L. 470
Loretz, O. 199
Lothal (Gulf of Cambay) 254, 256, 261

Lourandos, H. 438
Louvre Museum (Paris) 120, 123, 124, 212, 213
Love, M. W. 463
Lowe, G. W. 463, 469
Lower Magdalena, plant cultivation 477
Lower Xiajiadian culture 287
Lowie, R. H. 489, 491
Loze, 360
Lu Fu, son of King Zhou 292
Luce, J. 158
Lucretius, metal working 17
'Lucy' 7
Lumbreras, L. 444, 451, 476, 482
Lumbreras, L. G. 492–508, 516, 523
Lumley, H. de 388, 391
Lung Hoa burials (South East Asia) 405
Luoyi, Zhou dynasty 292
Lustian and Gava cultures 355
Luther, Martin 66
Luwians (Anatolia) 219
Luxor temple (Egypt) 134, 143
Lycian civilization (Anatolia) 221–2
Lydian civilization (Anatolia) 221–2
Lynch, T. 443, 494, 515, 521, 523

McClure, H. 238
McGimsey, C. 442, 449
McGimsey, C. R. 479
Machalilla culture (Andes) 450, 493
McIntosh, J. R. 274
Mackay, E. J. H. 260, 262, 266
McNeish, R. 442, 443, 494
McNeish, R. S. 463, 515, 523
Madame Bovary 96
Maddin, R. 18, 22
Magan, Harappan culture 258
Magdalena (South America) 443, 478
Maghreb (Africa) 303
magic 10, 389, 450
Magnificent Gallery (Australia) Pl.16
Magura culture (Bulgaria) 345
Mahabharata, painted grey ware culture 274
Mahadevan, I. 260
Maigret, A. de 240
Maikop culture (North Caucasus) 332, 358–9
maize cultivation
    Andes 494, 515, 516, 518, 520
    Langunillas phase (Venezuela) 481
    Meso-America 463
    North America 442, 455
    Panama 479
Majiayao culture (China) 285
Majumdar, N. G. 266
Makarevich, 359
Makkay, J. 88, 89
Malamat, A. 203
Malambo culture (Venezuela) 449, 479, 481
Malamir texts, Iran 228
Malayan Neolithic people 410
Malaysia 409, 410–11
Malbran-Labat, F. 188, 189
Mallory, J. P. 42, 80–90
Mallowan, M. E. L. 189
Malmer, M. P. 386, 388, 390, 391
Maloney, B. 404

Malta, temples 335, 337
Malwa culture 269–70
Mandal, D. 274
Manetho 133, 136
Manethon see Eusebius
manicuaroid series (Venezuela) 480
Manishtushu (Akkad) 226
Mansuy, H. 403, 406
Mar Casado site (Brazil) 487
Marañón Andes 494, 497, 499, 500, 503
Marazzi, M. 156
Marcos, J. 493, 509
Marcus, J. 462, 467, 473
Margiana (Central Asia) 392, 394, 396, 398
Margueron, J. 174, 180, 191
Marhasi/Parahshi/Warahshi political entity (Iran) 226
Mari dynasty (Mesopotamia) 92, 168, 191–3, 195
Marianas Reed pottery (Micronesia) 412
Marib (Arabian Peninsula) 243
Marien, M. E. 371, 372
Marinatos, S. 157
marine gatherers
    Americas 442–3
    South America 477
marine resources
    Panama 479
    Venezuela 480
marine technology, Aegean 145
maritime activities
    Aegean 143, 145
    Eastern Old World 40
    Island South East Asia and the Pacific 408–13
    Mediterranean and Aegean 21
    Mycenaeans 338
    Syria and Palestine 201
    Western Indonesia and West Malaysia 410
Maritime Archaic culture (North America) 455
Markey, T. Indo-European 84
Markovin, V. I. 359, 363
Marmesse (France), bronze armour Pl.13
marriage, proto-Indo-European 86
Marshall, F. 309
Marshall, J. 247, 249
Marshall, M. 401
Martin, P. 440
Martynov, A. I. 422, 431
Marudvridha stream (Peninsular India) 276
Marut warriors, Peninsular India 277
Mas d'Azaïs (France), menhir statue Pl.15
MASCA calibration, Harappan dating 263
Masimov, I. S. 396–7
masks
    animal, Western Zhou (China) Pl.121
    religion, Americas 447
Masry, A. 239
Masset, - 15, 22
Massif Central (France) 324
Masson, V. M. 170, 257, 392–400
mathematics
    astronomy 25
    development 23
    Egypt 24–5, 121–2, 129
    Pythagorean 25
    Western Asia 24–5
Matthaus, H. 155

Matthiae, P. 192
Mau Escarpment (East Africa) 309
Mauritania **Pl.132**, 303, 317
Maxwell, M. 453, 457
Maya civilization (Meso-America) 45, 70–1, 462
Maya language 70–1, 73
Mazdaism (Iran) 103
Meadow, R. H. 247, 249
measurement
    see also weights and measures
    cubit **Pl.7**
    Egypt **Pl.7**, 121–2
    time 27–9
medicine
    Assyria 189
    beginnings 25
    Egypt, Middle Kingdom 129
    pharaonic Egypt 25–6
Medijana culture (Europe) 348
Mediterranean
    architecture 110
    culture 167
    maritime activity 21
    Phoenicians 342–3
Medvedskaya, I. N. 230
Medway, L. 410
Meehan, B. 434, 435, 438
megalithic cultures
    Baluchi 268–9, 272
    Peninsular India 272–4, **272**, 274
    Western Europe 336
megalithic monuments, Europe 334–5, 340
Meggers, B. J. 443, 449–50, 476, 478, 482
Megiddo, destruction of 197
Mehrgarh (Iran) 226–7, 247, 251, 257
Mekong River (South East Asia) 403
Melanesia 401, 411
Melena, H. 154
Melleart, J. 207
Mellink, M. 207
Meluhha (Iran) 226
Memnon, colossi of 134
Memphis 98, 133, 143
menhir statue, Mas d'Azaïs (France) **Pl.15**
Mentuhotep the Great, King of Egypt 125
Merenptah, King of Egypt 135, 142
Merodakh-Baladan II, King of Babylonia 230
Meroe, kingdom of Kush 142, 143
Meroitic language 73, 139
Merpert, N. Y. 357–63
Meso-America 441–2, 446–9
    genesis 462–73
    Olmec civilization **465**
Mesopotamia
    agriculture 176–7
    animal husbandry 176–7
    archeological sites **171**
    architecture 109, 173–5
    art 110
    Assyrian control 58
    astral cults 98
    'axial age' 35
    Babylonian control 178
    changing urbanization **173**
    city-states 172, 173, 175

    clay tablets 10
    culture 172
    cylinder seals 109
    development 46–9
    disintegration 178
    Elamite links 393
    entrepreneurs 178, 179
    epic poetry 93
    great codes 93
    Indus civilization 246, 250
    Iran 224, 226
    iron carburization 59
    justice 179–80
    Kassite period 182
    kin groups 174
    languages 71, 73, 172
    legends 10–11
    literature 180
    maritime activity 21
    mosaic-making 20
    occupational specialization 177
    palaces 174
    political organization 171, 172, 173, 175–6, 182
    post-Kassite period 185–6
    religion 175
    sculpture 109
    social organization 171, 172, 173
    technical innovations 177
    temples 173
    trade 177–8, 179, 257
    tree crops **Pl.9**
    Ur III Empire 178, 179
    urbanization 38, 172–3
    writing 24, 176
metallurgy
    see also bronze; copper; iron
    Aegean 143, 144
    Afghanistan 234
    Anatolia 205
    Andes 508
    Carpathian basin 354
    Central Asia 393–6, 398–9
    China 290, 293
    Danube area 354
    discovery 5, 6
    Eastern Europe 358, 361, 363
    Europe 320, 329–31, 332, 347–8, 351–3, 357–63
    Harappan 259
    Northern Europe 375
    Sardinia 340
    Scandinavia, development 375
    South Africa 315–16
    South East Asia 407
    Southern Europe 339
    Southern Siberia 423–4
    Troy II 208
    urnfield period 355
    West Africa 305
    Western Europe, Middle Bronze Age 368
Metropolitan Museum, New York 126–7
Mexican Valley basin sites 446–7
Mexico
    Mayan/Teotihuacan civilization 45
    Olmec art 111
Meyer, E. 27

Miao-Yao language 77
Miaodigou II culture (China) 280–1
Michelana complex, Lake Valencia basin 481
Michelsberg culture, Spiennes (Belgium) 328
microlithic technology, South Africa 310–11, 315
microlithic tradition, Northern steppess 287
Micronesia, Central Asia 412
Mid-Continent Archaic, Eastern North America 456–7
Midant-Reynes, B. 130, 132
middens
    Qurum (Ras al Hamra) 239
    Senegambia 305
    South Africa 311
Middle Bronze Age
    Aegean 152–8
    Anatolia 211, 212, 212–13, 213
    carved horn bit branch Pl.148
    Central Asia 395–6
    city-states 212
    clay figure group Pl.60
    clay vessel (Hungary) Pl.149
    culture 212
    Cyprus 168
    Eastern Europe 359–60
    Europe 330, 346–7
    footed vessel (Hungary) Pl.147
    gold ornament (Romania) Pl.145
    Hattian culture 209–10
    horn disk (Hungary) Pl.144
    Hurrians 212
    Palestine 195–7
    Syria 194–5
    vessel with handle (Hungary) Pl.143
    Western Europe 367–9
Middle Chinese language 78
Middle Cycladic, clay jug with swallows, Thera (Greece)
    Pl.47
Middle Geometric
    ivory female statuette (Greece) Pl.54
    krater from Kerameikos (Greece) Pl.53
Middle Palaeolithic 4
Middle Stone Age 4
Mierzanowice culture (Central Europe) 353
migration 10
    Aegean 152
    Anatolia 219, 220–1
    Austrocratic 273
    Central Asia 399
    Central Europe 350–1
    Central Old World 42
    Eastern Europe 360
    Jorwe culture 271
    proto-Indo-European 86
    stock-raising (Eastern Europe) 359
Mikhalich (Balkans) 345
military aristocracy, Central Asia steppes 398
military campaigns
    Assyria 186
    Egyptians in Syria 198
military democracy, Mesopotamia 47
Mina phase (Brazil) 481–2
Mina pottery (Brazil) 482
Minaeans (Arabian Peninsula) 244
minerals, South Africa 314
mining

see also flint mining
Assyrian Empire 63
copper 329, 330, 337
Cycladic islands 143
rock salt, Hallstatt (Austria) 329
Minoa
    art 17
    civilization, Aegean 104, 153–4, 157
    clay crater with flowers (Greece) Pl.50
    gold workings 17
    religion 104
    ritual vessels Pl.51, Pl.52
    statuette Pl.52
Minusinsk Depression (Siberia), metal artefacts 430
Minyan, Early Bronze Age 155
Miroschedjis Neo-Elamite I period, Iran 229
Mishra, V. N. 249
Mitanni
    Kingdom of
        culture 185
        decline 58
        establishment 182
        expansionism 58
        ironworking 59
        politics 198
        social and economic conditions 184
    Late Bronze Age 198
Mitchener, J. E. 67, 69
mnemonic (Sumerian) 75
Mochanov, Y. A. 422, 431
model boats, Denmark 53
models, Egyptian tombs 128
Modoc site, burials, Archaic period 457
Mohen, J. P. 369, 370, 524–5
    art and architecture 107–11
    Europe 321–32
    main trends 6–12
    music 112–13
    oral traditions and literature 92–3
    technology 15–22
    time measurement 27–9
    trade 52–6
Mohenjo-daro
    excavations 67
    Harappan culture 249, 254, 257–8, 261–3
    Indus 45
    Sind 251
Mokhtar, G. 133–6
Mokrin-Perjamos culture (Europe) 346
Monagrillo culture (Americas) 449, 478
money, code of Eshnunna 22
Mongolia 421–31, 428–30, 430
Mongoloids
    Central Asia 401
    Eurasian steppes 42
monotheism
    Akhenaton, Egypt 102
    Israel 99, 102, 105
monsoons, Arabian Peninsula 238
Monsu culture (Americas) 449, 477, 478–9, 481
La Montaña (Costa Rica) 449, 479
Monte Alban (North America) 442
monumental architecture, Egypt 118, 119
monumental art
    America 111

Egypt 120
Mesopotamia 110
Olmec period **471**
monuments, megalithic, Europe 334–6
Moon, J. 175, 180
Moor Sand wreck 369
Moora, K. A. 360
Moore, D. 412
Moorey, R. 177, 180
Moragas, C. 520, 523
moral doctrine, Egypt 128
Mori, F. 301
Morris, S. P. 162
Morrison, M. A. 184, 189
Morse code 66
mortuary cult, Scandinavian rock art 387–8
mosaic-making, Mesopotamia 20
Moseley, M. E. 444, 497, 509
Moses 92
    Covenant 99, 105
    dance 113
    law 93
    ten Commandments 102
mother with child, Neo-Hittite Phoenicianizing style
    (Turkey) **Pl.96**
motivation, humankind 11
moulds, Bronze Age (1600/1500–1200/1150 BC) 347
Mughal, M. R. 45, 250–3, 266–7
Mughal, R. 241, 246–64
Muhly, J. D. 18, 22, 201
Mujica, E. 520, 521, 523
mukarrib of Qataban, Arabian Peninsula 243
Müller-Karpe, H. 368
mummification, Egypt 124–5
mummified corpses, peat bogs, Northern Europe 324
Mummy Cave, Plains Archaic 457
Mumun pottery period, Korea 415–17
Munchaev, R. M. 358
Mundigak
    Afghanistan 232–3, 236
    Baluchistan 251
Mundigak (Iran) 226, 228, 231
Muñoz, I. 516, 523
Murghab delta, Bactrian-Margiana archaeological complex
    396
Murra, J. V. 39, 42
Murud Memom megalithic culture 272
Muscarella, O. W. 230
music
    see also dance
    Egypt, tomb paintings 112
    instruments **Pl.37**, 112
        Europe 371, 380, 383
        Northern Europe 112
    pentatonic system 113
    song and dance 112–13
    Western Europe, Late Bronze Age 371, 383
musician, stela of Djedkhonouioufankh **Pl.21**
Musti, O. 161
Muzzolini, A. 301
Myanmar language (Central Asia) 401
Mycenae
    civilization (Aegean) 153–8, 162, 168
    contacts with Southern Italy 338
    discovery 6

golden funerary mask (Greece) **Pl.44**
regional divisions 154
religion 104
trade 200, 338
wall-painting of woman (Greece) **Pl.43**
Mycerinus, King of Egypt 124
myrrh, South Arabian highlands 243
Myrzhik metallurgical centre (Central Asia) 399
mythology
    Americas 11
    art 107, 448
    Celtic 388, 390
    creation 101
    development 7, 10
    explanatory function 26
    fertility, rock art 387–8
    Greek 184
    Harappan trade 257
    Hittite 210
    Indo-European, rock art 388
    Indo-Iranian 399
    Meso-America 448
    Mycenaean 104
    Olmec iconography 467
    royalty and humankind 100
    Sumerian 174, 177
    Syria 194, 200
    warrior king 61
    Western Semite 101

Nabonidus, King of neo-Babylonian Empire 50
Nabopolassar (Babylonia) 50
Nadistuti (Peninsular India) 276
Nahuatl world, Meso-America 462
Namazga (Central Asia) 392, 394
Namazga III (Central Asia) 224, 225, 251
Namazga IV (Central Asia) 227, 394
Namazga-depe (Central Asia) 392, 395–6
names 11
Napata, Kingdom of Kush 142, 143
Napir-Asu, wife of Untash-Napirisha 229
Napirisha, Anshanite god 226, 228
Naqada culture 118
Naram-Sin 49, **Pl.68**
Narmar palette (Egypt) **Pl.22**
Navarrete, C. 466
navigation, Europe 331
Nderit ware (Kenya) **Pl.135**, 308
Neanderthal Age 4
Nebuchadnezzar I, King of Babylonia 185, 229
necropolises
    see also cemeteries; tombs
    Eastern Europe 361
    Egypt 127–8
    Europe 346, 347–9
    Syria 194
Needham, J. 24, 26
Nefertiti, Queen of Egypt 135, 141
Negritos 401, 410
Neo-Assyrian Empire 62, 63–4
Neo-Assyrian period, Arabian Peninsula 243
Neo-Assyrian period (Iran) 230
Neo-Babylonia
    empire 50
    writing 75

Neo-Elamite cuneiform script 76
Neo-Hittite art 221
Neo-Palatial period, Cyclades 157
Neolithic cultures 4
    Afghanistan 232
    Andes 492–500, 510
    Arabian Peninsula 238–9
    Central Asia 392–3
    China 45
    Cyprus 167
    East Africa 309–10
    Eastern Europe 361
    Marañón Andes 497
    medical treatments 25
    Mongolia 428–31
    pottery (Gabon) **306**
    scientific observation 23
    Siberia 421–2
    smelting 351
    South West China 287
Neolithic-Megalithic culture, Peninsular India 274
Netherlands 324, 366, 368
Neugebauer, O. 23, 26
Neumann, H. 177, 180
New Caledonia 411
New Guinea 411
New World 11, 38, 39, 45
    South America 476
    urban civilization growth 39
Newfoundland 455, 458
Ngovo group (Africa) 306–7
Niah caves (Central Asia) 410
Nicholas of Damascus 143
Niederberger, C. 442, 446–9, 462–73
Niemeyer, H. 516, 523
Niger (Gao) **303**
Nigeria (Africa) 303–4
Nigerkordogan language family 73
Nile
    floods 23, 27, 118, 119, 121–2
    historic and cultural importance 21, 44, 138
    maritime activity 21
Nile Valley 118–32, 307
Nilosaharan language family 73
Nimrud (Iraq) iron artefacts 18
Nishitani, T. 415–17
Nissen, H. 174, 176, 180
Njoro River Cave (Kenya) 309, 316
No Carlos (Venezuela) 480
nomads 10, 37–42
    Central Asia 400
    Central Europe 351
    Eurasian steppes 42
    Syria 194
Non Nok Tha bronze workings (South East Asia) 406–7
non-Semitic Sumerian languages 70
Nordic Bronze Age, transport 52–3
Nordic countries, ski and sleigh use 331
Normandy (France) 324
Norovlin-uula burial site (Mongolia) 429
North Africa, pastoral population emergence 37
North America 440–1, 453–5, 453–60, **454**
    Archaic culture 440–1, 453–60
North Caucasian, languages 89
North semitic 77

Northern Asia 421–31
Northern Europe 373–80
    fishing and hunting 324–6
    percussion instruments 112
    religion and art 382–91
    rock art 386–7
Norway 325, 374
Noua culture (Eastern Europe) 361
Noulet, J. B. 406
Nova Zagora site (Europe) 346
novels, Egypt, Middle Kingdom 129
Novgorodova, E. A. 430, 431
Nubia **119**
    A-Group culture **Pl.26**
    culture 129–32, 139–40, 302
    Egypt 138–44
    Fortress of Buhen **Pl.27**
    geography 130, 138
    language 73
    temple of Wadi es Sebua **Pl.34**
    wildlife 130
Nubians, physiology 138–9
numeral systems **Pl.6**, 24–5, 76
numerology, Babylon 22
Núñez, L. 443, 510–22
Nuñez Regueiro, V. 481
Nuraghi culture (Sardinia) 340
Nurrum Sin, King of Akkadia 226
Nusanto Maritime Trade Network (Central Asia) 409

O-Luan-Pi Park site (Taiwan) 408–9
Oates, J. 239, 243
Oaxaca Valley (Mexico) 441, 464
Obediente, M. S. 440–4, 476–84
Obelisk temple (Syria) 195
Obenga, T. 138–44, 299
objets d'art, Early Bronze Age 207
Obobogo (Yaounde Africa) 306
Oceania (Central Asia) 411
ochre-coloured pottery (OCP), Post-Indus Cultures 271–2
Ochre-grave culture (Central Europe) 351
O'Connell, J. F. 411, 433, 438
Oded, B. 202
Odyssey 104, 164, 219–20
Oelsner, J. 184, 189
Ofrendas, Chavín pottery 451
Okladnikov, A. P. 422, 426–8
Old Copper Culture
    Lake Forest Archaic 456
    North America 441
Old Egyptian language 72
Old English language 84
Old Persian language 75–6
Old Prussian language 80
Old Testament, Book of Daniel 50
Oliveros, J. A. 463
Olmec culture (Mexico) 73
    art 111, 447–8, **448**
    chronology (table) **468**
    mouth art 467
    pottery **467**, **471**, 473
    society 442, 446
Olmstead, A. T. 186, 189
Olympia (Aegean) 164

Olympic Games 93
Oman (Persian Gulf) 239, 241–2, 258
Oppenheim, A. L. 30, 35, 173, 180, 189, 190, 257
oracles
    bone, Yin ruins (China) **Pl.118**
    Chavín temple (Andes) 505
    inscriptions, Shang 291
oral traditions 92–3
Ordos region (China) 227, 295
    Orient
    Iron Age beginnings 58
    ironworking technology 58–9
Orinoco (Venezuela) 443, 481
ornaments
    gold, Middle Bronze Age (Romania) **Pl.145**
    Mongolia 429
    Philippines 409
Orontes River (Syro-Palestine) 199
Ortega, E. 483
Orthmann, W. 212
Oshara tradition (Americas) 455
Oshibkina, S. V. 361
Osinovoe Ozero culture (Siberia) 422
Osten, - von der 207
Otomani culture 330, 346
Otomani/Fuzesabony-Unetice period, Central Europe 353–4
Otroschenko, V. V. 361
Otuma site (Peru) 497
Owen, D. I. 184, 189
ownership, emergence 4, 9
ox-drawn plough, Ethiopia 307

Pacific 401–13
Page, D. L. 158
Pakistan
    Indus civilization 247
    Post-Indus Cultures 266, 268, 276
    pre-Vedic religion 101
palaces
    Erlitou culture 283
    King Zimri-Lim, Syria 195
    Kish 27, 174
    Mesopotamia 174
    Sargon II, Khorsabad **Pl.I**
    Shang City (China) **Pl.III**
    Syria 192–3, 195
Palaeoarctic tradition (North America) 453
Palaites (Anatolia) 219
Palau (Micronesia) 412
Palawan cave sites (Philippines) 409
Paleolithic Age, Huanghe Valley 280
Palermo Stone 28, 119, 120, 130
Palestine **192**, 193–201
Palmieri, A. 207
Palongcheng site (China) 295
Pampa region (Argentina) 490–1
Pan-Hellenic culture (Aegean) 164
Panajitov, I. 359
Panama
    Aguadulce rock shelter 479
    Bicromo en Zonas tradition 479
    Cerro Mangote site 449, 479
    Cerro Punta civilization 479
    food production 442, 479–80

    Mongarillo site 479
    pottery 479
Pandya, S. 256
Panionion, Aegean 164
Pantalica culture, second millennium BC 339
Pantel, A. G. 483
Pantheon of Ugarit (Syro-Palestine) 200
Papua New Guinea, Melanesia 411
papyrus 72, 95, 129
    Turin 133
Papyrus Harris 136
Paracin culture (Europe) 348
Paradis, L. 469
Paraíso site (Peru) 497
Paraná River 489
Paranaíba (Itaparica) culture (Brazil) 488, 489
parchment 95
Pargiter, F. E. 11
Parkhai cemetery (Central Asia) 395
Parmenides 93
Parpola, A. 260, 274
Parpola, S. 189, 190
Parr, P. 244
Parrot, A. 189, 190, 191, 195
Pastaza phase (Brazil) 482
pastoralism 37
    Africa 313
    Central Europe 352
    nomadic, Eurasia 38
Pasupati seal (Harappa) 260
Patagonia (Argentine) 490–1, 510
Patanne, E. P. 410
Patterson, T. 443–4, 497, 509
Pauranic history, India 11
Pautreau, J. P. 368, 372
Pawley, A. 401
Peacock, B. A. V. 410–11
Pearsall, D. 493, 509
peasants, late Bronze Age 32
peat bog mummies, Northern Europe 324
Pecica culture (Carpathian basin) 353
Pedro Garcia complex (Venezuela) 481
Peirce, C. S. 66
Peleset group, Syria and Palestine 201
Pelon, O. 147, 148
Penard stage, United Kingdom 369
pendant, cast bronze (Hungary) **Pl.152**
'Peoples of the Sea' 58, 59, 221
Pérez, J. 521, 523
Pericles 93
Period of Transformation, Iran 227–8
perioikoi, fringe dwellers 162
Peroni, R. 334–44
Persian Gulf 50, 224, 226–7
Persian Makran Waghador megalithic culture 272
Persians, Cyprus 169
Peru 492, 494–506, 510
    Las Aldas site 496, 499
    Chavín art 111
    Los Chinos site 496
    crafts 495
    Las Culebras site 496, 498
    cultivation 444
    diet 494
    dwellings 497

Huaca Prieta 494–8
 Otuma site 497
 pottery 500
 priests 498
 pyramids 496–7, 499, 500
 religion 499
 Rio Soco site 497
 Sechin Alto 500
 textiles 495, 497
pestles and stone plates (Venezuela) 481
Petrie, Sir William Flinders 6, 140
petroglyphs 65, 385, 386
Pettinato, G. 241
Phaistos Disk (Greece) Pl.41
pharaohs see Egypt
Philippines, Central Asia 409
Phillipson, D. W. (United Kingdom) 299–319
Phoenicians
 Aegean 159, 163
 alphabet 67, 73–4, 77–8, Pl.79
 cities 202
 Cyprus 169
 maritime trade 21
 Mediterranean 56, 342–3
 trade 202
Phrygian culture
 Anatolia 221
 fibulae (Turkey) Pl.100
 vase (Turkey) Pl.99
 vessel (Turkey) Pl.98
Phu Lon copper mine (Mekong) 406
Phung Nguyen culture (South East Asia) 405
physico-chemical dating 6
Piaçaguera site (Brazil) 487
Piana, E. L. 490, 491
Piankhy, King of Nubia 136
P'iankova, L. T. 399
pictographs 53, 74
 Argentine Patagonia 490–1
 China 78
 North American Indian 66
 Uruk (Iraq) 54
Piggot, V. C. 406
Piña Chan, R. 470
Pinto, M. 450
Piperno, D. 442
Piperno, M. 178, 181
Pirak (Iran) 228, 230
Pirenne, J. 243–4
Pit-Grave culture (Central Europe) 352
Pitkin, H. 65, 69
'pitted-ware' culture (Scandinavia) 374
Plains Archaic (Americas) 457
plant cultivation 6
 Andes 492
 Archaic period 441, 444, 460
 Argentina 490
 Australia 433
 Brazil 489
plant gathering
 Andean Western valleys 520
 Archaic period 441, 444, 460
plants
 medicinal, Brazil 488
 processing, South America 478, 480

Plato 93
Platon, N. 146, 148, 154, 157–8
Playa phases, Meso-American civilization 463
Pleiner, R. 17, 22
Pleistocene ice-age (South East Asia) 401–2
Pliny 17, 138, 331
ploughs
 changing design 41
 development 38, 40–1
 Europe 326
 invention 5
Podzuweit, C. 212
poetry
 Aegean 163–4
 Egypt, Old Kingdom 128
 epic 47, 93, 100
 Meso-America 462
Pohorilenko, A. 467
Poisson, G. 89
Poitou marsh (France) 321
Poland
 Lausitz culture 378, 379
 Unetice culture 375
poleis
 Aegean 162
 monarchy 46
polis
 Aegean 161–2
 China 43
politics
 Chavín period (Andes) 503
 Egypt 121, 128–9
 Meso-American Civilization 472–3
 Mesopotamia 171–3, 176, 178
 Mycenaeans 153
 Southern Europe 334–5
 Syria and Palestine 198, 201–3
pollen analysis
 Indus civilization 249
 South East Asia 404
Polome, E. Indo-European 84
Poltavkin Centre (Eastern Europe) 359
Polynesia 37, 413
Ponce, C. 521, 523
Ponce Sanginés, C. 508, 509
Pookajorn, S. 404
Popova, T. B. 360–1
populations
 Archaic period 457
 Australia 435
 Eastern Europe 357
 preliterate 3
 United Kingdom 324, 365
 Western Asia 15
Port aux Choix cemetery (Newfoundland) 455, 458
Porter Weaver, M. 470
Poseidon sanctuary (Aegean) 164
Posner, R. 66, 69
Possehl, G. L. 45, 263
post glacial cultural traditions, Arctic and sub Arctic 453
Post-Indus civilization 266–78
 copper hoards 269
 Painted Grey Ware 275
post-Kassite period (Mesopotamia) 185–6
post-Mature Harappan phenomenon (Iran) 227

post-Pleistocene neolithic development (Meso-America) 463–5
Postgate, N. 175, 180, 188, 190
potatoes, Andes 516–17, 521
Potemkina, T. M. 398
Potier, M.-H. 234
potters wheel, China 284
pottery
    Achallan-type 493
    Afghanistan 236
    Africa 301, 303–10, 308, 315–16
    Americas 442–3, 449–51
    Andes 482, 492, 493, 496, 498, 499
    Andronovo culture 425
    Arabian Peninsula 239, 241–2
    Argentina 490
    Balkans 346–7
    bell-shaped, France **365**
    Brazil 481–2, 489
    Central Asia 393–6, 398–9, 403–4, 408–12
    Central Europe 350
    Chalmun, Korea 415
    China **Pl.110**, 281–2, 284–7, 290, 293, 295
    Crete 146
    East Africa 309–10
    Europe 327, 347–9
    Harappan 256
    invention 4
    Iran 225, 228–31, 229
    Japan **Pl.160**, 418
    Korea 415–17
    li (China) **Pl.126**
    Meso-America 464
    Mongolia 428, 429
    Olmec culture **467**, 473
    Panama 479
    Peru 500
    pioneering, New World 39
    Puerto Hormiga, South America 478–9
    Scandinavia 374
    South America 476, 478
    Tumulus period 355
    Uruk period 177
    Valdivian (Ecuador) 450, 478, 493, 498
    Venezuela 481
Potts, D. 240–2
Poulson, J. 412
Poursat, J. C. 155, 158
Poverty Point (Mississippi) 441, 459
Powell, B. B. 163
power relations, Assyria 183
power sharing 9
Pozdniakovo culture (Eastern Europe) 361
Pozorski, S. 496, 509
Pozorski, T. 496, 509
prayer, Mesopotamia 100
pre-Harappan, Indus civilization 253
pre-Lusatian culture, Tumulus period 355
pre-Vedic religion, India and Pakistan 101
prehistory 3
preliterate populations 3
Pretty, G. L. 437
Preziosi-Getz, P. 146, 148
Priam 219, 220
Priese, K. H. 142, 144

priests 31–2, 98, 99, 498
primates, first 3
private sector, Egypt 44
proper names 11
prophets 10–11
proto-Chinese 79
proto-Classic phase, Americas 446
proto-Dravidian language 67, 260
proto-Elamite language 67
proto-Elamite period (Iran) 224–7
proto-Greeks, Aegean 152
proto-Indic writing 67
proto-Indo-European culture 85–6
proto-Indo-European languages 81–2, 81–9
proto-Indo-Hittite 84
proto-Indoaryan language 67
proto-Mayan, languages 70
proto-Palatial period, Crete 157
proto-Syrian urban culture 192
proto-urban cultures
    Indus civilization 251
    Sicily and Italy 341
Prous, A. 489, 491
Pryakhin, 360
public works, Chavín period (Andes) 500, 502–3
Pucara ceremonial centre, Andes 521
Puerto Hormiga (South America) 477–9
Puglisi, S. M. 207
Punjab (Indus civilization) 253–4
Punt (Africa) 302, 314
Purukusta of the Purus, Peninsular India 277
Puzur-Kutik-Inshushinak, ruler of Awan 226
Pye, M. E. 463
pygmies (Zaire) 314
Pylos, Aegean 153
Pyramid Texts 121, 125, 128
pyramids
    Americas 442
    Andes 521
    Egypt 6, **Pl.17**, 108, 123–4
    Peru 496–7, 499, 500
Pythagorean mathematics 25

Qadesh (Tell Nebi Mend) 199
Qala'at al Bahrain, Arabian Peninsula 242–3
Qatna (Mishrife) **Pl.77**, 199
Qijia culture (China) 285–6
Qijiaping site (China) 285
Qinglongquan III cultures, China 286
Qinweijia cemetery (China) 286
quanat technique 242, 399
Quanrong tribes (China) 292
quasialphabetic script 75
queenship, Hittites 215
Quetta Valley (Baluchistan) 251
Qujialing culture, Huanghe Valley 286
Qurayyah (Arabian Peninsula) 244

radiocarbon dating 254, **512**
Raffino, R. 519, 523
Rahman, A. 266–78
Rahman Dheri, Gomal Valley 252
Raikes, R. L. 249
Rainey, A. F. 198
Rajasthan (Indus) 253–4

Rajpur Parsu copper hoards 271
Ramaswamy, C. 249
Ramesses I, King of Egypt 135
Ramesses II, King of Egypt **Pl.35**, 135, 142, 199
Ramesses III, King of Egypt 136, 201
Ramesses IV-XI, Kings of Egypt 136, 142
Ramesses V, King of Egypt **Pl.36**, 136, 142
Ramesside period, Egypt 135
Rancho Peludo site (Venezuela) 481
Ranere, A. 442, 479
Rao, S. R. 256, 259–61
Ratnagar, S. 256–7
Ravines, R. 513, 523
Reade, J. E. 188, 190
Real Alto site (Andes) 477, 493
Rector, M. 65–8, 95–6
Red Corded Ware Culture (Asia) **404**, 408–9, 458
Red Ochre Culture, Archaic period 458
Red Sea, minerals 302
red ware (China) 283
red ware pottery (Arabian Peninsula) 241
Reed, W. 244
Reichel-Dolmatoff, G. 443, 449, 477–8
Reilly, F. K. 470
Reinecke, W. F. 23–6
Reisner, G. A. 130, 132, 139, 140, 144
reliefs
    Alaca Hüyük city walls (Turkey) **Pl.90**
    Deir el Bahari **302**
    rock, Hittite sanctuary (Turkey) **Pl.91**
religions
    see also cults; monotheism
    Achaean and Mycenaean 104
    Aegean 162–3
    Africa 317
    Americas 446–52
    Andes 504, 522
    animal worship 428
    art 98–105
    Babylonian 99–100
    China 104–5, 291–2, 294
    Cretan-Mycenaean 104, 158
    Cyclades 158
    development 4, 11, 98–105
    Druids 332
    Egypt 101, 121, 124–5
    Europe 332, 334–5, 371, 377–8, 382, 384–91
    Harappan culture 260–1
    Hattic 210, 211
    Hittites 100, 216
    Homer 163
    Indo-European 102–4
    Meso-American 409, 462, 470
    Mesopotamia 100, 175
    Minoan 104
    Mongolia 428
    Mycenaean 104
    Northern Europe 382–91
    oral traditions 92–3
    Palestine 200–1
    Peru 499
    priests 31–2, 98, 99, 498
    proto-Indo-European 86
    rock art, Europe 384–91
    shamanism 389, 427

solar beliefs 98
Sumerian 99–100
supernatural 4–5, 10
Syria 200–1
Renaissance, spelling reform 68
Renfrew, C. 143, 144, 145, 148
    Asiatic hypothesis 89
    dating debates 28, 29
    language origins 83, 86–7, 88, 90, 350
Renger, J. 179, 180
rhetoric, oral tradition 92–3
rhetra, enactment oracle 161
Rhine Valley 324
Rhône culture 337
Rib-Addi of Byblos, Syria and Palestine 199
Ries, J. 98–105
Rift Valley (Africa) 300, 306
Rigveda document (Indus) 276
Rimantene, - 360
Río Guayas (Ecuador) 492
Rio Soco site (Peru) 497
Ritchie, W. A. 456–9
rites of passage, Andes 522
ritual objects
    China 291
    Hattian standard (Turkey) **Pl.80**, **Pl.81**
    Venezuela 480
    vessels
        Hittite style (Turkey) **Pl.89**
        Late Minoan (Greece) **Pl.51**
        rock crystal, Late Minoan (Greece) **Pl.52**
        silver, Turkey **Pl.92**
rituals
    Akkadians 100
    Chavín temple 505
    dance 113
    grave, Northern Europe 376–7
    Northern Europe 380
    oral tradition 93
Riverine Archaic (North America) 456–7
Riverton culture, Wabash Valley 456
roads 56
Roaf, M. 239
Robbins, M. 458
Roberts, N. 38, 43
Roccati, A. 130, 131, 132
rock art 4, 6, 107, 108
    Africa **Pl.136**, 301, 303, 305, 307–8, 312, 316–17, **318**
    Amenemhat III **Pl.18**
    Arabian Peninsula 239
    Arakoukam, Algeria **Pl.130**
    Armenia **55**
    Australia **Pl.16**, **Pl.162**, 436
    Bronze Age ships **Pl.12**, **Pl.159**
    Celtic 388, 390
    dance 113
    Egypt **Pl.133**
    eland and hunter, Transkei region (South Africa) **Pl.136**
    Ethiopia **307**
    Europe 383, 384–9, **384**
    Gobi Desert 428–9
    Hallstat culture 387, 388, 390
    Hittite sanctuary **Pl.91**
    Italy **Pl.137**, **Pl.156**, 336, 385

Jubba (Saudi Arabia) **Pl.103**
Karasuk period 426
magic 389
Magnificent Gallery (Australia) **Pl.16**
Northern Europe 325, 377–8
ox-drawn plough **308**
picture language 385
purpose and meaning 387–9
Scandinavia 380
shamans 389
ships 331, 380, 386–7, 388
social role 389–91
South Africa **312**
Sweden **Pl.159**
Tasmania **Pl.161**
Tassili **Pl.129**
Ulzit *somon* 428–9
rock sanctuary, Kurangum 229
rock shelters
    South Africa 311, 316–17
    South East Asia 403–4
    West Africa 305
Rodriguez, M. E. 468, 480
Rogers, D. 477
Rollig, W. 200, 202–3
Romance languages 76
Rome
    birth 341–2
    empire 47
    Indo-Europeans 80, 104
Romero, L. A. 480
Romulus 103–4
Rondon, J. 480
Ronquillo, W. P. 409
Ronquin tradition (Venezuela) 481
rope-making, Egypt 21, **21**
Roquin Barrancas tradition (Venezuela) 449
Rosenberg, C. 498
Rosetta Stone 72
Ross, E. J. 251
rotating wheel, China 282
Rothenberg, B. 16, 22
Rouse, I. 449, 480–1
Roux, G. 170, 182–9
Rowe, J. 451
royalty 100
    see also kingships
    Aegean 161
    China 45
    divine powers 98–9
    Israel 102
    Peninsular India 277
Ruiperez, M. C. 154
Rupar, Harappan burials 261
Russian Federation 325
Rutkowski, B. 158
Rzucewo culture, Bay of Gdansk 374

Saba 243
Sabatinovka culture (Eastern Europe) 361
sacral kingship 98–9
Sacred Lake (Syria) 193
sacrifice
    Indo-Europeans 103
    Peninsular India 277–8

Shang dynasty 291
Sader, H. 202
Safronov, V. A. 87, 89
Saggs, H. W. F. 186, 190
Sahara (Africa) 300–3, 313
sail, invention 5
St John River sites (Venezuela) 481
Sakellariou, A. 159, 161
Sakellariou, M. 152–64
Sakkara, tomb reliefs 21
Salamis (Cyprus) **Pl.62**, 169
Sali, S. A. 270
Salim, M. 276
Sall, B. 299
salmon fishing, North America 453–5
Salonen, A. 176, 180
salt
    Africa 314
    Europe 329
    sea 368
Samaria 62
Samaritan alphabet 77
samhita text, Peninsular India 276
Samoa, Polynesia 413
San Lorenzo (Gulf of Mexico) 442, 468, 470
San people (South Africa) 311–12
sanctuaries
    Aegean 164
    Central Asia 394
    Eastern Europe 361
    Syria 191–2
Sandars, N. K. 201
Sangmeister, E. 364
Sankalia, H. D. 270
Sanoja, M. 442–3, 477, 480–1, 483
Sanskrit languages 70, 79
Santoni, M. 266
Santoro, C. 519, 520, 523
Sapalli phase (Bactria) 396
Saqqara, tombs 133
Sarai Kala (Indus) 252, 267
Sarasvati (India) 276
Sardinia 340
Sargon, King of Akkad 48–9, 172, 177, 226, 257
Sargon II, King of Assyria **Pl.1**, 60–1, 62, 63, 64, 230–1
Sargon the Great, bronze head from Nineveh **Pl.63**
Sarianidi, V. 232–7
Sarianidi, V. I. 392–3, 396–9
Sarkar, S. S. 274
Sauer, J. 242
Saussure, F. de 66
savannah regions (Congo basin) 310
Säve-Söderbergh, T. 129, 132, 140, 144
Savithri, R. 257
Savvateev, J. A. 387, 391
Sawalda culture 269–70
Sayles, E. B. 440
scalpulimancy, China 282, 294
Scandinavia
    ancient monuments 373
    arrowheads and battleaxes 374
    Central Europe 352
    pottery 374
    rock art 389
    weaponry 375–6

Schachermeyr, F. 201
Schiappacasse, V. 516, 523
Schleswig-Holstein, weaponry 375–6
Schliemann, H. 6, 144, 206, 209
Schmitz, P. I. 443
Schneckenberg-Glina culture (South-Eastern Europe) 346
Schrapp, - 37
Schubart, H. 366, 367, 372
science
    see also technology
    Assyria 189
    Bronze Age foundations 23
    development 23–6
    Europe 334–7
    Greek 24
    medical, beginnings 25
    Neolithic Age 23
    prehistory 3
scribes
    Assyria 189, 213
    Egypt **Pl.8**, **Pl.19**, 22, **Pl.30**
scripts *see* writing
sculpture
    Bronze Age, Northern Europe 378
    Cyclades and Crete 158
    Egypt 108–9
    Meso-America **467**
    Mesopotamia 109
    Northern Europe 380
    Olmec 470
    statues
        Enkomi (Cyprus) **Pl.61**
        Goudea **Pl.11**
        Lanzón (Andes) 504
        menhir, Mas d'Azaïs **Pl.15**
        pharaonic Egypt 121
        Ramses V (Egypt) **Pl.36**
        Tuthmosis III **Pl.29**
    statuettes
        Abikhil **Pl.20**
        bronze, Europe 383–4
        bronze male (Greece) **Pl.57**, **Pl.58**
        bronze (Quatna) **Pl.77**
        female, Middle Geometric (Greece) **Pl.54**
        Greek snake goddess **Pl.50**
        gypsum (Eshnunna) **Pl.67**
        Hattian **Pl.86**
sea power, Greece 56
sea shell implements, Cuba 483
sea-ports, Indus civilization 248
seals
    Central Asia 399
    cylinder
        Akkadia **Pl.68**
        Babylonia 184
        Bactria **Pl.102**
        Kalibangan **Pl.107**
        Mesopotamia 109
        Sumirapa of Tuba **Pl.73**
        Syria **Pl.72**, **Pl.74**, **Pl.75**, 194
        Dilmun type (Kuwait) **Pl.106**
        gold, Bactria, North Afghanistan **Pl.101**
        Iran 224–5, 227
        Pasupati (Harappa) 260
Sebekhotep, King of Thebes 133

Sebeknefru, Queen, Egypt 133
Sechin Alto pyramid (Peru) 500
sedentism 37, 308, 463
Seidl, U. 184, 190
Seima-Turbino type (Eastern Europe) 361
Seistan (Afghanistan) 232, 236, 250
Sekenenre, King of Egypt 134
Semenov, V. A. 424, 431
Semites
    Nile delta 133
    religion 99, 100–1
    Syria 73, 191, 193
Semitic languages 70, 73–7, 83
Seneca 138
Sennacherib, King of Assyria 50, 60, 230–1
sepulchres, Egypt 124, 127, 128
serfdom, Assyria 34
Serovo culture (Siberia) 422
Sesostris I, King of Egypt 22, 131, 138
Sesostris III, King of Egypt 27, 127, 141
Setaou 142
Sethnakhte, King of Egypt 136
Seti I, King of Egypt 135, 142
Seti II, King of Egypt 135
settlements
    Aegean 143–4
    Andes 492–3, 495–7, 510, 513–16, **514**, **515**, 519, 520
    Archaic period 458–9
    Brazil 486–7, 487
    corded-ware, Northern Europe 374
    Etruria, Early Iron Age 341
    Europe 326–9, 363, 374, 379
    Indus 45, 247–9, 253
    Jomon culture (Japan) 417–18
    Koban cultures 363
    Korea 415, 417
    Mongolia 428
    Northern Asia 423
    Otomani/Fuzesabony-Unetice period 354
    Palestine 195
    Peruvian coast 494
    Scandinavia 376
    Siberia 421, 422–3
    South Africa 316
Shabaka stele 98
Shaffer, - 232, 236
shaft and chamber culture (Eastern Europe) 359, 361
Shah Billawal culture 272
Shah, U. P. 256
Shahdad (Iran) 225–6
Shahri Sokhta (Iran) 225–6
Shalmaneser I, King of Assyria 59
Shalmaneser III, King of Assyria 59, 230
Shalmaneser V, King of Ashur 50
shamanism
    Glazkovo culture 427
    rock art 389
Shamesh **Pl.70**
Shami Damb londo ware 269
Shamshi Adad I of Assyria 227
Shanbei culture (China) 287
Shandong I Longshan complex (China) 281
Shandong Longshan culture (China) 284–5
Shang City (China) 45, **Pl.111**, 289
Shang Dynasty (China) 45, 289–92

calendar 291–2
    culture 24, 280, 282–4, 286, 288, 291
Shang Longshan culture 284
Shang state (China) 286, 291
Shang-Zhou civilization 286
Shaposhnikova, O. G. 359
Sharafutdinova, - 361
Sharer, J. 466
Sharma, R. S. 274
Shaw, T. 303
shell adzes, Micronesia 412
shell deposits, Venezuela 480
shell middens, Senegambia 305
shell mounds
    Brazilian coast 487
    Korea 415
shellfish-gatherers
    Andes 492, 493, 494
    Brazil 486–8
shepherd-farmers, Andes 517–18, 520, 521
Sheri Khan Taraki occupation, Indus civilization 253
Sherrat, A 87
Sherrat, S. 87
Sherratt, A. G. 37–42
Shi Huangdi, Emperor of China 78
Shield Archaic, Boreal Archaic 455–6
Shimashki dynasty (Iran) 226–7
ships
    building 53
    rock art Pl.12, Pl.159, 331, 380, 386–7, 388
    rock painting Pl.159
    Scandinavia Pl.159, 380, 386–7, 388
    wrecks 369
Shiversky stage (Eastern Siberia) 427
Shixia culture (South China) 287
Shnirelman, V. 89
Shortugai (Afghanistan) 232
Shoshenq, King of Egypt 136
Shulgi, King of Ur 49
Shutruk dynasty, Iran 229
Shutruk-Nakhkhunte II, King of Assyria 230
Siberia
    Afanasievo culture 423–4, 424
    Neolithic culture 421
    Okunev culture 424, 425
    Shiversky stage 428
Sicily 338, 339, 341
silk, Shang dynasty 291
silk road, Iran 227
Similaun Man 324, 325, 336
Simoes, M. 443, 481–2
Sind (Indus)
    Harappan trade 257
    Indus civilization 248, 251
    Post-Indus Culture 267
Singh, G. 249
Singh, P. 270–1
Sino-Tibetan language group 77
Siret, L. 366
Siswal (India) 254
situla, silver Urartian Pl.97
Siwa culture (China) 295
skiing equipment 53, 331
Skrdstrup woman 377
slash and burn agriculture

Americas 442
    Eastern Europe Middle Bronze Age 360
    Meso America 462
slaves
    Shang dynasty 291
    Zhou dynasty 294
sledges
    Egypt 21
    Nordic countries 331
smelting, lowland South East Asia 407
Smenkhare, King of Egypt 135
Smith, B. D. 460
Smith, C. 443
'Snake Goddess', Late Minoan statuette (Greece) Pl.50
Snarkis, M. 479
Snefru, King of Nubia 130
Snodgrass, A. 201
Snodgrass, A. M. 18, 22, 159, 163
snow, long distance travel 53
social development 6, 7, 44–7, 524
    Andean coast 495
    Central Europe 353–4
    Meso-America 447
social relations 8–9
society
    Anatolia 207
    Andronovo culture (Siberia) 426
    Australia 432, 438
    Babylonia 183–5
    Central Asia 393
    China 291, 294
    Europe 332
    Kerma (Nubia) 131
    Meso-American Civilization 472–3
    rock art, Europe 389
    Southern Europe 334–7
    stratification 4, 5, 8, 9
    urban, emergence of 15
    Valdivian (Andes) 493
socio-economics
    Europe 337–8, 383
    Iron Age 33
socio-politics
    Africa 317
    Bronze Age 30–3
    Iron Age 33–5
    Pucara (Andes) 521
    Syria and Palestine 199–201
Socrates 93
soldiers, model, 11th dynasty (Egypt) Pl.25
Solheim, W. G. II 401–13
Sollberger, E. 171, 181
Solomon, King of Israel 102, 136, 203
soma drink, Peninsular India 277
Somalia 307
Sono, T. 450, 498, 509
Sood, R. K. 249
Sophists 93
sorcerers, rock art 389
sorghum food, Africa 301
Sosnitsa culture (Eastern Europe) 361
South Africa 108, 310–13, 314–15
South America 476–84
    Camelidae species 519
    Eastern region 486–91

northern 442–4
South-West 510–22
western region 492–508
South East Asia 401–3, **402**, 408–13
  lowlands 403–5
  uplands 403–5
Southern Europe
  cultural development 343
  second millennium BC 337–40
  third millennium BC 334–7
Southern Mongoloids (Central Asia) 401
Spain 337, 341
Spalinger, A. 199
Sparta (Aegean) 162, 164
spears, Australia 436
Spencer, R. 440–1
Sphinx, Giza (Egypt) 108
Spiennes (Belgium) 328
Spondylus mollusc, Andes 498–9
Spriggs, M. 412
Stacul, G. 267–8
Stager, L. E. 201, 203
staging posts, Israel 56
'Standard of Ur' **Pl.69**
Starostin, S. A 89
state, Zhou (China) 286, 289, 292, 294
states
  beginnings 161
  central Andes 500
  development 4, 7, 9–10, 11, 44
  emergence 524
  Iran 224
  Mesopotamia 46–7
statues/statuettes see sculptures
Stavrianopoulou E. 153
steale, sculpture, Meso-America 448
steatite seals, Harappan arts 259
Stein, A. 249, 269
Stein, D. 185, 190
Steinkeller, P. 172, 181
stelae
  Djedkhonouioufankh, musician playing harp **Pl.21**
  Estremadura (Spain) 370
  Naran-Sin **Pl.64**
  Neo-Hittite Aramean art (Turkey) **Pl.95**
  Shabaka 98
  Val Camonica (Italy) **Pl.157**
steppes
  Central Asia 398–9
  Central Europe 351–2
  China 287
  cultures 89, 351–2, 357, 359
  Eastern Europe 357, 359
  Eurasia 42
  invasions 90
  theory 89
Stirling, M. 466
stock-breeding
  Afansievo tribes 424
  Andronovo tribes 425
  development 4, 5
  Eastern Europe 359, 361
  Northern Asia and Mongolia 431
Stolper, M. 183, 189
Stoltman, J. B. 459

stone artefacts
  Africa 303–4, 306, 309
  Archaic period, Americas 441–2, 456, 458
  Argentine Pampa 490–1
  lowland South East Asia 407
  Okunev culture 424
  rasp and potsherd (Kintampo) **305**
  Siberia 422
  Tamsagbulag (Mongolia) 428
stone walled compounds, Africa 303
stone working
  Europe 327
  South Africa 314–16
  tool kit, West Indies 483
Stonehenge (United Kingdom) 23, 98, 107, 324, 332
  astronomers temple 365
  North-East **Pl.5**
  trilithons **Pl.4**
The Story of Sinuhe (Egypt) 129
Stothern, K. 476
Stothert, K. 493, 509
Strabo 17–18, 129, 138
Strettweg (Austria), bronze chariot 107
Strommenger, E. 184, 189, 190
Stronach, D. 187, 190
Strong, W. 495
Struever, S. 460
Subbrao, B. 270
subsidence, settlement patterns 249
subsistence economy
  emergence 37
  Meso-American Civilization 463–4
Sudan (East Africa) 302, 308
Sudas, King of Bharata 276–7
Sukkalmah dynasty 226–7
Sulaiman ranges (Iran) 248
Sulimirski, T. 89
Sumbar cemetery, Bactrian-Margiana archaeological
  complex 398
Sumer
  beginnings of history 27
  calendar 27
  culture 177, 199
  'freedom' law **179**
  gods 99
  measurement 22
  Syria and Palestine 199
Sumerian King List 49, 172, 174, 225
Sumerian languages 71, 73, 75
Sumerian script 72–3, 76, 191
Sumerian-Akkadian dictionaries 76
Sumirapa, King of Tuba, cylinder impression **Pl.73**
Sundara, A. 273
sunflower cultivation 460
supernatural, beliefs 6, 10
Suppiluliumas, King of the Hittites 182, 214, 215
sura drink, Peninsular India 277
Suraj, B. 253, 272
Surkotada (Indus) 254, 256, 261
Susa (Iran) 21, 224–9
Sveshnikov, - 359
Swadling, P. 411
Swat grave culture, Iran 230
Swat Valley, Post Indus culture 267, 275
Sweden 325

battleaxes 374
boat-axe culture 374
pottery 374
Stockhult hoard, Scania **Pl.155**
swords
proto-Hallstattian, United Kingdom 371
Western Europe 369
syllabic scripts, Greece 154
symbols
proto-Indo-European 71–2
rock art, interpretations 390–1
Syria 191–203, **192**
Bronze Age 191–201
city-states 135
cylinder seals **Pl.72, Pl.74, Pl.75**
prince plaque **196**
trade routes 50
Syro-Palestinian coalition 182, 198

Tabon caves (Central Asia) 410
Tadmur (Palmyra), Syria and Palestine 199
Taip I, Bactrian-Margiana archaeological complex 397
Taiwan 408–9
Talamanca phase, Americas 442
Talayots culture (Balearic Islands) 340
Tall-i Malyan walls (Anshan) 226
Taluqan basin (Afghanistan) 233
Tanshishan culture (China) 287
Tanzania 308
Taosi site (China) 281–2
Tapenkeng culture (Taiwan) 408–9
Tarague site (Guam) 412
Tarakai Qila, Bannu basin 253
Tarble, K. 481
Tarragó, M. 519, 523
Tartusi, M. 481
Tasic, N. 345–9
Taylour, W. 155–6
Tazabagyad culture (Central Asia) 398
tazura monuments (Africa) 306
technology
see also science
Aegean 143, 155, 160
Africa 315–17
Central Asia 394
Europe 330–1, 334–7, 383
iron-making 18
Kerma (Nubia) 139
Korea 417
Meso-America 464
Mesopotamia 177
pottery, Anatolia 208
Shang dynasty 290, 292
Urnfield period 355
weights and measures 21–2
writing 21–2
tectonic disturbance 263
Tehucan Valley (North America) 441–2
telestai, landowners 154
Tell Abraq, Arabian Peninsula 241–2
Tell Armar, dagger blade 18
Tell el-Amarna (Egypt) 134, 135
Tell Khuera (Syria) 192
Tell Mardikh (Syria) 192
Tell Yarmouth (Palestine) 193

Tell-el-Daba, Egypt 133
Tello, J. C. 498, 500, 503, 509
tells, Balkans, Europe 345
temples
Americas 442, 450
Andes 498, 499, 503–5
Egypt 123–4, 134
Iran 229
Malta 335
Mesopotamia 173
Syria 194
Wadi es Sebua (Nubia) **Pl.34**
Teopantecuanitlan site (Meso-America) 472
Teotihuacan civilization (Mexico) 45
Tepe Hissar (Iran) 225, 268
Tepe Yahya (Iran) 228
Tepti-ahar, King of Susa and Anshan 228
Tequendama period 477
Terada, K. 498, 509
terracotta, Central Asia 394–5
textiles
Andes 495, 497, 502, 513, 520
Peru 495, 497
Ur 177
Thai language 77
Thailand prehistoric period 403
Thalpi (Uttar Pradesh) grey ware culture 274
Thapar, B. K. 246–64, 253, 266–78
Thapar, R. 270, 274
Thapsos complex (Sicily) 339
theatre, oral tradition 93
Thebes (Egypt) 133, 134, 153
Theocharis, D. R. 143, 144, 148
Theocratic Formative phase, Americas 446
Thermi (Lesbos) 345
Thiel, W. 201
Thieme, P. 85
Thinite period (Egypt) 119–21
Thomsen, M. L. 75
Thracians, Troy VIIb2 220
Thrane, H. 373–80
throne, 'Royal Tomb' at Salamis (Cyprus) **Pl.62**
Tibetans 77
Tibeto-Burman languages 77
Tibeto-Myanmar languages (Central Asia) 401
Tiglath-Pileser I, King of Assyria 184, 202, 220
Tiglath-Pileser III, King of Assyria 50, 63, 202, 230–1
Tigris and Euphrates Valley 171–80
Tikriti, W. 240
Tilemsi Valley, Sahara 303
Tillya Tepe (Afghanistan) 236
Timashqi (Damascus) 199
timber frame culture (Eastern Europe) 361, **362**
time
acceleration 524
measurement 11, 27–9, 122
Timna, metallurgical installations 16
Timna tombs, Arabian Peninsula 242–3
Timor sites (Central Asia) 410
tin 16, 233, 300
Tischler, J. 82
Tisza-Maros settlements, Europe 353
Tiye, Queen of Egypt 134, 141
Tlapacoya art, Americas 447
Tlapacoya-Zohpilco site (Meso-America) 446–7

Tlatico art, Americas 447
tobacco (Brazil) 482
Tocharian language 84
Tochi River (Indus) 253
Togolok phase, Margiana 396
Toldense culture (Argentine) 490
Tolstoy, P. 469
tombs
    Arabian Peninsula 240–1, 243–4
    Central Asia 393, 396, 400
    Ebla (Syria) 194
    Egypt 108, 127–8, 135
    Europe 332, 346, 347–9, 361
    Jiangsu Province 286
    Sakkara 21
    Syria 194
    Taosi (China) **Pl.109**
    Valley of the Kings 108, 135
Tonga (Polynesia) 413
tools
    Afghanistan 234
    Americas 456, 458–9
    Andronovo culture 425
    Argentine Patagonia 490–1
    Australia 435–6
    Brazilian coast 487
    Bronze Age 347
    Central Asia 393, 395
    Europe 328, 332, 383
    iron 59, 60
    Iron Age A 371
    Japan **Pl.160**, 419–20
    Korea 415, 416–17
    Late Bronze Age **Pl.2**
    Majiayao culture 285
    Meso America 464, 477, 480
    Mongolian tribes 429
    Neolithic, Siberia 421, 422, 423
    Northern Asia 423
    Scandinavia, Bronze Age 376
    Shandong Longshan culture 284
    Siberia 423, **427**
    South East Asia 408–10
    Tamsagbulag stone 428
    Valdivian (Andes) 493
    Venezuela 480
topography, Central Asia 392
torres culture, Corsica 340
Tosi, M. 178, 181, 240–1, 258
totemism, rock art 389
towns, Bactrian-Margiana archaeological complex 397
Toynbee, Sir Arnold 11
trade
    Aegean 143, 159, 160–1
    Africa 302
    Anatolia 213
    Andes 520, 521, 522
    Assyrian Empire 49–50, 63–4, 213
    Beaker People 365
    caravan, Andes 521, 522
    development 5, 8, 9
    Egypt 63
    Europe 321, 331–2, 338
    Harappan culture 257–8
    Hittites 216

    Iran 227
    Kassite Babylonia 184
    'Land of Punt' **302**
    long distance 52–7, 302
    merchants 32, 56
    Meso-America 473
    Mesopotamia 48, 177–8, 178, 179
    Mycenaea 338
    North America 455
    Palestine 196, 200
    Peru 500
    Philippines 409–10
    South Africa 314–15
    Syria 191–2, 193–5, 200
    Troy II 208
    Western Asia 62–3
Trandiliense hunters (Argentine) 490
transitional groups, Eastern France 369
transport 20–1
    boats 21
    Europe 331
    Okunev culture 425
    proto-Indo-European 86
    sledges 21, 331
    states **52–6**
    wheel 20–1
    wheeled vehicles 21
trappers, Scandinavian rock art 389
travel
    long distance 52
    merchants 56
    pictographic 53
    snow 53
treaties
    Aramaen states 202
    Hattusidis III and Rameses II 215
tree crops
    development 37
    Mesopotamia **Pl.9**
Treuil, R. 153–4
Trialeti culture (Caucasus) 228
Tribes and Temples book, Meso-America 466
Trigger, B. G. 130, 132
trilithons, Stonehenge (UK) **Pl.4**
Trinidad 482–3
Tripolje, European affinity 89
Trojan Horse 220
Trojan War 164, 205, 219–20
Troy (Anatolia) 144–5
    art 212
    copper and gold metallurgy 16
    cultue 208
    culture 219
    Cyprus culture 168
    discovery 6
    earthquake 219
    ethnic origins 212
    Middle and Late Bronze Age 155
    pottery 206
    town plan **32**
    wooden horse 220
Troy I (Anatolia) 205, 206
Troy II (Anatolia)
    art 212
    culture 208

town plan 208–9, **209**
Troy III (Anatolia) 209
Troy IV (Anatolia) 209
Troy VI (Anatolia) 154, 219
Troy VII (Anatolia) 155
Troy VIIa (Anatolia) 219–20, 349
Troy VIIb (Anatolia) 220, 349
Troy VIII (Anatolia) 220
Trundholm (Denmark) 107, 377, 383, 388
Trziniec culture (Central Europe) 353, 361
Tshitolian tradition (Congo) 310
Tuck, J. A. 455, 458
Tukulti-Ninurta I, King of Assyria 59
tumuli
     Amorica, Middle Bronze Age 367
     Central Europe 354–5
     Mamun pottery period, Korea 417
     Northern Europe 376–7
Turbana period (Americas) 449
Tureng Tepe (Iran) 227–8, 230
Turin papyrus 133
Turner, C. G. 401
Turrialba site, Costa Rica 449
Tutankhamen, King of Egypt 6, 135, 141
     alabaster head rest (Egypt) **Pl.32**
     gilded chapel (Egypt) **Pl.31**
     iron-bladed dagger 59
     treasure 109
Tuthalia IV, King of the Hittites **218**
Tuthmosis I, King of Egypt 134, 141
Tuthmosis II, King of Egypt 134, 139
Tuthmosis III, King of Egypt 134, 139, 141, 143, 182, 198
     statue **Pl.29**
Tuthmosis IV, King of Egypt 134, 198
Tutiscanyo cultures (Americas) 443, 450, 482
Twosnet, Queen of Egypt 135
Tylecote, R. F. 17, 22
Tyre (Syro-Palestine) 64, 202

Ubaid period, Iran 224
Ugarit (Syria) 199
     cuneiform alphabet 77
     Early Bronze Age 193
     goddess of fertility **Pl.78**
     Pantheon 200
Ulf, C. 161
Ulu Burun, wreck 52
Umbú culture, Brazil 489
Umm an-Nar culture (Arabian Peninsula) 226, 240–1
UNESCO, Aswan high dam 130
Unetice culture 353, 354, 375
United Kingdom 324, 328, 332
     Bush Barrow 332
     'Celtic fields' 367–8
     Early Bronze Age 365, **366**
     fossil field systems 41
     Middle Bronze Age 368
     population 324, 365
     Stonehenge **Pl.4**, **Pl.5**, 23, 98, 107, 324, 332, 365
     Wessex culture 365, 372
United Nations 80
Untash-Napirisha, King of Elamite 228–9
Upanishadic thought, India 99
Upanishads 103
Ur

aerial photo **Pl.65**
bronze metallurgy 16
invention of the wheel 21
iron artefacts 18
royal tombs 174, 178, 332
standard **Pl.69**
third dynasty 49, 75, 178, 179, 194, 226–7
Ur-Mammon ziggurat 20
Urabarriu 451
Uralic language 89
Urarta (Anatolia) 81, 221
Urartian civilization (Anatolia) 221
Urartu (Armenia) 50
urban civilizations
     Andes 496, 500, 502
     Bronze Age 30–1
     Central Asia 395–6
     China 39–40, 45
     development 7, 8, 9
     emergence 38, 524
     Indus Valley 40
     New World 39
     Peru 499
     Western Asia 15
     Western Old World 40
urbanization
     Egypt 118
     Greece 144
     Greek cities 104
     Indus civilization 246–7
     Mesopotamia 172–3
     Palestine, Early Bronze Age 193
Urmia lake region, Iran 230
urnfield cultures, Europe 355, 372, 382–3
urns **Pl.153**, 348
Urtak 230
Uruguay River 489
Uruk period (Iran) 177, 224–6
ushabti figures 128

Vadetskaya, E. B. 424, 431
Vakhsh culture (Central Asia) 398
Valchitran gold hoard 347
Valdivia culture
     Ecuador 493, 498
     Guayas basin 450
     Santa Helena Peninsula 476
     tribal society 477
Valley of the Kings (Egypt) 108, 135
Valley of Mexico (Meso-America) 446–7, 450
Valley of Oaxaca (Meso-America) 446–7
Valley of Sarasvati, painted grey ware culture 274
van Beek, G. 242, 245
Vanden Berghe, L. 229
Vandersleyen, C. 141, 144
Vansina, J. 318
Vaphio (Greece) **Pl.45**
Las Varas shell deposits (Venezuela) 480
Vargas, I. 443, 478, 480–1, 483
Varna (Bulgaria) 332, 347
vase, marble, Early Cycladic (Greece) **Pl.39**
Vasilev, I. B. 361
Vasishta, priest 276
vassalage, Egypt 63
Vatin culture (Banat) 346

Vats, M. S. 260, 262, 266
Vedic literature (Peninsular India) 274–6
Vegas hunter-gatherers (South America) 476–82, 493
vegetation, evolution, Europe 321–4
vehicles 21, 42
Veloz Maggiolo, M. 443, 481, 482–3
Venezuela 492
    hunter-gatherers 480–1
    sea level rise 442
Venice (Italy) 321
La Venta (Gulf of Mexico) 442, 470–2
Venus, Valdivian culture 450
Vercoutter, J. 141, 144
Vernus, P. 120, 132
vessels
    bell-shaped, Early Bronze Age (Hungary) Pl.142
    clay, Middle Bronze Age (Hungary) Pl.149
    footed, Middle Bronze Age (Hungary) Pl.147
    hanging, Early Bronze Age (Hungary) Pl.141
    long distance travel 52
    Middle Bronze Age (Hungary) Pl.143
    Olanic art (Mexico) Pl.169
Vickery, K. D. 460
Victory Stela of Naram-Sin Pl.64
Viet Nam (South East Asia) 401
Vietnamese language 78
Vieyra, M. 186, 190
villages
    Americas 440–4
    Andes 492–4, 496, 498, 517–22
    China 45
    development 4
    Europe 326
    Jomon culture (Japan) 418
    Neolithic 5
Villard, P. 58–64
Vinette ceramics, Archaic period 459
Vinkovci culture (Europe) 346
Vishnu Mittre 249, 257
Vistula basin, Central Europe 352
Vlachos, G. 161
Vogt, B. 241–2
Volcanic Sand-Tempered ware (Micronesia) 412
Volga-Urals centres, Late Bronze Age Eastern Europe 360
Volkov, V. V. 429, 430, 431
Voznesenovkoe culture (Siberia) 423
Vucedol culture (Europe) 345–6

Wadi el Barramiya rock engravings 302
Wadi es Sebua temple (Nubia) Pl.34
Wadi Hammamat, slave expeditian 22
Wadi Suq period (Arabian Peninsula) 241–2
Waetzoldt, H. 177, 181
Wagner, E. 481
wagon, Armenia 54
Waldbaum, J. C. 18, 22
wall-paintings
    bull leaping (Greece) Pl.49
    Cyclades and Crete 157
    flotilla from Thera (Greece) Pl.46
    woman, Mycenae (Greece) Pl.43
walls, Aegean 162
Walsh, G. L. 436, 438
Walter, H. 144, 148
Waniek (Melanesia) 411

Wapanucket site (North America) 458–9
warfare
    Egypt 47
    horses 58, 60–1
    Mesopotamia 47
    Peninsular India 277
    professionalization 62
    proto-Indo-European 85–6
Warren, P. 146, 149
warrior king myth 61
warrior stelae, Estremadura (Spain) 370
warriors 31
    Bronze Age 354
    Bronze and Early Iron Age 61
    Late Bronze Age Europe 341
wars 4, 5
    chariots, Central Asia 399
    Egypt, 17th dynasty 133, 134
    Nebuchadnezzar I 229
wealth
    centralization, late Bronze Age 31
    Egypt 118
weaponry
    Andronovo culture 425
    Australia 435–6
    Central Europe 351
    Europe 327, 331, 332, 341
    iron 18, 59
    Mamun pottery period, Korea 417
    megalithic cultures 273
    Neolithic culture, Siberia 421
    Northern Europe 375–6
    Peninsular India 277
    rock art 385–6, 387
    Scandinavia 375
    Schleswig-Holstein 375–6
    Southern Europe 336
    Tumulus period 355
    Urnfield period 355
    Western Europe 368
weaving, invention 4
Webb, W. S. 457–9
Wedel, W. R. 457
Wedt, W. E. 497
weights and measures
    development 15
    Greek 154
    Harappan culture 258
    new techniques 21–2
    Sumer 22
Weisgerber, G. 243, 245, 258
Welch, D. 407
well, Alto Salaverry (Peru) 499
Wen Wang, Count of the West 292–3
Wenamun (Unamun) adventures, Egyptian tale 201
Wessex culture (United Kingdom) 365, 372
West Indies, food production 482–3
West Semitic language 76, 76
Western Asia
    Assyrian ascendency 58
    astronomy 25
    economic changes 58–9
    farming development 38
    Harappan trade 257
    horse domestication 60

iron introduction 58
mathematics 24–5
medical science 25
pastoralist lifestyle 37
political changes 185
population expansion 15
power relations 183
socio-economic structure 30–3
strategic resources control 62–4
trade 62–3
urban emergence 15
Western Europe
    Early Bronze Age 365–7
    Late Bronze Age 369–72
    Middle Bronze Age 367, 367–9
wetter climate theory, Indus civilization 249
wheel 5, 20, 21, 53–4, **55**, 331
wheeled vehicles 21, 41, 42, **55**
Wheeler, M. 249–50, 254, 257–9, 261–3
Wheeler, Sir Mortimer 6
White, J. P. 411, 433, 438
Whitehouse, D. 236
Whitelam, K. 201
Wietenberg culture (Carpathian basin) 353
Wilheim, G. 198
Wilkerson, S. J. K. 460
Willandra Lakes (New South Wales) 432
Willey, G. 442, 445, 449, 479
Willey, G. R. 46, 51
William, D. 130, 132
Williams, C. 499, 509
Wilson, J. A. 136, 137
Winnett, F. 244
Winter, M. 464
Winters, H. D. 440, 456, 458
Wisconsinan glacial period, North America 453
wisdom literature, Egypt, Middle Kingdom 128–9
Wissmann, H. von 243
women
    Greece 154
    South East Asia 405
wood working, Europe 327
wooden artefacts
    Africa 316, 318
    Gwisho Hotsprings **311**
Wooden Horse of Troy 220
woodland culture, North America 441
wool-bearing sheep, emergence 38
Woolley, Sir Leonard 8, 194
World Heritage List 432
Wright, J. V. 456
Wright, R. 170, 171–80, 236
writing
    see also alphabets; hieroglyphics; petroglyphs
    alphabetic 66
    Americas 447
    Aramaic 67
    Atlantic Europe 371
    Carolingian 68
    China 71–2, 111, 291
    civilization 96
    cuneiform 171
    demotic 72
    development 15, 21–2, 24, 30, 65
    Eblaite 192

Egypt 119, 120
Egyptian hieroglyphic 26
emergence 3
evolution 65–8
Gothic 68
Greek 93, 154
Harappan 67
Hittite 215
idoegraphic 66
importance 116
Indic 67
Indus 260
invention 8
Latin 68
Linear A **Pl.42**, 67
linguistic elements **67**
literature 95–6
logographic 66
Meroitic 139
Meso-America 463, 473
Mesopotamia 24, 176
North Africa **74**
oral tradition 93
origins 65–8
sources 6, 10
Sumerian 66–7, 99, 191
syllabic 154
Syria and Palestine 200
typology 67
Western Asia **74**
Wu Ding, King of Shang 295
Wu Wang, Zhou dynasty 292, 294
Wucheng, Shang and Western Zhou period 295
Wurm, S. A. **70–7**

Xia dynasty, China 283, 289
Xiajiadian cultures (China) 287, 295
Xibeigang burial area, Shang dynasty 290
Xibo (China) 289
Xingan grave (China) 295
Xinjiang (China) 291
Xinle culture (China) 287

Yadin, Y. 196
Yahweh
    Covenant 102, 105
    cult 203
    kingship 99
yams 304–6, 313–14
Yangi Kala burial grounds (Central Asia) 396
Yangshao culture (Huanghe Valley) 280–1, 283, 285
Yayoi culture (Japan) **412**, 417, 418
Yaz culture (Central Asia) 399
year, nomenclature 27
Yen, D. E. 403
Yin ruins (China) 289
    Anyang city, aerial view **Pl.112**
    bronze axe **Pl.119**
    bronze ritual vessel **Pl.113**
    bronze vessel mould **Pl.114**
    ivory cup **Pl.117**
    jade elephants **Pl.116**
    jade human figurine **Pl.115**
    oracle bone **Pl.118**
    ritual vessel **Pl.113**

Shang dynasty 289–91
Ymyyakhatakhskaya culture (Siberia) 422
Yonian philosophers (Greece) 35
Yuan-shan culture (South East Asia) 409
Yuangjiang River (South East Asia) 402–3
Yueshi culture (China) 285
Yugoslav Danube basin inroads, Bronze Age 345
Yukon (North America) 453
Yule, P. 147, 149
Yunkimun pottery (Korea) 415

Zacatenco site (Meso-America) 469
Zaehner, R. C. 399
Zagarell, A. 176, 181
Zagros, Iran 224–5, 227, 229, 231
Zaisanovka culture (Northern Asia) 423
Zalavruga (Russian Federation) 325
Zapotecs, Oaxaca, Meso America 462, 465
Zarif Kuruna (Peshawar Valley) 268
Zarins, J. 238–9
Zegarra, J. 498, 509
Zeidler, J. A. 493, 509
Zeravshan Cemetery (Central Asia) Steppe Bronze Age 398

Zevallos Menendez, C. 476
Zhimin, A. 280–8
Zho Wang, King of Zhou 295
Zhou Dynasty 286, 289, 292–4
    animal mask Pl.121
    bronze vessel Pl.125
    laquer *dou* (China) Pl.123
Ziegler, C. 118–32
ziggurat
    Iran 228
    moon god Nana Pl.66
Zimbabwe (Africa) 311
Zimmermann, J. L. 162
Zipacon site (Bogota) 449–50
Zlatar, V. 516, 523
Zoba (Aramaen states) 202
zooliths, Southern Brazil 488
Zoroaster, Iran 35, 103, 105
Zuckerman, S. 274
Zuto Brdo Girla Mare culture (Europe) 347
Zvelebil, K. 88
Zvelebil, M. 88–9

Plate 167 Jadeite head from Tenango del Valle (State of Mexico), 23 cm in height. (Courtesy National Museum of Anthropology, Mexico.)

Plate 168 Monument 34 of San Lorenzo (Veracruz), Basalt sculpture representing a half-kneeling personage with hollowed disks at the shoulders, probably made to hold movable arms (cf. Coe and Diehl 1980: 340–343), 79 cm in height. (Courtesy National Museum of Anthropology, Mexico.)

Plate 169 Black vessel from Tlatilco with Olanic excised motifs dominant in the graphic repertoire of Phase I. (Courtesy National Museum of Anthropology, Mexico.)

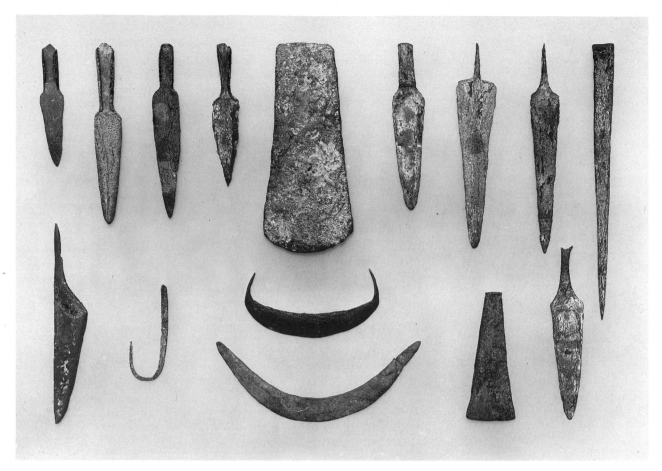

Plate 165 Copper artefacts of the Old Copper culture. Upper left: hafted spear points. Upper centre: tanged spear points. Lower left: fish-hook. Lower centre: ulu-shaped knives. Lower right: small cet. (Courtesy Milwaukee Public Museum, USA.)

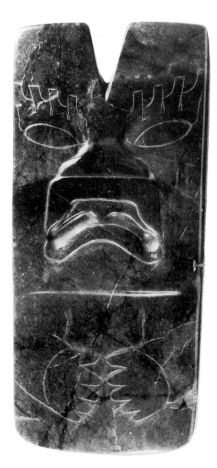

Plate 166 Jadeite celt from Oaxaca with incised human/feline motif, 22 cm in height. (Courtesy National-al Museum of Anthropology, Mexico.)

Plate 163 Stencil art and an engraved vulva in the Carnavon Gorge National Park, Queensland. The artefact on the left is a ground-edge stone axe hafted into a wooden handle, Australia. (Photo J. Flood.)

Plate 164 A dingo painted in red ochre with white outline at Lightning Brothers site west of Katherine, Northern Territory. Australia. (Photo J. Flood.)

Plate 161 Rock engravings or petroglyphs at Mt Cameron West on the north-west coast of Tasmania. Archaeological evidence suggests that these unique deeply sculptured circles belong to the Holocene rather than the Pleistocene epoch. (Photo R. Edwards).

Plate 162 A *mimi* hunter with barbed spear and spear-thrower in a rock painting in Kakadu National park, Northern Territory. Australia. (Photo R. Edwards.)

Plate 160 Class 2 tools: 1, clay figurine. Middle Jomon. Nishinomae Site, Yamagata Prefecture. H 45 cm: 2, Stone rod. Middle Jomon. Osakai Cave site, Toyama Prefecture. Length 98.2 cm; 3, Stamp-shaped stone objects. Final Jomon. (From right) Kinsei Shrine site, Suganuma site, and Miyanomae site, Gifu Prefecture. H 8.0 cm (right); 4, Chrysalis-shaped stone objects. Final Jomon. Ienoshita site, Gifu Prefecture. L 23.0 cm (right); 5, Clay earrings. Final Jomon. Kayamo site, Gunma Prefecture. D 5.0 cm (middle). Ritualistic features: 6, Stone alignment with a standing stone. Late Jomon. Ohyu site, Akita Prefecture. H 80 cm. Jomon pottery: 7, Jomon pottery style with flame-like design. Middle Joman. Umataka site, Iwanohara site and Sanka site, Niigata Prefecture. H 27.0 cm (right.) Japan. (photo T. Kobayashi)

Plate 158 Vallée des Merveilles (Alpes-Maritimes, France). Bronze Age engravings on the 'Chef de tribu' rock. (photo J.-P. Mohen)

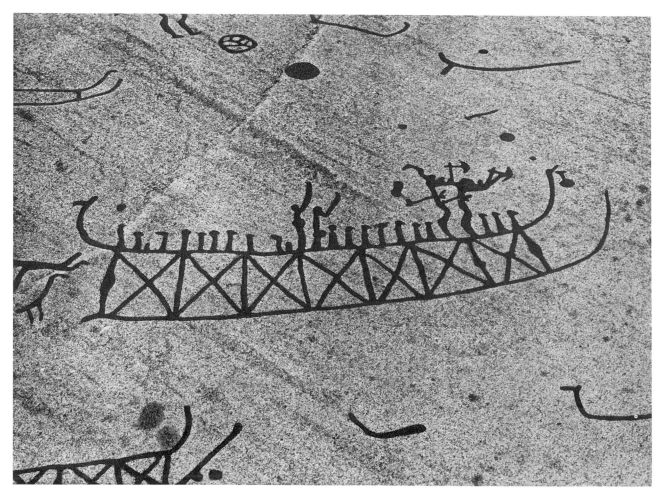

Plate 159 Site of Vitlycke I near Tanum in Swedish Bohuslän. Bronze Age ships. (Photo Eric Coquenguiot.)

Plate 156 Rock painting from Naquane, Grande Roche, Val Camonica (northern Italy), second millennium BC. (Photo WARA, Centro Camuno di Studi Preistorici, Italy.)

Plate 157 Anthropomorphic stela with a symbolic composition featuring a stag, two halberds, a torque necklace, five daggers and a set of antlers, from Paspardo, Capitello dei due pini, Val Camonica; end of third millennium BC. (Photo WARA, Centro Camuno di Studi Preistorici, Italy.)

Plate 152 Cast bronze pendant. The outer surface is ribbed, the inner surface smooth. H 12.4 cm; d 14.8 cm. Late Bronze Age. Kisterenye-Hárshegy (Department of Nógrád, Hungary) (after Kovács, 1977.)

Plate 153 Urn. Clay. The rim is decorated with a shell pattern. A band of incised parallel lines encircles the neck and on the shoulder festooned incisions form shell-like protuberances between the handles. H 57 cm; orifice d 38.5 cm; base d 15 cm. Late Bronze Age. Gava Culture. Poroszló-Aponhát (Department of Heves, Hungary) (after Kovács, 1977.)

Plate 154 Bronze object, possibly the hub-cap from a funeral car. In two parts. A truncated cone superimposed on the main disc is decorated with series of lines and arcs, and pierced with two holes for a lock-pin, one end of which is shaped like a three-headed bird. A second, almost identical object was discovered at the same time. H 8.1 and 8.5 cm; pin length 13.8 and 14.2 cm. Late Bronze Age. Nagybobróc (Bobrovec, Slovakia) (after Kovács, 1977.)

Plate 155 Hoard from Stockhult, Scania (Statenshistoriska Museum, Stockholm, Sweden.)

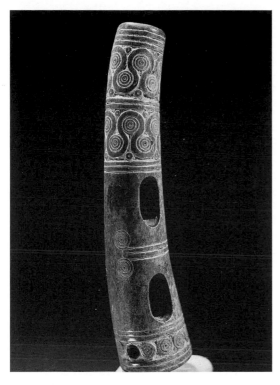

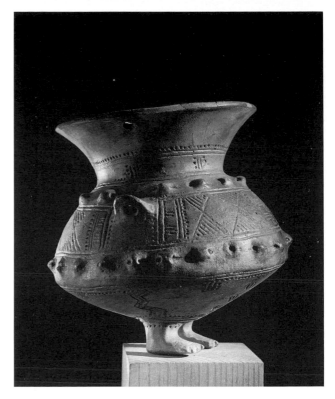

Plate 148 Carved horn bit branch with two oval holes for the mouth piece and two round holes, one up and one down, in a plane perpendicular to the first ones, for the bridle attachments. Decorated with frets and concentric circles. L 9 cm; upper d 1.3 cm; lower d 2 cm. Middle Bronze Age. Vatya Culture, Hungary. (after Kovács, 1977.)

Plate 149 Vessel with base in the form of human feet. Clay. The shoulder and body are decorated with a series of small knobs, and the remaining surface is decorated with incised lines and points. The rim and the two handles are perforated for hanging. H 10.5 cm; orifice d 9.5 cm. Middle Bronze Age. Vatya Culture. Iváncsa (Department of Fehér, Hungary) (after Kovács, 1977).

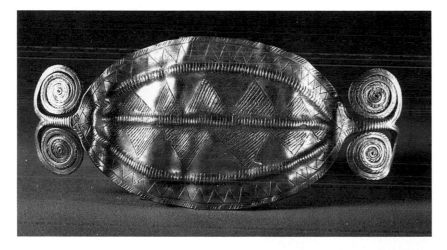

Plate 150 Wide bracelet in gold plate. Engraved geometrical design, with two flattened spirals at each extremity. L 17.5 cm; w 7.8 cm; weight 161.92 g. Late Bronze Age. Part of a hoard discovered at Bodrogkeresztur (Department of Borsod-Abaúj-Zemplén, Hungary) (after Kovács, 1977.)

Plate 151 Gold chain. Only 81 of the original 86 ridged links have survived. Link d 1.8–3.4 cm; total weight 328.08 g. Late Bronze Age. Part of a hoard from Szarvaszó (Sarasau, Romania) (after Kovács, 1977.)

Plate 143 Vessel with handle. Clay. Decorated with nick-edged serpentine and spiral finger marks and with engraved triangles encircling the base. H 15.5 cm; orifice d 9.8 cm; based 9 cm. Middle Bronze Age. Füzesabony Culture. Megyaszó (Department of Heves, Hungary) (after Kovács, 1977.)

Plate 144 Horn disk, possibly the base of a whip handle. A nicked band encircles five interlaced engraved spirals. D 5.2 cm; thickness 0.4 cm. Middle Bronze Age. Füzesabony Culture. Füzesabony (Department of Heves, Hungary) (after Kovács, 1977.)

Plate 146 Bracelet decorated with bulls' heads. Gold with silver overlay on the outer edge and triangular incrustations on the bulls' heads. The outer surface is divided with a series of notched bands; the inner surface bears a fretwork design. External d 10.8 cm; internal d 6.9 cm; weight 611.84 g. Origin unknown, but probably Transylvania (after Kovács, 1977.)

Plate 145 Disc-shaped gold ornament. The quartered surface is covered with an embossed design. The outer edge of one quarter is decorated with stylized birds. D 13 × 13.5 cm; depth 2.4 cm; weight 82.31 g. Middle Bronze Age. Ottlaka (Grăniceri, Romania) (after Kovács, 1977.)

Plate 147 Four-handled footed vessel. Clay. Decorated with engraved lines and zigzags, and protuberances surrounded by etched circles. H 15 cm; orifice d 20.5 cm; base d 9.5 cm. Middle Bronze Age. Füzesabony Culture. Tiszafüred-Majoroshalom (Department of Szolnok, Hungary) (after Kovács, 1977.)

Plate 138 Stone mould for casting bronze sceptre shafts, from the village of Pobit Kamak, Razgrad district; late Bronze Age. (photo Hans Mayer.)

Plate 139 Cart from Dupljaya. (Courtesy National Museum, Belgrade, Federal Republic of Yugoslavia.)

Plate 141 Hanging vessel. Clay. The surface is decorated with chalk-encrusted engraved lines; h 13.5 cm; orifice d 9.2 cm; base d 4 cm. Early Bronze Age. Nagyrév Culture. Nagyrév (Department of Szolnok, Hungary) (after Kovács, 1977.)

Plate 140 Idol from a cremation cemetery at Korbovo near Kladovo. (Courtesy National Museum, Belgrade, Federal Republic of Yugoslavia.)

Plate 142 Bell-shaped vessel. Clay. The surface is decorated with stamped bands alternating with plain, which gives a feeling of rhythm; H 10 cm; orifice diameter 6 cm. Early Bronze Age. Bell-beaker civilization. Tököl (Department of Pest, Hungary) (after Kovács, 1977.)

Plate 135 Nderit ware pottery bowl from central Kenya. (Photo D. W. Phillipson.)

Plate 136 Rock painting of eland and hunter in the Transkei region of South Africa. (Photo P. Vinnicombe; Courtesy Natal University Press.)

Plate 137 Farming scene: person guiding a plough drawn by two horses and five people digging, from Bedolina, Pistunsi, Val Camonica; second millennium BC. (Photo WARA, Centro Camuno di Studi Preistorici, Italy).

Plate 131 Rock engraving of boat, animals and people in the Wadi el-Barramiya, eastern desert of Egypt. (Photo Gerald Fuchs.)

Plate 132 Neolithic stone houses at Dhar Tichitt, Mauritania. (Photo Augustin Holl.)

Plate 133 Neolithic potsherds with seed-impressions of cultivated cereals, Oued Chebbi, Mauritania. (Photo Sylvie Amblard.)

Plate 134 Rock shelters at Ele Bor, northern Kenya. (Photo D. W. Phillipson.)

Plate 129 Rock painting of cattle-herders, Sefar, Tassili. (Photo K.H. Striedter.)

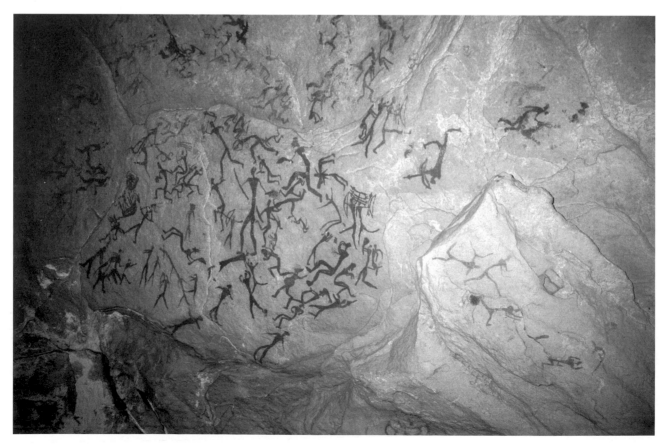

Plate 130 Rock painting at Arakoukam, Algeria. (Photo L. N. Viallet.)

Plate 128 A view in the Ahaggar highlands of southernmost Algeria, showing the location of a characteristic painted cave. (Photo F. Soleilhavoup.)

Plate 125 Western Zhou bronze vessel from Lintong with an inscription about the conquest of the Shang by Wu Wang. (Courtesy Institute of Archaeology, Chinese Academy of Social Sciences, Beijing.)

Plate 126 Pottery *li* with patterns painted after baking; Lower Xiajiadian culture. (Courtesy Institute of Archaeology, Chinese Academy of Social Sciences, Beijing.)

Plate 127 Huge bronze human figure from Guang-han County, Sichuan Province; h 2.60 m. (Courtesy Institute of Archaeology, Chinese Academy of Social Sciences, Beijing.)

Plate 119 Yin bronze axe (*yue*) with a human mask from Yidu County, Shandong Province; h 0.35 m. (Courtesy Institute of Archaeology, Chinese Academy of Social Sciences, Beijing.)

Plate 120 Foal-shape *zun* vessel with an inscription about the Zhou king attending a ceremony of parting adult foals from mother horses. (Courtesy Institute of Archaeology, Chinese Academy of Social Sciences, Beijing.)

Plate 121 Western Zhou jade animal mask from Chang'an County, Shaanxi Province; h 0.52 m. (Courtesy Institute of Archaeology, Chinese Academy of Social Sciences, Beijing.)

Plate 122 Western Zhou glazed pottery jar from Luoyang municipality, Honan Province; h 0.27 m. (Courtesy Institute of Archaeology, Chinese Academy of Social Sciences, Beijing.)

Plate 123 Restored Western Zhou laquer *dou*. (Courtesy Institute of Archaeology, Chinese Academy of Social Sciences, Beijing.)

Plate 124 Rubbing of the inscription on a basin (*shi giang pan*), Western Zhou dynasty. (Courtesy Institute of Archaeology, Chinese Academy of Social Sciences, Beijing.)

Plate 113 Bronze ritual vessel from the Yin ruins near Anyang city. (Courtesy Institute of Archaeology, Chinese Academy of Social Sciences, Beijing.)

Plate 114 Mould of a bronze vessel (*fang-yi*) from the Yin ruins; h 0.25 m. (Courtesy Institute of Archaeology, Chinese Academy of Social Sciences, Beijing.)

Plate 115 Squatting jade human figurine from the Yin ruins near Anyang city. (Courtesy Institute of Archaeology, Chinese Academy of Social Sciences, Beijing.)

Plate 116 Jade elephants from the Yin ruins. (Courtesy Institute of Archaeology, Chinese Academy of Social Sciences, Beijing.)

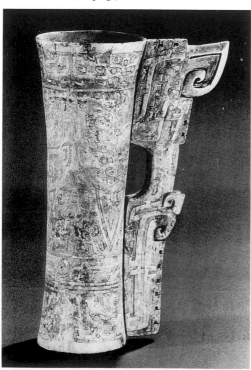

Plate 117 Ivory cup inlaid with turquoise from the Yin ruins near Anyang city. (Courtesy Institute of Archaeology, Chinese Academy of Social Sciences, Beijing.)

Plate 118 Oracle bone with inscriptions from the Yin ruins near Anyang city. (Courtesy Institute of Archaeology, Chinese Academy of Social Sciences, Beijing.)

Plate 110 Pottery *gui* and *li* from Keshengzhuang in Chang'an County, Shaanxi Province. (Photo An Zhimin.)

Plate 111 Palace foundation in the ruined Shang city at Yanshi. (Courtesy Institute of Archaeology, Chinese Academy of Social Sciences, Beijing.)

Plate 112 Aerial view of the Yin ruins near Anyang city. (Courtesy Institute of Archaeology, Chinese Academy of Social Sciences, Beijing.)

Plate 108 Kalibangan: close view of a grave showing an extended skeleton with pottery, period II (Harappan). (Photo B. K. Thapar.)

Plate 109 Large-sized tomb at Taosi in Xianfen County, Shanxi Province. (Photo An Zhimin.)

Plate 105 Lihyanite inscription from Hereibh, north-western Saudi Arabia. (Photo A. R. al-Ansary.)

Plate 106 Kalibangan: general view of an excavated north/south-running thoroughfare in the lower city, period II (Harappan). (Photo B.K. Thapar.)

Plate 107 Kalibangan: cylinder-seal and its impression, period II (Harappan). (Courtesy Archaeological Survey of India.)

Plate 101 North Afghanistan. Gold seal with a winged goddess and lions from the plundered tombs of Bactria. (Photo V.I. Sarianidi.)

Plate 102 North Afghanistan. Stone cylinder seal from the plundered tombs of Bactria. (Photo V.I. Sarianidi.)

Plate 103 Rock art from Jubba (northern Saudi Arabia) showing a line of animals following humans, superimposed by large humans, two carrying caprid. (Photo A.R. al-Ansary.)

Plate 104 Dilmun-type seals from Failaka, Kuwait. (Photo A. R. al-Ansary.)

Plate 97 Cultural scene from an Urartian situla. Silver. Urartian style, eighth century BC. (Photo E. Akurgal.)

Plate 98 Phrygian vessel. Clay. Transitional style, *c.* 730 BC. From Alışar. The Anatolian Civilizations Museum, Ankara. (Photo E. Akurgal.)

Plate 99 Phrygian vase. Clay. Ripe Phrygian style, *c.* 700 BC. From Gordion. Archaeological Museum, Istanbul. (Photo E. Akurgal.)

Plate 100 Phrygian fibulae. Bronze. Ripe Phrygian style, *c.* 700 BC. From Gordion. The Anatolian Civilizations Museum, Ankara. (Photo E. Akurgal.)

Plate 93 The goddess Kupaba. Fragment of an orthostat relief. Basalt; h 82 cm. from Kargamis. Neo-Hittite art, Traditional style, eighth century BC. The Anatolian Civilizations Museum, Ankara. (Photo E. Akurgal.)

Plate 94 Detail from an orthostat relief of a chimaira, the hybrid figure consisting of a lion and a human head. Basalt. Neo-Hittite art, Traditional style, eighth century BC. From Carchemish. The Anatolian Civilizations Museum, Ankara. (Photo E. Akurgal.)

Plate 95 Tomb stela of Tarhunpias. From Maras. Basalt. Neo-Hittite Aramaean style, about 700 BC. Musée du Louvre, Paris, France. (Photo E. Akurgal.)

Plate 96 Nursing mother with child from the western series of an orthostat on the north portal at Karatepe near Adana. Basalt. Neo-Hittite Phoenicianizing style, about 700 BC. (Photo E. Akurgal.)

Plate 90 Orthostat relief from the city walls of Alaca Hüyük. King and queen offering a libation before an altar and a bull relief, symbol of the weather-god. Basalt; h 126 cm. Hittite imperial style, fourteenth century BC. The Anatolian Civilizations Museum, Ankara. (Photo E. Akurgal.)

Plate 91 Rock reliefs of the Hittite open-air sanctuary in Yazilikaya, Boghazköy. Basalt. Procession of twelve gods, on the west wall of rock chamber B. Hittite imperial style, thirteenth century BC. (Photo E. Akurgal.)

Plate 92 The frieze on the rim of a ritual silver vessel in the form of a stag, symbol of the sun-goddess Arinna. The scene depicts a libation probably offered to Hepat. Hittite imperial style, fourteenth/thirteenth century BC. Found in Central Anatolia. (Photo E. Akurgal.)

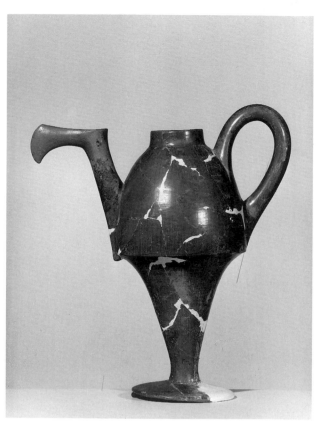

Plate 87 Jug. Clay with reddish-brown slip; h 39.8 cm. Hittite style of the Hittite principalities, eighteenth century BC. From Kültepe. The Anatolian Civilizations Museum, Ankara (Hirmer Fotoarchiv, Munich, Germany.)

Plate 88 Beaker-jug. Clay with reddish-brown slip; h 35.8 cm. Hittite style of the Hittite principalities, seventeenth century BC. From Alaca Hüyük. The Anatolian Civilizations Museum, Ankara (Hirmer Fotoarchiv, Munich, Germany.)

Plate 89 A pair of ritual vessels in the form of bulls representing Serri and Hurri, the two sacred animals of Tesup, the weather-god. Clay with reddish-brown slip; h 90 cm. Hittite imperial style, sixteenth century BC. From Boghazköy. The Anatolian Civilizations Museum, Ankara. (Photo E. Akurgal.)

Plate 86 Hattian female statuette. Silver and gold; h 24.4 cm. Hattian style, 2100–2000
BC. From Hasanoğlan, near Ankara. The Anatolian Civilizations Museum, Ankara.
(Photo E. Akurgal.)

Plate 82 Clasp with fitted pin. Gold; l 13 cm. Hattian style, 2100–2000 BC. From Alaca Hüyük. The Anatolian Civilizations Museum, Ankara (Hirmer Fotoarchiv, Munich, Germany.)

Plate 83 Twin idol. Sheet gold; h 3.1 cm. Hattian style, 2100–2000 BC. From Alaca Hüyük. The Anatolian Civilizations Museum, Ankara (Hirmer Fotoarchiv, Munich, Germany.)

Plate 84 Flagon. Gold; h 15.3 cm. Hattian style, 2100–2000 BC. From Alaca Hüyük. The Anatolian Civilizations Museum, Ankara (Hirmer Fotoarchiv, Munich, Germany.)

Plate 85 Jug with view of its base. Gold; h 17.7 cm. Hattian style, 2100–2000 BC. From Horoztepe. The Metropolitan Museum, New York (Hirmer Fotoarchiv, Munich, Germany.)

Plate 79 Sam'al/Zincirli. Relief of Kilamuwa, king of Sam'al in northern Syria, *c.* 850 BC, with a Phoenician inscription (Bildarchiv Preussischer Kulturbesitz, Berlin, Germany.)

Plate 80 Ritual standard in the form of a stag symbolizing the chief Hittite female divinity, sun-goddess Arinna, the spouse of the weather-god. Bronze inlaid with silver, h 52 cm. Hattian style, 2100–2000 BC. From Alaca Hüyük. The Anatolian Civilizations Museum, Ankara (Hirmer Fotoarchiv, Munich, Germany.)

Plate 81 Ritual standard representing the cosmos. The figurine of a deer, the symbol of a Hittite female divinity, under the celestial vault is supported by a pair of bull's horns, the attribute of the Hittite weather-god. Bronze; h 23 cm. Hattian style, 2100–2000 BC. From Alaca Hüyük. The Anatolian Civilizations Museum, Ankara (Hirmer Fotoarchiv, Munich, Germany.)

Plate 76 Pectoral from Byblos. Decorated with the Egyptian falcon, this precious object forms part of the funerary equipment of the royal tombs of the early centuries of the second millennium found in the coastal city. It is probably a local copy from Egyptian models and not, as in the case of some other objects, a gift sent to Byblos (Gebal or Gubla) by the pharaohs of the Middle Kingdom. Gold leaf work in repoussé; h×l: 10×20.5 cm. Lebanon. (Courtesy Musée du Louvre, Paris, France; photo R.M.N.)

Plate 77 Bronze statuette, probably from Qatna. This figure, enthroned in a royal costume edged with a thick trimming of fur, wears an ovoid tiara with several superimposed rows of horns. It has therefore been suggested that he represents a god-king, or a person who played the role of patron divinity of his kingdom, in this case Qatna, one of the major cities of Amorite Syria. Eighteenth-seventeenth centuries BC; bronze; h 17 cm. (Courtesy Musée du Louvre, Paris, France; photo R.M.N.)

Plate 78 Ugarit. Ivory: Seated goddess of fertility, demonstrating the mastership of the ancient Syrians in this field and also the influence of Aegean art on the Levant. Syria. (Bildarchiv Preussischer Kulturbesitz, Berlin, Germany.)

Plate 72 Syrian cylinder seal with gold mount. The engraved picture, with a cartouche bearing the owner's name, shows a meeting between representatives of two generations of Syrian gods: Baal, the young and impetuous storm god, addresses a more passive figure holding vases from which water is pouring. These attributes, which denote the water god, the sage Ea, in Mesopotamia, seem to apply in a Syrian context to the god El, father of the gods of Ugaritic mythology. Hematite and gold, eighteenth century BC; h × d: 4.2 × 1 cm. (Courtesy Musée du Louvre, Paris, France; photo R.M.N.)

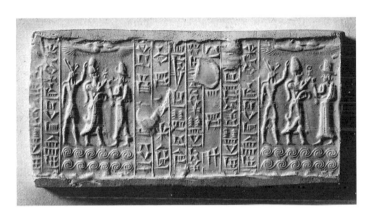

Plate 73 Impression of a cylinder of Sumirapa, king of Tuba. In a long cartouche, the king swears his devotion to the storm god Adad (Addu), the moon god Sin and Ishtar, goddess of love and war. He is shown in the centre, wearing an ovoid tiara and a long fur-trimmed garment, paying homage to the 'great Syrian goddess'. Egyptian influence is clearly discernible in the presence of the large winged solar disc, the figure reminiscent of Horus, Egyptian protector of royalty, and the life sign carried by the king. Seventeenth century BC; h 4 cm. (Courtesy Musée du Louvre, Paris, France, photo R.M.N.)

Plate 74 Impression of Syrian cylinder-seal: scene of homage being paid to the 'great Syrian goddess', who seems to have close ties with the monarchy. Addu (Baal) leads the procession, brandishing his weapons and holding his bull on a leash. He is followed by a goddess whose gesture of revealing her genitals shows her to be the personification of the female principle, ready for the sacred rite of marriage, a pledge of fecundity and fertility. The armed god bringing up the rear of the procession is a less common figure, probably Reshef, lord of the underworld and patron of warrior kings, like his Mesopotamian counterpart, Nergal. *c.* 1700 BC; hematite; h × d: 2.1 × 1 cm. (Courtesy Musée du Louvre, Paris, France; photo R.M.N.)

Plate 75 Impression of Syrian cylinder-seal of Hyksos period. Following the conquest of Egypt by the Hyksos, the different Syrian kingdoms took over many features of Egyptian culture, adapting them to fit their own concerns. The owner of this seal, for example, wearing Egyptian-style headgear and clothes, is blessed by the familiar figure of falcon-headed Horus, crowned with the *pshent*. The inscription in Egyptian hieroglyphics corresponds to the owner's name and the 'contentment' formula. Seventeenth century BC; green jasper; h × d: 2 × 1 cm. (Courtesy Musée du Louvre, Paris, France; photo R.M.N.)

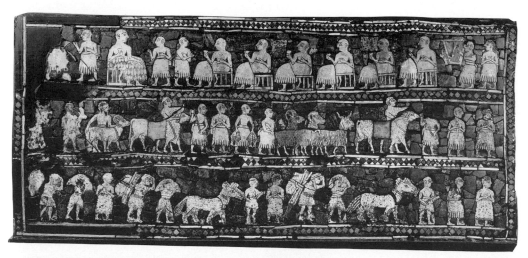

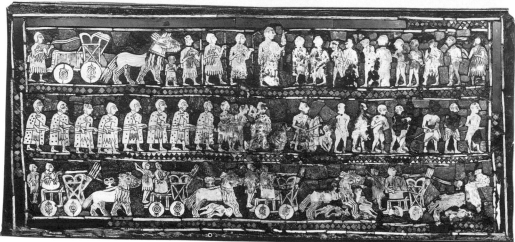

Plate 69 The so-called 'Standard of Ur' from the Royal Cemetery of Ur, *c.* 2685 BC: a mosaic of shell, lapis lazuli and carnelian, resources which had to be imported into Mesopotamia, h 0.20 m. The top view is thought to depict the 'peace side' and the bottom view the 'war side'. British Museum, London, United Kingdom (Hirmer Fotoarchiv, Munich, Germany.)

Plate 70 The sun god Shamash (seated), god of justice, presenting the 'law of the land' to Hammurabi (1792–1750 BC). Musée du Louvre, Paris, France. (Photo C. C. Lamberg-Karlovsky.)

Plate 71 Ebla (Tell Mardikh): stone ritual basin from temple D. Compartmentalized basins provide a valuable record of north Syrian sculpture from the beginning of the second millennium. The outer surface is decorated with bas-reliefs of mythological or religious subjects: a ritual banquet involving the king and queen, a peaceful procession of horned animals, a naked hero with a lion's head controlling two lions. Parallels have been drawn between these bas-reliefs and the iconography of Cappadocian seals dating from the period of Assyrian trading posts. Limestone, nineteenth century BC; h × l × w: 64 × 117 × 79 cm. (Courtesy Aleppo Museum, Syria.)

Plate 66 The ziggurat of the moon god Nana. Built by Ur–Nammu, king of Ur, *c.* 2112–2095 BC. (Hirmer Fotoarchiv, Munich, Germany.)

Plate 67 Gypsum statuette of a man holding a goblet from the Abu Temple at Eshnunna, *c.* 2900 BC. (Photo Hirmer Fotoarchiv, Munich, Germany.)

Plate 68 Akkadian cylinder-seal depicting a procession presenting gifts to a deity. (Photo C.C. Lamberg-Karlovsky.)

Plate 65 Aerial photograph of the Sumerian city of Ur. The Ziggurat of the moon god Nana is in the foreground. (Photo G. Gerster.)

Plate 63 Bronze head from Nineveh which is probably that of Naram-Sin rather than Sargon. Baghdad Museum, Iraq (Hirmer Fotoarchiv, Munich, Germany.)

Plate 64 Sandstone 'Victory stela' of Naram-Sin 2254–2218 BC, king of the Akkadian empire and grandson of Sargon, h 2 m. Discovered at Susa, the stela depicts Naram-Sin standing atop the vanquished enemies. Musée du Louvre, Paris, France (Hirmer Fotoarchiv, Munich, Germany.)

Plate 59 Tabular idol, red lustre ware, end of third millennium. Cyprus. (Courtesy Musée du Louvre, Paris, France.)

Plate 60 Group of clay figures surrounding a trough, engaged in washing? bread-making? or a ritual ceremony? Middle Bronze Age. Cyprus. (Courtesy Musée du Louvre, Paris, France.)

Plate 61 Bronze statue from Enkomi of an armed god standing on a base in the form of a copper ingot, twelfth century BC. Cyprus. (Courtesy Cyprus Museum, Nicosia.)

Plate 62 Ivory throne from a 'Royal Tomb' at Salamis, end of the eighth century BC. Cyprus. (Courtesy Cyprus Museum, Nicosia.)

Plate 55 Late Geometric krater from Dipylon with representation of funerary procession, c. 740 BC, h 1.23 m; Athenian fabric. (Courtesy German Archaeological Institute, Athens, Greece.)

Plate 56 Bronze horse found at Olympia, h 0.85 m; Argive fabric. (Courtesy German Archaeological Institute, Athens, Greece.)

Plate 57 Late Geometric bronze statuette from Olympia, h 0.15 m. (Courtesy German Archaeological Institute, Athens, Greece.)

Plate 58 Late Geometric bronze statuette found at Olympia, h 0.144 m; Argive fabric. (Courtesy German Archaeological Institute, Athens, Greece.)

Plate 50 Late Minoan faience statuette of the 'Snake Goddess'. (Courtesy Archaeological Museum of Herakleion, Greece.)

Plate 51 Late Minoan stone ritual vessel (rhyton) in the shape of a bull's head. (Courtesy Archaeological Museum of Herakleion, Greece.)

Plate 52 Late Minoan ritual vessel (rhyton) of rock-crystal. (Courtesy Archaeological Museum of Herakleion, Greece.)

Plate 53 Middle Geometric krater from Kerameikos, h 0.515 m; Athenian fabric. (Courtesy German Archaeological Institute, Athens, Greece.)

Plate 54 Middle Geometric ivory statuette, Greek adaptation of the Oriental prototype of Astarte, h 0.24 m; Athenian fabric. (Courtesy German Archaeological Institute, Athens, Greece.)

Plate 47 Middle Cycladic clay jug with painted decoration of swallows from Thera. (Courtesy National Archaeological Museum, Athens, Greece.)

Plate 48 Middle Minoan clay crater with flowers in relief. (Courtesy Archaeological Museum of Herakleion, Greece.)

Plate 49 Wall painting of bull-leaping. (Courtesy Archaeological Museum of Herakleion, Greece.)

Plate 46 Wall painting of the flotilla from Thera. (Courtesy National Archaeological Museum, Athens, Greece.)

Plate 42 Clay tablet with inscriptions in the Linear A script.
(Courtesy Archaeological Museum of Herakleion, Greece.)

Plate 43 Wall-painting of a woman from Mycenae. (Courtesy National
Archaeological Museum, Athens, Greece.)

Plate 44 Golden funerary mask from Mycenae. (Courtesy National Archaeological Museum, Athens, Greece.)

Plate 45 Golden cup from Vapeio with scene showing the catching
of a bull. (Courtesy National Archaeological Museum, Athens,
Greece.)

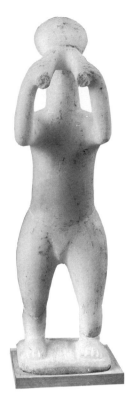

Plate 37 Early Cycladic marble figurine of a harp-player; h 0.225 m. (Courtesy National Archaeological Museum, Athens, Greece.)

Plate 38 Early Cycladic marble statue of a female figure; h 1.52 m. (Courtesy National Archaeological Museum, Athens, Greece.)

Plate 39 Early Cycladic marble vase. (Courtesy National Archaeological Museum, Athens, Greece.)

Plate 40 Early Cycladic clay container (pyxis) with painted linear decoration; h 0.72 m. (Courtesy National Archaeological Museum, Athens, Greece.)

Plate 41 The Phaistos Disk with hieroglyphic writing. (Courtesy Archaeological Museum of Herakleion, Greece.)

Plate 35 Ramses II crowned by Horus and Set. Abu Simbel, Small Temple. (Courtesy Centre of Documentation and Studies on Ancient Egypt, Cairo, Egypt.)

Plate 36 Statue of Ramses V offering a *naos*. (Courtesy Egyptian Museum, Cairo, Egypt.)

Plate 33 Great Temple, Abu Simbel. (Photo G. Mokhtar.)

Plate 34 Temple of Wadi es Sebua, Nubia. (Photo G. Mokhtar.)

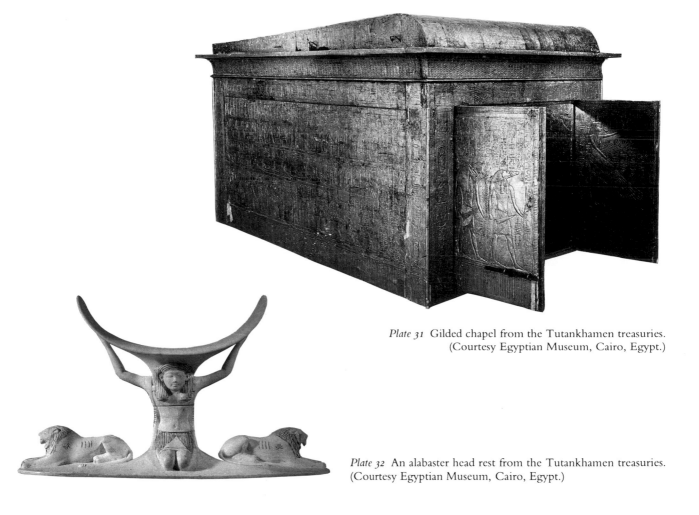

Plate 30 The famous scribe and architect Amenhotep, son of Hapu, 18th dynasty. (Courtesy Egyptian Museum, Cairo, Egypt.)

Plate 28 King Hor, 13th dynasty. (Courtesy Egyptian Museum, Cairo, Egypt.)

Plate 29 Statue of Thuthmosis III. (Courtesy Egyptian Museum, Cairo, Egypt.)

Plate 31 Gilded chapel from the Tutankhamen treasuries. (Courtesy Egyptian Museum, Cairo, Egypt.)

Plate 32 An alabaster head rest from the Tutankhamen treasuries. (Courtesy Egyptian Museum, Cairo, Egypt.)

Plate 26 A-Group culture, Nubia.
(Photo Scandinavian Joint Expedition.)

Plate 27 Fortress of Buhen, Nubia. (Photo Rex Keating.)

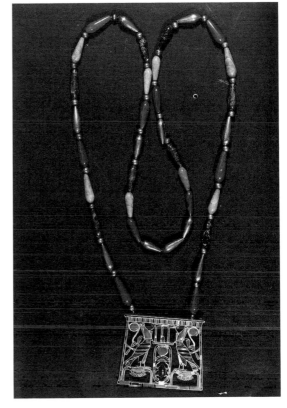

Plate 23 Detail from the Book of the Dead of Nebqued, *c.* 1320 BC. Painted papyrus, l 13 cm. Illustrated formulae for transforming oneself into heron or phoenix. (Courtesy Musée du Louvre, Paris, France; photo R.M.N.)

Plate 24 A collar from the Middle Kingdom found at Illahun. (Courtesy Egyptian Museum, Cairo, Egypt.)

Plate 25 Model of soldiers from the 11th dynasty. Myshty tomb at Asyût. (Courtesy Egyptian Museum, Cairo, Egypt.)

Plate 21 Stela of Djedkhonouioufankh, *c.* 1000–900 BC Painted wood, h 29.4 cm. Amon's musician, accompanying himself on the harp, sings a hymn in praise of the god Horakthi. (Courtesy Musée du Louvre, Paris, France; photo R.M.N.)

Plate 20 Seated alabaster statuette of Abikhil, superintendent of the temple at Mari, *c.* 2800–2685 BC. (Hirmer Fotoarchiv, Munich, Germany.)

Plate 22 Narmer Palette; slate. (Courtesy Egyptian Museum, Cairo, Egypt.)

Plate 17 The pyramids of Giza. (Hirmer Fotoarchiv, Munich, Germany.)

Plate 18 Volcanic-rock portrait of Amenemhat III, king of Egypt 1842–1797 BC. (Courtesy Fitzwilliam Museum, Cambridge, United Kingdom.)

Plate 19 Scribe, sitting cross-legged, painted limestone. (Courtesy Musée du Louvre, Paris, France; photo R.M.N.)

Plate 13 Bronze armour from Marmesse, Haute Marne (France); ninth–eighth century BC. (Courtesy Musée des Antiquités Nationales, Saint Germain-en-Laye, France.)

Plate 14 Detail from the Book of the Dead of Nebqued, c. 1320 BC. Painted papyrus, l 15 cm. Nebqued followed by his mother and wife. (Courtesy Musée du Louvre, Paris, France; photo R.M.N.)

Plate 15 Statue menhir, Mas d'Azaïs, Montlaur, Aveyron (France). End of third millennium BC. (Courtesy Musée des Antiquités Nationales, Saint Germain-en-Laye, France.)

Plate 16 Rock design in Magnificent Gallery, Laura, Cape Town Peninsula, North Queensland. The larger-than-lifesize white human figure wears a 'love-pendant' and is considered to derive from love-magic ritual. The thin dark red figure behind is a spirit figure or Quinkan. (Photo J. Flood.)

Plate 10 Fortifications of the Hittite Empire, 1450–1200 BC. (Photo E. Akurgal).

Plate 11 Statue of Goudea seated, *c.* 2150 BC. Dark green diorite; 45 × 22 cm. (Courtesy Musée du Louvre, Paris, France; photo R.M.N.)

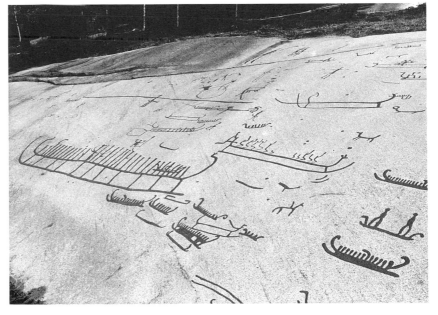

Plate 12 Site of Vitlyke I near Tanum in Swedish Bohuslän. Bronze Age ships. (Photo Eric Coquenguiot.)

Plate 7 The cubit (525 mm), an ancient Egyptian measure of length. (Courtesy Museo Egizie, Turin, Italy.)

Plate 8 Egyptian scribes drawing up the accounts for a burial ground. Mastaba of Akhethotep, 5th dynasty of the Old Kingdom, 2450–2290 BC. (Courtesy Musée du Louvre, Paris, France; photo R.M.N.).

Plate 9 Tree crops in Mesopotamia: relief from the palace of the Assyrian king Sennacherib, showing Babylonian captives and their guards passing along a riverbank with date-palms, *c.* 700 BC. (Courtesy Ashmolean Museum, Oxford, United Kingdom.)

Plate 4 Stonehenge. Trilithons.
United Kingdom (Photo J.-P. Mohen)

Plate 5 Stonehenge from the North East.
United Kingdom (Photo J.-P. Mohen)

Plate 6 Painted bas-relief of Nefertiabet showing a table for funerary gifts (Egypt, 2700 BC). The scene contains many figures from the Egyptian hieroglyphic numbering system: at lower right, the hieroglyph for 1,000 is repeated four times. (Courtesy Musée du Louvre, Paris, France.; photo R.M.N.)

Plate 1 Assyria, 721–705 BC: palace of Sargon II at Khorsabad. Decoration from Courtyard VIII: transport of cedar wood logs. Gypsum; h 4 m. (Courtesy Musée du Louvre, Paris, France; photo R.M.N.)

Plate 2 Bronze hoard. Part of a hoard of tools and jewellery. Late Bronze Age. Jászkarajenö (Department of Pest, Hungary) (after Kovács, 1977.)

Plate 3 Bronze foundry debris from Fort-Harrouard (Eure-et-Loir, France); 1300–1000 BC. From top left: terracotta moulds for pins and spearhead; chalk moulds for ring, axehead and anvil; baked clay tuyère; fragments of crucible and spearheads. (Courtesy Musée des Antiquités Nationales, Saint Germain-en Laye, France; photo D. Vigears.)

PLATES